LEO BAECK INSTITUTE
YEAR BOOK

2001

The *Repräsentantensaal* of the *Jüdische Gemeinde* in Berlin

By courtesy of the Library of the Staatliche Museen zu Berlin, Kunstbibliothek

LEO BAECK INSTITUTE

YEAR BOOK
2001

WITHDRAWN

XLVI

BERGHAHN BOOKS • OXFORD
PUBLISHED FOR THE INSTITUTE
LONDON • JERUSALEM • NEW YORK

FOUNDER EDITOR: ROBERT WELTSCH (1956–1978)
EDITOR EMERITUS: ARNOLD PAUCKER (1970–1992)

Editorial office: Leo Baeck Institute
4 Devonshire Street, London W1W 5LB
www.leobaeck.co.uk

THE LEO BAECK INSTITUTE
was founded in 1955 for the study of the history and culture of German-speaking Central European Jewry

The Institute is named in honour of the man who was the last representative figure of German Jewry in Germany during the Nazi period

LEO BAECK INSTITUTE

JERUSALEM: 33 Bustanai Street
LONDON: 4 Devonshire Street
NEW YORK: 15 West 16th Street

© Leo Baeck Institute 2001
Published by Berghahn Books
www.berghahnbooks.com
ISBN 1 57181 553 8

J. A. S. Grenville
EDITOR

Raphael Gross
ASSOCIATE EDITOR

Helen McEwan   Gabriele Rahaman
ASSISTANT EDITORS

ADVISORY BOARD

Great Britain:	Marianne Calmann	London
	David Cesarani	London/Southampton
	Ian Kershaw	Sheffield
	Jeremy Noakes	Exeter
	Peter Pulzer	Oxford
	Bernard Wasserstein	Glasgow
Germany:	Werner T. Angress	Berlin
	Wolfgang Benz	Berlin
	Ursula Büttner	Hamburg
	Michael Graetz	Heidelberg
	Arno Herzig	Hamburg
	Stefi Jersch-Wenzel	Berlin
	Monika Richarz	Hamburg
	Reinhard Rürup	Berlin
United States:	Christopher Browning	Tacoma
	Vicki Caron	Cornell
	Peter Gay	Yale
	Marion Kaplan	New York
	Hillel J. Kieval	St. Louis
	Steven Lowenstein	Los Angeles
	Michael A. Meyer	Cincinnati
	Jehuda Reinharz	Brandeis
	Ismar Schorsch	New York
	David Sorkin	Madison
	Fritz Stern	New York
	Guy Stern	Wayne State
Israel:	Steven Aschheim	Jerusalem
	Avraham Barkai	Lehavoth Habashan
	Evyatar Friesel	Jerusalem
	Hagit Lavski	Jerusalem
	Robert Liberles	Beersheva
	Paul Mendes-Flohr	Jerusalem
	Chaim Schatzker	Haifa
	Shulamit Volkov	Tel-Aviv
	Robert S. Wistrich	Jerusalem
	Moshe Zimmermann	Jerusalem

Contents

Preface by John Grenville and Arnold Paucker   IX

I. JEWS IN THE AGE OF METTERNICH

EDWARD TIMMS: The Pernicious Rift: Metternich and the Debate about Jewish Emancipation at the Congress of Vienna...   3

NIALL FERGUSON: Metternich and the Rothschilds: "A Dance with Torches on Powderkegs"?   19

ROBERT J. W. EVANS: Progress and Emancipation in Hungary during the Age of Metternich   55

EDA SAGARRA: Grillparzer, the Catholics and the Jews: A Reading of *Die Jüdin von Toledo* (1851)   67

RITCHIE ROBERTSON: Karl Beck: From Radicalism to Monarchism   81

II. GENDER AND BOUNDARIES OF THE JEWISH COMMUNITY IN NINETEENTH-CENTURY GERMANY

DEBORAH HERTZ: The Lives, Loves, and Novels of August and Fanny Lewald, the Converted Cousins from Königsberg   95

MARIA BENJAMIN BAADER: When Judaism turned Bourgeois: Gender in Jewish Associational Life and in the Synagogue, 1750–1850   113

TILL VAN RAHDEN: Intermarriages, the "New Woman", and the Situational Ethnicity of Breslau Jews from the 1870s to the 1920s   125

DAGMAR HERZOG: Telling Ethnic and Gender History Together: A Comment...   151

PANELLISTS' RESPONSES TO DAGMAR HERZOG   159

III. PHILOSOPHY, RELIGION AND POLITICS

HENRI SOUSSAN: The *Gesellschaft zur Förderung der Wissenschaft des Judentums*, 1902–1915   175

DAVID N. MYERS: Hermann Cohen and the Quest for Protestant Judaism   195

ULRICH TEMPEL: Religion and Politics in the Berlin Jewish Community: The Work of the *Repräsentantenversammlung*, 1927–1930   215

IV. ASPECTS OF ANTISEMITISM

GERD KORMAN: When Heredity met the Bacterium: Quarantines in New York and Danzig, 1898–1921   243

ALAN T. LEVENSON: The German Peace Movement and the Jews: An Unexplored Nexus   277

V. MEMOIR

CHANAN BENHAR: 107 Days on the SH-7: Experiences and Events of the
    Last Large Refugee Transport from the *Reichsgebiet*   305

VII.   BIBLIOGRAPHY FOR 2000   333

VIII.   LIST OF CONTRIBUTORS   473

IX.   INDEX   476

ILLUSTRATIONS

The *Repräsentantensaal* of the *Jüdische Gemeinde* in Berlin ... ... Frontispiece
Klemens von Metternich ... ... p. 4
Fanny von Arnstein ... ... p. 6
Salomon von Rothschild ... ... p. 21
Salomon von Rothschild's railway ... ... p. 43
Salomon von Rothschild with a rail map ... ... p. 43
Fanny Lewald ... ... p. 97
August Lewald ... ... p. 97
Jewish boys and girls being confirmed together ... ... p. 122
Main office of the *Jüdische Gemeinde* in Berlin, Oranienburger Strasse ... ... p. 218
Repräsentantensaal ... ... p. 221
Kibetzer cartoon ... ... p. 246
Jewish immigrants approaching Ellis Island, New York ... ... p. 275
Bertha von Suttner ... ... p. 280
Ludwig Quidde ... ... p. 283
Friedrich Wilhelm Foerster ... ... p. 287
Heinrich Coudenhove-Kalergi ... ... p. 294
Cover of Chanan Benhar's diary ... ... p. 304
Author's map of the route taken by the SH-7 ... ... p. 321

Permission to reprint was sought for all illustrations. Copyright holders who could not be ascertained will receive permission fees and acknowledgements if they contact the Leo Baeck Institute.

The Editor

Preface

The great majority of Germany's Jews in the twentieth century were not recent immigrants but had lived for several generations in the German lands. Even today we still do not feel at ease when we speak of different races using the ambiguous term ethnicity. To refer to German Jews as an "ethnic minority" in Germany is a mistaken notion still frequently to be found in contemporary writing. The large population movements in the nineteenth and twentieth centuries in and out of the German lands were a striking phenomenon of the times. The relatively small number of Jewish newcomers from Russia and the Habsburg empire into Germany paled in significance when compared with the great geographical shifts of people that then occurred. It was antisemitism that exaggerated their impact and importance. Immigrants of a different culture, generally not assimilated in the first generation, provide a ready-made weapon for those who wish to stir up strife and hatred. Vicious were the exaggeration and claim that a pure German culture and people being bastardised and subverted by alien "undesirables". In fact immigrants enrich culturally and materially the society which they have joined. The history of the German Jews provides an object lesson of how fragile civilisation really is and how we need to continue to be on our guard against those elements wishing to destroy it, especially by people attacking immigrants and those considered different to themselves.

The labours of the Leo Baeck Insitute and especially of the *Year Book* are not, however, just directed towards the negative. The growing acceptance and prosperity of German Jewry from the eighteenth century until at least the First Word War suggests another picture of relationships which is too often neglected. The contents of this *Year Book* bear convincing evidence how fruitful that relationship was.

This *Year Book* also emphasises how researchers are turning to new issues neglected for far too long. The role of gender to which a whole section is devoted is a striking example. The philosophy and inner life of Judaism has been one of the constant fields of enquiry published in the *Year Book*. For advice and help the editor for the past nine years has relied on the *Year Book*'s Associate Editor, Professor Julius Carlebach. Previous prefaces had been written by us both. His death, just as the *Year Book* goes to press, is a most grievous personal and professional loss.

Professor Julius Carlebach, a long-term member of the Executive of the London Leo Baeck Institute, died on 16 April 2001 at the age of 78. He was born in Hamburg in 1922, scion of the famous orthodox rabbinical family Carlebach. Julius came to England with a Kindertransport in 1939. In the war he served in the Royal Navy. Post-war he worked with the children of the Norwood Jewish Orphanage, later taking up a post in Kenya where he also acted as rabbi to the Jewish community in Nairobi. He continued to work with young people and with the homeless in Africa and, when back in Britain, with young people in trouble. After completing his studies in criminology at Cambridge he embarked on a distinguished academic career as a sociologist and a Judaist, with numerous publications to his credit. When he retired from the University of Sussex he was offered the Rectorship of the newly-founded Hochschule für Jüdische Studien in Heidelberg which, in a tenure of almost a decade, he turned into an eminent seat of Jewish learning. With the appointment of a new editor of the *Year Book* in 1992, Julius became an indispensable Associate Editor; his deep knowledge of Judaism had previously been essential to the *Year Book* for which he served as adviser for some twenty years. He was a wise man and a kindly man, much beloved by his students and by his colleagues.

Professor Werner E. Mosse, of the well-known Mosse family – a name associated with the *Berliner Tageblatt* – was born in Berlin in 1918 and died on 30th April 2001, at the age of 83. He was the Chairman of the London Leo Baeck Institute for some twenty years. Werner came to England in 1933, went to St. Paul's School in London and to Corpus Christi, Cambridge, where he read history, taking a Double First in 1939. After war-time internment in Canada, he served in the British Army as a Liaison Officer in Italy. Returning to academic life, from a Senior Lectureship at Glasgow he moved to a professorship at the University of East Anglia. He was a versatile historian, (a specialist in Russian history) and became deeply involved in the work of the London Leo Baeck Institute when he was appointed in 1960 as the Editor-in-chief of a series of symposium volumes on the development of the "Jewish Question" in modern Germany, the first three of which were edited in collaboration with Arnold Paucker. These firmly put the Institute on the international academic map. Quite apart from Werner's own trenchant monographs, almost all the conferences of the London institute, with their resulting conference volumes, were due to his initiative. A brilliant editor and an inexhaustible source of ideas, he inspired and guided our work for so many years. Even our next "Oxbridge" conference – at Clare College, Cambridge – was originally his conception, and will now be dedicated to his memory.

Julius Carlebach and Werner Mosse are deeply mourned by us all.

John Grenville   *Arnold Paucker*

As in previous years the Editor wishes to express the gratitude of the Institute to the unswerving support of the *Bundesministerium des Innern* and the *Ständige Konferenz der Kultusminister der Länder in der Bundesrepublik Deutschland* which make it possible for the *Year Book* to be affordable and so continue to enjoy a wide distribution throughout the world.

Jews in the Age of Metternich

The Pernicious Rift: Metternich and the Debate about Jewish Emancipation at the Congress of Vienna[1]

BY EDWARD TIMMS

Historians have argued that the principal error committed at the Congress of Vienna was Article 13 of the Federal Act – the Act which created the German Federation. This article appeared to promise constitutional reform, but actually had the effect of inhibiting the emergence of democracy in Germany. It took the form of a single-sentence declaration: "In all German states a constitution based on the estates will come into being." ("In allen deutschen Staaten wird eine landesständische Verfassung stattfinden.") The progressive implications of the word "Verfassung" ("constitution") were nullified by the reference to the system of "estates" ("Stände"), the representatives of traditional elites. Moreover, the insistence on the independence of more than thirty German states, each retaining its own sovereignty, frustrated the longing for national unity. Article 13 thus proved an empty promise, and during the following decades Metternich, through his control of the Federation, frustrated all attempts to introduce more liberal government.

However, the Federal Act also contained a flaw of a rather different kind, embodied in Article 16, which dealt with Jewish civil rights. This, too, appeared to hold out the promise of reform:

> Die Bundesversammlung wird in Berathung ziehen, wie, auf eine möglichst übereinstimmende Weise, die bürgerliche Verbesserung der Bekenner des jüdischen Glaubens in Teutschland zu bewirken sey, und wie insbesonderheit denselben der Genuß der bürgerlichen Rechte, gegen die Uebernahme aller Bürgerpflichten, in den Bundesstaaten verschafft und gesichert werden könne. Jedoch werden den Bekennern dieses Glaubens, bis dahin, die denselben von den einzelnen Bundesstaaten bereits eingeräumten Rechte erhalten.[2]

> The Federal Assembly will consult about the ways in which the civic improvement of members of the Jewish faith may be achieved in Germany in as uniform a way as possible and more specifically how they can be granted and guaranteed the enjoyment of civil rights in return for their acceptance of all civic duties. Until this occurs, the members of that faith will still retain the rights which have already been granted them by the individual states of the Federation.

---

[1]The essays in this section were originally presented as papers at a conference on "Progress and Emancipation in the Age of Metternich: Jews and Modernization in Austria and Germany 1815–1848", held at the Centre for German-Jewish Studies at the University of Sussex in April 1999. The Editor wishes to thank Dr. J. A. Hughes of Sussex University for assisting with the editing of the articles in this section.
[2]Salo Baron, *Die Judenfrage auf dem Wiener Kongreß: Auf Grund von zum Teil ungedruckten Quellen dargestellt*, Berlin and Vienna 1920, pp. 169–170.

Klemens von Metternich

The convoluted phrasing was to have even more fateful consequences for progress and emancipation in Germany than the delusive promise of a constitution. Article 16 reads like a commitment to the implementation of full civil rights, but its ambiguities become all too evident when its genesis is reconstructed and its phrasing decoded.

The Congress of Vienna, attended by representatives of the German states as well as the major European powers, provided an opportunity to sweep away the discriminatory laws which had for centuries imposed such burdens on German Jews. The first tentative steps had already been taken during the preceding forty years: by Joseph II with his edict of toleration in 1781, by Napoleon, when he extended the emancipatory principles of the French Revolution to the French-occupied territories of the Rhineland and parts of northern Germany, and by King Fredrick William's famous edict of 1812 in Prussia. These reforms created a powerful momentum for change, and the Congress provided an opportunity to extend these reforms throughout the German-speaking lands. The Prussian delegation was led by Prince Karl von Hardenberg, the enlightened reformer who had prevailed on Fredrick William to sign the Edict of 1812, abolishing at a stroke the most onerous restrictions on the Jews of Prussia. Hardenberg was supported by a man of even more liberal outlook, the educational reformer Wilhelm von Humboldt. If the Prussians and the Austrians, briefed by representatives of the Jewish communites from Vienna, Prague and Frankfurt am Main, succeeded in joining forces, there seemed no reason why civil rights should not be extended to Jewish citizens throughout the new German

Federation. This, as Salo Baron showed in his pioneering monograph on the Jewish Question at the Congress of Vienna, was a moment of unprecedented opportunity.[3]

Baron's book prompts reflection not only on the debate about Jewish civil rights at the Congress of Vienna, but also on the significance assigned to it in German historiography. Rather surprisingly, this debate has been marginalised by mainstream historians. There are scores of books about the congress, but very few that acknowledge the long-term implications of Article 16. There are dozens of analyses of the diplomacy of Metternich, but scarcely any discussion of his involvement with the debates about Jewish emancipation. It is hard to find a single reference to this question in the monumental two-volume biography of Metternich by the Austrian historian Heinrich von Srbik, which runs to fourteen hundred pages. It is the glamour of foreign policy that has fascinated the historians, even those who have experienced the consequences of anti-Jewish discrimination. Henry Kissinger's study of Metternich's diplomacy, *A World Restored*, does not make a single reference to the issue of Jewish civil rights. British commentators have been equally cavalier. In Harold Nicholson's *The Congress of Vienna* the matter is barely mentioned, while in Alan Palmer's 400-page biography of Metternich it is dismissed as if it were no more significant than the new regulations for the navigation of the Rhine.[4] Even in more specialised studies like David Sorkin's *The Transformation of German Jewry 1780–1840* the debates about Jewish emancipation at the Congress of Vienna are summarised in a couple of paragraphs.[5] One of the few historians to review the matter in any detail is Enno E. Kraehe in his two-volume study, *Metternich's German Policy*. But this, too, deals mainly with the territorial and constitutional questions which preoccupied the statesmen attending the congress, the partitioning of Saxony and the creation of the Federal Diet. Kraehe attaches no special significance to the efforts of Austria and Prussia to improve the position of the Jews, apart from noting that their efforts proved "inadequate".[6]

The reason for this neglect is not hard to understand. Historians can scarcely be expected to analyse events which did *not* happen, and the emancipation of the German Jews is the great "might-have-been" of the congress. We have to turn to more imaginative writers for a reminder that the most significant event may be what did not happen – the dog that did not bark in the night. One of the most illuminating accounts of the debate about Jewish emancipation is provided by by Hilde Spiel, the Austrian novelist who spent many years in exile in Britain and wrote an admirable biography of Fanny von Arnstein, *Fanny von Arnstein oder die Emanzipation: Ein Frauenleben an der Zeitenwende, 1758–1818*. As a Prussian Jewess married to an Austrian banker, Fanny became one of the great hostesses at the Congress of Vienna. After describing how the Arnstein salon became a meeting place for members of the political elite, especially the representatives of Prussia, Spiel recalls the

---

[3]*ibid.*, p. 85.
[4]Harold Nicholson, *The Congress of Vienna: A Study in Allied Unity 1812–1822*, London 1946, p. 216; Alan Palmer, *Metternich*, London 1972, p. 146.
[5]David Sorkin, *The Transformation of German Jewry 1780–1840*, New York 1987, pp. 33–34.
[6]Enno E. Kraehe, *Metternich's German Policy*, vol. II: 'The Congress of Vienna, 1814–1815', Princeton, NJ 1983, p. 382.

Fanny von Arnstein

two issues which were closest to Fanny's heart. The first, the Prussian claim to the territories of Saxony, dominated the whole congress, but it is the second question that is given greater prominence by Spiel:

> Die andere Frage war so nebensächlich, daß kaum jemand sie wichtig oder auch nur ernst nehmen mochte. Ja, als sie, nachdem die ersten Verhandlungen darüber im Herbst abgebrochen worden waren, Ende Mai noch einmal vor den Ausschuß deutscher Länder kam, fing der bayrische Graf Rechberg zu lachen an, "und das Gelächter wurde ansteckend und ging die Reihe herum bis auf ein paar". Der Gegenstand des Spottes waren, wie von alters her, die Juden. Ihre bürgerliche Gleichstellung, die in Preußen durchgeführt war, auf das übrige Deutschland auszudehnen, hatten sich Hardenberg und Humboldt zur Aufgabe gemacht.[7]

The second question was so marginal that hardly anyone regarded it as important or even took it seriously. Indeed, when it was once again placed before the German Committee in May [1815], after the first discussion of the matter the previous autumn had been adjourned, the Bavarian representative, Count Rechberg, began to laugh "and the mocking laughter proved infectious and spread to all those sitting around the table with a few exceptions". The targets of mockery were, then as from time immemorial, the Jews. Their civil emancipation, which had been achieved in Prussia, was to be extended to the rest of Germany: this was the task that Hardenberg and Humboldt had set themselves.

---

[7]Hilde Spiel, *Fanny von Arnstein oder die Emanzipation: Ein Frauenleben an der Zeitenwende, 1758–1818*, Frankfurt 1992, p. 429.

Spiel has not invented this scene (her quotation is taken from an authentic source).[8] But she uses it to show that Jewish civil rights were regarded as a trivial issue by most of the politicians who were engaged in creating a new Germany. They failed to recognise that the political evolution of Germany and the civil emancipation of the Jews were interdependent processes. Indeed, the frustration of proposals for Jewish civil rights at the Congress of Vienna resulted in an unresolved tension between reactionary and modernising agendas which was to resurface during the revolutionary upheavals of 1848.

In a famous speech to the Frankfurt National Assembly in 1848, the campaigner for civil rights, Gabriel Riesser, identified what he saw as the "pernicious rift" ("der verderbliche Riß") in the development of German democracy – the imposition of discriminatory laws on the Jewish minority. After Moritz Mohl, a Protestant deputy from Wurtemberg, had proposed that Jews should still be subject to discriminatory legislation, Riesser responded with an eloquent speech which culminated in the warning:

> Glauben Sie nicht, daß sich Ausnahmsgesetze machen lassen, ohne daß das ganze System der Freiheit einen verderblichen Riß erhalten, ohne daß der Keim des Verderbens in dasselbe gelegt würde.[9]

> You must not believe that you can enact discriminatory laws without the whole system of freedom suffering a pernicious rift and having implanted within it the seeds of its own destruction.

Riesser's analysis was to prove prophetic. His proposals for Jewish emancipation were so persuasive that they were approved by the National Assembly, some of whose leading members, like Riesser himself, were lawyers committed to the principle of civic equality.[10] But the Frankfurt reforms were blocked by the counter-revolution of 1849, and Jewish emancipation was delayed for a further twenty years – at grievous cost to the cause of German liberalism.

Riesser realised that it is necessary to return to the debates of 1815 if we are to understand the origins of that fateful rift. This is the crucial insight expressed in his pamphlet *Ueber die Stellung der Bekenner des Mosaischen Glaubens in Deutschland*, to which we shall have reason to return. Writing in 1831, Riesser describes Article 16 of the Final Act as "a point which has been neglected in an incomprehensible way" ("ein […] auf eine unbegreifliche Weise vernachlässigter Punkt").[11] If the debate about Jewish rights has tended to be ignored, this is because it was regarded as an internal matter which did not concern the other European powers that attended the Congress, led by Tsar Alexander, Talleyrand and Castlereagh. It was a matter for the German Committee and in that sense appeared rather parochial. But the discussions of the German Committee proved in the longer term to be of exceptional significance.

---

[8]See Baron, p. 156.
[9]*Stenographischer Bericht über die Verhandlungen der deutschen constituierenden Nationalversammlung zu Frankfurt am Main*, vol. III, p. 1757.
[10]See Frank Eyck, *The Frankfurt Parliament 1848–1849*, London 1968, pp. 241–245.
[11]Gabriel Riesser, *Ueber die Stellung der Bekenner des Mosaischen Glaubens in Deutschland* in Riesser, *Gesammelte Schriften*, Leipzig 1867–1868, vol. II, p. 54.

The congress lasted for almost nine months, but the work of the German Committee, whose principal task was to create a new constitution for the German Federation, was concentrated into two short and distinct phases. The first lasted from 14 October to 24 November 1814. During these six weeks the meetings were attended only by representatives of the leading German states: Austria, Prussia, Bavaria, Wurtemberg and Hanover. These meetings were suspended at the end of November as a result of the crisis over Prussian claims to Saxony and the problem of the future of Poland, which placed Prussia and Austria in antagonistic camps. The Saxon/Polish issue proved so divisive that it inhibited the discussion of other matters for a full five months, and the German Committee did not reassemble until May 1815, when it was expanded to include a dozen further members. Between 23 May and 10 June 1815 there followed eleven further meetings, crammed into an intensive period of twenty days, during which the status of the Jews was repeatedly discussed. The nature of these discussions can be clarified by reference to three competing models for Jewish emancipation, which may be termed "gradualist", "interventionist" and "particularist".

The first, associated with Christian Wilhelm Dohm, was the gradualist conception of "bürgerliche Verbesserung" – the theme of his famous book of 1783 arguing in support of the "civil improvement" of the Jews, as a precondition to their legal emancipation. Dohm did not himself attend the congress, but his ideas provided a defining framework for the discussions of the German Committee. It is his model of civic improvement that historians like Peter Pulzer have in mind when they speak of the "emancipation contract".[12] However, it is worth noting that the word "Emanzipation" was not commonly used in this context until the 1820s.[13] The word "emancipation" serves as a convenient shorthand for the movement to improve the social, economic and political rights of members of the Jewish faith, but it is important to analyse the precise arguments that were used to promote – or to frustrate – this process. There was a crucial ambiguity in the message to the Jews implied by the emancipation contract: only when your social and moral behaviour has improved will you be granted civil rights. This appeared to be a progressive principle, holding out the promise that equality could be attained through a protracted process of education. But the claim that Jews were not yet ready for German citizenship really meant that German Christians were not ready to accept Jews as fellow citizens, and the conditional model of civic improvement provided a pretext for postponing Jewish emancipation indefinitely.

With hindsight, it is easy to see that the pursuit of civic improvement would prove delusory, since – with every advance made by members of the Jewish community – the criteria for acceptance could be reformulated so that the final goal remained tantalisingly beyond reach. However, there was one person at the Congress of Vienna

---

[12]Peter Pulzer, 'Emancipation and its Discontents: The German-Jewish Dilemma', in *idem*, *The German-Jewish Dilemma: From the Enlightenment to the Shoah*, Lampeter 1999, p. 10.

[13]The phrase "Emanzipation der Juden" has been traced back to the pamphlet by Wilhelm Traugott, *Ueber das Verhältnis verschiedener Religionsparteien zum Staate und über die Emanzipation der Juden*, Jena 1828. See *Historisches Lexikon zur politisch-sozialen Sprache in Deutschland*, ed. Otto Brunner, Werner Conze and Reinhart Koselleck, 8 vols, Stuttgart 1972–1997, vol. II, pp. 178–185.

who already grasped the problem inherent in the gradualist model – Wilhelm von Humboldt, representative of Prussia. Humboldt was the most eloquent spokesman for the "interventionist" model of emancipation, since he perceived the fallacy inherent in gradualism. In a memorable analysis of the question of Jewish rights written in 1809, Humboldt had argued that Jewish emancipation should be achieved by means of a single "leap" – a "sudden declaration" that their rights should be identical with those of non-Jews. He summed up his arguments under three heads. The principle of unrestricted equality, he argues, is

> Gerecht: denn es läßt sich kein Rechtsgrund denken, warum der Jude, der alle Pflichten der Christen erfüllen will, nicht auch der Rechte teilhaftig sein soll.
>
> Politisch: denn diejenigen, die nicht viritim und persönlich, sondern aus Vorurtheil, und weil sie, als zu einer Classe gehörig, die Schuld ihrer Mitbürger tragen müssen, verachtet werden, zu der, selbst zur Moralität nötigen Achtung zu bringen, ist ein Sprung, eine plötzliche Erklärung nötig.
>
> Consequent: denn eine allmähliche Aufhebung bestätigt die Absonderung, die sie vernichten will, in allen nicht mit aufgehobenen Punkten, verdoppelt gerade durch die neue größere Freiheit, die Aufmerksamkeit auf die noch bestehende Beschränkung, und arbeitet dadurch sich selbst entgegen.[14]
>
> Legally just: for it is impossible to conceive of any legal reason why the Jew who is willing to fulfil all the duties of Christians should not also enjoy the same rights.
>
> Politically expedient: for in order to gain the respect which is necessary even for morality on behalf of those who are despised – not for any valid or personal reason, but as a result of prejudice and because, as members of a group, they have to bear the guilt of their brothers – a leap, a sudden declaration is needed.
>
> Logically consistent: for a gradual process of emancipation has the effect of confirming the separation which it is designed to remove, with respect to all the matters excluded from emancipation, and precisely as a result of the new increase in freedom it accentuates the restrictions which still remain, so that it becomes self-defeating.

Humboldt's style may be tortuous, but his argument is perceptive, especially on the self-defeating consequences of gradualism. He does not simply repudiate the "civic improvement" model but reverses its fundamental premise, arguing that political rights should come first and moral improvement will then follow.

The critique of gradualism was formulated even more incisively by Dr Carl August Buchholz, a young Christian lawyer from Lübeck who had made a study of all the emancipatory edicts of the recent past, which he published in 1815 under the title *Aktenstükke die Verbesserung des bürgerlichen Zustandes der Israeliten betreffend*. Buchholz also attended the congress, as representative of the Jewish communities of Hamburg, Lübeck and Bremen, and his essential argument was that the legal status of the Jews had to be reformed first. Using a striking metaphor he compares the position of the Jews to that of a person who has been unjustly imprisoned:

---

[14]Baron, pp. 82–83.

So wenig der unschuldig Eingesperrte, von seinem den Irrtum später erkennenden Richter, länger im Kerker um deswillen detiniert werden darf, weil er nun erst an den Gebrauch der Freiheit gewöhnt, und daß seinem Gemüt erst die nachteiligen Folgen der getragenen Sklavenkette verwischt werden müßten, so wenig darf es hier geschehen.

Just as the innocent prisoner should not be detained any longer by the judge who later recognises his mistake, simply because it will take some time for him to get used to his freedom and for his spirit to recover from the noxious effects of the chains which enslaved him, so equally here [in the matter of Jewish emancipation] there should be no delay.

Buchholz, a follower of Moses Mendelssohn and the universalist principles of the Enlightenment, went on to argue that the emancipation of the Jews should be carried out in a uniform way throughout Germany and that there was no reason why Jews should not also be admitted to positions in the civil service.[15]

When the congress began in autumn 1814, it looked as though these arguments would carry the day, since they had the backing of the most reform-minded politician to attend the congress, Humboldt's Prussian colleague Karl von Hardenberg. At the first meetings of the German Committee, only attended by the five leading states, Prussia seized the initiative, supported by Austria and Hannover, arguing for radical emancipation of the Jews. The representatives of Bavaria and Wurtemberg were opposed, but there was a real prospect of the reform being pushed through, not least because Metternich himself supported the moves towards emancipation. To understand his position, we must take a closer look at the lobbying that was going on behind the scenes, particularly by opponents of Jewish emancipation who were committed to a third and very different conception of civil rights, the "particularist" model.

"Particularism" is the English translation of "Kleinstaaterei", the principle that small independent states should be entitled to take their own decisions. Some of the German states of the early nineteenth century were very small indeed, one of the least significant being the free city of Bremen with a population of about 50,000. But it was precisely the representative of Bremen, Dr Johann Smidt, who emerged at the Congress of Vienna as the most forceful advocate of particularism. The basic position was that the Christian merchants of Bremen disliked the competition of Jews who had recently settled in their town and wanted to expel them. Being a lawyer, Smidt pitched his argument more plausibly, insisting that Bremen, like Lübeck and Hamburg, was entitled to determine its own principles of government. He was thus able to conceal the motives of religious prejudice and economic rivalry behind the claim that he was defending civic autonomy.

It may seem strange that a representative from the Hanseatic cities should have exerted such influence at the congress. But Hamburg, Bremen and Lübeck had been under French military occupation for several years, and it was a matter of principle that their territorial integrity should be restored. The insistence on the independence of the free cities placed Prussia and Austria in a dilemma when they attempted to restrict the right of the city councils to regulate their internal affairs. As soon as the French troops had withdrawn from Hamburg, Lübeck and Bremen, the local wor-

---

[15]*ibid.*, pp. 112–115.

thies set about the task of reversing the most significant political reforms introduced by the invaders: the provisions of Napoleon's civil code which emancipated the Jews. It is clear that the antagonism towards France had the effect of intensifying hostility towards France's alleged protégés, the Jews. A similar move was made by the city council of Frankfurt, where in December 1811 the Jews had been granted the same rights as their Christian fellow citizens. The representative of Frankfurt on the German Committee, Syndikus Danz, denounced this reform as a scandalous infringement of the rights of his Christian fellow citizens.[16]

These events filled the reformers with alarm, since Hardenberg's aim was to extend the Prussian emancipation Edict of 1812 to the whole of north Germany. On 4 January 1815 he sent a strong note to the Hanseatic cities through the Prussian emissary in Hamburg, Graf Grote, criticising the prejudices underlying anti-Jewish legislation:

> Die Schicksale der Juden in den übrigen Provinzen des nördlichen Deutschlands können seitdem [seit dem Edikt von 1812] dem preußischen Staat nicht gleichgültig seyn, weil durch die fortdauernde Bedrückung und gehässige Ausschließung von den Rechten, auf welche sie als Menschen einen Anspruch haben, der ihnen zum Vorwurf gemachte Zustand der Immoralität verlängert, und die Absicht unserer Regierung vereitelt wird, durch Teilnahme an allen bürgerlichen Rechten und Lasten, die Spuren eines Vorwurfs zu erlöschen, der nur aus einer verächtlichen und knechtischen Behandlung hervorgegangen ist. Auch hat die Geschichte unseres letzten Krieges wider Frankreich bereits erwiesen, daß sie des Staates, der sie in seinen Schoß aufgenommen, durch treue Anhänglichkeit würdig geworden.[17]

> Since the Edict of 1812 the destinies of the Jews in the other provinces of northern Germany cannot be a matter of indifference to the Prussian state, since their alleged condition of immorality is made to persist through their continuing oppression and malicious exclusion from the rights which they can claim as human beings. This also has the effect of frustrating the intention of our government to extinguish all traces of an alleged failing, which is merely a consequence of their demeaning and humiliating treatment, by granting them access to all civil rights and burdens. Moreover, the history of our last war against France has demonstrated that they are worthy of the state which has accepted them into its bosom through their loyal allegiance.

Three weeks later, on 26 January 1815, Metternich followed suit, sending a strongly-worded memorandum to the city councils of Hamburg, Bremen and Lübeck:

> In dem Augenblick, wo die jüdischen Glaubensgenossen eine nach liberalen Grundsätzen berechnete Bestimmung ihrer Verhältnisse und Rechte von dem hier versammelten Kongreß zu erwarten berechtigt sind, hat es mir nicht gleichgültig seyn können, die Bedrückungen zu erfahren, welche die jüdischen Einwohner in Hamburg, Bremen und Lübeck zu erleiden haben. Ich fühle mich um so mehr zur Theilnahme an ihrem Schicksal aufgefordert, als in der österreichischen Monarchie so wie in mehreren anderen Staaten Deutschlands die jüdischen Gemeinden schon längst sich einer den Forderungen der Menschlichkeit, dem Bedürfnis der Zeit und einem väterlichen Regierungs-System angemessenen Behandlung sich zu erfreuen haben, und der Druck, den die Häuser dieser Nation in einigen Orten in Deutschland leiden, auf die unter dem schützenden

---

[16] *ibid.*, p. 163.
[17] *ibid.*, p. 88.

Szepter Österreichs lebenden jüdischen Familien, der engen mit jenen bestehenden Handelsverbindungen wegen, eine höchst nachtheilige Einwürkung haben müßte.[18]

At the moment when the members of the Jewish faith are entitled to expect from the Congress here assembled a determination of their circumstances and rights in accordance with liberal principles, it cannot be a matter of indifference to me to learn of the oppression which the Jewish population of Hamburg, Bremen and Lübeck have to suffer. I feel all the more strongly called upon to sympathise with their fate because in the Austrian monarchy as in several other states of Germany the Jewish communities have long enjoyed a treatment which accords with the requirements of humanity, the demands of the age and a paternal system of government. Moreover, as a result of the close commercial ties which exist between them, the pressure which the houses of this nation are suffering in some places in Germany must have a highly disadvantageous effect on the Jewish families living under the protective sceptre of Austria.

Metternich goes on to appeal to the Hanseatic towns to cease their oppressive actions against the Jews and leave their existing rights intact until a final decision has been taken about the future constitution of Germany.

The reference to "liberal principles" in this memorandum will come as a surprise to those who regard Metternich as an incorrigible reactionary. It is clear that he and Hardenberg, invoking the principles of the Enlightenment, were taking a similar line on the question of Jewish civil rights, with a slight difference of emphasis. Basing their arguments on a humanistic concept of "Menschlichkeit", they also acknowledge the patriotism shown by Jews during the wars against France and the commercial importance of Jewish merchants and banking houses. Hardenberg invokes the Prussian edict of 1812 as the basis for reforms which should be extended to the other states of the German Federation. Metternich's position is more paternalistic, and he exaggerates the reforms already introduced under the benevolent sceptre of Austria, which were in reality far less liberal than in Prussia. But he did not hestitate to intervene on behalf of beleaguered Jewish communities, both during the congress and on subsequent occasions. At the Diet in Frankfurt and at the Congress of Aix-la-Chapelle of 1818 he made renewed attempts to improve the legal status of the Jews of Germany. And in 1840, during the Damascus Affair, Metternich threw the full weight of Austrian diplomacy behind the cause of the persecuted Jews of the Middle East. The conclusion reached by the most exhaustive study of this affair is that the "state that provided the Damascus Jews with their most consistent, and at times courageous, support was the Habsburg Empire".[19]

Metternich's reference to the "Jewish families" of Austria reflects his close rapport with the heads of the three leading banking houses of Vienna – Nathan von Arnstein, Bernhard von Eskeles and Leopold von Herz, all three of them already ennobled for their services to the state. The most interesting events at conferences often unfold behind the scenes, and this was certainly the case at the Congress of Vienna. When Wellington arrived in Vienna early in February 1815, Metternich

---

[18]*ibid.*, p. 92.
[19]Jonathan Frankel, *The Damascus Affair: "Ritual Murder", Politics and the Jews in 1840*, Cambridge 1997, p. 440.

almost immediately took both the Duke and the other principal British representative, Viscount Castlereagh, to visit Leopold von Herz.[20] The salons of Fanny von Arnstein and Cäcilie von Eskeles also formed the scene of very active lobbying on behalf of the Jewish cause, as well as that of Prussia. Metternich received a more formal appeal in support of Jewish rights, signed not only by Arnstein, Eskeles and Herz, but also by Lazar Auspitz of Brünn and Simon von Lämel of Prague. Their argument, in an extended memorandum dated 11 April 1815 and addressed to the Emperor, began by summarising the achievements of the Austrian Jews: the numerous workshops created by their industriousness in several provinces of the monarchy, their extensive factory buildings, the extent of their foreign trade connections, their sacrifice for the common good, their investment in the education of the young and, not least, the blood shed by Jews in defence of their fatherland which refutes the claim that they are unsuitable for military service. In short:

> Wir haben jede Probe bestanden: und wenn uns heute noch eine demütigende Scheidewand von anderen Staatsbürgern absondert, so besteht diese nur in veralteten Meynungen, oder blinder und grundloser Furcht vor einer dem kleinlichen Privatinteresse gefährlich scheinenden, für das ganze offenbar wohltätigen Concurrenz; in Ew. Majestät großer Seele ist diese Scheidewand längst darnieder gerissen.

> We have passed every test: and if today a humiliating barrier separates us from other citizens, this consists only in out-of-date opinions or blind and groundless fears of an economic competition which may appear threatening to small-minded private interests but is obviously beneficial to society as a whole; in Your Majesty's noble soul this barrier has long since been torn down.

On this basis they appealed both to the Emperor and to Metternich to support the proposals which were being put to the Congress to include "complete equality of rights between Jews and members of other faiths" ("vollständige Gleichheit der Rechte") in the new German constitution, including the German territories of Austria.[21] It is an eloquent document, based on general principles but also suggesting possible compromise solutions. It should be added that these interventions by the Jewish notables were not confined to words. Influential figures at the conference, most notoriously Friedrich von Gentz, also accepted substantial financial inducements in return for promises to support the Jewish cause.

It was not the intrigues of Gentz, but the principled arguments of Wilhelm von Humboldt that carried most weight during the debate about Jewish civil rights. In a letter to his wife on 4 June 1815, Humboldt describes how at meetings of the German Committee he pushed through the article promising improved rights for the Jews in the face of all opposition, even when Metternich had "almost given up the cause". This is the famous letter in which Humboldt recalls that he and his brother Alexander had been "defenders of Jewry" ("Schutzwehre des Judentums") ever since their childhood. But Humboldt also emphasises his more pragmatic motive: it will be better for Prussia if the provisions of the Edict of 1812 are extended throughout

---

[20] Baron, pp. 134–135.
[21] *ibid.*, pp. 141–144.

Germany, since otherwise there is a danger that a flood of Jews will want to move there from other states. In this same letter Humboldt describes how he has been briefed by a Jewish gentleman of the old school who has visited him a number of times and to whom he has taken a particular liking, Simon von Lämel. In contrast to Gentz, however, Humboldt refused to accept any remuneration.

Although Humboldt could be justly proud of his efforts to promote the cause of Jewish emancipation, the tortuous final stages of the debate about Jewish civil rights frustrated his fundamental aim. His intentions are most clearly expressed in the Prussian proposal for religious equality drafted on 30 April:

> Die drei christlichen Religionsparteien genießen in allen deutschen Staaten gleiche Rechte, und den Bekennern des jüdischen Glaubens werden, in so fern sie sich der Leistung aller Bürgerpflichten unterziehen, die denselben entsprechenden Bürgerrechte eingeräumt.
>
> The three Christian religious factions enjoy equal rights in all German states, and rights of citizenship are conceded to the members of the Jewish faith in so far as they submit to the fulfilment of all the duties of citizens.

This draft marked a breakthrough both in form and content. It included Jewish rights within the same framework as those of the Christian confessions, and the only condition it imposes is that equal rights presuppose the fulfilment of equal duties. When this draft was sent to Metternich, it was approved with minor modifications.[22] Unfortunately, the enlightened intentions of Hardenberg, Humboldt and Metternich were frustrated when the German Committee reconvened on 23 May 1815. The Committee was no longer dominated by the great powers, for it had been expanded to include a clutch of further members. Thus the opponents of reform, Bavaria and Wurtemberg, could now count on the support of the representatives of a dozen smaller German states, anxious to defend their autonomy. If Metternich had truly been an autocrat, he might have attempted to impose his views. Instead, the Committee became a disorganised convoy, obliged to advance at the speed of its slowest member, with the representatives of the smaller German territories resisting progress towards emancipation. Reformers like Humboldt might claim the moral high ground, but the obstructionists, led by Smidt, were the more effective tacticians.

The debates unfolded in the atmosphere of panic created by Napoleon's return to France. In March 1815 he had escaped from Elba and began to rally his troops, confronting the other European powers with the need for immediate concerted action both on the political and the military fronts. Suddenly, at a Congress which had become notorious for time-wasting, there was an urgent need to reach decisions. Under pressure of time, the proposals for Jewish civil rights were repeatedly amended by the German Committee and a compromise agreement emerged which found final expression in Article 16. This appeared to be a victory for the gradualist model: there would be no immediate transformation of the status of the Jews, but the matter would be debated again by the Diet of the German Federation, which was to meet in Frankfurt am Main, with the aim of introducing uniform legislation for the whole of Germany.

---

[22] *ibid.*, p. 150.

Metternich's intentions are clear from the letter which he wrote on 9 June 1815 to Buchholz, the representative of the Hanseatic Jews:

> Die auf dem Congress allhier versammelten hohen Mächte, auch für das Wohl der einzelnen besorgt, haben beschlossen, dass den jüdischen Glaubensgenossen in den deutschen Bundesstaaten die allgemeinen bürgerlichen Rechte zugesichert werden. Da aber die Zeitumstände die völlige Ausführung dieses Gegenstandes auf dem Congress in Wien unmöglich machten, so wurde vorläufig in der Bundesacte bestimmt und festgesetzt, dass auf dem deutschen Bundestage in Frankfurt am Main in Berathung gezogen werden soll, auf welche Art die allgemeinen bürgerlichen Rechte den israelitischen Gemeinden in Deutschland zu ertheilen sind und dass bis zum Ausgang dieser Berathung die den israelitischen Gemeinden in den verschiedenen Bundesstaaten bewilligten Freiheiten und Rechte aufrecht erhalten werden sollen.[23]

> The high powers assembled here at the Congress, also concerned for the well-being of individuals, have resolved that members of the Jewish faith in the states of the German Federation will be granted general civil rights. However, since pressures of time made it impossible to complete the implementation of this matter, it was resolved and recorded in the Federal Act that consultations should take place at the Federal Diet in Frankfurt am Main about the way in which general civil rights should be conferred on the Jewish communities in Germany and that pending the completion of this consultation process the freedoms and rights which have been granted to the Jewish communities in the various states of the Federation should be preserved.

Metternich's interpretation of Article 16 proved unduly optimistic. This statesman so celebrated for his diplomatic finesse had actually been outmanoeuvred by a provincial city councillor, Johann Smidt from Bremen. Smidt was not only a forceful negotiator but also a cunning draftsman, and it was one of the great misfortunes of the Congress that he was assigned the duty of actually drafting Article 16 in its final form. At the last moment he succeeded in inserting a change in the wording so miniscule that its significance passed unnoticed at the time, although it was to have the most momentous consequences. He replaced the phrase "rights granted in the individual states" with the phrase "rights granted *by* the individual states". Thus he smuggled the particularist principle back into the text and succeeded, at the stroke of a pen, in excluding from the agreement all the emancipatory measures which had been introduced not by the states themselves but under the French occupation – precisely the outcome which Metternich and Hardenberg had made such efforts to avoid. When Napoleon's forces withdrew from the Netherlands, the beneficent provisions of the French civil code were left intact and the rights of Jewish citizens preserved. But in Germany after 1815 the hatred of France which had inspired the War of Liberation became transferred to those who were perceived as France's protégés, and German nationalism became suffused with anti-Jewish sentiments.

We can now see more clearly the connections between the two flawed Articles in the Federal Act which undermined all hope of progress and emancipation. The backlash provoked by Article 13, the clause which frustrated political unity and constitutional government, features prominently in every history book: the nationalism

---

[23]*ibid.*, pp. 193–194.

of Arndt, Jahn and the Burschenschaften, the patriotic Wartburgfest of 1817 during which a procession of students solemnly burned the Federal Act, the assassination of Kotzebue by a fanatical student named Karl Sand in March 1819, and the Carlsbad decrees of August 1819, which imposed controls on the universities and censorship of the press throughout the German Federation. Srbik devotes some of his most eloquent pages to describing how frustrated patriots sought to mobilise the German university students and gymnastic clubs, much to the horror of Metternich, who denounced them as dangerous Jacobins.[24] But historians have failed to make the connection with the even more violent backlash associated with Article 16, which left the Jews exposed as potential targets for the resentments of the frustrated nationalists.

The debate about civil rights for the Jews did not remain confined to the committee room. It spilled over into the public arena and became a dominant issue in the press and the universities, city councils, churches and theatres. In February 1815, while the Congress was still in progress, Friedrich Rühs, Professor of History at the University of Berlin, published a pamphlet denouncing the 'Claims of the Jews to German Citizenship' – *Ansprüche der Juden auf das deutsche Bürgerrecht*. Once the battle to block Jewish emancipation had been won, there was a flood of further anti-Jewish publications. In 1816 a particularly virulent tirade was published by Friedrich Fries, Professor of Natural Science at Heidelberg, *Gefährdung des Wohlstandes und des Charakters der Deutschen durch die Juden*. At the same time the Senates of the most important German states and cities exploited the loophole in Article 16 to remove from the Jews the rights which they had so recently been granted.

Events in Frankfurt illustrate the consequences of the failure in Vienna most clearly. There were 3000 Jews living in the city, and as a result of the reforms of December 1811 over six hundred of them had been sworn in as full citizens. After the withdrawal of French troops their privileges were rescinded, and in October 1816 a new constitution was approved by the Senate which totally excluded them from citizenship. Among the many anti-Jewish tracts of this period was a pamphlet by two respected members of the Senate, *Ansichten und Bemerkungen über die bürgerlichen Rechts-Verhältnisse der Juden in der freyen Stadt Frankfurt am Main*. In a characteristic passage they declared that "the machinations of these money-grabbing nomads are solely directed towards the ruin of the Christians". ("Denn das Trachten dieser geldgierigen Nomaden ist nur auf das Verderben der Christen gerichtet"). Another typical publication was a play entitled *Jakobs Kriegstaten (Jacob's Military Eploits)*, by a Frankfurt parson named Gerhard Friedrich, a caricature of a cowardly Jew who is captured by the French and becomes a spy.[25] It was this post-Congress flood of anti-Jewish pamplets and plays, written by representatives of government, churches and universities, which prepared the ground for the anti-Jewish riots of August 1819. The riots were started by students at the University of Würzburg, but they quickly spread to other cities in German cities, including Frankfurt. Even more distressing were the developments in Prussia. Humboldt's view that the reforms in Prussia could only be consolidated if

---

[24]Heinrich Ritter von Srbik, *Metternich, der Staatsmann und der Mensch*, 3 vols, Munich 1957, vol. I, pp. 576–598.

[25]Rachel Heuberger and Helga Krohn, *Hinaus aus dem Ghetto. Juden in Frankfurt am Main 1800–1950*, Frankfurt 1988, pp. 33–35.

they were extended to the whole of north Germany proved justified, and during the following years the provisions of the Edict of 1812 were steadily eroded.

Rational views of history presuppose that great events must have great causes. The frustration of the proposals for Jewish emancipation at the Congress of Vienna was certainly an event with far-reaching consequences. It not only set back the cause of reform by several decades but threw a pall over Christian-Jewish relations in Germany from which they were never to recover. But this momentous outcome resulted not from some great confrontation between major powers, but from petty squabbling and double dealing in committee. Nothing could be more narrow-minded than the arguments used by Smidt, who described the appearance and behaviour of the handful of Jews he had encountered in Bremen as "something alien" ("etwas fremdartiges").[26] According to Salo Baron, there were only 21 Jews living in Bremen. But Smidt, in defending the particular interests of Bremen, succeeded in sabotaging Jewish rights throughout Germany.

It might be argued that Smidt and his allies on the German Committee were the instruments of larger historical forces, since educated opinion in Germany was not yet ready to grant equality to the Jews. It has been estimated that between 1815 and 1850 some 2,500 books, pamphlets and periodical essays were published in Germany on the Jewish question.[27] The evidence suggests that large sections of the Christian population regarded Jews with suspicion if not hatred. But this flood of publications was not the cause but the consequence of the diplomatic stalemate at the Congress of Vienna. One good law is worth a thousand pamphlets, and the Congress provided an unprecedented opportunity for changing the direction of German politics, at a time when the map of Europe was being radically redrawn. In 1814, and again in 1848, enlightened reforms were proposed that might well have carried the day. They were blocked, not simply by anti-Jewish prejudices, but by the constitutional arrangements of particularism, which resulted in a diffusion of power and a resistance to modern centralised government. Enlightened political leaders failed in their attempts to lead, leaving the question of emancipation unresolved in a way that appeared to endorse popular prejudices. Thus people were encouraged in the belief that Jews were unworthy of becoming full members of civil society. Under these circumstances, as Reinhard Rürup has perceptively observed, "it became possible to regard even the incontestable achievements and successes of Jews in the economy, scholarship and the arts less as contributions than as threats to German society as a whole".[28]

The failure of the emancipation debate at the Congress of Vienna resulted in a reinforcement of what may be called state-sanctioned or officially approved anti-semitism. In the aftermath of the Congress, an educated German Christian could despise the Jews with a good conscience, knowing that he had the law on his side, quite apart from the blessing of the churches. And in every small community in

---

[26]Baron, p. 105.
[27]Ritchie Robertson, *The 'Jewish Question' in German Literature, 1749–1939*, Oxford 1999, p. 54.
[28]Reinhard Rürup, 'Jewish Emancipation in Britain and Germany' in Michael Brenner, Rainer Liedtke and David Rechter (eds.), *Two Nations: British and German Jews in Comparative Perspective*, Tübingen 1999 (Schriftenreihe wissenschaftlicher Abhandlungen des Leo Baeck Instituts 60), p. 59.

Germany, parish-pump politicians could use the prevailing regulations to deny rights of residence to Jewish families and even prevent them from marrying and having children. The "particularist" solution to the Jewish question did not only mean that each of the thirty-seven states of the German Federation could make its own laws. It meant that local councillors in tiny towns like Heidingsfeld near Würzburg could prevent Jews from becoming residents, except under the most irksome conditions, invoking petty restrictions which remained in force until 1861.[29] In place of the liberal principles of Enlightenment, to which Hardenberg and Metternich had appealed, Germany was pervaded for most of the nineteenth century by a political culture based on discriminatory laws.

Those laws may be regarded as one of the defining features of the German *Sonderweg*. In the pioneering analysis which he published in 1831, Gabriel Riesser had argued that all citizens were entitled to equal rights as a matter of principle. He draws detailed comparisons with other countries, particularly France and England, where Jews are not singled out for discriminatory legislation. The Germans, in his view, are among the best educated of European peoples, but in Germany alone – among the advanced nations – Jews are denied civil rights. There is no other country in the world where the legal status of the Jews and the political condition of the country "form such a glaring contrast" ("in so grellem Widerspruch stehen").[30] He does not deny the reality of anti-Jewish sentiment, which he attributes primarily to economic envy and fear of competition. But in his conclusion he warns that the oppression of a defenceless minority creates a whole nation of underlings:

> Wohl ist es wahr, daß Druck und Ausschließung sittlich verderben; aber sie verderben den Unterdrücker mehr noch als den Unterdrückten. [...] Nur ein Volk von Knechten kann Gefallen finden an der Afterknechtschaft Weniger; nur eine kraftlose feige Nation kann in dem Gegensatz einer geringen Anzahl Unterdrückter ein Mittel der Spannung ihres Selbstbewußtseins, ein Reizmittel für ihre krankhafte Ohnmacht finden.[31]

> It may indeed be true that oppression and exclusion are morally damaging; but they are more damaging to the oppressor than to the oppressed. [...] Only a nation of slaves can take pleasure in the even greater enslavement of the few; only a lethargic cowardly nation can find, in the contrast with an oppressed minority, a means of raising its self-esteem and a tonic for its pathological impotence.

Riesser perceived that the health of the nation as a whole was threatened by the oppression of the Jewish minority. This is the analysis that was to inspire the great speech which he delivered at the Frankfurt National Assembly in 1848, denouncing the fateful rift that threatened the future of German democracy.

---

[29]Roland Flade, *The Lehmans–From Rimpar to the New World: A Family History*, Würzburg 1996, p. 51.
[30]Riesser, op. cit., p. 69.
[31]*ibid.*, pp. 83–84.

Metternich and the Rothschilds: "A Dance with Torches on Powder Kegs"?[1]

BY NIALL FERGUSON

I

On 3 April 1848, as he passed incognito through Arnhem on his way into English exile, Prince Klemens Wenzel Nepomuk Lothar von Metternich-Winneburg wrote a lengthy letter to his banker, Baron Salomon von Rothschild. He began by thanking Rothschild for the letter of credit he had sent him, and ended by saying he would turn to the Rothschild house in London if he needed further financial assistance – adding drily that he would not need much, as he "looked forward to living a truly *bürgerlich* life" there. The rest of his letter, however, was entirely given over to political reflections. These are worth quoting at length for the light they shed on one of the most extraordinary, yet hitherto largely neglected, relationships of the *Vormärz* era:

> What disorder the world has fallen into! You always used to ask me whether war was in sight. You always heard me reassure you that this was not the case and as long as *I* had the reins in my hands I would be able to vouch for political peace. The danger of the day was not on the field of political war, but of *social* war. On this field too I have held the reins in my hands as long as was humanly possible. On the day when that possibility ceased, I stepped down from the driver's seat, for being overthrown is against my nature. If I am asked whether that could have been avoided by what naive utopians call Reform, I reply with a categorical *No* – for the logical reason that the measures which *today* are called Reforms and which might, under some conditions, have had the merit of bringing improvements, could have had no more value, given the situation of society as it was, than a dance with torches on powder kegs. I have the ability to think and fortunately also the ability to act according to my convictions. My spirit follows a practical course and has always eschewed any kind of deceit. You, dear Salomon, have understood me for years. Many others have not.

---

[1] This paper draws on my book *The World's Banker: The History of the House of Rothschild*, London 1998. I would like to express my gratitude to Sir Evelyn de Rothschild, the Chairman of N. M. Rothschild & Sons Ltd., for giving me unrestricted access to the firm's pre-1918 archive in London (henceforth RAL), and to the archivists there, Victor Gray, Melanie Aspey and their assistants. I would also like to thank the archivists at the Archives Nationales, Paris (henceforth AN), the Centre for the Preservation of Historical and Documentary Collections, Moscow (henceforth CPHDCM) and the Frankfurt Stadtarchiv, as well as those at the other archives and libraries I used. I would like to thank Edward Timms and the other organisers of the conference on "Progress and Emancipation in the Age of Metternich: Jews and Modernization in Austria and Germany 1815–1848", held at the Centre for German-Jewish Studies at the University of Sussex in April 1999, at which the paper was first presented.

Things in France are only just beginning. Never before has there been a greater, more deep-seated confusion. Since the [Napoleonic] Empire, France has stood there like a crumbling building with an artificial covering. All its main structures were rotten through and through and were bound to weaken at the first blow. That blow has been Communism, which has spread like a rampant weed over the entire field. The conservatives in that country have relied on the opposition which the existing interests would put up against this evil; what they did not take into account was that on the day they were endangered these interests would be unable to put up resistance, as they would at that moment find themselves enfeebled.

The objective is revolution and destruction, without protecting the citizen ... The wreckers cannot stand up for their own doings, so they have chosen to call it the overthrow of the *Metternich* system. ... [H]owever, I can only stand on my own, i.e. the established tradition ... It is nonsense that freedom is attainable by way of any system, only wilful impostors and brainless folk can preach this gospel. The root of freedom is authority, not as an end in itself, but as a beginning. I am and always was a friend of freedom, therefore no friend of *systems*, consequently the overthrow of the Metternich system is likewise the overthrow of the Austrian Empire and of prosperity.

I am writing you this philosophical letter in order that you understand my view of the situation. ... I am today in the same state of equanimity and good humour that you have known for thirty and more years, since I have unswervingly wanted and sought the same thing, so that my spirit and conscience are in the utmost equilibrium.[2]

This remarkable document can be read as an epitaph for a partnership which was to the period before 1848 what the relationship between Bismarck and Bleichröder was to the period after.[3] Metternich biographers have long been aware of the Metternich-Rothschild link,[4] as have previous historians of the Rothschild family.[5] But until now this and other archival sources essential for a proper understanding of the Metternich-Rothschild relationship have been inaccessible. This paper seeks to delineate that relationship and to address a number of important questions it raises.

How far did the Rothschilds act as mere financial props for a "reactionary" regime in the Habsburg lands and beyond – a charge often levelled against the family by contemporary critics? Or were they able to use their financial leverage to accelerate the progress of Jewish emancipation and, more generally, the economic modernisation of the Habsburg lands? As will become clear, these are far from straightforward questions. If we define "emancipation" to mean the achievement of equal civil and political rights for all Jews, we exclude much that the Rothschilds consciously did on

---

[2]CPHDCM, 637/1/3/316, Metternich, Arnhem, to Salomon, Vienna, April 3, 1848. Cf. Frank Trentmann, 'New Sources on an Old Family: The Rothschild Papers at the Special Archive, Moscow – and a Letter from Metternich', *Financial History Review* (1995), pp. 76ff.
[3]See Fritz Stern, *Gold and Iron: Bismarck, Bleichröder and the Building of the German Empire*, Harmondsworth 1987.
[4]See A. Harman, *Metternich*, London 1932; Algernon Cecil, *Metternich, 1773–1859: A Study of his Period and Personality*, London 1933; H. du Coudray, *Metternich*, London 1935; Paul W. Schroeder, *Metternich's Diplomacy at its Zenith, 1820–2*, Austin 1962; Guillaume André de Bertier de Sauvigny, *Metternich and his Times*, London 1962; idem, *Metternich et la France après le congrès de Vienne*, Paris 1968; Alan Palmer, *Metternich: Councillor of Europe*, London 1972.
[5]The best account in this respect is Count Egon Corti, *The Rise of the House of Rothschild*, London 1928; idem, *The Reign of the House of Rothschild*, London 1928.

Salomon von Rothschild

behalf of their "poorer co-religionists", including the acquisition of privileges for themselves. If we regard the construction of an international bond market and a pan-European railway network as classic symptoms of modernisation, then no doubt the Rothschilds were agents of modernisation. But did these advances necessarily run counter to Metternich's conservative political programme?

II

The image of the Rothschilds as "underwriters" of the Holy Alliance dates from the early 1820s. In a letter to his wife in 1826, the itinerant German Prince Pückler-Muskau referred to Nathan Rothschild – the head of the London branch of the family and the *primus inter pares* of Mayer Amschel Rothschild's five sons – as "the chief ally of the Holy Alliance".[6] A British cartoon of 1824 satirised the Rothschild-founded Alliance Assurance Company as the "Hollow Alliance Fire and Life Preserving Office".[7] In 1821 Nathan even received a death threat because of "his connexion with foreign powers, and particularly the assistance rendered to Austria, on account of the designs of that government against the liberties of Europe".[8] To the Frankfurt-born poet Ludwig Börne, it was "unquestionable that most of the peoples

[6]Hermann Fürst von Pückler-Muskau, *Briefe eines Verstorbenen: Vollständige Ausgabe*, ed. Heinz Ohff, Kupfergraben 1986, p. 441.
[7]Alfred Rubens, *Anglo-Jewish Portraits*, London 1935, p. 299.
[8]*The Times*, Jan. 15, 1821.

of Europe would by this time be in full possession of liberty if the Rothschilds ... and others did not lend the autocrats the support of their capital".[9] In Heine's "Travel Sketches" too, "Rothschild I" appears alongside Wellington, Metternich and the Pope as a bulwark of reaction.[10] Although Heine later modified his opinions as he got to know James de Rothschild in Paris, other Germanophone writers continued to portray the Rothschilds in similar terms into the 1840s and beyond. Writing in 1846, the poet Karl Beck lamented "Rothschild's" refusal to use his financial power on the side of the "peoples" – and particularly the German people – instead of their detested princes.[11]

The Rothschilds certainly had the resources to give the Holy Alliance financial substance. When the Austrian Emperor remarked to his envoy in Frankfurt in 1817 that the eldest brother Amschel was "richer than I am," he was not being wholly facetious.[12] In 1815 the combined capital of the Rothschild houses in Frankfurt and London was at most £500,000. Three years later, however, the figure was £1.8 million and by 1828 it stood at £4.3 million.[13] These are astonishing figures: the Rothschilds' nearest rivals, the Barings, had total capital of less than £310,000 in 1828.[14] Moreover, by 1836 the Rothschilds' capital had increased again to more than £6 million.[15] This explains the family's dominance of the international capital market in the *Vormärz* period. Between 1818 and 1832 the London branch of the partnership accounted for at least 38 per cent of the total value of loans issued in London by foreign governments;[16] indeed, the bank's own figures suggest that this may be an underestimate.[17] The table below gives a breakdown of the loans issued by the London house between 1818 and 1846. Austria alone issued loans worth more than £3 million between 1818 and 1846 through the London Rothschilds; and this omits the substantial sums advanced to the Austrian government by the other Rothschild houses – beginning in 1820, when Salomon jointly organised two lottery loans worth 45 million Austrian gulden (c. £4.8 million) in partnership with David Parish. It was this transaction which persuaded Salomon to remain in Vienna on a more or less permanent basis.[18]

---

[9]Ludwig Börne, *Mittheilungen aus dem Gebiete der Länder- und Völkerkunde, zweiter Theil*, Offenbach 1833, pp. 142–155.
[10]S.S. Prawer, *Heine's Jewish Comedy: A Study of his Portraits of Jews and Judaism*, Oxford 1983, pp. 128f.
[11]Karl Beck, *Lieder vom armen Mann, mit einem Vorwort an das Haus Rothschild*, Leipzig 1846, pp. 4ff.
[12]RAL, XI/82/9/1/100, Amschel, Frankfurt, to James, Paris, April 30, 1817.
[13]CPHDCM, 637/1/8/1–7; also RAL, RFamFD, B/1, Articles of agreement between Messrs de Rothschild [Amschel, Nathan, Salomon, Carl, Jacob and Anselm], Aug. 31, 1825; CPHDCM, 637/1/7/48–52, Abschrift [Partnership agreement], Sept. 26, 1828; CPHDCM, 637/1/6/17, General Inventarium ... das gesamte Handelsvermögen, Sept. 26; CPHDCM, 637/1/6/44, 45, No. 4: General Capital [summary of total capital], Sept. 26.
[14]Philip Ziegler, *The Sixth Great Power: Barings, 1762–1929*, London 1988, p. 374.
[15]CPHDCM, 637/1/7/53–69, Vollständige Abschrift des Societäts-Vertrags ... Übereinkunft, July 30, 1836.
[16]Stanley Chapman, *The Foundation of the English Rothschilds: N. M. Rothschild as a Textile Merchant, 1799–1811*, London 1977, p. 20.
[17]J. Ayer, *A Century of Finance, 1804 to 1904: The London House of Rothschild*, London 1904.
[18]Corti, *Rise*, pp. 245–9.

Loans issued by the London Rothschilds, 1818–1846

Borrower	Total (£)	Percentage of total
Britain	44,938,547	29.2
France	27,700,000	18.0
Prussia	12,300,400	8.0
Russia	6,629,166	4.3
Austria	3,100,000	2.0
Naples	7,000,000	4.5
Holy Alliance*	29,029,566	18.8
Portugal	5,500,000	3.6
Brazil	4,486,200	2.9
Belgium	11,681,064	7.6
Other states**	5,843,750	3.8
Private sector	24,900,000	16.2
Total	154,079,127	100.0

* Prussia, Russia. Austria and Naples. ** Holland, Greece and Denmark.
Source: Ayer, *Century of Finance*, pp. 14–42.

As early as August 1820 the Bremen delegate to the German Confederation's Diet in Frankfurt had a conversation with his Austrian counterpart Count Buol which acutely identified the unrivalled extent of the Rothschilds' political influence in Europe:

> This house has, through its enormous financial transactions and its banking and credit connections, actually achieved the position of a real Power; it has to such an extent acquired control of the general money market that it is in a position either to hinder or to promote, as it feels inclined, the movements and operations of potentates, and even of the greatest European Powers. Austria needs the Rothschilds' help for her present demonstration against Naples, and Prussia would long ago have been finished with her constitution if the House of Rothschild had not made it possible for her to postpone the evil day.[19]

The Frankfurt banker Simon Moritz Bethmann could "well understand why the Rothschilds are such useful instruments for the [Austrian] government".[20]

Nor were government loans the only way the Rothschilds lent financial support to Habsburg rule. Before 1830 the Rothschild brothers' charity had been largely confined within the Jewish communities of Frankfurt, London and Paris. After 1830 Salomon made a point of contributing to causes which were regarded as good by the Habsburg elite. In the very dry summer of 1835, he offered 25,000 gulden towards the construction of an aqueduct from the Danube to the Vienna suburbs.[21] When Pest and Ofen were badly flooded three years later, he hastened to offer financial assistance for the

---

[19] Richard Schwemer, *Geschichte der Freien Stadt Frankfurt a. M. (1814–1866)*, Frankfurt am Main 1910–18, vol. II, pp. 149ff.
[20] Wilfried Forstmann, *Simon Moritz Bethmann, 1768–1826: Bankier, Diplomat und politischer Beobachter*, Studien zur Frankfurter Geschichte, ed. Frankfurter Verein für Geschichte und Landeskunde, Frankfurt am Main 1973, pp. 260–4.
[21] Corti, *Reign*, p. 166.

victims.[22] He donated 40,000 gulden to found an institute for scientific research in Brünn.[23] So frequently did Salomon act in this way that it was possible for a sentimental novella of the 1850s to portray him as a kind of Viennese Santa Claus.[24]

Moreover, the Rothschilds made a substantial contribution to Metternich's private finances. Although born into an aristocratic family with estates in the Mosel valley, Metternich was "cash-poor" for much of his long political career. Within a year of the Rothschilds' first meetings with him – in Paris during the 1815 peace negotiations[25] – he raised the possibility of a loan of 300,000 gulden with Amschel and Carl Rothschild in Frankfurt.[26] The arrangement he proposed was that the Rothschilds should advance him 100,000 gulden and sell a further 200,000 gulden of 5 per cent bonds to other investors, all secured on the new estate at Johannisberg which the Austrian Emperor had just given him. In fact, Carl was reluctant to lend so much to a single individual, no matter how wealthy,[27] and the brothers preferred at this stage to limit their generosity to routine banking services and occasional gifts, like the Wedgwood china Nathan sent Metternich in 1821.[28] In 1822, however, the brothers agreed to make a loan of 900,000 gulden.[29] And at Verona in 1823 Salomon furnished the prince with cash to meet his (considerable) personal expenses.[30]

This was just the beginning of a long financial relationship, the evidence of which can be found in the silver box, recently rediscovered in Moscow, where Salomon Rothschild kept Metternich's accounts and private financial correspondence. These long-lost bank statements show that between 1825 and 1826 Metternich was in a position to repay the loan of 1822.[31] However, no sooner had he done so – ahead of schedule – than a new loan for 1,040,000 gulden (c. £110,000) was arranged, roughly half of which the prince used to purchase a new estate at Plass.[32] The balance

---

[22]*ibid.*, p. 177.

[23]*ibid.*, pp. 234–239.

[24]Adolf Bäuerle, *Wien vor zwanzig Jahren: oder Baron Rothschild und die Tischlerstochter*, Pest –Wien – Leipzig 1855, esp. pp. 179–187.

[25]RAL, XI/109/2/1/63, Salomon, Paris, to Nathan, Sept. 10, 1815; RAL, XI/109/2/2/83, Amschel to Salomon and James, Sept. 17; RAL, T3/228, Metternich to MAR, Sept. 30.

[26]RAL, T31/238/4, XI/109/4, Carl, Frankfurt, to James, Paris, June 2, 1816; RAL, T33/375/2, XI/109/5B, Amschel, Frankfurt, to James, Dec. 18.

[27]RAL, T61/4/1, XI/109/6, Carl, Berlin, to Salomon, Nathan and James, Jan. 7, 1817; RAL, T61/9/1, XI/109/6, Carl to Amschel, Frankfurt, Jan. 10.

[28]RAL, T64/125/3, XI/109/9, Carl, Frankfurt, to Nathan and Salomon, April 7, 1818; RAL, T3/229, Metternich to Nathan, London, July 2, 1820; RAL, T52/4, Captain Bauer, Chandos House, to Nathan, London, July 22, 1821. Two years later, Nathan purchased a jewel-encrusted box from Metternich: RAL, T5/212, Salomon, Vienna, to Nathan, London, April 7, 1823.

[29]C. W. Berghoeffer, *Meyer Amschel Rothschild: Der Gründer des Rothschildschen Bankhauses*, Frankfurt am Main 1924, pp. 209ff.

[30]Corti, *Rise*, p. 311.

[31]CPHDCM, 637/1/18/23, Metternich's current account for the period Sept. 26, 1825 to June 30, 1826. Metternich had a gross income of 266,590 gulden for the three quarters covered by the statement, and outgoings totalling 78,164 gulden, leaving a credit balance of 188,426 gulden.

[32]CPHDCM, 637/1/18/3–11, "Vertrag ... zwischen seinem Durchlaucht dem hochgeborenen Herrn P. J. Fürsten Clemens, Wenzel, Lothar von Metternich Winneburg, Seinem k.k. Apostolischen Majestät Haus-, Hof- und Staatskanzler *einer-*, und dem Herrn Salomon Mayer Freiherrn von Rothschild ... *andererseits*", March 20, 1827; CPHDCM, 637/1/18/26, Metternich to MAR, March 20; CPHDCM, 637/1/18/22, Metternich current account for the period Feb. 16, 1826 to March 31, 1827; CPHDCM, 637/1/18/24,25, Untitled statement of Metternich's mortgage on Plass, 1827–1858.

sheet of the Vienna house shows that Salomon retained some 35,000 gulden of the bearer bonds issued by Metternich to pay for Plass, on top of which he owed an additional 15,000 gulden.[33] His total private debt to the Rothschilds grew in the succeeding two years to nearly 70,000 gulden.[34] In addition, the Frankfurt house advanced over 117,000 gulden to Metternich's son Victor.[35] When the prince married again in 1831, Salomon was on hand to help resolve the financial difficulties of his third wife, Countess Melanie Zichy-Ferraris.[36]

Nor did the Rothschilds confine themselves to loans and overdrafts. "Our friend Salomon's devotion always touches me," remarked Princess Melanie in her diary in May 1841, on receiving a present from him of American deer for their estate near Frankfurt. A few months later, she described a visit by "Salomon and James, their nephew Anthony and Salomon's son and finally Amschel, who made a great point of our coming to dine with him at Frankfurt next Tuesday. James brought me a pretty mother-of-pearl and bronze box from Paris, filled with sweets, which was all to the good". At Christmas in 1843, Salomon visited the Metternichs at Ischl, bringing "lovely things to the Metternich children, such as tempted their mother to play with them herself".[37]

Metternich was not the only eminent Austrian to put his private financial affairs in Salomon's hands. Another beneficiary was the prince's secretary, Friedrich Gentz, who had acquired the habit of selling political influence for cash long before he came into contact with the Rothschilds.[38] After an initial encounter in Frankfurt, Gentz met Carl and Salomon at Aachen in 1818. On 27 October he recorded in his diary that Salomon had handed him 800 ducats, supposedly the proceeds of a successful speculation in British stocks. A few days later, there were more "pleasant financial dealing with the brothers".[39] Gentz was soon paying regular visits to his new friends, whose apparently instinctive ability to make money deeply impressed him. He had regular business dealings with Salomon thereafter: a minor transaction in late 1820, a small loan at Laibach in 1821, a share in the Neapolitan loan of the same year, which quickly earned him 5,000 gulden. His diaries in this period make repeated references to "very agreeable communications" from Salomon; "important financial arrangements" with him; "a proof of real friendship" over breakfast; "matters which, although not so elevated [as diplomacy], were far more pleasant"; and "highly welcome financial transactions with the excellent Rothschild".[40] The pattern con-

---

[33]CPHDCM, 637/1/6/22, 25, Abschluß der Wiener Filial, June 30, 1828; AN, 132 AQ 3/2 No. 5, Balance, Vienna Filial of MAR, Sept. 26.
[34]CPHDCM, 637/1/18/34–6, Metternich to Salomon, March 8, 1829; CPHDCM, 637/1/18/39, Metternich current account for the period July 16, 1827 to March 31, 1829, which shows that Metternich's income in the accounting period was 6,922 gulden, his outgoings 76,320 gulden; CPHDCM, 637/1/18/40, Salomon to Metternich, Oct. 26, 1829.
[35]CPHDCM, 637/1/18/19, Ausweis, Dec. 30, 1829.
[36]Corti, *Reign*, pp. 54f.
[37]R. Metternich-Winneburg (ed.), *Aus Metternichs nachgelassenen Papieren*, Vienna 1880–1884, vol. IV, pp. 491, 493, 495.
[38]Richard Ehrenberg, *Große Vermögen*, vol. I: *Die Fugger, Rothschild, Krupp*, 3rd edn., Jena 1925, pp. 101ff.
[39]Paul R. Sweet, *Friedrich von Gentz* (Westport, Conn. 1970), p. 219; Golo Mann, *Secretary of Europe: The Life of Friedrich von Gentz, Enemy of Napoleon*, New Haven 1946, p. 256; Cecil, *Metternich*, pp. 154f.
[40]CPHDCM, 637/1/309, Gentz to Salomon, Dec. 17, 1820; CPHDCM, 637/1/309, same to same, Jan. 8, 1821; Corti, *Rise*, pp. 267, 294, 305–310, 322f., 368, 398; Ehrenberg, *Große Vermögen*, p. 107; Sweet, *Gentz*, p. 249; Coudray, *Metternich*, p. 246.

tinued throughout the decade. In 1829 Salomon lent Gentz 2,000 gulden "with the most amiable readiness", bringing his total debts to Salomon and other bankers to over 30,000 gulden. Such loans were regarded by Gentz as "donations pure and simple".[41] Indeed, according to one account, Salomon finally dispensed with the fiction that the money would ever be repaid by paying Gentz an annual retainer,[42] though this did not prevent Gentz from pleading for yet another loan of 4,500 gulden from Salomon, and gratefully settling for 500 gulden to tide him over.[43]

III

All this makes it exceedingly tempting to conclude that the relationship between Metternich and Salomon was the traditional eighteenth-century relation between prince and *Hofjude*. In return for financial favours for himself and his associates, it could be argued, Metternich rewarded Salomon with protection and privileges – as distinct from conferring rights on Jews in general, the essence of emancipation.

Protection was certainly needed. In Frankfurt the much-resented fact that the Rothschilds were now "richer than Bethmann" was widely seen as evidence of the need to restore the traditional legal restrictions on the Jewish minority.[44] In 1817 noisy crowds gathered outside Amschel's newly acquired garden, itself a symbol of Jewish social mobility, to mock his even more recent ennoblement, "chanting 'Baron Amschel' and all sorts of stupidities".[45] Caricatures were pinned to his door, and the Rothschilds' office windows were among those broken during the *Hep! Hep!* riots of 1819.[46] At around the same time, Amschel also received death threats.[47] Nor was such "anti-Rothschildism" confined to Frankfurt. Wherever the firm secured a large proportion of government business, local rivals often reacted with religiously-tinged attacks. In Vienna, for example, the 1820 lottery loan which Salomon arranged in tandem with David Parish was widely criticised as "a shameful Jewish ramp" because of the substantial profits the bankers stood to make.[48] Writing in the 1840s, Karl Beck too could not resist alluding to "Rothschild's ... interest-calculating brethren ... filling the insatiable money-bag for themselves and their kin alone!"[49]

Attacks like these do much to explain the Rothschilds' ambivalence about popular political participation. When Metternich expressed his disapproval of the riots – a disapproval which, of course, extended to all "outbreaks of the vulgar masses" – he did much to reinforce the family's sense that conservatism might offer them more

---

[41] Sweet, *Gentz*, pp. 283ff.
[42] Corti, *Reign*, pp. 69–71.
[43] Friedrich von Gentz, *Tagebücher von 1829–1831*, Vienna 1920, p. 151.
[44] RAL, T30, XI/109/2/2/170, Eva, Frankfurt, to Salomon and James, Paris, Nov. 15, 1815.
[45] RAL, T62/63/3, Amschel, Frankfurt, to Salomon, Paris, June 23, 1817.
[46] Paul Arnsberg, *Die Geschichte der Frankfurter Juden seit der Französischen Revolution*, Frankfurt 1983, vol. I, pp. 352f.; Rachel Heuberger and Helga Krohn, *Hinaus aus dem Ghetto ... Juden in Frankfurt am Main, 1800–1950*, Frankfurt am Main 1988, pp. 24ff.
[47] RAL, T62/63/3, XI/109/7, Amschel, Frankfurt, to Salomon, Paris, June 23, 1817; Corti, *Rise*, pp. 231ff.
[48] Corti, *Rise*, pp. 246–248. Parish himself was not Jewish.
[49] Beck, *Lieder vom armen Mann*, Leipzig 1846, pp. 4ff.

personal security than more popular forms of politics. This was especially true in Germany, where traditionally the Habsburg Emperor had given the Jews "protection" from the local populace. Imperial privileges were also essential for the Rothschilds in the absence of general emancipation. In Austria little had changed since the Tolerance Edict of 1782 (which had reduced economic restrictions somewhat): Jews continued to be denied the right to own land in the Empire, had to pay a special poll tax, were subject to marriage restrictions and, if born outside the Empire, required a special "toleration permit" to reside there, renewable every three years. They were also excluded from the civil service, though they could and did serve in the army and some had even become officers during the Napoleonic Wars. When Nathan Rothschild's son Lionel went on a tour through Germany in 1827, it was only in Vienna that he found the position of Jews so bad as to be noteworthy: "Jews are very much oppressed, they can hold no situation under Government nor possess any land property, not even a house in the town, they are obliged to pay a heavy tolerance tax, and must have a permission to hire lodgings."[50]

Perhaps the most important privilege the family acquired was the noble status conferred on them by the Emperor Francis II in 1817, as a reward for their role in paying British subsidies and French reparations payments to Austria.[51] The Rothschilds were not the first Jews to be elevated in this way: six other families had been ennobled (though all the others had converted to Christianity by 1848).[52] Nor did ennoblement by the Habsburg Emperor connote social elevation of the sort achieved two generations later, when Nathan's grandson Natty Rothschild was given a hereditary peerage by Queen Victoria. Like the Austrian currency, the Austrian nobility had been debased compared with its more exclusive British counterpart. On the other hand, ennoblement gave the brothers three valuable assets: the right to the prefix "von" ("de" in France and England), a coat of arms (albeit not quite the grandiose design they had originally hoped for) and, in 1822, the title "Freiherr" ("Baron" in France and England).[53]

However, the acquisition of noble status did not exempt the Rothschilds automatically from legal discrimination on the ground of their religion. Salomon had to write personally to Metternich in 1823, when his cousin Anton Schnapper wanted to move to Vienna to marry a relative of his senior clerk Leopold von Wertheimstein.[54] Ten years later he had to apply for renewal of "toleration" for another senior clerk, Moritz Goldschmidt, who was born in Frankfurt.[55] Salomon himself could only rent accommodation in Vienna, and his request in 1831 that he and his brothers be allowed "to convert part of the wealth with which a kind providence has blessed us into a form in which it will be remunerative whatever vicissitudes may befall us" was turned down – despite Salomon's ingenious argument that this would be "not wholly inconsistent with [the government's] own advantage, since it cannot regard

---

[50]RAL, RFam AD/1/2, Lionel, Journal [copy], April 1827, p. 59.
[51]See Hellmuth Rössler, *Graf Johann Philipp Stadion: Napoleons deutscher Gegenspieler*, vol. II: *1809 bis 1824*, Vienna – Munich 1966, pp. 169, 185.
[52]William O. McCagg Jr., *Jewish Nobles and Geniuses in Modern Hungary*, New York 1972, p. 58n.
[53]Corti, *Rise*, pp. 198–201, 302f.
[54]*ibid.*, pp. 333f.
[55]Corti, *Reign*, pp. 68f.

with indifference the possibility of attracting considerable capital sums to the country which will become subject to taxation".[56] It was not until 1837 that Metternich intimated the Emperor's willingness to grant him, as a special privilege, permission to own property in Vienna.[57] Salomon finally took advantage of this offer in 1842. His request to own real estate in the city was speedily granted, allowing him to buy the Hotel zum Römischen Kaiser in the Renngasse where he had long resided.[58] As he acknowledged, this – along with the grant of honorary citizenship which went with it – made him "a privileged exception in the midst of my fellow believers, who ... have the right to enjoy the same rights as those who belong to other religious confessions".[59] In 1843, when Salomon sought to buy an estate in Moravia, he was again obliged to adopt the tones of the humble but deserving *Hoffaktor*, listing his various financial contributions to the Empire as "adequate proof of his unshakeable devotion to the Austrian monarchy" and expressing his "most ardent desire to own property in a country whose rulers have shown him so many signal marks of their favour".[60] Again, the petition was granted, despite the reservations of the Moravian estates. As one official put it, Salomon's "position in society is so exceptional that he has been entirely removed from the ordinary circumstances of his co-religionists; his remarkable qualities and rare intelligence make it entirely inappropriate to apply strictly in his case the regulations in force with regard to other Israelites". The Lord Chancellor Count Inzághy was rather more candid: it was, he argued,

> highly desirable that Baron Rothschild should be more closely bound to the Imperial State of Austria by the investment of his money in real property in this country; and ... it would create a very strange impression abroad if his particular wish to settle permanently in that country, where he has been so actively engaged for a long period of years, and has been associated with the Government in more extensive and important transactions than has ever been the case before with a private individual, were to be refused after the special distinctions that have been conferred upon him.[61]

The estate Salomon duly purchased at Koritschau in Moravia, together with his property in Vienna, gave him real estate in the Empire worth 2 million gulden.[62]

It is against this background that Metternich's social intimacy with the Rothschilds must be understood. Contemporary comment suggests that social life in Vienna remained more segregated along religious lines than in Frankfurt, Paris, London or Naples, the other Rothschild cities. In the 1820s, Gentz remarked, the Jewish "aristocracy of money" tended to dine and dance together, apart from the aristocracy proper.[63] When the English writer Frances Trollope (the novelist's mother) visited Vienna in the 1830s, she encountered the same schism.[64] Nor should the ease of

---

[56]*ibid.*, pp. 42–46.
[57]*ibid.*, pp. 175f.
[58]*ibid.*, pp. 230f.
[59]Rudolf M. Heilbrunn, *Das Haus Rothschild: Wahrheit und Dichtung. Vortrag gehalten am 6. März 1963 im Frankfurter Verein für Geschichte und Landeskunde*, Frankfurt a. M. 1963, p. 33.
[60]Corti, *Reign*, pp. 232ff.
[61]*ibid.*, pp. 234–237.
[62]*ibid.*, pp. 251f.
[63]Hilde Spiel, *Fanny von Arnstein*, Oxford 1991, pp. 333f.
[64]Mrs Frances Trollope, *Vienna and the Austrians*, vol. II, London 1838, pp. 5–7, 103f., 220.

socialising with the Rothschild brothers be exaggerated. Salomon's employee Moritz Goldschmidt's son Hermann – a boy in the 1840s – remembered him as an impetuous, impatient, despotic man: "a brutal egoist, a man without wisdom or education, who despised those around him and took the opportunity to treat them ruthlessly [just] because he was rich". He ate and drank to excess and was habitually rude to everyone from his barber to the Russian ambassador. If the former was late in the morning – and Salomon habitually rose at 3 a.m. – he would be reviled as "an ass". If someone came into the office smelling slightly, Salomon would press his handkerchief to his nose, open the window, and shout: "Throw him out, the man stinks." "Why should I eat badly at your place, why don't you come and eat well at mine?" he was once heard to reply to a dinner invitation from the Russian ambassador. Another "highly placed personality" who asked for a loan received a blunt negative: "Because I don't want to." Salomon therefore "seldom went into high society, [because] he felt that because of his lack of education he would have to play a difficult and uncomfortable role".[65]

Yet it October 1821 Metternich – accompanied by his mistress, Princess Dorothea de Lieven – publicly accepted an offer of Rothschild hospitality, "taking soup" with Amschel in Frankfurt on his way back to Vienna from Hanover.[66] This was interpreted by some observers as a calculated gesture of support for the Frankfurt Jewish community at a time when conflict over the civil rights question was at its height. In 1825 his brother James played host to Metternich in Paris, throwing a lavish dinner for "the representatives of the Holy Alliance" which greatly impressed the *Constitutionnel* newspaper. It commented ironically:

> Thus does the power of gold reconcile all the ranks and all the religions. One of the more curious spectacles our time – rich as it is in contrasts – is that of the representatives of the Holy Alliance established in the name of Jesus Christ attending a banquet given by a Jew on the day that the law of sacrilege is being debated in the chambers.[67]

A year later, James was present at another equally grand soirée.[68] And in January 1836 the Metternichs dined with Salomon at his house in Vienna, along with Princess Marie Esterházy and a number of other distinguished guests, who were duly impressed by Rothschild's French chef.[69]

Metternich's motives are not hard to divine. The *Courrier Français* provided a revealing anecdote in connection with his visit to James's house in 1825: "An Englishman was asked how it could be that the ambassador of his nation had not been present at this diplomatic feast. 'Because', he replied, 'England has no need of money.'" In the same vein, when Count Kolowrat accepted an invitation from Salomon (evidently for the first time) in 1838, "some people of his own position in society told him that this was giving offence. 'What would you have me do?' he said. 'Rothschild attached such enormous importance to my coming that I had to sacri-

---

[65]Hermann von Goldschmidt, *Einige Erinnerungen aus längst vergangenen Tagen*, Vienna 1917, pp. 12–33, 35f.
[66]See Corti, *Rise*, pp. 290f.; Palmer, *Metternich*, p. 215; Harman, *Metternich*, p. 45.
[67]Bertier de Sauvigny, *Metternich et la France*, pp. 959f., 970.
[68]Comte Rudolf Apponyi, *Vingt-cinq ans à Paris (1826–50)*, Paris 1914, vol. I, pp. 6ff.
[69]Metternich, *Nachgelassene Papiere*, pp. 47, 324, 491, 493, 495.

fice myself to the interests of the service, as the State needs him.'"[70] As if to emphasise his financial leverage, Salomon declared expansively that his guest's presence had:

> "... given me as much pleasure today as if I had been given a thousand gulden, or had given them to a poor man." Thereupon Count Kolowrat replied, "Very well, give me the thousand gulden for a poor man who needs help, and has applied to me." Rothschild promised to do so and after dinner Count Kolowrat was given the thousand gulden.[71]

When the Metternichs dined with him, Salomon could not resist showing them the contents of his safe as a post-prandial treat. As was later said of the Papacy, when it turned to the Rothschilds for financial assistance: "The thesis is to burn M. de Rothschild: the hypothesis is to dine with him."[72]

IV

Yet there is a need to qualify this idea of the latter-day court Jew. In his famous essay 'On the Jewish Question', Marx quoted from the pamphlet on the subject by Bruno Bauer:

> "The Jew, who in Vienna, for example, is only tolerated, determines the fate of the whole Empire by his financial power. The Jew, who may have no rights in the smallest German states, decides the fate of Europe." This is no isolated fact [continued Marx]. The Jew has emancipated himself in a Jewish manner, not only because he has acquired financial power, but also because ... *money* has become a world power.[73]

Or, as Heine memorably put it, "Money is the god of our time and money is his prophet."[74] The Rothschilds' image as "bankers to the Holy Alliance" understated their relative autonomy as a multinational partnership with unrivalled resources; in particular, it understated their tendency to assess business opportunities in financial rather than political terms. As the table above shows, the Holy Alliance accounted for only 19 per cent of Rothschild bond issues in London, less than the amount raised for Britain and post-1830 France. Close scrutiny of the Rothschilds' involvement in Metternich's policy casts serious doubt in the idea that they were merely the purseholders of reaction.

In 1820–21 the order established at Vienna was challenged in Spain, Naples, Portugal, Piedmont and by Greeks throughout the Near East. In so far as they helped to finance Austrian intervention in Italy and French intervention in Spain, the Rothschilds perhaps do deserve to be thought of as financiers of reaction. Nevertheless, it is striking how independently the Rothschilds acted in each case. On

---

[70]Carl Friedrich Kübeck von Kübow, *Tagebücher des Kübeck von Kübow*, Vienna 1909, vol. I/2, pp. 779f..
[71]*ibid.*
[72]J. Derek Holmes, *The Triumph of the Holy See: A Short History of the Papacy in the Nineteenth Century*, London 1978, p. 148.
[73]Marx, Karl, 'On the Jewish Question', in *idem* and Friedrich Engels (eds.), *Collected Works*, vol. III: *1843–1844*, London 1975, esp. pp. 169ff.
[74]Heinrich Heine, 'Lutetia', in *Sämtliche Schriften*, vol. V, Munich 1971, p. 355.

the Italian peninsula, matters were at first sight straightforward: the Rothschilds supported Metternich's policy by lending to the various monarchical regimes which had his backing. As early as December 1820 the prince wrote to Salomon from Troppau alluding suggestively to a transaction involving 25 or 30 million francs "with respect to the future fate of the Kingdom of Naples".[75] The banker's initial response was positive. "Even our financiers, led by Parish and Rothschild," so the Austrian Finance Minister Stadion assured Metternich at Laibach in January 1821, "are only anxious to see our troops across the Po at the earliest possible moment, and marching on Naples."[76] Yet Salomon became suddenly unenthusiastic when Metternich and Nesselrode invited him to Laibach to discuss possible loans, the purpose of which was evidently to pay for intervention. Fearing a collapse in the price of Austrian bonds, he insisted that any loan should be raised by Ferdinand I only after his restoration to power in Naples, the proceeds to be used to reimburse the Austrian government for the costs of intervention. In the meantime he was prepared to offer nothing more than short-term advances.[77] Not for the first or last time in the nineteenth century, Austrian policy now threatened to be undermined by financial weakness. There were severe shortages of supplies at the front, while in Vienna Stadion despairingly foresaw a return to the fiscal and monetary morass of the Napoleonic period. Indeed, Salomon had to intervene in the market to prevent a slump in the price of "metalliques" (Austrian silver-denominated bonds).[78] By March 24, however, Naples had fallen, and the fourth Rothschild brother Carl hurried south to organise the now desperately needed Neapolitan loan from which the Austrians were to be reimbursed.

At this point, a conflict of interests emerged: the Austrian government wished to exact the maximum sum possible, but the Rothschilds had a low opinion of Neapolitan creditworthiness, and were willing to lend to the restored regime only at punitive rates, while the Bourbon regime itself faced the prospect of renewed unrest if it was burdened with onerous new debts. The first Neapolitan loan arranged by Carl amounted to 16 million ducats (around £2 million) at a discounted price of 60 (i.e. for every bond with a face value of 100 ducats, the Rothschilds paid just 60 ducats). To help meet the costs of the continuing Austrian occupation, a second loan was issued in November 1821 for 16.8 million ducats at a price of 67.3.[79] Two more loans followed, increasing the state's debt to around £13 million in all. Despite this increasing burden, the price of Neapolitan securities rose in Paris from 65 to 103, and in London there was considerable enthusiasm for the sterling-denominated bonds.[80] This successful stabilisation partly reflected the good relationship which had developed between Carl and the new Neapolitan Finance Minister, Luigi de' Medici, whose claim that the Austrians were unnecessarily prolonging the occupation and

---

[75]CPHDCM, 637/1/18/13–14, Metternich, Troppau, to Salomon, Abschrift, Dec. 21, 1820; Salomon to Metternich, undated, c. end Dec.
[76]Corti, *Rise*, pp. 253f.
[77]CPHDCM, 637/1/18/15, Metternich, Laibach, to Salomon, Vienna, Dec. 29, 1820; CPHDCM, 637/1/18/14, Salomon to Nesselrode, Laibach, Jan. 29, 1821; CPHDCM, 637/1/18/13–14, Salomon to Metternich, Laibach, Abschrift, Feb. 4, 1821.
[78]Corti, *Rise*, pp. 260–263.
[79]*ibid.*, pp. 267–274, 285–288.
[80]Rondo Cameron, *France and the Economic Development of Europe, 1800–1914*, Princeton 1961, pp. 408f.

overcharging for their presence Rothschild was inclined to support.[81] Even before the Congress of Verona in late 1822, it was obvious that the Austrians intended to recoup the costs of the invasion in full. Of 4.6 million gulden which Metternich demanded in August 1821 as payment for the actual invasion, 4 million had been received by the following February, and to this were added annual occupation costs of 9 million ducats. By 1825 Medici was accusing the Austrian government of deliberately profiting from the occupation and threatened to resign unless more than 1 million ducats were repaid. When the Viennese authorities stalled, Carl advanced the money to Medici – to Metternich's evident irritation.[82]

The financing of the Austrian intervention in Naples provides a classic illustration of the Rothschilds' ability, as a multinational entity, to play both ends against the middle. While Carl's establishment in Naples flourished on the strength of his ties with the Bourbon regime, the Austrian government found itself once again having to turn to Salomon. For no matter how much could be squeezed out of Naples, the costs of the military intervention there far exceeded what Stadion could raise in current revenue. There was no alternative but another loan.[83]

Vienna's dependence on the Rothschilds was further increased in 1823, when the British government, in an attempt to exert pressure on Vienna to end its occupation of Naples, raised the question of outstanding loans – now notionally totalling £23.5 million including interest – which dated back to the early stages of the war against revolutionary France. Once again, the Austrians had to turn to the Rothschilds, pressing Salomon to use his brother's influence in London to get the debt scaled down. When this had finally been achieved, the firm offered to organise yet another loan to pay the agreed sum of £2.5 million. Thirty million gulden of new metalliques were taken by the Rothschilds and their partners at an underwriting price of 82.33, and were soon trading at 93, yielding a substantial profit.[84] Another 15 million gulden loan followed in 1826.[85] Ultimately, then, the Austrian policy of intervention in Italy had yielded multiple profits for the Rothschilds. That was clearly more important to the brothers than the political outcome.

The outbreak of revolution in Spain raised more serious dilemmas. For two years after 1820, Ferdinand VII endured the Cortes constitution, and in that period the liberal government raised a number of loans. Although the Rothschilds – as Salomon hastened to reassure Metternich – were not at first involved in these, they were preparing to take a hand when, in July 1822, Ferdinand and his Ultra-royalist supporters unexpectedly attempted to overthrow the Cortes, calling for foreign intervention when their coup failed.[86] Soon after this, James was in touch with the Spanish financier Bertran de

---

[81]Corti, *Rise*, pp. 295ff., 375–376. Cf. Harold Acton, *The Bourbons of Naples*, London 1956, pp. 688, 699.
[82]Corti, *Rise*, pp. 376–380.
[83]*ibid.*, pp. 298–300, 324–327. See also Bertrand Gille, *Histoire de la Maison Rothschild*, vol. I: *Des origines à 1848*, Geneva 1965, pp. 96–103; Karl F. Helleiner, *The Imperial Loans: A Study in Financial and Diplomatic History*, Oxford 1965, p. 168.
[84]RAL, T5/212, XI/87/OB, Salomon, Vienna, to Nathan, London, April 7, 1823; RAL, T6/34, Metternich to Salomon, Nov. 17. Cf. Helleiner, *Imperial Loans*, pp. 171–175; Corti, *Rise*, pp. 322–323, 327–330.
[85]Gille, *Maison Rothschild*, vol. I, pp. 168f.
[86]RAL, T6/18, Belin [Rothschild agent], Madrid, to de Rothschild Frères, Sept. 23, 1822. In fact the Cortes loans were handled by the Paris bankers Laffitte and Ardouin & Hubbard: Corti, *Rise*, pp. 306ff., 312; Gille, *Maison Rothschild*, vol. I, pp. 108f., 132.

Lys, who hoped to forestall an invasion by reconstituting the government on less "exalted" (that is, radical) lines.[87] It was too late: in April 1823 a French expedition analogous to the Austrian invasion of Naples was launched under the leadership of Louis XVIII's surviving nephew, the Duc d'Angoulême.[88] Ever the pragmatist, James now offered his services to the French premier, the Comte de Villèle.[89] And just as military intervention had necessitated a new loan in Vienna, so too in Paris the government was obliged to fund its military adventure by borrowing.[90]

The difference between Naples and Spain was that after the restoration of the Spanish Bourbon (which had been achieved by the end of 1824), the Rothschilds declined to lend to his neo-absolutist regime without guarantees from the French government.[91] There were three reasons for this: the regime's refusal to recognise and redeem the bonds previously issued by the Cortes,[92] its refusal to repay France the costs of the invasion and, finally, the bankers' suspicion that any money lent to Ferdinand might be used in a last and doubtless vain attempt to recapture his former colonies in South America. As the Austrian ambassador in Paris shrewdly reported to Metternich: "Although the House of Rothschild may pretend that their sympathies are purely monarchist, the recognition of the engagements entered into by the Cortes Government, and the independence of the Spanish colonies, would provide a far wider field for his [Nathan's] financial enterprises and afford political security, the value of which they do not fail to appreciate."[93] In short, the Rothschilds' role in Spain had been ambivalent: initially showing signs of interest in the Cortes government, then financing the French invasion, but declining to bankroll the restored regime.

Their reaction to the revolution of 1830 also illustrates the brothers' political agnosticism. In Paris, James made the transition from Bourbon to Orleanist regime with the greatest of ease and shed no tears for the ousted monarch and ministers. He and his brothers also rushed to provide financial support for the new kingdom of Belgium as soon as Leopold of Saxe-Coburg – whom they had cultivated for some years – had accepted the throne. The Rothschilds' sole concern, once the danger of republicanism in France had faded, was the possibility that the revolutions might lead indirectly to a war between the great powers. It is easy to see why. A revolution – or even a reform crisis – primarily affected bonds in one country. As the 1790s had shown, a general European war would have caused a severe slump in the price of all government securities in all markets, with disastrous implications for the brothers' immense investment portfolio.

This helps explain why so many contemporaries believed that the Rothschilds not only favoured peace but also used their financial leverage to preserve it. Ludwig

---

[87]Corti, *Rise*, pp. 314ff.; Bertier de Sauvigny, *Metternich at la France*, pp. 729–733.
[88]RAL, T6/28, Dalberg, Paris, to Nathan, London, March 28, 1823.
[89]Jean Baptiste de Villèle, *Mémoires et corréspondance du comte de Villèle*, Paris 1888–1890, vol. III, pp. 429f.; vol. IV, p. 73.
[90]*ibid.*, vol. III, p. 535; vol. IV, pp. 212f., 228; Comte Pierre François Hercule de Serre, *Correspondance du comte de Serre 1796–1824, annotée et publiée par son fils*, Paris 1876, vol. IV, p. 566; François René, Vicomte de Chateaubriand, *Correspondance générale de Chateaubriand*, Paris 1913, vol. IV, pp. 315f.; vol. V, p. 16.
[91]RAL, Cataloguing Box [letter copy book Foreign Loans 1823–1831], Nathan, London, to "My Dear Brother", probably James, Paris, July 22, 1823; Chateaubriand, *Correspondance générale*, vol. V, p. 102.
[92]Villèle, *Mémoires*, vol. IV, p. 57.
[93]Corti, *Rise*, pp. 357f.

Börne, for example, explicitly argued that Rothschild sales of Austrian government bonds had limited Metternich's diplomatic room for manoeuvre in 1831, when the Prince was itching to check the spread of revolution in Belgium as well as Italy. Börne also implied strongly that the Rothschilds were keen to see France adopting a more pacific policy towards Austria.[94] Similar claims were made by political insiders too, for example by the Austrian diplomat Count Prokesch von Osten in December 1830: "It is all a question of ways and means and what Rothschild says is decisive, and he won't give any money for war."[95] Two years later the Austrian Finance Minister Baron Kübeck regarded Salomon as synonymous with "peace".[96] Nor was it only Austria which was perceived to be subject to Rothschild pressure: Metternich and his ambassador in Paris, Apponyi, alleged that the French government was even more susceptible. In Metternich's words: "The House of Rothschild ... for reasons that are natural although I cannot regard them as good, and certainly not as morally satisfactory, plays a much bigger part in France than do the foreign cabinets, except possibly that of England. The great vehicle in France is money ..."[97]

How much power over the policy of the great powers did the Rothschilds wield at this time? To answer this question, it is first necessary to distinguish their use of financial leverage – principally their ability to refuse loans to governments contemplating war – from the less tangible influence they were able to exercise in their capacity as a channel of diplomatic communication. This second function grew rapidly in importance in the course of the 1830s, though it had already begun to develop in the previous decade. In essence, statesmen and diplomats began to make use of the Rothschilds' network of communication because it was quicker than the official courier systems used for relaying diplomatic correspondence, and because messages of a non-binding nature could be sent from government to government indirectly via the brothers. It was in the 1820s that Metternich himself began to make use of the Rothschilds' courier service for important correspondence. From this point onwards, he and Salomon shared political news on a regular basis, the prince informing Salomon of Austrian intentions while the banker provided "Uncle" (his Rothschild codename) with news he received from his brothers. Thus Metternich made use of Salomon's couriers to Vienna and London at Pressburg in 1825.[98] When a minor crisis in Franco-Austrian relations blew up in 1826, it was a Rothschild courier who carried Villèle's placatory note to Metternich.[99] The Rothschilds also broke the news of the French revolution of July 1830 to Metternich, who was then in Bohemia.[100] It is not hard to see why the brothers were willing to provide this service: it gave them advance knowledge of foreign policy as it was being formed, and this in turn allowed them to make better-informed investment decisions.

---

[94]Börne, *Mittheilungen*.
[95]Corti, *Reign*, p. 10.
[96]Kübeck, *Tagebücher*, vol. I/2, p. 593.
[97]Bouvier, *Rothschild*, p. 52.
[98]See e.g. RAL, XI/109/10/1/11, Metternich, Pressburg, to Salomon, Vienna, Nov. 14, 1825; RAL, XI/109/10/1/12, Salomon, Vienna, to Metternich, Pressburg, Nov. 15.
[99]Bertier de Sauvigny, *Metternich et la France*, pp. 1157f.
[100]Karl von Mendelssohn Bartholdy (ed.), *Briefe von Friedrich von Gentz an Pilat: Ein Beitrag zur Geschichte Deutschlands im XIX. Jahrhundert*, Leipzig 1868, vol. II, pp. 288f.; Mann, *Secretary of Europe*, p. 298; Bertier de Sauvigny, *Metternich et la France*, p. 1361.

Between March 1831 and March 1832, there was a series of "flashpoints" when war involving more than one of the great powers seemed to come perilously close. On each occasion the Rothschilds worked frenetically to diminish the tension, using both their financial leverage and their role as an unofficial diplomatic channel. The first crisis raised the possibility not only of Austrian intervention in the Papal states but also of French moves in support of the revolutionaries; James and Salomon were much involved in the war of words which duly broke out between Paris and Vienna. Ultimately, Austria intervened not only in Modena (which the French tacitly accepted) but also in Bologna, in response to an appeal from Pope Gregory XVI; action which, after much prevarication, elicited a more or less direct threat of war from the French government – relayed, yet again, by James.[101] The second flashpoint came in August 1831 over Belgium. After months of uncertainty about the election of Leopold of Saxe-Coburg as King, the Dutch invasion of Belgium raised the possibility of a general war once more. But again the powers drew back. Neither Prussia nor Russia supported the Dutch move and the British government – after some tense negotiations – sanctioned the French decision to send an expeditionary force to Belgium, provided it withdrew once the Dutch had been driven out. It was only during October that the danger of war over Belgium gradually receded; though even the signing of the 24 Articles by Belgium on November 15 was far from the breakthrough it initially seemed, as Russia, Austria and Prussia took until May 1832 to ratify them, and the Dutch King continued to withhold his signature.[102] The third and final war scare came in February 1832, as a result of fresh unrest in the Papal States. Once again Austrian troops were called in, and once again the French sought to take a hand. Indeed, this time a French force was actually sent to occupy the port of Ancona – "a serious blunder", in James's view.[103] However, this was far less serious than the earlier crises (as the muted reaction of the markets testified) and there was never any real prospect of a serious breach between Paris and Vienna.

During each of these crises, the Rothschilds repeatedly argued against war. When Salomon returned to Vienna in early October 1830, it was in order "to impress upon Prince Metternich how important it now is to maintain peace", as "the issue of peace or war depend[ed] entirely upon" him.[104] This was a slight exaggeration, as Austrian influence over the Belgian question was limited; on the other hand, Russia (and possibly also Prussia) would be more likely to go on the offensive if a lead came from Vienna – that was the implication of the Carlsbad agreement of August 1830, which had reaffirmed the counter-revolutionary intent of the Holy Alliance. Over Italy, Metternich was unequivocal. He told Salomon in November 1830 that he was prepared "to send troops ... to keep the country quiet",[105] and he duly did so in both Modena and Bologna. Until April 1831 Salomon could do little more than relay Austrian intentions to Paris (in itself an important service as his letters to James

---

[101]RAL, XI/109/20/1/28, James, Paris, to Salomon, Vienna, undated, March 1831; RAL, XI/109J/J/31, James to Nathan, March 23; same to same, March 24; March 26; March 27; March 29; March 30.
[102]Details in Ferguson, *World's Banker*, pp. 253f.
[103]RAL, XI/109J/J/32, James, Paris, to Nathan, London, March 4, 1832.
[104]RAL, XI/109J/J/30A, Salomon, Paris, to Nathan, London, Oct. 10, 1830.
[105]RAL, XI/109/17/1/12, Lionel, Paris, to his parents, London, Nov. 28, 1830.

arrived as much as three days before Apponyi's official instructions). When the Tsar appealed for help in Poland, however, Salomon was able to exert real influence, forewarning Metternich's rival Count Kolowrat, who intervened "with uncharacteristic decisiveness" against such assistance.[106] By July he was able confidently to assure his brothers: "Strictly between ourselves, Austria will not make war, does not want war and is doing everything possible to avoid having a war ... I am convinced that even if England and France declared war on ... *Russia*, it would make no difference to Austria, we would stay ... neutral."[107] Even when he was away from Vienna, Salomon kept up the pressure on Metternich to avoid war. In March 1832 he wrote long and effusive letters from Paris, urging him not to overreact to Périer's decision to send troops to Ancona.[108] In November, when French troops were descending on Antwerp, Kübeck complained that "Prince Metternich is a veritable pendulum, swinging back and forth between Tatichev [the Russian ambassador in Vienna] and war, and Salomon Rothschild and peace."[109]

What made Metternich pay heed to Salomon was, needless to say, money. As early as November 1830 Salomon intimated to Gentz that, after the heavy losses suffered by himself and his brothers, there could be no question of their helping to finance a war.[110] When Metternich sent Austrian troops into Bologna, James backed up Périer's threat to intervene with an explicitly financial argument, evidently intended for official consumption. In the event of war, he asked, "how would Austria be able to pay the interest [on her debt]? ... Better not to risk one's entire capital".[111]

Yet Salomon did not occupy a monopolistic position. In the spring of 1830, when the Austrian government had issued a loan of 30 million gulden of 4 per cent metalliques, he had merely been one of a consortium of four issuing houses, along with Arnstein & Eskeles, Sina and Geymüller; and he had failed to wrest control of a planned conversion operation from the Frankfurt house of Bethmann.[112] In the wake of the revolution, he could not contemplate the idea of a new government loan being handled by his rivals. So when Metternich requested an issue of 36 million gulden of 5 per cent metalliques to finance intervention in Italy in March 1831, Salomon took a share.[113] Admittedly, a clause was inserted stating that the loan would have to be repaid within three months in the event of a war. But Salomon did nothing to oppose Metternich's covert borrowing of the 20 million francs which had been deposited with the Frankfurt house since 1815 in the name of the German Confederation.[114] Nor did he achieve much by a thinly veiled threat to withdraw financial support if Metternich did not ratify the 24 Articles relating to Belgium in early 1832:

---

[106]Kübeck, *Tagebücher*, vol. I/2, p. 382.
[107]RAL, XI/109/22/2/22, Salomon, Vienna, to his brothers, July 9, 1831.
[108]Corti, *Reign*, pp. 58–62.
[109]Kübeck, *Tagebücher*, vol. I/2, p. 593.
[110]Gentz, *Briefe an Pilat*, vol. II, p. 334.
[111]RAL, XI/109/20/1/28, James, Paris, to Salomon, Vienna, undated, March 1831.
[112]Corti, *Rise*, pp. 414–420.
[113]Kübeck, *Tagebücher*, vol. II/2, pp. 412ff.
[114]Corti, *Reign*, pp. 39f.

> Your Highness is aware that we have subscribed a quarter of the last loan of 50 million and have also purchased securities on the Bourse in order to maintain the price of metalliques, that we are carrying through other important financial operations, and that we are also negotiating new ones. As these are closely affected by the course of political events, and as I would like to see my brother happy and free from worry, I would humbly beg Your Highness to be pleased to let my manager ... know of your opinion as to the present situation and whether the Austrian Government will recognise Belgium and allow the statement to be ratified.[115]

Metternich hastened to reassure him "that, as the fundamental attitude and will of the Russian Tsar were very well known to him, he vouched for the fact that these, without a single exception, were as peaceful as those of the Austrian Emperor".[116] But these were soothing words; Austria did not ratify the articles for another three months.

Salomon's most explicit use of the financial lever came in June 1832, while he was in Paris. "I do not regard [it] with indifference", he wrote with uncharacteristic bluntness in a letter he ordered to be passed on to Metternich and Kolowrat, "... that Austria should issue a further metalliques loan during the year 1832, which God forbid":

> You know that, taking the sum of our holdings of metalliques at Frankfurt, Paris, London and Vienna ... the total amounts to several millions. Now ... if our firm were forced to sell ... what price could we expect to get? ... We should be forced to realise our metalliques, whether we wished to or not. What would the capitalists and the commercial world say to the issue of two metalliques loans in one year, when the payments in respect of the first loan are not due to be completed until December? Such action might produce a sharp fall in metalliques. The government would not be able to get further loans at a low rate of interest, a blow would be dealt at the credit of Austria's finances and the government would fail to achieve its object ... Moreover, what would the public say to a new loan? "There will be war – there must be a war, as Austria is issuing another loan." Even if we were not forced to sell, as we should be, prices would fall sharply and Austria's credit would be severely damaged ... [This is] my conviction as to what would happen if there were to be even a whisper of a suggestion that another loan should be issued this year.[117]

At first sight, this does indeed seem like the exertion of financial pressure with a view to limiting Metternich's room for aggressive manoeuvre. But it is important to realise that it came at a time of relatively low international tension: the Austrians had by now ratified the 24 Articles and the dispute over Ancona had been resolved. On closer inspection, it looks more like a primarily financial argument to avoid a slump in the price of Austrian bonds which would have been detrimental to the Vienna house's balance sheet. Salomon was not opposing a loan altogether; for purely technical reasons, he was arguing that "if it is essential to get money, it is much better to issue Treasury bills, and get in twelve millions of silver for the bank ... a procedure which costs the government hardly anything and provides it with money for six to eight months". A year later, he and the three other Vienna houses were perfectly happy to participate in another issue of metalliques worth 40 million florins, and in

---

[115]*ibid.*, pp. 56f.
[116]RAL, XI/109/5/2/4, Salomon, Vienna, to his brothers, Jan. 7, 1832.
[117]Corti, *Reign*, pp. 66ff.

1834 to a lottery loan of 25 million gulden.[118] In short, the idea that Salomon was able to impose a pacific policy on Metternich by financial means looks doubtful. On the other hand, there is ample evidence here that the relationship between the Rothschilds and Metternich was, in terms of power politics, a relationship between equals, no matter how deferential the tone of Salomon's letters.

A further illustration of this point can be found in the correspondence concerning Spain in the period of civil war during the 1830s. On the question of lending to the parliamentary regime, the brothers were divided: Nathan was evidently keen to play a bigger and more independent role in Spanish finances, while Salomon was generally opposed to involvement, primarily because of the intense pressure to which he was subjected by Metternich. Nathan's initial strategy seems to have been to secure some sort of agreement on the old Cortes bonds as the prelude to any new Spanish loan.[119] However, all the Spanish negotiators with whom the Rothschilds dealt carefully avoided giving a commitment on the issue.[120] After exceptionally convoluted and protracted negotiations, Nathan decided to ignore the warnings of Metternich, the Austrian ambassador Apponyi, the Russian ambassador Pozzo and no fewer than three French ministers (de Broglie, Rigny and Soult), all of whom strongly advised the Rothschilds to avoid Spain. On April 18 he offered to advance the Spanish government 15 million francs to pay the interest due at the end of June on its undeferred bonds. He had obtained no firm guarantee from Madrid that the Cortes bonds would be revalued, merely an empty promise that the issue would be raised when the Cortes met. Nor did he receive any security for his advance when the agreement was signed with the Spanish ambassador in Paris and a representative of the Bank of San Fernando on June 7.[121] As the Carlist-inclined Duke of Wellington sardonically observed, the Rothschilds were now well and truly "in the boat";[122] and, just as Metternich and the rest had predicted, "the boat" began to sink almost at once with the appointment of a new Finance Minister in Madrid, who reneged on the agreement.

Salomon now acted energetically to counter Nathan's arguments for intervention, ultimately going to extraordinary lengths to dissociate himself from his brother's actions in his correspondence with Metternich. The latter, in any case, had been kept well informed of Nathan's actions by the Austrian chargé d'affaires in London, Hummelauer, and a junior official named Kirchner who was supposedly assisting Nathan with his consular duties.[123] To clear himself of guilt by association, Salomon therefore had to write one of the most extraordinary of all Rothschild letters,

---

[118]RAL, XI/109/29/1/34, Anselm, Frankfurt, to James and Lionel, Paris, Jan. 29, 1833; RAL, XI/109/29/2/43, submission by MAR, Eskeles, Geymüller and Sina, Feb. 7; RAL, XI/109/31a/1/72, Nat, Vienna, to his parents, London, April 22, 1834; RAL, XI/109/31a/2/62, submission for loan, April 26; RAL, XI/109J/J/34, James, Paris, to Nathan and Anthony, April 26.

[119]RAL, XI/109J/J/31, James, Paris, to Nathan, London, Feb. 4, 1831; same to same, Feb. 5; June 6; July 2; Nov. 16; RAL, XI/109/20/1/14, Lionel, Paris, to his parents, London, March 23; RAL, XI/109/27/1/34, same to same, March 20, 1832.

[120]RAL, XI/109J/J/32A, James and Salomon, Paris, to Nathan, London, April 22, 1832; James and Salomon to Nathan and their nephews, Oct. 25; same to same, Oct. 27; RAL, XI/109/30/1/57, Lionel, Paris, to his parents, London, Dec. 23.

[121]RAL, XI/109/33/4/8, Agreement signed by Queen Regent, May 15, 1834.

[122]RAL, XI/109J/J/34, James, Paris, to Nathan, London, July 3, 1834.

[123]Corti, *Reign*, pp. 125–129, 139.

addressed to his senior clerk in Vienna, Leopold von Wertheimstein, but explicitly intended for Metternich's eyes. He began by claiming that the collapse in Spanish bond prices following the appointment of Toreno had been engineered by the Rothschilds as an act of "vengeance" for the losses he had caused them. According to accounts which Salomon enclosed, Nathan had sold no less than £2 million of Spanish bonds, ruining Toreno's credit and proving that the Rothschilds were now "confirmed enemies of Spain". Not only that, but Salomon and James had then gone to see Talleyrand, Guizot, Broglie and Louis Philippe himself to argue "that France's credit would go to the devil if they intervened, and that they would have to face a second and third revolution". There was therefore no question of the Rothschilds lending "a single farthing" more to Spain. As if to convince Metternich of his sincerity, Salomon's letter concluded by heaping abuse on his brother's head. "My brother Nathan Mayer," he wrote,

> is one of the ablest men as far as the Exchequer and price movements are concerned but has no special aptitude in other matters ... [H]e is a child in politics ... [and] believes that the Powers will be pleased by intervention ... In other matters that are not concerned with the Bourse, [he] is not particularly bright; he is exceedingly competent in his office, but, apart from that, between ourselves, he can hardly spell his own name. This brother of mine, however, is so disgusted with Spain that he can hardly bear himself, just like all of us, only perhaps he feels it more because he realises that he made the advance of 15,000,000 francs without asking any of his partners about it.

Nor was that all. Salomon even went so far as to suggest that Nathan's error had put the entire future of the brothers' partnership in jeopardy.

> I myself do not yet know when we brothers will meet; whether the affair of the Spanish Loan will cause a split we shall see. I am sixty, my brother at Frankfurt is sixty-two; I have only two children and if I live very carefully I can live on the interest of my capital; I have fortunately only to provide for my son, as my Betty is as rich as her father. I do not mean that I intend to give up business but only to see to it that I can sleep peacefully. The Spanish affair has completely ruined my nerves; it is not the loss of money, for, even if the whole 15,000,000 francs had been lost, my share would have been only 3,000,000, but the unpleasantness which we have had with this business. Now Nathan Mayer Rothschild has four grown-up sons, and Carl has two younger boys, so they manage on the basis of a dozen heads. Because my father has so disposed we shall probably have to remain together, but I must confess that it has all very much tired and exhausted
> Your,
> S. M. v. Rothschild.[124]

This was no mere charade: the Rothschilds' private correspondence indicates how strongly Salomon felt on this issue. As late as 1840, James could still tell his nephews:

> [W]e can't make a loan for Spain under our own name, unless a guarantee is provided by England and by France and ... nevertheless I tell you, my dear nephews, I don't want to have anything to do with it ... [I]t is only if the Governments provide us with the necessary guarantees that we can give the Northern Powers a reason, otherwise I can tell

---

[124] *ibid.*, pp. 131–135.

you, my dear nephews, that the first thing which my good Salomon will do will be to withdraw from the business. Do you think that this deal will generate a large enough profit to justify doing something like this?[125]

It has generally been assumed that on this issue Metternich's political power prevailed over the Rothschilds' financial interests. Armed with good-quality intelligence and making the most of Salomon's desire to acquire the title of Austrian consul for his son and nephews,[126] Metternich appears to have succeeded in scuppering the project of an Anglo-French guaranteed loan to Toreno's successor, Mendizábal. Like the British ambassador in Spain, Mendizábal assumed that the Rothschilds would back this project, not least because of his business links with James, with whom he had done business in Portuguese bonds.[127] But Nathan – apparently responding to Salomon's pressure – chose to leak the Anglo-French plan to Vienna and more or less deliberately allowed the project to fall through, leaving Mendizábal high and dry. Indeed, he told Palmerston that he had no confidence in the solvency of Mendizábal's government: when the British Foreign Secretary pointed out that the planned sale of crown lands would raise money, Nathan replied with a characteristically earthy image: "Yes, in time, but not in time for the May dividend. It is like telling me at seven o'clock when I want my dinner [that] there is a calf feeding in a field a mile off."[128] Contrary to the widespread expectation in diplomatic circles that they were eager to make such a guaranteed loan, Nathan and James were steadily withdrawing from the Spanish bond market altogether. Ultimately, despite pressure from the French government, they kept on selling, and bought Spanish bonds only in order to continue selling them; indeed, Nathan's last instructions to his sons before his untimely death in 1836 were to liquidate all their holdings of Spanish bonds. By 1837 the Rothschilds had more or less withdrawn completely from Spanish bonds. The Spanish Prime Minister was now "that stinking Mendizábal", whom James had "never trusted"; Spanish bonds – now trading as low as 19 – were simply "muck" or "shit".[129] The fact that Salomon moved so quickly after Nathan's death to secure for Lionel the Austrian consulship in London also seems to point to the importance of Metternich's leverage.[130]

However, although Metternich appeared to have won, the private Rothschild letters show that if France and Britain had intervened militarily – rather than just financially – the Rothschilds might well have resumed large-scale lending to Spain. In ditching Mendizábal Nathan was not merely bowing to pressure from Vienna. He was acting out of self-interest, on the ground that any loan to Spain was bound to fail in the absence of military intervention: no Spanish government could now afford to pay both the interest on its external debt and an army big enough to beat the

---

[125]RAL, XI/109J/J/40B, James, Paris, to his nephews, Feb. 28, 1840.
[126]Corti, *Reign*, pp. 168f.
[127]Roger Bullen and Felicity Strong (eds.), *Palmerston*, vol. I: *Private correspondence with Sir George Villiers*, London 1985, p. 316.
[128]*ibid.*, pp. 352–358, 294f., 434, 448, 554.
[129]RAL, XI/109J/J/36, James and Salomon, Paris, to their nephews, London, Sept. 14, 1836; James to his nephews, Sept. 18; same to same, Oct. 26; Nov. 2; Nov. 23; Dec. 5; Dec. 9; Dec. 13.
[130]Corti, *Reign*, pp. 147–152, 156ff., 169–174.

Carlists. Despite all that Salomon had said to Metternich, by March 1836 James was privately itching for France to intervene. As he put it to Nathan following an inconclusive meeting with Louis Philippe and Thiers:

> If we should be so fortunate that we, over here, decide to intervene [in Spain], this could make a difference for us of many hundreds of thousands of pounds sterling, and we could earn a great deal of money, because we could then calmly deal in bills, quicksilver and everything else ... I hope to God that they will indeed decide to intervene and you can then imagine how much business this will generate. I spoke so much [in favour of intervention] that my tongue nearly fell out of my throat.[131]

When the possibility of French intervention surfaced again in July, he and Lionel were again briefly enthused, only to be disappointed at the half-heartedness of the measures taken.[132] It was the same story when Thiers failed to overcome the King's opposition to intervention in the spring of 1837.[133]

On the other hand, it should not be assumed that the Rothschilds' refusal to back a full-scale loan to Mendizábal implied a complete withdrawal from Spanish finances. Before long, the practice of making advances on the mercury from the Almadén mines was resumed (despite Salomon's assurances to the contrary to Metternich), making sums of the order of £100,000 available to the government.[134] James also became increasingly interested in the revenue Spain was earning from Havana. In January 1837, a deal was proposed by Mendizábal which involved a buy-back of the deferred Cortes bonds in return for bills on Havana. Interestingly, the Rothschilds – Salomon included – were keen to do this, provided it could be kept secret.[135]

V

The Rothschilds, then, were far from being mere paymasters of the counter-revolution. Indeed, they were themselves agents of revolutionary change – a point which Heine came to appreciate sooner than most.

As is well known, railways made conservatives like Metternich uneasy: the "transformation in political and social conditions" which he saw as their inevitable consequence did not seem likely to assist him in defending the Central European status quo.[136] Yet it is a surprising fact that the first Rothschild railway was conceived (in

---

[131] RAL, XI/109J/J/36B, James, Paris, to Nathan and his nephews, March 19, 1836.
[132] RAL, RFamC/4/133, Lionel, Frankfurt, to James, Kreuznach, July 12, 1836; RAL, XI/109J/J/36, James, Kreuznach, to his brothers and nephew, July 14; James to Nat and Anthony, Aug. 17; RAL, RFamC/4/146, Lionel to Anthony and Nat, July 22.
[133] RAL, XI/109J/J/37, James, Paris, to his nephews, April 8, 1837; same to same, April 9; April 10; April 11.
[134] RAL, XI/109J/J/36, James, Paris, to Nathan and his nephews, London, April 12, 1836; same to same, April 30; James to Nat, June 4; James, Frankfurt, to Anthony, Paris, June 14; RAL, RFamC/4/140, Lionel, Frankfurt, to Anthony and Nat, July 17.
[135] RAL, XI/101/0–2/9, Mendizábal, Madrid, to deRF and NMR, Jan. 18, 1837; RAL, XI/101/0–2/10, deRF to Weisweiller, Madrid, Jan. 25; RAL, XI/101/0–2/11, same to same, Jan. 26; RAL, XI/101/0–4/10, March 22.
[136] James J. Sheehan, *German History, 1770–1866*, Oxford 1989, pp. 466ff.

1830) and constructed in Habsburg territory. It was not Salomon von Rothschild's own idea but that of a professor at the Vienna Polytechnic Institute named Franz Xavier Riepel, a mining expert who believed that the new technology of railways could be used to link the salt mines of Wieliczka in Galicia and the iron and coal mines of Moravian Ostrau (Ostrava) to the imperial capital more than 200 miles to the south-west. This was an ambitiously long line for the time.

Initially, the biggest obstacle to the scheme was political inertia in Vienna itself. On the basis of a report drafted by Riepel after his visit to England, Salomon submitted a petition to the Emperor to allow land to be acquired for the project. Predictably, it was shelved, the Crown Prince observing with true Habsburg insight that "Even the coach to Kagran isn't always full." The postal authorities also expressed reservations, fearing a threat to their monopoly. Undaunted, Salomon pressed on. He took over the horse-drawn railway line linking the Danube and the Gmündensee from an insolvent French engineer named Zola (the novelist's father), and commissioned Riepel to investigate the best possible route for the line to Moravia and Galicia.[137] Finally, in April 1835 – just six weeks after the death of the Emperor Francis – he felt ready to renew his appeal for imperial and royal backing. This time he was successful – an outcome which probably owed more to Metternich's and Kolowrat's decision to support the scheme than to the credibility of Salomon's claims that "the achievement of this great means of communication would be of benefit to the State and the public weal, no less than to those who join in the undertaking".[138]

It was agreed that a joint stock company should be set up to construct a line between Vienna and Bochnia (south-east of Cracow). As a second thought, to ensure that there would be no royal change of mind, Salomon suggested that the line be called the *Kaiser-Ferdinand-Nordbahn*. This appeal to royal vanity was successful. For good measure, he also sought – as he put it to Metternich – to "take such steps as may be appropriate to induce such statesmen as are the bearers of honoured names to place themselves as patrons at the head of this national undertaking". Specifically, he sought to enlist Metternich, Kolowrat and the head of the imperial Treasury, Count Mittrowsky, as board members. This use of noble names to lend respectability to new companies – in return for financial perks – was a device widely employed in England and elsewhere; in the Austrian case it was essential to overcome royal and bureaucratic opposition.[139]

In fact, the benefits of the *Nordbahn* – as the line was usually known – might well have ended up being greater for the "common weal" than for those who invested in it. The line was supposed to take ten years to build; the final stretch to Bochnia was not completed until 1858. It was supposed to cost 12 million gulden (£1 million), roughly 16,600 gulden per mile; the final figure was closer to 27,750 gulden. Yet – as so often in the history of railways – short-term benefits to investors tended to compensate for (or at least to distract from) such long-term cost overruns. From the

---

[137]Kurt Grunwald, 'Europe's Railways and Jewish Enterprise: German Jews as pioneers of railway promotion', *LBI Year Book XII* (1967), pp. 170ff.
[138]Haus-, Hof- und Staatsarchiv Wien, SMR to Austrian Kolowrat, April 15, 1835.
[139]Corti, *Reign*, pp. 92–99.

Salomon von Rothschild's railway

Salomon von Rothschild with a rail map

moment the concession was granted, demand for shares in the firm dramatically outstripped supply. Of 12,000 shares (each worth 1,000 gulden), Salomon retained 8,000, so that just 4,000 were offered to the public. There were 27,490 applications, driving the share price up well above par.[140]

These short-term capital gains help explain why other Austrian bankers hurried to compete – even when they realised better than Salomon the formidable practical problems involved. No sooner had Rothschild secured the Nordbahn concession than Sina petitioned to be granted the concession for the line from Vienna to Trieste, a petition which enjoyed some official support on the ground that Sina, unlike Salomon, was Austrian-born and hence a Habsburg subject. It is not wholly apparent why, after many years of amicable co-operation in the realm of Austrian bond issues, the major Vienna banks failed to co-operate over railways; but Salomon did not fire the first shot. Indeed, in allowing Sina and Arnstein & Eskeles substantial shareholdings in the *Nordbahn* and according them due influence on the company's provisional board of management, he was singularly accommodating. Unfortunately, the other bankers appear to have been intent on some sort of spoiling operation. At the second general meeting of the *Nordbahn*, Ludwig von Pereira (a partner at Arnstein & Eskeles) launched a well-researched technical critique of the engineering plans and financial projections, a move which succeeded in arousing the hitherto dormant anxieties of the Emperor. It was only with difficulty that Salomon and Riepel were able to rebut Pereira's criticisms, at least some of which, it must be said, were to prove quite justified.[141] The climax of this boardroom battle came in October 1836, when Salomon moved a resolution demanding that the building of the railway be commenced or the company liquidated. With 76 out of the 83 votes in favour, he was able to force Sina and Eskeles to resign.[142]

From the outset, Salomon had intended that the *Nordbahn* should be the basis for a succession of branch lines to the major cities on either side of it: indeed, his original petition had specifically mentioned subsidiary lines to Brünn, Olmütz and Troppau. Even while he was locking horns with Pereira – and before a single rail had been laid down – he therefore continued to secure supplementary concessions from the government to allow him to add further branches: to Pressburg, to Bielitz, to Deutsch-Wagram and so on.[143] Work finally began on the first stretch of line north from Vienna in 1837, and trains were running along the first section between Deutsch-Wagram and Florisdorf by the end of the following year.[144] It was not until 1839, however, that freight and passengers began to be carried between Vienna and Brünn, so that for more than two years the company was pouring money into materials and men (some 14,000 in all) for no return, and was kept going only by a Rothschild advance of some 8 million gulden. Small wonder Lionel felt it advisable to reassure Metternich that most English railways "will yield a profit of eight to ten per cent"; there was no sign at this stage that the Austrian line would do so, and its

---

[140]*ibid.*
[141]*ibid.*, pp. 100ff.
[142]*ibid.*, pp. 109–111.
[143]Österr. Verkehrsarchiv, SMR to Kaiser Ferdinand, Feb. 20, 1836; Salomon to Hofkanzlei, March 7; Präsidial-Erinnerung Wien, March 21.
[144]Corti, *Reign*, pp. 111f.

shares duly fell below par. As Salomon later recalled, the Nordbahn had required "the expenditure of large sums of money, and ... patient waiting; sacrifices that I was called upon to make, to the amount of several hundred thousand".[145]

Yet from 1841 onwards Salomon's senior manager Goldschmidt began to detect an improvement on his weekly visits to monitor traffic at the main terminus.[146] As had been the case in England, it was the unexpectedly large amount of passenger traffic – especially families of day-trippers on Sundays – which helped to boost receipts. As early as 1841, up to 10,000 people were regularly using the initial stretch of line from Vienna to the suburb of Vienna–Neustadt.[147] In 1843 the shares rose for the first time since their issue above par to 103; a year later they reached 129 and by 1845 they stood at no less than 228. This represented a huge if belated capital gain to the original investors – above all, to Salomon himself.[148]

Still, it would be unjust to Rothschild to suggest that he operated with the short-term speculative gains solely in mind. On the contrary, he genuinely does seem to have had an entrepreneurial vision of an integrated Austrian transport system. Not only did he envisage from the outset a railway which would link Galicia and Moravia to the imperial capital and southwards to Italy; he hoped also to extend his network into Hungary. Nor was Salomon content to dominate the development of the Habsburg railway system. He also pursued a strategy of "vertical integration", bringing together different stages in a particular economic process under a single corporate roof. As early as 1831, he saw the need to foster independent Austrian supplies of iron and steel, so that the development of the imperial railways would not be reliant on imports from the foundries of Britain. Although his first bid to purchase the Witkowitz Ironworks company in the Ostravian coalfields was unsuccessful (because as a Jew he was prohibited from owning land), he was able to lease the works indirectly from the Archibishop of Olmütz, Count Chotek, in 1841 by setting up a company in partnership with the banker Geymüller. When Geymüller went bankrupt soon after, Salomon petitioned again to be allowed to buy the works, and this time was successful. The Witkowitz works – the first in the Habsburg Empire to use the puddling process necessary for the production of rails – was to remain one of the Austrian house's principal industrial assets for almost a century.[149] At the same time, Salomon began to interest himself in coal mining.[150]

Finally, Salomon's vision of a rail link from Vienna to Trieste led him to expand Rothschild interests beyond land transportation into shipping, taking a leading role in the foundation of the Austrian Steamship Company or Austrian Lloyd in 1835. When the company got into difficulties in the 1830s, Salomon gave it the same life-saving injection of capital he gave the *Nordbahn* at the same time, in the form of a 500,000 gulden loan, in return for a mortgage on the company's seven steamers. As

---

[145]*ibid.*, pp. 232–234.
[146]Goldschmidt, *Erinnerungen*, pp. 33f.
[147]Victor L.Tapie, *The Rise and Fall of the Hapsburg Monarchy*, London 1971, p. 267.
[148]Corti, *Reign*, p. 112.
[149]*ibid.*, p. 232f.
[150]Ivan T. Berend and Györgi Ranki, *Economic Development in East-Central Europe in the 19th and 20th Centuries*, New York – London 1974, p. 100.

with the *Nordbahn*, the investment proved a sound one, with profits rising from around 82,000 gulden to nearly 370,000 gulden between 1841 and 1847.[151]

In short, from a strictly economic point of view the Rothschilds undoubtedly played the part of modernisers in the Habsburg lands before 1848.

VI

It is also misleading to portray Salomon von Rothschild as a mere "court Jew". This understates the exemplary significance which contemporaries attached to the Rothschilds' financial and social success. As early as 1817 other Frankfurt Jews were inclined to boast about the Rothschilds' wealth as a matter of communal pride.[152] When Salomon went to Pressburg in June 1844 to attend a meeting of the Central Hungarian Railway Company, he was greeted by a delegation from the local Jewish community. "Count Esterházy", the police observer reported,

> frustrated their intention of according the Baron a special welcome, as he would not allow the Jews to carry out their scheme of letting off forty rockets. They were restrained even from shouting their welcome which in view of the ill feeling between the citizens and the Jews here, might easily have led to a breach of the peace.[153]

The family sympathised with and encouraged this notion that Rothschild success was Jewish success. When Nathan was appointed Austrian consul, Amschel wrote: "Though it may mean nothing to you, it serves the Jewish interest. You will prevent the apostasy of quite a few Vienna Jews."[154] It was "a lucky thing for the Jews" according to Carl.[155] To James, the titles and other honours he and his brothers accepted were "a mark of distinction for our nation" – that is, for European Jewry.[156] The Rothschilds' ennoblement was widely interpreted in Frankfurt as a slap in the face for those in the town who wished to to reimpose the old disabilities on Jews. "[I]f one Jew is a Baron every Jew is a Baron": that was how they saw it in the *Judengasse*.[157]

Moreover – and this is a crucial point – the Rothschilds systematically used their influence to lobby on behalf of other Jews, as they had already done during the period of Napoleonic rule in western Germany. It was not self-interest which prompted their campaign to restore civil rights to the Jews of Frankfurt, after the city authorities reduced them to second-class *Schutzgenossen* (literally "protected comrades") in October 1816; for the Rothschilds themselves continued to enjoy privileged status. Even as they revoked the emancipation decree of 1811, the Frankfurt authorities

---

[151]Corti, *Reign*, pp. 165, 182–185.
[152]RAL, T27/204, XI/109/6, Amschel, Frankfurt, to James, Paris, Feb. 25, 1817; RAL, T62/21/1, XI/109/7, Carl, Frankfurt, to Salomon, Nathan and James, May 11.
[153]Corti, *Reign*, pp. 239ff.
[154]RAL, T64/326/3, Amschel, Frankfurt, to Nathan, London, April 19, 1818.
[155]RAL, T64/125/3, XI/109/9, Carl, Frankfurt, to Nathan and Salomon, London, April 7, 1818.
[156]RAL, T30/49/2, James to Hannah, Aug. 26, 1815.
[157]RAL, T33/262/1, XI/109/5B, Amschel, Frankfurt, to James, Paris, Oct. 19, 1816; RAL, T27/244, XI/109/6, Amschel to his brothers, March 11, 1817; RAL, T27/149, XI/109/6, Carl to his brothers, April 25. Technically, use of the title "Baron" was premature.

specifically cited Amschel's continued ownership of garden outside the ghetto as evidence of their enlightened attitude towards the Jewish community.[158]

As is well known, the Rothschilds had already attempted to get the question of the Frankfurt Jews discussed at the Congress of Vienna. They raised it again at Aachen; indeed, Amschel argued that Salomon should go there "not for business reasons but in the interest of the whole Jewry".[159] It was this issue that brought them into contact with Friedrich Gentz for the first time, as he and Metternich passed through Frankfurt on their way to the Congress.[160] After the "Hep" riots, James wrote a letter to the Vienna banker David Parish, evidently intended for Metternich's eyes, which explicitly used their financial leverage on behalf of the Jewish "nation":

> What can be the result of such disturbances? Surely they can only have the effect of causing all the rich people of *our nation* to leave Germany and transfer their property to France and England; I myself have advised my brother [Amschel] to shut up house and come here [to Paris]. If we make a start, I am convinced all well-to-do people will follow our example and I question whether the sovereigns of Germany will be pleased with a development which will make it necessary for them to apply to France or England when they are in need of funds. Who buys state bonds in Germany and who has endeavoured to raise the rate of exchange if it be not our nation? Has not our example engendered a certain confidence in the state loans so that Christian firms have also taken heart and invested part of their money in all kinds of securities? ... The object of the agitators at Frankfurt seems to have been ... to collect all the Israelites into a single street; if they had been successful in doing this, might it not have led to a general massacre? I need not point out how undesirable such an occurrence would be, especially at a time when our house might be holding large sums for the account of the Austrian or Prussian Court. It seems to me to be really necessary that Austria and Prussia should devise measures to be applied by the Senate at Frankfurt for energetically dealing with occurrences such as those of the 10th of this month, and thus making *each man* secure in his possessions.[161]

In the view of their avowed adversary, the Bremen delegate to the Frankfurt Diet, the Rothschilds were making full use of their financial leverage. Besides Austria and Prussia, "several minor states have also had recourse to this financial Power in their difficulties, which puts it in a strong position to ask for favours, especially for a favour of such an apparently trivial nature as the protection of a few dozen Jews in a small state".[162]

The brothers kept up the pressure in 1820, pressing Metternich to lean on Buol, who continued to support the Frankfurt authorities.[163] Significantly, when Salomon came to an "important financial arrangement" with Gentz in 1821, it was only after he had once again "bent his ear about the fatal Frankfurt Jews' affair".[164] In 1822 Amschel even wrote to Metternich's lover Princess Lieven "asking for the withdrawal of certain instructions towards [the Frankfurt Jews] that Count Münster must have sent to the Minister of Hanover".

---

[158]RAL, T32/209/1, XI/109/5B, Amschel, Frankfurt, to Salomon and Nathan, London, Sept. 19, 1816.
[159]RAL, T64/237/3, XI/109/9, Amschel, Frankfurt, to his brothers, undated, c. Sept. 1818.
[160]Isidor Kracauer, *Geschichte der Juden in Frankfurt am Main (1150–1824)*, vol. II, Frankfurt 1927, pp. 488, 499.
[161]Corti, *Rise*, pp. 233f. Emphasis added.
[162]Schwemer, *Geschichte*, vol. II, pp. 149ff.
[163]Corti, *Rise*, p. 290.
[164]Kracauer, *Geschichte der Juden*, vol. II, pp. 500ff.

This campaign was not a total failure. A year after his letter to Princess Lieven, for example, Amschel was able to celebrate the hostile Austrian delegate Buol's recall from Frankfurt and the arrival of the more sympathetic Münch-Bellinghausen.[165] And, writing from Berlin in March 1822, Heine detected "better prospects" that the Jews would win back their citizenship. Yet Princess Lieven's private reaction to Amschel's letter was revealing: it was, she told Metternich, "the funniest letter imaginable ... Four pages of sentiment, begging my help for the Jews of his town, and I, the patroness of the Jews! There is a kind of naive confidence in it all, which is at once laughable and touching."[166] If this was how Metternich felt too, the brothers' efforts in Vienna may have been less productive than they imagined. In the end, the Frankfurt authorities made only the most minimal concessions. Although there was to be no return to the ghetto – in itself a cause for relief rather than rejoicing – a plethora of restrictions on Jews remained, and their citizenship was clearly of the second-class variety. The new law confirming the "private citizen's rights" of the "Israelite citizens" (1824) excluded the Jews from political life as before; imposed restrictions on their economic activities; subordinated the community to a Senate commissioner; permitted, as before, only fifteen Jewish marriages a year (only two of which could be with outsiders); and restored the Jewish oath in the law courts.[167] Most of these rules – including the restriction on marriages to Jews from outside Frankfurt – remained in place until 1848. Indeed, the Frankfurt Jews did not secure full legal equality until 1864.

The Rothschilds were not much more successful in Austria itself. In January 1837 Salomon addressed a "special appeal" to Metternich concerning "the destiny of my co-religionists ... the hopes of so many fathers of families and the highest aspirations of thousands of human beings".[168] His specific request was that Jews in Austria be allowed to own land. But the government once again refused to grant any relaxation of discrimination – lest "the public ... suddenly draw the conclusion that full emancipation of the Jews is contemplated". The pattern was repeated elsewhere. On at least two occasions, Salomon protested through Metternich against ill-treatment of the Jewish community of Rome.[169] Probably the most effective action the Rothschilds took on behalf of their "poorer co-religionists" in this period concerned the Jews of Damascus, who were accused in 1840 of the murder of a Sardinian Capuchin friar named Father Tommaso and his servant Ibrahim. James de Rothschild made full use of his position as Austrian consul general in Paris to lobby for the release of the Jews accused of the crime.[170]

Such interventions gave lie to the charges which had been levelled at the Rothschilds in the 1830s of indifference to the fate of their fellow Jews.[171] For the

---

[165]Corti, *Rise*, p. 323.
[166]Princess Dorothea Lieven, *The Private Letters of Princess Lieven to Prince Metternich, 1820–1826*, London 1948, p. 126.
[167]Heuberger and Krohn, *Hinaus aus dem Ghetto*, p. 38.
[168]Corti, *Reign*, pp. 174f.
[169]*ibid.*, pp. 137–140, 176f. See also Muhlstein, Anka, *Baron James: The rise of the French Rothschilds*, London 1983, p. 105.
[170]Jonathan Frankel, *The Damascus affair: "Ritual murder", Politics and the Jews in 1840*, Cambridge 1997.
[171]Robert Liberles, 'The Aristocrat and the synagogue: The Rothschilds and Judaism', in Georg Heuberger (ed.), *The Rothschilds: Essays on the History of a European Family*, Sigmaringen 1994, pp. 95ff.

Rothschilds, however, the real significance of the Damascus affair can be understood only when it is set in its diplomatic context. For the Damascus affair presented James with an ideal opportunity to undermine the position of the French politician Adolphe Thiers, who had become premier a matter of weeks after the supposed "murder" of Father Tommaso. Similarly, Metternich welcomed the chance to challenge the French claim to defend the interests of Catholics in the Holy Land – hence his tolerance of James's conduct in the affair.[172]

This coincidence of interests was characteristic of the Rothschild-Metternich relationship in the 1840s. It was typical of the sense of mutual support that when Nathan's son Lionel was elected an MP in 1847 – the first step in the tortuous campaign to secure admission of Jews to the House of Commons – Metternich sent a letter of congratulation.[173] Did he perhaps fail to see that this was a victory for precisely that liberalism he had for so long sought to resist? By the same token, did the Rothschilds fail to see that their intimacy with Metternich might make them vulnerable to a general liberal advance?

VII

The 1848 revolutions had their roots in the 1847 economic crisis: they were as much a crisis of the financial as of the political order. As early as January of that year Metternich requested Salomon to return urgently from Paris "to contrive some plan which would ward off the crisis of the [financial] market".[174] By the end of September, it seemed that he had succeeded in "averting [an] immeasurable calamity".[175] However, the failure of the Haber bank in Frankfurt proved to have potentially disastrous implications for Eskeles, whom he owed 1 million gulden. With Metternich's instructions in mind, Salomon informed the Frankfurt house on December 23 that he and Sina had agreed to bail Eskeles out.[176]

The transmission mechanism which linked the economic crisis – of which Haber's failure was but one symptom – to the political crisis of 1848 was fiscal. All over Europe, the combination of rising expenditures (first on railways, then on social palliatives, finally on counter-revolutionary measures) and falling revenues (as earnings and consumption slumped) led inevitably to government deficits. Between 1842 and 1847, for example, Austrian expenditure rose by 30 per cent.[177] So deeply ingrained was Salomon's habit of lending to the government that, when he was approached for a new loan of 80 million gulden in February 1847, he "thanked God" for "an extremely good business".[178] It was to prove anything but that. Along with Sina and the foundering Eskeles, he had taken on 2.5 and 5 per cent bonds worth 80 million

---

[172]Details in Ferguson, *World's Banker*, chapter 14.
[173]RAL, T7/100, Salomon, Vienna, to Anselm, Frankfurt, Aug. 5, 1847.
[174]RAL, T7/135, James, Paris, to his nephews, London, Jan. 14, 1847.
[175]RAL, T7/101, Salomon, Vienna, to his son, Frankfurt, Sept. 18, 1847; RAL, T7/102, same to same, Sept. 19; RAL, T/103, Salomon to Metternich, Sept. 19; RAL, T/49, Charlotte, wife of Anselm, Paris, to her mother, Hannah, Sept. 27.
[176]RAL, T7/132, Salomon to MAR, Dec. 23, 1847.
[177]Calculated from B.R. Mitchell, *European Historical Statistics, 1750–1975*, London 1975, pp. 370ff.
[178]RAL, T7/94, Salomon, Vienna, to de Rothschild Frères, Feb. 15, 1847.

gulden nominal, in return for which the bankers had to pay the government 84 million in cash in instalments spread over five years.[179] This would have been good business only if five years of peace and prosperity had been at least probable.

Ostensibly, the government wanted the money to finance new railways: that was what Salomon told the Rothschilds' Russian agent when he tried to sell "a considerable sum" of the new bonds to the Tsar.[180] By November 1847, however, Austria was arming in preparation for intervention in Lombardy and Venetia, where insurrection seemed imminent. Salomon knew this because Metternich had told him. Yet instead of being alarmed he went so far as to offer more financial assistance.[181] Incredibly, he agreed to lend a further 3.7 million gulden in return for 4 per cent bonds, which he furthermore pledged not to sell on the already stretched market: they would, he promised Kübeck, remain "in his own safe" in return for interest of 4.6 per cent.[182] With short-term rates in London at this time standing at 5.85 per cent and the price of 5 per cent metalliques already ten points lower than they had been three years before, this was an extraordinary decision. Even as Salomon's proposal was being discussed, Kübeck was warning that intervention in Italy would lead to "the complete breakdown of our finances". "We are on the verge of an abyss," he told Metternich presciently.[183] Metternich was undaunted. When Salomon began to get cold feet in January, he angrily told him: "Politically, things are all right; the exchange [rate] is not. I do my duty but you do not do yours."[184]

As with his advance to Eskeles, Salomon's undertakings to the government were made without reference to the other Rothschild houses. "We have very curious letters from Vienna," Nathan's son Nat wrote to his brothers at around the same time:

> Our good Uncle is full of Austrian Metallics 2[.5]% & 5% & how he will get out on such markets the Lord knows – Prince Metternich takes our good Uncle in so that he may continue his financial operations, I fancy the F'furt house will find a little difference in their balance the next time they make it up.[185]

This was to prove a serious understatement. When the first efforts were made to compute Salomon's commitments in February 1848, the total approached 4.35 million gulden (around £610,000).[186] That was more than double the capital of the Vienna house in 1844. Now the Rothschilds too were on the edge of an abyss.

It was, needless to say, from a Rothschild courier that Metternich received the news of the fall of Louis Philippe. "Eh bien, mon cher, tout est fini," he is said to have commented, though his subsequent remarks to Salomon were more bullish.[187] It was

---

[179]Corti, *Reign*, p. 251; Gille, *Maison Rothschild*, vol. I, pp. 324f.
[180]AN, 132 AQ 5748/3M9, Salomon, Vienna, to Gasser, St Petersburg, April 4, 1847; Salomon to James and Anselm, Paris, May 1.
[181]Corti, *Reign*, p. 256.
[182]*ibid.*, pp. 245ff.
[183]Udo Heyn, 'Private Banking and Industrialization: The Case of Frankfurt am Main, 1825–1875', unpublished DPhil. thesis (University of Wisconsin, 1969), pp. 358–372.
[184]Alan Sked, *The Survival of the Habsburg Monarchy*, London – New York 1979, p. 113.
[185]RAL, XI/109/65B/2/12, Nat, Paris, to his brothers, London, undated, c. Jan. 1848.
[186]RAL, XI/109/65A/67, Salomon, Vienna, to his brothers, son and nephews, Feb. 12, 1848; RAL, XI/109/65A/93, Anselm, Frankfurt, to James, Feb. 17.
[187]Sheehan, *German History*, p. 662.

indeed all finished. On 13 March crowds of demonstrators clashed with troops outside the hall where the Lower Austrian Estates were meeting. The next day Metternich resigned, fleeing westwards in disguise and, as we have seen, with only a credit-note from his faithful banker Salomon to pay his family's passage to England.[188]

For his part, Salomon interpreted the revolution variously: as an avoidable political mishap attributable to the incompetence of Louis Philippe, the vanity of Princess Metternich and the irresponsibility of Palmerston, or a world-historical upheaval on a par not just with 1789 but with the Peasants' Wars, the Crusades and a biblical plague of locusts. Whichever it was, he regarded it as a divine test of his religious faith.[189] Unlike Metternich, he attempted to stay in Vienna. Despite regularly hearing the sound of "drumming in the streets" in the weeks after March 13, he did not quit the city until June, and then elected to settle with Amschel in less than tranquil Frankfurt.[190] His son Anselm hung on until October 6–7, when armed revolutionaries took up positions on the roof of the Rothschild offices following the lynching of Count Latour outside the War Ministry and the storming of the Arsenal, which was next door but one to the Rothschild office. So dangerous had the city become by this stage that when Moritz Goldschmidt returned to rescue the bank's papers, he had to disguise himself as a milkman.[191]

1848 marked the end of a thirty-year partnership between Metternich and Salomon von Rothschild. The denouement was revealing. The revolution had rendered Metternich not only powerless but also poor, as Carl's daughter Charlotte remarked:

> His castle at Johannisberg has been appropriated because he has not paid his taxes for the past nine years ... The Prince has never owned a large fortune. In his past youth he lived extravagantly and later had to settle the debts of his son. Now he has a large family to provide for and educate. His financial affairs have only recently been put in order by Uncle Salomon.[192]

Somewhat liberal in her own inclinations, Charlotte had little sympathy for the prince's plight and shared the Frankfurt partners' disinclination to give further financial assistance.[193] Yet her husband Lionel felt a sense of familial obligation to "Uncle". In June, Metternich was given a 323,000 gulden advance, secured against his (heavily depreciated) railway shares.[194] A further loan of 5,500 gulden to Princess

---

[188] CPHDCM, 637/1/316, Metternich, Arnheim, to Salomon, Vienna, April 3, 1848.
[189] RAL, XI/109J/J/48, Salomon, Vienna, to his brothers, son and nephews, March 3; same to same, March 4; March 8; March 16; March 19; March 21; March 22; March 23; RAL, XI/109/67, Salomon to Amschel, Frankfurt, April 4; RAL, XI/109/67, same to same, April 6; Salomon to James, April 22; Salomon to Amschel, May 16.
[190] RAL, XI/109/67, Anselm, Vienna, to Amschel, May 26, 1848; same to same, May 28; RAL, T8/54, Anselm to NMR, May 27; RAL, XI/109/67, Salomon to Amschel, June 8; RAL, XI/109/67/1, same to same, June 9; RAL, RFamP/D/1/2, ff. 132–133, Charlotte Diary, Aug. 21.
[191] RAL, XI/109/69A/2, Anselm, Sensing, to Lionel and Anthony, Nov. 5, 1848; same to same, Nov. 6; Nov. 7. Cf. Goldschmidt, *Erinnerungen*, pp. 36f.
[192] RAL, RFam P/D/1/1, Charlotte Diary, March 20, 1848.
[193] RAL, RFamP/D/1/2, ff. 115f., Charlotte Diary, Aug. 20, 1848.
[194] CPHDCM, 637/1/18/16, Extract from Metternich's current account, June 30, 1848.

Melanie appears in the Vienna house's books for November 1848, and by the following year the combined debts of the Metternichs stood at 216,500 gulden.[195] In addition, the repayments on the second half of the 1827 loan – which were supposed to be completed by 1859 – were rescheduled, so that a substantial sum was still outstanding at the end of the 1870s.[196]

In the same way, it was mainly the London Rothschilds who rescued the bankrupt house of Salomon von Rothschild. As Anselm discovered when he arrived in Vienna, his father's position was disastrous: in all, his obligations were closer to 8 million gulden. Salomon was in no position to pay such sums when they fell due, as the greater part of his assets were industrial shares which the revolution had rendered unsaleable.[197] He was, as he told his brothers, "in the most painful situation that ever existed".[198] Salomon pledged all his houses and estates as securities for the money he owed the Frankfurt house; but, as none of these were realisable, the valuation he gave them (5 million gulden) was purely notional.[199] There were bitter recriminations between father and son over the financial morass into which the Vienna house had sunk.

Yet, for all their differences, it did not take long for Anselm to start acting very much as his father had done before the revolution. He was keen from the outset to see Radetzky give "a good licking" to the Piedmontese armies.[200] And by late February 1849 he was beginning to receive the kind of inside information about Austrian diplomacy which his father had for so long taken for granted.[201] He was soon following in Salomon's footsteps by egging on Schwarzenberg against Piedmont.[202] Anselm also enthusiastically welcomed the Russian intervention in Hungary, conscious that Windischgrätz alone could not win.[203] As early as July 1849, he raised the idea of a new Rothschild loan to Austria, as well as urging the Paris house to provide the Russian army in Hungary with financial assistance.[204] He also began to involve himself in the efforts to stabilise the Austrian exchange rate, which war and the suspension of silver convertibility had seriously weakened.[205] By mid-

---

[195] CPHDCM, 637/1/11/1–16, Aufnahme [S. M. Rothschild] am 30. Nov. 1848, Nov. 30, 1848; CPHDCM, 637/1/12/34–7, Zusammenstellung [Vienna house], July 24, 1849.

[196] Berghoeffer, *Meyer Amschel*, pp. 209ff.; Palmer, *Metternich*, p. 318.

[197] RAL, XI/109J/J/48, Salomon, Vienna, to his brothers, son and nephews, March 2, 1848; same to same, March 10; RAL, XI/109/65, March 29; March 30; March 31; CPHDCM, 637/1/12/1–2, SMR to MAR, April 9.

[198] CPHDCM, 637/1/11/1–16, Aufnahme, Nov. 30, 1848.

[199] RAL, XI/109/67, Salomon, Vienna, to Amschel, Frankfurt, April 7, 1848; same to same, April 8; April 9.

[200] RAL, XI/109/67/1, Anselm, Vienna, to his cousins, London, June 21, 1848.

[201] RAL, XI/109/70/2, Anselm, Vienna, to James, Paris, Feb. 22, 1849; Anselm to his cousins, London, Feb. 27; RAL, XI/109/70/3, same to same, March 3.

[202] RAL, XI/109/70/3, Anselm, Vienna, to his cousins, London, March 20, 1849; Anselm to James, March 21.

[203] RAL, XI/109/71/1, Anselm, Vienna, to James, Paris, April 13, 1849; Anselm to his cousins, London, April 23; RAL, XI/109/71/2, same to same, May 2; May 5; May 29.

[204] RAL, XI/109/72/1, Anselm to James and Gustave, July 4, 1849.

[205] RAL, XI/109/71/3, Anselm, Vienna, to James and Gustave, June 16, 1849; Salomon, Vienna, to James, Paris, June 30. See also RAL, XI/109/73/3, James, Paris, to his nephews, London, Nov. 8.

September a small Austrian loan had been arranged in the form of a 71 million gulden issue of treasury bills.[206]

The commitment to the forces of monarchical reaction that these transactions implied aroused some disquiet among members of the family in France and London, where support for Hungary was widespread. Salomon's daughter Betty can hardly have been indifferent to the bitter sentiments expressed in Heine's pro-Magyar poem, "Germany in October 1849", a copy of which he sent her.[207] But Anselm had no time whatever for his English cousins' "uneasy" expressions of pro-Hungarian feeling, advising "your good English folks [to] stick to Ireland & its Potato crop, & keep their arguments for their objects".[208]

To the disappointed revolutionaries of 1848 – not least Marx – the moral was plain: "Thus we find that every tyrant is backed by a Jew ... In truth, the cravings of the oppressors would be hopeless and the practicability of war out of the question, if there were not ... a handful of Jews to ransack pockets."[209] Yet this over-simplified the nature of the relationship between the Rothschilds and the Metternichian system. The Rothschilds were more than mere bulwarks of reaction, just as Salomon von Rothschild was more than a court Jew. The sheer scale and international character of their wealth elevated them far above their eighteenth-century precursors. Nor were they ever unambiguous supporters of Metternichian policy. Sometimes their own economic interests ran counter to the prince's habitual strategy of "containment"; indeed, it was Salomon's cardinal mistake in 1847 to fail to see the conflict between his firm's solvency and the action Metternich intended to take in Italy. Above all, it was impossible for Metternich to rely as closely as he did on the Rothschilds for both personal and public finance without making at least some fundamental concessions to the forces of liberalism. "If I am asked" – as he wrote to Salomon as he fled incognito into exile – "whether [the revolution] could have been avoided by what naive utopians call Reform, I reply with a categorical *No*." Yet the concessions that Salomon had managed to wring from him – economic concessions in the form of his railway, social concessions in the form of his exemptions from anti-Jewish legislation – had implications that were (whatever Metternich might have told himself) progressive. In his 'Memorandum on Ludwig Börne' (1840), Heine had shrewdly identified the fundamental contradiction which underlay the Rothschild-Metternich relationship. "No one", he had argued, "does more to further the revolution than the Rothschilds themselves ... and, though it may sound even more strange, these Rothschilds, the bankers of kings, these princely pursestring-holders, whose existence might be placed in the gravest danger by a collapse of the European state system, nevertheless carry in their minds a consciousness of their revolutionary mission":

> I see in Rothschild one of the greatest revolutionaries who have founded modern democracy. Richelieu, Robespierre and Rothschild are for me three terroristic names, and they signify the gradual annihilation of the old aristocracy. Richelieu, Robespierre and

---

[206]RAL, XI/109/72/2, Anselm, Vienna, to James, Homburg, Aug. 4, 1849; AN, 132 AQ 5749/3M11, SMR to deRF, Aug. 18; RAL, XI/109/72/3, Salomon, Vienna, to his brothers and nephews, Sept. 19.
[207]RAL [formerly CPHDCM], 58-1-403/2, Heinrich Heine, 'Deutschland im Oktober 1849' [copy].
[208]RAL, XI/109/71/3, Anselm, Vienna, to his cousins, London, June 28, 1849.
[209]Quoted in Derek Wilson, *Rothschild: A Story of Wealth and Power*, London 1988, p. 117.

Rothschild are Europe's three most fearful levellers. Richelieu destroyed the sovereignty of the feudal nobility, and subjected it to that royal despotism, which either relegated it to court service, or let it rot in bumpkin-like inactivity in the provinces. Robespierre decapitated this subjugated and idle nobility. But the land remained, and its new master, the new landowner, quickly became another aristocrat just like his predecessor, whose pretensions he continued under another name. Then came Rothschild and destroyed the predominance of land, by raising the system of state bonds to supreme power, thereby mobilising property and income and at the same time endowing money with the previous privileges of the land.[210]

As he looked forward gloomily to his new "*bürgerlich*" existence in England, Metternich still dismissed the idea of political reform as "a dance with torches on powder kegs". Yet in banking with (and on) the Rothschilds he was, in his own way, playing with fire. The ease with which the Rothschilds were able to restore and indeed expand their business after the prince's fall was the best proof that they no longer needed him. In that sense, the "system of state bonds" did indeed prove as revolutionary as any of those political systems Metternich had sought to suppress – perhaps more so.

---

[210]Heinrich Heine, 'Ludwig Börne', in *Sämtliche Schriften*, vol. IV, Munich 1971, p. 28.

Progress and Emancipation in Hungary During the Age of Metternich

BY R. J. W. EVANS

When Metternich wrote home to Austria from his self-imposed Sussex exile at "Brigthen" on 30 March 1849, he commented about the nemesis of his regime twelve months before in his usual conceited and self-righteous fashion: "In the sphere where I was able to act, there was life, whereas everything else had been ailing for years. I believe that much would be on a different footing today if my practical views had not been met by the force of basic inertia."[1] This was a colourable account, to say the least, especially in regard to Hungary, which formed the locus of the State Chancellor's most intensive domestic activity in the years before 1848. Whereas the country took up a formidable amount of his time both inside the *Staatskonferenz* and outside it, it represented also Metternich's biggest failure.[2] He did, however, briefly achieve the near-impossible: unite Hungary and the rest of the Monarchy in common purpose, but at his own expense.

There was an extraordinary synergy between Austria and Hungary about revolutionary liberation in the spring of 1848. Progress concerted itself around Lajos (Louis) Kossuth, who first enunciated the demand for simultaneous freedoms in both halves of the Monarchy; and it continued with the overlapping programmes of German and Magyar reformers.[3] There was even more co-operation between Jews. Adolf Fischhof and Joseph Goldmark, like other early Viennese leaders of the Revolution, were Hungarian-born; both later gained election to the Austrian *Reichstag*. Journalists like Adolf Neustadt and Moritz Mahler made their careers in both countries. Such people helped bind together the two halves of the Monarchy in a distinctively amphibian way. At mid-century nearly half of Vienna's Jews had been born across the Leitha anyway; many of those came from families which had been comparatively recent immigrants to Hungary from Moravia and Bohemia.[4] They

---

[1]"Auf dem Gebiet, auf dem ich handeln konnte, herrschte Leben, auf allen anderen war es seit Jahren im Rückschritt. ... Ich glaube, daß manches heute anders stünde, hätte man meinen praktischen Ansichten nicht das einfache Gehenlassen entgegengestellt." *Metternich –Hartig. Ein Briefwechsel des Staatskanzlers aus dem Exil, 1848–51*, ed. F. Hartig, Vienna – Leipzig 1923, pp. 26–30. "Brigthen" must be a slip of the pen: the ex-Chancellor had already spent months there.
[2]Erzsébet Andics, *Metternich und die Frage Ungarns*, Budapest 1973, pp. 65ff. and *passim*, argues that from the 1830s Hungary came to absorb anything up to 80 per cent of the Chancellor's time.
[3]See, in general, R.J.W. Evans, 'Hungary and the Habsburg Monarchy, 1840–67: A Study in Perceptions', in *Etudes Danubiennes*, vol. II (1986), pp. 18–39.
[4]For this background, see William O. McCagg, *A History of Habsburg Jews, 1670–1918*, Bloomington – Indianapolis 1989, pp. 65ff., 123ff.; see also *idem, Jews in the Hungarian Economy, 1760–1945*, ed. by M.K. Silber, Jerusalem 1992, pp. 53–91.

seemed to embody a commitment to their own and other sorts of emancipation. They anticipated the coming role for the Jewish minorities – some five per cent of the whole population in each case – in both halves of the Monarchy during the second half of the century, as they conquered the commanding economic and intellectual heights of the liberal state.

Yet Hungary was also very different: beyond the *Landstrasse*, as Metternich notoriously put it, Asia began. Hungary's revolutionary paradigm in 1848 yielded a competent reforming ministry, just as Austria slipped into regional feuding and constitutional limbo; this regime was succeeded by civil war precisely as order began to return across the border.[5] Hungary furnished a different experience for Jews too, who found themselves both less and more a part of the new order. They were the target for serious disturbances: not just antisemitic tirades from some radical demagogues or from the likes of the militant priest Sebastian Brunner in Vienna, but street riots, even quasi-pogroms in places, the worst of them in the country's long-time chief city of Pressburg (Pozsony), where the local militia passively looked on, and in its new capital at Pest. There was general resistance to the participation of Jews in the national guard; and although some relaxation of the restrictions upon them had taken place since a diet resolution in their favour in 1840, no fresh civil rights were offered through the April Laws – the blueprint of progress in 1848. No Jew gained election to the liberal Hungarian assembly which met in July of that year.[6]

Yet when war broke out soon afterwards, Jews streamed into the ranks of the *Honvéd*, as many as 20,000 of them serving in its ranks. They made a major contribution behind the scenes too – including the design of the insurrectionist Kossuth banknotes. The cream of their younger intellectuals took the field, men such as Lipót Löw and Ignaz Einhorn. Their reward was the emancipation decree of 28 July 1849: a stillborn piece of legislation since the government which enacted it fell within a fortnight, but a foretaste of the future when Magyar fortunes should be restored.[7] Meanwhile Jews suffered conspicuous victimisation within the general *Gleichbeknechtigung* – as wits called it – when the revolution collapsed: not just a huge impost, but 40,000 cloaks, 40,000 trousers, 60,000 pairs of shoes, and 60,000 pairs of drawers (*gatya*) were requisitioned from the Jews of Pest alone.[8] The causes of all this lie in three basic aspects of the nineteenth-century Hungarian *Sonderweg*.

---

[5]For a brief narrative and bibliography of 1848–9, see R. J. W. Evans in *The Revolutions in Europe, 1848–9: From Reform to Reaction*, ed. Evans and H.Pogge von Strandmann, Oxford 2000, pp. 181–206.
[6]Béla Bernstein, *A negyvennyolcas magyar szabadságharc és a zsidók*, 2nd edn., Budapest 1939, pp. 29ff.; Lajos Venetianer, *A magyar zsidóság története*, Budapest 1922, pp. 164ff.; Mihály Horváth, *Huszonöt év Magyarország történelméből 1823–tól 1848-ig*, 2 vols., Geneva 1864, vol. II, pp. 669–71. Cf. the documentation in *1848–9 a magyar zsidóság életében*, ed. J. Zsoldos, Budapest 1948.
[7]János Beér (ed.), *Az 1848/49. évi népképviseleti országgyűlés*, Budapest 1954, pp. 869–873; cf., most recently, Ambrus Miskolczy, 'Szemere Bertalan napja: 1849. július 28.', *Aetas*, 1998, pp. 143–158. For individuals, here and later, P. Ujvári et al. (comp.), *Zsidó lexikon*, Budapest 1929, repr. 1987, s.vv.
[8]Bernstein, *Magyar szabadságharc*; Venetianer, *Magyar zsidóság története*, pp. 196ff.

The first of Hungary's specialities was the survival there into our period of what, for want of a better phrase, may be described as a feudal regime. The historic stalemate between king and noble estates, functioning ostensibly as executive and legislature respectively (with the judiciary in an intermediary position), left an executive which had to operate through the estates' administration and a diet which had effectively no powers of initiative. The terms of the balance were indeed gradually shifting, as baronial politics became outflanked on one hand by Habsburg centralism, as earlier essayed by Maria Theresa and Joseph II, and on the other by the increased power of the gentry, who would later spearhead a liberal reform movement. Meanwhile, however, the effect was a state authority which was uniquely weak by the standards elsewhere (outside the Ottoman realms, at least) in early nineteenth-century Europe.

The victims were the rest of society: peasants, of course, but more importantly for present purposes the crucial sector of towns and the associated trading and industrial activity. The royal free towns of Hungary (thirty to forty in total by this time) were on the whole stagnant and guild-dominated; the other boroughs, those subject at least formally to a landlord, remained too impotent and dependent to rival them. Commercial enterprise had to come from outside, and on sufferance. Since the expulsion of the Turks there had been scope mainly for the itinerant Balkan merchants known – whatever their actual ethnic origins – as "Greeks". But there were always some Jews too throughout the eighteenth century mostly in the extreme west of the country where they lived in small communities under aristocratic aegis, such as that of the Esterházys in Eisenstadt. Their numbers grew from a few thousands in 1700 to about 80,000 by 1800.

The first stage of emancipation for these Jews came, famously and fleetingly, under Joseph II. With the collapse of the Josephinist programme for Hungary, however, the Habsburgs were forced to retreat again, exercising leverage on the domestic society and economy largely through discriminatory tariff policies which lay outside the reach of the estates. The diet of 1790–1791 left the Jews to face decades of friction with local municipal authorities, which had the right to grant residence and work permits. The resultant interrelationships were too intricate for summary here, but we can note how urban magistracies, as represented by the *Rat*, or inner council (*belső tanács*), tended to be more sympathetic than the mass of the citizenry in the *Gemein*, or outer council (*külső tanács*).[9] From the 1820s things were complicated further by a major influx into the chief towns of Jews from the countryside (where replacements soon appeared, still mainly from the Bohemian lands). These immigrants now largely supplanted the increasingly assimilable and assimilated Greeks – seamlessly so, with the two groups being perceived in a similar way, as cunning (*ravasz*) for example, by their Hungarian neighbours. The clearest case is that of the burgeoning city of Pest (by contrast with its more sedate rival across the Danube,

---

[9]Dénes Oszetzky, *A hazai polgárság társadalmi problémái a rendiség felbomlásakor*, Budapest 1935; Géza Eperjessy, *A szabad királyi városok kézművesipara a reformkori Magyarországon*, Budapest 1988. The overall story of the stages of emancipation from the 1780s to 1849 is told in László Gonda, *A zsidóság Magyarországon, 1526–1945*, Budapest 1992, pp. 41–90.

Buda) where the numbers of artisans of all kinds more than doubled between 1828 and 1840, and those of Jewish masters and journeymen rocketed from under a hundred to more than a thousand in the six years after 1840.[10]

Jews took many of the new profits available, from a boom first in grain, then in wool, leather and other products. Thus the Pest merchants Samuel Wodianer and Moritz Ullmann became the prime exporters of wool and tobacco respectively.[11] Jews associated themselves with both progressive and profligate landowners, especially as innkeepers, millers and lessees (*árendások*) of other noble monopolies. The poet Petőfi, who helped restrain antisemitic crowds in 1848, recorded a little earlier in his diary, with a sigh, how he had just travelled for three days without meeting a non-Jewish publican.[12] "Have we seriously tried to establish contacts with other nations?" asked the great reforming aristocrat, István Széchenyi. "Would not our every product wither, if the Jews did not call to trade in it?" He put these questions in his *Hitel*, an epoch-making work on credit whose genesis was not unconnected with Széchenyi's own failure to secure a loan from the house of Arnstein in Vienna a few years before.[13]

A new commercial code enacted in 1840 realised some of Széchenyi's aspirations – but in the absence of domestic banking institutions it only exacerbated the lords' dependence on Jewish capital across the Austrian border, like that of the Biedermanns and Steiners who lent three-quarters of a million forints to the Batthyánys. As we now know, a syndicate of aristocrats heavily indebted to Salomon Rothschild in the 1840s included the enterprising landowners József Hunyady and Móric Sándor (whose daughter became Princess Pauline Metternich), as well as Széchenyi's eldest brother and the long-time Austrian ambassador in London, Paul Esterházy. Meanwhile the first major step was taken to release funds at home with the foundation of the *Pesti Magyar Kereskedelmi Bank* (Hungarian Commercial Bank of Pest) by one of those two richest Hungarian Jews of the day, Moritz Ullmann, whom we have already encountered.[14] Thus the Jews became a necessary element in any reform programme dedicated to raising the material condition of the country, as advanced by the Lower House of the diet from the beginning of the 1830s. But to understand their place in this scheme we need to take account of two further specifics, ethnic and religious, of our subject.

---

[10]Lajos Nagy, *Budapest története*. Vol. III: *A török kiűzésétől a márciusi forradalomig*, Budapest 1975, pp. 307ff. passim esp. pp. 386–388, 397–399; Klára Dóka, *A pest-budai céhes ipar válsága, 1840–72*, Budapest 1979; Vera Bácskai, *A vállalkozók előfutárai: nagykereskedők a reformkori Pesten*, Budapest 1989, summarised in *Jews in the Hungarian Economy*, pp. 40–49.
[11]Nagy, *Budapest története*, pp. 327f. Cf. in general, Péter Hanák in *Jews in the Hungarian Economy*, pp. 23–39.
[12]Sándor Petőfi, *Útirajzok, 1845–7*, Budapest 1962, p. 77.
[13]"Iparkodtunk e felettébb más nemzetekkel összeköttetést keresni? ... Nem száradna e sokra minden productuma, ha azt házánál nem keresné a' zsidó?": István Széchenyi, *Hitel*, Pest 1830, p. 140. András Gergely, *Széchenyi eszmerendszerének kialakulása*, Budapest 1972, pp. 83ff. (Arnstein).
[14]László Ungár, 'A magyar nemesi bírtok eladósodása 1848 előtt', *Századok*, vol. LXIX (1935), pp. 39–60; *Magyarország története*. Vol. V: *1780–1848*, ed. Gy. Mérei and K. Vörös, Budapest 1980, p. 580 (Batthyany); pp. 244, 323, 580, 910 (Ullmann); Niall Ferguson, *The World's Banker: The History of the House of Rothschild*, London 1998, p. 406.

Hungary was the most multinational country in Europe. Contemporaries possessed no firm statistics about this, and we can only extrapolate from subsequent ones (it is a striking index of the immateriality of the matter even in the later eighteenth century that the arch-absolutist Joseph II took no account of it). Yet there can be no doubt that the dominant ethnicity, the Magyars, with which most of the ruling noble strata – by now – identified themselves, formed only a minority in the country as a whole, though a much larger one than any of the rest, who were mainly Rumanians, Slovaks, Germans, Croats, Serbs, and Ruthenes. That Magyar relative majority is enhanced if we leave out of account in the current setting, since they contained few Jews, the largely separate realms of Croatia and Transylvania – though they are necessary for the whole picture of national rivalry in the area, in ways which cannot be entered into here.

The Magyars found themselves increasingly at odds with the other nationalities in an age of, on the one hand, Romantic search for identity and, on the other, successful pressure for advancement of the Hungarian language as the badge of a programme to modernise the entire Hungarian state. Thus clashes with Serbs erupted especially around 1790; then came an extended pamphlet war with "panslav" Slovaks from the 1820s; the Rumanian issue took on sharp contours by 1840, while relations with Croats dramatically deteriorated with the latter's so-called Illyrian campaign. Yet the underlying contest was still perceived as one between Magyardom, or Hungarianness, and the "Germans", which meant mainly authorities and influences emanating from Austria, but also the domestic German element as its (putative) supporters. In this context the Jews' chief rivals were precisely the local German or Germanised urban patriciates, especially in the royal boroughs with their municipal rights. One contrast may illustrate the point. Whereas the magistracy and guilds in Pressburg (here I advisedly use the German form of the place-name) waged an unrelenting and largely effective struggle over many decades to maintain the exclusion of Jews from the city's trading privileges, in the Magyar-dominated market town of Kecskemét, on the Great Plain, the only questions asked were about what they could contribute to the local economy.[15]

Jews thus constituted natural allies for a movement of political resistance to Vienna which was seeking both to assert national interests *vis-à-vis* Austria and to liberalise town government as the precondition before the existing exiguous municipal representation at the diet could be extended. It was *these* resentments which exploded when the lid came off the pot in early 1848; and Jews, for their part, felt alienated both from German burgherdom at home and from the torpid regime in Vienna which sustained its privileges and operated swingeing tariffs against the economy of the country as a whole. More broadly, Jews, given their close association with new forms of exploitation of landed estates, seemed to represent Magyar interests in the coun-

---

[15] Eugen Forbat, *Dejiny bratislavského obchodu v 18. a 19. storočí*, Bratislava 1959, esp. pp. 109ff., 238ff., 290ff., for Pressburg, where, however, the Pálffy family continued to protect Jews within the castle precinct. József Ö. Kovács, *Zsidók a Duna–Tisza közén. Társadalomtörténeti esettanulmányok, XVIII.–XIX. század*, Kecskemét 1996.

try at large. The sharp edge of this was felt by the other nationalities, especially by the Slovaks, who (with the Ruthenes) lived in areas of densest Jewish settlement. There are hints of antisemitism in the rhetoric of their leaders by 1848, both in the role of L'udevít Stúr as the diet representative for the decayed municipality of Krupina (Korpona; Karpfen) and in the attitudes of his principal lieutenant, the Protestant cleric Miroslav Hurban.[16] It comes as no accident that their bugbear, Count Károly Zay, the most prominent Magyarizer in Upper Hungary at that time, was also a noted philosemite.[17]

Thus Jews, by the same token, were obvious candidates for the programme of the rising Hungarian liberal opposition, with its slogan of "harmonisation of interests" (*érdekegyesítés*), opening up the constitution to a wider political nation. This was specifically the context for the diet campaign in 1839–40, which generated from the Lower House the proposal for their full equality – albeit as yet only on a par with the rest of non-noble society. It yielded a watered-down law offering the Jews free mobility (with certain reservations) and recognition of their religious sensibilities in the new commercial code. There followed pressure to commute the Toleration Tax, which achieved its aim by 1846, though the issue was by now a largely symbolic one: the tax had long been a relatively light burden anyway, and had remained unpaid since 1828 because of estates' obstruction.[18]

* * *

Thus far we have been in the realm of conventional wisdom. But the analysis tends to stay incomplete, and thus to distort. The "Jewish question" was not at the forefront of liberal minds. It emerged only desultorily and haltingly. That is clear, for example, from the work of the historian Mihály Horváth, who accords it scant treatment in his subsequent classic account of the *Vormärz* and none at all in his pioneering contemporary study of Hungarian trade and industry.[19] Széchenyi still reckoned the Jews Germanic – unsuited to meld with his Magyar "people of the East" – and he opposed their liberation on that ground. I quote from the note about a speech which he committed to his private diary: "It's a great error to believe that emancipation would turn the Jews into Hungarians, for they're too German in their attitudes, and it's highly doubtful whether they would mix with a genuinely oriental

---

[16]Karel Goláň, *Štúrovské pokolenie*, ed. F. Bokeš, Bratislava 1964, p. 157; omitted from the collections of his speeches in L'. Štúr, *Kde leží naša bieda?*, T.S. von Martin 1948, and *Dielo*. Vol. I: *Politické state a prejavy*, ed. by J. Ambruš *et al.*, Bratislava 1954. J.M. Hurban, *L'udovít Štúr*, Bratislava 1959, 558ff., and his 'Rozpomienky', ibid. pp. 645–783, passim. Cf. Ludwig Gogolák, *Beiträge zur Geschichte des slowakischen Volkes*, 3 vols., Munich 1963–72, vol. II, pp. 218ff.

[17]Bernstein, *Magyar szabadságharc*, pp. 18–20.

[18]The law on Jews (1840: XXIX) is in *Magyar Törvénytár. 1836–68. évi törvénycikkek*, ed. D. Márkus, Budapest 1896, pp. 175f.; the relevant part of the law on Bills of Exchange (1840: XV) is ibid. For the burden, cf. Gonda, *Zsidóság Magyarországon*, p. 75.

[19]Horváth, *Huszonöt év*; idem, *Az ipar és kereskedés története Magyarországban, a három utolsó század alatt*, Buda 1840, where Jews are mentioned only *en passant*, e.g. p. 190.

people."[20] And little Magyarization took place among the Jews themselves before the 1840s, when it came rather as a consequence than as a cause of noble patronage of their affairs.

For a fuller picture we need also to consider the third distinctive feature, or anomaly, of Hungary: its multiconfessionality, with five substantial separate churches which interacted with social and, especially, national divisions in intricate ways.[21] Some ethnic groups significantly defined themselves by religion: thus almost all Serbs were Greek Orthodox, Croats Catholic. But there were more cases where the two did not coincide, including crucially the Magyars themselves, split three ways (even if we leave out their residual Unitarian tradition). Moreover, the one predominant confession, the Roman Catholic (whose centrality is reinforced if the Greek Catholics are comprehended within it), had lately been weakened by the Habsburgs themselves. Ecclesiastical Josephinism, the intervention of the state in the organisation, and even the teaching and liturgy of the Church, had been a foreign implant in Hungary in the 1770s and 1780s. Yet it was only partly rescinded later and left Catholics disoriented. Both imperial-loyalist and ultramontane tendencies in the early nineteenth-century Church were vulnerable to charges of being unpatriotic. At the same time Joseph II's toleration edict fell into the same constitutional black hole as the first Jewish emancipatory measure. The Catholic establishment was strong enough to prevent the full equality of other faiths, but not to restore its former hegemony.

In an age of liberal and secular critique, this state of affairs both aggravated and mitigated the political situation. Fierce debates about clerical issues, notably mixed marriages and the religious education of ensuing children (the practice of demanding *reversales*), blocked the diet for weeks on end.[22] Yet at the same time long-standing traditions of at least *de facto* tolerance now bore fruit in the commitment of a substantial body of reformers to an interconfessional stance. So spokesmen for the rights of Jews appeared among the other religious minorities: the Lutheran Kossuth, say, or his aforementioned colleague Zay, who were already seeking to reconcile the two Protestant churches to each other. But those rights found a still more vital body of support among reform-minded Catholics, able to head off any kind of reaction from the clergy and undercut the force of popular prejudice. Széchenyi stood in this camp;

---

[20]"Man irre sich übrigens sehr, wenn man glaube, daß die Juden durch die Emanzipation zu Ungarn gemacht würden, denn sie sind zu deutsch gesinnt, und er zweifle sehr, daß sie mit den [sic] echten orientalischen Stamme vermischen werden." Széchenyi's own note on a speech of 20 April 1839: *Naplói*, ed. by Gyula Viszota, 6 vols., Budapest 1925–1939, Vol. V, pp. 271f., n. This needs to be set against the background, for Széchenyi, of the "traurige Wahrheit, daß der ungarische Stamm ... immer mehr und mehr verschwinde, und die Deutschen das Obergewicht verlangen." The psychological lability of all this is, of course, only enhanced by the fact that Széchenyi kept his diary mostly in German. Venetianer, *Magyar zsidóság története*, pp. 97–99, cites other comments of his on the Jews, some positive, but also the claim that emancipation in Hungary would be like pouring the contents of an ink pot into a soup dish, not an ocean as elsewhere. Cf. also George Barany, *Stephen Széchenyi and the Awakening of Hungarian Nationalism, 1791–1841*, Princeton 1968, pp. 358f.

[21]Cf. R. J. W. Evans, 'Religion und Nation in Ungarn, 1790–1849', in *Siebenbürgen in der Habsburgermonarchie, vom Leopoldinum bis zum Ausgleich*, ed. by Zs. K. Lengyel and U. A. Wien, *Siebenbürgisches Archiv*, Vol. XXIV, Cologne 1998, pp. 13–45.

[22]Horváth, *Huszonöt év*, vol. I, pp. 313ff., pp. 403–406, 609ff., vol. II, pp. 82ff., 197ff.; George Bárány, 'The Liberal Challenge and its Limitations: The Religious Question at the Diet of 1843–4', in *Hungary and European Civilization*, ed. by Gyula Ránki, Budapest 1989, pp. 31–77.

so did the emergent legal oracle, Ferenc Deák; so did Ödön Beöthy and István Bezerédj, liberal leaders in the west and east of Hungary respectively. So, even, did a few prominent priests, among them the noted Franciscan preacher Albach, who spoke in favour of Jews in his Lenten sermons at the time of the 1840 diet, and Horváth, who was shortly to become simultaneously bishop and minister of education in the revolutionary government, and hence one of the authors of the legislation of July 1849.[23]

***

This context should help us to identify more clearly the motivations for philosemitism in *Vormärz* Hungary. Certainly Jews, as we have observed, were taking their own increasingly marked share in modernisation; certainly those actions were welcome to patriotic nobles seeking their country's – and their personal – material advancement, *pari passu* with the liberal transformation of the Hungarian state under their own Magyar leadership. But a further crucial element was recognition of the Jews as a kind of moral touchstone, almost detached from the real issues of assimilation. They served as a yardstick for the programme widely designated by the words *polgárosodás* and its pair *polgárosítás*, active and passive modes of a term calqued on the notion of (*Ver*)*bürger*(*lichung*), which had at least as much to do with "civilization" as with *embourgeoisement*, and which still possessed the character of a future vision.

This is clear in the single most important work connected with the place of Jews in the Hungary of the period: Eötvös's *A zsidók emancipációjáról / Über die Emancipation der Juden*. Baron József Eötvös was another eminent lay Catholic intellectual, a somewhat *déclassé* aristocrat who attracted attention equally as literary lion and as political leader. His passionate speech in the Lower House at the 1840 diet carried the day for the emancipation bill. When that failed to become law except in highly diluted form, he published an extended version of his ideas.[24] He begins full of pathos in describing the situation of the Jews, a people "without fatherland", "without any centre to bring them together", isolated, vagrant, and above all persecuted by Christians for centuries. They are now victims, not of religious fanaticism any longer – significantly Eötvös thinks the historical antisemitic slanders a thing of the past – but of prejudice and selfishness. He refutes arguments that Jews are congenitally corrupted; that they threaten the nation or religion of others; even that they damage the livelihood of Christians. Simply allow them freedom, toleration, and fair competition, says Eötvös.

A zsidók emancipációjáról is an uplifting, though robustly argued, tract of moral liberalism. Some contemporaries undoubtedly became far more conscious of the practical utility of Jewish allies to the Magyar cause. Kossuth, for example, looked to their

---

[23]Sándor Takáts, *Hangok a múltból*, Budapest n.d., pp. 277–323, esp. 312 on Beöthy. Horváth, *Huszonöt év*, passim on Bezerédj. Ferenc Pulszky, *Életem és korom*, 2 vols., Budapest 1884, vol. I, p. 133. For Horváth himself, see Sándor Márki, *Horváth Mihály, 1809–78*, Budapest 1917.

[24]The diet speech was delivered on 31 March 1840. For the text, see József Eötvös, *Arcképek és programok*, ed. by I. Fenyő et al., Budapest 1975, pp. 351–355. The larger work first appeared in *Budapesti Szemle*, vol. II (1840), pp. 110–156. The German translation, by H. Klein, was published shortly afterwards. Cf. István Fenyő in his *Ábránd és valóság*, Budapest 1973, pp. 66–81.

rapid integration as a prerequisite for full emancipation; so did a number of conservative spokesmen. Beöthy stressed the need for their adequate education.[25] Yet a principled stand for the Jews as equal members of a society based on religious pluralism belongs to the characteristic ethos of the debate as orchestrated by the Hungarian national camp. And the opponents of the latter made the same connection with a contrary purpose: when a delegation from the city council of Pest went to Vienna in the mid-1840s to protest at the annulment of Jewish disabilities, the Austrian Chancery apparently told them that it would work to revoke the legislation if they could only ensure the failure of the patriotic protectionist campaign currently being led by Kossuth.[26]

* * *

The political argument over the Jews played itself out in the open constitutional forum which marked the public life of Hungary's ruling groups. What, finally, accompanied it on the ground, in everyday life, in the decades before the Revolution? Assimilation and even acculturation continued to be slow. By comparison with Germany and even Austria, Jewish communities in Hungary were mostly still small, often remote, and traditional. Of the quarter-million Jews resident there by the 1840s, an ever-larger proportion were recent immigrants from the *shtetl*s of Galicia. Yeshivot, especially that run at Pressburg by the Orthodox dynasty of Schreiber or Sofer, with its 500 students, flourished, alongside the ancestral rabbinate. Whereas more than a tenth of students at the Piarist *Gymnasium* and the university in Pest were Jewish by 1840, literacy rates across the country remained much lower than in the Austrian lands of the Habsburgs.[27]

Besides, the gentile world offered only limited encouragement. The new network of clubs known as "casinos" which sprang up from 1830 to further cultural and political change hardly welcomed them, despite the best efforts of their founder, Széchenyi; nor did the literary circles (*körök*), which arose no less suddenly in the 1840s.[28] The problem was, of course, precisely that Hungary's noble-led society had not yet delivered an environment in which more than a few Jews – Ullmanns or Wodianers say – could take their place, and those only after conversion and, in the latter case, a suitable name-change for "Wodianer" had earlier been "Weidmann". Whereas Salomon Rothschild was received with servile pomp when he visited

---

[25]On Kossuth: Venetianer, *Magyar zsidóság története*, pp. 150–153; Gonda, *Zsidóság Magyarországon*, pp. 69ff.; Michael K. Silber, 'The Historical Experience of German Jewry and its Impact on Haskalah and Reform in Hungary', in *Towards Modernity: The European Jewish Model*, ed. by J. Katz, New Brunswick and Oxford 1987, pp. 107–157, at 136f. For examples of conservatives: Venetianer, *Magyar zsidóság története*, p. 101; Gonda, *Zsidóság Magyarországon*, p. 68. For Beöthy: Márton Hegyesi, *Biharvármegye 1848–49-ben*, Nagyvárad 1885, pp. 24ff.

[26]Takáts, *Hangok*, p. 259.

[27]Nagy, *Budapest története*, pp. 386–388, 397–399 on students; overall Silber, 'Haskalah and Reform'.

[28]See the subtle analysis in Michael K. Silber, 'The Entrance of the Jews into Hungarian Society in *Vormärz*: The Case of the Casinos', in *Assimilation and Community: The Jews in Nineteenth-Century Europe*, ed. by J. Frankel and S.J. Zipperstein, Cambridge 1992, pp. 284–323; Takáts, *Hangok*, pp. 253f., 258, is more sanguine about the reception of Jews at least in the Nemzeti Kör.

Pressburg and Pest on railway business in 1844, the indigenous Pesti Magyar Kereskedelmi Bank, likewise seeking to profit in that area, hid its Jewishness behind an aristocratic façade.[29]

Hence the irony that Jewish acculturation in Hungary long remained largely an accommodation to German models, heavily influenced by the spirit of the Mendelssohnian Haskalah as modified in Vienna and Prague, and as introduced above all by the *maskil* rabbi Aron Chorin. A striking change was, however, already under way by 1848 with the first signs of widespread espousal of the Magyar language, which coincided with the emergence of more radical reformist currents inside certain Jewish communities. That could be observed first in those towns with existing Magyar majorities (such as Arad – long Chorin's own base – or Szeged, Nagyvárad or Pápa), and it derived strong impetus from the diet debate of 1840, particularly in Pest, and from the requirement of the law of that year that Jewish documents be recorded in the "living language employed in the fatherland".[30] The pamphlets of Daniel Ehrmann, with their fulsome praise for the "hochherzige Nation der Magyaren", are typical of their genre, and need to be set against the simultaneous want of confidence in their own culture which Hungary's Germans themselves began to feel in the chief cities. Now several societies were founded to teach Hungarian to the Jews, an activity enthusiastically promoted by the likes of Lipót Löw and Ignaz Einhorn, whom we have already met in a revolutionary context.[31] The latter was to become better known in the Magyar style which he assumed as Ede Horn; so did his contemporary Moses Bloch, subsequently a Calvinist theologian, linguist and critic under the name of Mór Ballagi.

Thus were set the lines for the decoupling of Jewish assimilation from its German and Austrian roots, and its reorientation towards an – often fervent – Hungarian patriotism. The process was confirmed, even catalysed, by the events of 1848–1849. Acceptance of a few leading members of local Jewish society might quickly bring over whole communities to the reform positions which two decades afterwards would be identified as those of Neolog Jewry. In future their Habsburg loyalty, which they still shared with their Austrian co-religionists, would be mediated by Hungarian constitutional and social traditions. This would form the basis for an extraordinary flowering of enterprise and creativity which, while it buttressed and enhanced the cosmopolitan contribution of Habsburg Jewry in general, was also shaped by a definite sense of place.

Even if the shadow of the original "mixed marriage" would never be completely erased, if the gentry could favour Jews while continuing to hold them at a safe dis-

---

[29]Takáts, *Hangok*, pp. 359–365, on Rothschild, who gave financial support to Hungarian religious communities and later 1,000 forints for a statue to the supportive Palatine József; cf. Ferguson, *The World's Banker*, p. 437. *Pesti magyar kereskedelmi bank, 1841–1941: száz esztendő emlékei*, Budapest 1941.

[30]Silber, 'Haskalah and Reform', pp. 133f.; id., 'Case of the Casinos', pp. 298–304. The law ordered the Jews to draw up "minden okleveleket és szerződéseket" in "a hazában … divatozó élő nyelven", a phrase to be set in the context of the contemporary statute for the Magyar language, 1840:VI.

[31]Daniel Ehrmann, *Betrachtungen über jüdische Verhältnisse*, Pest 1841. István Fried, 'Das deutschsprachige Bürgertum von Pest–Ofen in den 1840er Jahren', *Ungarn-Jahrbuch*, vol. XVIII (1990), pp. 19–42. Gonda, *Zsidóság Magyarországon*, 73ff. The best work on the overall process of Magyarization in the Hungarian capital in this period remains János Kósa, *Pest és Buda elmagyarosodása 1848-ig*, Budapest 1937, with lengthy treatment of the Jews at pp. 98ff.

tance, if acculturation always outran true assimilation: nevertheless the nineteenth-century trajectory of Hungarian Jewry affords a remarkable example of the coincidence of progress with emancipation.[32] There was some justice for Eötvös to reflect in later years — and more appositely than Metternich, with whom I began — that he had moved and shaken to good effect. As Eötvös put it in 1867, the year of the *Ausgleich*, and fulfilment of that full civil emancipation of the Jews for which he had so long campaigned: "I'm a real *zukunftmuzsikus* in politics; my whole life I've been playing the tunes which twenty years later every *suszter* boy would whistle."[33]

---

[32]The point is well made in several articles by Michael Silber, particularly in his 'Case of the Casinos'.
[33]Quoted in József Galántai, *Nemzet és kisebbség Eötvös József életművében*, Budapest [1995], p. 105.

Grillparzer, the Catholics and the Jews: A Reading of Die Jüdin von Toledo *(1851)*

BY EDA SAGARRA

Roman Catholic attitudes to Judaism and the Jews have received less scholarly attention from literary historians than the scale and significance of these relations would warrant. But to claim to help redress the balance, as it were, by placing Grillparzer's late play, *Die Jüdin von Toledo*, in such a context might seem misplaced. As a consistent critic of the Roman Catholic establishment, Grillparzer hardly seems a representative spokesman of that confession. In terms of the history of mentalities, one could well argue that Grillparzer is closer in this play to Lessing's *Nathan der Weise* than to his fellow Austrian Catholics in the age of Metternich. The editor of an important modern edition of the play even associates the leading male character, King Alphonso, with the figure of Lessing's Nathan.[1] However, there are grounds for suggesting that a significant concern of Grillparzer in *Die Jüdin von Toledo* was in fact to provide a critique of traditional Roman Catholic attitudes towards the Jews.[2] True, the setting of the play in Spain derives from his main source, Lope de Vega's play, *Las paces de los reyes, i la Judía de Toledo* (1616). But his decision to retain the Spanish setting was highly appropriate for such a critique, given the dynastic links between the Austrian and Spanish Habsburgs and, more significantly, Spain's image in the nineteenth century as a Roman Catholic state of rigorous orthodoxy, notorious for having expelled its ancient Jewish community in 1492. The fact that, unlike Grillparzer's other late plays, *Libussa* and *Ein Bruderzwist*, no part of *Die Jüdin* had been published at the time of its author's death, and that the poet was reticent in discussing it,[3] suggests that he was well aware of the seditious character of his critique in terms of the Austrian religious and political establishment. Indeed, few of Grillparzer's numerous satires on orthodox Roman Catholicism in various text types were published in his lifetime. But of his engagement in the topic, there is no doubt. In 1868, at the age of seventy-seven, as member of the *Herrenhaus* (the upper house of the Austrian parliament), he recorded his vote in favour of repealing the Concordat of 1855. Reflecting for a moment on what Hans Küng has identified as the many different paradigms of Roman Catholicism,[4] we can find grounds to sup-

---

[1]Franz Grillparzer, *Werke in sechs Bänden*, ed. by Helmuth Bachmaier, vol. III: *Dramen 1828–51*, Frankfurt am Main 1987, p. 868. All references to the play are to this edition.
[2]There is an extensive secondary literature on the play which documents the many and diverse readings of the work. W. E. Yates' article and bibliography in Walter Killy, *Literaturlexikon*, vol. IV, München 1989, pp. 346–351, provides a good introduction.
[3]"Grillparzer schwieg sich über das Stück aus", Bachmaier, *Dramen*, p. 846.
[4]Hans Küng, *Church and Change. The Irish Experience*, Dublin 1986, pp. 26ff.

port the argument that Grillparzer's critical stance associates him with a representative strand in Austrian Catholic thought. Much persecuted within the Austrian church (and state), this liberal or reformist strand of Austrian Catholicism was a consistent feature of her intellectual history. In the twentieth century, it has not been without impact on the wider Roman Catholic community.

How did the poet's Roman Catholic contemporaries in Austria and Germany between the defeat of Napoleon and the Revolution of 1848 regard the relationship between the Jews and the society in which they lived? An event in the contemporary book market can perhaps serve as an exemplary case. The years between the Congress of Vienna and the Revolution of 1848 were a time when that barometer of bourgeois opinion, the *Conversations-Lexikon* or general encyclopaedia, became a feature of popular culture in German-speaking lands. Initially, it was the product of secularised Protestant Germany. Only in the 1840s did a Catholic publisher follow suit and provide its readers with a source of information on various aspects of modern life, though strictly from an orthodox Roman Catholic perspective. The initiative occurred in the context of vigorous efforts by the church authorities, with the assistance of clergy and laity, aimed at creating a self-consciously Catholic reading culture for the educated and the yet-to-be-educated among them.[5] Between 1846 and 1850 Manz, a successful Catholic publishing firm with offices in Vienna, Silesia and the Bavarian towns of Regensburg, Landshut and Passau, published the ten-volume *Allgemeine Real-Encyclopädie für das katholische Deutschland* in Regensburg. The fifth volume includes an article of some eleven pages under the heading: *Judenthum*, the first ten of which were devoted to a reasonably dispassionate, chronological account of the history of the Jewish race from the earliest times to Germany in the 1840s. Given the manner in which contributors were hired to write such articles, it may well be that the body of the article was "lifted" from another source, which would explain the disparity between it and the last section. Be that as it may, the last page of the article strikes a completely discordant note, and continues without introduction or any attempt at justification:

> Bei dem Fanatismus, wovon die Juden selbst beseelt waren, kann man auch die Wahrheit jener Anschuldigungen, die meist zum Ausbruche der Volkswuth Veranlasssung gab: Kindermord, Entweihung geistlicher Heiligthümer, Durchstechung der Hostie u.s.w. nicht ganz in Abrede stellen.[6]

Within a few short lines we thus are confronted with a whole panoply of traditional Roman Catholic myths about the Jews. The only other perennially popular ones not included are the Jews as "crucifiers of Christ" and "Jewish pride" (the German term "*Verstocktheit*" is more offensive), – though the reader no doubt could feel that these were encompassed by the elliptical "etc.".

---

[5]A characteristic example of these initiatives was the so-called *Borromäusverein*, founded in the Rhineland in 1844 to provide guidance on books suitable for Catholics and to adjudicate on the products of the contemporary German literary market. The *Borromäusverein* published commented lists of new books at irregular intervals up to the first decades of the twentieth century.

[6]"Given the fanaticism characteristic of the Jews, the truth of these accusations which were often the source of outbursts of popular fury, namely: the murder of children, sacrilege, the piercing of the (sacred) host etc. cannot entirely be gainsaid." *Allgemeine Real-Encyclopädie*, vol. V, pp. 393f.

How can such irrationality be accounted for? A study of the historiography of the German Confederation in and well after the Metternich era, suggests a signal lack of awareness on the part of Catholics that their relations with the Jews were problematical. There is, however, abundant evidence of the existence of inherited and unreflective hostility or indifference among Catholics towards the Jews in their midst. Thus the poet Annette von Droste-Hülshoff, whose interest in the Westphalian Jewish community was stimulated by her Jewish doctor, Alexander Heimdorf, could yet write to her friend, Luise von Bornstedt, about the former Young German writer, Heinrich Laube: "Laube is surely a Jew – he has all the hallmarks of a Jewish writer, wit, intelligence, hatred for all inherited ways, especially the Christian and bourgeois [...] If he isn't a Jew, well, he ought to be."[7] Or she tells her sister, Jenny von Laßberg, of how their old nurse used to put out brightly coloured figurines in the form of "Jews" and "Jewesses" under the redcurrant bushes to frighten the birds.[8]

Even among mid-twentieth century historians, we find scant attention devoted to the topic. Thus the index to the third edition (1955) of Franz Schnabel's still standard *History of Germany in the Nineteenth Century*, volume 4: *Die religiösen Kräfte* contains but a single entry under 'Judaism' and one further one under 'hostility to the Jews' (*Judenfeindschaft*). The relevant (third) volume of the authoritative history of Bavaria, Max Spindler's *Handbuch der bayerischen Geschichte*, covering the period 1800, makes no reference to the Jews, Judaism, anti-Jewish feeling or antisemitism. Yet by that date, mainstream German historiography had already begun to focus attention on German-Jewish history, and more particularly on the phenomenon of antisemitism in nineteenth-century Germany. Moreover, this was almost a decade after the official Roman Catholic church had begun to confront its own deep-seated and endemic anti-Jewish prejudice, and to do so at the highest level. It was Pope John XXIII (1958–1963), initiator of the Second Vatican Council, who was instrumental in challenging inherited attitudes in a most tangible way, at a liturgical level. The conciliar decree, *Nostra Aetate,* of 28 October 1965, abolished the thousand-year-old prayer in the Roman Missal which had been customarily said on Good Friday, the feast of the Crucifixion. This had called on the faithful to pray for insight on the part of what the text had styled "the perfidious Jews". Perfidy encompasses both the notion of wickedness – the Jews as crucifiers of Christ – and obstinate pride, in refusing to acknowledge their guilt in this matter and accept the truth of Christianity.[9] *Nostra Aetate* went further than merely expunging so hurtful a reference. Instead, Roman Catholics were, and are to this day, exhorted to pray on that most holy day for "the Jews, who were the first to receive the word of God".[10]

---

[7]"Sagen Sie mir doch: ist der Laube nicht ein Jude? Er hat wenigstens alles, was die Schriftsteller dieses Volkes bezeichnet: Geist, Witz, Grimm gegen alle bestehende Formen, sonderlich die christlichen und bürgerlichen [...] kurz, ist er kein Jude, so verdiente er es einer zu sein." *Die Briefe der Annette von Droste-Hülshoff*, ed. by Karl Schulte Kemminghausen, Jena 1944, vol. II, p. 261.

[8]*ibid.*, vol. I, p. 531.

[9]Its older sense was "breaching the covenant" (by refusing to acknowledge Christ as the Messias).

[10]See: Austin Flannery (ed.), *Vatican Council II. The Conciliar and Post-Conciliar Documents*, Dublin 1975. See esp. the section 'Declaration on the Relations of the Church to Non-Christian Religions', p. 741: "... the Church [...] deplores all hatreds, persecutions, displays of antisemitism leveled at any time and from any source against the Jews".

The Metternich era was an era of paradox. There is much evidence of interest on the part of intellectuals and the wider public in the manners and customs of other peoples and other cultures, including the Jews. Yet, equally, a feature of the period is its frequent and rarely disguised institutional hostility to the Jews. Moreover, the authorities often showed pronounced reluctance to condemn popular violence against the Jews, such as that experienced in Bavaria in 1819 in the so-called *Hep! Hep!* movement.[11] Though such anti-Jewishness tended to be sporadic rather than systematic in nature, and though there were notable exceptions, the Metternich era was a period which witnessed the revival of traditional prejudice at virtually every level of Roman Catholic society. A profound change in the temper of the age is perceptible, a change shaped by the political events of the Napoleonic era, as they began to have an impact on the lives of ordinary people. The years spanning the late Enlightenment and the French revolutionary wars had initiated discussion of and legislation in favour of toleration and the granting of civic rights to the Jews. After 1815, those years began to be identified by German Roman Catholics with change, loss and threat. In Austria both the emperor Francis I (1804–1835) and the Austrian elite managed to associate the Enlightenment in the public mind with revolution and terror.[12] As Alexander Dru[13] argued cogently more than thirty years previously, the Roman Catholic church in Austria and Germany denied herself the fruits of the Catholic Enlightenment and reform by associating them with secularisation, anti-clericalism and subversion.[14] These historians articulate views which the Josephinist Grillparzer would have understood and with which he might have sympathised. The asperity of his recorded comments show him to have had little time for intellectuals, such as Friedrich Schlegel, who lent their considerable ability to promote the claims of the ultramontane church in Austria. But the important point is that even relatively apolitical Catholics came to associate the Napoleonic era primarily with loss, with the loss of familiar landmarks. Sometimes it was simply the destruction of monasteries and favoured places of pilgrimage. Or it could concern the abolition of old and familiar state boundaries which had shaped local allegiances for centuries. More generally, Catholics remembered that it was Napoleon who had abolished the Holy Roman Empire and the ecclesiastical territories. These had once made up a significant part of the political landscape of Catholic Germany, and their rulers had been, in general, benign if not always effective sovereigns of their subjects. In the decade and a half following mediatisation of the ecclesiastical territories, Jews were not infrequently accused of having made profits as middlemen in the sale of church land. Meanwhile, measures introduced by individual states in the Napoleonic era to ameliorate the lot of Jews aroused hostility. In the case of Humboldt's 1812 Edict of

---

[11] The slogan: *Hierusalem est perdita!* Jerusalem is destroyed! was invoked as a demagogic call to violence against the Jewish communities.
[12] Charles W. Ingrao, *The Habsburg monarchy (New approaches to European history)*, Cambridge 1984, pp. 220 and 230f.
[13] Alexander Dru, *The church in the nineteenth century: Germany 1800–1918*, Dublin 1963.
[14] On Grillparzer and the Catholic Enlightenment see Roger Bauer: 'Katholisches in der josephinischen Literatur' in Harms Klueting *et al.* (eds.), *Katholische Aufklärung – Aufklärung im katholischen Deutschland*, Hamburg 1993, pp. 260–270, esp. 268f.

Tolerance it earned Prussia in some parts of Catholic Germany the epithet: *das judenfreundliche Preußen.* (Prussia, friend of the Jews.)[15]

Toleration of religions other than Roman Catholicism became associated in the public mind with secularisation, and in the post-1815 decades the Roman Catholic church authorities in Germany invested considerable efforts into immunising their flock against the modern world, and especially against the modern secular press. This was often described in popular parlance as the "Jewish" press. At the same time, the church proved itself an apt pupil of this particular agent of modernity, developing at local, national and regional level its own network of Catholic press organs. These were designed to, and largely succeeded in, insulating Catholics in their reading culture from the rest of Germany and from much of the modern world. Nineteenth-century Roman Catholic authorities tended to regard modern life as characterised by an ever-increasing encroachment by the state on those areas which had traditionally and "more properly" belonged to the religious realm: marriage and the family, education and welfare. The growing influence of Rome was a feature of European countries with a substantial Roman Catholic population in the first half of the nineteenth century, and it was accompanied by an increasing clericalisation of the church. It was a fundamental feature of Restoration Europe, in France, Spain and Italy, as in Austria under Francis I, that it rested on a political understanding, ideologically underpinned, between the restored monarchy and the ultramontane Roman church. It is this unwritten "pact" between state and church, with its tacit denial and even reversal of the reforms of the Enlightenment, its elaborate propaganda apparatus for the tutelage of intellectuals, and its attraction for time servers and for cynics, which lies at the heart of Grillparzer's bitter and sustained critique of the Catholic church of his day. We find references to his stance in his unpublished diaries and other autobiographical writings, in his satiric poems and epigrams across almost the whole of his life.

This then is the politico-religious background to his unusual drama, *Die Jüdin von Toledo*, which is based on sixteenth-century sources, but which offers an original and modern perspective on an ancient theme. Only published and performed for the first time after his death, – and then in Stuttgart and Prague, rather than Vienna[16] – the gestation of the play covered more than half the poet's lifetime. It coincides nearly with Metternich's term of office, his flight to England and settling down in Brighton, that is, from 1816 to the early 1850s. Grillparzer first encountered the tale of the fair Jewess of Toledo in 1809 and in 1824 read Lope's play. It was not until 1839 that he wrote the first act and part of the second of his own drama, completing it between the winter of 1848 and some time in 1851. The particular interest of *Die Jüdin von Toledo* in terms of Roman Catholic-Jewish relations lies in the manner in which

---

[15]See Anita Bunyan, 'Reaktionen auf die britische Judenemanzipation im Deutschland des Vormärz', in Helmut Koopmann and Martina Lauster (eds.), *Vormärzliteratur in europäischer Perspektive I. Öffentlichkeit und nationale Identität*, Bielefeld 1996, p. 147. See also Edward Timms in this volume.

[16]The play had its first performance in Prague on 21 November 1872, in the year of Grillparzer's death. The Vienna premiere followed on the first aniversary of the poet's death on 21 January 1873, but was not a success. The great Hungarian-born actor, Joseph Kainz, playing the role of Alphonso, established *Die Jüdin* in the classicial repertoire in 1888, with Agnes Sorma as Rahel. They brought the production to Vienna in 1897 where it was received with acclaim.

Grillparzer incorporates in his play an historically aware, critical view of Catholic prejudice against the Jews. Equally prescient is the sense he conveys of Catholic self-legitimisation as persecutors of the Jews. It is precisely because Grillparzer was a Catholic by birth, culture and mentality, and not simply a critical outsider, that he could do so effectively. Grillparzer is not normally described as such. More usually he is identified as an anticlerical and even, in a recent monograph,[17] as a-religious. Sceptical he certainly was, as befitted his Josephinist formation. But he was not, despite his many scathing comments on church, papacy and prominent clerics, a secular anticlerical. As a Josephinist he actually approved of greater involvement by the clergy in the business of state, in the education and welfare of the people.[18] Grillparzer's own position as the critical observer, who is also in some senses an insider, provides an essential dimension of the play's religious and political context, reminding us of the cultural significance of confessional origins, even in secular society.[19] He may not share the sentiments of traditional Catholicism or its views on the Jews, indeed he may deplore them, but he fully understands the dynamics involved. In his play he presents that blend of ideology, mythology, power politics and the surviving vestiges of medieval ecclesiological thinking which in early modernism had been characteristic of the Christian state in its dealings with its Jews, and which was now re-emerging in Restoration Europe.

It was part of Grillparzer's intention in his historical drama of state and illicit love, to confront his potential audience with the implications of actual and inherited legislative and social policies towards the Jews. It is not without significance that the body of the play was written during and after the Revolution of 1848, when the issue of Jewish emancipation was highly topical, not least because of the high level of Jewish participation "on both sides of the barricades". But the nature of the subjects he addresses, and the manner in which he represented religion and the monarchy, made it unlikely that his play could have passed the censor in neo-absolutist Austria of the 1850s, even had Grillparzer wished to see it performed.

Though the older play differs in significant details, the poet's choice of Spain for the setting of his drama was certainly dictated by his principal source, Lope de Vega's *Las paces de los reyes, i la Judía de Toledo* of 1616. The drama's setting in Spain of the age of the *Reconquista*, the twelfth-century reconquest of the Iberian peninsula from the Moors, is critical to Grillparzer's intention. The *Reconquista* was underpinned by a thoroughly modern propaganda campaign. It formed part of the Crusading concept of "winning back" all the "civilised world" to Christianity, a process which involved the ideological vilification of the beliefs and the culture of the opponent. Thus the king's councillor Manrike speaks at one point in Act IV of the

---

[17] Ian F. Roe, *An Introduction to the Major Works of Franz Grillparzer, 1791–1872, Austrian Dramatist*, Studies in German language and Literature, vol. VII, Lewiston – Queenstown – Lampeter 1991, p. 210.

[18] The Josephinist ideal of the *pastor bonus* or shepherd of souls was actually incorporated by Grillparzer in his comedy *Weh' dem, der lügt* (1838) in the figure of Gregory, bishop of Tours, a man who much prefers simple pastoral duties to the social obligations of his post.

[19] A point made by Peter Stachel with reference to Bernhard Bolzano in: 'Die Bedeutung von Bolzanos "Wissenschaftslehre" für die österreichische Philosophiegeschichte. Ein Baustein zu einer Geschichte der pluralistischen Tradition der österreichischen Philosophie', in Heinrich Ganthaler and Otto Neumaier (eds.), *Bolzano und die österreichische Geistesgeschichte*, Salzburg 1997, p. 132 , note 76.

war being waged for the purpose of restoring the sacred order of things ("die heilige Ordnung", v.1238). Medieval Spain was ruled by a monarch who as king of Spain held the official title conferred on him by the Pope of "Most Catholic King". In his play Grillparzer, following Lope, assigns to Alphonso's English queen Eleonore[20] the chief impetus to the murder of Rahel the Jewess. But the king connives in the murder by default. Grillparzer, for all the protestations of his autobiography of his ignorance of the Catholic faith,[21] was well versed in Catholic theology and would no doubt have known that sins of omission are judged with the same rigour as sins of commission. Alphonso ultimately recognises this himself and accepts guilt in equal measure. In their treatment of the Jews, the royal pair, the generous-minded but weak-willed king and his harsh queen, are associated with that other Spanish royal couple, Ferdinand of Aragon and Isabella of Castile, authors of the notorious expulsion of the Jews from Spain in 1492. A sinister aspect of that act was that the Spanish rulers refused to accept the authenticity of Jewish conversion to Christianity, as Christian society had traditionally been ready to do, and as Central Europe in the first half of the nineteenth century, broadly speaking, still did. In a further anticipation of later nineteenth-century antisemitism, the fifteenth-century Spanish regime institutionalised the use of a biological term of vilification of the Jews, which helped to reify the object of persecution and popular hatred: the Spanish term of abuse for the Jews was *marannos*, or pigs. The same process of reification is operative at a key point in Grillparzer's play. In advising the queen and the court to sanction the judicial murder of Rahel, the most senior royal counsellor, Manrike, does not refer to Rahel by name nor even to her as a person. She is merely termed "jener Anstoß", or cause of offence, which must be removed ("entfernt", v.1241).[22] Were the king to oppose their intention, recourse would have to be made to "blut'ges Recht" (v. 1243), to the full force of the penal code. But, he avers, should they indeed have to have recourse to such measures, they would in fact be serving both the prince and the law.

Underlying such casuistry is the fact that the Jews are present in Christian society only on sufferance, that they have no real protection before the law. Such tolerance as does exist derives from the ruler's "protection" for those who, as their Christian critics freely admit, promote trade and increase profit throughout the land ("Handel und Gewinn im Land zerstreut", v. 284). At three different points in the play, Alphonso pledges the Jews his personal protection. "Hier ist Schutz" (v. 301), he calls to Rahel in Act I, when she flees from her supposed persecutors. In the second act he declares to Manrike's son Garceran that he wishes those to be unmolested ("unbelästigt", v.426), to whom he offers protection. Towards the end of the same act, he gives his word to Rahel that he can implement his pledge: "Dafür mein Wort! /

---

[20]England's later (deserved) European reputation for generosity towards her Jewish subjects allowed her advocates to forget that one of the first European monarchs to drive the Jews out of his realm was the English king, Edward I, in 1290.

[21]There are many contradictions in Grillparzer's own evidence on his religious socialisation, as attested in his autobiography, written in his sixties, and in the earlier autobiographical fragment, dated 1809, but evidently re-written much later, and in the conversations of his old age.

[22]See Borchmeyer's analysis of Grillparzer's subtle use of syntax to pinpoint the psychological process involved in 'Grillparzers *Die Jüdin von Toledo*' in Harro Müller-Michaels, *Interpretationen zu Werken von der Aufklärung bis zur Gegenwart*, vol. I: *Von Lessing bis Grillparzer*, Königstein, Taunus 1981, pp. 200–238, here p. 215.

Ich weiß zu schützen, wem ich Schutz gelobt" (v. 616f). Again, as he leaves Retiro for the court, he assures her that both it and she are well guarded: "Das Schloß ist fest!" (v. 1073). The irony is evident here, since the king proves impotent to prevent the murder and even the mutilation of her body. In addition to its dramatic function, the irony has the effect of questioning the validity of the traditional privilege system on which the Jews relied to permit them to go about their lives. It depends on one man, the ruler, who may, like Alphonso, prove fallible – as Jews over the centuries had learned to their cost.

The play portrays a society proud to call itself Christian, and one predicated on the assumption that society is, by definition, Christian. The *Reconquista* suppressed the fact that the Moors had developed a highly sophisticated society. By analogy the expulsion of the Jews in fifteenth-century Spain denied the cultural achievements of medieval Spanish Jewry, denied the fact that the Jews lived in a culture governed by strict rules and customs. This is indicated by Rahel's father Isak in his roundabout way in the first act, and exemplified by Esther throughout the play. Underlying the centuries-old hegemonial claims of the Roman Catholic church to incorporate "society", was the ecclesiological thinking of the thirteenth-century papacy, which had been elaborated in the decades following the reconquest of Spain from the Moors. Between the Fourth and the Fifth Crusades, the papacy developed that ecclesiological notion of human society which was to have such fateful consequences for the Jews both then and later. Society, according to this (novel) vision, was co-extensive with membership of the Christian church. Heresy, moreover, was defined by Innocent III (1198–1216) as the worst of sins, so vile that it could justify the withdrawal of basic civil rights. His successor Gregory IX (1229–1241) condemned the Talmud as heretical, and thus gave a most sinister weapon into the hands of the enemies of the Jews, which would in time be invoked by crusading spirits to justify extreme measures against the whole Jewish community.[23] It is revealing to know that, some years before he began to write his own play, Grillparzer had read (and commented at considerable length on) a study of Pope Innocent III, written from an ultramontane or strictly orthodox Roman Catholic perspective. This was one Friedrich Hurter's *Geschichte Innozenz III. und des Papsthums des dreizehnten Jahrhunderts*[24] which Grillparzer read in 1836, shortly after its publication. The poet's lengthy notes on the tome are peppered with acid comments on Innocent's modern apologist.[25] Hurter, a Swiss Catholic from Schaffhausen, subscribes unswervingly to the notion that the state is of its essence Christian, though he does stress Innocent III's guarantees for the "natural rights of the Jews" ("die natürlichen Rechte der Juden").[26] Hurter's advocacy of the modernity and rightness of Innocent III's decree opposing forcible conversion of the Jews, rests on the Augustinian concept, sporadically forgotten in medieval and early modern Christian states, of the Jews as precursors of Christ. He contrasts Innocent

---

[23]Jeremy Cohen, *The Friars and the Jews: The Evolution of Medieval Anti-Judaism*, Ithaca – London 1982, pp. 44f. and 67f.
[24]2 vols, Hamburg 1834–1835. Book 3 of vol. I contained a section entitled 'Innocenzens Verfügungen wegen der Juden', pp. 311–318.
[25]*Sämtliche Werke*, ed. by Peter Frank and Karl Pörnbacher, Darmstadt 1961–1965, vol. III: *Ausgewählte Briefe, Gespräche, Berichte*, pp. 957–968.
[26]Hurter, vol. I, p. 313.

III's position with the harsh anti-Jewish practice of some sovereigns and their populaces, citing in particular the kings of Spain and England as notorious examples. Hurter is conscious of the extreme topicality of the issue he is addressing.[27] But immediately prejudice asserts itself, undermining his argument. Thus he cites with approval the "shrewd" ("klug") reply of Archbishop Balduin of Canterbury to Richard II of England about the treatment of Jewish converts who lapse: no force should be used, but they should be left to their just deserts. If they wish to be the servants of Satan rather than God, so be it: "Hat er nicht Lust ein Diener Gottes zu werden, so mag er ein Diener des Teufels bleiben".[28] Similarly, Hurter sees no cause to comment on Innocent's quoted view: "Christi Tod hat die Gläubigen zu Freyen gemacht, das Judenvolk zu Knechten", that Christ's death had liberated believers but enslaved the Jews.[29] The notion of *Knechtschaft* or bondage points to an underlying assumption of the constitutional inferiority of the Jews in society, since society is by definition Christian. This, not surprisingly, is where Grillparzer takes issue with Hurter, whose lengthy work he had excerpted from so liberally. The real object of Hurter's resentment proves to be – as was the case with so many of his fellow orthodox Catholics of the Metternich era – modern liberal Jews, whom he defames as being at the whim of fashion but without a sense of values: "jene neuerungssüchtigen Mosaiten [...] welche in jede und keine Form schmiegen".[30] Hurter's hostility derives from the fact that the aspiration of secularised Jews to civic emancipation explicitly demanded the separation of state and church, or, as Hurter put it, such aspirations were led by the misguided attempt to eradicate Christianity from the state(s) and with it the so positive and all-embracing influence of Christian faith on the civil institutions of society.[31]

The significance of this work in the present context is twofold. It focused Grillparzer's attention on the historical dimension of Restoration thinking with regard to church-state relations and introduced him to a key period in the elaboration of the Roman Catholic church's ideological position with regard to the Jews. For it was above all the ecclesiological arguments of the thirteenth-century papacy which effectively excluded believing Jews from society, implicitly denying them protection unless they convert. It is not always remembered by historians when discussing the often problematical relationship between Jews and Christians in Metternich's Germany that the founding act of the German Confederation, the *Bundesakte* of June 1815, defined the new state as "Christian". Much Catholic (and Christian) opposition to Jewish civil rights in the Metternich era was predicated on this concept. A representative example of such attitudes is the protest of the former Prussian civil servant and later bishop of Mainz, Wilhelm Emmanuel von Ketteler (1811–1877), against the idea of equal civic rights for all, regardless of belief. The logic of such

---

[27]"Das Verhältnis der Israeliten zu den Christen, unter welchen sie wohnen, hat oftmals und in unseren Zeiten mehr als ehedem Stoff zu Erörterungen und Untersuchungen hergeben müssen." *ibid.*
[28]*ibid.*, p. 316
[29]*ibid.*, p. 314
[30]*ibid.*, p. 313
[31]"... [durch] das verkehrte Bestreben[geleitet], das Christentum gänzlich von den Staaten auszuschneiden [...] jenen gewinnbringenden oder durchströmenden Einfluß des christlichen Glaubens in seinem Zusammenhang mit der bürgerlichen Einrichtung der Gesellschaft". *ibid.*

demands, he claims, would be that the local Catholic hospital management board would have to accept "Jews and pagans".[32]

Given this context, it is a striking feature of Grillparzer's play that it is, in part, presented from the point of view of the Jews. This was not uncommon in the earlier part of the Metternich era, which produced a body of texts in popular literature which purported to offer insight in worlds unfamiliar to the *Biedermeier* reader. Such texts derived from the avid demand of the theatres – one authority on the period speaks of the "myriads of Jewish figures" peopling the stage in these years[33] – and also from lending libraries eager for reading material. The portrayal of Jewish figures on stage and in narrative literature could also be seen as an attempt by liberal writers to break down the barriers of ignorance and prejudice. In his own play, Grillparzer uses the Jews in his framing device, whereby the play opens and closes with the Jewish characters dominating the stage.[34] He also employs an interesting early example of stylising cultural difference through linguistic means, in that the Jews speak in Spanish trochaic verse and the Christian in (classical) blank verse. The exclusion of the Jews, of Rahel, her sister Esther and her father Isak, from the royal garden can be seen symbolically as the exclusion of the Jews from the protection of the state,[35] though the king disassociates himself from the law and encourages them to enter. The dramatist's presentation of his Jewish characters is at once traditional and novel. Traditional in the sense that he makes use of the long-established stage type of the (male) Jew as a comic figure. In the opening scene Isak blames Rahel's mother, whom he married for her riches, for his daughter's undisciplined character, asking himself whether his wife might not in fact have evaded his watchful eye and got involved with some Christian. As soon as Rahel is installed in the king's favour, however, he is ready to do a little blackmail, and when the murderers arrive, and again at the close of the play, he is concerned more with his gold than his daughter. Grillparzer correlates behaviour and social status, notably in the figure of the father. But Isak is a more rounded figure than is traditionally assumed. He knows that if he and his kind are to survive in so hostile an environment, and if he is to provide for his family, he must develop characteristics which make him either comical or repulsive to the Christians. As Alphonso himself points out, the demerits of the Jews are the fault of the Christians: "Was sie verunziert ist unser Werk" (v. 486). Isak has his merits too, though his virtues of cleverness, foresight and ingratiating patience: ("Klugheit [...] Vorsicht [...] das geschmeid'ge Warten", v. 829f) are the attributes of the weak pitted against the strong.

---

[32]"Wenn unsere Gesetzgebung vielleicht bald Juden und Heiden zu den städtischen Ämtern zulassen wird, was kann dann aus dem Geist einer kirchlichen Anstalt werden, die entweder solche Personen selbst oder unter ihrem Einfluß gewählte Subjekte in ihrem Curatorium zulassen muß." Wilhelm Emmanuel Freiherr von Ketteler, *Sämtliche Werke und Briefe. Im Auftrag der Akademie der Wissenschaften und der Literatur*, ed. by Erwin Iserloh, Mainz 1977ff, series 1, vol. II, p. 147.

[33]"In der Dramatik und auf der Bühne der Metternichschen Restaurationsepoche wimmelte es von Juden-Figuren, die als einzelne oder zu mehreren und manchmal sogar unter Ausschluß anderer dramatisch eingesetzt wurden." Horst Denkler in Hans Otto Horch and Horst Denkler (eds.), *Conditio Judaica. Judentum, Antisemitismus und deutschsprachige Literatur vom 18. Jahrhundert bis zum Ersten Weltkrieg*, Tübingen 1988, p. 149.

[34]Roger Bauer, "Die Jüdin von Toledo oder der verbotene Garten Eden", *Literarisches Jahrbuch der Görres-Gesellschaft*, vol. IXX (1978), pp. 277–287, here p. 278.

[35]Borchmeyer (p. 231, n. 22), in my view rightly, differs from Bauer in seeing the garden in political rather than religious terms.

Literary representation of the Jew in medieval and early modern literature tended to be gender-specific and so too here. Male Jews like Isak are frequently presented as physically unattractive, and in a Christian context as beyond redemption. When Alphonso tries to persuade himself to break with Rahel and marry her off to one of her own race, his jealous imagination immediately shrinks from seeing her in the arms of a member of her race, whom he stereotypes as having, "grubby hands and an obsession with money" ("mit schmutz'ger Hand und engem Wuchersinn", v. 1449). Literary Jewesses, by contrast, are more often than not attractive and occasionally feature as converts to Christianity – a surprising tradition, given the fact of Jewishness being inherited through the female line. Rahel, the Jewess of Toledo, for all the psychological realism of the poet's treatment of her, conforms to the well-established topos of European literature in that she is a "schöne Jüdin", a fair Jewess. Grillparzer goes much further than his predecessors in portraying Rahel's erotic fascination for the king. Particularly impressive is his capacity to portray this scenically and equally her awareness of the physical beauty and power of her body. Rahel is totally natural in this, natural as a child in her perceptions and her articulation of them, but she is as capricious and manipulative as only a child can be. She lives for the moment, heedless of what is to come, in stark contrast with her half-sister Esther, who is from the outset keenly aware of the danger from the Christian community to Rahel, the family and their race. The Jewish matriarch as centre of the family is embodied in the figure of Esther who exemplifies the literary topos of the plain but gifted unmarried girl, a *mulier fortis*, a valiant woman of Old Testament provenance. Rahel, who is more like an errant daughter than a sister, says of Esther that she is so strong, if she were a man she would be a hero (v. 975). Many of Esther's comments provide the perspective through which the author asks the audience or the attentive reader to interpret the action. She alone is master of irony in the play. In Act V, Manrike, who has been a driving force in the conspiracy against Rahel, tells Esther disdainfully: "Weib, wir sind Christen", to which she instantly responds: "Nun ihr habt's gezeigt" (v. 1796) "Wench, we are Christians". "As you've shown." Significantly, it is the king, who has been shown to be less prejudiced than his entourage, who comes closest at one point to her perspective. In an exchange with the young courtier Garceran, he makes an unusual reference to the abiding myth of the Jews as crucifiers of Christ, when he declares that "we [the Christians] crucify the Lord ten times a day by our sins while they, the Jews, did it but once".[36]

On account of Rahel's absence from the stage after Act III, earlier critics saw the play as falling into two distinct halves, the love tragedy and the drama of state, with the play's interest being seen in the drama of state. Older critics, even well before the Third Reich, did not even regard Rahel as a main character. Why then did Grillparzer change Lope's title? For the Spanish play centres on politics and is entitled *Las paces de los reyes, i la Judía de Toledo*, that is, the reconciliation of the king and queen, and the Jewess of Toledo, the last-named separated by a comma, as though she were a kind of appendage. Not so in Grillparzer's drama. Here the love interest and the Jewish interest are integral parts of the political play. Modern critical interest in Jewish

---

[36]"Wir kreuzigen täglich zehnmal den Herrn/ Durch unsre Sünden, unsre Missetaten/ Und Jene haben's einmal nur getan." (v. 506–508).

and feminist studies has placed Rahel back at the play's heart, where she belongs. The play has been seen in terms of traditional defamation of sensuality, the mutilation of Rahel's body as paradigmatic of a society which marginalised and exercised violence on Jews and women. Though absent from the stage after the third act, as the queen and the courtiers plot her murder, which takes place between Acts IV and V, Rahel remains *ex negativo* a powerful presence, and is invoked as such by Esther. The queen and the courtiers have forgotten her as a person; she has become for them but a mere incident. Even the king now translates her into an abstraction, as indeed "the Jews" are an abstraction for the Christian society, not real people of flesh and blood. Thus Rahel can be seen to function as an emblem of Christian society's treatment of its Jews, an indictment of its hypocrisy and casuistry, which cites "reason of state" and the force of the prejudice of "the people" in defence of an action or to justify the withdrawal of that protection of individual and group, which had been pledged by the ruler and on which feudal authority was predicated.

Grillparzer is at all times and in all his writings a political animal, and he does indeed put political issues at the heart of his play. Older interpretations focused on the fall, punishment and redemption of the king. Contemporary Grillparzer scholars are less ready to accept so affirmative a view. One can go further and see the political "message" of *Die Jüdin von Toledo* as being a critique of a society which, by analogy with the Austria of his own day, practised intolerance while underpinning it by an attempted revival of the medieval notion of society as Christian, with everyone else by definition non-persons. Grillparzer's abiding concern, as documented in his unpublished writings, with the relationship between church and state, his advocacy of freedom of conscience as part of the remit of the (modern) state, are well illustrated in the conversations recorded in May 1868 by Auguste von Littrow-Bischoff over another of his dramas with a Jewish theme, the unfinished *Esther*.[37] But the ending of his one completed "Jewish" play, on Rahel the Spanish Jewess and her family, which sees the Sibylline Esther, alone with her father on the stage in her devastated home, is difficult to reconcile with his measured optimism in the more liberal age of late 1860s Austria. Esther's bitter accusation against Christian amorality and hypocrisy, and her ringing curse invoked on the Christian community would have been a powerful note on which to end the play. But Grillparzer does not end his play here. At the sight of her father obsessed with his gold, he has Esther revoke her curse and instead utter a plea for mercy for Jews and Christians alike. "Faced with all that wretchedness, is that all you can think of?" she chides him. "If that be so, I take back the curse which I uttered, for you are guilty and so am I – and she. We are counted with them in the company of sinners. Let us forgive, that God may forgive us too."

> Denk ihr noch des?
> Im Angesicht des Jammers und der Not.
> Dann nehm' ich rück den Fluch den ich gesprochen,
> Dann seid Ihr schuldig auch und ich – und sie.
> Wir stehn gleich jenen in der Sünder Reihe.
> Verzeihn wir denn, damit uns Gott verzeihe. (v.1943–1948)

[37] *Sämtliche Werke* (*op. cit.* n. 25), vol. IV, pp. 974–983, especially pp. 978 and 980.

The evidence is not perhaps compelling, but, given the originality of the perspective which the poet offers here on Roman Catholic-Jewish relations, it is conceivable that Grillparzer wished Esther's valedictory words to offer an alternative to traditional responses to religious difference. Those responses had found expression, on the one hand, in the Old Testament traditional call for revenge for wrong wrought, and, on the other, to the policies of a Christian church which had become a powerful political institution and which over the centuries had translated its own intolerance of difference at a theological level into the systematic persecution of minorities.

Karl Beck: From Radicalism to Monarchism

BY RITCHIE ROBERTSON

For a short period in the late 1830s Karl Beck was inordinately famous as a radical poet. Karl Gutzkow called him a second Byron.[1] Friedrich Engels called him a second Schiller.[2] But within ten years both his poetry and his politics suffered a sharp decline. He deplored the 1848 Revolution as sinful and declared his loyalty to the young Emperor Franz Joseph. The rest of his life was spent in obscurity with the label of a renegade, which has always clung to him.

In taking a fresh look at Beck, I want to treat him above all as a case study in the problems of Jewish assimilation. Since we have little information about Beck's private life, the attempt to understand his political trajectory must be based on his poetry. And, though he is now forgotten except by literary historians, his poetry is not negligible. No less a critic than Siegbert Prawer has said of him: "Beck brings a strange, exotic element into German poetry, which we can see to be partly at least due to ghetto origins, though he likes to disguise it (in *Der fahrende Poet*, for instance) as Hungarian local colour, or in *Der Sultan* as Eastern fairy-tale. Beck, however, more openly and more directly than most, speaks of what it meant to be a Jewish poet and escape from what he felt, like many others, to be a restrictive atmosphere: that of orthodox Judaism as he had encountered it as a child."[3]

Beck was born in 1817 in Baja, then one of the largest Jewish communities in southern Hungary. When he was about twelve, his father, a businessman, moved to Pest, where Karl Beck attended a German-speaking Gymnasium. He first left home at the age of sixteen to study medicine in Vienna, but was forced by illness to return home, where he reluctantly entered on a business career. In 1835 or 1836, however,

---

[1] "Das kräftigste und hoffnungsvollste Talent unter den Jüngeren ist Karl Beck, der alle Mittel besitzt, ein deutscher Byron zu werden": Gutzkow quoted in Wolfgang Häusler, 'Politische und soziale Probleme des Vormärz in den Dichtungen Karl Becks', in Julius H. Schoeps, Imanuel Geiss and Ludger Heid (eds.), *Revolution und Demokratie in Geschichte und Literatur*, Duisburg 1979, pp. 235–258 (p. 245). This is the most important study of Beck; but see also Ruth Kestenberg-Gladstein, 'Karl Beck: Identitätsprobleme der ersten Assimilationsgeneration in deutscher Sprache', *Bulletin des Leo Baeck Instituts*, 60 (1981), pp. 51–66; Antal Mádl, 'Karl Beck. Ein Vermittler zwischen ungarischer, österreichischer und deutscher Literatur', in his *Auf Lenaus Spuren: Beiträge zur österreichischen Literatur*, Vienna and Budapest 1982, pp. 167–182; Jacob Toury, 'Moritz Saphir und Karl Beck – zwei vormärzliche Literaten Österreichs', in Walter Grab and Julius H. Schoeps (eds.), *Juden im Vormärz und in der Revolution von 1848*, Stuttgart and Bonn 1983, pp. 138–156. I am grateful to Kevin Hilliard and Andrew Webber for supplying me with photocopies.
[2] "Karl Beck ist ein Dichtertalent, wie seit Schiller keins aufgestanden ist": Engels, letter to Friedrich Graeber (24 April 1839), in Karl Marx, Friedrich Engels, *Über Kunst und Literatur*, ed. by Manfred Kliem, 2 vols., Berlin 1968, vol. II, p. 391.
[3] S. S. Prawer, 'Jewish contributions to German lyric poetry', *LBI Year Book VIII* (1963), pp. 149–170 (pp. 156–157).

he left home again, this time to study philosophy in Leipzig, where many young Austrian writers, including Moritz Hartmann, Ignaz Kuranda, Georg Karl Herloßsohn, and Alfred Meissner, had moved to avoid the restrictions of the Metternich government.

Seen from the outside, in sociological categories, Beck's career is in many ways typical of his generation of acculturated Jewish intellectuals from the Habsburg provinces, recently described by Hillel Kieval.[4] Like Moritz Hartmann, Leopold Kompert, and others, Beck received a secular education, moved to an urban centre (first Vienna, later Leipzig), and travelled more widely, in a manner that could symbolise his generation's sense of homelessness. He converted to Protestantism in 1843. He found himself torn between diverse possibilities of assimilation: whether by entering German-language culture or allying himself with a nationalist movement – in his case, Hungarian nationalism. Like Hartmann, who in 1848 was an extreme left-wing member of the Frankfurt Parliament, Beck espoused radical politics. Though the seriousness of his radicalism is debatable, his choice can be seen as an attempt to escape from marginality and outflank antisemitism by helping to found a society based on equality: in other words, a "revolutionary assimilation".[5] This aspiration helps to explain the often-noted prominence of Jews in the Vormärz and the 1848 Revolutions, especially in Vienna.[6] Beck's brothers also chose various forms of assimilation: Siegfried Beck, a businessman, converted to Catholicism, while Willi Beck shared Karl's early radicalism and worked as a caricaturist on Sigmund Engländer's satirical paper *Katzenmusik*.[7]

Beck, however, also illustrates another form of assimilation: the attempt to establish oneself in one's host society through the rapid rise to literary fame. This was Beck's aspiration from early on. In 1835, as an unwilling clerk in Pest, he wrote to his friend Jacob Kaufmann (also later well-known as a political poet):

> Ich habe wieder den dunkeln Mantel der Melancholie angezogen und dichte gewöhnlich bis nach Mitternacht. Während meine Nachbarn um diese Zeit der Sterblichkeit opfern, quält mich eine grosse Sorge: "*Unsterblichkeit*".[8]

To learn more about the tensions of assimilation, we must look closely at the poems that gave him his short-lived reputation. In Leipzig he made valuable contacts. The Young German journalist Ferdinand Gustav Kühne invited him to publish in the

---

[4]See Kieval, 'The social vision of Bohemian Jews: intellectuals and community in the 1840s', in Jonathan Frankel and Steven J. Zipperstein (eds.), *Assimilation and Community: The Jews in Nineteenth-Century Europe*, Cambridge 1992, pp. 246–283.
[5]See Jochanan Bloch, 'Sozialismus und Judentum', *Neue Deutsche Hefte*, 93 (May/June 1963), 86–113 (p. 102).
[6]See especially Salo W. Baron, 'The impact of the revolution of 1848 on Jewish emancipation', *Jewish Social Studies*, 11 (1949), pp. 195–248; Wolfgang Häusler, 'Demokratie und Emanzipation 1848', *Studia Judaica Austriaca*, 1 (1974), pp. 92–111; Reinhard Rürup, 'The European revolutions of 1848 and Jewish emancipation', in Werner E. Mosse, Arnold Paucker, and Reinhard Rürup (eds.), *Revolution and Evolution: 1848 in German-Jewish History*, Tübingen 1981 (Schriftenreihe wissenschaftlicher Abhandlungen des Leo Baeck Instituts 39), pp. 1–53.
[7]Häusler, 'Politische und soziale Probleme', p. 237.
[8]Letter of 24 July 1835 in Adolph Kohut, 'Ungedrucktes von Karl Beck', *Internationale Litteraturberichte*, 5 (1898), pp. 353–355, 375–376, 391–392, 404–406 (p. 354). I am grateful to Rudolf Muhs for drawing this article to my attention and giving me a photocopy.

Zeitschrift für die elegante Welt. Beck proudly told Kaufmann "dass meine Lieder in allen Zeitschriften mit ungeheuerem Beifall aufgenommen und gelesen werden", and added: "man nennt mich hier den magyarischen Dichter, der mit seinen Liedern wie ein Donner dreinschlägt."[9]

In the last week of 1837 the twenty year old Beck brought out his first collection of poems, *Nächte: Gepanzerte Lieder*. Contemporaries were impressed by the impetuous radicalism of these poems. Engels compared them to the taboo-breaking spirit shown by the young Schiller in *Die Räuber*. He went even further when, having compared Ludwig Börne to Lessing, he added: "möge ihm in Karl Beck der Goethe folgen!"[10] As soon as the poems had appeared, the publisher Julius Campe warned Heine, who was still suffering under the ban placed on his works by the Federal Diet two years earlier, that he must look to his laurels because of younger and more popular talents: "Eben in dieser Woche tritt ein junger Dichter auf – ein *Ungar* – gab ein Buch: Nächte, gepanzerte Lieder v. Carl Beck. Was sind das für Gedanken, welche Gesinnung; es tändelt nicht, es bereitet sich ernst vor."[11]

The tone of *Nächte* is set by Beck's most famous poem, 'Die Eisenbahn', written to mark the opening of the line between Dresden and Leipzig. Not only did he take a daringly contemporary subject – the first railway line in Germany, between Fürth and Nuremberg, had been opened only in 1835 – but he boldly made the train into the aggressive bearer of progress and liberty:

> Rasend rauschen rings die Räder,
> Rollend, grollend, stürmisch sausend,
> Tief im innersten Geäder
> Kämpft der Zeitgeist freiheitsbrausend.[12]

The poem gives drastic and onomatopoeic form to a concept frequent in *Nächte*, that of "die Zeit", the Age, the Present. In the opening poem, 'Der Sultan', the Oriental speaker tells us how he was roused from sensual pleasure and mindless reveries first by the elusive figure of Poetry and then by another allegorical female, to whom he yields despite his friends' warnings:

> Sie nennt sich Zeit, und ihres Sehnens Drang,
> Ihr Lieben, ihr Gebären, ihr Bestreben,
> Und ihre Märchen, mitternächtig, bang,
> Ich schrieb sie hin mit meinem rothen Leben. (*Nächte*, p. 8)

In the structure of Beck's first volume, the Age appears as a Sheherazade who entertains the Sultan with a number of "Märchen" or Tales, each comprising a number of "nights", in the manner of the Arabian Nights.

As a radical poet, Beck had to choose whether to follow the ironic, self-mocking style of Heine or the forthrightness of Börne, who had died in 1837, and he opted

---

[9] Letter of 9 September 1836 in Kohut, 'Ungedrucktes', p. 375.
[10] Engels, letter to Graeber, in Marx, Engels, *Über Kunst und Literatur*, vol. 2, p. 390.
[11] Campe, letter of 31 December 1837, quoted in Heine, *Sämtliche Schriften*, ed. by Klaus Briegleb, 6 vols., Munich 1968–1976, vol. VI/2, p. 435.
[12] Beck, *Nächte: Gepanzerte Lieder*, Leipzig 1838, p. 32.

unequivocally for the latter. The poem 'Vor Heine's Portrait' criticises Heine's irony for killing all true emotion:

> Du warst Dir selbst ein unbestochner Richter;
> Du ließest Dir das Herz zu Asche brennen,
> Und suchtest drin des Liedes Geisterlichter. (*Nächte*, p. 34)

A rare echo of Heine occurs in the poem 'Schillers Haus in Gohlis', which ends with the poet on his knees, addressing an unidentified passer-by in words from Schiller's play *Don Carlos*:

> Ich seufzte, bat: "O geben, geben Sie
> Gedankenfreiheit!"
> "Herr, sind Sie betrunken?" (*Nächte*, p. 28)

This *Stimmungsbruch* is evidently borrowed from the end of Heine's *Seegespenst*, where the Captain saves the dreamy poet from plunging over the ship's side by exclaiming "Doktor, sind Sie des Teufels?". But in Beck's poem, Schiller's Marquis Posa is placed alongside Börne:

> Dein Posa ist kein schaumgeborener Wahn:
> Ist Börne für die Menschheit nicht gefallen? (*Nächte*, p. 27)

The second section of *Nächte* is entitled "Die neue Bibel". The author of the new Bible is supposed to be Börne, who resolves:

> Ja, eine neue Bibel will ich schreiben,
> An die ein zweifelndes Jahrhundert glaubt. (*Nächte*, p. 77)

The poem 'Die Schöpfung' is headed "Börne schreibt die Bibel". Unfortunately Beck cannot juxtapose the events of the Bible with a coherent narrative of his own, so we have a series of loosely related poems which do not always gain anything from their Biblical titles (in contrast to Heine's later poem 'Adam der Erste'). The events of Genesis are given a revolutionary reinterpretation: a serpent identified with "die Zeit" urges the primal couple to eat from the tree of knowledge; the children born of the sons of earth and the daughters of heaven, "Riesenkinder", demand equality on earth (p. 100), and God, a terrified tyrant, resolves to destroy them all in the Flood, but Noah preserves the idea of freedom in his heart. Noah's son Ham, "der seines Vaters Blöße zeigt", attacks the Germans for their political indifference. In 'Der Dornbusch' (pp. 108–110), what speaks from the burning bush is the "Weltengeist", promising to rescue humanity from slavery; Börne is equated with Moses, and, instead of Aaron, the mediator between him and his people will be his pen. In 'Der neuen Bibel anderer Teil', the prophet Jeremiah is equated with the Austrian political poet Anastasius Grün (p. 137).

Beck's homage to Börne in *Nächte* did not convince everyone. Despite his initial admiration for the volume, Engels soon afterwards objected that Beck had misrepresented Börne, attributing to him an emotional "Weltschmerz" that was alien to Börne's firm and resolute character. "Nein, das ist Börne nicht, das ist nur ein unbestimmtes

Ideal des modernen Dichtens, aus Heinescher Koketterie und Mundtschen Floskeln zusammengesetzt, ein Ideal, vor dessen Realisierung uns Gott bewahren möge."[13]

When we look closely at the poems, we find other features that conflict with their radical assertiveness. Beck likes to stylise himself as a Byronic hero. The Sultan in the introductory poem describes himself as follows:

> Kein Gott, als Gott – der Dichter sein Prophet,
> Mein Koran ist das Buch der Weltgeschichte,
> Ich wende mich in brünstigem Gebet
> Nach Sonnenaufgang mit dem Angesichte.
> Ein Sultan bin ich, wild und sturmbewegt,
> Mein Heer – des Lieds gepanzerte Gestalten;
> Um meine Stirne hat der Gram gelegt
> Den Turban in geheimnisreiche Falten. (*Nächte*, p. 3)

The speaker is a Byronic hero, "wild und sturmbewegt", afflicted by "Gram" (a recurrent word), but also an Oriental who pays his devotions to the rising sun of Enlightenment. Byron was an exile from his own country who identified with the cause of Greek liberty and, in the verse-narratives he called 'Turkish tales', assumed a series of Oriental identities. In repeating Byron's Oriental move, Beck has the advantage of a Jewish identity to which the Oriental persona, as in the early writings of Heine, serves as a coded reference.[14] However, Beck's persona risks collapsing under this weight of meaning, as is apparent when we are told that melancholy is visible not in the lines on his forehead but in the folds of his turban – an image that does not withstand much scrutiny.

Along with his Byronic posturing, Beck expresses a lofty conception of poetry. In the poem 'Deutsche Buchhändlerbörse' the Leipzig book fair is represented as the profanation of a temple, where sacred art is commercialised:

> Zum Markte ist der Tempel umgewandelt –
> Der Gott wird ausgeboten und verhandelt. (*Nächte*, p. 22)

In the Biblical sequence, the act of creation is represented by a young man in a garret writing a poem, and the poet is imagined in sublime terms:

> Ein Gott ist der Poet! er kann aus Nichts
> Auf tausend Säulen sich ein All erbauen,
> Sein flammend Auge ist der Thron des Lichts,
> Und seine Wolkenschatten sind die Brauen. (*Nächte*, p. 80)

These two major themes of *Nächte*, political radicalism and poetic self-aggrandisement, stand in an uneasy relationship to the third, the situation of the Jews. Early in the book, the poem 'Die Juden auf der Messe' reminds us that the Jews are exiles from their own country, where the Turk now smokes his pipe on the ruins of past

---

[13]Marx, Engels, *Über Kunst und Literatur*, vol. 2, p. 416.
[14]See Michael Perraudin, 'Irrationalismus und jüdisches Schicksal. Die thematischen Zusammenhänge von Heines *Ideen. Das Buch Le Grand*', in Joseph A. Kruse et al. (eds.), *Aufklärung und Skepsis: Internationaler Heine-Kongreß 1997 zum 200. Geburtstag*, Stuttgart and Weimar, 1998, pp. 279–302.

civilisations. The Jews cannot see beyond their delusory religion and their small-minded commercialism:

> Ach nach Wundern fragt der Jude,
> Sieht in Wolken seinen Hort;
> Aber von der theuren Bude
> Geht er nicht um Welten fort. (*Nächte*, p. 42)

Beck speaks for the young generation of Jews who feel trapped in this little world of huckstering. One section of *Nächte* is headed 'Das junge Palästina', an implicit rejoinder to Wolfgang Menzel, who in 1835, in the *Morgenblatt für gebildete Stände*, had reported it as a widespread view that "das sogenannte junge Deutschland sey eigentlich ein junges Palästina".[15] Beck replies by presenting the situation of young Jews imprisoned in Orthodoxy:

> Im Kerker: Judentum bin ich gefangen,
> Und rüttle kraftlos an den Gitterstäben. (*Nächte*, p. 182)

While he depicts the poverty of the ghetto, Beck stresses the emptiness of the Jews' religion. They pray to "Dem Gott, aus Schlamm und Vorurtheil geknetet" (p. 177). The religious content of Judaism has been replaced by commercialism. The most extreme statement of this charge against the Jews comes in a poem which seems not to have been quoted so far in the secondary literature on Beck. It forms the sixty-second "night" of the volume:

> Ja, dich beglückt des Herzens stiller Glaube
> Daß du im *Himmel Alles* solltest werden;
> Doch vor den Menschen kriechst du jetzt im Staube,
> Und giltst als *Nichts* vor ihnen hier auf *Erden*.
>
> Du bist zerstreut, du mußt noch mehr zerstieben,
> Und nicht wie Austern fest beisammen hocken,
> Und nicht wie diese in den Flutgetrieben
> Zu Felsen eigensinnig dich verstocken.
>
> Was bist du jetzt? Nur Schatten, Nebelstreifen,
> Die nimmermehr die Ruhe finden können,
> Die am Kozytus auf und nieder schweifen,
> Und gern umsonst die Überfahrt gewönnen.
>
> Doch wird der kluge Fährmann sich bewahren –
> Begrüßt ihr ihn, so wird er Euch verlachen;
> Er will Euch nicht ins Reich der Ruhe fahren,
> Er nimmt Euch nicht in seinen schwanken Nachen.

---

[15]Quoted in *Politische Avantgarde 1830–1840: Eine Dokumentation zum 'Jungen Deutschland'*, ed. by Alfred Estermann, 2 vols., Frankfurt am Main 1972, vol. I, p. 295.

> Ihr würdet sonst zur Stelle spekulieren,
> Sofort ein Dampfboot auf Papiere gründen –
> Und seinen Posten dann der Mann verlieren -
> Und seinen Obolus und seine Pfründen. (*Nächte*, pp. 183–184)

The Jews suffer both from their false religion and their real commercialism. Both prevent them from attaining any real self-improvement. Commercialism is so deeply ingrained that even in the underworld Charon will not take them over in his boat, for fear they start modernising the infernal shipping and put him out of a job. Beck further shows how redundant Judaism is by placing the Jews within the framework of another mythology, the classical picture of the underworld, because it has cultural authority in the society to which he seeks assimilation.

In *Nächte*, then, Beck constructs a Jewish identity which is wholly negative. Jewishness is equated with confinement, degradation, hypocrisy, money-grubbing. Its counterpart is the myth of the sublime poet. Both are reconciled in the ideal figure of the Sultan, a poet and an Oriental who escapes from confinement and confronts real life. Thus Beck, like other Jewish writers of the early nineteenth century, constructs an ideal image of Jewishness which compensates for real discrimination and frustration but which only exists on paper. Other examples include the superhuman philosophical serenity of Berthold Auerbach's Spinoza and the suave, relaxed, sexually successful man of the world who is the narrator of Heine's Italian *Reisebilder*. These are Jewish identities which can be created on paper but cannot be lived.[16]

The success of *Nächte* widened Beck's horizons. Ottilie von Goethe invited him to Weimar. He promptly exploited his travels for his next book, *Der fahrende Poet*, which is loosely modelled, as contemporaries recognised, on Byron's *Childe Harold's Pilgrimage*. Like Byron's hero, Beck's persona undertakes a tour, though confined to Central Europe; starting from Hungary, he passes through Vienna and Weimar, where he pays homage to Goethe and Schiller, and ends at the Wartburg, where Luther was confined in 1519. The Weimar section is presented as having been composed in Goethe's house. The poems are all sonnets, some of them more personal and contemplative than the poems in *Nächte*, and Beck's self-doubt is often apparent: "Nennt man mich Dichter, so verhöhnt man mich" (p. 143). In the following years, we see him experimenting with identities. He returned to Jewishness in his unsuccessful Biblical drama *Saul* (1841), but did better with Hungarian material in his popular verse narrative *Janko, der ungarische Roßhirt* (1841). In the mid-1840s, however, he made a fresh start with social and Jewish themes.

The *Lieder vom armen Manne* (1846) astonished Beck's contemporaries by their drastic depictions of poverty. It may well be true, as Sol Liptzin says, that Beck was projecting his own situation: "self-pity led him to pity others".[17] At any rate, the volume gains its coherence, not from any vision of society, but from its presentation of the Jewish situation. The poems begin with a long poem addressed to Rothschild, meaning Salomon Mayer Rothschild, who managed the family's Vienna subsidiary. It very much follows the polemics against the Rothschilds by Börne, who in the seventy-sec-

---

[16]See Ritchie Robertson, *The 'Jewish Question' in German Literature, 1749–1939*, Oxford 1999, pp. 88, 90.
[17]Sol Liptzin, *Lyric Pioneers of Modern Germany: Studies in German Social Poetry*, New York 1928, p. 42.

ond *Brief aus Paris* accused them of being the true rulers of the world, with crowned heads paying them homage, and of using their wealth to suppress nationalist movements.[18] Beck similarly calls Rothschild the "Papst des Goldes".[19] He depicts the Rothschilds as successors to the Roman Empire:

> Verkühlet sind die römischen Blitze!
> Kein Heil mit drohender Degenspitze,
> Kein Solon und keine Helena
> Lenkt zaubergewaltig der Erde Zügel;
> Du siegst, o Herr, mit kaltem Geklügel,
> Der Könige König stehst du da! (*Lieder*, p. 3)

Another poem in this volume, 'Der Trödeljude', moves to the opposite end of the spectrum of Jewish life by depicting the harsh life of a Jewish pedlar who poignantly worries about his son having to lead a similar existence:

> Ein jüdisch Kind – auf deutscher Erde –
> Ich trug es kaum, du trägst es nie.
> Du willst des Christen Herz gewinnen,
> Und sinnst und strebst und weißt nicht wie.
> Er grollt, nicht um Jesu willen,
> Er grollt, bis Dein Athem stirbt,
> Weil Deine Hand um Geld und Güter
> Geschwinder und beglückter wirbt. (*Lieder*, p. 56)

By showing that modern antisemitism is really economic, despite its religious façade, Beck develops his portrayal of the modern world as governed by material forces. The Rothschilds, who command these forces and thus the world, are blamed for failing to help their fellow-Jews but instead keeping them in a miserable exile where they can think of nothing but trade. Addressing the financier in the informal "Du" form, he writes:

> Hast Du den eigenen Stamm befreit,
> Der ewig hofft und ewig duldet?
> Der lächelnd die schimpflichen Ketten verguldet,
> Ein fertiger Knecht, zu tragen bereit,
> Was er verschuldet und nicht verschuldet!
> Sie haben ihre Geschichte begraben,
> Es duften die Psalmen vergessen und wild,
> Wo blüht ihr Reich? Wo glänzt ihr Schild?
> *Doch einen König mußten sie haben!*
> Sie salbten *Dich* in Saus und Braus,
> *Du* ragtest über die Häupter hinaus,
> *Dir* waren die Blicke des Volkes hold,
> Denn *Du* besaßest – das schwerste Gold. (*Lieder*, pp. 19–20)

---

[18]Börne, *Sämtliche Schriften*, ed. by Peter and Inge Rippmann, 5 vols., Dreieich 1977, vol. III, pp. 482–492. For a selection of attacks on the Rothschilds by Börne and Heine, see Niall Ferguson, *The World's Banker: The History of the House of Rothschild*, London 1998, pp. 224–228.

[19]Beck, *Lieder vom armen Manne*, Leipzig 1846, p. 13.

Instead of educating his people, Rothschild leads them in the dance round the golden calf (*Lieder*, p. 21).

Beck therefore participates in the radical critique which identified modern Judaism with a shallow materialism. Similarly, Ludwig Börne, on his return from Berlin to Frankfurt, told Henriette Herz that the Jews there struck him as absurdly obsessed with money: "Drei Dinge sind, die sie zu schätzen wissen, erstens: Geld, zweitens: Geld, und drittens: Geld."[20] This is the substance of Marx's notorious essay 'On the Jewish Question' which has brought him the reputation of being a self-hating Jew.[21] Beck's criticism of the Rothschilds may be unjust: Niall Ferguson has shown how actively they supported their fellow-Jews, financing, for example, the inquiry into the Damascus blood libel.[22]

However, Beck has seldom received credit for his critique of the Rothschilds, for his *Lieder vom armen Mann* were attacked by Engels in a hilariously unfair review which deserves to be ranked among the great "Verrisse", alongside Macaulay's destruction of Robert Montgomery's poems and Mark Twain's essay on Fenimore Cooper.[23] Engels complained that Beck was too sympathetic towards the poor. Beck did not want the wealth of the Rothschilds to be swept away, but to be used for the benefit of the poor:

> Nicht die Vernichtung der wirklichen Macht Rothschilds, der gesellschaftlichen Zustände, worauf sie beruht, droht der Dichter; er wünscht nur ihre menschenfreundliche Anwendung. Er jammert, daß die Bankiers keine sozialistischen Philanthropen sind, keine Schwärmer, keine Menschheitsbeglücker, sondern eben Bankiers. Beck besingt die feige kleinbürgerliche Misère, den "armen Mann", den pauvre honteux mit seinen armen, frommen und inkonsequenten Wünschen, den "kleinen Mann" in allen seinen Formen, nicht den stolzen, drohenden und revolutionären Proletarier.[24]

It might be argued that Engels romanticises the revolutionary proletariat and that Beck's compassion is at least equally attractive. Certainly Beck had no theory, Communist or other, about how to improve the lot of the poor; devising theories was hardly his job as a poet. Engels, however, fails to recognise that the poems amount to a coherent critique of Jewish capitalism as a force which does especial harm to the Jews.

By the mid-1840s Beck's revolutionary élan had undoubtedly waned. Antal Mádl has shown how in revising his poems he toned them down, so that an original attack against "Tyrannen" was redirected against the softer target "Philister".[25] In 1848 Beck felt little, if any, enthusiasm for the revolutions. He annoyed Moritz Hartmann by writing to him on 24 December 1848: "Helfen Sie mit, der in den Revolutionsstürmen

---

[20]Börne, letter of 26 May 1805, in *Sämtliche Schriften*, vol. 4, p. 121. See Orlando Figes, 'Ludwig Börne and the formation of a radical critique of Judaism', *LBI Year Book XXIX* (1984), pp. 351–382.
[21]See Julius Carlebach, *Karl Marx and the Radical Critique of Judaism*, London 1978.
[22]Ferguson, *The World's Banker*, pp. 418–422.
[23]'Mr. Robert Montgomery', in Lord Macaulay, *Critical and Historical Essays*, 2 vols., London 1868, vol. I, pp. 122–132; Mark Twain, 'Fenimore Cooper's Literary Offenses', in *The Shock of Recognition*, ed. by Edmund Wilson, 2 vols., 2nd edn., New York 1955, vol. I, pp. 582–594.
[24]Engels, 'Deutscher Sozialismus in Versen und Prosa', in Marx, Engels, *Über Kunst und Literatur*, vol. 2, p. 203.
[25]Mádl, *Politische Dichtung aus Österreich 1830–1848*, Vienna and Budapest 1969, p. 116.

heimatlos gewordenen Kunst in meinen Blättern ein sicheres Nest zu bauen."[26] Besides preserving the autonomy of art, Beck had other preoccupations. In 1846 or earlier he had got to know a young woman called Julie Mühlmann. He described her in a letter to Kühne that demonstrates his own desire to settle down in his own household:

> Ich kenne auch wohl in Berlin ein 18jähriges Kind, dem ich gut bin, das ich für mich erziehe, es ist leidlich hübsch, besitzt 10 000 Thaler, hat Geist und Herz, liebt den Menschen in mir mehr als den Dichter und ist besorgter um meine Gesundheit als um meinen Namen.[27]

In 1848 Julie followed Beck to Vienna, where they married, but a few months later, in 1849, she died of cholera.

To his readers, ignorant of his private grief, it was in 1849, with the publication of his long poem addressed to the new Emperor, *An Franz Joseph*, that Beck seemed to have sold out completely. Certainly the poems address Franz Joseph in a tone of submissive flattery, quite unlike the political poet's self-image as tribune, and describe the Hungarian uprising as sinful:

> Ich weiß, es war die Sünde groß
> In Ungarland geworden.
> Es rangen sich schreiend aus ihrem Schooß
> Die Schuld und der Fluch, die Zwillinge, los.[28]

The purpose of the poems, however, is to plead for mercy towards the Hungarian revolutionaries, who were being hunted down, put on trial, and hanged, while their country was plundered, by troops under the notorious General Haynau (known as "General Hyena"). Whether the poems had any effect may be doubted. But would they have swayed the Emperor if they had been cast in tones of righteous indignation?

At all events, Beck had used up his inspiration. As poetry, *An Franz Joseph* is nothing. By the age of thirty he was a worn-out talent and a disappointed man. The remaining thirty years of his life were spent in Vienna and Budapest, where he was supported largely by the charity of his friends. Some volumes of poetry and short-lived editing projects failed to raise him from the literary oblivion in which he stayed till his death in 1879.

A revealing essay on Austria's political mission was found among Beck's papers after his death and published in part by Adolph Kohut. Here Beck espouses the civilising mission of German culture in the Austrian Empire:

> Die grosse politische Idee Österreichs, welche in alle nationalen Besonderheiten mächtig übergreift, die weltgeschichtliche Bedeutung der Monarchie *findet nur in unserer deutschen Muttersprache ihren entsprechenden Ausdruck*. Wie in Nordamerika das angelsächsische Idiom, so hat in Österreich die deutsche Sprache die Mission, einen mannigfaltig gemischten Völkerkomplex in einem grossen politischen Gedanken zu vereinigen.[29]

---

[26]Quoted from MS by Häusler, 'Politische und soziale Probleme', p. 256.
[27]Letter of 27 April 1846 in Kohut, 'Ungedrucktes', p. 376.
[28]Beck, *An Franz Joseph*, Vienna 1849, p. 36.
[29]Kohut, 'Ungedrucktes', p. 406. Emphasis in original.

And the elderly Beck revealed himself as an admirer of Bismarck, declaring: "*Wenn ein Deutscher einen Stern entdeckt, soll er ihn Bismarck taufen.*"[30] This attitude aligns Beck with other Jewish writers from the Austrian provinces who felt that the civilising mission of the Germans in Austria could be best conducted if Austria would learn from the example of Prussia, since 1871 the dominant region of a united Germany. Karl Emil Franzos, another Germanophile, thought the Austrian bureaucracy too corrupt to undertake its mission of spreading German culture in Galicia. Jakob Freud, the Galician-born father of Sigmund, on adopting the Gregorian calendar, also changed his date of birth from 18 December 1815 to 1 April – Bismarck's birthday.[31] And Fritz Mauthner, born in northern Bohemia, so worshipped Bismarck that he added to his autobiography the invocation: "sancte Bismarck, magister Germaniae, ora pro nobis."[32]

As a literary career, Beck's work might be hard to defend against the charge levelled by Moritz Hartmann in his doggerel round-up of the events of 1848, *Reimchronik des Pfaffen Maurizius* – the charge of merely following fashion. In the fifth "Caput" of his poem, entitled 'Apostel und Apostaten', Hartmann denounces "Carlos Beck" (another allusion to Schiller) for flattering the Emperor, and continues:

> Doch recht' ich nicht mit ihm. In Wien
> Ists jetzt zu kriechen auf den Knien
> Gewißlich sehr beliebte Mode,
> Und das war immer seine Methode
> Zu thun, was ihm die Mode befahl.
> Vor langer, langer Zeit einmal
> Sang er mit "*Börne*" spielendem Herzen,
> Dann war er vor den Iden des Märzen
> Republikaner und Sozialist –
> Nach Ungarns Fall ist er Monarchist.[33]

A slightly more charitable account might stress Beck's wish to escape from the constrictions of Jewishness. The revolutionary enthusiasm he expressed at the age of twenty need not be false, but it may well have been shallow. It enabled him to create a literary sensation and to forge for himself a literary identity which wavered between self-aggrandisement and insecurity. Although he rejected Jewish life, it provided much of his most convincing poetry. His early radicalism was an impassioned mood, not a settled conviction; his later monarchism seems even more shallow. To call him a "renegade" is unjust: it means treating him as first and foremost a political writer, when in fact he was a writer desperate for fame. He played the nationalist card without being a Hungarian, and the proletarian card without being a Socialist. The thread running through his work seems to be the desire for literary success as a means of escaping from the ghetto; but such success was granted him only in the short term. His later identification with Germany may be seen as an over-compensation for his sense of marginality, and as an example of the phenomenon that I have elsewhere called hyperacculturation.[34]

---

[30]*ibid*; emphasis in original.
[31]Ernest Jones, *Sigmund Freud: Life and Work*, 3 vols., London 1953–1957, vol. I, p. 2.
[32]Mauthner, *Erinnerungen I: Prager Jugendjahre*, Munich 1918, p. 349.
[33]Hartmann, *Reimchronik des Pfaffen Maurizius*, Frankfurt am Main 1849, pp. 220–221.
[34]Robertson, *The 'Jewish Question'*, pp. 345–378.

*Gender and Boundaries of the
Jewish Community in
Nineteenth-Century Germany*

The Lives, Loves, and Novels of August and Fanny Lewald, the Converted Cousins from Königsberg[1]

BY DEBORAH HERTZ

I

In 1937, the former literature professor Victor Klemperer was living with his wife Eva in their home in Dölzschen, a village near Dresden. He was then 56. He was born in 1881, the son of a Reform rabbi, and had converted to become a Lutheran when he was 31.[2] Klemperer and his wife would later be spared from receiving deportation orders for several years because Eva was Christian by descent. One day in October 1937 Klemperer recorded in his diary his thoughts about reading the memoir by the nineteenth-century novelist Fanny Lewald, which he had recently borrowed from his local lending library.[3] Eva was often ill and unhappy and he devoted many hours to reading aloud to her. Klemperer viewed Fanny Lewald through the lens of his own evolving German identity. On that day in 1937 he confided in his diary: "contempt and disgust and deepest mistrust with respect to Germany can never leave me now. And yet in 1933 I was so convinced of my Germanness."

Later in the same diary entry Klemperer elaborated on his reaction to reading Lewald's memoirs: "The memoirs of Fanny Lewald, written around 1860, are by far the most important for me." Klemperer went on to note that "seen from the present state of affairs, this Jewish penetration of German society, the part they played in Liberalism, in Young Germany is deeply moving".[4] Just exactly what he meant by the phrase "deeply moving" we shall never know. But we can easily imagine the broad contours of Klemperer's thinking. Fanny Lewald lived in an era when mastery of German language and literature and participation in German politics were exciting new projects, avidly taken up by many young Jews. Seven decades after Lewald

---

[1] The articles in this section originated as papers presented at the American Historical Association in Chicago in January 2000. They are followed by the comment of the panel chair. An interesting debate ensued which is reflected in the responses of the authors. Editor.
[2] See Victor Klemperer, *Curriculum vitae: Erinnerungen 1881–1918*, edited by Walter Nowojski, 2 vols., Berlin 1996. We can also now read his diaries from the pre-Nazi years *Leben sammeln, nicht fragen wozu und warum. Tagebücher 1918–1924*, edited by Walter Nowojski, Berlin 1996.
[3] The standard edition of the memoir is Fanny Lewald, *Meine Lebensgeschichte*, Berlin 1861–1862. The most recent complete edition is Ulrike Helmer (ed.), in the *Edition Klassikerinnen*, Frankfurt am Main 1998. An edited version with a useful introduction is Gisela Brinker-Gabler (ed.), *Fanny Lewald. Meine Lebensgeschichte*, Frankfurt am Main 1980. A short version of the autobiography is available in English. See Hanna Lewis (trans.), *The Education of Fanny Lewald: An Autobiography* (Albany, New York 1992).
[4] Victor Klemperer, *I Will Bear Witness: A Diary of the Nazi Years 1933–1941*, New York 1998, here pp. 239–240. The second volume bears the same title and covers the years 1942–45 and appeared in 1999.

published her memoir in the dark year of 1937 Victor Klemperer's German identity was constantly under attack. His diary tells the painful story of how that identity was also unravelling from within. Fanny Lewald's apparently harmonious identity must have seemed quite elusive to Klemperer in 1937.

This essay goes back several generations before Victor Klemperer's time to explore the lives and the literature of Fanny Lewald and her father's first cousin August Lewald.[5] Both Fanny and August had considerable fame and prominence in their own day. Both were prolific authors, she of a long list of novels, a memoir, and several volumes of social commentary. August was an actor, a theatre director, an editor, a playwright and also quite a prolific novelist. Sadly for him, August and his writings fell into obscurity during his lifetime. When he died at the age of seventy-eight in 1871 he was already a forgotten figure. Few have found him of interest since then.[6] It would no doubt be painful for him to discover that his friend Heinrich Heine is still supremely famous, and that other contemporaries such as his cousin's daughter Fanny Lewald, Rahel Levin Varnhagen and Ludwig Börne are known to a few specialists at least.

Fanny, in contrast, was very famous when she died, like August at seventy-eight, in 1889. Indeed, she was the highest-paid and best-selling German woman writer of her day.[7] Since then, attention to her life and her work has waxed and waned over the generations. Today her life story has again been re-discovered and there is considerable innovative scholarship probing her Jewish identity and her gender politics. We have new editions of several of her novels, as well as of her lengthy autobiography, the memoir that so "deeply moved" Victor Klemperer in 1937.[8] And one of her novels, indeed the very novel we explore in this essay, is now available online.[9]

Beyond their parallel careers as writers, Fanny and August shared other decisive life experiences. Both converted to the Lutheran church when they were teenagers. Fanny married a Christian by descent, and it is probable that August did the same. More to the point of this essay, both Lewald cousins published novels featuring converted characters. August's novel *Memoiren eines Banquiers* was published in 1836, and Fanny's novel *Jenny* was published seven years later, in 1843. *Memoiren eines Banquiers* was virtually Lewald's only publication in which he investigated Jewish themes, whereas *Jenny* was one of many books in which Fanny wrote about Jews and their special problems. Each novel provides a beautifully detailed panorama of the lives of thoughtful and ambitious Jews in the 1830s and 1840s. These novels give us the feel for the sophisticated way in which ex-Jewish intellectuals represented the act of conversion. Comparing what we know of the authors' own lives with the lives of their

---

[5]August Lewald is often referred to as Fanny Lewald's uncle. But he was her father's cousin, and thus her cousin "once removed".
[6]There is only one critical work on Lewald: see Ulrich Cruse, *August Lewald und seine zeitgeschichtliche Bedeutung*, Breslau 1933.
[7]This is the estimation provided by Dagmar Lorenz in her *Keepers of the Motherland: German Texts by Jewish Women Writers*, Lincoln, Nebraska and London 1997, p. 37.
[8]By far the most comprehensive new work on Fanny Lewald is Gudrun Marci-Boehncke, *Fanny Lewald: Jüdin, Preußin, Schriftstellerin*, Stuttgart 1998. See also Gabriele Schneider, *Fanny Lewald*, Reinbek bei Hamburg 1996; and Brigitta van Rheinberg, *Fanny Lewald. Geschichte einer Emanzipation*, Frankfurt am Main and New York 1990.
[9]See the full text of Lewald's *Jenny* at www.gutenberg.aol.de/lewald/jenny/jenny.htm.

Fanny Lewald

By courtesy of Mercedes Gurlitt

August Lewald

By courtesy of the Heinrich Heine Institut, Düsseldorf

fictional characters is fascinating. For we shall see that the two Lewald authors each created characters whose Jewish identity was often quite different from the Jewish identity of their creators.

Exploring the lives of the characters in the two novels brings texture and colour to our understanding of what conversion could mean in their times. The novels help us understand the subtle mixtures of motives Jews had for converting. We shall see that the reasons why the characters in the novels leave Judaism do not quite match the kinds of pragmatic motives which historians typically invoke when looking from afar. For instance, during these years the Prussian government required conversion for all high civil service posts, including professors, lawyers, and military officers. And undoubtedly this requirement was a very practical stimulus for many talented Jewish boys and men to become Christians. But career ambition does not push August Lewald's main character to convert. Indeed he remains in commerce long after he leaves Judaism.

Fanny Lewald's character Jenny does not fit the model of a wealthy woman whose conversion motives are pragmatic rather than spiritual.[10] On the contrary, after her conversion Jenny becomes increasingly sceptical about Protestant dogma. She decides to share her doubts with her beloved, who is training to become a Protestant pastor. He is appalled and cancels the engagement. So Jenny suffers in love because she takes religion seriously. In sum, both of these fictional characters help us refine the motives historians have employed hitherto.

Refining our analysis of motives is an important task, because we need to explain the dramatic rise in the proportion of Jews choosing conversion in these decades. We know a fair amount already about the Berlin statistics, thanks to the *Judenkartei* record of conversions compiled from the original Protestant parish registers during the Third Reich.[11] Of course we certainly may not assume that the Königsberg conversion pattern was identical to that of Berlin. But Berlin is close enough geographically to be of relevant interest. We know that during the decades when the two novels were published the absolute and also the proportional conversion rates in Berlin were both steadily increasing. Indeed, the rates were so high, especially among the wealthier Jews, that one scholar has recently argued that Berlin Jewry experienced a "family crisis" when most of the élite families in Berlin left Judaism during the 60 years between 1770 and 1830.[12] As the rates were rising, the composition of the converts was also shifting. During the eighteen twenties and thirties, the proportion of young men converting went up dramatically, whereas the proportion of women who became Christians fell considerably.[13] We can look to the novels in the hope that the

---

[10]This was an interpretation I frequently argued in my *Jewish High Society in Old Regime Berlin*, New Haven 1988. For a summary of new research in this field, see the *Preface* to the new edition of Deborah Hertz *Jewish High Society*, Syracuse 2001.

[11]For background on this unusual source see Deborah Hertz 'The Genealogy Bureaucracy in the Third Reich' in *Jewish History*, 11 (Fall 1997) pp. 53–78.

[12]See Steven Lowenstein, *The Berlin Jewish Community: Enlightenment, Family, and Crisis, 1770–1830*, New York 1994.

[13]I discuss these themes in my 'Theilhaber's 'Racial Suicide' or Scholem's "Flight of the Avant-Garde": Interpreting Conversion Rates in Nineteenth-Century Berlin', in Marc Lee Raphael (ed.), *The Margins of Jewish History*, Williamsburg, Virginia 2000.

imaginary characters we meet there might help us explain why so many Jews chose conversion in early nineteenth-century Germany, and especially why the rate of young men converting was so high in the 1830s.

II

August Lewald, the elder of the two cousins, was born in Königsberg in 1792. Königsberg, the capital of Prussia, was not only an important commercial centre but also home to a dynamic university and a lively intellectual scene. Because of its centrality in both politics and trade, Königsberg was a strategic city during the Napoleonic Wars. The Jewish community was relatively large, well-to-do, and intellectually avant-garde.[14] August was born into one of Königsberg's well-established and modern Jewish families. August's father Samuel Markus had been a successful merchant, but during these years fortunes could be made and lost all too quickly. Samuel Markus died when August was eight, and his widow inherited very little. As a teenager, August loved literature and the arts and was happy studying at a local *Gymnasium*. But because of the family's dire circumstances, when he was in his late teens he was sent by his mother to work in the banking and transport business of August's older first cousin David, who also lived in Königsberg. As was common for commercial apprentices, especially for those who were relatives, August moved in with the young couple, David and Zippora Markus.[15]

When David and his wife Zippora welcomed their teen-aged cousin August into their home and their business, they had only recently married. Their marriage had been delayed for years, because at this time Jewish families in Prussia were only allowed to have one child settle in the parental town. Neither David nor Zippora were the lucky child to receive permission to marry locally. The couple considered solving this dilemma by conversion. Zippora was actually very much in favour of leaving Judaism. But she was still a minor. Moreover "the usual threats of damnation and disinheritance were not spared" by Zippora's family as her daughter Fanny notes in her autobiography.[16] Finally, thanks to good connections and after a prolonged struggle, the couple obtained permission to marry. The years when August lived in his cousin's home were eventful. In 1811 David and Zippora's first daughter, Fanny, was born. That same year Königsberg suffered a devastating fire, and David Markus's business collapsed. In 1812, when he was 20, August became a Protestant and changed his family name from Markus to Lewald.

Two years later August left Königsberg to fight against France in the War of Liberation which had begun in March 1813. However, he was soon discharged

---

[14]A good survey of Königsberg's historic importance can be found in Marci-Boehncke, pp. 41–49. For a history of the Lewald family see Heinrich Spiero, 'Die Familie Lewald. Ein Beitrag zur Königsberger Familiengeschichte', in *Altpreussische Monatsschrift*, 48 (1911), pp. 318–324. August's uncle on his mother's side was Isaac Abraham Euchel (1756–1804), a major intellect in the Berlin *haskalah*.

[15]See Spiero, 'Die Familie Lewald', p. 320. For short biographical summaries of August Lewald's life, see the articles on him in the *Allgemeine Deutsche Biographie*, vol. 18, Leipzig 1880, pp. 512–513; and in the *Neue Deutsche Biographie*, vol. 14, Berlin 1968, pp. 408–409.

[16]See Brinker-Gabler, p. 37.

because of illness. When he recovered Lewald took on a family business assignment in Warsaw. Later he rejoined the fight against Napoleon, this time as the secretary for a Russian count who was a general in the Russian Army. After the war Lewald settled for a time in Breslau where he worked as an actor, a theatre director, and as an editor. It was in the Breslau years that he began to focus more directly on literary work and public intellectual enterprises editing a journal as well as publishing a play and a collection of sonnets under the pseudonym Kurt Waller.

Years of wandering followed as he lived in Vienna, Brünn, Bamberg, and Hamburg, working in various theatres as an actor and director. It was in Hamburg in 1828, when he was the director of a theatre, that August became friendly with Heinrich Heine. Heine at this point had been a convert for three years, and was just then becoming truly famous with his first poetry and prose publications. Heine encouraged Lewald to publish his first novel, and it was then that August decided to leave the theatre.[17] It was also in 1828 that Lewald, now 36, married a woman from Munich named Kathi. August and Kathi moved to Paris early in the eighteen thirties where they remained for several years. Heine too moved to Paris in 1831, and the two formerly Jewish writers were especially close in these years. Paris was an important haven for German liberals whose political and intellectual work was often banned at home in the German states.

In 1834 Lewald and his wife returned to Germany and settled in Stuttgart. When he published his novel *Memoiren eines Banquiers* in 1836 he was the influential editor of the journal *Europa* which he had founded a year before.[18] Lewald befriended an eclectic circle of intellectuals in these years, some of whom wrote for *Europa*. Apart from Heine, Lewald counted Richard Wagner and the novelist Berthold Auerbach among his friends. Lewald appointed Auerbach as the theatre and literature critic of *Europa*.[19] Auerbach had once planned to become a rabbi, and he seems to have been the only Jewish friend of Lewald who remained Jewish. In these years Lewald's work seems to have been quite profitable, as his lifestyle was rather lavish for a writer at that time.[20] A friend of Lewald's describes a visit to his home in 1840 as follows:

> Lewald lived then in the so-called *Bazar* on the Königstrasse and seemed to live in grand style. A servant in livery received me. ... Lewald was in his best years, had a full head of

---

[17] On Lewald's life in this era see Cruse, pp. 16–17, and S. S. Prawer, *Heine's Jewish Comedy: A Study of his Portraits of Jews and Judaism*, Oxford 1983, pp. 220 and 414. Lewald published a short portrait of Heine in 1836; see August Lewald, *Aquarelle aus dem Leben*, vol. I, Mannheim 1836, pp. 89–139.

[18] The original citation of *Memoiren eines Banquiers* lists August Lewald as the editor; the publisher was Scheible. This reference is from the unsigned review of the novel in *Blätter für literarische Unterhaltung*, no. 131, 11 May 1837, pp. 530–532. I am grateful to Professor Michael Schmidt for this reference. At the present time the easiest way to locate the novel is in August Lewald, *Gesammelte Schriften*, vol. 12 Leipzig 1846, pp. 125–388.

[19] On this period in Lewald's life see Cruse pp. 18–20. On Auerbach see David Sorkin, 'The Invisible Community: Emancipation, Secular Culture, and Jewish Identity in the Writings of Berthold Auerbach', in Jehuda Reinharz and Walter Schatzberg (eds.), *The Jewish Response to German Culture*, Hanover, New Hampshire and London 1985, pp. 100–119, here p. 103.

[20] Cruse, our major source on August Lewald's life, has no mention of the sources of his income. It may well be possible to reconstruct his income from primary sources. For a survey of archival material on August Lewald, see the web site www: library.byu.edu/~rdh/prmss/l-m/lewaldau.html.

dark hair, a well-trimmed moustache, and from his delicately rosy face beamed his beautiful, soulful eyes. He wore a silk robe in the Persian style.[21]

III

At first glance Lewald's *Memoiren eines Banquiers* certainly appear to be a memoir and the title seems to confirm this. Lewald frequently mentions various real historical individuals in the book, especially writers. Moreover, there are quite a few exact parallels between the narrator's life and Lewald's life. Both were born into wealthy Jewish merchant families in East Prussia in the late eighteenth century, and both lost their fathers in youth or young adulthood. Both were teenagers during the dramatic years of the Napoleonic occupation and the War of Liberation. Both Lewald and his novel's narrator were ardent German patriots. Both were passionate about the arts and literature. Both author and narrator travelled constantly, and both converted.

So there are many good reasons to think that the volume is indeed a memoir. But when we compare Lewald's life story more closely with the life story of his narrator, we see that *Memoiren eines Banquiers* is actually a novel, a novel written to appear as a memoir.[22] Amidst the many parallels between Lewald's life and the narrator's life, there are crucial differences between the fictional and the historical stories. In a variety of ways the narrator leads a much more Jewish life than Lewald himself did. In reality August Lewald broke with the old way of life much earlier and much more sharply than does the narrator of his novel. For one thing, the narrator remains a banker, whereas Lewald left commerce behind when he left his cousin David's house at the age of twenty-two. The novel's narrator also remains more Jewish in love than Lewald seems to have been. In the novel, the narrator marries a Jewish woman who is the daughter of one of his business contacts. It is not until they have been married for several years that they both converted to become Catholics. Lewald's narrator is also more Jewish in his social life than was Lewald himself. Lewald's friends were almost exclusively Christians by birth or by conversion. In contrast, his narrator suffers because he fails to make lasting ties to the Christian acquaintances he invites to his home after his conversion.

Lewald's novel has one major theme, which is the narrator's quest for *Bildung*. As he tells the story of his life, the narrator returns again and again to the challenges facing wealthy Jewish merchants who seek to become *gebildet*. By this Lewald meant a set of qualities and behaviours that might be described with the words moral, sensitive, autonomous, educated, cultured, and refined. *Bildung* in this sense should not be equated with high culture skills or performances. *Bildung* could not be purchased or learned in a school. Anxiety about *Bildung* was by no means limited to Jewish intellectuals in Lewald's time. The question of whether employment in commerce or

---

[21]The description appeared in Friedrich Wilhelm Hackländer, *Der Roman meines Lebens*, in his *Ausgewählte Werke* vol. 19, Stuttgart 1881–1882, p. 150. The quote appears in Cruse, pp. 21–22. The translation is my own. I am grateful to my Sarah Lawrence College colleague Roland Dollinger for his kind advice.

[22]I am grateful to Sander Gilman, who brought the novel to my attention in his *Jewish Self-Hatred: Anti-Semitism and the Hidden Language of the Jews*, Baltimore and London 1986, here pp. 143–144. Gilman suggests that August Lewald's book is a memoir.

even in the state civil service was compatible with acquiring *Bildung* was a very pervasive concern for many intellectuals in this setting. Jewish intellectuals may well have been especially haunted by the difficulty of becoming *gebildet*. Indeed, two of Lewald's peers also wrote fictional works in these very same years exploring the difficulties Jews have in achieving *Bildung*.

August Lewald's friend Heinrich Heine published *Die Bäder von Lucca* (The Baths of Lucca) in 1829. This was a fictional essay in the form of a travelogue, forming part of the volume *Reisebilder Dritter Teil*. In *Die Bäder von Lucca* Heine created two eminently mockable characters, Gumpelino and his servant Hyacinth. The setting is Gumpelino's palace in an Italian spa town. Gumpelino and Hyacinth are satirised for their futile attempts to hide their "Jewish" values and habits under the cloak of Catholicism and romantic high culture.[23] And Lewald's friend Berthold Auerbach published two novels in these years featuring Jewish intellectuals who sought intellectual authenticity outside traditional Judaism. His novels *Spinoza* (1837) and *Dichter und Kaufmann* (Writer and Merchant) (1840) tell the life stories of Baruch Spinoza and Ephraim Kuh, both Jewish intellectuals who struggled to find some kind of community outside the Jewish circles which each had tried to leave.[24]

In Lewald's *Memoiren eines Banquiers* the author is highly aware of his duty to draw the reader into the novel's historical setting. The narrator frequently pauses his narrative to deliver heartfelt mini-lectures analysing social trends and policy issues of the day. Readers looking for a riveting plot and complex character development may therefore be disappointed. Reading the novel it becomes clear why Lewald lies neglected on the shelf and Heine is still in print. But the historian is in luck. Indeed, we can learn much from the book about Jewish life in the years of the Napoleonic wars and in the *Biedermeier* era. Our narrator opines about various Jewish personalities, habits, and practices. He reports on conversations between various social types in his world, from New York to Paris, to Frankfurt to Berlin. He recounts stories of real life encounters in drawing rooms and coffeehouses, on promenades, and during long trips in carriages. The level of detail is nothing short of fabulous.

Memoiren eines Banquiers begins with a letter from Alvaro de la Torre, a Spanish banker in Cadiz, who had been the business colleague of the narrator. In de la Torre's introduction the narrator is not named, and indeed he remains anonymous throughout the book. His Spanish friend tells the tragic story of how the narrator completed his manuscript and was planning to leave banking to become a writer full time, just before he died in a shipwreck in 1836. Then the memoir itself begins. The narrator announces at the very beginning of the book that his will be the first account of how rich Jewish merchants raised their families in the second half of the eighteenth century. He identifies himself as a former banker who will describe a traditional way of life, which to his mind scarcely exists any more.

After a short flashback to his childhood, the narrator begins to tell us his life story. He begins in the year after his father's death, when, as a young adult, he establishes

---

[23]To read the work in English, see Heine's *The Prose and Poetical Works*, transl. by Charles Leland, New York 1900. For commentary, see Prawer, p. 133, as well as Jeffrey Sammons, *Heinrich Heine: A Modern Biography*, Princeton 1979, pp. 141–146.
[24]See Sorkin, p. 107.

his own semi-independent branch of the family business. The French occupation of eastern Prussia was just beginning then, which places the novel's action in the months just after June 1807. The narrator's family has arranged for him to marry the oldest daughter of the richest Jewish family in the town. But before the wedding the bride's father goes bankrupt in a scandal involving debased coinage. Minting and distributing debased coins was one of the few methods governments could employ in this era to balance their books. For more than a century there had been quite a strong tradition in Prussia of Jewish merchants producing and distributing debased coinage. In this episode the narrator's future father-in-law had become wealthy overnight by distributing debased English coins. The occupying French administration arrests him. The narrator has little patience for the business practices of his bride's father.[25] We see here an emerging left-wing critique of the way that some Jews in commerce were growing wealthy under the chaotic circumstances of the Napoleonic occupation.

The bad luck experienced by his prospective bride's family continues. Just as their father is embroiled in the scandal, one of the sons in the family commits suicide. As a result of so many troubles, our narrator's family cancels the engagement. His would-be bride's family moves away. Our narrator believes that the bride's brother committed suicide because he was in love with a Christian woman and was afraid that his family might punish him if he converted and married her. Here Lewald points to a common problem experienced by many of his relatives and peers at the time. There was no civil marriage in Prussia until 1874. Before then an ethnic intermarriage involving individuals of Jewish and Christian descent would have to be a marriage between two individuals who both professed the same religion. It was very unlikely that the religion that would unite such a mixed couple would be Judaism. To be sure, conversion to Judaism was not explicitly forbidden by Prussian law. But after 1814 converts to Judaism could be, and indeed were, banished from Prussia by a cabinet order from the king.[26] Therefore, becoming a Christian so as to be able to marry a Christian was a very plausible motive for conversion in this setting.

But not every Jew facing this situation considered conversion an appropriate response. Indeed, one of August Lewald's uncles, Solomon Lewald, was unhappy with the idea of converting in order to marry a Christian woman. In 1813 he had made a public appeal to government officials for permission to marry a woman of Christian descent in a civil ceremony but his petition was denied.[27] The most celebrated attempt to fight for the right of Jews to marry Christians in a civil ceremony was made by Dr. Ferdinand Falkson, also from Königsberg, during the eighteen forties.[28]

After his engagement comes to an end the narrator remains unmarried for quite a while, travelling about Germany on business excursions. His wandering life comes

---

[25] See August Lewald, *Memoiren*, pp. 169–171.
[26] See Christopher Clark, 'Jewish Conversion in Context: A Case Study from Nineteenth-Century Prussia', in *German History*, 14 (1996), pp. 281–296, here p. 281. See also Clark's immensely useful *The Politics of Conversion: Missionary Protestantism and the Jews in Prussia 1728–1941*, Oxford 1995.
[27] Solomon Lewald "wollte 1813 als erster ungetaufter Jude in Königsberg eine Mischehe mit der christlichen Deutschen Eleonore Hoser schließen, erhielt aber keine behördliche Erlaubnis dazu" as cited in Gerhard Kessler, 'Judentaufen und judenchristliche Familien in Ostpreußen', special publication of *Familiengeschichtliche Blätter/Deutscher Herold*, vol. 36 (1938), p. 28.
[28] See Dagmar Herzog, *Intimacy and Exclusion: Religious Politics in Pre-Revolutionary Baden*, Princeton 1996, p. 94.

to an end when he marries the daughter of a rich Polish Jew he has met on his travels. His romance with this young woman is quite ardent. He takes great joy in this, especially because for a long time he had been certain that he would not find a female soulmate, as he was "too sentimental" to marry in the manner expected of a Jewish banker.[29] Marrying for love, or at least falling in love, is for him an experience that aids *gebildet* individuals in their personal development. In his view, the practice of arranged marriages, so common among the Jewish élite of this era, created suffering for young adults denied the opportunity to marry for love.

After the couple is married the narrator joins his father-in-law's grain business. During the year 1814 – the last year of the Napoleonic occupation of Prussia – the narrator's father-in-law continues to sell supplies to the French army and administration. This angers our narrator, for he has become an ardent patriot secretly funding the anti-Napoleonic resistance. When Prussia regains her sovereignty in 1814 the father-in-law is arrested for treason and a scandal ensues. He loses his good name and his fortune. The narrator and his wife even lose the wife's dowry. But their marriage survives.[30] Our narrator loves his wife, and they live in comfort, mixing socially mainly with their extended families. Although from the outside they may appear to be leading rather traditional lives, they are beginning to neglect many rituals and no longer keep the dietary laws, for instance.

In September 1814, after Napoleon's defeat, the couple moves to Vienna. There they live in an apartment in the home of a Catholic family with whom our narrator has become acquainted through business. It is at this point that the narrator and his wife decide to convert. At first he is disinclined to leave Judaism. We who have read thus far wonder why he hesitates at all. He is not spiritually or ritually engaged, and he has shared with his readers so many of the ways he is critical of negative behaviour he identifies as Jewish. But as he tells the story, he hesitates about actually converting. He pauses because of the experience of one of his relatives who has converted, only to spend his days lonely and in poverty.[31]

But a converted friend continues to persuade our narrator, and eventually he and his wife decide to become Catholics. Although they both study with a priest, the narrator thinks little of the quality of this religious instruction. Later his wife will become rather devout.[32] But nowhere in his pages does Lewald's narrator ever describe intense spiritual experiences. Rather, he remembers how high his hopes were that with his conversion his children would be guaranteed "a bourgeois existence".[33] The couple decide to keep the conversion a secret from the wife's family. Although he has described himself as having been ambivalent about converting in the first place, after the conversion the narrator's tone changes. Now he reminds his readers how enthusiastic he was right after the ceremony, so happy that "behind me was the Talmud and its ponderous and hairsplitting interpreters, far away from me

---

[29] For example, see August Lewald, *Memoiren*, p. 202.
[30] August Lewald, *Memoiren*, p. 246.
[31] A reference to his previous hostility to converts can be found on p. 232 of August Lewald, *Memoiren*.
[32] *Memoiren eines Banquiers* is to some extent autobiographical. This section foreshadows Lewald's own conversion to Catholicism, of which he was to become a devout adherent.
[33] We should, I think, interpret this formulation as a reference to civil rights. The phrase appears in August Lewald, *Memoiren*, p. 237.

was the muck and the pain of Jewish life". He expects that "now I will be lovingly accepted by the community of Christians".[34]

Considering his litany of irritations about the traditional Jewish lifestyle we are not really surprised that the narrator has chosen to leave Judaism. We have already learned about his objections to Jewish business and marriage practices. He also dislikes Jewish prayer and Jewish food. And to intensify his isolation, the narrator tends to be quite critical of other assimilated Jews and former Jews who seem so much like him from the outside. This is how he describes his experience of Jewish worship. He asks his readers to imagine themselves

> [I]n a medium-sized room, filled with many prayer stands against which leant muttering Jews, densely pushed together, swaying to and fro, like trees rustling in the wind. ... It was a thick, dark, moving mass, full of jarring noise, a sinister sea. ... The gloomy racket, the heat, the unpleasant odour in this room usually made me somewhat faint and I had to seek freedom outside before the service was ended.[35]

Jewish food also displeases the narrator. He makes a connection between the aesthetics of the food and his revulsion for the religious "police state" which enforces the dietary laws. He is surprised and rather appalled at the situation he finds himself in when, in his travelling years, he is invited to dine at a wealthy Jewish home in Frankfurt. Impressed that many of the guests are prominent Christians, he wonders "what faces those elegant ladies and gentlemen will make when they start to taste the food cooked in the oriental manner, strongly spiced with garlic" alongside the "overly peppered roasts, the saffron-coloured soups and the sweetened vegetables. For in the home where I dined, the style of the food was decidedly old-testament."[36] Our narrator regularly labels various daily habits as either Jewish or Christian. For instance when he notes with pleasure that his wife keeps their home very tidy, he calls her style of housekeeping "Christian".

We see another example of how August Lewald's narrator disdains other Jews by his reaction to a contemporary play called *Unser Verkehr* (The Company We Keep) written by the Breslau physician Karl Alexander Sessa. Sessa's farce was meant to open in July 1815 in Berlin, but was postponed until September. Because riots against the Jews had been announced to coincide with the opening of the play, Chancellor Hardenberg refused permission to allow the satire to be staged. But pressure mounted as the actors performed segments to private audiences and the play was revised. Hardenberg agreed, and *Unser Verkehr* opened in September at the Berlin Opera House. The play became an immediate hit in Berlin, and was later also immensely popular when it played in other towns across Germany.[37]

Sessa's farce mocks the various exploits of a provincial Jewish family whose children have embraced the German language, German dress, and German cultural habits with laughable over-enthusiasm. The parents send their son Jacob out into the

---

[34] August Lewald, *Memoiren*, pp. 237–238.
[35] August Lewald, *Memoiren*, p. 152.
[36] The dinner is described in August Lewald, *Memoiren*, p. 184.
[37] See Hans-Joachim Neubauer, 'Auf Begehr: Unser Verkehr. Über eine judenfeindliche Theaterposse im Jahre 1815', in Rainer Erb and Michael Schmidt (eds.), *Antisemitismus und jüdische Geschichte: Studien zu Ehren von Herbert Strauss*, Berlin 1987, pp. 313–327.

world with a bag of debased coins. He becomes a soldier in the War of Liberation against France in 1813, but proves to be a coward in battle. Eventually Jacob becomes engaged to the daughter of a wealthy family on the basis of a false rumour he himself spreads about having won the lottery. When the truth comes out, he is rejected by his prospective in-laws. The mock Yiddish accents make all the Jewish characters' aspirations humorous. The play had a huge impact, well beyond those who managed to see it in person. The text itself was available for purchase in numerous pirate editions, and prints featuring caricatures of the play's characters were rapidly produced by satirical artists in various towns.[38]

Historians have interpreted *Unser Verkehr* as an expression of how widespread antisemitic criticism of assimilated Jews was in the years just following the Vienna Congress. Therefore Lewald's readers today will be rather surprised to read that the narrator in Lewald's novel actually declares *Unser Verkehr* a "masterpiece". Lewald's view in *Memoiren eines Banquiers* is that the behaviour satirised in *Unser Verkehr* was absolutely true to type.[39] Through his narrator's voice Lewald seems to be attacking other Jews who do not succeed in their attempts to look and sound like Christian Germans. Elsewhere in the novel the narrator notes how less assimilated Jews usually think he is a Christian by birth. We must wonder whether it was pleasurable for August Lewald to have his narrator concur with Sessa's satire of his fellow Jews. We must ponder Lewald's narrator's public sympathy with a play which is now casually labelled as antisemitic.

Sometime after their conversion, the couple leave Vienna and return to East Prussia. Now one of the narrator's ambitions is to avoid typically Jewish commercial transactions. He vows to ban all "supplying, money loaning and currency exchange" from his *Comptoir*.[40] At this point he stands mid-way in his journey away from Jewish life. He is a formerly-Jewish banker of the Catholic faith searching for a way to remain in commerce. And our narrator also hopes that now that they are Christian, he and his wife will be able to mix easily with their Christian neighbours. He is ambitious but not a sycophant. It is a major disappointment to him, however, that after their conversion they do not seem to make lasting friendships or even succeed in establishing some kind of social life with very many Christians.

Eventually our narrator becomes more and more despondent about his social life. The prominent Christians whom he invites to his well-appointed home never invite him back. He decides to stop inviting them rather than accept relationships that are not mutual. Eventually the couple drift back to a social life with Jews who have also converted or those contemplating conversion. The emergence of such a network seems to be an important shift. For when they first converted the couple kept their change of faith a secret from the wife's family. Now it seems that a new social space was developing, a space which could protect converts from the painful disappointments of attempting to truly enter established Christian circles.

The narrator's Jewish identity is highly complex. His rejection of Jewish life is at one level aesthetic. He has an idea of what is modern and proper, and is critical of

---

[38] Some of the caricatures made and sold of the characters in *Unser Verkehr* are reproduced in Peter Dittmar, *Die Darstellung der Juden in der populären Kunst zur Zeit der Emancipation*, Munich, London, New York and Paris 1992, pp. 199–217.

[39] His discussion is in August Lewald, *Memoiren*, p. 168.

[40] See August Lewald, *Memoiren*, p. 240.

Jewish life because it is disordered and crude. One of the strongest themes of the novel is that any involvement in commerce can never be reconciled with being *gebildet*. It is because the narrator is convinced that any involvement in commerce is incompatible with achieving *Bildung* that he ultimately leaves commerce, just at the time when he is completing the manuscript of the memoir.

The narrator is fully aware that among his own generation of educated Jews some are fighting for a new form of prayer and for a new relationship to the wider worlds of politics and high culture. At one point in his travels the narrator befriends an impoverished Jewish intellectual who tries to make a living as a preacher for a new Reform temple. The narrator has a kind of distant pity for this friend but certainly does not share his friend's enthusiasm for reforming Judaism. Ultimately his friend dies in loneliness and poverty.[41]

In spite of all of the frustrations caused by conversion the narrator is strongly in favour of it, even in the mid-1830s when he is completing his memoir. He sharply warns any Jewish readers of his book of the pain involved in remaining Jewish:

> Poor young man, if you love your home town, or if you do not wish to leave your parents, or if you wish to assist your fellow citizens by working as a physician or as an enlightened businessman, you are bound to suffer because of your origins, and you should weep bitter tears because of this your entire life. No person will embrace you as their own, the circles of those with *Bildung* are closed to you, you are rejected, despised and satirised.[42]

At the end of the tale we are left with a bitter feeling. The timing of the narrator's death in a shipwreck suggests that Lewald could not imagine a way for his narrator to find happiness, even after he had left the commercial world. Although our narrator once had high hopes for a new life as a Christian, these hopes are largely disappointed. But the narrator, and undoubtedly August Lewald as well, are still strongly in favour of conversion.

There are several messages for historians in this novel. Jews considering conversion at that time might well have decided to become Christians even if they were all too aware that other Jews, in life or in fiction, were failing to find acceptance in Christian circles. They might have wanted to pursue prestige careers, to intermarry or to acquire new friends in spite of the obvious difficulties. *Memoiren eines Banquiers* alerts us to the importance of a social network which included both converts and other Jews. We do not yet know how typical such circles were then. But socialising between Jews and converts may well have been important in the complex causation of the high conversion rates of the era. When families routinely ostracised converts and the convert found no alternative familial circle, conversion could well lead to isolation and loneliness. Indeed such a fate had been the narrator's original deterrent to converting in August Lewald's novel. But when Jews who were still Jewish socialised with converts, conversion became a much less dramatic life change than it was in settings where families closed ranks and shut out the converts. Let us now turn to Fanny Lewald, August's cousin's daughter, and explore how she faced similar challenges in life and in her novel *Jenny*.

---

[41]See August Lewald, *Memoiren*, pp. 175–180.
[42]August Lewald, *Memoiren*, p. 229.

IV

In 1836, when August Lewald published *Memoiren eines Banquiers*, Fanny was twenty five years old. To her own dismay, she was still living in her family home in Königsberg, the eldest of seven siblings. Her father had recovered from a business setback, and by the middle of the eighteen thirties he owned a wine distribution firm and had been elected as the first Jewish city council member in Königsberg. By then he and Zippora had also changed the family name to Lewald. In 1836 David and Zippora were still Jewish, but Fanny's two brothers and Fanny herself had become Lutherans.[43] In principle neither parent was opposed to conversion. Indeed Fanny's mother Zippora often expressed regret that she and David had not converted long before they married.[44] But David feared that the more traditional Jews whom he relied on in business would shun him if he and his wife left Judaism. Here David seems to be acting in accordance with his cousin August's narrator's view that if one was in commerce it was altogether more fitting to be Jewish. David Lewald's rather self-interested financial reason to remain Jewish reminds us to beware the pat truism that it was the converts who held pragmatic motives and the loyalist Jews who were selfless and principled.

As for the children, David and Zippora felt that their sons should be converted as youngsters, since entering into the educational system as a Christian would be more harmonious than converting just before applying for a post for which it was required. There also seems to have been a view current in these circles that by converting the children before they were fully autonomous, one did them the favour of removing the aura of hypocrisy from the ritual. As for his daughters, the Lewald parents felt that they wanted them to wait until it was clear whom they would marry. Premature conversion could narrow rather than widen a young woman's marriage choices.

But Fanny's life had not proceeded along the neat lines imagined by her parents. When she was a teenager she had fallen in love with Leopold Bock, a theology student. This romance altered her picture of what kind of woman she would become. Gradually, with difficulty, she convinced herself that she should become the sort of woman who could be happy as a pastor's wife in a small village. In the beginning neither of her parents opposed the match, and it was of course expected that Fanny would become a Lutheran before the eventual marriage. But then David Lewald changed his mind and insisted that the couple break their engagement. His motivation was, according to one account, a rumour that Leopold's parents were not happy that their son planned to marry a woman of Jewish descent. Fanny was left particularly forlorn, for her father never explained why he cancelled her engagement. She became even more distraught when Leopold, whom she still loved, became very ill and died. To console Fanny, her parents allowed her to continue as planned with her conversion. Fanny Lewald became a Lutheran in 1830 when she was nineteen. As things turned out, Fanny never became enthusiastic about Lutheran Christianity and later regretted converting.

David Lewald's decision to forbid his daughter to marry Leopold was undoubtedly a complex one. It is important for us to note that he did not desire an intermar-

---

[43]See Schneider, pp. 10–38.
[44]Noted in Marci-Boehncke, p. 151.

riage for his daughter under conditions which might become painful or embarrassing. Yet even without the intermarriage he did approve her conversion. This episode teaches us to beware of thinking that conversion and intermarriage were always in tandem for women in this era. Lewald's change of heart about his daughter's planned intermarriage is an important historical moment for us to understand.

At the age of twenty-five Fanny was immensely frustrated with her life. She was single, smart, and ambitious, but her father forbade any work outside the home. Although he had taken great care with her education he would not allow her to work as a governess, one of the few paid positions open to educated single women of the middle or even upper classes. But she did begin to write. And this is where her father's cousin August played a decisive role in her life. The two cousins were in correspondence, and August published selections from her letters and in this way August pushed Fanny into becoming a published author. In 1840, when the new Prussian King Frederick William IV was crowned in Königsberg, Fanny sent a long letter to August describing the gay atmosphere in town. He printed the letter in *Europa*, and her public career as a writer was launched.

Only three years after her *Europa* articles, Lewald published two novels, both in 1843, and both anonymously. Reception of the books was positive from the start, and soon Fanny received her father's permission to claim authorship of the two novels and publish henceforth under her own name. Four years later, in 1847, Fanny moved to Berlin and established herself as a publishing author. When she was thirty-four she met the Christian writer Adolf Stahr. Much later, in 1855 when he had obtained a divorce, she and Stahr married. Together they hosted a salon in Berlin during the late 1850s and 1860s, and Fanny became a public intellectual fighting for liberal and early feminist causes.

In her novel *Jenny* (1843), Fanny Lewald created characters who either opposed conversion in principle or suffered tragedy in connection with a conversion. The narrative of the life of the Meier family begins in 1832. In the book we follow the fate of the two siblings in the family. Jenny, the main character in the novel, converts to marry Reinhard, a candidate for the Lutheran ministry, when she is in her teens. After her conversion, she realises that she was acting in bad faith by publicly accepting the Trinity and the Incarnation. Her father has trained her to a "Spinozistic identification of God with Nature and of religion with morality" and in a bold, honest letter she shares her true beliefs with Reinhard.[45] Reinhard has already experienced doubts about his engagement with Jenny, as his mother has warned him that Jenny is trouble, because she has become too 'enlightened' by too much male company. Reinhard is furious with Jenny for not sharing his beliefs and he breaks off their engagement.

Jenny's brother Eduard also has his doubts about the attractions of Christianity. He is trained as a physician, but in order to become the director of a clinic, he would have to convert. Eduard has a second motive for becoming a Christian: he is in love with Fanny's close friend Clara, who is of Christian descent. But his petition to marry her in a civil marriage is rejected. Eduard does not believe in Christian doc-

---

[45]This formulation was penned by Ritchie Robertson, in *The 'Jewish Question' in German Literature 1749–1939: Emancipation and its Discontents*, Oxford 1999, p. 93.

trine and refuses to be baptised for pragmatic reasons such as intermarriage or professional advancement. The character of Eduard in *Jenny* was later thought to have been based on three of Fanny Lewald's real-life friends: the liberal physician Johann Jacoby who rejected conversion, her cousin Eduard Simson who did actually convert, and a Dr. Kosch, also a Königsberg physician, who had appealed for permission to marry a Christian in a civil marriage.[46]

As for Eduard's sister Jenny, she falls in love with Count Walter eight years after Reinhard's break with her. They have a truly equal relationship. The count, moreover, is philosemitic and is actually proud to marry a woman of Jewish descent. Several of his aristocratic friends, however, do not agree that marrying Jenny is a good idea and challenge the count to a duel which he does not survive.[47] Jenny dies of shock. Lewald seems to be issuing a warning. There may be well-meaning, even heroically dedicated Christians who are ready to help converted Jews. But tragedy awaits those Jews who convert and the Christians who marry them. As for Jenny's brother Eduard, he goes on to devote himself to the cause of Jewish political emancipation.[48]

Jenny helps us understand the differences between Jewish men and Jewish women's experiences in this era. Fanny Lewald suggests that it was more difficult for women to shape their lives according to principle than it was for men. Jenny is critical of inauthentic conversion, but she – unlike her brother – is never able to define a public role for herself that reflects her authentic convictions. Jenny's encounters with the Christian world are almost always relational. She suffers when Christians treat her or her loved ones harshly. That she should die at the end of the novel, whereas Eduard is just beginning his heroic career as a fighter for Jewish rights, highlights the gender difference in their fates. In this regard Fanny Lewald's novel tells us much more about women and conversion than did her cousin August's novel. August Lewald is of course critical about the Jewish marriage system. But his narrative pays scant attention to the experiences of the narrator's wife, and indeed it is unclear if she is still alive when he dies at the end of his memoir.

V

In conclusion it can be said that the two novels explore characters who wonder about whether or not to convert. Both novels are set in the world of the Jewish élite of East Prussia in the early nineteenth century. And early death in extreme circumstances is another theme common to these novels, for the narrator in *Memoiren* and Jenny Meier in *Jenny* both die young.

But beyond these external similarities, the stance of the two novels is fundamentally different. In *Jenny* Fanny Lewald challenges both the motivations for and the

---

[46]See Marci-Boehncke, p. 252.

[47]*Jenny* was published anonymously by Brockhaus in 1843. David Lewald had made an agreement with his daughter that her first two novels would not have her name on them. For interpretation of the novel, see Heinrich Spiero, *Geschichte der deutsche Frauendichtung seit 1800*, Leipzig 1913, p. 26. There is a summary of the plot of the novel in Hildegard Fulde, *Studie zum jungdeutschen Frauenroman*, Doctoral Thesis, University of Tübingen 1931, pp. 42–43.

[48]See van Rheinberg, p. 174,

profit from conversion. In contrast the narrator in August Lewald's *Memoiren* provides what we might be described as an existential endorsement of conversion. Perhaps August is using his narrator in *Memoiren* to describe difficulties that he had not in fact experienced in his own life. The narrator's dilemmas may also reflect some dimension of his own experience. But however we account for his position, there is no doubt that Lewald's narrator is endorsing conversion.

In contrast, the two main characters in Fanny's novel approach conversion more critically. And indeed it is a major accomplishment of the novel to point to an honourable path that was neither conversion nor traditional Judaism. Eduard is a rather new figure on the literary and on the historical landscape. Eduard is a proud Jew who refuses conversion. His decisions show that honour and Judaism might go together in the struggle for Jewish civil rights. Indeed it is Eduard's refusal to convert which is the opening move in his own growing commitment to the struggle for Jewish civil rights. At this juncture the character Eduard closely resembles Gabriel Riesser who made a similar decision in the late 1820s in Hamburg. In addition to providing a new model of Jewish behaviour, Fanny Lewald's tone in *Jenny* is much more critical of Christians. Her character Jenny loses in love twice, both times because the Christian man or the Christian world is prejudiced or narrow-minded.

Comparing Fanny's heroic Eduard in *Jenny* to August's troubled and unhappy narrator in *Memoiren*, the question arises why the fundamental stance of the two novels is so different. Fanny's novel follows August's by only seven years, and both novelists obviously had much in common. They were only seventeen years apart, each was in mid-life when they wrote their novel and both were obviously similar in terms of their family experiences and in their liberal and patriotic politics. Yet August was in favour of conversion while ultimately Fanny was not. To explain the contrast between these two novels on the issue of conversion it might be helpful to look beyond these two individual lives. We need to know how much of the contrast between the narrator in *Memoiren eines Banquiers* and Eduard in *Jenny* can be explained by new developments in Jewish political life, especially by the work of Riesser.

The lives and the novels by the two Lewalds do in the end provide some tantalising pointers as to why the conversion rates were so high in early nineteenth century Prussia. For one thing there are men in both novels who could only marry the woman they loved if they became Christian before the wedding. Although conversion in order to intermarry was perhaps more pervasive among the motives attracting women to convert, men could indeed have this motive too. We know from statistics regarding Berlin that in the 1820s and 1830s the male intermarriage rate shot up to become considerably higher than the female rate.[49] Secondly, the appearance in the novel of social groups which include converts and Jews considering conversion suggests another possible reason why conversion rates shot up in these years. An intermediate social space such as this would protect converts from exclusion from the traditional Jewish and the Christian side. And when we learn how willing Fanny's parents were to have their sons convert at a young age, we see a motivation that might help explain the large number of infant and child conversions of these decades.

---

[49]See my article, 'Theilhaber's Racial Suicide', *passim*.

Reading August Lewald's *Memoiren* stimulates us to think more deeply about when and how *Bildung* came to be associated with Judaism and Jewish life. Historians who argue that it was in the early decades of the nineteenth century when the *Bildungsideal* began to be integrated into Jewish practice and identity may well be describing the vast majority of Jews then and there.[50] But it is also possible that the incorporation of the *Bildungsideal* into Jewish life did not emerge until the second half of the nineteenth century. In either case both novels illustrate how the struggle to become *gebildet* could be extremely painful at the individual level of experience. The character of the narrator in *Memoiren eines Banquiers* also provokes debate of what constitutes self-hatred in life as well as in literature. August's narrator's manifold critiques of the paths taken by all possible relatives, friends, and colleagues made for a rather cramped emotional life. We must however examine whether self-hatred is the term which best captures the particular historical features of Lewald's narrator's psychological and social struggles. Perhaps, had Victor Klemperer had the opportunity to read August's as well as Fanny's work he might have found an even more poignant reference to his own suffering in the Nazi years.

---

[50]See Marion Kaplan, 'Women and the Shaping of Modern Jewish Identity in Imperial Germany', in Shulamit Volkov (ed.), *Deutsche Juden und die Moderne*, Munich 1994, pp. 58–61.

When Judaism Turned Bourgeois: Gender in Jewish Associational Life and in the Synagogue, 1750–1850

BY MARIA BENJAMIN BAADER

In pre-modern Jewish society, Talmud Torah and *Halakhah* formed the bedrock of Jewish culture and Jewish life. The study of Torah and *halakhic* observance structured Jewish society internally and also defined the boundaries of the Jewish community towards the outside. In the last decades of the eighteenth century and in the nineteenth century Jews in German lands integrated into the surrounding society by joining the emerging middle classes. They embraced, first, Enlightenment and, later, middle-class value systems and life-styles, and rabbinical learning and Jewish law successively lost its central status in Jewish society and culture. New, competing practices transformed Judaism. Modern scholarship, most importantly in the form of *Wissenschaft des Judentums*, displaced rabbinical learning.

Synagogue worship, family life, and communal organisation experienced dramatic reconfiguration, and new forms of bourgeois religiosity took hold. In a process of transformation that overturned the foundations of what had constituted Jewish civilisation since Antiquity, Jews renegotiated what it meant to be Jewish. Jews in German lands struggled for emancipation, and they began to think of themselves as German and of Judaism as a religion; they rebuilt communal institutions in modern frameworks; they adapted ritual and worship to bourgeois sensibilities, or sometimes they just abandoned Jewish practice in the *halakhic* sense; some Jews in Germany converted to Christianity without severing all ties to their Jewish families, friends, and acquaintances. As German Jews engaged in redefining difference and in creating community in ways that were meaningful in modern society, they reconfigured Judaism and thereby also revolutionised the gender system of Jewish culture.

Women had been excluded from the practices that stood at the core of Jewish culture since the Talmudic period. Religious study, participation in rabbinical discourse, and the prescribed cycles of prayer and worship constituted a male domain. In fact, these practices defined Jewish masculinity and male superiority within rabbinical Judaism. The construction of gender differentiation and gender hierarchy within pre-modern Jewish society rested on the exclusion of women from rabbinic study and Hebrew prayer.[1] This article focuses on how German Jews reset the parameters of Jewish culture, when they

---
[1] For a full discussion of the social and cultural implications of women's exclusion from the Torah and the house of study see Daniel Boyarin who suggests that the exclusion of women from religious learning, rather than the gendered division of private and public spheres of participation in the economic realm, formed the basis for gender differentiation and gender hierarchy within pre-modern Jewish society, *Unheroic Conduct: The Rise of Heterosexuality and the Invention of the Jewish Man*, Berkeley 1997.

recast their associational life and synagogue worship in the late eighteenth and the early nineteenth centuries. Voluntary associations and synagogues no longer primarily constituted places in which Jewish men pursued rabbinical study and engaged in ritually prescribed prayer, but associations and synagogues turned into sites of bourgeois self-expression and representation. Thereby, Jews in German lands undermined the framework that had organised gender difference in pre-modern Jewish society. Consequently, women moved into the world of modern Jewish associations and occupied more prominent and visible positions in public worship.

In the last decades of the eighteenth century, Jewish women began to found female voluntary societies, because the religious practices from which they had been excluded in rabbinical culture lost importance. In fact, between 1745 and 1870, at least 136 Jewish women's associations operated throughout the German lands. In 1810, when no similar non-Jewish or Christian organisation existed, Jewish women in at least sixteen urban as well as rural Jewish communities ran independent women's associations. Only in the years from 1812 to 1814, during the wars against the Napoleonic occupation, did non-Jewish women create their own charitable organisations, most notably the *Vaterländische Frauenvereine* (patriotic women's clubs). Yet, many of these early women's associations were short-lived, and non-Jewish women in Germany did not found more permanent networks of female associations before the 1830s.[2] By then, Jewish women's voluntary societies were well established. The history of Jewish women's associations, however, does not seem to reach back to pre-modern Jewish society. Evidence of organised female benevolence in the pre-modern Jewish communities of Central and Western Europe is rare, and the extent of women's involvement in the world of early modern *ḥevrot* (traditional Jewish voluntary associations) remains hard to assess.[3] My investigation of Jewish associational life in the late eighteenth and early nineteenth cen-

---

[2]E. Gatz, *Kirche und Krankenpflege im 19. Jahrhundert. Katholische Bewegung und karitativer Aufbruch in den preussischen Provinzen Rheinland und Westfalen*, Munich – Paderborn – Vienna 1971; Rebekka Habermas, 'Weibliche Religiosität – oder: Von der Fragilität bürgerlicher Identitäten', in Klaus Tenfelde and Hans-Ulrich Wehler (eds.), *Wege zur Geschichte des Bürgertums. Vierzehn Beiträge*, Göttingen 1994, pp. 131–132; Alfred Kall, *Katholische Frauenbewegung in Deutschland. Eine Untersuchung zur Gründung katholischer Frauenvereine im 19. Jahrhundert*, Paderborn – Munich – Vienna – Zurich 1983; Heidrun Merk, 'Von ehrbaren Frauenzimmern, honetten Weibspersonen und liebreizenden Mägden. Weibliche Lebenszusammenhänge in Frankfurt 1760–1830', in Viktoria Schmidt-Linsenhoff (ed.), *Sklavin oder Bürgerin. Französische Revolution und Neue Weiblichkeit 1760–1830*, Frankfurt 1989, pp. 277–278; Catherine Prelinger, *Charity, Challenge, and Change: Religious Dimensions of the Mid-Nineteenth-Century Women's Movement in Germany*, New York – Westport CO – London 1987; Sabine Rumpel-Nienstedt, '"Thäterinnen der Liebe" – Frauen in Wohltätigkeitsvereinen', in Carola Lipp (ed.), *Schimpfende Weiber und patriotische Jungfrauen. Frauen im Vormärz und in der Revolution 1848/49*, Moos – Baden-Baden 1986, pp. 206–226; Klaus Tenfelde, 'Die Entfaltung des Vereinswesens während der industriellen Revolution in Deutschland (1850–1873)', in Otto Dann (ed.), *Vereinswesen und bürgerliche Gesellschaft in Deutschland, Historische Zeitschrift, Beiheft 9*, Munich 1984, pp. 76–77.

[3]We know about a female burial society in 1692 in Prague, but it is not completely clear whether this women's *ḥevrah* was an auxiliary of the men's association or an independent organisation. Jacob R. Marcus, *Communal Sick-Care in the German Ghetto*, Cincinnati 1947, p. 136. A depiction on a pitcher of the Prague *ḥevrah Qaddisha*' from 1783/84 shows a group of women under a funeral cortege of men. Anne Alter, 'Armut und Wohltätigkeit in der Kunst der Aschkenasim', in Jüdisches Museum der Stadt Frankfurt am Main (ed.), *Zedaka: Jüdische Sozialarbeit im Wandel der Zeit. Ausstellung im Berlin Museum*, Frankfurt a. Main 1992, p. 47. In 1698, a Jewish women's society in Hamburg provided dowries for poor girls, and it seems that gravestones at the Bingen cemetery mention activities of women in pre-modern associations. Erika Hirsch, *Jüdisches Vereinsleben in Hamburg bis zum Ersten Weltkrieg. Jüdisches Selbstverständnis zwischen Antisemitismus und Assimilation*, Frankfurt a. Main 1996, p. 28; Martina Strehlen, interview, summer 1997. In Italy, a women's association was listed as early as 1617 as one of the eight *ḥevrot* in Rome and already a century earlier, a burial society

turies in the German lands suggests that the process of social and cultural embourgeoisement of German Jewry shifted the gender organisation of Jewish society and paved the way for the proliferation of female Jewish voluntary associations.

The early modern *hevrot* of Central and Western Europe were male prayer circles whose members aspired to fulfill the *mitsvot* (religious commandments) of studying Torah, giving charity (*zedakah*), and performing "acts of loving-kindness" called *gemilut hesed*.[4] The care of the dead ranked highest among the deeds of *gemilut hesed*. In fact, the first *hevrah* to emerge north of Italy was the *hevrah Qaddisha'* (burial society) in 1564 in Prague, and from there the institution spread fast through the communities of early modern Ashkenaz.[5]

Soon, Jewish men pursued rabbinical learning in newly founded Talmud Torah societies, which established schools and educated the poor, and in larger communities a variety of specialised associations, such as sick-care societies (*hevrot biqqur holim*) or dowry associations (*hakhnasat kallah*), came into being. Previously, it appears, the ritual washing, dressing, and burying of Jewish corpses was left to the initiative of the family of the deceased and to professionals who were either employed by the community or operated independently. For the sick, the needy, and the poor who died, the Jewish community cared directly without the intermediary of a *hevrah*.[6] In the sixteenth century, however, Jewish voluntary societies began to fulfill these social functions in the framework of new patterns of religiosity. In fact, the rise of men's *hevrot* in Western and Central Europe was closely connected to the process of intensification and individualisation of religious life among early modern Ashkenazi Jewry. The formation and the spread of burial societies in particular appears to have been propelled by the innovation from Lurianic Kabbalah of studying Mishnah in a house where the seven days of mourning, the *shiv'ah*, were being observed. In a similar vein, charity held a new, central place in the ethical system of the Kabbalah.[7]

---

in Northern Italy had admitted female members. Andreas Reinke, *Judentum und Wohlfahrtspflege in Deutschland. Das Jüdische Krankenhaus in Breslau 1726–1944*, Hanover 1999, p. 33; David Ruderman, 'The Founding of a Gemilut Hasadim Society in Ferrara in 1515', in *AJS Review*, 1 (1976), p. 236.

[4] Avigdor Farine, 'Charity and Study Societies in Europe of the Sixteenth-Eighteenth Centuries', in *Jewish Quarterly Review*, 64 (1973), pp. 164–165; Jacob Katz, *Tradition and Crisis: Jewish Society at the End of the Middle Ages*, New York 1993, pp. 134–136.

[5] 'Armenwesen', in Georg Herlitz and Bruno Kirschner (eds.), *Jüdisches Lexikon*, vol. I, Berlin 1927, p. 476; Salo W. Baron, *The Jewish Community: Its History and Structure to the American Revolution*, Philadelphia 1948, vol. I, pp. 348–350; Sylvie Anne Goldberg, *Crossing the Jabbok: Illness and Death in Ashkenazi Judaism in Sixteenth- through Nineteenth-Century Prague*, Berkeley – Los Angeles – London 1996, p. 303; Marcus, *Communal Sick-Care*, pp. 67–68; Reinke, pp. 32–33. In Italy, Jewish voluntary societies existed earlier, and their social and religious character differed significantly from that of their counterparts in Central and Western Europe. While *hevrot* in Northern Ashkenaz found their organisational model in medieval guilds, Italian-Jewish societies emerged in the milieu of expanding Christian confraternities and neighbourhood associations. In both cases however, *hevrot* developed in ways dissimilar from their Christian environment. Farine, pp. 16–47 and 164–175; David Ruderman, 'The Founding of a Gemilut Hasadim Society in Ferrara in 1515', in *AJS Review* 1 (1976), pp. 233–267.

[6] Goldberg, pp. 75–86; Katz, pp. 134 and 319; Marcus, *Communal Sick-Care*, pp. 3–54 and 141. For the contested view that burial societies appeared in medieval Spain and Germany independently see Baron, pp. 352 and 360.

[7] Goldberg, pp. 86–90 and 194. While this interpretation is uncontested for Ashkenazi Jewry in Western and Central Europe, Italian *hevrot* emerged before the popularisation of Kabbalistic ideas and practices. See Ruderman, note 5.

We can safely assume that every male burial society used the services of women to perform the washing, dressing, and guarding of female corpses. Independent female ḥevrot, however, seem to have been founded only in exceptional cases. Although the promulgation of printed literature in Yiddish gave women some access to the world of early modern Jewish piety, women stayed on the periphery. When women gathered in order to perform the burial rites for a deceased woman, they were expected to recite Psalms. Surely, during the night-watch over a dead body, women engaged in communal prayer. They may also have read and discussed religious texts in Yiddish. Indeed, from the early eighteenth century on, women who visited the sick and performed death-bed and burial rituals could have recourse to a body of literature, including burial manuals and collections of *teḥinnot*, individualised prayers in Yiddish.[8] However, women were excluded from the study of rabbinical texts such as the Mishnah and they could not form a prayer quorum. Their marginalisation in the culture of Jewish learning and worship pre-empted the full-scale formation of female associational life in early modern Europe.[9] Women's ḥevrot thus did not constitute a common feature of pre-modern Jewish society. Rather, female Jewish voluntary associations sprang up in the late eighteenth century, when new social trends and cultural ideals transformed Jewish associational life.

In the late decades of the eighteenth century, young Jewish men in Germany began to found a new type of Jewish association. The most prominent and the most fashionable among these societies were the *Gesellschaft der Freunde* (Society of Friends) in Berlin and Königsberg and the *Gesellschaft der Brüder* (Society of Brothers) in Breslau.[10] Other Jewish "youth ḥevrot" emerged in Dresden, Heidelberg, Prague, and other German and Central European towns. In these associations, unmarried Jewish men established mutual-aid ḥevrot, most of them sick-care societies. While the new societies belonged within the orbit of early modern religious ḥevrot, their statutes included provisions that constituted a significant departure from previous Jewish associations. The members of this new type of ḥevrah still engaged in acts of *gemilut hesed*, such as visiting the sick, burying the dead, and poor relief and most "youth ḥevrot" held prayer services and study sessions.[11] In some of these societies however, including the *Gesellschaft der Freunde*, membership now entitled the individuals to receive medical care and financial benefits when they were sick or in need. This new practice marked an important shift. Previously, sick-care societies had offered their members spiritual support in illness and death, but had not dispensed monetary benefits. When a member of a ḥevrah had received a financial contribution, this had constituted an act of charity rather than a payment to a self-respecting member. In the emerging type of mutual-aid sick-care societies, a generation of young men

---

[8]Marcus, *Communal Sick-Care*, pp. 137–138.
[9]Farine, pp. 27–28.
[10]David Sorkin, *The Transformation of German Jewry, 1780–1840*, Oxford 1987, pp. 116–120.
[11]The activities of the *Gesellschaft der Freunde*, probably being the most modern and secular of these "youth ḥevrot", seem not to have included religious study or worship and its benevolent acts were restricted to its members. However, the society made itself responsible for providing a decent burial for its members, who were required to visit each other in case of sickness. See Ludwig Lesser, *Chronik der Gesellschaft der Freunde in Berlin*, Berlin 1842, pp. 10–12, 15, 25–27, 40, 47–48, 66, and 71.

expressed a new self-confidence and created a framework that provided them with adequate medical care and with financial support while sick and convalescent.[12]

In the course of the following decades, mutual-aid and charitable societies spread and existing ḥevrot shifted their focus from religious study and prayer to self-help, philanthropy, and civil commitment. While members of a ḥevrah had previously performed acts of zedakah and gemilut hesed in order to acquire spiritual benefits and had been most concerned with the care of the dead, nineteenth-century Jewish associations directed their attention increasingly towards the needs of the living. Ideas of reward in the 'olam ha-ba' (world to come) disappeared from the statutes of Jewish associations, and in their place, Enlightenment and bourgeois values such as friendship, self-help, Menschenliebe, morality, respectability, civil responsibility, and patriotic commitment gained prominence. While many of these organisations still functioned in the framework of traditional Jewish associational life and fulfilled religious functions such as performing or at least providing burial rites for their members, they also saw themselves as modern voluntary associations.

At this juncture, as practices of male prayer and study moved to the background within Jewish associational life, as mutual-aid and philanthropic features came to the fore, and as the rhetoric of the statutes shifted from religious values to ideas of Enlightenment brotherhood and social responsibility, Jewish women founded ḥevrot that paralleled male associations in form, purpose, content, language, and range of activity. (A difference was that some male ḥevrot kept private synagogues or retained practices such as study sessions at certain Jewish holidays such as Shavu'ot and Hosha'na' Rabbah, the seventh day of Sukkot. Moreover, Talmud Torah societies remained an exclusively male domain.)

Typically, a women's sick-care or sick-benefit association would be established within a few years after Jewish men founded a male ḥevrah of the same type in which Jewish learning was no longer central. In one of the earliest foundings in Frankfurt, for instance, five married women in 1761 established the *Israelitische Frauenkrankenkasse* (Israelite Women's Sick Fund) and thereby followed the example of two previously erected sick-care associations of Jewish men, founded in 1738 and 1758.[13] More than hundred years later, in 1860, the Jewish women of the small town of Grünstadt in the Rhineland-Palatinate established what appears to have been the first women's association of that Jewish community: a female sick-care society which paralleled the male Jewish sick-care society of Grünstadt founded in 1851.[14] In other communities, such as in Schnaittach in Franconia, Jewish women's associations combined self-help, sick-care, and philanthropy, while Jewish men ran a ḥevrah Qaddisha' and a Talmud Torah society, or other associations with distinctly religious character. The

---

[12]Marcus, *Communal Sick-Care*, pp. 143–159.

[13]Paul Arnsberg, *Die Geschichte der Frankfurter Juden seit der Französischen Revolution*, vol. II, *Struktur und Aktivitäten der Frankfurter Juden von 1789 bis zu deren Vernichtung in der nationalsozialistischen Ära*, Frankfurt 1983, pp. 122–123; Arno Lustiger, *Jüdische Stiftungen in Frankfurt am Main: Stiftungen, Schenkungen, Organisationen und Vereine mit Kurzbiographien jüdischer Bürger dargestellt von Gerhard Schiebler*, Frankfurt 1988, pp. 139–140; Josef Unna, 'Die israelitische Männer- und Frauen-Krankenkasse ("Kippestub") in Frankfurt a. M.', in *Bulletin des Leo Baeck Instituts*, 8, Nos. 29–32 (1965), pp. 227–230; *Gesellschaftsvertrag der Krankenkasse für Frauen zu Frankfurt am Main*, Frankfurt 1820, pp. III-IV.

[14]Central Archives for the History of the Jewish People, Jerusalem, PF IV, folder 71.

Schnaittach *Frauenverein* thus cared for every sick woman in the community and distributed money to the poor, whereas the male benevolent society formed a study and prayer circle which assisted its members in sickness and death and also gave charity to the needy of the community.[15] In Hamburg, Jewish men had already established a burial society in 1670.[16] In the eighteenth century, male Talmud Torah and sick-care associations followed, death-benefit chests and sick-benefit societies appeared, and existing associations expanded their realm of activities.[17] Jewish women's societies, however, emerged in Hamburg only in the second decade of the nineteenth century in the form of welfare societies.[18] In fact, before the 1850s, most Jewish women's associations did not perform burial rites. As a rule, in the nineteenth century and earlier, Jewish men in Germany founded a burial society as soon as a community established a cemetery. Women assisted the members of male burial societies in caring for the female deceased. Yet independent women's burial societies emerged only slowly.

While pre-modern, overwhelmingly male Jewish associations had focused on burial rites as well as on practices of rabbinical study and prayer, women entered the world of *ḥevrot* – now modern voluntary associations – as Jewish associational life turned bourgeois. Under the impact of social and cultural embourgeoisement of Jewish society, ideas of civil morality, self-improvement, respectability, friendship and middle-class philanthropy superseded religious values and practices. In new types of Jewish associations, religious learning and prayer lost its central place, and Jewish women either replicated these novel male associations or established benevolent societies parallel to men's societies which still bore the characteristics of early modern *ḥevrot*. In late eighteenth- and nineteenth-century Jewish society, the proliferation of women's associations became possible, because what had marked women as marginal in traditional Jewish society, namely the exclusion from Torah study, no longer exercised its normative function. The fact that comparable non-Jewish women's societies emerged only decades after Jewish women's associations did, underscores this interpretation. The transformation of Jewish society from a culture of male learning and ritual observance to a modern Judaism informed by bourgeois values, thus redefined the units of Jewish social organisation. During this process, women moved from the periphery of Jewish associational life to a more prominent position. The Jewish community renegotiated its boundaries with the surrounding German society, and the changing cultural practices of German Jews restructured the gender organisation within the Jewish community. In this way, German Jewry also transformed the regulation of inclusion and exclusion within the community of worshippers.

From rabbinical times on, the synagogue had been the centre of Jewish communal as well as religious life. It was not only the place where Jewish men congregated

---

[15] Central Archives, S 135, folder 7, and N 22a, folder 13.
[16] Salomon Goldschmidt, *Geschichte der Beerdigungs-Brüderschaft der deutsch-israelitischen Gemeinde in Hamburg: Zur Jahrhundertfeier der Neugründung 1812*, Hamburg 1912, pp. 17–18.
[17] Hirsch, pp. 25–35 and 364–365.
[18] Edgar Frank, 'Zum 125jährigen Bestehen der Beerdigungs-Brüderschaft der Deutsch-Israelitischen Gemeinde zu Hamburg', in *Jahrbuch für die jüdischen Gemeinden Schleswig-Holsteins und der Hansestädte*, 8 (1936/37), pp. 99–100; Goldschmidt, p. 44; Hirsch, p. 39; Rainer Liedtke, *Jewish Welfare in Hamburg and Manchester, c. 1850–1914*, Oxford 1998, pp. 164–165.

twice a day in order to say the ritually prescribed prayers, but a synagogue was also always a *beit midrash*, a house of study, where Jewish men engaged in the learning of rabbinical literature, most importantly the Talmud. And the reading of the Torah, the Five Books of Moses, stood at the centre of the Jewish service. Women had no direct access to the Torah. They could neither participate in the communal study of rabbinical literature, nor were they entitled to read from the Torah publicly. Furthermore, most women lacked the education in the Hebrew language that would have permitted them to do so. Even though regular synagogue attendance constituted a form of female piety, Jewish women's synagogue devotion took place on the margins of public Jewish worship. Seated in women's sections and in women's galleries removed from the main sanctuary, women cultivated a distinct type of Jewish religiosity.[19]

From the early modern period to the first decades of the nineteenth century, a whole literature in Yiddish catered to Jewish women in the German lands. Jewish women had access to the world of Jewish texts and could find spiritual and moral guidance in books such as the *Ze'enah u-Re'enah*, a Yiddish Bible translation with commentary, ethical tracts, religious manuals, and *tehinnot*. As opposed to men's prayers in Hebrew, *tehinnot* had no fixed formulas. While Jewish law called upon men to recite standardised Hebrew prayers each morning and evening and at set times of the week and the Jewish calendar, *Halakhah* did not regulate women's prayer correspondingly. Some *tehinnot* constituted Yiddish prayers which a woman could say or read while attending a synagogue service in which men recited the Hebrew liturgy; some *tehinnot* enabled women to address God when they celebrated Jewish holidays or participated in communal fasts; many *tehinnot*, however, were supplicatory prayers in which women asked for divine assistance when pregnant, during the sickness of a family member, the absence of the husband, or at occasions such as a drought. *Tehinnot* could be petitions for sustenance and livelihood; they related to specifically female religious practices when visiting a cemetery and at *Ro'sh Ḥodesh*, the Jewish new moon celebration; and they offered Yiddish formulae for women who observed the three female *mitsvot*: *niddah* (laws of sexual purity), the lighting of candles on Shabbat and holidays, and the discarding of a piece of the dough when baking bread.[20] Thus, Jewish women had a rich body of Yiddish literature to draw upon, and married women at least were expected to attend synagogue services as far as their domestic duties allowed. The reading of devotional literature in Yiddish, however, by no means carried the same weight as the study of rabbinical texts, and the

---

[19]Rachel Biale, *Women and Jewish Law: An Exploration of Women's Issues in Halakhic Sources*, New York 1984, pp. 10–43; Susan Grossman and Rivka Haut, 'Introduction: Women and the Synagogue' and Emily Taitz, 'Women's Voices, Women's Prayers: Women in the European Synagogues of the Middle Ages', in Susan Grossman and Rivka Haut (eds.), *Daughters of the King: Women and the Synagogue*, Philadelphia 1992, pp. 3–11, 59–71; Shoshana Pantel Zolty, *"And All Your Children Shall Be Learned": Women and the Study of Torah in Jewish Law and History*, Northvale, NJ 1993.

[20]Shmuel Niger, 'Yiddish Literature and the Female Reader', in Judith R. Baskin (ed.), *Women of the Word: Jewish Women and Jewish Writing*, Detroit 1994, pp. 70–90; Arthur Posner, 'Literature for Jewish Women in Medieval and Later Times', in Leo Jung (ed.), *Woman*, New York 1976, pp. 63–83; Anne Sheffer, 'Beyond Heder, Haskalah, and Honeybees: Genius and Gender in the Education of Seventeenth- and Eighteenth-Century Judeo-German Women', in Peter Haas (ed.), *Recovering the Role of Women: Power and Authority in Rabbinic Jewish Society*, Atlanta, GA 1992, pp. 85–112; Chava Weissler, *Voices of the Matriarchs: Listening to the Prayers of Early Modern Jewish Women*, Boston 1998.

recitation of *tehinnot* did not constitute prayer in the *halakhic* sense, in which Jewish men were required to recite formulaic, time-bound, Hebrew prayers. In early modern religious culture, women, who were excluded from Talmud Torah and from the obligation to say the Shema', stayed at the periphery of public Jewish devotion.[21] As long as *Halakhah* and rabbinical learning delineated the parameters of Jewish worship, the community of worshipers consisted by definition exclusively of men.

This changed in the nineteenth century, when concepts of bourgeois religiosity eclipsed the Jewish culture of male learning and ritual in the synagogue. Groups of progressively-minded individuals and families in Seesen, Berlin, Hamburg, and Frankfurt initiated the first Reform services at the beginning of the nineteenth century. Soon Jewish community boards as well as the governments of German states – with, initially, the exception of Prussia – enforced bourgeois standards of decorum and aesthetics in synagogues throughout Germany, and prescribed innovations such as weekly sermons in the German language, choirs, and confirmation ceremonies. The introduction of organs into the service and prayer-book reform developed into highly divisive issues and were rejected by those Jews who began to organise themselves in modern Orthodox frameworks.[22] By the second half of the nineteenth century, however, the character of synagogue devotion in Germany had changed dramatically, whether Jewish communities fell ideologically into the camp of Reform or modern Orthodoxy. Rather than being based on active and spontaneous participation in prayer, Jewish worship had developed into carefully orchestrated spectacles, in which the worshipper expected to be emotionally aroused and spiritually uplifted by edifying sermons and by the well-trained voices of a choir.[23] German-language sermons, indeed, comprised one of the earliest and most widely adopted innovations. Previously, the communal rabbi had given sermons only on High Holidays and on special occasions, and these sermons in Yiddish had served to explicate *Halakhah* and to expound Torah and rabbinical literature. In the nineteenth century, weekly sermons in German fulfilled a radically different purpose. Delivered by university-trained rabbis or gifted preachers, sermons were intended to promote morality and *Bildung*.[24] As self-respecting Germans whose

---

[21]The Shema' constitutes the centrepiece of the daily prayers that men are required to say according to Jewish law. Biale, pp. 17–21; Shaul Stampfer, 'Gender Differentiation and Education of the Jewish Woman in Nineteenth-Century Eastern Europe', in Antony Polonsky (ed.), *From Shtetl to Socialism: Studies from Polin*, London – Washington 1993, pp. 187–211, see in particular pp. 194–195.

[22]Steven M. Lowenstein, 'The 1840s and the Creation of the German-Jewish Reform Movement', in Werner E. Mosse, Arnold Paucker, and Reinhard Rürup (eds.), *Revolution and Evolution: 1848 in German-Jewish History*, Tübingen 1981 (Schriftenreihe wissenschaftlicher Abhandlungen des Leo Baeck Instituts 39), pp. 255–297; Michael A Meyer, *Response to Modernity: A History of the Reform Movement in Judaism*, New York – Oxford 1988, pp. 25–142.

[23]Michael A. Meyer, '"How Awesome is this Place!" The Reconceptualisation of the Synagogue in Nineteenth-Century Germany', in *LBI Year Book XLI* (1996), pp. 51–63. For modern Orthodoxy see Mordechai Breuer, *Modernity within Tradition: The Social History of Orthodox Jewry in Imperial Germany*, New York 1992, pp. 43–45 and 160–162; Robert Liberles, *Religious Conflict in Social Context: The Resurgence of Orthodox Judaism in Frankfurt am Main, 1838–1877*, Westport, CT 1985, pp. 140–148.

[24]*Bildung* literally means "formation" and can be translated as "education". The term, however, has a moral and religious connotation and its meaning is closer to "self-cultivation" or "harmony of personality." See Reinhart Koselleck, 'Einleitung – Zur anthropologischen und semantischen Struktur der Bildung', in Reinhart Koselleck (ed.), *Bildungsbürgertum im 19. Jahrhundert*, vol. II, *Bildungsgüter und Bildungswissen*, Stuttgart 1990, pp. 11–46; Rudolf Vierhaus, 'Bildung', in Otto Brunner, Werner Conze, and Reinhart Koselleck (eds.), *Geschichtliche Grundbegriffe. Historisches Lexikon zur politisch-sozialen Sprache in Deutschland*, vol. I, Stuttgart 1972, pp. 508–551.

highest goal consisted in the balanced cultivation of the heart and the intellect, Jewish men and Jewish women came to consider a spiritually uplifting, well-phrased sermon as indispensable for their religious experience in the synagogue.[25] In particular, Jewish women formed a devoted audience for popular preachers such as Joseph Wolf in Dessau and Gotthold Salomon in Hamburg.[26] In fact, Jewish women appreciated sermons, choirs, hymns, and decorous services, and Jewish leaders actively promoted synagogue attendance for girls and women.[27] Women were not only seen as being particularly well-equipped for the emotionalised religiosity of modern Judaism, but their prominence in Jewish culture also increased as a new emphasis on mothers' roles in the moral, intellectual, and religious development of their children took hold in nineteenth-century German society. Thus, it seemed essential that the female sex be exposed to the beneficial influence of synagogue devotion. According to Orthodox as well as Reform rabbis, the religious experience in the modern synagogue developed and sustained inner beauty and morality among Jewish daughters, wives, and mothers. German rabbis encouraged women and girls to attend services on a regular basis, and they introduced religious education for girls.[28]

In a growing number of Jewish communities, girls participated in newly established programmes of religious instruction. Typically, such an instruction culminated in a public confirmation ceremony in the synagogue.[29] Confirmation ceremonies offered women an unprecedented degree of inclusion in public Jewish worship. Boys as well as girls demonstrated their familiarity with the principal tenets of the Jewish religion in a pre-arranged and well-rehearsed public examination, and they pledged their loyalty to the values of the Jewish tradition in a confession of faith.[30] In some synagogues, Jewish boys continued to undergo the customary male rite of passage, the *Bar Mitzvah*, in addition to the newly introduced confirmation ceremony. In other communities, however, confirmation ceremonies replaced *Bar Mitzvah* celebrations, thus abolishing gender hierarchy in the ritual which marked the transition to Jewish adulthood.[31]

The shift from the *Bar Mitzvah* to the confirmation ceremony clearly exemplifies the transformation of Judaism from rabbinical culture to modern Jewish religiosity. *Bar Mitzvah* means literally "son of commandment" and it refers to the coming of

---

[25]Alexander Altmann, The New Style of Preaching in Nineteenth-Century Germany', in Alexander Altmann (ed.), *Studies in Nineteenth-Century Jewish Intellectual History*, Cambridge, MA 1964, pp. 65–116.

[26]D. Caro, 'Über die Würde der Frauen in Israel', in *Allgemeine Zeitung des Judenthums*, vol. I, No. 87 (21 October 1837), p. 370; Ludwig Philippson, 'Aus meiner Knabenzeit', in *Allgemeine Zeitung des Judenthums*, vol. LI, No. 47 (24 November 1887), p. 750; Gotthold Salomon, *Selbst-Biographie*, Leipzig 1863, pp. 49–50, 70–72.

[27]Paul Diamant (ed.), *Minna Diamant 1815–1840: Ihre Freunde und Verwandten. Ein Briefwechsel aus der Biedermeierzeit*, Tel Aviv 1964, pp. 41–43; Philippson, p. 750.

[28]Michael Hess, Darstellung der Töchterschule des jüdischen Philantropins in Frankfurt am Main, in *Sulamith*, vol. III, No. 2, (1811), pp. 177–185; Samuel Holdheim, *Geschichte der Entstehung und Entwicklung der jüdischen Reformgemeinde in Berlin*, Berlin 1857, pp. 190–193.

[29]The first confirmation ceremonies were held in schools or private homes, but within a few decades, confirmation ceremonies in the synagogue were introduced in most Jewish communities in Germany. Meyer, *Response to Modernity*, pp. 34–39, 50, 102, 119, 150, 154 and 157.

[30]Siegfried Däschler-Seiler, *Auf dem Weg in die bürgerliche Gesellschaft. Joseph Maier und die jüdische Volksschule im Königreich Württemberg*, Stuttgart 1997, pp. 245–271.

[31]Philippson, p. 750; David Philipson, *The Reform Movement in Judaism*, 2nd ed., New York 1931, p. 456; Immanuel Heinrich Ritter, *Geschichte der jüdischen Reformation*, Berlin 1858, vol. III, p. 47.

Jewish boys and girls being confirmed together.
Engraving, Germany, late 19th century.

Photograph from Ashkenaz: The German Jewish Heritage, Yeshiva University Museum, 1986–1988.

age of the thirteen-year old Jewish male in the *halakhic* framework. When an adolescent becomes a *Bar Mitzvah* he assumes full responsibility for all the ritual obligations of a Jewish man.

In the *Bar Mitzvah* ceremony during the synagogue service, he is called to publicly read from the Torah scroll for the first time in his life. The *Bar Mitzvah* celebration marks the access of the Jewish male to the Torah, which he is expected to study by immersion in rabbinical literature. Modern Jewish religious instruction, as German Jews introduced it in the nineteenth century, did not focus on rabbinical literature. Rather than studying Talmud and learning to recite the Torah in the traditional manner, Jewish boys and girls were familiarised with the tenets of what German Jewry believed constituted the Jewish faith. New types of German-language catechism books introduced Jewish children to the moral principles of the Jewish religion in a well-organised manner. Boys and girls learned about biblical history, the Jewish calendar, and the basic concepts of rabbinical Judaism in a scientific framework.[32] In the religious schooling which the Reform movement offered, daily ritual observance played a secondary role. Modern Orthodox leaders, conversely, remained ideologically committed to *Halakhah* and expected children to grow up as observant Jews. Yet, modern Orthodox religious education changed significantly too. According to the curriculum which the leader of modern Orthodoxy, Samson Raphael Hirsch, introduced in Frankfurt, Talmud learning for boys lost in emphasis, and girls as well as

---

[32]Däschler-Seiler, pp. 199–245; Jacob J. Petuchowski, 'Manuals and Catechisms of the Jewish Religion in the Early Period of Emancipation', in Altmann, pp. 47–64.

boys received extensive Bible instruction. Moreover, Hirsch paid increasing attention to the formation of the heart and character of the students and emphasised moral values. In the same vein as Reform Judaism, modern Orthodoxy valued women's supposedly outstanding sense for religiosity highly. Hirsch, in fact, ascribed to women a crucial role in securing the faithfulness of their families. In order to fulfill their mission as Jewish mothers and wives, he considered a modern-type religious education as indispensable for girls.[33]

Religious instruction and confirmation ceremonies began to include girls as study of Torah and practice of *Halakhah* ceased to constitute the dominant framework for Jewish culture. Women moved into the synagogue, as bourgeois sensitivities transformed Jewish worship. Although the reading of the Torah during the service remained a male privilege, innovations such as weekly sermons in German language and well-trained choirs, as well as the aesthetisation of the service displaced practices of male learning and prayer. In time, Jewish worship no longer primarily offered Jewish men the opportunity to fulfill their ritual obligations, but synagogue services became an edifying performance that an orderly and well-dressed audience attended in awe. The newly emotionalised religiosity of nineteenth-century German synagogues addressed Jewish women as much as Jewish men, and thus included women in a redefined community of worshipers.

In pre-modern Jewish society, *Halakhah* had structured Jewish life and had delineated the boundaries of the Jewish community. Religious learning and time-bound, formulaic prayer had stood at the core of Jewish culture. Access and exclusion to these practices had regulated gender differentiation and gender hierarchy, as women's access to the Torah was severely restricted. Thus, synagogues and Jewish voluntary associations in German lands had constituted male spaces, and Jewish women's religious and social practices had held a secondary and marginal status. In the late eighteenth and the nineteenth centuries, *halakhic* observance and male learning declined, and bourgeois values and sensitivities came to shape Jewish worship, Jewish associational life, and other spheres of Jewish existence. During this process, the exclusion of women from the central sites of Jewish life subsided. Jewish women founded female sick-care and benevolent associations which paralleled male institutions, and they gained greater inclusion in modernised synagogue services and in Jewish religious instruction. The embourgeoisement of Jewish culture and religion decentralised what had formed the organising principle of Judaism since the Talmudic period. As German Jews recreated their communities while integrating into the German middle classes, they redefined Jewish life according to the parameters of a non-Torah centred, bourgeois Judaism, and they displaced the gender order of pre-modern Jewish society.

---

[33]Breuer, pp. 122–123.

Intermarriages, the "New Woman", and the Situational Ethnicity of Breslau Jews from the 1870s to the 1920s

BY TILL VAN RAHDEN

In most models of ethnic relations, intermarriages mark the final step towards integration. Linear concepts of assimilation equate mixed marriages with structural or total assimilation. The more open the private sphere is for friendships across religious and ethnic boundaries, the more likely intermarriages are.[1] Despite the merits of these linear concepts of integration and assimilation, this essay argues that they are less useful for an analysis of marriages between Jewish and non-Jewish Breslauers because they ignore the gendered nature of intermarriages and do not do justice to the complex identities of Breslauers who intermarried.

Intermarriages in Breslau indicate close and sometimes amicable relations between Jews and other Breslauers. While in the possibly more widespread short-term love affairs between Jews and non-Jews, the ties of friendship could be ephemeral and efforts were often made to keep the relationship secret, the partners in Jewish-Christian marriages chose to make their bond both permanent and public. The unique nature of marriage as a social form of intimacy reflects a mixture of private and public aspects. Whereas men and women could conceal casual sexual relations or a "flirt", a marriage had consequences for their families, their friends and their social life.

At no point during the Imperial period was it considered "normal" for Jews in Breslau to marry other Breslauers. Such marriages differed markedly from those within the Jewish community, being regarded by most contemporaries as, at best, a curiosity. That the percentage of mixed marriages quadrupled during the Wilhelmian era does not alter this fact. Although during the Weimar Republic the occurrence of marriages between Jews and non-Jews remained at a high rate, the

---

[1] Eliott R. Barkan, 'Race, Religion and Nationality in American Society. A Model of Ethnicity from Contact to Assimilation', in *Journal of American Ethnic History* 14, 2 (1995), pp. 52, 54 and 56; David M. Heer, 'Intermarriage', in Stephen Thernstrom (ed.), *Harvard Encyclopedia of American Ethnic Groups*, Cambridge, MA 1980, pp. 513–521. For a broader analysis of relations between Jews and other Breslauers, see Till van Rahden, *Juden und andere Breslauer: Die Beziehungen zwischen Juden, Protestanten und Katholiken in einer deutschen Großstadt von 1860 bis 1925* (Kritische Studien zur Geschichtswissenschaft, vol. 139), Göttingen 2000; for a thoughtful and stimulating analysis of Jewish-Gentile relations generally, see Marion A. Kaplan, 'Friendship at the Margins: Jewish Social Relations in Imperial Germany', forthcoming in *Central European History*; readers may contact the author at Till.van-Rahden@Uni-Koeln.de.

mixed marriage continued to be stigmatised as exceptional, unusual and indeed inappropriate. As marriages between Jews and other Germans were regarded as particularly reprehensible by antisemites during the Imperial period, the Weimar Republic and above all under National Socialism, it came to be an important focus of enmity, especially because the daily lives of such couples exposed the senselessness of the antisemitic Utopia of an "Arian *Volksgemeinschaft*". However courageously many non-Jewish women and men may have tried to protect their partners after January 1933, as of that date such marriages had become a way of life without a future.[2]

In the historiography on German Jewry, the subject of Christian-Jewish marriages has usually been discussed in the context of the debate on Jewish assimilation. Like conversion to Christianity, mixed marriages were regarded as an expression of "radical assimilation".[3] In her path-breaking study on Jewish women in Imperial Germany, Marion Kaplan separates her discussion of Jewish marriage strategies from her cursory remarks on Christian-Jewish marriages. According to the dominant view, those who intermarried severed all ties with the Jewish community, just like those who converted to Christianity. Although Jacob Toury concedes that the Jewish-Christian marriage was a sign of "complete social integration", he argues that it necessarily implied the "ultimate rejection of Judaism".[4]

In contrast to this traditional perspective, Kerstin Meiring has recently argued that intermarriages indicated "the transformation of German Jews into an ethnic community with a new, ... vital identity".[5] Meiring's probably is a more fruitful approach. Rather than limit myself to a discussion of the nexus between assimilation and the rising number of marriages between Jews and other Breslauers, I will try to place their history in the context of gender history (especially the rise of the "New Woman"), the history of the middle class, and family history. Only at the end of my remarks will I address the familiar debates about mixed marriages and argue that we would do well not to equate intermarriages with a rejection of Jewishness on a par with conversions.

This analysis of the marriages between Jews and other Breslauers will proceed in four steps. My initial task will be to demonstrate how the historiographical debate on

---

[2]Nathan Stoltzfus, *Resistance of the Heart. Intermarriage and the Rosenstrasse Protest in Nazi Germany*, New York 1996; Beate Meyer, *Jüdische Mischlinge. Rassenpolitik und Verfolgungsgefahr 1933–1945*, Hamburg 1999.
[3]Todd M. Endelman, *Radical Assimilation in English Jewish History, 1656–1945*, Bloomington, IN 1990.
[4]Marion A. Kaplan, *The Making of the Jewish Middle Class: Women, Family, and Identity in Imperial Germany*, New York 1991; Jacob Toury, *Soziale und politische Geschichte der Juden in Deutschland 1847–1871: Zwischen Revolution, Reaktion und Emanzipation*, Düsseldorf 1977, p. 123; see also Marsha L. Rozenblit, *The Jews of Vienna 1867–1914: Assimilation and Identity*, Albany, NY 1984, pp. 127–146; Shulamith Volkov, *Die Juden in Deutschland 1780–1918*, Munich 1994, pp. 56–57; Victor Karady, *Gewalterfahrung und Utopie: Juden in der europäischen Moderne*, Frankfurt 1999, pp. 48–52; Paula Hyman considers "intermarriage and conversion" as the "most-extreme manifestations of assimilation"; see her *Gender and Assimilation in Modern Jewish History*, Seattle 1995, p. 19; According to Jacob Katz mixed marriage was "tantamount to defection from the Jewish family and society" for "marrying out of faith led ... to a conversion to Christianity": idem, *Out of the Ghetto: The Social Background of Jewish Emancipation 1770–1870*, Cambridge, MA 1973, reprint. New York 1978, p. 205.
[5]Kerstin Meiring, *Die Christlich-jüdische Mischehe in Deutschland 1840–1933*, Hamburg 1998, p. 10. For a provocative review of Meiring see Yfaat Weiss, 'Deutsche, Juden und die Weder-Nochs. Neuerscheinungen zum Thema deutsch-jüdische Mischehen', in *WerkstattGeschichte*, 27 (2000), pp. 73–82. Although Weiss raises important objections, her overall critique does not quite do justice to the qualities of Meiring's work.

mixed marriages reproduces contemporary discourses and stereotypes. The second step will involve a comparative social history of both mixed marriages and intra-Jewish marriages in which the factors of social origin, age at marriage, the living conditions of the marriage partners (particularly of women) and the role of the witnesses to the marriage will be analysed. In the third section, the argument will be put forward that the increase in marriages between Jews and other Breslauers after the turn of the twentieth century was related to the rise of the so-called "New Woman". In the fourth and final step, we will return to the initial question and consider what Jewish-Christian marriages can tell us about the relationship between Jews and other Breslauers and about the changing nature of Jewish community-building in Germany.

THE NEGATIVE IMAGE OF THE "MIXED MARRIAGE" (*MISCHEHE*) IN CONTEMPORARY DEBATES AND HISTORICAL RESEARCH

The so-called "mixed marriage" (*Mischehe*) contrasts starkly with the nineteenth- and twentieth-century ideal of purity and homogeneity. Any marriage between two partners from different religious, ethnic or racial groups ran counter to the modernist impulse to classify all individuals unambiguously. The mixed marriage became a symbol in which fascination and loathing went hand in hand. It is for this reason that such marriages – be they between Catholics and Protestants, Jews and Christians or whites and blacks – became a focus of public debates that led to anti-miscegenation laws in the German colonies or the USA.[6]

Read against the background of the ideal of purity and homogeneity and of the impulse to classify, the seemingly bizarre contemporary comments on marriages between Jews and other Germans begin to make sense. For many Jewish and Gentile contemporaries alike, intermarriages were a sign of moral decay. Impoverished aristocrats or swanky lieutenants married rich Jewish women for their fortunes and together they made it onto the front page of the *Simplicissimus*.[7] In its treatment of the subject, the publication played on common stereotypes. Shortly after the introduction of civil marriage ceremonies between Jews and other Germans, Emanuel Schreiber, a well-known Reform rabbi and former student of Abraham Geiger, condemned such unions as being typically marriages for money. Although he was not opposed to such marriages on principle, he claimed that it would be a long time before "mixed marriages would also be happy ones... [s]o long as the Christian barons, officers and artists only hunt for rich Jewesses to obtain the means with which to keep their insistent creditors at bay or to enable them to continue to live prodigal

---

[6]Robert C. Young, *Colonial Desire: Hybridity in Theory, Culture, and Race*, London 1995; Peggy Pascoe, 'Miscegenation Law, Court Cases, and Ideologies of "Race" in Twentieth-Century America', in *Journal of American History* 83 (1996), pp. 44–69; Cornelia Essner, '"Wo Rauch ist, da ist auch Feuer": Zu den Ansätzen eines Rassenrechtes für die deutschen Kolonien,' in *Rassendiskriminierung, Kolonialpolitik und ethnisch-nationale Identität*, ed. by Wilfried Wagner, Münster 1992, pp. 145–160.

[7]See the cartoon in Ruth Gay, *Geschichte der Juden in Deutschland*, Munich 1993, p. 191. Since 1890, such "misalliances" between Jewish women on the one hand and officers or aristocrats on the other, had been a favourite subject of serialised novels in Jewish weekly newspapers; see Meiring, *Mischehe*, pp. 51 and 53.

lives more easily; as long as Jews are only sought after for their riches..., neither we nor any unprejudiced person – be he Jew or Christian – can welcome the mixed marriage as a blessing."[8] The orthodox weekly, *Der Israelit*, emphasised the connection between mixed marriages and the dissolution of traditional gender roles. That young, unmarried women went "to the theatre and to concerts, to balls and celebrations" and attempted to claim public space reflects the "complete lack of religious education" among German Jews. To illustrate this "moral neglect", the paper's Breslau correspondent reported in March 1892 that three young women from that city's "most respected Jewish families" had engaged in sexual relations with Breslau officers. However, while the correspondent strongly condemned the women's behaviour as immoral, he simultaneously evoked the sexual fantasies of the readers by describing the events in detail. The "young girls ... entered into a thoroughly light-minded, hair-raising relationship with several officers". Together, he reports, they rented a villa in the neighbouring town of Kleinburg in order to be able to surrender themselves to their "nefarious doings" – that is, "if the parental home did not also serve this purpose from time to time". In view of the dissolution of the gender order, the correspondent continued, "our gaze is involuntarily drawn back to the halcyon days when morality and chastity formed the basis of true Jewish womanhood" when young women avoided public space and "lived quiet, retiring virginal lives in Jewish houses under the watchful eye of their mothers and knew nothing of life beyond that which would prepare them for their future, circumscribed field of activity".[9] The more "the family represented ... one of the final markers of Jewish difference within the larger society", the more threatening to their communities' survival marriages between Jews and other Germans seemed to Jewish leaders.[10]

In academic discussions, too, intermarriages symbolised moral decay. The sexologist Max Marcuse argued that a great number of those who intermarried were "neurotics", and that intermarriages reflected "psychological deformity" leading to "a no-doubt often-disrupted family life". Similarly, the sociologist Werner Sombart insisted that children of intermarriages lacked "mental balance". The Rabbi and historian Arnold Tänzer and the Jewish doctor-cum-demographer Felix Theilhaber issued an even more alarming verdict, arguing that the offspring of intermarriages frequently went on to a life of crime.[11] Elswehere Theilhaber characterised mixed marriages as one of the "saddest and mistaken institutions" of his time. Jews who entered into mixed marriages "had little interest in the family as such" but rather used their marriages "to pursue any number of other possible objectives". "They usually hail from the wealthiest circles," continued the pioneer ideologue of the racialist branch of

---

[8]Emanuel Schreiber, *Die sociale Stellung der Juden: Offenes Sendschreiben an Herrn Dr. Maass-Breslau*, Königsberg 1877, pp. 12–13.

[9]*Der Israelit*, 33, No. 20 (10 March 1892), pp. 393–394, here 393. On the connections between the gender-specific limits of public space and notions of sexuality, see Judith M. Walkowitz, *City of Dreadful Delight: Narratives of Sexual Danger in Late-Victorian London*, Chicago 1992.

[10]Sharon Gillerman, 'The Crisis of the Jewish Family in Weimar Germany. Social Conditions and Cultural Representation', in *In Search of Jewish Community: Jewish Identities in Germany and Austria, 1918–1933*, ed. by Michael Brenner and Derek J. Penslar, Bloomington, IN 1998, pp. 178–179.

[11]Marcuse, Sombart, Tänzer and Theilhaber are cited in Walter Hanauer, 'Die jüdisch-christlichen Mischehen', *Allgemeines Statistisches Archiv* 17 (1928), pp. 56–58. On the relationship between "racial hygiene" and the discussion on "mixed marriage" in general, see Meiring, *Mischehe*, pp. 58–65.

Zionism, "in which intentional or physically existing impotence or infertility is only too common."[12]

Another testimony to mixed marriages symbolising a diffuse sense of crisis is its representation in memory – at least among those (almost exclusively upper-middle-class) Jews whose recollections are recorded. According to Eugen Altmann, the high rate of intermarriage did not indicate "good relationships", since such "marriages between Christians and Jews had a different basis than that which would have been expedient with regard to the objectives of a mixing based on ethical motives". Mixed marriages "were entered into by representatives of unequal social categories, in which the Jew provided the material advantage". So confident was Altmann of the accuracy of his judgement that he went so far as to quote some percentages: "In 95 of every 100 cases" it was the "Jewish man who wed a Christian girl, usually his so-called "affair", who in most cases had not so much as set foot in his parents' house until the wedding day".[13]

Conflating his dislike of left liberals and mixed marriages, the Breslau Zionist Willy Cohn argued that it was "no coincidence that some Aryan democrats intermarried, as inconsistency was the essence of both left liberals and racial intermarriage".[14] Zionists and Reform Jews, liberal non-Jews and antisemites concurred in their negative assessments, an eclectic and jarring alignment that reflected widespread gender anxieties and resembled middle-class views of working-class – especially female – sexuality.[15]

Historians have done very little to question these legends. Monika Richarz notes a "high incidence of intermarriages between Jewish women and members of the aristocracy". Dirk Blasius blames the relatively high divorce rate in Jewish-Christian marriages on "a long tradition of instability in Christian-Jewish marriages". Hannah

---

[12]Felix A. Theilhaber, *Der Untergang der deutschen Juden: Ein volkswirtschaftliche Studie*, Munich 1911, pp. 98–117, quotations on pp. 113–115, Theilhaber urgently called for an analysis of the "increased hedonism, effeminacy, nervosity, perversity and criminality of converts and products of mixed marriages", p. 116.

[13]Eugen Altmann, 'Mein Leben in Deutschland vor und nach dem 30. Januar 1933', Houghton Library, Harvard University, Manuscript Collection 'My Life in Germany Before and After January 30, 1933', p. 14.

[14]Willy Cohn, *Verwehte Spuren: Erinnerungen an das Breslauer Judentum vor seinem Untergang*, ed. by Norbert Conrads, Cologne 1995, p. 281. Altmann and Cohn characteristically tempered their misgivings about Jewish-Christian unions when commenting upon mixed marriages among persons of their own acquaintance; Altmann had only good things to say about his brother's wife, who came from a family of Protestant pastors and estate owners, and Cohn reported benevolently on the Königsberg cultural journalist Ludwig Goldstein, the son of a Jewish-Christian marriage, and on the union between the "very pleasant" Lola Landau and Armin Wegner, "well-known for his travel accounts"; Altmann, 51; Cohn, *Spuren*, pp. 325 and 37. For an assessment similar to Cohn's see Albert Reibmayr, 'Ueber den Einfluß der Inzucht und der Vermischung auf den politischen Standpunkt einer Bevölkerung', *Politisch-Anthropologische Revue*, vol. 1 (1901), No. 1, quoted by the Breslau Zionist Aron Sandler in his *Anthropologie und Zionismus: Ein Populärwissenschaftlicher Vortrag*, Brünn 1904, pp. 41–42

[15]For negative middle-class assessments of working-class sexuality see Carola Lipp, 'Die Innenseite der Arbeiterkultur. Sexualität im Arbeitermilieu des 19. und frühen 20. Jahrhunderts', in *Arbeit, Frömmigkeit und Eigensinn*, ed. by Richard van Dülmen, Frankfurt 1990, pp. 215–220; Cornelia Usborne, 'The New Woman and Generational Conflict: Perceptions of Young Women's Sexual Mores in the Weimar Republic', in *Generations in Conflict: Youth Revolt and Generation Formation in Germany, 1770–1968*, ed. by Mark Roseman, Cambridge 1995, pp. 150–154; Derek S. Linton, 'Between School and Marriage. Young Working Women as a Social Problem in Late Imperial Germany', *European History Quarterly* 13 (1988), pp. 387–408.

Arendt and, more recently, Todd Endelman have argued that the statistics on intermarriage are misleading, because many of the "Christian" partners in mixed marriages were really converts from a Jewish background. Contrary to Arendt and Endelman but likewise without documentation, Alan Levenson, who recently completed a dissertation on intermarriage, claims that intermarriage led to "a severance of ties with the Jewish world".[16] The question therefore remains to be answered: What do the archival sources – which include the municipal statistics, a quantitative analysis of the records of the Breslau registrar's office and the small number of extant self-testimonies – tell us about the marriages between Jews and other Breslauers?

A SOCIAL HISTORY OF CHRISTIAN-JEWISH MARRIAGES

The rising rate of intermarriage in Breslau mirrored patterns found in other large German cities. Between the 1870s and the mid-1920s the intermarriage rate among Breslau Jews quadrupled, from nine to 39%, peaking at 53% during the war.[17] Unlike in other major German cities, Jewish men in Breslau were only slightly more likely to choose a non-Jewish partner than were Jewish women. It thus seems improbable that intermarriage reflected a sexual disparity amongst Breslau Jewry, a demographic force that would have pressured either Jewish men or women to marry outside the Jewish fold. Between 1899 and 1908, the gender ratio among Jews marrying Catholics remained evenly divided, whereas Jewish women accounted for 51.4% of all Jewish-Protestant intermarriages. In the war and post-war years, however, the sexual ratio of Breslau Jews opting for intermarriage converged with national trends, with Jewish men accounting for about 55% of all Jewish-Catholic and all Jewish-Protestant intermarriages.[18] The fact that the number of mixed marriages rose conspicuously after the turn of the century shows that friendly and intimate relations between Jews and other Breslauers had become more common.

The history of Jewish-Christian marriages in Breslau contradicts both contemporary stereotypes and much of the recent historiography. Contrary to Arendt's and Endelman's speculations, Jewish-Gentile marriages generally involved spouses of exclusively Jewish or Christian backgrounds. Of over 350 intermarriages recorded between 1905 and 1920, only twenty involved Jewish converts to Christianity in the role of the Christian spouse. Nor were impoverished aristocrats typical candidates

---

[16]Monika Richarz, 'Jewish Social Mobility in Germany During the Time of Emancipation (1790–1871)', in *LBI Year Book XX* (1975), p. 70; see also: Lamar Cecil, 'Jew and Junker', *ibid.* p. 49, who asserts that the Berlin Jewish high society entertained Junkers in order to match their daughters with aristocratic grooms; Dirk Blasius, *Ehescheidung in Deutschland*, Frankfurt 1992, p. 159. Todd M. Endelman, 'Conversion as a Response to Anti-semitism in Modern Jewish History', in *Living with Antisemitism: Modern Jewish Responses*, ed. by Jehuda Reinharz, Hanover, NH 1987, p. 79; Hannah Arendt, *The Origins of Totalitarianism*, New York 1964, p. 64. Although Arendt does not footnote her argument, a possible source might be Arthur Ruppin, *Die Soziologie der Juden*, vol. 1, Berlin 1930, p. 219. Alan T. Levenson, 'Reform Attitudes, in the Past, Toward Intermarriage', *Judaism* 38 (1989), pp. 321, 330.

[17]Walter Hanauer, 'Die jüdisch-christlichen Mischehen', *Allgemeines Statistisches Archiv* 17 (1928), p. 517. In compiling statistics on mixed marriages, one must take into account that unions between Jews and non-Jews were not counted as mixed when one member of the couple had converted to the other's religion. (Hanauer, p. 526f.).

[18]H. Philippsthal, 'Die jüdische Bevölkerung Breslaus', *Breslauer Jüdisches Gemeindeblatt*, 8 (1931), p. 67.

for Jewish-Christian marriages. Not one of the more than 600 Christian-Jewish marriages registered in the city of Breslau between 1874 and 1920 involved an aristocrat marrying a Jewish woman. Nor were dashing officers very common: Indeed, for the entire Imperial period, there are only two recorded cases of such men entering into mixed marriages in Breslau; and only one of them – the Protestant First Lieutenant Simundt – married into a respected upper-middle-class Jewish family. The female partner to this marriage, which took place in March 1882, was Margarete Rosalie Sachs, the Breslau-born (1859) daughter of the banker Siegmund Sachs and his wife Ottilie (neé Immerwahr). Admittedly Simundt was likely to have been of Jewish origin himself, having been born in Berlin 1846 as the son of the merchant Samuel Simon.[19]

One of the most notable characteristics of mixed marriages in Breslau during this period is that working-class and lower-middle-class Jews were more likely to intermarry than were middle-class Jews, a phenomenon that is especially striking in the case of Jewish women.[20] This contrast was particularly pronounced at the beginning of the Imperial period but became noticeably less so after 1890, although it was still evident in 1920 (see Table 1). Between 1874 and 1894, the two decades following the introduction of civil marriage, 73% of Jewish women in intra-Jewish marriages had fathers with middle-class or upper-middle-class professions, while 20% came from lower-middle-class families and only 7% from lower-class ones. For the same period, the social origins of those Jewish women who married Christians differed markedly. Among these women, not 73% but only 35% came from upper-middle-class households, 43% from lower-middle-class ones and no less than 17% from lower-class families.

By 1914 and above all during the war and in the immediate post-war period, the differences between the social backgrounds of Jewish women in mixed marriages and those who married Jewish men had begun to narrow. While the percentage of women in intra-Jewish marriages who were of upper-middle-class origin remained virtually unchanged until 1920 – at 75% – the percentage of women from this background who married non-Jewish men rose from 35% at the beginning of the Imperial period to over 45% between 1890 and 1910 and finally to 55% during and after the First World War.

The contrast between those Jews who married a Jewish partner and those who married a non-Jewish spouse appears even more stark if income rather than profession is used as a marker – a phenomenon that is especially pronounced in the case of Jewish women (see Table 2).[21] Among those Jewish women in the survey who mar-

---

[19]Marriage between Simundt and Margarete Rosalie Sachs, Archiwum Państwowe we Wrocławiu (hereafter APW), Urzad stanu cywilnego (hereafter USC), Standesamt Breslau I, 28 March 1882.

[20]The following is based on an analysis of all Jewish-Christian marriages in Breslau between 1874 and 1920. Sources: Marriage records of Breslau registrar's offices I and II, 1874–1894, (APW, USC Wrocław) and marriage records of Breslau registrar's offices I–IV 1905–1920, now at Urzad stanu cywilnego, Wrocław. For Catholic-Protestant mixed marriages there has so far been only one study, on the city of Bonn. It shows that the likelihood of a mixed marriage was much higher in the lower class than in the upper middle class: Gabriele Müller-List, *Die Sozialstruktur der evangelischen Einwohner Bonns im 19. Jahrhundert*, Bonn 1980, pp. 152–166, and 219–225. I would like to thank Kerstin Meiring for her help in analysing the marriage registers of 1874–1894.

[21]Unfortunately, it is impossible to analyse the income stratification for the years after 1882, since to do so one would need to combine an analysis of the marriage registers with that of the tax lists, which would only make sense if one included all Jewish earners of income, as occurred for 1876.

Table 1: The Social Origins of Jewish Women in Intra-Jewish and Mixed Marriages in Breslau, 1874–1894 and 1905–1920

Social status of the brides' fathers	1874 to 1894 Intra-Jewish Marriages No.	%	Jewish-Christian Marriages No.	%	1905 to 1920 Intra-Jewish Marriages No.	%	Jewish-Christian Marriages No.	%
Upper- middle-class stratum	322	72.7	36	35.6	171	75	79	53.7
Of these: "merchant"	246		28		146		59	
Middle and lower-middle-class stratum	88	19.9	43	42.6	45	19.8	47	32.0
Lower-class stratum	29	6.5	17	16.8	6	2.6	15	10.2
Others	4	0.9	5	5.0	6	2.6	6	4.1
Total	443	100	101	100	228	100	147	100

Sources: Marriage records of Breslau registrar's offices I and II, 1874–1894, (Archiwum Państwowe we Wrocławiu, Urzad stanu cywilnego, Wrocław) and marriage records of Breslau registrar's offices I–IV 1905–1920, now at Urzad stanu cywilnego, Wrocław.

Table 2: Annual Income of Jewish parents in Jewish-Christian Marriages and Intra-Jewish Marriages in Breslau 1874–1881, 1875 and 1881.

Income in Marks	Jewish-Christian Marriages Husband's Parents No.	%	Wife's Parents No.	%	Intra-Jewish Marriages Husband's Parents No.	%	Wife's Parents No.	%
Under 1,100	2	33.3	12	60.0	9	37.5	10	12.7
1,100 – 2,749	1	16.7	3	15.0	9	37.5	20	25.3
2,750 – 9,200	3	50.0	4	20.0	5	20.8	34	43.0
Over 9,200	–	–	1	5.0	1	4.2	15	19.0
Unknown	30		28		127		72	
Total	36		48		151		151	

Sources: see Table 1 and Akta miasta Wrocławia, K 150: Class tax roles, City of Breslau 1876 (35 vol.). Percentages refer only to those cases for which information on income is available.

ried Christian men in the years between 1874 and 1881 and for whom information on paternal income is available, 60% hailed from proletarian families earning less than 1,100 marks annually. Only a quarter came from middle or upper-middle-class households with a yearly income of more than 2,750 marks. Jewish women who married Jewish men, on the other hand, generally came from the higher-income brackets: only 13% of their fathers earned less than 1,100 marks annually, while 40% were well-to-do men who brought home between 2,750 and 9,200 marks a year; indeed a further 20% were very wealthy men whose yearly earnings exceeded 9,200 marks. At the very top of the economic scale, the contrast is particularly clear. Only one Jewish woman from a very wealthy family entered into a mixed marriage. Rosa Pringsheim (born 1835), the daughter of the wealthy banker Siegmund Pringsheim (yearly income: 170,000 marks), married the municipal court judge (*Stadtgerichtsrat*) Bernhard Englaender in September 1876. Although a convert to Christianity, Englaender, like his bride, had been born into a Jewish family from the city of Oppeln. Nevertheless, despite his conversion to Protestantism – a move made mostly likely for career purposes – he sought his future wife within the Jewish community, just like those Jewish sons who had remained true to their religion.[22]

Similarly, the annual income of Jewish men who married outside their faith lay considerably below that of those who wed a Jewish spouse (Table 3). In the case of men, it is more expedient to use their own income as a basis for comparison rather than that of their fathers. Due to their more advanced age at marriage, it is difficult to classify the parental households of grooms with any degree of precision, as their fathers were often already deceased or the families had moved away from Breslau. Of those Jewish husbands of Christian women for whom tax information is available, only 18% had an annual income of over 2,750 marks – fully 60% of them falling into the decidedly lower-class bracket of those earning less than 1,100 marks per annum. In contrast, Jewish men in intra-Jewish marriages were better off financially. Among this group, 28% presided over a "middle-class" income, while the percentage of those earning less than 1,100 marks hovered at around 50%.

The unusual case of Theodor Stahl – the only incidence in the records of a Jewish groom in a mixed marriage who could be classified as "wealthy" – is the exception

Table 3: Annual Income of Jewish grooms in Jewish-Christian Marriages and Intra-Jewish Marriages in Breslau 1874–1881, 1875 and 1881

Income in marks	Jewish-Christian Marriages		Intra-Jewish Marriages	
	No.	%	No.	%
Under 1,100	13	59.1	61	53.0
1,100 – 2,749	5	22.7	22	19.1
2,750 – 9,200	3	13.6	26	22.6
Over 9,200	1	4.6	6	5.2
Unknown	14		36	
Total	36		151	

Sources: see Table 1 and Akta miasta Wrocławia, K 150: Class tax roles, City of Breslau 1876 (35 vol.). Percentages refer only to those cases for which information on income is available.

[22] Marriage between Bernhard Englaender and Rosa Pringsheim, APW, USC, Standesamt Breslau II, 26 September 1876; on Siegmund Pringsheim's income, see APW, AMW K 150, Bezirk 20, No. 259 and APW, AMW K 146, vol. 21.

that proves the rule of how uncommon interfaith marriages were among the Jewish upper middle class. Born in Breslau in 1813, Stahl earned roughly 17,000 Marks in 1881. Six years earlier, at the age of 62, he had married Emilie Haertel, then aged 27, the Breslau-born daughter of a Protestant gardener. Beyond their considerable age difference, this case is remarkable in that the couple had already lived together prior to their marriage. This strongly suggests that the ceremony that took place in May 1875 represented the legalisation of a pre-existing common-law marriage – a step that only the introduction of the civil marriage had made possible. Yet another aspect worthy of mention is the fact that, whether voluntarily or under pressure from her husband, Emilie Haertel converted to Judaism after the wedding. This would belie the supposition that for Stahl, the decision to enter into a mixed marriage would necessarily have implied the breaking of all his ties to Judaism.[23]

Although a higher degree of antisemitism among the middle classes might partially account for the contrast between those Jews who married a Jewish partner and those who chose to marry a non-Jewish spouse, their different marriage strategies are a more significant factor. For the middle classes to a higher degree than their working-class counterparts, marriage served to maintain and augment cultural, social, as well as economic capital. It was primarily the *Bürger* and the *Bürgerin* who had family fortunes to win or lose in marriage. In his novel, *Jenny Treibel* (1892), Theodor Fontane ridiculed middle-class marriage behaviour through the character of the *Gymnasium* teacher Schmidt: "They are continually liberalising and sentimentalising, but it is all a farce; when the time comes to show one's colours, gold is all that counts."[24] No doubt young middle or upper-middle-class men and women were afforded some measure of choice. But their scope of action was limited by their parents, relatives and friends, through the latters' ability to initiate such marriages. Anna Auerbach (born 1863), one of five daughters of the wealthy industrialist Wilhelm Silbergleit, recalled in 1905 that even as children, it had been impossible for her sisters and her "to choose acquaintances independently, let alone friends". In her father's house, "a brusqueness that can only be described as aristocratic" dominated the daily routine; one "which only intensified as we girls approached marriageable age".[25]

In this sense, the (upper) middle-class marriage remained an arranged one, despite the ideal of the marriage for love. Even as the practise of marrying for money and as a means of capital accumulation fell increasingly into disrepute, the politics of marriage played an important role in the bourgeoisie's establishment of itself as a class. For in middle-class marriages, it was not only money that circulated, but also the honour of the families involved. To a far greater extent than in lower-class families,

---

[23]Marriage between Theodor Stahl and Emilie Haertel APW, USC, Standesamt Breslau II, 6 May 1875; Haertel's conversion and Stahl's financial situation are evident from the tax list; see APW, AMW K 151, Bezirk 19, No. 697. The Lutheran shopgirl Anne Ottilie Schüttke, who married the Jewish merchant Moritz August Brandy, whose annual income was 3,600 marks, in July 1875 converted to Judaism after her marriage; see APW, USC, Standesamt Breslau I, 6 July 1875 and APW, AMW, K 150, Bezirk 11, No. 603.

[24]Theodor Fontane, *Frau Jenny Treibel*, in *Werke in drei Bänden*, ed. by Kurt Schreinert, vol. 1, Munich 1968, p. 903.

[25]Anna Auerbach, 'Die Chronik der Familie Silbergleit, geschrieben aus Anlaß des 70. Geburtstages der Mutter am 21. November 1905', ME 600, LBI, NY, 21. On Wilhelm Silbergleit's financial circumstances, see APW, AMW, K 151, Bez. 19, No. 2577, and Staatssteuerrolle APW, AMW, K 146, Bd. 21, No. 3071.

the bourgeois marriage was integrated into a system of strategic "marriage alliances". It was also supposed to serve the purpose of insuring and increasing the economic capital of the family and above all its honour.[26] Without attempting to deny the significance of "economic motives in the search for a marriage partner", Anne-Charlott Trepp has recently argued that for the early nineteenth century, the topos of the "arranged marriage" obscures the "real scope of action and choices available to women in choosing a husband". Trepp rightly warns us against being taken in by the overly simplistic image of "polarised gender characters". Nevertheless, her own analysis shows that even at this time, the ability to choose could only be exercised on a playing field on which parents and relatives defined and enforced the rules.[27]

With Jewish-Gentile intermarriages still a relatively recent phenomenon, members of the middle classes were wary of taking the risky road of intermarriage. "For all of us daughters," recalled Anna Auerbach of her childhood and youth in the 1870s and 1880s, "the prospect of marrying a converted Jew was unlikely, and a Christian of German blood thoroughly out of the question".[28] "Marrying out of faith was not done", Steffi Granby (née Klinenberger), the daughter of a Breslau factory owner, has confirmed for her own generation.[29]

As long as middle-class marriages remained a way to secure and enhance social status, Jewish, Protestant, and Catholic middle-class parents tried to monitor the loves and sexual lives of their sons and especially their daughters to a much higher degree than in working-class families.[30] With good reason Mary Jo Maynes has ques-

---

[26]David Sabean, 'Die Ästhetik der Heiratsallianzen. Klassencodes und endogame Eheschließung im Bürgertum des 19. Jahrhunderts', in *Historische Familienforschung: Ergebnisse und Kontroversen. Festschrift Michael Mitterauer*, eds. Josef Ehmer et al., Frankfurt 1997, pp. 157–170; Kaplan, *Making*; Andrea Hopp, *Jüdisches Bürgertum in Frankfurt am Main im 19. Jahrhundert*, Stuttgart 1997, p. 194f. On the Catholic bourgeoisie see Thomas Mergel, *Zwischen Klasse und Konfession: Katholisches Bürgertum im Rheinland im 19. Jahrhundert*, Göttingen 1994, pp. 82–87, esp. 83f.; more generally, see Peter Borscheid, 'Geld und Liebe. Zu den Auswirkungen des Romantischen auf die Partnerwahl im 19. Jahrhundert', in *Ehe, Liebe, 'Tod: Zum Wandel der Familie, der Geschlechts- und Generationsbeziehungen in der Neuzeit*, eds. Peter Borscheid and Hans-Jürgen Teuteberg, Münster 1983, pp. 112–134; Gunilla-Friederike Budde, *Auf dem Weg ins Bürgerleben: Kindheit und Erziehung in deutschen und englischen Bürgerfamilien*, Göttingen 1994, pp. 25–43, esp. 31–36. Traditional Jewish forms of matchmaking may have promoted the establishment of bourgeois marriage patterns among German Jews; see Jacob Katz, *Tradition and Crisis: Jewish Society at the End of the Middle Ages*, 1958, newly transl. and with an afterword and bibliography by Bernard Dov Cooperman, New York 1993, pp. 113–124; Jacob Goldberg, 'Jewish Marriage in Eighteenth-Century Poland', *Polin* 10 (1997), pp. 1–37. The main difference lay in the early age at marriage among pre-modern Jewry. Steven Lowenstein, however, argues that by 1800 Ashkenazi Jews had already adopted the late age at marriage of the "European Marriage Pattern"; see his 'Ashkenazic Jewry and the European Marriage Pattern', *Jewish History* 8 (1994), pp. 155–175.

[27]Anne-Charlott Trepp, *Sanfte Männlichkeit und selbständige Weiblichkeit: Frauen und Männer im Hamburger Bürgertum 1770–1840*, Göttingen 1996, pp. 88–103, quotations, pp. 88 and 103.

[28]Anna Auerbach, 'Die Chronik der Familie Silbergleit', LBI, NY, S. 66; Arnold Bernstein, 'Erinnerungen, 1888–1964', LBI, NY, ME 55, S. 31: "Intermarriage was looked upon with contempt, more so by Jews than by gentiles." Among Königsberg Jews, too, "there was a general disapproval of mixed marriages"; Stefanie Schüler-Springorum, *Die Jüdische Minderheit in Königsberg, Preußen 1871–1945*, Göttingen 1996, p. 92.

[29]Steffi Granby, letter to the author, London, 18 March 1996; her father Sigmund Klinenberger owned a clothing factory in Breslau (letter of 9 September 1995). I would like to thank Steffi Granby for sharing her memories of Jewish-Gentile relations in Breslau with me. See also Hopp, *Jüdisches Bürgertum*, p. 213.

[30]Heidi Rosenbaum, *Formen der Familie: Untersuchungen zum Zusammenhang von Familienverhältnissen, Sozialstruktur und sozialem Wandel in der deutschen Gesellschaft des 19. Jahrhunderts*, Frankfurt 1982, pp. 348–350.

tioned the notion that working-class sexuality was "necessarily freer, more spontaneous, or somehow less [a] product of their society and culture" than middle-class sexuality.[31] Nevertheless working-class Jewish men and women had more opportunities to mingle with other Breslauers than did middle-class Jews, be it at work, at dances or through neighbourly contact. Here they could establish intimate and possibly sexual relations without parental monitoring or consent.[32] As a young man at the turn of the century, Adolf Riesenfeld, the son of a middle-class Jewish family, was at once fascinated and repelled by the gender relations among his lower-class contemporaries. "On muggy evenings I would often stroll along the promenade [the *Liebichshöhe*]", he recalled in his journal in October 1917. "On pleasant evenings, thousands of couples would be wandering up and down the street. Many men and girls also came alone, searching for contact and often finding it. Most of them were salesgirls and seamstresses, less often factory workers or housemaids. There was also the occasional prostitute, mostly of the second-class variety. The better set avoided the streets at this time, when behaviour was not always impeccable."[33]

The importance of dowries further limited the possibilities for middle-class women to individually choose a partner. The fact that working-class Jewish women were much more likely to intermarry than middle-class women must be read against this background. As late as the early Weimar years, dowries continued to play a critical role in intra-Jewish marriages. Middle-class fathers who could afford to provide their daughters with considerable dowries often used them to control the latter's choice of spouse. The fathers of working-class women, however, whose income was more modest, lacked this means of exerting pressure. Thus the larger the dowry, the less room there was for individual agency on the part of the young woman.[34]

The Riesenfeld family of Breslau provides an interesting example of the marriage strategies of the city's Jewish bourgeoisie. The father, who was born in 1853, was the owner of a successful Breslau shipping company; according to tax records, he earned 20,000 Marks in 1905. In the spring of 1901, his eighteen-year-old daughter met the man who would become her first husband, the thirty-five-year-old Moritz Goldman,

---

[31] Mary Jo Maynes, *Taking the Hard Road: Life Course and Class Identity in Nineteenth-Century French and German Workers' Autobiographies*, Chapel Hill, NC 1995, p. 150.

[32] See Maynes, *Taking the Hard Road*, pp. 129–151, esp.136–139; Rosenbaum, *Formen*, p. 425; Ulrich Linse, '"Animierkneipen" um 1900. Arbeitersexualität und Sittenreform', in *Kirmes – Kneipe – Kino: Arbeiterkultur im Ruhrgebiet zwischen Kommerz und Kontrolle 1850–1914*, ed. by Dagmar Kift, Paderborn 1992, pp. 83–118; Marianne Friese, 'Familienbildung u. Heiratsstrategien im Bremischen Proletariat des 19. Jahrhunderts', in *Familie und Familienlosigkeit: Fallstudien aus Niedersachsen und Bremen vom 15. bis 20. Jahrhundert*, ed. by Jürgen Schlumbohm, Hanover 1993, p. 230f.; to a more limited extent also Borscheid, 'Geld', p. 132. Premarital sex was common among the lower classes; about 50% of the working-class women in Hanover-Linden were pregnant at marriage: Heide Rosenbaum, *Proletarische Familien: Arbeiterfamilien und Arbeiterväter im frühen 20. Jahrhundert zwischen traditioneller, sozialdemokratischer und kleinbürgerlicher Orientierung*, Frankfurt 1992, p. 134. Ulrich Linse estimates that two-thirds of working-class women were pregnant at their weddings, and thus that almost all of them would have engaged in premarital sexual relations: idem, 'Arbeiterschaft und Geburtenentwicklung im Deutschen Kaiserreich von 1871', *Archiv für Sozialgeschichte* 12 (1972), p. 206.

[33] Adolf Riesenfeld, 'Memoiren', LBI, NY, vol. 1, entry for 25 October 1917; on the "hypocritical erotic life" of upper middle-class Jewish sons in turn-of-the century Breslau, see Cohn, *Spuren*, p. 86.

[34] For the best analysis of dowries, see Kaplan, *Making*; see also Hopp, *Jüdisches Bürgertum*, pp. 195–197 and 202f.; for a brief account of dowries among the Protestant and Catholic upper middle class, Budde, *Auf dem Weg*, pp. 28–30.

at the home of her uncle Samuel in Oppeln. In his memoirs, her brother Adolf comments ironically that his future brother-in-law's visit to the Oppeln relatives had "by chance" coincided with hers. Grete must have made a good impression on Moritz Goldmann, her brother recalls, "for as the material side" – that is, the dowry – "found favour with [...] Goldmann, the bands of Hymen were eagerly tied by the relatives. And as Grete's primary interest lay in soon becoming a bride, [...] she put up no resistance. Indeed, she had all the less reason to do so as Goldmann lived in Berlin and purportedly had an income of 10–15,000 marks. Thus, with regard to the most important thing, an agreement was already reached before the marriage candidates had even met for a second time."[35]

The marriage, which began in the autumn of 1901, had already fallen apart by January 1902. The Riesenfeld family was then left with a problem: a divorced nineteen-year-old daughter who was also expecting a child. It was, recalls Adolf Riesenfeld, "the particular desire of the parents that Grete, after the break up of her first marriage, should find a new life-partner". This time, the role of the marriage broker was played not by the uncle but by a "business and gambling friend" of his father's. This friend had a distant relation living in Vienna, a university-trained apothecary who wanted to go into business for himself and had hoped to obtain the necessary starting capital "from the other side". Grete's father offered the prospective son-in-law a dowry of 30,000 marks, in compensation for marrying a divorced woman with a child from her first marriage. This was, as Adolf Riesenfeld rightly observed, a "quite considerable sum for a young man with a monthly income of some 300 crowns [approximately 250 marks]". After the financial negotiations were completed at the end of 1904, Adolf Riesenfeld continues, "this gentleman then came to my parents' house and was invited to dinner". He made a "good impression on my parents and everyone else", including his sister Grete, so that nothing more stood in the way of her second marriage.[36]

Similar conditions governed Adolf Riesenfeld's own experience of choosing a partner. Although many of his friends went to the more fashionable Reifsche School of Dance, at which both Jewish and non-Jewish upper-middle-class children took lessons together, Riesenfeld chose to attend the exclusively Jewish Baersche Dance School. "From the *Drachenfels* the mothers looked on", recalls Willy Cohn, a contemporary of Riesenfeld's at Baersche School, and stared with "gaping eyes" at the wooing efforts of the sons of the bourgeoisie. It was in this atmosphere that Riesenfeld met his future wife, the then sixteen-year-old "Mieze" Eckmann. "A lively girl," he remembered in his autobiography, "quite plain, but charming and very restrained" – qualities that particularly attracted him. After paying a "formal visit" on the Eckmann family, Adolf Riesenfeld expressed his satisfaction at the financial situation of his prospective father-in-law, Leopold Eckmann, a junior partner at the thriving S. Sternberg Fertiliser Company.[37] However, as long as Adolf Riesenfeld continued

---

[35]Riesenfeld, 'Memoiren', vol. 1, entry for 27 January 1917.
[36]*ibid.*, vol. 1, entry for 26 February 1941.
[37]*ibid.*, vol. 1, entries for 16 and 17 February 1941. On the two dancing schools see also Cohn, *Spuren*, p. 84f.: "In those days [1906] there were two dancing masters in Breslau, the baptised Jew Reif and the unbaptised Jew Baer. Reif's dancing lessons were considered more refined. They were also attended by my sister. For Jewish reasons I however refused, and went to Baer, even at the risk of appearing less refined."

to earn his living as a commercial traveller, the two could not officially get engaged. Only in 1909, when he had advanced to the position of partner in his father's firm, were they finally free to marry, which they proceeded to do in November of that year. The Eckmanns offered him a dowry of 15,000 marks, part of which was invested in his family's shipping company, the other part used to furnish the young couple's flat.[38]

Nevertheless, there was also a gender-specific difference between the experiences of the two siblings. While for Grete Riesenfeld Goldmann, premarital sexual relations of any kind were out of the question, her brother, like other middle-class young men, was allowed to indulge in sexual encounters between puberty and marriage.[39] Between 1905 and 1909, during his extended engagement, Adolf had a string of love affairs with lower-class women. Despite his true and deep attachment to Mieze, Riesenfeld recalled, it was for him "a matter of course" that he should also seek "adventures elsewhere". Already at sixteen, during his apprenticeship at his father's company, he began a "flirtation" with a young female employee at the firm. Forty years later, Adolf noted that it was "still a mystery to me what I could have talked about with these girls and later on in the numerous other relationships I had with proletarian women". Such affairs were nevertheless far from uncommon: "Nearly all of my friends had such relationships, and most of these lower-class girls were very adept at assuming the superficial social polish that enabled them to circulate with confidence in a completely different milieu."[40]

Not all of these women were Christian. Around 1905 Riesenfeld met Dora Weiss, a seventeen-year-old Jewish industrial worker at an umbrella factory located next to his office. After the two had gone on numerous trips together to "the theatre, Liebich's music hall, cafés and [on] evening strolls", the young woman's parents invited him to dinner on the occasion of a Jewish holiday. However, as the family lived in "very modest circumstances" according to Riesenfeld, their efforts to "introduce me into their family in no way corresponded with my intentions. I therefore informed her straight out that there could be no talk of marriage, I myself being already engaged". Thereafter Dora Weiss' parents forbade her to see him and furthermore reproached the young man by letter. However, neither at the time (1906) nor in hindsight did Adolf Riesenfeld appear to suffer any pangs of conscience: "It was already clear to me then," he wrote in 1942, "that Dora's mother had encouraged this harmless flirtation in the hopes that I would bind myself to her daughter in some more serious way." In any event, her parents would certainly have welcomed "an engagement with a young man from a well-off and respectable bourgeois family".[41]

The more unlikely it was that an affair would lead to marriage – that is, if the woman was non-Jewish and from a lower-class background – the less complicated it

---

[38]Riesenfeld, 'Memoiren', vol. 2, entry for 16 January 1942.
[39]Rosenbaum, *Formen*, pp. 348–350; Michelle Perrot (ed.), *A History of the Private Life*, vol. 4: *From the Fires of Revolution to the Great War*, Cambridge, MA 1990, pp. 150–151 and p. 159: "Virginity remained the most precious form of capital."
[40]Riesenfeld, 'Memoiren', vol. 2, entry for 16 October 1941. Since almost all of his friends were Jewish, Riesenfeld's sexual affairs with non-Jewish women were by no means unusual. Around 1900 the usual period of engagement was two years; Budde, *Auf dem Weg*, p. 37.
[41]Riesenfeld, 'Memoiren', vol. 2, entry 1 January 1942.

was for Riesenfeld. This casts doubt on Eugen Altmann's thesis that in "95 of every 100" cases of a Jewish man marrying a Christian woman, he was marrying his mistress. Indeed, it was precisely outside of their usual circles of acquaintance that Riesenfeld and his friends sought their affairs. Only in this way could these relationships be kept secret from their parents, remain non-binding and be broken off without any risk to the man's reputation.[42] Indeed, the precondition for Riesenfeld's intimate and sometimes also sexual relationships with women from the lower class was that there be no question of marriage. This rule applied most strictly to non-Jewish women. In the autumn of 1907 Riesenfeld began working as a commercial traveller for a company in Dresden. There he struck up a friendship with a female colleague, the approximately eighteen-year-old clerk Johanna Schindler. "Hanne", as Riesenfeld still referred to her in his memoirs, started out as "a good chum and unqualified admirer". Although she initially refused sexual relations, Riesenfeld managed to persuade her to become his lover in the "deeper sense of the word" by threatening to drop her otherwise. In contrast to the relationship with Dora, this one appears to have received the approval of the young woman's parents. "Her mother", Riesenfeld recalled, "must have known what was happening and did not interfere with her child's wishes." The relationship with Johanna Schindler lasted until the end of March 1908, when Riesenfeld returned to Breslau in order to take up a position in his father's firm. Although at the time of departure his girlfriend believed herself – albeit mistakenly – to be pregnant, there was no question of their getting married. Nevertheless, Riesenfeld claims in his memoirs that had she been pregnant, he would have "helped her to the best of my abilities".[43]

At the same time, middle class women also tended to have a more sheltered adolescence than members of the working class, with strict mores limiting the opportunity for casual sexual relationships.[44] In 1914, shortly after her twentieth birthday, Lola Landau, the daughter of a wealthy Jewish doctor from Berlin, met her first husband Siegfried Marck, a *Privatdozent* in philosophy at the University of Breslau, during a holiday trip to the Silesian mountains. With both sets of parents supervising their flirtation and encouraging their engagement, sense and sensibility rather than romance characterised the affair. "I would like to read Plato with you" was Siegfried Marck's way of proposing to her: "Do you like the idea?" While young Lola did like the idea in 1914, she soon became disenchanted, and by 1919 their marriage had failed.[45] In 1917, when riding a crowded streetcar in downtown Breslau, she encountered the man who would become her second husband, the non-Jewish writer Armin T. Wegner. "On the last platform I noticed a striking figure," she recalls in her autobiography, with a face "fair as if cut from a noble stone, and possessing a perfectly

---

[42]A similar observation is made by Lynn Rapaport: "The anonymity gained by crossing over to the German world, and the lack of pressure from or surveillance by family, friends, and community", the cultural sociologist argues, "creates a situation conducive to sexual liaisons"; see her *Jews in Germany after the Holocaust: Memory, Identity, and German-Jewish Relations*, New York 1997, p. 232f.

[43]Riesenfeld, 'Memoiren', vol. 2, entry for 6/7 January 1942, 68f., 72f., 74 and 78f.

[44]Budde, *Auf dem Weg*, pp. 39–40, and passim; Reinhard Sieder, *Sozialgeschichte der Familie*, Frankfurt, 1987, pp. 204–205; Lipp, 'Die Innenseite der Arbeiterkultur', pp. 222–224, 228, 230; Gerhard A. Ritter and Klaus Tenfelde, *Arbeiter im Deutschen Kaiserreich*, Bonn 1992, pp. 619, 623, 626–627.

[45]Lola Landau, *Vor dem Vergessen: Meine Drei Leben*, Berlin 1987, p. 15.

symmetrical beauty". Meeting sporadically in literary circles and at political meetings of the peace movement, they secretly carried on a passionate romance. Whereas her husband, who himself was involved with a female student, was willing to separate, Lola Landau's father tried to prevent her from both divorcing and remarrying a non-Jew through emotional blackmail. "If you get divorced to marry this person", Theodor Landau remonstrated, "you might as well be dead. For me you won't exist anymore."[46] Even if Lola Landau's autobiography – written in response to her grief following Armin Wegner's death in 1978 – reveals the complex workings of memory, and even if their marriage was far from representative, the Breslau marriage records convey a similar picture.

CHRISTIAN-JEWISH MARRIAGES AND THE "NEW WOMAN"

The rising number of mixed marriages developed in tandem with an independent and assertive "New Woman". Women as much as men who intermarried were arguably pioneers of more egalitarian relations between the sexes, relations that undermined traditional gender hierarchies. Marriage records reflect that both Jews and Gentiles who intermarried – particularly Jewish women – were more independent of their families, more adventurous and rebellious than partners in intra-Jewish marriages. They were far more likely than women in intra-Jewish marriages to have worked professionally and far less likely to still be living with their parents.[47] In an age when premarital sex for women was taboo, about a quarter of intermarried couples had actually shared an apartment with their partner before marrying.[48] Jewish women who entered mixed marriages did so because they wanted to; intra-Jewish marriages, in contrast, continued to conform to the pattern of strategic marriage alliances.

Whereas women in intra-Jewish marriages rarely worked, many intermarried women, both Jewish and Gentile, pursued a professional career, mostly as workers or petty clerks, at least until their marriage (Table 4). In an age when members of the upper and the lower middle class tended to look down on working women, many of these Jewish women entered a profession because their parents were too poor to sup-

---

[46]Landau, *Vor dem Vergessen*, pp. 15; 64–65, and 145. Theodor Landau later developed an "interest and respect" for Armin Wegner, but nevertheless continued to treat him as an "unwelcome son-in-law, a stranger formally addressed by his last name". (*ibid.*, p. 239)

[47]Between 1905 and 1909 40% of all intermarried Jewish women had jobs, in contrast to only 10% of all women in intra-Jewish marriages (1919–1920: 50% to 20%). It was unusual for women to have a job before marrying and reflected badly on their families. Adolf Asch, a Jewish lawyer from Posen, notes in his memoirs that "it was generally looked down upon for young ladies to have a paid occupation. Even less wealthy parents and poorer widows kept their daughters at home without a profession in order to avoid a decline in the family's reputation", quoted in *Jüdisches Leben in Deutschland*, ed. by Monika Richarz, vol. 2, p. 230.

[48]Presumably as a live-in couple. On the taboo of premarital sex see Budde, *Auf dem Weg*, p. 40; Ute Frevert, *Frauen-Geschichte: Zwischen Bürgerlicher Verbesserung und Neuer Weiblichkeit*, Frankfurt 1986, pp. 130–131; Franziska Lamott, 'Virginität als Fetisch. Kulturelle Codierung und rechtliche Normierung der Jungfräulichkeit um die Jahrhundertwende', in *Tel Aviver Jahrbuch für deutsche Geschichte* 21 (1992), pp. 153–170. 24% of all Jewish women marrying a Gentile groom between 1905 and 1909 had lived with their future husbands, in contrast to only 4 % of all women in intra-Jewish marriages.

port them between leaving school and entering marriage.[49] These women had many opportunities to mingle with non-Jewish colleagues at the workplace. Their parents could hardly monitor these contacts, not the least because their daughters were economically independent and because they lacked a substantial dowry as a means of control. Lower-class Jews, complained the *Jüdische Volkszeitung* in April 1917, fell prey much more easily to "the slogans of the enemies of religion", particularly when, by virtue of their profession, they lived "in social circles dominated by the uneducated and non-Jews".[50]

Table 4: Percentage of Women "Out to Work" before Marriage.

Year of Marriage	Intra-Jewish Marriages				Jewish-Christian Marriages							
					Jewish Women				Non-Jewish Women			
	Out to Work		Without Profession		Out to Work		Without Profession		Out to Work		Without Profession	
	No.	%	No.	%	No.	%	No.	%	No.	%	No.	%
1874–1884	17	8.9	197	92.1	22	43.1	39	56.9	20	44.4	25	55.6
1885–1894	23	10.0	206	90.0	19	47.5	21	52.5	31	64.6	17	35.4
1905–1909	9	11.0	73	89.0	20	40.0	30	60.0				
1914–1918	14	28.6	35	71.4	23	45.1	28	54.9				
1919–1920	15	20.8	57	79.2	15	50.0	50	50.0				

Sources: see Table 1

Mothers and fathers whose children intermarried also lacked another means of control, because their sons and especially their daughters were also less likely to be living with their parents. Many women who intermarried had actually shared an apartment with their partner before marrying (Tables 5–8). This was remarkable in an age in which premarital sex was taboo for women and the "*wilde Ehe*" (common-law marriage) was considered "a major cause of depravity ... among the lower classes".[51] From the beginning to the end of the Imperial period and into the post-war

---

[49]On women's employment as a flaw in bourgeois and petty bourgeois circles, see Hopp, *Jüdisches Bürgertum*, p. 162; see also Paula E. Hyman, 'Jüdische Familie und kulturelle Kontinuität im Elsaß des 19. Jahrhunderts', in *Jüdisches Leben auf dem Lande: Studien zur deutsch-jüdischen Geschichte*, eds. Monika Richarz and Reinhard Rürup, (Schriftenreihe wissenschaftlicher Abhandlungen des Leo Baeck Instituts 56), Tübingen 1997, p. 262f.

[50]'Nicht hinunter – sondern hinauf', *Jüdische Volkszeitung* 26 April 1917, p. 1.

[51]On premarital sexuality as a taboo, see Franziska Lamott, 'Virginität als Fetisch'; Budde, *Auf dem Weg*, p. 40; on the debate in the 1830s and 1840s on "concubinage" as "one of the chief causes of the ruin of the lower classes of the population", see Ute Gerhard, *Verhältnisse und Verhinderungen: Frauenarbeit, Familie und Rechte der Frauen im 19. Jahrhundert. Mit Dokumenten*, 1978; Frankfurt 1981, pp. 351–360, and Lynn Abrams, 'Concubinage, Cohabitation, and the Law. Class and Gender Relations in Nineteenth-Century Germany', *Gender and History* 5 (1993), pp. 81–100. In Prussia, "living in sin" (*wilde Ehe*) was still a punishable offence in the Weimar Republic if it caused a public nuisance; see the article 'Konkubinat', in *Meyers Lexikon*, vol. 6, Leipzig 1927, p. 1672f.

era, only 5% of partners in intra-Jewish marriages had shared living quarters beforehand. Of Jewish women in mixed marriages in the years between 1874 and 1894, in contrast, 37% had lived together with their future husbands before the wedding. For Jewish men who married non-Jewish women, a full 50% had previously "lived in sin". The contrast between intra-Jewish and mixed marriages narrowed after the turn of the century, as the trend grew more conservative. Nevertheless, between 1905 and 1909 still a quarter of all Jewish women and a third of Jewish men entering mixed marriages had previously lived with their future spouses in common-law marriages – a period during which 50% of Jewish women entering intra-Jewish marriages had never lived outside of their parents' home. Of course, a good many Christian-Jewish couples never legalised their relationship. Indeed, the sharp increase in the rate of mixed marriages during the war years clearly suggests that common-law marriages between Jews and other Breslauers were far from infrequent.

Table 5: Living Status of Jewish Women before Marriage 1874–1884 and 1885–1894.

	1874–1884				1885–1894			
	Jew.-Christian Marriages		Intra-Jewish Marriages		Jew.-Christian Marriages		Intra-Jewish Marriages	
Living Status	No.	%	No.	%	No.	%	No.	%
With parents	15	25%	149	70%	7	33%	143	62%
By themselves	24	39%	53	25%	6	29%	86	38%
With future spouse	22	36%	12	6%	8	38%	–	–

Sources: see Table 1.

Table 6: Living Status of Jewish Women before Marriage 1905–1909 and 1919–1920.

	1905–1909				1919–1920			
	Jew.-Christian Marriages		Intra-Jewish Marriages		Jew.-Christian Marriages		Intra-Jewish Marriages	
Living Status	No.	%	No.	%	No.	%	No.	%
With parents	11	22%	42	51%	11	37%	31	39%
By themselves	27	54%	37	45%	15	50%	67	57%
With future spouse	12	24%	3	4%	4	13%	3	4%

Sources: see Table 1.

Table 7: Living Status of Jewish Men before Marriage 1874–1884 and 1885–1894.

	1874–1884				1885–1894			
	Jew.-Christian Marriages		Intra-Jewish Marriages		Jew.-Christian Marriages		Intra-Jewish Marriages	
Living Status	No.	%	No.	%	No.	%	No.	%
With parents	–	–	24	11%	1	3%	29	13%
By themselves	19	42%	178	83%	19	50%	200	87%
With future spouse	26	58%	12	6%	18	47%	–	–

Sources: see Table 1.

Table 8: Living Status of Jewish Men before Marriage 1905–1909 and 1919–1920.

	1905–1909				1919–1920			
	Jew.-Christian Marriages		Intra-Jewish Marriages		Jew.-Christian Marriages		Intra-Jewish Marriages	
Living Status	No.	%	No.	%	No.	%	No.	%
Parents	2	3%	9	11%	4	9%	10	13%
By themselves	51	66%	70	85%	32	68%	67	83%
With future spouse	24	31%	3	4%	11	23%	3	4%

Sources: see Table 1.

The respective ages of the spouses at marriage and especially their age difference also suggest that the partners in intermarriages formed a part of a different social group than those in intra-Jewish marriages (Tables 9 and 10).[52] Between 1874 and 1884, the average age at marriage of Jewish women who chose a Gentile groom was 29 years, in contrast to their sisters in intra-Jewish marriages, who were on average 25 years old. Although the contrast was less marked after the turn of the century, the average age at marriage of women who intermarried was still two years higher (28 between 1905 and 1909) than that of women in intra-Jewish marriages (26 in 1905). More importantly, women who married outside of their faith were much closer in age to their husbands than were women in intra-Jewish marriages. Whereas only a few intermarried women were ten or more years younger than their grooms, in almost a third of all intra-Jewish marriages the husband was at least ten years older than his wife. In intra-Jewish marriages the age difference re-enforced the gender inequality enshrined in the legal order.

Finally, a look at the witnesses at the wedding ceremonies suggests that intermarriage tended to be an individual choice, whereas spouse selection in intra-Jewish marriages remained influenced by the families of both spouses (Table 11). As

---

[52]On the nexus between marriage age and gender hierarchies see Budde, *Auf dem Weg*, pp. 40–43; Hopp, *Jüdisches Bürgertum*, pp. 168–169 and pp. 205–208; Leonore Davidoff and Catherine Hall, *Family Fortunes: Men and Women of the English Middle Classes, 1780–1850*, London 1987, p. 323.

Table 9: Average Age at Marriage and Age Differences between Spouses.

Year of Marriage	Average Ages of Spouses									
	Jewish-Christian Marriages						Intra-Jewish Marriages		
	Jewish Men			Jewish Women					
	Husb.	Wife	Differ.	Husb.	Wife	Differ.	Husb.	Wife	Differ.
1874–1884	34.3	26.6	7.7	30.2	28.6	1.6	32.8	25.3	7.5
1885–1894	35.3	29.8	5.5	27.6	26.4	1.2	32.8	25.6	7.2
1905–1909	33.7	27.2	6.5	30.2	28.1	2.1	32.8	26.0	6.8
1914–1918	34.9	28.3	6.4	31.2	28.5	2.7	36.5	29.1	7.4
1919–1920	37.2	30.1	7.1	31.7	28.0	3.7	35.4	27.9	7.5

Sources: see Table 1.

Table 10: Age Differences in Percentages (Percentage of marriages in which the husband is X years older).

| Year of Marriage | Age Differences between Husbands and Wives in Years (x < 0 when the wife was older) ||||||||||||
| | Jew.-Christian Marriages, Husband Jewish |||| Jew.-Christian Marriages, Wife Jewish |||| Intra-Jewish Marriages ||||
	< 0	0–5	6–10	> 10	< 0	0–5	6–10	> 10	< 0	0–5	6–10	>10
1874–1884	15.6	33.3	22.2	28.9	45.6	29.5	14.8	13.1	11.2	30.8	27.6	30.4
1885–1894	16.7	29.2	37.5	16.7	30.0	50.0	12.5	7.5	10.0	30.6	33.6	25.8
1905–1909	14.3	40.2	19.5	26.0	26.0	48.0	16.0	10.0	11.2	31.8	30.8	26.2
1914–1918	12.3	36.0	30.7	21.0	33.3	39.2	11.8	15.7	10.2	38.8	24.5	26.5
1919–1920	11.6	55.1	18.8	14.5	15.2	63.0	10.9	10.9	9.7	27.8	33.3	29.2

Sources: see Table 1.

Hartmut Zwahr has argued, the choice of godparents in Christian families reflects "a substantial part of the social origins and environment of the respective families".[53] The same is true for witnesses at wedding ceremonies. Whereas family members served as witnesses in half of intra-Jewish marriages at the beginning and two-thirds at the end of the Imperial period – reflecting their influence on the choice of partner, the witnesses at Christian-Jewish marriages tended to be neighbours, co-workers or friends. If the fathers of the bride and groom were still alive, it was usually they who, in intra-Jewish marriages, served as witnesses to their children's mar-

---

[53] Hartmut Zwahr, *Zur Konstituierung des Proletariats als Klasse: Strukturuntersuchungen über das Leipziger Proletariat während der industriellen Revolution*, Berlin 1978, pp. 165.

Table 11: Witnesses at Jewish-Christian Weddings and at Intra-Jewish Weddings: 1874–1884, 1905–1909, 1914–1918 and 1919/1920.

	1874–1884				1905–1909 and/or 1905				1914–1918 and/or 1919/1920			
	Jew.-Chr.		Jew.-Jew.		Jew.-Chr.		Jew.-Jew.		Jew.-Chr.		Jew.-Jew.	
	No.	%	No.	%	No.	%	No.	%	No.	%	No.	%
I Parents	54	25	217	50	52	23	84	51	41	28	78	55
II Relatives	–	–	–	–	19	8	22	13	14	9	19	13
III Neighbours	23	11	33	8	18	8	5	3	10	7	8	6
IV Co-workers	17	8	1	0,2	42	19	24	15	27	18	24	17
V Friends	120	56	177	41	95	42	29	18	56	38	13	9
Total	214				226		164		148		142	

Sources: see Table 1.

riages at the registry office. Father and son and father and daughter gathered before the registrar, making it clear that the marriage into which the children were about to enter was also a strategic alliance between two families.

Whereas the majority of intra-Jewish marriages continued to be arranged, those Jews – particularly women – who chose a Gentile spouse seem to have been an independent lot, listening less to family members than to their hearts. Even if Lola Landau did not explicitly mention intermarriage in a programmatic article of 1929, she was probably recalling her own two marriages when she sharply contrasted the "economic institution of bourgeois marriage" to the "companionate marriage". The latter united "the economically and intellectually independent woman ... with her informed views and mature heart, to the man as a comrade".[54]

After the turn of the century, Christian-Jewish and intra-Jewish marriages came more closely to resemble one another. In the case of Breslau, the discrepancies in terms of age at marriage, social background and age difference between the partners began to narrow. This may in part be a reflection of the fact that, compared to the beginning of the Imperial era, mixed marriages had lost some of their stigma of inappropriateness. Even among the middle class, Christian-Jewish marriages had become a possibility. Simultaneously, however, the middle-class strategy of forging marriage alliances between families via their sons and especially their daughters was eroding. The marital behaviour of young men and – to an even greater extent – young women came more closely to resemble that of lower middle-class and lower class Jews. While in other respects the lower-class population became more middle class during this period, the marital behaviour of the Jewish bourgeoisie of Breslau became less so with the rise of the "New Woman".

---

[54]Lola Landau, 'Die Kameradschaftsehe', *Die Tat* 20 (11 February 1929), pp. 831–835; translated as 'The Companionate Marriage', *The Weimar Republic Sourcebook*, eds. Anton Kaes, Martin Jay, and Edward Dimendberg, Berkeley 1994, pp. 702–703; for the general context see Usborne, 'The New Woman', pp. 137–163; Frevert, *Frauen-Geschichte*, pp. 146–199.

Around 1910 the first serious conflict over the issue of mixed marriages took place within the Jewish community. Although those opposed to such marriages ultimately won the day, other, more differentiated voices also entered in the debate – voices that maintained the distinction between mixed marriage and conversion.[55] At the general meeting of the Israelite Charity Hospital and Burial Society (*Israelitische Kranken- und Verpflegungs-Anstalt und Beerdigungsgesellschaft*) in June 1909, members of the Zionist Club put forward the motion that doctors who had "left Judaism or the *Synagogengemeinde* or were in mixed marriages or whose children had left Judaism before reaching the age of majority" should be excluded from employment at the Jewish Hospital. Those in favour of the motion were represented by the lawyer Felix Hirschberg, who, as a candidate for the orthodox Society for the Advancement of the Interests of Judaism (*Verein zur Förderung der Interessen des Judentums*), had lost to the Association of Liberals (*Liberalen Verein*) during community elections the previous December.[56] "The problem lies just as much with mixed marriages as with leaving the *Gemeinde*", Hirschberg argued, thereby defending a position that still predominates in the historiography. David Mugdan of the Religious Liberals (*Religiös-Liberalen*) represented the opposing viewpoint, arguing that the Jewish Hospital – although it received neither state nor municipal funding – should also choose its doctors solely on the basis of their qualifications. The liberal rabbi of the community, Jacob Guttmann, attempted to mediate. Anyone who had left the Jewish *Gemeinde* he argued, "has ... forfeited the right to occupy a position that is financed through the contributions of his former co-religionists". Nevertheless, although he strongly condemned conversion, his stand on mixed marriage was more moderate. "If someone marries a Christian out of love but still remains true to Judaism, he should not be seen as being either unworthy or unfit to be an employee of a Jewish Hospital." Guttmann succeeded in winning over the Society's board – in which liberals held the majority – to his position. The last word, however, was had by the members' assembly. Here the Zionist and orthodox wings joined forces and, continuing to set mixed marriage on a par with conversion, outlawed the hiring of Jewish doctors married to non-Jews. This policy remained in force in the hospital throughout the Weimar Republic. In October 1927, a doctor applying for a position as head of the ophthalmology department was obliged to testify that he was "not engaged to marry a Christian lady nor was [he] intending to do so".[57]

Even though it was higher than in intra-Jewish marriages, the rate of divorce in mixed marriages remained low. The intermarriage of the Breslau Jew Franz Ungerleider and the Protestant Gabriele Jakubczik, who had married on April 3, 1920 and got divorced on June 26 the same year, was anything but typical. True, in intra-Jewish marriages divorce was much less likely than in mixed marriages: only

---

[55]On what follows see Andreas Reinke, *Judentum und Wohlfahrtspflege: Das jüdische Krankenhaus in Breslau 1744–1944*, Hanover 1999, pp. 234–237.

[56]On Hirschberg's candidacy in December 1905 see *Jüdisches Volksblatt*, 11, 1905, p. 489. In December 1909 he succeeded in being elected to the synagogue administration, from 1918 on he belonged to the Breslau synagogue congregation's board of directors and in 1921 he became chairman of the regional chapter for Middle and Lower Silesia of the *Centralverein deutscher Staatsbürger jüdischen Glaubens*; see Aron Heppner, *Jüdische Persönlichkeiten in und aus Breslau*, Breslau 1931, 21, and *Im Deutschen Reich*, 27, 1921, p. 300.

four percent of all Breslau intra-Jewish couples married in 1905 obtained a divorce, compared to 11% of intermarriages between 1905 and 1909. Yet even among intra-Jewish couples wed in 1920, 18% successfully filed for divorce, reflecting the other side of the often over-hasty wartime weddings and the marriage epidemic of the post-war period which affected intra-Jewish marriage and intermarriage alike. And whereas 30% of all post-war intermarriages eventually led to divorce, had it not been for Nazi anti-Jewish policies, the number of terminated intermarriages may well have remained at little over 20%.[58] The fact that about four out of five Jewish-Gentile intermarriages remained intact may not indicate that they were all harmonious relationships; it does, however, suggest that these women and men struggled to make their marriages work and, generally speaking, they succeeded.[59]

CHRISTIAN-JEWISH MARRIAGES AND THE SITUATIONAL ETHNICITY OF BRESLAU JEWS

It is misleading to equate intermarriage with a desire for total assimilation. After the introduction of civil marriage ceremonies in 1874, Jews and other Germans could marry out of faith without having to convert. Jewish men and women who wanted to sever all ties with their Jewish background could, of course, still convert, and we can speculate endlessly about how many Jews chose total assimilation. All Jewish spouses in contemporary intermarriage statistics consciously chose not to convert. To them, marrying out of faith simply did not equal a rejection of their Jewishness comparable to conversion.[60] Whereas some Jewish partners in mixed marriages converted after marrying, their number is likely to be rather small, as it would have been easier for them to "assimilate" totally if they had converted beforehand.

In addition, some Christian partners in mixed marriages converted to Judaism after the wedding, even though it is difficult to estimate their significance in quantitative terms. Many of those who had formerly been Protestants, and about whom the Protestant church of Silesia kept precise records, doubtless belonged to this group. In any event, in the whole of Silesia, 46 Protestant men and women converted to Judaism in the years between 1880 and the turn of the century; 80 between

---

[57]Quoted in Reinke, *Judentum*, p. 236 n. 174.

[58]For the case of Ungerleider/Jakubczik see USC, Standesamt Breslau, Standesamtsbezirk IV, 3 April 1920. Among couples who intermarried during World War I, only one out of five ended up filing for divorce. On divorces in the early Weimar years see Blasius, *Ehescheidung in Deutschland*, pp. 157–159; Richard Bessel, *Germany after the First World War*, Oxford 1993, pp. 231–33; Usborne, 'The New Woman', p. 154.

[59]The resistance of non-Jewish spouses to Nazi policies also attests to the tenacious bonds formed in intermarriages; see Nathan Stoltzfus, 'Widerstand des Herzens. Der Protest in der Rosenstraße und die deutsch-jüdische Mischehe', *Geschichte und Gesellschaft* 21 (1995), pp. 218–247, and *Resistance of the Heart: Intermarriage and the Rosenstrasse Protest in Nazi Germany*, New York 1996; for examples from Breslau, see Eugen Altmann, 'Mein Leben in Deutschland vor und nach dem 30. Januar 1933', Houghton Library, Harvard University, Manuscript Collection "My Life in Germany Before and After January 30, 1933", 51, and Anita Lasker-Wallfisch, *Inherit the Truth 1939–1945: The Documented Experiences of a Survivor of Auschwitz and Belsen*, London 1996, 50–51; a fascinating inside view of the difficulties facing these marriages can be gleaned from the diary of Victor Klemperer, *Ich will Zeugnis ablegen bis zum letzten: Tagebücher 1933–1945*, 2 vols. (Berlin, 1995).

1900 and 1918; and 52 in the decade from 1918 to 1927.[61] In February 1922, a twenty year-old Protestant industrial worker named Gertrud Luise Springer, the daughter of Hermann Springer, a Breslau hatter, married the twenty-five-year-old Jewish coachman Benno Breslauer, the son of a master tailor. Both children of this marriage – a son born in 1926 and a daughter born the following year – were Jewish from birth. Their mother converted to Judaism after her marriage. Gertrud Breslauer remained true to her adopted religion until 1941, when she was obliged to quit the Breslau *Gemeinde* in order to protect her husband and children.[62]

Indeed, the religion of the children born of mixed marriages cautions against equating such marriages with conversion. Not all of the children born of mixed Christian and Jewish parentage were lost to Judaism. At least on paper, a considerable minority of them were raised Jewish.[63] If one looks at the religion of the children produced in all Jewish-Christian marriages recorded in Breslau, some 30% were nominally Jewish in the years 1890 and 1910 and as many as 35% in 1900. In contravention of the *Halachic* tradition but in line with the patriarchal family structure, it is the religion of the father that appears to be decisive. Until the turn of the century, mixed marriages involving Jewish men did not pose any demographic threat to the Breslau Jewish community. On the contrary, in 1890 more than half of all children born of marriages between Jewish men and Christian women – be they Catholic or Protestant – were registered as Jewish. Nevertheless, the proportion of Jewish children in such marriages gradually declined: by 1900, it was only in the case of marriages between Jewish men and Protestant women that the majority of such children were Jewish. After the turn of the century, the majority of children of mixed parentage were raised Christian even if the father was Jewish. If the mother was Catholic, only a quarter of children were Jewish; if she was Protestant, a third.

In the case of Jewish women who intermarried, the result – at least until around 1900 – was a net demographic "loss" from the perspective of the Jewish community. Only 4% of children born to a Jewish mother and a Protestant father were Jewish in 1890; if the father was Catholic, then all of the children were Christian. Yet already by 1900, the picture had changed. In that year, 20% of all such children were nominally Jewish; ten years later, this figure had risen to 24%. In contrast to the period around 1890, the independence and self-confidence that characterised Jewish women who intermarried began, at the close of the Imperial era, to find expression in the religion of their children.

More important than these demographic number games so popular among contemporaries is the fact that the question of whether marriages between Jews and other Breslauers were "Christian" or "Jewish" cannot do justice to the plurality of identities among parents no less than children. Especially children of intermarriages

---

[60]Marsha Rozenblit has made a similar argument for Vienna; *Jews*, p. 129.

[61]*Statistische Mittheilungen aus den deutschen evangelischen Landeskirchen, 1880–1897*, Stuttgart 1883–1899; 1900–1909, Stuttgart 1902–1927 (for the years 1880–1925); *Kirchliches Jahrbuch für die evangelischen Landeskirchen Deutschlands* 56 (1929), p. 90 (for 1926 and 1927).

[62]USC, Standesamt Breslau I, 9 Feb. 1922 (No. 137); the marriage licence notes the religion of the children and that Gertrud Springer left the Breslau syngagogue congregation in 1941. For further information on the children, USC, Geburtsregister, Standesamt Breslau III, 1926, no. 250 and 1927, no. 1196.

often hesitated to consider themselves unambiguously as either "Christian" or "Jewish." When the son of a Jewish-Christian couple who had been baptised as Protestant had to write a school essay on "What I Know about My Ancestors" at the age of sixteen in 1929, he noted proudly that he was a "hybrid of nations and races".[64] In the everyday life of these families, Jewish and Christian became inextricably entwined. Even children who were nominally raised as Christians often participated at family gatherings of their Jewish relations.[65] Being Jewish remained a meaningful option for the three children of Lola Landau and Armin T. Wegner. Addressing his daughter Sybille as "My child! My little Jewess!" Armin Wegner urged her to defend both her *Judentum* and *Deutschtum* when she entered school.[66]

For some Jews, choosing a Gentile spouse represented the ultimate break with Jewish tradition. For others, it constituted one variety of what has been termed situational ethnicity, a concept that emphasises the high degree to which ethnicity is bound to social situations. Although for intermarried Jews their Jewishness was more problematic and fragile than for other Jews, it may well have been important and meaningful to them in some situations, such as family gatherings or religious celebrations, whereas in others it was not. Certainly their Jewishness was a new and unfamiliar sight and as such a disturbing phenomenon to both Jewish and Gentile observers, but it was also one of many ways in which to be Jewish in early twentieth-century Breslau.

As long as research into Christian-Jewish marriages analyses them exclusively in the context of radical assimilation, it cannot do justice to this aspect of the relationship between Jews and other Germans. Unlike conversion, mixed marriage cannot be equated with a rejection of Judaism. Jewish men and women who married Christian partners were experimenting with new forms of Jewish identity – gropingly and searchingly, perhaps, but in general successfully. Before the turn of the century, it was primarily lower-middle-class and lower class Jews who entered mixed marriages. However, with the emergence of the "New Woman" around 1900, the numbers of Jewish middle-class sons and daughters choosing to marry Christians rose, although the Jewish-Christian marriage remained primarily a lower-class and lower-middle-class phenomenon. Among the middle-class, the choice of a partner remained integrated into a system of strategic marriage alliances in which religious boundaries were not crossed, be it among Jews, Protestants or Catholics.

That the number of intermarriages rose considerably in Bismarckian Breslau and especially after the turn of the century indicates that relations between Jews and other Breslauers could be casual and intimate. Jewish-Gentile sociability was not limited to semi-public spaces (such as associations) and did not end at the doorstep. Neighbourly or collegial contacts between Jews and other Breslauers could develop into friendships, love affairs, long-term relations, or even marriages. The fact that Breslau intermarriage rates quadrupled between the 1870s and the early 1920s suggests that the city's social life offered ample opportunities to meet and mingle across

---

[63]The remarks that follow are based on *Breslauer Statistik* vol. 15, 4 (1884), p. 140; vol. 22 (1903), p. 89*; vol. 27 (1909), p. 151; vol. 33 (1914), p. 78*.
[64]Helmut Krüger, *Der halbe Stern: Leben als deutsch-jüdischer "Mischling" im Dritten Reich*, Berlin 1993, pp. 10–11.

religious and ethnic divides. Like so many other aspects of Europe's multicultural and multiethnic heritage, we must, to borrow Prasenjit Duara's felicitous phrase, rescue the history of intermarriages from the nation.[67] The story of marriages between Jews and other Breslauers cannot be told within frameworks that continue to be indebted to the modernist ideal of purity and homogeneity. Rather, it is best understood within transcultural emplotments of turn-of-the century European history that employ unfamiliar terms such as diasporas, borderlands, hybridity, and multiculturalism.[68]

[65]On the following, see especially Meiring, *Mischehe*, pp. 129–138.
[66]Landau, *Vergessen*, p. 274.
[67]Prasenjit Duara, *Rescuing History from the Nation: Questioning Narratives of Modern China*, Chicago 1995.
[68]See John R. Gillis, 'The Future of European History', *Perspectives: American Historical Association Newsletter* 34,4 (April, 1996), p. 5; Samuel Moyn, 'German Jewry and the Question of Identity. Historiography and Theory', *LBI Year Book XLI* (1996), pp. 291–308; Shulamit Volkov, 'Minderheiten und der Nationalstaat. Eine postmoderne Perspektive', in *Geschichte und Emanzipation. Festschrift Reinhard Rürup*, eds. Michael Grüttner et al., Frankfurt 1999, pp. 58–74.

Telling Ethnic and Gender History Together: A Comment

BY DAGMAR HERZOG

The project of bringing together ethnic and interethnic history with gender history in fruitful and mutually illuminating ways has gone through several stages since the 1980s. One early and indispensable move was to emphasise the double burden experienced by those who occupied the disempowered poles of more than one power inequity; African-American women and Jewish women were the subjects of some of the most significant of these studies. Another important move was to think about the parallel exclusions of blacks, Jews and women from the Enlightenment ideal of universal equality. Although the Enlightenment, and indeed also the French Revolution, held out the promise of equality and liberty for all, the supposedly universal, abstract, rights-bearing individual was initially imagined – depending on geographical context – as a (white, Christian) man. When they sought to claim equality for themselves, blacks, Jews and women were each in turn, and repeatedly, rebuffed on the grounds of their "difference" from the imagined norm.

Particularly in the late 1980s and early 1990s, and at least partially under the influence of poststructuralist thinking about language in the broadest sense as a system of meaning-making through differentiation, scholars moved towards a growing understanding of both the instability and the mutual constitutiveness of different categories of identity. For anyone who has been paying attention to trends in the fields of Modern European and especially U.S. history it has become standard operating procedure to take note of and analyse the ways in which, depending on the concrete historical situation being discussed, class, gender, race, sexuality and/or ethnicity served to construct each other. We have become acutely aware, for instance, that not just class but also classifications of ethnicity and race fundamentally shaped who came to be counted as a lady (or in some cases even as a woman) and who did not, and whose manhood was or was not in doubt; we are more and more attuned to how much ideological labour has gone (and still goes) into making identity categories appear coherent.[1] In the German

---

[1] For some recent examples of conceptually path-breaking work, focused on race and gender relations in the U.S., but definitely also relevant for other geographical contexts, see: Evelyn Brooks Higginbotham, 'African-American Women's History and the Metalanguage of Race', in *Signs* vol. 17, No.2 (1992), pp. 251–274; Gail Bederman, '"Civilization," the Decline of Middle-Class Manliness, and Ida B. Wells's Anti-Lynching Campaign', in *Radical History Review*, 52 (Winter 1992), pp. 5–30; Ann duCille, 'The Unbearable Darkness of Being: "Fresh" Thoughts on Race, Sex, and the Simpsons', in Toni Morrison and Claudia Brodsky Lacour (eds.), *Birth of a Nation'hood: Gaze, Script, and Spectacle in the O.J. Simpson Case*, New York, 1997, pp. 293–338; and Kendall Thomas, '"Ain't Nothin' Like the Real Thing": Black Masculinity, Gay Sexuality, and the Jargon of Authenticity', in Wahneema Lubiano (ed.), *The House that Race Built*, New York, 1998, pp. 116–135.

and Austrian contexts, furthermore, we have also recently become more sensitive to the mutual constitutiveness of antisemitism and homophobia – a dynamic especially evident as the homo/hetero divide acquired growing salience at the turn of the nineteenth to the twentieth century.[2] And meanwhile, those occupying the dominant positions within the key oppositional pairings men/women, whites/blacks, Christians/Jews, and heterosexuals/homosexuals, have also come in for increasingly valuable critical scrutiny. Gender historians have been so busy demonstrating the centrality of gender issues to all the classic concerns of historians – from war and high politics to class formation and colonialism – that gender history is losing its distinct boundaries as a subfield. Increasingly, to do good gender history is simply to do good history.

Yet how best to theorise the multiple and intricate interconnections between ethnic and gender history has remained an open question. We often call for a greater integration of ethnic and gender history, and/or lament the absence of attention to gender in recent and ongoing work in German Jewish studies, but it seems that we have not spent adequate time articulating the ways in which different categories of analysis are connected. One of the most exciting things about the three papers presented at the panel on "Gender and the Boundaries of the Jewish Community in Nineteenth-Century Germany" is precisely how each on their own, and in juxtaposition with each other, they point the way out of some of our current conceptual impasses.

The papers are able to do that because in each case both the evidence and the arguments expand our understanding of what gender history can be about. All of the papers demonstrate the value of more capacious thinking about the fluidities of individual and group identities; all of them present evidence that complicates conventional assumptions about where to locate the dividing line between the public and the private realms; and all of them deal with phenomena – family life, friendship, associational life, romantic longing, imaginary identifications – whose impact on identity formation is profound and which need urgently to be made more analytically visible.

Each of these thought-provoking papers pushes against the available ways of thinking about nineteenth-century German Judaism. In each case the richness of the papers also prompts the reader to want to know more about a number of the topics that are being addressed. For example, in the case of Deborah Hertz's paper on 'The Lives, Loves, and Novels of August and Fanny Lewald, the Converted Cousins from Königsberg', it would be interesting to hear a fuller discussion of why the term "self-hatred" may not be the best descriptor for the special pain of the narrator in August Lewald's novel. What might some better terms be? How can we distinguish the kinds of comments about his fellow Jews that this character makes from other kinds of

---

[2]See Sander L. Gilman, 'Sigmund Freud and the Sexologists: A Second Reading', in Roy Porter and Mikulas Teich (eds.), *Sexual Knowledge, Sexual Science: The History of Attitudes to Sexuality*, Cambridge 1994, pp. 323–349; Daniel Boyarin, 'Freud's Baby, Fliess's Maybe: Homophobia, Anti-Semitism and the Invention of Oedipus', *GLQ: A Journal of Lesbian and Gay Studies*, vol. 2, Nos. 1 and 2 (1995), pp. 115–147; Eric L. Santner, *My Own Private Germany: Daniel Paul Schreber's Secret History of Modernity*, Princeton 1996; and Dagmar Herzog, 'Psychoanalysis, History, and *My Own Private Germany*', in *History and Theory*, vol. 39, No. 1 (2000), pp. 67–76.

intra-Jewish hostilities? Secondly, with regard to both August and Fanny Lewald, it would be interesting to learn more about the broader contexts – across time and across ethnic and ideological space – for the characters' perspectives and the authors' own lived perspectives. With respect to chronology and periodisation, what are the main shifts over time in the language and terms of what is called Jewish self-hatred, which motifs move in and which move out of focus? With respect to ethnicity and ideology, how much are August's narrator's remarks about traditional Jews part of a broader intergenerational rhetoric in which young Christians are also criticising their parents?

And finally: why does August Lewald's narrator seem to show so little awareness that his historical moment is also the moment of emergence of a liberal Jewish pride movement which refused the terms on which Gentiles had condescended to tolerate Jews? Hertz notes that the character of Jenny's brother in Fanny Lewald's novel is based on the Jewish rights activist Gabriel Riesser who was, in addition to being a well-known politician and publicist, a leading spokesman for that liberal Jewish pride movement. But where is August's recognition that Gentile and Christian culture was not something so very great to aspire to? Or to put it another way, where is the insight into the instability and weakness of the dominant ideal? It is worth quoting Riesser himself on this point, to clarify that this perception does not depend on hindsight. In an essay from 1831, for example, Riesser dissected German Gentiles' "craven arrogance" and "pleasure in oppressing". "Only a slave-people," he remarked, "can take delight in the greater enslavement of a few; only a feeble cowardly nation can find in the contrast of a tiny number of oppressed a means for rousing its sense of self-worth, a means for stimulating it in its sickly impotence."[3] Quite aside from what we might want to notice about the interesting masculinism in this observation, it would also be helpful to know where ultimately both of the Lewalds should be placed in relationship to *this* contemporaneous Jewish perspective.

Maria Baader's paper, 'When Judaism Turned Bourgeois. Gender in Jewish Associational Life and in the Synagogue, 1750–1850', also raises crucial questions. Among other things it would be useful to learn more about class, especially about class dynamics within German Jewry and about the connections between the embourgeoisement of values and embourgeoisement in financial terms. What about associational life and religious life among poor Jews?

Baader's insistence on Jews' agency in the revitalisation of Judaism is particularly impressive; this is an extremely valuable point which just cannot be emphasised enough. However, it would still be helpful to learn more about internal debates among Jews over what the drawing-in of women into a redefined Jewish religious and cultural life meant to them. For example, it could be argued that it is also a boon for men when women are allowed more rights, or when women are included in new ways. This was already remarked upon critically at the time. I am thinking, for instance, of how in the 1840s Orthodox Jews mocked Reform Jews for their so "chivalrous" desire to "break a Talmudic lance in honor of the Jewess"; the

[3]Gabriel Riesser, 'Über die Stellung der Bekenner des mosaischen Glaubens in Deutschland: An die Deutschen aller Konfessionen' (1831), in *idem, Eine Auswahl aus seinen Schriften und Briefen*, Frankfurt 1913, quoted in Dagmar Herzog, *Intimacy and Exclusion: Religious Politics in Pre-Revolutionary Baden*, Princeton 1996, p. 135.

Orthodox critics were well aware of the possible advantages to men of this sort of self-styled male feminism.[4] It would be good to know, in short, based on the broader evidence Baader's research has been uncovering, what different constituencies at the time had to say about the new roles for women in Jewish communal life. Reconstructing these internal Jewish debates would be important as well for fleshing out Baader's own larger argument about the connections between changes in gender history and changes in Jewish history, with broad relevance for scholars in a whole range of fields. Furthermore, and perhaps most importantly for the purpose of locating intersections between Baader's and the other two papers: we need to understand better how to assess the extent to which the changes in German Judaism emerged out of impulses internal to Judaism and the extent to which they were responses to Gentile stereotypes about Jews. To this end, it would be valuable to hear more about the texture of the discussion within the Jewish community at that time about the underlying causes of these changes.

If Hertz's paper is most dramatically about painful tensions *among* Jews (although fantasies of Gentile life figure prominently in these conflicts), and Baader's paper is about creative Jewish self-renewal, Till van Rahden's paper, 'Intermarriages, the "New Woman", and the Situational Ethnicity of Breslau Jews from the 1870s to 1920s', puts the issue of interethnic relations squarely at the center of its analysis. One small question I have concerns what may or may not be a sort of weird essentialising – Occidentalising and Orientalising – going on in the Wegner/Landau love affair, both in Lola's rapturous description of Armin's face on the streetcar and in Armin's addressing of his daughter as "meine kleine Jüdin", my little Jewess. What can these moments tell us about the role of problematic stereotypes in the innermost erotic intensities of some human beings? Are there echoes here with some of the evidence Hertz discusses, and if so what do we make of that? And yet to say that there is "internalisation" of stereotypes going on would also be too simplistic, for these are stereotypes that are being loved and used, that are identity-shaping, not identity-destroying. The point is that the quotes do not just speak for themselves; more analysis is needed.

I would also like very much to hear more about changing masculinity during the period covered by van Rahden's paper. What are the male parallels – Jewish and Gentile – to the New Woman, and what does that have to do with the prevalence of interethnic marriage? For example, in view of the growing scholarship on the turn-of-the-century stereotype of the supposedly effeminate Jewish man, it would be useful to know more about whether and how that stereotype worked at the grassroots in Breslau. Was there such an imaginary figure, and if so, was he considered less sexist or more sexist? More or less sexy? Or did class-based identities supersede ethnic ones? At the same time, van Rahden's account of Jewish women within interethnic marriages becoming increasingly self-confident in insisting on Jewish childrearing is quite significant and it would be interesting to hear more about "the new Gentile man" who was comfortable with that. On a different but related note, the question

---

[4]See the critical review of Reform rabbi Samuel Holdheim's *Die religiöse Stellung des weiblichen Geschlechts im talmudischen Judenthume*, Schwerin 1846, in *Der Orient. Literaturblatt*, 20 August 1846, pp. 538–42, quoted in Herzog, *Intimacy and Exclusion*, p. 100.

of changing forms of religiosity among both Jews and Christians should be further explored. What was it about these changes that permitted intermarriage to coexist with the persistence of religious affiliations and intensities? What has happened by the late nineteenth and early twentieth century to the transformation in Judaism towards "faithification" (for want of a better term) that Baader identified? In this context one may also ask whether the happy coexistence of Jewish and Christian religious rituals within the same extended family Gad Beck describes so well in the early pages of his memoirs, *Und Gad ging zu David*, held true for Breslauers as well, and if so how van Rahden would periodise that moment of happy harmony.[5]

The contrasts between Hertz's unsettling account of August Lewald's ugly compendium of anti-Jewish complaints, Baader's analysis of the calm acceptance of the modernisation of both religious culture and gender relations, and van Rahden's inspiring stories of romantic love and self-confident maintenance of ethnic identity despite intermarriage are themselves revelatory. Reading the three papers together brings into sharp relief both the complexity of questions of individual and group identity, and the utter non-inevitability of historical developments. Considering the three papers in conjunction with one another also suggests some directions that historians of ethnic and gender relations might usefully take in the years to come. All three papers, for example, showed that ethnic group coherence is no static or self-evident matter, but rather a process in perpetual flux and elaboration. But it would be good to be even more self-conscious about this. What might it mean, for instance, to bring into German Jewish studies the feminist theorist Judith Butler's brilliant observation that a seemingly coherent identity "operates ... not as the ground of politics but as its effect"?[6] In other words, it is not that people have identities and then make politics; rather, politics are made, and out of that process identities emerge. Or, as cultural studies and ethnic studies theorist Stuart Hall put it recently, "identity is at the end, not the beginning, of the paradigm". Hall points out that what we really need to focus on are processes of identification, and those do not work in any simple or obvious way.[7] As Hertz's paper, for example, shows, individuals do not always feel they fit where they supposedly belong, while for others – as van Rahden's paper demonstrates – a sustaining identity can come precisely from the boundary-crossing between groups. Meanwhile we should not assume that the only individuals we need to explain are the ones who are somehow peculiar, who seek to break free from identification with the group to which they are designated to belong, that is, the overt malcontents or cheerful hybrids. We should be just as interested in making visible the emotional mechanisms by which people stay within groups, for that, too, is not at all self-evident. The collective self-transformations Baader documents are important testimony to the fact that staying within a group does not mean staying the same as one once was.

Along related lines, one of the most stimulating aspects of these papers is the way they draw our attention to as yet inadequately understood elements of identity. As

---

[5] Gad Beck, *Und Gad ging zu David: Die Erinnerungen des Gad Beck 1923 bis 1945*, Munich 1997, pp. 14–16.
[6] Judith Butler, 'Gender Trouble, Feminist Theory, and Psychoanalytic Discourse', in Linda J. Nicholson (ed.), *Feminism/Postmodernism*, New York 1990, p. 339.
[7] Stuart Hall, 'Subjects in History: Making Diasporic Identities', in Lubiano, pp. 291–292.

sexuality scholar Eve Sedgwick articulated more eloquently than anyone else, the terms race, class, and gender (as well as ethnicity, religion, nationality, and sexual orientation) remain exceedingly crude tools with which to describe the actual similarities and differences between people. Sedgwick is also the theorist who has worked most effectively to make visible the important issue of vicarious identifications.[8] Not only is it the case that people really do have the most profound emotional investments in things and people they are "not supposed" to have, it is also a fact that we do not as yet have a fully satisfactory language for talking about this phenomenon. The key theoretical point here is that it is precisely those more elusive aspects of identity that have not been elevated to the status of official identity categories (belief or disbelief in a particular conception of God, for example, or a specific experience of loss and bereavement, or a distinctive personal style) which are often of greatest relevance and consequence in permitting identifications.

In addition to taking the variegated quality of human subjecthood seriously, we would also do well to reconsider our conventional assumptions about where the lines are drawn between private and public domains and between self and other. It is probably no coincidence that once again it is scholars of sexuality and race who seek to map out new conceptualisations of these issues. Lauren Berlant argued most persuasively in the context of theorising contemporary sexual politics that the usual casual invocations of the terms public and private completely underdescribe the ways those realms are continually mediated to each other. Among other things, Berlant asks, "How can we think about the ways attachments make people public, producing transpersonal identities and subjectivities, when those attachments come from within spaces as varied as those of domestic intimacy, state policy, and mass-mediated experiences of intensely disruptive crises?"[9] Although the reference to mass media clearly makes this a comment about the present, the relevance for studies of the past is still strong. Along similar lines, Thomas Holt argued in the context of analysing racism in the U.S. that we are still a long way from understanding what he – building on the work of Leora Auslander and Alf Luedtke – calls "the levels problem", the need to think through more clearly the "linkage between the social and the individual" (particularly in view of the insight that "the formation of the human subject" always already involves the social, and indeed "that the individual self is already imbricated in the social"). Holt calls for historical work that will "elaborate the nexus between the remote or global levels of [human] experience and its immediate or micro-local expressions". Or as Auslander, cited by Holt, puts it: "The challenge ... is to simultaneously grasp the manifestations of the very large and abstract structures and transformations of the world in the small details of life ... and, finally, to analyse how concrete and mundane actions in the everyday may themselves transform the abstract structures of

---

[8]Eve Kosofsky Sedgwick, 'Introduction: Axiomatic', in *Epistemology of the Closet*, Berkeley 1990, pp. 22–26, 61–63.

[9]Lauren Berlant, 'Intimacy: A Special Issue', in *Critical Inquiry*, vol. 24, No. 2 (Winter 1998), p. 283. See also Lauren Berlant and Michael Warner, 'Sex in Public', *ibid.*, esp. p. 560; and for a lucid exposition of related points see also again Butler, pp. 333–337.

polity and economy."[10] Each of the three papers offers ample evidence of these phenomena of public-private and structural-individual imbrication, and can help us deepen our understanding of how global-local nexuses work.

Just as we are still seeking clearer ways to talk about selves and contexts, identificatory processes, as well as motives and possibilities for individual and collective transformations, it seems we are also searching for a more refined conceptual apparatus for talking about the intricate mechanisms by which developments in gender history are connected with and mediated to and through developments in ethnic and interethnic history. Scholars of gender relations in particular – and among them especially Joan Scott, Mary Poovey, Ann Stoler, and again Berlant – have spent a great deal of time thinking about how struggles over one set of power relations are displaced onto or allegorised in another set, often by circuitous, overdetermined and even internally contradictory routes.[11] My own work shows just how messy and confusing this can be: conflicts over sexual matters can have consequences for interethnic relations, as when intra-Christian conflicts over sex and marriage in the 1830s shaped non-Jewish liberals' attitudes about Jewish rights in the 1840s.[12] But conversely, intergenerational tensions over the meanings and lessons of the Holocaust became displaced onto and played out in the realms of sexual politics in the 1960s–1970s.[13] This circuity and complexity of interconnection between ethnic and gender history is also what all of the papers discussed here, explicitly and implicitly, are getting at. But it is also evident how difficult this quickly becomes. In Baader's paper, for instance, changes in Judaism made possible changes in gender relations; in van Rahden's work, the causation is opposite: changes in gender roles made possible changes in Judaism. Baader says that Jews renegotiated what it meant to be Jewish, that they reconfigured Judaism and thereby also revolutionised the gender system of Jewish culture. Van Rahden, by contrast, demonstrates that we cannot understand the way intermarriages coexisted with ongoing commitments to Judaism without understanding the reorganisation of gender relations symptomatically grouped

---

[10]See Thomas C. Holt, 'Marking: Race, Race-Making, and the Writing of History', in *American Historical Review*, vol. 100, No. 1 (February 1995), pp. 7–13. This section draws extensively on Luedtke's pioneering work in "daily life history", esp. Luedtke, 'Polymorphous Synchrony: German Industrial Workers and the Politics of Everyday Life', in *International Review of Social History*, 38 (1993), Supplement, pp. 39–84. Note in this context also the remarks of Anthony Appiah about the Self-Other binarism being "the last of the shibboleths of the modernizers that we must learn to live without", for: "if there is a lesson in the broad shape of this circulation of cultures, it is surely that we are all already contaminated by each other." Kwame Anthony Appiah, 'Is the Post- in Postmodernism the Post- in Postcolonial?', in *Critical Inquiry*, vol. 17, No. 2 (Winter 1991), p. 354.

[11]See Joan Wallach Scott, *Gender and the Politics of History*, New York 1988; Joan Wallach Scott, *Only Paradoxes to Offer: French Feminists and the Rights of Man*, Cambridge, MA 1996; Mary Poovey, *Uneven Developments: The Ideological Work of Gender in Mid-Victorian England*, Chicago 1988; Ann Laura Stoler, 'Carnal Knowledge and Imperial Power: Gender, Race, and Morality in Colonial Asia', in Joan Wallach Scott (ed.), *Feminism and History*, Oxford 1996, pp. 209–266; and Lauren Berlant, 'Collegiality, Crisis, and Cultural Studies', in *Profession 1998* (New York: Modern Language Association of America, 1998), pp. 105–116.

[12]Dagmar Herzog, 'The Rise of the Religious Right and the Recasting of the "Jewish Question": Baden in the 1840s', in *LBI Year Book XL* (1995), pp. 185–208.

[13]Dagmar Herzog, 'Sexuelle Revolution und Vergangenheitsbewältigung', in *Zeitschrift für Sexualforschung*, vol. 13, No. 2 (June 2000), pp. 87–103; and Dagmar Herzog, '"Pleasure, Sex, and Politics Belong Together": Post-Holocaust Memory and the Sexual Revolution in West Germany', in *Critical Inquiry*, vol. 24, No. 2 (Winter 1998), pp. 393–444.

under the heading of the emergence of "the New Woman". It is precisely this kind of complexity that needs to be spelled out more clearly.

In sum, with more self-conscious reflection on the instability and non-inevitability of identities and the mutual imbrication of public and private realms, and with sustained attention to the extraordinary variety of ways the daily intimate relations between men and women, men and men, women and women, parents and children, are also absolutely key places for the playing out of the "great dramas" of politics, religion, and minority-majority relations, gender history can be made freshly relevant for German Jewish studies, and for many other fields. By focusing on associations, on friendships, on attachments and rivalries, on yearnings and animosities, and on families and ethnic enclaves as sometimes objects of desire but sometimes also emotionally unsafe places, these papers move us in enormously productive directions.

Response to Dagmar Herzog

BY DEBORAH HERTZ

Reading Dagmar Herzog's comment, I feel somewhat like Monsieur Jourdain in Jean Baptiste Molière's satiric play *Le Bourgeois Gentilhomme*. The play mocks a boorish businessman who hires a tutor to help him achieve greater cultivation. Monsieur Jourdain is told by his tutor that "one can only express oneself in prose or verse". The would-be gentleman concludes to his great surprise that "Upon my word! I have spoken prose for more than forty years without knowing anything about it."[1] Like the *bourgeois gentilhomme*, after reading Herzog's comment I now realise that August and Fanny Lewald, as well as the converts in their novels, all had fluid, unstable identities. Neither I nor the two Lewalds used Herzog's terms to describe their identities or the identities of their fictional characters. But Herzog's language is absolutely appropriate and helps us raise our analysis to a higher level.

Herzog's attention to the complexity of how individuals created their identities may help us to gain more insight into some of the dilemmas faced by the Jews of modern Germany. For too long historians working though this history have assumed that particular individuals or groups had either a Jewish *or* a German identity. Rigid bipolar interpretations have long been favoured in our field, long before the Nazis made it just about impossible to feel Jewish and German at the same time.[2] Thus the readers of the *Leo Baeck Institute Year Books* may well be the prime patients for even a small dose of Herzog's postmodern tonic.

Herzog's point here encourages us to ponder the apparent paradox that Jewish identity could continue to evolve after conversion. The paradox is explained in part by the fact that conversion became ever more popular in the nineteenth century. Obviously, in these decades religion was becoming a less salient way of interpreting the world for many educated Jews in Europe. Before the nineteenth century, when many converts were motivated by spiritual experiences, it would be logical to see baptism as the confirmation of an inner shift in religious feelings. But in nineteenth-century Germany few converts seemed to have been in search of new religious experiences when they left Judaism. A subtle mix of pragmatic and cultural attractions seems to have motivated most of the converts in this setting. Thus it was probably quite rare for a new Christian religious identity to replace a previous Jewish identity. When converts remained in close contact with their still-Jewish friends and relatives, they could continue to feel Jewish loyalties and sentiments. Indeed in his *Memoiren*

---

[1] Jean Baptiste Molière, *The Plays of Molière in French with an English Translation*, vol. 7, Edinburgh 1907, p. 117.
[2] For a welcome change of paradigm, see Paul Mendes-Flohr, *Germans and Jews: A Dual Identity*, New Haven 1999.

eines Banquiers August Lewald introduced us to a fictional setting where familial and social ties were maintained between converts and Jews.

Sometimes the Jewish identity that remained after conversion was stormy, tormented, and unhappy. Indeed, one of the thorniest issues facing all those who seek to interpret post-conversion Jewish identities is to decide whether the notion of self-hatred is at all a useful concept for this project. Herzog has not made my life any easier by asking me to clarify whether this label should be applied to August Lewald. Herzog's question is important, and indeed it is so important that it is the only one of her many stimulating questions I can address in this short piece. For if we decide to use the term for either Lewald or his fictional personae, we are surely opening the door to using self-hatred to describe other Jews or former Jews. But we must proceed with caution, because the legacy of the term self-hatred and the debate around its use are frankly rather daunting.

Before we even begin to look at the variety of possible terms, we need to recount which of Lewald's own behaviors come under consideration for our task. Lewald himself had few if any still-Jewish friends. Apart from *Memoiren eines Banquiers* he rarely published fiction or journalism either about Jews or for Jewish causes. He certainly never pleaded the case for Jewish civil rights in his writings. As for the narrator he created in his novel, we have seen that he pretends not to be Jewish in public settings. He thinks *Unser Verkehr* is a "masterpiece". Lewald's narrator is unhappy with the prayer style, the food, and in general what he calls the "muck and pain" of Jewish life. And he pities rather than admires Jews who dedicate themselves to religious reform.

How shall we describe Lewald and his narrator? Let us begin by considering some less loaded terms than self-hatred. First, let us examine the distinction Hannah Arendt made between a pariah and a parvenu. With this juxtaposition she was seeking to contrast Jews excluded from desirable Christian circles to Jews who found an entrée into such circles. We might describe Lewald and his narrator as struggling to leave the pariah status and become successful parvenus. Lewald himself appears to have been a successful parvenu, whereas his narrator was still a pariah when he died in the shipwreck and bequeathed his Spanish banker friend his life story.[3]

Another possible way to think about Lewald or his narrator would be as non-Jewish Jews. To Isaac Deutscher, who coined this term, a non-Jewish Jew might be seen by others as Jewish. But on the inside the non-Jewish Jews possessed no inner Jewish identity and was committed to universal human liberation rather than specifically Jewish aims.[4] Deutscher's label has the advantage that very little moral or psychological judgement is embedded in it. Deutscher's approach can inspire us to create other non-judgmental labels for Jews like Lewald. Thus we might also describe Lewald as post-Jewish or secular. In our day Lewald might fit well in the Ethical Culture movement, whose members espouse universal humanistic values and are not affiliated with Judaism or any version of Christianity. Alternatively, the contemporary usage of "unaffiliated Jew" might also be appropriate for Lewald and his narrator.

---

[3]For a useful discussion of Arendt's interpretation of Rahel Varnhagen see the introduction in Liliane Weissberg, (ed), *Rahel Varnhagen: The Life of a Jewess*, Baltimore and London 1997, pp. 3–69

[4]See Isaac Deutscher, 'The Non-Jewish Jew', in *The Non-Jewish Jew and Other Essays*, London 1968.

Finally, before considering the self-hatred label, there is the notion of anti-Judaism. With this term we mean a critique of the Jewish religion, as distinct from a critique of those born into the Jewish people. Anti-Judaism should not be equated with anti-Jewish sentiments or actions. Here the term Jewish, as opposed to the term Judaism, is to be understood in ethnic rather than in religious terms. An anti-Judaism stance might be held by a Jew or by a Christian. Take an example from Lewald's era. In 1793, the philosopher Johann Fichte published an essay about the French Revolution. In the essay Fichte argued against granting Jews in Prussia civil rights, as they had received in 1791 in France. He wrote: "To give them the rights of citizenship, I see no other way than to cut off all their heads in one night and to replace them with others in which there is not a single Jewish idea."[5] Shall we call Fichte's statement antisemitic, or should we call it an expression of anti-Judaism?

We might interpret Fichte's demand to mean that Jewish values, languages and loyalties should be left behind by Jews when they became citizens of a nation state. Perhaps Fichte meant that only Jews who had shed Jewish ideas in the widest sense should be allowed to join the larger body politic. Fichte's formulation actually remained salient and controversial for many decades after he published these words in 1793. Indeed it was precisely Fichte's model for Jewish citizenship that would later anger German Zionists who came of age at the time of the First World War. One of Gershom Scholem's critiques of the assimilation pattern in Germany was that Jews so rarely articulated any Jewish values, images, or ideas when they created works of secular high culture.[6] As for Lewald and perhaps his narrator as well, we could describe them as anti-Judaism with ease.

Regarding Fichte's sentence as an expression of anti-Judaism rather than describing it as being antisemitic means that we consider Fichte as not *really* calling for the actual murder of real Jews. According to this interpretation the term antisemitism should be reserved for views that call for discrimination or worse towards those born Jewish, whatever ideas are in their heads. The notion of anti-Judaism is in fact especially important in the study of converts. By their conversion they gave an outward sign of a willingness to shed Jewish beliefs. If, as in the Nazi era, converts were not truly accepted as new Christians, it was because the dominant form of discrimination then and there was ethnic and not religious.[7]

Mention of the ubiquitous term antisemitism brings us at last to the self-hatred label. For self-hatred is often understood as internalised antisemitism. First introduced by Theodor Lessing in his book *Der jüdische Selbsthass* (1930), the term was frequently used during the 1960s in the United States.[8] In that setting the label was applied by various pundits, most of them Jewish, to describe other Jews who inter-

---

[5]The essay in question was 'Beiträge zur Berichtigung der Urtheile des Publicums über die französische Revolution', in J.H. Fichte (ed.), *Johann Gottlieb Fichtes sämmtliche Werke*, vol. VI, Berlin 1845 (reprint. Berlin 1965), p.247–248.
[6]See Gershom Scholem 'Against the Myth of German-Jewish Dialogue'; 'Once More: The German-Jewish Dialogue'; and 'Jews and Germans' in idem, *Judaism in Crisis: Selected Essays*, New York 1976, pp. 61–92.
[7]For more details see my 'The Genealogy Bureaucracy in the Third Reich', in *Jewish History*, 11 (Fall 1997) pp. 53–78.
[8]On Lessing see Lawrence Baron, 'Theodor Lessing: Between Jewish Self-Hatred and Zionism', in *LBI Year Book XXVI* (1981), pp. 323–40.

married, or who were critical of Israeli policies, or even those who disdained to follow Orthodox practice.[9] Used in this way the term is indeed "a clumsy term of attack, intended to foreclose, not open discussion".[10] But in recent years academics across a range of disciplines have brought new respectability to the notion of self-hatred. The prime rescuer of the term is Sander Gilman with his publication in 1986 of *Jewish Self-Hatred: Anti-Semitism and the Hidden Language of the Jews*.[11] Since Gilman's pioneering study, several biographers of major intellectuals of Jewish descent have freely described their subjects as having been self-hating.[12]

But problems persist. Todd Endelman convincingly argued that the term is often used far too broadly, confusing self-criticism of Jewish practices with description of a feeling state that is "pathological, disturbed, and unhealthy."[13] Endelman suggested that historians avoid trying to discover the inner individual psychology of self-hatred. We rarely have sufficient evidence for such claims either way. Even in cases where we do, it is difficult to draw conclusions about large groups based on evidence from a few individuals. Endelman notes that historians would do better to explore how inner feelings were expressed in published words or actions. He argued that historians need to look at the external conditions in various settings which made self-hatred more or less common. Endelman concluded that in the modern era, public statements of self-loathing were much more common among Jews in Germany than such public statements were in Britain. He argues that the cause of the pervasive public displays of self-hatred in the combination of external prejudice and internal lack of Jewish practices, loyalties, and identities.[14]

This certainly rings true for the narrator of the *Memoiren eines Banquiers*. Certainly, many of the comments Lewald's narrator makes could be interpreted as self-hating. Yet his tone reveals anguish at his hard choices. The quotations Endelman uses tend to be more arrogant, more snide and more confident than the words of Lewald's narrator. We might choose to distinguish between the narrator's self-hating statements and his post-Jewish statements. As self-hating we could class his remarks about *Unser Verkehr*, and as post-Jewish we could class his remarks about Jewish services and Jewish food.

One key issue to consider is who the intended and the real readership was for a possibly self-hating document. A good test of whether public statements criticising other Jews were self-hating or not might be whether more Jewish Jews found the comments offensive. For instance Fanny Lewald's family was apparently aghast at Heine's *Die Bäder von Lucca*. Unfortunately, here we cannot enter into a sustained analysis of whether Lewald's friend Heine was self-hating, in life or in literature.

---

[9]Here I follow closely the narrative provided by Todd Endelman in his 'Jewish Self-Hatred in Britain and Germany', in Michael Brenner, Rainer Liedtke and David Rechter, (eds.), co-ordinated by Werner E. Mosse, *Two Nations: British and German Jews in Comparative Perspective*, Tübingen 1999 (Schriftenreihe wissenschaftlicher Abhandlungen des Leo Baeck Instituts 60), pp. 331–363.
[10]Endelman, p. 331.
[11]Sander Gilman, *Jewish Self-Hatred: Anti-Semitism and the Hidden Language of the Jews*, Baltimore 1986.
[12]For some recent biographies with this theme, see David Cesarini, *Arthur Koestler: The Homeless Mind*, New York 1998; Elzbieta Ettinger, *Rosa Luxemburg: A Life*, Boston 1990: and Frank E. Manuel, *A Requiem for Karl Marx*, Boston 1997.
[13]Endelman, pp. 334–335.
[14]Endelman, p. 340.

What is fascinating in the Lewald case is to think about the significance of Lewald's decision to embed the narrator's critiques in a novel which is pretending to be a memoir. After all it is his narrator who expresses the critiques of Jewish life, not Lewald in his own name. He must have wanted to distance himself from the content of his narrator's views.

In sum we must retain our caution about the label self-hating. We could try out the idea that in life August Lewald was a post-Jewish parvenu, whereas his fictional narrator is at times a self-hating pariah. At the end of the day we may choose to admit that our choice of terms often seems inescapably subjective. For those who value ethnic particularity will usually label those who give up much to achieve assimilation as self-hating. And those who value assimilation will tend to sympathise with the understandable anguish of individuals who seek to change their life position in a setting where owning their ethnic heritage was felt as more painful than denying that identity.

Response to Dagmar Herzog

BY MARIA BENJAMIN BAADER

Dagmar Herzog proposes to employ conceptual frameworks of gender studies in order to create a Jewish scholarship in which the interlinking of gender history, ethnic and interethnic history opens new perspectives. I suggest, in fact, that the transformation of the gender order of Jewish society and the transition of Judaism from a Torah- and *Halakhah*-centered culture to a culture of bourgeois religiosity constituted closely interrelated processes. In my brief contribution, I describe the new forms of bourgeois Judaism, without however relating these changes to the social and economic position of the men and women involved in the new trends. As is well established, in the first half of the nineteenth century German Jews as a group achieved an outstanding degree of upward social mobility. While German Jewry consisted of a largely impoverished population in the late eighteenth century, by the mid-nineteenth century at least half of Jewish families had attained a middle-class income level and formed part of the commercial middle class as well as of the *Bildungsbürgertum*. In 1870, mass poverty had disappeared in the Jewish communities and German Jews had overwhelmingly adopted middle-class value systems and life-styles.[1]

The cultural embourgeoisement of German Jewry, although connected to the socio-economic upward mobility of the Jewish population, followed its own dynamics and often preceded the rise of the income level of individuals and families. In fact, the social and cultural formation to which scholarship refers as *bürgerlich*, and into which German Jews began to integrate and acculturate during the Enlightenment, in itself did not constitute a class in any meaningful sense of the word. Bourgeois ideas and practices in Germany rather emerged in the second half of the eighteenth century in the *Bildungsbürgertum*, a heterogenous stratum of civil servants, Protestant pastors, teachers, professors, doctors, lawyers – and Jews, – who often socialised with segments of an enlightened nobility. Thus, scholars such as Jürgen Kocka propose to understand nineteenth-century German *Bürgertum* not as a class but as a culture, unified by a shared belief-system in personal achievement hon-

---

[1]Avraham Barkai, 'The German Jews at the Start of Industrialisation: Structural Change and Mobility 1835–1860', in Werner E. Mosse, Arnold Paucker, and Reinhard Rürup (eds.), *Revolution and Evolution: 1848 in German-Jewish History*, Tübingen 1981 (Schriftenreihe wissenschaftlicher Abhandlungen des Leo Baeck Instituts 39), pp. 123–156; Monika Richarz (ed.), *Jüdisches Leben in Deutschland. Selbstzeugnisse zur Sozialgeschichte 1780–1871*, Stuttgart 1976, (Veröffentlichung des Leo Baeck Instituts), pp. 31–44; Jacob Toury, 'Der Eintritt der Juden ins deutsche Bürgertum', in Hans Liebeschütz and Arnold Paucker (eds.), *Das Judentum in der deutschen Umwelt 1800–1850*, Tübingen 1977 (Schriftenreihe wissenschaftlicher Abhandlungen des Leo Baeck Instituts 37), pp. 139–242; Jacob Toury, *Soziale und politische Geschichte der Juden in Deutschland 1847–1871. Zwischen Revolution, Reaktion und Emanzipation*, Düsseldorf 1977, pp. 100–114.

oured by economic success, in associations of equals, in *Bildung* and aesthetics, and in specific standards of family life and gender roles. Bourgeois culture, however, was not class-neutral, but bound to the social strata of the *Bildungsbürgertum* and the middle classes, to economic change, and ultimately to capitalism. Bourgeois ideology and bourgeois life forms certainly possessed class-related dimensions.[2]

For German Jewry, social and cultural embourgeoisement included a rising socio-economic position as well as the adaptation of bourgeois cultural norms and life styles with the goal of civil emancipation. The transformation of Jewish culture from a coherent social and religious system delineated by *Halakhah*, Talmud Torah, and the fulfillment of *mitsvot* to a modern, bourgeois religion formed part of this process. As Jews embraced bourgeois values, beliefs, and practices, they left the framework of rabbinical Judaism behind, while they aspired to integration and upward mobility. The mutual-aid and benevolent associations I have described illustrate this dynamic. Overwhelmingly, they were not founded by Jewish men and women who had already reached a comfortable socio-economic status. Rather, the founders and members of sick-care societies, for instance, organised themselves in mutual-aid associations in order to create a financial stability that could serve them as springboard for socio-economic improvement. For members of these societies, sickness no longer needed to lead to financial crisis and business failure.

In the "youth ḥevrot" of the late eighteenth century, such as the *Gesellschaft der Freunde* in Berlin, sons from well-off local families mixed with greater numbers of young Jewish men who had arrived in the urban centres more recently. These associations provided their members with opportunities to put novel ideas such as delayed burials into practice and they allowed unmarried men to assume leadership positions from which they were barred in the established ḥevrot. For those members, however, who possessed no strong family ties in the city, a mutual-aid society fulfilled a more basic function too. Their residence rights were precarious; they lacked family support; and in case of sickness or need they depended on communal charity boards which only reluctantly assisted foreigners and newcomers.[3] Thus, membership in a mutual-aid society could play a significant role in helping a young and ambitious person to succeed economically and professionally. Certainly, joining a voluntary association required having enough financial strength to pay the admission fee as well as the weekly or monthly contributions. In the founding statutes of the *Ḥevrat Esrat Nashim* (Association for the Help of Women) of Emmendingen, a small community in Baden, the women reported that they had wanted to create a benevolent society for some time, but had been short of the necessary funds. Finally, in 1823, the Jewish women of Emmendingen established an association that bore some of the features of an early modern *ḥevrah* and which distributed charity to non-members, but that also guaranteed its members financial support and personal care in sickness.[4]

---

[2] Jürgen Kocka, 'Bürgertum und Bürgerlichkeit als Probleme der deutschen Geschichte vom späten 18. zum frühen 20. Jahrhundert', in Jürgen Kocka (ed.) *Bürger und Bürgerlichkeit im 19. Jahrhundert*, Göttingen 1987, pp. 21–48.
[3] Ludwig Lesser, *Chronik der Gesellschaft der Freunde in Berlin*, Berlin 1842, pp. 6–7; Jacob R. Marcus, *Communal Sick-Care in the German Ghetto*, Cincinnati 1947, pp. 146–148; Jacob Rader Marcus, 'The Triesch Hebra Kaddisha', *Hebrew Union College Annual*, 19 (1945–46), pp. 175–176.
[4] Central Archives for the History of the Jewish People, Jerusalem, Ga/S 222.5.

The men and women who established the Jewish mutual-aid societies of the late eighteenth and the early nineteenth centuries did not belong to the destitute members of the Jewish communities. Very often, however, they had just stepped out of poverty into a still unstable but more hopeful existence. By founding and joining voluntary associations with mutual-aid functions, German Jews expressed their aspiration to further improve their economic situation and to raise their social status. In this project of embourgeoisement, economic considerations and the desire to embrace contemporary German notions of respectability and civil virtues were closely connected. As I have pointed out above, religious ideas of reward in the afterlife and the fulfilment of the *mitsvot* of Talmud Torah, *zedakah*, and *gemilut hesed* had stood at the centre of early modern *ḥevrot*. In modern Jewish voluntary societies, these values moved into the background. A passage from the 1832 annual report of the Hamburg *Verein für Krankenpflege* (Association for Sick Care) makes this shift explicit:

> ... the light of a better enlightenment and nobler civilization has spread since then [the foundation of older institutions of benevolence]; in the place of a welfare that seeks retribution is the higher love of mankind and only foundations which owe their inception to the latter can now render to the educated and refined individual [*Gebildeter*] what was formerly rendered by compassion alone.[5]

The claim to be *gebildet*, and Enlightenment or bourgeois concepts of honour played an important role in the new type of mutual-aid societies such as the *Verein für Krankenpflege*. In fact, the members of mutual-aid societies and of benevolent associations did not perceive themselves as either recipients nor as dispensers of charity. Rather, they declared themselves to be committed to the ideal of *Menschenliebe* and to the welfare of humanity. A member of a modern Jewish voluntary association asserted his or her position as a useful and worthy member of German society. *Menschenliebe*, often also designated by its Greek term, philanthropy, involved assisting one another in mutual-aid societies as well as aiding members of the larger Jewish community in benevolent associations without mutual-aid features. The boundaries between these two types of associations were fluid, and all voluntary societies engaged in improving the social and economic position of Jews on the individual and the communal level. Mutual-aid and benevolent associations formed part of the strategy of embourgeoisement, when, in the last decades of the eighteenth and the first half of the nineteenth centuries, German Jews pursued economic stability, social upward mobility, and cultural integration.

During this process, Jewish culture underwent a dramatic transformation, and women moved from the marginal position that they had held in rabbinical Judaism to new prominence. Women, however, did not receive "more rights". Neither in the *halakhic* legal framework nor in nineteenth-century German society were women emancipated. Rather, women gained greater recognition in Jewish society and culture, because the legal and cultural system that had determined their inferior status, namely *halakhic* Judaism, ceased to be the axis of Jewish life. Women continued to be exempt from the duty of performing active, time-bound *mitsvot*, most important among them the obligation of reciting standardised Hebrew prayers three times a

---

[5] Quoted in Rainer Liedtke, *Jewish Welfare in Hamburg and Manchester, c. 1850–1914*, Oxford, 1998, p. 193.

day.⁶ In nineteenth-century Germany, women could not be counted in a Jewish prayer quorum, the *minyan*, and they could not form women's prayer groups which would qualify as *minyanim*. Women did not gain access to the culture of rabbinical learning and they could not participate in the reading of the Torah in the synagogue. Thus, Jewish women remained excluded from the religious practices that had stood at the centre of Jewish associational life and Jewish worship for centuries.

Even Reform Judaism did not cede to women the privileges and duties that men held in rabbinical Judaism, and the efforts of some Reform leaders to emancipate women within *Halakhah* did not lead to success. After Abraham Geiger had called for the removal of "the distinction between the duties for men and women" and for the end of "the spiritual minority of women" in 1837, the rabbinical conference of 1845 considered a petition by Samuel Adler that demanded equality of women in Jewish law. Yet, rather than taking a vote on the petition, the assembly appointed a Committee on the Religious Status of Women in Judaism.⁷ Over the course of the following year, the committee prepared a report in which it suggested to fully emancipate women within *Halakhah*. Most importantly, it advocated including women into the obligation of performing time-bound *mitsvot* and to count them in a *minyan*. The following rabbinical conference in Breslau, however, again failed to discuss the question of women. The report on the position of women in Judaism was read out at the assembly and then published with the proceedings of the rabbinical conferences.⁸ Nevertheless, the report and Samuel Adler's petition, which formed the only full-length Hebrew treatise in the publications of the three rabbinical conferences, proved to have virtually no impact. For more than a century after the rabbinical conferences in Germany, the demand of emancipating women in *halakhic* Judaism did not attract any support.⁹

Women's status in modern Judaism rose without women being emancipated in the *halakhic* or any other legal or formal framework. Rather, women moved from a marginal to a more central position within Jewish society and culture, because *Halakhah* lost the all-defining power it used to hold in Jewish society. Cultural and religious practices other than rabbinical learning and Hebrew prayer began to take precedence, and these practices included women. Synagogue devotion that emphasised emotionalised religiosity, morality, and *Bildung* addressed women as well as men; religious instruction that treated Judaism as a faith rather than a legal and scriptural sys-

---

⁶See Rachel Biale, *Women and Jewish Law: An Exploration of Women's Issues in Halakhic Sources*, New York 1984, pp. 10–43, here in particular p. 17.
⁷Abraham Geiger, 'Die Stellung des weiblichen Geschlechts in dem Judenthume unserer Zeit', in *Wissenschaftliche Zeitschrift für jüdische Theologie*, 3 (1837) pp. 1–14, quoted here after Gunther W. Plaut, *The Rise of Reform Judaism: A Sourcebook of its European Origins*, New York 1963, p. 253; *Protokolle und Aktenstücke der zweiten Rabbiner-Versammlung, abgehalten in Frankfurt am Main, vom 15ten bis zum 28ten Juli 1845*, Frankfurt 1845, pp. 167–170, 334–348, and 379–381.
⁸*Protokolle der dritten Versammlung deutscher Rabbiner, abgehalten zu Breslau vom 13. bis 24. Juli 1846*, Breslau 1847, pp. 253–266, here p. 253; the report was also published in *Literaturblatt zum Israeliten des 19. Jahrhunderts*, 1 (1846), pp. 206–212, and in *Die Reform des Judenthums*, 1 (1846), pp. 65–69 and 73–75.
⁹Only Samuel Holdheim attempted to pursue the issue further. See Samuel Holdheim, *Die religiöse Stellung des weiblichen Geschlechtes im talmudischen Judentum. Mit besonderer Rücksicht auf eine diesen Gegenstand betreffende Abhandlung des Dr. Adler*, Schwerin 1846; and David Philipson, *The Reform Movement in Judaism*, 2nd ed., New York 1931, p. 473.

tem included boys and girls; female voluntary societies arose when Jewish associations no longer focused on Talmud study and Hebrew prayer, but embraced bourgeois ideas of philanthropy and civil responsibility. This transformation of religious and cultural values took place in modern Orthodoxy as well as in Reform Judaism.

Orthodox leaders defended Jewish ritual law as immutable, opposed changes in *Halakhah*, and ridiculed Reformers for attempting to base women's emancipation on Talmudic sources. Modern Orthodoxy, though, also embraced notions of Judaism being essentially a system of moral codes in which women as mothers and wives played an outstanding role. As I have outlined above, Orthodox synagogues too became sites of decorous, emotionalised devotion.

Even though Orthodoxy rejected the introduction of organs and confirmation ceremonies in the synagogue, concepts of edification and *Bildung* displaced the exclusively male culture of Talmud study and Hebrew prayer circles in German Orthodoxy as it did in the Reform movement. Different from Reform rabbis who amended *Halakhah* in order to adapt Judaism to life in modern society, and different from many German Jews who simply dropped ritual observance as well as practices of prayer and religious study, modern Orthodox Jews remained committed to *halakhic* observance. In German Orthodoxy, bourgeois sensibilities of religion and new modes of worship did not entirely replace *halakhic* Judaism. The novel values and practices of nineteenth-century religiosity, however, decentered the culture of rabbinical learning and Hebrew prayer which had stood at the heart of a male-defined Judaism for centuries also in the Orthodox Jewish community. This fundamental shift occurred in nineteenth-century German-Jewish society as a whole, regardless which stance Reform or Orthodox Jews took towards Talmudic law and observance. And women's marginal position in Jewish culture and society subsided in all segments of German Jewry, exactly because the increased integration that women enjoyed in modern Jewish culture was not an emancipation of the female sex within *Halakhah*. Rather than receiving rights and being granted equal status with men, women gained greater inclusion in Jewish religious culture, because the practices that had excluded them – rabbinical learning and Hebrew prayer – and that had marked their inferiority and marginality in Jewish society, ceased to define the parameters of Jewish religion and Jewish social organisation.

Thus, the restructuring of the gender order in Jewish society formed part of a larger process of transformation that comes into focus when we explore the positions of men and women in Jewish culture. In my investigation, the gender analysis operates as a prism which allows us to examine a whole range of complex historical dynamics anew. The emergence and proliferation of Jewish women's voluntary associations in the late eighteenth and early nineteenth centuries, for instance, beautifully illustrates the interaction of internal and external forces in the process of modernisation of Jewish society. The character of male Jewish societies changed as their members adopted the value system of their environment. Enlightenment and bourgeois ideas of self-help, civil responsibility, and philanthropy displaced the traditional concept of the *ḥevrah* as primarily a prayer and study circle. This development is in line with our understanding of German Jewry's acculturation to the surrounding society. Jewish women, however, began to found their own associations without having non-Jewish models. The emergence of significant numbers of female Jewish voluntary societies rather resulted from changes *within* Jewish culture, while this culture adjusted to nineteenth-century German society. The marginal position of women in Jewish associational life waned, because access to and exclusion from Talmud Torah and Hebrew prayer no longer regulated the gender organisation in the German-Jewish community.

Here, patterns of a social order peculiar to Jewish society and cultural and political impulses from German gentile society coalesced into one historical phenomenon: the formation of female Jewish voluntary associations. By investigating this development, we are able to discern how gender history interrelates with the dynamics at work in the interplay between inner-Jewish processes and the impact of external cultural trends.

Herzog suggests that "we are ... searching for a conceptual apparatus for talking about the intricate mechanisms by which developments in gender history are connected with and mediated to and through developments in ethnic and interethnic history".[10] Indeed, while for feminist scholarship the categories of race and ethnicity have proved to be extremely rich loci for investigating the workings and constructions of gender, the study of gender in Jewish historiography still is a largely uncharted terrain. We possess a substantial body of scholarship on gender in biblical and rabbinical Jewish society, and issues of gender and Jewish identity in the twentieth century are fairly well explored.[11] Moreover, scholars have investigated how gender, antisemitism, and conceptions of the Jewish body have been historically interrelated.[12] Paula Hyman analysed the gender dynamics in the history of Jewish assimilation in modern Europe and in North America, and Marion Kaplan laid new ground

---

[10] Comment, Dagmar Herzog.

[11] For biblical and rabbinical history see Susan Ackerman. *Warrior, Dancer, Seductress, Queen: Women in Judges and Biblical Israel*, Garden City, NY 1998; Mieke Bal, *Death and Dissymetry: The Politics of Coherence in the Book of Judges*, Chicago 1988; Daniel Boyarin, *Carnal Israel: Reading Sex in Talmudic Culture*, Berkeley – Los Angeles – Oxford 1993; Howard Eilberg-Schwarz, *God's Phallus and Other Problems for Men and Monotheism*, Boston 1994; Judith Hauptman, *Rereading the Rabbis: A Woman's Voice*, Boulder, CO 1997; Tal Ilan, *Jewish Women in Greco-Palestine: An Inquiry into Image and Status*, Tübingen 1995; Ilana Pardes, *Countertraditions in the Bible: A Feminist Approach*, Cambridge, MA 1992; Miriam Peskowitz, *Spinning Fantasies: Rabbis, Gender, and History*, Berkeley 1997; Michael L. Satlow, *Tasting the Dish: Rabbinic Rhetorics of Sexuality*, Atlanta 1995; For modern Jewish history see Sylvia Barack Fishman, *A Breath of Life: Feminism in the American Jewish Community*, New York 1993; Harry Brod (ed.), *A Mensch among Men: Explorations in Jewish Masculinity*, Freedom, CA 1988; Susan Glenn, *Daughters of the Shtetl: Life and Labor in the Immigrant Generation*, Ithaca 1990; Moshe Hartman and Harriet Hartman, *Gender Equality and American Jews*, Albany 1996; Susannah Heschel (ed.), *On Being A Jewish Feminist: A Reader*, New York 1983; Jessica Jacoby, Claudia Schoppmann, and Wendy Zena-Henry (eds.), *Nach der Shoa geboren. Jüdische Frauen in Deutschland*, Berlin 1994; Marion Kaplan, *Between Dignity and Despair: Jewish Life in Nazi Germany*, New York 1998; Melanie Kaye/Kantrowitz and Irena Klepfisz (eds.), *The Tribe of Dina: A Jewish Women's Anthology*, Montpellier, VT 1986; Bonnie J. Morris, *Lubavitcher Women in America: Identity and Activism in the Postwar Era*, Albany 1998; Carol Rittner and K. John Roth (eds.), *Different Voices: Women and the Holocaust*, New York 1993; Naomi Seidman, *A Marriage Made in Heaven: The Sexual Politics of Hebrew and Yiddish*, Berkeley 1997; Sidney Stahl Weinberg, *The World of our Mothers: The Lives of Jewish Immigrant Women*, Chapel Hill – London 1988; Barbara Swirski and Marilyn Safir (eds.), *Calling the Equality Bluff: Women in Israel*, New York 1991.

[12] Jonathan Boyarin and Daniel Boyarin (eds.), *Jews and Other Differences: The New Jewish Cultural Studies*, Minneapolis 1997; Sander Gilman, *Freud, Race, and Gender*, Princeton, NJ 1993; Sander Gilman, *Jewish Self-Hatred: Anti-Semitism and the Hidden Language of the Jews*, Baltimore – London 1986; George Mosse, *Nationalism and Sexuality: Middle-Class Morality and Sexual Norms in Modern Europe*, Madison 1985.

in her study on the Jewish family and Jewish culture in Imperial Germany.[13] From the European Middle Ages to the second half of the nineteenth century, however, Jewish historical scholarship has not only been slow to advance our knowledge of women's lives and women's experiences, but conceptually sophisticated work on the gender organisation of Jewish society remains rare.[14] While Herzog proposes to retell Jewish history as a history in which gender history permeates ethnic and interethnic history, I argue for treating Jewish society and culture as a formation that has negotiated its distinctiveness, not last, by its gender organisation. In fact, the scholar of Talmudic culture, Daniel Boyarin, has laid out a model for theorising gender differentiation and gender hierarchy in Jewish society, in which he reads the Jewish concepts of masculinity and femininity as "queer" in relation to Western models of gender identities. Jews deployed this "queerness", according to Boyarin, as a strategy of cultural resistance. Moreover, Boyarin created a narrative of how the gender order of Jewish culture transformed, when Jews integrated and acculturated to modern society.[15]

Certainly, gender identities and gender identifications are highly specific to their cultural context, and the social categories of man and woman emerge in a multifarious interplay of factors internal and external to a culture. In Jewish history, we have just began to understand that gender constitutes a conceptual language for examining some of the central questions of our field anew. Or, as the historian Joan Scott formulated it more than a decade ago:

> Gender, then, provides a way to decode meaning and to understand the complex connections among various forms of human interaction. When historians look for ways in which the concept of gender legitimizes and constructs social relationships, they develop insight into the reciprocal nature of gender and society and into the particular and contextually specific ways in which politics constructs gender and gender constructs politics.[16]

If we succeed to apply this programme to Jewish history, if we explore how gender, the character of Jewish textual traditions and of Jewish social organisation, and the social, political, and cultural frameworks of gentile societies were implied into each other, an entirely new dimension of Jewish history may evolve.

---

[13]Paula E. Hyman, *Gender and Assimilation in Modern Jewish History: The Roles and Representation of Women*, Seattle – London 1995; Marion A. Kaplan, *The Making of the Jewish Middle Class: Women, Family, and Identity in Imperial Germany*, New York – Oxford 1991.

[14]For exceptions see Dianne Ashton, *Rebecca Gratz: Women and Judaism in Antebellum America*, Detroit 1998; Michael Galchinsky, *The Origin of the Modern Jewish Woman Writer: Romance and Reform in Victorian England*, Detroit 1996; Deborah Hertz, *Jewish High Society in Old Regime Berlin*, New Haven – London 1988; Dagmar Herzog, *Intimacy and Exclusion: Religious Politics in Pre-revolutionary Baden*, Princeton, NJ 1996; Renee Levine Melammed, *Heretics of Daughters of Israel?: The Crypto-Jewish Women of Castile*, New York 1999; Ada Rapoport-Albert, 'On Women and Hasidism: S.A. Horodecky and the Maid of Ludmir Tradition', in Ada Rapoport-Albert and Steven J. Zipperstein (eds.), *Jewish History: Essays in Honor of Chimen Abramsky*, London 1988, pp. 495–525; Stampfer, pp. 187–211; Chava Weissler, '"For Women and for Men Who Are Like Women": The Construction of Gender in Yiddish Devotional Literature', in *Journal of Feminist Studies in Religion*, 5 (1989), pp. 7–24; Chava Weissler, *Voices of the Matriarchs: Listening to the Prayers of Early Modern Jewish Women*, Boston 1998; Shaul Stampfer, 'Gender Differentiation and Education of the Jewish Woman in Nineteenth-Century Eastern Europe', in Antony Polonsky (ed.), *From Shtetl to Socialism: Studies from Polin*, London – Washington 1993.

[15]See note 1of the author's main article.

[16]Joan Wallach Scott, *Gender and the Politics of History*, New York 1988, pp. 45–46.

Response to Dagmar Herzog

BY TILL VAN RAHDEN

Dagmar Herzog's comment provides us with an extremely stimulating outline for the future study of intermarriages and raises a number of important questions. I agree with almost everything she says. Any substantive answer would require considerable research and I very much look forward to historical studies addressing Herzog's research agenda. Thus, my aim here is not to answer her questions but to suggest possible research avenues that might eventually lead to answers or at least help us pose a somewhat different set of questions.

I found Herzog's comment especially important because it helps us understand the limits of my own approach. In my essay, I employed the methodology of quantitative social history – an approach which provides us with limited evidence about the micro-dynamics of identity-shaping and identity-destroying within the everyday life of Jewish-Christian marriages. As Victor Turner noted many years ago, however, although numbers can never tell us the whole story, they are useful because they point us to places where we can look for narrative traces that will help us understand the many and possibly contradictory histories of marriages between Jews and other Germans.[1] Future scholars of Jewish-Christian marriages would therefore do well to bear in mind that the vast majority of Jews and other Germans who decided to intermarry did not belong to the middle classes. Rather than situating the history of intermarriages within the history of the middle classes we should try to interpret them within the history of conceptions and practices of gender, sexuality, religion and ethnicity among the lower-middle and the working classes.

A second reason why we are still a long way from answering Herzog's questions is that our knowledge about the history of Protestant-Catholic marriages is even more limited than that about marriages between Jews and Christians in Imperial and Weimar Germany. Only a comparative perspective will be able to cover the many facets of a highly complex phenomenon and will enable us to identify the differences and similarities between Protestant-Catholic and Jewish-Christian marriages and thereby to understand the unique nature of marriages between Jews and other Germans. It is, for example, remarkable in itself that contemporary parlance sometimes used two different concepts, such as "*gemischte Ehen*" versus "*Mischehen*", in order

---

[1]Victor Turner, *Vom Ritual zum Theater. Der Ernst des menschlichen Spiels*, 1989; Frankfurt 1995, p. 95: "Obwohl ... Zählen und Messen auch etwas Irritierendes hat ... erzählten mir diese Zahlen [die Turner im Rahmen seines Feldaufenthaltes bei den Ndembu gesammelt hatte] wenn nicht eine Geschichte, so doch wenigstens, wo sich Geschichten finden ließen.".

to distinguish between the two forms of intermarriage.[2] Tilmann Bendikowski's literally path-breaking essay on Protestant-Catholic marriages reaches a very similar conclusion as I did in my study of marriages between Jews and other Breslauers. In contrast to contemporary observers that often depicted these marriages as symbols of religious misery and moral decay, those who intermarried as well as their children often remembered their families as rather happy and successful.[3]

Another reason for our inability to analyse the history of Jewish-Christian marriages has to do with the fact that our knowledge about everyday relations between Jews and other Germans between the mid-nineteenth century and the 1930s remains limited until today. We are left with the task of excavating how gender, class, as well as antisemitism affected the cultural and social interactions that occurred in the structures of everyday life. It is only within the broader context of relations between Jews and other Germans generally that we can do justice to the history of Jewish-Christian marriages.

---

[2]See Kerstin Meiring, *Die Christlich-Jüdische Mischehe in Deutschland 1840–1933*, Hamburg 1998, pp. 29–33, esp. p. 32.
[3]Tilmann Bendikowski, 'Großer Kampf um kleine Seelen. Konflikte um konfessionelle Mischehen im Preußen des 19. Jahrhunderts', *Jahrbuch für Westfälische Kirchengeschichte* 91 (1997), pp. 87–108, esp. p. 93.

Philosophy, Religion and Politics

The Gesellschaft zur Förderung der Wissenschaft des Judentums, *1902–1915**

BY HENRI SOUSSAN

By the end of the nineteenth century, German Jewry found itself in the midst of an "organisational renaissance".[1] The most prominent and widely researched organisation representing this trend was the *Centralverein deutscher Staatsbürger jüdischen Glaubens*, founded in 1893. Another organisation, however, which has so far escaped the attention of academic evaluation, the *Gesellschaft zur Förderung der Wissenschaft des Judentums*,[2] belongs in this category. The *Gesellschaft* was something of an enigma, insofar as it was an organisation which attempted to breach the political boundaries of Jewish status and bring Jewish scholarship into German society; it represented, and was an active participant in, the "coming-out" of Jewish studies into the German academic arena. This fact alone makes the *Gesellschaft* unique. The desire to establish Jewish studies on this level had been repeatedly disappointed, and the point at which an organisation was prepared to take on this task marked a crucial episode in the history of German Jewry. The first part of this article concerns itself with the main reasons for the foundation of this society, as well as the goals that the founders had set themselves. The second part outlines the main activities and discusses the organisational structure, and the approach applied by the society to achieve those goals.

Within the sphere of Jewish adult education, a significant indication of the organisational renaissance was an increased interest in Judaism, manifesting itself mainly in the successful establishment of nationwide *Vereine für jüdische Geschichte und Literatur*. The driving force behind the popular-scientific *Literaturvereine* movement was Gustav Karpeles, editor of the *Allgemeine Zeitung des Judentums*. By 1900, the *Vereine* "consisted

---

*This paper is based on my Ph.D. thesis, to be submitted soon, entitled *The Gesellschaft zur Förderung der Wissenschaft des Judentums*. I would like to thank my supervisors, Professor Julius Carlebach and Professor Edward Timms, for their sympathetic editorship and encouragement in the preparation of this article. Professor Julius Carlebach passed away as this article went into production. Since the beginning of my research, Professor Carlebach had given me inestimable support in my endeavors. He was and is a source of great inspiration. Space limitations force me to restrict the topic to the years leading up to the First World War, although the *Gesellschaft* officially existed until November 1938. 1915 is, however, a very appropriate place to end the article, as it marked a definite close of era in the organisation's development; the majority of the founders had passed away, turning the leadership over to a new generation of board members.
[1] Peter Pulzer, *Jews and the German State. The political History of a Minority*, Oxford and Cambridge, MA 1992, p.13.
[2] Recently Dieter Adelmann has written, on part of the activities of the *Gesellschaft*. See idem, 'Die 'Religion der Vernunft' im 'Grundriss der Gesamtwissenschaft des Judentums' ', in *Tradition and the Concept of Origin in Hermann Cohen's Later Work*, ed. by Helmut Holzney, Gabriel Motzkin, and Hartwig Wiedebach, Hildesheim 2000.

of 12,149 members in 131 societies".[3] Success notwithstanding, Karpeles lamented the poor state of *Wissenschaft des Judentums*, which he expressed in the *Literarische Jahresrevue* which prefaced each volume of the national organisation's *Jahrbuch*. His main criticism was directed against the widening gulf between scholarship and the education of the people:

> The academic study of Judaism has taken on a position of respect; it has achieved much more than its enemies will ever admit. But one facet... remains neglected within this great work: the education of the [Jewish] people... Scholarship has secluded itself more, particularly in the last decades, from any contact with people than [ever] before...[4]

The seeming disparity between an organisational renaissance and a crisis of learning can be explained in the following terms: renewed interest and enthusiasm for Jewish studies highlighted the fact that the field of Jewish studies had little or nothing to offer the non-scholar. German-Jewish scholarship had reached a state of confusion in which research was extremely specialised and particularist. This phenomenon was not limited to the Jewish sphere but was part of the general impression of a "crisis of learning" at the German universities, which began to emerge roughly ten years before the turn of the nineteenth century.[5] At that time, German scholars had begun to voice their concerns about a widening gap between learning and the practical application of learning (*Lehre und Leben*), as well as the ever-increasing specialisation of studies. Eduard Spranger scornfully called contemporary learning a "sum of specialised disciplines", in which positivist theory reigned supreme. In his jubilee article of 1928, Ismar Elbogen focuses on the same issue:

> The scholarly research of Judaism is a child of the nineteenth century ... it had its great time, but did not remain at the pinnacle ... covering new territory, buoyed by the pleasure of the explorer, the scholars laid discovery upon discovery without processing the results. Bricks were heaped upon one another, but there was never a building, seldom [even] a harmoniously toned mosaic. One detail after another, but seldom [ever] a summary. Specialisationism siezed the upper hand, [it was] lost in minutiae ... The educated, even the theologians, barely took notice of this work..."[6]

Karl Jaspers went a step further, maintaining that German academics felt a justifiable sense of guilt, insofar that they had failed as "bearers of tradition". This last statement suggests that it was the inherent responsibility of the intellectuals to educate the public. The entire intellectual climate at this time was saturated with *fin de siècle* pessimism of varying degrees.

This feeling of dissonance between learning and practice as well as the super-specialisation of subject matter within German academia was as acutely felt by Jewish scholars, who had effectively formed the same kind of academic inner sanctum,

---

[3]Jacob Borut, '*Vereine für jüdische Geschichte und Literatur* at the End of the Nineteenth Century', in *LBI Year Book XLI* (1996), p. 89.
[4]Gustav Karpeles, 'Literarische Jahresrevue', in *Jahrbuch für jüdische Geschichte und Literatur*, 2 (1899), pp. 21–25.
[5]See also Fritz Ringer, 'Academics in Germany', in *LBI Year Book XXXVI* (1991), p. 208.
[6]Ismar Elbogen, 'Zum Jubiläum der Gesellschaft zur Förderung der Wissenschaft des Judentums', in *Monatsschrift für Geschichte und Wissenschaft des Judentums* 72 (1928), p. 3.

albeit exterior to the universities. To be sure, the divide between *Lehre und Leben* may have been experienced even more strongly by Jewish theologians than by their non-Jewish counterparts, as this dichotomy was a new phenomenon in the Jewish world, bringing with it the disorientation inherent in any new cultural phenomenon. It must be pointed out that roughly until the Mendelssohnean era, Jewish study went hand in hand with the practice of the religious precepts to a greater or lesser degree. From the moment that Jews began to integrate into the larger society, and to adopt the *Weltanschauung* of their German environment, many began to abandon the adherence of stringent religious practice, leaving behind them knowledge about their own religion and culture. Within a very short time, perhaps two generations, familiarity with Jewish religion and its practice shifted from the majority, if not the entirety, to the Jewish clergy and a few Jewish theologians. The obligation to "enlighten" the Jewish population, estranged from its own culture and religion, was thus a burden assumed from a very early stage, and reflects the statement by Jaspers regarding the responsibility of scholars noted above.

The lack of awareness about Jewish religion and culture was initially addressed by the *Literaturvereine*. Karpeles purported to overcome this obstacle to ethnic identity by creating a link between scholarly research and the general public, in presenting the public with results of research.

> The ... Jew often faces abuse and ridicule of his beliefs and culture and even internalises those prejudices, and ... does not know that they are based on a corruption of historical facts and is at a loss at how to react to them. This dearth of knowledge was countered by the *Literaturvereine*.[7]

The matter of the transmission of knowledge was not a purely 'academic' problem for Jewish activists, but carried with it a more lofty ideology. The lack of the most basic knowledge about Judaism and Jewish culture was believed to strengthen the attraction towards Christianity and was felt to be directly responsible for conversions from Judaism to the Christian faith, particularly among the more highly educated.

This impression was not unfounded. In absolute numbers, conversions to Christianity between 1870 and 1900 numbered approximately 11,000. This might seem a negligible percentage, considering a Jewish population of over 500,000, but the fact that university educated Jews accounted for 36% of all conversions meant that they were overrepresented by about ten to one.[8] Two additional points are noteworthy: first, that the period of increased antisemitism at the end of the century caused a rise in conversions, and second, that over two thirds of the conversions at this time were to Protestantism.[9] The latter can be at least partially explained by the numerous publications brought out by Protestant theologians at the turn of the century, which extolled the virtues of Protestantism/Christianity, while diminishing the worth of Judaism.

---

[7]Rabbi Eschelbacher in *Jahrbuch für jüdische Geschichte und Literatur*, 7 (1904), p. 2.
[8]Eduard Baneth, lecturer at the *Lehranstalt für die Wissenschaft des Judentums* and one of the founders of the society mentions as one of the main concerns and goals of the new organisation: 'to stop the horrendous loss of educated Jews' and holds that one of the duties of the *Wissenschaft des Judentums* is to missionise amongst Jews in order to prevent conversion to Christianity. cf. *Protokoll der konstituierenden Sitzung der Gesellschaft zur Förderung der Wissenschaft des Judentums*, 2 November 1902.
[9]cf. Michael A. Meyer (ed.), *Deutsch-Jüdische Geschichte in der Neuzeit*, vol. 3, Munich 1997, p. 20f.

Perhaps the most significant publication creating awareness of the need for a central organisation to further and strengthen *Wissenschaft des Judentums* was the work of the prominent theologian Adolf von Harnack. *Das Wesen des Christentums* was based on a series of lectures he had given at the University of Berlin, and published in 1899. Harnack was the acknowledged leader of Protestant theology in Germany, and the popular style of his book won it an enormous audience. Judaism was presented as an elementary stage on the path to Christianity, which liberated Judaism from its ritualistic and nationalistic attributes, while rabbinical Judaism was seen as a step down, a primitive and superstitious form of worship. The book highlighted the disadvantaged situation of Jewish scholarship versus Protestant scholarship, disregarding research of rabbinical literature and painting "a dark Jewish background in order to make the picture of Jesus shine ever brighter". In short, the book was a devastating attack on Judaism because it portrayed the Jewish religion as being intrinsically unworthy, beyond any possible correction. The Jewish newspapers of the time reflected the depressed mood which pervaded the aftermath of *Das Wesen des Christentums*, condemning the inability of Jewish scholars to find a swift and adequate reply. Although the most famous, von Harnack's was not the only publication of this type to be brought out at that particular time. This attitude was particularly demoralising to Jewish scholars, as they came from the exalted forum of the university. The belief in the necessity of university recognition led to the conclusion that a concerted effort to revitalise *Wissenschaft des Judentums* within an organisational framework would help to achieve this goal.[10]

Further, the resurgence of antisemitism in the 1880s forced the realisation that the work of Jewish scholars in the various fields of *Wissenschaft des Judentums* had not resulted in a more objective treatment of the Jewish religion by theologians.[11] Anti-Jewish prejudice still prevailed, and the optimistic belief that antisemitism would gradually diminish began to give way to a more realistic appraisal of the current socio-political atmosphere, and awareness that a concerted effort was required to counteract it.

Much more, therefore, was required of Jewish scholars than of their Christian counterparts. The requirement of addressing the obstacles of transmission of knowledge, antisemitism, and socio-academic recognition vexed *Wissenschaft des Judentums*, which still had no central body to mobilise it. The *Vereine für jüdische Geschichte und Literatur* could satisfy the need for a comprehensive *Wissenschaft des Judentums* only to a limited extent. While it is true that they were instrumental in spreading knowledge to the larger public, they were not in the position to develop or support any new research, but merely to disseminate that which already existed.[12] Karpeles himself realised that this major challenge could not be met by the *Vereine*:

> Especially in our time, when the most vital religious questions are on the agenda – when Judaism is attacked, slandered, and degraded on a daily basis in newspapers and journals,

---

[10]See Alfred Jospe, 'The Study of Judaism in German Universities before 1933', in *LBI Year Book XXVII* (1982) pp. 295–323.
[11]The battle for scholarly attention was described by Christian Wiese in his recently published work *Wissenschaft des Judentums und protestantische Theologie im wilhelminischen Deutschland*, Tübingen 1999 (Schriftenreihe wissenschaftlicher Abhandlungen des Leo Baeck Instituts 61).
[12]Martin Philippson in *Jahrbuch für jüdische Geschichte und Literatur*, 7 (1904), p. 4.

even by men who claim to be knowledgable and are accepted as such – it is precisely in this time that an educational description of Judaism has become a pressing necessity. Our educated vacillate between Haeckel and Harnack, between the all-negating natural science and a Protestant theology which degrades Judaism; between one world view which deconstructs any religion, and another one which lowers Judaism to the level of a national cult.[13]

Increased Jewish activism, as a reaction to the social and political antisemitism of the 1880s, played a significant role in the realisation of the need for a systematic and comprehensive approach to *Wissenschaft des Judentums*.

In the summer of 1902, the *Allgemeine Zeitung des Judentums* printed an appeal (*Aufruf*) to create a new association to further *Wissenschaft des Judentums*. Rabbi Leopold Lucas, then Rabbi of Glogau in Silesia, is closely connected to the appeal for this new organisation, believing it would remedy many of the problems that Jewish scholarship was suffering in Germany. Lucas had tried for some time to gain support for such an organisation. In 1897, during his studies in Berlin, he had given a lecture to this effect at the *Akademischer Verein für Jüdische Geschichte und Literatur*.[14] Born in 1872 in Marburg, Lucas had studied history, oriental studies and philosophy under Heinrich von Treitschke, Adolf von Harnack, Eduard Zeller, and Bernhard von Kugler in Berlin and Tübingen. At the same time he attended the *Lehranstalt für die Wissenschaft des Judentums* in Berlin, where he received his rabbinical ordination in 1898. In 1899 Leopold Lucas took the position of Rabbi of Glogau, succeeding Benjamin Rippner (1842–1898).

Even after his move to Glogau, Lucas never gave up his intention of creating a Jewish scholarly organisation. He presided over the local *Verein für jüdische Geschichte und Literatur* and lectured on numerous occasions. In the winter of 1900 to 1901, the first external lecturer to give a talk to the *Literaturverein* in Glogau was Martin Philippson, and the following year both Philippson and Gustav Karpeles lectured in Glogau.[15] As both men were influential in German-Jewish affairs and were on the board of the *Verband der Literaturvereine*,[16] one can assume that Lucas approached them with plans for his new organisation.[17] In particular Martin Philippson's support was of great importance for the success of the project. The oldest son of Ludwig Philippson and a historian by training, he was then chairman of the *Deutsch-Israelitischer Gemeindebund* and member of the Curatorium of the *Lehranstalt für die Wissenschaft des Judentums* in Berlin.[18]

---

[13]Gustav Karpeles in *Jahrbuch für jüdische Geschichte und Literatur*, 5 (1902), pp. 20–22.

[14]Founded in 1882 at Berlin University, this student organisation was the first German fraternity to include the word 'Jewish' in its title, a statement of bold self-identification in the antisemitic atmosphere pervading the university. Placards announcing initial meetings were defaced or torn down. See *LBI Year Book VIII* (1963), pp. 267–268.

[15]'Bericht über die Tätigkeiten der Vereine' in *Jahrbuch für jüdische Geschichte und Literatur* 5 (1902), p. 25.

[16]Since 1898 Martin Philippson contributed the 'Jahresrückblick' and Gustav Karpeles the 'Literarische Revue' in the *Jahrbuch für jüdische Geschichte und Literatur*.

[17]Leopold Lucas intensified his attempts to found the *Gesellschaft* since the end of 1901. See L. Lucas, 'Zum 25jährigen Bestehen der Gesellschaft zur Förderung der Wissenschaft des Judentums', in *Monatsschrift für Geschichte und Wissenschaft des Judentums* 71 (1927), p. 321.

[18]See Johanna Philippson, 'The Philippsons, a German-Jewish Family', in *LBI Year Book VII* (1962), p. 110f.

After having received the support of Philippson, Lucas prepared his first appeal, which had to be retracted due to resolute opposition from the German-Jewish scholarly establishment. Rabbi Lucas had criticised the poor state of the discipline in too outspoken a manner.[19] Nevertheless, the idea had excited sufficient interest for a new appeal to be drafted, which was composed by Hermann Cohen in close collaboration with Lucas.[20] This appeal was signed by many of the leading scholars of the *Wissenschaft des Judentums*, which led to the founding of the *Gesellschaft* on 2 November 1902.[21]

The founders emphasised that their activity was not understood to be an attempt to segregate Jews from the larger German culture. Rather, the *Gesellschaft* was to be viewed as a temporary step on the road to acceptance in German society, their ultimate goal. This thought is carefully expressed by Martin Philippson, who justifies the need to create Jewish organisations within German society as a reaction to the segregationist and anti-Jewish politics of many German *Vereine*, from which Jews were often excluded. According to this view, the creation of Jewish organisations was actually a means of reducing tension between Jews and non-Jews:

> One should understand us correctly. Of course we do acknowledge with joy all that we owe to German culture ... But we nevertheless are conscious of our human dignity and pride, and each offence hurts us and arouses in us justified anger. We are absolutely convinced that the future reconciliation (*Wiederannäherung*) of the Christian majority to the Jews...will happen much easier and sooner if the Jews keep to themselves for the time being, thereby eliminating any reason for social frictions and complaints of Jewish obstrusiveness.[22]

A similar tone is discernible in the *Aufruf*. The goal of furthering *Wissenschaft des Judentums* was a necessity for the self-preservation of the Jewish people and as much a "holy duty to our religion", as it was a "duty to science and general [German] culture". The position that the investigation of Jewish culture and religion was in the interest of humanity in general and German society in particular was maintained.

On the other hand, the appeal entitled '*An unsere Glaubensgenossen*' was clearly addressed to Jews only, and translated into English and Hebrew in order to secure support from Jews in other countries. This underlined the conviction that the time for scholarly cooperation in the field of *Wissenschaft des Judentums* had yet to arrive. Although Christian theologians had contributed to the scholarly investigation of Judaism, particularly in the area of Bible criticism, their prejudiced viewpoint had prevented them from a neutral, value-free examination of post-exilic Jewish literature.

The authors of the *Aufruf* recognised correctly that the social climate indicative of academic acceptance was extremely unfavorable. Zunz's dictum that the Jewish (social) Ghetto would only fall after the Ghetto of *Wissenschaft des Judentums* has been dismantled still stood central to the founding ideology of the *Gesellschaft*. However, the founders were realistic enough to recognise that a development such as their

---

[19]See *Allgemeine Zeitung des Judentums* 66, No. 45 (7 November 1902), p. 532. To date the author has been unsuccessful in locating this important document.
[20]Lucas, 'Zum 25jährigen Bestehen der Gesellschaft zur Förderung der Wissenschaft des Judentums', in *Monatsschrift für Geschichte und Wissenschaft des Judentums* 71 (1927), p. 321.
[21]See *Allgemeine Zeitung des Judentums* 66, No. 34 (22 August 1902), pp. 398f.
[22]Martin Philippson, *Jahrbuch für jüdische Geschichte und Literatur*, 7 (1904), pp. 2f.

organisation envisaged would not occur in the foreseeable future[23]. They were not, as in the past, prepared to wait for this event, as the hopeful assertion that German Liberalism would give way to academic acceptance was undermined by increased antisemitism. The *Aufruf* is conspicuous for its use of a reactive vocabulary such as *"Abwehr"* and *"Verteidigung"*. This confrontational approach must be seen as part of the general trend towards "Jewish activism", intended to bolster resolve and ethnic pride.[24]

The *Gesellschaft* aimed to create an *Ersatz*-forum for the as yet unattainable university chair in Jewish Studies. The initial practical step was the drawing up of certain goals to provide a framework for the furtherance of *Wissenschaft des Judentums*. Primarily, these goals involved financial planning and investment, which effected for the first time a phenomenon we will call professionalisation. These included the financial support of promising scholars, on whose continued study and research the field of Jewish Studies depended, and the support and publication of comprehensive literature. Annual assemblies were planned for the purpose of discussing pertinent developments and coordinating organisational strategies. And a monthly journal would be published.

At the meeting of the executive board on the 21 and 22 April 1903, the society planned their most ambitious project, the *Grundriss der Gesamtwissenschaft des Judentums*. This was to be a series of scholarly works which would encompass the entire field of *Wissenschaft des Judentums*. The *Grundriss* was divided into the four categories of linguistics (*Sprachwissenschaft*), history and literary history (*Geschichtliche und literaturgeschichtliche Fächer*), systematic subjects (*Systematische Fächer*) and practical subjects (*Praktische Fächer*).[25]

The plan for this encyclopaedic project came from Gustav Karpeles, and was enthusiastically acclaimed by the members of the society. Martin Philippson called the *Grundriss* "the greatest Jewish literary enterprise in centuries".[26]

---

[23]See *Allgemeine Zeitung des Judentums* 66, No. 45 (7 November 1902), p. 532: "... die Noth der Zeit lehrt uns aber, daß diese unsere Emanzipation noch weit im Felde sein dürfte ...".
[24]Jakob Boruth, 'Der Central-Verein und seine Vorgeschichte', in *Jüdischer Almanach 1996*, p. 99.
[25]These subjects were further divided into the following sub-categories: A. Sprachwissenschaft: 1. Hebräische Sprachlehre: a.) Biblisches Hebräisch b.) Neuhebräisch; 2. Aramäische Sprachlehre; 3. Geschichte der hebräischen Sprachwissenschaft. B. Geschichtliche und literargeschichtliche Fächer: I. Biblische Zeit: 1. Einleitung in die Bibel, 2. Biblische Altertümer, 3. Geschichte des Volkes Israel bis zum babylonischen Exil, 4. Jüdisch-hellenistische Literatur (einschl. Apokryphen), 5. Geschichte der Bibelexegetischen Literatur. II. Talmudische Zeit: 1. Einleitung in den Talmud, 2. Talmudische Altertümer, 3. Geschichte vom babylonischen Exil bis zum Abschluss des Talmud, 4. Geschichte der talmudischen Literatur: a.) Geschichte der Halacha, b.) Geschichte der Haggada. III. Nachtalmudische Zeit: 1. Geschichte vom Abschluss des Talmuds bis auf die Gegenwart: a.) bis Mendelsohn b.) seit Mendelsohn, 2. Wirtschaftsgeschichte, 3. Geschichte der Literatur: a.) der rabbinischen, b.) der religionsphilosophischen c.) der übrigen (poetischen, mystischen etc.) IV. Geschichtliche Hilfswissenschaften: 1. Geographie von Palästina, 2. Chronologie, 3. Quellenkunde, 4. Epigraphik, Paleographie und Numismatik. C. Systematische Fächer: 1. Systematische Theologie, 2. Ethik und Religionsphilosophie, 3. Ethik der praktischen Religionsvorschriften, 4. Apologetik, 5. Geschichte der jüdischen Religion, a.) im Allgemeinen, b.) Geschichte der jüdischen Sekten, 6. Vergleichende Religionswissenschaft: a.) Judentum und Christentum b.) Judentum und Islam. D. Praktische Fächer: 1. Praktische Theologie (einschl. Gemeindeverwaltung und Vereinswesen), 2. Homiletik, 3. Pädagogik, 4. Liturgik. See *Monatsschrift für Geschichte und Wissenschaft des Judentums* 48 (1904), pp. 60–63.
[26]Martin Philippson in *Jahrbuch für jüdische Geschichte und Literatur* 7 (1905), p. 2.

Although the project was never even close to being finished, the attempt to encompass all of Jewish scholarship within one comprehensive framework is worthy of recognition. The *Grundriss* exemplified the trend to systematise scholarship in order to present the interested lay public with readable results. Obviously this plan was only conceivable through the mutual cooperation of a great number of scholars in the field, consequently one of the main achievements for which the *Gesellschaft* can be commended. Although only nine works were ever published within the scope of the *Grundriss*, many of those produced became standard works in Jewish scholarship.

> The goal of the *Germania Judaica* [project] is to list in alphabetical order all provinces and localities within the German Empire where Jews have settled from earliest times until the Contracts of Vienna or where outstanding Jews have lived ... by briefly describing their history and achievements based on existing sources, and presenting this in an understandable form to the general reader.[27]

The decision to undertake this work, a comprehensive history of German Jewry from its first settlement, was made as early as 1903. Leadership of the project was given to Markus Brann, with Professor Aaron Freimann as co-editor and Heinrich Gross, after whose *Gallia Judaica* the enterprise was modelled. The *Arbeitsplan* (itinerary) for the *Germania Judaica* was drafted in December 1904 according to the instructions of the ailing Professor Steinschneider. The *Arbeitsplan* was sent to a number of Jewish and non-Jewish scholars for evaluation and advice, and the first volume was expected to be published five years later.[28] In January 1907 Brann presented the completed Index of the first volume to the *Gesellschaft's* board of directors.[29] However, the first part of the first volume, *Von den ältesten Zeiten bis 1238, A-L*, was not published until the end of the 1916. The *Gesellschaft* had initially purported to engage a number of historians to write up individual articles, but it became clear that the majority of those who had arranged to contribute were unable to meet the agreed deadlines. The fact that the majority of collaborators were "on average, men of the most diverse vocations"[30] and worked on Jewish studies merely in their free time and not as professional scholars was the main reason for the repeated delay in the publication. The fact that many had no appropriate access to adequate libraries and other required documentation meant that the list of contributors had to be rearranged. The articles were technically ready for publication at the end of 1913, however, the outbreak of the war postponed this event. Although the critique by the *Theologische Literaturzeitung* was harsh, stating that the project was "[a] failure in [both] plan and execution",[31] the first part of *Germania Judaica* was well received in the Jewish press.[32]

One of the main obstacles to scholarly investigation of rabbinical texts was the lack of critical editions of post-exilic religious literature. In order to remedy this, the

---

[27]See '1. Sitzung der Komission der Germania Judaica 13.06.1905', in *Monatsschrift für Geschichte und Wissenschaft des Judentums* 49 (1905), p. 508.

[28]'3. Jahresbericht der Gesellschaft zur Förderung der Wissenschaft des Judentums', in *Monatsschrift für Geschichte und Wissenschaft des Judentums* 50 (1906), pp. 125–127.

[29]'Ausschußsitzung 4. Januar 1907' in *Monatsschrift für Geschichte und Wissenschaft des Judentums* 51 (1907), p. 117.

[30]*Germania Judaica*, Band I,1 *Von den ältesten Zeiten bis 1238, A-L*, 1916, p. xi.

[31]*Theologische Literaturzeitung* 43. Jg. No. 15/16 (27 July 1918), p. 212.

[32]See '16. Jahresbericht der Gesellschaft zur Förderung der Wissenschaft des Judentums (1918)', p. 9: "The [*Germania Judaica*] received favourable reviews by competent judges."

society planned to produce a *Corpus Tannaiticum*, which would "collect all existing texts of the tannaitic period in philologically faultless editions". As an introduction to this series, Professor Eugen Mittwoch was elected to assemble a dictionary of Mishnaic Hebrew.

Of great importance was the decision of the *Gesellschaft* to take over the prestigious *Monatsschrift für Geschichte und Wissenschaft des Judentums*.[33] The journal was in financial difficulties at the time, with indications that it would not have been able to continue had the society not supported and reorganised its structure.[34]

In contrast to Christian theologians, a university career was generally closed to Jewish scholars. This academic non-recognition and the resulting professional insecurity effectively prevented most Jews from making a career of the academic study of Judaism. Only the few lecturers at the Jewish theological seminaries could hope for even a partial university career. The fault lay at least in part with the seminaries, which saw the education of rabbis as their main responsibility. There was no allowance made for the systematic education of theologians in the field, who could in turn have assured the continuity of *Wissenschaft des Judentums*, comparable with the self-procreation of Protestant theology through the work of Christian scholars.

This gave rise to the need for a professional framework for Jewish scholarship. The main obstacle to a career in Jewish studies was financial. In the great majority of cases, scholars had to finance their own projects through to completion, often dependent on sponsorship within the Jewish community or even paying their own publication fees. Jewish scholarship was not a financially viable field. The *Gesellschaft* concluded that financial support was crucial if scholars were to choose to continue to research and study in the field. It was therefore one of their stated objectives to support scholars financially in order to create an incentive to promising students to continue their studies[35].

The compensation of scholars for contributions was a novelty in the development of Jewish Studies in Germany. Whereas in the past contributions for articles in the *Monatsschrift für Geschichte und Wissenschaft des Judentums* were expected to be written without financial gain for the authors, the *Gesellschaft* remunerated every contribution to the journal. It was further possible to receive a subsidy for works that were deemed to be of scientific value. Jewish scholars could approach the *Gesellschaft* for annual subsidies or sponsorship for research trips. In order to qualify for a subsidy, the scholars had to submit research proposals to a committee which would decide on the basis of strictly scientific guidelines. The prerequisites for a subsidy were that the work had to "present the results of [existing] research" or "contain essential new results of research". Additionally, the research had to be related to one of the following subjects: systematic theology, ethics and religious philosophy, Hebrew language study and Bible exegesis, Talmud and codices, history (political, legal, economic, or cultural), literary and religious history, practical theology, or apologetics. In order to

---

[33] From 1904 each volume of the journal included the subtitle: *Organ der Gesellschaft zur Förderung der Wissenschaft des Judentums.*
[34] Ismar Elbogen, 'Ein hundertjähriger Gedenktag unserer Wissenschaft', in *Monatsschrift für Geschichte und Wissenschaft des Judentums*, 66 (1922), p. 97.
[35] 'Satzung des Vereins Gesellschaft zur Förderung der Wissenschaft des Judentums § 11', in *Monatsschrift für Geschichte und Wissenschaft des Judentums* 65 (1921), p. 381.

decide about the scientific value of individual applications and to guarantee a high academic standard, twelve *Fachkommissionen* (topic committees) were appointed, consisting of three to five members.[36] There were many notable examples of scholars who received such assistance, among them Professor Krauss (*Talmudische Archäologie*), Dr. Horowitz (*Epigraphik*), Ismar Elbogen (*Liturgik*), and Rabbi Dr. S. Klein (*Geographie Palästinas*). In addition, travel expenses to and from meetings were reimbursed by the *Gesellschaft*. In order not to have to rely on purely voluntary administrative help, the *Gesellschaft* decided to hire Dr. Nathan Max Nathan as secretary.[37]

With the crisis of learning in recent memory, one aspect stressed throughout the existence of the society was that *Wissenschaft des Judentums*, while striving for the highest scientific standard[38] must nevertheless become more accessible to the interested non-specialist lay person. The *Grundriss* stated unequivocally that "in addition to the precise scientific nature within this enterprise, [the objective was] the comprehensive quality of the publications for the educated non-expert public in particular".[39] Each member of the *Gesellschaft* received a free copy of the popular *Jahrbuch für jüdische Geschichte und Literatur*.[40] This tension between popularisation and strict scholarship determined the activities of the *Gesellschaft* throughout its existence.

Hand in hand with the professionalisation of the discipline went the attempt to exclude religious conflicts. Realising that *Wissenschaft des Judentums* had often been a point of contention in the past between conservative and progressive streams within the German-Jewish community, the *Gesellschaft* repeatedly stressed its religious neutrality. Armed with a guarantee of complete academic freedom, the organisation sought to facilitate the cooperation of scholars of different ideological backgrounds, emphasising that "every author will be granted complete freedom in the accomplishment of his project, and [the author] must assume the responsibility for the contents ..." The *Gesellschaft* had made every effort to attract Orthodox scholars to join and support the organisation, and the guarantee of near-autonomy eventually did enable some, such as Professor Landauer, Professor Ginzberg and Rabbi Eppenstein to contribute.[41] In 1913 the Orthodox rabbi of the Frankfurt community, Rabbi

---

[36]See '1. Jahresbericht der Gesellschaft zur Förderung der Wissenschaft des Judentums', in *Monatsschrift für Geschichte und Wissenschaft des Judentums* 48 (1904), pp. 52–64. Altogether there were twelve *Fachkommissionen* covering the following subjects: Systematische Theologie, Ethik und Religionsphilosophie, Hebräische Sprachwissenschaft, Bibelexegese, Talmud und Kodices, Geschichte bis zur Zerstörung des zweiten Tempels, Geschichte von der Zerstörung des zweiten Tempels bis zum Ende des Gaonats, Geschichte vom Ende des Gaonats bis zum Zeitalter Mendelsohns, Geschichte vom Zeitalter, Mendelsohns bis auf die Gegenwart, Litteratur- und Religionsgeschichte, Praktische Theologie (Pädagogik), Apologetik.
[37]See 'Ausschußsitzung der Gesellschaft zur Förderung der Wissenschaft des Judentums vom 24. Juni 1912', in *Monatsschrift für Geschichte und Wissenschaft des Judentums* 56 (1912), pp. 511–512.
[38]'Satzung des Vereins Gesellschaft zur Förderung der Wissenschaft des Judentums § 9', in *Monatsschrift für Geschichte und Wissenschaft des Judentums* 65 (1921), p. 381.
[39]See *Monatsschrift für Geschichte und Wissenschaft des Judentums*, 47 (1903), p. 572.
[40]'Satzung des Vereins Gesellschaft zur Förderung der Wissenschaft des Judentums § 10', in *Monatsschrift für Geschichte und Wissenschaft des Judentums*, 47 (1903), p. 572.
[41]The idea came from Gustav Karpeles, who had for many years lamented the lack of Jewish reaction to the ever-increasing Christian attacks on the fundamental principles of Jewish faith and culture resulting in part from the generally unsystematic and uncoordinated work by the Jewish scholarly community. A committee consisting of Gustav Karpeles, Professor Bacher, Professor Cohen, Rabbi Dr. Güdemann, Rabbi Dr. Bloch, Rabbi Dr. Kroner, Rabbi Dr. Lucas and Professor Philippson decided to limit the *Grundriss* to 36 monographs, with the option to expand at a later stage if deemed necessary.

Nehemia Nobel became a member of the executive committee.[42] The *Gesellschaft* maintained that *Wissenschaft des Judentums*, as all other science, must be completely *wertfrei* (free of bias) and was thus not ever to be used as a tool in the inner-Jewish conflicts between conservative and progressive factions. Moreover, contemporary records show that the *Gesellschaft* went to great lengths not to become involved in religious communal strife. To cite but one example, we need only look at the petition of acknowledged leader of Liberal Judaism, founder and president of the *Vereinigung der Liberalen Rabbiner Deutschlands* and a vice-president of the *Vereinigung für das Liberale Judentum*, Rabbi Heinemann Vogelstein (1841–1911). Vogelstein requested a subsidy on behalf of the *Liberale Rabbinerverband* to begin circulation of a periodical in order to promote Liberal Judaism through new discoveries in the field of *Wissenschaft des Judentums*. The *Gesellschaft* flatly refused, although the petitioner was himself a founding member of the *Gesellschaft* and author of a part of the *Grundriss*.

In spite of the *Gesellschaft*'s attempts to avoid the religious arena, Rabbi Lucas admits to having failed to convince any Orthodox "authorities" to collaborate initially, as they claimed that "common ground for cooperation was non-existent".[43] This initial refusal of involvement may have been due to internal pressure. Over time the *Gesellschaft* was able to overcome this somewhat, and eventually did receive active support from many members of the Orthodox "camp".[44] It is also possible that the Orthodox shied away from the sheer number of Conservative/Liberal founders. Upon examination, we can note that all twenty signatories of the *Aufruf*, without exception, are affiliated with either the Liberal *Lehranstalt* in Berlin, the conservative *Jüdisch-Theologisches Seminar* in Breslau, or the corresponding seminary, the *Landesrabbinerschule* in Budapest. Similarly, the participants at the founding assembly (save for Orthodox Rabbi David, who opposed the founding) were exclusively former students of either the *Lehranstalt* or the *Jüdisch-Theologisches Seminar*, or connected with the movements represented by these institutions. The assembly included strong supporters of the extreme Liberal wing like the leading Liberal Rabbi Heinemann Vogelstein and Professor Ludwig Geiger. Here there was one exception. One of the most conspicuous absences from the *Grundriss* enterprise was that of the eminent lecturer of the Orthodox *Rabbinerseminar*, Professor Jacob Barth. Although he had initially agreed to write a monograph on Hebrew linguistics, the Orthodox Professor ultimately decided against becoming involved with the *Gesellschaft*. He defended his position with the statement that the condition for his participation had been that his work would not be associated with the contributions of his Liberal colleagues, who clearly dominated the project

To be sure, the *Gesellschaft* did not publish solely uncontroversial books. In fact many publications were judged in the Jewish press according to their position towards one of the religious trends. For instance, Martin Philippson's three volume

---

[42]'Ausschußsitzung der Gesellschaft zur Förderung der Wissenschaft des Judentums vom 31.12.1913', in *Monatsschrift für Geschichte und Wissenschaft des Judentums* 58 (1914), pp. 126–128.

[43]*Jüdische Presse*, 33, No. 45 (7 November 1902), p. 438. Rabbi Lucas seemed to be somewhat preoccupied with this failure, as he recalled it in a celebratory article in 1927. See Leopold Lucas 'Zum 25jährigen Jubiläum der Gesellschaft zur Förderung der Wissenschaft des Judentums', in *Monatsschrift für Geschichte und Wissenschaft des Judentums* 71 (1927), pp. 321–331.

[44]Examples include Rabbi Samuel Klein, Rabbi Salomon Funk and Rabbi Heinrich Brody.

series, *Neueste Geschichte des Jüdischen Volkes*, while praised in the Liberal *Allgemeine Zeitung des Judentums*, was soundly damned by the critics of the leading Orthodox newspaper, *Der Israelit*.[45] The author was sharply attacked for having ignored the neo-Orthodox contribution to German-Jewish culture.[46] Even the more moderate Orthodox newspaper, *Die Jüdische Presse*, was critical of Philippson's portrayal of recent Jewish history.[47] Examination of contemporary reviews indicate that his work was evaluated mainly on the basis of the manner in which he portrayed the early conflict between Reform and Orthodoxy in Judaism, and how he rated their respective achievements and roles in modern society. Nevertheless, the volumes were acknowledged by many, including the non-Jewish theologians: "For the historiography of modern Judaism as well as for the consideration of the Jewish problem in general, the work of Philippson constitutes a very valuable contribution."[48]

Many Orthodox scholars did over time receive subsidies from the *Gesellschaft* in order to further their scientific work, including Rabbi Joseph Carlebach and Rabbi Louis Lewin.[49] Although Professor Jacob Barth had withdrawn his offer of active collaboration with the *Gesellschaft*, this did not prevent him from joining the organisation as a paying member. Likewise over time, the *Rabbinerseminar* in Berlin acquired membership, as did its director, Professor David Hoffmann. Finally, in 1912 when a revision of the original plan of the *Grundriss* became necessary, the list of contributors included Rabbi Heinrich Brody, a former graduate of the *Rabbinerseminar*.[50] Brody set to work on *Neuhebräische Poesie* and Professor Alexander Marx, himself a former student of the *Rabbinerseminar*, agreed to contribute *Nachbiblische jüdische Literatur bis zum Erlöschen des Gaonats*[51] to the *Grundriss* effort.

This project was planned in 1904 as a conglomerate of articles to commemorate the 700th anniversary of Maimonides's death. It was the earliest example of the cross-over effect of *Wissenschaft des Judentums*, or true cooperative effort between Orthodox and Liberal scholars. Out of twelve articles written for the first volume of the Maimonides's biography, four were by Orthodox scholars and rabbis. Other authors included Hermann Cohen,[52] the lecturer of the *Lehranstalt für die Wissenschaft*

---

[45] The review ends with the not very flattering words: "No man of science … [but] a fanatic wrote this book. May God protect us from the third volume", cf. *Der Israelit* 51, No. 5 (3 February 1910), p. 2.

[46] *Der Israelit* 51, No. 4 (27 January 1910), pp. 1–3 and No. 5 (3 February 1910), pp. 1f.

[47] Although his effort is acknowledged, he is attacked for having taken too biased a standpoint. The review is noteworthy that it ends by admitting that the work will become a standard work within Philippson's circle ("seinen Parteigenossen") meaning Liberal German Jews. See *Die Jüdische Presse*, 38, No. 47 (21 November 1907), p. 472.

[48] The author, Koft, wrote an untitled book review on Caro's *Sozial- und Wirtschaftsgeschichte der Juden im Mittelalter und der Neuzeit* and Philippson's *Neueste Geschichte des Jüdischen Volkes*, vol. 1, in *Historisches Jahrbuch* XXXI, Munich 1910, p. 357.

[49] Rabbi Louis Lewin (1868–1941), a graduate of the *Rabbinerseminar*, published regularly in the Orthodox *Jahrbuch der Jüdisch Literarischen Gesellschaft*, mainly on the history of Jews in Poland. He was also among the first scholars to receive financial support for the printing of his work, *Geschichte der Juden in Lissa. Die Landessynode der grosspolnischen Judenschaft*, was published by the *Gesellschaft* in 1926.

[50] Brody wrote a Hebrew article on the "Sefer ha-Tarshish" in *Jahrbuch der Jüdisch Literarischen Gesellschaft* XVIII:1ff. He published in the *Monatsschrift für Geschichte und Wissenschaft des Judentums* respectively.

[51] See '10. Jahresbericht der Gesellschaft zur Förderung der Wissenschaft des Judentums (1913)', in *Monatsschrift für Geschichte und Wissenschaft des Judentums* 57 (1913), pp. 119–125.

[52] His contribution is entitled 'Charakteristik und Ethik Maimunis', in *Moses ben Maimon. Sein Leben, seine Werke und sein Einfluß*, vol. 1, Leipzig 1908.

des Judentums Ismar Elbogen,[53] the Rabbi of the Liberal congregation *Brüdergemeinde* of Posen, Philipp Bloch, who also took a leading role in the *Vereinigung der Liberalen Rabbiner Deutschlands*,[54] serving as chairman for many years. The conservative Rabbi Jakob Guttmann wrote *Der Einfluß der maimonidischen Philosophie auf das christliche Abendland*, and the head of the (conservative) *Israelitisch-theologische Lehranstalt* in Vienna, Adolf Schwarz, contributed the article *Das Verhältnis Maimunis zu den Gaonen*. The editors included Professor of the *Landesrabbinerschule* Rabbi Willhelm Bacher, historian and successor of Heinrich Graetz at the *Jüdisch-Theologisches Seminar* in Breslau Markus Brann, the Chief Rabbi of Denmark David Simonsen, and the vice chairman and Rabbi Jakob Guttmann. Maimonides proved to be an excellent example of a neutral forum in which scholars from different backgrounds could cooperate, as he was esteemed as no other Jewish historical personality in all Jewish circles.[55]

Perhaps the most compelling example of the cross-over effect in the *Wissenschaft des Judentums* is embodied in its last chairman, the orientalist Eugen Mittwoch (1876–1948). Mittwoch was another former student of the *Rabbinerseminar* and a prominent member of the separatist *Agudas Jisroel* community in Berlin. Having been involved from the very onset with the activities of the *Gesellschaft*, Mittwoch was among the first to receive an annual subsidy to support his reseach for *Wörterbuch der Mischnasprache*. He was assigned to write the work *Epigraphik* for the *Grundriss*, and in addition was a member in several committees. In 1930 he was officially asked to represent the *Gesellschaft* at a rally of the organisation *Schomre Schabbos*, a group whose stated objective was the strengthening of Shabbat observance among Jews, particularly those engaged in trade.[56] In 1934 Mittwoch assumed chairmanship of the *Gesellschaft*.

While it has become clear that many Orthodox scholars had no compunction about contributing to an academic enterprise such as the *Gesellschaft*, it is equally important not to extrapolate that fact. The impression should not arise that the *Gesellschaft* was slowly being taken over by the Orthodox, but instead that there was a surprising consensus among scholars that collaboration, at least in one forum, had become possible. This cross-communal activity was a model for a possible co-operation in the field of the academic study of Judaism, even when certain limitations had to be set in order to preserve the cohesion of this religiously heterogeneous organisation.

---

[53]His contribution is entitled 'Der Ritus im Mischne Thora' in *Moses ben Maimon. Sein Leben, seine Werke und sein Einfluß*, W. Bacher, M. Brann, D. Simonsen… Jakob Guttmann, 2 vols., 1908, 1914.

[54]His contribution is entitled 'Charakteristik und Inhaltsangabe des More Nebuchim' in *ibid*.

[55]The list of contributors to the first volume, published in 1908, contains diverse personalities, including the orientalist Israel Friedländer (1876–1920). A graduate of the *Rabbinerseminar*, he wrote the two parts of the first Maimonides project (published in 1908), *Die arabische Sprache des Maimonides* and *Der Stil des Maimonides*. Another co-author of the Maimonides biography was the Orthodox rabbi and scholar Ferdinand Rosenthal (1838–1921). Rosenthal, who studied with Esriel Hildesheimer at the Eisenstadt *Yeshivah* and at Berlin and Leipzig universities served for many years as Rabbi of Breslau. His contribution is entitled *Die Kritik des maimonidischen Buches der Gesetze durch Nachmanides*. Finally Orthodox Rabbi Simon Eppenstein published *Beiträge zur Pentateuchexegese Maimunis*.

[56]Board meeting (8 December 1930) of the *Gesellschaft zur Förderung der Wissenschaft des Judentums* in *Monatsschrift für Geschichte und Wissenschaft des Judentums* 74:479 (1930): "Professor Mittwoch participated as representative of the *Gesellschaft* in an activity [by the organisation] *Schomre Schabbes*, World Union for the protection of Sabbath observance; a unified action in defense of the continuity of the Sabbath, endangered by calendar reform."

Additionally, many publications were put out by the *Gesellschaft* which became standard reference works for Liberal Judaism, including Leo Baeck's *Wesen des Judentums*, Kaufmann Kohler's *Grundriss einer systematischen Theologie des Judentums*,[57] Hermann Cohen's *Religion der Vernunft aus den Quellen des Judentums*,[58] and the above-mentioned *Neueste Geschichte des Jüdischen Volkes*.[59]

While the *Aufruf* initially received much attention, by 1904 Rabbi Lucas comments on "the great difficulty of interesting wider circles in our work, and convincing them to support it ..."[60] Rabbi Lucas wrote *Wissenschaft des Judentums und Wege ihrer Förderung* in 1905, following the receipt of a significant number of letters in which the signatories expressed a disconcerting lack of clarity about the meaning and objectives of the *Gesellschaft*.[61] The *Gesellschaft* took public relations very seriously, and outreach was consistent in the years leading up to the First World War. The repeated appeal for more support also shows the challenge of maintaining the interest of the lay public. Trips to Worms, Frankfurt and Breslau were frequent, with meetings with political representatives of city councils in order to initiate contact with potential members. Expanding membership was initially achieved through personal "propaganda"; existing members recruited new ones. Subsequently, advertisements were placed in newspapers with the purpose of attracting new members and keeping the public informed of activities. The *Gesellschaft*'s board sought to maintain contact with existing members, and to this effect adopted the practice of holding annual assemblies, where elections were held and any points of issue could be raised. In keeping with German academic tradition, the meetings always included a scholarly lecture. The annual assemblies were generally announced in the Jewish press in an additional effort to draw wider recognition.

Prominent members often delivered public lectures, mainly in the framework of the *Vereine für jüdische Geschichte und Literatur*, on behalf of the *Gesellschaft*. Consequently, the *Gesellschaft* engaged *Vertrauensmänner* (agents) in numerous cities and countries, who had the duty of "advertising" activities and collecting membership fees.

The society's statutes define three membership possibilities: *Stifter*, or sponsors who had donated an amount once of at least 1000 marks; *Immerwährende Mitglieder*, sponsors who had donated a one-time amount of at least 300 marks; and *Mitglieder*, regular members paying an annual membership fee of 8 marks.[62] A member could be an individual or a group, the latter category being the most common form of membership. Membership included, free of additional charge, the *Monatsschrift für Geschichte und Wissenschaft des Judentums* and the *Jahrbuch für jüdische Geschichte und Literatur*. All other publications put out by the *Gesellschaft* could be purchased at a discount of 70% off the cover price. *Stifter* and members paying at least 100 Marks per year received one free copy of

---

[57]Kaufmann Kohler, *Grundriss einer systematischen Theologie des Judentums*, Leipzig 1910.
[58]Herman Cohen, *Religion der Vernunft aus den Quellen des Judentums*, Leipzig 1919.
[59]c.f. note 48, 3 vols, Leipzig 1910, 1910, 1911.
[60]See '3. Jahresbericht der Gesellschaft zur Förderung der Wissenschaft des Judentums (1905)', in *Monatsschrift für Geschichte und Wissenschaft des Judentums* 50 (1906), pp. 125–127.
[61]Rabbi Lucas also lectured on numerous occasions within the *Vereine für jüdische Geschichte und Literatur* in order to attract new members to the *Gesellschaft*.
[62]'Satzung der Gesellschaft zur Förderung der Wissenschaft des Judentums §3', in *Monatsschrift für Geschichte und Wissenschaft des Judentums* 65 (1921), p. 381.

any book published by the *Gesellschaft*.⁶³ In order to distribute as much literature as possible, the society acquired books in bulk to offer them to members at reduced prices.

The membership fluctuation shows an almost linear increase in membership up to the outbreak of the First World War, reflecting the increased interest in the *Gesellschaft* (see Table 1) In examining the statistics table, it must be kept in mind that they represent neither the absolute distribution, nor the literary output of the *Gesellschaft*. Since numerous Jewish communities and organisations, themselves with many members, joined the organisation collectively, the real distribution of the *Gesellschaft*'s literature and the *Monatsschrift* was much higher. Nevertheless, they can be indicative of certain trends in the volume of the organisation. The membership development shows that up until World War One, a steady increase in membership can be observed, illustrating the success of the organisation. As a result of the war, however, membership declined slightly for the first time in 1915. This was due to three factors: the economic hardship of members, the fact that former members were now living in "enemy countries" and could no longer be counted as members, and the service and deaths of members on the battlefields.⁶⁴ Perhaps less significantly, propaganda for new members ceased during the war years. During the war years, the board attempted to stabilise membership by taking personal economic hardships into consideration, through the reduction of membership fees or even exemption from payments.

The *Gesellschaft* considered its work to be of great importance to Christian scholars, and the board viewed Christian membership as an encouraging sign of long-awaited inter-faith relations. The *Gesellschaft* was always interested in non-Jewish reactions to their work. When an Australian priest wrote a letter to the *Gesellschaft* expressing his honour at having been accepted as a member, the entire letter, which was full of praise for the work of the *Gesellschaft*, was read to the committee.⁶⁵ When a publication received a good review or was commented upon positively by Christian critics, the *Gesellschaft* always made mention of it in their annual report. The annual report of 1914 was decidedly positive and optimistic and reflects the impact of the society's activities on Christian scholars. One of the most prominent Christian members was Nikolaus Müller, Professor of Theology at the University of Berlin. Müller was involved with the *Gesellschaft* from a very early stage; in the spring and fall of 1906, 1907, and 1909 the organisation financed Müller's travels to Rome for the purpose of researching a rediscovered Jewish catacomb, even paying for the workmen needed to free the necropolis from debris.⁶⁶ Because the owners of the plot and the Italian authorities repeatedly blocked Müller's investigations, he felt compelled to publish his preliminary research results in 1912 under the title *Die Jüdische Katakombe am Monteverde zu Rom, der älteste bisher bekannt gewordene jüdische Friedhof des Abendlandes*. Müller unfortunately died before he could publish the remainder of his work. At this time, the Faculty of the New Testament Studies in Berlin contacted the *Gesellschaft*

---

⁶³'Satzung der Gesellschaft zur Förderung der Wissenschaft des Judentums §10', in *Monatsschrift für Geschichte und Wissenschaft des Judentums* 65 (1921), p. 381.
⁶⁴'13. Jahresbericht der Gesellschaft zur Förderung der Wissenschaft des Judentums', in *Monatsschrift für Geschichte und Wissenschaft des Judentums* 59 (1915), pp. 311–316
⁶⁵*Monatsschrift für Geschichte und Wissenschaft des Judentums* 71 (1927), p. 156.
⁶⁶Nikolaus Müller, *Die jüdische Katakombe am Monteverde zu Rom*, Leipzig 1912, p. 20.

Table 1: Membership Development of the *Gesellschaft*, 1903–1915

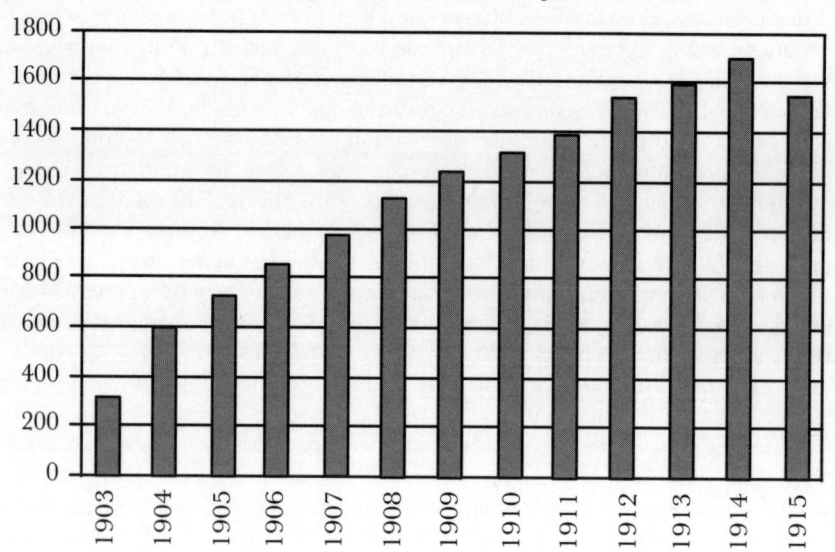

Year	Members
1903	~310
1904	~600
1905	~720
1906	~850
1907	~970
1908	~1120
1909	~1230
1910	~1310
1911	~1380
1912	~1520
1913	~1580
1914	~1680
1915	~1530

Source: Annual reports of the *Gesellschaft*.

for the purpose of collaborating on a new, more complete edition of Müller's work. On 17 July 1915 the contract for the publication was signed between Philippson and the Faculty of the New Testament Studies in Berlin. The preparatory works leading to the publication included such eminent Christian scholars as the Professors A. Deißmann, Greßmann, and H.L. Strack, as well as the Jewish scholars Otto Hirschfeld, and Eugen Mittwoch, who advised the publisher, Nikos Bees, on questions of Judaica.[67] Indeed this project was hailed in the Christian press as "a beautiful sign of the productive cooperation between Jewish and Christian scholars".[68] The claim made in the 10th annual report that the publication was one of the "finest achievements of our society so far" illustrates the enthusiasm which Müller's participation created in the circles of the *Gesellschaft*.[69]

In a strictly business sense, the *Gesellschaft* as an organisation was only a moderate success. In truth, it depended strongly on the financial support of the Jewish communities and the B'nai B'rith lodges. In the first quarter of 1903 the three communities of Breslau, Frankfurt am Main and Berlin each contributed 1000 marks, enabling the organisation to launch itself. The first annual report counted forty-three communities, which had joined collectively, as did the *Deutsch-Israelitischer Gemeindebund* and many of the local *Vereine für jüdische Geschichte und Literatur*. Altogether the organisation received around 8,500 marks in donations by the end of the first

---

[67] Nikolaus Müller, *Die Inschriften der jüdischen Katakombe am Monteverde zu Rom*, Leipzig 1919, pp. V-IX.
[68] *Theologische Literaturzeitung*, 47. Jg., No. 7 (8 April 1922), p. 152f.
[69] '10. Jahresbericht der Gesellschaft zur Förderung der Wissenschaft des Judentums', in *Monatsschrift für Geschichte und Wissenschaft des Judentums* 57 (1913), pp. 119–125.

year.[70] An additional 10,000 marks was contributed by wealthy members, Martin Philippson's brother *Generalkonsul* Franz Philippson making the most generous donation of 5 000 Marks. This money was put into an account whose interest would benefit the *Gesellschaft*.

The following annual reports show the financial development, based on the annual contributions of members and the income from sales of the *Monatsschrift* and any other publications.

Table 2: Financial Development of the *Gesellschaft*, 1905–1915

Source: see table 1.

The financial development of the society until the First World War is relatively stable with an average annual income of just above 30,000 Marks.[71] Although the *Gesellschaft* did complain about insufficient funds at times, the table indicates a fairly steady income. Nevertheless, only five years after its founding, the *Gesellschaft* was so short of funds that it was unable to pay any subsidies for that year.[72] The annual reports repeatedly state that many worthy projects had to be refused subsidies, and the number of applications for scholarly grants exceeded the financial commitments which the *Gesellschaft* could maintain.

---

[70]'1. Jahresbericht der Gesellschaft zur Förderung der Wissenschaft des Judentums', in *Monatsschrift für Geschichte und Wissenschaft des Judentums* 48 (1904), pp. 52–64.

[71]The significantly higher income in 1910 is due to an additional payment by Edmond de Rothschild, Franz Philippson and Marie Errera, amounting to 14,000 marks, after a special effort was made on the part of the society to secure additional finances for the *Corpus Tannaiticum*.

[72]'Ausschußsitzung der Gesellschaft zur Förderung der Wissenschaft des Judentums 23.12.1907' in *Monatsschrift für Geschichte und Wissenschaft des Judentums* 52 (1908), p 127.

The founding and development of the *Gesellschaft zur Förderung der Wissenschaft des Judentums* must be viewed against the backdrop of the organisational renaissance of German Jewry at the turn of the nineteenth century. There was nothing unusual in the establishment of interest groups during this time, of which the *Gesellschaft* was certainly one. Interest groups, however, generally exist for the benefit of the group's members. What made the *Gesellschaft* unusual was the fact that one of its primary motives was to facilitate entry into a society which had hitherto been closed to German Jews. Its founding sent a strong signal, to Jews and non-Jews alike, that the time had come for social change in the form of intellectual communication and acceptance. Obviously this was an arduous process, although the prominent examples of trans-cultural cooperation show that the *Gesellschaft* did succeed in realising this goal to some extent.

The promotion of *Wissenschaft des Judentums* had become as much a means of combating scholarly antisemitism as one of self-preservation. It was this twofold obective of an "inner and outer mission" that for the first time unified scholars from across the religious spectrum in a scholarly enterprise of such a large scale. In one way, the success of the *Gesellschaft*'s actvities were therefore measured by the interest with which Christian academic readership judged their publications, and the annual reports never fail to mention a positive critique from a non-Jewish source. The last annual report before the outbreak of the First Word War indeed marks the culmination of the attempt to gain scholarly recognition pointing to a promising modification of theological prejudice towards Jewish scholarship:

> That our toil is not useless is proven by the reception of our works in the scholarly world and by the competent judgement of significant scholars. The aforementioned work by Elbogen *Der jüdische Gottesdienst* is described as "epoch-making" by the *Theologische Rundschau* and in the *Theologische Literaturzeitung* as an "outstanding scholarly work", through which the author has "earned himself lasting scholarly merit". The *Theologische Literaturblatt* calls *Tradition und Tradenten* by Bacher, published by us and mentioned in our last annual review, "a masterpiece of scientific work, which will instruct talmudists and Christian theologians alike". Another critic writes of the same publication: "Through publishing this work, the Gesellschaft zur Förderung der Wissenschaft des Judentums has added to its prior merits another immeasurable one. Only a decade ago, the publication of such a work would have been impossible. The Christian as well as the Jewish scholarly world had indeed reason to be thankful to the Gesellschaft for having dared to publish this work in such a critical time."
>
> This is how the work of our Gesellschaft is being evaluated and we are noting these judgements with satisfaction."[73]

APPENDIX: THE APPEAL

To our co-religionists! The conviction of the individual concerning the significance of the truth of Judaism as well as the appreciation of our teachings and our history by fellow citizens of another faith stand in direct proportion to the position taken by

---

[73]'13. Jahresbericht der Gesellschaft zur Förderung der Wissenschaft des Judentums (1914)', in *Monatsschrift für Geschichte und Wissenschaft des Judentums* 59 (1915), pp. 311–316.

Wissenschaft des Judentums. Wissenschaft des Judentums gave former generations security and hope, and constantly provided our champions with the direction for defence and deflection.

Our scholarship has not only not lost its significance in modern times, but its problems have been expanded and become even more defined through the general methods of scholarship. We acknowledge that the free scholarly investigation of our literature is one of the most vivid and deepest sources of general culture, of the spiritual and especially of the ethical progress of humanity, and should be acknowledged as such in every civilised State (Kulturstaat). Those scholars who are teaching Wissenschaft des Judentums at the universities have indeed produced laudable achievements, which we have not failed to acknowledge. Nevertheless we cannot overlook that their prejudice against Judaism does taint their objectivity and that their knowledge usually extends to the [church] canon but not to the later souces of Judaism. But we can neither forego a purely objective judgement, nor, for the sake of the later development of our religion and our history, can we renounce academic acknowledgment. To take a stand [for this principle] is a duty of self-preservation; the holiest duty towards our religion, but equally a duty towards science and general culture.

Zunz in his deep wisdom has pronounced that our ghetto will only disappear when the ghetto of our scholarship ends. Our confidence must also directed towards the goal that chairs for our scholarship, free of all bias [against us], will be established at universities; however these troubled times teach us that our emancipation is still far away. Therefore we are called upon to help ourselves and to create an organisation, the grandeur of which matches the significance and duties of our scholarship. We are planning a Gesellschaft zur Förderung der Wissenschaft des Judentums. This organisation shall primarily support talented young people, who have completed their university education as well as one of the theologial seminaries, and whose inclination and vocation drives them towards scholarly work. [These] will be endowed with sufficient stipends, in order that we may be assured of a support base of adequate teachers, which we desperately need in order to educate our theologians and present our scholarship with dignity. Furthermore we demand solid and comprehensive works, covering the whole of our scholarship, which will be promoted and generously supported by our society. Thirdly, the Gesellschaft shall hold annual assemblies, as is customary in other academic branches, where the representatives of our field will meet to debate the state of research, and coordinate necesssary measures. Finally it seems necessary to publish a journal or to support an existing publication, in which valuable monographs will find a place and appropriate publicity, and where thorough and unbiased reviews of new publications in the field will be presented.

We are announcing an assembly for interested circles on Sunday the 2 of November at 10:00 am in Berlin, Wilhelmstrasse 118, where the preparations and the founding of the society will take place.

We do not doubt that our co-religionists will recognise and cherish the importance of our plan, and will support it wholeheartedly. Out of the enthusiasm for the study of our precepts, which was always part of our religion, may there develop a new strong scholarly life.

Director Dr. Adler, Prof. Dr. Bacher, Dr. Baneth, Director Dr. Bärwald, Dr. Brann, *Geheimrat* Prof. Dr. Cohen, Prof. Dr. Geiger, Chief Rabbi Dr. Güdemann, Rabbi Dr. Guttmann, Dr. Karpeles, Rabbi Dr. Kayserling, Kirchenrat Dr. Kroner, *Geheimrat* Prof. Dr. Lazarus, *Geheimrat* Dr. Mayer, Prof. Dr. Philippson, Prof. Dr. Schwarz, Chief Rabbi D. Simonsen, Rabbi Dr. Vogelstein, Rabbi Dr. Weisse, Rabbi Dr. Werner.

All correspondence etc. to be addressed to Rabbi Dr. Lucas, Groß-Glogau (Lower Silesia).[74]

---

[74]*Allgemeine Zeitung des Judentums* 66, No. 34, (22 August 1902), p. 398f. Author's translation, as are all quotations from the German.

Hermann Cohen and the Quest for Protestant Judaism

BY DAVID N. MYERS

Eighty years after his death, the great German-Jewish philosopher, Hermann Cohen (1842–1918), is in the midst of a most impressive scholarly afterlife. New editions of his writings, a steady stream of monographic studies, and a spate of doctoral dissertations devoted to him have recently appeared. The net effect of this literary profusion is to reclaim the reputation of one of German Jewry's leading intellectual personalities prior to the Weimar Republic, as well as to return Cohen to the centre of contemporary Jewish thought. The field of Jewish thought itself seems to be in the midst of a rather energetic period, as it brushes off its post-Holocaust languor and finds a voice in the polyphony of postmodern intellectual culture.

The renewed interest in Hermann Cohen certainly belongs to this broader current, but also has to do with more biographically specific factors, some of which are responsible for Cohen's posthumous retreat into obscurity. To begin with, Cohen was alternately mentor, polemical target, and intellectual foil to the extraordinary cadre of German-Jewish intellectuals – e.g. from Martin Buber and Franz Rosenzweig to Gershom Scholem and Walter Benjamin – that has attracted so much attention in recent decades.[1] One of the more iconoclastic members of this illustrious fraternity, Leo Strauss, recalled that "I grew up in an environment in which Cohen was the center of attraction for philosophically minded Jews who were devoted to Judaism; he was the master whom they revered."[2] Nonetheless, for many occasional students of these Jewish intellectuals, Hermann Cohen's name is a faint memory or even unknown.

Part of Cohen's obscurity stems from the fact that the neo-Kantian philosophical system with which Cohen's name is so closely linked, and which dominated European philosophy for well over a half century from the 1860s, fell into desuetude shortly after Cohen's death. This is not to suggest that neo-Kantianism died an easy death. Its adepts were involved in a pitched battle following the First World War with the new cadre of thinkers who sought to shift the focus of philosophical discourse from epistemological to ontological matters. The symbolic battleground on which neo-Kantianism gave way to the new current was the conference of French and

---

[1] Gershom Scholem reports that although he and Walter Benjamin ultimately became disappointed in Cohen, they attended his classes at the Lehranstalt für die Wissenschaft des Judentums in Berlin, admired him, and read his Kantian writings carefully. See Scholem's account in *Walter Benjamin: The Story of a Friendship*, trans. Harry Zohn, Philadelphia 1981, p. 59.

[2] See Strauss' introductory essay to the English version of Cohen's Jewish *magnum opus*, *Religion of Reason*, Atlanta 1995, p. xxiii.

German philosophers held in Davos, Switzerland in March/April 1929 at which Martin Heidegger delivered a sharp renunciation of neo-Kantianism as represented by Hermann Cohen's student, Ernst Cassirer.

In the throes of these swirling polemical debates, Cohen's close collaborator at the University of Marburg, Paul Natorp, counselled that the time was not right to undertake a synthetic assessment of Cohen's life and work.[3] Notwithstanding this advice, a number of studies of Cohen's work were produced in the twenties, including extended analyses of his philosophical system by two students, Walter Kinkel and Jakob Klatzkin.[4]

If Natorp believed that the time was not right for a full assessment of Cohen in the 1920s, prospects did not improve much in the subsequent decade.[5] In fact, there were few serious discussions of Hermann Cohen's thought for decades until after the Second World War. The star of neo-Kantianism had faded in the constellation of European philosophy and Cohen's great faith in the progressive force of reason – as well as his belief in the utter compatibility of *Deutschtum* and *Judentum* – seemed hopelessly naive in an era dominated by the Nazi terror.

One of the earliest and most sustained post-Holocaust efforts to revive the Cohenian legacy belonged to the German-born American philosopher and rabbi, Steven Schwarzschild. Schwarzschild inaugurated his life-long interest in Cohen with a 1955 dissertation devoted in large part to Cohen's philosophy of history.[6] In a series of subsequent essays over some three decades, Schwarzschild, who unabashedly identified himself as a "Marburg neo-Kantian", sought to call attention to and invigorate Hermann Cohen's philosophical commitment to "ethical idealism".[7]

A similar interest in the content of Cohen's teachings, and the very possibility of an ethically grounded idealism, has informed the indefatigable efforts of the Zurich-based scholar, Helmut Holzhey. As founder of the Hermann Cohen Archive in Zurich, Holzhey has overseen a vast enterprise of Cohen scholarship involving the republication of Cohen's collected writings, the supervision of numerous doctoral dissertations on Cohen, and his own substantial analyses of Cohen's philosophy, particularly his study of Cohen and Paul Natorp. The intense concern which Holzhey and his European students have evinced in Cohen's work reflects a renewed estimation of the philosophical merits of neo-Kantianism. Their systematic excavation of Cohen's *oeuvre* itself bears a powerful ethical charge to salvage a liberal-minded, rationalist world-view deeply unsettled by Nazism and seemingly at odds with the postmodern sensibility.[8]

---

[3]Natorp's advice to Kinkel is mentioned in the excellent exhibition catalogue assembled by Franz Orlik, *Hermann Cohen (1842–1918): Kantinterpret, Begründer der "Marburger Schule", Jüdischer Religionsphilosoph*, introduced by Reinhard Brandt, Marburg 1992, p.184.

[4]See Jakob Klatzkin, *Hermann Cohen*, Berlin 1921 and his later Hebrew volume, *Hermann Cohen: Shitato be-musar u-mishnato be-Yahadut*, Berlin 1923, as well as Walter Kinkel, *Hermann Cohen. Eine Einführung in sein Werk*, Stuttgart 1924.

[5]One of the last systematic treatments in this period was Simon Kaplan's doctoral dissertation, *Das Problem der Geschichte im System der Philosophie H. Cohens*, Berlin 1930. Two years later, Joseph Soloveitchik, the great Orthodox jurist and philosopher, published *Das reine Denken und die Seinskonstituierung bei Hermann Cohen*, the fruit of his earlier doctoral dissertation research at the University of Berlin.

[6]"Two Modern Jewish Philosophies of History: Nachman Krochmal and Hermann Cohen", unpublished dissertation, Hebrew Union College, Cincinnati, Ohio, 1955.

[7]Quoted in Menachem Kellner (ed.), *The Pursuit of the Ideal: Jewish Writings of Steven Schwarzschild*, Albany, NY 1990, p. 6.

[8]See the brief, but helpful, introduction to Holzhey's work by Peter A. Schmid and Simone Zurbuchen, *Grenzen der kritischen Vernunft. Helmut Holzhey zum 60. Geburtstag*, Basel 1997, pp. 7–8, 10.

Under the dark shadow of the Holocaust it is understandable that some will continue to hold Cohen's persistent aspiration to reconcile – for instance, Judaism and modernity or Jewishness and Germanness – in low regard, even as a betrayal of a core Jewish loyalty. And yet, as increasing scholarly attention is focused on the vibrant cultural world of European Jewry prior to the Shoah, and as we are urged to resist the impulse to "backshadow" that compels us to regard past events or actors as necessary links in a causal chain leading to the Holocaust, then we would be well advised to consider anew not only the philosophical achievements, but also the intriguing cultural-historical predicament of Jews such as Hermann Cohen.[9] Particularly in a world in which divided or hybrid identities are widely acknowledged and even celebrated, Hermann Cohen's concerted attempts to demonstrate the affinity between seemingly distinct thought systems and identities bespeaks an important experiment in cultural engineering in a highly complex social milieu.

We need not deny Gershom Scholem's famous claim that the German-Jewish dialogue was one-sided.[10] After all, it is hard to find Christian thinkers contemporaneous with Cohen who sought to demonstrate that their German-Christian identity was identical to Judaism.[11] More common were those who asserted that ancient Judaism formed a part, if largely superseded, of their own Christian identity. In this regard, Cohen had regular exchanges with Protestant theologians throughout his career, but few genuine partners in his search for a reconciliation of Jewish and German-Christian cultures. But it is precisely the unrequited quality of his attempted reconciliation that interests us, for it sheds light on and adds poignancy to his predicament as a German-Jewish intellectual.

The aim of this essay is to explore Hermann Cohen's textured engagement with German culture, with a particular focus on his desire to fuse diverse traditions into what might be called Protestant Judaism. What is intriguing is that while Cohen had few Protestant partners in this endeavour, he nonetheless belonged to an historical moment in which the principle of reconciliation (*Versöhnung*) was central to the activity of Protestant intellectuals in Germany. He himself embraced the term as a tool of theological clarification to describe the nature of the relationship between humans and God.[12] At the same time, Cohen understood the term in a broader, less technical sense – as a bridge between traditional religion and modern culture. It is a

---

[9]The critique of "backshadowing" animates Michael André Bernstein in *Foregone Conclusions: Against Apocalyptic History*, Berkeley 1994.

[10]According to Scholem, "(t)his dialogue died at its very start and never took place". Gershom Scholem, 'Against the Myth of the German-Jewish Dialogue' in Werner J. Dannhauser (ed.), *On Jews and Judaism in Crisis*, New York 1976, p. 62.

[11]Leo Strauss, however, observed a countervailing trend in which "the German spirit, turning to Jewish tendencies, makes them alive within itself…" This comment surfaced in a review of Rudolf Otto's *Das Heilige*, a text which manifested precisely that tendency of which Strauss spoke. See the review in *Der Jude*, 7 (1922–1923), pp. 240–242.

[12]Cohen wrote an essay on 'Die Versöhnungsidee' in 1890–1892 in which he addresses not the contemporary cultural manifestations of *Versöhnung*, but typically "the prophetic concept of man's reconciliation with God". See the English version of this essay excerpted in *Reason and Hope: Selections from the Jewish Writings of Hermann Cohen*, trans. Eva Jospe, New York 1971, p. 200. It is interesting to bear in mind Amos Funkenstein's point that the term "accommodation", a conceptual cognate of "reconciliation", came to indicate in modern times the "emancipation of the secular from transcendental connotations". Amos Funkenstein, *Perceptions of Jewish History*, Berkeley 1993, p. 98.

similar understanding that undergirded the contemporaneous enterprise of *Kulturprotestantismus*.[13] This term, which seems to have surfaced initally in the last years of the First World War, was first applied as a pejorative reference to liberal Protestants who had subordinated the integrity of religious experience to the demands of modern culture. However, the term also came to assume a more neutral connotation as a descriptor for a set of intersecting religious and social values embraced by liberal Protestants in Germany from the last third of the nineteenth century through the first third of the twentieth. The opening statement of the newly founded *Deutscher Protestantenverein* in 1863 spoke of the need for "a renewal of the Protestant church in the spirit of evangelical freedom and *in harmony with the general cultural development of our age*".[14] Accommodating Protestantism to the spirit of the time required careful calibration of political and social, as well as theological, positions. Hence, those who operated under the aegis of *Kulturprotestantismus* tended to espouse a liberal version of nationalism which envisaged the German state as a *Rechtsstaat*, motivated by a strong sense of righteousness and justice. That is not to say that *Kulturprotestanten* necessarily believed that Christianity, as a religion of the spirit, should intervene in the affairs of a political state. Christianity's influence should be both broader and more diffuse, bestowing upon society its most exalted spiritual values. In this respect, *Kulturprotestantismus*, as George Rupp has noted, was "an expression of the Christian ethical imperative to inform and shape the whole of life so that it realizes the ultimately religious significance which is its ground and end".[15]

The point of this digression to *Kulturprotestantismus* is not merely to note its contemporaneity with Hermann Cohen. It is to suggest that Cohen shared much with its adepts: the commitment to the preeminence of the ethical in understanding the spirit of religion; the conviction in the compatibility between ethical-religious values and modern social norms; and the belief that the German state, with its ethical and cultural legacy, was the most enlightened form of political expression ever developed, not to mention the catalyst for a global confederation of nation-states that heralded the messianic era. Given Cohen's adherence to these articles of faith, it does not seem unreasonable to designate him an exemplar of a *jüdischer Kulturprotestantismus*. Seemingly oxymoronic, this term captures the tension-filled position that Hermann Cohen, and many German Jews, occupied as they passed frequently and often imperceptibly into German society, only to be reminded periodically of the discrete boundaries around their Jewish group allegiance.

---

[13]As early as 1865 the Heidelberg theologian Richard Rothe declared that the primary goal of a newly formed group of liberal Protestants into the "Deutscher Protestantenverein" was the "Versöhnung von Religion und Kultur". Quoted in Friedrich Wilhelm Graf, 'Kulturprotestantismus. Zur Begriffsgeschichte einer theologiepolitischen Chiffre', in *Archiv für Begriffsgeschichte*, 28 (1984), p. 217. Uriel Tal notes that Rothe sought to cleanse Protestantism of its irrational elements in a manner consistent with modern science. See Uriel Tal, *Christians and Jews in Germany: Religion, Politics, and Ideology in the Second Reich, 1870–1914*, translated by Noah J. Jacobs, Ithaca, NY 1975, p. 162.

[14]Graf, 'Kulturprotestantismus', pp. 216–217, my emphasis.

[15]George Rupp, *Culture-Protestantism: German Liberal Theology at the Turn of the Twentieth Century*, Missoula, Montana 1977, p. 9.

BETWEEN WITTENBERG AND DESSAU

It has been noted that Hermann Cohen's birthplace of Coswig lies between Wittenberg, home of Martin Luther, and Dessau, birthplace of Moses Mendelssohn.[16] These two locales symbolised the poles between which Cohen's intellectual world-view was forged. It is hardly surprising that Moses Mendelssohn would have inspired Cohen. Not only was Mendelssohn a contemporary and philosophical colleague of Cohen's master, Immanuel Kant, he also exemplified the very Enlightenment-era reconciliation between Judaism and modernity that Cohen so valued in his life's work.

Cohen's attraction to Luther would seem somewhat more complicated, given the latter's periodic anti-Jewish outbursts.[17] And yet, Luther was one of the most storied heroes in Cohen's philosophical pantheon. For Cohen, Luther was the prototypical German patriot, and a pioneering influence in the formation of German language and cultural identity. More significantly, Cohen identified in Luther's Reformation a principle – namely, that religion was a function not of ecclesiastical authority but of individual conscience – which resonated deeply with his own and Mendelssohn's philosophical tenets.[18]

That the legacy of Protestantism left a deep imprint on Cohen was acknowledged by Franz Rosenzweig in his introduction to Cohen's collected Jewish writings. In 1924 Rosenzweig observed, with Hermann Cohen uppermost in mind, that "all modern Jews, and German Jews more than any others, are Protestants".[19] Rosenzweig's observations have been echoed by later readers of Cohen. Hans Liebeschütz, in an excellent historical essay on Hermann Cohen, called attention to Cohen's "radically liberal interpretation" of Luther which bespoke a deep and abiding sympathy with Protestantism.[20] More recently, Jacques Derrida made this point more explicit by referring to Cohen as a "Judeo-Protestant".[21]

The roots of Cohen's hybrid identity, hinted at by Derrida, reach back to his formative experience in the town of Coswig. As one of a handful of Jews in the town, Cohen was raised in an environment dominated by the Protestant Church. The powerful cultural presence of Protestantism continued to inform Cohen's self-understanding as a Jew throughout his life. Cohen's "protestant" vision assumed the form

---

[16]See E. Steinthal, 'Aus Hermann Cohens Heimat' in *Allgemeine Zeitung des Judentums*, 82 (April 1918), p. 222; see also Martha Cohen's introduction to the first edition of *Religion der Vernunft*.

[17]On Luther's derogatory attitudes toward Jews, see his 1543 text, 'Concerning the Jews and their Lies' excerpted in Jacob R. Marcus (ed.), *The Jew in the Medieval World*, New York 1983, pp. 167–169.

[18]See Cohen's 1915–1916 essay 'Deutschtum und Judentum', in Bruno Strauß (ed.), *Hermann Cohens Jüdische Schriften*, vol. 2, Berlin 1924, pp. 241–243. (Hereafter *Jüdische Schriften*). See also the illuminating comments in Hans Liebeschütz, 'Hermann Cohen and his Historical Background', in *LBI Year Book, XIII* (1968), p. 13.

[19]See Franz Rosenzweig's introduction to *Jüdische Schriften*, vol. 1, Berlin 1924, p. xxviii.

[20]Liebeschütz argues that Cohen's reading of Luther reflected the influence of the school of Protestant theology associated with Albrecht Ritschl, teacher of both Friedrich Nietzsche and Ernst Troeltsch. Both the Ritschlian school and Cohen sought to immunise theological truths against the advances of historicism, in large measure by resorting to Kant. Liebeschütz, p. 13.

[21]Jacques Derrida, 'Interpretation at War: Kant, the Jew, the German', in *New Literary History*, 22 (1991), p. 54. Cohen's essay 'Deutschtum und Judentum', reinforced the author's long-held belief that there was a complete union of interests between German and Jewish identities.

of an unwavering commitment to a Judaism of ethical perfection rather than ritual observance. It also prompted him to construct an intellectual and spiritual genealogy – a "Platonico-Judeo-Protestant axis" according to Derrida – which commenced with the Biblical prophetic tradition and included Plato, Maimonides, Luther, and Kant before culminating in the modern German Jew represented by Cohen himself.[22] Before exploring the contours of this genealogy, it might be helpful first to retrace Cohen's early path from cantor's son to Neo-Kantian philosopher.

Hermann Cohen was born on July 4, 1842 in Coswig, a small town in central Germany that belonged at the time to the principality of Anhalt-Bernburg. Situated on the banks of the Elbe River, this town hosted a tiny Jewish community that numbered some eleven families at the beginning of the nineteenth century. In 1800, twenty-three years after gaining the right of settlement, the Jews of Coswig were permitted to construct a synagogue on Domstrasse that was renovated in 1843. This institution assumed a dominant role in Hermann Cohen's early life. Indeed, the family lived on the same street, since Cohen's father served as cantor at the synagogue, as well as teacher of the town's Jewish youth.

The Cohen household reflected the traditional piety of the parents, Gerson and Friederike (née Salomon). On the Sabbath, the family welcomed passing Jewish travellers into their home during which time the father would engage the visitors in Talmudic discussion.[23] Hermann Cohen's deep Jewish ethos – the sense of tribal affinity that would later manifest itself in his activist stance against antisemitism – was born in this intimate ambience. So too was his often-ignored, yet expansive Jewish knowledge, which enabled the mature Cohen to draw freely on ancient and medieval Jewish sources.

Cohen's father oversaw his son's Jewish education.[24] He began to teach Hermann Hebrew from the age of three and a half, and continued to instruct him in Jewish subjects even after the young Cohen had left to attend the non-Jewish grammar school (*Gymnasium*) in Dessau at age eleven. Much later in life, when Gerson moved to Marburg, Hermann Cohen, then a renowned philosophy professor, would fill in for his ailing father as the *shaliah tsibur* (prayer leader) at the local synagogue.[25] Even though Cohen *fils* did not lead a scrupulously observant life, his reverence for Jewish tradition and ritual, as personified by his father, remained firm. Franz Rosenzweig acknowledged this point in the closing sentence of his introduction to Cohen's Jewish writings when he recalled that Cohen's great Jewish book, the posthumously published *Religion der Vernunft*, was dedicated neither to a philosophical school nor to a leading intellectual influence, but rather to the man who bestowed on him a grounded sense of German-Jewish identity: his father.[26]

If Hermann Cohen's allegiance to Jewish religion was forged in the insular confines of Jewish Coswig, his equally steadfast faith in the virtue of Protestant ethics

---

[22]Derrida, p. 61.
[23]Hermann Cohen, 'Der polnische Jude', first published in *Der Jude* (June 1916) and republished in *Jüdische Schriften*, vol. 2, p. 163.
[24]Steinthal, p. 223.
[25]*ibid*.
[26]Rosenzweig, introduction to *Jüdische Schriften*, vol. 1, p. lxiv.

and German culture was born there as well. By his own account, he grew up in an environment largely free from expressions of anti-Jewish sentiment. His father typified the sense of social optimism which this environment yielded and to which his son would later give telling expression. The traditionalist *melamed* felt at home in the Gentile surroundings of the town; he was friendly with Protestant teachers who respected his learning and regarded him as a colleague. He was also a proud German patriot, who at the outbreak of the Franco-Prussian War, prayed for his country along with fellow Coswig residents in the town's church.[27]

The example of the father's patriotism left an indelible imprint on Hermann Cohen. Throughout his life, Cohen remained convinced that Germany was the most enlightened nation known to humanity, a beacon of humanism to the rest of the world. While for many Jewish contemporaries, not to mention later critics, this view appeared contrived, it emerged quite naturally from Cohen's formative environment. In fact, Cohen was a classic representative of the kind of German Jew, ever loyal to the cherished *Bildungsideal*, to whom George Mosse has famously called attention.[28]

This ideal was fortified during Cohen's many years of learning and teaching in German academic institutions. At the *Herzogliches Gymnasium* in Dessau, where Cohen was the first Jewish student admitted, he was in a class with eleven others boys, of whom seven went on to study Protestant theology. After four years of study at the *Gymnasium*, Cohen went to study at the new *Jüdisch-Theologisches Seminar* established in Breslau in 1854. This decision was a fitting Jewish parallel to the study of Protestant theology, and perhaps already reflected Cohen's vision of the proximity, even confluence, of Judaism and Protestantism.

At Breslau, the fifteen-year-old Cohen began to study with some of the most distinguished Jewish scholars in nineteenth-century Germany: Jakob Bernays, Heinrich Graetz, and Zacharias Frankel. Each of these scholars exerted a deep, though not necessarily favourable, impression on Cohen. The classicist Bernays was a powerful intellectual personality, and yet, Cohen recalled fifty years later "there was no living, creative, constructive thought at work in this powerful machine".[29]

Bernay's sober and dispassionate attitude stood in contrast to Heinrich Graetz, who taught Talmud and history. Graetz was then in the midst of writing the first volumes of what would become the most important historical survey of the Jews of the century, the eleven-volume *Geschichte der Juden*. Unlike Bernays, Graetz possessed an untamed "impulsivity" which informed "his interesting and lively presentation of the great men of our literature" and which, Cohen once recalled, "elevated us to our spiritual heights".[30]

---

[27]Steinthal, p. 223.
[28]See the classic exposition in George L. Mosse, *German Jews beyond Judaism*, Bloomington 1985. For critical perspectives on Mosse's view of the dominance of *Bildung* in German-Jewish culture, see Klaus L. Berghahn (ed.), *The German-Jewish Dialogue Reconsidered: A Symposium in Honor of George L. Mosse*, New York 1996.
[29]My emphasis. See Cohen's recollection, 'Ein Gruss der Pietät an das Breslauer Seminar', in *Jüdische Schriften*, vol. 2, p. 421.
[30]*ibid.*, p. 420.

Notwithstanding Graetz's powerful effect on him, Cohen decided to leave rabbinical studies after four years.[31] He immediately took up the study of philosophy and philology at the *Königlich Preussische Universität* in Breslau, proving himself to be an outstanding student. But like many university students in Germany, Cohen pursued his studies at more than one university. In 1864 he left Breslau and moved to Berlin to study at the *Friedrich-Wilhelms-Universität*. While continuing his work in philosophy, Cohen also became enthralled with the new academic discipline of *Völkerpsychologie* developed by the renowned Jewish scholar Heymann Steinthal. This field entailed an historically grounded approach to the psychology of groups. In particular, practitioners sought to comprehend the spirit of a people by examining its language, myths, religion, ethics, and public institutions.[32] Under Steinthal's tutelage, Cohen began to make use of the historical and philological tools of this new discipline. Indeed, his first published article on Plato's theory of ideas, reflecting his use of these tools, appeared in the journal edited by Steinthal and another prominent Jewish scholar, Moritz Lazarus: the *Zeitschrift für Völkerpsychologie und Sprachwissenschaft*.[33]

Simultaneous with his training in *Völkerpsychologie* in Berlin, Cohen also became an enthusiastic supporter of a new philosophical movement that was gaining considerable momentum in the 1860s, and whose rallying cry was "back to Kant".[34] The movement had strong support in Berlin where Cohen was studying. In fact, various scholars have noted the strong links in this period between the *Völkerpsychologie* school and Berlin neo-Kantians such as Adolf Trendelenburg.[35] Consistent with this link, Cohen increasingly focused his intellectual energies on the philosophy of Immanuel Kant, even though he did not abandon altogether the methods of *Völkerpsychologie* for at least a decade, that is, not until the late 1870s. Cohen's new interest in Kant culminated in a book and a long article in 1871, both of which revealed a lively interest and bold confidence in intervening in the bitter disputes that had erupted among the new cohort of Kant interpreters.[36]

---

[31]On later occasions, Cohen proved less reverential toward Graetz, castigating his erstwhile teacher for his overly partisan, i.e. nationalistic, presentation of Jewish history. See, for example, Cohen's 1880 response to Heinrich von Treitschke's attack on Graetz (in which Cohen adds a few unflattering remarks of his own), 'Ein Bekenntnis in der Judenfrage', reprinted in *Jüdische Schriften*, vol. 2, pp. 73–94. See also Cohen's commemorative essay on the centenary of Graetz's birth, 'Grätzens Philosophie der jüdischen Geschichte', *ibid.*, 3, p. 203–212. I discuss Cohen's relationship to Graetz in a chapter on Cohen in my forthcoming book, *Beyond History: Anti-Historicism in Modern Jewish Thought*.

[32]See Ingrid Belke's introduction to Moritz Lazarus, *Moritz Lazarus und Heymann Steinthal. Die Begründer der Völkerpsychologie in ihren Briefen*, vol. 1, Tübingen 1971, p. lii.

[33]See, for instance, Cohen's 1866 essay, 'Psychologische Entwicklung der platonischen Ideenlehre', reprinted in *idem*, *Kleine philosophische Schriften*, edited by Albert Görland and Ernst Cassirer, Berlin 1927, pp. 30–87.

[34]See, for instance, Herbert Schnädelbach, *Philosophy in Germany, 1831–1933*, trans. Eric Matthew, Cambridge 1984, pp. 76 and 100; or Henri Dussort, *L'école de Marbourg*, Paris 1963, p. 37. The return to Kant movement sought to navigate between the perceived metaphysical excesses of the previously dominant Hegelianism and the hyper-empiricism of the new positivism. By reviving the Kantian legacy of "transcendental logic", the neo-Kantians thereby aimed to recast the focus of philosophical inquiry from metaphysics to epistemology without surrendering to a lifeless scientism.

[35]See, for instance, Andrea Poma, *The Critical Philosophy of Hermann Cohen*, trans. John Denton, Albany, NY 1997, pp. 4–5, 269–270.

[36]Cohen's article, 'Zur Kontroverse zwischen Trendelenburg und Kuno Fischer', originally published in 1871 in the *Zeitschrift für Völkerpsychologie und Sprachwissenschaft*, was reprinted in Cohen's *Kleine philosophische Schriften*. His first major book-length study of Kant, *Kants Theorie der Erfahrung*, was also published in 1871.

In fact, it was Cohen's book from 1871, *Kants Theorie der Erfahrung*, that attracted the attention of Friedrich Albert Lange, the philosopher renowned for his 1866 study, *Geschichte des Materialismus*.[37] Lange was a newly appointed professor at the Protestant university of Marburg. He endeavoured to bring Cohen to Marburg, first by convincing his colleagues to accept Cohen's *Kants Theorie der Erfahrung* as an *Habilitationsschrift* (equivalent to a second doctorate and qualifying its holder for a professorial position). Lange also lobbied to gain Cohen an academic appointment to the university. He first had to convince his colleagues that Cohen, as a Jewish instructor of philosophy in a Protestant university, would not be hostile to Christianity. Lange reportedly asked Cohen if there was "any serious difference between us in regard to Christianity". Cohen's answer was telling, offering an early articulation of his deeply held Protestant Jewish sensibility: "No, because what you call Christianity – I call prophetic Judaism."[38] Shortly thereafter, Cohen was appointed *Privatdozent* at Marburg in 1873; three years later, he succeeded the recently deceased Lange as the chair holder in philosophy.

It was at this point that Hermann Cohen began to develop, along with his Protestant colleague Paul Natorp, the distinct tradition of neo-Kantianism that would come to be known as the Marburg School. It is important to note here that one of the most confusing features of neo-Kantianism is the fact that various and diverse groups of thinkers laid claim to its mantle. Hence, the Southwest or Baden school of neo-Kantians, which included thinkers such as Wilhelm Windelband and Heinrich Rickert, was particularly interested in utilising Kantian categories to establish a stable protocol for the study of history. The Marburg School of neo-Kantians, by contrast, did not share this emphasis, and was at times antagonistic to contemporary historical study. Its main objective was to affirm that human consciousness was the source of all things knowable, including experience. In rejecting the existence of a noumenal realm beyond consciousness, the Marburg School was careful to maintain that thought was not a matter of mere subjectivity. On the contrary, Cohen and his colleagues devoted considerable attention to the function of science and scientific method in framing human knowledge. Even more distinctively, Hermann Cohen and his colleagues in Marburg held that one of the chief goals of philosophy, as a scientific enterprise, was to clarify the central role of the ethical in human thought and behavior. This emphasis on the ethical not only distinguished the Marburg tradition of neo-Kantianism, but also undergirded Hermann Cohen's vision of the juncture of Jewish and Protestant ideals.

---

[37] It is a measure of Lange's magnanimity that he vigorously supported Cohen's cause notwithstanding Cohen's sharp disagreement with him over the significance of materialism in the history of philosophy. While Cohen dismissed materialism as a brief episode in antiquity, Lange called Cohen's *Kants Theorie der Erfahrung*, "one of the most significant achievements to emerge in the field of philosophy in the last years". Quoted in Orlik, *Hermann Cohen: Kantinterpret*, p. 54. See also Poma, pp. 58–59.

[38] Cohen expressed gratitude to Lange "without whose aid I would not have been able to became a university lecturer" *ibid.*, p. 54. For an account of Cohen's exchange with Lange, see Jehuda Melber, *Hermann Cohen's Philosophy of Judaism*, New York 1968, p. 82.

AT HOME IN MARBURG?

At first glance, Marburg would seem to have been an unlikely site for a Jewish thinker to expound a philosophical system marked by the quest for a universal ethics. Home to the oldest Protestant university in Germany (founded in 1527), Marburg was a small provincial town in Hesse. The university possessed a long tradition of tolerance, extending back to its early history as a centre of Calvinist dissent. In the early eighteenth century, the theologian Christian Wolff, shunned by other German universities and feared by some Marburg professors themselves, was invited to teach at Marburg.[39] During this century, the fortunes of the university first improved – with a dramatic rise in student attendance – and then declined as a result of financial difficulties.

By the early nineteenth century, the university had regained some lustre through such scholars as Carl von Savigny, who was the moving force behind the "historical school of law" (*historische Rechtsschule*). Among Savigny's students were the brothers Jacob and Wilhelm Grimm who devoted themselves to the collection and analysis of German folk traditions.[40] The university also was home to a jurist, Silvester Jordan, who authored a new liberal constitution in 1830 intended to replace the despotic rule of Kurfürst Wilhelm in Hesse-Kassel.[41] However, Wilhelm's son, Prince Friedrich Wilhelm, paid only lip service to the new constitution, and sought to stifle political expression at the university. At this point, the university's fortunes began to sag under the oppressive weight of Friedrich Wilhelm's control.

This rather gloomy period in the university's history came to an end in 1866, the year in which Prussia annexed a number of northern German states, including Hesse. Prussian rule inaugurated a new era of openness and free thought for the Marburg institution. In 1872, Hermann Cohen's mentor, F. A. Lange, joined the university, and shortly thereafter, began his efforts to bring Cohen to Marburg. Cohen, in turn, worked in tandem with Paul Natorp to attract an excellent and diverse cadre of students that included Ernst Cassirer, José Ortega y Gasset, and even the author Boris Pasternak.

These efforts to transform Marburg into a major centre of neo-Kantian philosophy were matched by vital activity in the field of theology. Wilhelm Herrmann, with whom Cohen conversed on theological matters, was appointed professor of theology in 1879. Like Cohen, Herrmann drew promising young students to Marburg through his sharp intellect and liberal inclinations. Indeed, many of the most important names in Protestant theology – Karl Barth, Martin Rade, Adolf von Harnack, and Julius Wellhausen – studied, taught or worked in Marburg at one point or another in the turn-of-the-century period.

It is clear that the Prussian annexation of Hesse gave impetus to an impressive bout of growth at the university, particularly in the fields of philosophy and theology.

---

[39]For a detailed discussion of the university in this period, see H. Hermelink and S.A. Kaehler, *Die Philipps-Universität zu Marburg, 1527–1927*, Marburg 1927, p. 388ff. Drawing on Dussort, Judy Deane Saltzman also provides a good summary of Marburg's history in *Paul Natorp's Philosophy of Religion within the Marburg Neo-Kantian Tradition*, Hildesheim 1981, pp. 32–34.

[40]See Hermelink and Kaehler, *Die Philipps-Universität zu Marburg*, 477, as well as Ingeborg Schnack, 'Die Philipps-Universität zu Marburg 1527–1977', in Wilfried Frhr. von Bredow (ed.), *450 Jahre Philipps-Universität Marburg*, Marburg 1979, pp. 92–94.

[41]Hajo Holborn, *A History of Modern Germany, 1840–1945*, Princeton 1969, p. 24.

And yet, the arrival of the Prussians also introduced another, countervailing current with direct consequences for Hermann Cohen: namely, the rise of a vigorous new antisemitism which found adherents among the rural farmers and peasants of Hesse.[42] The chief agitator was Otto Böckel, a librarian at the University of Marburg who came to know the country peasants through his work collecting German folk songs and tales.[43] Böckel forged a unique brand of populist politics that combined anti-Prussian, anti-clerical, and antisemitic sentiments. Campaigning under the slogan "Against Junkers and Jews", Böckel became the first openly antisemitic candidate elected to the *Reichstag* (1887).

Hermann Cohen was acutely aware of the rising chorus of antisemitic voices in his midst. He had himself been embroiled some years earlier in the infamous controversy occasioned by the historian Heinrich von Treitschke's attack on Heinrich Graetz.[44] In that earlier episode, Cohen challenged von Treitschke's claims that the Jews of Germany were unassimilable, by stating that there was hardly "any difference between Israelite monotheism and Protestant Christianity".[45] At the same time, Cohen criticised his former teacher, Heinrich Graetz, in bitter terms, accusing him of a "frightening perversity of emotional judgments".[46] The ferocity of Cohen's comments regarding a fellow Jew brought down upon him widespread condemnation within the German-Jewish community in 1880–1881, and prompted his one-time teacher, Heymann Steinthal, to break off contact with him.[47]

As controversial as it was, Cohen's response to Treitschke rested on a premise that would later serve him in his role as a public figure in Jewish communal affairs: namely, that antisemitism was as alien to an enlightened German nation as Judaism was compatible with it. In Cohen's mind, von Treitschke violated the former principle, whereas Graetz denied the basic confluence of Germanness and Jewishness. He, by contrast, held firm to both principles which undergirded his subsequent career as an activist in German-Jewish defense work.

One of the most apposite instances of such activism was Cohen's role in an antisemitic episode in Marburg shortly after Otto Böckel was elected to the *Reichstag*. In 1888 Cohen was summoned by a judge to serve as an expert witness in the trial of a local teacher who had been accused of defaming the Jewish religion. Pitted against

---

[42]Richard Levy notes that while many Hessian peasants greeted the arrival of the Prussians with fear and apprehension, the Jewish population "openly welcomed the annexation of Electoral Hesse by Prussia". The resulting gap in attitude helps explain the rise of antisemitism in the region. See Richard S. Levy, *The Downfall of the Anti-Semitic Political Parties in Imperial Germany*, New Haven 1975, p. 53. See also Rudy Koshar, *Social Life, Local Politics, and Nazism. Marburg, 1880–1935*, Chapel Hill, NC 1986, p. 65.

[43]On Böckel's activities, see Levy, pp. 39–48 and Peter Pulzer, *The Rise of Political Anti-Semitism in Germany and Austria*, Cambridge, MA 1988, p. 102.

[44]Von Treitschke published his attack on Graetz, 'Ein Wort über unser Judenthum', in 1880. On the dispute, see Michael A. Meyer, 'Great Debate on Antisemitism: Jewish Reactions to New Hostility in Germany 1879–1881', in *LBI Year Book XI* (1966), pp. 137–170 and *idem*, 'Heinrich Graetz and Heinrich von Treitschke: A Comparison of their Historical Image of the Modern Jew', in *Modern Judaism*, 6 (1986).

[45]See Cohen's response to von Treitschke in 'Ein Bekenntnis' in *Jüdische Schriften*, vol. 2, p. 74; originally published as a separate pamphlet in Berlin in 1880.

[46]Cohen, 'Ein Bekenntnis', p. 76.

[47]See Dieter Adelmann, 'H. Steinthal und Hermann Cohen', in *Hermann Cohen's Philosophy of Religion*, eds. Stéphane Moses and Hartwig Wiedebach, Hildesheim 1997, pp. 2–3.

the well-known Göttingen orientalist Paul de Lagarde, Cohen took a page out of the history of medieval disputations by defending the integrity of the Talmud, particularly by asserting that it was not antagonistic to non-Jews. On the contrary, Cohen argued, the Talmud was full of charitable sentiments towards Gentiles. Moreover, Cohen sought to demonstrate not only that moral precepts were prominently represented in the Talmud, but that "in many places in the Talmud one notices the tendency to shift the centre from law to ethical teachings".[48]

Cohen's assertion of the primacy of the ethical in Judaism would become a standard feature of his intellectual project. In the case before us, it served as a successful tool to uphold the virtue of Judaism against antisemites; Cohen's testimony in the Marburg trial proved persuasive enough to help convict the antisemitic agitator. In broader terms, the primacy of the ethical resonated deeply with Cohen's neo-Kantianism. At the same time, it formed the basis of Cohen's protestant vision of Judaism, a sensibility born in his native Coswig and reinforced in his adopted Marburg.

Notwithstanding the outbreak of antisemitism in Hesse in the 1880s, Cohen shared with Protestant colleagues such as Herrmann, Natorp, and Wellhausen a number of important pillars of the liberal Protestant edifice they laboured to build. For example, Wilhelm Herrmann not only placed ethics at the centre of his theological investigations, but also sought to show the fundamental compatibility between New Testament morality and Kantian ethics.[49] In parallel fashion, Hermann Cohen aimed to demonstrate that a rational and universal ethical system was anchored in biblical, and especially, as we shall see, prophetic sources. The affinity between the two religious traditions was hardly foreign to Cohen. He declared, "just as Protestantism has thrown off the yoke of ecclesiastical tradition", so too ethical Judaism had thrown off the onerous yoke of rabbinic law.[50]

At one level, it was inevitable that Cohen would adopt the conceptual language of the broader Protestant milieu. After all, it was he who belonged to a minority religious community seeking to demonstrate its compatibility with a sometimes hostile majority culture. His Protestant colleagues neither felt nor demonstrated the need to render Protestantism compatible with Judaism. And yet, as we noted at the outset, they spoke a language deeply resonant with Cohen's own harmonising impulses: the language of reconciliation, particularly between traditional religious faith and modern society.

Within this broader discursive world of theological and social reconciliation, Hermann Cohen was at home in a Protestant culture; but his lingering Jewish loyalties prevented him from becoming fully of that culture. It is the resulting position of

---

[48]Cohen's brief in the trial, 'Die Nächstenliebe im Talmud', was published in Marburg in 1888 and reprinted in his *Jüdische Schriften*, vol, 1, p. 158; see also the editor's notes on this episode *ibid.*, pp. 338–339.

[49]See Rupp, *Culture-Protestantism*, p. 38. William Kluback offers a detailed analysis of the Cohen-Herrmann relationship, including a discussion of their shared interest in ethics as well as the important philosophical differences between them. See William Kluback, 'Friendship without Communication: Wilhelm Herrmann and Hermann Cohen', in *LBI Year Book XXXI* (1986), pp. 317–338.

[50]Cohen, 'Ein Bekenntnis', quoted in Uriel Tal, *Christians and Jews in Germany*, p. 62. See also Gabriel Motzkin, 'Hermann Cohen's Integration of Science and Religion', in *Archives de Science sociale des Religions* 60/1 (July-September 1985), p. 44.

liminality which suggests that Cohen was the formulator of a deeply held and uniquely conceived *jüdischer Kulturprotestantismus*.[51] That which Cohen shared with *Kulturprotestanten* themselves was the belief that an enlightened German nation and an enlightened ethical culture were consonant, if not identical.[52] Their shared concern for a socially responsible nation suffused by noble ethical values rested on a spiritual lineage whose heroes included Martin Luther and Immanuel Kant. By contrast, what distinguished Cohen from his Protestant contemporaries were their respective views of the provenance of this spiritual lineage, and hence of much of Western civilisation. Whereas Christian thinkers cast their gaze quite naturally on early Christianity, Hermann Cohen focused his attention on prophetic Judaism. A good part of the intricacy of our story stems from the fact that Protestant scholars themselves demonstrated considerable interest in the Israelite prophets in this period – and, in fact, stimulated Hermann Cohen's own curiosity in the subject.

FROM THE PROPHETS TO KANT: THE LINEAGE OF PROTESTANT JUDAISM

Cohen's designation of the prophets as the starting point of the ethical tradition that framed Western history was hardly his invention. On the one hand it represented an extension and refinement of mid-nineteenth-century liberal Jewish thought, most notably that of the Reform rabbi and scholar, Abraham Geiger, for whom the prophets represented the most exalted expression of Jewish morality.[53] On the other, it owed much to the surrounding non-Jewish intellectual culture. Indeed, Cohen's interest in the essential, and essentialising, features of the prophets paralleled the strong desire of many nineteenth and early twentieth-century Protestant thinkers to define the essence of Christianity.[54] The most famous expression of this desire came in Adolf von Harnack's series of lectures at the University of Berlin from 1899–1900. Later published as *Das Wesen des Christentums*, Harnack's lectures argued for the indispensability of history in yielding a nuanced understanding of Jesus, his followers, and the roots of early Christianity. A good number of theological opponents, including Martin Kähler, Cohen's colleague Wilhelm Herrmann, and later Karl Barth, challenged the view that

---

[51]Cohen was here exemplary of the "double aim" which Uriel Tal identifies in German Jewry: "to integrate completely into their environment as full-fledged Germans and at the same time preserve their separate existence." Tal, *Christians and Jews*, p. 17.
[52]See Tal's excellent discussion of liberal Protestant attitudes toward the state in the late nineteenth century in Tal, *Christians and Jews*, pp. 167–176.
[53]In surveying the evolution of Reform Judaism in the latter half of the nineteenth century, Michael A. Meyer notes that the "message of Israel's ancient Prophets, universalised beyond its original context, became for Geiger, as for the Reform movement, the most viable and important component of Judaism." Michael A. Meyer, *Response to Modernity: A History of the Reform Movement in Judaism*, New York 1988, pp. 95–96.
[54]See Tal, *Christians and Jews*, p. 203. Susannah Heschel argues that it was a Jewish scholar, Abraham Geiger, who actually prompted the intense Protestant interest in the essence of Christianity through his scholarly conclusion that Jesus was and must be considered a Jew. Though derivative, Protestant theology *per* Heschel failed to acknowledge Geiger. See Susannah Heschel, *Abraham Geiger and the Jewish Jesus*, Chicago 1998, pp. 9–10.

history *per se* could ever penetrate to the core of their religious tradition.[55] The essence of Christianity, they maintained, defied historicisation altogether.

In the midst of this intense debate over the essence of Christianity, Protestant historians, in particular, developed an interest in the Israelite prophets as an early link in the chain of Christianity's evolutionary development. One of the most illuminating cases was another of Hermann Cohen's Marburg colleagues and friends, Julius Wellhausen, the famous Biblical scholar. Much of what Cohen came to know and identify with the prophets was derived from his reading of Wellhausen and other Protestant Biblical scholars for whom the prophets represented the spiritual heights of Israelite religion.[56] Yet, Cohen rejected one of the fundamental tenets of this group of scholars: the idea that the prophets represented the terminal stages of *Spätjudentum* (late Judaism), whose spiritual embers were rekindled by the new and true Israel, Christianity. In this respect, Cohen had a great deal of ambivalence for the work of Wellhausen, a man whom he liked and admired. On one hand, Cohen believed, as he noted in a eulogy for Wellhausen in 1917, that his colleague truly grasped the "ethical foundation and universalism of the prophets".[57] On the other hand, Cohen could not understand why Wellhausen's studies "concluded with the political history of Israel and turned just as quickly to the history of the Arabs". "How could he end the history of Israel so abruptly", Cohen inquired, "without even devoting attention, as a philologist, to the language of the Mishna?"[58] The familiar neglect by Christian scholars of rabbinic Judaism proved irksome to Jewish students of antiquity generally, but in the specific case of Hermann Cohen unsettled his vision of an ecumenical bond between Jews and Christians.

The divergences between Cohen and Wellhausen regarding the Israelite prophets offer a revealing glance into the nature of Cohen's immersion into Protestant intellectual culture. While Cohen relied on Protestant scholarship for a nuanced understanding of the historical context of the prophets, he could not accept the theological claim that the prophets passed on the mantle of Israel's spiritual leadership to Christianity. Rather, he insisted on the ongoing relevance, and at times the ethical superiority, of a Judaism rooted in the prophetic tradition. But even while making this Judeocentric move, Cohen paralleled the thrust of some contemporaneous Protestant thinkers such as Wilhelm Herrmann and the later dialectical theologians who sought to dig through later historical manifestations of Christianity and locate its essence in antiquity. Hence, Cohen attempted to situate the essence of Judaism – its ethical grandeur – in the ancient prophets, and neglected subsequent rabbinic writings including the Talmud, codes, and commentaries.[59] For it was the prophets

---

[55]See Tal, *Christians and Jews*, p. 204, as well as Uriel Tal, 'Theologische Debatte um das 'Wesen' des Judentums', in Werner E. Mosse (ed.), *Juden im Wilhelminischen Deutschland, 1890–1914*, Tübingen 1976 (Schriftenreihe wissenschaftlicher Abhandlungen des Leo Baeck Instituts 33), pp. 599–632.

[56]According to Hans Liebeschütz, "it was the work of Wellhausen and his school, which gave the prophetic message its definite place in Cohen's interpretation of Judaism." Hans Liebeschütz, pp. 21–23.

[57]See Cohen's eulogy, 'Julius Wellhausen: Ein Abschiedsgruss', first published in the *Neue Jüdische Monatshefte* and reprinted in *Jüdische Schriften*, vol. 2, p. 464.

[58]*ibid.*, p. 464.

[59]A notable exception was Cohen's intervention in defense of the Talmud in Marburg in 1888, typically focused on the centrality of ethics.

who first – and most profoundly – grasped that monotheism was "an exclusively moral teaching."[60]

If the prophets were the progenitors of a sublime ethical system, their spiritual heirs tended not to be rabbis but philosophers, not all of whom were Jewish. Cohen was particularly intrigued by Plato, whom he regarded as adumbrating the principles of Kantian idealism. In fact, Cohen regarded Plato, along with the Israelite prophets, as "the two most important sources of modern culture", indeed as "the spiritual leaders of humanity".[61] Cohen did not mean to suggest that the prophets and Plato were identical, but rather that their complementarity laid the foundation for social progress in the modern world. The prophets' social consciousness contained the "pure source of religion".[62] But the prophetic mind knew nothing of scientific thought or reason. It was here that Plato innovated, not merely by introducing scientific perception, but by effecting a synthesis of science and morality (*Wissenschaft und Sittlichkeit*). Without science, Cohen declared, "there could be no perception, no idea, no idealism". Science provided the logical scaffolding for ethics, and thus enabled the human quest for the Good. In pioneering this momentous fusion of science and ethics, Plato had achieved a measure of "historical eternity" (*geschichtliche Ewigkeit*).[63]

Those who qualified for historical eternity in Cohen's scheme imparted a message that was not wedded to a single historical context, but which reflected the quest for a timeless and universal state of perfection.[64] While the foundations of this tradition were grounded in antiquity, the most important medieval exponent was Moses Maimonides, the great medieval Jewish scholar. Cohen's labors to include Maimonides's in his grand spiritual lineage led him to a reading quite distinct from other scholars. That is, he did not emphasise Maimonides' renown as a legal decisor or his acumen as a philosopher operating in the Aristotelian mould. He rather argued that the Maimonidean system reflected a strong Platonic thrust, particularly in its preoccupation with ethics. In making this claim, Cohen creatively re-interpreted Maimonides, upending the carefully delineated hierarchy of perfections set out in the last chapter of the *Guide of the Perplexed* (3:54).[65] Thus, Cohen seems to transpose or at least blur the fourth and final perfection of the Maimonidean system, rational virtues, and the penultimate perfection, moral virtues. The effect was to proclaim the pinnacle of the Maimonidean system as ethical, not intellectual, perfection.[66]

---

[60]Hermann Cohen, 'Der Stil der Propheten', in *Jüdische Schriften*, vol. 2, p. 263.

[61]See Cohen's posthumously published lecture from 1916, "Das soziale Ideal bei Platon und den Propheten", in *Jüdische Schriften*, vol. 1, pp. 306 and 330.

[62]*ibid.*, p. 310.

[63]*ibid.*, p. 309. For elaboration, see Pierfrancesco Fiorato, *Geschichtliche Ewigkeit. Ursprung und Zeitlichkeit in der Philosophie Hermann Cohens*, Königshausen 1993, especially chapter 3.

[64]It is appropriate here to recall the distinction, favoured by Kant, between the "historisch" and the "geschichtlich", that is between empirical and *a priori* notions of history. See Yirmiahu Yovel, *Kant and the Philosophy of History*, Princeton 1980, p. 240.

[65]See Moses Maimonides, *The Guide of the Perplexed*, ed. by Shlomo Pines/Leo Strauss, vol. 2, Chicago 1963, p. 635.

[66]According to Cohen, Maimonides adumbrated his own view that "God is not a God of metaphysics...but is rather the God of ethics." See Cohen's important essay, 'Characteristik der Ethik Maimunis', originally published in Wilhelm Bacher, Marcus Brann, and David Simonsen (eds.), *Moses ben Maimon: Sein Leben, seine Werke und sein Einfluss*, vol. 1, Leipzig 1908, and reprinted in *Jüdische Schriften*, vol. 3, p. 289.

In the process, Maimonides is transformed by Cohen into "the standard-bearer of Protestantism in medieval Judaism".[67] This anachronistic designation reflects Cohen's view that the great Spanish-Jewish philosopher understood the essence of Judaism to be its ethical ideals rather than its dogmas, prescriptions, or institutions. Hence, Maimonides was an appropriate precursor to Martin Luther, who also occupied a central place in Cohen's lineage. Luther's rejection of ecclesiastical authority and institutions redirected religious responsibility to the domain of the individual's conscience.[68] Indeed, in Luther, and the Reformation he heralded, Cohen located the core ingredients of the German nation he so admired – a nation rooted in the values of ethical autonomy, moral rectitude, and philosophic inquiry. This vision of Germany – and of Luther – revealed a highly selective historical approach. Rather than place Luther in a specific historical context, Cohen folded him into a sweeping trajectory of grand ethical thinkers who lay the foundation for Western civilisation.[69]

A similar selectivity informed Cohen's discussion of Immanuel Kant. Despite Kant's denigration of Judaism as mere "statutory laws", Cohen saw Kantianism as compatible, indeed deeply consonant, with Judaism. In the first instance, this consonance resulted, Cohen wrote in a 1910 essay on 'The Inner Relations of Kantian Philosophy to Judaism', from the "rejection of eudaemonism and all its varieties". That is, both Kant and Judaism exhibited steadfast "opposition to egoism, selfishness, and above all the horizon of individualism".[70] By contrast, both acknowledged fealty to the universal force of reason and to the higher goal of ethical progress which issued from it. This overarching ethical thrust led Kant and Jewish philosophers to conclude that the "essence of God is morality and only morality".[71] Moreover, it yielded a "social idealism...that stands in close connection to messianism".[72] It was precisely this link between social idealism and messianism that drew ancients (the prophets and Plato), medievals (Maimonides), and moderns (Kant) together into a fraternity of ethical grandeur.[73] And it was this fraternity which aspired to and attained a measure of "historical eternity".

DEUTSCHTUM UND JUDENTUM: A FUSION OF CULTURAL HORIZONS?

We have already seen that the lineage of ethical grandeur that Hermann Cohen developed embraced not only illustrious individual thinkers, but also entire cultural traditions. This point is perhaps most evident in Cohen's notorious '*Deutschtum und*

---

[67]See Cohen, 'Deutschtum und Judentum', in *Jüdische Schriften*, vol. 2, p. 244.
[68]See Liebeschütz, p.13.
[69]As Hans Liebeschütz has noted, Cohen's discussion of Luther was not beholden to "the collection of single facts from the life in Wittenberg in the sixteenth century." *ibid*.
[70]Cohen, 'Innere Beziehungen der Kantischen Philosophie zum Judentum', *Jüdische Schriften*, vol. 1, pp. 290 and 292.
[71]*ibid.*, p. 294.
[72]*ibid.*, p. 301.
[73]In eulogising his teacher, Ernst Cassirer wrote of Cohen that "(w)e encounter three fundamental moments in the thought of this great rationalist: Plato, Kant, and prophecy." See Cassirer's comments in the *Vossische Zeitung*, 18 May 1920, quoted in Orlik, *Hermann Cohen. Kantinterpret*, p. 156. Jacques Derrida, meanwhile, writes of the "Platonico-Judeo-Protestant axis" in Cohen's thought, Derrida, p. 61.

Judentum', the title given to a pair of long essays from 1915–1916 in which Cohen's harmonising instincts were at their most expansive. Written in the midst of the First World War, Cohen's essays argued that German Jews were – and deserved to be – fully at home in their fatherland. This message was addressed to world, and particularly American, Jewry, whose support Cohen hoped to elicit for the German war effort. Cohen argued that the "German spirit" had immeasurably enriched Jewish intellectual and cultural life in Germany; German Jews, in turn, exerted a nearly singular influence on the intellectual and cultural life of world Jewry.[74]

While appealing to Jews abroad, Cohen was also trying to convince many at home – Jews attracted to Zionism and non-Jews attracted to antisemitism – that the locus of Jewish collective fulfillment was Germany. His claim that the Jewish and German spirits were closely entwined relied on his identification of a set of intersecting idealisms: the prophetic sense of hope for social betterment and the Protestant-German advancement of philosophical-scientific thought. The point of intersection was a rationalist ethics that impelled the human quest for perfectibility – and hence the messianic process – forward.

The idea of messianism, as distinct from a personal messiah, was a central concept in Cohen's lexicon. Although its source lay in prophetic Judaism, its renewed force owed to the "the humanity of the German spirit" which pushed toward the unity of all mankind.[75] Cohen's ability here and elsewhere to filter out xenophobic, racist, and antisemitic elements of German political culture in conceiving of this idealised view of the German spirit was an astonishing feat of repression for which he was sternly castigated in his day and subsequently.[76] At one level, this instinct reflected the social pressures toward conformity that German Jews regularly encountered and internalised. At another level, Cohen's neglect issued from the deep-seated, we might even say intoxicated, faith that there was "a kindred spirit linking Germanness and Jewishness" and, moreover, that this spirit would set in motion a global political realignment toward a harmonious confederation of nations. In so doing, this spirit, with its Judeo-Protestant-German pedigree, would stimulate human progress toward "eternal peace".[77]

In chronological terms, Hermann Cohen's '*Deutschtum und Judentum*' represents the climax of his life-long pursuit of cultural and spiritual reconciliation. The essays were written a few years prior to Cohen's death, after he had moved to Berlin and assumed a position of prominence in Jewish intellectual circles there. And yet, Cohen's ecumenical language seemed out of touch with the hardened realities of the War years. The German-Jewish symbiosis of which he was a most fervent adherent, not to mention its most dedicated theorist, was assaulted by antisemites who insisted with new vigour that Jews were not serving their country in proportionate numbers and, in fact, could never be true members of the German nation. And as Cohen discovered in his debate with Martin Buber in 1916, Jewish intellectuals in Germany,

---

[74]Cohen, 'Deutschtum und Judentum (II)', p. 316.
[75]Cohen, 'Deutschtum und Judentum (I)', p. 267.
[76]For a convenient inventory of critical responses to 'Deutschtum und Judentum', see the editor's notes in *Jüdische Schriften*, vol. 2, p. 476.
[77]Cohen, 'Deutschtum und Judentum (I)', p. 290.

especially Zionists, often regarded Cohen's words as antiquated and disconnected from the new spirit of Jewish nationalism.[78]

Perhaps even more disappointing to Cohen than Buber's Zionist polemic was the failure of liberal Protestant intellectuals to affirm his millennial vision. It bears repeating that for all of his extensive interaction with and immersion in Protestant culture, Cohen had no real Christian partner in his spiritual journey toward a Protestant Judaism. This may come as little surprise to those familiar with theological discourse of the period, but a final example illustrates the gap between Cohen and *Kulturprotestanten* of his day. I am referring to Cohen's exchange, shortly before his death, with one of the most storied Protestant historians and theologians of the day, Ernst Troeltsch.

Uriel Tal and now Susannah Heschel have reminded us that, in the context of German-Jewish history, one's logical allies do not always become one's close friends; quite to the contrary, relations between liberal Jews and liberal Christians were often deeply strained.[79] In the case before us, Cohen and Troeltsch seemed to share a great deal, both in terms of their conception of an enlightened German polity and in their faith in an enlightened monotheistic religious tradition.[80] And yet, real and sharp divergences surfaced between them that symbolised the chasm between liberal Protestantism and liberal Judaism.

The dispute between Cohen and Troeltsch centred around a recurrent concern of both thinkers, the Israelite prophets.[81] An important and contiguous problem was

---

[78]Important excerpts of the debate between Buber and Cohen are included in Paul Mendes-Flohr and Jehuda Reinharz (eds.), *The Jew in the Modern World*, New York 1995, pp. 571–577. See also Moses Glückson's essay 'Hermann Cohen und das nationale Judentum' in *Neue Jüdische Monatshefte*, 3 (March 1919), pp. 231–235, cited in Jörg Hackeschmidt's helpful essay 'Die hebräischen Propheten und die Ethik Kants: Hermann Cohen in kultur- und sozialhistorischer Perspektive', *Aschkenas*, 1 (1995), p. 129. It is important to recall that Buber himself supported the German war effort for which he was ridiculed and excoriated by younger generations of German Zionists.

[79]Tal, *Christians and Jews*, p. 220. Susannah Heschel, meanwhile, offers a withering critique of liberal Protestant circles in turn-of-the-century Germany, accusing them of lack of originality, disingenuousness, and powerful anti-Jewish animus. See Heschel, p. 226.

[80]According to Wendell S. Dietrich, "(t)wo major proposals emerge on the late nineteenth-century German religious and intellectual scene-proposals for revising classic Western religious traditions in the interests of enhancing their credibility in the modern world:" namely, those of Cohen and Troeltsch. See Wendell S. Dietrich, *Cohen and Troeltsch: Ethical Monotheistic Religion and Theory of Culture*, Atlanta 1986, p. 5.

[81]There may also have been an overlay of personal suspicion involved in the relationship between Cohen and Troeltsch, particularly from Cohen's side. In 1913, Troeltsch dedicated the second volume of his collected writings to his mentor Paul de Lagarde, the noted nineteenth-century Orientalist. Lagarde, as already mentioned, was none other than Hermann Cohen's adversary in the 1888 trial of a man accused of defaming Judaism in Marburg. It was Lagarde who was called upon to defend the accuracy of the anti-Jewish defamations. Moreover, he was notorious for his frequent fulminations against Jews as alien and antagonistic to the German nation. See Jacob Katz's discussion of Lagarde in *From Prejudice to Destruction: Anti-Semitism, 1700–1933*, Cambridge, MA 1980, pp. 305–306, or George L. Mosse, *Toward the Final Solution: A History of European Racism*, Madison, Wisc. 1975, pp. 100–101. Although Troeltsch did distance himself from Lagarde's antisemitism, he did appreciate Lagarde's "essentially historical, and not speculative, comprehension of religion." Ernst Troeltsch, *Gesammelte Schriften*, vol. 2, Tübingen 1913, p. viii. Still, debates abound about the extent to which Troeltsch may have succumbed to an anti-Jewish bias himself. A particularly controversial indictment can be found in Constance L. Benson, *God and Caesar: Troeltsch's Social Teaching as Legitimation*, New Brunswick, NJ 1999, pp. 92–93. For a more tempered, though hardly flattering discussion, see Robert Rubanowice, *Crisis in Consciousness: The Thought of Ernst Troeltsch*, Tallahassee 1982, p. 126

Hermann Cohen and the Quest for Protestant Judaism 213

how best to understand, in an historicist age, the inspired values and texts of a given religious tradition. The historian Troeltsch fired the opening salvo in this affair with a lecture in 1916 on 'The Ethos of the Hebrew Prophets'.[82] Troeltsch argued that only an historical approach to religion (*eine religionsgeschichtliche Methode*) could generate serious investigation of the Israelite prophets. Troeltsch eschewed "a transcendental-rationalist" method, an unmistakable reference to Hermann Cohen's Marburg school of neo-Kantians.[83] Troeltsch's preferred strategy was to contextualise, or localise, the ethics of the prophets. Hence, he averred that "the ethics of the prophets is not the ethics of humanity, but rather of Israel (as reflected) in the undifferentiated unity of ethics, law, and morality that is particular to all ancient peoples." Challenging the image of the prophets as bearers of a universal message, Troeltsch rejected any equation between their ethical message and modern notions of "humanity and freedom or, less, democracy and socialism".[84] Israelite prophecy was born and bred in the rural ambience of ancient Palestine, far removed from the more sophisticated urban cultures of the day; it was in this rural context that "an oriental-religious messianic dream" was born.[85] And it was only by moving beyond this environment that Christianity was able to revive prophetism, leading to a "profundity and interiority of pure human feeling" unmatched by either Judaism or Islam.[86]

When Troeltsch offered these remarks in 1916, he was immediately challenged by a member of the audience, Benzion Kellermann who was a liberal rabbi and neo-Kantian student of Cohen's. Kellermann tried to publish his critical response in the same journal, *Logos*, in which Troeltsch published his lecture, but was rebuffed. Undeterred, Kellermann came out with a seventy page rebuttal to Troeltsch in 1917 entitled *Der ethische Monotheismus der Propheten und seine soziologische Würdigung*.[87] Later in the same year, Hermann Cohen printed a brief reply to Troeltsch, '*Der Prophetismus und die Soziologie*', that summarised many of Kellermann's main points.

Despite its brevity, Cohen's retort bristles with scornful disdain. It commences with a strong indictment of contemporary historiography whose materialist tendencies reduce all cultural achievements to social and economic conditions, and in so doing, remain blind to the "pure spiritual forces" that guide history.[88] Troeltsch's essay on Israelite prophecy masquerades as sociology, a discipline which Cohen ranks higher on the methodological ladder than history. But even the sociological approach of Ernst Troeltsch comes up far short. It grasps the ethics of Israelite prophets merely as a function of a rural "peasant mentality". Troeltsch's attempt to contextualise the prophetic impulse transforms "the universalism of the (Israelite) God into the particularism of a tribal god". "With this," Cohen laments, "Judaism as a religion is destroyed."[89]

---

[82]Troeltsch, 'Das Ethos der hebräischen Propheten', *Logos*, 6 (1916/17), pp. 1–28.
[83]Troeltsch, 'Das Ethos', p. 28. See Dietrich's discussion of the distinction between Troeltsch's Baden neo-Kantianism and Cohen's Marburg version in Dietrich, pp. 56–57.
[84]Troeltsch, 'Das Ethos', pp. 15 and 18.
[85]*ibid.*, pp. 24–25. See also Dietrich, pp. 38–39.
[86]Troeltsch, 'Das Ethos', pp. 26 and 28.
[87]Benzion Kellermann, *Der ethische Monotheismus der Propheten und seine soziologische Würdigung*, Berlin 1917.
[88]Cohen, 'Der Prophetismus und die Soziologie', originally published in the *Neue Jüdische Monatshefte*, 22 (25 August 1917), and reprinted in *Jüdische Schriften*, vol. 2, p. 398.
[89]*ibid.*, p. 399.

Cohen's outrage at the content of this lecture was matched by his outrage at the timing. How, in a time of rising antisemitism, could Troeltsch dare present such a flawed perspective on Israelite prophecy, which Cohen dismissively referred to as "supposed scholarship"?[90] Troeltsch had not only misunderstood the ethical mission of the prophets; he himself had violated, Cohen implied, the ethical mission of the scholar. But perhaps his gravest sin was that he had frustrated the ultimate act of reconciliation which Cohen hoped to effect between Jews and Protestants.

Hermann Cohen's vision of a Protestant Judaism did not survive much beyond his death in 1918. The succeeding Weimar period produced a wide range of particularist Jewish expressions that departed from Cohen's synthetic ideal. And the destruction of German Jewish culture during the Holocaust meant that no indigenous school of thought arose to perpetuate Cohen's thought. But we need not judge Cohen as naive or disloyal. Rather, we would do well to appreciate the sincerity of his conviction, the range of his erudition in diverse traditions, and the trying circumstances that fueled his desire for a Protestant Judaism. Above all, we should recall the predicament of this exceptional German-Jewish figure who was as unwilling to surrender his Jewish faith as he was to surrender the myth of a German-Jewish symbiosis.[91] For it not only forces us to acknowledge the rich complexity of the processes tucked neatly into a facile term like assimilation,[92] it also illumines, in appropriately nuanced fashion, the broader condition of modern Western Jews, ever straining to achieve a balance between the poles of particularism and universalism.*

---

[90] *ibid.*, p. 400.

[91] Jacques Derrida suggests that "a ruptivity, a dissociative and irruptive power" always lurked beneath such an attempted synthesis, Derrida, p. 44.

[92] For a brilliant, if underappreciated, complication of the term, see Gerson Cohen's 1966 commencement address at the Hebrew Teachers College, *The Blessing of Assimilation in Jewish History*, Brookline, MA 1966.

*The author would like to thank Nomi Maya Stolzenberg and Eugene Sheppard for their helpful reading of this essay.

Religion and Politics in the Berlin Jewish Community: The Work of the Repräsentantenversammlung, 1927–1930

BY ULRICH TEMPEL

"The end of the Liberal Party's domination – huge success for the Jewish People's Party." This is how the *Jüdische Rundschau* described the results of the election to the *Repräsentantenversammlung* of the Berlin Jewish community on 16 May 1926.[1] The traditionally dominant religious Liberal community representatives lost their absolute majority at this election and had to make do with ten of the twenty-one *Repräsentantensitze*.[2]

Divergent views concerning the meaning and activities a Jewish community should hold and undertake existed between the Liberals and the Zionist-influenced Jewish People's Party (JVP). While the Liberals emphasised the religious character of the community, the JVP represented the concept of the *Volksgemeinde* and supported the broadening of the community's scope of activities.[3] This article attempts to discover what effect these differing preconditions had on communal policy (*Gemeindepolitik*) under the changing majority. To this end, the discussions at the forty-three sessions of the *Repräsentantenversammlung* between July 1927 and December 1930 have been compiled and analysed on the basis of sources available in order to contribute to an understanding of the complex constitutional structure of the community and, in particular, of the intellectual debates concerning the further development of the Jewish community in the Weimar Republic.

The experiences of Jews in Weimar Germany differed greatly. At the beginning of the Weimar Republic German Jews looked back on decades which were shaped by an increasing tendency towards German bourgeois culture. This was accompanied by a considerable climb in social and economic status. Moreover, the Weimar constitution endorsed the full equal rights of Jews. The rights of the Jewish community as a religious community and one which embodied public law were strengthened and

---

[1]'Die Berliner Gemeindewahlen', in *Jüdische Rundschau*, (18 May 1898), p. 289.
[2]On the situation of the Jewish minority in the Weimar Republic, see Moshe Zimmermann, *Die deutschen Juden 1914–1945*, München 1997; Michael Meyer (series ed.), *Deutsch-jüdische Geschichte in der Neuzeit, vol. IV: Aufbruch und Zerstörung 1918–1945* by Avraham Barkai, Paul Mendes-Flohr, Munich 1997.
[3]On the JVP see Michael Brenner, 'The Jüdische Volkspartei. National-Jewish Communal Politics during the Weimar Republic', in *LBI Year Book XXXV* (1990), pp. 197–219.

state aid was granted.[4] On the other hand, Jews in the Weimar Republic felt confronted by an increase in antisemitism. The unsettling experience of the war and the immediate post-war years resulted in a general disorientation amongst the population. To many of those who were looking for scapegoats, Jews were a particularly useful target of blame. German Jews established extensive strategies of defence against antisemitism. The main thrust of this was carried out by the *Centralverein deutscher Staatsbürger jüdischen Glaubens* (C.V.) which sought to suppress antisemitism through education (*Aufklärung*) and legal means. However, there was no permanent union between Liberal Jews and Zionists in fighting antisemitism during the Weimar Republic.

THE BERLIN JEWISH COMMUNITY

There were more than 170,000 Jews living in Berlin in the 1920s; Berlin was thus one of the cities in the world with the largest proportion of Jews in its population.[5] The Berlin Jews had played a considerable part in the development of the city ever since the late seventeenth century. In the nineteenth and twentieth centuries Jews contributed in a variety of ways to the rapid rise of Berlin into a metropolis.[6] The rate of growth of the Jewish population was in close relation to that of the population in general. In the years between 1871 and 1933 about four per cent of the population was Jewish. In 1910 there were circa 144,000 Jews in Berlin, by 1925 there were 172,672, which represented an increase of circa twenty per cent.[7] Approximately thirty per cent of the Jewish population of Germany was located in Berlin in the mid 1920s. During the Weimar Republic Berlin was also the centre of East European Jews who had emigrated to Germany.

The Jews differed considerably in comparison with the general population in terms of their economic activity. In the mid twenties half of the Jewish population

---

[4]See Trude Maurer, 'Die Juden in der Weimarer Republik', in Dirk Blasius, Dan Diner (eds.), *Zerbrochene Geschichte*, Frankfurt a. Main 1991, pp. 102–120; Peter Gay, 'In Deutschland zu Hause ... Die Juden der Weimarer Zeit', ed. by Arnold Paucker, *Die Juden im Nationalsozialistischen Deutschland/The Jews in Nazi Germany 1933–1943*, ed. by Arnold Paucker, Tübingen 1986 (Schriftenreihe wissenschaftlicher Abhandlungen des Leo Baeck Instituts 45), pp. 31–43.

[5]The history of the *Jüdische Gemeinde zu Berlin* during the Weimar Republic is in its initial stages. This is mainly due to the loss of the community's archive and the scattering of its remains around the globe (particularly to the USA and Israel). It is only in the last few years that attempts have been made to broaden our knowledge of the history of the community using these existing documents. A thesis by Gabriel Alexander entitled *Berlin Jewry and their community during the Weimar Period, 1919–1933* was submitted to the Hebrew University in Jerusalem in 1995. Three articles which draw on this study and an English language summary were useful for my investigation of the activities of the *Repräsentantenversammlung*, for which I am grateful. C.f. Gabriel Alexander, 'Die Entwicklung der jüdischen Bevölkerung in Berlin zwischen 1871 und 1945', in *Tel Aviver Jahrbuch für deutsche Geschichte*, vol. XX (1991), pp. 287–314; idem, 'Die jüdische Bevölkerung Berlins in den ersten Jahrzehnten des 20. Jahrhunderts: Demographische und wirtschaftliche Entwicklungen', in Reinhard Rürup (ed.), *Jüdische Geschichte in Berlin. Essays und Studien*, Berlin 1995, pp. 117–148; Gabriel Alexander, 'Die Demonstration der Erwerbslosen in der Repräsentantenversammlung', ed. by Hermann Simon, Jochen Boberg, *"Tuet auf die Pforten". Die Neue Synagoge 1866–1995*, Berlin 1995, pp. 154–164. In addition, the catalogue ed. by Reinhard Rürup in connection with an exhibition project in 1995 and an accompanying volume of essays contains valuable information, *Jüdische Geschichte in Berlin. Essays und Studien*, Berlin 1995.

[6]idem, Introduction in *Essays und Studien*, pp. 5–12.

[7]Alexander, 'Die jüdische Bevölkerung Berlins', pp. 118–120, p. 141, Table 1.

of Berlin was employed in trades. When compared to the rest of the *Reich* the proportion of self-employed amongst those Jews in work was very large, while the proportion of Jewish manual workers stood at only ten per cent.[8]

Berlin became a centre for Jewish culture during the Weimar Republic. During this time the Jewish adult education system was developed considerably. The first and largest Jewish *Volkshochschule* (adult education college) in Germany was built in Berlin. The Jewish library system experienced a noticeable increase in the twenties. In January 1933 the Jewish Museum was opened, which had developed out of the art collection of the Jewish community. As well as being a centre for German-speaking Jewish culture, Berlin also became a centre for new Hebrew and Yiddish culture.[9] The Berlin Jewish community, which supported many Jewish associations and clubs through its organisational and financial means was located at the heart of Jewish life in Berlin. Exact membership numbers are not available. 130,000 people joined the electoral list of the *Repräsentantenversammlung* in 1930.[10] The number of tax paying members for 1930 is recorded as 64,513. Community members whose *Reich* taxes were less than 75 Reichsmark did not pay community taxes.[11]

The Jewish community was built along similar lines to a city community in terms of its body of self-administration. At the head was the *Gemeindevorstand* (community council) and the *Repräsentantenversammlung* whose members worked together in the *Verwaltungskommissionen* (management committees). The *Vorstand* (board) departments were headed voluntarily by the members of the *Gemeindevorstand* who led the administrative apparatus of the community. During the Weimar Republic this administrative apparatus grew considerably because of the increasing involvement of the community in economic and social affairs.[12] The Jewish community employed circa 1500 members of staff in 1933.[13]

There was an element of centralisation and decentralisation working side by side in many of the community's spheres of activities. This was most evident within the sphere of welfare. In April 1922 the department of welfare was made into a "head organisation" (*Spitzenorganisation*) by bringing together various *Verwaltungskommissionen*. And the city was also divided into welfare districts headed by district committees. The districts and the welfare department strove for a balanced division of authority between them.[14]

The community maintained sixteen community synagogues in 1930. The number of synagogue places available in that year was 23,277. For the festival services roughly the same number again could be secured by hiring meeting halls. In 1929 the community donated circa 266,000 Reichsmark in order to subsidise private synagogue

---

[8]*ibid*, pp. 133–135.
[9]See Michael Brenner, *The Renaissance of Jewish Culture in Weimar Germany*, London 1996; Michael Brenner, 'Zwischen Ost und West: Berlin als Zentrum jüdischer Kultur in der Weimarer Republik', in Rürup (ed.), *Essays und Studien*, pp. 197–214.
[10]Alexander, 'Die jüdische Bevölkerung Berlins', p. 120.
[11]'Verwaltungsbericht des Vorstandes der Jüdischen Gemeinde zu Berlin 1926–1930', in *Gemeindeblatt der Jüdischen Gemeinde zu Berlin* 20, No. 11 (1930), pp. 17–40, here pp. 18–19.
[12]'Organisation der Jüdischen Gemeinde und der Synagogengemeinde Adass Isroel', in *Jüdisches Jahrbuch für Groß-Berlin. Ein Wegweiser durch die jüdischen Einrichtungen und Organisationen Berlins*, Berlin 1926, pp. 54–61; Heinemann Stern, *Warum hassen Sie uns eigentlich?*, Düsseldorf 1970, pp. 114–120.
[13]Kurt Wilhelm, 'The Jewish community in the Post-Emancipation Period', in *LBI Year Book II* (1957), p. 69.
[14]'Jüdische Wohlfahrtspflege in Groß-Berlin', in *Jüdisches Jahrbuch für Groß-Berlin* (1926), pp. 83–113.

Main office of the Jüdische Gemeinde in Berlin, Oranienburger Strasse

By courtesy of the Gidal Bildarchiv im Steinheim Institut, Duisburg

associations (*Synagogenvereine*). This paid for the rabbis and choirmasters and contributed towards the cost of rent.[15] The *kashrut* committee of the community was responsible for everything concerned with obtaining foodstuffs and goods for the rituals. Overall supervision was in the hands of the rabbinate, and in addition to this, inspectors and kosher slaughterers (*Schächter*) were appointed.[16]

The most important point of contact between the community and its members was the *Gemeindeblatt der Jüdischen Gemeinde zu Berlin*, which was published in 1930 with a circulation of 79,000 copies.[17] It was a free monthly paper delivered to households which published information about community administration and different Jewish organisations, as well as contributions of a popular scholarly nature. In this way the large number of those community members who did not take an active part in community life, and who did not read any other Jewish newspapers, were provided with basic Jewish knowledge. In 1928 Leo Winz took over the technical directorship of the community paper. Before this he had edited the illustrated monthly *Ost und West*. Latin script was introduced and the number of pages increased, not least because of the extensive advertisement pages in each issue, and it was highly illustrated.[18]

[15]'Verwaltungsbericht', in *Gemeindeblatt* 20, pp. 19–24.
[16]'Kultus- und Ritualwesen', in *Jüdisches Jahrbuch für Groß-Berlin* (1926), pp. 70–75.
[17]'Verwaltungsbericht', in *Gemeindeblatt* 20, p. 27.
[18]Brenner, 'Zwischen Ost und West', p. 202.

DIE REPRÄSENTANTENVERSAMMLUNG DER JÜDISCHEN GEMEINDE ZU BERLIN

"We are so to speak a small parliament of a public-legal corporation",[19] Hans Goslar characterised the *Repräsentantenversammlung* of the Jewish community in this way. The position of the *Repräsentantenversammlung* had already been described on 23 July 1847 in article 46 of the Law Concerning the Relationship with Jews:

> Through its election and the law, the *Repräsentantenversammlung* has the authority and the obligation to represent with conviction and conscience the synagogue community in accordance with this prescription, without consulting the whole community or departments thereof and to pass binding resolutions for the community.[20]

This law fixed the number of representatives to 21 (section 40) and the period between elections to six years (section 41). Every three years half of the representatives were to leave office and a "replacement election" (*Ergänzungswahl*) was to be held (section 42). Even the position of the *Gemeindevorstand* was decided on in 1847; it was to arrange the concerns of the community, to put into practice the decisions of the *Repräsentantenversammlung* and to represent the community to a third party (section 44).

This law formed the framework for the statute of the community and was approved in 1861. At the end of the nineteenth century a Revised Statute for the Jewish Community in Berlin was agreed upon, which – with a few additions – remained valid during the Weimar Republic.[21] The statute lays down the working procedure for the representation of the community (*Gemeindervorstand* and *Repräsentantenversammlung*), the election rules, the type of decisions and the work of the *Verwaltungskommissionen*. In the procedure of the *Repräsentantenversammlung* adopted on 28 May 1899, the obligations of the representatives and the work of the committees were also regulated. Of great importance, in particular for narrow majorities, was the requirement that in case of a tied vote, the vote of the chair would be the deciding one.[22] The demand from all sides for a new statute was not successful during the Weimar Republic. Far-reaching changes to the statutes were, however, passed in 1929. The number of representatives increased to forty-one, the length of service was fixed to four years, and the rotation of office was disbanded.[23]

A sumptuous hall for the representatives was built in the New Synagogue at *Oranienburger Straße* 30. Situated behind the middle section of the street façade under the dome, it is visible from outside through the two-storey leaded tracery windows.[24]

---

[19] Hans Goslar, on Session on 4 April 1929, *Gemeindeblatt* 19, No. 5 (1929), p. 252.
[20] Ismar Freund, *Die Rechtstellung der Synagogengemeinde in Preußen und die Reichsverfassung*, Berlin 1926, p. 49 (Appendix).
[21] *Revidirtes Statut für die Jüdische Gemeinde zu Berlin*, Berlin 1896.
[22] *Geschäftsordnung für die Repräsentanten-Versammlung der jüdischen Gemeinde zu Berlin*, passed in the session on 28 May 1899.
[23] See Ismar Freund, 'Das neue Statut der Jüdischen Gemeinde', in *Gemeindeblatt* 20, No. 2 (1930), pp. 61–63. The title of this article is misleading because the article really only deals with amendments to statutes.
[24] "Dieser Saal ist durch die Raumproportionen, das stark wirksame Motiv der Fensterarchitektur und durch die umlaufende Empore, die zwischen schlanke kannelierte Einsäulen gespannt ist, als ein auffällig kostbares Gehäuse geformt." See Robert Graefrath, 'Denkmalpflegerische Gesichtspunkte beim Wiederaufbau', in Simon, Boberg (eds.), "*Tuet auf die Pforten*", pp. 63–83, here p. 78.

There was a large horseshoe-shaped table around which the representatives sat. At the open end of the horseshoe the table of the *Gemeindevorstand* was situated.[25] The sessions of the *Repräsentantenversammlung* were public, but there was only a small visitors' gallery. The *Jüdisch-liberale Zeitung* was repeatedly reminded of the unfriendly visitor conditions. Space on the gallery was limited; again and again visitors had to turn back because not even standing room was available:

> But there is really a great deal of idealism in stepping up onto the gallery and being present at the high meeting. For the remarks of some of the older representatives are inaudible, and the gallery is so narrow and small that it is impossible to allow a stranger to enter. …Today visitors sit there breathing in, their chins leaning on the barrier attempting to lip-read the speakers so that they can at least in this way work out the contents of the discussion because they cannot hear it. But even this is no longer possible because the representatives and community leaders without exception surround themselves in a thick fog of cigarette smoke. Naturally this smoke rises directly upwards, and when about thirty people puff away for hours you can imagine that the visitors' eyes will start to water and that they will not only no longer hear anything, but not see anything either. There is really nothing else left for them to do than to get out as quickly as possible. The representatives, however, are not allowed to drive away members of the public in this way. The time has therefore come for the gallery of the assembly hall to be rebuilt in a modern style.[26]

This vivid description makes it quite clear how events in the *Repräsentantenversammlung* were of great interest to those in the community and the Jewish press. This interest grew after the First World War because Jewish parties had proliferated and the right to vote in the *Repräsentantenversammlung* was quickly democratised, urged on by the JVP and through the introduction of proportional representation in all public bodies.[27] The first representative elections in the Berlin community after the First World War were already conducted according to the principles of proportional representation, although only twelve of the twenty-one seats were taken in 1920. Four representatives of the JVP entered the *Repräsentantenversammlung* in 1920 for the first time.[28]

THE PARTIES IN THE *REPRÄSENTANTENVERSAMMLUNG* AND THE ELECTIONS OF 1926

During the Weimar Republic the Jewish party system fanned out considerably. While it was predominantly those in favour of and those against religious reform who opposed each other in the nineteenth century, Zionism brought with it a new movement, which also influenced the work of the community. Added to this came parties, some of which made it their business to overcome existing opposition in a new insti-

---

[25]The one-time stenographer of the *Repräsentantenversammlung*, Alexander Szanto, gave an accurate description of the hall and the seating plan; see Monika Richarz (ed.), *Jüdisches Leben in Deutschland. Selbstzeugnisse zur Sozialgeschichte 1918–1945*, Stuttgart 1982 (Veröffentlichung des Leo Baeck Instituts), pp. 217–218.

[26]Heinz Levy, 'Gegenwartsfragen der Berliner Repräsentantenversammlung', in *Jüdisch-liberale Zeitung* (16 November 1928).

[27]Barkai, Flohr, *Aufbruch und Zerstörung*, p. 77.

[28]Max Birnbaum, *Staat und Synagoge 1918–1933. Eine Geschichte des Preussischen Landesverbandes jüdischer Gemeinden*, Tübingen 1981 (Schriftenreihe wissenschaftlicher Abhandlungen des Leo Baeck Instituts 38), p. 16.

Repräsentantensaal

By courtesy of the Staatliche Museen zu Berlin, Kunstbibliothek

tution, and others which were above all politically orientated organisations.[29] Six parties and groupings stood in the 1926 elections to the *Repräsentantenversammlung*: the Liberals, the Conservatives, the JVP, the *Religiöse Mittelpartei* (Religious Centre Party), the *Poale Zion* and the *Bund jüdischer Arbeitnehmer*, an association of Jewish workers which played a marginal role.

The *Gemeindearbeit* (community work) of the Liberals based on the institutional framework of the *Liberaler Verein für die Angelegenheiten der jüdischen Gemeinde zu Berlin*, founded in 1895, was particularly active in the run-up to the community elections and tried to waken religious interest amongst those community members who had distanced themselves from active community life. The main focus of the Liberal's *Gemeindearbeit* was considered to be the tasks embodied in the statute of the community – ensuring a religious service, religious education and charity work. The status of the community as a *Religionsgemeinde* (religious community) was of fundamental importance to the Liberals. Any political activities in the eyes of the Liberals were dismissed as being adverse to the community.[30] The Conservatives represented the Orthodox Jews who had remained in the main community after the founding of the separate *Adass Jisroel* community, in order to add more weight to traditional Judaism. The Conservatives were a small party in the *Repräsentantenversammlung* during the Weimar Republic and in 1926 they only won one seat.[31] In 1919 the *Berliner Zionistische Vereinigung*, the *Misrachi-Ortsgruppe Berlin*, the *Neuer Jüdischer Gemeindeverein* and the *Verband der Ostjuden* came together to form the *Jüdische Volkspartei* (JVP).[32] The June 1920 programme of the JVP begins with the party statement: "The Jewish People's Party strives to bring together all those attempting to preserve the strengths of Judaism within the Berlin Jewish community to make it a true community of the people."[33] The central demands of the JVP were the democratisation of community elections and a broadening of the social institutions, the opening of more Jewish schools, and the introduction of a more traditional service.[34]

The existence of two smaller parties highlights particularly the broadening of the intra-Jewish party system. The *Poale Zion* represented the German wing of the international Socialist-Zionist Workers' Party founded in 1907, and was closely connected with the JVP in Berlin.[35] The *Religiöse Mittelpartei* was founded in 1924 based on an organisation that had already existed before the First World War and was brought to life again by rabbis who strove to overcome the intra-Jewish conflicts, but it quickly came into conflict with the Liberals.[36]

---

[29]Included amongst the first group are the *Religiöse Mittelpartei* and the *Überparteiliche Vereinigung für die Gesamtinteressen und die Einheit des Judentums* founded in 1930, and in the second group the *Poale Zion* and the *Vereinigung nationaldeutscher Juden*.

[30]Michael E. Meyer, 'Von Moses Mendelssohn bis Leo Baeck: Die Bedeutung Berlins für die jüdische Reform', in Rürup (ed.), *Essays*, pp. 37–52, here p. 50; Heinrich Stern, 'Liberale Gemeindearbeit', in *Jüdisches Jahrbuch 1930*, pp. 22–32.

[31]Moritz A. Loeb, 'Konservatives Judentum', in *Jüdisches Jahrbuch 1930*, pp. 42–47.

[32]*Jüdisches Lexikon*, vol. IV, 2, Spalte (Sp.) 1243.

[33]Jehuda Reinharz (ed.), *Dokumente zur Geschichte des deutschen Zionismus 1882–1933*, Tübingen 1981 (Schriftenreihe wissenschaftlicher Abhandlungen des Leo Baeck Instituts 37), p. 276.

[34]Brenner, 'The Jüdische Volkspartei', p. 223.

[35]Georg Salomon, 'Grundsätzliches zur Gemeindearbeit der Poale Zion', in *Jüdisches Jahrbuch 1930*, pp. 46–47.

[36]Fabius Schach, 'Die Religiöse Mittelpartei', in *Jüdisches Jahrbuch 1930*, pp. 37–41.

The elections to the *Repräsentantenversammlung* on the 16 May 1926 represent a central event in the history of the Jews in the Weimar Republic. The Liberals lost their absolute majority in the community parliament of the largest and most significant of the Jewish communities in Germany. However, this result did not come as such a surprise. At the elections to the *Preußischer Landesverband jüdischer Gemeinden* (PLV) in 1925 the Liberals in Berlin only gained a tiny lead on the non-Liberal parties. In individual towns after 1925, community elections could be avoided through election compromises based on the PLV elections, but negotiations to this end broke down in Berlin.[37] The long-standing struggle, particularly by the *Jüdischer Frauenbund* (Jewish Women's Association), to grant women the vote at community elections was achieved in 1925. Creating the new lists of candidates proved to be so time-consuming a job that the elections which were actually due at the end of 1925 were postponed until May 1926 as a result.[38] After the first counting of votes, the Liberals won ten seats, the JVP eight, the RMP two and the Conservatives one.[39] Fourteen months passed between the election and the first meeting of the *Repräsentantenversammlung* on 14 July 1927. The reason for this delay was due to the amount of election disputes brought by the Liberals which required investigating by the police.[40] In 1927 the state authorities confirmed the number of votes cast. (See table 1).

Table 1: Distribution of votes in 1927

	Votes	*Seats*	*Representatives*
Liberals	23110	10	5
Jüdische Volkspartei	16330	7	4
Religiöse Mittelpartei	5541	2	1
Conservatives	2901	1	–
Poale Zion	2142	1	–
Bund jüdischer Arbeitnehmer	287	–	–

Source: *Jüdische Rundschau*, 18 May 1926, p. 289, and 13 April 1927, p. 216

The only difference to the first count was that Oskar Cohn entered the *Repräsentantenversammlung* as a representative and not as deputy of the *Poale Zion* thereby causing the JVP to lose a seat.[41]

The *Jüdische Rundschau* published a list of the candidates before the elections, for the most part listing their jobs. There were thirty-five nominations for the JVP, of whom the proportion of university graduates came to 54.3%. The percentage of graduates amongst the Liberal candidates stood at 39.1%.[42] Thereby a prominent

---

[37]Birnbaum, *Staat und Synagoge*, pp. 125–126.
[38]*ibid.*
[39]*Gemeindeblatt* 16, No. 6 (1926), p. 125.
[40]Birnbaum, *Staat und Synagoge*, p. 126.
[41]'Der neue Kurs in der jüdischen Gemeinde. Abrechnung und Ausblick', in *Jüdische Rundschau*, (10 May 1927), p. 266.
[42]On the list of candidates see, 'Bekanntmachung betreffend Repräsentantenwahl', in *Jüdische Rundschau* (11 May 1926), p. 278. The percentages are found in Jacob Toury, 'Zur Problematik der jüdischen Führungsschichten im deutschsprachigen Raum 1880–1933', in *Tel Aviver Jahrbuch für deutsche Geschichte* 16 (1987), p. 275.

feature of Jewish leadership is clear – the strong influence of university-educated individuals. The majority were lawyers, also editors, rabbis, doctors and civil servants.

SOME OF THE MAIN PERSONALITIES IN THE *REPRÄSENTANTENVERSAMMLUNG*

Heading the JVP list was Alfred Klee (1875–1943), one of the most important representatives of the older generation of German Zionists, who considered the work of the community as fundamental. Klee held office as chairman of the *Zionistische Vereinigung für Deutschland* (ZVfD) from 1920 to 1921, but stepped down after numerous differences of opinion with the majority of the executives of the committee. From 1925 until it disbanded (1938) Klee was Vice-president of the *Preußischer Landesverband jüdischer Gemeinden*. As a member of the JVP in Berlin he had represented his party in the *Repräsentantenversammlung* since 1920. He left his mark on many of its sessions with his sharp and often sarcastic comments. In 1938 Klee left for the Netherlands and in 1943 he was deported to Westerbork.[43] In second place on the JVP list stood Heinrich Loewe (1869–1951), librarian at the University library of Berlin and, after emigrating, head of the City Library of Tel Aviv. He was also an editor and a publisher and was one of the most important representatives of the Jewish renaissance. He counts amongst one of the first Zionists in Germany.[44] Hans Goslar (1889–1945) represented the Zionist federation *Misrachi* in the *Repräsentantenversammlung*, which belonged to the JVP, and he was placed third on the JVP list.[45] He was born in 1889 in Hanover, attended the *Handelshochschule* in Berlin and worked as an economics journalist. The Prussian *Ministerpräsident* Otto Braun entrusted him with the construction of the press office of the Prussian Ministry. As the head of this project, he was given the title of *Ministerialrat* in 1926. Goslar developed comprehensive publication activities in different fields. He was an advocate of economic activity for Jewish communities, he propagated the view of marrying early and fought against mixed marriages. Zionism, according to Goslar, was something which could be realised in the Diaspora, not just in Palestine, "through the complete and resolute adaption of one's life to Jewish fundamental principles by the spiritual relocation of home".[46] Hans Goslar was often the target of antisemitic attacks, but he was also sharply criticised by patriotic German (*nationaldeutsche*) Jews. In 1938 he lost his citizenship, and in 1943 he was deported to Westerbork along with his father-in-law Alfred Klee. He died in Bergen-Belsen in the spring of 1945.

Oskar Cohn (1869–1934) won a seat in the *Repräsentantenversammlung* for the *Poale Zion*, which was closely connected to the JVP.[47] In 1912 he was elected to the *Reichstag*

---

[43]Birnbaum, *Staat und Synagoge*, p. 17.

[44]See Inka Bertz, *"Eine neue Kunst für ein altes Volk". Die Jüdische Renaissance in Berlin 1900 bis 1924*, Berlin 1991, see p. 6 for biographical notes on Heinrich Loewe.

[45]See Trude Maurer, 'Auch ein Weg als Jude und Deutscher: Hans Goslar (1889–1945)', in Julius H. Schoeps (ed.), *Juden als Träger bürgerlicher Kultur in Deutschland*, Sachsenheim 1989, pp. 193–239.

[46]Hans Goslar, 'Der moderne Jude und der Staat', in *Der Jude* 9, *Sonderheft Antisemitismus und jüdisches Volkstum*, (1925), p. 108, cited in Maurer, 'Hans Goslar', p. 202.

[47]See Ludger Heid, 'Oskar Cohn – ein deutsch-jüdischer Parlamentarier zwischen Sozialismus und Zionismus', in Julius H. Schoeps (ed.), *Menora. Jahrbuch für deutsch-jüdische Geschichte*, Munich 1995, pp. 201–232.

for the SPD, became the speaker in his party for legal issues and was one of the founding members of the USPD. Already during the First World War he took on the concerns of the East European Jews. Cohn was an SPD member of the Prussian *Landtag* until 1924 and became heavily involved in fighting discrimination and expulsion of East European Jews. It is still not known why Cohn stepped out of "big" politics. Some explanations have been his own personal experience of antisemitism, but also hostilities within his own party.[48]

After the head of the list, Hugo Sonnenfeld, resigned the Liberal *Fraction* in the *Repräsentantenversammlung* was led by Moritz Türk (1859–1929) until 1929. He was born in Vilna and moved to Berlin via Thorn with his parents.[49] He later became a member of the *Reformgemeinde*. As a teacher, he became particularly involved in educational issues and clashed with Alfred Klee. Alexander Szanto provides a vivid description of the oft recurring constellation:

> The vocal duels between Dr. Klee and Professor Türk were always of the highest level, and for the objective observer it was a pleasure, an aesthetic joy, to hear them. Already in their outward appearance the two men could not have been more different: Alfred Klee, sharp, agile, aggressive, with gesticulating arms and hands, in the manner of the well-versed advocate who slings his sentences suggestively and glares at his counterpart from behind his dark black horn-rimmed glasses – Professor Türk, placid and easy-going with an imperturbable calm, his arguments made in sonorous tones underlined by tiny hand movements, already having thought about formulating his sentences in perfectly executed style, shaped by inner logic.[50]

After Moritz Türk's death in 1929, Kurt Fleischer, twenty years younger, took over the leadership of the Liberal faction. He had stood in eleventh place on the list until Hugo Sonnenfeld left office and then he entered the group of representatives. Fleischer was a surgeon and gynaecologist, and he got involved in, amongst others, the boards of the Jewish hospital and the *Prinzregentenstraße* Synagogue.[51] Heinrich Stern (1883–1951), who was second on the Liberal's list, belonged to the moderate wing of the Liberals. Stern held important positions within central Jewish organisations. He was the chairman of the *Vereinigung für das liberale Judentum* and a board member of the C.V. He worked as a lawyer in Berlin and was able to emigrate to England in 1938.[52]

In 1926 two women were elected to the *Repräsentantenversammlung* – Lina Wagner-Tauber (1874–1936) and Bertha Falkenberg (1876–1946). The latter was chairwoman of the *Jüdischer Frauenbund* in Berlin and was placed third on the Liberal's list in 1930.[53] Moritz A. Loeb (1862–1935) played a central role in the discussions of the *Repräsentantenversammlung*. He was the only Conservative delegate. Loeb was the chairman of the Berlin *Verein zur Erhaltung des überlieferten Judentums*. In the 1920 elections

---

[48]*ibid.*, p. 224.
[49]Walter Breslauer, 'Was war uns Türk?', in *Jüdisch-liberale Zeitung*, (4 September 1929).
[50]Cited in Alexander, 'Die Demonstration der Erwerbslosen', p. 162.
[51]'Dr. Kurt Fleischer zum 50. Geburtstag', in *Jüdisch-liberale Zeitung*, (10 June 1931).
[52]Birnbaum, *Staat und Synagoge*, p. 43.
[53]See Larissa Dämmig, 'Bertha Falkenberg – Eine Spurensuche', in *Leben mit der Erinnerung. Jüdische Geschichte in Prenzlauer Berg*, Berlin 1997, pp. 24–28.

he stood as a Liberal-Conservative Alliance candidate, but in the run-up to the 1926 elections he moved closer to the JVP.[54]

THE WORK OF THE *REPRÄSENTANTENVERSAMMLUNG*

In the twenties there was a column in the *Gemeindeblatt der jüdischen Gemeinde zu Berlin* called '*Aus der Repräsentantenversammlung*'. The numbers of representatives and community leaders who attended the sessions was listed followed by the minutes of these sessions.[55] Minutes and comments were also printed in the *Jüdische Rundschau* and the *Jüdisch-liberale Zeitung*.[56] These were not printed on a regular basis, were of differing lengths, and were impartial in their interpretations of the discussions. The minutes in the *Gemeindeblatt* generally present a far more detailed picture; personal attacks on general politics were left out, however, which also led to greatly varying opinions in the *Repräsentantenversammlung*. Publishing the minutes allowed for a wide dissemination of the speeches. The speeches of the *Repräsentantenversammlung* were made for the public, which gave rise to criticism of the somewhat unproductive marathon speeches.[57]

The last months of 1927 and the first weeks of 1928 were beset by heavy discussions in the community about the arrangement for future co-operation. There was an agreement amongst the non-Liberals to strive for concerted action in personal affairs and in all fundamental points of community policy.[58] In connection to this the Liberals spoke of a "block" directed against them, or even of a "Zionist dictatorship".[59] The reason for the great controversy was the different decisions regarding staff, above all resulting from the new majorities. The non-Liberals held the chair of the *Repräsentantenversammlung* and also held the majority in the *Gemeindevorstand*.

In February 1928 the new *Gemeindevorstand* made an appeal to the community members which appeared on the first page of the *Gemeindeblatt*. The *Gemeindevorstand* urged the members to finally contribute "to the peace of the community". It promised to do everything "to bring the community out of the passionate party battles and

---

[54]Loeb drew up a text a few weeks before the 1930 elections in which he called to account the Liberal faction as well as the JVP, and he demanded far-reaching reforms, see Moritz A. Loeb, *Um die Zukunft der Berliner Jüdischen Gemeinde*, Berlin 1930; Birnbaum, *Staat und Synagoge*, pp. 16–17.

[55]The minutes are only on the public sessions of the *Repräsentantenversammlung* and follow the meetings in chronological order. The length of the minutes varies greatly. They can be from one to thirteen pages long, and sometimes this includes adverts amongst them. Unimportant orders of the day are noted in a few sentences and the resulting decisions are reported. The contributions by individual participants for the important discussions are given, either indirectly, or the name is given followed by several passages of the speech.

[56]The *Jüdische Rundschau*, founded as the *Israelitische Rundschau* in 1895, was the most important newspaper of the German Zionists. In 1928 it had a circulation of 10,000 copies and was printed twice a week, cf. Barbara Suchy, 'Die jüdische Presse im Kaiserreich und in der Weimarer Republik', in Julius H. Schoeps (ed.), *Juden als Träger bürgerlicher Kultur in Deutschland*, Stuttgart 1989, pp. 167–191, here p. 186; the *Jüdisch-liberale Zeitung* was the organ of the *Vereinigung für das liberale Judentum*. C.f. Barkai, Flohr, *Aufbruch und Zerstörung*, p. 90.

[57]Aron Sandler, in Richarz (ed.), *Jüdisches Leben in Deutschland*, p. 191.

[58]Loeb, *Um die Zukunft*, p. 5.

[59]'Vor den Vorstandswahlen in der Berliner Jüdischen Gemeinde', in *Jüdisch-liberale Zeitung* (14 October 1927). (The *Jüdisch-Liberale Zeitung* was published without page numbers.)

restore calm and peace once again".⁶⁰ This unconventional measure by the *Gemeindevorstand* makes clear how serious the conflict of interests had become.

The situation inside the community improved during the course of 1928, but differences of opinion remained. Added to this was the problem of the non-Liberal party alliance being unstable. It soon became apparent that the differences in their policies – aside from the rejection of Liberal policies – was great. This was particularly clear as regards education policy. The JVP and the Conservatives were in favour of extending the Jewish school system, but there were great differences on how this was to be brought about, particularly with regard to the actual educational content.⁶¹ There were further differences concerning the nature of cultural affairs. The Conservatives wanted full autonomy for all religious groups of the community in questions of culture, while the JVP felt that this would risk the unity of the community. It was therefore no great surprise that in 1929, at the same time as the handing over of the chair of the community to Georg Kareski, secret agreements were made between the Liberals and the JVP. The Liberals declared their willingness for the community to take on the private primary school of the *Jüdischer Schulverein* in *Rykestraße*, and to agree to the funding of a chair at the Hebrew University in Jerusalem. The JVP promised the Liberals that a new election would already take place at the end of 1930.⁶² Through this settlement at the beginning of 1929 some of the points of conflict between the Liberals and the JVP could be side-lined. Moritz A. Loeb and the representatives of the RMP felt that they had been betrayed by these secret agreements and voiced strong reproaches against the JVP.⁶³ The ensuing ballots resulted in changing majorities and the partners of the JVP felt that they were only conditionally duty-bound to them now.

The granting of the budget was the central function of the *Repräsentantenversammlung*. The discussions over the budget were traditionally the high point of the session; besides fixing expenditure for the new budget year, it was possible to attend to fundamental problems of community policy. During the period under examination there was a continual increase in the extent and importance of the budgetary discussions. In 1929 and 1930 there was a general discussion and separate discussions on the individual sections of the budget which lasted several days.

The budget consisted of six sections which were also sub-divided. The first three sections were connected to the main areas of concern of the community – culture, education and welfare. The General Jewish Affairs section only came into being in 1924 and primarily involved generous subsidies to the *Preußischer Landesverband*. There were also sections on financial and general administration.⁶⁴ The budget increased steadily between 1927 and 1930. The largest budgetary fields were welfare and culture, which both constituted circa thirty per cent. Welfare received the highest subsidies. The biggest relative increase in outgoings between 1927 and 1930 was in education, whose expenditure rose by forty per cent to about one and a half million Reichsmark.⁶⁵

---

⁶⁰*Gemeindeblatt* 18, No. 3 (1928), p. 47.
⁶¹Session on 17 January 1929, in *Gemeindeblatt* 19, No. 3 (1929), p. 122.
⁶²*ibid.*, pp. 118–127; Loeb, *Um die Zukunft*, p. 5.
⁶³Cf. session on 17 January 1929 *op. cit.*; Loeb, *Um die Zukunft*, p. 5.
⁶⁴Loeb, *Um die Zukunft*, p. 11; 'Steuer und Etat', in *Jüdisches Jahrbuch 1926*, pp. 62–68.
⁶⁵Loeb, *Um die Zukunft*, p. 11.

Table 2: Outgoings 1926–1930

	1926	1927	1928	1929	1930
Kap. I. Kultus	RM 2 441 426,-	RM 2 559 884,-	RM 2 763 800,-	RM 3 198 307,-	RM 3 535 558,-
Kap. II. Schulwesen	RM 1 002 022,-	RM 1 093 142,-	RM 1 126 600,-	RM 1 394 800,-	RM 1 535 500,-
Kap. III. Wohlfahrtswesen	RM 2 602 125,-	RM 2 706 318,-	RM 2 886 100,-	RM 3 264 100,-	RM 3 606 398,-
Kap. IV. Allg. jüd. Angelegenheiten	RM 333 000,-	RM 406 000,-	RM 415 000,-	RM 405 000,-	RM 518 000,-
Kap. V. Vermögensverwaltung	RM 967 000,-	RM 899 000,-	RM 502 000,-	RM 967 500,-	RM 708 028,-
Kap. VI. Allgemeine Verwaltung	RM 1 662 444,-	RM 1 662 444,-	RM 1 697 800,-	RM 1 796 700,-	RM 1 781 200,-
Gesamtbetrag	RM 9 008 017,-	RM 9 264 310,-	RM 9 401 500,-	RM 11 026 407,-	RM 11 684 836,-

Table 3: Contributions 1926–1930, gross and as a % of tax contributions[66]

	1926 RM	%	1927 RM	%	1928 RM	%	1929 RM	%	1930 RM	%
Kap. I. Kultus	915 000,-	17,7	1 096 000,-	19,-	1 188 000,-	20,-	1 488 000,-	23,-	1 575 020,-	23,3
Kap. II. Schulwesen	794 000,-	15,2	884 000,-	15,4	886 000,-	15,-	1 208 000,-	18,-	1 262 890,-	18,-
Kap. III. Wohlfahrtswesen	1 688 000,-	31,8	1 757 000,-	30,6	1 666 000,-	28,-	1 594 000,-	24,-	1 918 400,-	27,3
Kap. IV. Allg. jüd. Angelegenheiten	333 000,-	6,-	406 000,-	7,2	415 000,-	7,-	455 000,-	7,-	543 000,-	7,7
Kap. V. Vermögensverwaltung	396 000,-	15,3	695 000,-	12,3	532 000,-	9,-	730 000,-	11,-	504 030,-	7,2
Kap. VI. Allg. Verwaltung	780 000,-	14,-	875 000,-	15,5	1 208 000,-	21,-	1 114 000,-	17,-	1 232 000,-	17,5

[66]These tables are found in Loeb, *Um die Zukunft*, p. 11.

The most important building project between 1927 and 1930 was undisputedly the construction of the synagogue in *Prinzregentenstraße*. The planning permission was granted in spring 1928. There was a large-scale discussion on the 26 April 1928 in the *Repräsentantenversammlung* on the subject of granting the monies. The building of this synagogue would provide the large number of the Liberal community members in the boroughs of Wilmersdorf and Schöneberg with a synagogue. The Liberal Heinrich Stern commented that with the growing significance of the social work of the community, "the concern for the worship of God is one of our most noble duties".[67] Representatives of the JVP were dubious as to whether a building of the type planned was really necessary and financially justifiable. The Conservative Moritz A. Loeb was particularly opposed to the building on grounds of the anticipated strain on the community's finances. This important building project was in no way supported unanimously. There were 15 votes in favour, 2 against, and four abstentions.[68] However, it could not be said that there was a blockade on Liberal policies as five of the votes in favour came from outside the Liberal camp.

One of the most important community institutions was the cemetery in Weißensee. The cemetery committee made an effort to treat the different religious groups of the community equally. The non-Liberal representatives of the *Gemeindevorstand* and the *Repräsentantenversammlung* tried to implement different changes in the cemetery. The attempt to abolish the opening times of the cemetery on the Sabbath and on holidays failed. But a prayer hall – considered to be a luxury by the Liberals – was built enabling representatives of the priestly caste of Cohen to take part in funeral ceremonies.[69] In many of the comments raised by the representatives the great significance of the cemetery to the community and its members was mentioned. In the discussion over the granting of funds to build the *Prinzregentenstraße* synagogue, the Liberal Wilhelm Marcus maintained: "There are only two things which unite the community with its members today: the *Gottesdienst* and the cemetery."[70] Samson Weiße, rabbi and RMP representative, stated in the budget debate of 1930: "For us Jews the cemetery is a place of piety, and for many a connection between individual and universal Jewishness."[71]

THE ECONOMIC SITUATION OF THE JEWISH MINORITY AND THE RELIGIOUS DEBATES IN THE COMMUNITY

Hyper-inflation in 1923 and the Depression after 1929 also had their effect on the economic activities of German Jews.[72] The Jewish minority in Berlin, as in the whole of the *Reich*, differed from the general population with regard to the division of indi-

---

[67]Session on 26 April 1928, in *Gemeindeblatt* 18, No. 6 (1928), pp. 175–178, quote by Heinrich Stern on p. 176.
[68]*ibid*.
[69]'Diskussion über den Antrag auf Schließung der Friedhöfe an Sabbaten und Feiertagen' in the session on 5 December 1927, in *Gemeindeblatt* 18, No. 1 (1928), p. 11; 'Diskussion über den Antrag auf Umbau der Bethalle' in the session on 23 May 1929, in *Gemeindeblatt* 19, No. 7 (1929), pp. 349–351.
[70]Session on 26 April 1928, in *Gemeindeblatt* 18, No. 6 (1928), p. 176.
[71]Session on 27 February 1930, in *Gemeindeblatt* 20, No. 4 (1930), p. 188.
[72]Zimmermann, *Die deutschen Juden*, pp. 16–17. It is still debated today whether these events had a particularly drastic effect on the Jewish population.

vidual economic groupings and their social structure. This is particularly noticeable in the field of trade and on account of the fact that the number of self-employed and employed was significantly higher than compared to the rest of the population.[73]

"The (present) time ... is marked by economic need, which has also presented the community with new and difficult problems", reads the *Verwaltungsbericht der jüdischen Gemeinde zu Berlin* in 1930.[74] During this time the Jewish communities received more and more appeals for help. The *Repräsentantenversammlung* devoted itself to numerous large discussions on the economic situation of the community members. The problems faced by the particularly badly hit middle class were discussed in depth. Furthermore, the various forms of economic antisemitism were pointed out. Jewish employers were asked to employ Jewish staff and the *Gemeindevorstand* requested that all tasks of the community would be carried out by Jewish companies.

The judgement on the causes of the economic crisis were quite different for the Liberals and the JVP. Alfred Klee was convinced that a particular Jewish economic need existed which could not be compared with the general economic situation.[75] The Liberals rejected, or greatly diminished, the emphasis on a specific Jewish economic need. Despite these deeply differing opinions, both sides were agreed that the existing community welfare system would need extending. One development was that the direct offers of aid were further increased at the end of the twenties. Meals were provided for free, coal delivered to those in need, and warm rooms ("*warme Stuben*") were set up during the winter months.[76] In the last proper session of the 1926 *Repräsentantenversammlung* on 14 December 1930, extensive measures for winter aid for the poorer Jewish population were promised.[77] Of great significance – in particular for the Jews of Berlin's centre – was the opening of the polyclinic in *Linienstraße*, which had been commissioned by the JVP.[78]

"*Produktive Fürsorge*" became the most important field of the welfare work of the community during the Weimar Republic. In 1930 this included an employment office, career advice, clothes and a cookery school.[79] All parties of the *Repräsentantenversammlung* were strongly in favour of the *Arbeitsgemeinschaft der jüdischen Arbeitsnachweise*, founded in 1923, being taken on by the community budget. The employment office was integrated into the welfare department of the community on 1 January 1929.[80] The expansion of the employment office was seen as an urgent task by all factions of the *Repräsentantenversammlung*. Oskar Cohn of the *Poale Zion* described it as the "core of productive welfare" in the budget discussions of 1929.[81]

---

[73]*ibid.*, p. 14.
[74]'Verwaltungsbericht', in *Gemeindeblatt* 20, p. 17.
[75]Cf., for example, session on 1 May 1930, in *Gemeindeblatt* 20, No. 6 (1930), p. 296.
[76]'Verwaltungsbericht', in *Gemeindeblatt* 20, p. 30.
[77]Session on 14 December 1930, in *Gemeindeblatt* 21, No. 1 (1931), pp. 20–23.
[78]'Verwaltungsbericht', in *Gemeindeblatt* 20, p. 31; *Jüdisches Jahrbuch 1930*, p. 19; The JVP bill on the building of a *Poliklinik* was passed "with a large majority" in the session on 11 October 1928, in *Gemeindeblatt* 18, No. 12 (1928), pp. 434–435.
[79]'Verwaltungsbericht', in *Gemeindeblatt* 20, p. 32.
[80]*ibid.*
[81]"*Kernstück produktiver Fürsorge*", Oskar Cohn, in the session on 12 June 1929, in *Gemeindeblatt* 19, No. 8 (24. July 1929), p. 401.

Religion and Politics in the Berlin Jewish Community 231

In 1930 the employment office was divided into five departments: business, freelance, commercial, unskilled work, career advice. The statistics published in 1930 of the activities of the employment office record the continued increase in the number of those seeking work and they give a picture of the achievements of the employment office. (See table 4).

Table 4

Year	Those seeking employment	Those who found work
1926	9 138	4 334
1927	9 409	5 865
1928	10 151	5 560
1929	11 543	5 896
1930 (to 30 Sept.)	10 102	3 587

Source: *Verwaltungsbericht* 1930, p. 82.

As well as demands for the extension of the employment office, there are many examples in the minutes on initiatives to support the credit bank which had been founded in Berlin in 1924. Representatives on all sides regarded it as one of the most important means of fighting the economic plight of the middle class, and contributions were made to it over and over again.[82]

The activities of the community with regard to employment were considered to be one of the main concerns of the Jewish community by the JVP as well as the Liberals. They both supported an emphatic commitment by the community to improve the economic situation of its members and thus disregarded their difference in opinion over the question of the particular burden on the Jewish minority due to the economic situation. Within the realm of religious practice there was a similar relationship between far-reaching differences of opinion but the preparedness to work closely together in order to solve various issues.

The entry of the JVP into community life, their election successes and influence on communal policy was felt as threatening to the unity of the community by some Liberals who saw the make-up of the community being threatened by Zionist-political aims. Religious differences and political arguments regarding the duties of the Jewish community were closely related since the beginning of the twentieth century. Because the JVP felt more closely connected to the Orthodox Jews with regard to religion, some of the Liberals called for the founding of their own community, or at least the strict division of religious administration, during the months of great controversy in 1927 and 1928.[83] However, the community had grown and was able to protect itself despite these difficulties.

The unity of the community was maintained against a backdrop of weighty differences in opinion over the outcome of the development process of the Jewish com-

---

[82] *Jüdisches Jahrbuch 1926*, p.101; Julius Hartog, 'Jüdische Kreditinstitute in Deutschland', in *Jüdisch-liberale Zeitung* (24 July 1929).
[83] 'Die Krise in der Berliner Gemeinde', in *Jüdisch-Liberale Zeitung* (30 December 1927); 'Aus der Berliner jüdischen Gemeinde. Die Liberalen in der Opposition', in *Jüdische Rundschau* (6 January 1928), p. 11; Moritz Rosenthal, 'Ist die Einheitsgemeinde noch möglich?', in *Jüdisch-liberale Zeitung* (13 January 1928).

munities in Germany since the middle of the nineteenth century. The Liberals took stock of an overwhelmingly positive result. According to Moritz Türk it was precisely thanks to the "reforms in religious practice which were introduced in the nineteenth century ... that Jewry in Germany was preserved".[84] Heinrich Loewe, however, characterised the reforms of the nineteenth century as "a growing assimilation (*Angleichung*) to Christianity, with the result that Judaism had begun to disintegrate.[85] Alfred Klee formulated his negative impressions rather vividly: "What have they achieved by their reforms? Nothing! The synagogues with the most beautiful organs and choirs stand empty."[86]

Besides these differences in the evaluation of religious-Liberal developments, there were also diverging opinions in dealing with the varied religious needs within the Berlin community. Traditionally, contested issues concerning ritual were decided on by majority decisions in the *Repräsentantenversammlung*. The Liberals in particular had benefited from this ruling, but by 1926 the situation had changed. At the beginning of the parliamentary term the Liberals – in agreement with the Conservative Moritz A. Loeb – proceeded to erect two separate committees on culture (*Kultuskommissionen*). In January 1928 a Liberal motion that a mixed deputation should advise on the setting up of the committees was even accepted, but these endeavours quickly ran aground. At the discussions on issues of culture all parties declared almost as a leitmotif that they did not want to block decisions which affected the other side.

A particularly difficult question for the community committee was how far synagogues could be used for events, including services, on work-free Sundays. In order for the community to bring back those who had withdrawn from active community life, the Liberal faction made an application to hold "religious ceremonies" (*religiöse Feierstunden*) in two synagogues on Sunday mornings in winter "at whose centre point a speech is held in which current issues are treated in the spirit of Jewish religion, framed by a short organ piece".[87] Alfred Klee rejected the application on fundamental grounds in order to oppose "the beginning of the change to Sundays" which, according to his perception, would inevitably lead to a Sunday service. Klee's reasons were manifold: on the one hand, such an "age-old Jewish tradition" would be broken thereby losing a distinctive characteristic of Judaism, on the other, the Sunday service to him signified a "moment of assimilation and conformity, his introduction signifies a split between us and the greater majority of Jews in the whole world".[88] The Liberals rejected the connection between the establishment of *Feierstunden* with the question of Sunday worship.

Opinions in this matter were very different. The endeavour, however, undoubtedly led to both sides strengthening their connection to members of the community. The Liberal proposal was rejected, but a commission was agreed upon. At the beginning of 1930, therefore, a report over the "first Sunday holy hour in Berlin" was made in the *Jüdisch-liberale Zeitung*. In this, reference is made again of the discussion in the *Repräsentantenversammlung* and its continuation in the *Gemeindevorstand*. The event

---

[84]Session on 28 June 1928, in *Gemeindeblatt* 18, No. 8 (1928), p. 240.
[85]Session on 11 October 1928, in *Gemeindeblatt* 18, No. 12 (1928), p. 432.
[86]Session on 18 February 1929, in *Gemeindeblatt* 19, No. 4 (1929), p. 179.
[87]Session on 20 September 1928, in *Gemeindeblatt* 18, No. 11 (1928), p. 384.
[88]*ibid.*

took place in the *Brüdervereinshaus* – not in a synagogue. After a harmonium recital and a choral concert, Rabbi Seligmann from Frankfurt am Main gave a lecture on the 'Foundations of religious belief'.[89]

Perhaps the most important discussion in the *Repräsentantenversammlung* on the question of culture was the debate about a *Gemeindevorstand* bill 'Concerning the Ending of Gender Divisions in the *Prinzregentenstraße* Synagogue' in February 1929. Experts among the community rabbis were instructed to offer their judgement in this matter.[90] The *Gemeindevorstand* came to a compromise, which was not in any way binding, based on their findings that married women and female family members could sit next to their husbands or relatives.[91] This bill, which presented something essentially new for the community, led to a large-scale discussion in the *Repräsentantenversammlung*. Heinrich Stern of the Liberals put forward three arguments in favour of lifting the ban on gender divisions. He pointed out that in other countries, such as America, sitting together had been normal practice for many years, and therefore it was time for Germany to adopt this custom also. Stern continued to argue that this change corresponds to "the spirit of the age", that "the Jewish woman, like other women [ought to be] freed from prejudice and her shackles which centuries of development has imposed on her". For his third point he expressed the expectation that sitting together could strengthen the ties between the family and the community and could further consolidate the "Jewish sense of community".[92]

These three points were rejected by the JVP. America's experience could in no way be definitive. Alfred Klee made it clear that it was precisely under the Zionists that equality for women was advanced. It was not considered with contempt in the traditional practice of worship, but rather the opposite, it showed respect to women. In response to the third point he argued that all reforms hitherto had not led to a revival of the service.[93] Arthur Rau of the JVP argued on the fundamentals: his rejection did not rest on considerations of religious law, but on the "conviction that that which is to happen here contradicts basic tenets of Judaism".[94]

Surprisingly the bill was passed. Oskar Cohn and Moritz A. Loeb abstained and declared their abstentions with the conviction that they were absolutely unable to comment on religious issues or in matters which concerned the other [political] direction. What was noticeable about the discussion was the fact that the debate, which once again highlighted the deep-seated differences between the parties, was conducted within a calm and serious atmosphere. The *Jüdische Rundschau* spoke of a "spirit of real co-operation", and Hugo Ostberg summarised it thus in the *Jüdisch-liberale Zeitung*: "Everyone respected the other's point of view ... so that the negotiations ran according to an appropriate and pleasant fashion, that it can be recommended as exemplary for forthcoming sessions."[95]

---

[89]'Erste Sonntagsweihestunde in Berlin', in *Jüdisch-liberale Zeitung*, (26 February 1930).
[90]This expert advice was announced in the *Jüdisch-liberale Zeitung* (22 February 1929).
[91]Session on 18 February 1929, in *Gemeindeblatt* 19, No. 4 (1929), p. 175.
[92]*ibid.*, pp. 175–176.
[93]*ibid.*, pp. 178–179.
[94]*ibid.*, p. 177.
[95]'Berliner Jüdische Gemeinde. Aus der Repräsentantenversammlung', in *Jüdische Rundschau* (22 February 1929), p.94; Hugo Ostberg, 'Schafft getrennte Kultuskommissionen!', in *Jüdisch-liberale Zeitung* (22 February 1929).

LIBERAL AND NATIONAL-JEWISH OPINIONS ON THE SCHOOL SYSTEM AND THE COMMITMENT TO PALESTINE

Two subject areas caused sharp differences in the *Repräsentantenversammlung*. There were wide differences in opinion with regard to what extent the community should commit itself to the scope of the school system in general, and, to the question of which interpretation the Jews in Germany should follow with regard to Zionist *Aufbau* in Palestine, and how far the Berlin community should become involved. The Liberals found themselves divided on the question of a general school system. Because of their belief in far-reaching integration of the Jewish minority into the non-Jewish environment, they rejected denominational schools as a matter of principle. On the other hand, a community boys' and a girls' school had existed since the nineteenth century, the maintenance of which was written into a statute. The JVP was in favour of a considerable expansion of the community's general school system. Over and above that Oskar Cohn, for example, saw "education and bringing to life the concept of the unity of the Jewish people"[96] as one of the tasks of the Jewish school. Such demands stood in great contradiction to Liberal opinions.

After their promotion to public educational establishments in 1923, both *Mittelschulen* were forced to phase out the lower classes in the following years. For this reason the community began to build two separate private *Volksschulen* in 1927.[97] Moritz Türk pointed out that this decision contradicted the Liberal principle of rejection of denominational schools, but which the Liberals wanted to prevent out of piety particularly with regard to the *Knabenschule*, rich in tradition, which was closing down due to a lack of pupils.[98] In his great budget speech of 1930, the community chair, Georg Kareski, proudly announced that the general schools of the community were developing well. The number of pupils attending the community *Volkschulen* had risen threefold to 1200 since 1927.[99] This development was traced back to 1929 when the private *Volkschule* of the *Jüdischer Schulverein* was taken over by the community as part of the agreements between Liberals and JVP.

The community *Mittelschulen* fell into a deep crisis at the end of the twenties. On the one hand, more and more pupils from Jewish families were pushing for graduation from a higher school, on the other hand, these schools were religious-Liberal in outlook, so that children from Orthodox families switched to the *Adass Jisroel* community school system. One of the central demands of the JVP therefore, was that the community build a higher school. "We cannot accept responsibility for entrusting activity in this area to the special community", Georg Kareski said in June 1929.[100] The decision to build a higher school in west Berlin was made by the *Gemeindevorstand* at the same session. At the next session, therefore, Moritz Türk announced that the Liberals would oppose the founding of a higher school with all their might.[101]

---

[96]Session on 28 June 1928, in *Gemeindeblatt* 18, No. 8 (1928), p. 238.

[97]Jörg H. Fehrs, *Von der Heidereutergasse zum Roseneck. Jüdische Schulen in Berlin 1712–1942*, Berlin 1993, pp. 258–259.

[98]Session on 28 June 1928, in *Gemeindeblatt* 18, No. 8, (1928), p. 240.

[99]'Der neue Gemeindehaushalt', in *Gemeindeblatt* 20, No. 3 (1930), p.121.

[100]By special community, he meant *Adass Jisroel*. Session on 6 June 1929 in *Gemeindeblatt* 19, No. 7 (1929), p. 355.

[101]Session on 12 June 1929, in *Gemeindeblatt* 19, No. 8 (1929), p. 400.

Religion and Politics in the Berlin Jewish Community

In a similar vein fundamental differences of opinion between the Liberals and the Zionists arose over the meaning and the extent of Jewish involvement in Palestine and its consequences on the life of Jews in Germany. These differences found their first high point in the declaration of the executive (*Hauptvorstand*) of the C.V. in February 1928. The Zionists were reproached in the so-called Mecklenburg-Resolution for bringing "the achievements of their hundred-year long struggle for emancipation into serious danger".[102] There were two events of prime importance in 1929 which forced the discussion and led to sharp separation. First, the decision over the question of the expansion of the Jewish Agency to include non-Zionist members, and secondly, the reaction from both camps to unrest in Palestine in August 1928. The debates were conducted within the large Jewish organisations, and also reached the *Repräsentantenversammlung*. The Jewish Agency was founded on the basis of article 4 of the Palestine Mandate treaty in 1922 and it had the task, as political representative, of collaborating in the *Aufbau* and development of Palestine.[103] In the mid twenties Zionist organisations discussed whether this committee should be opened to non-Zionist members in order to obtain greater support. Those in favour started negotiations with leading non-Zionists and convinced the Zionist movement at the XVI Zionist Congress in Zürich in 1929.

As a condition for Liberal co-operation, Heinrich Stern demanded a declaration from the Zionists that the non-Zionists could continue to remain members of their home countries in a national and legal sense, and that they did not have to see themselves as belonging to a Jewish nation (*Volk*).[104] The discussions between prominent representatives of Zionist and Liberal organisations remained fruitless. The C.V. and the *Vereinigung für das liberale Judentum* refused to work with the Jewish Agency in February and March 1929. Members of these organisations were permitted to be involved in the Jewish Agency in a private capacity.[105]

On 12 June 1929 the chairman of the *Repräsentantenversammlung*, Julius Stern, informed it of the *Gemeindevorstand*'s decision to dispatch two members of the executive as representatives of the community to the initiative committee for the expansion of the Jewish Agency.[106] In the following session the Liberal faction demanded that the *Gemeindevorstand* withdraw this delegation. Kurt Fleischer explained this request and the opposing view of many Liberals in this matter:

> The Liberal movement is prepared to co-operate, naturally not by abandoning its fundamental Jewish view, but on the basis of particular demands. We want to co-operate in Palestine [in turn] for a corresponding concession of a particular influence on the work in Palestine and the respect for our non-national settlement plans whereby Palestine is not the Jewish homeland settlement above all others. Attempts that we have made have been unsuccessful.[107]

---

[102]'Innerjüdische Debatte im C-V. Die antizionistische Resolution angenommen', *Jüdische Rundschau* (17 February 1928), p. 98.
[103]C.f. *Jüdisches Lexikon*, vol. III, Berlin 1929, Sp. 246–249.
[104]Heinrich Stern, 'Zur Frage der Agency', in *Jüdisch-liberale Zeitung* (4 January 1929).
[105]C.f. Sabine Pfennig- Engel, 'Der Streit zwischen CV und ZVfD. Die innerjüdische Diskussion am Ende der Weimarer Republik (1928–1933)', in *Tribüne* 25 (1986), pp. 143–154, here p. 152.
[106]Session on 12 June 1929, in *Gemeindeblatt* 19, No. 8 (1929), p. 396.
[107]Session on 26 June 1929, in *Gemeindeblatt* 19, No. 9 (1929), p. 469.

The principle of working together therefore existed, but was seen by many Zionists as connected to the unacceptable (to them) rejection of the supremacy of Palestine. The board memeber, Arthur Lilienthal, explained the conflict which many Liberals found themselves facing:

> We must not and cannot lie that we too feel emotionally connected to Palestine, and that something joyful resonates within us at the mention of Palestine which does not occur at the mention of other countries. It must however be stated quite categorically that our Jewishness is completely separate from our work for Palestine.[108]

The representatives of the other factions voted unanimously in favour of community co-operation with the initiative committee of the Jewish Agency and in this way turned down the Liberal request.

In August 1929 there were heavy clashes between Arabs and Jews in Palestine which resulted in deaths and injuries. The cause of the clashes was the disputed rights on the Wailing Wall in Jerusalem. The *Repräsentantenversammlung* passed a unanimous resolution on 12 September 1929 in which the events in Palestine were mourned and the Berlin community conveyed to "the Jews in Palestine conscious of their shared fate their deepest sympathies". The resolution stated that Jewish work in Palestine could "only be carried out in harmony between Jews and Arabs".[109] The Jewish Agency in the meantime published an appeal, *Hilfe durch Aufbau*, which called for special assistance. A passage referring to the XVI Zionist Congress was put at the beginning of the appeal and unleashed strong opposition from some Liberals:

> The great task of the unity of Jews for the Palestine-*Aufbau* has been achieved in Zürich. Alongside the representatives of Zionist organisations, the representatives of Jewish communities from all countries have ceremoniously committed themselves to working together with all their strength on the establishment of the Jewish national homeland in Palestine."[110]

In reaction to this appeal a group of anti-Zionist German Jews published their own appeal in which they spoke out against the events in Palestine "being used by the Zionist, that is to say, the Jewish-national party system, to increase agitation". Their appeal ended with the statement: "We see an error in the establishment of a Jewish-national homeland which endangers the emancipation achieved by the pioneers of German Jewry and the religious-moral tasks of Jewry in humanity."[111] The phrasing makes perfectly clear the radical criticism the signatories had towards Zionist activities. The emphasis on the "Jewish nation" and the work of the "national homeland" struck them as self-sacrificing work now that political equality had been achieved. In their opinion what was special about Jewry was precisely its non-national, religious-ethical character.

Both appeals were the object of much argument in the *Repräsentantenversammlung* on 24 October 1929. In a Liberal question it was stated that a member of the *Gemeindevorstand*, Ismar Freund, had raised attacks against the signatories of the anti-

---

[108] *ibid.*, p. 471.
[109] Session on 12 September 1929, in *Gemeindeblatt* 19, No. 10 (1929), p. 521.
[110] 'Das Jüdische Palästinawerk "Hilfe durch Aufbau"', in *Jüdische Rundschau* (13 September 1929), p. 473.
[111] Cited in Hugo Ostberg's speech in the session on 24 October 1929, in *Gemeindeblatt* 19, No. 12 (1929), p. 650. Also printed in Rürup (ed.), *Bilder und Dokumente*, p. 229.

Zionist appeal in a sermon. The Liberals asked how the *Gemeindevorstand* thought it could prevent such incidents taking place in future.[112] The discussion immediately turned to the central points of both proclamations. Heinrich Stern rejected the Jewish Agency's appeal because he sensed the unjustified impression that the whole Jewish world stood behind the construction work in Palestine. He disapproved of the "appeal battle" which had ensued, and at the same time made it clear that the anti-Zionist appeal had only been a reaction to the appeal by the Jewish Agency.[113] Hugo Ostberg, who held a decidedly anti-Zionist viewpoint, declared the Zionist idea of establishing a "national homeland" in Palestine, in his opinion, to have failed. According to him, Palestine could have a future as "homeland for impoverished Jews" but not as a "centre of Jewry".[114] Alfred Klee described the anti-Zionist announcement as "unheard of provocation" and the signatories "as a detached small group, which did not recognise the signs of the time".[115]

Both of the discussions show clearly how deep seated the ideological differences concerning the evaluation of Zionist involvement in Palestine was. But the clear position of the JVP politicians in favour of the goals of Zionist *Aufbau* in Palestine in no way resulted in them organising practical communal policy geared towards activities there.[116] Direct support for *Aufbau* in Palestine was presented by the decision reached within the framework of the agreement negotiated in January 1929. The community announced it would fund a chair at the Hebrew University. In turn, the JVP was able to secure that despatch of a community representative to *Keren Hajessod* would not occur, which was later cause for criticism by the ZVfD.[117] A further reference to Zionist *Aufbau* in Palestine can be seen in the contents of the community paper. Since 1928, the organ of the *Gemeindevorstand*, the *Gemeindeblatt* had reported on the events in the Jewish world and several articles were directly dedicated to the developments in Palestine.[118]

ALL-EMBRACING WORK TO MAINTAIN THE COMMUNITY

This article has shown how the discussions in the *Repräsentantenversammlung* mirrored the opinions of the three traditional branches of community work: welfare, culture and education. The amount of work achieved in these areas increased dramatically during the Weimar Republic. The JVP did not undertake any attempts to break up the institutional framework of the community, but rather it attempted to increase some of its areas of activity and work together with the Liberals.

During the Weimar Republic the representatives were confronted by new tasks parallel to their commitment to the traditional areas of community work and aside along with clarification of their relationship to Zionist *Aufbau* in Palestine. The rise

---

[112]'Die Palästina-Debatte in der Gemeinde-Stube', in *Jüdische Rundschau* (1 November 1929), p. 575.
[113]Session on 24 November 1929 in *Gemeindeblatt* 19, No. 12 (1929), p. 648.
[114]*ibid.*, p. 651.
[115]*ibid.*, p. 649.
[116]Barkai, Flohr, *Aufbruch und Zerstörung*, p. 80.
[117]Yehoyakim Cochavi, 'Liberals and Zionists on the Eve of National-Socialist Seizure of Power', in *LBI Year Book XXXIX* (1994), pp. 113–129, here p. 122. *Keren Hajessod* was set up as the central fund for *Aufbau* in Palestine. C.f. *Jüdisches Lexikon*, vol. III, Berlin 1929, Sp. 654–656.
[118]C.f. Brenner, *The Jüdische Volkspartei*, p. 226; Barkai, Flohr, *Aufbruch und Zerstörung*, p. 80.

of antisemitism was noted and the community asked itself how far it could contribute to its decline. To active members of community politics, however, Jews in Germany and particularly in Berlin appeared to be threatened 'from the inside' by increasing old age, the growing number of "mixed marriages" (*Mischehen*) and the rising numbers of those "*Indifferenten*", as those community members were known who neither attended service nor took part in community elections.[119] In the face of these developments, the different camps were prepared to work together to maintain Jewry. Zionists and Liberals held different views on how to react to antisemitism in Germany. While the C.V., influenced by Liberal Jews, saw the only solution to the effective struggle against antisemitism to lie in education and resistance work, many Zionists criticised what they considered to be the fruitless work of the C.V. along with its anti-Zionist stance, and pleaded for a well-organised 'united front' of all Jews in Germany to be established.[120]

These disputes particularly between the C.V. and the ZVfD, spilled over into the *Repräsentantenversammlung*. In February 1930, Alfred Klee spoke that it might be necessary for the community to take up the resistance struggle more vigorously, because the people in the C.V. excluded those with his world view.[121] The Liberal Sally London represented the uncompromising wing of the C.V.: "The political resistance struggle against antisemitism assumes one spiritual-intellectual foundation: that Jews belong to the German people."[122] According to his point of view, all resistance work should have been left to the C.V.

On Kurt Fleischer's request, the *Repräsentantenversammlung* concerned itself with 'Measures to Educate Christian Society Against Hatred of Jews' in January 1930. In the debate, the differences mentioned above between Liberals and Zionists on the formulation on the basis for resistance activity as well as their readiness to work together on the community level were clear. The Liberals in particular sketched many possibilities for working together in a wide range of public relations activities. Fleischer recommended lectures and tours through Jewish welfare institutes and to cemeteries. Negotiations with church and state authorities were to establish prerequisites for joint activities.[123]

It is particularly noteworthy that both sides described their starting positions with regard to community activities in a self-confident and attacking manner. The Liberal Moritz Rosenthal said: "We want to show the non-Jewish circles ... that Judaism is a religion upon which the world must be proud." Hans Goslar emphasised: "We do not want to be 'put up with' (*geduldet*). We must make the public much more aware of the fact that we are descendants of the world's oldest culture (*Kulturvolk*)."[124] In summing up, a Liberal member of the community executive described the debate as "*wichtig und hochstehend*", and the *Jüdische Rundschau* also spoke of a high level discussion.[125] In unanimously accepting the motion, the Berlin Jewish community resolved

---

[119]Session on 6 June 1929, *Gemeindeblatt* 19, No. 7 (1929), p. 360.

[120]C.f. Pfennig-Engel, 'Der Streit zwischen CV und ZVfD', p. 147; Birnbaum, *Staat und Synagoge*, pp. 216–217.

[121]Session on 27 February 1930, in *Gemeindeblatt* 20, No. 4 (1930), p. 193.

[122]Session on 20 March 1930, in *Gemeindeblatt* 20, No. 5 (1930), p. 244.

[123]Session on 9 January 1930, in *Gemeindeblatt* 20, No. 3 (1930), pp. 131–132.

[124]*ibid.*, pp. 133–134.

[125]*ibid.*, p. 136; 'Aus der Berliner Gemeinde. Sitzung der Repräsentanten-Versammlung', *Jüdische Rundschau* (14 January 1930), p. 31.

to participate "through its organisations in the education of Christian society" and developed many activities to this end. These were to have had the goal of providing the opportunity "especially for the older school and academic youth ... to lose their prejudices against Judaism and to learn its values".[126]

The demographic development of German Jewry since the nineteenth century pointed to certain peculiarities, particularly the increasing ageing of the Jewish population. Contemporaries were convinced that Jewry in Germany was in danger.[127] The concerned voices did not go unnoticed; both in the central Jewish organisations and in the Berlin community strategies were thought out which would strengthen Jewry in Germany. Measures were discussed again and again in order to be influential on developments in the short term. To this end, for example, the representatives asked the *Gemeindevorstand* on 11 October 1928 to set up a new office of statistics which would have an accurate overview of the demographics.[128] Youth clubs were to be opened and Jewish marriages were to be financially supported. The setting up of a Jewish marriage agency was also discussed.[129]

In February 1927 the welfare committee of the Prussian *Landesverband* established a Political Population Committee (*Bevölkerungspolitischer Ausschuß*), which was to work on the demographic problems of a low birth rate and late marriages resulting in the ageing of German Jewry. The high point of the committee's activities was a conference on 24 February 1929 in Berlin.[130] The discussions of the conference were continued in the Berlin *Repräsentantenversammlung* on 14 March 1929. Moritz Türk, who was also chair of the welfare committee, put forward a comprehensive catalogue of demands, at the centre of which stood a call for an active policy of accommodation by the community. Better housing should be provided for the families from East European Jews in Berlin and the officials of the community. Türk also proposed the payment of child benefit and the setting up of day centres. At the beginning of his speech he pointed out that the Liberal proposal had the aim of "significantly increasing the work of our community".[131] The community leader, Kareski, recognised the need for these far-reaching tasks, but did not see how they could be realised without raising taxes. Moritz Türk thanked all those who had taken part in the discussion at the end of the debate and expressed joy that the Liberal proposal had found such approval. There was universal acceptance of the proposal to establish a mixed deputation.[132] Two months after this debate, however, Alfred Klee made known that the *Gemeindevorstand* had to decline from making means available for the political population measures.[133] The fact that these far-reaching demands were made by the Liberals is surprising. In any case, the debate reveals the general party struggle to

---

[126]Session on 9 January 1930, in *Gemeindeblatt* 20, No. 3 (1930), pp. 131–132.
[127]See in particular, Felix Theilhaber, *Der Untergang der deutschen Juden. Eine volkswirtschaftliche Studie*, 2nd edn., Berlin 1921. Theilhaber was placed in position 21 on the list for the *Jüdische Volkspartei* for the elections to the *Repräsentantenversammlung*. C.f. *Gemeindeblatt* 16, No. 5 a (1926).
[128]Session on 11 October 1928, in *Gemeindeblatt* 18, No. 12 (1928), p. 433.
[129]Session on 11 October 1928, in *Gemeindeblatt* 18, No. 12 (1928), p. 428.
[130]Birnbaum, *Staat und Synagoge*, pp. 190–191.
[131]Session on 14 March 1929, in *Gemeindeblatt* 19, No. 5 (1929), pp. 236–239.
[132]*ibid.*, p. 246.
[133]Session on 23 May 1929, in *Gemeindeblatt* 19, No. 7 (1929), p. 348.

secure the existence of Jewry in Germany, and also a trust typical of its time of seeking to solve questions of population and social policy comprehensively.[134]

During the time in question, there was one matter of concern which united all factions in working together – the support and involvement of the younger generation in the work of the community. The representatives were fundamentally in agreement that this was of steadily growing importance for the community in the face of demographic development. The most important institutional decision in connection to this was the new organisation of the youth and welfare office of the community. In 1929 *Jugendpflege* (youth welfare) was moved from the field of welfare to a new youth welfare committee (*Jugendpflegeausschuß*).[135] The statutes were adopted in the *Repräsentantenversammlung* in December 1929.[136] Arthur Lilienthal, the deputy community chair who was appointed at the same time as the new department was created, saw how the field of youth welfare offered the possibility of learning "to work together with those of different points of view".[137]

The support of sporting activities was seen as a main request in the field of youth welfare by all representatives. There had been attempts in the *Repräsentantenversammlung* since spring 1928 to build a sports ground. In February 1929 two Liberals and two JVP representatives each introduced a bill on this matter. The Liberal Sally London demanded: "Jewish youth must have a sports ground as quickly as possible, and I mean the youth of all parties."[138] The realisation of this plan dragged along considerably, however. In May 1931, at the last meeting of the 1926 *Repräsentantenversammlung*, Kareski announced that the sports ground would be opened in June.[139]

In conclusion it is clear that despite the ideological differences, there were great agreements when it came to practical community work and in relation to the goal of communal policy: the Liberals and the JVP made efforts to strengthen community organisations and to secure Jewish existence in Germany.*

---

[134]On social policy see, Detlev J. K. Peukert, *Die Weimarer Republik. Krisenjahre der Klassischen Moderne*, Frankfurt a. Main 1987, p. 138.
[135]'Verwaltungsbericht', in *Gemeindeblatt* 20, p. 33–34.
[136]Session on 12 December 1929, in *Gemeindeblatt* 20, No. 2 (1930), p. 80.
[137]Arthur Lilienthal, 'Jugend und Gemeinde', in *Jüdisch-liberale Zeitung* (25 June 1930).
[138]Session on 18 February 1929, in *Gemeindeblatt* 19, No. 4 (1929), p. 181.
[139]Session on 7 May 1931, in *Gemeindeblatt* 21, No. 6 (1931), p. 199.

*I would like to thank Professor Reinhard Rürup for his support and encouragement. I am also indebted to the staff at the *Bibliothek der Jüdischen Gemeinde zu Berlin* for their help.

Aspects of Antisemitism

When Heredity Met The Bacterium: Quarantines in New York and Danzig, 1898–1921

BY GERD KORMAN

I

Recent careful examinations of American quarantines placed on incoming migrants have found that public health officials were potent carriers of bigotries rooted in the larger society;[1] but usually historians have not paid sufficient attention to the complex challenges facing quarantine units in action. By examining the work of quarantine health officials dealing with migrating Jews from East Central Europe this analytical narrative seeks to show in detail important structural circumstances within which acts of bigotry manifested themselves between the 1890s and 1920s.

The narrative also has a larger agenda. Connections between public health quarantines and bio-cultural determinisms have long participated in the construction of public enemies. For instance in the 1980s, during the early years of the AIDS panic in the United States, public health officials could take for granted a citizenry that had long trusted in abstract empirical scientific knowledge and, for half a century, in the disease curing power of pharmacology's sulfa drugs and other antibiotics. Even so, in the first moments of panic all sorts of calls for screens and quarantine impacted on public policy discussions in ways reminiscent of the years between the 1890s and 1920s. During those years biological determinisms from the past had remained in the saddle. Even as modern public health programmes were becoming dramatically successful in fighting disease, they remained affected by hierarchies of bio-cultural notions, especially in apprehensions about immigrants as agents of dangerous contagious diseases.

That is one reason why this article focuses on Jews. The other reason derives from the evidence about Jews and disease in the places and times covered by this study. To be sure, there were other quarantines, involving, for example, resident Chinese and Italians; and in the months after the First World War potential incomers from Italy were at least as much an object of concern among American advocates of immigration restriction as were the Jews in Poland. But, in part, because of a typhus epidemic in that war-torn country, the association between disease and bio-cultural assumptions about Jews retained its traditional particularity in Western Europe and in the United States.

[1]Alan M. Kraut, *Silent Travelers: Germs, Genes, and the "Immigrant Menace"*, New York 1994, pp. 84–95, 303–305; Howard Markel, *Quarantine! East European Jewish Immigrants and the New York City Epidemics of 1892*, Baltimore 1997, *passim*.

During the 1890s, within a Darwinian framework, the young revolution of the germ theory of disease was well under way, but in the public health arena, as in biology and medicine in general, older convictions and practices were still competing with new concepts and bacteriological findings. In Philadelphia quarantine practitioners continued to treat ships from abroad as miasmatic vessels, that is as the primary "source of disease", in comparison to individual passengers as the potential pathogenic agent.[2] Even so, at the century's turning, advocates of the new were demonstrating to their own satisfaction the effectiveness of applied bacteriological knowledge in efforts to control and even stop the spread of a dangerous epidemic: a transformed urban water supply, more or less free of disease-causing germs, was one of their most powerful defences against deadly pathogens.

By the era of the First World War, victory was in the hands of bacteriologists and their diagnostic tools. Unfortunately, the new laboratory scientists, let alone the medical establishment, had failed to find reliable cures for the specific life-threatening contagious bacilli such as cholera, tuberculosis, or typhus now being observed under the microscope and diagnosed in the person migrating to the United States.[3] Guardians of public health and national integrity may have adopted the new scientific discourse. But as emergency response teams in fear of killer epidemics, as guards standing at border crossings, or as campaigners for restrictive immigration legislation, these guardians followed a traditional rule of survival: safe is better than sorry, especially when the incomer or resident "foreigner" seemed to match a harmful or dangerous ethnic or racial profile.

New tools of diagnosis had clearly outstripped pharmacological efforts to cure infected patients and to eliminate contagious diseases before sulfa drugs and other antibiotics came into use during the Great Depression and the Second World War. There was thus a significant gap leaving all sorts of decisions affecting public health to administrative and political "solutions", These were reached often in the face of experience or of new scientific findings, especially in times of real or imagined panics about contagion; they usually remained soaked in biological determinisms which, in no small measure, were shaped by popular forms of neo-Lamarckism.

It is therefore important to appreciate that most practitioners of biology and medicine, while working in a Darwinian mode, seemed to have taken for granted all sorts of notions about the inheritance of natural as well as of acquired characteristics. While preoccupied with Sigmund Freud's Jewishness, Yosef Hayim Yerushalmi's insight illuminates an entire bio-cultural landscape. "Deconstructed into Jewish terms what is Lamarckism if not the powerful feeling that, for better or worse, one cannot really cease being Jewish, and this not merely because of current antisemitism or discrimination, and certainly not because of the Chain of Tradition, but

---

[2]Edward Mormon, 'Guarding Against Alien Impurities: The Philadelphia Lazaretto, 1854–1893' in *Pennsylvania Magazine of History and Biography*, 108 (April, 1984), p. 151.

[3]William H. McNeill, 'The Flu of Flus', in *New York Review of Books*, 47 (10 February 2000) p. 29; Martin V. Melosi, *The Sanitary City: Urban Infrastructure in America from Colonial Times to the Present*, Baltimore 2000, pp.103–204; Richard J. Evans, *Death in Hamburg: Society and Politics in the Cholera Years 1830–1910*, New York 1990, pp. 262–284.

because ones fate in being Jewish was determined long ago by the Fathers, and that often what one feels most deeply and obscurely is a trilling wire in the blood." Freud, in writing about the Land of Israel, was more circumspect : " we hail from there ... our forebears lived there for perhaps a whole millennium ... and it is impossible to say what heritage from this land we have taken into our blood and nerves."[4]

Indeed, in an era when so much public sentiment in governing circles wanted to restrict immigration from "barbaric lands", to use a phrase popular with labour leader Samuel Gompers, changing biological concepts about contagion and quarantine were easily influenced by traditional assumptions of moral agency, race, nationality, class, and religion. Howard Markel, a physician and historian of the typhus and cholera panics in New York City in 1892, recently put this point sharply when he wrote of a "mentality of quarantine" when "the infectious disease become[s] the enemy but so, too, do ... human beings (and their contacts)". Such a mentality contains the driving energy to use police power "to do everything possible to prevent the spread of an epidemic, often at the neglect of the human or medical needs of those labelled contagious."[5]

II

On July 28,1911, *Der Kibetzer*, a New York Yiddish-language *Punch*, published a cartoon[6] showing cholera as an angel of death hovering between sky and water over New York harbour, facing Ellis Island and the United States chief immigration control officer, who is alarmed at the prospect of losing his deportation work to the killer. It clutches an immigrant steamship in each of its bony hands and dumps passengers from one of them into the open mouth of a nearby overflowing crematorium – a crematorium in New York Harbor, chimneys belching black smoke in Liberty's Bay!

Obviously *Der Kibetzer* spoke most directly to migrating Jews in steerage, who could hardly be expected to appreciate the concerns of class and ethnicity-conscious officials guarding national borders from potential lethal enemies. After the American Civil War

---

[4]Yosef Hayim Yerushalmi, *Freud's Moses: Judaism Terminable and Interminable*, New Haven 1991, p. 31, but see also p. 52, and pp. 87–90; Richard J. Bernstein, *Freud and the Legacy of Moses*, New York 1998, pp. 110–113; Peter J. Bower, *Evolution: The History of an Idea*, Berkeley 1983, pp. 243–256; *The Eclipse of Darwinism*, Baltimore 1983, 1992, pp. x and xv, p. 89, p. 284 ; Ernst Mayr, *The Growth of Biological Thought: Diversity, Evolution and Inheritance*, Harvard 1982, pp. 356–357; George. L. Mosse, *Toward the Final Solution: A History of European Racism*, New York 1978, pp. 16,18–19, 35. Neo-Lamarckism had its own national contexts. For the United States see Alpheus S. Packard, *Lamarck: The Founder of Evolution: His Life and Work*, New York 1901, *passim*; George W. Stocking Jr., *Race, Culture, and Evolution: Essays in the History of Anthropology*, New York 1968, pp. 234–269. For examples of Lamarckian-like biological determinisms in earlier contexts and public health paradigms see Conway Zirkle, 'The Early History of the Idea of Acquired Characteristics and of Pangenesis', in *Transactions of the American Philosophical Society*, 35, Pt. 2 (1946), pp. 91–151.
[5]Markel, pp. 185–186; Charles E. Rosenberg, *The Care of Strangers:The Rise of America's Hospital System*, New York 1987, pp. 297–309.
[6]The author wishes to thank the late Professor John J. Apple of Michigan State University for sending him a copy of this cartoon. He is the author of 'Jews in American Caricature: 1820–1914', in *American Jewish History*, 21 (September 1981), pp. 103–133. His extensive collection of original cartoons and slides are in the John and Selma Apple Collection of Michigan State University Museum in East Lansing.

246 Gerd Korman

Der Kibetzer, 28 July 1911

The Yiddish caption of this cartoon – loosely translated – reads as follows:

Poor Williams!

Deadly Cholera grabs each ship even before it approaches Ellis Island and hurls it into the crematorium. [The immigration Chief Inspector William] Williams stands at the edge of the ocean and his heart cries out for the unfortunate victims. He says: "If cholera continues for long I won't have anyone to send back. I'll lose my job. Oh! how I feel for the poor, unfortunate victims."

cholera epidemics had broken out while, on German railways, Jews migrated towards Prussian heartlands. There, the recently formulated germ theory of disease was being used to reshape public health perspectives about guarding the national border. This led to intensified efforts for devising protective screens. With sealed railway carriages, Germans organised steam-powered *Wanderstrassen*, which included medical control points and ended at guarded overseas passenger terminals and kosher kitchens in Hamburg's harbour. To migrating Jews and their justified sense of paranoia it was all but self-evident that Russian, Austro-Hungarian and German officials and clerks at border crossings, railway stations, and harbour facilities usually conspired to examine each person and each piece of Jewish baggage as if each was especially fit for a special quarantine. Mary Antin dramatically recalled her medical examination amidst hissing steam. She was stripped naked in front of strangers in white uniforms apparently threatening her in German. This Russian-Jewish girl, a first generation migrant among her people en route to the American promised land, was so frightened she expected to be murdered. She then realised that there was no German policy to do away with her. "Hurry, hurry or else…" she had heard, losing the crucial subsequent phrase called out by the sanitising attendant in white: "or else you'll miss the train."[7]

At the end of the journey across the Atlantic, the health service in New York's harbour became the final threat. Its web of detection spanned the United States Marine Hospital Service, hospital ships, disinfection barges, outlying beaches, and harbour islands. If a steamer came into the Lower Bay flying the yellow flag signalling cholera victims on board, physicians and their bacteria hunting helpers, with a "police boat patrol" hovering "about all day", went to work protecting the republic from the threat in steerage. Each passenger, was now regarded as a potential killer and isolated for the duration of lethal potency. Some died on board ship or in quarantine.

Many remembered, years after the event, as reported by the *New York Times*, the "Cholera scare in 1893. On Aug. 4, the *Karamania* arrived and reported three deaths from cholera on the voyage. The passengers were quarantined on Hoffman Island. The survivors were released on Aug. 24. There were 430 alive of the original list of 471." Eighteen years later, the crematorium was still burning bodies "as a sanitary precaution", to quote a small fragment in another *New York Times* story from 1911 about the delivery of two urns of ashes from Swinburne Island which was also controlled by public health officials.[8]

Jews had good reason to fear European and American public health policies. For centuries they had often been entangled in the bio-cultural obsessions of different times and places.[9] When the *Kibetzer* cartoon appeared in 1911, its publication co-

---

[7] Mary Antin, *From Plotzk to Boston*, New York 1985 [Reprint from 1894], pp. 37 and 41–43.
[8] *New York Times*, 6 August 1893; 23 July 1911; 1 August 1911.
[9] John Block Friedman, *The Monstrous Races in Medieval Art and Thought*, Cambridge, MA 1981, pp. 31–32, 54–55, 69, 88; Davyd Greenwood, *Nature, Culture, and Human History: A Bio-Cultural Introduction to Anthropology*, New York 1977, pp. 38–41,107–126; B. Netanyahu, *The Origin of the Inquisition in Fifteenth Century Spain*, New York 1995, pp. 1082–1084 and 1145; Henry Kamen, 'The Secret of the Inquisition', in *New York Review of Books*, vol. 43 (1 February 1996), pp. 4–6; Carlo Cipolla, *Miasmas and Disease: Public Health & the Environment in the Pre-Industrial Age*, Yale:1992, pp. 4–5; David S. Katz, *The Jews in the History of England 1485–1850*, Oxford 1996, p. 108; David B. Davis, 'Jews and Blacks in America', in *New York Review of Books*, 46 (2 December 1999), p. 58; John Efron, *Defenders of the Race: Jewish Doctors & Race Science in Fin-De-Siècle Europe*, New Haven 1994, pp. 6–7; Yerushalmi, *Freud's Moses*, pp. 32–33; . Sander L. Gilman, *The Case of Sigmund Freud: Medicine and Identity at the Fin De Siècle*, Baltimore 1993, pp. 11–20.

incided with commercially profitable mass transport linking Europe with the ports of the Atlantic basin. Jews migrated west in their hundreds and thousands, from the Duchy of Poznan within the German Empire, from Galicia in Austro-Hungary, from the Russian Empire and from Lithuania in the decade before the First World War. They crossed great divides of nations, cultures, class, and of border screens separating one state from another. They encountered hostile stereotypes. In addition to intensifying nervous apprehensions among receiving populations about the impact of the Jew on their political economy and in the face of new forms of anti-assimilation pressures, there was wide-spread apprehension among frustrated, upwardly mobile Jews whose families, decades earlier, had come from Poznan and other western parts of East Central Europe regarding the influx of poor and unassimilated Jews that might threaten their own status. It was also assumed that, as migrants from the Asiatic East, Jews were potential carriers of dangerous diseases and epidemics.[10]

For the guardians of a receiving nation and neighbourhood who were already preoccupied with criteria of genuineness, trustworthiness and reliability these arrivals stimulated efforts to modernise old profiles for Jews. Conveniently at hand were changing national biomedical cultures in Europe and America. Articulate doctors were often at the cutting edge, as in the case of Sigmund Freud who rejected much of the race thinking so popular among his fellow physicians. The writings of Jews in this group demonstrate the point especially well. German and Austrian authorities, in part because they were convinced about the uniquely diseased nature of each Jew's body and mind, usually presented deaf ears and blind eyes to the work of Jewish colleagues. They consistently ignored what they considered inherently untrustworthy Jewish evidence which, in fact, challenged many of the negative findings about Jews in particular and race in general.[11] On the other hand Jewish physicians almost always reflected their own versions of Lamarckian beliefs. Euro-American physicians among Freud's contemporaries still attributed to Jewish men and women all sorts of peculiar characteristics and habits.[12] Experts continued to construct Jews as being impervious to the different climates and lifestyles in which they lived. Racial immunity or "a hereditary aversion to liquor" protected them from alcoholism; they also had not succumbed to plague and pestilence "to the same extent ... as had non-Jews". In similar fashion, but usually determined by the current events of their practice, doctors often made assumptions about the Jewish stranger or neighbour next door, widely believing all sorts of things, for instance that they were not as susceptible as Gentiles to typhus, tuberculosis, cholera, measles, scarlet fever, diphtheria, or croup. They believed that Jews suffered from diabetes, lung and bronchial problems, haemorrhoids, cancer "but neither penile nor uterine,

---

[10]Jack Wertheimer, *Unwelcome Strangers: East European Jews in Imperial Germany*, New York, Oxford 1987, pp. 14–15 and 24–26. Between 1905 and 1914 over 700,000 Jews left German ports. Between 1871 and 1914, 5.8 million non-Germans left North Sea ports legally. Of these as many as one half were probably Jews, *ibid*. See also Shulamit Volkov, 'The Dynamics of Dissimilation: Ostjuden and German Jews'; Steven E. Aschheim, 'The Myth of "Judaization" in Germany', in Jehuda Reinharz and Walter Schatzberg (eds.), *The Jewish Response to German Culture: From the Enlightenment to the Second World War*, Hanover, New England 1985, pp. 195–211 and pp. 212–241.

[11]Efron, *passim*.

[12]This was particularly true of doctors who were convinced of significant connections between mental illness and sexual practices, Efron, p. 7.

due to male circumcision", conjunctivitis, trachoma, and colour-blindness in proportions significantly higher than non-Jews.[13] Indeed, in Germany's influential biomedical culture social construction of disease and illness led to the general conclusion that Jews, though as individuals belonging to the white race, collectively constituted a separate race – pure, bifurcated, mixed, or racially separate by virtue of its unique religious community.[14]

This kind of construction was embedded in the perspective of profile-oriented physicians who were charged with the responsibility of guarding the nation's well-being and integrity. The long period of conflict and uncertainty over fundamental questions of inheritance had precluded the quick establishment of a body of verified knowledge which would effectively challenge popular and professional beliefs and convictions from the past. On the one hand there was the continuing impact of beliefs that should have been discarded, as Ernst Mayr stressed when he evaluated the opposition to August Weismann's work among biologists: his "revolutionary rejection of soft inheritance encountered great hostility. It was attacked not only by the neo-Lamarckians, who reached the height of their influence in the 1880s and 1890s, but even by orthodox Darwinians who continued to accept Darwin's occasional reliance on the effects of use and disuse". Weismann, according to Mayr "had probably, up to the 1930s, more adherents in England than in ... [his] home country. Near universal acceptance did not occur until the 1930s and 1940s."[15]

On the other hand there was bacteriology and its findings. Once organisms were isolated, identified, and linked to specific contagious human diseases such as anthrax, tuberculosis and cholera the new approach was ready-made for emerging interventionist governments trying to cope with the impact of a steam-powered international economy. In the United States, public health officials had started to treat all passengers "as potentially pathogenic". At Prussian control points, official campaigns "assumed the guise of a systematic war against an identifiable enemy carried out under the clear direction and supervision of specialist medical scientists. Even the avoidance of personal contact was now given scientifically validated form in the destruction of the bacillus through medically approved actions such as washing, disinfection, boiling water, and so on". In other words, while believing in the inheritance of personal and collective characteristics, be they "natural" or "acquired", the practitioners modern scientific eye now looked upon each traveller as a potential killer.[16]

In the United States these convictions and patterns of perceptions in public health policies, existed in an environment of deeply rooted and widely accepted forms of American bio-cultural obsessions. Beyond the imposed "normal" separation of blacks and whites, self appointed guardians of an idealised white Anglo-American society used a terrifying lynching crusade in the "deep south" to institutionalise post Civil War segregation throughout America's southern region. Having first been devastated by cam-

---

[13] *ibid.*, p. 27.
[14] *ibid.*, pp. 16–26.
[15] Richard Quain *et al.*, *A Dictionary of Medicine*, New York 1883, p. 532; Mayr, pp. 356–357; Nancy Stepn, *The Idea of Race in Science: Great Britain 1800–1960*, Hamden 1982, pp. 85–86.
[16] Evans, pp. 271 and 477; Rosenberg, p. 140ff.; Mormon, p. 151. For a careful discussion of this complex subject in Germany see Paul Weindling, *Health, Race and German Politics between National Unification and Nazism, 1870–1945*, New York 1989, pp. 11–269.

paigns of pacification, indigenous Americans were penned up in patrolled reservations. The republic also continued to manifest its special hostility towards Chinese migrants by adopting and sustaining special laws of exclusion applicable only to them.[17]

So it is not surprising when in 1892, New York City, scared by fear of epidemics involving typhoid, typhus and cholera, struck incoming Jews from Europe with special force. Jews were arriving in the city in much larger numbers than ever before. The sanitary inspectors, physicians, and a special police force in the city's Division of Contagious Diseases in the Health Department were mobilised to protect the metropolis from catastrophe. They were also Jew-conscious germ-chasing officials with extraordinary powers, akin to the authority of a few state and federal officials who could impose martial law. It was the kind of empowerment and enforcement which caused panicky outcries in the Yiddish press comparable to Mary Antin's fear of being murdered in Prussia.[18]

III

In fact the screens and quarantines were applied under the guise of the supposed public good. Public health officials thus felt justified to routinely use all sorts of protective procedures. Cremation was one of them. The crematorium on the artificial Swinburne Island in the Lower Bay of New York harbour had been authorized in 1888, when, under the impact of miasma theory, burial grounds still remained suspect of contagious virulence. New York's public health officials had managed to persuade the state legislature and governor to pay for "a crematory ... for the incineration ... of the bodies of persons dying at Quarantine for contagious or infectious diseases".[19]

Many remembered, years after the event, the cholera scare in 1893, as told by the *New York Times*. The vessel *Karamania* – already mentioned in connection with that episode – carried mostly Italians, and so did two other ships which had actually contributed to the death toll of forty-one on board ship in quarantine. The two urns of ashes – also mentioned in reports by the same paper – were the remains of a former New York City street cleaning commissioner who had died of yellow fever "his body had been cremated as a sanitary precaution". The oven had been busy, but not as a special weapon of public policy against Jews or any other group. New York law specified that the "health officer ... shall cause to be incinerated ... the bodies of persons dying at the quarantine hospital from the infectious diseases, except of persons

---

[17]John Carey, *The Intellectuals and the Masses: Pride and Prejudice among the Literary Intelligentsia 1880–1939*, New York 1992, *passim*; Asa Briggs, *Victorian Cities*, London 1963, pp. 168–234; Paul Boyer, *Urban Masses and Moral Order in America 1870–1920*, Harvard 1978, pp. 123–283; Joel Williamson, 'Wounds Not Scars: Lynching, the National Conscience, and the American Historian', in *Journal of American History*, 83 (March 1997), pp. 1236–1238; Leon F. Litwack, *Trouble in Mind: Black Southerners in the Age of Jim Crow*, New York 1998, pp. 179–341.

[18]Markel, *passim*. Reporting on the coerced removal by health inspectors, a *New York World* account talked of the Jewish "patients ... ignorant and already cowed by oppression" as individuals "being hurried to execution for all they knew". The Yiddish-language *Arbeiter Zeitung* reported "alarming screams and outcries as if ... children and relatives were being taken to the slaughterhouse", Markel, pp. 50 and 52.

[19]J.M. Hawley to Abraham Hewitt, April 2,1888, N.Y. Attorney General's Office to F.L. Dallon, 25 May 1889, Folders: Health Dept, 1888, OF-1892, Box 88-GH-21, NYC Municipal Archives (hereafter MA).

whose religious views as communicated by them while living, or by their friends within twenty-four hours after their decease, are opposed to cremation."[20]

Incineration of private property was another procedure. During the cholera scare of the spring and summer of 1892, as part of an emergency disinfection sweep, Manhattan's health officials had the legal authority to take and destroy private belongings without restitution or compensation. So when a Mrs. McGrath was hit by typhoid fever the city burnt her "bed and Featherbedding". A year later she lodged a formal complaint in vain to the Mayor for, she claimed, she was still without a "bed to sleep nor anything to cover". Hermann M. Biggs, the distinguished Chief Inspector of Pathology, Bacteriology & Disinfection, confirmed that her bedding had been exposed to infection and was "destroyed in accordance with the directions of the Board [of Health] governing such cases". Therefore, the Board informed the Mayor's Office, it "cannot approve of any claim for payment for the same".[21]

And the city's dog pound protected citizens from stray dogs suspected of rabies by gassing them, allegedly a less cruel method of killing than the shooting of captured animals. There is an "airtight Box made of Wood and lined with zink the size of 9 ft long 5 ft wide and 3 ft 6 in high into which a $1\frac{1}{2}$ in gas pipe is connected to supply the ordinary illuminating Gas, and the capacity," reported the Keeper to Mayor Hugh J. Grant, "for holding about 120 Dogs ... when they are put in. The gas is turned on allowing about Eighty feet of Gas to fill the box, which takes about four minutes, by that time the Dogs are asphixiated, after which we allow them to remain in the box for about ten minutes, and then we draw off the gas by a 4 in ventilating pipe and a draught valve on the bottom of the box."[22]

Fumigation and quarantine were also enforced when the threat from germs did not come from foreign incomers; indeed, the treatment of returning soldiers, who had served in battle under the American flag, best reveals normal emergency responses by health officials. At the close of the Spanish-American War, when segregated black and white American soldiers from abroad were believed to pose a health threat, including Theodore Roosevelt's "Rough Riders" and young Harvard men who belonged to élite families, the public good was served by isolating them in Montauk, at the opposite end of Long Island.[23]

---

[20] *New York Times*, 4 September 1892, 6 August 1893, 23 July, 1 and 3 August 1911; Deed to the NY Quarantine Station and copy of passages of New York State law governing the activities of the Station, in Hugh Smith Cumming, U.S. Surgeon General to L. E. Cofer, 25 February 1921. The Quarantine Station's correspondence for this period is part of the collection generated by the Treasury Department. Accession # 65A-233, 330–8300, Box 509093, RG 90, National Archives, Bayonne, NJ (Hereafter NA/B).

[21] M. Jackson, MD to Hon. Thomas Gilroy, 28 August 1893, Hermann M. Biggs to Chas. G. Wilson, 1 September 1893, Secretary, Health Department to William Holly Esq., 5 September 1893, Folder: Health Dept, OF-1892, Box 88-GH-21, MA.

[22] 5 July 1892. The Mayor had requested the information to answer a question put to him by the president of the Board of Commissioner in the District of Columbia. On 30 June 1892 he wanted to know how New York killed its impounded animals because he had complaints about the "alleged cruelty" in shooting them. *ibid.*, GHJ-8, MA.

[23] *New York Journal*, 1 September 1898, in Jeff Healy (ed.), *Bully: Colonel Theodore Roosevelt, The Rough Riders and Camp Wikoff*, Montauk 1998, pp. 5 and 196–200; see also Elting E. Morison *et al.*, *The Letters of Theodore Roosevelt*, Cambridge, MA 1951, II, pp. 842–843, 851, 852, 854, 855, 865; *New York Times*, 4 August 1898; *Annual Report of the Supervising Surgeon-General of the Marine Hospital Service of the United States*, Washington 1899, pp. 622–623.

Some 22,000 of these soldiers, having been quickly evacuated from Cuba, were delivered into the hands of officials entrusted with the guardianship of the nation. From the start there were problems of organisation and preparedness. Doctors George M. Magruder and his deputy Joseph P. Kinyoun, in command of the assigned federal quarantine unit, had to navigate among competing authorities such as their own surgeon general in the Department of the Treasury, the army's surgeon general, officials in the navy in charge of transports and patrol boats, the secretary and his assistant secretary of the War Department, the health officials in New York City, and the governor of New York. Initially Magruder reported, "it was proposed to place the detention hospital in charge of officers of [his] Marine Hospital Service, but to avoid complications which threatened and to prevent the unsatisfactory and inefficient work which too often attends division of authority, it was considered best to adhere rigidly" to the decision "that my authority over troops and vessels should terminate when the yellow flag was hauled down". In fact, just before the transports began to land, issues of rank, jurisdiction, pride, prestige, and professional competition between ranking Marine Hospital Service doctors and army doctors all but dictated the arrangements that Magruder glossed over in his final report. His jurisdiction, however, would stop at the waters edge.[24]

A harbinger about preparations had come a few weeks before the first transport arrived at Montauk's Wikoff Camp. The *Concho* was quarantined for three days at Hampton Roads, Virginia with many typhoid victims on board, amongst them soldiers from the Cuban coast struggling with "exhausting malarial fever" and many others "recovering from the yellow fever hospitals at Sibonay". From there the transport sailed into quarantine in New York harbour, which meant the *Concho* would be handled like a vessel carrying immigrants diagnosed as suffering from illness or being suspected of harboring a contagious disease. Upon arrival the *Concho* was thoroughly disinfected. It was decided that "most of the officers and passengers might be landed later while all but fifty-nine of the others, too ill to be moved, should be taken to Hoffman and Swinburne Islands". At Swinburne that day one of the soldiers died of typhoid fever. The *Times* reported that his "body will be encased in a hermetically sealed casket and brought to the city". The vessel with its soldiers remained in quarantine but, unlike the very ill taken from immigrant ships, the soldiers on Hoffman and Swinburne were moved to new quarters at the quarantine station on Staten Island.

The *Times* also reported the reactions of some of the quarantine employees. They described conditions comparable to steerage in summer time. "Emaciated men lay on hard bunks, burning with fever. Some had only undershorts or a pair of drawers." In other words the *Concho*, and later some of the other transports had not been properly equipped or staffed to transfer the returning soldiers, including some of the sons of the richest and most influential Americans. Dr. Monae Lessing of the Red Cross, although appreciating the military emergency, was appalled: "Everybody apparently supposed that the vessel had proper stores. But there were no medicines, no disinfectants, no ice, no fresh water, no mattresses, little covering. The men ... were put between decks to sleep on hard bunkers, where little fresh air could reach them." In

---

[24]*ibid.*, p. 625; George M. Magruder to Surgeon General Walter Wyman, 17 August 1898., MHS, RG 90, National Archives (hereafter NA).

other words the vessel was a breeding box for the contagious diseases so feared by the quarantine service.[25]

Soldiers from a battle zone rife with malaria, yellow fever, typhoid, and typhus were arriving at a U.S army camp which did not have the necessary infrastructure in place. As happens so often with surges of contagion threatening to endanger public health, emergency response groups found themselves stretched well beyond their expectations; for besides incompetence, neglect, and capriciousness they had no or very little control over the infrastructures and the logistics required to fight such an emergency. The Long Island Rail Road had to extend its rail connections to a long sought terminus in Montauk. The *World* and the *New York Herald* reported:

> About three hundred men appeared on the scene yesterday, with horses and cart and picks and shovels. The railroad, which stops short eight miles before it reaches the tip of the Point where the troops were to be unloaded, sent down carloads of lumber and ties and railroad iron. The workmen had to bring food for themselves and their horses, for there was none to be had in the wilderness. These men have been rapidly laying down tracks, making roadways and putting up houses. ... Linemen are [also] at work stringing wires between [nearby] Bridgehampton and this place. ... There is now one direct wire between here and New York, but within two days there will be four wires in service.[26]

But according to a summer resident from nearby Southampton, who at the time was a national senior official and field agent of the Red Cross, work on tent and store house construction, as well as on reliable water facilities was so far behind schedule that Camp Wikoff remained unprepared for days after the troops started to arrive. Indeed, a few months after the closing of the camp, the Red Cross official was still appalled by what had happened to the general hospital: it was "constructed day after day, almost over the heads of the sick men"; work "was going on almost until the day when the order came to clear out the hospital".[27] By early September, many a local resident feared the camp was a veritable breeding ground for typhoid and typhus. So did doctors. Nicholas Senn, an army doctor criticised his colleagues and superiors:

> All the conditions for an epidemic were in place. Water pumps were failing even as doubts about the reliability of the well water itself remained. Poor discipline led to exposure to human and animal waste. Stagnant pools of water near the soldiers' tents were filled with excrement from horses. Flies abounded. Wagons carried uncovered stacked loaves of bread through the dust covered camp. And there was no working hospital laundry to prevent the accumulation of "foul linen" – in the end they had to be burnt.[28]

Another doctor, visiting the Presbyterian and Bellevue Hospital, after having visited the camp, exploded to a reporter for the *New York Times*. Disinfection at the camp is a "farce. The whole camp is infected with disease." Typhoid fever takes two weeks to develop. That's why typhoid cases have shown up in the city's hospitals; these were brought by soldiers from Montauk who had never been hospitalised or who had been

---

[25] *New York Times*, 1–3 August 1898.
[26] Healy, pp. 25–27, 32–37.
[27] At the time Townsend was acting as volunteer field agent. *American National Red Cross Relief Committee Reports, 1898–1899*, pp. 227–228.
[28] *Red Cross Report*, p. 226.

furloughed, free to try to walk the streets of Manhattan. "Proper sanitation is what they don't understand there." The spread of typhoid fever "is perfectly preventable … just as much as cholera, and yellow fever".[29]

Obviously, contagious diseases had been a serious problem at Wikoff. Yellow fever had not been the culprit; it had been the "other sick", the "ordinary cases of sickness, such as malarial fever, typhoid fever, etc." that had presented the danger to all those who feared them, especially typhoid fever and typhus, illnesses often difficult for even a trained eye to diagnose with precision or tell apart one from the other. Ninety-eight out of the one hundred and fifty soldiers who died, and were buried, at Wikoff had their cause of death listed as typhoid.[30]

Against this background it is clear that the quarantine imposed on Jews a few years earlier had been part of the routine of quarantine but it had been quarantine with a difference. In March 1892 victims of typhus in one Jewish residential quarter had been traced to a recently arrived vessel from Europe. Upon them, on other Jewish passengers, and on the nearby Jewish places they frequented, swooped quarantine officials along with the ruthlessness, incompetence, and capriciousness so characteristic of the emergency response efforts. In no time at all, and given the prejudice towards impoverished recent arrivals living in unsanitary overcrowded conditions, all sorts of anti-Jewish language made its way into official reports. According to Cyrus Edson, Manhattan's chief sanitary inspector and quarantine enforcer, Jews were "phlegmatic, dull, and stupid … sullen and suspicious". When it "comes to a question of disease, they will … do anything … and lie with the most magnificent elaboration as to all matters touching their own sickness or those of their neighbors". Indeed, reports Markel, who studied this quarantine closely, "the popular perception among many native born New Yorkers was that the Lower East Side was a breeding ground for pestilential disease".[31]

But the quarantines achieved a measure of success. In the Spring of 1892, typhus in the Jewish Lower East Side remained contained. In 1898, yellow fever did not spread from Cuba to the mainland, and disease from the sick interned at Wikoff was also contained. Officials claimed police control had helped. For example, around the troop carriers military discipline kept intruders out, even an eager patriotic physician from Springfield, Massachusetts. He had tried to bring food packages to "his boys", the 2nd Regiment of Massachusetts Volunteers, on board the returning, now quarantined, troop carrier *St. Louis*. As his launch in the Long Island sound started to come alongside, he faced rifles ready to fire at him if he did not turn away.[32]

This incident with the doctor pointed to three important differences between Wikoff and the way public health officials related to Jewish immigrants. The doctor,

---

[29] *New York Times*, 2, 3, 4, 5 September 1898; *Red Cross Report*, p. 237. See also A. R. Tooth, a medical service worker in the camp, protesting to Wyman about standards of health and control: 23 August 1898, MHS, RG 90, NA.

[30] Healy, pp. 499–508.

[31] Markel, p. 33. See also *ibid.*, pp. 50–59, 62–75, 113, 119, 132–133 for other anti-Jewish references during the following months and year.

[32] David Clark MD, Springfield, Mass., to General Greenville M.Dodge, President of Commission for Investigation of Conduct of War, 3 October1898; Magruder, Camp Hutton, La., to Surgeon General Walter Wyman, October 14,1899, Marine Hospital Service, RG 90, NA.

technically an agent of Springfield's Auxiliary Branch of the Massachusetts Volunteers Aid Association, sent a long complaint to Washington about Wikoff's quarantine enforcements. Its senior quarantine officer responded with a point by point refutation: the physician's treatment by the officer in charge was an act flowing from authorised public health policies designed to protect the republic.

Secondly, albeit only on its own terms, the army had encouraged care packages and all sorts of other assistance from the "outside". It eagerly sought and received the help of the American Red Cross for fresh water supplies and other perishables. The field commanders even accepted its female nurses and other personnel, although the officer in charge "like all army surgeons of the old school ... was prejudiced against them;" without them the camp would have been hard pressed to cope with the army's unpreparedness to handle embarking troops from inspected ships. It also allowed the Red Cross to distribute care packages from friends and relatives of the encamped soldiers. In addition there were many visitors, parents or siblings from afar and patriotic residents from nearby.[33]

Implicit was the most important difference. In comparison to Jewish immigrants associated with contagious diseases, the soldiers were not held responsible for their illnesses or circumstances, not in the camp, not in stations of the Long Island Railroad, and not on Manhattan's streets, where some of them collapsed. They were not considered phlegmatic, dull, or stupid. Indeed Roosevelt made certain that he and his fellow soldiers were perceived as heroes as did President William McKinley who, having visited the site, launched an investigation of the Wikoff experience. (It found no evidence of unusual negligence or incompetence in the activities of any federal agency involved.) Blame was assigned to military officialdom and circumstances, or sometimes to incompetent doctors or the enforcers of quarantine rules.[34]

The different approach was not limited to the 1890s; it remained embedded in the quarantine structure. Indeed events a few years later foreshadowed the future. Notwithstanding the experiences and criticisms of the quarantines on Long Island, under Surgeon General Wyman's authority, the well trained and respected bacteriologist, Dr. Joseph P. Kinyoun who had long been a deputy to Wyman and who had worked at Wikoff, imposed a punishing quarantine against bubonic plague on San Francisco's Chinese and Japanese residents. Before a federal court order ended it, his race-based cordon sanitaire was reminiscent of Edson's emergency decrees for Jews of the Lower East Side.[35]

IV

In 1911, the *Kibetzer*'s cartoonist and his kinfolk had assumed that there was hostility among European and American officials towards themselves as Jews. Since the end of the century, the proportion of those kept out for medical reasons had gone up from less than 2% to 57% in 1913, and up to 69% three years later. More important

---

[33]*Report of the Supervising Surgeon-General*, p. 621; *Red Cross Report*, pp. 229–230.
[34]Healy, pp. 61–72, 75, 138–140, 231–248.
[35]Kraut, pp. 79–96

still, especially from the perspective of the new incomer, there were the explosions of suspicion about distrusted immigrants and deadly contagious diseases understood in terms of germ theory. In this new perspective ghettos were seen as dangerous breeding grounds with a difference, presumed worst in San Francisco among the Chinese, but presumed present also in Philadelphia and New York among Italians and Jews. Still, in spite of the rise of modern political anti-Semitism there were also many reasons for being hopeful. By 1911 many more Jews had arrived and, together with older immigrants, they were acquiring more economic and political influence, especially in New York City where most of them were concentrated and where they shared with everyone else expectations about the control or even elimination of lethal epidemics.[36]

But the law of unintended consequences had also been at work. Within a few years after 1911 there were indicators of profound change for the worse, especially from the perspective of any individual not protected by citizenship. Such persons were akin to creatures in the wild, fair game to any predator. Patriotic public health practices from the past persisted, becoming ever deeply enmeshed in the policies of the United States and of European countries preoccupied with the defence of perceived national cultures. Despite the advent of more reliable diagnoses of contagious diseases and of more experiences with fumigation and quarantine techniques, particularly in the years of war and revolution after 1914, profile screening continued to be used for selected incomers perceived as potential transmitters of typhus, typhoid, or cholera. In the absence of reliable protective vaccinations, or the availability of sulfa drugs and antibiotics of a later generation, fear of diagnosed harmful bacteria mingled easily with rising tides of xenophobia, race consciousness, and inflammatory metaphors.

Indeed, in these years all sorts of hierarchies were emerging in European and American biological politics. Once the twentieth century science of genetics started to explain biological mechanisms for inheritance, Koch's kind of campaign to identify and contain, if not to control harmful bacteria in the human body, served as one influential model for achieving ideal states of public health for an envisioned national body politic; programmes of social hygiene and race institutes compared their "genuine nation" to a healthy human body and campaigned for policies that would protect their nation against particular groups of human organisms.[37] Between 1914 and 1921, war and revolution often intensified such perspectives. Moments of triumph for self determination, often in the aftermath of blood soaked battles, brought refugees in flight from regions associated with epidemics of contagious diseases. These were ideal conditions constructing and reconstructing public enemies, for propagating old and new metaphors with which individuals and peoples distanced themselves from each other: snakes and cattle, weeds and parasites mingled easily

---

[36]*ibid.*, p. 66.
[37]Weindling, pp. 270–395; Stefan Kuehl, *The Nazi Connection: Eugenics, American Racism, and German National Socialism*, New York 1994, pp. 13–48, 65–76; Michael Burleigh and Wolfgang Wippermann, *The Racial State: Germany 1933–1945*, New York 1991, pp. 23–43; Goetz Aly, Peter Chroust, and Christian Pross, *Cleansing the Fatherland: Nazi Medicine and Racial Hygiene*, Baltimore 1994, pp. ix–xiii, and *passim*. See also the late Detlev J. L. Peukert in Thomas Childers and Jane Caplan (eds.), *Reevaluating the Third Reich*, New York 1993, pp. 234–249.

with bacteria, germs, and after 1917 with "nits and cooties", that is with lice and vermin often associated with Jewish migration from Eastern Europe.[38]

V

Because so much of the post-war East European steerage migration headed for New York from battle zones in which typhus raged, the inadequate capacity of its port to handle the incomers reverberated throughout overseas medical control arrangements. The need for improvements had been obvious for some years but since 1916 the harbor's quarantine station was caught in a transfer process between the state of New York and the federal government. The final arrangements were not completed until 1 March 1921. Until then funds for expanding and modernising the facilities were not available.

In the event, the quarantine station, technically owned by New York but managed by Dr. Leland E. Cofer, a federal employee on loan to the station, was ill equipped for the task at hand. It was run down because New York, according to Cofer, had spent "very little money" on the station in "recent years". The buildings "are all in poor conditions and require extensive repair". The station had also found it hard to recruit personnel. According to Cofer the rate of pay at the station was lower than at local hospitals even though the work was more "exposed and strenuous". Fear of contagion was a constant problem:

> [B]efore almost any kind of help will come to this station, the fear of quarantinable diseases must be quieted and a natural aversion to isolation on [the] Islands must be overcome. The result is that instead of having persons apply for position at this station we are continuously advertising for help in papers and in other ways hunting up persons for employment here.[39]

On its two quarantine islands there was just not enough room to meet the demand. "It is necessary that the capacity of the Station [100 sick with quarantinable disease and 1600 in detention for observation] should at least double throughout," Cofer wrote in a report for the president of the New York Academy of Medicine. Experience had taught that when several vessels arrived at the same time

---

[38] On metaphors for humans and insects during the First World War see for example Edmund P. Russell III, "'Speaking of Annihilation': Mobilizing for War Against Human and Insect Enemies, 1914–1945', in *Journal of American History*, 82 (March 1996), pp. 1512–1513. Years earlier "vermicides" – "a group of anthelminties" – were used to kill "intestinal worms". After the First World War "Verminicide" was on the market in England for killing "vermin". For examples of the specific use of "verminous" with this meaning see the following: the first was written about English conscripts to explain typhus in the trenches, "The continuance of lousiness evidently depends upon a low standard of life. ... It has been stated that the infection was started by new recruits who came from verminous slums, and the crowding together by troops and the limited facilities for bathing gave the parasites every condition favorable to multiplying and spreading." Folder Report I–XXXIX, Box 35, in Strong Papers "Infection with Vermin", 1. The second was applied to Bolsheviks. Alfred E. Cornebise, *Typhus and Doughboys: The American Polish Typhus Relief*, Delaware 1982, p. 136 . The word "verminous" like "vermin" has a long pedigree which includes the following use in 1830: "Both in Russia and Poland I believe ... [Jews] are a verminous population preying upon others" as well as this one in 1899: "In 'verminous persons' the hair is sometimes matted together by pus, nits, scales and scabs." *The Compact Edition of the Oxford English Dictionary*, II, Oxford 1971, pp. 3614, 4084.

[39] L. E. Cofer to R. H. Creel, Asst. Surgeon, General Bureau of the Public Health Service, Treasury Dept., 17 November 1920, RG 90, NA/B

the station needed observation space for around 3,500 patients instead of the available 1,600. "In past winter when twelve ships arrived with typhus on board and eight with small pox," the station had to make "vessels ... lie at anchor in Quarantine with their personnel aboard, which not only constituted faulty quarantine methods, but was a personal hardship to the passengers involved and a distinct financial loss to the steamship companies and the community in general on account of the withdrawal from regular schedule of passenger vessels."[40]

Passengers had little choice and did not rebel.[41] They were confined in run-down, inadequate quarantine facilities where personnel used procedures marked by incompetence and sloppiness. Cofer had to admit to the Surgeon General that "lousy passengers were turning up in Ellis Island after having been inspected at Quarantine". He identified his problems in detail: "immigrants are caused to scrub up their bodies just before arrival at this port when they are caused to put on clean undershirts and then it would appear that the infested undershirt formerly removed is put back on the immigrant over the still clean undershirt and the immigrant naturally shows up lousy at the Ellis Island inspection." Mattresses and blankets presented another problem for which neither the budget nor the facilities allowed obvious solutions: "it has been found that immigrants accounted for as clean from this Station after spending two or three nights on probably already infested mattresses and under infested blankets can show up an increased ratio of uncleanliness at Ellis Island ... It would be a big project to send them through steam chambers. It could be done," he informed Washington, "but we are already overtaxed with 6–700 in quarantine. There is also the matter of time for tying up the vessel ..." And, Cofer reminded his superiors, even though he was offering "125.00 [dollars] a month without quarters and subsistence" he was unable to find additional men or women "to train in examining these people for body vermin".[42]

In these circumstances Cofer was also apprehensive about the streams of migrants now heading his way from Eastern Europe. They were returning to pre-war levels but with plague and typhus fever. These "were reported as existing especially in Russia and Poland to an alarming degree. Asiatic cholera was reported in the Crimean and other ports of the Ukraine." While he did not expect an immediate problem in New York, he was nervous: "if the report was true that there were 250,000 cases of typhus fever in Poland and 40,000 cases existing in the City of Lomberg [sic], then it was not unlikely that the foreign ports of departure would become infected."[43]

The interaction of structural circumstances in New York, when combined with apprehension if not fear of the post-war migrations, especially of Jews from Poland, prompted the Public Health Service to install a rigorous control system. At ports of embarkation with hinterlands or contact with regions associated with contagious diseases, U.S. quarantine officers were expected to quarantine and clear all passengers

---

[40]Cofer to E. W. Lewinsky-Corwin, 3 May 1921 with undated report attached, NA/B.
[41]In contrast 38 crew members of the *Antigone* rebelled in New York harbour. Report attached to letter from Cofer to Creel, 22 June 1921, NA/B.
[42]Cofer to Cumming, 28 April 1921, NA/B.
[43]Leland F. Cofer, Report of the Health Officer of the Port of New York, 1 July 1920–28 February 1921, Typescript copy NA/B.

headed for the United States. At American ports, a "most rigid system of medical examination of arriving passengers from Europe and thorough fumigation of vessels was inaugurated. Not only were vessels quarantined and persons exposed to infection detained when actual quarantinable diseases were found on arriving ships," reported Cofer in March 1921, "but extraordinary precautions were taken, as follows: In the first place, persons arriving from places suspected of infection with typhus were required to be deloused. Persons arriving from places where cholera was known to exist were required to submit to bacteriological examination of discharge prior to admission, and vessels from plague infected or suspected ports were required to be fumigated for rat destruction."[44] Clearly, the more effective and reliable the clearance procedures abroad the less pressure on the quarantine station in New York; and for that reason conditions in New York radiated outwards throughout the entire quarantine system at foreign ports of embarkation.

VI

In those circumstances, which in some ways are comparable to events associated with Wikoff and New York City in the years around 1898, thousands of returning soldiers and migrating Jews were heading for quarantine in or near Danzig. After 1917, and for different reasons, the Baltic port city received special attention. Victorious diplomats and generals at Versailles in April and May 1919 and again in the summer of 1920 focused on this old Prussian commercial centre, its hinterland, and its rail connections to Warsaw, especially the section running from Thorn to Danzig.[45] American and European immigration restrictionists also watched its affairs. As opponents of Southern and East European migrants, they feared the aftermath of war. Restrictionists were convinced it would bring a resumption of mass migration towards the west. Until Americans adopted a new immigration law with its ceilings and race-based quotas – these were expected to all but stop Polish Jews from emigrating after May 1921, when the new law was to go into effect – concern focused in the intervening months on Danzig.

The returning soldiers consisted of a special army unit which had been deployed in Poland. It was an odd collection of about 12,000 soldiers who shared one characteristic: they were all Polish-American residents of the United States who, once America had joined the war, had been encouraged by officials of an emerging Polish government to fight for the newly independent Poland as volunteers in a Polish Legion. With its distinctive uniform this force had been attached to the French army, but after the armistice the Legion served in Poland under General Joseph Haller in his campaigns against Germans, in disputed territory subject to plebiscites, and against Bolsheviks, who were fighting Poles for sovereignty over the western Ukraine. In late 1919, during a lull in the fighting, these "Haller men", were discharged into limbo until early 1920 when a joint

---

[44] *ibid.*

[45] Arno J. Mayer, *Politics and Diplomacy of Peacemaking*, New York 1967, pp. 95, 599–603, 759. There were some suggestions that Germany's border with Poland would be fixed to the west of that railway line so that the Allies could intervene in Poland independent of German policies. In August of 1920 Bolshevik units came within 30 kilometers of Warsaw.

resolution of Congress authorised the "Secretary of War to use such army transports as may be available to bring back to the United States from Danzig, Poland, such residents of the United States of Polish origin as were engaged in the war on the side of the allied and associated powers." By March, the U.S. army's transportation service, operating out of Antwerp, took charge of the men's embarkation from Danzig and transfer to the United States, while in Poland the American Ambassador, his military attache, and his consul in Warsaw handled citizenship verification, organisational procedures, and arrangements for quarantine control prior to the troops boarding ship.[46]

The quarantine control for the soldiers was assigned to the American Polish Relief Expedition. It consisted of another group of American soldiers who were in Poland as part of a larger effort to help the Polish government fight the widespread typhus epidemic in order to establish around Poland a cordon sanitaire. (The epidemic had been raging since 1916, when most Poles were, and would remain until the end of 1918, under German military occupation.) The American efforts had diverse elements to it, including the work of the Jewish Joint Distribution Committee, and, as part of the strategic goals of the relief programme, that of a scientific Red Cross mission, staffed by Harvard biologists keen on studying the typhus vector. The quarantine unit, now also heading for the vicinity of Danzig, was part of an emergency response detachment which had been formed after the armistice agreement. Its French headquarters were in Paris, its Polish centre of operations in Warsaw. It was led by Colonel Harry L. Gilchrist, a fifty-year-old physician with an MD from Western Reserve and training at the Army Medical School.[47]

Fighting among Poles, Ukrainians, and Bolsheviks had been most disruptive and had put an end to the important eastern part of the cordon sanitaire against typhus, threatening to do the same in the west. Retreating soldiers, reported Gilchrist to his superiors, destroyed much of the anti-typhus fighting equipment and, as large proportions of soldiers "were filthy and verminous", they "reinfected large parts of Poland which had been [made] free of the disease". Gilchrist's view of the future was bleak: without immediate aid, he insisted, "suffering will be intense and all Europe will be threatened with a terrible Typhus Fever Epidemic".[48]

The men connected with the Danzig embarkations knew what to keep out of the United States and were experienced to execute quarantine orders under the most chaotic of conditions. Gilchrist's number two, Doctor Lee R. Dunbar, was in charge. He had been head of the Bathing and Delousing Division of the American Third Army, and had most recently been posted to Lublin as an adviser to Polish health officials. He arrived on 18 March 1920 with the expectation that his first contingent would have to be ready to embark within a few weeks for the first troop carrier was due to arrive in Danzig on 23rd March.[49]

---

[46]Cornebise, pp. 101–102;. H. H. Ben Sasson (ed.), *A History of the Jewish People*, Cambridge Mass., 1976, p. 954; Joseph T. Hapak, 'Selective Service and Polish Army Recruitment During World War I', in *Journal of Ethnic History*, 10 (Summer 1991), pp. 38–60; Nancy Gentile Ford, '"Mindful of the Traditions of His Race": Dual Identity and Foreign-Born Soldiers in the First World War American Army', in *Journal of Ethnic Studies*, 16 (Winter 1997), pp. 36–57.
[47]Cornebise, p. 153, n11.
[48]*ibid.*, pp. 113–119, 136.
[49]*ibid.*, pp. 103–104.

At first, Dunbar's military operation was obliged to make the final screen, delousing, and clearance for embarkation within Danzig, using the Danzig-Troyl plant, which the German army had operated.[50] The Polish American soldiers coming to him were arriving from two quarantine camps in Polish territory south of the city. They were run by two of Gilchrist's other medical officers. At these camps the men were supposed to have been bathed, deloused, isolated from new arrivals, and then dispatched to Dunbar at Danzig for the final pre-boarding procedures.[51]

But in practice there were all sorts of problems and after two transports had left for America another camp site was established as the final clearance centre before embarkation from Danzig. One reason was that the quarantine and delousing measures were not fool proof. The first two ships, the *Antigone* and the *Pocahantes*, sailed without risk free assurances, and indeed two typhus cases developed en route to the United States. When the *Pocahantes* arrived in New York, her crew and passengers were placed in quarantine for eleven days.[52] For another, the arrangements ran foul of the conflicting micro-jurisdictions then governing Danzig and its hinterland. During one major transfer of Haller's men into the city, Dunbar had failed to obtain barrack space from the British authorities then running municipal affairs in Danzig. Troops on the Thorn line were held up for many hours; so long in fact that on their train food was running out while Polish and British officials worked out the details which would be least offensive to the tense German Danzig population suspicious of any Polish troop movement through their city.[53]

Within a month after his arrival in Danzig, Gilchrist ordered Dunbar and his men to shut down the Troyl operation. He sent them about 100 kilometres south of the port city to a new site, Camp *Gruppe*, near the main railway line between Danzig and Warsaw which was of such concern to post World War I belligerents, and also to Jews seeking to leave Poland. For the time being *Gruppe* was "most congenial" to the professionals persuaded by the quarantine mentality. Geographically it was comparable to Wikoff. It was in a pine forest isolated from population centres yet connected via a camp siding to a reliable rail system. It was superior to Montauk. As a former German artillery site it had the required housing facilities. In addition, this quarantine camp had one command structure. It was in the hands of a military emergency response team dedicated to keeping typhus out of the United States.[54]

Indeed, it was ideally suited for experimenting with the American quarantine mentality in action, especially after some deficiency in supplies, equipment and staffing were overcome. Haller's men would come in from the initial staging camps, placed into *Gruppe*'s "dirty camp" and then, following inspection, bathing, and delousing, isolated in the "clean" camp. At its peak of efficiency, in response to sailing schedules out of Danzig, Dunbar could delouse more than a thousand soldiers each day.[55]

---

[50]*ibid.*, p. 106.
[51]*ibid.*, pp. 105–106.
[52]John H. Linson to Rupert Blue, 29 May 1920, Correspondence of the Assistant Surgeon of the Public Health Service of Danzig, Poland, 1920–1921, Reel 1, Records of the Public Health Service, Record Group 90, National Archives (hereafter Reel 1).
[53]Cornebise, p. 105.
[54]*ibid.*, p. 106.
[55]*ibid.*, p. 110.

Military discipline reinforced quarantine procedures. The troops were marched in and commanded to pay strict obedience to the rules. Violators were pulled out of the company sailing for home; they were left free to remain in Poland, but unless they complied with standing quarantine orders, they would remain ineligible for government transport. Within that framework troops had to follow the routine, from the first hair inspection, to check if each man had been properly clipped and shaved, to their last camp inspection, to check for nits and lice. Dunbar commanded and Polish-American soldiers obeyed: into the delouser, stripped with clothing into a steriliser; into a bath with strong soap; into a clean bathrobe and to a doctor: he checked for infectious diseases, lice and nits on "scalp, axillary, pubic, and anal region". Cleared, each soldier was then marked with an indelible stamp and sent with fresh socks and underwear to join his company which, as a unit, marched into a clean barrack.[56] In the next few days there were more general inspections, more baths and specific inspection for lice and nits; and early on the morning of their departure for embarkation at Danzig the soldiers heading for home returned to the delouser for their final bath and inspection.[57]

Strict rules also governed the rail journey to the Baltic harbour. Within forty-eight hours of departure on a camp siding boxcars were prepared: swept out, scrubbed, dried, and then sprayed with a five per cent creol solution. Twenty-four hours later the waiting train and its boxcars were ready for the soldiers who had been cleared, stamped with "Deloused, Camp *Gruppe*" on their left forearm, and segregated in a special section of the camp. En route to Danzig, United States quarantine officers and a small detachment of enlisted men maintained the isolation from the general population. By late July some 11,000 "clean" Polish-American soldiers had sailed for home.[58]

VII

Reminiscent of the difference between Camp Wikoff and the earlier treatment of Jews in New York City, their processing now was also different than it was for Polish-Americans at Camp *Gruppe*. In the wake of World War I – typhus – the cooties and nits to the American Public Health Service, had become the epidemic threatening from Eastern Europe. Between 1919 and 1921, fuelled by the forged "Protocols of Zion" and the immigration restriction campaigns in the United States, fear of Jews and typhus once again combined with special potency, indeed now with greater clarity: potentially, Jews carried the identifiable bacterium invariably found in the faeces of lice.[59]

Migrating Jews had also focused on Danzig, for until Riga was opened to commercial transport it was the nearest available oceanic harbour from which they could

---

[56]*ibid.*, pp. 107–108. Each man was issued special soap with which to wash his dirty clothing and uniform.
[57]*ibid.*, p. 108.
[58]Some 8,000 sailed from *Gruppe*. Almost 3,000 had sailed before *Gruppe* had been set up. The departure of about 1,000 men was delayed because of fear that Bolshevik troops would sever the Warsaw–Danzig rail line. *ibid.*, pp. 109–111. See also Linson to Blue, 29 May and 28 July 1920, Reel 1.
[59]On the Protocols see Norman Cohn, *Warrant for Genocide: The Myth of the Jewish World-Wide Conspiracy and the Protocols of the Elders of Zion*, New York 1967), *passim*. See also John Higham, *Strangers in the Land: Patterns of American Nativism*, New Brunswick 1955, pp. 264–311.

emigrate. Its strategic location in the months when the Allies blockaded German ports was coming to an end. During most of the period from late 1919 to May of 1921, Danzig, previously controlled by the defeated Central Powers, was the only former German port open to civilian shipping on the Baltic and on the North Sea. Until November 9,1920 it was under Allied control; then it turned into a Free City under the emerging authority of the League of Nations.

In other words, the way out to America was through a city and across boundaries supercharged with metaphors derived from competing nationalisms and revolutionary zeal, intense antisemitism, and the biological determinism from pre-war years. Danzig's hinterland was surrounded by the new controversial Polish Corridor and by a strip of territory that in a plebiscite in June 1920 chose overwhelmingly to remain part of East Prussia. In addition internal politics in Danzig and nearby towns was in turmoil because of competing local German and Polish revolutionary militias and the interventions in their affairs by units of the German army.[60]

Responses to typhus fighting efforts invariably tangled with all sorts of experiences and stereotypes, including those brought from across the ocean and those from inflamed war-time Polish xenophobic passions. Americans in Poland reported about Jews with the kind of detail and intensity usually missing from comments about ordinary Catholics in Poland. Catholics were Poles. Jews on the other hand were not identified as Jewish Poles or Polish Jews – they were seen as stereotypical figures along the lines of traditional antisemitic stereotypes.

One cool assessment of the Polish situation came from Richard P. Strong, Harvard's leader of the Red Cross typhus mission: He thought it was difficult to mount an effective campaign against the epidemic because "not enough [Poles] have died to realize it is an emergency. ... Indeed the general attitude of many of the people in Poland is hostile to anti-typhus work, perhaps," he suggested, thus echoing a widely held opinion, "because often during the German occupation the people were compelled to submit to the necessary delousing measures which were applied by the Germans with military severity."[61]

Gilchrist had positive impressions about Poles in charge of the anti-typhus campaign; but field reports from Paris and those coming into Warsaw told a different story. Poles were "less than helpful", "hopeless, helpless", "dilatory", "inefficient", "thieving", incapable of keeping promises, "always quarrel[ling] amongst themselves", their trains were unsanitary, and no matter what they said, they were men who did not "really know what they are doing".[62] From Lvov came a report reflecting the general problem: strict rules and procedures on paper but "in practice things were carried out in a perfunctory manner, largely due to the low salaries paid to the various workers."[63] And in rural areas near Bedzin and Krakow doctors were often

---

[60] F. L. Carsten, *Revolution in Central Europe 1918–1919*, Berkeley 1972, pp. 14–15, 271–276; Paul Robert Magocsi, *Historical Atlas of East Central Europe*, Seattle 1993, pp. 28,126–127,130–131.
[61] Richard P. Strong et al., *Typhus fever with Particular Reference to the Serbian Epidemic*, Harvard 1910, p. 106; Richard F. Strong Papers, Box, 35–36(b-d), Rare Book Room, Harvard Medical School Library; Cornebise, p.122.
[62] *ibid.*, pp. 35, 36, 48, 53.
[63] *ibid.*, p. 115.

diagnosing typhus as influenza "to allay the fears of the people". Then, in violation of modern practices, they treated their patients with alcohol and coffee.[64]

Apparently the American typhus fighter was ignorant of Jewish practices in life-threatening situations or he was indifferent to the kinds of experiences Jews had had during the war and were having within the new xenophobic Poland and in its eastern border lands. Pogroms by belligerents were commonplace, particularly in the Ukraine. Still, there were differences and that meant by comparison in particular instances, Soviet soldiers offered the best chance for survival. "On ocasion, an entire settlement would follow retreating Red soldiers." Much of this was known at the time.[65]

From Tarnopol and elsewhere came reports by American typhus fighters of doctors and other Jews working with the Bolsheviks, stripping Poles of hospital equipments and supplies when the Bolsheviks retreated, and then retreating en masse towards the East.[66] From the town of Busko came news of Jewish distrust of medical institutions and authorities.

> [There] is considerable Typhus in the town [of Busko], particularly among the Jews. They are afraid to go to the hospital and use all means to keep the disease among them hidden [because they believe] that at the hospital they would not be able to live according to their religion – that they would be required to eat what the others ate – that they could never eat with their hats on and that if one of them died there he could not be buried according to his religion. This belief is being overcome and the hospital now has ten Jews as patients.

The American official persuaded Busko to require a "fine of 500 rubles from anyone who hid or attempted to his case of typhus". All to no avail: "it did not prove very effective as the Jews, who were afraid of the hospital, bribed the police and kept their sick hidden."[67]

Perhaps the most revealing document came from Robert C. Snidow, a coastal artillery officer turned by Gilchrist into a typhus fighter who was insensitive to differences in lifestyle among the inhabitants, to extreme poverty, and to religious rules governing diet and ritual bathing. The report came from June 1920, when, as a test for operational planning, Gilchrist decided to send some of his men into a town which Polish authorities had identified as the "dirtiest" one in Poland. They chose the 7000 residents of Garwolin, 70% of whom were Jewish.

> In some of the small houses of from two to three rooms, as many as fifty people sometimes lived, cooking, eating, and sleeping as well as carrying on their industries in the

---

[64] *ibid.*, p. 117.

[65] In the very months when field reports were being filed by Gilchrist's people, there were special investigations and regular press reports about all kinds of civilian attacks against Jews: in new Poland's alleys, streets, and courtyards of towns; on railways running amongst them; about military pogroms in the places being contested by armies and roving bands. See for example the pages of the English *Jewish Chronicle*, the New York *Forward*, the *New York Times* for 1920, and Peter Kenez, *Civil War in South Russia, 1919–1920*, Berkeley 1977, pp. 166–177.

[66] This perceived conduct by Jews, reported the sympathetic historian of the American typhus fighters "accounts, at least in part, for the American dislike of Polish Jews". Cornebise, *Typhus and Doughboys*, pp. 116–117.

[67] *ibid.*, p. 117.

same small room. Typically ... the furniture would consist of a dirty table, one or two chairs, THE pot, spoons, THE washbowls, a couple of beds in the corners – during the daytime piled high with pillow and bedding which served for distribution over the floors at dusk, and the great flat tiled stove which served to heat and cook potatoes and water during the day and at night formed the base for the bedding and pillows of the patriarch and his wife who slept on the honored and warmest spot. One family or patriachate, was observed who served the repasts in [sic] the little brother of the conventional triangular pig trough of America pouring the potatoes and water into the trough after which the common spoon the tribe took turns in helping themselves to a great mouthful retiring to the outskirts to chew and swallow it. [...] In almost all of the house areas would be found after much search an open latrine which they jealously guarded from us by all kinds of disguises and camouflage as the product therefrom would be used after the harvest to put on their small patches in the outskirts of town. Most of the drinking water was obtained from a sluggish creek at the edge of the town, which a mill dam rendered more sluggish and sometimes covered the yards of some of the houses, turning them into reeking swamps." Bathing habits were atrocious: " In the first preliminary council we were assured by the priest, the rabbi and mayor and later confirmed by two doctors that not a soul in to town had had a bath for over a year. This statement we considered conservative and I personally doubt if water had touched the persons of most of them since the departure of the Germans during whose occupation they were required to bathe at least once a week, when they could be caught.[68]

Quarantine procedures for the Jews coming through Danzig were affected not only by passions and policies being generated in Poland; American officials, themselves informed about Jews in Poland by information reported by Gilchrist and his men, were also in webs of information coming from Germany and the United States. At a time when their government placed all sorts of obstacles in the way of Polish Jews eager to cross the border, Danzig's American officials read German claims and reports. These included the charge that Polish medical information regarding typhus and its control was unreliable, and that Jewish migrants from Poland and neighboring states occasionally brought "small pox" across the border.[69]

On the face of it these claims and counter claim were all about the relative medical and scientific reliability of the German and Polish public health establishments. In fact, it was also a difference driven by legacies from the past of a united Germany: chauvinism, antisemitism, and restrictionist migration policies intersecting with public health policies of neo-Lamarckian orientated biomedical cultures. All had been intensified by the war and the upheavals in its wake: Poles were primitive; incoming Jews were carriers of cholera or typhus.[70]

Albeit in an unusual set of circumstances, Jews themselves revealed the hold of these kinds of convictions. Jews in Poland had constituted a problem not only for

---

[68]*ibid.*, pp. 121–122, and 174, n.17, with its reference of reports from Snidow to Gilchrist, Warsaw, *circa* October 1920. No doubt some of the tone of this report was determined by efforts to make the claimed clean-up achievements of the unit look good. Snidow had been demoted from captain to First Lieutenant. *ibid.*, p. 119.
[69]See for example Linson to Blue, 15 November 1920, Reel 1.
[70]The 1918 flu pandemic, which indiscriminately killed millions in Europe and America, seems not to have influenced public officials and their profiles in the web of information in which Danzig found itself.

German authorities but, as was well known at the time, also for many German Jews who had reasons of their own for keeping the Polish Jew out of Germany: he was no longer like them, not Western, but primitive, a threat to their place in a Germany in convulsion.

The Jewish migrants had often included war-time "guest" workers who at war's end had been sent back to Poland. Now they wished to return, often to rejoin the family they had been forced to leave behind. German authorities insisted this return flow across the war-torn eastern frontier had to be stopped in order to protect the general public from typhus, cholera, and even small pox. To some Jewish observers, however, the rational appeared tainted coming as it did in the midst of defeat, revolutionary turmoil, and a high tide of antisemitism, perhaps at a post-war peak between 1919 and 1921.[71] Leading politically active German Jews, including Albert Einstein and others sympathetic to Zionism and other forms of Jewish peoplehood, opposed any kind of anti-Jewish discrimination by a German government. Besides, went one of their arguments, a majority of the Jews from Poland wanting to come into Germany were of *"deutscher Abstammung"*, that is of German extraction.[72]

Another German-Jewish argument focused their campaign on typhus. The Jewish critics knew what the quarantine officials at *Gruppe* knew: typhus could be contained, managed, and stripped of its virulence before the migrants would be allowed to mingle with Germany's residents. But at that point a group of German-Jewish physicians who were Zionists, and involved with this campaign, argued against such a public health effort. Colleagues among German physicians, including German-Jewish ones, could not be trusted to be scientifically honest when it came to making diagnoses about an incoming Jew from Poland; they would abuse public health arguments to keep those Jews out of Germany.[73]

Quarantine officials in Danzig received constant bulletins from their superiors in Washington then being bombarded by a veritable "nordomania" media blitz.[74] Their attitudes usually resonated positively with those among Americans in Warsaw screening the flow of Jewish immigrants from Warsaw. This was especially the case between July and December when over 20,000 Jews, about 90% of all the emigrants then traveling from Warsaw went into and through Danzig.[75] They had come as railway passengers, crossing the fluid national and city borders protected by suspicious guardians, observing or engaged in the war between Poland and Russia over future

---

[71] Werner Jochmann, *Gesellschaftskrise und Judenfeindschaft in Deutschland 1870–1945*, Hamburg 1991, pp. 99–170. See also the column 'Foreign and Domestic News' in the *Jewish Chronicle* for 1920.

[72] Einstein published his defense of the migration of "Ostjuden" in the *Berliner Tageblatt. Jüdische Rundschau*, 6 January 1920.

[73] Evidence for this interplay of Jewish workers, antisemitism, public health positions, Zionists and German border policies is in files F4/28 and Z3/ 202, 203 in the Central Zionist Archives in Jerusalem and in Trude Maurer, 'Medizinalpolizei und Antisemitismus: Die deutsche Politik der Grenzsperre gegen Ostjuden im Ersten Weltkrieg', in *Jahresbücher für Geschichte Osteuropas*, 33 (1985), pp. 205–229, where she cited these and related files. See also *idem, Ostjuden in Deutschland, 1918–1933* , Hamburg 1986, pp. 57, 258.

[74] Henry L. Feingold, *A Time for Searching: Entering the Main Stream 1920–1945*, Baltimore 1992, pp. 1–28. I thank him for the expression "nordomania".

[75] Between October 1920 and 1 January 1921, Linson sent Rupert Blue, his superior, weekly reports of emigrants going through Danzig's migration camp. The quarantine men at Danzig visited *Gruppe* and typhus control stations in Warsaw. J. H. Linson to Blue, 10 May 1920, Reel 1.

state boundaries. These guards were no less hostile than the capricious and officious Polish and American clerkdoms in Warsaw that had reluctantly approved the Jews' departure in the first place; some, like John C. White, American chargé d'affairs in the Polish capital, tried unsuccessfully to prevent American-Jewish organisations, such as the Hebrew Immigrant Aid and Sheltering Society (HIAS) from aiding Jewish immigrants in transit. On July 9, 1920 he put the point in classic diplomatic language: "In as much as practically all of the immigrants who pass through Danzig are of decidedly inferior types physically, mentally and morally and, because their insanitary habits, constitute a menace to the health of all with whom they come in contact, it is my opinion that efforts to stimulate their emigration to the United States should be discouraged."[76]

These sort of expressions were part of the contentious discourse in the corridors of the Department of State and in the halls of Congress during the hearings about the legislation designed to stop the very Jewish migrants trying to board ship in Danzig. In the spring and summer of 1920, at the height of the typhus epidemic and military crisis in Poland, consular survey reports had been sent to Washington about potential European migrants. In the fall and winter, the leadership in the House of Representatives, fighting for the new law in Senate hearings requested summaries of those reports and presented them to the senators. In the summaries Jews from Poland, whether in the new Poland or in its neighbouring countries and their Atlantic ports, received special attention by virtue of the dangerous attributes ascribed to them. They were the only group repeatedly identified with contagious diseases as well as threatening social, political, and economic characteristics.

The timing of this presentation, at the end of 1920, was significant. Albeit not a demonstrable fact at the time, the presentation occurred after the typhus epidemic in Poland had started to ebb. It had climbed from 1916 to a peak in mid-1920, and dropped just as sharply as it had spiked a few years earlier when Germany had occupied the country.[77] Here, from the spring of 1920, are summaries from Warsaw about emigrants expecting to travel to the United States. (There were similar ones from Romania, Austria, Germany, the Netherlands, and one from France about a form of cholera.)

> [The emigrants are] physically deficient, wasted by disease and lack of food supplies ... mentally deficient ... socially undesirable. ... Eighty five to ninety percent lack any conception of patriotism or national spirit and the majority of this percentage is mentally incapable of acquiring it. ... At the moment 90 per cent may be regarded as a low estimate of the proportion representing the Jewish race among emigrants to America from Poland. The unassimilability of these classes politically, is a fact too often proved in the past to bear any argument. ... Many of these persons have ... quarantinable diseases and come from typhus infected areas. They are filthy and ignorant and the majority are ver-

---

[76] Linson to Surgeon J.W. Kerr, 9 July 1920, Reel 1. As described below, White was denouncing the work of HIAS, in Danzig's Troyl Camp, accusing it of spending on a large scale to help Jewish immigrants to the United States by advancing money to those who could not pay for passage. See also the more nuanced claims of U.S. Immigration Commissioner Anthony Caminetti. United States Senate, *Hearings of the Emergency Committee on Immigration, 1921*, Microfiche copy, pp. 574–577.

[77] Sidney Brooks, 'America and Poland 1915–1925', in *American Relief Bulletin*, Series 2, No.44 (April 1925), page between pp. 48–49 for the graph 'Spread and Conquest of Typhus in Poland'.

minous. Persons who come into contact with these prospective emigrants [in any European port] are obliged owing to their unsanitary conditions, to take the greatest precaution to avoid contamination. ... Some emigrants are objecting to "certain sanitary provisions such as removal of beards and clipping of hair.

The summer reports were similar. "Reports indicate 34,538 cases of typhus in Galicia and Poland in 1916, 43,485 in 1917, 97,082 in 1918, and 232,206 in 1919, and the first two month of 1920, 16,500. Typhus situation in Poland shows little improvement despite active campaign against it. Refugees from infected region in Russia are constantly pouring into Poland. ... All emigrants who pass through Danzig are decidedly inferior type, physically, mentally, and because of their sanitary habits constitute a menace to the health of all with whom they come into contact. ... Crowds collecting in Warsaw for the purpose of procuring necessary papers to enable them to emigrate are alleged to be a menace to the health of Warsaw." A report from early fall sent a message about the coming dangerous tidal wave: It was alleged some 350,000 "Polish subjects of the Hebrew race" wanted to go to America – in the next three years five million of them. "It is impossible to overestimate the peril of the class of emigrants coming from this part of the world, every possible care and safeguard should be used to keep out the undesirables."[78]

VIII

There were important differences between practices involving the returning Polish-American soldiers and Jewish immigrants. As in the case of Wikoff, at *Gruppe*, too, the governing assumption controlling quarantine procedures was one of 'can do', with time, discipline, adequate staff and support, and with the cooperation of the troops and their commanders. In neither camp was there any doubt that typhus was containable and that, with quarantine, it was a contagion that could be stripped of its virulence. To be sure, Wikoff had all sorts of serious problems with its quarantine practices on the camp side of the shore line, and at *Gruppe* too there were lapses. But among the enforcing public health authorities there was no doubt that the population of the American republic was secure in its hands. When there was needless suffering among the troops, or gaps in the quarantine screens, critics pointed to the army's logistical incompetence or the incompetence of some of its officers in Washington or in the field. During the time of Wikoff, typhus-infected soldiers were not held responsible for collapsing in railway stations of the Long Island Railroad or on of the sidewalks of Manhattan; it was the army physicians at Wikoff who had not acted in line with public health knowledge about how best to control and contain the contagious disease. During *Gruppe*, the troops were Polish-Americans, whose kinfolk in the United States were subjected to all sorts of discriminations, especially in media campaigns by steel magnates struggling with post-war labour unrest – Poles in the work force, they proclaimed, were fodder for radicals organising strikes. Indeed, an American military intelligence report about these returning soldiers from Haller's army said they "are not on the whole, a desirable element. Most of them have come

---

[78] *Emergency Committee on Immigration, 1921*, pp. 8–21.

from the large manufacturing [centres] such as Chicago, Buffalo, Pittsburgh, and are what we would consider in our own army a rough crowd."[79] When they filed past quarantine inspectors, it was obvious, that there was something about the soldier's tunic and his American military service papers that served him well: both intersected to his benefit with medical information obtained from him in terms of the germ theory of disease. And more. The commander at *Gruppe* not only welcomed the Red Cross and YMCA, HIAS-like voluntary organisations, to help the army provide for soldiers' personal needs. He also instituted special dental programmes to assure the best of health for his Polish-American charges when they returned to civilian life in their home towns.[80]

Public authority in Danzig treated migrating Jews quite differently.[81] To begin with, Poland did not cloak the migrants with the protective shield of citizenship. Jews had little if any recourse to any government when harassed or exploited. It was a radicalisation of normal conditions experienced by most people engaged in long distance migration across foreign borders, especially at the places where they actually crossed national frontiers. Within the turmoil brought on by war and revolution, the formation of news states, and what some at times called "permanent pogroms," hazards of travel and currency exchange threatened to strip Jews of their belongings, their beards and side locks, and often left them all but penniless by the time they arrived at the Baltic Port.

For the exit through Danzig now involved new American procedures at designated US consulates or embassies and at ports of embarkation. In comparison to pre-war days, migrating civilians needed a visa stamped into their passport and required the twelve day quarantine which had become mandatory at *Gruppe* early on. Both requirements caused days of delay far from home, well beyond the control of the migrants. Indeed, the delays served as an important engine of exploitation. At the beginning of migration, when migrants had to "wait for steamers" the lodgings available to migrating Jews were in the hands of Danzig's German landlords; and they charged unregulated rents by the day.[82]

In the late spring of 1920, Troyl, the very place that Gilchrist had ordered evacuated a few weeks earlier, became the site of the transit camp for Jewish migrants coming in from Warsaw. They and the various Americans who screened or worked with the immigrants had to somehow manage with the same public authorities from whose authority Gilchrist had removed himself. In practice this meant that American

---

[79]Quoted in Cornebise, p. 101.

[80]*ibid.* This dental work was probably part of the larger effort made by the U.S. Army to provide social uplift and Americanisation exposure for immigrant soldiers. Ford, pp. 40–42. For a larger context of this work see Gerd Korman, *Industrialization, Immigrants, and Americanizers: the View from Milwaukee*, Madison 1967, pp. 65–202.

[81]For responses among Jews in Danzig to the migration crisis see the following in the Central Archives for the History of the Jewish People, Hebrew University (hereafterCAHJP): Eliyahu Stern, "The History of the Jews in Danzig. 1840–1943", PhD Dissertation, Hebrew University 1978; Dr. J. Kurt Nawratzki,"Yiddische Auswanderung über Danzig", Typescript Report, nd; Nawratzky to Zionistisches Zentral Bureau in London, 17 August 1920; Summary Notes: Danzig Comitee für Wanderarmenfürsorge, 11 April 1920, Danzig Jewish Immigration Committee, 15 April 1920.

[82]Frances Kellor, *Emergency Committee on Immigration, 1921*, pp. 422–429; Report of the European Commission of HIAS, Typescript, 11 August 1920, HIAS Archives, Institute for Jewish Research [YIVO]; (hereafter HIAS).

consular officials, public health physicians, and representatives of private organisations, such as the Hebrew Immigrant Aid Sheltering Society had to improvise on an ad hoc basis and negotiate with competing local authorities, steamship and railway organisations, manufacturers and suppliers of delousing equipment.

Sooner or later, quarantine drove everybody's agenda because the isolation required each migrant to stay in one guarded place for twelve days. Once HIAS became engaged, it focused on the same jugular issues as had the military, transportation and housing officials, but first, in the Polish capital, together with the Joint Distribution Committee, it tried to break the passport and visa bottlenecks which were rife with antisemitism, graft, and corruption. ("The question of Polish clerks who don't like Jews and mistreat our people terribly is one continuous problem.") In Warsaw HIAS representatives met the American consul whose "very small quarters," could not possibly "handle with any degree of expedition the large and ever increasing number of application for visas." When the consul informed them he was negotiating a lease for a bigger office, they were also told that the landlord demanded $10,000, a rent advance of three years, before signing a lease with the consul. The problem was that the Department of State had approved the lease but had funds for only the first year; and efforts to obtain a loan from a local banker had proved futile. So the consul "applied to us for a loan of $5200 upon which he was willing to pay interest. We, of course, advanced the money without any interest at all. We felt it a privilege to be of assistance to our government in so great an emergency." Still, six or eight weeks "elapsed before passports were issued to immigrants, sometimes only after heart wrenching decisions splitting migrating families. ... We found that fully 90 per cent of the [newly required affidavits of support] which had been sent from America were lost in the mail never reaching the addressees." In Rotterdam and Antwerp the bottlenecks were worse.[83]

HIAS was more successful in solving problems of transport and lodging. Its representatives managed to obtain from the Polish government special immigrant trains running from Warsaw to Danzig, a twelve hour journey fraught with all sorts of problems but much shorter and safer than two weeks of "misery" to ports in Western Europe, where at journey's end the immigrants, with their Yiddish, Polish, and German, arrived in places where they did not know the language. In the absence of constant, direct civilian passenger traffic between the Baltic port and the United States, HIAS arranged with the Cunard and White Star steamship companies to run "small steamers to English ports where they would be transferred to the big liners going to America"; a similar arrangement would send immigrants to the United States via Le Havre.[84] Both options raised all sorts of complaints, against HIAS and about effective American quarantine control during these migration transfers from one European port to another.

In the absence of the kind of military arrangements governing the establishment of Wikoff and *Gruppe*, HIAS moved into the vacuum by dealing with German, English and Polish public authorities regarding the use of the vacant facility that the Germans had used for prisoners during the war. No one seemed to own it. The

[83]Report of the European Commission, pp.15–17, HIAS.
[84]*ibid.*, pp. 21–22.

Germans and English were each prepared to let HIAS rent it, so to speak, as long as the Poles were not involved; and the Poles for their part dealt with HIAS on those terms. "Everybody claimed to be the owners of the camp. Finally we came to an understanding with the [Polish] authorities of Danzig by which we could use the camp for Jewish immigrants." Poles "were to manage the camp whilst we were to regulate prices. It was agreed that the immigrants should be charged 16 marks for a night's lodging which included ... transporting baggage from the railroad station to the camp and from the camp to the steamer. Food, including any medicine that may be necessary was charged at the rate of 22 marks a day per person."[85] In addition to these charges, the Polish Commission of Danzig, charged for the city a fixed fee of 20 marks for delousing. These fees were "to be paid by each immigrant," that is by HIAS in the event the immigrants could not afford to pay the fees.[86]

These arrangements occurred in the shadow cast by quarantine officials of the American Public Health Service who in the face of the typhus epidemic went into an emergency mode. On 20 May 1920, Hugh Smith Cumming, its Surgeon General, notified Assistant Surgeon General Rupert Blue, in Paris, that John H. Linson, who had recently been transferred from Marseilles to Danzig,

> and others like him are to delouse emigrants and supervise fumigation of vessels. ... Until there has been a material decline in the typhus rate in Central Europe, I think that all emigrants from European ports should prior to embarkation, be thoroughly deloused, and that steamship companies at the respective ports should provide adequate facilities in the way of barracks, bath houses, etc. to accomplish this purpose.

Cumming would send these types of warnings throughout the year.[87] A few days later Linson himself went to Warsaw to discuss the typhus situation with Gilchrist, who had just returned from a general inspection tour. He told him that practically no delousing was being done: there were shortages of coal, no food for patients, sterilisers were rusting, hospitals were practically empty. Linson told Blue that medical officers were urging that removal of hair, "especially the whiskers, is an essential part of the delousing process."[88] For the Jewish immigrants this part of the delousing procedure was symbolically threatening and rife with indecent conduct. Militant "Westernized" Jews in Europe and America had long mocked beards and side locks; and in these weeks of pogroms and random hooliganism, physical attacks on Jews often included ripping out or cutting those facial hairs. There were repeated reports of women being photographed while taking delousing baths. But, of course, the formal quarantine procedure was onerous enough; indeed, HIAS officials, who compared "scientific requirements" in the quarantine procedures at Ellis Island thought Danzig's requirements were "cruel. They are not civilized." In Danzig the "American

---

[85] *ibid.*, pp. 22–23. High prices, complex negotiatons with city officials and the camp director, and the delays from quarantine imposed all sorts of burdens on Danzig's Jewish organisations. Dr.[Rabbi] Kelter, Comitee für Wanderarmenfürsorge, 11 April and 12 June 1920, CAHJP; *Denkschrift des jüdischen Comitees*, 11 October 1920.

[86] *ibid.*, pp. 22–23.

[87] H. S. Cumming to Blue, 20 May 1920, Reel 1. See also *ibid.*, 13 October 1920 and Public Health circulars; one was concerned with bubonic plague in Mediterranean ports.

[88] Linson to Blue, 10 May 1920, Reel 1.

doctor has charge of it. He is very strict. He will not give a certificate to any man or women who has lice or who is affected by anything. In the examination he says cut off your hair or you cannot go." Women acquiesced, reported a HIAS observer, "rather than go back to their home. They agree to cut their hair. The hair on the body was to be removed by a certain lime to boil off the hair. Many persons did not know how to stand while the lime was on. If the lime gets wet it burns the skin." After September 4, women or religious men who objected to shaving apparently could opt for a treatment using a mixture of "equal parts kerosene and vinegar for at least one hour."[89]

At the time, in the tense days of summer, the immigrants and HIAS related to quarantine in much the same spirit that merchants, concerned about their quarantined cargoes, had historically related to it. If they could not get rid of it entirely, they tried to reduce the length of the isolation, if only because each day locked up was one more day of expense and of all sorts of losses from collateral damage.[90] "There is a great deal of bitterness among the people while in quarantine. When the people have to stay in quarantine for 12 days they want to go to the city. When they come back they are told that those five days you were away do not count at all. They are kept the same as prisoners. When they come back they are told your days start from now on."[91]

To complicate matters, by late summer there was American pressure to shut down the Troyl camp. All sorts of problems existed and motives were mixed. Linson did not want to continue to sponsor a delousing establishment "in which sanitation, personal comfort and humane treatment are ignored"; for such conditions where both sexes "crowded together in dirty and uncomfortable barracks ... [would] promote the spread of contagious diseases" and "immoral relations between the sexes"; and with winter coming, the "poorly clad and underfed" women and children, who at the time were the "majority of ... immigrants constituted a special problem." But Linson obviously recognised the impact of these conditions on the flow of migration: "It is not unreasonable to assume that the volume of immigration through Danzig will be greatly affected by the unpleasant experience through which so many immigrants are passing."[92]

On August 30, the Public Health Service did temporarily withdraw its approval, thus holding up the delousing and disinfection process of 190 passengers in the camp. When it did recertify, for the sake of those immigrants, new rules were required of the city: Linson demanded and got "the assistance of ... four persons because in the past the bathing and disinfection at the Troyl camp has been notoriously inefficient": one record keeper for the clothing being processed, which now had to remain in steam sterilisers for 40 minutes at 100°C; one man and one woman for supervising the bathing of each immigrant, who now had to stay in the shower for at least 5 minutes "using soap freely and paying special attention to hair" – this procedure included the use of

---

[89]Report of the European Commission 1, HIAS; A. Surgeon to Blue, 4 September 1920, Reel 1.
[90]On merchants and cargoes see for example, Evans, pp. 372–379. In 1917 Cofer wrote Booth & Co., Inc., steamship agents of New York, that the "use of cyanide gas is being perfected to a point where in the not distant future it will be possible to fumigate vessels in one-third or even one-fourth the time that was formerly required in sulphur fumigation." Cofer to Lawson, Sandford, 10 May 1917, NA/B.
[91]Report of the European Commission, 1, HIAS.
[92]Linson to HIAS and Karlsberg Spiro & Co., 2 September 1920. Memo: Ein- und Auswandererlager, Danzig, Troyl, 21 September 1920 and Linson to Doctor Haralson, 2 November 1920, Reel 1.

acetic acid to "kill the nits" which were then removed with fine tooth combs and finger nails by friends of passengers or the woman hired to do so; and one examiner for patrolling the entire process. Linson also insisted that in future, after receiving their cleaned clothing, each immigrant go directly to the departing steamer.[93]

The tight sailing schedules of those steamers could intensify frustrations and anxieties as capricious conduct and control of departure permits by American doctors took its toll. "On the second day of July, Friday," reported a HIAS official,

> I went to the ticket office of ... [a representative for the Cunard Line]. I was told tomorrow there will be a steamer going to England. The steamer will stay only two hours in Danzig. He said that if we had the immigrants that are through with the quarantine, we should have them ready and they will take them on. In order that they should be able to go, they have to get a certificate from the doctor. There was no doctor there since it was 4 oclock. I was told the doctor was in his bathing place, about forty miles away. We hired an automobile and rushed over there. We found him in a hotel playing. ... We told him the story. ... He said his business hours are over. We explained that there is a shortage of steamers and now we can take away 250 immigrants. He said he cannot do anything. For the people to remain meant that the longer they stay the more they suffer. This man did not move from his place.[94]

Even as the the Public Health Service continued its high alert warnings, by year's end Linson was forced to admit that his Jews had not been verminous. In a note to an inquiring fellow physician in the Service, he wrote there was no typhus fever in Danzig. "We have had only two suspected cases since the opening of the camp. In fact I must confess that I have never yet seen an authentic case of typhus fever."[95] In New York's quarantine station in the meanwhile the tone about the migration out of Poland was also beginning to change. To be sure, in the spring of 1921, Blue is still pressing his officers in Europe to "secure cleaner ships" and in New York and other oceanic ports officials are asked to be prepared in the case of typhus for quarantining passengers for twelve days; for it was clear to him: "Absolute control ... is not possible at foreign ports."[96] But, in line with Linson's experience, Blue now "did not believe that any restrictions should be imposed against emigrants departing from Poland or the Baltic regions"; no cases had been reported since March.[97]

No doubt the epidemic had passed its peak – the medical charts were falling back to their pre-1916 levels. Yet two other factors were now in play. The Emergency Immigration Act was scheduled to go into force at the end of the month: it would stop all mass migration out of Europe in general, out of eastern and southern Europe in particular. And bacteriologists had closed in on typhus: Arthur Felix and Edmund Weil had described a diagnosis of typhus that used the patient's blood serum,[98] and

---

[93]Memo: Ein- und Auswanderer Lager, Danzig, Troyl, 21 September 1920 reporting the hire of Kitty Scheffler as stenographer and assistant in checking the delousing at Troyl, and Linson to Doctor Haralson, 2 November 1920, Reel 1.
[94]Report of the European Commission, 17, HIAS.
[95]Linson to Doctor Haralson, 2 November 1920, Reel 1.
[96]Blue to Cofer, 9 May 1921; J. Perry, Acting Surgeon General to Cofer, 19 May 1921; Cofer to Blue, 10 June 1921, Reel 1.
[97]Blue to Cofer, 9 May 1921, Reel 1.
[98]Arthur Felix and Edmund Weil, 'Zur serologischen Diagnose des Fleckfiebers', in *Wiener klinische Wochenschrift*, 29 (13 January 1916), pp. 33–35.

within a few years the laboratory test was being used successfully for screening and confirming typhus in ways similar to diagnostic tests for cholera among passengers arriving at Atlantic ports. So on 22 June 1921 the Medical Superintendent of the Department of Health, at Canada's quarantine station at Gross Isle, in Montmagny, Quebec, could confirm, for the Medical Officer in Charge, at the United States Quarantine Station in New York, that yes indeed there was typhus fever aboard the *Oristano*. His station had used the Felix- Weil test to prove that "we had really to deal with cases of typhus fever. ... [It] has given us entire satisfaction."[99]

IX

In comparison with returning troops, the quarantine treatments and experiences of migrating Jews from new Poland and old Russia had been similar but different. Both groups had shared all sorts of uncertainties brought on by the exigencies of war or post-war problems. They had also been victims of conflicting chains of command, incompetence, ignorance, capriciousness, corruption, and the snarls of bureaucracy. They had all suffered needlessly from indifference to or perhaps tolerance of human suffering by officials masking ignorance and serving under the cloak of guardianship of the republic. The obvious differences in the treatment between incoming soldiers and incoming Jews need not be restated in these concluding remarks.

Some implications of these differences deserve to be teased out. In the absence of sulfa drugs or other antibiotics, the darker sides of quarantine mentalities in America's liberal democracy had changed during a critical moment, when heredity had met the bacterium. Clearly, after WWI, the more modern and professional public health service insisted on testing when in doubt rather than on imposing quarantine. But all along, there had remained significant gaps between diagnoses and cures of threatening contagious diseases.

In the neo-Lamarckian biomedical culture of these years the gaps had been ready-made for acts of biological politics. These would shield the returning soldier in the service of the republic, even as they were targeting Jews in anti-immigration campaigns and within legitimate structures of quarantine. While still believing in the inheritance of personal and collective characteristics, be they "natural," or "acquired," especially during times of emergency, in the name of the republic's public good, the practitioners' modern scientific eye now fixed each traveller as potentially pathogenic, that is as a potential killer. With that gaze local and federal American health authorities, at home and abroad, helped to shape anti-immigrant rhetoric that could be group specific, enforce confinements, evictions, burning of private belongings, and when fearing dogs, enforce orders to kill them with gas.

Indeed, in late nineteenth and early twentieth century, in their totality these kinds of efforts by United States officials had important consequences, some certainly unanticipated. Especially while a typhus epidemic was raging in Poland, they may

---

[99] 12 June 1921. By then J. E. Holt Harris, director of the laboratory at the New York Quarantine Station had been reporting regularly about his "Weil-Felix" reactions. L. E. Cofer to R. H.Creel, Asst. Surgeon, 17 November 1920, NA/B.

Jewish immigrants approaching Ellis Island, New York

By courtesy of The Wiener Library, London

well have contributed to the complex process by which quarantine-connected health officials helped to build part of the platform on which American public officials responded to a German fascist regime reconstructing the Jew as the new old mortal enemy of modern civilised society.[100]

---

[100]William W. Hagen, 'Before the "Final Solution". Toward a Comparative Analysis of Political Anti-Semitism in Inter war Germany and Poland', in *Journal of Modern History*, 68 (June 1996), pp. 351–352; Saul Friedländer, *Nazi Germany and the Jews: The Years of Persecution*, New York 1997, pp. 39–40, 207–210; Charles Meier, 'Introduction', in Thomas Childers and Jane Caplan (eds.), pp. xii–xv.

The German Peace Movement and the Jews: An Unexplored Nexus

BY ALAN T. LEVENSON

Jewish support for the American peace movement is proverbial, if anecdotal.[1] Like many historical phenomena, this one appears to be over-determined. To begin with, the left-of-centre orientation of the majority of American Jews makes them better candidates for a left-of-centre movement. Jews also played an active role in the 1960s counter-culture, an important breeding ground for the contemporary peace movement. One may also note that a tiny and historically oppressed minority has good reason to champion the cause of right versus might. All of these reasons probably have some merit, but they fail to account for the little-known fact that Jews played a disproportionately great role in European peace movements too. One additional factor, therefore, needs emphasising. Jews have been made to feel welcome in the peace movement, which has opposed antisemitism since its inception. This essay examines four founders of the peace movement in German-speaking lands: Bertha von Suttner (1843–1914), Ludwig Quidde (1858–1941), Heinrich Graf Coudenhove-Kalergi (1859–1906) and Friedrich Wilhelm Foerster (1869–1966). The focus will not be on their peace activities, an area that has been well researched, but on how these non-Jewish peace activists thought about Jews and Judaism. Three observations will be elaborated here: one, the peace movement in Germany was home to a number of outspoken anti-antisemites; two, the peace movement created an institutional culture where Jews and Gentiles collaborated freely and as equals; three, German peace activists favoured a progressive, at times radically progressive, resolution of the ubiquitous so-called "Jewish Question".

Before investigating these figures, the level of Jewish involvement in the peace movement needs to be addressed. Nobody in Germany kept statistics on this, but Jews were identifiably active at the leadership level. The organisational spirit of the *Deutsche Friedensgesellschaft* (German Peace Society) was Alfred Hermann Fried (1864–1921), a dynamic bookseller and publisher. Fried was born, bred and buried in Vienna, but he was the son of two Hungarian Jews. When Bertha von Suttner engaged in a correspondence campaign to get the Berlin chapter of the *Deutsche Friedensgesellschaft* off the ground, Max Hirsch (1823–1905) and Gustav Karpeles (1848–1909) served as her whips. Hirsch, elected three times to the Reichstag, was a nephew of the famous rabbi and journalist Ludwig Philippsohn. Hirsch was a mem-

---

[1]Gordon Scott Clark, Disarmament Director of Green Peace, private communication. This article is dedicated to Mr. Clark and his colleagues in the peace movement.

ber of several organisations, none of them Jewish. Karpeles, a well-known journalist and literary historian, belonged to a family active in many areas of Jewish life, and played an important role in the Society for Jewish History and Literature.[2] Von Suttner's diary entry of 10 September 1892 approved of Karpeles' desire to work behind the scenes, lest the initiative for a Berlin chapter appear "too Jewish".[3] Despite the tacit agreement between Christian and Jewish supporters of the peace movement to underplay the Jewish role, the list of prominent Jews was still a long one: Eduard Löwenthal, Heilberg, Arnhold, Leopold Sonnemann, Lina Morgenstern, W. A. Berendsohn, E. J. Gumbel, Bernhard Dernburg and Bloch.[4] *Die Friedensbewegung* (*The Peace Movement*), a 1922 publication, contained sixty-four contributors, at least nine of whom were Jewish and five of whom were non-Jewish who had publicly opposed antisemitism. Just over half the contributors came from German-speaking lands (*deutscher Kulturbereich*). All of the German contributors were liberals, several were feminists, and a dozen emigrated in 1933.

The contributors to *Die Friedensbewegung* were patently among the organisation's most famous members. Were Jews in the rank and file of the *Deutsche Friedensgesellschaft* similarly represented as in the leadership? There seems no way of knowing for certain, but circumstantial evidence inclines us towards this conclusion. Studies of the *Liga für Menschenrechte* and the *Bund Neues Vaterland*, peace society splinter groups, demonstrate that these organisations had many members of Jewish descent.[5] Roger Chickering's detailed examination of the Frankfurt, Königsberg and Danzig peace societies indicates that *Kaufleute* formed the single-largest group, followed by the intelligentsia, while "clergymen and blue-collar workers were conspicuous chiefly by their absence."[6] Karl Holl, the leading scholar on German pacifism, also describes a group very similar in composition to German Jewry at large:

> Although the masses of members remain generally anonymous in the sources, the independent entrepreneurs, albeit of lesser success, and the small salespersons made up the greatest percentage. Following that, academic or non-academic educated [*Gebildete*] intellectuals, among them several writers and journalists – a diffuse category which also included a number of teachers in the adult education movement [*Volkshochschule*]. To the third largest group belonged those occupied in the free professions, above all doctors, lawyers and pharmacists.[7]

[2]On the Jewish Society for Jewish History and Literature see Jacob Borut, *"A New Spirit Among Our Brethren in Ashkenaz." German Jewry's Change in Direction At the end of the 19th Century*, (Hebrew), Jerusalem 1999.
[3]Bertha von Suttner, *Lebenserinnerungen*, Berlin 1970, pp. 306–307.
[4]Karl Holl, *Pazifismus in Deutschland*, Frankfurt am Main 1988, p. 84. Holl lists another set of Jewish and Jewish-born pacifists who fled Hitler on pp. 204–205. Significantly, Jews were deeply involved in the *Deutsche Friedensgesellschaft* both at the beginning and end of its existence. Unlike groups which started out as integrated and became entirely Jewish (e.g. the *Freie Wissenschaftliche Vereinigungen*), the *Deutsche Friedensgesellschaft* remained a meeting ground of Christians and Jews.
[5]Richard Cohen, *The German League for Human Rights in the Weimar Republic*, Ph.D. dissertation, State University of New York, Buffalo 1989, p. 50 and *passim*.
[6]Roger Chickering, *Imperial Germany and a World Without War. The Peace Movement and German Society, 1892–1914*, Princeton 1975, p. 74. Chickering takes issue with Istvan Deak's characterisation of the pre-war peace society as comprising well-heeled professors, journalists and Jews, but demonstrates only that Deak overestimates the economic status of peace activists. Chickering, moreover, offers no explanation why salesmen in general should be inclined to pacifism.
[7]Holl, *Pazifismus*, p. 54.

While the xenophobic ranting of German nationalists who derided the *Deutsche Friedensgesellschaft* as Western, un-German, and Jewish cannot be taken at face value, the theme of Jewish participation is so consistent that it should not be dismissed altogether as negative evidence.[8] As a matter of fact, most of the peace activists who wrote against antisemitism were less chauvinistically German and more cosmopolitan in orientation than the average German. Since global disarmament and restraining nationalist excess were central to the programme of the peace movement, it comes as no surprise that the movement regarded itself as international in orientation. Certainly any German reactionary would have felt as out of place in a *Deutsche Friedensgesellschaft* meeting as would a Jewish tailor at a meeting of the nationalistic *Alldeutscher Verband* (Pan-German League). In a society that was becoming more antisemitic, especially in the social arena from the 1890s onward, the German peace movement went against the general current of the era. To put it more pointedly, participating in the *Deutsche Friedensgesellschaft* meant collaborating with Jews as allies and as equals. While this prospect might have been revolting to some "Aryans", to others it seemed quite a natural, even positive development.

Bertha von Kinsky, brought up in an impoverished Austrian aristocratic family with a tradition of military service, rejected her conventional background early on in life. Turning down a marriage proposal by the poet Heinrich Heine's younger brother, she worked briefly as a secretary to chemist Alfred Nobel. After marrying the relatively unsuccessful novelist Arthur Gundaccar von Suttner – against the wishes of his family – the couple became part of the impoverished nobility who did not quite rank in the social circles of the Hapsburg court. After several earlier failures to establish a career, Bertha had found her vocation as an author. Her novel *Die Waffen nieder!* (*Lay Down Your Arms!*) (1889), an international bestseller, inspired many figures in the peace movement. One of these, her old employer, Alfred Nobel, endowed the prize that bears his name at her suggestion. Alfred Fried, another admirer, became the organisational head of the movement until his death in 1921 and served, to some degree, as von Suttner's public relations agent. *Die Waffen nieder!* also made Bertha a celebrity. Showcased at every important peace conference, she enjoyed the admiration of world rulers, including Tsar Nicholas II. At the first International Peace Congress at the Hague in 1899 she was the undisputed star of the show. Although peace activism took up the best part of her efforts, von Suttner supported herself through her writing and promoted a variety of unpopular causes including feminism, anti-antisemitism, animal rights and Zionism.

Her support for Zionism, quite an unusual stance for someone also associated with the liberal *Abwehrverein*, emerged from her friendship with the Viennese journalist who brought Zionism to political life, Theodor Herzl. Von Suttner and Herzl, authors of utopian novels, champions of unpopular causes were kindred spirits.[9] Herzl's particular brand of Zionisim – liberal, modern and culturally European rather than specifically Jewish – helps explain *their* affinity. In any event, the goals of

---

[8]Holl, *Pazifismus*, pp. 83–94; Dieter Riesenberger, *Geschichte der Friedensbewegung in Deutschland. Von den Anfängen bis 1933*, Göttingen 1985, p. 246.

[9]Alan T. Levenson, 'Theodor Herzl and Bertha von Suttner: Criticism, Collaboration and Utopianism' in *The Journal of Israeli History*, 15:2 (1994), pp. 213–222.

Bertha von Suttner

European Jewry, whether liberal or nationalist, could be reconciled to her vision of a league of nations, all guided by progressive principles. This ultimate goal made it possible for her to fight for Jewish equality within Europe and also to support Herzl's liberal, modern concept of a Jewish state. Bertha von Suttner won the first Nobel Peace Prize in (1903) and lost her husband in (1906). Somewhat out of place in a peace movement that had become increasingly based on grass-roots organising as opposed to dramatic personal appeals, Bertha von Suttner died just seven days before the outbreak of the great war she had tried to prevent.

As Steve Beller has demonstrated, there were few areas of cultural life in Vienna in which Jews did not participate heavily. The liberal, intellectual circles of Vienna, the von Suttner's social sphere, forged their outlook on the "Jewish Question".[10] Von Suttner's connection with the journal *Nouvelle Revue* put her in touch with the well-known authors Max Nordau and Lucienne Halevy. Brigitte Hamann's excellent biography of Bertha von Suttner does not dwell on the impact of these Jewish contacts, but it is a fact that von Suttner reacted stridently to the pogroms that began in 1881. Closer to home, the rise of Karl Lueger (Vienna's antisemitic mayor) provoked Bertha to a fictional response. Von Suttner had skewered antisemites in her early novels *Daniela Dormes* and *Schach der Qual*. Baron Arthur and Baroness Bertha von Suttner shared the aspirations of Viennese liberals: they aimed to create a rational, lawful society in which each person would be judged equally. But that universal goal

---

[10]Steve Beller, *Vienna and the Jews. A Cultural History*, Cambridge 1989.

did not stop von Suttner from taking up particularist causes, feminism and anti-antisemitism among them. Her outlook on the "Jewish Question" in the early 1890s can be seen in the preface she wrote for James F. Simon's aggressive call for Jewish self-defence, *Wehrt Euch!! Ein Mahnwort an die Juden*.[11]

> The main thing is: all conflicts of opinion must – in the name of reason and in the name of law – be removed from the untenable terrain of Jew or non-Jew. No one should ignore the vague reproach 'You are a Jew' when it is launched against him. No one should let it go without a response, but rather: one should force the assailant to the wall: 'Yes, I am, just as you are a Christian ... what of it?'[12]

Bertha von Suttner consistently avoided the stereotypical dichotomy of "Jew" and "Aryan". She also refused to enter into the rhetorical game of conceding Jewish defects and demanding improvement in exchange for equality. Like most liberals (Jewish and Christian alike) the von Suttners tended to underestimate the centrality and utility of antisemitism to the forces of reaction. Still, von Suttner refused to underestimate the viciousness of antisemites, contending that they intended the physical destruction of Jews.[13] In a biting comment, Suttner noted that the political economists who blamed everything on the stock market wished to solve the problem by "hanging 3,000 Jews. Or better yet: turning all the Jews into artificial fertilizer. The last [proposal] was only meant in jest. The gentlemen also have a sense of humor."[14]

For Bertha von Suttner, the connection between anti-antisemitism and peace activism was obvious: "I fight against antisemites even as against war – for they represent the same spirit."[15] The "spirit" von Suttner attacked was militarism, brutality and cruelty, the weapons employed by the antisemites in their disappointingly successful campaigns. Von Suttner berated fellow liberals – Jewish colleagues included – for not being aggressive or insistent enough in forwarding their basic principles. Appalled by the Russian pogroms, the Liberal disaster in the elections of 1891, and the continued success of Karl Lueger, the Suttners helped establish an Austrian branch of the *Verein zur Abwehr des Antisemitismus* (Society for the Defence Against Antisemitism). The German branch of the *Abwehrverein* was founded in 1890 as a response to a wave of antisemitism that swept over Germany. It allied itself solidly with the Left Liberal parties. The Austrian branch also comprised left-of-centre figures, though without direct connection to a particular party. Both branches of the

---

[11]Bertha von Suttner, preface to James F. Simon, *Wehrt Euch!! Ein Mahnwort an die Juden*, Berlin 1893 (*Beware! An Appeal to the Jews!!*). This tract played a significant role in galvanising the *Centralverein deutscher Staatsbürger jüdischen Glaubens*, a Jewish self-defence organisation. As the *Centralverein* and the Zionists became rivals for German Jewish loyalties, it is a nice irony that von Suttner offered both organisations her support. The scholarly literature on the *Centralverein* is immense, but the best treatments of the C.V. during the Imperial and Weimar periods remain, respectively, Ismar Schorsch, *Jewish Reactions to German Antisemitism, 1870–1914*, New York 1972, pp. 117–148 and Arnold Paucker, *Der jüdische Abwehrkampf gegen Antisemitismus und Nationalsozialismus in den letzten Jahren der Weimarer Republik*, Hamburg 1968.

[12]Suttner, in Simon, *Wehrt Euch!! Ein Mahnwort an die Juden*, p. vi.

[13]See, for example, Bertha von Suttner, *Memoiren*, Bremen 1965, p. 176; Brigitte Hamann, *Bertha von Suttner. Ein Leben für den Frieden*, München–Zurich 1986, pp. 194–321.

[14]Cited in Leopold Schaffer (ed.), *Vermächtnis und Mahnung zum 50. Todestag Bertha von Suttners*, Bonn 1964, pp. 71–72.

[15]Cited in Hamann, pp. 212–213.

Abwehrverein comprised a high-class membership consisting of, among others, scholars from all disciplines, well-known jurists and physicians and the mayor of Berlin. Collectively, the *Abwehrverein* disseminated anti-antisemitic propaganda, reported on antisemitic outbreaks as well as the governmental responses and took antisemites to courts of law.[16] Given the von Suttners' pivotal role, it comes as no surprise that membership in the Austrian *Abwehrverein* and in the Austrian peace movement overlapped considerably.[17]

Ludwig Quidde, the son of a well-off Bremen merchant and well-educated mother, overcame a serious speech impediment and became a distinguished student at *Gymnasium* level. Quidde attributed his political views to his parents; they were clearly well formed by the time he arrived at the University of Göttingen. Despite a very small Jewish student body (between one and two per cent), Göttingen became a hotbed of antisemitism. Although Göttingen lagged behind the University of Berlin, the centre of the antisemitic movement, four hundred Göttingen students signed the Anti-Semite's Petition. Quidde organised a counter-petition, which garnered one hundred and sixty-eight signatures. As the student body seethed, the university officialdom did not hesitate to take sides; they disbanded the committee against antisemitism on 25 June 1881. Liberal students responded by forming a *Freie Wissenschaftliche Vereinigung* (FWV). These free fraternities, open to all religious denominations, became an important chapter in the lives of many liberally inclined Christian and Jewish students throughout Germany. Quidde played a significant role in establishing the Göttingen model.[18] Nor did his advocacy of Jewish-Christian amity end with his role in the FWV.

Quidde's anonymous 1881 pamphlet, *Die Antisemitenagitation und die deutsche Studentenschaft* (The Antisemitic Agitation and German Students) caused an enormous stir.[19] When Quidde's authorship was revealed, he was challenged to several duels, one of which he accepted despite his moral opposition to duelling. He survived the ordeal and received his doctorate the next year with a thesis on the fifteenth century Prussian King Sigismund.[20] *The Antisemitic Agitation and German Students*, his only extended statement on antisemitism, proved that the twenty-three year old Quidde appreciated the dangers of the new movement better than the majority of his elders.

---

[16]On the German *Abwehrverein*, see the articles by Barbara Suchy, 'The Verein zur Abwehr des Antisemitismus (I)–From its Beginnings to the First World War', in *LBI Year Book XXVIII* (1983), pp. 205–240; idem, 'The Verein zur Abwehr des Antisemitismus (II)–From the First World War to its Dissolution in 1933', in *LBI Year Book XXX* (1985), pp. 67–103. On the Austrian *Abwehrverein*, see Jacques Kornberg, 'The Austrian Verein zur Abwehr des Antisemitismus: An Analysis of A Failure' in *Proceedings of the Eleventh World Congress of Jewish Studies*, 3 (1994), pp. 77–84; idem, 'The Response to Antisemitism in the 1890s: The Austrian Verein zur Abwehr des Antisemitismus', in *LBI Year Book XLI* (1996), pp. 161–196. Kornberg contends that the failure of the Austrian branch to ally itself closely with the Left Liberal party in Austria doomed it to relative impotence. The German organisation dissolved itself in the summer of 1933; the Austrian branch fizzled out by the end of the 1890s.
[17]Hamann, pp. 202–203.
[18]Konrad Jarausch, *Students, Society and Politics in Imperial Germany*, Princeton 1982, p. 271. On the *Freie Wissenschaftliche Vereinigungen*, see Keith Pickus, *Constructing Modern Identities. Jewish University Students in Germany 1815–1914*, Detroit 1999, pp. 75–80.
[19]Ludwig Quidde, *Die Antisemitenagitation und die deutsche Studentenschaft*, Göttingen 1881.
[20]Brigitte Maria Goldstein, *Ludwig Quidde and the Struggle for Democratic Pacifism in Germany, 1914–1930*, Ph.D. dissertation, New York University 1984, pp. 17–18.

Ludwig Quidde

By courtesy of Deutsches Historisches Museum, Berlin

Quidde warned that the ideals of the collegiate generation were no longer framed by the expectations of 1848, but by the bloody successes of Bismarck in the 1860s and 1870s. He pointed to a generation gap that led older liberals to underestimate the strength of the antisemitic movement and overestimate the powers of progress and *Bildung*. For Quidde, a generation of nationalist chauvinists had come to maturity and the Anti-Semite's Petition represented a preview of other, greater demands to come.[21] Quidde explained the antisemitic movement primarily as a varied reaction to the excesses of the 1870s, the *Gründerzeit*: "It [the antisemitic movement] is a reaction against the economic and therefore also against political and religious Liberalism."[22] Quidde recognised that religious prejudices had been transformed into hostility against scepticism, materialism, cosmopolitanism and a secular spirit in general – even by people who themselves were products of those transformations.

Quidde proposed stealing the antisemites' fire – combating the negative developments in Germany derisively called judaised (*verjudet*) by the reactionaries. This anti-antisemitic tract steered clear of any expressions that could be called philosemitic. Quidde engaged in the standard liberal explanation of Jewish concentration in finance as the product of Christian compulsion in the Middle Ages. But he also

---

[21]Quidde, *Die Antisemitenagitation*, pp. 11–12. Quidde was both right and wrong on this point. The failure of the Antisemite's Petition to find any response from Bismarck doomed that particular form of initiative. The political demands of the antisemitic parties also met with failure. On the other hand, antisemites certainly succeeded in broaching a variety of radical solutions incomparably more violent and extreme than in the opening salvos of Treitschke and Stoecker.

[22]Quidde, *Die Antisemitenagitation*, p. 5.

denied that the demonstration he helped organise should be considered pro-Jewish. He distanced the goals of Liberalism from the defense of Jewry as such, recognised the undeniable racial difference between "us and our Jewish fellow citizens", and ended his essay by calling antisemitism the new Pharisaism.[23] Quidde also noted the rising number of Jewish students as a cause for tension, without mentioning that the number of Jewish students at Göttingen was miniscule.[24] Quidde clearly had rhetorical considerations on his mind when he took care not to appear too pro-Jewish as Paul Dulon, the organiser of the petition at Göttingen, derided the opponents of the petition as philosemites. Although Quidde clearly disdained antisemites, nobody reading this pamphlet would have been struck by signs of his empathy for Jews. In 1881, Quidde on the "Jewish Question" sounds very much like a member of the Liberal mainstream.

1882 was a momentous year for Quidde. In addition to completing his doctorate, Quidde married Margarete Jacobson (1858–1940), whose Jewish father was the prominent ophthalmologist Julius Jacobson (1828–1889).[25] Quidde, now blessed with a talented wife and a handsome dowry, became deeply involved in liberal politics in Munich where the young couple settled.[26] Quidde's association with the myriad of Left Liberal parties began in the first decade of the twentieth century and lasted until the *Deutsche Demokratische Partei* fused with the anti-pacifist and antisemitic *Jungdeutscher Orden* in 1930.[27] The Left Liberal parties in Munich before the war enjoyed the support of the influential *Frankfurter Zeitung*, published by Leopold Sonnemann (1831–1909), one of a trio of important liberal, Jewish newspaper publishers.[28] Quidde was a significant figure in Bavaria's Left Liberal politics, pushing the party toward pacifism and, no doubt, supporting its anti-antisemitic inclinations. In 1895, three years after the *Deutschkonservative Partei* (German Conservative Party) adopted the Tivoli Programme, which gave an antisemitic orientation to a major party for the first time, the *Deutsche Volkspartei* (German People's Party) declared itself to be a party of peace.[29] That same year, Quidde's career as a mainstream politician and as an academic with professional standing came to a dramatic end with the publication of his biting satire *Caligula* (1894). Ostensibly a study of Caius Caligula's brief reign of terror, the thinly veiled target of Quidde's work was none other than Kaiser Wilhelm II. Quidde's notoriety, and subsequent jailing for *lèse-majesté*, consigned to him the role of outsider, a role not unsuited to participation in Germany's marginalised peace movement.

Despite his long association with Left Liberal parties, Quidde's principal energies were devoted to the German peace movement. Quidde clearly considered anti-

---

[23]These statements are found in Quidde, *Die Antisemitenagitation*, pp. 16, 5, 7 and 18, respectively.
[24]Pickus, p. 71.
[25]Julius Jacobson, Quidde's Jewish father-in-law, is mentioned in Siegmund Katznelson, *Juden im deutschen Kulturbereich*, p. 513.
[26]Margarethe Quidde became a noted musicologist and animal rights activist.
[27]Karl Holl, introduction to Ludwig Quidde, *Der deutsche Pazifismus während des Weltkrieges, 1914–1918*, Boppard am Rhein 1979.
[28]Hans Ullstein, Rudolf Mosse and Leopold Sonnemann were all liberal, Jewish newspaper magnates, sympathetic to the peace movement. The prominence of Jews in the press was a perpetual antisemitic target; newspapers such as the liberal, business-orientated *Frankfurter Zeitung* were derided by critics as *Judenpresse* ("Jew papers").
[29]Goldstein, p. 20.

semitism a less critical enemy than militarism, but he never lost his early contempt of the former. "Antisemitism and pacifism are mutually exclusive. Absolutely. The Peace Society is the sworn opponent of any form of racism, also of antisemitism."[30] More revealing than these occasional anti-antisemitic comments is the fact that Quidde worked with Jews throughout his decades-long career as a peace activist. Alfred Fried disagreed with Quidde's conception of pacifism, but the Bremen merchant's son and the irascible Viennese Jew seem to have worked together without any problems. Quidde participated in the *Bund Neues Vaterland*, an association of anti-war intellectuals who banded together in 1914. The two most prominent members of the *Bund* were Albert Einstein, already famous for his contribution to physics, and Eduard Bernstein, the formulator of Revisionist Socialism. Both men were assimilated Jews, but with pronounced Jewish loyalties. Bernstein spoke movingly of the Jewish spiritual contributions to socialism. Einstein became an avid Zionist and was offered the Presidency of the State of Israel. The German government disbanded the *Bund* in 1916, adding another mark of disrepute to Quidde's name.

Times of war have been a challenge to the modern peace movement, forcing difficult choices between principles and popular opinion, as the nation redefined dissent as treason. When World War I broke out, Quidde lost much respect in the international peace community for denying that the Central Powers bore sole responsibility despite the invasion of neutral Belgium. Quidde, furthermore, defended military service as a patriotic duty. Quidde insisted that the movement should focus on a postwar settlement that would render future conflict impossible. Trying to force this issue, Quidde used his years of service to call a meeting in Berne, but the results were the exact opposite of what he had expected. Sandi Cooper writes: "Quidde's hope that a meeting of the Berne executive board would produce a joint statement on the war backfired. In many ways, the meeting was the epitaph of the peace movement in Europe that flourished in the nineteenth century."[31]

Quidde's post-war career as a peace activist proved even more frustrating. Younger men such as Friedrich Wilhelm Foerster found Quidde antiquated: still committed to the defunct ideals of 1848, and not nearly confrontational enough for the rougher era of the 1920s. Although he won a Nobel Peace Prize in 1927, Quidde was marginalised in the German peace movement he had done so much to found. Quidde reacted to the rise of Nazism with horror, but also with desperation, naively clinging to Hitler's specious claims about desiring peace, and earning Quidde the contempt of old friends such as the Junker Conservative turned Left Liberal Hellmut von Gerlach. Quidde's thoughts on Hitler's antisemitism have to be imagined, and despite Quidde's partly Jewish wife, none of his biographers have much to say about the dilemma of being married to a "first-degree *Mischling*" in the 1930s.[32] Perhaps, as Graf Harry Kessler suggested, Quidde was watching his words for his wife's sake. As in 1914, Quidde faced the pacifist's dilemma of confronting an all-powerful and immoral ruler. Kessler entered this note in his diary on 6 April 1933:

---

[30]"Interview mit Ludwig Quidde' in *Die Wahrheit* (15 May 1928), cited in Goldstein, pp. 18–19.
[31]Sandi Cooper, 'The Re-Invention of the "Just War" Among European Pacifists before the First World War' in Harvey Dyck (ed.), *The Pacifist Impulse in Historical Perspective*, Toronto 1996, p. 387.
[32]Goldstein neglects to mention the fact of Quidde's marriage to a Jewish woman and relegates his essay on antisemitism to a footnote.

Breakfast with Quidde. He is not a fugitive and wants to return to Germany. He told of the truly horrible flight of [Hellmut] Gerlach from Berlin and then through Munich over the Swiss border without a passport. He is of the opinion that only a military overthrow [*Militärputsch*] can free us from the brown pest. It is a remarkable transformation of the situation, that he, an old pacifist, must place his hopes on the military.[33]

What can be inferred regarding Quidde's personal "comfort level" with Jews? Family and institutional contacts suggest that Quidde had no Jewish problem whatsoever; he collaborated with Jews personally and politically for sixty years. Letters to and from Albert Einstein in 1930–1931 regarding Oscar Wassermann, the director of the *Deutsche Bank* and a peace proponent, highlight the ease with which Quidde enlisted Jewish support.[34] Nevertheless it is also worth noting that the "Jewish Question" remained a peripheral one to Quidde. In 1928, on the occasion of numerous interviews on his reception of the Nobel Peace Prize, only rarely did Quidde bother to mention antisemitism as a prompt to pacifism or democracy. Quidde reacted viscerally against antisemitism, but appears to have regarded the Jewishness of so many collaborators as incidental to their common goals. Formally, Quidde's position on the "Jewish Question" was classically liberal; informally, he moved in a mixed social circle with apparent ease.

Like Ludwig Quidde, Friedrich Wilhelm Foerster was a product of the educated middle-class, the *Bildungsbürgertum*. Born in Berlin to a Friesian mother and a Silesian father, his parents brought Friedrich up in the classical German spirit of Alexander von Humboldt and the early Goethe. Despite his mother's family connection to General von Moltke, Foerster's parents were opponents of Bismarck's "blood and iron" politics and opposed to the Prussianisation of Germany. Wilhelm Foerster (1832–1921), Friedrich's father, was a famous astronomer, a founder of the Society for Ethical Culture, and a sympathiser with von Suttner's peace activities. He was also a signatory of the 1914 Manifesto to Europeans a counter-manifesto to the nationalistic Manifesto to the Civilised World in which ninety-three intellectuals defended Germany's invasion of neutral Belgium. The Manifesto to Europeans, brainchild of Georg Nicolai, garnered four signatures in all, including Albert Einstein's and the elder Foerster's.[35] Friedrich Wilhelm seems to have imbibed the political convictions of his parents. Shortly after obtaining his doctorate in Freiburg, Foerster spent three months in jail on a charge of *lèse-majesté*.

By the outbreak of the First World War, Foerster had received his doctorate, his *Habilitation*, and had already taught at Zurich, Vienna and Munich. He had also become one of the leading voices of German pacifism, an opponent of the war, and afterwards, a proponent of accepting the Versailles Treaty. He defended the Jewish-born Kurt Eisner, the idiosyncratic and controversial ruler of the post-war Bavarian Republic. Foerster unequivocally denounced the Jew-baiting Right who sought Eisner's ruin as deflecting the true responsibility for the German tragedy: a willingness to worship political and military power, a new paganism without the tolerance or

---

[33]Harry Graf Kessler, *Tagebücher, 1918–1937*, Frankfurt a. M.: 1961, p. 714.
[34]The Quidde–Einstein correspondence is located in the Einstein Archive, Manuscript Division, National and University Library, Jerusalem, documents 48–052 to 48–054.
[35]Otto Nathan and Heinz Norden (eds.), *Einstein on Peace*, New York 1960, pp. 1–7.

Friedrich Wilhelm Foerster

By courtesy of Professor Franz Pöggeler

universality of the paganism of antiquity.[36] The 1920s and 1930s saw Foerster emerge as a leading figure among the radical peace activists, a champion of the unpopular cause of admitting Germany's war guilt, editor of the left-wing journal *Menschheit* (Humanity). From the outskirts of the German academy, Foerster contributed to what would become the field of philosophy of education. Foerster fled to the United States in 1933, ultimately settling in Switzerland until his death in 1966.

Quidde's anti-antisemitism stemmed from a visceral revulsion against reactionary forces and an unfashionable association with the classic liberalism of the 1848 generation. Foerster's initial orientation toward the Jewish Question may have been similarly shaped by classic liberalism, but his mature perspective was stamped by his deep-seated Christian convictions. Rejecting the arch-rationalism of his parents' household, Foerster embraced religion, though he stayed clear of any institutional association. As to Foerster's early relations with Jews, they cannot be reconstructed. He attended a *Gymnasium* in Berlin with a high percentage of Jewish students and recorded his disgust at the ultra-nationalism of German students at the University of Vienna in 1913–1914, where he was then teaching.[37] Opportunities to befriend Jews were therefore not lacking in his school years in Berlin and Vienna. Foerster's only specific remarks about his personal encounters however, are found in his largest and most problematic work, *The Jews*. Foerster announces in his introduction:

---

[36]Friedrich Wilhelm Foerster, *Erlebte Weltgeschichte, 1869–1953. Memoiren*, Nuremburg 1953, pp. 211–214.
[37]Friedrich Wilhelm Foerster, *Mein Kampf gegen das militaristische und nationalistische Deutschland*, Stuttgart 1920, p. 10.

> Throughout his long life the author has had exceptional opportunities of working with Jews[:] German, Slavonic and American. He has enjoyed relations of close friendship with them and shared with them in a community of cultural work. When therefore the anti-Semitism which broke out at the end of the last century proved to be a phenomenon of cumulative intensity, he could only regard it as something that went utterly contrary to his own feelings – feeling of friendship for Jewry and of admiration for the ethical principles that guided Jewish life.[38]

That Foerster failed to write anything similar to the above-cited lines before the Second World War is not that surprising – next to being Jewish, having Jewish friends and being regarded as "philosemitic" was the surest way of losing credibility when participating in public discussion of the "Jewish Question". As noted above, understating the Jewish factor served an important role even in a dissident liberal group like the peace movement. Foerster's chronology in this passage deserves comment. Not unlike Jews who found their identity with the rise of antisemitism ("Jews by the grace of Stoecker"), Foerster connected his own pro-Jewish feelings to the resilience of antisemitism in the 1890s.

Whenever and however the groundwork had been laid, Foerster's first published analysis of the "Jewish Question" appeared in his *Politische Ethik und Politische Paedagogik* in 1913.[39] Stressing that no European peoples have been in as symbiotic a relationship as Aryans and Jews, Foerster adopted the almost irresistible German urge to divide Jews into two groups: the admirable pious and "religiously highly disciplined Jew", and the uprooted modern Jew. Foerster's preference for the first category, obviously driven by his own religious convictions, would prove to be problematic. The Jews with whom Foerster collaborated in the peace movement were, overwhelmingly, the secular Jews that Foerster described in his essay as guilty of either overbearing egotism (*Hochmut*) or cringing (*Kriecherei*). Foerster ultimately managed his awkward categories by assigning all idealistically motivated Jews to the category of the admirable and "highly disciplined". Thus the Jews within the movement, though hardly traditional, were dubbed authentic Jews by Foerster by dint of their idealistic fidelity to the cause of peace.

Foerster employed other dichotomies besides pious and impious, arrogant and servile. Contemporary Jews, opined Foerster, had learned a sense of competitive, productive sense of honour (*das fordernde Ehrgefühl*), but not yet a sense of sacrificial honour (*das opfernde Ehrgefühl*).[40] The Jews could climb higher than all other peoples, but they could also sink lower, and so on.[41] Foerster's tendency to dichotomise established a language of difference that he consistently employed when discussing Jewry; this language remained unaffected by the events of the following forty years. His

---

[38] Friedrich Wilhelm Foerster, *The Jews*, translated by Brian Battershaw, London 1961, pp. ix–x. Foerster's *Weltgeschichte*, p. 275 notes a humorous interchange between himself and a relative, then *Reichskanzler* Georg Michaelis. The latter chided Foerster for publishing his articles in a "Jewish paper". Foerster responded that he had long held these ideas and that the Jewish papers were better than the antisemitic rags favoured by the reactionaries.
[39] Friedrich Wilhelm Foerster, *Politische Ethik und Politische Paedagogik*, 4th edition, Munich 1920 (Political Ethics and Political Pedagogy).
[40] *ibid.*, p. 384.
[41] *ibid.*, p. 370.

"dichotomitis" does not appear to be a malady in his own eyes – on the contrary. Antisemitism's failure to understand these competing tendencies in the Jew precluded it from apprehending the true solution to the "Jewish Question": an alliance with the best part of Jewry to convert the degenerate part. Foerster's Christian beliefs claim centre-stage, but the vocabulary of liberal assimilationism and even of racial thinking inject themselves into his 1913 solution to the "Jewish Question":

> Only through Christ and in Christ will the Jewish Question be solved. Neither expulsion nor exclusion, nor mere assimilation and sham conversion can resolve the terrible intrinsic difficulties of this problem. Only when both the Jew and the Christian "assimilate" with their entire souls to the spirit of Christ will the true assimilation of the Jewish people and the Aryan race become possible and capable of life.[42]

In *Mein Kampf gegen das militaristische und nationalistische Deutschland* Foerster assessed the possibilities for a more pacific Germany in the wake of Versailles. One key to Germany's future, in his view, would be found in the treatment of the "Jewish Question". Citing Paul Seippel's words that the Dreyfus Affair was the overture to the French victory on the Marne, Foerster pronounced: "How we treat the Jews will be the way we are judged [by the world]".[43] The East European Jews (*Ostjuden*), in particular, would be a critical testing point. Germany, Foerster maintained, could handle the problem in a way that would make all of Europe grateful, or, in a way that could poison the international atmosphere. Practically, it seemed suicidal not to align Germany's economic reconstruction to the energy and practical nature of the Jews.[44] Foerster once again divided Jews into good and bad. Here, Foerster contrasted the degenerate ghetto Jew (the *Ostjude*) with the noble and inwardly free, acculturated German Jew. He seemingly had no awareness that the *Ostjuden* were patently closer to the "religiously disciplined" Jew he had praised in his *Politische Ethik und Politische Paedagogik*. In any case, Foerster believed that the *Judenfrage* would be a gauge of Germany's post-First World War identity and warned against allowing the antisemites to set the agenda. Foerster insisted that Christians of good will should work with German Jewry to acculturate the *Ostjuden*. Foerster viewed German Jews as partners in the colonialising enterprise of civilising *Ostjuden*, not an unheard of theme for anti-antisemites.[45] Other than the references to post-war conditions, this work mainly repeats the analysis of his 1913 essay. The language of difference remains predominant; perhaps even more insistently than before the war, Foerster linked Germany's future with that of European Jewry.

Foerster's opposition to antisemitism clearly preceded the Nazi years. It cannot be grouped with the sort of *ex-post facto* philosemitism that stemmed from a bad con-

---

[42]Foerster, *Mein Kampf gegen*, p. 255. The original reads: "Nur durch Christus und in Christus wird die Judenfrage gelöst. Weder Ausstoßung und Aussperrung, noch bloße Assimilierung und äußerliches Taufen kann den ungeheuren inneren Schwierigkeiten des Problems irgendwie gerecht werden. Erst wenn beide, der Jude und der Christ, sich von ganzer Seele dem Geist Christi "assimilieren", ist die wirkliche Assimilierung des jüdischen Volkes mit den arischen Rassen möglich und lebensfähig."
[43]*ibid.*, pp. 252–253.
[44]*ibid.*, p. 254.
[45]Tacitly, this acknowledged just how foreign the *Ostjuden* were perceived to be, creating a zone of Jewish difference that could be affirmed despite the assimilation of German Jews.

science and a desire to demonstrate repentance to the Western powers.[46] Precisely this track record of anti-antisemitism and his accompanying self-identification as pro-Jewish make Foerster's post-World War II reflections on the fate of German Jewry so troubling. Regarding the Jews, Foerster did not learn much from the Second World War; the events from 1939–1945 confirmed rather than shook his opinions. In Foerster's case this confirmation occurs despite his insistence on the enormity and uniqueness of the crime and his own profound feelings of remorse. Relating a medieval prophecy that Germany would be a land in which a great crime would one day be perpetrated, Foerster wrote in his memoirs:

> Must I disclose to my countrymen, when and where this deadly crime actually took place? It was committed in Auschwitz, where millions of Jews were gassed. They were not millions of victims that resulted from a German-Jewish war, no, it was a great murder, which had never before been committed in the entire history of the world. Who can take away from me the consciousness of this great guilt? ... [W]e Germans benefited [from Jews] for hundreds of years, in our culture, in our economy, in our scholarship, in our medicine and in the world of friendship. ... No one can do it. But even worse is the fact that this great guilt has been submerged in silence.[47]

Despite these moving words, Foerster's *Die jüdische Frage* offers a good example of what troubles many Jews – scholars and laypersons alike – about philosemitism. Published in Germany in 1959, *The Jews* attempts to be a spiritual reparation for the indescribable wrong suffered by the Jewish people.[48] Given that intention, it is not surprising that the glorification of Jewish culture and a lachrymose presentation of the external history of the Jews dominated his presentation. Foerster warmly praised the piety of the Jews from time immemorial, devoting a chapter to the medieval pietists. Foerster quoted the many admonitions from Judah the Hasid's moral classic, *Sefer Hahasidim,* at length. The reasons for this choice of Jewish texts, the only text to be discussed at length in *The Jews,* seem apparent. First, the medieval Hasidim were *German,* allowing Foerster to stress the antiquity and earnestness of German Jewry. Second, the religious thrust of the Hasidim, or at least those sections which Foerster read in German translation, was moral. Contrary to the typical presentation of Judaism as mired in legal technicalities, *Sefer Hahasidim* evidences an acute moral sensitivity toward Jews and gentiles.[49] Equally impressive to Foerster, as to many well-meaning Gentiles and Jews, was the Jews' willingness to commit martyrdom for their beliefs.[50] The long history of Jewish suffering, which culminated in what Foerster called "the National Socialist epilogue", demonstrated the tenacity with which Jews clung to the Ten Commandments and God's Kingship.

The lachrymose history of Jewish suffering, standard fare for anti-antisemites, did not lead Foerster to a deep reappraisal of Christianity. Foerster acknowledged that

---

[46]Frank Stern, *The Whitewashing of the Yellow Badge,* Oxford 1992, *passim.*
[47]Foerster, *Weltgeschichte,* p. 642; idem, *Deutsche Geschichte und Politische Ethik,* Nuremberg 1961, p. 198.
[48]Foerster, *The Jews,* p. viii.
[49]Foerster either neglects to mention (or simply does not know) that the Hasidim were an elitist, sectarian and ascetic group extremely critical of the Jewish mainstream. They were also far more concerned with legal matters than Foerster assumes.
[50]Foerster, *The Jews,* p. x.

the Church's record of anti-Judaism had been "not consistently reassuring", but safely categorised the transgressions of the past as not truly Christian in spirit.[51] This rhetorical manoeuvre, well-honed by Christian apologists, failed to do justice to both the ancient past (e.g. the demonisation of Jews beginning in the Gospels and carried on by the Patristic Fathers) and also the recent past (e.g. the German Christians who sought to eradicate Jewish influence from Christianity under the Nazi aegis). Einstein, an admirer of Foerster's who helped secure him entry into the United States and a pension, chided Foerster on this point: "Christianity – taken as an abstract notion – may rightly be considered as the principle of moral good, of real human progress. The [Christian] churches, however, in the name of Christian principles, have served ... apocalyptic darkness (*apokalyptische[n] Nächten*) more than the eternal goals of humanity."[52] Foerster eagerly acknowledged that the "Jewish Question" was really a "Christian Question". But this seems to have meant little more to him than that Christians ought to stop blaming on Jews "faults for which they themselves bear ultimate responsibility".[53] A really thorough consideration of the role played by Jews and Judaism in mainstream Christian thought does not take place.[54]

There is something terrifyingly unsurprising about the Nazi Holocaust in Foerster's analysis. Despite Foerster's terming it the "epilogue" of Jewish persecution, it appears as another in a long line of martyrdom suffered willingly by the Jews for their faith. Inadvertently, Jews become objects acted upon in the moral history of progress and regress, a theme Foerster had already developed before the First World War. In a metaphor that Foerster used in his 1913 essay and repeated in 1959, he wrote: "They [the Jews] were like penguins on some uninhabited island which sailors can kill by the thousands for no better reason than the prompting of an evil whim."[55]

The sociologist Zygmunt Bauman has employed the neologism "allosemitism" to describe the allocation of a special vocabulary to address the radical otherness of the Jews. For Bauman, discussions of Jews are thus supercharged before a particular valence, either positive or negative, is assigned. Allosemitism is radically ambivalent, for it may manifest itself as hatred or love of Jews, but tends to be intense and extremely malleable.[56] In Foerster's case, the prevailing tendency is philosemitic, but

---

[51] Foerster still insisted in 1920 that "only through Christ and in Christ" can the Jewish problem be solved. *Mein Kampf gegen*, pp. 255.

[52] Letter, Einstein to Foerster, 13 March 1938, document, 53–085 of the Foerster-Einstein correspondence, Einstein Archive, Manuscript Division, National and University Library, Jerusalem.

[53] Foerster, *The Jews*, p. 124.

[54] Foerster continued to regard Jews as the spiritual wellspring of western civilization, as a people chosen by God for a special mission. Richard Rubinstein's *After Auschwitz*, Indianapolis 1966, forcefully exposed the dark underside of this evaluation. Rubinstein concluded that the idea of being the chosen people, an idea initiated by ancient Israel and adopted by both Christianity and rabbinic Judaism, lay at the source of the Jews' special treatment through the ages. It provided a theological explanation for the Jews' long history of suffering. For devout Christians the Jews' suffering – somehow – had to be part of the Divine scheme of redemption. Rubinstein concluded, in light of Auschwitz, that the myth of being the chosen people needed to be dispensed with altogether.

[55] Foerster, *The Jews*, p. 126. (Did penguins subconsciously remind Foerster of the Orthodox Jewish males of Eastern Europe, who dressed exclusively in black and white and (at least in stereotype) walked with a peculiar gait?)

[56] Zygmunt Bauman, 'Allosemitism: Premodern, Modern, Postmodern', in Bryan Cheyette and Laura Marcus (eds.), *Modernity, Culture and 'the Jew'*, Cambridge 1998, pp .143–156; idem, *Modernity and the Holocaust*, Ithaca 1991, pp. 31–60.

the negative potential lies just beneath the surface. Discussing Walther Rathenau and Albert Ballin, two very prominent figures in Wilhelminian Germany, Foerster criticised their German nationalism as a betrayal of their Jewish mission:

> Both in one way or another lived to see that their treason to their own best principles had been completely [in] vain. Both were to live through the hour when they received their parting kick and when it suddenly became plain to them that they had consecrated their brains and strength to a Germany that did nothing but squander its enormous moral and spiritual inheritance.[57]

One may find Foerster's anti-militarism admirable and still recognise that he ultimately validated the shabby treatment Rathenau and Ballin received on the basis of some reputed "treason" to Jewish values. But how *could* either Rathenau or Ballin betray a Jewish tradition that was really no part of their assimilated upbringing? And how could Foerster really expect highly assimilated German Jews to be free from the flaws that plagued Germany in general? The very subtitle of the chapter, 'Jews and Christians give way (*weichen*) to Nationalism', shows a lack of proportion on Foerster's part, as if the two groups were equally important in determining Germany's course. Bauman's words about the unbridgeable divide between "the Jew as such" and "the Jew next door" apply nicely to Foerster. However well Foerster knew German Jewry from his youth in Berlin, from his studies in Vienna, or from his activities in the peace movement, he was able to disconnect that knowledge from some ideal, abstract, essentialised Jew, constructed out of his own private theology. How else to account for the damning discussion of Ballin and Rathenau, the citations to the deeply ambivalent novelist Gustav Freytag, the metaphor of penguins done to death, and the persistent dichotomy between "good" and "bad" Jews? As Bauman suggested, the language of radical difference (allosemitism) invited the segregation of the facts of history which Foerster recognised from a pre-existing construction of *Judentum*. Even the Shoah did not force a fundamental reappraisal on Foerster's part.[58]

A similar balancing act between praising and damning can be found in Foerster's discussion of modern Israel near the end of *The Jews*. Foerster noted the extraordinary practical difficulties involved in the building of a new Jewish nation, and then takes a different tack:

> Yet all this can do no more than serve the purpose of recreating the material conditions of a new Israel. By this I mean a Jewish nation, which, in the midst of a world concerned almost exclusively with materialistic things, will remain faithful to its historic mission, a Jewish nation in a word, which will provide within itself the political center where its religious and ethical vocation will be turned into a lasting reality.[59]

---

[57]Foerster, *The Jews*, p. 132.
[58]Foerster discussed Ballin and Rathenau twice in *Weltgeschichte*, pp. 272–273 and in *The Jews*, pp. 132–134. In the latter treatment, Foerster juxtaposed Ballin and Rathenau with the orthodox Jewish businessman R. E. May, whose annual report Foerster described as "quite as much an annual of ethics as it was a survey of trade". By adding May's example I suspect that Foerster was trying to ameliorate the judgment on Jewish complicity on the rise of German nationalism in his *Erlebte Weltgeschichte*. Regrettably, he does this by simply reverting to the "bad Jew" versus "good Jew" model.
[59]*ibid.*, p. 145.

Casting the mantle of the prophets upon a new, weak, tiny and beleaguered nation made sense given Foerster's idealisation of the powers inherent in the individual Jew and collective Jewry, but, of course, hardly corresponded to reality. Foerster engaged in the typically modernist gesture of overloading the entity "Jew" with whatever significance he wanted. What makes Foerster unusual, in the modern setting, is the generally positive valence he assigns to the ideal Jew. Nevertheless, the spring is set for deep disappointment should the Jews fail to live out their divinely appointed role.

Fundamentally, this combination of high expectation and anticipatory disappointment stems from Foerster's traditional Christian soteriology. He criticised Christianity's failure to incorporate the Jewish legacy appropriately: ignorance of Christianity's Jewish roots, ignorance of Judaism's ethical and spiritual qualities, too much focus on the person of Jesus and not enough commitment to the Old Testament idea of God as Judge. Ultimately, however, Foerster bounced the question back to the Jews, "How can we explain the fact…that the Jews for centuries unhesitatingly chose death for themselves, for their wives and for their children, rather than embrace the Christian Faith?"[60] Foerster wished to highlight the affinity of Judaism and Christianity. Yet Foerster seemed strikingly unable to imagine Judaism's ability to be spiritually adequate on its own. Once again, Foerster intended the following statement to be philosemitic:

> Now it is a very extraordinary thing that the greatest counterpoise to this Aryan split between spirit and life should be found in the particular genius of Jewry. Because of this it is only through the conjunction in Christianity of Semitic and Aryan elements that something truly human could come into existence. Naturally I am speaking here of the earthly and cultural foundations of the life of Christianity.[61]

When Christianity succeeds fully in being Christian, the Jew will cease to be a Jew. This was Foerster's initial solution to the Jewish Question in 1913, and it was his solution in 1959.

More than any other figure examined here, Heinrich Coudenhove-Kalergi belongs to a bygone era. A Bohemian nobleman with ancient lineage on both sides of his family, Coudenhove received a Jesuit education, earned a doctorate of law, and entered the Austrian diplomatic service. At thirty-six, married to a Japanese woman and the father of two boys, he retired from public service to manage the family estates left to him by his father. Besides the considerable practical demands of running a manorial estate, Coudenhove educated his children, composed bedtimes prayers for the family, engaged in eclectic correspondence, and studied religion and philosophy. He also supported the nascent Austrian peace movement and prohibited his sons from playing with toy soldiers, quite a statement for a former big-game hunter who appeared in the Austrian equivalent of *Sports Illustrated*. An uncommonly energetic scholar, Coudenhove earned a second doctorate (in philosophy) from the University of Prague at age forty-two, mastered sixteen languages, and produced a considerable literary legacy. *The Essence of Antisemitism* (1901), begun as Coudenhove's doctoral thesis at Prague university became his most successful work. *Antisemitismus*

---

[60]*ibid.*, pp. 146, 145–153.
[61]*ibid.*, p. 139.

Heinrich Coudenhove-Kalergi

was reissued in 1923 with a biographical sketch; reissued again in 1929 by his son Richard who also wrote a long afterword; and reissued a further three times between 1932–1935, with a total print run of 22,000 copies. Translated into English as *Antisemitism Through the Ages* in 1935, *Antisemitismus* was reissued once again in 1992 in German with a new introduction by Coudenhove's granddaughter Barbara. With the possible exception of Jean-Paul Sartre's *Reflexions sur la question juive*, no single non-literary anti-antisemitic work can claim such a successful publication history, certainly none in the German language. Coudenhove's premature death in 1906 at the age at forty-five silenced the voice of a promising progressive.

Coudenhove was a private scholar without many Jewish contacts and distant from the daily politics of the "Jewish Question". He was, in his son's words, a conservative in his respect for tradition, a liberal in his advocacy of tolerance and a socialist in his hatred of social injustice.[62] Coudenhove was an unusual man and *Antisemitism* has more than a few quirks. Despite a deep study of Western and Eastern religions, Coudenhove commenced his work with an impassioned defense of Catholicism as the best of all religions, totally irrelevant to the theme and incongruous with the tone of the remainder of the work. The original 1901 edition also contains a long poem devoted to religious toleration, excised in succeeding editions. For all its many peculiarities, *Antisemitism* is a remarkable work. Coudenhove began with the standard denial of Jewish ancestry, but with a twist:

---
[62]Richard Coudenhove-Kalergi, 'Biographie' in Heinrich Coudenhove-Kalergi, *Antisemitismus. Von den Zeiten der Bibel bis Ende des 19. Jahrhunderts,* Vienna and Munich 1992, pp. 43–44.

Anybody who writes or utters the slightest word about Israel which is not unfavourable is at once cried down as a Jew or as a freemason. This expedient will have no effect in my case. There is not the slightest trace of Jewish blood in my genealogical tree. *Had this been the case, instead of concealing the fact, I would candidly and most joyfully have proclaimed it, because I would have felt proud of a possible kinship with the noblest men and women who ever wandered on this planet.*[63]

Denial of Jewish roots seems to have been a necessary patent of reliability when discussing the "Jewish Question"; Coudenhove subverted that shibboleth with the unabashed Judeo-enthusiasm of a convert. As he wrote at the conclusion of the work:

I confess that among my Christian friends and acquaintances I can call to mind only three were inspired by Philo-Semitism. I confess that I have myself been a theoretical Anti-Semite. ... Had I been asked a few years ago, when I decided to study the Jewish question and to write a book on it, whether this work would turn out Anti-Semitic, my answer to this question would most probably have been in the affirmative. A serious and, as I believe, a thorough study of the subject has taught me better.[64]

Coudenhove's study of antisemitism was as he described it: serious and thorough, and one could add, written with verve and passion. These were the features that made *Antisemitisus* an anti-antisemitic "classic", despite its profound inconsistencies.

Coudenhove's principal thesis is that religious intolerance lies at the root of the phenomenon. He proved this point directly, through an historical inventory of Christian Jew-hatred, and indirectly, through a variety of claims. He laid special emphasis on the first (negative) exposure to Judaism through early religious education and very ostentatiously walked out of the Ronsperg Church every Good Friday when the service reached the passage regarding the perfidy of the Jews.[65] For Coudenhove, racial differences were a fraud; the Jews comprised many different races as did contemporary Europeans. One could speak of Semitic languages, but not of Semitic peoples. Even in the Graeco-Roman past the Jews' minority religious beliefs and practices caused the social animosity of pagans, but only with the advent of Christianity did this hatred exceed the normal limits of xenophobia. Other nations, such as the Parsees and the Armenians have also survived through the ages without a state; Jews in non-Western parts of the world have been treated more or less like any other minority. Coudenhove's rational analysis contained a distinct demystifying tendency in. But the contrary tendency is just as strong. Coudenhove seems to have been in a quandary between what he says he was trying to do, namely to engage in an empirical investigation into the nature of antisemitism, and a deeply-seated traditional religious vantage point on Jewish difference. The first contradiction, therefore, is a common one in philosemitic discourse: whether to describe Jews and Judaism in natural or supernatural terms. Coudenhove described Jewish martyrdom as a "supernatural divine greatness".[66] He followed Renan's verdict that

---

[63]Heinrich Coudenhove-Kalergi, *Anti-Semitism Throughout the Ages*. Authorised English translation by Angelo S. Rappoport, London 1935, p. 21 (my italics). All quotes, unless otherwise noted, are from this translation.
[64]*ibid.*, p. 222.
[65]Richard Coudenhove-Kalergi, *Ein Leben für Europa*, Cologne and Berlin 1966, pp. 44.
[66]Heinrich Coudenhove-Kalergi, *Anti-Semitism*, p. 157.

"the best of all men have been Jews and the most wicked of men have also been Jews". He noted that: "Anybody who remembers that the Lord Jesus Christ was born among this nation will not wonder at its differing so greatly from all other nations."[67] Coudenhove thus replaced Jesus' death at the hands of Jews, with Jesus' birth from a Jewish mother. Accepting Jewish difference as a reality, Coudenhove gave it a positive spin.

Ultimately for Coudenhove, antisemitism had been a pan-Christian phenomenon cutting across denominational borders. Coudenhove clearly objected to the widespread tendency to equate antisemitism with medievalism and medievalism with the Catholic Church, thus letting other Christians off the hook. Although he devoted several pages to indicting the Dominicans' role in Jew-hatred from the thirteenth century until the present day, he defended the Popes as posting a generally favourable record in opposing antisemitic assaults.[68] Regarding Protestant antisemitism, Coudenhove uttered a judgment that would probably have been rejected by most contemporaries, but which seems more plausible in light of the Holocaust:

> If we compare the attitude of Luther and of the Protestant Church in the Middle Ages [sic] towards the Jews with that of the Roman Church, it becomes strikingly evident that the latter behaved towards this unfortunate people comparatively more humanely and tolerantly than did the Protestant Church. Nothing is more unjust than the assertion that strict Protestantism is more enlightened, progressive and tolerant than the Roman Church.[69]

Religious intolerance in all its forms drew sustenance from monotheism and the Hebrew Scriptures. Thus Judaism, in its more Orthodox forms, initially created the intellectual climate for oppression and martyrdom. Although Coudenhove did not have a positive view of Orthodox Judaism, he did not take this potentially antisemitic turn of argument very far, nor did he suggest that Jewry was responsible for its own suffering. Individuals and institutions carry the responsibility for their deeds. Coudenhove concluded that there needed to be a move back to an *Ur-Religion* that preceded these visions and which recognised that love of one's neighbour is the true basis for faith. His introductory poem 'Enoch' imagined a pre-Judeo-Christian figure as a potential basis for a common religious faith, without the intolerance that monotheism inevitably bred. Spinoza's influence on Coudenhove appears very pronounced here on several counts. Coudenhove prescribed philosophy for the élite and religion for the masses; he argued that there can only be one universal truth overarching all religions and "proved" Catholicism's superiority by showing that no other religion had performed so many deeds of "charity, pity and compassion".[70] Here is the second contradiction: a committed Catholic convinced of his tradition's superiority, turns out, on closer inspection, to share the views of a renegade Jew from Amsterdam.

Spinoza, in his *Tractatus theologico-politicus* (1670), considered Jesus the most perfect representative of human beings. So did Coudenhove, for whom Jesus epitomised the moral imperative to love one's neighbour. Both Christians and Jews needed to be led

[67] ibid., p. 195.
[68] ibid., pp. 91–97.
[69] ibid., pp. 104
[70] ibid., pp. 21–22.

in that direction. How will the modern Jew be led to Jesus? By Reform Judaism, answered Coudenhove, "the noblest, and most beautiful rejuvenation of Judaism and the greatest imaginable simplification of Monotheism". Coudenhove did not expect imminent religious conversion. Indeed, he thought the talmudic doctrine that the pious of all the nations would have a share in the world to come superior to the doctrines of Christianity and Islam. Nevertheless, Jesus represents a religious ideal that will ultimately win over Jews, precisely because they are so smart and admirable. "[I]t is my firm conviction that it is only a question of time when all educated Jews with their capacity for education and their love of knowledge will hail and adore Christ, our Lord, as one of the best, greatest and holiest men of their nation, while persisting at the same time in their aversion for Christianity."[71] Reform Judaism, to Coudenhove, was everything religion should be: ethical, universal, international and cosmopolitan. The Reform Jewish mission, as Coudenhove saw it, would be to cure humanity of the poison of religious fanaticism.[72] In a view both pluralistic and ironic, Coudenhove concluded that the world needed Jesus Christ and Reform Judaism for its salvation. Coudenhove thus combined traditional Christian supersessionism regarding Jesus as a religious archetype with a Reform view of "mission".

Reform Judaism and Zionism, bitter enemies in 1901, were considered by Coudenhove as equal partners in the solution to the "Jewish Question." Reform, as noted in the preceding paragraph, had a role to play in the bridging of remaining gaps between Jews and Christians in Western Europe. With the vast exodus carried out by Zionists, Coudenhove expected the remaining Jewish population to be small and easily assimilable. But Zionism had a critical role to play: rescuing Eastern European Jews from the clutches of the Tsar. However much the Christian states would be impoverished by the Jewish exodus (and Coudenhove listed the impressive contributions made by Jews in all fields), Christians had a moral duty to help the Zionists. Eastern European Jews, Coudenhove held, would be prepared to emigrate. "It is not true what the Anti-Semites say that the Jews would not go. ... Try it gentlemen, work for Zionism, and you will soon see how crowds of Jews will emigrate."[73] Sympathy with Zionism from the antisemitic impulse of getting the Jews of Europe was not a new phenomenon. Aiding Zionism out of a moral impulse to help solve the Jewish problem, despite the loss it would entail for Christian Europeans – that was something unusual. For a committed Christian like Coudenhove to be both pro-Reform and pro-Zionist on the basis of what each movement could contribute to furthering an internal *Jewish* agenda was unusual in the extreme.

If empathy with the Jewish condition was one of the lessons Heinrich Coudenhove-Kalergi and Mitsu Aoyama of Castle Ronsberg, Bohemia wished to teach their children, they succeeded admirably. Richard Graf Nikolaus Coudenhove-Kalergi (1894–1972), founded and inspired the pan-European League, a forerunner of the contemporary European Union. His activism in the peace movement began before the First World War. In the 1922 collection *Die Friedensbewegung* mentioned above, Richard contributed the article on Judaism in the section 'Ways to

---

[71]Heinrich Coudenhove-Kalergi, *Antisemitismus*, p. 291.
[72]*ibid.*, pp. 219–220.
[73]*ibid.*, pp. 208–209.

Peace'. That a Catholic should be chosen to write this section probably says something both about the secular loyalties of Jews in the movement and also about their Judaic limitations. In the same section Albert Einstein contributed the essay on Science, and Ernst Toller on Revolution, so suppressing the Jewish involvement in the movement could not have been a motive here. His remarkable two-page essay probably expresses what at least some non-Jewish peace activists thought about Judaism. The "text" Coudenhove used was not the élite texts of Judaism, but the history of the Jewish people. A believer in Jewish "world mission" like his father, Coudenhove argued that the realisation of Jewish justice was socialism; Jewish abstention from power politics was pacifism. Jews, claimed Coudenhove, were the first European people to disarm, albeit unwillingly. The most ancient cultural people (*Kulturvolk*), Jews were more mature. Like adults, Jews resorted to words; like children, Europeans resorted to violent conflict. In Richard Graf Coudenhove's estimation the Jews, to use an analogy employed by Disraeli and Nietzsche on earlier occasions, were a second European nobility. His conclusion is a remarkable statement that takes many antisemitic imputations and boldly calls them virtues. It is doubtful that the following statement would have been penned in his father's day by a *supporter* of Jewry. The First World War had made the Jews' enemies bolder, but, in this instance, also their friends:

> The diaspora made the Jews into an international people. From this curse came a blessing. Excluded from narrow nationalism the best among the Jews found their fatherland in the world, their patriotism in humanity. The world-mission of the Jews is the rebuilding of a destroyed world-community through a new cosmopolitanism, pacifism and socialism. They are precursors of a coming, denationalised humanity. Their goal is: to love each other instead of hating each other, to build rather than to destroy, to unite instead of dividing. Under the sign of their prophets humanity will be led out of Egyptian bondage of capitalism and militarism into the praiseworthy future land of freedom and peace.[74]

Richard Coudenhove continued his contribution to anti-antisemitism with the updating and republishing of his father's work in the 1920s and 1930s. Richard's revisions of *Antisemitism* were really independent essays, one of which was published by the Paneuropa Press in 1937 under the title *Judenhass!* Although Richard Coudenhove shared his father's detestation of religiously-based antisemitism, his appraisal of post-war antisemitism forced him to emphasise other factors and new realities. The mass emigration of Eastern European Jews, the rise of Bolshevism, and the impoverishment of Europe, Coudenhove sensibly argued, created the context for antisemitism in the post-war period. Germany, not Russia, had become the world-capital of antisemitism, to his deep dismay. Following in his father's footsteps, Coudenhove urged Western Jews to support Zionism. Contrary to their fears, the exodus of Eastern European Jews would make the "Jewish Question" easier to resolve by reducing the number of Jews who would remain in Europe and become fully integrated into their respective nations.

---

[74] Richard Coudenhove-Kalergi, 'Judentum' in Kurt Lenz and Walter Fabian (eds.), *Die Friedensbewegung*, Berlin 1922, p. 74.

As with all the figures discussed in this essay, Richard Coudenhove believed that a progressive solution to the Jewish plight could be found. He considered the persecution of Jews the "essence" of Nazi Germany's revolution and recognised that the Churches' opposition to the Nazis was driven mainly by Nazism's anti-Christian, not anti-Jewish, implications. Nevertheless, Richard Coudenhove, as late as 1935, still saw assimilation and national exodus as the two alternatives to solving the Jewish problem in Germany. Physical annihilation was as unthinkable for this conscientious and cosmopolitan Christian as it was for European Jewry.

The following table may help to emphasise our first conclusion:

QUIDDE	Bremen *Bildungsbürgertum*	Marginalised Academic	Secular, Liberal, Assimilationist
VON SUTTNER	Austrian aristocracy	Novelist	Secular, Liberal, Federation of Nations
FOERSTER	Berlin *Bildungsbürgertum*	Marginalised Academic	Devout Christian, Assimilationist
COUDENHOVE	Austrian aristocracy	Marginal Academic	Devout Catholic, Federation of Nations

The variety of anti-antisemitism evidenced by the figures discussed above was considerable. Foerster and Heinrich Coudenhove were thoroughly influenced by their Christian beliefs; Quidde and Suttner, deeply moral individuals, were resolutely secular. Suttner and Coudenhove, aristocratic inhabitants of the multi-national Austro-Hungarian Empire, envisioned a solution that gave play to Jewish contributions both within the land of their birth (assimilationism) and also the Jewish homeland (Zionism). Quidde and Foerster, middle-class North Germans, ultimately endorsed assimilationism, though without the impatience and intolerance of diversity typical of most German liberals. The three men held doctorates; Bertha von Suttner, as a women, was excluded from attending university. Quidde married a Jew, Suttner had numerous Jewish friends; Heinrich Coudenhove knew Jews mainly through epistolary exchanges. Von Suttner, Quidde and Foerster worked with Jews in the *Deutsche Friedensgesellschaft* and other organisations, as did Richard Coudenhove. It seems the precise positions they held on the "Jewish Question" were less important than their very participation in a movement offering a haven for Jewish-Christian collaboration.

In *German Jews Beyond Judaism*, the late George Mosse stressed the role Jews played in organisations and in intellectual life that, *prima facie*, were not Jewish at all.[75] Mosse further argued that certain domains such as, for instance, Goethe scholarship and commemoration, or the Frankfurt Institute for Social Research became predominantly Jewish. The examples adduced here support Mosse's first claim, if not his second. Christians (by birth and by conviction) constituted the majority of the *Deutsche*

[75]George L. Mosse, *German Jews Beyond Judaism*, Bloomington–Cincinnati 1985.

Friedensgesellschaft and, with the exception of Alfred Fried, the bulk of its visible leadership. Nevertheless, scholars have neglected the presence and/or significance of the large number of Jews in the movement.[76] Consequently, scholars have failed to sufficiently acknowledge the tight nexus between peace activism and anti-antisemitism, although that nexus seemed obvious to the four figures discussed above. The casual way in which both Arthur von Suttner in 1894 and Hellmut von Gerlach in 1937 equated the two positions is telling:

> "Before we will be able to achieve peace from the outside, we must produce peace within. For this work, we [the *Abwehrverein*] and you [the *Friedensbewegung*] work entirely on the same side."[77]

> "As a younger man I was an antisemite, because I knew no Jews, so was I, until about 1900, a militarist, because I knew no pacifists."[78]

The names on peace publications, the socio-economic composition of the movement, the prominence of Jewish peace activists in the public arena, the presence of such outspoken anti-antisemites must have made it clear to contemporaries – friends and foes alike, that here was a place that welcomed Jews as Jews.

What role did the *Deutsche Friedensgesellschaft* play as a vehicle for *Jewish* identity? An investigation into this matter would be well worth undertaking. I would conjecture that a wide and imprecise range of Jewish identity could probably be found among Jewish members. Just as the precise view of non-Jews on the "Jewish Question" mattered less than their possessing a generally anti-antisemitic outlook, so I suspect, Jews who shared the basic goals of the *Deutsche Friedensgesellschaft* would have been welcome whatever their own brand of Jewishness. No doubt, the highly acculturated were more represented than the highly observant, who tended to be less political than the Jewish mainstream. The Jews in the *Deutsche Friedensgesellschaft* may not have been talmudic scholars, but figures such as Albert Einstein, Eduard Bernstein and Gustav Karpeles certainly had a healthy Jewish identity. But again, this should not be overemphasised: just as the Christian anti-antisemites differed in their view of Jewry, so did the Jewish members.

What does this investigation suggest about placing the *Deutsche Friedensgesellschaft* within the framework of German Left Liberalism? The consensus is that nineteenth century liberalism defended Jews *qua* citizens-in-general, not *qua* Jewish-citizens. In Germany, leading Liberals such as Theodor Mommsen spoke out against a German-Jewish *Mischkultur* and rarely deviated from a projection of complete Jewish assimilation: German Jews were ultimately expected to become indistinguishable from other Germans. That position, at least publicly, was the bottom-line. This "ideal" Liberal ideology, however, needs fleshing-out in a social context. Dagmar Herzog's *Intimacy and Exclusion* and Keith Pickus's *Constructing Modern Identities* present two examples, namely the *Mannheimer Montag-Verein* (Mannheim Monday club) and the

---

[76]Karl Holl introduces the pivotal figure of Alfred Fried as "einen jungen, ehrgeizigen Österreicher, der soeben in Berlin sein Glück als Journalist und Verleger versuchte". Holl, *Pazifismus*, p.42. Only one pertinent fact remains unstated: Fried's Jewishness.
[77]Arthur von Suttner in the *Abwehrverein* circular *Freies Blatt* (15 May 1894), cited in Hamann, p. 194.
[78]Hellmut von Gerlach, *Von Rechts nach Links*, Zurich 1937, p. 261.

Freie Wissenschaftliche Vereinigungen, respectively) of settings where Christians and Jews socialised as equals.[79] Certainly the Christian as well as many Jewish members of these organisations expected complete assimilation and entertained ambivalent views about Jewish difference. Nevertheless, I would conclude that how these organisations functioned mattered more than what they said. The *Deutsche Friedensgesellschaft* offers a third example of a liberal context in which the term "neutral society" is justified.[80]

A final thought on the contemporary application of this study is surely not inappropriate. In the modernist mindset, one's religious and ethnic community was supposed to be irrelevant to political affinities, and a political organisation felt compelled to fight for the good of society – often at the expense of being able to fight openly for the particular segments of that society. In the postmodern era that we now inhabit, a progressive movement can oppose antisemitism, racism and sexism without fear that it compromises its avowedly universal mission. This article offers evidence that this subterranean tendency had been part of the *Deutsche Friedensgesellschaft* from the start.

[79]Pickus, pp. 75–80; Dagmar Herzog, *Intimacy and Exclusion*, Princeton 1996, esp. pp. 112–115.
[80]In a self-revision well-known to students of German-Jewish history, the late Jacob Katz abandoned the term "neutral society", employed in his path-breaking *Out of the Ghetto*, Cambridge, Mass. 1973, for the term "semi-neutral society". Katz thus intended to highlight the majoritarian impulse of the emancipationist view of the future. Katz was undoubtedly correct in general, I refer here only to some exceptions to his rule.

Memoir

Chanan Benhar

107 Tage mit der SH7

107 Days on the SH-7

BY CHANAN BENHAR

Editor: We are publishing, in shortened and translated form, this remarkable account of the Gestapo-organised illegal immigration to Palestine by one of the survivors of the Patria. It is based on the journal kept by Chanan Benhar which he saved when he jumped off the sinking Patria in the bay of Haifa. The author explained that he made some additions, "what at the time of the English I could not write". There is no question, however, that the manuscript is overwhelmingly a copy of the original journal. Fascinating and new are the details of the journey down the Danube and the varying attitudes of the Bulgarians, Romanians and Yugoslavs, generally only distinguishable by degrees of inhumanity. What a contrast the helpfulness of the Greeks! The harrowing crossing in an overcrowded and unsuitable boat to Haifa is graphically told. The behaviour of the British in Haifa who would not let them land and were torn between sympathy for the refugees and anxiety about Arab reactions, is here naturally condemned. But at least the refugees' lives were saved as the authorities would not have turned them back. The ardent desire of these pioneers to settle in Erez Yisrael, their stoicism, and bravery, makes this account a worthy tribute to all who perished on the Patria and to the survivors, as intended by the author.

From my Journal: Experiences and Events of the Last Large Refugee Transport from the Reichsgebiet.

In memory of our *Hawerah* Ruth Effenburger, may she rest in peace, who lost her young life when the *Patria* sank, and to the more than 250 *maapilim* who perished.

Glossary of some of the terms that may not be familiar to all readers:

Bethar	Revisionist movement
Haluz	Pioneer
Haluzim (plural)	
Hawer	Comrade, friend (male)
Hawerim (plural)	
Hawerah	Comrade, friend (female)
Haweroth (plural)	
Hachsharah	Preparation and education of the *Haluzim*
Ha We	In the journal, Hans Wedel, leader of the *Maccabi Hazair*
Yishuw	The Jewish inhabitants of Palestine
Maapil	Illegal immigrants
Maapilim (plural)	
Maccabi Hazair	The young Maccabis
Vatik	Older *Hawer*, comrade, companion
Vatikim (plural)	

It appeared likely that no further special Aliyah transport would be allowed to leave Germany for Palestine after the 17 November 1939. The reason being that the previous transport SH-6 which had left Germany in the spring of 1939 with hundreds of young pioneers from various agricultural training camps had been trapped in the frozen Danube in Yugoslavia. Also, with Italy's entry into the war the conflict spread to the Balkans. Finally, it was a matter of finance. We did not have the necessary foreign exchange to organise and equip the transport by sea.

Nevertheless our *Hehaluz* representatives and the Palestine Office worked non-stop to organise a new transport for young Jewish emigrants who had trained and prepared themselves for a new life in Palestine. Telegrams were sent to relatives in neutral countries, above all the USA, for funds for the transport. Every emigrant needed about $80. Thanks to the co-operation of the 'Joint' and the Palestine Office in Berlin and Vienna it was possible to raise the necessary funds to make Transport SH-7 possible.

There were constant problems with the Gestapo. The immediate concern of our Palestine Office in Berlin was to ensure, first of all, facilitating the immigration of the *hawerim* who were held in concentration camps because they were stateless or of Polish origin. The negotiations were almost hopeless. It required much effort and bribery to enable just a few to free themselves from the claws of the Gestapo. For months the outcome of all this was uncertain. We, the *hawerim* who for so long had prepared ourselves in Germany as pioneers for Palestine (*hachsharah*), could hardly wait for the time to leave. Every time our rucksacks were packed we thought it would just be a matter of a few days for the call to come to depart. After some more waiting a letter turned up to say that it was not possible whilst hostilities raged for the departure of *SH-7* to take place. For one thing no ships were available that could take us to the Black Sea. Then another letter from Geneva advised us against proceeding and expressed much scepticism about our preparations. There were no Marks or Dollars available. Nor could the 'Joint' help out. No country on the Danube would give us a visa allowing us to pass through. At the same time the Gestapo put pressure on the Palestine Office and deported all the stateless *hawerim* to Slovakia where they were interned in Patronka camp. Again and again our emigration was postponed. This only depicts some of the difficulties which postponed and prevented our emigration, problems of which we were aware in our *hachsharah*. All the difficulties the Palestine Office had to cope with were not our concern; we were busy with the harvest. We no longer really believed in our emigration. Nor, after all, was there any point pursuing other openings. Who would want to take us?

My own affidavit for eventual immigration to the USA had a number that would become valid six years later. We were told that we would have to reckon on staying on our *hachsharah* – perhaps until the end of the war.

THE BEGINNING OF THE ALIYAH

10 August 1940. The greater part of the harvest of the Ellguth farm have been brought in. During the lunch break in the dining room – I can still remember it to this day – it is announced that the SH Transport will depart. A few minutes later we

re-receive an express telegramme from the post office at Stein informing us to be ready for departure. Really this time it is true! The list with names setting out the various groups are ready. We still can't believe it. The first group from the farm are all ready to leave about 5pm. Off to Vienna by rail to meet another group of *hawerim* from the agricultural factory Ahrensdorf. It is Transport No.7 with transport organisers from Berlin and representatives of the *Maccabi-Hazair* Association.

11 August 1940. Sunday. Paul Jentes is in charge of our group. [Group No. 1 responsible for discipline and order.] We also meet and get to know *hawerim* from other training camps, and together we form a group responsible for looking after the transport on its way to Vienna.

12 August 1940. Early Monday morning the train enters Vienna *Ostbahnhof* to be met by representatives from the transport organisation. All goes very smoothly and to our great astonishment we are all accommodated in the Oesterreischicher Hof, exchanging a camp bed for a hotel bed! Some in our group are taken to the hotel König von Ungarn. It could not be better!

13 August 1940. We are all kept busy today for within a few hours we have 100 rooms – a whole wing of the Central Hotel to get ready to receive additional groups: it means setting up beds, chairs, tables etc. When one takes into account that these hotel rooms stayed empty for a whole year collecting dirt and dust we did a good job preparing for the arrival of our friends. There were just a few hotel employees, and they would have needed days to accomplish this. The transport organisers were accommodated in the Oesterreischicher Hof with other emigrants in various other hotels. The transport from the German controlled areas numbered five hundred. These in turn were divided into fifteen groups each headed by a group leader. The transport also included thirty-five per cent older *hawerim* (*Vatikim*), yet we, the younger ones preparing for new careers, were in the majority. This included Groups 2 and 3 consisting mainly of boys and girls none older than 17 years. Those in charge of the transport and of all the *hawerim* who belonged to Group 1 came directly under the transport organisers who in turn were made up of leading Zionists. Almost all of us stayed in various hotels in Vienna: Stalener Hof, Hotel Triest, Hotel zu den Drei Kronen, Währinger Hof, Belvedere, Hotel Terminus, Hotel Wandel. There were no problems with the hotel owners, because all of this was partly supported by the Gestapo. By the 18th August 1940 all of us on orders of the Gestapo had to leave German controlled areas. It is amazing to think that thanks to the pressure of the Gestapo the SH Transport became a reality. 120 *hawerim* stayed together in the Oesterreischicher Hof two to a room, the lucky ones had a room to themselves with bath.

14 August 1940. First day for the group to assume responsibility: seeing to correspondence, helping where necessary, ensuring good behaviour whilst visiting the city which means that no one when walking through the streets of Vienna draws needless attention to himself. We do not want to be subject to unpleasant comments. The lady owner of a delicatessen shop close to our hotel who noticed that we were persecuted called us in to her shop and gave us food without asking us to surrender

ration coupons. She was probably told about us by the owner of the hotel. Our main responsibility was to take members of the group in small numbers – so as not to be unduly noticed – from our hotel for our lunch at the *Griechenbaiszel*. At our disposal was a total of RM 6500; each *Hawer* received RM 15 for personal use. In addition the cost of necessary provisions, e.g. pocket torches, lighting fuel etc., had to be met. Our stay in Vienna is costing the *Reichsvereinigung* about RM 4000 a day. Not surprisingly for five hundred people accommodated in hotels in full comfort it obviously does cost that much. Where else were they to stay? Every day brings something unexpected. More *hawerim* arrive daily in Vienna, and on 19 August 1940 a total of five hundred Jews had left Germany; the demands of the Gestapo have been met. The various groups under the direction of Herr Mali have made a start with organising lessons. We are all eager to learn Hebrew. We have formed discussion groups, and in very small groups we visited the grave of Theodor Herzl buried here in Vienna, where his idea of a Jewish state originated. We have also met other young Jews, yet among us some unease has manifested itself. Why the delay, what are we doing here in Vienna? But those who have looked beyond the immediate problems ought to be glad that so far everything has passed rather smoothly. We had been given food coupons and have enough to eat. But these are only minor matters. Our journey is delayed with daily "minor matters" such as the *Tulcea*, which has first to reach Sulima before the *Donaudampfschiffahrtsgesellschaft* (DDSG) will place its ships at our disposal. Slovakia has made the issuing of visas to pass through its territory dependent on Jews expelled from Germany being joined by Jews at present in Patronka concentration camp. Our ship has also to fly a neutral flag, since Greece has declined to allow her flag to be flown. Attempts to negotiate with Spain failed. Finally our ship has to fly the flag of Panama which is probably not aware of this. Thus our departure is delayed from one day to another. Yet it is bearable for we could hardly complain about our accommodation and food here in Vienna …

26 August 1940. "What are these lousy Jews doing in our Vienna Hotels?" Gestapo Eichmann railed, and we were given one hour precisely to clear out of "his hotels". Again there was much work for our organisation. Within a very short time new accommodation had to be found for five hundred people. The Vienna Jewish community made classrooms in Jewish schools available, but there were no beds or washing facilities – just floor space. Some of us despaired. This was the start of what life would be like for the SH emigrants – good preparation for what lay in store. Crammed sleeping space on the floor, and on the ships it would hardly be any better. Now we had to move into classrooms of schools located in *Kastellix Gasse* 35, *Grüne Torgasse*, *Haasgasse* 10, *Krummbaum Gasse* 8, *Ferdinands Gasse* 23. The Jewish children had enforced holidays and we had bed bugs for the first time …

27 August – 1 September 1940. Slowly we acquired back ache from sleeping on the hard floors. We were not permitted to go out. We read books, studied, talked and took walks in the school yard and garden and were bored for days on end.

2 September 1940. It was tough going. We could hardly get any sleep, and we were lucky not to fall ill under these conditions. Surely it could not last much longer. The

visas from Slovakia had now come with the help of the Gestapo! Buses had come, but had returned empty. Why?

3rd September, 1940. Today – at long last. Early morning the buses are back, and this time we will board them with our luggage to be taken to the *Ostbahnhof* goods station. There a special train was drawn up. Group 1 with Paul Jentes in charge had to move the luggage from the buses to the train. With all the luggage transferred, the train left at 11am. On its way to Marchegg at the border watched over all the way by the SS! They wanted to make sure that we all left the country. On reaching the frontier at lunch time we had to leave the train with our luggage, which had been thrown anywhere when it was loaded onto the train. The long platform led to the customs hall and we waited with our rearranged luggage for ten hours. For us young ones who had come from the *hachsharah* camps this was not a problem with our luggage not weighing more than 8 kilos. We were hardly searched, not being suspected of smuggling. We had undertaken in writing before leaving our *hachsharah* that we did not carry any gold or valuables. But the *vatikim* had a lot more luggage and possessions and were subjected to a thorough search. Since this was a lengthy process we *haluzim* had permission from the Gestapo to help with carrying their luggage. Soon we were looked upon as serving porters taking luggage from the customs building after it had been searched back onto the train – no break for us, 10 hours non-stop. Those who came from the *hachsharah* were dealt with quickly, but the *Vatikim* were searched and subjected to vicious treatment by the Nazi customs officers. Almost all the books were confiscated, even prayer books. All that carried on until 10pm. Back on the train and on to the Slovakian border where customs stamped 'J' on our passports. We reached Bratislava at about 11pm, and the quay at midnight with the Danube steamer *Uranus* waiting for us. The five hundred from Patronka concentration camp had already boarded, now five hundred of us as well as a hundred Jews from Vienna made it a total of 1,100 Jewish emigrants. Being well organised our embarkation went smoothly. This cannot be said for the 100 from Vienna. Loading all the luggage was completed by 4 o'clock in the morning. The hard work earned us the "best places" that were left on the small steamer; the whole upper deck with no roof. No bugs on the wooden planks, but plenty of fleas! We were all famished!! Now that we were on board and just about to get some sleep the ship's sirens woke us after just one hour with all the engine noises to go with it …

4 September 1940. With the fog gone we had a clear view across the Danube. Getting up early we listened to an Orthodox group singing '*Leshalom*'. Another similar looking steamer could be seen. As we drew nearer we recognised the *Helios* crammed with people we know – all illegal emigrants from Czechoslovakia heading for Palestine. They chant "Judah, Judah" and hundreds sing across the Danube:

> *We are illegal emigrants*
> *The A-li-ya Beth*
> *We move over land and cross the oceans*
> *Chance is our travel plan*
> *Good fortune our pilot*
> *We have to land somewhere*
> *For there is no turning back for us.*

We sail down the Danube and look across green fields and forests. People peacefully pursue their work. They wave to us. We are heading for freedom. Those over there have no idea how we feel. We have left our homes, parents, brothers and sisters. Left behind are our relatives who were not so lucky to be on our transport. We are heading for our new homeland, the land of our fathers. They don't know what it means to escape Nazi tyranny. Those people who wave to us from the windows of their homes, they don't know what it means, "*Lehitraoth bearzenu!*". We rejoice ... for us a new life begins. No matter what the future holds, we will persevere. "Because for us there is no turning back." On and on we steam passing towns and villages as we approach Budapest. It's 3 o'clock in the afternoon. What magnificent views: Old palaces, fine buildings ... a peaceful city its inhabitants wave to us from the bridges. Do they know how closely crammed we are on board, do they know that instead of two or three persons per cabin, three times as many are on the *Uranus* all over the ship. Even the dining room is now turned into a large sleeping area for girls where they lie next to each other like sardines only finding sleep in turns. Along the gangways of the middle decks the designated stewards keep an eye on the queues lining up for their food. Patiently they wait to receive a ladle of warm soup. Do those who watched us from the bridges of Budapest see that? But why should they bother about our fate? They wave to us and we wave back. We sing Hebrew songs, but do they understand them? We have thrown off our yoke and servitude! We are liberated and are heading for the country of our fathers, we journey to our *hawerim* and *haluzim* to build a new home. We take on all hardships and deprivations. We are still young. One day we will set foot on land because for us there is no turning back.

Late in the afternoon we leave Budapest behind us, and are approaching the frontier of Yugoslavia where we stop to complete all formalities. We hope here to send a letter to our relatives. We don't have the right currency, and our paid-for return-coupons remain with those who promised to post our letters. Sailors of the *Uranus* or employees of the DDSG were boarding the ship. Letters which did get as far as the post office were never received by our parents.

Lemonade, beer, cigarettes, biscuits could be purchased on board in exchange for special bank notes issued on the *Uranus*. Those who can remember the concentration camp "shops" where necessities were sold to the inmates, will know what goes on here as far as profiteering is concerned. It was sensible that those in charge did not let each one of us have more than 5 RM, rather than the 45 RM that actually were to be given to each one of us, a reserve that was used to buy iron rations in the form of tinned food. Unfortunately some of us did not behave the way that was to be expected, for they would queue more than once when food was given out. With the issuing of food cards this malpractice came to an end. During the early days there were difficulties and disputes among the various groups who came from the *Reich*, and those from Patronka and Vienna. They were dealt with by the *Haganah* formed by all inclusive representations to solve problems ... Gradually national backgrounds faded into the past, we merged into one group of *hawerim* with one aim.

The *Haganah* made itself responsible for calm and order ... Night watches were set up, and the passage along the corridors leading to the toilets was organised. Some parts of the ship were cordoned off to ensure that food brought on board reached the kitchen. The heavy luggage had been loaded on the upper deck, mainly crates and large trunks belonging to the emigrants from Vienna and those from Patronka who did not bother about weight limitation. All that had to be looked after. Our dear travel companions failed to see that they could not have all their luggage with them, for there was only just enough room along the ship's corridors, let alone the cabins.

5 September 1940. We cheered up as the days passed and we approached Belgrade in the late sunny afternoon ... Belgrade was in the midst of celebrating its King's birthday; we for our part wanted to release our anger for again having to cart all those heavy bags to the custom sheds and back to the ship ...

We passed Belgrade lit in all its splendour. We lost sight of the *Helios* which was sailing behind us in the growing darkness of the evening. The bridges and palaces of Belgrade grew more distant. Calm returned on the *Uranus*. We were settling down finding our own little corner on the ship's bare planks. There was still some whispering among those who found it difficult to sleep after all the commotion. The *Haganah* patrolled the upper and middle decks. A gentle call, a change of guard and a whispering of German and Viennese accents could be heard.

6 September 1940. Another day begins. Announcement that we are to pass through the 'Iron Gate'. As we approach we see steep bare cliffs on both sides so narrow that we could almost touch them ... After a few hours ... we see vineyards and villages conveying normal life on both banks of the Danube, and over there are some fishermen. What do they think of us? Would they know that we are 1,100 refugees on a small "excursion steamer" crammed together like sardines in a tin? On we sail.

Again another rumour which some heard already. Kladowo must be located just beyond the hills where our *hawerim* from a previous transport were left stranded unable to proceed, because in the severe winter the Danube had frozen over. Then their money ran out. Everyone had to leave the ship to be interned in a camp in Kladowo by the Yugoslavs. People wave to us with flags and pieces of cloth. Are those our *hawerim* from the 'Kladowo'? Too distant to hear us ... it's a shame we cannot help. They have no prospect of continuing. Only three quarters of a year ago we lived together ... What will become of them? We are depressed. Will we suffer the same fate? We sail on, we cannot do otherwise. Our duties keep us busy and give us no time to reflect as we are heading for our final destination. As if Kladowo was not awful enough, shortly before reaching the landing place Russé in Bulgaria, we noticed a ship bopping up and down in the middle of the Danube outside territorial waters full with emigrants clinging to the ship's railings. They wave to us and call but we cannot hear them. Binoculars reveal the ship's name. It is the *Pencho*. Again another story of Jewish tragedy. We are told by those *hawerim* who came from Patronka that those over there belong to the *Bethar* movement. For a long time now they have been floating around the Danube aimlessly. The crew had abandoned them. They have no money left to continue on their journey, and the countries bordering the Danube have refused them transit. A Jewish fate. First the 'Kladowo', now the *Pencho*. We are approaching the ship, but our ship's engine makes it impossible to hear them. Speaking in chorus we call: "Do you want to go to Erez?" They reply: "We want to go with you, help us, take us with you." We have no answer, how can we take them with us? We call: "Are you hungry?" The reply emphatically "Yes", and again: "Help us, take us on board."

It is so tragic. Abandoned in no man's water in the middle of the Danube outside territorial waters watched over by Romanian and Bulgarian police with a yellow flag flying from the ship's mast indicating quarantine. We cannot come to them and they cannot come to us. Why is there so much suffering in this world, why? What have we done to deserve this, only because we are Jews? Is this to be the fate of a whole people.

... We are anchoring in Russé to take on supplies. The *Pencho*'s weak lights still showing for us to see ...

We sail to the opposite shore to Giurgiu on the Romanian side of the Danube. Up to Russé the Uranus travelled in the no man's water of the Danube ... Since our transit visas have not arrived, the Romanians send us back to Russé. We have to wait!

7 September 1940. We are again in Russé. We cannot continue. We are told that this time it can last days. At least our transport organisers had now time to care about the unfortunate refugees stranded on the *Pencho*. Application to the Giurgiu authorities was made to bring help to these refugees. But the authorities in Giurgiu were not inclined to help. We in turn on the *Uranus* started to collect funds. Some of the women with us had husbands on the *Pencho* to whom they wrote letters. Negotiations with the Romanians and our captain ended in failure. Not even the husbands on board of the *Pencho* were given permission to join their wives who were with us here. The answer was "danger of epidemic". We could unfortunately do no more than collect cigarettes, cheese, tinned fish to be sent to them from our provisions.

In the course of the day, to our surprise, the whole 'Jewish Danube fleet' landed in Russé. The *Hechaluz* had brought together 4000 refugees from Central Europe to be transported all at the same time on four Danube ships: the *Uranus*, *Helios*, *Schönbrunn*, and *Melk*, all reaching Russé unable to move on. Some of the refugees on the *Schönbrunn* had passports which had expired and thus could not come with us. The *Melk* carried expelled refugees from Danzig. They were taken by the Gestapo via Marchegg to Bratislava. Now all of us here just had to wait for what was to come. During the night our most senior organiser, the leader of the *Maccabi* groups, Hans Wedel, tried to make contact with the *Pencho* using a morse lamp. He hoped to convey to the men on the *Pencho* that their wives were on the *Uranus*. Perhaps they could find a way to join them.

8 September 1940. Sunday. Yesterday one of the *vatik*'s died of a heart attack. Our doctor could not help. His funeral is today. Ten of us making a *minjaam* were permitted on land for his funeral in a Jewish cemetery, the first occasion to be allowed on land was for this sad ceremony.

9 September 1940. At long last the Romanians allow us to proceed and, after saying a sad farewell to the *Pencho*, we sail on. A few brave men jumped into the water trying to reach us, but the Romanian police began shooting and drove them back!

Once again in Guirgiu we left all the food we collected with the Romanians to be passed on to the refugees on the *Pencho*. Would they receive it? – God and the Romanians only know! At long last the *Uranus* sails downstream with the Danube getting broader passing fields and meadows and pretty little homes with people again waving to us. Actually this is quite a beautiful journey – if only it had taken place in different circumstances. We were not quite as free as we thought. For how did these SS boats which now circle around us get here to ensure that we did not return? "For us there is no return!"

10 September 1940. Closer and closer we come to our final destination on the Danube. We recognise the delta. We reach Tulcea about lunch time. We spot large, elegant cruise liners. Which one will be ours, which will be the one to take us to Palestine? But these cannot really be our ships – they are luxury ships. Are we likely to be transported in such luxury? There – beyond them – that is where they are! We can hardly believe it. Three ships to sail on the high sea; little fishing vessels are anchored there. Two of these are even smaller than our *Uranus*. One is a little larger. How on earth are we to accommodate 4000 refugees who embarked from the just about manageable Danube ships. It is just not possible to find room for 1000 people on an 800 ton steamboat on which 30 fishermen had enough room. I saw boats in Hamburg harbour which could take 500 passengers but they were 10,000 tons or larger. And now we are to be transported on these miniature boats?

We had to sail under the hated swastika whilst on the Danube. The ships over there fly the Panama flag. We only had one wish: away from those German ships – on to those small ships.

11–13 September 1940. But it is not going to happen that fast. Our organisers in charge of the transport did not wish to assume responsibility for the safety of 4000 refugees on these three small ships. In Tulcea negotiations took place with the representatives of the *Hechaluz*. They inspect the ships and confer how to solve the problem. Perhaps an additional ship will be put at their disposal. How else can 4000 people be accommodated? The ships flying the flag of Panama are the following:- *Pacific* approx. 800 tons, *Milos* approx. 700 tons, *Atlantic* approx. 1400 tons.

The names of the ships have all been changed. They may have had different ones sailing under the Greek flag. Everyone only has one wish; everyone wants to be on the larger ship, everyone wants to be on the *Atlantic*, being better, larger and more seaworthy. But how many are to board it? With an additional one or two ships the problem would be solved! On Friday evening we, the youth groups, held an *Oneg Shabath* in the large sleeping hall previously the dining hall of the *Uranus*. The girls had moved their sleeping bags to one side. We were all singing Hebrew songs making it a happy atmosphere ... Our negotiators returned looking serious ... Erich Frank, the leader of our transport from the *Reichsgebiet* made the following announcement: "*Hawerim!* Tomorrow we begin boarding. I emphasise all 1,125 from the *Uranus* will be transferred to the *Pacific*. Our most testing time has come. Living conditions we least expected are facing us. We were lied to in Vienna. The ship has no kitchen for us. The galley is available for the crew only and out of bounds for us. And just two toilets near the cabins. Latrines on the deck will be constructed by our builders from the Paderborn group. Sleeping space is available for only half of us, and here also the builders will add places wherever they can find them. Pregnant women and those with children will be accommodated in cabins that can be found. Four times as many will have to be placed in them, but additional cabins will also be built. In 10 minutes those in charge of the various groups will meet to hand in passports!" This is all Erich had to say.

How are we to manage? There was hardly any room on the *Uranus* and now it will be worse. Sardines are better off. On the large *Uranus* we had just about some room in cabins and on gangways, on various decks and under the stairs. Every space was used to find a place to sleep. Washing facilities were just about adequate and there were two large kitchens. And now we are to board a smaller ship with no sanitary facilities, no kitchen, no lifeboats and inadequate sleeping places and sail with this vessel on to the high seas. There are no other ships now or later.

Erich also added that the Danube ships had to be vacated by tomorrow evening. Last minute discussions with those in charge of various groups took place on the *Uranus*, and we all meet for instructions and to receive our passports which are required for boarding. Paul Jentes already on the *Pacific* called out: "It is much worse here than you were told by Erich. It is up to all of us whether we can keep our nerves. Accept light-heartedly the conditions as they are. This will have a calming effect on the women and elderly. The *Haganah* will get up at 5 am, get your personal belongings together and be ready for boarding at 7 am to ensure a smooth transfer ..."

14 September 1940. Today we transfer with all our belongings and supplies. Both ships are side by side. Now we can see how small the *Pacific* really is. Luggage and crates are stowed deep down under the bunker next to the coals. The Paderborn group, the first to board, organises the places to be occupied. Every inch of space is utilised. Plank beds everywhere 42 cm apart. Not even sardines can be closer. Only the upper deck and the captain's cabin are left unoccupied. 300 of us have to sleep in the open, exposed to all weather – and yet we still do not leave.

There was still no provision for coal or any crew on board. That worried us. Sometimes the captain came on board, but mostly he stayed in Tulcea. Now for the first time we experienced what it is meant to be on a ship which is bopping up and down constantly moving from side to side and from stern to bow. With its broad keel the *Uranus* just floated on the Danube like a duck, but the *Pacific* with its painted keel as all high sea ships, is subject to changes of currents. What will it be like on the open sea? Every time some passengers were leaning over the railing the ship turned with them and, on hearing the order "*Sporti*", they had to go to the other side to keep the boat on an even keel. We had to keep close watch to prevent the ship from capsizing. We also had to watch so that not too many came on deck. Many, nevertheless, came up for fresh air to escape the bad oppressive air down below.

15 September 1940. First day on the *Pacific*. So little space that one cannot take one step without disturbing someone else, bumping against someone or stepping on them. For an outsider it must be impossible to visualise what it is like to cope with such inhuman conditions. And how did we fare with the food situation at first? For a small piece of dry bread and half a cup of tea one had to queue up somewhere in the centre of the ship. The air there was fetid and one was glad to be back on deck even if it rained.

16 September 1940. Today for the first time I went to the latrine. It is best not to eat anything then one need not go there. Although everything was well organised and buckets were attached to ropes to collect water from the sea for flushing, the whole

business was repulsive. This place is used by thousands of passengers. And this was by no means the worst. The space we have for sleeping on deck is the best as long as it is not raining, and many of our young people stealthily make their way up there during the night to escape the heat and stench down below. It is a terrible ordeal for the mothers with their small children who are crowded into overflowing cabins. Nobody who has not experienced it can not imagine what it is like. And how were the sick to be accommodated? There were no separate rooms for the sick! One can only heap praise on our nurses who untiringly found their way to the sick among the vast number of people.

17 September 1940. Another night passed. Non-stop rain, and those of us who slept on deck left in a panic for cover. All the luggage had to be taken down. But where to? And where to find sleep, for there was nowhere else? The bunkers were overflowing with people despite the sickening air. How are we to go on? There is still as yet no date for departure. Tonight for the first time we had some warm food for supper: potato soup. In the afternoon our Paderborn group placed two large vessels for washing in the middle of the deck and also took care of the firewood. Now it was possible to cook kosher and non-kosher food separately... Small boats come daily from Tulcea. The Romanian police watch over the *Pacific*, still anchored in the middle of the Danube.

18 September 1940. Only small boats were permitted to bring drinking water. But how? A fisherman in a boat not larger than a lifeboat three-quarters full with "drinking water" in which he stood in his bare feet passed the water to us in a bucket. Our *hawerim* filled our tanks with this water. *Bon appetit*! But why worry? Paul pointed out the water will be boiled first. Other fishermen bring white bread for which we pay with good money. It looks good but is mouldy and smells musty. But we cannot select our suppliers. We have to deal with those the Romanian police service permit to pass!

19 September 1940. A fine day. All the buckets have been taken over by our *Haweroth* to do the washing. But we too wanted to have a good wash and did not want to wait. So we just put on our bathing trunks and jumped into the Danube and swam and bathed. The Romanian police watching our ship looked the other way. Now that we were bathing under police supervision, despite the strong current we just could not resist swimming to the *Atlantic* anchored only 100 metres away from us, where we saw the worse conditions than we had to live in on the *Pacific* with more than 1700 people crammed together, worse than the little more than 1000 of us on our ship.

Our food improved daily. Those in charge of provisions provide boxes of macaroni and our *haweroth*, who at their *hachsharah* had worked in the kitchens, made special efforts to do their best with the little at their disposal producing a tasty hot meal. For supper we either had bread with cheese and a slice of salami, for breakfast tea, marmalade and the issue of our daily bread issue. Paul Jentes's orders could be heard throughout the ship, even as far as the shore: each group to keep good order ... The crew had still not come on board, only the captain ...

20 September 1940. For a change we had watermelon for lunch, 1/6th of a slice each. Again we are swim in the Danube and more of us cross over to the *Atlantic* with

some of its passengers crossing over to us. With all that good weather we felt like were convalescing. We are getting used to our way of life. Fishermen trade with us. The Romanians make the best bargains offering cigarettes, sweets, biscuits, all paid for with good money. Those who came from Patronka camp with a lot of luggage exchanged clothing for cigarettes – a flourishing trade ...

22 September 1940. One of our agents from Tulcea tells us that the *Völkischer Beobachter* reported that 4000 Jews had starved to death on the Danube. If this turns out to be true, what will our relatives left behind think?

24 September 1940. The Romanians influenced by the Nazis forbade us to bathe today. We had not the slightest intention to enter Romania illegally! ...

1 October 1940. In my diary the publisher has printed "1938" the Sudeten German area has been liberated. My own entry 8 o'clock in the morning ... A ship like ours comes slowly upstream. It is the *Rosita – Panama*. Now we will soon sail on. Our representatives have not lied to us after all. Up to now we have been cheated by Mr. Goldner and Mr. Staufer who should have looked after our transport. Not to mention Mr. Weinstock, our supplier who for exorbitant payment was supposed to look after our supplies. But I really know little about the machinations of all these "gentlemen" who enriched themselves at our expense ...

2 October 1940. *Erev Rosh Hashana*, the eve of the new year. The sky is cloudy. The crew now come on board with their own belongings and food supplies. We have to vacate the bridge and find somewhere else to sleep which we do gladly. The crew are Greeks and only speak their own language. They make a lively impression on us and check over the ship ready for departure...

3 October 1940. *Rosh Hashana*. But we are at work on this holiday all the same. Those sixty sacks we had stacked on the front deck yesterday have to be moved again, so that the crew can get to the anchor chains. We realise that, but where to put the sack? The Paderborn people have an idea: use the large air shaft between the bunker and deck. A wooden rack is built and placed in the air shaft to store the sixty sacks. No doubt this will cut off the air to our *hawerim* down below the bunker, and there are a lot of complaints ...

4 October 1940. Today our second day of new year. Only two years ago we celebrated the service in the synagogues of Berlin, Magdeburg, Leipzig, Munich... and other cities with Jewish communities. All were destroyed by the Nazis. Where will our relatives go today to pray? The religious groups on our ship are holding a joint service on the back deck ... The Romanian 'Iron Guard' would not permit bread to be delivered today. They want to force us in this war to leave. As if we did not want to. These Romanian Nazis!!

5 October 1940. We are supposed to continue our journey. What is stopping it? Everything is in order – isn't it? But there are always problems that prevent depar-

ture, from the beginning of our journey. The crew made new demands. They want more dollars to be paid in advance to make sure that they are getting it now not at the end of the journey. They know if caught by the English it will be taken away from them and that they will face heavy penalties in Palestine. We were not permitted to leave Germany with more than $4 each. These were put into a joint account administered by the transport committee.

6 October 1940. Still not enough provisions on board. Mr. Weinstock is being urged by the Romanians to get on with it. Perhaps we will shortly depart ...

7 October 1940. The great day has come. All morning preparations are underway for departure. The crew finally checks the six lifeboats. The luggage that was smuggled into the ship must be removed. The pulleys of the anchor are greased, smoke comes out of the funnel and the captain is in good humour. At 12.30 the anchor is raised and very slowly the *Pacific* makes a turn towards the centre of the Danube, and sailing through the middle of the delta makes her way to the Black Sea port of Sulina. It's 4 o'clock now at Sulina where we stop once more. Paul takes the opportunity to scoop "drinking water" from the Danube into a large vessel. Half an hour later we have "sweet" salt water coffee ... We pass Sulina, but again the captain drops anchor.

8 October 1940. The captain gives the order to sail on. The sea is calmer. At long last we leave the grey-brown water of the Danube behind us and enter the grass green waters of the Black Sea ...

9 October 1940. We wash ourselves in the salt water which we have scooped from the sea ... In the afternoon the captain changes course to North West. In the evening we reach the bay of Cap Caliacre on the Bulgarian coast. The captain announced that he was waiting for the *Atlantic* so that we can take two additional stokers on board.

10 October 1940. We remain in the bay. Glorious warm weather. The captain, Erich and Hans have taken a small boat to go on land. They want to know what had happened to the *Atlantic* which is supposed to have run aground as she was about to leave Tulcea. We made the most of the beautiful weather to bathe in the bay. On our own – no strangers, no police boats, just us.

At last the captain, Erich and Hans returned. They got nowhere. The nearby radio station was supposedly demolished by the Romanians before they evacuated this area. Quarrels among Balkan states. That did not bother us. We enjoyed ourselves, happy to be in this beautiful bay with all its beautiful colours – red, white and green. In the afternoon a Bulgarian coastal security boat approaches to take us to the port of Warna to the control check point. The ship enters the port in the evening. The captain informs them that the compass is not working ... Our transport leaders use the time to stock up with provisions and drinking water.

11 October 1940. Fog, fog, fog. Gradually Warna, bathed by the sun, emerges from the fog. We can see a large harbour and imposing ships that make us jealous.

Substantial houses come into view. ... A beautiful beach slowly comes to life with bathers. They are far away from us. Now police, customs and medical officers are coming on board. The Bulgarian officials are more polite than the Romanians. Their English is better, making it easier to communicate.

12 October 1940. Today is our most important religious day, *Yom Kippur*, the Day of Atonement. The religious groups are praying all day. Observing tradition, we fast. A terrible storm is raging beyond the harbour ... We are glad to be here inside the harbour. A change of attitude is noticeable as regards the port officials. They are not as friendly as I described them to be yesterday. They want to force us to take twenty-two expelled passengers. Jewish refugees – but where to place them? Our ship is full. There is not even space for a needle, and now another twenty-two people with all their luggage? Erich and Hans negotiate with the authorities. They make conditions: a compass, a dynamo, provisions for taking ten passengers. Phone call to Stauffer in Tulcea. At last there is agreement. The *Atlantic* and *Milos* have supposedly already passed through the Bosphorus. Is that true??

13 October 1940. The Bulgarians deliver provisions to take on board. We are pleased. Our journey does not proceed. A storm is raging and it would be dangerous to leave. In addition the Bulgarians are not prepared to let us go. Though protected in the harbour, the *Pacific* is rolling dangerously. Much sea sickness on board ...

14 October 1940. I hand a letter to my father with a prepaid coupon to a Bulgarian policeman to post. Hopefully the letter will be delivered??? There is no prospect today that we will sail. Erich and Hans negotiate with the Jewish Community. It is planned to bring twenty Jewish *Haluzim* from Sofia to join us, provide us with coal, bread, and a compass.

15 October 1940. The necessary dynamo is delivered. The new compass is to follow. In the afternoon Gerda and Wolf are married on board according to Jewish custom. Tomorrow we are to leave with twenty additional *haluzim* on board.

16 October 1940. ... Those Bulgarian swines! No *haluzim*, but forty-one passengers are forced on board by guards with arms. Protests from us are of no avail. There is no resistance. We are unarmed and their rifles are aimed at us. They are worse than the Nazis. I shout at them ... Overloaded, the ship leaves the harbour ... No insurance company would have agreed to take a *Groschen* from us. Where can such conditions exist? An 800-ton boat with almost 1200 people and six lifeboats each of which could hold at most twenty people!! As the anchor is raised it is damaged with a large piece breaking off the quay wall. No returning to these crooks. Never again to Warna. After half an hour we are on the high seas. The sea is becoming restless and by the evening full storm. The decks are cleared. There is room only on the lower staircases. We cannot find sleep, but who can under these conditions? I sneak onto the upper deck looking at the stars and the main mast and I am able to see with what force the ship is thrown about. It looks so dangerous one fears the ship could capsize. Waves sweep over the deck, and I rush below to save myself. The cries of the women

and children in the bunkers are drowned by the din of the storm. It gets so much worse around midnight that the captain steers towards the coast to seek shelter in a bay. The anchor is dropped but not even that can prevent the ship from being tossed about.

17 October 1940. There are many who were sea sick during the night. During that night Wolfi and Gerda become parents. A sweet baby girl on board, born in freedom, attended by Dr. Friedenthal and nurse Deborah despite the storm. All day the bay protects us from the angry sea ...

18 October 1940. Early morning the anchor is raised again and we are setting sail for the Bosphorus. Now we are sailing beside the Turkish coast ... We pass the Golden Horn but are not allowed to stop. A Turkish pilot comes on board as we enter it and pass the splendid buildings of Constantinople approaching the Sea of Marmara which we enter and the pilot leaves us and we steam through the peaceful Sea of Marmara.

19 October 1940. Afternoon. We leave the greater part of the Dardanelles behind us and we see carved in stone in the mountains GALLIPOLI 18 III 1915 in memory of the First World War. Here on the peninsula to the north of the Dardanelles the English and French landed and were beaten back by combined German and Turkish armies. Many Jews fought with the Germans and died there. "The gratitude of your fatherland will always be with you!"

In the evening, on entering the Aegean, we are already in Greek territorial waters. Now we have nothing to fear, for the Greeks are kind to us. That we learnt from other transports which passed here before us. The representatives of the *Hechaluz* in Geneva, Switzerland, are kept informed and I am sure know all about us, but Erich and Ha We keep us in the dark whenever we ask about it... We can understand that because our *hachsharah* is to remain as secret as possible. That is why our transport has not been designated as an *Aliyah* transport to Palestine. As mentioned before, we call ourselves *Aliyah-Beth* (Immigration B) meaning entering Palestine illegally, not legally. Yet this did not mean that we left Germany illegally, but quite legally and with the assistance of and under pressure from the Gestapo... Because the English blocked immigration by us Jews to their Palestine Mandate since early 1939, the *Hechaluz* found a way out: legal emigration from German occupied Europe, illegal immigration to Palestine.

23–24 October 1940 ... The Greeks now bring us sufficient drinking water – it is not how it was in Tulcea, but now the water comes in large casks. We can now wash properly. The *Haweroth* wash their hair and the sun dries it quickly. The Greeks on Crete are very, very nice to us.

25 October 1940. The weather is hot and humid. A motor boat approaches. Who is the passenger? A representative (Herr Lewy) of the *Hechaluz* comes on board the *Pacific* and negotiates with Erich and Hans. Remaining here has its reasons. A little later we have the representative's Athens address and note it for all eventualities. One can't

know what will happen – more about that later. Soon boats come to bring 900 loaves of freshly baked bread, masses of biscuits, potatoes and vegetables. Now we don't have mouldy biscuits from Tulcea, which our cooks roasted to make them more edible.

26 October 1940. A gentle spring rain at night. In the morning we load up again with coal. Boats with young people circle our boats and sing folk songs to us, and we sing Hebrew songs. The coastal police allow us to bathe in the magnificent bay... For the first time we feel free! After such a long time we are once more respected. The Greek people are good to us, so kind to us, it must be repeated again and again.

27 October 1940 ... Herr Lewy comes on board. We carry two heavy suitcases for him. Now we know why we were given his address. The heavy suitcases contain our stamped passports with the 'J'. Now we are stateless. We cannot return to Germany and the English cannot send us back to Germany. I don't think Herr Lewy will take the passports to Athens. Erich won't tell. Our passports will most probably meet the fate of a seaman's death. We could not care less.

31 October 1940. All the coal is gone. Erich orders all wood not needed to be used for fuel. Only the Paderborn group is allowed on deck to work with hammer and saw; with no one there they cut up lifeboats and wooden railings ... latrines and anything made of wood, like cabin doors, wooden hatches, planks etc., all fuel for the ship's boilers. Next in line are unnecessary wooden staircases. The ship seems to go faster and faster...Rolf and I watch on the upper deck. No railings, no life boats, no stairs – nothing made of wood is left. High on the mast the captain has attached an emergency distress signal. We need help. Will it come? We cannot continue for much longer. There is light ahead of us. We call Ha We. The light comes ever closer. Ha We knows what it is; it is the morning star which glows so brilliantly. We wait and are on the look out. Will we be seen? Will help come in time? Again lights appear and vanish in the distance Are they U-boats? English coast guards? English warships? What are they going to do to us on discovery? All of a sudden on the horizon there are black shadows; is it land? Yes or perhaps only clouds? Dawn breaks slowly. There in the distance mountains can be seen. Could that be Lebanon? Or ?? Soon we know for certain. It is the 1 November 1940, 4 o'clock in the morning. Ahead of us is land!! As we come closer we clearly spot settlements in the distance ... Ahead of us is Haifa!! The news spreads like wildfire throughout the ship. No control boat, no police or warship in sight. No Englishmen. We are not detained or arrested. Is it possible to enter Haifa without being apprehended in the middle of the war? Perhaps the English are still asleep. All of Haifa fast asleep, just smoke from the factory chimneys. The *Pacific* manages to enter the bay under her own steam. The captain drops anchor. To enter the harbour right away seems to be a dangerous gamble for the captain. There could be mines. The danger is too great. We stay 350 metres outside the entrance of the harbour waiting and hoping that someone will come. The emergency light is still on the main mast, above it the yellow quarantine flag. We are bound to be seen, just as we can see the harbour! We wait till 11am. At long last a police boat comes out of the harbour. About time!! The harbour police is boarding the ship confiscating the ship's papers. They asked after the *Milos* and *Atlantic*. How

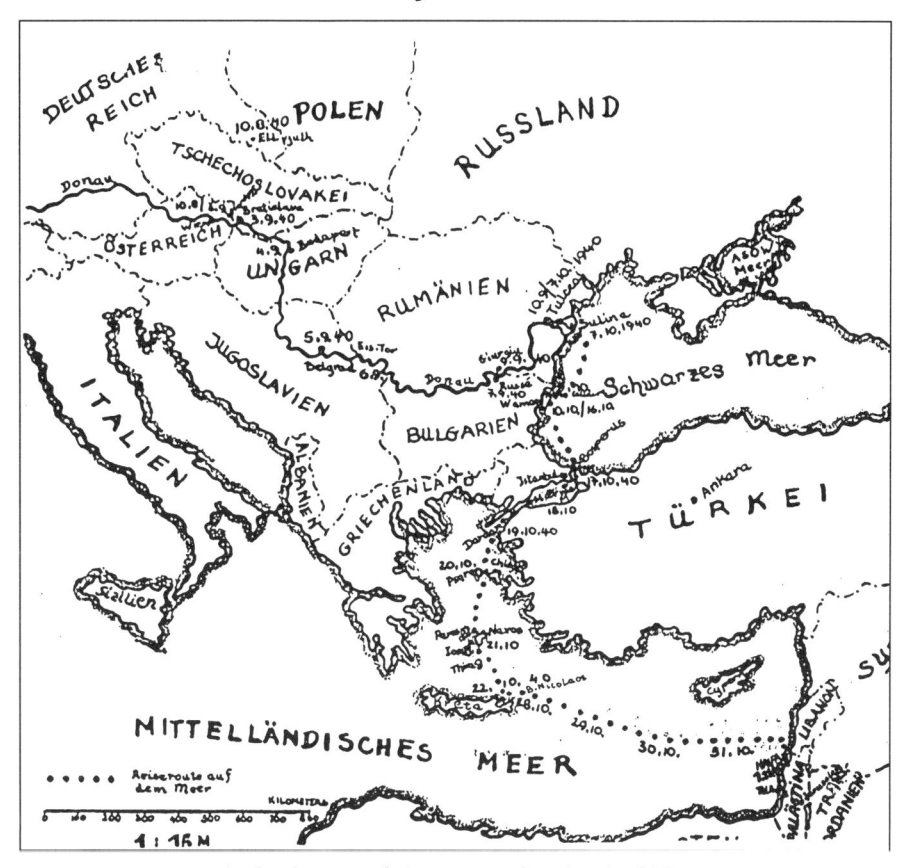

Author's map of the route taken by the SH-7

well they are informed! We are the first of the three ships to have reached our destination. We are happy and sing, planning where to go, which *kibbutz* to join once we disembark. Erich gives instructions to distribute the greater part of the provisions among all passengers. Everyone gets a large piece of sausage, rusks and bread. Even fat rations are distributed, and one can eat one's fill again. Nothing else is happening. The English leave the ship but leave guards on board. Again a boat approaches us at 1pm. This time it is the harbour doctor. He wants to assure himself that there is no epidemic on board. It's no use. The yellow flag stays on the mast!

Now a pilot joins the police on board and the anchor is let down once more. This is where we are to stay. The captain and the crew are taken away by the English police, placed under arrest and taken to a prison in Akko. Charged with aiding illegal immigrants, they are released six months later. We wave to the captain and crew as they leave. They are lucky to step on land already, but what will happen to us? Are we also to be taken to Akko or interned in Athlit, a camp we heard about – who knows? The English have brought with them two Arab policemen to guard us. We talk to them whenever the English don't look. All are polite to us but the English are cold and keep aloof. Opposite us is Akko. One of the Arabs comes from there. When we ask him what he thinks is going to happen to us, he replies that he does not know. For the first time we are in quarantine. The conversation with the Arab is in broken English. We hope that the *Yishuw* are aware of our arrival. We also hope that they will take care of us. We are getting our belongings in order and Papa Schuster takes stock of our provisions. "I cannot distribute everything you good people, we are not on land yet, but whoever is hungry can by all means come and see me. There is enough good salami." Yes, it was good to know that he played safe with our supplies. And this business involving lemons lies in the past. That happened in Tulcea. This was the 1 of November 1940. Arrival in Palestine – a date we shall always remember even if we are not permitted to set foot here.

2 November 1940. Last night it rained. Shortage of space required us to sit on the iron steps to catch some sleep. Waking early we are eager to witness what is going on, and what is going to happen to us. A small tug with dock labourers, mostly Arabs, leaves the harbour to bring us drinking water, crates of oranges and freshly baked bread. We are not allowed to talk to them. The English keep watch. There were no Jews among the dockers. The English do not allow any workers from the *Yischuw* to come to us. The *Pacific* is anchored in such a way that we have a full view of Haifa, and yet so distant that we can hardly observe life on land. People that far away look like match sticks. We can see streets that lead to Mount Carmel but can hardly identify anything else. Houses appear small with windows the size of tiny points. This was our first impression of Haifa.

3 November 1940. The English return with tugs. They bring plenty of water, oranges and bread. One of the Arabs thinks that soon we will disembark. Papa Schuster distributes tins of oil sardines. We can hardly be better off. But the sardines now make us need the latrines, the few that are left most having been burnt days ago. Getting there was awful. Some of us did not make it all the way. There is so little space on the *Pacific* causing much overcrowding. Medical inspectors came and left, and still we are not allowed to leave the ship!!

Just look – far out there a small ship rocked by the waves is approaching! We recognise the *Milos* ...

It is getting dark. John Bull, as I call the English, has work on hand. This time they approach the ship, and the pilot guides it 100 metres close to us. We call and wave, but the *hawerim* on the *Milos* have no news about the *Atlantic*.

4 November 1940. All day we wait for a decision from the English ... It is getting unpleasant on the *Pacific*. There is so little room, since almost all of the wooden plank beds are no longer there. We take it in turn to sleep on deck, on the floor, in corridors and bunkers. Since the captain is no longer there, we have taken over his cabin ...

5 November 1940. All night heavy rain. Fast asleep on deck, a sudden cloud burst hits us. Within seconds we were completely drenched with all our blankets. We fled the deck down to the stinking bunkers – where else to go? We had to jump over people sitting or sleeping. When only can we leave the ship? Who is negotiating with the English? I have a feeling that our organisers have no intention to represent us. Only Dr. Friedenthal draws the attention of the English authorities to the catastrophic conditions here on board. He tells them that he will no longer assume responsibility for the health of his passengers. But the English can see for themselves under what conditions we live here on the *Pacific*. We are waiting for a decision from the highest authorities. There is talk that the first passengers, 300 women, will leave the *Pacific*.

6 November 1940. Today the first women are disembarking. We are excited. They are supposed to be taken to a large troopship where there is ample room. Over there in the harbour is a large French boat, it is said that it is called the *Patria*. For us another 14 days in quarantine. Again we help, dragging the luggage of our women from the bunker to the tugs which will bring them to the 'luxury' *Patria*. With the tugs steaming to and fro all the women and their children were transferred by the afternoon. At long last we ourselves have enough room now for a good night's sleep.

7 November 1940. Papa Schuster distributes the last provisions among us. There is a great deal of confusion on the *Patria* Paul Jentes now also disbands the groups responsible for order. Now it is up to the English to assume responsibility for keeping order. Ha We is telling me that this is in order to put pressure on the English. The greater the confusion, the better. The English will only be too glad to get rid of us, hence we will have a better chance at last to get ashore. Today it is the turn of our *haweroth* from the youth groups to be taken to the *Patria*. No women are left on the *Pacific* now. At midday it is the older *hawerim*'s turn, and there is a good chance we too will leave the *Pacific* tomorrow.

8 November 1940. It is Friday and quite early the tugs return. There is no breakfast anymore, but we all have enough bread, sardines and sausage for everyone to have his fill. We are so excited, we don't feel like eating. At long last it is our turn. As usual we are the last. We pass our rucksacks and luggage to the dockers and jump into the tugs, and making a wide birth we sail through the harbour entrance towards the large ship. It is the *Patria* moored to the breakwater wall. Ladders on the side of the *Patria* enable us to board the ship. We have to go through customs control. We have no passports. The contents of our rucksacks and luggage are subject to search. – What are they looking for? We are then shown the way to a large and spacious bunker. The smell tells us that horses were the previous occupants. The bunker was clean. Plank beds had been set up not three above each other as on the *Pacific* but just at floor level. Now there was room for everyone. Lighting was adequate with everyone finding his own place to sleep. We made our own beds. … Everything was more spacious now than we ever expected. However, since we were no longer organised in groups, there was now a great deal of confusion, especially when meals were given out. We queued twice or three times which annoyed the English and the cooks. The food was good and ample.

9 November 1940. On board many English soldiers are guarding us. With their rifles they walk up and down making themselves look important. We avoid them and talk to them only a little. They think they are guarding black natives from the jungle. We are not natives, and some of us have a better command of the English language than they have, not to mention the academics who are with us. We are writing letters to our relatives in Palestine and look for ways of posting them. Ulla approaches us beaming and tells us that the fair-haired policewoman is not English, but her cousin from Haifa; she has already spoken to her – this is our first contact with land. Today doctors from the health commission are going to vaccinate us against smallpox and tetanus.

11 November 1940. The English police have our transport lists. German-speaking C.I.D. officials interrogate the *hawerim* individually. Questionnaires are filled in with all our personal details... After our fingerprints are taken we sign the document. Anyone who wished to provide information about German military camps or airstrips could do so ... but most *hawerim* kept silent. We have left all relatives behind us in Germany. Why should we endanger them? ...

13 November 1940. Last night two of our *hawerim* jumped into the water and swam to land. They were caught by the English and were taken to prison in Akko, so we were told. At least they have landed!!
   The confusion we cause is so great today that the cooks refused to issue any more food. Erich and Ha We and other organisers show understanding, and resume responsibility for maintaining order. The English and their guards can breathe again. Meals are punctually given out and we queue up only once.

14 November 1940. There is a variety show this afternoon on the *Patria*. We did not know we had so many talented people. ... We are slowly beginning to "feel at home" on the *Patria*, but rumours persist that we are going to be deported and spoil our pleasure. Why deport us? We are not enemies of England, not spies. We fled from the Nazis, why are we not allowed ashore?

15 and 16 November 1940. We can hardly believe it, and don't want to. But all denials are useless. The *Haganah* in Haifa has been in touch with our transport organisers. They have our passenger lists. They smuggled newspapers to us. Slowly the truth emerges that there is no chance for us to step ashore on the land of our fathers. Did we make this dangerous journey for no avail??? ... In the evening during darkness two of our *hawerim* from the youth group jump overboard. It seems they have reached land for the following day nothing is said, or do the English just keep silent?? Today is the 16 November – a Saturday. ... Ha We calls us to hold a general protest meeting on deck for 8.30pm. Although we are not permitted by the English to be on deck after 7pm, we all assemble there all the same to protest in unison with Hebrew songs calling loudly "*Hawerim, hawerim* help us. We don't want to be taken to Australia." We shout and roar again and again. Perhaps someone will hear us. The English were surprised by our demonstration watching us from the gangways above, which they had occupied. But what else could they do against so many people – protest? We only assumed the English wanted to shove us off to Australia, we were not sure.

17 November 1940. After our demonstration two more *hawerim* jumped overboard and swam to the shore. Hopefully they made it this time. The English have their Sunday today, and none of them can be seen apart from a few soldiers making their rounds. Sometimes we talk to them. What are they to do? Their orders are to guard us. They would rather have a beer …

18 November 1940. Tugs with coal come along in the early hours of the day. The English seem to be in a hurry. Ha We and two *hawerim* of the Paderborn group come to our sleeping bunker. They unscrew the screws of a large air shaft near our sleeping place. They climb down, but we pretend not to have seen anything.

19 and 20 November 1940. Life goes on as before on the *Patria*, but there is something in the air!? Some *hawerim* become rebellious picking quarrels with the English who hit out with their truncheons. There are lots of complaints. We get medical certificates to prove that we were beaten. A religious service and prayers today on 20 November followed by a 24-hour hunger strike starts at noon. On land at 12 o'clock a general strike starts in *Yishuw*. … We now know that the *Yishuw* have the lists with our names, and that our *hawerim* try everything to obtain permission for us to land. No more coal is coming.

21 November 1940. Our transport organisers have copies of the *Palestine Post* which has reports by the British government about the refugees on the *Patria*. After a joint meeting attended by the organisers of the *Patria* and *Milos*, a translation of the article from the *Palestine Post* is made available together with a counter statement. I copy these carefully as well as the signatures of the three transport leaders: Hans Rabl, Erich Frank and Kronenberger. At 9 o'clock Ha We calls us together. This time while we sing our groups walk to the bread oven. Our task is to cordon off the oven, so that Ha We and Ziwa, a nice looking *Hawerah* from the Bielefeld group, have time to talk to a Jewish docker who is to repair the oven. Ha We and Ziwa pretend to be in love with each other. They also share oranges with the docker. We are still singing and suddenly Ziwa takes a small bag hanging beside the door leading to the oven and walks quickly towards her cabin. We carry on singing. Ha We has not given us the signal that the undertaking has been completed. A few minutes later Ziwa comes back with the empty bag which she returns to the same place where she found it. We don't ask questions, we have seen nothing. … We are duty-bound to keep silent, and that we do!

TO THE *MAAPILIM* ON THE STEAMBOAT *PATRIA*!

We have received information about the official publication which appeared in the *Palestine Post* dated 21.11.1940 which was also broadcast on the radio. The announcement goes as follows: Earlier this month two steamers with altogether 1771 Jewish passengers on board were intercepted by a police patrol boat on the Palestine coast and taken into the harbour of Haifa. There can be no doubt that these persons were illegal immigrants, that is people who intend to enter Palestine breaking well known laws in doing so. His Majesty's Government has sympathies for refugees from

German-controlled areas, but H.M. Government is responsible for the administration of Palestine, and must ensure that the laws of the land are not broken with impunity. Furthermore, it must be considered as undesirable if Jewish illegal immigrants are again admitted taking account of the current local situation as this would bring about a threat to English interests in the Middle East. H.M. Government has therefore decided that the passengers of the *Pacific* and *Milos* are not to be given permission to land, but to be deported to a British colony as soon as they can be safely transported there and the necessary building preparations can be made. They will be held there until the end of the war. Their final destiny will be subject to discussion at the end of the war, but it is not suggested that they should settle in the colony they are being sent to now, nor should they be allowed to come to Palestine. Similar steps will apply to ships in future with passengers on board intending to enter Palestine illegally.

The following remarks are in reply to the above announcements:
1) Our transport boats, the *Pacific* and *Milos*, have not been "intercepted" by police boats, but sailed of their own free will into the bay of Haifa. Their intention was to place themselves under the protection of the Palestine Government and the Jewish *Yishuw* of Erez Israel.
2) We are refugees driven from our homes and were unable to land anywhere without breaking immigration laws. In addition to existing laws, people everywhere were opposed to our immigration, except for the Jewish population of our national home who receive us with open arms. This is one of the many reasons we have come to Palestine.
3) We have not been given an adequate opportunity to explain how our transports were put together, and reasons why the apprehension that illegal Jewish immigration may be resumed is unwarranted.
4) We state that there is no enemy of England amongst us, even less so enemies of Palestine. We are friends of England and are here as enemies of Germany. Thus we do not understand how our arrival can be construed to be a threat to English interests in the Middle East.
5) 80% of our *maapilim* have close relatives in Palestine, but no relatives in a British colony. Many hundreds of us have prepared ourselves for years to start a new life in Erez Israel, not in a British colony. In the name of many hundreds of selected *hawerim*, we say that a greater hardship is imposed on Jews deported from Erez Israel than being expelled from Germany, a country from which we are estranged.
6) We put our faith in the efforts of our brothers in Israel, England and the USA to succeed in lifting the terrible *Geserah* that H.M. Government has placed over us.

Kronenberger, Erich Frank, Hans Rabl.
On board the *Patria* 21.11.1940.

22 November 1940. The weather is fine. No signs that we are to be deported today. We are not giving up hope. Ha We says that all is lost. He calls upon several young *Aliyah hawerim* to jump overboard this evening. There is a reason, for the English do not send those under 18 to prison in Akko if they are caught. With great ado in the

evening while it is dark they jump into the water one after the other and try to reach land. All of them are caught and are put behind bars on board the ship.

23 November 1940. The English announce a collective punishment. As far as they are concerned too many last night jumped overboard. We must not leave our bunkers after 5 o'clock in the afternoon! This time they even count us again and again. They suspect that some passengers have reached land after all. We keep silent. Again we get rebellious, and John Bull makes use of batons and we make numerous complaints. We are no longer silent but growing more challenging towards the English police, singling out a rather stout one. But they soon withdraw to the promenade deck and let us shout below deck. Only armed soldiers keep guard on deck.

24 November 1940. There is tension in the air. There is something going on. No English officer is to be seen. We are queuing up for our meal. The French cooks are all right. After all they cannot help us. They don't know much about the immigration policy of the English. The crew of the *Patria* is nice to our children. We have nothing against them. We are waiting and waiting. It is grim to have to wait, not knowing for what. … Late afternoon the *Atlantic* enters the bay of Haifa. Tugs bring timber to the *Patria*. The English make preparations to transfer the refugees from the *Atlantic* to the *Patria*. This time we offer no opposition, nor do we help. Early tomorrow the transfer of the *Atlantic* passengers will begin. With 4000 people on the *Patria* there will be even less room for all of us!!

25 November 1940. Day 107 on board the *SH-7*
The transport organisers have ordered a protest demonstration to take place at 9 o'clock on the main deck. Those in charge of discipline are responsible for everyone to be on deck. There are to be no shirkers. All must be on deck!! Of all people I have to have a temperature, and I cannot join in the protest. Our bunker is almost empty and I am lying on my plank bed. Just before 9 o'clock Ha We and Moritz, a member of the Paderborner group, enter the bunker and see me lying on my bed. "Are you still not on deck?" I say I have a temperature, but that is not accepted. Temperature or not I was ordered to be on deck and I get dressed hurriedly. Moritz, opens the air shaft again, and mocks me saying I am rather spoilt with a temperature today of all days.

 I quickly join the other *hawerim* on deck. Adi tells me that when Heini raises his hand at 9 o'clock as many *hawerim* as possible will jump overboard with a lot of commotion. This time more than fifty *hawerim* jump into the water in order to distract and obstruct the soldiers. This could have a good outcome despite my fever. Should I also jump? I am undecided. In any case, I have left my dollars downstairs. They are not to get wet. Now we are all on deck and start singing! At exactly 9 o'clock Heini raises his hand. We shout "Go!" And over twenty *hawerim* and *Haweroth* climb over the railing and jump 10 metres down into the water making as much noise as possible followed by another group close behind – then the sound of a terrible explosion is heard. The whole ship shudders, and slowly, very slowly the ship begins to turn on its side. More and more *hawerim* jump over the railing into the water. A soldier next to me with his rifle wants to stop me jumping. In the turmoil I shout at him in English: "Throw your rifle away, we are sinking. There is a hole in the ship." As soon as he heard me, he threw his rifle away in a panic and jumped over the railing into the water. Those of us *hawerim* still on deck kept calm, but from below we could hear the piercing screams of women and children who feared that an air attack had taken place.

The ship was keeling over to one side by 10 degrees. I was running towards the swing doors leading to the cabins and bunkers searching for Margot and Ruth. Just as I want to go through the door, Ha We comes from the other side. I asked him about Margot and Ruth, and he replied that he had seen them on the right side of the deck, and that he was about to check quickly to see that nobody was left in the bunkers. Those were his last words before he disappeared through the swing doors forever. Now it was perhaps five past 9. The ship listed so heavily already that running and maintaining balance was no longer possible. I wanted to reach the deck and came across some *hawerim* who were still quickly trying to recover their luggage. They were running down to the bunker but never came up again...

I was again on deck. Large chunks of beams and planks were sliding into the water. The *Patria* tilted more and more on her side. Glass and porcelain began to break. The kitchen must have been below me. *Hawerim* still kept jumping into the water from the sloping deck. From below the panic-like screaming increased. I was afraid that the ship's boilers would explode, and with the railing only two metres from the water I decided to jump. Many *Hawerim* were swimming in the water, and I saw very many of them drowning before my own eyes. All ships in the harbour sounded their sirens to raise the alarm. Barges, life boats and cutters raced towards us to save what could still be saved. The boats first picked up those who could not swim. Heini's little son who could swim was caught in the propeller of a tug and drowned. I was already close to the quay wall when I was picked up by a cutter which returned to the *Patria* to save more passengers. A horrible sight unfolded before us. Everywhere shipwrecked people in the water calling for help. On the ship itself one could see *Hawerim* climbing towards the right side to save themselves. When the tug was full with those it could save it returned to the quay wall whence we were taken to large warehouses. These the dockers had quickly made ready to receive us. We undressed to dry out and were not ashamed to do so. Women were on one side, we on the other. It was shortly after 10 o'clock. From everywhere those who were saved were bought into the hall, and I looked for Ruth and Margot. But no one had seen them. In the meantime it turned 11 o'clock. Women came from Haifa *Yishuw* bringing us clothing and blankets which had been collected in a hurry. They returned with large tea urns and distributed sweet milk tea and biscuits. I saw Paul Isai at the entrance of the warehouse we were in. He was quite dry and behaved as if he did not belong to us. He calls to me "Hans come with me! I know somebody who will get us out of the harbour." I did not want to because I wanted to wait for Margot and Ruth. Paul disappeared round the corner. It is now 12 o'clock. – Margot walks through the warehouse door. She is quite dry. I was pleased and immediately asked her for Ruth. It was then she told me that she and Ruth saved themselves as the *Patria* was tilting on her side by rushing to the right passage gang of the upper deck. As the water came ever closer to the deck Ruth called upon Margot to jump together with her into the water. But Margot said that she could not swim and refused to jump. Ruth urged her several times to jump, but all entreaties were in vain. Then Ruth jumped into the water by herself. Margot could still see a large ship plank hitting Ruth's head. Ruth went under and did not come up...

As the ship was almost completely lying on its left side Margot climbed on to the curved end of a large air shaft lying about one metre above the water, waiting for a lifeboat to collect her. She also told me that there were still many saved passengers on the breakwater. She saw that dockers were breaking open the upper walls of cabins with large welding torches in order to save the trapped refugees who were unable to save themselves through the small window hatches.

The army and police closed the harbour gates and occupied the whole harbour area to prevent further escapes by the *Maapilim*. Ambulances collected the wounded and took them to hospitals. Many suffered from shock. In the harbour itself there was great turmoil, and all the time more and more of those rescued were landed. The warehouses and halls were filling up. Among the saved were the first passengers the English had just transferred from the *Atlantic*. Now we are all shipwrecked. We have left all our belongings on the *Patria*. Everything has gone down with her. All we have saved is what we have on us. My small diary had remained almost dry is in my trouser pocket. Just the cover is wet, and the saltwater has made some blemishes on several pages.

The memory of the 107 days on our *Aliyah* will stay with me. Only in the evening buses came to take us to the internment camp Athlit. There we get blankets and a warm meal. We are directed to the barracks, and everyone is given a bed. After a few days we hear the following announcement:-

H.M. GOVERNMENT PARDONS US – WE ARE ALLOWED TO STAY!

Epilogue:
Today, after 40 years, I am copying this diary and add what at the time of the English I was unable or permitted to write.

Today we are the "survivors" of the *Patria* – Israelis living in a free country. We have helped to build and create this country. We have weathered and left behind us hard times. But our children and grandchildren are growing up in freedom, the very freedom we so much longed for.

POSTSCRIPT AND OBSERVATIONS.

1) The sinking (capsizing to one side) of the *Patria* took about 10 minutes. Panic broke out on deck as well as below deck. Many drowned for they would not follow the order for all to be on deck at 9 o'clock, and thus could not get out of their cabins in time. Those refugees whose cabins were on the left side of the *Patria* were the ones who suffered most. Over 250 *Haweroth* and *hawerim*, younger and older ones, drowned within minutes. Families were torn apart. The incident resulted in great tragedy.
2) The fate of the *Maapilim* on the *Atlantic* and *Patria*.
   We, the shipwrecked of the *Patria*, were taken to the prison camp Athlit in the evening of the 25 November and interned there. The refugees from the *Atlantic*

were also taken there on the 5 December 1940, but brought to a special part of the camp which a few days earlier had been surrounded by a double fence of barbed wire. We were not allowed to go over to them. Both inside and outside the camp armed English soldiers were on guard. Machine guns were placed in position directed towards our barracks. In the evenings we were not allowed to leave them – not even to go to the toilets! On the 6 December 1940 those refugees who on the 25 November had jumped overboard into the water joined us in the camp. Before that they were held in the prisons of Haifa and Akko.

During the night of the 8 to the 9 December 1940 terrible screams were heard coming from the barracks that housed the refugees of the *Atlantic*. The English brutally forced them to leave the barracks to be brought to Haifa and then put on transport ships to be deported to Mauritius. Our barracks were temporarily barricaded by the English, and guards kept watch so that nobody could leave them. This was one of the cruellest actions taken by the English which we were ever to witness. – We shall never forget it. On the 27 December 1940 we were able to identify the engagement ring of Ruth Effenberger – now it is certain that Ruth is no longer alive. Ruth is the only *Hawerah* of our group whom we have to mourn. – She was always so lively and she wanted to go to the *kibbutz* with all of us.

From 14 July 1941 onwards the English camp administration started to release the first women and children. Daily groups of 10 to 40 *Hawerim* were released from Athlit and taken to their prepared destinations on buses organised by the *Sochnuth*. – By the end of 1941 all the *Maapilim* had been released from Athlit!

3) On the 25 November 1980 a great many people took part in a ceremony to commemorate the fortieth anniversary of the sinking of the *Patria*. Hundreds of those who were rescued with their relatives met at the graves of all those who lost their lives and were thus not able to come to the land they had hoped to enter. Later we all gathered in the community hall to listen to several speakers, among them the *hawer* from the *Haganah* who smuggled the bomb on the *Patria*.

Muniah was from the *Haganah* in Haifa. When the representatives of the *Yishuw* came to the conclusion that, despite several petitions to H.M. Government, the *Maapilim* on the *Patria* would be deported to a British colony in a few days, the *Haganah* was charged with delaying by all means possible the departure of the *Patria* in order to gain more time for further negotiations!

Muniah continued to explain that the plan was to attach a small mine held in a small container to the side of the *Patria*. The resulting hole caused by the explosion would delay the departure of the *Patria*. This plan had to be abandoned. The swimmers could not be fitted adequately to approach the ship submerged without being noticed. The danger of being discovered by the English was too great.

A second plan was to attach a grenade onto the ship's propeller which was to explode as the propeller turned. That plan also was abandoned. After detailed deliberations at the headquarters of the *Haganah*, Muniah was authorised to smuggle a small mine on board and to get in touch with the *Haganah* on board the *Patria*. For this purpose Muniah was assigned part of a construction group to repair the bread oven of the *Patria*. He described how on the 21 November 1940 he had hidden a small mine in his bread bag so cleverly that neither the Arab nor the English policemen at the harbour gate thought it necessary to examine his bag thoroughly. Muniah had smeared a fried egg on the mine itself and put it in bread on which he placed his coffee flask. That is how he reached the harbour without being stopped.

His second problem was how to smuggle the mine on board. The bag containing the mine was hidden in a sand bag and so was surrounded by sand on all sides. Together with building material: building stones, cement, sand bags, the bag with the mine was brought on board. They had to pass the English secret agents who "examined" all the sacks with steel spikes. As luck would have it they did not hit the mine otherwise we would all have been blown up, and the ship would not have been further damaged. Under the watchful eyes of the English, Muniah still managed to take the mine to the oven. From then on there was no problem for the *Haganah* on board to get hold of it. The mine was to explode the same day but the ignition was faulty. Ha We informed Muniah who was still working at the oven. In the evening Muniah made his report to his superiors, and after consulting with the engineers of the *Haganah* a new fuse was prepared. The next day the fuse was smuggled on board again hidden with building material passing the secret police. On the 25 November at 9 o'clock, Moritz attached the mine below our sleeping quarters on the left side wall of the *Patria* having first set the fuse.

The *Haganah* had calculated that the mine would only blow a small hole in the side of the *Patria* so that she would have to be repaired first before being able to depart. This would then enable the representatives of the *Yishuw* to continue negotiations. After the unexpected consequence of the explosion resulting in the death of over 250 people, the *Haganah* set up an investigation that came to the following conclusion:

The *Patria*'s superstructure looked to have been well maintained. Her outer walls below water were decayed and completely corroded. The reason was the ship's owners criminal neglect, refusing to assume responsibility for the ship's maintenance. The force of the explosion tore out a whole wall weakened by rusty rivets creating a six square metre hole through which vast quantities of water flooded the *Patria*. It was irresponsible on the part of the English to build bunkers intended for taking on refugees in such a bad way that they could not be hermetically sealed in the event of flooding. That is why it was possible for the *Patria* to tilt on one side and sink within a few minutes. It was lucky, despite the catastrophe that the width of the *Patria* was greater than the depth of the harbour. That is why hundreds of non swimmers were saved by being on the right side of the *Patria* which rose above the water.

A special mention is due to an unknown marine officer who forced his way to reach the boilers of the ship, and by opening the valves prevented the boilers from exploding. He paid with his life for his courageous deed.

Publications on German-speaking Jewry

A Selected and Annotated Bibliography of Books and Articles 2000

Compiled by

BARBARA SUCHY and ANNETTE PRINGLE

The Bibliography is supported by grants from:

Friends of Bat Hanadiv Foundation
Sheldon and Suzanne Nash Fund
The Rayne Trust
Robert Bosch Stiftung
The Ruben and Elisabeth Rausing Trust

Leo Baeck Institute
4 Devonshire Street
London W1N 2BH

CONTENTS

		Page
I.	HISTORY	
	A. General	335
	Linguistics/Western Yiddish	340
	B. Communal and Regional History	
	1. Germany	341
	1a. Alsace	353
	2. Austria	353
	3. Central Europe	354
	4. Switzerland	356
	C. German-Speaking Jews in Various Countries	357
II.	RESEARCH and BIBLIOGRAPHY	
	A. Libraries and Institutes	359
	B. Bibliographies, Catalogues and Reference Books	361
III.	THE NAZI PERIOD	
	A. General	362
	B. Jewish Resistance	390
IV.	POST-1945	
	A. General	390
	B. Education and Teaching. Memorials and Remembrance	395
V.	JUDAISM	
	A. Jewish Learning and Scholars	397
	B. Perception and Identity	401
	C. Jewish Life and Organisations. Genealogy	403
	D. Jewish Art and Music	405
VI.	ZIONISM and ISRAEL	405
VII.	PARTICIPATION in CULTURAL and PUBLIC LIFE	
	A. General	408
	B. Individual	412
VIII.	AUTOBIOGRAPHY, MEMOIRS, LETTERS	426
IX.	GERMAN-JEWISH RELATIONS	
	A. General	429
	B. German-Israeli Relations	431
	C. Church and Synagogue	432
	D. Antisemitism	432
	E. Noted Germans and Jews	436
X.	FICTION and POETRY	438
	INDEX	441

BIBLIOGRAPHY 2000

Includes books and articles published in 2000 as well as supplementary books and articles published in 1998 and 1999 and not yet listed in the previous bibliographies.

Owing to the wealth of studies on the history of German-speaking Jewry and antisemitism which appeared in 2000, Section VII (Participation in Cultural and Public Life) and Section IV B (Post-1945/Education and Teaching. Memorials) had to be curtailed.

Preference has been given to entering as many publications as possible and, to this end, review essays have been cut somewhat. All titles are fully indexed: names, places, periodicals, titles (in some cases), subjects.

Communal and regional histories are listed either in Section I B (Communal and Regional History), or in Section III (The Nazi Period), depending on their main focus.

Autobiographies and memoirs are listed either in section III (The Nazi Period), or in Section VIII (Autobiography, Memoirs, Letters), again depending on their main focus.

(B.S.)

I. HISTORY

A. General

38410. ARENDT, HANNAH: *Die verborgene Tradition.* Essays. Frankfurt am Main: Jüdischer Verlag, 2000. 184 pp. [First publ. 1975; cont. 11 essays orig. written in the 1940s in the US in German, one in English. On general aspects of Jewish history, enlightenment, "Jewish question", Zionism; also on Heine and Kafka.] [See also No. 12974/YB XXI and No. 38704.]

38411. ASCHHEIM, STEVEN E.: *Brothers and strangers: the East European Jew in German and German Jewish consciousness, 1800–1923.* Madison: The Univ. of Wisconsin Press, 1999. XXXI, 331 pp., bibl., illus., notes, index. [For orig. edn. in 1982 and details see No. 19204/YB XXVIII.]

38412. BERGHAHN, KLAUS L.: *Grenzen der Toleranz. Juden und Christen im Zeitalter der Aufklärung.* Köln: Böhlau, 2000. VIII, 304 pp., footnotes, bibl. [Incl. 11 chaps.: Christlicher Judenhaß im Zeitalter der Toleranz. Eisenmengers 'Entdecktes Judentum' (12–21). Jüdischer Alltag unter den Deutschen. Die Judenedikte des 18. Jahrhunderts (23–45). Aufklärung und Judentum: das Zeitalter der Toleranz (46–68). Der Casus des "edlen Juden" als Muster der Vorurteilskritik. Lessings 'Die Juden' (69–82). Der Freundschaftskult des 18. Jahrhunderts und die Anfänge eines christlich-jüdischen Dialogs (83–101). Von Shylocks Tragödie zu Nathans Märchen (102–126). Eine Denkschrift für aufgeklärte Monarchen. Christian Wilhelm Dohms 'Über die bürgerliche Verbesserung der Juden'(127–149). Von der Last in zwei Welten zu leben. Moses Mendelssohns 'Jerusalem' (150–182). Hebräer oder Juden (183–231; deals with Goethe, Herder, Kant, Fichte, Saul Ascher). Gesellige Assimilation. Die jüdischen Salons in Berlin 1780–1806 (232–262). Wiederkehr des Verdrängten. Die Entstehung des modernen Antisemitismus zur Zeit der Emanzipation (263–294).]

38413. BLÖMER, URSULA/GARZ, DETLEF, eds.: *"Wir Kinder hatten ein herrliches Leben ...": Jüdische Kindheit und Jugend im Kaiserreich 1871–1918.* Oldenburg: BIS-Verlag, 2000. 321 pp., illus., footnotes, gloss., index, bibl. [Cont.: Vorwort: Schatten auf der Kindheit bei den deutschen Juden (Friedrich Wißmann, 7–18). Historical introductions dealing with Imperial Germany, Weimar Republic, antisemitism, militarism and schools by Ursula Blömer, Detlef Garz, Esther Schwarz, Andrea Djuren,

Nicole Hummel and Ilse Heinke. 27 childhood memoirs taken from the 260 autobiographies collected 1939–1940 by Gordon Willard Allport (et al.) at Harvard University, written by German-Jewish émigré participants in a competition; incl. also short biographies of the memoir writers.]

38414. BRENNER, MICHAEL: *Jüdische Kultur in der Weimarer Republik.* Aus dem Engl. übers. von Holger Fliessbach. München: Beck, 2000. 316 pp., notes (240–276), bibl. 277–298), index. [Orig. American edn. publ. in 1996 with the title 'The renaissance of Jewish culture in Weimar Germany', for details see No. 33638/YB XLII.]

38415. BRENNER, MICHAEL: *Wie jüdisch waren Deutschlands Juden? Die Renaissance jüdischer Kultur während der Weimarer Republik.* Vortrag im Gesprächskreis Geschichte der Friedrich-Ebert-Stiftung aus Anlass des 85. Geburtstages von Frau Prof. Dr. Susanne Miller in Bonn am 18. Mai 2000. [Hrsg. von Dieter Dowe]. Bonn: Historisches Forschungszentrum, 2000. 47 pp., illus. (Reihe Gesprächskreis Geschichte, H. 32.)

38416. BRÜLLS, HOLGER: *Kulturelle und nationale Identität deutscher Juden und der Stil gründerzeitlicher Synagogenarchitektur.* [In]: Mitteldeutsches Jahrbuch für Kultur und Geschichte, Bd. 7, Köln, 2000. Pp. 137–153, notes, illus. [See also No. 38562.]

38417. CAPLAN, GREG: *Militärische Männlichkeit in der deutsch-jüdischen Geschichte.* [In]: Die Philosophin. Forum für feministische Theorie und Philosophie, Bd. 22, Tübingen, 2000. Pp. 85–100, footnotes.

38418. CHASE, JEFFERSON S.: *Inciting laughter: the development of "Jewish humor" in 19th century German culture.* New York; Berlin: Walter de Gruyter, 2000. VIII, 330 pp., footnotes, bibl. (313–325), index. (European cultures, 12.) [Deals with the development of "Judenwitz" and its manifestation in literature. Incl. the writings of Ludwig Börne, Heinrich Heine, Moritz Gottlieb Saphir.]

38419. CRESTI, SILVIA: *Nation, Volk und Rasse. Zu einer jüdischen Auseinandersetzung in der Weimarer Republik.* [In]: Aschkenas, Jg. 10, H. 1, Wien, 2000. Pp. 366–364, footnotes. [On a debate in 'Neue jüdische Monatshefte', 'Der Morgen' and 'Der Jude' on race, integration and antisemitism.]

38420. *Die Landjudenschaften in Deutschland als Organe jüdischer Selbstverwaltung von der frühen Neuzeit bis ins neunzehnte Jahrhundert. Eine Quellensammlung.* Hrsg. von Daniel J. Cohen. Bd. 2. (Fontes ad res judaicas spectantes.) Jerusalem: Israelische Akademie der Wissenschaften; Göttingen: Akademie der Wissenschaften zu Göttingen. 1997. Pp. 733–1377. [Incl. the sections: II. Mittelrheinlande und Hessen. III. Franken. IV. Pfalz-Saarland. For vol. 1 see No. 34680/YB XLXXX.]

38421. ERLER, HANS/EHRLICH, ERNST LUDWIG, eds.: *Jüdisches Leben und jüdische Kultur in Deutschland. Geschichte, Zerstörung und schwieriger Neubeginn.* Frankfurt am Main, 2000, 267 pp., notes. [Incl.: Vorbemerkung (eds., 7–12). Judenrecht vom Codex Theodosianis bis zu den Anfängen der Emanzipation (Christine Magin, 13–43). Jüdische Kultur vor der Aufklärung (Carsten Wilke, 44–76). Deutschjudentum: Bildungskonzeptionen von Moses Mendelssohn bis Franz Rosenzweig (Daniel Krochmalnik, 77–99). Jüdisches Leben zwischen Aufklärung und Restauration (Stefi Jersch-Wenzel, 100–119). Judentum und Liberalismus in Deutschland: Ein Rückblick (George L. Mosse, 120–137). Judentum und Sozialdemokratie: Moses Hess – Karl Marx – Ferdinand Lassalle – Eduard Bernstein (Hans Erler, 138–173). Die Kultur der osteuropäischen Juden im Deutschland der Weimarer Republik (Ludger Heid, 174–201). Further contribs. are listed according to subject.]

38422. *Fighting for the fatherland: the patriotism of Jews in World War I.* An exhibition of the Leo Baeck Institute, New York. Catalogue essay by Jay Winter. New York: LBI New York, 1999. 14 pp., illus.

38423. *Forum Vormärz Forschung.* Jahrbuch 1998, Jg. 4 [with the title] *Juden und jüdische Kultur im Vormärz.* Red.: Horst Denkler, Norbert Otto Eke, Hartmut Steinecke. Bielefeld, 1999. 1 vol., footnotes. [Incl.: Zur Einführung (eds., 1–13). Die Aufklärung im jüdischen Denken des 19. Jahrhunderts: Rahel Levin Varnhagen, Ludwig Robert, Ludwig Börne, Eduard Gans, Berthold Auerbach, Fanny Lewald (Heidi Thomann Tewarson, 17–61). Jüdische Akkulturationsvorstellungen im Vormärz (Arno Herzig, 63–70; on Alexander Haindorf). "Annehmen oder Ablehnen …?" Der Jurist Heinrich Simon als Vorkämpfer des Rechtsstaats (Gabriele Schneider, 71–89; H.S., 1805 Königsberg – 1860 Berlin). "In diesem Hause immer fremd". Carl Spindlers historischer Roman

'Der Jude' (Wolfgang Beutin, 91–109; novel publ. 1753). Verwahrungen aufklärerischer Vernunft. Literatisch-publizistische Strategien in Börnes Schutzschriften für die Juden (Bernhard Budde, 111–140). Georg Weerths Juden-Bild (Uwe Zemke, 141–163). Zur Freundschaftskultur von Prager und Wiener Juden im Vormärz. Briefe aus dem Umfeld von Moritz Hartmann (Sigurd Paul Scheichl, 165–180). "Judenwitz" – zur Semantik eines Stereotyps in der Literaturkritik des Vormärz (Gunnar Och, 181–199). Fanny Lewald and Bismarck: forty-eighter turned monarchist? (Irene Stocksieker Di Maio (233–250).

——— GRAB, WALTER: *Zwei Seiten einer Medaille: Demokratische Revolution und Judenemanzipation.* [See No. 39434.]

38424. GRAETZ, MICHAEL, ed.: *Schöpferische Momente des europäischen Judentums in der frühen Neuzeit.* Heidelberg: Winter, 2000. XV, 364 pp., footnotes. [Incl.: Einleitung (ed., VII-XV). Zur Zäsur zwischen Mittelalter und Neuzeit in der jüdischen Geschichte (Michael Graetz, 1–18). Jewish Amsterdam's impact on modern Jewish history (Yosef Kaplan, 19–62). Creative ambiguities and Jewish modernity (Eleazar Gutwirth, 63–73). Kreativität und Traditionsgebundenheit (Mordechai Breuer, 113–120; on orthodoxy). Kontinuität und Wandel in der hebräischen Dichtung der frühen Neuzeit (Johann Maier, 139–160). A reconsideration of Jewish modernity (Gershon David Hundert, 321–332). Also essays on Italian and Polish developments. Further essays pertaining to German lands are listed according to subject.]

38425. GRÖZINGER, KARL E.: *Zahlen, die auf das Ende deuten. Jüdische Endzeithoffnungen als Spiegel der Generationen.* [In]: Menora, Bd. 11, Berlin, 2000. Pp. 209–227, notes.

38426. GRAETZ, HEINRICH: *Die Konstruktion der jüdischen Geschichte.* Hrsg. von Nils Römer. Düsseldorf: Parerga, 2000. 90 pp., footnotes. (Jüdische Geistesgeschichte, Bd. 2.) [Orig. publ. 1846; incl.: Nachwort (ed., 79–90).]

38427. HAGEN, WILLIAM W.: *Mord im Osten. Die polnischen und anderen osteuropäischen Pogrome von 1918–1919 im Verständnis der zeitgenössischen deutschen Juden.* [In]: Deutsche Umbrüche im 20. Jahrhundert. Hrsg. von Dietrich Papenfuß und Wolfgang Schieder. Köln: Böhlau, 2000. Pp. 135–146, footnotes.

38428. HANSLOCK, ANDREAS: *Die landesherrliche und kommunale Judenschutzpolitik während des späten Mittelalters im Heiligen Römischen Reich Deutscher Nation. Ein Vergleich der Entwicklungen am Beispiel schlesischer, brandenburgischer und rheinischer Städte.* Berlin: Wiss. Verl. Berlin Gaudig und Veit, 2000. 272 pp., footnotes, bibl. Zugl.: Potsdam, Univ., Diss., 1999. [Deals with Glogau, Stendal, Frankfurt an der Oder, Mainz, Speyer, Worms.]

38429. HEIL, JOHANNES: *"Boden der Vergangenheit"? Antiquierte Barbarei: Mittelalterliche Pogrome im neuzeitlichen Gedächtnis.* [In]: Aschkenas, Jg. 10, H. 1, Wien, 2000. Pp. 9–41, footnotes. [Examines how non-Jewish writers from the pre-enlightenment period til the mid-19th cent. dealt with medieval persecutions of Jews; also on Heine and Börne and some Jewish historians from early 19th cent.]

38430. HELLER, MARVIN H.: *Moses Benjamin Wulff – Court Jew (1661–1729).* [In]: European Judaism, vol. 33, No. 2, London, autumn 2000. Pp. 61–71, notes.

38431. HENZE, BARBARA: *Vor gut 650 Jahren: Der Mord an den Juden im Oberrheingebiet.* [In]: Freiburger Diözesan-Archiv, Bd. 120 (Dritte Folge, Zweiundfünfzigster Band), Freiburg, 2000. Pp. 109–121, footnotes. [On the pogroms 1348/49.]

38432. HÖDL, SABINE/LAPPIN, ELEONORE, eds.: *Erinnerung als Gegenwart: Jüdische Gedenkkulturen.* Berlin: Philo, 2000. 236 pp., illus., notes. [Incl. papers given at an international conference held in Vienna, July 1999; cont. (some titles abbr.): Vorwort (eds., 7–10). Sachor – Erinnern im jüdischen Denken durch die Jahrtausende (Albert H. Friedlander, 11–32). Name und Nachruf in Memorbüchern (Aubrey Pomerance, 33–54). Drei Wege jüdischer Geschichtsauffassung in der ersten Hälfte des 20. Jahrhunderts (Michael Brenner, 55–78; on Isaak Markus Jost, Heinrich Graetz, Simon Dubnow, Salo Baron, Jizchak (Fritz) Baer, Ben-Zion Dinur, Gershom Scholem). Gedanken zu Samuel Josef Agnons "Nur wie ein Gast zur Nacht" (Gershon Shaked, 79–88). Die Chiffre Sommerfrische als Erinnerungstopos (Albert Lichtblau, 89–128; based on memoirs by

Austrian Jews, also on antisemitism). Nieder here nor there. Memorial projects (Melissa Gould, 129–148). Die Wiener Jahrhundertwende und die Konstruktion jüdischer Identitäten in der Zweiten Republik (Matti Bunzl, 149–172). Bringschuld, Erbe und Besitz. Jüdische Museen nach 1945 (Cilly Kugelmann, 173–192). Der Wettbewerb um die Erinnerung an die Shoa: Institutionen, Ideologien und Interessen (Moshe Zimmermann, 193–210). Gedächtnisraum Graz, zeitgeschichtliche Erinnerungszeichen im öffentlichen Raum von 1945 bis zur Gegenwart (Heidemarie Uhl, 211–232).]

38433. HOFFMANN, STEFAN-LUDWIG: *Brothers or strangers? Jews and Freemasons in nineteenth-century Germany.* Transl. by Pamela Selwyn. [In]: German History, Vol. 18, No. 2, London, 2000. Pp. 143–161, footnotes. [Examines the attitudes and behaviour of German Freemasons towards Jews and their admission to the lodges.]

38434. JONAS, HANS: *Unsere Teilnahme an diesem Kriege. Ein Wort an Jüdische Männer.* [In]: Jüdischer Almanach 2001 des Leo Baeck Instituts, Frankfurt am Main, 2000. Pp. 79–91. [First publ. of manuscript, found in the LBI New York: H.J. calling on Jews to join the British Army in Palestine; also in this issue: "Ein 'bellum Judaicum' in des Wortes tiefster Bedeutung". Hans Jonas' Kriegsaufruf 1939 im Kontext seiner Biographie und seines philosophischen Denkens (Christian Wiese, 92–107).]

38435. *Illustrierte Geschichte des Judentums.* Hrsg. von Nicholas de Lange. Aus dem Engl. von Christian Rochow. Frankfurt am Main: Campus Verl., 2000, 462 pp., illus., bibl., indexes. [Orig. edn. publ. 1997; incl.: Auf dem Weg in die Moderne, David Sorkin (223–280). Die schwärzeste Stunde (Michael A. Marrus, 281–330; on antisemitism and the Nazi period).]

38436. KAMPMANN, CHRISTOPH: *Die Petition des Salomon Hirsch und die Würzburger "Hepp-Hepp"-Krawalle von 1819: Zur frühen Verwendung des Begriffs "Judenemanzipation" in der publizistischen Debatte.* [In]: Jahrbuch für Fränkische Landesforschung, Bd. 60, Neustadt (Aisch), 2000. (Festschrift Rudolf Endres. Zum 65. Geburtstag gewidmet von Kollegen, Freunden und Schülern, hrsg. von Charlotte Bühl und Peter Fleischmann.) Pp. 417–434, footnotes.

38437. KAUFMANN, URI R.: *Das Judentum. Neue "Staatskirche" und Produktivierungsinstrument in Südwestdeutschland 1809–1870.* [In]: Zwischen "Staatsanstalt" und Selbstbestimmung. Kirche und Staat in Südwestdeutschland vom Ausgang des Alten Reiches bis 1870. Hrsg. von Hans Ammerich und Johannes Gut. Stuttgart: Thorbecke, 2000. Pp. 295–329, footnotes.

38438. HERZIG, ARNO: *Max Kayser (1853–1888). Der erste jüdische Abgeordnete der deutschen Arbeiterbewegung.* [In]: Bert Becker/Horst Lademacher, eds.: Geist und Gestalt im historischen Wandel. Facetten deutscher und europäischer Geschichte 1789–1989. Festschrift für Siegfried Bahne. Münster, New York: Waxmann, 2000. Pp. 105–111, footnotes.

38439. LÄSSIG, SIMONE: *Sprachwandel und Verbürgerlichung. Zur Bedeutung der Sprache im innerjüdischen Modernisierungsprozeß des frühen 19. Jahrhunderts.* [In]: Historische Zeitschrift, Bd. 270. München, 2000. Pp. 617–667, footnotes.

38440. LOTTER, FRIEDRICH: *Zur Stellung der Juden im Frankenreich der Merowinger und Karolinger.* [In]: Aschkenas, Jg. 10, H. 2, Wien, 2000. Pp. 525–533, footnotes. [Review essay.]

38441. MEYER, MICHAEL A., ed.: *German-Jewish history in modern times.* New York: Leo Baeck Institute, 2000. 40 pp., illus., ports., facsims.

38442. MITTLEMAN, ALAN: *Continuity and change in the constitutional experience of the German Jews.* [In]: Publius, Vol. 30, No. 4, Philadelphia, Fall 2000. Pp. 43–70, notes. [Discusses the changes and modernisations in the constitutional development of German-Jewish communities after emancipation, seen in the context of general German constitutional law. Author tries to show that modern statutes implemented by Jewish communities were based both on German forms of administration and on traditional communal ordinances practised by Ashkenazi Jewry going back to the Middle Ages.]

38443. MOMMSEN, THEODOR: *"Auch ein Wort über unser Judentum" (1880).* [In]: Deutsche Geschichte in Quellen und Darstellung. Band 8. Kaiserreich und Erster Weltkrieg 1871–1918. Hrsg. von

Rüdiger vom Bruch und Björn Hofmeister. Stuttgart: Philipp Reclam jun., 2000 (Universal-Bibliothek Nr. 17008.). Pp. 193–196.

38444. NIEWYK, DONALD L.: *The Jews in Weimar Germany.* New Brunswick, NJ: Transaction Publishers, 2000. VIII, 229, bibl. [Orig. publ. in 1980, for details see No. 16918/YB XXVI.]

38445. ROEMER, NILS HOLGER: *The historicizing of Judaism in 19th-century Germany: scholarly discipline and popular historical culture.* New York: Columbia Univ., Diss. 2000. Typescript, 277 pp.

38446. RÜRUP, REINHARD: *Jewish history in Berlin – Berlin in Jewish history.* [In]: Leo Baeck Institute Year Book XLV, Oxford, 2000. Pp. 37–50, footnotes.

38447. SCHOCHAT, ASRIEL: *Der Ursprung der jüdischen Aufklärung in Deutschland.* Aus dem Hebräischen von Wolfgang Jeremias. Mit einem Vorwort von Michael Graetz. Frankfurt am Main/New York: Campus Verl., 2000. (Campus Judaica, Bd. 14.) 476 pp., footnotes, bibl., index. [Orig. edn. publ. 1960.] [Incl.: Vorwort. Von einer Ideen- zu einer Sozialgeschichte der jüdischen Aufklärung (Michael Graetz, 7–14).]

——— SCHULTE, CHRISTOPH: *Saul Ascher's Leviathan, or the invention of Jewish orthodoxy in 1792.* [See No. 39258.]

38448. SCHULIN, ERNST: *Nationalismus und jüdische Geschichtsschreibung in Deutschland.* [In]: Geschichtsdiskurs. Bd. 3: Die Epoche der Historisierung. Frankfurt am Main: Fischer Taschenbuch Verl., 2000. Pp. 198–217, notes.

38449. SCHULTE, CHRISTOPH: *Der Messias der Utopie. Elemente des Messianismus bei einigen modernen jüdischen Linksintellektuellen.* [In]: Menora, Bd. 11, Berlin, 2000. Pp. 251–278, notes.

38450. SIEG, ULRICH: *Jüdische Intellektuelle und die Krise der bürgerlichen Welt im Ersten Weltkrieg.* Stuttgart: Stiftung Bundespräsident-Theodor-Heuss-Haus, 2000. 31 pp., notes. (Kleine Reihe/Stiftung Bundespräsident-Theodor-Heuss-Haus, 7.)

38451. SORKIN, DAVID: *The transformation of German Jewry 1780–1840.* Detroit: Wayne State Univ. Press, 1999. XI, 255 pp., notes (131–173), gloss., index. [For 1987 edn. and details see No. 23906/YB XXXIII.]

38452. SORKIN, DAVID: *The Berlin Haskalah and German religious thought: orphans of knowledge.* London; Portland, OR: Vallentine Mitchell, 2000. X, 191 pp, bibl. essay (175–178). (Parkes-Wiener series on Jewish studies, 4.) [Cf.: Review (Ritchie Robertson) [in]: Journal of Jewish Studies, Vol. 51, No. 2, Cambridge, Autumn 2000, pp. 354–355.]

38453. *Synagogen in Deutschland.* Eine virtuelle Rekonstruktion. Bonn: Kunst- und Ausstellungshalle der Bundesrepublik Deutschland, 2000. 79 pp., illus., chronol., map, bibl. [Catalogue of exhibition, held in Bonn May 17 – July 16, 2000, showing computer-based virtual reconstruction of 11 synagogues no longer existant; incl. contribs. on German synagogues by Salomon Korn and Marc Grellert, also on the reconstruction project realised by architecture students of the Techn. Univ. Darmstadt (Manfred Koob).]

38454. TOCH, MICHAEL: *Jewish women entrepreneurs in the 16th and 17th century economics and family structure.* [In]: Jahrbuch für Fränkische Landesforschung, Bd. 60, Neustadt (Aisch), 2000. (Festschrift Rudolf Endres. Zum 65. Geburtstag gewidmet von Kollegen, Freunden und Schülern. Hrsg. von Charlotte Bühl und Peter Fleischmann.) Pp. 254–262, footnotes.

38455. TREUE, WOLFGANG: *Aufsteiger oder Außenseiter? Jüdische Konvertiten im 16. und 17. Jahrhundert.* [In]: Aschkenas, Jg. 10, H. 2, Wien, 2000. Pp. 307–336, footnotes. [Focuses on Worms, Deutz, Coburg, Frankfurt am Main.]

38456. *Über das Mittelalter.* [Title issue of] Wiener Jahrbuch für jüdische Geschichte, Kultur & Museumswesen, hrsg. von Gerhard Milchram im Auftrag des Jüdischen Museums der Stadt Wien, Bd. 4, 1999/2000/5760. Wien, 2000. [Incl.: Über das Mittelalter. Einleitung (Gerhard Milchram,

7-8), Die Wirtschaftsgeschichte der Juden im Mittelalter: Stand, Aufgaben und Möglichkeiten der Forschung (Michael Toch, 9–24). Die "Weisen Österreichs". Einflüsse, Bedeutung und Ausstrahlung (Shlomo Spitzer, 25–40). Die christlich-jüdische und die jüdisch-christliche Problematik im Mittelalter (Kurt Schubert, 41–54). Begegnungen zwischen Christen und Juden (Klaus Lohrmann, 55–70). Bet haKnesset, Judenschul. Die mittelalterliche Synagoge als Gotteshaus, Amtsraum und Brennpunkt sozialen Lebens (Martha Keil, 71–90); further articles are listed according to subject.]

38457. VOIGTS, MANFRED: *Von der Nation zur Einheit der Menschheit? Zur Dialektik des jüdischen Messianismus in der modernen Geschichte.* [In]: Menora, Bd. 11, Berlin, 2000. Pp. 279–297, notes.

38458. VOLKOV, SHULAMIT: *Antisemitismus als kultureller Code.* Zehn Essays. 2., durch ein Register erw. Aufl. München: Beck, 2000. 238 pp., notes. [For first ed. publ. 1990 with the title 'Jüdisches Leben und Antisemitismus im 19. und 2o. Jahrhundert' see No. 26970/YB XXXVI.]

38459. WILKE, CARSTEN: *Vom Berufsbild des modernen Rabbiners.* [In]: Forschung, Das Magazin der deutschen Forschungsgemeinschaft, H. 1, Weinheim, 2000, Pp. 20–22, illus.

38460. *Wissensbilder. Strategien der Überlieferung.* Hrsg. von Ulrich Raulff und Gary Smith. Berlin: Akademie, 1999. VII, 378 pp., footnotes, index. (Einstein-Bücher.) [Incl. (selected essays): Blut und Glauben. Über jüdisch-christliche Symbiose (David Biale, 145–168). Die Dialektik der Assimilation (Amos Funkenstein, 203–220). Wissensbilder im modernen jüdischen Denken (Paul Mendes-Flohr, 221–240).]

——— *Wissenschaft vom Judentum: Annäherungen nach dem Holocaust.* Hrsg. von Michael Brenner und Stefan Rohrbacher. [See No. 39141.]

Linguistics/Western Yiddish

38461. ALTHAUS, HANS PETER: *nebbich.* [Part 2.]. [In]: Jiddistik-Mitteilungen, Nr. 23, Trier, April 2000. Pp. 10–25, notes, bibl. [For part 1 see No. 37198/YB XLIV.]

——— APTROOT, MARION: *Jiddische Sprache und Literatur.* [See in No. 39141]

38462. DREEßEN, WULF-OTTO: *Horant als 'Schadchen'?* [In]: Jiddistik-Mitteilungen, Nr. 23, Trier, April, 2000. Pp. 1–9, notes. [Deals with a Yiddish manuscript from the late 14th cent.]

38463. GROSSMAN, JEFFREY: *The discourse of Yiddish in Germany from the Enlightenment to the Second Empire.* Rochester, NY: Camden House, 2000. 258 pp., illus., notes, index. (Studies in German literature, linguistics, and culture.) [Deals with the uses of Western Yiddish in German literary and cultural texts.]

38464. JAEGER, ACHIM: *Ein jüdischer Artusritter: Studien zum jüdisch-deutschen "Widuwilt" ("Artushof") und zum "Wigalois" des Wirnt von Gravenberc.* Tübingen: Niemeyer, 2000. VII, 465 pp., footnotes, bibl. (413–456), index. (Conditio Judaica, 32.)

38465. *Jiddische Bücher und Handschriften aus den Niederlanden.* Eine Ausstellung der Abteilung für Jiddische Kultur, Sprache und Literatur Heinrich-Heine-Universität Düsseldorf und des Menasseh ben Israel Instituut voor joodse sociaal-wetenschappelijke en cultuurhistorische studies, Amsterdam in Zusammenarbeit mit der Bibliotheca Rosenthaliana Universiteitsbibliotheek Amsterdam und der Universitäts- und Landesbibliothek Düsseldorf. Amsterdam;Düsseldorf: Privately printed, 2000. 64 pp., illus, facsims., bibl. [Incl. contribs. by Marion Aptroot, Mirjam Gutschow, Riety van Luit, Emile Schrijver, Shlomo Berger.]

38466. KERLER, DOV-BER: *The origins of modern literary Yiddish.* New York: Oxford Univ. Press; Oxford: Clarendon Press, 1999. XIII, 347 pp, illus. (Oxford modern languages and literary monographs.)

38467. *The language and culture Atlas of Ashkenazic Jewry.* Vol. III: *The Eastern Yiddish – Western Yiddish Continuum.* Prepared and publ. under the aegis of an editorial collegium Marvin I. Herzog (Ed.-in-chief), Vera Baviskar, Ulrike Kiefer, Robert Neumann, Wolfgang Putschke, Andrew Sunshine and Uriel Weinreich. Tübingen: Niemeyer, 2000; New York: Yivo Inst. for Jewish Research, 2000. X, 378 pp., illus., maps, indexes. [Title and index also in Hebrew.] [Cf.: Besprechung (Erika Timm) [in]: Jiddistik-Mitteilungen, Nr. 24, Trier, Dez. 2000, pp. 18–22, notes.]

38468. SCHULZ, ARMIN: *Die Zeichen des Körpers und der Liebe. "Paris und Vienna" in der jiddischen Fassung des Elia Levita.* Hamburg: Kovac, 2000. 100 pp. (Poetica. Schriften zur Literaturwissenschaft, Bd. 50.) [Deals with a frequently adapted love story from the 16th cent.] [Cf.: Besprechung (Wulf-Otto Dreßen) [in]: Jiddistik-Mitteilungen, Nr. 24, Trier, Dez. 2000, pp. 23–26.]

38469. *Das Schwedisch lid: ein westjiddischer Bericht über Ereignisse in Prag im Jahre 1648.* Original- und lateinschriftlich ediert, mit Einleitung und Kommentar versehen und hrsg. von Simon Neuberg. Hamburg: Buske, 2000. 107 pp., footnotes, facsims., bibl. (jidische schtudies, Bd. 8.)

38470. SOXBERGER, THOMAS: *"Vos Vin farmogt" Jiddische Drucke des 16.-18. Jahrhunderts in der Österreichischen Nationalbibliothek.* [In]: Jiddistik Mitteilungen, Nr. 24, Dez. 2000, Trier, 2000. Pp. 1–9, footnotes.

38471. TIMM, ERIKA: *Das jiddischsprachige literarische Erbe der Italo-Aschkenasen.* [In]: Schöpferische Momente des europäischen Judentums in der frühen Neuzeit [see No. 38424]. Pp. 161–175.

—— TURNIANSKY, CHAVA: *The events in Frankfurt am Main (1612–1616) in 'Megillas Vints' and in an unknown Yiddish "historical" song.* [See No. 38522.]

B. Communal and Regional History

1. Germany

38472. BADEN. BAUMANN, ULRICH: *Zerstörte Nachbarschaften: Christen und Juden in badischen Landgemeinden 1862–1940.* Hamburg: Dölling und Galitz, 2000. 341 pp., illus., maps, tabs., notes (252–285), bibl. (303–317), indexes. (Studien zur jüdischen Geschichte, Bd. 7.) Zugl.: Univ., Freiburg/Br., Diss., 1998. [Cf.: Besprechung (Armin Bergmann) [In]: Zeitschrift für Geschichtswissenschaft, Jg. 49, H. 3, Berlin, 2001, pp. 255–256.]

—— BADEN-WÜRTTEMBERG. KAUFMANN, URI R.: *Das Judentum. Neue "Staatskirche" und Produktivierungsinstrument in Südwestdeutschland 1809–1870.* [See No. 38437.]

38473. BERGHEIM. FRIEDT, GERD: *Die hebräischen Epitap[h]en von den Grabsteinen der jüdischen Friedhöfe in Bergheim/Erft und Bergheim/Paffendorf.* [In]: Geschichte in Bergheim. Jahrbuch des Bergheimer Geschichtsvereins e.V., Bd. 9, Bergheim, 2000. Pp. 130–151, illus., name lists, plan.

—— BERLIN. BERADT, MARTIN: *Die Strasse der kleinen Ewigkeit.* Roman. Mit einem Essay und einem Nachruf von Eike Geisel. [See No. 39564.]

38474. BERLIN. BILSKI, EMILY D.: *Berlin Metropolis: Jews and the new culture.* Berkeley, CA: Univ. of California Press, 2000. 284 pp., illus.

38475. BERLIN. DOMKE, PETRA: *Synagogen in Berlin.* Berlin: Homilius, 1999. 26 pp., illus. (Der historische Ort, Nr. 21.). [Guide book, also available in English; incl. historical overview.]

38476. BERLIN. HELAS, HORST: *Juden in Berlin-Mitte. Biografien – Orte – Begegnungen.* Hrsg. vom Verein zur Vorbereitung einer Stiftung Scheunenviertel Berlin e.V. Berlin: trafo verl., 2000. 303 pp., notes, illus., bibl., facsims.

38477. BERLIN. JEWISH MUSEUM. BLUMENTHAL, W. MICHAEL: *Daniel Libeskind and the Jewish Museum of Berlin.* New York: Leo Baeck Institute, 2000. 12 pp. (The Leo Baeck Memorial Lecture 44.)

38478. BERLIN. JEWISH MUSEUM. BLUMENTHAL, W. MICHAEL: *Wir wollen nicht nur Bilder an die Wand hängen. Wie man Geschichte anfaßt: Noch zwölf Monate bis zur Eröffnung des Jüdischen*

Museums in Berlin und sechs Antworten auf bange Fragen. [In]: 'FAZ', Nr. 189, Frankfurt am Main, 16. Aug. 2000. P. 47.]

38479. BERLIN. JEWISH MUSEUM. DORNER, ELKE: *Daniel Libeskind: Jüdisches Museum in Berlin.* Berlin: Gebr. Mann, 2000. 111 pp., illus. [Incl. two interviews with Libeskind.]

38480. BERLIN. JEWISH MUSEUM. LACKMANN, THOMAS: *Jewrassic Park.* Wie baut man (k)ein Jüdisches Museum in Berlin. Berlin: Philo, 2000. 248 pp., illus., notes. [Deals with the history of the new Berlin Jewish museum, its architect, Daniel Libeskind, and its various conceptions against the background of the complex relations between Germans and Jews; incl. also contribs. by Vera Bendt, Rolf Bothe, Amnon Barzel, Tom Freudenheim and W. Michael Blumenthal.]

38481. BERLIN. KOPPENFELS, JOHANNA VON: *Jüdische Friedhöfe in Berlin.* Berlin: Berlin-Ed., 2000. 71 pp., illus. (Berliner Ansichten, Bd. 15.)

38482. BERLIN. RISS, HEIDELORE: *Ansätze zu einer Geschichte des jüdischen Theaters in Berlin 1889 – 1936.* Frankfurt am Main, New York: Lang, 2000. 270 pp. (Europäische Hochschulschriften: Reihe 30, Theater-, Film- und Fernsehwissenschaften, Bd. 81.) Zugl: München, Univ., Diss., 1997.

—— BERLIN. RÜRUP, REINHARD: *Jewish history in Berlin – Berlin in Jewish history.* [See No. 38446.]

38483. BERLIN. SIMON, HERMANN: *Das Berliner Jüdische Museum in der Oranienburger Straße: Geschichte einer zerstörten Kulturstätte.* Teetz: Hentrich und Hentrich, 2000. 185 pp., illus.

38484. BERLIN. THIEL, JENS: *Paul Abraham. Ein vergessener Mitarbeiter der Preußischen Akademie der Wissenschaften.* [In]: Die Preußische Akademie der Wissenschaften zur Berlin 1914–1945. Hrsg. von Wolfram Fischer [et al.]. Berlin: Akademie Verlag, 2000. Pp. 435–458, footnotes, bibl. [P.A., 1886 Berlin – 1943 Auschwitz, jurist, historian, scholar of legal history, 1910–1939 compiler/author of the "Vocabularium Iurisprudentiae Romanae".] [Also in this vol.: "Arisierung", Nazifizierung und Militarisierung. Die Akademie im „Dritten Reich" (Peter Th. Walther, 87–120.]

38485. BERLIN. WILHELMY-DOLLINGER, PETRA: *Die Berliner Salons. Mit historisch-literarischen Spaziergängen.* Berlin, New York: de Gruyter, 2000. IX, 429 pp., illus., no footnotes etc.] [Incl. Rahel Varnhagen, Henriette Hertz and many other Jews.]

38486. BERLIN-TREPTOW. TATZKOW, MONIKA/HENICKE, HARTMUT unter Mitarbeit von MARINA BLUMBERG: *Arthur Müller. Leben, Werk, Vermächtnis.* Ein jüdisches Familienschicksal. Fragmente. Berlin: Proprietas-Verlag, 2000. 176 pp., illus., facsims., plans, side notes, indexes. [Deals also with aryanisation and restitution.] [A.M., orig. Aron Cohn, 1871 Stuhm, West Prussia – Jan. 19, 1935 Berlin, grain agent, industrialist, airplane pioneer, founder of the Luft-Verkehrs-Gesellschaft AG in Berlin-Johannisthal, after World War I: AMBI-Waggon- und Apparatebau AG.]

38487. BERLIN-WEISSENSEE. PROKASKY, JUDITH: *Das jüdische Kriegerdenkmal in Berlin-Weißensee. Suche nach Identität und Kampf gegen das Vergessen.* [In]: Menora, Bd. 11, Berlin, 2000. Pp. 103–118, notes. [On the memorial erected 1927 in the Jewish cemetery.]

38488. BERNKASTEL-WITTLICH. RASKIN, ALEXANDER: *Bibliographie zur Geschichte der Juden im Kreis Bernkastel-Wittlich.* Trier: Paulinus, 2000. XII, 131 pp. (Schriften des Emil-Frank-Instituts, Bd. 3.)

38489. BORNHEIM. WOLFF, CLAUDIA-MARTINA: *Die Juden in Bornheim vom Beginn der Französenherrschaft (1794) bis in die Zeit des Nationalsozialismus.* [In]: Heimatblätter des Rhein-Sieg-Kreises, Jg. 66–67, Siegburg, 1998–1999. Pp. 93–156, notes, illus., list of names.

38490. BRANDENBURG. HOMANN, URSULA: *Juden in Brandenburg.* [In]: Tribüne, Jg. 39, H. 155, Frankfurt am Main, 2000. Pp. 174–186.

38491. BRESLAU. RAHDEN, TILL VAN: *Juden und andere Breslauer.* Die Beziehungen zwischen Juden, Protestanten und Katholiken in einer deutschen Großstadt von 1860 bis 1925. Göttingen:

Vandenhoeck & Ruprecht, 2000. 382 pp., footnotes, tabs., bibl. (333–370), indexes (names, places, subjects).] (Kritische Studien zur Geschichtswissenschaft, Bd. 139.) Zugl.: Bielefeld, Univ., Diss., 1998/99. [Incl. the sections: I. Die Sozialstruktur von Juden, Protestanten und Katholiken von der Mitte des 19. Jahrhunderts bis zum Ersten Weltkrieg. II. Grenzgänger. Juden im allgemeinen und im jüdischen Vereinswesen Breslaus III. Jüdisch-christliche Ehen, die 'Neue Frau' und die situative Ethnizität der Breslauer Juden. IV. Einheit, Vielfalt und Differenz. Juden, Protestanten und Katholiken im Breslauer Schulwesen. V. Liberalismus und Juden, Antisemitismus und jüdische Gleichberechtigung.] [Cf.: Besprechung (Uffa Jenden) [in]: Zeitschrift für Geschichtswissenschaft, Jg. 49, H. 5, Berlin, 2001, pp. 470–471.]

——— BRESLAU. RAHDEN, TILL VAN: *Words and actions. Rethinking the social history of German antisemitism, Breslau, 1870–1914.* [See No. 39529.]

38492. BRESLAU. ZIATKOWSKI, LESZEK: *Die Geschichte der Juden in Breslau.* Deutsch von Barbara Kocowska. Wroclaw: Wydawnictwo Dolnoslaskie, 2000. 132 pp., illus., facsims., bibl., index. [Publ. simultaneously in Polish.]

38493. BRODENBACH. GIESING, GEORG: *"Wir sind doch ein Leut'". Auf der Suche nach dem jüdischen Viehhändler Siegfried Forst aus Brodenbach.* Briedel/Mosel: Rhein-Mosel-Verlag, 2000. 128 pp., illus., facsims. [Brodenbach on the Moselle, south of Koblenz.]

38494. BURG. BRÜLLS, HOLGER: *Die Synagoge in Burg. Kleinstädtischer Synagogenbau und jüdische Emanzipation im 19. Jahrhundert.* [In]: Menora, Bd. 11, Berlin, 2000. Pp. 341–368, notes. [Burg: near Magdeburg.]

38495. CASTROP. WANDELT, HARALD: *Von der ersten Niederlassung bis zur Jewish Trust Corporation – jüdisches Leben in Castrop-Rauxel (1722–1952).* Dortmund: Univ., Diss., 1998. 254 pp., illus., facsims. [Cf.: Besprechung (Dietmar Scholz) [in]: Vestische Zeitschrift, Bd. 97/98, Recklinghausen, 1999, pp. 382–386.]

38496. CELLE. SCHÜTZ, SIEGFRIED.: *"Hinsichtlich meiner Persönlichkeit aber bin ich fast gar nicht gekannt". Die "Erklärung" des Salomon Philipp Gans.* [In]: Festgabe für Dieter Neitzert zum 65. Geburtstag. Hrsg. von Peter Aufgebauer [et al.]. Bielefeld: Verlag für Regionalgeschichte, 1998. Pp. 363–398, footnotes, port. [Deals with an autobiographical text of a Celle lawyer written 1843.]

38497. CHEMNITZ. NEUBERT, ANDREAS: *Wohlfahrtspflege der Juden in Chemnitz. Betrachtet im Zeitraum von 1871 bis 1942.* Chemnitz: Techn. Univ., Philos. Fakultät, Mag.-Arbeit, 1999. 135, XXIX pp., footnotes, bibl. [Available at the Bibliothek Germania Judaica, Cologne.]

38498. COESFELD. ASCHOFF, DIETHARD: *Minderheit in Coesfeld – Die Juden.* [In]: Coesfeld 1197–1997. Beiträge zu 800 Jahren städtischer Geschichte. Im Auftrag der Stadt Coesfeld hrsg. von Norbert Damberg. Bd. 2. Münster: Ardey, 1999. Pp. 1143–1214, notes. [Incl. the Nazi era.]

38499. COLOGNE. GECHTER, MARIANNE/SCHÜTTE, SVEN: *Ursprung und Voraussetzungen des mittelalterlichen Rathauses und seiner Umgebung.* [In]: Walter Geis/Ulrich Krings, eds.: Köln: Das gotische Rathaus und seine historische Umgebung. Mit Beiträgen von Christoph Bellot [et al.]. Köln: Bachem, 2000. Pp. 69–173, illus., plans, notes. [Incl. section: "Die Entwicklung des jüdischen Viertels, der Synagoge und der Mikwe" (107–139).]

38500. COLOGNE. GRÜBEL, MONIKA: *Seit 321: Juden in Köln.* Kurzführer. [Hrsg.: Synagogengemeinde Köln]. Köln: Synagogengemeinde, 2000. 63 pp., illus.

38501. COLOGNE. HAGSPIEL, WOLFRAM/MADER, RUTH: *Helmut Goldschmidt: Porträt eines ungewöhnlichen Kölner Architekten.* [In]: Polis, Jg. 12, H. 2, Wuppertal, 2000. Pp. 34–39, illus. [H.G., Oct. 16, 1918 Cologne, architect, lives in Cologne.]

38502. COLOGNE. KOBER, ADOLF: *Grundbuch des Kölner Judenviertels 1135–1425. Ein Beitrag zur mittelalterlichen Topographie, Rechtsgeschichte und Statistik der Stadt Köln.* Bearb. von Adolf Kober. Mit einer Karte des Judenviertels. Nachdruck der Ausgabe Bonn 1920. Düsseldorf: Droste, 2000. 232 pp.

38503. COTTBUS. SCHARNHOLZ, LARS: *Kaufhaus Schocken Cottbus*. Leipzig: Diekmann, 2000. 103 pp., illus.

38505. CRONHEIM (FRANCONIA). ROSSMEISSL, RALF: *Mikrokosmos Cronheim. Ein Dorf – drei Religionen*. Mit einem Beitrag von Evelyn Gillmeister-Geisenhof über Trachten in Cronheim. Hrsg.: Kreisverband der Arbeiterwohlfahrt Roth-Schwabach e.V. Schwabach: Kreisverband d. Arbeiterwohlfahrt Roth-Schwabach, 2000. 185 pp., illus., facsims., footnotes. [Incl.: VI. Die jüdische Krone Cronheims zwischen Integration und Vertreibung (79–179); also on the cemetery in Bechhofen.]

38506. DARMSTADT. STEINBECK, UDO: *Jüdische Spuren in Darmstadt*. H. VII. Darmstadt: U. Steinbeck [privately printed], 2000. 35 pp.

38507. DIERSBURG. *Diersburg: Die Geschichte einer jüdischen Landgemeinde 1738–1940*. [Hrsg.]: Historischer Verein Mittelbaden, Mitgliedergruppe Hohberg. Haigerloch: Verlag Medien und Dialog, 2000. 235 pp., illus., facsims., notes, bibl. [Cont. contribs. by Cornelius Gorcka, Reinhard Krauß, Igor Lindner, Bernd Rottenecker, Uwe Schellinger, Axel Scheurig, Gisela Stoffel, Jürgen Stude; list of names and plan of the cemetery; incl. essay on life and work of Isaak Blum (1833 Diersburg – 1903 Frankfurt am Main), educator and scientist.]

38508. DITHMARSCHEN. REHN, MARIE-ELISABETH: *Juden in Norderdithmarschen im Spiegel von Niederlassungsgesuchen des 19. Jahrhunderts*. Hrsg. von Erhard Roy Wiehn. Konstanz: Hartung-Gorre, 2000. 178 pp., facsims., docs., map, footnotes, bibl.

38509. DRESDEN. *Alter jüdischer Friedhof in der Dresdner Neustadt*. [Dokumentation der Projektgruppe Pegasus des Gymnasiums Großzschachwitz]. Hrsg. von einem Autorenkollektiv unter der Leitung von Frank Thiele. Dresden: Hille, 2000. 136 pp., illus.

38510. EAST FRIESLAND. ADAMS, HERMANN: *Die Geschichte einer ostfriesisch-jüdischen Familie oder: die Einwohner verrieten nichts*. [Nachträge und Ergänzungen zu der Schrift: Juden in Ihrhofe]. [Westoverledingen, Lüdeweg 52]: [H. Adams], 2000. 16 pp.

38511. EAST PRUSSIA/WEST PRUSSIA. *Zur Geschichte und Kultur der Juden in Ost- und Westpreußen*. Hrsg. von Michael Brocke, Margret Heitmann und Harald Lordick. Hildesheim, New York: Olms, 2000. 660 pp., footnotes, tabs., illus., bibl., indexes (Netiva, Bd. 2.) [Incl.: Vorwort (eds., 9–11), Grundzüge der staatlichen Entwicklung in Ost- und Westpreußen (Klaus-Eberhard Murawski, 13–37). Juden im Ermland (Aloys Sommerfeld, 41–65). Aus der Geschichte der jüdischen Gemeinde zu Johannisburg/Ostpreußen (Andreas Kossert, 67–86). Die jüdische Gemeinde Ortelsburg. Ein Beitrag zur Geschichte der Juden in Masuren (Andreas Kossert, 87–123). Juden in (Märkisch) Friedland. Aspekte ihres Gemeindelebens in Polen und Preußen (Dorothea Elisabeth Deeters, 125–163). Die Danziger, Zoppoter und Gdinger Juden im 20. Jahrhundert. Ein historischer Vergleich (Gregorz Berendt, 187–201). Einigkeit macht stark. Der Verband der Synagogen-Gemeinden Ostpreußens (Horst Leiber, 205–215). "Liebe zur Gemeinde erwächst erst aus dem Gefühl der Sicherheit". Der Verband der Westpreußischen Synagogengemeinden 1897–1922 (Margret Heitmann, 217–237). "..., daß sie sich mit Stolz Juden nennen". Die Erziehung jüdischer Kinder in Ost- und Westpreußen im 19. Jahrhundert (Jörg H. Fehrs, 239–279). Entwicklungen und Strukturen. Jüdische Wohlfahrtspflege in Ost- und Westpreußen im 19. Jahrhundert (Harald Lordick, 281–303). Die ostpreußischen "Söhne des Bundes". Zur Geschichte des Ordens B'nai B'rith (Horst Leiber, 305–315). Demographie und Statistik der Juden in Ostpreußen im 19. Jahrhundert (Stefan Hartmann, 319–341). Die Juden im südlichen Westpreußen (Regierungsbezirk Marienwerder) im 19. Jahrhundert. Zahl und soziale Schichtung (Kazimirz Wajda, 343–357). Jüdisches Wirtschaftsleben in Ost- und Westpreußen (Konrad Fuchs, 359–375). Der Aufstieg der jüdischen Familie Friedländer in Königsberg (Andrea Ajzenstejn, 377–395). "Im Glauben, meiner speziellen Heimat einen großen Dienst zu leisten". Bethel Henry Strousberg und der Eisenbahnbau in Ostpreußen (Klaus-Eberhard Murawski, 397–403). Isaak Abraham Euchel. Ein jüdischer Aufklärer in Königsberg (Andrea Ajzensztejn, 405–423). Jüdische Studenten, Doktoren und Professoren der Königsberger Universität im 19. Jahrhundert (Manfred Komorowski, 425–443;incl. name list), Fanny Lewald. Eine Königsberger Demokratin (Gabriele Schneider, 445–459). Jüdische Politiker aus Ost- und Westpreußen (Helmut Neubach, 461–483). "... daß ich mit vielen Banden an Königsberg fest und gern hänge". Hugo Haase – eine Skizze (Ludger Heid, 485–509). Hannah Arendt und Königsberg (Stefanie Schüler-Springorum, 511–529). Benennen aber ist eine fortwährende Aufgabe. Von den literarischen Möglichkeiten geschichtlicher Erkenntnisvermittlung am Beispiel von Johannes Bobrowskis Roman "Levins Mühle" (Kerstin Huizinga, 533–543). Die "Atmosphäre eines Narrenhauses". Eine Ritualmordlegende um die Ermordung des Schülers Ernst Winter in Konitz (Bernhard Vogt, 545–577). Judentum im Spiegel von ostpreußischem Heimatschrifttum aus der Zeit nach 1945 (Klaus-Eberhard Murawski, 579–596).]

38512. ELBERFELD. *"... hoch auf dem Engelnberg". Der Alte Jüdische Friedhof in Elberfeld.* Eine Dokumentation mit Beiträgen von Christine Dämgen [et al.] und Texten von Fritz Jorde und Else Lasker-Schüler. Hrsg.: Trägerverein Begegnungsstätte Alte Synagoge Wuppertal e.V. Wuppertal: Trägerverein Begegnungsstätte Alte Synagoge Wuppertal, 1998. 71 pp., illus. [Incl. list of gravestones.]

38513. EMSLAND. POLLE, THEODOR: *Ein Jahrhundert jüdisches Leben in Herzlake/Bakerde.* [In]: Emsländische Geschichte, Jg. 8, Meppen, 1999. Pp. 122–131.

38514. ESENS. *Das August-Gottschalk-Haus in Esens.* Zwei Aufsätze zur Erinnerung. Esens: Ökumenischer Arbeitskreis Juden und Christen in Esens, 2000. 48 pp., illus. [Esens: East Friesland near Aurich. Cont.: August Gottschalk und die jüdische Volksschule in Esens (Gerd Rokahr, 5–24; on the Jewish teacher and cantor A.G., (1870–1927). Ein Haus in der Burgstraße (Wolfgang Ritter, 25–48; deals with the Jewish school, its fate during the Nazi era and its present function as a Jewish museum and memorial site.]

38515. FLÖRSHEIM/MAIN. SCHIELE, WERNER: *Juden in Flörsheim am Main.* Die Geschichte einer Minderheit auf dem Lande. Flörsheim am Main: Heimatverein Flörsheim am Main 1924 e.V., 1999. 512 pp., illus., facsims., footnotes, family trees, bibl. (491–512). [Also on the cemeteries in Wickerbach.]

38516. FRANCONIA. DIPPOLD, GÜNTER: *'Nur mit Kraft und Gewalt kann gegen diese verstockte Nation gewirkt werden'. Die Haltung fränkischer "Polizeibehörden" zu Juden im frühen 19. Jahrhundert.* [In]: Jahrbuch für Fränkische Landesforschung, Bd. 60 [with the title] Festschrift Rudolf Endres. Hrsg. von Charlotte Bühl und Peter Fleischmann. Neustadt (Aisch), 2000. Pp. 404–416. footnotes.

38517. FRANCONIA. SCHERG, LEONHARD: *Jüdisches Leben im Main-Spessart-Kreis.* Orte, Schauplätze, Spuren. [Hrsg.: Förderkreis Synagoge Urspringen e.V.] Haigerloch: Medien und Dialog, 2000. 50 pp., illus., map. (Orte jüdischer Kultur, 15.)

38518. FRANCONIA. STIMPFIG, KARL ERNST: *Die Juden in Leutershausen, Jochsberg, Colmberg und Wiedersbach: eine Dokumentation.* Leutershausen: Majer, 2000. XIX, 247 pp., illus.

38519. FRANCONIA. WACHTER, CLEMENS: *Neue Literatur zur Geschichte der Juden in Nürnberg, Fürth und der Fränkischen Schweiz.* [In]: Mitteilungen des Vereins für Geschichte der Stadt Nürnberg, Bd. 86, 1999. Nürnberg, 1999. Pp. 211–217. [Review essay.]

38520. FRANKFURT am Main. *Die jüdischen Schüler des Kaiser-Friedrichs-Gymnasium 1888–1933.* Begleitdokumentation zur Ausstellung im Heinrich-von-Gagern-Gymnasium, Am Tiergarten 6-8, 60316 Frankfurt/Main. 19. März – 5. April 2000. Recherche und Realisierung: Petra Bonavita. Frankfurt am Main: Privately printed, 2000. 117 & 5 pp., facsims. [Incl. lists of names.]

38521. FRANKFURT am Main. *Ostend. Blick ein jüdisches Viertel.* Mit Beiträgen von Helga Krohn [et al.]. Erinnerungen von Wilhelm Herzfeld [et al.]. Frankfurt am Main: Jüdisches Museum Frankfurt am Main, 2000. 238 pp. [Selected essays (titles partly abbr.): Die Israelitische Religionsgesellschaft in Frankfurt am Main (Matthias Morgenstern, 42–47). Synagoge Friedberger Anlage (19. August 1907 – 9. November 1938) (Salomon Korn, 48–57). Erziehung zu "Menschen, Juden und Bürgern". Schule und Ausbildung (Helga Krohn, 64–77). Das Ostend als Zentrum ostjüdischer Zuwanderer (Ernst Benz, 90–95). "Bar Kochba oder Zions letzte Stunde" – Ein Blick auf das kulturelle Leben (Helga Krohn, 124–127). "Auf einem der luftigsten und freundlichsten Punkte der Stadt, auf dem Röderberge, sind die jüdischen Spitäler" (Helga

Krohn, 128–143). Jüdische Großhändler und Fabrikanten im Ostend (Simone Mergen, 144–157). Im Nationalsozialismus. Einführung zu biographischen Beiträgen (Helga Krohn, 158–161). Jüdische Jugend im Dritten Reich (Yaakov Zur, 162–165). Wer war Herschel Grynszpan? (Lutz van Dick, 166–175). Zwischen Hoffnung und Enttäuschung – Familie Freund auf der Suche nach einer Auswanderungsmöglichkeit (Moshe Ayalon/Helga Krohn, 176–187). Herbert Stein. Bookseller, Jerusalem. Von der Battonnstraße zur King George Street – Eine Erinnerung (Wolf von Wolzogen, 208–221). "Alte Frankfurter gibt es hier sehr wenig …". Die jüdische Gemeinde nach Kriegsende (Cilly Kugelmann, 222–227). Neubeginn nach der Zerstörung. Zur Lebenssituation einer jüdischen Familie im Frankfurter Ostend nach 1945 (Carola Seiz, 228–231).]

38522. FRANKFURT am Main. TURNIANSKY, CHAVA: *The events in Frankfurt am Main (1612–1616) in 'Megillas Vints' and in an unknown Yiddish "historical" song.* [In]: Schöpferische Momente des europäischen Judentums in der frühen Neuzeit [see No. 38424]. Pp. 121–137.

——— FRANKFURT am Main. WEBER, ANNETTE, ed.: *"Außerdem waren sie ja auch Menschen". Goethes Begegnung mit Juden und Judentum.* [See No. 39548.]

38523. FRANKFURT am Main. WOLGAST, EIKE: *Frankfurt – das christliche Umfeld jüdischen Lebens im 16. und 17. Jahrhundert.* [In]: Schöpferische Momente des europäischen Judentum in der frühen Neuzeit [see No. 38424]. Pp. 97–111.

38524. FRANKFURT am Main. *Forschung Frankfurt.* Wissenschaftsmagazin der Johann Wolfgang Universität Frankfurt am Main. Jg. 18, H. 3 [with the issue title] Sonderband zur Geschichte der Universität. Frankfurt am Main, 2000. 216 pp., illus. [Selected articles dealing with Jewish professors at Frankfurt univ. and their expulsion in 1933 are listed in chap. VII.]

38525. FRANKFURT am Main. MONTGELAS, PETER JANUS GRAF VON: *Arthur von Weinberg. Ein Frankfurter Bürger – Jude und Mäzen.* [In]: Tribüne, Jg. 39, H. 156, Frankfurt am Main, 2000. Pp. 69–70.

38526. FREUDENBERG. HEIDT, GÜNTHER/LENNARTZ, DIRK S.: *Fast vergessene Zeugen. Juden in Freudenberg und im Saar-Mosel-Raum.* Norderstedt: Libri books on demand, [2000]. 560 pp., illus., facsims., footnotes, tabs., lists, bibl. (541–559).

38527. FÜRTH. PURIN, BERNHARD: *Erinnerung braucht einen Ort. Das Jüdische Museum Franken in Fürth.* [In]: Bayerische Blätter für Volkskunde, Jg. NF 2, H. 1, Würzburg, 2000. Pp. 37–44, illus.

38528. GIESSEN. OESTERLE, JENNY RAHEL/STEIN, CHRISTINE: *Die "Commerzienrat Heichelheim-Stiftung" in Gießen und ihr Stifter Siegmund Heichelheim.* [In]: Mitteilungen des Oberhessischen Geschichtsvereins Giessen, N.F., Bd. 84, Gießen, 1999. Pp. 141–158, footnotes, illus. [S.H., 1842 Gießen – 1920 Gießen, banker.]

38529. GÖTTINGEN. MANTHEY, MATTHIAS/TOLLMIEN, CORDULA: *Juden in Göttingen.* [In]: Göttingen. Geschichte einer Universitätsstadt. Bd. 3: Von der preußischen Mittelstadt zur südniedersächsischen Großstadt 1866–1989. Hrsg. von Rudolf von Thadden [et al.]. Göttingen: Vandenhoeck & Ruprecht, 1999. Pp. 675–760, illus., footnotes. [Covers the period from 1866 till the post-1945 era.]

38530. HAIGER. *Das Schicksal der Haigerer Juden.* [Hrsg.: Gesellschaft für Christl.-Jüd. Zusammenarb. Dillenburg e.V., Red.: Klasse 10 R1 der Johann-Textor-Schule in Haiger, Daniela Dörr [et al.].] Dillenburg: Ges. für Christl.-Jüd. Zusammenarb., [1999]. 30, XVIII pp., illus.

38531. HAIGERLOCH. JEGGLE, UTZ, ed.: *Erinnerungen an die Haigerlocher Juden.* Ein Mosaik. Tübingen: Tübinger Vereinigung für Volkskunde, 2000. 432 pp., illus., facsims., footnotes, lists. (Untersuchungen des Ludwig-Uhland-Instituts der Universität Tübingen, Bd. 92.) [Based on the investigations of the "Projektgruppe Haigerloch"; also contribs. by Helmut Gabeli, Angelika Haak, Michael Hermann, Klaus Mohr, Klaus Schubert on the history of the Haigerloch Jews from the 16th cent. to the Nazi period. Incl. list of deportees.]

38532. HALLE. ZIMMERMANN, CORNELIA: *Juden im Wirtschaftsleben der Stadt Halle im 19. und 20. Jahrhundert.* [In]: Menora, Bd. 11, Berlin, 2000. Pp. 369–376, notes.

38533. HAMBURG. BRÄMER, ANDREAS: *Judentum und religiöse Reform: Der Hamburger Israelitische Tempel 1817–1938.* Mit einem Vorwort von Michael A. Meyer. Hamburg: Dölling und Galitz, 2000. 304 pp., illus., footnotes, docs., bibl. (285–297), gloss., index. (Studien zur Jüdischen Geschichte, Bd. 8.) [Incl. 43 docs. relating to the history of the reform synagogue.]

38534. HAMBURG. KLEßMANN, ECKART: *M.M. Warburg & Co. Die Geschichte eines Bankhauses.* Hamburg: Dölling und Galitz, 2000. 206 pp., illus., facsims. [Covers the period 1798–1998.]

38535. HAMBURG. LIEDTKE, RAINER: *Zur mäzenatischen Praxis und zum kulturellen Selbstverständnis der jüdischen Wirtschaftselite in Deutschland: Die Hamburger Warburgs im ersten Drittel des 20. Jahrhunderts.* [In]: Großbürger und Unternehmer. Die deutsche Wirtschaftselite im 20. Jahrhundert. Hrsg. von Dieter Ziegler. Göttingen: Vandenhoeck & Ruprecht, 2000. Pp. 187–203, footnotes. (Bürgertum. Beiträge zur europäischen Gesellschaftsgeschichte, Bd. 17.).

38536. HAMBURG. STUDEMUND-HALÉVY, MICHAEL: *Biographisches Lexikon der Hamburger Sefarden. Die Grabinschriften des Portugiesenfriedhofs an der Königstraße in Hamburg-Altona.* Hamburg: Christians, 2000. 906 pp., illus., gloss., bibl., indexes. (Hamburger Beiträge zur Geschichte der deutschen Juden, Bd. 22.) [Incl. introd. essays on the history of the Sephardi community, on language and art of gravestones, chronol.; documents all Hamburg and Altona Portuguese Jews buried in Hamburg between 1611–1878; Hebrew, Portuguese and Spanish epitaphs with German translation, also short biographical annotations.]

38537. HAMBURG. STUDEMUND-HALÉVY, MICHAIL: *L'imprimerie séfarade a Hambourg et la censure Protestante et Rabbinique.* [In]: Revue des études juives, T. 159 (3–4), Louvain, juillet-dec., 2000. Pp. 485–500, footnotes. [In 1621 the Hamburg rabbi Isaac Attias transl. into Spanish the work by the Karaite scholar Isaac Abraham Troki 'Hizuk emunah', of which a Hebrew and German version already existed. This led to a polemic between Attias and the Lutheran Johannes Müller who considered Troki's writings dangerous to the Lutheran cause.]

38538. HAMELN. GELDERBLOM, BERNHARD: *Sie waren Bürger der Stadt. Die Geschichte der jüdischen Einwohner Hamelns im Dritten Reich. Ein Gedenkbuch.* 2. überarb. Aufl. Hameln: C.W. Niemeyer, 1997. 164 pp., docs., illus., facsims., index (159–160). (Beiträge zur Geschichte des jüdischen Lebens in der Stadt Hameln und im Kreis Hameln-Pyrmont.)

38539. HAMELN. GELDERBLOM, BERNHARD: *Von Christen und Juden in Hameln. Ein Gang durch 700 Jahre gemeinsamen Lebens.* Hameln: Gesellschaft für Christlich-Jüdische Zusammenarbeit in Hameln e.V., 2000. 41 pp.

38540. HENNEF. *Die jüdische Gemeinde Hennef-Geistingen.* Hrsg. von der Stadt Hennef durch Gisela Rupprath. Red.: Stadtarchiv Hennef. Hennef: [Stadt Hennef], 1999. 137 pp., illus., facsims., docs., bibl. [Cont. contribs. by Helmut Fischer and personal memoirs by Hannelore Jacoby.]

38541. HESSE. HEINEMANN, HARTMUT: *Forschungen zur Geschichte des Judentums in Hessen.* [In]: Ulrich Reuling/Winfrid Speitkamp, eds.: Fünfzig Jahre Landesgeschichtsforschung in Hessen. Marburg: Selbstverlag Hess. Landesamt für gesch. Landeskunde [et al.], 2000. Pp. 351–360, footnotes. [Review essay.]

38542. HESSE. LOTZE, SIEGFRIED: *Juden rund um den Reinhardswald in der frühen Neuzeit. Zur Vorgeschichte der "Judenbuche" der A. von Droste-Hülshoff.* [In]: Jahrbuch 2001 Landkreis Kassel, Kassel, 2000. Pp. 25–32, illus., bibl., notes. [Also in this vol.: "Kaddisch" – oder: Mein letztes Konzert (Meta Frank, 13–14).]

38543. HESSE. ZINK, WOLFGANG SE'EV: *Synagogenordnungen in Hessen. Formen, Probleme und Ergebnisse des Wandels synagogaler G'ttesdienstgestaltung und ihrer Institutionen im frühen 19. Jahrhundert.* Originale Archivdokumente hessischer Staaten und preußisch-rheinländischer Enklaven mit Einbeziehung des Königreiches Württemberg. Aachen: Verl. Mainz, 1998. 2 vols. 896 & [Ergänzungsband] 142 pp., footnotes, facsims., docs., gloss., bibl. Zugl.: Potsdam, Univ., Diss., 1998.

38544. HÖXTER. DEVENTER, JÖRG: *Die Juden und das Rathaus in Höxter.* [In]: Jahrbuch Kreis Höxter 1999, Höxter, 1999. Pp. 177–183.

38545. HOFGEISMAR. *Vertraut werden mit Fremden: Zeugnisse jüdischer Kultur im Stadtmuseum Hofgeismar.* 2., vollst. überprüfte, erg. und erhebl. erw. Aufl. Hrsg.: Verein für hess. Geschichte e.V. Kassel 1834, Zweigverein Hofgeismar. Hofgeismar: Stadtmuseum, 2000. 78 pp., illus. [Incl.: Vorwort (Helmut Burmeister/Michael Dorhs, 5–6). "Gut Purim, ihr lieben Leut' …". Die Helmarshäuser Synagoge und ihre Feste (Meta Frank, 7–17, notes). Ein Sabbat in Niedermeiser (Louis Rosenthal, 19–26, notes). Also bibl. related to Jews in Hofgeismar, Kassel and Wolfhagen (Michael Dorhs, 53–78).]

38546. HOLZHAUSEN (HESSE). THIERLING, MAGDA: *Zum Gedenken an Richard Hammerschlag (1886–1940).* [In]: Jahrbuch 2001 Landkreis Kassel, Kassel, 2000. Pp. 32–42, illus., notes.

38547. HORB (NECKAR). *Schattenrisse. Eine Annäherung an die Geschichte der jüdischen Gemeinde von Horb a.N.* Hrsg.: Martin-Gebert-Gymnasium Horb a.N./Otto-Hahn-Gymnasium Nagold. Beiträge: Johannes Becker [et al.]. Horb/Nagold: Privately printed, 2000. 221 pp., illus., facsims., name list, bibl. [Documents also Horb cemetery with photographs, inscriptions and annotations.]

38548. HUNSRÜCK. *Versöhnung braucht Erinnerung. Juden in Kirchberg/Hunsrück.* Dokumentation aus der Sammlung von Ernst Fuchß, Kirchberg. Mit einem Aufsatz "Die jüdische Schule in Kirchberg/Hunsrück" von Gustav Schellack. Eingel. und bearb. von Manfred Stoffel. Kirchberg: Presbyterium der Evang. Kirchengemeinde, 2000. 162 pp., illus., bibl. (Schriftenreihe zur Geschichte der Stadt Kirchberg, Bd. 2.)

38549. INGOLSTADT. *Ingolstädter Gesichter. 750 Jahre Juden in Ingolstadt.* [Ausstellung im Stadtmuseum Ingolstadt vom 26.6. bis 15.10.2000.] [Hrsg. von] Theodor Straub, Alisa Douer. Ingolstadt: Stadt Ingolstadt, Kulturreferat, 2000. 264 pp., illus.

38550. KAISERSESCH. WAGENER, HARALD: *Die Geschichte der Juden in Kaisersesch.* Kaisersesch: [Wagener, Koblenzer Str. 50], 1998. 11 pp., illus., bibl. [Print-out from: http://titan.informatik.uni.bonn.de/wagener; available also at the Bibliothek Germania Judaica, Cologne.]

38551. KAMP-LINTFORT. *Jüdische Einwohner in den heutigen Kamp-Lintforter Ortsteilen Hoerstgen und Kamp.* Hrsg.: Stadt Kamp-Lintfort. Bearb.: Albert Spitzner-Jahn. 2., erw. Aufl. Kamp-Lintfort: Stadt Kamp-Lintfort, 2000. 21 pp. [Cont. only names and birth and death dates.]

38552. KASSEL. *Synagogen in Kassel.* Ausstellung im Stadtmuseum Kassel anlässlich der Einweihung der neuen Synagoge im Jahr 2000. bearb. von Esther Haß, Alexander Link und Karl-Hermann Wegner. [Hrsg.: Stadtmuseum Kassel]. Marburg: Jonas, 2000. 110 pp., illus., facsims., notes, bibl. [Incl.: Einführung. Museum und Synagoge (Karl-Hermann Wegner, 7–12). 8 essays, some also dealing with the history of the Jews of Kassel in the 19th and 20th cent., by Dietrich Krause-Vilmar, Jutta Schuchard, Albrecht Rosengarten, Karl-Hermann Wegner, Anke Schmeling, Alfred Jacoby, Esther Haß, Eva Schulz-Jander.]

38553. KIPPENHEIM. SCHELLINGER, UWE: *Albert Weill (1867–1950) aus Kippenheim.* Eine biographische Spurensuche nach dem Vater von Kurt Weill. [In]: Geroldsecker Land, H. 42, 2000. Pp. 161–178, illus., notes. [A.W., 1867 Kippenheim – Dec. 30, 1950 Nahariya, cantor, composer, lived from 1898 in Dessau, emigr. 1936 to Palestine.]

38554. KLEINHEUBACH. HOLL, BERNHARD: *Die Geschichte der jüdischen Gemeinde zu Kleinheubach.* Kleinheubach: Heimat- und Geschichtsverein Kleinheubach, 1998 [?]. 208 pp., illus., facsims., lists. [First part (13–41) incl. facsim. reprint of the history of the Jews of Kleinheubach by the Protestant pastor Gottlieb Wagner, publ. 1933. Kleinheubach/Main, near Michelstadt.]

38555. LANGENDERNBACH. MINK, PETER-JOSEF: *Das Leben der Juden in Langendernbach von den Anfängen bis zur Zeit des Nationalsozialismus.* [In]: Nassauische Annalen, Bd. 110, Wiesbaden, 1999. Pp. 265–296, footnotes.

38556. LOWER SAXONY. *Christen und Juden. Blickwechsel. Juden und Christen*. Eine Ausstellung in Niedersachsen. Hrsg.: Ursula Rudnick. Essen: Klartext, 2000. 156 pp., illus., facsims. [Incl. contribs. on the history of Jews in Lower Saxony from the beginning to the present; also Luther, Christian-Jewish dialogue, antisemitism.]

38557. MAINZ. DROBNER, MARTINA: *Zur Entwicklung der Mainzer Jüdischen Gemeinde im Kontext gesamtgesellschaftlicher Prozesse des 19. Jahrhunderts*. Frankfurt am Main; New York: Lang, 2000. 410 pp., illus., footnotes, docs., bibl. (329–346), index. (Europäische Hochschulschriften: Reihe 19, Volkskunde, Ethnologie: Abt. A, Volkskunde, Bd. 52.) Zugl.: Mainz, Univ., Diss., 1999.

38559. MALSCH (nr. Karlsruhe). MAIER, LOUIS: *Schweigen hat seine Zeit, Reden hat seine Zeit*. Ein Sohn spricht vom Leben und Schicksal der Jüdischen Gemeinde in Malsch. Hrsg. von der Gemeinde Malsch. Übers. von Sally Laws-Werthwein und Donald Werthwein. Ubstadt-Weiher: Verlag Regionalkultur, 2000. 192 pp., illus. [Author, b. 1924 in Rastatt, psychotherapist, emigr. 1940 via Russia and Japan to the US, lives in Maryland.]

38560. MESCHEDE. OERTEL, W.: *Die Alte Synagoge Meschede. Der fünfeckige Stern – ein jüdisches Symbol?* [In]: Jahrbuch Hochsauerlandkreis, Brilon, 1999. Pp. 109–112.

38561. MICHELSTADT. GRÖZINGER, KARL E.: *Seckel Löw Wormser – der Ba'al Schem von Michelstadt*. Zum 150sten Tage seines Todes. [In]: Aschkenas, Jg. 10, H. 1, Wien, 2000. Pp. 157–176, footnotes.

38562. MÖNCHENGLADBACH. BRÜLLS, HOLGER: *Die Mönchengladbacher Synagoge von 1883*. Großstädtischer Synagogenbau im gründerzeitlichen Rheinland und die Ästhetik des jüdischen Gottesdienstes im 19. Jahhundert. [In]: Rheinisch-Westfälische Zeitschrift für Volkskunde, Bd. 16, Bonn, 2000. Pp. 171–215, illus., footnotes. [See also No. 38416.]

38563. MONDORF. BUSCH, HANS-ULRICH: *Die Synagogengemeinde Mondorf*. [In]: Heimatblätter des Rhein-Sieg-Kreises, Jg. 66–67, Siegburg, 1998–1999. Pp. 157–203, illus., notes. [Incl. list of names.]

38564. MOSELKERN. BACKHAUSEN, MANFRED: *Juden in Moselkern*. [In]: Jahrbuch für den Kreis Cochem-Zell 2001. Cochem, 2000. Pp. 159–161, illus.

38565. MOSELLE. SCHUMANN, HENRY: *Mémoire des communautés juives de Moselle*. Présentation historique de Pierre-André Meyer. Metz: Editions Serpenoise, 1999. 88 pp., illus., map, notes. [Account goes back to the middle ages, and covers some parts of Alsace-Lorraine.]

38566. MÜNSTER. ASCHOFF, DIETHARD: *Quellen und Regesten zur Geschichte der Juden in der Stadt Münster 1530–1650/1662*. Münster: LIT, 2000. 365 pp., indexes. (Westfalia Judaica, Bd. 3.1.) [Incl.: Anhang: Der Prozeß des Gerhard Schroderken gegen den Juden Jakob 1554 Januar 20 – Dezember 17 (281–304).]

38567. MUNICH. FLEISCHER, MANFRED/NEUMEIER, GERHARD: *Jüdische Akademiker und Unternehmer in München vor dem Ersten Weltkrieg*. Geographische Herkunft und Strukturen der Zuwanderung. [In]: Zeitschrift für bayerische Landesgeschichte, Bd. 63, H. 1, München, 2000. Pp. 80–121, footnotes.

38568. NEUWIED. BAMBERGER, NAFTALI BAR-GIORA: *Der jüdische Friedhof in Neuwied-Niederbieber*. Memor-Buch Hrsg.: Deutsch-Israelischer Freundeskreis Neuwied e.V. Neuwied: Neuwieder Verlagsges., 2000. 534 pp., illus., docs, bibl., indexes (401–497). [Incl. historical essays on the Jews of Neuwied and the cemetery by the author (revised by Barbara Runkel); also list of names of Nazi victims. Photo-documentation of all gravestones, incl. Hebrew inscriptions, German translations and annotations; 6 indexes related to family names, first names, plan of cemetery, dates of death, places, symbols, professions, position/status, 401–497). Author died shortly before completion of the book.] [Cf.: Zum Tode von Naftali Bar Giora Bamberger sel. A. (Jürgen Sielemann) [in]: Maajan, Jg. 14, H. 54, Zürich, 2000. Pp. 1581.] [N.B.-G. Bamberger, July 22, 1919 Hamburg – Jan. 15, 2000 Stuttgart, son of Hamburg rabbi Pinchas Selig Bamberger, Hebrew scholar, Judaist.]

38569. NONNENWEIER (Baden). BOLL, GÜNTER: *Die ersten Generationen der jüdischen Familie Wertheimer von Nonnenweier*. [In]: Die Ortenau, Bd. 80, Offenburg/Baden, 2000. Pp. 229–236, illus., notes.

38570. NÜMBRECHT. VOGLMAYR, ANNE: *Mein Name ist Meta Herz. Erinnerungen an die jüdische Gemeinde Nümbrecht*. Nümbrecht: Martina Galunder-Verlag, 2000. 152 pp., illus., facsims., bibl. [Nümbrecht: Rhineland; incl. the Nazi period.]

38571. NUREMBERG. ROSENBERG, LEIBL: *Spuren und Fragmente. Jüdische Bücher, jüdische Schicksale in Nürnberg*. Nürnberg: Israel. Kultusgemeinde/Stadtbibliothek Nürnberg, 2000. 211 pp., illus. (Ausstellungskatalog der Stadtbibliothek Nürnberg, 102/2000.) [Exhibition catalogue; on confiscated books from the former "Stürmer" library, now owned by the Jewish community, and on their original owners.]

38572. OFFENBURG. DZIALOSZYNSKI, SAMUEL/RUCH, MARTIN: *Der Gute Ort. Der jüdische Friedhof in Offenburg*. Book on demand: Historymarketing.de, 2000. 139 pp., illus. [Documents the German inscriptions on more than 300 gravestones, incl. translations of Hebrew inscriptions.]

38573. OFFENBURG. RUCH, MARTIN: *Der letzte Offenburger Rabbi. In memoriam Bernhard Gries (1917–1938)*. [In]: Die Ortenau, Bd. 80, Offenburg/Baden, 2000. Pp. 261–268, facsims., illus.

38574. OLFEN. ALTHOFF, GERTRUD: *Geschichte der Juden in Olfen*. Jüdisches Leben im katholischen Milieu einer Kleinstadt im Münsterland. Mit einem einleitenden Beitrag von Diethard Aschoff. Münster: LIT, 2000. IV, 289 pp., illus., facsims., footnotes, geneal. (Geschichte und Leben der Juden in Westfalen, 4.) [Incl.: Juden in Olfen bis zum Beginn der Preußenzeit (1568–1816) (Diethard Aschoff, 3–37).]

38575. PALATINATE. HOMANN, URSULA: *Juden in Rheinland-Pfalz*. [In]: Tribüne, Jg. 39, H. 153, Frankfurt am Main, 2000. Pp. 179–191.

38576. PALATINATE. KUKATZKI, BERNHARD: *Bibliographie zur pfälzisch-jüdischen Geschichte. Berichtsjahr 1999*. Mit Nachträgen aus den Vorjahren. Schifferstadt: Privately printed, 2000. 46 pp., illus., facims.

38577. PALATINATE. KUKATZKI, BERNHARD: *Die pfälzischen Juden und ihre Beteiligung an der Revolution 1848/49 – "Keine Juden, sondern nur noch israelitische Mitbürger"*. [In]: Die Pfalz und die Revolution 1848/49. Band II. Hrsg. von Hans Fenske [et al.]. Kaiserslautern: Institut für pfälzische Geschichte und Volkskunde, 2000. Pp. 193–220, footnotes, facsim., port.

38578. PALATINATE. KUKATZKI, BERNHARD: *Steinerne Zeugnisse jüdischen Lebens in der Verbandsgemeinde Rockenhausen: Synagogen, Schulen, Friedhöfe und Ritualbäder in Dielkirchen, Marienthal, Rathskirchen, Rockenhausen, Teschenmoschel und Würzweiler*. Landau i.d. Pfalz: [Ges. f. Christl.-Jüd. Zusammenarbeit Pfalz], 2000. 66 pp., illus, bibl.

38579. PALATINATE. *Sachor. Beiträge zur jüdischen Geschichte und zur Gedenkstättenarbeit in Rheinland-Pfalz*. Jg. 10, H. 18 & 19. Bad Kreuznach, 2000. 2 issues, illus., facsims., notes, index. [H. 18 (82 pp.) incl. contribs. on the Jews in Dausenau, Mülheim/Moselle, Obermoschel, Deidesheim, Mutterstadt, by Kurt Bruchhäuser, Uwe F.W. Bauer, Albrecht Martin, Michael Tilly, Hans-Jürgen Becker. H. 19 (81 pp.) incl. contribs. on the Jews in Lahnstein, Worms (on the teacher Herta Mansbacher), Zweibrücken, Bretzenheim/Nahe, by Hubertus Seibert, Fritz Reuter, Bettina Hübschen, Hans Schneider. Both issues incl. also contribs. on projects, exhibitions, conferences, German-Israeli youth contacts, memorials and commemorations, book reviews.]

38580. RECKLINGHAUSEN. BORGGRAEFE, PETER: *Christianus Gerson aus Recklinghausen und Johannes Buxtorf aus Kamen – zwei Beispiele humanistischer Gelehrsamkeit im Reformationszeitalter*. [In]: Vestischer Kalender 2000, Jg. 71, Recklinghausen, 2000. Pp. 86–90, illus. [Ch. Gerson, author of 'Der Juden Thalmud fürnembster Inhalt und Widerlegung', first publ. 1607, converted in 1600.]

38581. RENDSBURG. STEINER, ELKE: *Rendsburg Prinzessinstrasse*. Die Geschichte einer jüdischen Kleinstadtgemeinde. [Rendsburg: Privately printed, 2000]. 48 pp., bibl. [Based on the history of the Jews of Rendsburg and a fictionalised story of a family; hand-written "comic book", illustrated with wood-cuts by the author.]

38582. RENDSBURG, JUDISCHES MUSEUM. DETTMER, FRAUKE: *Aus den Sammlungen des Jüdischen Museums Rendsburg (1)*. [In]: Rendsburger Jahrbuch 2000, Jg. 50, Rendsburg, 2000. Pp. 183–187, illus.

38583. RHINELAND. PRACHT-JÖRNS, ELFI: *Jüdisches Kulturerbe in Nordrhein-Westfalen. Teil II: Regierungsbezirk Düsseldorf*. Köln: Bachem, 2000. VIII, 695 pp., illus., footnotes, bibl., gloss., index, maps. (Beiträge zu den Bau- und Kunstdenkmälern im Rheinland, Bd. 34,2.)

38584. ROMMERSKIRCHEN. SCHMITZ, JOSEF: *Jüdische Familien am Gillbach: Herkunft und Schicksal*. Rommerskirchen: Gemeinde Rommerskirchen, 1999. 128 pp. (Beiträge zur Geschichte der Gemeinde Rommerskirchen, Bd. 3.)

38585. SACHSEN-ANHALT. HOMANN, URSULA: *Juden in Sachsen-Anhalt*. [In]: Tribüne, Jg. 39, H. 154, Frankfurt am Main, 2000. Pp. 202–214.

38586. SALZSCHLIRF (BAD). LISTMANN, ANJA: *Beinahe vergessen. Jüdisches Leben in Bad Salzschlirf*. Hünfeld: Rhön Verlag, [2000]. 180 pp., facsims., docs., notes, family trees, bibl. [Incl. the Nazi period, also on the post-war DP-camp.]

38587. SALZWEDEL. BLOCK, ERNST: *Wir waren eine glückliche Familie. Zur Geschichte und zu den Schicksalen der Juden in Salzwedel/Altmark*. Hrsg.: Museen des Altmarkkreises Salzwedel. Uelzen: C. Beckers Buchdruckerei, 1998. 164 pp., illus. (Museen des Altmarkkreises Salzwedel, Schriften zur Regionalgeschichte, Bd. 1.)

38588. SCHWABEN. FASSL, PETER, ed.: *Geschichte und Kultur der Juden in Schwaben II. Neuere Forschungen und Zeitzeugenberichte*. Red.: Gerhard Willi. Stuttgart: Jan Thorbecke Verl., 2000. 444 pp., footnotes, indexes (Irseer Schriften, Bd. 5.) [Extended and corrected (year of publ.) entry of No. 37331/YB XLV. Cont. the sections: Biographische Aspekte (15–86). Beiträge zur Orts- und Landesgeschichte (87–228). Beiträge zur Volkskunde (229–284). Kunst und Kultur (285–318). Die Zeit des Nationalsozialismus (319–422).]

38589. SCHWABEN. ULLMANN, SABINE: *Der Streit um die Weide. Ein Ressourcenkonflikt zwischen Christen und Juden in den Dorfgemeinden der Markgrafschaft Burgau*. [In]: Mark Häberlein, ed.: Devianz, Widerstand und Herrschaftspraxis in der Vormoderne. Studien zu Konflikten im südwestdeutschen Raum (15.-18. Jahrhundert). Konstanz: UVK Universitätsverlag Konstanz, 1999. (Konflikte und Kultur – Historische Perspektiven, 2.) Pp. 99–136, footnotes.

38590. SELIGENSTADT (nr. Hanau). FICHTNER, DIETRICH: *... und wollten so gerne bleiben: ein Rundgang zu den Häusern der Seligenstädter Juden*. Hanau: CoCon-Verl., 2000. 80 pp., illus.

38591. SILESIA. SCHIEWITZ, LUCIAN: *Aspekte jüdischen Kulturlebens in Schlesien und das Phänomen Max Tau*. [In]: "Ein symbolisches Leben". Beiträge anläßlich des 100. Geburtstages von Max Tau (1897–1976) [see No. 39391]. Pp. 202–216, footnotes.

38592. SÖTERN. BIER, THOMAS: *Der Judenfriedhof zu Sötern*. [In]: Mitteilungen des Vereins für Heimatkunde im Landkreis Birkenfeld und der Heimatfreunde Oberstein, Jg. 73, Birkenfeld, 1999. Pp. 197–205, notes, bibl.

38593. SOLINGEN. *"... daß ich die Stätte des Glückes vor meinem Tode verlassen müßte". Beiträge zur Geschichte jüdischen Lebens in Solingen*. Hrsg.: Manfred Krause/Solinger Geschichtswerkstatt e.V. Solingen: Selbstverlag Solinger Geschichtswerkstatt e.V. 373 pp., illus., facsims., notes, bibl. [Cont.: Einleitung (ed., 10–18), Auseinandersetzung mit der Vergangenheit: Schulprojekte (contribs. by Wilhelm Bramann/Michael Sandmöller, Olaf Link, Sebastian Schwenk/Horst Sassin, Victor Pankratius, Jürgen Beese; on the cemetry and the synagogue). Jüdische Familien (contribs. by Wilhelm Bramann, Sebastian Schwenk, Marc-René Hagner, Patrick Hagner, Lutz Peters, Horst Sassin; on the Coppel and Leven families and on Emil Kronenberg). Solinger Juden vor 1933 (contribs. by Ralf Zurek, Horst Sassin). Solinger Juden in der NS-Zeit (contribs. by Horst Sassin, Wilhelm Bramann, Margit Tamar Rudzi, Sabine Ebert, Emine Kavalli, Pia Weck). Die jüdische Gemeinde nach 1945 (contribs. by Ulrike Schrader, Leonid Goldberg). Auseinandersetzung mit der Vergangenheit (contribs. by Wilhelm Bramann, Manfred Krause).

Anhang (bibl., Horst Sassin). Kurzbiographien Solinger Juden 1933–1945 (Aline Poensgen). A CD-rom is attached to the book.]

38594. SOLINGEN. SASSIN, HORST: *Die Lehrer und Vorbeter der Israelitischen Synagogengemeinde Solingen.* [In]: Zeitschrift des Bergischen Geschichtsvereins, Bd. 98, Jg. 1997/1998, Neustadt an der Aisch, 2000. Pp. 167–2000, footnotes, illus.

38595. STRALSUND. *Die Keibel-Cohns. Zur Geschichte der Juden in Stralsund.* [Authors: Gitte Struck, Thomas Waschk, Henryk Pich]. Stralsund: Mückenschwein, 1998. 183 pp., illus., facsims. [Book combines personal memoirs, historical overview and introduction to Judaism, its history, rites and ceremonies.]

38596. TELGTE. FREESE, WERNER, ed.: *Geschichte der Stadt Telgte.* Münster: Ardey-Verl., 1999. 740 pp. [Incl.: Jüdisches Leben in der frühen Neuzeit. Geschichte des alltäglichen Gegen-, Neben- und Miteinanders von Minderheit und Mehrheit (Michael Hohlstein). Jüdisches Leben in preußischer Zeit (Andreas Determann, Susanne Freund).]

38597. THURINGIA. LITT, STEFAN: *Territoriale Organisationsformen der Juden in Thüringen während der Frühen Neuzeit.* [In]: Aschkenas, Jg. 10, H. 1, Wien, 2000. Pp. 245–253, footnotes.

38598. THURINGIA. VOGEL, BERNHARD: *Spuren, die in die Zukunft weisen – Zeugnisse jüdischer Kultur in Thüringen.* [In]: "Hinauf und Zurück/in die herzhelle Zukunft". Deutsch-jüdische Literatur im 20. Jahrhundert. Festschrift für Birgit Lermen [see No. 39217]. Pp. 147–159, notes.

38599. TRIER. KANN, HANS-JOACHIM: *Neue Erkenntnisse zur alten Trierer Synagoge (1859–1944).* [In]: Kurtrierisches Jahrbuch, Jg. 39, Trier, 1999. Pp. 365–385, footnotes, illus.

38600. UPPER SILESIA. FUHRMANN, HORST: *Von solchen, "die noch östlicher wohnen" – Deutsche, Polen, Juden im Oberschlesien des 19. Jahrhunderts.* [In]: Reich, Regionen und Europa in Mittelalter und Neuzeit. Festschrift für Peter Moraw. Hrsg. von Paul-Joachim Heinig [et al.]. Berlin: Duncker & Humblot, 2000. Pp. 497–514, footnotes.

38601. USINGEN (Taunus). BIERWIRTH, JOACHIM: *Die jüdischen Einwohner von Usingen. Materialien zur Rekonstruktion insbesondere ihrer älteren Geschichte.* Neu-Anspach: GeoHist-Verl. 2000. 86 pp., illus.

38602. VERSMOLD. BECKMANN, V.: *Synagogenbau und Antisemitismus (1822–1900). Zur Geschichte der Synagogen der jüdischen Gemeinde Versmold.* [In]: Ravensberger Blätter, Jg. 1999, Bielefeld, 1999.

38603. VIENNA. LOHRMANN, KLAUS: *Die Wiener Juden im Mittelalter.* Berlin: Philo, 2000. 192 pp., illus., side notes, bibl., index. (Geschichte der Juden in Wien, Bd. 1.)

38604. WAREN. BENKENDORF, ARNE/ROTHER, DOROTHE/KNIESZ, JÜRGEN: *Jüdisches Leben in Waren zwischen Emanzipation und Vernichtung.* [Issue title of]: Chronik. Schriftenreihe des Warener Museums- und Geschichtsvereins, H. 16, Waren, 1999. 215 pp., illus.

38605. WARENDORF. ESTER, MATTHIAS M.: *Die jüdische Minderheit in Warendorf im 19. und 20. Jahrhundert.* [In]: Paul Leidinger, ed.: Geschichte der Stadt Warendorf, Bd. 2. Die Stadt Warendorf im 19. und 20. Jahrhundert: Politik, Wirtschaft, Kirchen. Warendorf/Münster, 2000. Pp. 651–690, notes, illus., facsims.

38606. WEILBURG/Lahn. HOOS, HANS-HELMUT: *Die Stadt Weilburg und ihre Juden.* [In]: Nassauische Annalen, Bd. 110, Wiesbaden, 1999. Pp. 237–264, footnotes.

38607. WESTPHALIA. LUTTER, WALTER E.: *Der Todtenhof in Körbecke ein (fast vergessener) Jüdischer Friedhof.* Erinnerung und Dokumentation. Mit einem Beitrag von Maria Sperling. Möhnesee: Privately printed, [2000]. 137 pp., illus., facsims., maps, tabs., footnotes, bibl. [Incl. several family trees; available at the Bibliothek Germania Judaica, Cologne.]

38608. WESTPHALIA. RIDDER, THOMAS: *Synagogen in Westfalen.* Münster: Landschaftsverband Westfalen-Lippe, 2000. 48 pp., illus.

38609. WITTEN. AHLAND, FRANK: *"... weit weg vom Antisemitismus, obgleich nicht weit vom Kohlenstaub." Probleme der Integration der Wittener Juden im Kaiserreich.* [In]: Jahrbuch des Vereins für Orts- und Heimatkunde in der Grafschaft Mark, Bd. 100, Dortmund, 2000. Pp. 149–183, footnotes.

——— WÜRZBURG. KAMPMANN, CHRISTOPH: *Die Petition des Salomon Hirsch und die Würzburger "Hepp-Hepp"-Krawalle von 1819: Zur frühen Verwendung des Begriffs "Judenemanzipation" in der publizistischen Debatte.* [See No. 38436.]

38610. WUPPERTAL. SCHRADER, ULRIKE/JAKOBS, HILDEGARD: *Ma towu ... Alte Gebetbücher der Jüdischen Kultusgemeinde.* Hrsg.: Trägerverein Begegnungsstätte Alte Synagoge Wuppertal e.V./Jüd. Gemeinde Wuppertal. Wuppertal: Privately printed, 2000. 50 pp., illus. [Authors trace the former owners of some of more than 100 prayerbooks and tell their stories.]

38611. ZEILITZHEIM. TANNENBAUM, WILLIAM Z.: *A town on the Volkach: The acculturation of the Jews of Zeilitzheim in the nineteenth century.* [In]: Leo Baeck Institute Year Book XLV, Oxford, 2000. Pp. 93–117, footnotes, tabs. [Zeilitzheim: Lower Franconia.]

1a. Alsace

38612. BENBASSA, ESTHER: *Geschichte der Juden in Frankreich.* Aus dem Französ. von Lilli Herschhorn. Berlin: Philo, 2000. 322 pp., footnotes, chronol., gloss., bibl., index. [Orig. publ. 1997; incl. chapt. on the Jews on Lorraine (with Metz) and Alsace.]

38613. HONIGMANN, PETER: *Nichtstaatliches Schriftgut einer Grenzregion am Beispiel der Archivaliensammlung der Gesellschaft für die Geschichte der Israeliten in Elsass-Lothringen.* [In]: Archive im zusammenwachsenden Europa. Referate des 69. Deutschen Archivtags und seiner Begleitveranstaltungen 1998 in Münster veranstaltet vom Verein deutscher Archivare. Siegburg: Schmitt, 2000. (Der Archivar, Beiband 4.). Pp. 131–140, footnotes. [On an archival collection founded by Rabbi Moses Ginsburger, at present kept in the Archives Départementales du Bas-Rhin, Strasbourg.]

38614. WEIß, GERHARD: *Alexander Weills "Sittengemälde aus dem elsässischen Volksleben" (1847): volkskundliche Zeugnisse, literarische Kunstwerke und emanzipatorische Botschaften.* [In]: Heine-Jahrbuch 2000, Stuttgart, 2000. Pp. 164–183, illus., notes. [A.W., orig. Abraham W., May 11, 1818 Schirrhofen, Alsace – April 18, 1899 Paris, rabbi, journalist, author, friend of Heinrich Heine, wrote and publ. in German, in later life in French.]

2. Austria

38616. BIENENFELD, FRANZ RUDOLF. ADUNKA, EVELYN: *Franz Rudolf Bienenfeld. Ein Pionier der Menschenrechtsgesetze.* [In]: David, Jüdische Kulturzeitschrift, Jg. 12, Nr. 45, Wien, Juni 2000. Pp. 10–16, notes. [F.R.B., 1886 Vienna – 1961 London, jurist, writer, emigr. 1939 to London.]

38617. GRAZ. ZIEGERHOFER, ANITA: *"Laßt Haß der Feinde den Amboß sein, der unsre Einheit schmieden hilft". Ein sozial- und rechtshistorischer Streifzug durch die israelitische Kultusgemeinde Graz 1877 bis 1939.* [In]: Geschichte und Gegenwart, Bd. 17, Graz, 1998. Pp. 77–90.

——— HÖDL, SABINE/LAPPIN, ELEONORE, eds.: *Erinnerung als Gegenwart: Jüdische Gedenkkulturen.* [See No. 38432.]

——— HÖDL, KLAUS, ed.: *Jüdische Identitäten: Einblicke in die Bewußtseinslandschaften des österreichischen Judentums.* [See No. 39152.]

38618. HOHENEMS. DENMAN, HUGH: *The languages of the Jews in Hohenems.* [In]: Stammbaum, Issue 16, January 2000. New York, 2000. Pp. 1–5, footnotes, illus.

38619. HOHENEMS. *Hohenems re-visited: meeting of descendants of Jewish families from Hohenems, August 1998 = Begegnungen in Hohenems.* [Hrsg.: Jüd. Museum Hohenems]. Hohenems: Jüd. Museum [1999]. 112 pp., illus. [All texts in English and German; incl. personal memoirs.]

38620. LOHRMANN, KLAUS: *Zwischen Finanz und Toleranz: Das Haus Habsburg und die Juden.* Ein historischer Essay. Graz: Verl. Styria, 2000. 232 pp., illus., bibl.

38621. NEUNKIRCHEN (NÖ). MILCHRAM, GERHARD: *Heilige Gemeinde Neunkirchen.* Eine jüdische Heimatgeschichte. Wien: Mandelbaum, 2000. 206 pp., illus., facsims., bibl., notes. [Incl. list of Nazi victims.]

38622. VIENNA. DALINGER, BRIGITTE: *Begegnungen mit Dibbukim. Chassidische Mystik im modernen Wiener Theater zwischen 1880 und 1938.* [In]: Menora, Bd. 11, Berlin, 2000. Pp. 229–250, notes.

38623. VIENNA. HELGERT, HEIDRUN/SCHMID, MARTIN A.: *Die mittelalterliche Synagoge auf dem Judenplatz in Wien. Baugeschichte und Rekonstruktion.* [In]: Wiener Jahrbuch für jüdische Geschichte, Kultur & Museumswesen, Bd. 4, 1999/2000/5760, Wien, 2000. Pp. 91–110.

38624. Vienna. *Illustrierte Neue Welt.* Nr. 10/11 [with the issue title] *Das jüdische Wien.* Wien, Okt./Nov. 2000. 1 issue, illus. [Incl.: Editorial (Joanna Nittenberg, 5); contribs. on the period 1890–1938 (Anton Legerer, 7–20; on the social life of Jews in Vienna, as well as statistics, policies, Jewish identity, B'nai B'rith, the Jewish Museum, the library, Hakoah, the Zionistic Youth Kibbuzim of Vienna, immigrants). Contribs. on the post-1945 period (Daniela Davidovits, 6–7, 26–41; on Jewish life in Austria today, immigrants' life, schools, synagogues, youth and sport organisations, Jewish community, cultural life, antisemitism, professions, Austrian politics). Entartete und verfemte Komponisten (Beate Hennenberg, 22–23).]

38625. VIENNA. MITCHELL, PAUL/SCHÖN, DORIS: *Zur Bauforschung im Misrachihaus. Ein Haus der Judenstadt im Verlauf der Jahrhunderte.* [In]: Wiener Jahrbuch für jüdische Geschichte, Kultur & Museumswesen, Bd. 4, 1999/2000/5760, Wien, 2000. Pp. 111–122.

38626. VIENNA. POHANKA, REINHARD: *"... keinen Sitz, Haus noch Niederlaß ...". Der Judenplatz in Wien. Eine Geschichte.* [In]: Projekt: Judenplatz Wien [see No. 39090]. Pp. 119–131.

38627. VIENNA. WEISER-VARON, BENNO: *Reminiscences from Vienna.* [In]: Midstream, Vol. 46, No. 4, New York, May-June 2000. Pp., 11– 15. [Author, born in Vienna, recently participated in an Erich Fried symposium, which brought back memories from his pre-Anschluss life in Vienna.]

38628. VIENNA. *Zwischen Ost und West: Galizische Juden und Wien.* Hrsg. von Gabriele Kohlbauer-Fritz im Auftrag des Jüdischen Museums Wien. Wien: Jüd. Museum der Stadt Wien, 2000. 160 pp., illus., footnotes. [Catalogue book for exhibition with the same title, Nov. 7, 2000 – Feb. 18, 2001; incl. (some titles abbr.): Vorwort (Karl Albrecht-Weinberger, 6–7). Galizien in Wien (Yoram Kaniuk, 8–20). Zur Migration osteuropäischer Juden bis zum Beginn des Ersten Weltkriegs (Almut Meyer, 21–31). Ein Kaddisch zur Erinnerung an Ludwipol (Jacob Allerhand, 32–37). Der königliche Hof und seine Mitglieder. Ein kleiner Staat im Staate (David Assaf, 38–56; on Hasidic courts). Zaddik und Starez – Gurus in Altösterreich (Elias Ungar, 57–63). Mein Großvater aus Drohobyc (Claudia Erdheim, 64–74). Soma Morgenstern – Leben und Schreiben im Schatten der Geschichte (Raphaela Kitzmantel, 75–80).]

38629. *Wegweiser für Besucher der jüdischen Friedhöfe und Gedenkstätten in Wien, Niederösterreich, Burgenland, Steiermark und Kärnten.* Hrsg. vom Verein "Schalom". Wien: Verein Schalom, 1999. 100 pp., illus.

3. Central Europe

38630. BOHEMIA. GUNDACKER, FELIX: *Matrikenverzeichnis der jüdischen Matriken Böhmens.* Wien: F. Gundacker, 1998. VI, XII, 94 pp.

38631. BOHEMIA & MORAVIA. OTTO, ANTON [et al.] *Die Juden im Sudetenland.* Prag: Ackermann-Gemeinde/Ceská Krestanska Akademie, 2000. 351 pp., notes. [Title and all texts also in Czech; incl.: Einführung (Anton Otto, 9–12). Grussworte an die Teilnehmer der Konferenz: Die Juden im Sudetenland (Zdenek Prosek, 13–16). Tausend Jahre jüdische Geschichte in Böhmen und Mähren (Ferdinand Seibt, 17–46). Von Schönerer zum Genozid ? (Alena Misková, 47–86). Der Antisemitismus im sudetendeutschen katholischen Milieu 1918–1938 (Jaroslav Sebek, 87–99). Die deutschen Juden und ihre Wahl politischer Parteien (Fred Hahn, 100–110). Die nationale Strömung in der deutschen Gesellschaft und ihre Beziehung zu den Juden (Stanislav Biman, 111–118). Sudetenjuden oder Juden im Sudetenland? Versuch einer Problembestimmung (Dieter Schallner, 119–139). Die Juden im Sudetenland und ihre Schicksale nach dem Münchner Abkommen – 1938 (Helena Krejcová, 140–152). Die Juden in Nordostböhmen – Aufstieg und Untergang (Rudolf M. Wlaschek, 153–164). Die Juden in Südböhmen in den Jahren 1918–1945 (Jiri Dvorak, 166–203). Einige Anmerkungen zur Position der Juden im Gau Sudetenland 1938–1945 (Ludomir Kocourek, 204–216). Die jüdische Gemeinde in Aussig/Usti nad Labem im 19. und 20. Jahrhundert (Vladimir Kaiser, 235–254). Die jüdische Gemeinde im Teplitzer Raum in den Jahren 1850–1938 (Kvetoslava Kocourková, 255–269). Schulalltag mit jüdischen Lehrern und Mitschülern (Johanna von Herzogenberg, 270–276). Juden in der Tschechoslowakei (Peter Brod, 277–292). Die Schicksale der Teschener Juden nach 1945 (Jozef Szymecek, 293–311). Die gegenwärtige Situation der jüdischen Gemeinden in der Tschechischen Republik (Tomas Kraus, 312–322).]

38632. BUDAPEST. FROJIMOVICS, KINGA [et al.]: *Jewish Budapest: monuments, rites, history.* Ed. by Geza Komoroczy. Budapest; New York: Central European Univ. Press. (Distrib. by Plumbridge Distributors, Plymouth), 1999. XII, 597 pp., illus., maps, ports. (Atlantic studies on society in change, No. 101.) [Covers the history of the Jewish community in Budapest, incl. the Nazi period.]

38633. CZERNOWITZ. BARTFELD-FELLER, MARGIT: *Nicht ins Nichts gespannt. Von Czernowitz nach Sibirien deportiert. Jüdische Schicksale 1941–1997.* Hrsg. von Erhard Roy Wiehn. Konstanz: Hartung-Gorre, 1998. 108 pp., illus., facsims.

38634. CZERNOWITZ. BARTFELD-FELLER, MARGIT: *Wie aus ganz anderen Welten. Erinnerungen an Czernowitz und die sibirische Verbannung.* Hrsg. von Erhard Roy Wiehn. Konstanz: Hartung-Gorre, 2000. 72 pp., illus. [M. B.-F., b. 1923 in Czernowitz, 1940 deported by the Soviets to Siberia, in 1990 emigr. from Tomsk to Israel.]

38635. CZERNOWITZ. *Czernowitz: Die Geschichte einer ungewöhnlichen Stadt.* Hrsg. von Harald Heppner. Köln: Böhlau, 2000. X, 225 pp., illus., notes (183–216), index. [A collection of 10 essays; incl.: Die jüdische Gemeinde von Czernowitz (David Sha'ary, 103–128).]

38636. CZERNOWITZ. HOROWITZ, BERNHARD & LAURA MIT EDITH POMERANZ: *Stimmen der Nacht. Gedichte aus der Deportation in Transnistrien.* Vorworte von Andrei Corbea-Hoisie [et al.]. Hrsg. von Erhard Roy Wiehn. Konstanz: Hartung-Gorre, 2000. 84 pp., illus. [Personal memoirs in rhyme on the deportation by the Romanians of the Horowitz family from Czernowitz to Berschad (Ukraine) in Nov. 1941; written between 1941 and 1945.]

——— HAHN, HANS HENNING/STÜBEN, JENS, eds.: *Jüdische Autoren Ostmitteleuropas im 20. Jahrhundert.* [See No. 39253.]

38637. KIEVAL, HILLEL J.: *Languages of community: the Jewish experience in the Czech lands.* Berkeley: Univ. of California Press, 2000. XI, 311 pp., map, appendix, notes (235–283), bibl. 285–306, index. [Incl. chaps. [titles abbr.]: The Jews of Bohemia and Moravia to 1918. Enlightenment and tradition in Jewish Prague, 1780–1830. Intellectuals and community in the 1840s. Jewish culture and the invention of a tradition (Golem). Education and national conflict: Germans, Czechs, and Jews. Jan Hus and the prophets: fashioning a Czech Judaism at the turn of the century. Ritual murder as political discourse in the Czech lands. Masaryk and Czech Jewry: the ambiguities of friendship.]

38638. PRAGUE. GOLDBERG, SYLVIE ANNE: *Von der (Prager) Judenstadt zum jüdischen Prag.* [In]: Schöpferische Momente des europäischen Judentums in der frühen Neuzeit [see No. 38424]. Pp. 217–227.

38639. PRAGUE. REINER, ELCHANAN: *A biography of an agent of culture: Eleazar Altschul of Prague and his literary activity.* [In]: Schöpferische Momente des europäischen Judentums in der frühen Neuzeit [see No. 38424]. Pp. 229–248.

38640. PRAGUE. SPECTOR, SCOTT: *Prague territories: national conflict and cultural innovation in Franz Kafka's fin de siècle.* Berkeley: Univ. of California Press, 2000. [Distrib. in UK: Wiley]. XIV, 331 pp., illus, ports., map. (Weimar and now: German cultural criticism, 21.) [Deals with German-Jewish intellectuals in Prague at the beginning of the 20th century and explores the social, cultural and ideological context in which they worked. Incl. Franz Kafka, Egon Erwin Kisch, Max Brod, Hugo Bergmann, Franz Werfel.]

38641. *Viersprachenland am Pruth – Bukowina I & II.* [Issue title of] Zwischenwelt [formerly: Mit der Ziehharmonika], Jg. 17, Nr. 2 & 3, Wien, Juli & Nov. 2000. 2 issues. [Selected articles in Nr. 1: Bukowina 1850 bis 1918: Österreichs Osterweiterung (Hannes Hofbauer, 16–19). Czernowitz (Kurt Rein, 20–22). Kein "Bukowiner Poet" – Karl Emil Franzos (Andrei Corbea-Hoisie, 23–25). "Wir waren ein Herz und eine Seele ..." (Georg Drozdowski). Zu den deutsch-jüdischen Wechselseitigkeiten in Czernowitz bis 1940 (Günther Guggenberger, 40–43, notes.) Deutsch – die Muttersprache der meisten Bukowiner Juden (Edith Silbermann, 44–45). Der junge Celan und die Sprachen der Bukowina und Rumäniens (Heinrich Stiehler, 46–51, port., tabs., notes). Jüdische Autorinnen der Bukowina im zwanzigsten Jahrhundert (Amy Colin, 57–62, notes). Der letzte Heimkehrer – Erinnerungen von Josef Kinsbrunner. Aufgezeichnet und vorgestellt von Cécile Cordon (63–67). Selected articles in Nr. 2: Rumänische Sonderwege. Pogrome und Hilfsaktionen. Überlebenschancen unter dem antisemitischen Regime (Mariana Hausleitner, 9–14, notes). "Die Marken meiner Wege waren Mythen": Mythologisierung des Todes in der Holocaust-Lyrik von Immanuel Weißglas (Peter Rychlo, 19–25, notes). Deutschsprachige Gedichte von Emigranten im Exil (Helmut Braun, 30–33). Behaust nur im Wort. Der Bukowiner Dichter Alfred Kittner (1906–1991) (Walter Engel, 40–44).]

4. Switzerland

—— ALTERMATT, URS: *Katholizismus und Antisemitismus. Mentalitäten, Kontinuitäten, Ambivalenzen. Zur Kulturgeschichte der Schweiz 1918–1945.* [See No. 39498.]

38642. BASLE. EGGER, FRANZ: *Basel und die Juden im 17. Jahrhundert.* [In]: Israelitisches Wochenblatt, Jg. 100, Nr. 33, Zürich, 18. Aug. 2000. Pp. 17–19, illus.

38643. BERN. *Reiz und Fremde jüdischer Kultur. 150 Jahre jüdische Gemeinden im Kanton Bern.* Hrsg. im Auftrag des Collegium generale von Georg Eisner und Rupert Moser. Bern; New York: Peter Lang, 2000. 199 pp., illus., facsims. (Collegium Generale Universität Bern, Kulturhistorische Vorlesungen 1998/99.) [Incl.: Einleitung (Georg Eisner, 7–10). Antisemitische Vorurteile gegen Einstein (Armin Hermann, 87–102). Zwischen Öffnung und Abwehr: Hundert Jahre Berufungs- und Beförderungspraxis an der medizinischen Fakultät der Universität Bern (Urs Boschung, 103–142). Jüdisches Universitätsleben in Bern: Zwischen Sozialismus und Zionismus, Antisemitismus und Nationalsozialismus (Franziska Rogger, 143–180). Der Berner Prozess um die "Protokolle der Weisen von Zion" (Erwin Marti, 181–200). Further selected essays are listed according to subject.]

38644. *Israelitisches Wochenblatt.* Sondernummer [with the title] *100 Jahre iw".* Zürich, 24. Nov. 2000. 1 issue. [Incl.: iw in Zürich. Sprachrohr einer beredten Minderheit (Felix Rom, 14–15). Herzl und Bialik (Heinrich Urbach, 16–23; reprint from an article by the Chief Rabbi of Sarajevo orig. publ. 1945). "Zionismus war immer schon ein Thema" (Claire Wohlmann-Mayer, 24–25; personal recollections). Reiche publizistische Tradition (Pierre Heumann, 87–91; deals with the history of the Jewish press). Man wollte es einfach nicht glauben (Gerhart Riegner, 59–66; on his role in informing the US about the mass annihilation plans of the Nazis). Also facsim. articles and advertisements of previous vols.]

38645. STUTZ, HANS: *Der Judenmord von Payerne.* Zürich: Rotpunktverl., 2000. 137 pp. [Deals with the murder of a Jewish cattle dealer by a member of the Swiss Nazi party in Payerne, Canton Vaud, in 1942.]

C. German-Speaking Jews in Various Countries

38646. ARGENTINA. GÖRTZEN, ANTJA: *Opposition durch Literatur? Deutsche Exilliteratur 1933–1945 im Argentinischen Tage- und Wochenblatt. Mit einem Ausflug in die pseudonyme Seelenlandschaft Paul Zechs.* Berlin: Logos, 1999. 276 pp. Zugl.: Trier, Univ., Diss., 1999.

38647. AUSTRALIA. FINNANE, ANTONIA: *Far from where? Jewish journeys from Shanghai to Australia.* Carton South, Vic.: Melbourne Univ. Press, 1999. XIX, 267 pp., illus., maps, notes (245– 253), bibl. (254–260), index. [Personal accounts of mainly German- and Austrian-Jewish refugees who went to Shanghai and later emigr. to Australia.]

38648. AUSTRALIA. KIRCHHOF, ASTRID M.: *From Germany and Austria to Australia: experiences of Jewish women refugees in the 1930s.* [In]: Australian Jewish Historical Society Journal, Vol. 15, part 2, Sydney, 2000.

38649. BRAZIL. FISCHER, GUDRUN: *"Unser Land spie uns aus". Jüdische Frauen auf der Flucht vor dem Naziterror.* Mit einem Interview mit Anita Prestes und einem kritischen Nachwort des Verlages. Unter Mitarbeit von Susanne Behrend [et al.]. Berlin: Verlag Olga Benario und Herbert Baum, 2000. 219 pp., ports., illus., gloss., map, bibl. [Incl. 11 interviews and chap. on the German and the German-Jewish emigration to Brazil; critical epilogue refers to interview with Anita Prestes, a Brazilian communist, daughter of Olga Benario.]

38650. BRAZIL. FURTADO KESTLER, IZABELA MARIA: *Rivalisierende österreichische Gruppen im brasilianischen Exil.* [In]: Zeitgeschichte, Jg. 27, H. 6, Salzburg, 2000. Pp. 405–413, notes.

38651. EXILE. BEHMER, MARKUS, ed.: *Deutsche Publizistik im Exil 1933 bis 1945.* Personen – Positionen – Perspektiven. Festschrift für Ursula E. Koch. Münster, LIT, 2000. 423 pp., footnotes, index. (Kommunikationsgeschichte, Bd. 11.) [Incl. (selected articles pertaining to Jewish émigrés, some titles abbr.): Die Emigration aus dem nationalsozialistischen Deutschland. Ursachen, Phasen und Formen (Horst Möller, 46–57). Sanary, Hauptstadt der deutschen Literatur im Exil (1933–1940). Bericht eines Zeitzeugen (Pierre-Paul Sagave, 58–73; on Lion Feuchtwanger and Ludwig Marcuse). On the illegal press in France (Pierre Albert). Der Weg des Journalisten Fritz Heymann aus Nazi-Deutschland in das Amsterdamer Exil (Julius H. Schoeps, 83–94). Hermann Schwab: Orthodoxer Jude, liberaler Publizist (Guy Stern, 95–107). Benedikt Fred Dolbin, der Portraitist eines halben Jahrhunderts (Hans Bohrmann, 134–144). Walter Trier (1890–1951) (Maike Furbach-Sinani, 155–172). "Der Tag danach". Eine Exildebatte um Deutschlands Zukunft (Markus Behmer, 223–244; on a controversy in 1939 in 'Das Neue Tage-Buch', a Paris exile paper, ed. by Leopold Schwarzschild). Rückkehr nach Sibirien oder die Macht. Das Schicksal des KPD-Funktionärs, SPD-Politikers und Journalisten Leo Bauer (Klaus Arnold, 331–353). One further article is listed according to subject.]

38652. GREAT BRITAIN. DOVE, RICHARD: *Journey of no return: five German-speaking literary exiles in London, 1933–1945.* London: Libris, 2000. IX, 308 pp., illus., ports., notes (267–289), bibl. (290–300), index. [Incl. Alfred Kerr, Robert Neumann, Karl Otten, Stefan Zweig. Chaps. are entitled: The flight of intellectuals: departure. The waiting room (1933–1936). Isolation or integration (1936–1939): aspects of appeasement. Enemy aliens (1939–41): the phoney war and internment. No man's land (1941–45): writers without language. Return journey: 'once an emigré, always an emigré: the reception of exile literature in post-war Germany.]

38653. GREAT BRITAIN. SIEBER, PETER: *The Newcastle-upon-Tyne hostel for Jewish refugee girls.* London: Wiener Library: unpublished manuscript No. 4184, 2000. 10 pp., illus., ports. [On the hostel designed as a temporary refuge for girls after the events of 1938. Groups, mainly German- or Austrian-Jewish (some Czech), stayed in the hostel from 1939–1945, incl. period of evacuation to Cumbria.]

38654. LATIN AMERICA. SAINT SAUVEUR-HENN, ANNE: *Zukunftspläne für Österreich aus der Sicht der Lateinamerikaemigranten.* [In]: Zeitgeschichte, Jg. 27, H. 6, Salzburg, 2000. Pp. 397–404, notes.

38655. LIECHTENSTEIN. BIEDERMANN, KLAUS [et al.]: *Pfadfinderschaft und jüdische Kinder zur Zeit des Nationalsozialismus in Liechtenstein*. [In]: Jahrbuch des Historischen Vereins für das Fürstentum Liechtenstein, Bd. 99, Vaduz, 2000. Pp. 216–230, illus., footnotes, bibl.

38656. POLAND. ANDRZEJEWSKI, MAREK: *Zur deutschsprachigen Emigration in Polen 1933 bis 1939*. [In]: Exile im 20. Jahrhundert. Hrsg. im Auftrag der Gesellschaft für Exilforschung von Claus-Dieter Krohn [et al.]. München: ed. text + kritik, 2000. (Exilforschung. Ein Int. Jahrbuch, Bd. 18.). Pp. 138–156, notes. [Refers also to Jewish émigrés.]

38657. POLAND. DEETERS, DOROTHEA-ELISABETH: *Jüdische Gemeinden im Spannungsfeld innerchristlicher Machtkämpfe.* [In]: Beiträge zur ostdeutschen Kirchengeschichte. Folge 2, Düsseldorf, 1997 [publ. 1998]. Pp. 84–95, footnotes. [Deals with Jews in Deutsch-Krone, Friedland, Heinrichsdorf and elsewhere in Poland in the 18th cent.]

38658. TURKEY. *Haymatloz. Exil in der Türkei 1933 – 1945*. Eine Austellung des Vereins Aktives Museum und des Goethe-Institutes mit der Akademie der Künste, 8. Jan. bis 20. Feb. 2000. Red.: Sabine Hillebrecht. Berlin: Verein Aktives Museum, 2000. 235 pp., illus., notes, bibl. [Incl.: Grußwort (Walter Jens, 6–7). Geleitwort (Barbara John, 8–9). Prolog – Exil in der Türkei (Christine Fischer-Defoy, 10–20). 'Vogelfrei'. Die Verfolgung der Emigrantinnen und Emigranten in der Türkei durch das Deutsche Reich (Christiane Hoss, 130–155). Der Wahrheit eine Gasse. Franz von Papen und die Rettung der Juden (Christiane Hoss, 160–161). Vertürken? Die deutschen Emigranten zwischen heimisch werden und fremd bleiben (Sabine Hillebrecht, 162–171). Die Spuren der deutschsprachigen Exilanten in der Türkei (Ayhan Bakirdögen, 210–211). Also contribs. on individual Jews among the exiles.]

38659. USA. BOLKOSKY, SIDNEY M.: *Detroit's reaction to the Holocaust and the new immigrants.* [In]: Judaism, Vol. 49, New York, Summer 2000. Pp., 309–321, notes. [Examines the reactions of the Detroit Jewish community to the plight of the German Jews in the 1930s, and how the community rose to the post-war challenge when Holocaust victims began arriving in Detroit.]

38660. USA. CROWE, CAMERON: *Hat es Spass gemacht, Mr. Wilder?* München: Diana-Verl., 2000. XXI, 372 pp., indexes, list of films. [Deals with Wilder's American films.]

38661. USA. FRANK, WERNER L.: *The Frank Family: immigration of German Jews to the Mid-West in the nineteen thirties*. [In]: Western States Jewish History, Vol. 32, No. 2–3, Santa Monica, CA, Spring 2000. Pp. 130–161. [Describes the emigration of the Arthur Frank family from Germany to Chicago, IL. during the 1930s and their efforts to build a new life.]

38662. USA. GEHRING-MÜNZEL, URSULA: *The emigration of German Jews to America in the 19th century.* New York: Leo Baeck Institute, 2000. 20 pp. (LBI Occasional Paper.)

38663. USA. HARTENSTEIN, ELFI: *Jüdische Frauen im New Yorker Exil.* 10 Begegnungen. Dortmund: edition ebersbach, 1999. 127 pp., ports.,

38664. USA. ROSEN, EVELYN BODEK: *The Philadelphia Fels, 1880–1920: a social portrait*. Madison, NJ: Farleigh Dickinson Press, 2000. 231 pp., illus., notes (188–217), bibl. (218–225), index. [Story of a German-Jewish family from Kaiserslautern who went to Philadelphia in 1848 and became prominent in business and philanthropy.]

38665. USA. STEPHAN, ALEXANDER: *"Communazis": FBI surveillance of German émigré writers*. Transl. by Jan van Heurck. New Haven, CT: Yale Univ. Press, 2000. XXI, 362 pp., illus. [Incl. Leonard Frank, Fritz Kortner, Franz Werfel and many other German-Jewish refugees. For orig. German edn. see No. 32703/YB XLI.] [Cf.: Watched by the G-men (Martin Kettle) [in]: The Guardian, London, Sept. 22, 2000, pp. 6–7.]

38666. USA. *The "Unacceptables". American foundations and refugee scholars between the two wars and after*. Bruxelles, New York: P.I.E.-Peter Lang, 2000. 1 vol. (Euroclio: Etudes et documents, No. 18.) [Cont. articles by Guiliana Gemelli, Claus-Dieter Krohn, Christian Fleck, Reinhard Siegmund-Schultze, Rosario J. Tosello, Paola Zambelli, Diane Dosso, Pnina G. Abir-Am, Giovanni Paoloni, Albert Müller.]

38667. USA/CANADA. *Lebenswege und Lektüren. Österreichische NS-Vertriebene in den USA und Kanada.* Hrsg. von Beatrix Müller-Kampel unter Mitarbeit von Carla Carnevale. Tübingen: Niemeyer, 2000. VI, 352 pp., ports., bibl., index. [Cont.: Lebenswege und Lieblingslektüren österreichischer NS-Vertriebener in den USA und Kanada (ed., 1–19). Interviews (with bibl. annots.) with: Walter Herbert Sokel, Peter Heller, Herbert Lederer, Hans Eichner, Egon Schwarz, Harry Zohn, Dorrit Claire Cohn, Ruth Klüger, Evelyn Torton Beck. Book attempts to answer why former Austrians devoted their professional life to German literary studies.]

II. RESEARCH AND BIBLIOGRAPHY

A. Libraries and Institutes

—— ASCHOFF, DIETHARD: *Quellen und Regesten zur Geschichte der Juden in der Stadt Münster 1530–1650/1662.* [See No. 38566.]

38668. BARKAI, AVRAHAM: *The C.V. Archives in Moscow. A reassessment.* In]: Leo Baeck Institute Year Book XLV, Oxford, 2000. Pp. 173–182, footnotes.

38669. BUNDESARCHIV. BRACHMANN-TEUBNER, ELISABETH: *Die Neubearbeitung des Gedenkbuches "Opfer der Verfolgung der Juden unter der nationalsozialistischen Gewaltherrschaft in Deutschland 1933–1945". Eine Zwischenbilanz.* [In]: Klaus Oldenhage [et al.], eds.: Archiv und Geschichte. Festschrift für Friedrich P. Kahlenberg. Düsseldorf: Droste, 2000. (Schriften des Bundesarchivs, Nr. 57.) Pp. 275–290, footnotes.

38670. THE CENTRAL ZIONIST ARCHIVES JERUSALEM: *A 15. List of files of the papers of Max Bodenheimer and the Bodenheimer family.* [Jerusalem: The Central Zionist Archives], 1999. 2 vols., XX, 154 pp.; XX, 155–300 pp., illus., facsims. [Vol. II incl. introduction and biographical notes. also bibl.] [M.I.B., March 12, 1865 Stuttgart – July 19, 1940 Jerusalem, Zionist activist, lawyer, emigr. 1933 from Cologne via the Netherlands to Palestine.] [Available at the Bibliothek Germania Judaica, Cologne; also at the LBI London.]

38671. DEUTSCHES EXILARCHIV 1933–1945/DIE DEUTSCHE BIBLIOTHEK: *Archivalien des deutschen Exilarchivs 1933–1945: Bestandsübersicht.* [Red.: Marie-Luise Hahn]. Frankfurt am Main: Die Dt. Bibliothek, Dt. Exilarchiv 1933–1945, 2000. 55 pp.

38672. DUISBURG UNIVERSITY: *Judaica- und Hebraica-Bestände in der Gerhard-Mercator-Universität Duisburg.* Eine Übersicht mit Benutzungshinweisen von Manfred Komorowski. Duisburg: Univ.-Bibl., 2000. 17 [24] pp.

38673. INSTITUT FÜR GESCHICHTE DER JUDEN IN ÖSTERREICH, ST. PÖLTEN. GRÖBL, LYDIA/HÖDL, SABINE/STAUDINGER, BARBARA: *'Austria Judaica'. Geschichte der Juden in Österreich von 1520 bis 1670. Projektbericht.* [In]: Mitteilungen des Instituts für österreichische Geschichtsforschung, Bd. 108, H. 1–2, Wien, 2000. Pp. 139–143, footnotes. [On the recently started Austrian equivalent to the historico-topographical project 'Germania Judaica IV'.]

38674. INSTITUT FÜR GESCHICHTE DER JUDEN IN ÖSTERREICH, ST. PÖLTEN: *Aschkenas. Zeitschrift für Geschichte und Kultur der Juden.* Hrsg.: Friedrich Battenberg, Hans Otto Horch, Markus J. Wenninger in Verbindung mit dem Inst. für Gesch. der Juden in Österreich. Jg. 10, H. 1 & 2. Wien: Böhlau, 2000. 612 pp., footnotes, indexes. [H. 1 incl.: Aufsätze (9–41). Kleinere Beiträge (245–270). Literatur- und Forschungsberichte (273–276). Rezensionen und Buchanzeigen (277–300). Projektberichte (301–305). H. 2 cont.: Aufsätze (307–502). Kleinere Beiträge (503–523). Forschungs- und Literaturberichte (525–538). Rezensionen und Buchanzeigen (539–544). Projektberichte und Veranstaltungshinweise (575–580). Individual contribs. dealing with German-speaking Jewry are listed according to subject.]

38675. LEO BAECK INSTITUTE: *Jüdischer Almanach 2001/5761 des Leo Baeck Instituts.* Hrsg. von Anne Birkenhauer. Frankfurt am Main: Jüdischer Verlag, 2000. 199 pp., illus., notes. [Incl.: Zu diesem

Almanach (ed., 7–9); essay by David Grossman, contribs. on a documentary film about the Jews in the Ukraine (Nicole Hess), on Yiddish poets in Shanghai (Irene Eber), and on a South African Yiddish novel (Astrid Starck-Adler). Articles pertinent to German-Jewish history are listed according to subject.]

38676. LEO BAECK INSTITUTE: *Leo Baeck Institute Year Book 2000*. Vol. XLV. Ed.: J.A.S. Grenville, assoc. ed.: Julius Carlebach, assist. eds.: Helen McEwan, Gabriele Rahaman. Oxford: Berghahn, 2000. 425 pp., frontis., illus., footnotes, bibl. (243–416), general index (505–518). [Cont.: Preface (eds.). Essays are arranged under the sections: I. Jewish philosophy and politics in the enlightenment. II. Jewish acculturation and scholarship. III. Jewish identity in art and music. IV. Research from the 'Osobyi' archive in Moscow. V. Future research (207–229; cont. introd. (J.A.S. Grenville) and contribs. by Avraham Barkai, David Sorkin, Stefi Jersch-Wenzel, Robert Liberles, Werner T. Angress, Marion Kaplan, Michael A. Meyer, Christopher Browning, Evyatar Friesel, Ian Kershaw, Jeremy Noakes, Guy Stern, Chaim Schatzker). Further contribs. are listed according to subject.]

38677. LEO BAECK INSTITUTE, LONDON: *Report of activities 2000*. London: Leo Baeck Institute, Feb./March 2000. 24 pp.

38678. MOSES MENDELSSOHN ZENTRUM FÜR EUROPÄISCH-JÜDISCHE STUDIEN.: *Menora*. Jahrbuch für deutsch-jüdische Geschichte 2000. Bd. 11 [with the title] Geschichte, Messianismus und Zeitenwende. Im Auftrag des Moses Mendelssohn Zentrums für europäisch-jüdische Studien hrsg. von Julius H. Schoeps, Karl E. Grözinger, Willi Jasper und Gert Mattenklott. Red.: Willi Jasper, Olaf Glöckner, René Schreiter. Berlin: Philo, 2000. 1 vol., 390 pp., notes, index. [Cont.: Einführung (eds., 9–12). Essays are arranged under the sections: I. Erinnern und Vergessen. Deutsch-jüdische "Normalität"? II. Mystik, Messianismus und Zeitenwende. III. Regionalgeschichtliche Beiträge: Sachsen-Anhalt. Individual essays are listed according to subject.]

38679. OFFE, SABINE: *Ausstellungen, Einstellungen, Entstellungen. Jüdische Museen in Deutschland und Österreich*. Berlin: Philo, 2000. 365 pp., illus., footnotes, bibl. (325–361). [Examines critically the concepts underlying German- and Austrian-Jewish museums.]

38680. SCHWEIZERISCHES BUNDESARCHIV: *Inventare. Flüchtlingsakten 1930–1950*. Thematische Übersicht zu Beständen im Schweizerischen Bundesarchiv. Bearb. von Guido Koller und Heinz Roschewski. Leitung: A. Kellerhals-Maeder. [Bern]: Schweizerisches Bundesarchiv, 1999. 309 pp.

38681. STAATSBIBLIOTHEK ZU BERLIN: *Verleihung des Max-Herrmann-Preises an Dr. Cécile Lowenthal-Hensel*. [In]: Mitteilungen [der] Staatsbibliothek zu Berlin – Preußischer Kulturbesitz, N.F.9, Nr. 2, Berlin, 2000. Pp. 213–227. [Incl.: Grußwort (Antonius Jammers, 213–217). Der Max-Herrmann-Preis (Winfried Sühlo, 217–219). Laudatio (219–225). Dankrede (Cécile Lowenthal-Hensel, 225–227).] [Max Herrmann, 1865 – 1942 (Auschwitz), prof. of theatre and literature, president of several literary societies, founder and compiler of "Bibliothek deutscher Privat- und Manuskriptdrucke", since 1938 part of the Staatsbibliothek.] [Cécile Lowenthal-Hensel, archivist, editor, great-granddaughter of Fanny and Wilhelm Hensel, founder of the Mendelssohn-Archiv and the Mendelssohn-Gesellschaft.]

38682. WIENER LIBRARY, LONDON. GABEL, GERNOT: *Die "Wiener Library" in London 1939–1999*. [In]: Buch und Bibliothek, Jg. 52, H. 1, Bad Honnef, 2000. Pp. 45–49, illus.]

38683. WIENER LIBRARY, LONDON. BARKOW, BEN, comp.: *Testaments to the Holocaust: series two: the Wiener Library thematic press cutting collection, 1933–1945*. Guide Woodbridge, CT: Primary Source Media, 1999. [76] leaves.

38684. ZENTRUM FÜR ANTISEMITISMUSFORSCHUNG, BERLIN.: *Jahrbuch für Antisemitismusforschung 9*. Hrsg. von Wolfgang Benz für das Zentrum für Antisemitismusforschung der Technischen Universität Berlin. Red.: Werner Bergmann, Johannes Heil, Mona Körte. Geschäftsführende Red.: Juliane Wetzel. Frankfurt am Main; New York: Campus, 2000. 300 pp., notes. [Incl.: Vorwort (Wolfgang Benz, 7–9). Essays are arranged under the sections: Rechtsextremismus (11–107; on right-wing cases in Germany and Russia). Antisemitismus (108–181; also on English and South-African antisemitism). Auseinandersetzung mit der Vergangenheit (182–280; on

Polish, German, US-American and Japanese aspects of Holocaust remembrance). Selected essays are listed according to subject.]

B. Bibliographies, Catalogues and Reference Books

38685. BEINART, HAIM: *Geschichte der Juden. Atlas der Verfolgung und Vertreibung im Mittelalter.* [Übers. und teilweise Bearb. der dt. Ausgabe: Klaus Lohrmann]. Augsburg: Bechtermünz, 1998. 144 pp., illus., maps, bibl., indexes. [Orig. publ. in Israel 1992. Covers persecutions up to the mid-17th century.]

38686. BOLBECHER, SIGLINDE/KAISER, KONSTANTIN: *Lexikon der österreichischen Exilliteratur.* In Zusammenarbeit mit Evelyn Adunka, Nina Jakl, Ulrike Oedl. Wien: Deuticke, 2000. 761 pp., ports., bibl. (746–755), indexes.

38687. COHEN, SUSAN SARAH, ed.: *Antisemitism.* An annotated bibliography. Vol. 12, 1996. [Publ. by] The Vida Sassoon International Center for the Study of Antisemitism/The Hebrew University of Jerusalem. München: Saur, 2000. IX, 527 pp., indexes. (The Felix Posen Bibliographical Project of Antisemitism.]

38688. *Deutsche biographische Enzyklopädie (DBE).* Hrsg. von Walther Killy u. Rudolf Vierhaus. München; New Providence: Saur. 1995–2000. 10 vols.: A–Z, 4 vols.: Nachträge, name index, place index., profession index.

——— EDELHEIT, ABRAHAM/EDELHEIT, HERSHEL: *History of Zionism: a handbook and dictionary.* [See No. 39197.]

38689. GESELLSCHAFT ZUR ERFORSCHUNG DER GESCHICHTE DER JUDEN E.V.: *Dokumentation: Arbeitsgebiete und Veröffentlichungen der Mitglieder der GEGJ e.V.* Im Auftrag der Gesellschaft zur Erforschung der Geschichte der Juden e.V. bearb. von Friedhelm Burgard und Antje Hansen. Trier: GEGJ e.V., 2000. 288 pp.

38690. *The Holocaust Chronicle.* Contributors: Marilyn Harran [et al.]. Lincolnwood, IL: Publications International, 2000. 765 pp., illus., chronol., facsims., maps, appendixes.

——— KLAWITER, RANDOLPH J.: *Stefan Zweig: an international bibliography.* Addendum I. [See No. 39417.]

——— KUKATZKI, BERNHARD: *Bibliographie zur pfälzisch-jüdischen Geschichte. Berichtsjahr 1999.* Mit Nachträgen aus den Vorjahren. [See No. 38576.]

38691. *Lexikon deutsch-jüdischer Autoren.* Bd. 8: Frie-Gers. Red. Leitung: Renate Heuer. Unter Mitarbeit von Gudrun Jäger, Manfred Pabst, Birgit Seemann, Siegbert Wolf. München: Saur, 2000. 406 pp. (Archiv Bibliographia Judaica.)

38692. MEDOFF, RAFAEL/WAXMAN, CHAIM I.: *Historical dictionary of Zionism.* Lanham, MD: Scarecrow Press, 2000. XXIX, 238 pp., maps. (Religions, philosophies, and movements series, 31.)

38693. *Metzler Lexikon der deutsch-jüdischen Literatur.* Jüdische Autorinnen und Autoren deutscher Sprache von der Aufklärung bis zur Gegenwart. Hrsg. von Andreas B. Kilcher. Stuttgart: Metzler, 2000. XX, 664 pp., illus. [Incl. an introd. essay by the ed. (I-XX).]

38694. *Neues Lexikon des Judentums.* Hrsg. von Julius H. Schoeps. Red. des Moses-Mendelssohn-Zentrums, Julius H. Schoeps [et al.]. Überarb. Neuausg. Gütersloh: Gütersloher Verl.-Haus, 2000. 896 pp., illus.

38695. POLLMANN, VIKTORIA: *NS-Justiz, Nürnberger Prozesse, NSG-Verfahren.* Auswahlbibliographie. Frankfurt am Main: Fritz Bauer Institut, 2000. 96 pp. (Verzeichnisse, Nr. 4.)

——— PRACHT-JÖRNS, ELFI: *Jüdisches Kulturerbe in Nordrhein-Westfalen.* Teil II: Regierungsbezirk Düsseldorf. [See No. 38583.]

38696. *Publications on German-speaking Jewry*. A selected and annotated bibliography of books and articles 1999. Compiled by Barbara Suchy and Annette Pringle. [In]: Leo Baeck Institute Year Book XLV, London, 2000. Pp. 243–414, index (names, places, periodicals, subjects, 377–414).]

38697. *Quellen zur Geschichte der Juden in den Archiven der neuen Bundesländer*. Hrsg. von Stefi Jersch-Wenzel und Reinhard Rürup. Bd. 5. Geheimes Staatsarchiv Preußischer Kulturbesitz Teil II: Sonderverwaltung der Übergangszeit 1806–1815, Zentralbehörden ab 1808, Preußische Parlamente 1847–1933, Preußische Armee (bis 1866/1867), Provinzialüberlieferungen, Provianzial- und Lokalbehörden, Nichtstaatliche Provenienzen und Archivische Sammlungen. Bearb. von Kurt Metschies unter Mitarbeit von Waltraud Elstner [et al.]. Red.: Bernd Braun und Manfred Jehle. München: Saur, 2000. XVII, 480 pp., indexes (persons; places, 441–480). [For previous vols. see Nos. 33943/YB XVII and 37456/YB XLV.]

38698. ROZETT, ROBERT/SPECTOR, SHMUEL, eds.: *Encyclopedia of the Holocaust*. Publ. jointly by Yad Vashem and Facts on File. Jerusalem: Jerusalem Publ. House, 2000. VIII, 528 pp., illus., tabs., facsims., index.

——— STUDEMUND-HALÉVY, MICHAEL: *Biographisches Lexikon der Hamburger Sefarden. Die Grabinschriften des Portugiesenfriedhofs an der Königsstraße in Hamburg-Altona*. [See No. 38536.]

38699. WENDLAND, ULRIKE: *Biographisches Handbuch deutschsprachiger Kunsthistoriker im Exil. Leben und Werk der unter dem Nationalsozialismus verfolgten und vertriebenen Wissenschaftler*. Teil 1 & 2. München: Saur, 1999. 2 vols. XLII, 813 pp. Zugl.: Hamburg, Univ., Diss., 1996.

38700. WIRTZ, STEFAN/KOLBE, CHRISTIAN: *Enteignung der jüdischen Bevölkerung in Deutschland und nationalsozialistische Wirtschaftspolitik*. Annotierte Bibliographie. Frankfurt am Main: Fritz Bauer Institut, 2000. 56 pp., index.

III. THE NAZI PERIOD

A. General

——— AACHEN. DÜWELL, KURT: *Exil und Remigration von RWTH-Professoren (1933–1953)*. [See No. 39222.]

38701. AHRENSBÖK. WOLLENBERG, JÖRG: *Ahrensbök – eine Kleinstadt im Nationalsozialismus. Konzentrationslager – Zwangsarbeit – Todesmarsch*. Mit Beiträgen von Norbert Fick und Lawrence D. Stokes. Bremen: Edition Temmen, [2000]. 271 pp., facs., illus. [Incl. personal recollections of Jewish inmates of the Fürstengrube concentration camp.]

38702. AMKRAUT, BRIAN DAVID: *Let our children go: Youth Aliyah in Germany, 1932–1939*. New York: New York Univ., Diss., 2000. [Typescript], 437 pp.

38703. APLERBECK/DORTMUND. KIRCHHOFF, HANS-GEORG: *Die jüdische Gemeinde Aplerbeck und ihre Vernichtung*. [In Heimat Dortmund, Stadtgeschichte in Bildern und Beiträgen, Jg. 14, Dortmund, 1999.

38704. ARENDT, HANNAH: *Vor Antisemitismus ist man nur noch auf dem Monde sicher*. Beiträge für die deutschjüdische Emigrantenzeitung "Aufbau" 1941–1945. Hrsg. von Marie Luise Knott. München: Piper, 2000. 244 pp., bibl., index. [Incl.: Nachwort (ed., 285–221).] [See also No. 38410.]

38705. *"Arisierung" im Nationalsozialismus. Volksgemeinschaft, Raub und Gedächtnis*. Hrsg.: Fritz Bauer Institut. Frankfurt am Main: Campus, 2000. 312 pp., notes, illus., tabs. (Jahrbuch 2000 zur Geschichte und Wirkung des Holocaust.) [Cont. (some titles abbr.): Einleitung (Irmtrud Wojak/Peter Hayes, 7–13). "Arisierung" als gesellschaftlicher Prozeß. Verhalten, Strategien und Handlungsspielräume jüdischer Eigentümer und "arischer" Erwerber (Frank Bajohr, 15–30). Antisemitische Wirtschaftspropaganda und völkische Diktaturpläne in den ersten Jahren der Weimarer Republik.

Anhang: Gegenüberstellung der Verfassungsentwürfe (Susanne Meinl, 31–58). Die "Arisierung" der Wirtschaftselite. Ausmaß und Verlauf der Verdrängung der jüdischen Vorstands- und Aufsichtsratsmitglieder in deutschen Aktiengesellschaften (1933–1938) (Martin Fiedler, 59–84). Die "Arisierungen" der Degussa AG. Geschichte und Bilanz (Peter Hayes, 85–124). Zur "Arisierung" von Immobilien durch Städte und Gemeinden 1938–1945 (Wolf Gruner, 125–157). Antijüdische Maßnahmen im Protektorat Böhmen und Mähren und das "Jüdische Zentralmuseum" in Prag (Jan Björn Potthast, 157–200). Die Enteignung "jüdischen Eigentums" im Reichskommissariat Ostland 1941–1944 (Martin Dean, 201–218). Zwangsarbeit von Juden in Arbeits- und Konzentrationslagern (Hermann Kaienburg, 219–240). Belzec – Das vergessene Lager des Holocaust (Michael Tregenza, 241–268). "Dieses Atelier ist sofort zu vermieten". Von der "Entjudung eines Berufsstandes" (Rolf Sachsse, 269–286; on photojournalists). Vorhanden/Nicht-Vorhanden. Über die Latenz der Dinge (Harald Welzer, 287–308).]

38706. AUGSBURG. BERNHEIM, ERHARD: *"Halbjude" im Dritten Reich. Die Erinnerungen des Augsburger Fabrikanten Erhard Bernheim*. Erhard Bernheim, Gernot Römer (Hrsg.) Augsburg: Wißner, 2000. 68 pp., illus. (Lebenserinnerungen von Juden aus Schwaben, Bd. 3.)

38707. AUSCHWITZ. FRANKFURTER, BERNHARD, ed.: *The meeting: an Auschwitz survivor confronts an SS physician*. Transl. from the German by Susan E. Cernyak-Spatz. Syracuse, NY: Syracuse Univ. Press, 2000. XVIII, 192 pp., illus., maps. (Religion, theology, and the Holocaust.) [Interviews conducted with former SS physician Hans Wilhelm Münch and the survivor Dagmar Ostermann, and conversations between them. For orig. edn. and more details see No. 32748/YB XLI.]

38708. AUSCHWITZ. NEUFELD, MICHAEL/BERENBAUM, MICHAEL, eds.: *The bombing of Auschwitz: should the allies have attempted it?* New York: St. Martin's Press, 2000. 350 pp., notes. [Cont. 15 contribs. reflecting both sides of the issue, based on a conference at the US Holocaust Museum in 1993.] [Cf.: Review (Abraham Edelheit) [in]: Jewish Book World, Vol. 18, No. 3, New York, 2000, pp. 33–34.]

38709. AUSCHWITZ. *Standort- und Kommandanturbefehle des Konzentrationslagers Auschwitz 1940–1945*. Hrsg. im Auftrag des Instituts für Zeitgeschichte von Norbert Frei, Thomas Grotum, Jan Parcer, Sybille Steinbacher und Bernd C. Wagner. München: Saur, 2000. 604 pp., maps, footnotes, bibl., indexes. (Darstellungen und Quellen zur Geschichte von Auschwitz, Bd. 1.)

38710. AUSCHWITZ. STEINBACHER, SYBILLE: *"Musterstadt" Auschwitz. Germanisierungspolitik und Judenmord in Ostoberschlesien*. München: Saur, 2000. 419 pp., footnotes. (Darstellungen und Quellen zur Geschichte von Auschwitz, Bd. 2.) [Deals also with the history of the town of Oswiecim/Auschwitz and its Jewish population, which was in part German-speaking.]

38711. AUSCHWITZ. TICHAUER, ERWIN R.: *Totenkopf und Zebrakleid. Ein Berliner Jude in Auschwitz*. Bearb. und mit einem Nachwort versehen von Jürgen Matthäus. Berlin: Metropol, 2000. 212 pp., illus., notes. (Bibliothek der Erinnerung, Bd. 5.) [E.T., 1920 Berlin – 1996 New York, prof. of engineering and bio-mechanics, 1943 deported to Auschwitz; his fictionalised hitherto unpubl. recollections were written 1949–1950 in Australia.]

38712. AUSCHWITZ. WAGNER, BERND C.: *IG Auschwitz. Zwangsarbeit und Vernichtung von Häftlingen des Lagers Monowitz 1941–1945*. München: Saur, 2000. 378 pp., illus., tabs., footnotes, bibl., index. (Darstellungen und Quellen zur Geschichte von Auschwitz, Bd. 3.)

38713. AUSTRIA. DOHLE, OSKAR: *Die Chronik der Linzer Judenschule, Mai-November 1938*. [In]: Historisches Jahrbuch der Stadt Linz 1997, (1999). Linz, 1999 [sic]. Pp. 409–423, illus.

38714. AUSTRIA. GRUNER, WOLF: *Zwangsarbeit und Verfolgung: Österreichische Juden im NS-Staat 1938–45*. Innsbruck: Studien-Verlag, 2000. 356 pp., illus., tabs., lists, maps, bibl. (328–339), index (341–356; persons, firms, places). (Der Nationalsozialismus und seine Folgen, Bd. 1.)

38715. AUSTRIA. KWIET, KONRAD: *"Wenn ein Wiener da ist, kann uns nicht viel passieren"*. Zum Anteil der Österreicher am Holocaust. [In]: Projekt: Judenplatz Wien [see No. 39090]. Pp. 216–230.

38716. AUSTRIA. LEMKE, UTE: *Deutsche Exilpresse im österreichischen Ständestaat – gab es denn das?* [In]: Zeitgeschichte, Jg. 27, H. 6, Salzburg, 2000. Pp. 378–385, notes.

38717. AUSTRIA. LOACKER, ARMIN/PRUCHA, MARTIN, eds.: *Unerwünschtes Kino. Der deutschsprachige Emigrantenfilm 1934–1937.* Wien: Filmarchiv Austria, 2000. 211 pp., illus., facsims.. [Deals with Austrian film productions made by exiles from Nazi Germany.]

38718. AUSTRIA. MERTZ, PETER: *Glücklich ist, wer vergisst. Arisierungen und Enteignungen in Österreich.* [In]: Die Zeichen der Zeit/Lutherische Monatshefte, Jg. 3, H. 1, Hannover, 2000. Pp. 40–41, illus.

38719. AUSTRIA. NEUGEBAUER, WOLFGANG: *Die jüdischen Euthanasieopfer in Österreich.* [In]: Jahrbuch 2000 [des] Dokumentationsarchivs des österreichischen Widerstandes (DÖW), Wien, 2000. Pp. 134–141.

38720. AUSTRIA. SCHWEIGER, ANDREAS: *David Herzog. Erinnerungen eines Rabbiners 1932–1940.* Auf Grundlage einer Diplomarbeit. Hrsg. von Walter Höflechner. Graz: Akad. Dr.-und Verl.-Anst., 1997. XXXIV, 80 pp., illus., bibl. (Publikationen aus dem Archiv der Universität Graz, Bd. 32.) [D.H., 1869 Tyrnau, Slovakia – 1946 Oxford, historian, Landesrabbiner of Styria and Carinthia until flight from Graz to the UK after Anschluss 1938.]

38721. AUSTRIA. THUMSER, REGINA: *"Ernst ist das Leben, heiter ist die Kunst." – Kabarett im Österreich der Zwischenkriegszeit.* [In]: Zeitgeschichte, Jg. 27, H. 6, Salzburg, 2000. Pp. 386–397, notes. [Focuses on Jimmy Berg (orig. Symson Weinberg).]

38722. *Ausbeutung, Vernichtung, Öffentlichkeit: Neue Studien zur nationalsozialistischen Lagerpolitik.* Hrsg. im Auftrag des Instituts für Zeitgeschichte von Norbert Frei, Sybille Steinbacher und Bernd C. Wagner. München: Saur, 2000. 335 pp., footnotes, bibl. (299–320), indexes. (Darstellungen und Quellen zur Geschichte von Auschwitz, Bd. 4.) [Incl. articles on Mittelbau-Dora (Jens-Christian Wagner, 11–42), Jewish slave labour for the SS 'Ostindustrie GmbH' (Jan Erik Schulte, 43–74), forced labour for Volkswagen, concentrations camps Hinzert, Stutthof, Soldau (Gabriele Lotfi, 209–230), mass murder in Ukraine (Dieter Pohl, 135–174), in the Soviet Union (Christian Gerlach, 175–208). Also: Gerüchte, Wissen, Verdrängung: Die IG Auschwitz und das Vernichtungslager Birkenau (Bernd C. Wagner, 231–248). Justizmord und Judenmord: Todesurteile gegen Judenhelfer in Polen und der Tschechoslowakei 1942–1944 (Bernward Dörner, 249–264). "… nichts weiter als Mord." Der Gestapo-Chef von Auschwitz und die bundesdeutsche Nachkriegsjustiz (Sybille Steinbacher, 264–298).]

38723. BACHRACH, SUSAN D.: *The Nazi olympics: Berlin 1936.* Boston: Little, Brown, 2000. 128 pp., illus., facsisms., map, ports., chronol., appendix, bibl., index. [Incl. Jewish athletes some of whom, for propaganda reasons, were allowed to participate in the games.]

38724. BAJOHR, FRANK: *Verfolgung aus gesellschaftsgeschichtlicher Perspektive. Die wirtschaftliche Existenzvernichtung der Juden und die deutsche Gesellschaft.* [In]: Geschichte und Gesellschaft, Jg. 26, H. 4, Göttingen, 2000. Pp. 629–652, footnotes.

38725. BANKIER, DAVID, ed.: *Probing the depths of German antisemitism: German society and the persecution of the Jews, 1933–1941.* New York; Oxford: Berghahn Books in association with Yad Vashem and the Leo Baeck Institute, Jerusalem, 2000. 585 pp., notes, index of names and places. [Cont. (titles. abbr.): Introd.: Overall explanations, German society and the Jews (Yehuda Bauer, 3–18). Acquiescence? (Heide Gerstenberger, 19–35). The double consciousness of the Nazi mind and practice (Leny Yahil, 36–53). The mixed marriage: a guarantee of survival or a reflection of German society during the Nazi regime? (Beate Meyer, 54–77). Public welfare and the German Jews under National Socialism (Wolf Gruner, 78–107). Local administration and Nazi anti-Jewish policy (Uwe Lohalm, 109–146). The Germans: "an anti-Semitic people": the press campaign after 9 Nov. 1938 (Herbert Obenaus, 147– 180). Violence against Jews in Germany 1933–1939 (Michael Wildt, 181– 211). The minister of economics and the expulsion of the Jews from the German economy (Albert Fischer, 213–225). The "aryanization" of Jewish companies and German society (Frank Bajohr, 226–245). The attack on Berlin department stores after 1933 (Simone Ladwig-Winters, 246–269). The German population and the Jews (Otto D. Kulka,

271–281). Popular attitudes to National Socialist antisemitism (Christl Wickert, 282–295). German work and German workers: the impact of symbols on the exclusion of Jews in Nazi-Germany (Alf Lüdtke, 296–311). The German-Jewish relationship in the diaries of Victor Klemperer (Susanne Heim, 312–327). Reaction of the Jewish press in Germany to the Nuremberg Laws (Joseph Walk, 329–338). The final years of the Centralverein (Daniel Fraenkel, 339–359). The "emigration effort" or "repatriation" (Yfaat Weiss, 360–370). Jewish leadership and Jewish resistance (Arnold Paucker and Konrad Kwiet, 371–394). Jewish daily life in wartime Germany (Marion Kaplan, 395–413). The Catholic anti-Jewish prejudice (Walter Zwi Bacharach, 415–430). German Protestants and the persecution of the Jews in the Third Reich (Ursula Büttner, 431–461). The German resistance to Hitler and the Jews (Peter Hoffmann, 463–477). 20 July and the "Jewish Question" (Christof Dipper, 478–499). American diplomatic records regarding German public opinion during the Nazi regime (Richard Breitman, 501–510). German Social Democrats and the Jewish Question (David Bankier, 511–532). British policy, allied intelligence and Zionist dilemmas in the face of Hitler's Jewish policies (Shlomo Aronson, 533–569).]

38726. BARTROP, PAUL ROBERT: *Surviving the camps: unity in adversity during the Holocaust.* Lanham, MD: University of America, 2000. XIII, 209 pp., maps, notes, bibl.(189–204), index. (Studies in the Shoah, 23.) [Author deals with psychological and historical elements which contributed to survival, uses Bruno Bettelheim, his experiences and theories as an example.]

38727. BAUER, MARKUS: *Exil und Galut.* Zum jüdischen Selbstverständnis nach 1933. [In]: Exile im 20. Jahrhundert. Hrsg. im Auftrag der Gesellschaft für Exilforschung von Claus-Dieter Krohn [et al.]. München: ed. text + kritik, 2000. (Exilforschung. Ein Int. Jahrbuch, Bd. 18.). Pp. 37–51, notes.

38728. BAYREUTH. *Physische und behördliche Gewalt. Die "Reichskristallnacht" und die Verfolgung der Juden in Bayreuth.* Hrsg. von der Geschichtswerkstatt Bayreuth. Ekkehard Hübschmann, Helmut Paulus, Siegfried Pokorny. Bayreuth: Bumerang-Verl., 2000. 259 pp., illus.

38729. BEKER, AVI, ed.: *The plunder of Jewish property during the Holocaust: confronting European history.* Basingstoke: Macmillan, 2000. 336 pp., map, notes, index.

——— BELGIUM. SCHREIBER, MARION: *Stille Rebellen. Der Überfall auf den 20. Deportationszug nach Auschwitz.* [See No. 39011.]

38730. BENZ, WOLFGANG: *Der Moskauer Schriftstellerkongreß 1934.* Literarische und politische Erinnerungen. [In]: Zeitschrift für Geschichtswissenschaft, Jg. 48, H. 7, Berlin, 2000. Pp. 624–632, footnotes. [Incl. German- and Austrian-Jewish participants; also in this issue : Freundschaft in einem Sommer. Ernst Toller in Moskau (Ruth Körner, 633–641; personal recollections of author, née Elisabeth Schwarz, later E. Passer, written in the 1960s).]

38731. BENZ, WOLFGANG: *Deutschland war ein Land, aus dem man floh.* Rede zur Eröffnung der Jahrestagung der Gesellschaft für Exilforschung, Wien, 24.3.2000. [In]: Zwischenwelt [formerly: Mit der Ziehharmonika], Jg. 17, Nr. 1, Wien, Mai 2000. Pp. 5–7. [Incl. an unpubl. text by Ruth Körner; see also in No. 38730.]

38732. BERGEN-BELSEN. WENCK, ALEXANDRA-EILEEN: *Zwischen Menschenhandel und "Endlösung": Das Konzentrationslager Bergen-Belsen.* Paderborn: Schöningh, 2000. 444 pp., footnotes, maps, bibl. (402–435), index. (Sammlung Schöningh zur Geschichte und Gegenwart.) Zugl.: Münster, Univ., Diss., 1997.

38733. BERLIN. HALLEY, ANNE: *Before the deportation – a German-Jewish fate: Edith Marcuse, 1898– 1945.* [In]: The Massachusetts Review, Vol. 40, No. 4, Amherst, Winter 1999/2000. Pp. 521–549. [Story of the Marcuse family from Berlin, the merchant Carl and his wife Paula, and their three children Ludwig, Johanna, and Edith, a writer. Incl. excerpts from her diary written before deportation 1943.]

38734. BERLIN. HERZBERG, HEINRICH: *Dienst am höheren Gesetz. Dr. Margarete Sommer und das "Hilfswerk beim Bischöflichen Ordinariat Berlin".* Berlin: Servi, 2000. 224 pp., illus., facsims., notes (183–208), chronol., index. [Deals with the help and rescue for Catholic and other "non-aryans"]

38735. BERLIN. MARKUS, JUDITH: *Das Vaterland*. [In]: Zwischenwelt [formerly: Mit der Ziehharmonika], Jg. 17, Nr. 4, Wien, Dez. 2000. Pp. 33–36. [Author, born 1926, tells about her childhood years in Berlin until she left her family with a Kindertransport to Sweden; lives in Amsterdam. Her memoirs: *Het vaterland. Kinderjaren in Berlin*. Amsterdam: Nijgh & Van Ditmar, 2000. 1 vol.]

38736. BERLIN. MEYER, BEATE/SIMON, HERMANN: *Juden in Berlin 1938–1945*. Begleitband zur gleichnamigen Ausstellung in der Stiftung "Neue Synagoge Berlin – Centrum Judaicum", Mai bis August 2000. Berlin: Philo, 2000. 356 pp., illus., tabs., notes, index. [Cont. (some titles abbr.): Einleitung (eds., 9–16). Das Jahr 1938 (Hermann Simon, 17–32). Die "Juni-Aktion" 1938 in Berlin (Christian Dirks, 33–43). Eine merkwürdige Begebenheit in Schloß Bellevue (Frank Schirrmacher, 44–50). Flucht und Vertreibung der deutschen Juden 1933–1941 (Michael Schäbitz, 51–76). "Arisiert" und ausgeplündert. Die jüdische Fabrikantenfamilie Garbáty (Beate Meyer, 77–88). "Wir waren von allem abgeschnitten". Zur Entrechtung, Ausplünderung und Kennzeichnung der Berliner Juden (Albert Meirer, 89–106). Zwischen "Leben in Brasilien" und "Aus den Verordnungen". Das Jüdische Nachrichtenblatt 1938–1943 (Clemens Maier, 107–128). "Trotzdem". Zionisten in Berlin (Chana C. Schütz, 129–146). Zwangsarbeit (Diana Schulte, 147–158). "Gebt unsere Männer frei!" (Diana Schulte, 159–170). Deportation (Beate Meyer, 171–178). "Jeder Mensch hat einen Namen" (Rita Meyhöfer, 179–198). Die Opernsängerin Therese Rothauser (Alexandra von Pfuhlstein, 197–203). Zum Schicksal der Familie Scheurenberg (Christian Dirks, 204–214). Das Poesiealbum der Ruth Schwersenz (Karin Wieckhorst, 215–232). Der Fahndungsdienst der Berliner Gestapo (Christian Dirks, 233–258). Vom Überleben der Familie Frankenstein in der Illegalität 1943–1945 (Barbara Schieb, 259–279). Das Beispiel Hans Rosenthal (Michael Schäbitz, 280–290). Die Reichsvereinigung der Juden in Deutschland und die Jüdische Gemeinde zu Berlin 1938–1945 (Beate Meyer, 291–337). Die Gebäude der Oranienburger Straße 28–31 (Diana Schulte, 338–348).]

38737. BERLIN. OWINGS, ALISON: *Eine andere Erinnerung: Frauen erzählen von ihrem Leben im "Dritten Reich"*. Aus dem Amerik. von Kay Dohnke. Mit einer Vorbemerkung von Elke Fröhlich. Berlin: Ullstein, 1999. 601 pp. [Incl. chaps. about a Jewish woman and a woman who sheltered a Jewish woman.]

38738. BERLIN. SCHIEB, BARBARA: *Nachricht von Chotzen. "Wer immer hofft, stirbt singend"*. Berlin: Ed. Hentrich, 2000. 286 pp., illus., facsims., footnotes, bibl. (Publikationen der Gedenk- und Bildungsstätte Haus der Wannseekonferenz, Bd. 9.) [Documents the fate of various members of the Chotzen family in Berlin during the Nazi era; incl. letters from the ghetto of Riga and Theresienstadt.]

38739. BERLIN. TOSCH, KARIN: *Erwerbungen der Preußischen Staatsbibliothek aus jüdischem Besitz, 1933–1945. Überprüfung beschlagnahmter Bücher im allgemeinen Druckschriftenbestand*. [In]: Mitteilungen [der] Staatsbibliothek zu Berlin, N.F. 9, Nr. 1, Berlin, 2000. Pp. 119–123, tabs.

38740. BIEGE, BERND: *Helfer unter Hitler. Das Rote Kreuz im Dritten Reich*. Reinbek b. Hamburg: Kindler, 2000. 287 pp., illus., notes (243–276), bibl., index. [Incl. chap.: Das Rote Kreuz und der Holocaust (85–98).]

38741. BLUMESBERGER, SUSANNE: *"Die Haare kraus, die Nasen krumm". Feindbilder in nationalsozialistischen Kinderbüchern*. Am Beispiel von "Mutter, erzähl von Adolf Hitler" von Johanne Haarer. [In]: biblos, Jg. 49, H. 2, Wien, 2000. Pp. 247–268, footnotes, illus.

38742. BOCHUM. SCHNEIDER, HUBERT: *Bochum 1933: Die Situation auf dem Städtischen Schlacht- und Viehhof und die Geschichte der jüdischen Viehhändlerfamilie Block*. [In]: Bert Becker/Horst Lademacher, eds.: Geist und Gestalt im historischen Wandel. Facetten deutscher und europäischer Geschichte 1789–1989. Festschrift für Siegfried Bahne. Münster, New York: 2000. Pp. 331–346, footnotes.

—— BRACHMANN-TEUBNER, ELISABETH: *Die Neubearbeitung des Gedenkbuches "Opfer der Verfolgung der Juden unter der nationalsozialistischen Gewaltherrschaft in Deutschland 1933–1945". Eine Zwischenbilanz*. [See No. 39100.]

30743. BRAKELMANN, GÜNTER: *Hans Ehrenberg. Ein judenchristliches Schicksal in Deutschland*. Bd. 2: Widerstand – Verfolgung – Emigration 1933–1939. Waltrop: Spenner, 1999. 481 pp., bibl. H.E., bibl. (Schriften der Hans Ehrenberg Gesellschaft, Bd. 4.) [For vol. 1 see No. 35512/YB XLIII.]

38744. BRECHTKEN, MAGNUS: *Apologie und Erinnerungskonstruktion – Zum zweifelhaften Quellenwert von Nachkriegsaussagen zur Geschichte des Dritten Reiches. Das Beispiel Madagaskar.* [In]: Jahrbuch für Antisemitismusforschung 9, Frankfurt am Main; New York, 2000. Pp. 134–252, notes. [Analyses the post-war testimonies of the Madagascar Plan protagonists such as Adolf Eichmann, Franz Rademacher, Viktor Brack.]

38745. BROWNING, CHRISTOPHER R.: *Nazi policy, Jewish workers, German killers.* Cambridge; New York: Cambridge Univ. Press, 2000. XI, 185 pp., map, bibl., [Six essays, orig. presented as lectures at Cambridge Univ.; incl. testimonies of victims, focus on the motives of the perpetrators.] [Cf.: Inside, outside (Omer Bartov) [in]: The New Republic, Vol. 222, No. 15, Washington, DC, April 10, 2000, pp. 41–45. Review (Johan Ahr) [in]: History, Vol. 28, No. 3, Washington, DC, 2000, p. 120. Deadly policy enacted (John Jacobs) [in]: Jewish Chronicle, London, Aug. 11, 2000, p. 24.]

38746. BREYSACH, BARBARA: *Das stellvertretende Zeugnis als Problem polnischer und deutscher Holocaust-Literatur.* [In]: Jahrbuch für Antisemitismusforschung 9, Frankfurt am Main; New York, 2000. Pp. 182–195, notes.

38747. BUCHENWALD. HEMMENDINGER, JUDITH/KRELL, ROBERT: *The children of Buchenwald: child survivors of the Holocaust and their post-war lives.* Jerusalem, New York: Gefen, 2000. 191 pp., illus., appendixes, ports., facsims., bibl. [Tells the story of the 426 children who survived Buchenwald from many different countries, incl. Germany, Czechoslovakia, Hungary, who made a new life in France, America, and Israel.]

38748. BURLEIGH, MICHAEL: *Die Zeit des Nationalsozialismus.* Eine Gesamtdarstellung. Aus dem Engl. übers. von Udo Rennert und Karl Heinz Siber. Frankfurt am Main: S. Fischer, 2000. 1080 pp., notes (953–1039), maps, bibl., indexes. [Incl. chap.: Leben in einem Land ohne Zukunft. Deutsche Juden und ihre Nachbarn 1933–1939 (324–396); "Eiserne Zeiten, eiserne Besen". Der Rassenkrieg gegen die Juden (656–768).]

38749. BUGAJER, RICHARD: *Mein Schattenleben. Eine Jugend im Ghetto und KZ.* Hrsg. von Reinhard Engel. Wien: Czernin, 2000. 174 pp., illus., notes. [Incl.: Postscriptum des Herausgebers: Lernen und Liebe (153–158).] [R.B., 1928 Kielce – 1998 near Korfu, physician, imprisoned in the Ghetto of Lodz, Auschwitz and several slave labour camps until May 1945. After liberation lived in Vienna.]

38750. CHAPMAN, FERN SCHUMER: *Motherland: beyond the Holocaust: a daughter's journey to reclaim the past.* New York: Viking, 2000. 190 pp., illus.

38751. CHARGUÉRAUD, MARC-ANDRÉ: *Tous coupables? Les démocraties occidentales et les communautés religieuses face à la détresse juive 1933–1940.* Genève: Labor et Fides; Paris: Cerf, 1998. 303 pp. [Cf.: Besprechung (Bruno Ackermann) [in]: Schweizerische Zeitschrift für Geschichte, Vol. 49, Basel, 1999. Pp. 578–580 [in French].]

38752. CHURCH. KLINKHAMMER, LUTZ: *Pius XII., Rom und der Holocaust.* [In]: Quellen und Forschungen aus italienischen Archiven und Bibliotheken. Bd. 80, Tübingen, 2000. Pp. 668–678, footnotes.

38753. CHURCH. LEWY, GUENTER: *The Catholic Church and Nazi Germany.* New York: Da Capo, 2000. XXVII, 416 pp. [Orig. publ. in 1964; incl. chap. on 'The Jewish question'.]

38754. CHURCH. PHAYER, MICHAEL: *The Catholic Church and the Holocaust, 1930–1965.* Bloomington: Indiana Univ. Press, 2000. 328 pp., illus., notes, bibl., index. [Deals also with the Vatican and Pope Pius XII.]

38755. COHN, FREDERICK G.: *A lucid interval.* London: Premier Fois Publications, 1999. 1 vol. [Fictionalised memoirs of a young refugee who was interned with his elder brother in Britain and Canada.]

38756. COLOGNE. *Kalk im Nationalsozialismus.* Köln: Der Oberbürgermeister, Amt für Weiterbildung, Volkshochschule, Geschäftsstelle Kalk, 2000 [?]. 132 pp., illus., facsims. (Einschnitte.) [Incl.: Vorwort (Horst Matzerath, 6). Ein weißer Fleck: Juden in Kalk (8–27).] [Kalk: part of Cologne.]

38757. COLOGNE. WERTHEIM, CLAUS ALBERT: *The past is indestructable: My childhood memoirs including a history of the Wertheim family*. Cedar Grove, NJ, USA: Privately printed, 2000. 71 pp., facsims., family tree. [Available at the Bibliothek Germania Judaica, Cologne.] [Author, b. 1927 in Berlin, went to live in Cologne 1931, emigr. 1940 via Switzerland to the US.]

38758. CONFESSING CHURCH. GERLACH, WOLFGANG: *And the witnesses were silent: the Confessing Church and the persecution of the Jews*. Slightly rev. edn., transl. and ed. by Victoria J. Barnett. Lincoln: Univ. of Nebraska Press, 2000. XI, 304 pp., tabs., gloss., notes (237–286), bibl., index. [For orig. German edn. see No. 24204/YB XXXIII.]

38759. CRANE, CYNTHIA: *Divided lives: the untold stories of Jewish-Christian women in Nazi Germany*. New York: St. Martin's Press, 2000. XI, 372 pp., notes (343–357), bibl. (359–372), index. [Collection of essays by survivors, dealing with mixed marriages and the persecution of their offspring.] [Cf.: Review (Mark Rotella et al.) [in]: Publisher's Weekly, Vol. 247, No. 45, New York, Nov. 6, 2000, pp. 80–81.]

38760. CZECHOSLOVAKIA. BARTOS, JOSEF: *Die Arisierung jüdischen Vermögens in Olmütz im Jahre 1939*. [In]: Theresienstädter Studien und Dokumente 2000, Prag, 2000. Pp. 282–296.

38761. CZECHOSLOVAKIA. BONDY, RUTH: *Chronik der sich schließenden Tore. Jüdisches Nachrichtenblatt – Židovské Listy (1939–1945)*. [In]: Theresienstädter Studien und Dokumente, 2000, Prag, 2000. Pp. 86–106.

38762. CZECHOSLOVAKIA. ECKERT, RAINER: *Emigrationspublizistik und Judenverfolgung. Das Beispiel Tschechoslowakei*. Frankfurt am Main, New York: Lang, 2000. 346 pp., bibl. [Deals with the refugees from Nazi Germany and their activities until 1939.]

38763. CZECHOSLOVAKIA. HÁJKOVÁ, ALENA: *Ursprung und Zusammenarbeit einer Personenkartei der Juden aus der Zeit des Protektorats*. [In]: Theresienstädter Studien und Dokumente, 2000, Prag, 2000. Pp. 343–352.

38764. CZECHOSLOVAKIA. PRIBYL, LUKÁS: *Das Schicksal des dritten Transports aus dem Protektorat nach Nisko*. [In]: Theresienstädter Studien und Dokumente 2000, Prag, 2000. Pp. 297–342.

38765. DACHAU. KERSTEN, LEE: *'The Times' and the concentration camp at Dachau, December 1933 – February 1934: an unpublished report*. [In]: Shofar, Vol. 18, No. 2, West Lafayette, IN, Winter 2000. Pp. 101–109, footnotes. [Discusses a long report on Dachau which 'The Times', London, received and which the editor decided not to publish.]

38766. DeCOSTE, FREDERICK, ed.: *The Holocaust's ghosts*. Edmonton: Univ. of Alberta Press, 2000. XIX, 568 pp., illus., facsims., appendix (538–554), endnotes, index. [A collection of essays dealing with aspects of art, politics, law and education in the context of the Holocaust.]

38767. *Die Philipps-Universität Marburg im Nationalsozialismus. Dokumente zu ihrer Geschichte*. Hrsg. von Anne Christine Nagel, bearb. von Anne Christine Nagel und Ulrich Sieg. Stuttgart: Franz Steiner Verl., 2000. X, 563 pp., footnotes, bibl., indexes. (Pallas Athene. Beiträge zur Universitäts- und Wissenschaftsgeschichte, Bd. 1) [Also on antisemitism and the expulsion of Jews.]

38768. DINER, DAN: *Beyond the conceivable: studies on Germany, Nazism and the Holocaust*. Berkeley: Univ. of California Press, 2000. 286 pp., notes (231– 272), index. (Weimar and now, 20.) [Cont.: Part I: Political ideology and historical context (4 essays). Part II: Perceptions of the Holocaust (5 essays, some on the issue of "Judenräte"). Part III: Holocaust narratives (4 essays).]

38769. DISSELNKÖTTER, ANDREAS: *Schoah und Literatur*. [In]: Tribüne, Jg. 39, H. 156, Frankfurt am Main, 2000. Pp. 57–64, footnotes. [On a conference held in Dresden, May 2000, with the title: Erinnerte Shoah. Die Literatur der Überlebenden.]

38770. DOLGESHEIM (Hesse). SEIBERT, WINFRIED: *Dolgesheimer Mord. Der Tod des Juden Julius Frank im Frühjahr 1933*. Frankfurt am Main: Brandes und Appel, 2000. 154 pp., illus., facsims., notes, bibl.

38771. DOMINICAN REPUBLIC. HOFELLER, ERNEST B.: *Timetable to nowhere: A personal history of the Sosua settlement.* [In]: Leo Baeck Institute Year Book XLV, Oxford, 2000. Pp. 233–242, illus. [Personal memoirs of author about his time in the Dominican Republic, 1940–1943.]

38772. DORA. NEANDER, JOACHIM: *"Hat in Europa kein annäherndes Beispiel". Mittelbau-Dora – ein KZ für Hitlers Krieg.* Berlin: Metropol, 2000. 220 pp., illus., tabs., plan, footnotes, bibl.

38773. DORA. SELLIER, ANDRÉ: *Zwangsarbeit im Raketentunnel. Geschichte des Lagers Dora.* Aus dem Französ. übers. von Maria-Elisabeth Steiner. Lüneburg: zu Klampen, 2000. 627 pp., illus., maps, lists, bibl., index. [Preface by Eberhard Jäckel (9–10). Incl. list of prisoners.]

38774. DRESDEN. BRENNER, HENNY: *Mit den Bomben kam die Rettung. Als erstes rissen wir den Judenstern ab.* Eine Erinnerung an Dresden im Februar 1945. [In]: 'FAZ', Nr. 78, Frankfurt am Main, 3. April 1999. P. II, Beilage.

38775. DÜLMEN. MÖLLERS, H.: *Für eine Synagoge gehalten und verwüstet. Die evangelische Kapelle am Flugplatz Borkenberge.* [In]: Dülmener Heimatblätter, Jg. 46, Dülmen, 1999.

38776. DÜREN & JÜLICH. WALLRAFF, HORST: *Nationalsozialismus in den Kreisen Düren und Jülich. Tradition und "Tausendjähriges Reich" in einer rheinländischen Region 1933 bis 1945.* Hrsg. vom Kreis Düren, der Stadt Düren und der Stadt Jülich. Düren: Hahne & Schloemer, 2000. XIV, 604 [84] pp., illus., bibl., index. [Deals also with the fate of the Jews.]

38777. DÜSSELDORF. BERSCHEL, HUGO: *Polizeiroutiniers und Judenverfolgung.* Die Bearbeitung von 'Judenangelegenheiten' bei der Stapo-Leitstelle Düsseldorf. [In]: Paul, Gerhard/Mallmann, Klaus-Michael, eds.: Die Gestapo im Zweiten Weltkrieg. 'Heimatfront' und besetztes Europa. Darmstadt: Wiss. Buchgesellschaft, 2000. pp. 155–178, footnotes.

38778. DÜSSELDORF. MOß, CHRISTOPH, ed.: *Briefe der Düsseldorfer Familie Glücksmann. Schicksal einer christlich-jüdischen Familie 1939–1945.* Düsseldorf: Mahn- und Gedenkstätte Düsseldorf; Archiv der Ev. Kirche im Rheinland, 2000. 180 pp., illus., facsims., notes, gloss., index. (Schriften des Archivs der Ev. Kirche im Rheinland, Nr. 27.)

38779. EVAN, GERSHON: *Winds of life: the destinies of a young Viennese Jew, 1938–1958.* Riverside, CA: Ariadne Press, 2000. 377 pp., illus. [Author describes his childhood in Vienna under the Nazis, survival of Buchenwald, and later of the sinking of the SS Patria and subsequent imprisonment by the British, four years in the British army in Palestine, two years in the Israeli army. In 1958 he moved to the US, lives in San Francisco.]

38780. EXILE. BHATTI, ANIL/VOIGT, JOHANNES H., eds.: *Jewish exile in India: 1933–1945.* New Delhi: Manohar Publs., 1999. 195 pp. [Cont. papers given at a symposium at the Centre for German Studies, Jawaharlal Nehru Univ., March 1995; dealing with political, sociological and cultural aspects of the German immigration; incl. Alex Aronsen, Willy Haas, Walter Kaufmann, Margarete Spiegel.]

38781. EXILE. FRANKE, JULIA: *Unerwartet im selben Boot: politische Exilanten und jüdische Emigranten aus Deutschland im Paris der dreißiger Jahre.* [In]: Beiträge zur Geschichte der Arbeiterbewegung, Jg. 42, H. 2, Berlin, 2000. Pp. 3–19, footnotes.

38782. EXILE. KIRCHHOF, ASTRID MIGNON: *From Germany & Austria to Australia: experiences of Jewish women refugees in the 1930s.* [In]: Australian Jewish Historical Society Journal, Vol. 15, Part 2, Sydney, 2000.

——— FILM. BRENNER, PETER J.: *Der deutsche Jude. Lion Feuchtwangers Roman 'Jud Süß' und Veit Harlans Verfilmung des "Jud Süß"-Stoffes.* [See in No. 39217.]

38783. FILM. KNILLI, FRIEDRICH: *Ich war Jud Süß.* Die Geschichte des Filmstars Ferdinand Marian. Mit einem Vorwort von Alphons Silbermann. Berlin: Henschel, 2000. 208 pp., bibl., index. [Biography of the non-Jewish actor F.M., deals also with the background of the Nazi propaganda film 'Jud Süß'.]

38784. FILM. TEGEL, SUSAN: *"The demonic effect": Veit Harlan's use of Jewish extras in Jud Süss (1940)*. [In]: Holocaust and Genocide Studies, Vol. 14, No. 2, Oxford, Fall 2000. Pp. 215–241, notes. [Jewish extras were recruited in Lublin and Prague to portray 'Ostjuden'.]

38785. FINAL SOLUTION. BREITMAN, RICHARD: *Heinrich Himmler: der Architekt der "Endlösung"*. Aus dem Amerik. übers. von Karl und Heidi Nicolai. Zürich: Pendo, 2000. 435 pp. [For orig. edn. publ. 1991 see No. 28272/YB XXXVII.]

38786. FINAL SOLUTION. HERBERT, ULRICH, ed.: *National Socialist extermination policies: contemporary German perspectives and controversies*. Oxford; New York: Berghahn Books, 2000. XXII, 336 pp., notes, index. [For orig. German edn. in 1998 and more details see No. 36257/YB XLIV.]

38787. FINAL SOLUTION. LONGERICH, PETER: *The Wannsee Conference in the development of the 'Final Solution'*. London: The Holocaust Ed. Trust, 2000. 29 pp., illus. (Hol. Ed. Trust Research Papers, vol. 1, No. 1.)

38788. FINAL SOLUTION. LOZOWICK, YAACOV: *Hitlers Bürokraten. Eichmann, und seine willigen Vollstrecker und die Banalität des Bösen*. Aus dem Engl. von Christoph Münz. Zürich: Pendo, 2000. 407 pp., notes (350–386), bibl., index.

—— FINAL SOLUTION. RIEGNER, GERHART: *Man wollte es einfach nicht glauben*. [See in No. 38644.]

38789. FLÖRSHEIM/MAIN. BECKER, PETER: *Mirjam und andere Erzählungen*. Illustriert von Judith Gall-Amslgruber. Flörsheim: Becker, 2000. 268 pp., illus. [Based on authentic research, stories deal with Jewish families in Flörsheim during the Nazi era.]

38790. *Flüchtlingspolitik und Fluchthilfe*. Berlin: Verlag der Buchläden Schwarze Risse, Rote Strasse, [2000]. 187 pp., notes, index. (Beiträge zur nationalsozialistischen Gesundheits- und Sozialpolitik, 15.) [Incl.: Die illegale Einwanderung nach Palästina. Politische, nationale und persönliche Aspekte (1939–1941) (Dalia Ofer, 9–38). Einige Pläne zur Auswanderung deutscher Juden nach Albanien (Artan Puto, 39–46). Fluchthilfe aus Südfrankreich. Das 'Centre américain de secours' in Marseille, 1940/41 (Anne Klein, 47–90). Hitlerflüchtlinge in den Niederlanden unerwünscht. Die Politik der niederländischen Regierung gegenüber den deutschen Flüchtlingen 1944–1940 (Johan van Merrienboer, 91–106). Vertreibung, Raub und Umverteilung. Die jüdischen Flüchtlinge aus Deutschland und die Vermehrung des "Volksvermögens" (Susanne Heim, 107–138).]

38791. FORCED LABOUR. BLOXHAM, DONALD: *"Extermination through work": Jewish slave labour under the Third Reich*. [Title issue of]: Holocaust Educational Trust, Vol. 1, No. 1, London, 1999–2000. 37 pp., illus., port., facsim., gloss., notes. [Deals with Jewish slave labour in Germany and the occupied countries; incl. section on the perpetrators: both the Nazi authorities and private industry.]

38792. FRAIMAN, SARAH: *The transformation of Jewish consciousness in Nazi Germany as reflected in the German-Jewish journal 'Der Morgen', 1925–1938*. [In]: Modern Judaism, Vol. 20, No. 1, New York, Feb. 2000. Pp. 41–59, notes.

38793. FRANCE. ANDRIEU, CLAIRE, ed.: *La persécution des juifs de France 1940–1944 et le rétablissement de la légalité républicaine*. Paris: Mission d'étude sur la spoliation des Juifs de France, 1999. 531 pp., facsims, tabs. [Incl. official texts of laws and orders issued by the German occupation forces which affected many German-Jewish refugees.]

38794. FRANCE. FRANKE, JULIA: *Paris – eine neue Heimat? Jüdische Emigranten aus Deutschland 1933–1939*. Berlin: Duncker & Humblot, 2000. 423 pp., illus., footnotes, tabs., chronol., lists, bibl. (364–414), index (persons, subjects, 417–423). (Zeitgeschichtliche Forschungen, Bd. 5.). Zugl.: Freiburg (Br.), Univ., Diss., 1999.

38795. FRANCE. MEYER, AHLRICH: *Die deutsche Besatzung in Frankreich 1940–1944*. Widerstandsbekämpfung und Judenverfolgung. Darmstadt: Wiss. Buchgesellschaft, 2000. 279 pp., notes (271–276), index.

38796. FRANCE. PHILLIPS, ALASTAIR: *The camera goes down the streets. 'Dans les rues' (Victor Trivas, 1933) and the Paris of the German émigrés.* [In]: Modern & Contemporary France, Vol. 8, No. 3, Abingdon (UK), 2000. Pp. 325–334, notes. [Deals with a film about émigrés, set in Paris.]

38797. FRANCE. PRUTSCH, URSULA: *Der "Aufruf zum Misstrauen" durch "prophetischen Pessimismus". Joseph Roths Exilpublizistik im 'Pariser Tageblatt' und 'Pariser Tageszeitung'.* [In]: Österreich in Geschichte und Literatur mit Geographie, H. 2, Wien, 2000. Pp. 93–108.

38798. FRANK, ANNE. *Alles Liebe, Otto: das Erbe Anne Franks. Der Briefwechsel zwischen Cara Wilson und Otto Frank.* Mit einem Vorw. und einer Lebensskizze Otto Franks von Buddy Elias. [Übers. aus dem Engl. von Helga Paul]. Basel: Perseus-Verl., [1999?]. 169 pp., illus. [Orig. publ. 1995, see No. 32848/YB XLI.]

38799. FRANK, ANNE. ENZER, HYMAN AARON/SOLOTAROFF-ENZER, SANDRA, eds.: *Anne Frank: reflections on her life and legacy.* Foreword by Bernd Elias. Urbana, Chicago: Univ. of Illinois Press, 2000. XXVII, 285 pp, illus., chronol., appendixes, notes, bibl. (251–259), index. [Collection of essays on different aspects of A. F.'s life.]

38800. FRANK, ANNE. LEE, CAROL ANN: *Anne Frank. Die Biographie.* Aus dem Englischen von Bernd Rullkötter und Ursel Schäfer. München: Piper. 2000. 414 pp., illus., notes (367–405), bibl., index. [For English orig. edn. see No. 37579/YB XLV.]

38801. FRANK, ANNE. PRESSLER, MIRJAM: *A hidden life.* Transl. from German by Anthea Bell. London: Dutton, 2000. 176 pp., illus., chronol., notes, bibl., index.

—— FRANKFURT am Main. *Ostend. Blick in ein jüdisches Viertel.* [See No. 38521.]

38802. FRANKENTHAL, HANS: *Verweigerte Rückkehr. Erfahrungen nach dem Judenmord.* Unter Mitarbeit von Andreas Plake, Babette Quinkert und Florian Schmaltz. Frankfurt am Main: Fischer Taschenbuch Verlag, 1999. 189 pp., illus., gloss. (Lebensbilder. Jüdische Erinnerungen und Zeugnisse.). Orig.-Ausg. [First part of book deals with persecution, deportation to Auschwitz, forced labour, death march, second part with the author's return to his home town Schmallenberg and his experience with restitution matters and Nazi trials.]

—— FRIEDLANDER, ELIZABETH. PAUCKER, PAULINE: *Die Bauersche Giesserei und die Elisabeth Schrift. Georg Hartmann/Elizabeth Friedlander: Ein Briefwechsel.* [See No. 38912.]

38803. FRÖNDENBERG. KLEMP, STEFAN: *"Richtige Nazis hat es hier nicht gegeben": eine Stadt, eine Firma, der vergessene mächtigste Wirtschaftsführer und Auschwitz.* 2., völlig überarb. Aufl. Münster: LIT, 2000. 482 pp., illus., tabs., footnotes, map, bibl., index. [Incl. chaps.: Judenverfolgung (293–320). Also on forced labour.] [Fröndenberg: nr. Unna, Westphalia.]

38804. GANN, CHRISTOPH: *Raoul Wallenberg: so viele Menschen retten wie möglich.* München: Beck, 2000. 273 pp., illus.

38805. GERA. SIMSOHN, WERNER: *Juden in Gera III. Judenfeindschaft in der Zeitung. Leben, Leiden im NS-Staat, Folgen, 1933–1945.* Hrsg. von Erhard Roy Wiehn. Konstanz: Hartung-Gorre, 2000. 222 pp., illus., footnotes. [Incl. list of names.]

38806. *Geschichte der Kaiser-Wilhelm-Gesellschaft im Nationalsozialismus.* Bestandsaufnahme und Perspektiven der Forschung. Hrsg. von Doris Kaufmann. Göttingen: Wallstein, 2000. 767 pp., footnotes, index. [Vol. 1 incl.: "Vordenker der Vernichtung". Wissenschaftliche Experten als Berater der nationalsozialistischen Politik (Susanne Heim, 77–91). Das Blut von Auschwitz und das Schweigen der Gelehrten (Benno Müller-Hill, 189–227); vol. 2 incl.: Emigration und Wissenschaftswandel als Folgen der nationalsozialistischen Wissenschaftspolitik (Mitchell Ash, 610–631).]

38807. GLADBECK. SAMEN, M.: *Die Reichsprogromnacht* [sic] *vom 9./10. November 1938 in Gladbeck.* [In]: Gladbeck – Unsere Stadt, Jg. 27, Gladbeck, 1999.

38808. GOGGIN, JAMES/GOGGIN, EILEEN BROCKMAN: *Death of a "Jewish science": psychoanalysis in the Third Reich.* West Lafayette: Purdue Univ. Press, 2000. XVI, 242 pp., notes, bibl., index. [Incl. the exclusion of Jewish analysts from the profession.]

38809. GOLDHAGEN DEBATE. BERGMANN, PETER E.: *Daniel Goldhagen in Germany: an exploration in German historiography* [In]: Historical Reflections, Vol. 26, No. 1, Waterloo, Ont., Spring 2000. Pp. 141–159, notes.

38810. GOLDHAGEN DEBATE. ELEY, GEOFF, ed.: *The "Goldhagen effect": history, memory, Nazism – facing the German past.* Ann Arbor: Univ. of Michigan Press, 2000. VII, 172 pp., footnotes, index. (Social history, popular culture, and politics in Germany.) [Cont.: Ordinary Germans, Nazism and Judeocide (Geoff Eley, 1–32). Reception and perception: Goldhagen's Holocaust and the world (Omer Bartov, 33–88). The "Goldhagen effect": memory, repetition, and responsibility in the new Germany (Anita Grossmann, 89–130). Austrian non-reception of a reluctant Goldhagen (Pieter Judson, 131–150). Reflections on the reception of Goldhagen in the United States (Jane Caplan, 151–161).]

38811. GOLDHAGEN DEBATE. GONEN, JAY Y.: *The roots of Nazi psychology: Hitler's utopian barbarism.* Lexington: Univ. of Kentucky Press, 2000. 224 pp., notes, bibl. (213–218), index. [Author shares Goldhagen's contention that antisemitic ideology was the basis for the Holocaust.]

38812. GOLDHAGEN DEBATE. KÖTT, MARTIN: *Goldhagen in der Qualitätspresse.* Eine Debatte über "Kollektivschuld" und "Nationalcharakter" der Deutschen. Konstanz: UVK Medien, 1999. 142 pp., footnotes, bibl., index. (Journalismus und Geschichte, Bd. 3.)

38813. GOLDSMITH, MARTIN: *The inextinguishable symphony: the true story of music and love in Nazi Germany.* New York: Wiley, 2000. VI, 346 pp., illus., facsims., map, bibl. (337–340), index. [On Günther and Rosemarie Goldschmidt from Sachsenhagen, after 1933 as musicians actively involved in the 'Jüdischer Kulturbund', later emigr. to the US, where R.G. after the war made a new career in St. Louis.]

38814. GROHS-MARTIN, SILVIA: *Silvie.* New York: Welcome Rain, 2000. VI, 373 pp., illus., facsims., index. [Author, Vienna-born actress, dancer, escaped to Switzerland, later went to Holland where she followed a successful acting career; from there deported via various camps to Ravensbrück. After liberation emigr. to the US.]

38815. GRUNER, WOLF: *Die NS-Judenverfolgung und die Kommunen.* Zur wechselseitigen Dynaminisierung von zentraler und lokaler Politik 1933–1941. [In]: Vierteljahrshefte für Zeitgeschichte, Jg. 48, H, 1, München, 2000. Pp. 75–126, footnotes.

38816. GURS. WIEHN, ERHARD ROY, ed.: *Camp de Gurs 1940. Zur Deportation der Juden aus Südwestdeutschland. 60 Jahre danach zum Gedenken.* Konstanz: Hartung-Gorre, 2000. 188 pp., illus., bibl. [Incl. personal memoirs of 13 deportees; also: Zur Oktoberdeportation 1940 und ihren Folgen (ed., 161–174).]

38817. HAFNER, GEORG M./SCHAPIRA, ESTHER: *Die Akte 'Alois Brunner': Warum einer der größten Naziverbrecher noch immer auf freiem Fuß ist.* Frankfurt am Main; New York: Campus, 2000. 327 pp., illus., notes (301–319), bibl., index. [Also avaiblable as a TV film.]

38818. HAHN-BEER, EDITH mit SUSAN DWORKIN: *Ich ging durchs Feuer und brannte nicht.* Eine außergewöhnliche Lebens- und Liebesgeschichte. Aus dem Englischen von Otto Bayer. Bern: Scherz, 2000. 287 pp., illus. [Orig. title: 'The Nazi officer's wife', publ. 1999. Author, b. 1914 in Vienna, jurist, tells how she survived with false identity in Brandenburg, marrying 1943 an "Aryan" German.]

38819. HAMBURG. BAUMBACH, SYBILLE [et al.], eds.: *Rückblenden. Lebensgeschichtliche Interviews mit Verfolgten des NS-Regimes in Hamburg.* Hamburg: Ergebnisse Verl., 1999. 475 pp., footnotes. (Forum Zeitgeschichte, Bd. 7. Hrsg. von der Forschungsstelle für Zeitgeschichte in Hamburg. Red.: Frank Bajohr.) [Incl.: Die Verfolgung Hamburger Juden aus lebensgeschichtlicher Perspektive (Sybille

Baumbach, 13–129). Grenzgänger zwischen "Normalität" und Verfolgung – Die Situation "jüdischer Mischlinge" in der NS-Zeit (Beate Meyer, 130–205).]

38820. HAMBURG. LEHBERGER, REINER/RANDT, URSULA: *"Aus Kindern werden Briefe"*. *Dokumente zum Schicksal jüdischer Kinder und Jugendlicher in der NS-Zeit*. Hrsg. von der Behörde für Schule, Jugend und Berufsbildung. Red.: Uwe Reiner. Hamburg: Behörde für Schule, Jugend und Berufsbildung, 1999. 65 pp., illus. (Geschichte – Schauplatz Hamburg.)

38821. HANSEN-SCHABER, INGE/SCHMEICHEL-FALKENBERG, BEATE, [et al.], eds.: *Frauen erinnern. Widerstand – Verfolgung – Exil 1933–1945*. Mit einem Vorwort von Christa Wolf. Berlin: Weidler, 2000. 248 pp., footnotes. [Cont. (some titles abbr.): 1. Einführung in die Thematik (15–38; contribs. by Inge Hansen-Schaberg, Hiltrud Häntzschel). 2. Zur Aufarbeitung von traumatisierenden Erfahrungen und Erinnerungen (39–100; contribs. by Hanna Papanek, Bea Green, Hanna Blitzer, Susanne Berglind, Marianne Kröger). 3. Probleme des Erinnerns und Auswirkungen der Traumata (101–154; contribs. by Ute Benz, Adriane Feustel on Alice Salomon, Silvia Schlenstedt on Ilse Blumenthal-Weiss, Ariane Huml on Barbara Honigmann). 4. NS-Geschichte im individuellen und kollektiven Gedächtnis (155–243; incl.: Frauen im Exil – Frauen in der Exilforschung. Zur kurzen Geschichte der Frauenexilforschung (Beate Schmeichel-Falkenberg, 155–160). Zur Erinnerungskultur in Deutschland (Wolfgang Benz, 161–163). Also contribs. by Christine Labonté-Roset, Gabriele Knapp, Birgit Rommelspacher, Inge Deutschkron, Simone Barck, Juliane Wetzel.]

38822. HARDMAN, ANNA: *Women and the Holocaust*. [In]: Holocaust Educational Trust, Vol. 1, No. 3, London, 1999–2000. 36 pp., illus., notes. [Deals mainly with the historiography of the subject, author also uses case studies from Auschwitz-Birkenau, incl. German-Jewish women.]

38823. HAUSLEITNER, MARIANA: *Von der Inklusion zur Exklusion: Juden in Ungarn und Rumänien vor 1945*. [In]: Minderheiten, Regionalbewusstsein und Zentralismus in Ostmitteleuropa. Hrsg. von Heinz-Dietrich Löwe, Günther H. Tontsch und Stefan Troebst. Köln: Böhlau, 2000. Pp. 139–160, footnotes. [Deals also with German-speaking Jews. Incl. Engl. and French summaries.]

38824. HEPP, MICHAEL: *Deutsche Bank, Dresdner Bank – Erlöse aus Raub, Enteignung und Zwangsarbeit 1933–1945*. [In]: 1999. Zeitschrift für Sozialgeschichte des 20. und 21. Jahrhunderts, Jg. 15, H. 1, Köln, 2000. Pp. 64–116, footnotes, tabs. [German and English summaries, pp. 225–226. Deals with the participation of the two major German banks in the Nazi plunder of the Jews.]

38825. HESSE. KIRCHHOFF, WOLFGANG: *Über Widerstand und Verfolgung von Medizinerinnen und Medizinern in Hessen 1933–1945*. [In]: Antifaschismus. Hrsg. von Frank Deppe [et al.]. Mit Beiträgen von Georg Auernheimer [et al.]. Heilbronn: Distel Verl., 1996. Pp. 176–183.

38826. HIRSCH, BENJAMIN: *Hearing a different drummer: a Holocaust survivor's search for identity*. Macon, GA: Mercer Press, 2000. XIII, 235 pp., illus., facsims. [Memoirs of a Frankfurt-born Jew who before the war was sent to France, where he survived in hiding; after liberation went to the US.]

38827. HISTORIOGRAPHY. GRZYWATZ, BERTHOLD: *Zeitgeschichtsforschung und Geschichte der NS-Verfolgten in der deutschen Nachkriegspolitik*. [In]: Zeitschrift für Geschichtswissenschaft, Jg. 48, H. 11, Berlin, 2000. Pp. 1012–1036, footnotes.

38828. HISTORIOGRAPHY. LEITZ, CHRISTIAN: *Holocaust research: the current position*. [In]: History Now, Vol. 6, No. 1, Christchurch (New Zealand), 2000. Pp. 24–28. [Review essay on current Holocaust historiography with special attention to the reception of Goldhagen's book and other studies about the participation of the Wehrmacht and police in the Holocaust.]

38829. HISTORIOGRAPHY. METZLER, GABRIELE: *Doppelte Vergangenheit. Zur Auseinandersetzung mit Diktatur und Holocaust in Deutschland*. [In]: Historisches Jahrbuch, Jg. 120, Freiburg, 2000. Pp. 396–420, footnotes.

38830. HITLER, ADOLF. KERSHAW, IAN: *Hitler 1936–1945: nemesis*. New York: Norton, 2000. XLVI, 1115 pp., illus., ports., gloss., maps, notes, bibl. [German edn.: Hitler 1936–1945. Aus dem Engl.

von Klaus Kochmann. Stuttgart: Deutsche Verlags-Anstalt, 2000. 1343 pp., illus., ports., gloss., maps, notes (1089–1294), bibl. (1295–1327), index. For vol. 1 see No. 36336/YB XLIV.] [Cf.: The road to destruction (Richard Gott) [in]: New Statesman, Vol. 13, No. 625, London, Oct. 2, 2000, pp. 51–53.]

38831. HITLER, ADOLF. ZEHNPFENNIG, BARBARA: *Hitlers 'Mein Kampf'*. Eine Interpretation. München: Fink, 2000. 348 pp., notes (315–341), bibl. Zugl.: Hamburg, Univ., Habil.-Schr., 1998. [Deals also with H.'s antisemitism.]

38832. HOLOCAUST. BARTOV, OMER, ed.: *The Holocaust: origins, implementation, aftermath*. London; New York: Routledge, 2000. X, 300 pp., notes, bibl., index. (Rewriting histories.) [Collection of 13 articles, all prev. publ., with a new introd. by the ed.]

38833. HOLOCAUST. FINKELSTEIN, NORMAN G.: *The Holocaust industry: reflections on the exploitations of Jewish suffering*. London; New York: Verso, 2000. 150 pp. [Cf.: Reflections on Finkelstein (Katherine Klinger) [in]: The Jewish Quarterly, Vol. 47, No. 3, London, Autumn 2000, pp. 77–79. A unique event? (Hyam Maccoby) [in]: TLS, London, Sept. 1, 2000, p.25.]

38834. HOLOCAUST. *Text+Kritik*. H. 144 [with the issue title]: *Literatur und Holocaust*. München, Okt. 1999. 97 pp., notes. [Incl. (some titles abbr.): Anmerkungen zu Geschichte und Gegenwart des jüdisch-nichtjüdischen Verhältnisses in den Täterländern (Robert Schindel, 3–8). Im Sog der Erinnerungskultur. Holocaust und Literatur – 'Normalität' und ihre Grenzen (Jan Strümpel, 9–17). Kommentar. Holocaust: Sprechen (Marcel Beyer, 18–24). Der Holocaust in der Lyrik nach 1945 (Hermann Korte, 25–47). Deutschsprachige jüdische Autoren und der Holocaust (Anat Feinberg, 48–58). Die Kryptotheologie der Walser-Bubis-Debatte (Micha Brumlik, 59–66). Das Unbehagen an wissenschaftlicher Zurichtung von 'Holocaust-Literatur' – mit Blick auf Carl Friedmans Erzählung "Vater" (Irmela von der Lühe, 67–78). Literaturwissenschaft und Literaturgeschichte nach dem Holocaust (Stephan Braese/Holger Gehler, 79–95).]

38835. HOLOCAUST. *Visual culture and the Holocaust*. Ed. and with an introd. by Barbie Zelizer. New Brunswick, NJ: Rutgers Univ. Press, 2000. VII, 364 pp., illus., index. [Incl. the depiction of the Holocaust in art, television, video, film, architecture, and photography.]

38836. HOLOCAUST. *Witness: voices from the Holocaust*. Ed. by Joshua M. Greene and Shiva Kumar in consult. with Joanne Weiner Rudof. Foreword by Lawrence L. Langer. New York; London: The Free Press, 2000. XXX, 270 pp., illus., ports., facsims., video refs. [Publ. in association with the Fortunoff Video Archive for Holocaust testimonies at Yale Univ. Cont. excerpts from eyewitness accounts, incl. many from German Jews, collected by the Fortunoff Video Archive.]

38837. HOLOCAUST. KNOPP, GUIDO: *Holokaust*. In Zusammenarbeit mit Vanessa von Bassewitz [et al.]. Redaktion: Alexander Berkel [et al.]. München: Bertelsmann, 2000. 415 pp., illus., bibl., index. [Based on a TV documentary series.] [Cf.: Holokaust, sagte Herr K. Bescheidener Vorschlag, einen Begriff einzudeutschen (Eberhard Jäckel) [in]: 'FAZ', Nr. 191, Frankfurt am Main, 18. Aug. 2000, p. 47; pleads for writing "Holokaust" in German.]

38838. HOLOCAUST. LAUCKNER, NANCY A./JOKINIEMI, MIRIAM, eds.: *Shedding light on the darkness: a guide to teaching the Holocaust*. New York; Oxford: Berghahn Books, 2000. XXIII, 261 pp., bibl., index. [Collection of essays, on the teaching of the Holocaust and related subjects in the Germanistic departments of American universities. Incl. (titles abbr.): Teaching the Holocaust in a program of German literature and culture (Dagmar C. G. Lorenz, 59–76). The Holocaust and resistance in German literature (Gisela Brude-Firnau, 92–106). A course on Jewish-German relations (Karen Remmler, 124–139). Witness Grete Weil (Laureen Nussbaum, 157–176). A graduate seminar on the Holocaust and the Third Reich as reflected in postwar German literature (Nancy A. Lauckner, 174–189). The Nazi period, the Holocaust and German-Jewish issues as integral subjects in a German language course (Karin Doerr, 191–199).]

38839. HOLOCAUST. NIEWYK, DONALD/NICOSIA, FRANCIS R., eds.: *The Columbia guide to the Holocaust* [sic]. New York: Columbia Univ. Press, 2000. XII, 473 pp., maps, tabs., bibl. index.

38840. HOLOCAUST. POHL, DIETER: *Holocaust. Die Ursachen, das Geschehen, die Folgen.* Freiburg: Herder, 2000. 188 pp., bibl. (Herder Spektrum, Bd. 4835.).

38841. HOLOCAUST. ROSENFELD, ALVIN H.: *Ein Mund voll Schweigen.* Literarische Reaktionen auf den Holocaust. Aus dem Amerik. Englisch übers. von Annette und Axel Dunker und mit einem Vorwort von Dieter Lamping. Göttingen: Vandenhoeck & Ruprecht, 2000. 237 pp., notes (203–210), bib. (211–233), index. [Revised, updated and augmented edn. of the orig. edn. publ. 1988 with the title 'A double dying': reflections on Holocaust literature. Incl. chap. on the abuse and exploitation of the holocaust.]

38842. HOLOCAUST DENIAL. HIGH COURT OF JUSTICE. QUEEN'S BENCH DIVISION: *The Irving judgement: David Irving v. Penguin Books and Prof. Deborah Lipstadt.* London: Penguin Books, 2000. XIII, 348 pp. [Cf.: The battle may be over — but the war goes on (Neal Ascherson) [in]: The Observer, London, April 16, 2000, p. 19.]

38843. HOLOCAUST DENIAL. MENASSE, EVA: *Der Holocaust vor Gericht. Der Prozess um David Irving.* Berlin: Siedler, 2000. 191 pp., notes, index.

38844. HOLOCAUST DENIAL. SHERMER, MICHAEL/GROBMAN, ALEX: *Denying history: who says the Holocaust never happened and why do they say it?* Foreword by Arthur Hertzberg. Berkeley: Univ. of California Press, 2000. XVIII, 312 pp., illus., ports., facsims., tabs., notes, bibl. (287–304), index. [Surveys the main authors, journals, institutions who engage in Holocaust denial; incl. David Irving, the Leuchter report, the Journal of Historical Review.] [Cf.: Diabolical blindness (Arnold Ages) [in]: Midstream, Vol. 46, No. 6, New York, Sept.-Oct. 2000, pp. 394.]

38845. HOLOCAUST DENIAL. WANDRES, THOMAS: *Die Strafbarkeit des Auschwitz-Leugnens.* Berlin: Duncker und Humblot, 2000. 338 pp. (Strafrechtliche Abhandlungen, N.F., Bd. 129.) Zugl.: Regensburg, Univ., Diss., 1999.

38846. *Holocaust chronicles: individualizing the Holocaust through diaries and other contemporaneous personal accounts.* Ed. by Robert Moses Shapiro. Introd. by Ruth R. Wisse. Hoboken, NJ: Ktav, 1999. XVIII, 302 pp., frontis., illus., facsims., index. [A collection of papers orig. presented at a conference at Yeshiva Univ., New York in 1996.]

—— *The Holocaust chronicle.* [See No. 30690.]

38847. *The Holocaust and the book: destruction and preservation.* Essays on the Nazi campaign against the written word. Ed. and with introd. by Jonathan Rose. Amherst: Univ. of Massachusetts Press, 2000. VI, 314 pp., illus., notes, bibl.(295–310).(Studies in print culture and the history of the book.) [Essays on the burning, looting and censoring of books, as well as on the Nazi destruction of libraries throughout occupied Europe.]

38848. HOLUB, ROBERT C.: *The memories of silence and the silence of memories: post-war Germans and the Holocaust.* [In]: German Politics and Society, Vol. 18, No. 1, Berkeley, CA, Spring 2000. Pp. 105–123. [Incl. reviews of 'Stated memory' (Theodor Fox, see No. 37843/YB XLV), and 'The language of silence' (Ernestine Schlant, see No. 38942).]

38849. HOLZMAN, HELENE: *"Dies Kind soll leben". Die Aufzeichnungen der Helene Holzman 1941–1944.* Hrsg. von Reinhard Kaiser und Margarete Holzman. Frankfurt am Main: Schöffling & Co., 2000. 384 pp., frontis., illus., map, plan, chronol., bibl., index. [Incl.: Anhang (ed., 343–384; incl. short biography of H.H.).] [H.H., née Czapski, Aug. 30, 1891 Jena – Aug. 25, 1968 Gießen, painter, art and German teacher, daughter of a Jewish father and a non-Jewish mother, in 1923 went with her husband, the Jewish book dealer Max Holzman, to Kaunas, Lithuania, where she survived the war while her husband and daughter were murdered in 1941. Memoirs were written between Sept. 1944 and Aug. 1945.]

38850. JAPAN. MAUL, HEINZ EBERHARD: *Japan und die Juden.* Studie über die Judenpolitik des Kaiserreiches Japan während der Zeit des Nationalsozialismus 1933–1945. Meckenheim: H.E. Maul [privately printed], 2000. 349 pp., footnotes, docs., bibl. (287–326), gloss. Bonn:

Univ., Diss., 2000. [Deals also with refugees from Nazi occupied countries in Harbin and Shanghai.]

38851. JENA. ZIMMERMANN, SUSANNE: *Die Medizinische Fakultät der Universität Jena während der Zeit des Nationalsozialismus.* Berlin: Verl. f. Wiss. und Bildung, 2000. XIII, 223 pp., footnotes, bibl., indexes. (Ernst-Haeckel-Haus-Studien, Bd. 2.) [Deals also with the fate of Jewish students and faculty members.]

38852. JOHNSON, DANIEL: *What Victor Klemperer saw.* [In]: Commentary, Vol. 109, No. 6, New York, June 2000. Pp. 44–50. [Discusses how K.'s diary provides a portrait of tyranny, and of the ordinary Germans who failed to resist it.]

38853. JUREIT, ULRIKE: *Einnerungsmuster. Zur Methodik lebensgeschichtlicher Interviews mit Überlebenden der Konzentrations- und Vernichtungslager.* Hamburg: Ergebnisse Verl., 1999. 425 pp., footnotes, bibl. (Forum Zeitgeschichte, Bd. 8. Hrsg. von der Forschungsstelle für Zeitgeschichte in Hamburg. Red.: Frank Bajohr.)

38855. KATER, MICHAEL H.: *Ärzte als Hitlers Helfer.* Mit einem Geleitwort von Hans Mommsen. [Aus dem Amerik. von Helmut Dierlamm und Renate Weitbrecht]. Hamburg: Europa Verl., 2000. 576 pp., notes (412–522), bibl., index. [For orig. edn. see No. 27312/YB XXXI. Incl. chap.: Die Verfolgung der jüdischen Ärzte (291–359).]

38856. KATER, MICHAEL H.: *Composers of the Nazi era: eight portraits.* New York; Oxford Univ. Press, 2000. XIII, 399 pp., notes (285–377), index. [Incl.: Kurt Weill – a survivor on two continents (57–85). Arnold Schoenberg – musician of contrasts (183–210); deals also with exile.]

38857. KESSLER, HERBERT ZWI: *Der Weg ins Ungewisse. Von Berlin nach Holland und Belgien. Erinnerungen eines jüdischen Flüchtlingskindes 1928–1945.* Hrsg. von Erhard Roy Wiehn. Konstanz: Hartung-Gorre Verl., 2000. 510 pp., illus., facsims., footnotes. [Author lives in Israel.]

38858. KILLIUS, ROSEMARIE: *Sei still, Kind! Adolf spricht.* Gespräche mit Zeitzeuginnen. Leipzig: Militzke, 2000. 253 pp., ports. [Incl. interviews with Etty Gingold and Lilli Segal.]

38859. KINDERTRANSPORT. *Recollections of child refugees from 1938 to the present: Kindertransports: Scotland's child refugees.* Ed. and compiled by Rosa M. Sacharin. Glasgow: Scottish Annual Reunion of Kinder, 1999. 101 pp., illus., facsims., ports. [Incl. c. 30 personal recollections of mostly German- or Austrian-Jewish refugees aged from 4–17 years in 1938. Book was instigated by the Reunion of Kindertransport (ROK) formed in 1990 to celebrate the 50th anniversary of the Kindertransport.]

38860. KINDERTRANSPORT. *Into the arms of strangers: stories of the Kindertransports.* The British scheme that saved 10.000 children from the Nazi regime. Ed. by Mark Jonathan Harris and Deborah Oppenheimer. Preface by Richard Attenborough. Introd. by David Cesarani. New York; London: Bloomsbury, 2000. XIII, 292 pp., illus., facsims., ports., bibl. [German edn.: Kindertransport in eine fremde Welt. Aus dem Amerik. von Jerry Hofer. München: Goldmann, 2000. 444 pp., illus.] [Personal recollections of children who were part of the Kindertransports. Based on the feature-length documentary film.]

38861. KINDERTRANSPORT. *Sixtieth anniversary of the Kindertransport. 1939, 1999.* [London: Privately printed, 1999]. 184 pp., illus., facsims. [Incl.: How it all started (Bertha Leverton, 5.). Collection of articles, speeches, memoirs, name lists, publ. on the occasion of the Kindertransport reunion in London, June 1999. Obtainable at the Imperial War Museum, London.]

38862. KLÜGER, LEO: *Lache, denn morgen bist du tot. Eine Geschichte vom Überleben.* Aus dem Schwedischen von Verena Reichel. Mit 17 Abbildungen. München: Piper, 2000. 361 pp., illus. [L.K., born 1921 in Vienna, fled 1938 to Belgium, 1940 to France, from 1942–1945 imprisoned in various concentration camps. Lives in Sweden.]

38863. KÖPKE, MONIQUE: *Mit dem Nachtzug nach Paris. Ein jüdisches Mädchen überlebt Hitler in Frankreich.* Erkelenz: Altius, 2000. 413 pp., illus., facsims., docs., notes. [Cf.: Ein Denkmal für die Eltern.

Kindheit im französischen Exil – ein Rückblick voller Liebe und voller Zorn (Florian Sendtner) [in]: Süddeutsche Zeitung, Jg. 56, Nr. 162, München, 17. Juli, 2000, p. 10.] [M.K., née Monika Lehmann, b. 1925 in Berlin, emigr. 1933 with her father, the art historian and Communist Ernst Lehmann-Lukas to Paris, escaped in 1942 to Switzerland. Her Mother (née Zippert) and her father were deported from Gurs resp. Rivesaltes to Auschwitz. Lives in Boston. Incl. numerous family letters.]

38864. KOENIG, ERNEST: *Im Vorhof der Vernichtung.* Als Zwangsarbeiter in den Außenlagern von Auschwitz. Hrsg. und mit einem Nachwort versehen von Gioia-Olivia Karnagel. Frankfurt am Main: Fischer Taschenbuch-Verl., 2000. 181 pp., illus. (Lebensbilder. Jüdische Erinnerungen und Zeugnisse.) Orig.-Ausg. [Author, b. 1914 in Vienna, grew up in Moravia, studied in Prague and Paris, imprisoned there in 1940 by the French police, deported 1942 to Auschwitz, slave labourer in Laurahütte and Blechhammer, after liberation emigr. to the US, from 1951 civil servant, from 1959 US diplomat in Bonn, Brussels and Paris. Lives nr. Washington, DC.]

38865. KOPPER, CHRISTOPHER: *Wirtschaftliche Selbstbehauptung im sozialen Ghetto. Jüdische Wirtschaftsbürger im "Dritten Reich".* [In]: Großbürger und Unternehmer. Die deutsche Wirtschaftselite im 20. Jahrhundert. Hrsg. von Dieter Ziegler. Göttingen: Vandenhoeck & Ruprecht, 2000. Pp. 204–214, footnotes. (Bürgertum. Beiträge zur europäischen Gesellschaftsgeschichte, Bd. 17.).

38866. KRAMER, HELGARD, ed.: *Die Gegenwart der NS-Vergangenheit.* Berlin: Philo, 2000. 349 pp., footnotes. [Cont. 16 essays, mostly dealing with former Nazi perpetrators and other aspects of "Vergangenheitsbewältigung"; selected essays: Von Theresienstadt nach Auschwitz (Trude Simonsohn, 199–220; personal recollections of Prague-born German-speaking author, who lives in Frankfurt am Main). "Ausgelassene" Gefühle. Analysen lebensgeschichtlicher Interviews mit versteckten jüdischen Kindern (Birgit Schreiber, 239–254). Generationenkonflikte und deutsches Selbstverständnis. Sozialpsychologische Aspekte der Goldhagen-Debatte (Birgit Rommelspacher, 314–328).]

38867. KRAUSE, KUNO: *Dolores & Imperio. Die drei Leben des Sylvin Rubinstein.* Köln: Kiepenheur & Witsch, 2000. 272 pp., illus. [Story of the twin Flamenco dancers Maria and Sylvin Rubinstein from Brody, Galicia, b. 1914 in Moscow to a Jewish actress and a Russian aristocrat, trained at a Warsaw dance school, performed in Berlin and other European cities before 1933, fled to Poland after 1933, later to Lithuania. S.R. survived with the help of a German officer, himself involved in the resistance, joined a local resistance group, went to Berlin in 1943 with fake identity. Has lived in Hamburg-St. Pauli since the 1950s.]

38868. KÜHN-LUDEWIG, MARIA: *Johannes Pohl (1904–1960). Judaist und Bibliothekar im Dienste Rosenbergs.* Eine biographische Dokumentation. Hannover: Laurentius, 2000. 334 pp., illus., facsims., footnotes, bibl., index. (Kleine Historische Reihe, Bd. 10.)

38869. LAQUEUR, WALTER: *Geboren in Deutschland. Der Exodus der jüdischen Jugend nach 1933.* Berlin: Propyläen, 2000. 472 pp., illus.

38870. LASKER-WALLFISCH, ANITA: *Inherit the truth: a memoir of survival and the Holocaust.* New York: Thomas Dunne Books/St. Martin's Press, 2000. 176 pp., illus., facsims., docs., index. [Memoirs of a young girl from Breslau who survived Auschwitz (where she was a cellist in the camp orchestra) and Bergen-Belsen. For orig. English edn. and details see No. 34086/YB XLII.]

38871. *The last days.* Ed. by Steven Spielberg and Survivors of the Shoah Visual Foundation. Preface by Steven Spielberg. Introd. by David Cesarani. London: Weidenfeld & Nicolson; New York: St. Martin's Press, 1999. 240 pp., illus., facsims., maps. [Companion vol. to documentary of the same name by James Moll. Film portrays the last year of World War II and the accelerated programme of the destruction of Hungarian Jewry as narrated by 5 survivors. Incl.: Introduction (David Cesarani, 15–51); the foundation was founded in 1994 by Spielberg to record the testimonies of survivors, eyewitnesses, bystanders, liberators and rescuers.]

38872. LEIPZIG. LAWFORD-HINRICHSEN, IRENE: *Music publishing and patronage: C.F. Peters, 1800 to the Holocaust.* Kenton, UK: Edition Press, 2000. XXIV, 332 pp., illus., ports. facsims., geneal. tab., bibl. (319–323), index. [History of the prestigious Leipzig music publishing house C.P. Peters, owned by the Abraham-Hinrichsen family for several generations until the Nazi period. Incl. November Pogrom, aryanization, emigration, the murder of Max Abraham and his nephew Henry Hinrichsen in Auschwitz.]

38873. LENZ, WILHELM: *Die Handakten von Bernhard Lösener, "Rassereferent im Reichsministerium des Innern.* [In]: Klaus Oldenhage [et al.]: Archiv und Geschichte. Festschrift für Friedrich P. Kahlenberg. Düsseldorf: Droste, 2000. Pp. 684–699, footnotes.

38874. LIEBERT, ELISABETH: *Aspekte der deutschen mittelprächtigen Gesellschaft am Ende der zwanziger Jahre in diesem Jahrhundert.* [In]: Die Mahnung, Jg. 47, Berlin, 1. Feb. 2000. P. 7. [Memoirs dealing with the author's Jewish school friend.]

38875. LÖRRACH. SEILER, LUKREZIA, ed.: *Was wird aus uns noch werden? Briefe der Lörracher Geschwister Grunkin aus dem Lager Gurs, 1940–1942.* Zürich: Chronos, 2000. 128 pp., illus., facsims., notes (118–124), bibl.

38876. LOESER, HANS: *Early memoirs of Hans Loeser 1920–1946: Germany – England – America.* Cambridge: Unpubl. MA thesis, Univ. of Cambridge; privately printed, 1999. 125 pp. [Author, born in Kassel, emigr. 1937 to England, 1940 reunited with family in US, enlisted in 1942 and served in Europe and with the Military Govt. in Germany.]

38877. LONDON, LOUISE: *Whitehall and the Jews, 1933–1948: British immigration policy, Jewish refugees and the Holocaust.* Cambridge; New York: Cambridge Univ. Press, 2000. XIII, 313 pp., illus., appendixes, bibl., index. [Cont. chaps (some titles. abbrev.): Introd. Immigration control and administration. Control without visas; refugee immigration 1933– 1938. New restrictions after the "Anschluss". From "Kristallnacht to the outbreak of war. Refugees from Czechoslovakia. Wartime policy: 1939–1942. Response to the Holocaust. Post-war decisions. Conclusion.]. [Cf.: Whitehall and the refugees: the 1930s and the 1990s (Louise London) [in]: Patterns of Prejudice, Vol. 34, No. 3, London, July 2000. pp. 17–26, footnotes. Paper, camparing British refugee policies of the past and present, given at the book launch for 'Whitehall and the Jews'.] [Cf.: Review article (Tom Lawson) [in]: Journal of Refugee Studies, Vol. 13, No. 4, Oxford, Dec. 2000, pp. 431–432. Review (William D. Rubinstein) [in]: The English Historical Review, Vol. 115, No. 464, Oxford, 2000, pp. 1362–1363.]

38878. LUDWIGSHAFEN (Kreis). SCHEPUA, MICHAEL: *Nationalsozialismus in der pfälzischen Provinz. Herrschaftspraxis und Alltagsleben in den Gemeinden des heutigen Landkreises Ludwigshafen 1933–1945.* Mannheim: Palatium, 2000. XIII, 998 pp., footnotes, maps, tabs., bibl. (945–986), index. (Mannheimer historische Forschungen, Bd. 20.) [Incl. chap. entitled 'Vom Boykott zum Holocaust: Die Verfolgung der jüdischen Bevölkerung' (533–608).]

38879. LÜBECK. *"Hoffentlich klappts alles zum Guten ...". Die Briefe der jüdischen Schwestern Bertha und Dora Lexandrowitz (1939–1941).*: Bearb. und kommentiert von Heidemarie Kugler-Weiemann und Hella Peperkorn. Neumünster: Wachholtz, 2000. 175 pp., illus., facsims., notes (145–165), bibl., index. (Quellen und Studien zur jüdischen Bevölkerung Schleswig-Holsteins.) [Incl. letters written by two sisters from Lübeck before deportation to a family in Shanghai.]

38880. MÄCHLER, STEFAN: *Der Fall Wilkomirski. Über die Wahrheit einer Biographie.* Zürich: Pendo, 2000. 366 pp., notes (329–362), bibl.

38881. MAIWALD, STEFAN/MISCHLER, GERD: *Sexualität unter dem Hakenkreuz: Manipulation und Vernichtung der Intimsphäre im NS-Staat.* Hamburg: Europa-Verl., 1999. 287 pp. [Incl. chap.: "Rassenschande – Angriff auf die Reinheit des deutschen Blutes".]

38882. MANNHEIMER, MAX: *Spätes Tagebuch.* Theresienstadt – Auschwitz – Dachau. Mit 14 Abbildungen, Anmerkungen von Wolfgang Benz und einem Nachwort von Ernst Piper. Zürich: Pendo, 2000. frontis., 127 pp., illus., notes (117–121). (Geschichte des 20. Jahrhunderts.) [M.M., b. 1920 in Neutitschein, Czechoslovakia, deported 1943 to Auschwitz, then to Warsaw as a slave labourer, later to Dachau, lives nr. Munich, painter (with the name ben jakov), chairman of Lagergemeinschaft Dachau e.V.]

38883. MANN, MICHAEL: *Were the perpetrators of Genocide "ordinary men" or "real Nazis"?: results from fifteen hundred biographies.* [In]: Holocaust and Genocide Studies, Vol. 14, No. 3, Oxford, Winter 2000. Pp. 331–366, notes.

38884. MARUM-LUNAU, ELISABETH: *Auf der Flucht in Frankreich. "Boches ici, Juifs là-bas".* Der Briefwechsel einer deutschen Familie im Exil 1939–1942. Ausgewählt und kommentiert von Jacques Grandjonc, für die deutsche Ausgabe übers. und erw. von Doris Obschernitzki. Teetz: Hentrich & Hentrich, 2000. 296 pp., footnotes, illus., facsims., chronol., bibl., index. [First publ. in French 1997.] [E.M.-L., 1910 Karlsruhe – 1998 New York, daughter of the Social Democratic politician Ludwig Marum (murdered 1934).]

38885. MATTHÄUS, JÜRGEN: *Antisemitic symbolism in early Nazi Germany, 1933–1935.* [In]: Leo Baeck Institute Year Book XLV, London, 2000. Pp. 183–203, illus., footnotes. [Based on the C.V. files in the Osobyi archives in Moscow.]

38886. MEDOFF, RAFAEL: *A foolish encroachment upon the Allied High Command? American Jewish perspectives on requesting U.S. military intervention against the Holocaust.* [In]: Modern Judaism, Vol. 20, No. 3, Baltimore, Oct. 2000. Pp. 299–314, notes.

38887. Mühlheim (Main). SCHNEIDER, HANS C.: *Die Gemeinde braucht mich. Leopold Isaak und die Seinen. Der letzte Vorsteher der jüdischen Gemeinde Mühlheims.* Hrsg. vom Geschichtsverein Mühlheim am Main e.V. Hanau: CoCon-Verl., 2000. 112 pp., illus. (Zur Geschichte der Stadt Mühlheim, Bd. 17.)

38888. MÜLLER, REINHARD: *Der Fall Werner Hirsch. Vom KZ Oranienburg in die Moskauer Lubjanka.* [In]: Int. wissenschaftliche Korrespondenz zur Gesch. der deutschen Arbeiterbewegung (IWK), H. 1, Berlin, 2000. Pp. 34–61, footnotes. [W.H., Dec. 7, 1899 Berlin – June 10, 1941 Moscow (Butyrka prison), son of a Jewish father, KPD functionary, journalist, from March 1933 to 1934 imprisoned in German concentration camps, thereafter emigr. to the Soviet Union, 1935 imprisoned in Moscow.]

38889. MÜNSTER. HERZOG, EMMY: *Leben mit Leo. Ein Schicksal im Nationalsozialismus.* Münster: Aschendorff, 2000. 184 pp., illus. [Author tells about her life with her first husband Leo Steinweg, with whom she emigr. to the Netherlands; lived in hiding in Utrecht until betrayal in 1942 when L.St. was deported to Auschwitz.]

38890. MÜNSTERLAND. TEUBER, WERNER: *"Wohin sollten wir denn gehen?". Juden im Oldenburger Münsterland.* [In]: Nationalsozialismus im Oldenburger Münsterland. Beiträge zum 2. Studientag des Geschichtsausschusses für das Oldenburger Münsterland. Cloppenburg: Heimatbund Oldenburger Münsterland, 1999. (Die Blaue Reihe, 5.) Pp. 112–124, illus. [Book incl. also an essay on the concentration camp in Vechta (Albrecht Eckhardt, 89–99).]

38891. MUNICH. RAPPL, MARIAN: *"Arisierungen" in München.* Die Verdrängung der jüdischen Gewerbetreibenden aus dem Wirtschaftsleben der Stadt 1033–1939. [In]: Zeitschrift für bayerische Landesgeschichte, Bd. 63, H. 1, München, 2000. Pp. 80–121, footnotes.

38892. MUNICH. *"... verzogen, unbekannt wohin". Die erste Deportation von Münchner Juden im November 1941.* Hrsg. vom Stadtarchiv München. Zürich: Pendo, 2000. 175 pp., illus., tabs.

38893. NAOR, SIMHA: *Leben nach Auschwitz.* Eine Tagebucherzählung. [In]: Zwischenwelt [formerly: Mit der Ziehharmonika], Jg. 17, Nr. 1, Wien, Mai 2000. Pp. 35–40. [Introd. by Kurt Kreiler. Autobiographical story is set shortly after liberation.] [S.N., orig. Stella Silberstein, 1899 Vienna – 1994 Haifa, Auschwitz survivor.]

38894. NETHERLANDS. AALDERS, GERARD: *Geraubt! Die Enteignung jüdischen Besitzes im Zweiten Weltkrieg.* Aus dem Niederl. von Stefan Häring. Köln: Dittrich, 2000. 435 pp., notes, bibl., indexes. [Incl. the property of refugees.]

38895. NETHERLANDS. BACHMANN, MARTIN: *Geliebtes Volk Israel – Fremde Juden: Die Nederlandse Hervormde Kerk und die "Judenfrage", 1933–1945.* Münster: LIT. 340 pp., footnotes, docs., bibl.

(379–430), indexes. (Geschichte, 15.) Zugl.: Wuppertal, Univ., Diss., 1996. [Also on refugees, Westerbork.]

38896. NETHERLANDS. BOVENKERK, F.: *The other side of the Anne Frank story: the Dutch role in the persecution of the Jews in World War II.* [In]: Crime Law and Social Change, Vol. 34, No. 3, Dordrecht, Boston, 2000. Pp. 237–258, notes.

38897. NEUENGAMME. HERTZ-EICHENRODE, KATHARINA, ed.: *Ein KZ wird geräumt. Häftlinge zwischen Vernichtung und Befreiung: Die Auflösung des KZ Neuengamme und seiner Außenlager durch die SS im Frühjahr 1945.* Katalog zur Wanderausstellung. Bd. 1: Texte und Dokumente. Bd. 2: Karten. Bremen: Ed. Temmen, 2000. 381; 117 pp. [Incl. contribs. by Detlef Garbe and Nina Holsten.]

38898. NEWMAN, RICHARD (with KAREN KIRTLEY): *Alma Rosé: Vienna to Auschwitz* Portland, OR: Amadeus Press, 2000. 407 pp., illus., ports., facsims., geneal. tab., gloss., plans, notes (329–361), bibl. (362–375), index. [Incl. list of members of the Auschwitz orchestra of women.] [A.R., 1906 Vienna – 1943 Auschwitz, daughter of Justine (sister of Gustav Mahler) and Alfred Rosé, (first violinist of the Vienna Philharmonic), musician, deported to Auschwitz where she directed an all women's orchestra until she was killed.]

38899. *New German Critique.* Spring-Summer 2000. No. 80 [with the issue title] *Holocaust.* Ithaca, NY, Spring- Summer 2000. 1 issue, notes. [Incl. (titles condensed): History, memory, and the historian (Saul Friedländer, 3–15). Historical consciousness in Germany after the Genocide (Michael Naumann, 17–28). Germany as victim (Omer Bartov, 29–40). Rescreening "the Holocaust": the children's stories (David Bathrick, 41–58). "The arrogance of youth": the Goldhagen-debate in Germany as generational conflict (Axel Körner, 59–76). Austria's recycling of the Nazi past and its European echoes (Lutz Musner, 77– 91). Touching tales of Turks, Germans, and Jews (Leslie A. Adelson, 93– 124). The return of the gaze: stereoscopic vision in Jünger and Benjamin (Carsten Strathausen, 125–148).]

38900. *"Niemand zeugt für den Zeugen" Erinnerungskultur und historische Verantwortung nach der Shoah.* Hrsg. von Ulrich Baer. Frankfurt am Main: Suhrkamp, 2000. 278 pp., footnotes. [Cont.: Einleitung (ed., 7–31), Intellektuelle Zeugenschaft und die Shoah (Geoffrey Hartman, 35–52). Die Zeit der Erinnerung. Zeitverlauf und Dauer in Zeugenaussagen von Überlebenden des Holocaust (Lawrence Langer, 53–67). Zeugnis ablegen oder Die Schwierigkeit des Zuhörens (Dori Laub, 68–83). Trauma als historische Erfahrung: Die Vergangenheit einholen (Cathy Caruth, 84–98). Der Ort und das Wort (Claude Lanzmann, 101–118). Überlegungen zu drei 'Ravensbrück' (Pierre Vidal-Naquet, 119–132). Die Aufgabe der Zeugenschaft. Das Holocaust-Zeugnis der Alina Bacall-Zwirn (Jared Stark, 133–155). Identitätspolitik als politische Ästhetik. Peter Weiss' 'Ermittlung' im amerikanischen Holocaust-Diskurs (Robert Cohen, 156–172). Im Zeitalter der Zeugenschaft: Claude Lanzmanns 'Shoah' (Shoshana Felman, 173–193). Der Film als Zeuge. 'Nazi Concentration Camps' vor dem Nürnberger Gerichtshof (Lawrence Douglas, 197–218). Der entleerte Blick: Gewalt im Visier (Bernd Hüppauf, 219–235). Zum Zeugen werden. Landschaftstradition und Shoah oder Die Grenzen der Geschichtsschreibung im Bild (Ulrich Baer, 236–254). Trauma-TV: Video als Zeugnis. Zwölf Schritte jenseits des Lustprinzips (Avital Ronell, 255–273).]

38901. NOVEMBER POGROM. BLASCHKE, OLAF: *Die "Reichspogromnacht" und die Haltung der katholischen Bevölkerung und Kirche.* Mentalitätsgeschichte als Schlüssel zu einem neuen Verständnis? [In]: Zeitschrift für Religions- und Geistesgeschichte, Jg. 52, H. 1, Leiden, 2000. Pp. 47–74, footnotes.

38902. NOVEMBER POGROM. PERELS, JOACHIM: *Wendepunkt in der Politik des Judenhasses. Die Reichspogromnacht und die Komplizenschaft der Gesellschaft.* [In]: Licht und Schatten. Der 9. November in der deutschen Geschichte und Rechtsgeschichte. Symposium der Arnold-Freymuth-Gesellschaft, Hamm, am 14. Nov. 1999. Hrsg.: Franz-Josef Düwell. Baden-Baden: Nomos, 2000. (Juristische Zeitgeschichte, Bd. 9.) Pp. 59–70, footnotes.

38903. NUREMBERG TRIALS. WEINDLING, PAUL: *From international to zonal trials: the origins of the Nuremberg Medical Trials.* [In]: Holocaust and Genocide Studies, Vol. 14, No. 3, Oxford, Winter 2000. Pp. 367–389, notes.

38904. OESTREICHER, FELIX HERMANN: *Ein jüdischer Arzt-Kalender.* Durch Westerbork und Bergen-Belsen nach Tröbitz. Konzentrationslager-Tagebuch 1943–1945. Transkription von Anneliese Nassuth-Broschmann und Maria Goudsblom-Oestreicher. Hrsg. von Maria Goudsblom-Oestreicher und Erhard Roy Wiehn. Konstanz: Hartung-Gorre, 2000. 288 pp., illus., facsims., docs.. [F.Oe., 1894 Karlsbad – 1945 Tröbitz, emigr. 1938 to Amsterdam.]

38905. ONDRICHOVÁ, LUCIE: *Fredy Hirsch.* Von Aachen über Düsseldorf und Frankfurt am Main durch Theresienstadt nach Auschwitz-Birkenau. Eine jüdische Biographie 1916–1944. Aus dem Tschech. von Astrid Prackatsch. Konstanz: Hartung-Gorre, 2000. 104 pp., frontis., illus., facsims., notes, bibl. (Konstanzer Schriften zur Schoáh und Judaica, Bd. 8.) [F.H. (orig. Alfred), 1916 Aachen – 1944 Auschwitz, active in the Jewish youth movement (JPD, later Makkabi Hatzair, then Hechaluz), in 1935 went to Prague, later to Moravia, after deportation to Theresienstadt, where he worked as educator and youth leader, trying to save children.]

38906. ORTENAU. HANß, KARL: *"Ihre Seele sei eingebunden im Bündel des Lebens": Verzeichnis der aus der Ortenau am 22. Oktober 1940 deportierten Juden, die im Internierungslager Gurs (Südfrankreich) verstorben und auf dem dortigen Friedhof bestattet sind.* [In]: Die Ortenau, Bd. 80, Offenburg/Baden, 2000. Pp. 251–260, notes.

38907. ORTMEYER, BENJAMIN: *Schulzeit unterm Hitlerbild.* Analysen, Berichte, Dokumente. Frankfurt am Main: Brandes & Apsel, 2000. 223 pp., notes (185–210), bibl. [New edn. with new publ., for orig. edn. see No. 35152/YB XLIII. Incl. chaps. on Jewish school children.]

38908. PAETZ, ANDREAS/WEISS, KARIN, eds.: *"Hachschara".* Die Vorbereitung junger Juden auf die Auswanderung nach Palästina. Potsdam: Verlag für Berlin-Brandenburg, 1999. 94 pp., footnotes. [Cont.: Vorwort (eds., 7–8). Contribs. by Ulrich Tromm (9–28; on Markenhof, Kirchzarten-Burg), Sieghard Bußenius (29–40; on Brüderhof nr. Harksheide), Herbert Fiedler (41–46; on the Begegnungsstätte Hachschara – Landwerk Ahrensfelde e.V.), eds. (on Hachschara places in Brandenburg), Juha Tiusanen (on Hachschara places in Denmark).]

38909. PAPEN, PATRICIA VON: *'Scholarly' antisemitism during the Third Reich: the Reichsinstitut for Research on the 'Jewish Question'.* New York: Columbia University, Diss., 1999. [Typescript] III, 390 leaves, bibl.

38910. PARKER, CLARE: *Klara's story.* As told by Clare Parker. Privately publ. [1999]. 116 pp., illus., ports. [Memoirs of a Hungarian-Jewish woman, who survived Auschwitz and Mauthausen as a child. Incl. life under post-war communist rule and eventual flight with father to England.]

38911. PATZELT, PETER: *Ein Bürokrat des Verbrechens. Hans Hinkel und die "Entjudung" der deutschen Kultur.* [In]: Deutsche Publizistik im Exil 1933 bis 1945 [see No. 38651]. Pp. 307–317, footnotes.

38912. PAUCKER, PAULINE: *Die Bauersche Giesserei und die Elisabeth-Schrift. Georg Hartmann/Elizabeth Friedlander: Ein Briefwechsel.* [In]: Philobiblon. Eine Vierteljahrsschrift für Buch- und Graphiksammler, Jg. 44, Stuttgart, Dez. 2000. Pp. 270–291, frontis., illus., footnotes. [E.F., data see No. 36827/YB XLIV.]

38913. PETROPOULOS, JONATHAN: *The Faustian bargain: the art world in Nazi Germany.* New York: Oxford Univ. Press, 2000. XVII, 395 pp., illus., facsims., notes (281–349), bibl. (351–376), index. [Incl.: Jews as artdealers and critics, persecution of Jewish artists, the seizure of art by the Nazis, the Nazi concept of "degenerate art", and the plundering of art in occupied countries.] [Cf.: After the panzers, the plunderers (George Steiner) [in]: The Observer, London, April 16, 2000, p.12. Review (James J. Sheehan) [in]: Dimensions, Vol. 14, No. 2, New York, 2000, pp. 42– 45, illus.]

38914. PHILIPPSBURG. WILDMANN, MANFRED/WIEHN, ERHARD ROY, eds.: *Und flehentlich gesegnet. Briefe der Familie Wildmann aus Rivesaltes und Perpignan. Jüdische Schicksale aus Philippsburg 1941–1943.* Konstanz: Hartung-Gorre, 1997. 204 pp., illus., facsims.

38915. PLACZEK, ADOLF K.: *Traumfahrt mit der Familie.* Frankfurt am Main: Jüd. Verlag, 1999. 73 pp. [On a family from Vienna.]

——— POLLMANN, VIKTORIA: *NS-Justiz, Nürnberger Prozesse, NSG-Verfahren.* Auswahl-Bibliographie. [See No. 38695.]

38916. POSNER, LOUIS: *Through a boy's eyes: the turbulent years 1926–1945.* Santa Ana, CA: Seven Locks Press, 2000. XV, 285 pp., illus., gloss., bibl. [Author, b. Berlin, 1926, describes his early years in Nazi Germany. Fled in 1938 to Belgium, subsequently sent to a labour camp from which he escaped; on recapture deported to Auschwitz and eventually liberated by the Russians. Now lives in California.]

38917. POTSDAM. *"Überall spontane antijüdische Aktionen".* Erinnerungsfenster zum 60. Jahrestag der Reichspogromnacht in Potsdam. Ein Projekt des Studienganges Kulturarbeit an der Fachhochschule Potsdam. Die Projektgruppe: Anke Bröskamp [et al.]. Projektbetreuer: Hermann Voegen. Potsdam: FHP, Presse- und Informationsstelle, 1999. 21 pp., illus.

38918. PRAGUE. RUPNOW, DIRK: *"Ihr müßt sein, auch wenn ihr nicht mehr seid…" Das "Jüdische Zentralmuseum" in Prag 1942–1945.* [In]: Theresienstädter Studien und Dokumente, 2000, Prag, 2000. Pp. 192–214.

38919. PRAGUE. RUPNOW, DIRK: *Täter, Gedächtnis, Opfer: Das "Jüdische Zentralmuseum" in Prag 1942–1945.* Wien: Picus, 2000. 231 pp., illus., footnotes, bibl. [Incl.: Vorwort (Dan Diner, 9–11). Deals with the museum founded in 1942 by the SS; also on the earlier Jewish museum in Prague and its post-1945 development.]

38920. PROSECUTION OF NAZI CRIMES. BOBERACH, HEINZ: *Die Beteiligung des Bundesarchivs an der Verfolgung und Wiedergutmachung nationalsozialistischen Unrechts in den sechziger Jahren.* [In]: Klaus Oldenhage [et al.], eds.: Archiv und Geschichte. Festschrift für Friedrich P. Kahlenberg. Düsseldorf: Droste, 2000. (Schriften des Bundesarchivs, Nr. 57.) Pp. 265–274, footnotes.

38921. PROSECUTION OF NAZI CRIMES. *Der Nationalsozialismus vor Gericht. Die alliierten Prozesse gegen Kriegsverbrecher und Soldaten 1943–1952.* Mit Beiträgen von Rainer A. Blasius [et al.]. Hrsg. von Gerd Ueberschär. Frankfurt am Main: Fischer Taschenbuch Verlag, 2000. 319 pp., notes, docs., bibl., index. (Die Zeit des Nationalsozialismus.) Orig.-Ausg. [Cf.: Besprechung (Gerhard Stuby) [in]: 1999, Zeitschrift für Sozialgeschichte des 20. und 21. Jahrhunderts, Jg. 15, H. 2, Köln, 2000, pp. 134–137.]

38922. *Rassismus, Faschismus, Antifaschismus.* Forschungen und Betrachtungen. Gewidmet Kurt Pätzold zum 70. Geburtstag. Hrsg. von Manfred Weißbecker [et al.] Köln: Papyrosssa, 2000. 570 pp., notes. [Incl.: Revisionismus als Antisemitismus. Motive der Realitätsverleugnung des Holocaust (Wolfgang Benz, 14–24). "Judentum und Kriminalität" – Rassistische Deutungen in kriminologischen Publikationen 1933–1945 (Robert G. Waite, 46–62). Die NS-Führung und die Zwangsarbeit für sogenannte jüdische Mischlinge (Wolf Gruner, 63–79); further selected articles are listed according to subject.]

38923. REBHUN, ZE'EV: *Autumn 1939 – Yamin Noraim: Memorial Book for East European Jews who lived in Germany.* Jerusalem: Erez, 1999. XX, 220 pp., illus.

38924. RENDSBURG. GLADE, FELICITAS: *Ernst Bamberger – Wilhelm Hamkens. Eine Freundschaft in Mittelholstein unter dem NS-Regime.* Rendsburg: Kreisverein Rendsburg für Heimatkunde und Geschichte e.V., 2000. 281 pp., illus., notes (223–254), bibl., index. (Rendsburger Jahrbuch, Beihefte Bd. 1.) [E.B., April 30, 1885 Frankfurt am Main – Dec. 6, 1941 Remmels (suicide before deportation), surgeon, 1922 -1938 director of a private clinic for surgery in Rendsburg. W.H., jurist, Landrat of Rendsburg (Kreis), since 1929 member of the NSDAP and high Nazi functionary, during the Nazi era Regierungspräsident of Schleswig-Holstein.]

38925. RENSMANN, LARS: *Jüdische Selbstverwaltung im NS-Staat.* [In]: Freiburger Rundbrief, N.F., Jg. 7, H. 1, Freiburg, 2000. Pp. 28–33, footnotes. [Review essay.]

38926. RESCUE OF JEWS. GÖRGEN, HERMANN: *Ein Leben gegen Hitler: Geschichte und Rettung der "Gruppe Görgen". Autobiographische Skizzen.* Mit Vorworten von I. Bubis, O. Lafontaine und M. Abelein.

Red.: Ursula Meissner/Hermann Görgen. Münster: Lit, 1997. IV, 248 pp., footnotes. [H.G. helped 48 refugees to escape to Brazil.]

38927. RESCUE OF JEWS. KRANZLER, DAVID: *The man who stopped the trains to Auschwitz: George Mantello, El Salvador, and Switzerland's finest hour.* With a foreword by Senator Joseph I. Lieberman. Syracuse, NY: Syracuse Univ. Press, 2000. XXV, 341 pp., illus. notes (259-314), bibl. 315-321), index. (Religion, theology, and the Holocaust.) [Story of George Mantello, First Secretary of the El Salvador Consulate in Geneva from 1942 to 1945, where he launched a press campaign against the daily deportations of Hungarian Jews to Auschwitz; saved numerous lives by distrib. Salvadoran citizenship papers.]

38928. RESCUE OF JEWS. LAND-WEBER, ELLEN: *To save a life: stories of Holocaust rescuers.* Urbana, IL: Univ. of Illinois Press, 2000. IX, 331 pp., illus., facsims., maps, bibl. (303-310) index. [Deals with the Netherlands, Poland, Czechoslovakia; recounts individual stories through interviews, incl. German-Jewish refugees.]

38929. RESCUE OF JEWS. *Ministers of compassion during the Nazi period. Gertrud Luckner and Raoul Wallenberg.* Sixth Monsignor John M. Oesterreicher Memorial Lecture. South Orange, NJ: The Institute of Judaeo-Christian Studies, 2000. 40 pp. [Incl.: Gertrud Luckner: resistance and assistance. German woman who defied Nazis and aided Jews (Elizabeth Petuchowski, 4-19). Raoul Wallenberg and the Jews of Hungary (John F. Morley, 23-40).]

38930. RESCUE OF JEWS. PETUCHOWSKI, ELIZABETH: *Gertrud Luckner: Widerstand und Hilfe.* [Aus dem Amerik. von Alwin Renker]. [In]: Freiburger Rundbrief, N.F., Jh. 7, H. 4, Freiburg, 2000. pp. 242-259, footnotes.

38931. RESCUE OF JEWS. ROSENBERG, ERIKA, ed.: *Ich, Oskar Schindler.* Die persönlichen Aufzeichnungen, Briefe und Dokumente. Mit 39 Fotos und zahlreichen faksimilierten Dokumenten. München: Herbig, 2000. 448 pp., frontis., footnotes, index. [Incl. Schindler's famous list (facsim.) of 801 names, some of them German Jews.]

38932. RESCUE OF JEWS. TSCHUY, THEO: *Dangerous diplomacy: the story of Carl Lutz, rescuer of 62,000 Hungarian Jews.* Foreword by Simon Wiesenthal. Grand Rapids, MI; Cambridge: Eerdmans, 2000. XIV, 265 pp., illus. gloss., maps. [C.L., Swiss Consul General in Budapest, worked together with Raoul Wallenberg to save Jews by issuing them foreign passports. Knowledge of his actions was suppressed by the Swiss authorities; he has only recently been honoured.]

38933. RESISTANCE BY NON-JEWS. WEGNER, ARMIN T.: *Letter to Hitler* [In]: Journal of Genocide Research, Vol. 2, No. 1, Basingstoke, Hants., 2000. Pp. 133-144. [Reproduces in the orig. German and in English a letter which W. (husband of Lola Landau) had written to Hitler in April 11, 1933, protesting against Nazi treatment of the Jews. See also No. 39324.]

38934. REUBAND, KARL-HEINZ: *Gerüchte und Kenntnisse vom Holocaust in der deutschen Gesellschaft vor Ende des Krieges.* Eine Bestandsaufnahme auf der Basis von Bevölkerungsumfragen. [In]: Jahrbuch für Antisemitismusforschung 9, Frankfurt am Main; New York, 2000. Pp. 196-233, notes.

38935. RHEINAU. HIRSCHBERG, GERD: *Von Rheinau über Gurs nach Auschwitz. Stationen der Vernichtung der jüdischen Gemeinden Neufreistett und Rheinbischofsheim.* [In]: Die Ortenau. Bd. 80, Offenburg/Baden, 2000. Pp. 237-250, illus., notes. [Rheinau: Neufreistett and Rheinbischofsheim.]

38936. *Richard Wagner im Dritten Reich. Ein Schloss Elmau-Symposion.* Hrsg. von Saul Friedländer und Jörn Rüsen. München: Beck, 2000. 373pp., notes, indexes. [Incl. (some titles abbr.): Vorwort (eds., 9-10). Zum Symposion von Schloss Elmau (Dietmar Müller-Elmau, 11-14). "Wagner im Dritten Reich" (Jörn Rüsen, 15-23). Richard Wagner – Das Werk neben dem Werk. Zur ausstehenden Wirkungsgeschichte eines Großideologen (Joachim Fest, 24-39). Über einen Aspekt des Zusammenhangs von Richard Wagner mit Hitler und dem Dritten Reich (Udo Bermbach, 40-65). Renaissance und Instrumentalisierung des Mythos. Richard Wagner und die Folgen (Dieter Borchmeyer, 66-91). Die Dramaturgie der Alterität (David J. Levin, 92-108). Wagners Aktualität für den Nationalsozialismus (Reinhold Brinkmann, 109-141). Wagner-

Interpretation im Dritten Reich (Jens Malte Fischer, 142–164). Hitler und Wagner (Saul Friedländer, 165–178). Zu Winifred Wagner (Nike Wagner, 179–193). Wagners Bayreuth und Hitlers München (David Clay Large, 194–211). Zum Wandel des Wagnerbildes im Exil (Horst Weber, 212–229). Wagner-Kult und nationalsozialistische Herrschaft. Hitler, Wagner, Thomas Mann und die "nationale Erhebung" (Hans Rudolf Vaget, 264–282). Wagner, Hitler und historische Prophetie (Paul Lawrence Rose, 283–308). Richard Wagners antisemitische Werk-Idee als Kunstreligion und Zivilisationskritik und ihre Verbreitung bis 1933 (Hartmut Zelinsky, 309–341). Über Wagner sprechen. Ideologie und Methodenstreit (Marc A. Weiner, 342–361).]

—— *Richard Wagner und die Juden*. Hrsg. von Dieter Borchmeyer, Ami Maayani und Susanne Vill. [See No. 39560.]

38937. ROSEMAN, MARK: *A past in hiding: memory and survival in Nazi Germany*. London: Allen Lane; New York: Holt, 2000. XIII, 525 pp., illus., maps, notes (502–552), bibl.(553–563), index. [Account based on interviews, war-time letters and diaries of Marianne Strauss-Ellenbogen (1920 Essen – 1996 Liverpool). Went into hiding in 1943, after 1945 emigr. to the UK. Also on her family history and the fate of various family members under the Nazis.]

38938. ROTHSCHILD, M.H.: *Transforming our legacies: heroic journeys for children of Holocaust survivors and Nazi perpetrators*. [In]: Journal of Humanistic Psychology, Vol. 40, No. 3, Beverly Hills, CA, Summer 2000. Pp. 43–55.

—— ROZETT, ROBERT/SPECTOR, SHMUEL, eds.: *Encyclopedia of the Holocaust*. [See No. 38698.]

38939. RUHR. KELLER, MANFRED/SCHNEIDER, HUBERT/WAGNER, JOHANNES VOLKER, eds.: *Gedenkbuch. Opfer der Shoa aus Bochum und Wattenscheid*. Mit Beiträgen von Udo Arnoldi, Andreas Halwer und Irmgard Hantsche. Bochum: Kamp, 2000. 64 pp., illus., bibl..

38940. SAFRIAN, HANS: *Expediting expropriation and expulsion: the impact of the "Vienna Model" on anti-Jewish policies in Nazi Germany, 1938*. [In]: Holocaust and Genocide Studies, Vol. 14, No. 3, Oxford, Winter 2000. Pp. 390–414, notes. [Examines the influence of Austrian anti-Jewish legislation on the Nazi government; in Nov. 1938 decrees and laws orig. crafted in Vienna, were implemented throughout Germany.]

38941. SCANDINAVIA. LORENZ, EINHART: *Zwischen dem Geist Nansens und der Furcht vor einer "Judeninvasion". Fremdenpolitik und Asylpraxis gegenüber jüdischen Flüchtlingen in Skandinavien*. [In]: "Ein symbolisches Leben". Beiträge anläßlich des 100. Geburtstages von Max Tau (1897–1076) [see No. 39391.]. Pp. 245–262, footnotes.

38942. SCHLANT, ERNESTINE: *The language of silence: West German literature and the Holocaust*. New York: Routledge, 1999. X, 277 pp., notes (245–261), bibl. (262–272), index. [Analyzes critically works by non-Jewish authors from the first post-1945 decade to post-unification; incl. chap.: The Jewish presence in contemporary Germany.] [Cf.: A daughter's hard questions (Matt Bai) [in]: Newsweek, Vol. 135, No. 4, New York, Jan. 24, 2000, pp. 50–51, illus. See also Sch.'s essay with the same title [in]: Dimensions, Vol. 14, No.2, New York, 2000, pp. 21–28, illus., notes.]

38943. SCHLESWIG-HOLSTEIN. HARCK, OLE: *Jüdische Vergangenheit – jüdische Zukunft*. Hrsg. Landeszentrale für Politische Bildung Schleswig-Holstein. Kiel, 1998. 117 pp. (Gegenwartsfragen, 80.).

38944. SCHWELM. RUDOLPH, H.: *Ignoriert, beschimpft, gekränkt, erpreßt. Von der Ausgrenzung zur Verfolgung jüdischer Menschen im Dritten Reich*. [In]: Der Schwelmer Heimatbrief, Bd. 75 (1997/1998), Schwelm, 1999. Pp.

38945. SEBNITZ. BERGMANN, HERBERT: *Juden in Sebnitz und ihr Schicksal*. Sebnitz-Hinterhermsdorf: Fremdenverkehrsbetriebe, 1999. 8 pp., illus.

38946. SEIDLER, EDUARD: *Kinderärzte 1933–1945. Entrechtet – geflohen – ermordet*. Pediatricians – victims of persecution 1933–1945. Im Auftrag der Deutschen Gesellschaft für Kinderheilkunde und

Jugendmedizin. Bonn: Bouvier, 2000. 492 pp., illus., indexes, bibl. [Most texts also in Engl.; incl. biographical documentation.]

38947. SHANGHAI. ARMBRÜSTER, GEORG/KOHLSTRUCK, MICHAEL/MÜHLBERGER, SONJA, eds.: *Exil Shanghai 1938–1947. Jüdisches Leben in der Emigration.* Teetz: Hentrich & Hentrich, 2000. 272 pp., notes, illus., index. [Incl.: Vorwort (Arnold Paucker, 7–9). Contribs. by Sonja Mühlberger, Steve Hochstadt, David Kranzler, Barbara Geldermann, Gerhard Krebs, Pan Guang, Astrid Freyeisen, Christiane Hoss, Helga Embacher, Margit Reiter, Michael Philipp, Georg Armbrüster, Dagmar Yü-Dembski, Christian Taaks, Michael Kohlstruck; a CD-rom is attached to book containing lists of foreigners, 1944.]

38948. SHANGHAI. FREYEISEN, ASTRID: *Shanghai und die Politik des Dritten Reiches.* Würzburg: Königshausen und Neumann, 2000. 544 pp., illus., footnotes., bibl. Zugl.: Würzburg, Univ., Diss., 1998. [Deals also with refugees in Shanghai from Nazi-occupied countries.]

38949. SILBERMANN, ALPHONS/STOFFER, MANFRED: *Auschwitz: Nie davon gehört?* Berlin: Rowohlt, 2000. 237 pp., tabs. [Based on a survey; on the 2nd and 3rd post-1945 generations' knowledge about the Nazi crimes.]

38950. SIRGES, THOMAS/SCHÖNDORF, KURT ERICH, eds.: *Haß, Verfolgung und Toleranz.* Beiträge zum Schicksal der Juden von der Reformation bis in die Gegenwart [see No. 39533]. [Incl. five contribs. dealing with different aspects of the Nazi period: Antisemitismus in der Sprache des Nationalsozialismus (Kurt Erich Schöndorf, 101–118). Nordeuropa und die jüdischen Flüchtlinge aus Hitler-Deutschland nach 1933 (Einhart Lorenz, 119–134). Auschwitz und anderswo. Gedanken über politische Großverbrechen (Jost Hermand, 135–152). Eine Annäherung an Auschwitz als Ortschaft/"Zeitschaft" in Prosatexten von Jean Améry, Ruth Klüger, George Tabori und Peter Weiss (Elin Nesje Vestli (153–170). "Hitlers willige Vollstrecker". Die Rezeption des Goldhagen-Buchs in Deutschland (Thomas Sirges, 171–210).]

38951. *So viel Phantasie hat niemand besessen: Szenische Collage der Spielschar am Essener Helmholtz-Gymnasium nach 'ZehnNullNeunzig in Buchenwald, ein jüdischer Häftling erzählt' von Rolf Kralovitz/Walter Meckauer Kreis.* Hrsg. von Frank Herdemerten. Köln: Walter-Meckauer-Kreis, 2000. 104 pp., illus. [For Rolf Kralovitz's book see Nos. 33984/YB XLII and 33984/YB XLIV.]

38952. SPAIN. BÖCKER, MANFRED: *Antisemitismus ohne Juden. Die Zweite Republik, die antirepublikanische Rechte und die Juden. Spanien 1931– bis 1936.* Frankfurt am Main, New York: Lang, 2000. 392 pp., illus. (Hispano-americana. Bd. 23.) [Deals also with German-Jewish refugees.]

38953. STARGARDT, NICHOLAS/MERCER, BEN: *Children and the Holocaust: an interview with Nicholas Stargardt.* [In]: Limina: A Journal of Historical and Cultural Studies, Vol. 6, Sydney, 2000. Pp. 1–11. [Interview with Australian historian N. Stargardt on his recent research on children under the Nazis.]

38954. STAUBER, RONI: *Confronting the Jewish response during the Holocaust: Yad Vashem – a commemorative and a research institute in the 1950s.* [In]: Modern Judaism, Vol. 20, No. 3, Baltimore, October 2000. Pp. 277–298, notes. [Discusses Yad Vashem's dealings with historians of the Holocaust in its quest to find an authentic account which could be transl. into Hebrew. At the time both Gerald Reitlinger and Raul Hilberg were rejected by Yad Vashem for depicting the Jews as passive victims.]

38955. STEINBACH, PETER: *Antisemitismus und Widerstand.* [In]: Tribüne, Jg. 39, H. 154, Frankfurt am Main, 2000. Pp. 120–138.

38956. STETTIN. AMBROSE, KENNETH: *The suitcase in the garage. letters and photographs of a German Jewish family, 1800–1950.* London: K. Ambrose [privately printed], 1999. 1 vol., illus., facsims., bibl. [Based on numerous letters and other documents, author relates the history of his family, the Abrahamsohns in Stettin, their fate during the Nazi era; also on the Cronbach, Buss and Waldauer families.] [Available at the Bibliothek Germania Judaica, Cologne.]

38957. *Studia nad faszyzmem i zbrodniami hitlerowskimi.* Vol. XXIII. Breslau: Wydawnictwo Uniwersytetu Wrocławskiego Sp. z.o.o., 2000. 419 pp., illus., annot. (Acta Universitatis Wratislaviensis No.

2207.). [Incl.: Die Wirtschaftspolitik des Senats der Freien Stadt Danzig im Verhältnis zur jüdischen Bevölkerung der Stadt (1933–1939) (Grzegorz Berendt, 199–230). Principles of anti-Semitic policy of the Nazi party before 1933 (Marek Maciejewski, 321–336). Die Holocaust-Kontroverse. Wirklichkeit oder Mythos? (Karol Jonca, 383–419).]

38958. STUTTHOF. LANDE, PETER W.: *Register of German Jews in Stutthof concentration camp, 1944–1945*. Washington, DC: United States Holocaust Memorial Museum, 2000. 60 pp.

38959. SWITZERLAND. ALBERS-SCHÖNBERG, HEINZ: *Die Schweiz und die jüdischen Flüchtlinge: 1933–1945. Eine unabhängige Studie*. Stäfa: Gut, 2000. 255 pp., bibl.

38960. SWITZERLAND. BATTEL, FRANCO: *"Wo es hell ist, dort ist die Schweiz". Flüchtlinge und Fluchthilfe an der Schaffhauser Grenze zur Zeit des Nationalsozialismus*. Zürich: Chronos, 2000. 375 pp., illus., tabs., map, chronol., bibl. (Schaffhauser Beiträge zur Geschichte, Bd. 77/2000.) [Section 3 is entitled: Jüdische Flüchtlinge (119–276); also incl. name lists of Jewish refugees.]

38961. SWITZERLAND. BORNSTEIN, HEINI: *Insel Schweiz. Hilfs- und Rettungsaktionen sozialistisch-zionistischer Jugendorganisationen 1939–1946*. Zürich: Chronos, 2000. 281 pp., illus., facsims., docs., bibl., notes, gloss. [First publ. in Hebrew 1996; incl. a preface by Yehuda Bauer (9–12). Book is based on the author's own active involvement in the rescue work of the Swiss Zionist youth organisations.] [H.B., b. 1920 in Basle, emigrated 1947 to Palestine, lives in the Kibbuz Lehavot Habashan.]

38962. SWITZERLAND. BOURGOIS, DANIEL: *Das Geschäft mit Hitlerdeutschland. Schweizer Wirtschaft und Drittes Reich*. Aus dem Französischen von Birgit Althaler. Zürich: Rotpunktverl., 2000. 297 pp., illus., notes, bibl. [Incl. chap.: Asylpolitik und Antisemitismus (179–242).]

38963. SWITZERLAND. *Die Schweiz und die Flüchtlinge zur Zeit des Nationalsozialismus*. Unabhängige Expertenkommission Schweiz – Zweiter Weltkrieg. Projektleitung Gregor Spuhler. Autorinnen und Autoren: Valérie Boillat [et al.]. Bern: Unabhängige Expertenkommission Schweiz – Zweiter Weltkrieg; BBL/EDMZ, 1999. 360 pp., bibl. (331–349).)

38964. SWITZERLAND. FISCHER, MONIKA: *"Retten Sie wenigstens mein Kind". Zeitzeugen des Zweiten Weltkrieges berichten*. Zürich: Schweizerisches Jugendschriftenwerk, 2000. 63 pp., illus.

38965. SWITZERLAND. FISCHER, ELMAR: *Abwehr im Innern: zur schweizerischen Flüchtlingspolitik im Zweiten Weltkrieg*. [In]: Zeitschrift für Geschichtswissenschaft, Jg. 48, H. 3, Berlin, 2000. Pp. 214–238, footnotes.

——— SWITZERLAND. *Flüchtlingsakten 1930–1950. Thematische Übersicht zu Beständen im Schweizerischen Bundesarchiv*. [See No. 38680.]

38966. SWITZERLAND. INDEPENDENT COMMITTEE OF EXPERTS SWITZERLAND, ed.: *Switzerland and refugees in the Nazi era*. Berne: BBL/EDMZ, 1999. 5 vols., illus., tabs., maps, diagr. [Report transl. from German and French orig. texts.]

38967. SWITZERLAND. KERNEN, JEAN-MARC: *L'origine du tampon "J": une histoire de neutres*. [In]: Schweizerische Zeitschrift für Geschichte, Vol. 50, No. 1, Basel, 2000. Pp. 45–71, notes, appendix. [Compares the positions of the Swedish and Swiss governments towards the exodus of Jews from Austria following the Anschluss, in relation to the German order of Oct. 5, 1938 to stamp a "J" on the passports of Jews.]

38968. SWITZERLAND. KOLLER, GUIDO: *Der J-Stempel auf schweizerischen Formularen*. [In]: Schweizerische Zeitschrift für Geschichte. Vol. 49, Basel, 1999. Pp. 371–374, footnotes.

38969. SWITZERLAND. KREIS, GEORG: *Die Rückkehr des J-Stempels. Zur Geschichte einer schwierigen Vergangenheitsbewältigung*. Zürich: Chronos, 2000. 210 pp., illus., notes (181–210), bibl. (173–180). [One part of book deals with the "J-Stempel" in the context of Swiss refugee policy during the late 1930s and 1940s, the other part deals with post-1945 debates in Switzerland and Swiss anti-semitism.]

38970. SWITZERLAND. KREIS, GEORG: *Zur schweizerischen Verwendung von J-Stempeln*. [In]: Schweizerische Zeitschrift für Geschichte, Vol. 49. Basel, 1999. Pp. 351–370, footnotes. [Incl. comment by Guido Koller (367–370).]

38971. SWITZERLAND. LAMBELET, JEAN-CHRISTIAN: *Die Macht der Mythen. Politik und Praxis der Schweiz gegenüber Flüchtlingen im Zweiten Weltkrieg.* [In]: 'NZZ', Nr. 192, Zürich, 19./20. Aug. 2000. Pp. 55–56.

38972. SWITZERLAND. SPIRA, HENRY: *L'attitude de la Suisse envers les réfugiés juifs 1939–1945*. [In]: Schweizerische Zeitschrift für Geschichte. Vol. 49, Basel, 1999. Pp. 273–279, footnotes.

38973. SWITZERLAND. SPUHLER, GREGOR/LUDI, REGULA, eds.: *La suisse et les réfugiés a l'époque du national-socialisme*. Paris: Fayard, 2000. 471 pp., notes, index. [Deals with Swiss refugee policy during the Nazi period and states that only a small number of all foreigners admitted were German Jews, some of whom were handed back to the German authorities.]

38974. SWITZERLAND (JEWISH ASSETS). INDEPENDENT COMMITTEE OF EXPERTS SWITZERLAND, ed.: *Report of dormant accounts of victims of Nazi persecution in Swiss banks*. Bericht über nachrichtenlose Konten von Opfern des Naziregimes. Paul A. Volcker, chairman. Berne: Staempfli, 1999. 1 vol., various pagings, appendixes, bibl. [Also in French transl.]

38975. SZITA, SZABOLCS: *Verschleppt, verhungert, vernichtet. Die Deportation von ungarischen Juden auf das Gebiet des annektierten Österreich 1944–1945.* Vorwort: György Konrád. Übers. aus dem Ungar.: Agnes Schmidt und Winfried Schmidt. Wien: Eichbauer, 1999. 279 pp., illus.

38976. TAUTZ, JOACHIM: *'Es ist vergeblich, für sie zu leben und zu sterben. Sie sagen: er ist ein Jude'. Antisemitismus und nichtjüdische Bevölkerung in der Zeit der nationalsozialistischen Herrschaft.* [In]: Uwe Meiners [et al.], eds.: Fremde in Deutschland – Deutsche in der Fremde. Schlaglichter von der Frühen Neuzeit bis in die Gegenwart. Begleitband zu einer gemeinsamen Ausstellung des Museumsdorfes Cloppenburg [et al.]. Cloppenburg: [Museumsdorf Cloppenburg], 1999. Pp. 249–256, notes.

38977. TEICHERT, CARSTEN: *Chasak! Zionismus im nationalsozialistischen Deutschland 1933–1938*. Köln: Elen-Verl., 2000. 560 pp., footnotes, gloss., bibl. (514–555), index. [Also on pre-1933 Zionism in Germany.] [Cf.: Sei stark! Studien zum Zionismus in der Nazizeit (Joachim Schlör) [in]: 'NZZ', Nr. 82, Zürich, 7./8. April 2001, p. 54.]

38978. THERESIENSTADT. DUTLINGER, ANNE D., ed.: *Music and education as strategies for survival: Theresienstadt, 1941–1945.* New York: Herodias, 2000. 202 pp., illus., bibl., notes, index.

38979. THERESIENSTADT. KÁRNY, MIROSLAV/KEMPER, RAIMUND, HRSG.: *Theresienstädter Studien und Dokumente. 2000.* In Zusammenarbeit mit Martin Niklas. Prag: Institut Theresienstädter Initiative, Academia, 2000. 364 pp., illus. [Incl.: Das Gestapo-Polizeigefängnis Kleine Festung Theresienstadt (Marek Poloncarz, 11–26). Dokumente über die Schicksale der jüdischen Häftlinge in der Theresienstädter Kleinen Festung (27–65). Kaltenbrunners Reise nach Theresienstadt und der Prominententransport im April 1945 (Miroslav Kárny, 66–85). Arbeit in der Falle. Die Arbeitszentrale im ersten Jahr der Existenz des Ghettos Theresienstadt (Anita Tarsi, 107–122; about an album of drawings by Leo Haas). Dienst am Ghetto und Kulturtat. Ein Tatsachenbericht von Philipp Manes (Klaus Leist, 123–150; deals with a report by a Berlin Jew kept in the Wiener Library, London). Der Theresienstädter Hechalutz. Aus den Erinnerungen von Berl Herskovic (151–163). Als Maurice Rossel zu reden begann. "Auch heute würde ich ihn unterschreiben…" (164–191; interview with Claude Lanzmann by M. Rossel, former Red Cross delegate on his visit to Theresienstadt in June 1944). Further contribs. are listed according to subject.]

38980. THERESIENSTADT. ROVIT, REBECCA: *The Brundibar project: memorializing Theresienstadt children's opera.* [In]: A Journal of Performance and Art, No. 65, Balitmore, May 2000. Pp. 111–122. [On the children's opera "Brundibar" by Hans Krasa, first written and performed in Theresienstadt, and a recent series of productions in Germany aimed at remembering its author and the Jews who first performed it.]

38981. THERESIENSTADT. *Theresienstädter Gedenkbuch. Die Opfer der Judentransporte aus Deutschland nach Theresienstadt 1942–1945.* Hrsg.: Institut Theresienstädter Initiative. Prag: Academia, 2000. 89,895 pp. [Incl.: Geleitwort (Václav Havel, 5). Theresienstadt 1941–1945 (Miroslav Kárny, 15–44). Die Vorbereitung und die Quellen des Theresienstädter Gedenkbuches (Michal Frankl, 45–54). Deportationsgebiete (55–72). Chronologische Übersicht der Judentransporte nach und aus Theresienstadt (73–89). Die Opfer der Deportationen aus den einzelnen Gebieten (1–770). Personenindex (771–895).] [Cf.: Besprechung (Peter Witte) [in]: Fritz Bauer Institut, Newsletter, Jg. 10, Nr. 20, Frankfurt am Main, Frühjahr 2001, pp. 44–45.]

38982. TRAVERSO, ENZO: *Auschwitz denken. Die Intellektuellen und die Shoah.* Aus dem Franz. von Helmut Dahmer. Hamburg: Hamburger Edition, 2000. 368 pp., footnotes, index. [Orig. publ. 1997. Deals a.o. with Franz Kafka, Walter Benjamin, Hannah Arendt, Günther Anders, Theodor Adorno, Paul Celan, Jean Améry.]

38983. *Ungleiche Paare.* [In]: Damals, Jg. 32, H. 3, Stuttgart, 2000, 63–67. [Deals with "mixed marriages".]

38984. VIENNA. ANDERL, GABRIELE: *"Störungen sind zu vermeiden". Emigration und Vertreibung aus Wien 1938–1945.* [In]: Projekt: Judenplatz Wien [see No. 39090]. Pp. 132–152.

38985. VIENNA. BARTA-FLIEDL, ILSEBILL/POSCH, HERBERT: *invent/arisiert. Enteignung von Möbeln aus jüdischem Besitz.* Mit Fotografien von Arno Gisinger und einem Beitrag von Monika Schwärzler. Wien: Turia+Kant, 2000. 144 pp., illus., lists. (Museen des Mobiliendepots, No. 7.) [Catalogue book for exhibition held in the 'Museum Kaiserliches Hofmobiliendepot', Vienna, Sept. 7 – Nov. 19, 2000; deals with the confiscation of 8 properties in 1938, the contents of which were registered and stored in the "Mobiliendepot" and, after 1999, returned to their original owners or their heirs.]

38986. VIENNA. CZERNIN, HUBERTUS: *Jahr des Erwachens: eine jüdische Geschichte.* Wien: H. Czernin [Privately printed], 2000. 55 p. (Die Bibliothek des Raubes, Bd. 4.) [On "aryanisation" and restitution.]

—— VIENNA. *Das jüdische Wien.* [See No. 38624.]

38987. VIENNA. KERSCHBAUMER, GERT: *Meister des Verwirrens – Die Geschäfte des Kunsthändlers Friedrich Welz.* Wien: Czernin, 2000. 207 pp. [Deals also with W.s involvement with Jewish "aryanised" property.]

38988. VIENNA. KRIST, MARTIN: *Vertreibungsschicksale. Jüdische Schüler eines Wiener Gymnasiums 1938 und ihre Lebenswege.* Wien: Turia + Kant, 1999. 202 pp.

38989. VIENNA. RABINOVICI, DORON: *Instanzen der Ohnmacht. Wien 1938–1945. Der Weg zum Judenrat.* Frankfurt am Main: Jüd. Verlag, 2000. 495 pp., notes (428–490), index. [The first chap. discusses Holocaust denial; incl. chaps. on November Pogrom, deportations.] [Cf.: Besprechung (Bernhard Kuschey) [in]: Österreichische Zeitschrift für Politikwissenschaft, Jg. 30, H. 1, Baden-Baden, 2001, pp. 112–114.]

38990. VIENNA. SCHAFRANEK, HANS: *V-Leute und "Verräter". Die Unterwanderung kommunistischer Widerstandsgruppen durch Konfidenten der Wiener Gestapo.* [In]: Int. wissenschaftliche Korrespondenz zur Geschichte der deutschen Arbeiterbewegung (IWK), H. 3, Berlin, 2000. Pp. 300–349, footnotes. [Incl. Jews among the traitors and resistance groups.]

38991. VIENNA. SPITZER, SHLOMO: *Jüdische Lebens- und Leidensgeschichte am Judenplatz.* [In]: Projekt: Judenplatz Wien [see No. 39090]. Pp. 190–198.

38992. WALSER-BUBIS-DEBATE. ESHEL, AMIR: *Vom eigenen Gewissen. Die Walser-Bubis-Debatte und der Ort des Nationalsozialismus im Selbstbild der Bundesrepublik.* [In]: Deutsche Vierteljahrsschrift für Literaturwissenschaft und Geistesgeschichte, Jg. 74, Bd. 73, Stuttgart, 2000. Pp. 333–360, footnotes.

38993. WALSER-BUBIS-DEBATE. HIEBER, JOCHEN: *Unversöhnte Lebensläufe. Zur Rhetorik der Verletzung in der Walser-Bubis-Debatte.* [In]: "Hinauf und Zurück/in die herzhelle Zukunft". Deutsch-jüdische Literatur im 20. Jahrhundert. Festschrift für Birgit Lerman [see No. 39217]. Pp. 543–559.

38994. WALSER-BUBIS-DEBATE. TABERNER, STUART: *A manifesto for Germany's 'new right'? Martin Walser, the past, transcendence, aesthetics and 'Ein springender Brunnen'*. [In]: German Life and Letters, Vol. 53, No. 1, Oxford, Jan. 2000. Pp. 126–141, footnotes.

38995. WANNSEE CONFERENCE. LONGERICH, PETER: *The Wannsee Conference in the development of the "Final Solution"*. [In]: Holocaust Educational Trust, Vol. 1, No. 2, London, 1999–2000. 29 pp., illus., facsims., ports., gloss., endnotes. [Deals also with stages in the Nazi persecution of the Jews prior to 1941 and the transition to policy of genocide in summer 1941.]

38996. WATT, RODERICK H.: *Landessprache, Heeressprache, Nazisprache? Victor Klemperer and Werner Krauss on the linguistic legacy of the Third Reich*. [In]: Modern Language Review, Vol. 95, part 2, Belfast, 2000. Pp. 424–437.

38997. WEISS, YFAAT: *Citizenship and ethnicity. German Jews and Polish Jews, 1933–1940. Staatsbürgerschaft und Ethnizität. Deutsche und polnische Juden, 1933–1940*. Jerusalem: The Hebrew University Magnes Press; Leo Baeck Institute, 2000. 309 pp., footnotes, index, bibl. [In Hebrew, title transl.]

38998. WEISS, YFAAT: *Deutsche und polnische Juden vor dem Holocaust. Jüdische Identität zwischen Staatsbürgerschaft und Ethnizität 1933–1940*. Aus dem Hebr. übers. von Matthias Schmidt. München: Oldenbourg, 2000. 252 pp., footnotes, bibl. (231–246), gloss., index. (Schriftenreihe der Vierteljahrshefte für Zeitgeschichte, Bd. 81.) [Incl. chap. on antisemitism in Germany and Poland in the 1930s.]

38999. WERMUTH, HENRY: *Atme, mein Sohn, atme tief. Die Überlebensgeschichte*. Aus dem Engl. von Henry Wermuth. München: Droemer Knauer, 2000. 319 pp., illus. [Memoirs of a Frankfurt born Jew; for orig. edn. and details see No. 30664/YB XXXIX.]

39000. WETZEL, JULIANE: *Gesetze verändern das Leben. Die Auswirkungen der "Nürnberger Gesetze" auf das Verhältnis von Bürgern jüdischer und nichtjüdischer Herkunft in Deutschland*. [In]: Jüdisches Leben und jüdische Kultur in Deutschland [see No. 38421]. Pp. 202–216, notes.

39001. WEISS, VOLKMAR: *Zur Vorgeschichte des arischen Ahnenpasses*. Teil 1. [In]: Genealogie, Jg. 50, Bd. 25, H. 1–2, Neustadt/Aisch, Jan.-Feb. 2000. Pp. 417–436, footnotes.

39002. WIEVIORKA, ANNETTE: *Mama, was ist Auschwitz?* Aus dem Französ. von Manfred Flügge. Berlin: Ullstein, 2000. 80 pp. [Orig. edn. publ. 1999.]

———— WIRTZ, STEFAN/KOLBE, CHRISTIAN: *Enteignung der jüdischen Bevölkerung in Deutschland und nationalsozialistische Wirtschaftspolitik 1933–1945*. [See No. 38700.]

39003. WURM, SIEGFRIED: *Die finanzielle Vernichtung der Juden im Dritten Reich. Wie vollzog sich der Griff der Nationalsozialisten nach dem jüdischen Vermögen? (Eine dokumentarische Skizze)*. Berlin: Kronen Verlag, 1999. 151 pp., footnotes, facsims., docs., appendixes (72 pp.), bibl.

39004. WYMAN, DAVID S.: *Das unerwünschte Volk. Amerika und die Vernichtung der europäischen Juden*. Aus dem Amerik. von Karl Heinz Siber. Frankfurt am Main: Fischer Taschenbuch Verlag, 2000. 511 pp., notes (407–482), bibl. (496), index (499–511). Erweiterte Neuausgabe. [Incl.: Nachwort zur Neuausgabe (387–403). First publ. 1984, first German edn. see No. 23281/YB XXXII.]

39005. ZIMMERMANN, MOSHE: *Deutsche Juden und 'deutsche' Umbrüche*. [In]: Deutsche Umbrüche im 20. Jahrhundert. Hrsg. von Dietrich Papenfuß und Wolfgang Schieder. Köln: Böhlau, 2000. Pp. 19–29. [Deals mainly with the Nazi period and its impact on German Jews.]

39006. ZWEIBRÜCKEN. VOLKSHOCHSCHULE ZWEIBRÜCKEN, ed.: *Zweibrücken unter dem Hakenkreuz: Stationen jüdischen Lebens*. [Erstellt vom Arbeitskreis "Zweibrücken unter dem Hakenkreuz"]. Hrsg.: Michael Staudt. Zweibrücken: VHS, 2000. 183 pp., illus.

B. Jewish Resistance

39007. BRÜNING, JENS: *Zum Tode von Hermann Adler.* [In]: europäische ideen, H. 118, Berlin, 2000. Pp. 19–20. [H.A., Oct. 2, 1911 Deutsch-Diosek, Hungary, – Feb. 18, 2000 Basle, teacher in Upper Silesia, author of 'Gesänge aus der Stadt des Todes', fled 1934 to Czechoslovakia, 1938 to Poland, later to Wilna, Lithuania, where he organised, together with the German sergeant Anton Schmid, the escape of 350 Jews from the ghetto, fled after Schmid's execution to Hungary, deported to Bergen-Belsen. See also No. 39009.]

39008. COPPI, HANS: *Der Mythos "Rote Kapelle" oder wie die Politik sich der Geschichte bemächtigte.* [In]: Rassismus, Faschismus, Antifaschismus [see No. 38922]. Pp. 244–259, notes.

39009. LUSTIGER, ARNO: *Feldwebel Anton Schmid. Um den Preis des Lebens: Die Rettung von Juden aus Wilna und die Hilfe beim jüdischen Widerstand.* [In]: 'FAZ', Nr. 128, Frankfurt am Main, 3. Juni 2000. P. III, Beilage. [See also No. 39007.]

39010. ROBBINS, CHRISTOPHER: *Test of courage: the Michel Thomas story.* New York; London: The Free Press, 2000. XV, 382 pp., illus., ports., maps, notes, bibl. (339–369), index. [First Engl. edn. publ. 1999 by Century.] [M. Thomas, born in Poland in 1914, linguist and teacher, moved to Breslau as a child, later fled to France where he studied and joined the French Resistance.]

39011. SCHREIBER, MARION: *Stille Rebellen. Der Überfall auf den 20. Deportationszug nach Auschwitz.* Mit einem Vorwort von Paul Spiegel. Berlin: Aufbau, 2000. 352 pp., illus., bibl. [Based on authentic documents, interviews and publ. material, author describes the background to the attack by a young Jewish resistance group from Brussels on the 20th deportation train from Mechelen to Auschwitz, April 19, 1943, leading to the escape of 231 deportees; deals also with numerous refugees from Germany and Austria. Incl.: transportation list of the 20th deport. train (1631 names).]

39012. STEINDLING, DOLLY: *Hitting back: An Austrian Jew in the French resistance.* Introd., epil., and annot., by Haim Avni. Ed. by Haim Avni and Susanna Steindling. Baltimore: Univ. Press of Maryland, 2000. 239 pp., notes (228–239). (Studies and texts in Jewish history and culture.) [Author fled Vienna in 1938, went via Switzerland and Belgium to Paris, from there he was sent to Gurs and other French camps, after escaping survived the war as a member of the French Resistance. Returned to Vienna after the war and became a bank manager.]

39013. URBAN-FAHR, SUSANNE: *Juden im Widerstand gegen die Schoah.* [In]: Tribüne, Jg. 39, H. 154, Frankfurt am Main, 2000. Pp. 138–148.

IV. POST-1945

A. General

—— AUSTRIA. FLECK, CHRISTIAN/MÜLLER, ALBERT: *Front-stage and back-stage: the problem of measuring post-Nazi antisemitism in Austria.* [See No. 39506.]

39014. AUSTRIA. GREMLIZA, HERMANN L., ed.: *Braunbuch Österreich. Ein Nazi kommt selten allein.* Hamburg: KVV konkret, 2000. 168 pp. (Konkret Texte 26.) [Incl.: Die goldenen siebziger Jahre oder: Bruno Kreiskys Staatstheater (Erwin Riess, 86–97). "Wir verfolgen, wen wir wollen!" Rassismus und Antisemitismus in Österreich seit 1986 (Heribert Schiedel, 98–116).]

—— AUSTRIA. HÖDL, KLAUS, ed.: *Jüdische Identitäten: Einblicke in die Bewußtseinslandschaften des österreichischen Judentums.* [See No. 38432.]

—— AUSTRIA. MARIN, BERND: *Antisemitismus ohne Antisemiten. Autoritäre Vorurteile und Feindbilder.* [See No. 39522.]

39015. AUSTRIA. OERTEL, CHRISTINE: *Juden auf der Flucht durch Austria*. Jüdische Displaced Persons in der US-Besatzungszone Österreichs. Wien: Eichbauer, 1999. 182 pp., illus., bibl.

39016. AUSTRIA. *Another country? Austria's past and present*. [Issue title of] Patterns of Prejudice, Vol. 34, No. 4, London, Oct. 2000. 1 issue, footnotes. [Incl. papers given at a seminar held at the Wiener Library in London, June 11, 2000. Selected essays: Contours of memory in post-Nazi Austria (Robert Knight, 5–11; deals with antisemitism at the time of the Anschluss and in post-war Austria.) The return of the repressed: is Austria a racist society? (Felix de Mendelssohn, 13–22; expresses the personal view of a psychoanlayst who as a survivor returned from Britain to Vienna.) Further contribs. on the resurgence of openly expressed antisemitism, the Haider election, and the problem of facing up to the past.]

39017. BAVARIA. SNOPKOWSKI, SIMON: *Zuversicht trotz alledem. Erinnerungen eines Überlebenden in Deutschland*. München: Olzog, 2000. 143 pp., illus. [Author, b. 1925 in Myschkow near Katowice, Poland, surgeon, survived three years of forced labour in various concentration camps, lived 1945–1949 in the Landsberg DP-camp, since then in Munich; active in Jewish community life of Bavaria.]

39018. BERLIN. MESHULASH BERLIN, ed.: *DAVKA. Jüdische Visionen in Berlin/Jewish visions in Berlin*. Berlin: AvivA, 1999. 141 pp., illus. [All texts German and Engl.]

39019. BERLIN. RÖHRS, CHRISTINE-FÉLICE: *Jüdin sein kam lange nicht in Frage*. DDR-Produkte: Wie Irene Runge und ihr Jüdischer Kulturverein in die Bundesrepublik hineinwuchsen. [In]: Die Zeit, Nr. 10, Hamburg, 2. März 2000. Pp. 16–17, port. [I.R., née Alexan, born 1942 in New York, sociologist, author, daughter of German-Jewish Communists, lives since 1949 in Berlin (East), co-founder of the Jüdischer Kulturverein in Berlin.]

39020. BRECKNER, ROSWITHA/KALEKIN-FISHMAN, DEVORAH/MIETHE, INGRID, eds.: *Biographies and the division of Europe*. Experience, action, and change on the 'Eastern side'. Opladen: Leske + Budrich, 2000. 387 pp., footnotes. [Incl.: Intergenerational dialog in families of Jewish communists in East Germany: a process-oriented analysis (Bettina Völter, 139–158). Doing "being Jewish": constitution of "normality" in families of Jewish Displaced Persons in Germany (Lena Inowlocki, 159–178). Tricky hermeneutics: public and private viewpoints on Jewish migration from Russia to Germany (Ingrid Oswald/Viktor Voronkov, 335–348). "We are similar in that we're different": social relationships of young Russian Jewish immigrants in Israel and Germany (Yvonne Schütze/Tamar Rapoport, 349–366).]

39021. BRUMLIK, MICHA: *Deutschlands Juden*. [In]: Blätter für deutsche und internationale Politik, Jg. 45, H. 11, Bonn, 2000. Pp. 1287–1289.]

39022. CRAMER, ERNST J.: *Germany and the Jews at the turn of the millennium*. New York: Leo Baeck Institute, 2000. 16 pp. (The Leo Baeck Memorial Lecture, 43.)

39023. DIAMANT, ADOLF: *Geschändete jüdische Friedhöfe in Deutschland 1945 bis 1999*. Mit einem Nachwort von Julius H. Schoeps. Potsdam: Verlag für Berlin-Brandenburg, 2000. 95 pp., footnotes, bibl.

39024. DORFMAN, RIVKA & BEN-ZION: *Synagogues without Jews and the communities that built and used them*. Foreword by Dr. Joseph Burg. Philadelphia: Jewish Publication Society, 2000. XIV, 353 pp., illus., gloss., plans, appendix, bibl. (335–342), index. [Authors went in search of lost synagogues and tell the stories of over thirty Jewish communities in various countries, incl. Austria, Czechoslovakia, Hungary from the past to present-day. Book cont. over 300 photographs of either remains or renovations of synagogues.]

39025. FRANKFURT am Main. *Dokumentation*. [In]: Tribüne, Jg. 39, H. 156, Frankfurt am Main, 2000. Pp. 89–96. [Incl. speeches by Paul Spiegel and Salomon Korn about Ignatz Bubis at the renaming the Frankfurt Jewish community centre after Bubis on the first anniversary of his death (Aug. 13, 2000).]

39026. *50 Jahre Zentralrat der Juden in Deutschland*. Ansichten, Standpunkte und Perspektiven. [In]: 'Allgemeine', Jg. 55, Nr. 15, Berlin, 19. Juli 2000. Pp. 9–55, illus. [Incl. 29 contribs. dealing with the post-1945 history of Jews in Germany and their present situation.]

39027. GEIS, JAEL: *Übrig sein – Leben "danach". Juden deutscher Herkunft in der britischen und amerikanischen Zone Deutschlands 1945–1949*. Berlin: Philo, 2000. 485 pp., footnotes, bibl. (449–474), gloss., index.

39028. GILMAN, SANDER L.: *America and the newest Jewish writing in German*. [In]: The German Quarterly, Vol. 73, No. 2, Riverside, CA, Spring 2000. Pp. 151–162, notes. [Deals with German-Jewish historians. Incl. the Goldhagen debate and the response by German historians.]

39029. GRÜNBERG, KURT: *Liebe nach Auschwitz. Die Zweite Generation*. Jüdische Nachkommen von Überlebenden der nationalsozialistischen Judenverfolgung in der Bundesrepublik Deutschland und das Erleben ihrer Paarbeziehungen. Tübingen: edition diskord, 2000. 315 pp., footnotes, tabs., bibl. (291–311). (Psychoanalytische Beiträge aus dem Sigmund-Freud-Institut, Bd.5), Zugl.: Hannover, Univ., Diss., 1999.

39030. HALLE. HOMANN, URSULA: *Cohn Hanacha zum Beispiel. Die jüdische Gemeinde zu Halle an der Saale*. [In]: Die Zeichen der Zeit/Lutherische Monatshefte, Jg. 3, H. 4, Hannover, 2000. Pp. 32–34, illus..

39031. HARTEWIG, KARIN: *Zurückgekehrt: die Geschichte der jüdischen Kommunisten in der DDR*. Köln: Böhlau, 2000. VII, 646 pp., illus., footnotes, bibl. (624–637), index. [Cf.: Rote Assimilation (Michael Wuliger) [in]: 'Allgemeine', Jg. Nr. 23, Berlin, 9. Nov. 2000, p. XI. Kommunisten. DDR. Jüdisch (Irene Runge) [in]: Jüdische Korrespondenz, Jg. 11, Nr. 2, Berlin, Feb. 2001, p. 1.]

39032. HESSE. *"... wohnen auf der verfluchten deutschen Erde" – jüdisches Leben in Südhessen nach 1945: die DP-Lager in Lampertheim, Lindenfels, Bensheim, Dieburg und Babenhausen sowie die Anfänge der Jüdischen Gemeinde Darmstadt*. Beiheft zur Ausstellung des Hessischen Staatsarchivs Darmstadt, 26.10.1998 – 18.12.1998. [Text: Dietrich Kohlmannslehner. Red. Bearb.: Thomas Lange]. Darmstadt: Hess. Staatsarchiv, 1998. 56 pp., illus. (Ausstellungskataloge des Hess. Staatsarchivs Darmstadt, 18.)

39033. HESS, RAINER/KRANZ, JARDEN: *Jüdische Existenz in Deutschland heute: Probleme des Wandels der jüdischen Gemeinden in der Bundesrepublik Deutschland infolge der Zuwanderung russischer Juden nach 1989*. Berlin: Logos-Verl., 2000. 264 pp. (Zugl.: Frankfurt am Main, Univ., Diss., 2000.).

39034. HILLIARD, ROBERT L.: *Von den Befreiern vergessen*. Der Überlebenskampf jüdischer KZ-Häftlinge unter amerikanischer Besatzung. Aus dem Engl. von Andreas Simon. Frankfurt am Main; New York: Campus, 2000. 240 pp., illus. [Orig. publ. 1997 with the title 'Surviving the Americans'. Deals mainly with the hospital St. Ottilien nr. Landsberg.]

39035. *Jüdische Gemeinden in Europa zwischen Aufbruch und Kontinuität*. Hrsg. von Brigitte Ungar-Klein. Unter Mitarbeit von Piroska Lonyai-Kelemen. Wien: Picus, 2000. 199 pp., illus. [Cont. lectures given at a symposium org. by Jüdisches Inst. für Erwachsenenbildung, Oct. 1998. Incl.: Von der bitteren Erfahrung zum gesunden Selbstbewußtsein: Jüdisches Leben in Österreich nach 1945 (Marta S. Halpert, 33–38). Die Russen kommen. Der demographische Umbruch in den jüdischen Gemeinden Deutschlands (Cilly Kugelmann, 51–64).]

39036. KORN, SALOMON: *Noch keine Normalität möglich*. [In]: Tribüne, Jg. 39, H. 155, Frankfurt am Main, 2000. Pp. 96–108.

39037. KORN, SALOMON: *Erbschaft der Nachgeborenen*. [In]: Jüdisches Leben und jüdische Kultur in Deutschland [see No. 38421]. Pp. 252–262, notes.

39038. KRUSE, JÜRGEN/LERNER, MARKUS: *Jüdische Emigration aus der ehemaligen Sowjetunion nach Deutschland. Aspekte eines neuen Migrationssystems*. Hrsg. von den Abteilungen Humangeographie und Geoinformatik des Instituts für Geographie der Universität Potsdam. Potsdam: Abt. Humangeographie und Geoinformatik des Inst. für Geographie der Univ., 2000. 161 pp., tabs., bibl. (Praxis Kultur- und Sozialgeographie, Bd. 22.)

39039. KRUSE, ANDREAS/SCHMITT, ERIC: *Wir haben uns als Deutsche gefühlt. Lebensrückblick und Lebenssituation jüdischer Emigranten und Lagerhäftlinge*. Darmstadt: Steinkopf, 2000. X, 286 pp., footnotes, illus., tabs., bibl., index. [Based on interviews with 5 people living in Germany.]

39040. LAU, JÖRG: *Was heißt hier jüdisch? Der Zentralrat der Juden wählt am Wochenende einen neuen Vorsitzenden – wohl zum letzten Mal einen Holocaustüberlebenden.* [In]: Die Zeit, Nr. 2, Hamburg, 5. Jan. 2000. Pp. 9–13, illus. (Dossier.)

39041. LORENZ, DAGMAR, C. G.: *Discovering and making memory: Jewish cultural expression in contemporary Europe.* [In]: The German Quarterly, Vol. 73, No. 2, Riverside, CA, Spring 2000. Pp. 175–178, notes. [Incl. Germany.]

39042. MECKLENBURG-VORPOMMERN. GUNDLACH, CHRISTINE: *Ein bißchen anders bleibt man immer. Jüdische Zuwanderer in Mecklenburg-Vorpommern vorgestellt von Christine Gundlach.* Schwerin: Thomas Helms, 2000. 207 pp., gloss., bibl. (Schriften aus dem Max-Samuel-Haus, 2.) [Incl.: Statt eines Vorworts: Ein historischer Rückblick (Frank Schröder, 7–11). Menschen sind Antwort. Menschen sind Fragen (Christine Gundlach, 193–198). 27 interviews with resp. essays by immigrants from the former Soviet Union who live in Rostock, Schwerin and Wismar.]

39043. MÜLLER-COMMICHAU, WOLFGANG: *Jüdische Erwachsenenbildung im heutigen Deutschland.* Köln: Böhlau [in Kommission], 1998. 128 pp., footnotes.

39044. MUNICH. KAUDERS, ANTHONY: *Catholics, the Jews and democratization in post-war Germany, Munich 1945–1965.* [In]: German History, Vol. 18, No. 4, London, 2000. Pp. 461–484, footnotes.

39045. *New Jews in a new Germany.* [Section title of] European Judaism, vol. 33, No. 2, London, Autumn 2000. 1 issue, notes. [Incl.: Editorial (Albert H. Friedlander, 1–3). Between appropriation and keeping our distance: German attitudes towards the Jewish theme (Joachim Schlör, 4–19). Coming home to a foreign land (Michael Daxner, 30–26). Germany, my Germany (Jens Reich, 27–37). Identity structures of religious Jews in post-war Germany (Andrea Zielinski, 38–44).]

39046. PROSECUTION OF NAZI CRIMES. *Geschichte vor Gericht. Historiker, Richter und die Suche nach Gerechtigkeit.* Hrsg. von Norbert Frei, Dirk van Laak und Michael Stolleis. München: Beck, 2000. 187 pp., notes, index. [A collection of 8 essays dealing with various aspects of "Vergangenheitsbewältigung", historiography of the Nazi period, prosecution of Nazi crimes by Dirk van Laak, Irmtrud Wojak, Michael Wildt, Dieter Gosewinkel, Jörgt Requate, Manfred Hildermeier, Gerald D. Feldman, Harold James, Henry Rousso, Raphael Gross, Michael Stolleis.]

39047. PROSECUTION OF NAZI CRIMES. TIMM, ANGELIKA: *Der Eichmann-Prozeß – eine Zäsur für den Umgang mit der Schoah in der DDR.* [In]: Rassismus, Faschismus, Antifaschismus [see No. 38922]. Pp. 340–356, notes.

39048. RESTITUTION. KNIGHT, ROBERT, ed.: *"Ich bin dafür, die Sache in die Länge zu ziehen".* Die Wortprotokolle der österreichischen Bundesregierung von 1945 bis 1952 über die Entschädigung der Juden. Wien: Böhlau, 2000. 256 pp., footnotes, docs., notes, bibl., indexes. [Incl. preface of 1st edn. (publ. 1988) and a new preface.]

39049. RESTITUTION. KROIS, ISABELLA: *Die Restitution von Kunst- und Kulturgütern am Fall der Familie Rothschild aus zeithistorischer und rechtlicher Sicht.* Wien: Verl. Österreich, 2000. 154 pp., bibl. (Juristische Schriftenreihe, Bd. 173.)

39050. RESTITUTION. SCHOENFELD, GABRIEL: *Holocaust reparations: a growing scandal.* [In]: Commentary, Vol. 101, No. 2, New York, Sept. 2000. Pp. 25–34. [Author discusses whether the pursuit of restitution through US-based Jewish organisations is damaging Jewish interests and breeds antisemitic feelings.]

39051. RESTITUTION. *Wiedergutmachung und Kriegsfolgenliquidation. Geschichte – Regelungen – Zahlungen.* Von Hermann-Josef Brodesser, Bernd Josef Fehn, Tilo Franosch, Wilfried Wirth. München: Beck, 2000. XVII, 251 pp., footnotes, chronol., bibl. (XV-XVII). [Cont. 3 sections: Die Entwicklung des Wiedergutmachungs- und Kriegsfolgenrechts. Die Regelungen und Leistungen im einzelnen. Heute diskutierte Fragen.]

39052. RESTITUTION. WINKLER, ULRIKE, ed.: *Stiften gehen. NS-Zwangsarbeit und Entschädigungsdebatte.* Köln: PapyRossa, 2000. 272 pp., notes. [Incl.: Ressentiment und Rancune: Antisemitische Stereotype in der Entschädigungsdebatte (gruppe 3 frankfurt a.m., 251–271).]

39053. RESTITUTION. WOGERSIEN, MAIK: *Die Rückerstattung von ungerechtfertigt entzogenen Vermögensgegenständen.* Eine Quellenstudie zur Wiedergutmachung nationalsozialistischen Unrechts aufgrund des Gesetzes Nr. 59 der britischen Militärregierung. Inauguraldissertation. [Münster]: Privately printed, 2000. 369 pp., footnotes, bibl., suppl. (22 pp.). [Available at the Bibliothek Germania Judaica, Cologne.]

39054. RHEINZ, HANNA: *Warum wir bleiben, wo wir sind. Aus dem Wörterbuch des neuen alten jüdischen Lebens in Deutschland.* [In]: Kursbuch 141, Berlin, 2000. Pp. 105–125.

39055. ROLNICK, JOSH: *Totally normal?* [in]: Moment, Vol. 25, No. 1, New York, Feb. 2000. Pp. 56–62, illus., notes. [Deals with the state of Jewish life in Germany today, and its struggle to become "normal".]

39056. ROSHWALD, A.: *After the Holocaust: rebuilding Jewish lives in post-war Germany.* [In]: European History Quarterly, Vol. 30, No. 3, London, 2000. Pp. 431–442, notes.

39057. ROSENBERG, RICHARD: *Eine Säule der jüdischen Gemeinschaft. 50 Jahre Zentralrat der Juden in Deutschland.* [In]: Tribüne, Jg. 39, H. 156, Frankfurt am Main, 2000. Pp. 15–19.

39058. RUNGE, IRENE: *Sind Einsichten Ansichtssache? Oder: Das Verkennen der jüdischen Frage.* [In]: Rassismus, Faschismus, Antifaschismus [see No. 38922]. Pp. 357–364, notes.

—— SCHAFRANEK, HANS: *V-Leute und "Verräter". Die Unterwanderung kommunistischer Widerstandsgruppen durch Konfidenten der Wiener Gestapo.* [See No. 38990.]

39059. SCHMIDT, WALTER: *Jüdisches Erbe in der DDR.* [In]: Rassismus, Faschismus, Antifaschismus [see No. 38922.]. Pp. 311–339, notes.

39060. SCHNEIDER, RICHARD CHAIM: *Wir sind da! Die Geschichte der Juden in Deutschland von 1945 bis heute.* Berlin: Ullstein, 2000. 499 pp., gloss. [Cont. an historical overview (pp. 13–51) and interviews with 34 people, some of whom no longer live in Germany.]

39061. SCHOEPS, JULIUS H.: *"Nil inultum remanebit". Die Erlanger Universität und ihr Umgang mit dem deutschjüdischen Remigranten Hans-Joachim Schoeps (1909–1980).* [In]: Zeitschrift für Religions- und Geistesgeschichte, Jg. 52, H. 3, Leiden, 2000. Pp. 266–278, footnotes.

39062. SCHWABACH. TOBIAS, JIM G.: *Das Jüdische Kreiskomitee Schwabach 1946–1949: "Wartesaal" für Israel oder Übersee.* [In]: Wohlstand, Widerstand und Wandel. Schwabach 1945 bis 1979. Hrsg. von Sandra Hoffmann-Rivero [et al.]. Schwabach: Privately printed, 2000. Pp. 9–18, illus., facsims., footnotes.

39063. SPIEGEL, PAUL: *Bald 120 000 Juden in Deutschland.* [In]: Tribüne, Jg. 39, H. 153, Frankfurt am Main, 2000. Pp. 97–100.

39064. VIENNA. ADUNKA, EVELYN: *Die vierte Gemeinde. Die Geschichte der Wiener Juden von 1945 bis heute.* Berlin: Philo, 2000. 568 pp., illus., side notes, bibl., gloss., index. (Geschichte der Juden in Wien, Bd. 6.)

—— VIENNA. *Das jüdische Wien.* [See No. 38524.]

—— *Wissenschaft vom Judentum: Annäherungen nach dem Holocaust.* Hrsg. von Michael Brenner und Stefan Rohrbacher. [See No. 39141.]

B. Education and Teaching. Memorials and Remembrance

——— *Antisemitismus unter Jugendlichen.* Fakten, Erklärungen, Unterrichtsbausteine. Hrsg. von Dietmar Sturzbecher und Ronald Freytag. [See No. 39499.]

39065. AUSTRIA. KNIGHT, ROBERT: *Contours of memory in post-Nazi Austria.* [In]: Patterns of Prejudice, Vol. 34, No. 4, London, 2000. Pp. 5–11. [Discusses post-war Austrian response to the Holocaust and the Nazi era, and Austria's seeming exemption from responsibility for Nazi crimes; also mentions the Waldheim affair. Also in this issue: The return of the repressed: is Austria a racist society (Felix de Mendelssohn).]

39066. BERLIN, HOLOCAUST MEMORIAL. LAMMERT, NORBERT: *Viele Fragen sind noch nicht beantwortet, aber: Die Debatte ersetzt das Mahnmal nicht.* [In]: Die Politische Meinung. Jg. 44, Osnabrück, 1999. Pp. 5–10.

39067. BERLIN, HOLOCAUST MEMORIAL. RAUTHE, SIMONE: *Das Denkmal für die ermordeten Juden Europas. Facetten einer Kontroverse 1988–1999.* [In]: Christoph Roolf und Simone Rauthe, eds.: Projekte zur Geschichte des 20. Jahrhunderts. Deutschland und Europa in Düsseldorfer Magister- und Examensarbeiten. Neuried: ars una, 2000. Pp. 126–141, footnotes.

39068. BERTSCH, FRANZ: *Nationalsozialismus und Holocaust: ein fester Bestandteil des Schulunterrichts in Deutschland.* Bonn: Inter Nationes, 2000. 10 pp. (IN press/Inter Nationes: Basis-Info, Nr. 22, Kultur.) [Engl. edn.: National socialism and the holocaust: an integral part of school education in Germany.]

39069. BLUMENTHAL, W. MICHAEL: *Der Holocaust und die Öffentlichkeit. Über den schwierigen Weg zu einer Ethik des Gedenkens.* [In]: Menora, Bd. 11, Berlin, 2000. Pp. 69–79.

39070. BRUCHFELD, STÉPHANE/LEVINE, PAUL A.: *Erzählt es euren Kindern. Der Holocaust in Europa.* Übers. und Bearb. der deutschen Ausg. von Robert Bohn und Uwe Danker. München: C. Bertelsmann Jugendbuchverlag, 2000. 160 pp., illus. [Allein gelassen. Ein Buch soll Jugendliche mit dem Holocaust konfrontieren (Jasper von Altenbockum) [in]: 'FAZ', Nr. 56, Frankfurt am Main, 7. März, 2000, p. 10.]

39071. EHRLICH, ABRAHAM: *Das Gebot Auschwitz zu überleben.* Köln: Seippel, 2000. 321 pp., bibl. [On the challenges Nazism and its crimes present for Judaism, the Jews as well as for the Germans and the Christian churches; stresses lack of interest in past history and the necessity for keeping up public awareness in order to learn from the past.]

39072. EHRLICH, ERNST LUDWIG: *Umgang mit den Juden im Religionsunterricht.* [In]: Jüdisches Leben und jüdische Kultur in Deutschland [see No. 38421]. Pp. 229–239, notes.

39073. HAMBURG-HARBURG. YOUNG, JAMES E.: *Das Mahnmal verschwindet.* [In]: Jüdischer Almanach 2001 des Leo Baeck Instituts 2001. Frankfurt am Main, 2000. Pp. 40–56, illus. [First publ. 1994; on the memorial in Hamburg-Harburg, erected in 1986, invisible since 1993. Also in this issue: Die unendliche Bewegung der Erinnerung (Esther Shalev-Gerz, 57–64, illus.; on her own memorial projects).]

39074. HERF, JEFFREY: *Abstraction, specificity, and the Holocaust: recent disputes over memory in Germany.* [In]: German Historical Institute London, Bulletin, Vol. XXII, No. 2, London, 2000. Pp. 20–35. [Review article.]

39075. HETTLING, MANFRED: *Die Historisierung der Erinnerung – Westdeutsche Rezeptionen der nationalsozialistischen Vergangenheit.* [In]: Tel Aviver Jahrbuch für deutsche Geschichte, Vol. 29, Gerlingen, 2000. Pp. 357–378, footnotes.

——— HÖDL, SABINE/LAPPIN, ELEONORE, eds.: *Erinnerung als Gegenwart: Jüdische Gedenkkulturen.* [See No. 38432.]

39076. KÖLSCH, JULIA: *Politik und Gedächtnis.* Zur Soziologie funktionaler Kultivierung von Erinnerung. Wiesbaden: Westdeutscher Verl., 2000. 271 pp., bibl.. [Incl. commemorating the Novemberpogrom (Nov. 9) and the Holocaust (Jan. 27).]

39077. KOWALCZUK, ILKO-SASCHA: *Literaturbericht: "Vergangenheitsbewältigung", Erinnerung und Geschichtspolitik in Deutschland.* [In]: Jahrbuch Extremismus & Demokratie, Jg. 12, Baden-Baden, 2000. Pp. 325–349. [Reviews 22 books.]

39078. *Lernen aus der Geschichte.* Projekte zu Nationalsozialismus und Holocaust in Schule und Jugendarbeit (Medienkombination): ein wissenschaftliches CD-Rom-Projekt mit Begleitbuch/ Learning from history: the Nazi era and the Holocaust in German education. Hrsg. von Annette Brinkmann [et al.]. Bonn: ARCult-Media-Verl., 2000. 67; 60 pp. plus CD-Rom. [All texts in German and English.]

39079. MARIENFELD, WOLFGANG: *Die Geschichte des Judentums in deutschen Schulbüchern.* Hannover: [Univ. Hannover, Fachbereich Erziehungswissenschaften], 2000. 65 pp., illus., facsims. (Theorie und Praxis, Bd. 72.)

39080. MÉTRAUX, ALEXANDRE: *Die Darstellbarkeit der Shoah – Zum Antagonismus zwischen Erinnern und geschichtswissenschaftlicher Rekonstruktion.* [In]: Tel Aviver Jahrbuch für deutsche Geschichte, Vol. 29, Gerlingen, 2000. Pp. 283–292, footnotes.

39081. NEUMANN, KLAUS: *Shifting memories: the Nazi past in the new Germany.* Ann Arbor: The Univ. of Michigan Press, 2000. X, 333 pp., illus., gloss., notes (267–319), bibl. (321–323). [Discusses how different German communities and towns came to terms with their Nazi past, either by writing local histories, or creating memorials and commemorations. Cities given as examples incl. Salzgitter, Celle, Hildesheim.]

39082. OFFENBACH. *Erinnerung bewahren, Zukunft gestalten.* 50 Jahre "Gesellschaft für Christlich-Jüdische Zusammenarbeit Offenbach am Main e.V." [Red.: Ernst Buchholz.]. Offenbach: Ges. für Christl.-Jüd. Zusammenarbeit Offenbach am Main e.V., 2000. 74 pp.

——— OFFE, SABINE: *Ausstellungen, Einstellungen, Entstellungen. Jüdische Museen in Deutschland und Österreich.* [See No. 38679.]

39083. PRIMOR, AVI: *Kollektives Gedächtnis in Israel, Deutschland und Europa.* [In]: Menora, Bd. 11, Berlin, 2000. Pp. 29–39.

39084. RAULFF, ULRICH: *Mäßig seriös. Was kostet das Gedenken? Ein Gespräch mit Reinhard Rürup.* [In]: 'FAZ', Nr. 223, Frankfurt am Main: 2000. P. 53.

39085. SACHSEN-ANHALT. *Gedenkorte für die Opfer des Nationalsozialismus in Sachsen-Anhalt. Eine Übersicht.* [Red.: Werner Binger]. Oppin: Wenzel, 1999 [?]. XII, 132 pp., illus., maps, bibl., index.

39086. SCHOEPS, JULIUS H.: *Die Last der Geschichte. Nationalsozialismus und Judenmord in der Erinnerung der Deutschen.* [In]: Menora, Bd. 11, Berlin, 2000. Pp. 13–25.

39087. SILBERMANN, ALPHONS: *Das "Auschwitz-Loch" im Gedächtnis der Deutschen.* [In]: Menora, Bd. 11, Berlin, 2000. Pp. 169–179. [Summarises the results of a survey; see also No. 38949.]

39088. TATERKA, THOMAS: *Mythen und Memoiren im "Antiglobkestaat". Konturen des zwischen Buchenwald und Auschwitz gespaltenen Lagerdiskurses in der DDR.* [In]: Menora, Bd. 11, Berlin, 2000. Pp. 119–167, notes.

39089. *Unterricht über den Holocaust/Teaching the Holocaust.* [Issue title of] Internationale Schulbuchforschung, Jg. 22, H. 1, Braunschweig, 2000. Ed.: Falk Pingel. 168 pp., tabs., footnotes. [Cont. papers presented at a conference in Turin, Italy, May 2000. Selected papers: Einleitung/Introduction (ed., 7–10). National Socialism and the Holocaust in West German school books (ed., 11–30). DDR-Geschichtsbilder. Zur Interpretation des Nationalsozialismus, der jüdischen Geschichte und des Holocaust im Geschichtsunterricht der DDR (Stefan Küchler, 31–48). Developing reflective citizens: the role of Holocaust education (William R. Fernekes (73–88). Um vom Unsagbaren zu reden … Didaktische Anmerkungen zur Behandlung der Geschichte der Juden im österreichischen Geschichtsunterricht (Reinhard Krammer, 109–126). Further contribs. deal with Holocaust education in the US (Matthias Heyl), in Israel (Nili Keren), in Russia (David Poltorak/Viatcheslav Leshchiner) and the Holocaust Memorial Museum in Washington (Wolfgang Böge). All contribs. incl. English, German and French summaries.]

39090. VIENNA. WIESENTHAL, SIMON, ed.: *Projekt: Judenplatz Wien. Zur Konstruktion von Erinnerung.* Wien: Zsolnay, 2000. 256 pp., illus., notes. [A collection of 15 essays mostly dealing with the Vienna Holocaust memorial, its history and controversial debates. Other essays are listed according to subject.]

39091. VOEGELIN, ERIC: *Hitler and the Germans.* Transl., ed. and with introd. by Detlev Clemens and Brendan Purcell. Columbia, MO: Univ. of Missouri Press, 1999. VIII, 285 pp., footnotes. [Author's semester lectures given at Munich Univ. in 1994; lect. discuss Germans' treatment of their Nazi past.] [A 294–page typescript of E. V.'s lectures is available in the E. V. papers at the Hoover Institution, Stanford, CA.]

39092. VOGEL, HANS-JOACHIM: *Zur Notwendigkeit des Erinnerns.* Über den Umgang mit der jüngeren deutschen Geschichte. Baden-Baden: Nomos, 2000. 32 pp. (Veröff. der Potsdamer Juristischen Gesellschaft, Bd. 5.)

39093. WARENDORF. ESTER, MATTHIAS M.: *Gedenken und Erinnern an Warendorfer Juden nach dem Holocaust.* Beispiele und Beobachtungen 1970–1999. [In]: Warendorfer Schriften, H. 28–29, Warendorf, 1999. Pp. 181–215, illus., notes. [Also in this issue: Die jüdische Familie Metz in Warendorf (A. Smieszchala, 319–321).]

39094. WINTER, JAY: *The generation of memory: reflections on the "memory boom" in contemporary historical studies.* [In]: German Historical Institute, Washington, DC: Bulletin, issue 27, Washington DC, 2000. Pp. 69–92.

39095. *Wir kneten ein KZ: Aufsätze über Deutschlands Standortvorteil bei der Bewältigung der Vergangenheit.* Hrsg.: Wolfgang Schneider. Hammburg: KKV konkret, 2000. 177 pp. (Konkret: Texte, 24, 2000.) [Incl.: Vorwort: Wenn die Deutschen Auschwitz nicht erfunden hätten, hätten sie Auschwitz erfinden müssen (Hermann L. Gremliza, 7–12). 6 essays, some dealing with the Holocaust memorial debate, Goldhagen debate and other aspects of Vergangenheitsbewältigung.]

39096. YOUNG, JAMES E.: *At memory's edge: after-images of the Holocaust in contemporary art and architecture.* Newhaven, CT: Yale Univ. Press, 2000. VIII, 248 pp., illus., facsims., plans, bibl., notes, index. [Also by the same author: Daniel Libeskind's Jewish Museum in Berlin: the uncanny arts of memorial architecture [in]: Jewish Social Studies, Vol. 6, No. 2, Bloomington, IN, Winter 2000, pp. 1–23, notes.]

39097. ZUCKERMANN, MOSHE: *Gedenken, Kunst und Kulturindustrie.* [In]: Menora, Bd. 11, Berlin, 2000. Pp. 81–102, notes. [Deals with the problems of remembrance and memorials concerning the November Pogrom and Holocaust.]

V. JUDAISM

A. Jewish Learning and Scholars

39098. ALEXANDER, ISAAK. SPEICHER, ANJA, ed.: *Isaak Alexander.* Schriften. Ein Beitrag zur Frühaufklärung im deutschen Judentum. Frankfurt am Main; New York: Lang, 1998. 259 pp., footnotes, indexes. (Judentum und Umwelt, Bd. 67.) [A.I., 1722 in Regensburg – beginning of the 19th cent., Regensburg, rabbi, publ. from the 1770s in German.]

39099. BENJAMIN, WALTER. BOCK, WOLFGANG: *Walter Benjamin – die Rettung der Nacht: Sterne, Melancholie und Messianismus.* Bielefeld: Aisthesis-Verl., 2000. 474 pp., illus. Zugl.: Bremen, Univ., Habil.-Schr., 1996.

39100. BRÄMER, ANDREAS: *Rabbinical scholars as the object of biographical interest: an aspect of Jewish historiography in the German-speaking countries of Europe (1780–1871).* [In]: Leo Baeck Institute Year Book XLV, Oxford, 2000. Pp. 51–79, footnotes.

39101. BREUER, ISAAC. BIEMANN, ASHER D.: *Isaac Breuer: Zionist against his will?* [In]: Modern Judaism, Vol. 20, No. 2, New York, May 2000. Pp. 129–146, notes.

39102. BUBER, MARTIN. BARZILAI, DAVID: *Homo Dialogicus. Martin Buber's contribution to philosophy.* Jerusalem: The Hebrew University Magnes Press; Leo Baeck Institute, 2000. 330 pp., notes, indexes, bibl. [In Hebrew, title transl.]

39103. BUBER, MARTIN. BERTMAN, MARTIN A.: *Buber's mysticism without loss of identity.* [In]: Judaism, Vol. 49, No. 1, New York, Winter 2000. Pp. 80–92, notes.

39104. BUBER, MARTIN. GELLMANN, JEROME: *Buber's blunder: Buber's replies to Scholem and Schatz-Uffenheimer.* [In]: Modern Judaism, Vol. 20, No. 1, New York, Feb. 2000. Pp. 20–40, notes. [Buber's exchange with Scholem and Schatz-Uffenheimer on Hasidism.]

39105. BUBER, MARTIN. SCHMIDT, GILYA G.: *Martin Buber's conception of the relative and the absolute life.* [In]: Shofar, Vol. 18, No. 2, West Lafayette, IN, Winter 2000. Pp. 18–26, notes.

39106. BUBER, MARTIN. URBAN, MARTINA: *In search of a 'narrative anthology': reflections on an unpublished Buber manuscript.* [In]: Jewish Studies Quarterly, Vol. 7, No. 3, Tübingen, 2000. Pp. 252–288, footnotes. [Deals with a hitherto unpubl., undated, handwritten essay (25 pp.) on Sabbatai Zvi: *Zur Geschichte des Messianismus.* Ms. is held in the Buber collection of the National and Univ. Library, Jerusalem.]

39107. COHEN, HERMANN. HERMANN COHEN ARCHIV AN DER UNIVERSITÄT ZÜRICH, ed.: *"Religion der Vernunft aus den Quellen des Judentums". Tradition und Ursprungsdenken in Hermann Cohens Spätwerk. "Religion of reason out of the sources of Judaism". Tradition and the concept of origin in Hermann Cohen's later work.* Internationale Konferenz in Zürich 1998. Hrsg. von Helmut Holzhey, Gabriel Motzkin und Hartwig Wiedebach. Hildesheim, New York: Georg Olms Verl., 2000. XI, 460 pp., footnotes. (Philosophische Texte und Studien, Bd. 55.) [Cont. 23 articles.]

39108. COHEN, HERMANN. IDELSOHN, ABRAHAM ZWI: *Erinnerungen an Hermann Cohen.* [In]: Jüdischer Almanach 2001 des Leo Baeck Instituts, Frankfurt am Main, 2000. Pp. 65–72, notes. [Obit., first publ. in Hebrew 1918. Also in this issue: Nachbemerkung zu Abraham Zwi Idelsohns "Erinnerungen" (Hartwig Wiedebach, 73–78).]

——— COHEN, HERMANN. SHEAR-YASHUV, AHARON: *Darstellung und kritische Würdigung von Hermann Cohens Stellung zum Zionismus.* [See No. 39195.]

——— COHEN, HERMANN. WIEDEBACH, HARTWIG: *Das Problem eines einheitlichen Kulturbewußteins. Zur Person des deutsch-jüdischen Philosophen Hermann Cohen.* [See No. 39144.]

39109. COHEN, HERMANN: *Die Messiasidee.* [In]: Menora, Bd. 11, Berlin, 2000. Pp. 321–339. [Lecture given in 1892, first publ. 1924.]

39110. DEUBER-MANKOWSKI, ASTRID: *Der frühe Walter Benjamin und Hermann Cohen: Jüdische Werte, Kritische Philosophie, vergängliche Erfahrung.* Berlin: Vorwerk 8, 2000. 399 pp., footnotes, bibl. Zugl.: Berlin, Humboldt-Univ., Diss., 1999.

39111. DIENEMANN, MAX: *Liberales Judentum.* Neudr. der Ausg. Berlin 1935. Hrsg. von Jan Mühlstein. Berlin: Jüdische Verl.-Anst., 2000. 69 pp.

39112. FRANKEL, ZACHARIAS. BRÄMER, ANDREAS: *Rabbiner Zacharias Frankel: Wissenschaft des Judentums und konservative Reform im 19. Jahrhundert.* Hildesheim; New York: Olms, 2000. 479 pp., frontisp., footnotes, bibl. Z.F. (433–448), bibl. (449–476), index. (Netiva, Bd. 3.). Zugl.: Berlin, Freie Univ., Diss., 1996.

39113. FREIES JÜDISCHES LEHRHAUS. GYSLER, CAROLINE: *Das 'Freie Jüdische Lehrhaus' in Frankfurt. Ein Beitrag zum jüdischen Selbstverständnis in der Weimarer Republik.* Köln: Univ. Köln, Hist. Seminar, M.A. Thesis, 1999. 115+7 pp., footnotes. [Available at the Bibliothek Germania Judaica, Cologne.]

39114. GUTTMANN, JULIUS. *Die Philosophie des Judentums von Julius Guttmann.* Mit einer Standortbestimmung von Esther Seidel und einer biographischen Einführung von Fritz Bamberger. Berlin: Jüdische Verlagsanstalt Berlin, 2000. 447 pp., notes, index. [Cont.: Julius Guttmann – Philosoph des Judentums (Fritz Bamberger; first publ. 1963). Die Philosophie der Judentums (Julius Guttmann, 41–396; first publ. 1933). Julius Guttmanns Philosophie der Judentums – eine Standortbestimmung (Esther Seidel, 397–442).] [J.G., April 15, 1880 Hildesheim – May 19, 1950 Jerusalem, prof. of philosophy at the Berlin Hochschule für die Wissenschaft des Judentums, 1930 at Hebrew Union College, Cincinnati, emigr. 1934 to Palestine and became prof. at Hebrew Univ.]

39115. HESCHEL, ABRAHAM JOSHUA. HEYMEL, MICHAEL: *A witness to the existence of God: music in the work of Abraham J. Heschel.* [In]: Judaism, Vol. 49, No. 4, New York, Fall 2000. Pp. 399–410, notes.

39116. HOMOLKA, WALTER, ed.: *Traditionelles Judentum in der Moderne leben: Die Neo-Orthodoxie im 19. Jahrhundert am Beispiel eines religionsphilosophischen Fragmentes von Simon May aus Hamburg.* Egelsbach: Hänsel-Hohenhausen, 1999. 1 Microfiche. (Deutsche Hochschulschriften, Alte Reihe, 3220.) (Monographien zur Wissenschaft des Judentums.) [Manuscript: IV, 71 pp.]

39117. JAKOBOVITS, IMMANUEL. SHASHAR, MICHAEL: *Lord Jakobovits in conversation.* London; Portland, OR: Valentine Mitchell, 2000. 202 pp., frontis., index of names. [I.J., 1921 Königsberg – 1999 London, Chief Rabbi of Great Britain from 1967–1991.]

39118. KRELL, MARC A.: *Schoeps vs. Rosenzweig: transcending religious borders.* [In]: Zeitschrift für Religions- und Geistesgeschichte. Jg. 52, H. 1, Leiden, 2000. Pp. 25–37, footnotes.

39119. LEVENSON, ALAN T.: *Modern Jewish thinkers.* Northvale, NJ: Jason Aronson, 2000. 352 pp. [Incl. Martin Buber and Abraham Heschel.]

39120. MAIMON, SALOMON. DAMKEN, MARTIN: *Theoretischer und praktischer Gott oder: Zweierlei Universalismus und die unübersehbaren Folgen.* Versuch einer Annäherung an Salomon Maimons vielfach zerrissene Einstellung zum Judentum. Berlin: M. Damken [privately printed], 2000. 97 pp., footnotes, bibl. [Available at the Bibliothek Germania Judaica, Cologne.]

39121. MAIMON, SALOMON. FEINER, SHMUEL: *Solomon Maimon and the Haskalah.* [In]: Aschkenas, Jg. 10, H. 2, Wien, 2000. Pp. 337–359, footnotes.

39122. MENDELSSOHN, MOSES. ENGEL-HOLLAND, E.J.: *Die Seele.* [In]: Aschkenas, Jg. 10, H. 1, Wien, 2000. Pp. 265–270, footnotes. [Deals with an article by Friedrich Niewöhner on Mendelssohn's Hebrew booklet 'HaNefesh'; see No. 37157/YB XLV.]

39123. MENDELSSOHN, MOSES. HILFRICH, CAROLA: *"Lebendige Schrift".* Repräsentation und Idolatrie in Moses Mendelssohns Philosophie und Exegese des Judentums. München: Fink, 2000. 188 pp., footnotes, bibl. (179–184), index. Zugl.: Jerusalem, Hebr. Univ., Diss., 1998.

39124. MENDELSSOHN, MOSES. HORWITZ, RIVKA: *'Kabbalah' in the writings of Mendelssohn and the Berlin circle of 'maskilim'.* [In]: Leo Baeck Institute Year Book XLV, Oxford, 2000. Pp. 3–24, footnotes.

39125. MENDELSSOHN, MOSES. KROCHMALNIK, DANIEL: *Tradition und Subversion in der Hermeneutik Moses Mendelssohns.* [In]: Trumah 9, Berlin, 2000. Pp. 63–102, footnotes.

39126. MENDELSSOHN, MOSES. *Moses Mendelssohn im Spannungsfeld der Aufklärung.* Hrsg. von Michael Albrecht und Eva J. Engel. Stuttgart-Bad Cannstatt: frommann-holzboog, 2000. 284 pp., facsims., index. [Incl. (some titles abbr.): Mendelssohns mathematische Hypothese zum Problem des Handelns wider besseres Wissen (Michael Albrecht, 13–36), Moses Mendelssohn und seine Konkurrenten um den Preis der Preußischen Akademie für 1763 (Cornelia Buschmann, 37–50). Literaturkritik als Wissenschaft und Kunst (Eva J. Engel, 51–72). Ein vergessener "Anti Phädon" aus dem Jahr 1771 (Günter Gawlick, 73–88). A Jewish reading of Moses Mendelssohn's response to Lavater (Robert A. Jacobs, 89–100). Rechtsphilosophisches zur Kant/Mendelssohn-Kontroverse über das Völkerrecht (Hermann Klenner, 101–118). Moses Mendelssohn und die zeitgenössische Mathematik (Hans Lausch, 119–136). Kausalität und Induktion bei Hume und Mendelssohn (Astrid von der Lühe, 137–158). Moses Mendelssohn und der musikalische Diskurs der Aufklärung (Laurenz Lütteken, 159–194). Mendelssohn und die Sprachtheorien der Aufklärung (Ulrich Ricken, 195–242). Moses Mendelssohn's biblical exegesis (David Sorkin, 243–276).]

39127. PELLI, MOSHE: *Literature of Haskalah in the late 18th century.* [In]: Zeitschrift für Religions- und Geistesgeschichte, Jg. 52, H. 4, Leiden, 2000. Pp. 333–348, footnotes. [Deals with the revival of Hebrew literature in late 18th-cent. Germany.].

39128. ROSENZWEIG, FRANZ. GRÜMME, BERNHARD: *Franz Rosenzweig: Denker der unbedingten Verantwortung.* [In]: Stimmen der Zeit. Bd. 218, Freiburg i.Br., 2000. Pp. 327–336, notes.

39129. ROSENZWEIG, FRANZ. *Selections: philosophical and theological writings.* Transl., ed. and with notes and comments by Paul W. Franks and Michael L. Morgan. Indianapolis, IN: Hackett, 2000. XII, 165 pp, notes.

39130. ROSENZWEIG, FRANZ. *Ninety-two poems and hymns of Yehuda Halevi.* Transl. by Thomas Kovach, Eva Jospe, and Gilya Gerda Schmidt. Ed. and with an introd. by Richard A. Cohen. Albany, NY: State Univ. of New York, 2000. IX, 283 pp. [First Engl. edn. of Rosenzweig's 1927 transl. and commentaries on Halevi's poems.]

39131. ROSENZWEIG, FRANZ. RUBINSTEIN, ERNEST: *An episode of Jewish romanticism: Franz Rosenzweig's 'The star redemption'.* Albany: State Univ. of New York Press, 1999. XIII, 306 pp., notes, bibl. (271–293), index. (SUNY series in Judaica.) [Incl. chaps. on the relationship between Rosenzweig and Leo Baeck, and between Leo Baeck and Friedrich von Schelling.]

39132. ROSENZWEIG, FRANZ. WOLF, ARNOLD JACOB: *Current theological writing: Franz Rosenzweig and religious music.* [In]: Judaism, Vol. 49, No. 4, New York, Fall 2000. Pp. 479–483.

39133. SCHOLEM, GERSHOM. *Gershom Scholem: Literatur und Rhetorik.* Hrsg. von Stéphane Mosès und Sigrid Weigel. Köln: Böhlau, 2000. 201 pp., footnotes. [Cont. 6 essays by Stéphane Mosès, Sigrid Weigel, Moshe Idel, Pierre Bouretz, Thomas Macho, Andreas B. Kilcher.]

39134. SCHOLEM, GERSHOM. KAUFMANN, DAVID: *Imageless refuge for all images: Scholem in the wake of philosophy.* [In]: Modern Judaism, Vol. 20, No. 2, Baltimore, May 2000. Pp. 147–156, notes. [Also in this issue: Presenting and representing Gershom Scholem: a review essay (Daniel Abraham, 226–243, notes).]

39135. SCHOLEM, GERSHOM. LÖWY, MICHAEL: *L'intellectuelle moderne et son ancêtre hérétique: Gershom Scholem et Nathan de Gaza.* [In]: Diogène, No. 190, Paris, Avril-Juin 2000. Pp. 148–153, footnotes.

39136. SCHOLEM, GERSHOM. SCHMIDT, CHRISTOPH: *Der häretische Imperativ: Überlegungen zur theologischen Dialektik der Kulturwissenschaft in Deutschland.* Tübingen: Niemeyer, 2000. 189 pp., footnotes, bibl. (177–186), index. (Conditio Judaica, 31.) [Contrasts the concepts of political theology of Carl Schmitt and Gershom Scholem; also on Hermann Cohen.]

39137. SCHOLEM, GERSHOM. TWARDELLA, JOHANNES: *Gershom Scholem: Prophet und Wissenschaftler.* [In]: Aschkenas, Jg. 10, H. 2, Wien, 2000. pp. 513–523, footnotes. [Based on Sch.'s diaries.]

39138. STEGMAIER, WERNER, ed.: *Die philosophische Aktualität der jüdischen Tradition*. Frankfurt am Main: Suhrkamp, 2000. 527 pp., footnotes. [Selected essays: Mendelssohns Projekt: Vier Herausforderungen (Yirmiyahu Yovel, 331–350). Sokratisches Judentum. Moses Mendelssohns Metamorphose (Daniel Krochmalnik, 351–375). Argumentatio ad hominem: Kant und Mendelssohn (Josef Simon, 376–399). Das Prinzip des Ursprungs in Hermann Cohens 'Religion der Vernunft aus den Quellen des Judentums' (Reiner Wiehl, 403–413). Aus der Sicht des Bleibenden. Franz Rosenzweigs Philosophie des Christentums (Micha Brumlik, 415–428).]

39139. VOIGTS, MANFRED: *Weltgeschichte oder Augenblick? Messianische Zeit bei Franz Rosenzweig und Walter Benjamin*. [In]: Selbstorganisation. Jahrbuch für Komplexität in den Natur-, Sozial- und Geisteswissenschaften, Bd. 10, Berlin, 1999. Pp. 237–326, footnotes.

39140. WEINBERG, JECHIEL JACOB. SHAPIRO, MARC B.: *Between the Yeshiva World and modern orthodoxy. The life and works of Rabbi Jehiel Jacob Weinberg*. London, Portland, OR: The Littman Library of Jewish Civilization, 1999. 283 pp. [Cf.: Der Rektor der [sic] Rabbinerseminars (Yizhak Ahren) [in]: Israelitisches Wochenblatt, Jg. 101, Nr. 9, Zürich, 2. März 2001, pp. 39–41.] [J.J.W., 1884 Lithuania – 1966 Switzerland, rabbi, talmudic scholar, lived in Germany since World War I, 1924 lecturer, 1934 rector at the Berlin Rabbinical Seminary.]

39141. *Wissenschaft vom Judentum: Annäherungen nach dem Holocaust*. Hrsg. von Michael Brenner und Stefan Rohrbacher. Göttingen: Vandenhoeck & Ruprecht, 2000. 240 pp., notes (207–239). [Cont.: Vorwort (eds., 7–10). Das erste Jahrhundert der Wissenschaft des Judentums (1818–1919) (Ismar Schorsch, 11–24). Wissenschaft des Judentums in der Weimarer Republik und im "Dritten Reich" (Christhard Hoffmann, 25–41). Jüdische Studien im internationalen Kontext (Michael Brenner, 42–57). Jüdische Studien ohne Gewißheiten (Joseph Dan, 58–69). "Jüdische Studien" oder "Judaistik" in Deutschland. Aufgaben und Strukturen eines "Faches" (Karl Erich Grözinger, 70–84). Judaistik an deutschen Universitäten heute (Margarete Schlüter, 85–96). Entwicklung eines Faches – Die universitäre Lehre in der Judaistik (Andreas Gotzmann, 97–110). Antisemitismusforschung (Wolfgang Benz, 111–120). Talmud und Rabbinische Literatur (Günter Stemberger, 121–133). "Jüdische" Philosophie – Eine philosophisch-bibliographische Skizze (Giuseppe Veltri, 134–163), Jüdische Geschichte (Stefan Rohrbacher, 164–176). Jüdische Kunst (Hannelore Künzl, 177–188). Jiddische Sprache und Literatur (Marion Aptroot, 189–197). Jüdische Literatur (Dieter Lamping, 198–206).]

B. Perception and Identity

39142. AUSLÄNDER, ROSE. KRISTENSON, JUTTA: *Identitätssuche in Rose Ausländers Spätlyrik. Rezeptionsvarianten zur Post-Schoah-Lyrik*. Frankfurt am Main; New York: Lang, 2000. 353 pp., footnotes, bibl. (Beiträge zur Literatur und Literaturwissenschaft des 20. Jahrhunderts, Bd. 19.) Zugl.: Kiel, Univ., Diss., 1999.

39144. COHEN, HERMANN. WIEDEBACH, HARTWIG: *Das Problem eines einheitlichen Kulturbewußtseins. Zur Person des deutsch-jüdischen Philosophen Hermann Cohen*. [In]: Aschkenas, Jg. 10, H. 2, Wien, 2000. Pp. 417–441, footnotes.

39145. FELDMAN, LINDA E./ORENDI, DIANA: *Evolving Jewish identities in German culture*. Foreword by Sander L. Gilman. Westport, CT: Praeger, 2000. XVII, 210 pp., illus., facsims., notes, bibl. (198–200), index. [Deals with pre-Hitler and post-war German-Jewish literature concerned with Jewish identity: i.e. Franz Kafka, Irene Dische, Esther Dischereit. Incl. chaps.: The new expatriates: three American-Jewish writers in Germany today (Diana Orendi, 179–186). An entrepreneur of victimhood: Jewish identity in the confessions of a Stasi informant (Denis M. Sweet, 187–195).]

39146. FISCHER, BARBARA: *Nathans Ende? Von Lessing bis Tabori: zur deutsch-jüdischen Rezeption von "Nathan der Weise"*. Göttingen: Wallstein, 2000. 184 pp., illus., bibl.

39147. FRAIMAN, SARAH: *Judaism in the works of Beer-Hofmann and Feuchtwanger.* New York; Bern: Lang, 1998. 254 pp., footnotes, bibl., index. (Studies in German Jewish history, vol. 3.). Brandeis Univ., doctoral thesis, 1996.

39148. GEIGER, ABRAHAM. KOLTUN-FROMM, KEN: *Historical memory in Abraham Geiger's account of modern Jewish identity.* [In]: Journal of Contemporary History, Vol. 35, No. 1, London, 2000. Pp. 109–126, notes.

39149. GOODMAN-THAU, EVELINE: *Sehen, Sein und Sagen. Zur Lesbarkeit religiöser Erfahrung.* [In]: Selbstorganisation. Jahrbuch für Komplexität in den Natur-, Sozial- und Geisteswissenschaften, Bd. 10, Berlin, 1999. Pp. 275–308, footnotes. [On Gershom Scholem Hermann Cohen, Walter Benjamin, Ernst Cassirer.]

39150. HERTZBERG, ARTHUR. *"Für mich ist der Jude, der Jude sein will!"* Religion, Assimilation und Auserwähltheit – Was ist jüdische Identität? Eine Debatte über Arthur Hertzbergs Buch "Wer ist Jude?" [In]: 'Allgemeine', Jg. 55, Nr. 8, Berlin, 2000. P. IX. [Excerpts from a television debate about: Arthur Hertzberg: *Wer ist Jude? Wesen und Prägung eines Volkes.* In Zusammenarbeit mit Aron Hirt-Mannheimer. Aus dem Amerik. von Udo Rennert. München: Hanser, 2000. 360 pp.; participants of the debate: Arthur Hertzberg, Dan Diner, Alfred Grosser, Michael Stürmer, Christoph Türcke; see also: Erwähltheit und Leiden. Ein neuer Versuch über die Schwierigkeit, Jude zu sein (Julius H. Schoeps) [in]: Die Zeit, Nr. 13, Hamburg, 23. März, 2000, p. 27.]

39151. HILSENRATH, EDGAR. ZANTHIER, AGNIESZKA VON: *Julian Stryjkowski und Edgar Hilsenrath. Zur Identität jüdischer Schriftsteller nach 1945.* Essen: Verlag Die Blaue Eule, 2000. 251 pp., footnotes, bibl. (Literaturwissenschaften in der Blauen Eule, Bd. 31.) Zugl.: Duisburg, Univ., Diss., 1996.

39152. HÖDL, KLAUS, ed.: *Jüdische Identitäten: Einblicke in die Bewußtseinslandschaften des österreichischen Judentums.* Innsbruck: Studien-Verl., 2000. 336 pp., notes. (Schriften des David-Herzog-Centrums für Jüdische Studien, Bd. 1.) [Cont.: (some titles abbr.): Problems of Jewish identity in modern Central European history (Steven Beller, 15–48). Mental illness and the Jewish woman in turn of the century Vienna (Alison Rose, 49–70). Confronting anti-semitism and antifeminism in turn of the century Vienna: Grete Meisel-Hess and the modernist discourses on hysteria (Helga Thorson, 71–94). Juden und Nervosität (Georg Hofer, 95–120). Was haben Ostjuden mit Afro-Amerikanern gemein? (ed., 121–140). Sprache und Identität: Disparate Gefühle der Zugehörigkeit (Desanka Schwara, 141–170). Tempest in a teapot? Yiddish Socialist periodicals in the Austrian First Republic (Jack Jacobs, 171–188). Kaisertreu: The dynastic loyalty of Austrian Jewry (David Rechter, 189–208). Christlich-jüdische Liebesbeziehungen als Motiv in deutschsprachiger jüdischer Erzählliteratur zwischen 1870 und 1920 (Petra Ernst, 209–242). Deutschsprachig-jüdische Identität in Sydney, Australien 1933–1973 (Birgit Lang, 243–270). Jüdische Identität in der österreichischen Nachkriegsliteratur. Peter Henisch, Robert Schindel, Robert Menasse und Doron Rabinovici (Andrea Kunne, 271–306). Notizen zum Verhältnis zwischen nichtjüdischen und jüdischen Österreichern nach 1945 (Heinz P. Wassermann, 307–336).]

39153. JAFFÉ, ROBERT. ARONSFELD, C.C.: *Der Selbsthaß des Robert Jaffé.* [In]: Freiburger Rundbrief, N.F., Jg. 7, H. 1, Freiburg, 2000. Pp. 34–37. [R.J., 1870 Gnesen – 1911 Berlin (suicide), writer, converted to Christianity, author of the novel 'Ahasver' (1900).]

39154. KROBB, FLORIAN: *Selbstdarstellungen. Untersuchungen zur deutsch-jüdischen Erzählliteratur im neunzehnten Jahrhundert.* Würzburg: Königshausen & Neumann, 2000. 206 pp., footnotes, bibl., index.

39155. KUH, ANTON. KILCHER, ANDREAS: *Physiognomik und Pathognomik der jüdischen Moderne. Anton Kuhs anarchistische "Sendung des Judentums".* [In]: Aschkenas, Jg. 10, H. 2, Wien, 2000. Pp. 361–388, footnotes. [Deals with an essay publ. 1821.] [A.K., July 12, 1890 Vienna – Jan. 28, 1941 New York, journalist, lived 1925–1933 in Berlin, fled 1938 from Vienna to the US.]

39156. LASKER-SCHÜLER, Else. KRUG, MARINA: *Die Figur als signifikante Spur: eine dekonstruktive Lektüre zu den Gedichten "Esther" sowie "David und Jonathan" aus dem Zyklus "Hebräische Balladen" von Else Lasker-Schüler.* Spurenlegung. Für eine dekonstruktive & feministische Theorie des Lesens. Frankfurt am

Main; New York: Lang, 2000. XI, 252 pp., footnotes, bibl. (Europ. Hochschulschriften: Reihe 1, Deutsche Sprache und Literatur, Bd. 1771.) Zugl.: Hamburg, Univ., Diss., 1997.

39157. MAIMON, SALOMON. LIBRETT, JEFFREY S.: *Stolen goods: cultural identity after the counter-enlightenment in Salomon Maimon's autobiography (1792)*. [In]: New German Critique, No. 79, Ithaca, NY, Winter 2000. Pp. 36–66, footnotes.

39158. MORUZZI, NORMA CLAIRE: *Asking the questions, telling a story*. [In]: The German Quarterly, Vol. 73, No. 2, Riverside, CA, Spring 2000. Pp. 179–184, notes. [On Hannah Arendt and her conflict between intellectual and personal identity. Author reflects on questions of German-Jewish identity in the context of her own and H. A.'s experience.]

39159. ROSENZWEIG, FRANZ. GÖRTZ, HEINZ-JÜRGEN: *"Autobiographische Konfession". Franz Rosenzweigs Gedanke einer "erzählenden Philosophie"*. [In]: Selbstorganisation. Jahrbuch für Komplexität in den Natur-, Sozial- und Geisteswissenschaften, Bd. 10, Berlin, 1999. Pp. 257–276, footnotes.

39160. SCHÖNBERG, ARNOLD. KANGAS, WILLIAM: *The ethics and aesthetics of (self)representation: Arnold Schoenberg and Jewish identity*. [In]: Leo Baeck Institute Year Book XLV, Oxford, 2000. Pp. 135–169, footnotes.

39161. SCHRUFF, HELENE: *Wechselwirkungen. Deutsch-jüdische Identität in erzählender Prosa der "Zweiten Generation"*. Hildesheim; New York: Olms, 2000. 262 pp., footnotes, bibl. (245–259), index. (Haskala, Bd. 20.) Zugl.: Berlin, Freie Univ., Diss., 1998 u.d. Titel: Jüdische Identität in erzählender Prosa der "Zweiten Generation" in Deutschland und Österreich. [On Maxim Biller, Barbara Honigmann, Esther Dischereit, Doron Rabinovici, Robert Schindel, Lothar Schöne, Rafael Seligmann.]

39162. SREBERNY, ANNABELLE: *Travelling tales: routes and roots in my Jewish identity*. [In]: The Jewish Quarterly, Vol. 47, No. 4, London, Winter 2000– 2001. Pp. 53–58, illus. [Author's mother went to England on a Kindertransport. Author discusses the problems of being a second-generation survivor.]

39163. WALLAS, ARMIN A.: *Mythos Osten. Die Suche nach den orientalischen Grundlagen jüdischer Identität zu Beginn des 20. Jahrhunderts*. [In]: Geschichtliche Mythen in den Literaturen und Kulturen Ostmittel- und Südosteuropas. Hrsg. von Eva Behring [et al.]. Stuttgart: Steiner, 1999. (Forschungen zur Geschichte und Kultur des östlichen Mitteleuropa, Bd. 6.) Pp. 137, footnotes.

39164. WEISS, PETER. BERGH, MAGNUS: *Wofür wir keinen Namen hatten. Der geheime Teil von Peter Weiss' Autobiographie in der "Ästhetik des Widerstandes"*. [In]: 'FAZ', Nr. 54, Frankfurt am Main, 4. März 2000. P. IV, Beilage.

39165. WERFEL, FRANZ. SAJAK, CLAUß PETER: *Der hartnäckige Wanderer. Franz Werfel im Spannungsfeld von Judentum und Katholizismus*. [In]: Freiburger Rundbrief, Jg. 7, H. 2, Freiburg, 2000. Pp. 91–98, footnotes.

C. Jewish Life and Organisations. Genealogy

39166. ABOLING, SABINE: *Das Epitheton 'Jude' bei Pflanzen – Jüdische Kultur im Spiegel botanischer Volksnamen*. [In]: Aschkenas, Jg. 10, H. 1, Wien, 2000. Pp. 273–276, illus.

39167. *Avotaynu. The International Review of Jewish Genealogy*. Vol. XVI, Nos. 1–4. Teaneck, NJ, 2000. 4 issues. [Incl. contribs. on German-Jewish families and their genealogical source material.]

39168. BERGBAUER, KNUT: *Jüdische Jugendbewegung in Deutschland von ihren Anfängen bis zur Shoah*. [In]: Sozialwissenschaftliche Literatur-Rundschau, Jg. 23, H. 41, 2000. Pp. 23–36. [Review essay.]

39169. *Chronik der Familie Hirschland*. Aufgestellt durch Albert J. Phiebig, Berlin 1936/1937. Ergänzt 1996/1999 Herbert Schüürmann, 46446 Emmerich. [H. Schüürmann: Typescript, [2000?]. 1 vol., illus., facsims., docs., bibl. [Lists all descendants of the Hirschland family from Steinheim, later Essen; available at the Bibliothek Germania Judaica, Cologne.]

39170. DROV, DAGMAR: *Heilpädagogik im deutschen Judentum*. Eine Spurensicherung 1873–1942. Mit einem Essay von Shimon Sachs. Hrsg. von Bernd Schröder. Münster: LIT, 2000. 155 pp., notes (107–134), bibl. (135–147), index, suppl. (I-XXXI). (Münsteraner Judaistische Studien, 7.) [Incl. 27 short biographies of people engaged in Jewish education of the mentally and physically handicapped; also: Zur Stellung des behinderten Menschen in der jüdischen Überlieferung (Shimon Sachs, V-XXXI, bibl. Shimon (Walter) Sachs).]

39171. GILLIS-CARLEBACH, MIRIAM: *Jedes Kind ist mein Einziges: Lotte Carlebach-Preuss. Antlitz einer Mutter und Rabbiner-Frau*. Veränd. Neuaufl., neu durchges. und bearb. Aufl. Hamburg: Dölling und Galitz, 2000. 374, [16] pp., illus., bibl. [For 1st edn. see No. 29875/YB XXXVIII.]

39172. JANESCH, JÜRGEN: *Deutsch – Jiddisch – Hebräisch. Sprachdebatten des Kölner "Israelitischen Gemeindeblattes"*. Köln: Univ., Inst. für Deutsche Sprache und Literatur, 2000. (Schriftl. Hausarbeit.). 89 pp., footnotes, bibl. [Available at the Bibliothek Germania Judaica, Cologne.]

39173. JOSEPHU, JOHANNA: *Jüdische Jugendorganisationen vor 1938 und nach 1945: ein soziologischer Vergleich*. Wien: WUV, 2000. 268 pp., illus. (Dissertationen der Universität Wien, Bd. 64.) Zugl.: Wien, Univ., Diss., 1998.

39174. KIRCHNER, PAUL CHRISTIAN: *Jüdisches Ceremoniell. Beschreibung jüdischer Feste und Gebräuche*. Leipzig: Reprint-Verlag, 1997. 226 pp., illus. [28 pp.], footnotes. [Reprint of the 1734 edn.]

39175. KUCHENBECKER, ANTJE: *Zionismus ohne Zion. Birobidjan: Idee und Geschichte eines jüdischen Staates in Sowjet-Fernost*. Berlin: Metropol, 2000. 272 pp., footnotes, bibl. (249–272). (Reihe Dokumente, Texte, Materialien/Zentrum für Antisemitismusforschung der Techn. Univ. Berlin, Bd. 32.) [Incl.: Das Programm der Produktivierung (46–56).]

39176. LAPPIN, ELEONORE: *Der Jude 1916–1928: jüdische Moderne zwischen Universalismus und Partikularismus*. Tübingen: Mohr Siebeck, 2000. XI, 456 pp., footnotes, bibl., index. (Schriftenreihe wissenschaftlicher Abhandlungen des Leo-Baeck-Instituts, 62.)

39177. *Maajan – Die Quelle*. Zeitschrift für jüdische Familienforschung. Organ der Schweizerischen Vereinigung für jüdische Genealogie [und der] Hamburger Gesellschaft für jüdische Genealogie e.V. Jg. 14, H. 1–4. Zürich, 2000. 4 issues.

39178. MAYER, PAUL YOGI: *Jüdische Olympiasieger*. Sport – Ein Sprungbrett für Minoritäten. Kassel: Agon Sportverlag, 2000. 192 pp., frontis., illus., facsims., footnotes, list of names, bibl. [Incl. German-speaking countries and chaps.: 'Olympia – Minoritäten – Judentum' (13–28); and '1936: Berlin – Juden unerwünscht' (54–101).]

39179. REMY, NAHIDA: *Das jüdische Weib*. Mit einer Vorrede von Prof. Dr. M. Lazarus. Reprint der Ausgabe von 1892. Hrsg. von Esther Sharell. Frankfurt am Main: Cultura Judaica, 1999. 328 pp. [Incl.: Zum Geleit (ed., 3 pp.).] [N.R., (1894–1928), novelist, playwright, wife of Moritz Lazarus, converted 1895 to Judaism; first publ. 1891.]

39180. ROTH, JOSEPH: *The wandering Jews*. Transl. by Michael Hofmann. Preface by Elie Wiesel. London, Granta Books, 2000. 146 pp. [First Engl. edn. of an extended essay on the Jews of Eastern Europe, first publ. in 1927.]

39181. SCHUMACHER, CHRISTINA: *Der Versuch einer historischen Biographie zu Regina Jonas*. Köln: M.A. Thesis, 2000. 105 pp., footnotes, bibl. (91–104). [Available at the Bibliothek Germania Judaica, Cologne.]

39182. *Stammbaum*. The Journal of German-Jewish Genealogical Research. Issues 16–18. New York: Leo Baeck Institute, Jan. & June & Dec. 2000. 3 issues. [Incl. contribs. on new publs., projects and other material relevant to the genealogy of German-speaking Jewry by Peter Lande, Annette Haller, Edward Salier, Hans George Hirsch, Robert A. Weinberg, Werner L. Frank, George E. Arnstein et al.]

39183. TOCH, MICHAEL: *Gedenken und Gedächtnis: die Familienerinnerungen von Erna Strassberger.* [In]: Mitteilungen des Instituts für Österreichische Geschichtsforschung, Bd. 107, Heft 1–4, München 1999. Pp. 166–169, footnotes. [Deals mainly with the Toch family.]

39184. WALLET, BART: *Religious oratory and the improvement of congregants: Dutch-Jewish preaching in the first half of the nineteenth century.* [In]: Studia Rosenthaliana, Vol. 34, No. 2, Amsterdam, 2000. Pp. 168–193, footnotes. [Also on rabbis from German-speaking countries and on Yiddish.]

39185. ZELLER, SUSANNE: *Jüdische Ethik in der sozialen Arbeit.* [In]: neue praxis. Zeitschrift für Sozialarbeit, Sozialpädagogik und Sozialpolitik, Jg. 28, Nr. 6, Neuwied, 1998. Pp. 540–558, footnotes.

D. Jewish Art and Music

39186. KLEMMER, CLEMENS: *Salomons Tempel. Symbolistik und Erinnerung im modernen Synagogenbau der jüdischen Gemeinden in Deutschland.* [In]: Menora, Bd. 11, Berlin, 2000. Pp. 41–67, notes. [Also on post-1945 synagogues.]

39187. KNAPP, ALEXANDER: *The influence of German music on United Kingdom synagogue practice.* [In]: Jewish Historical Studies. Transactions of the Jewish Hist. Society of England, Vol. 35, 1996–1998, London, 2000. Pp. 167–197, scores, notes. [Discusses the development of German-Jewish music, incl. synagogue song. Refers to cantor Salomon Sulzer.]

39188. KOGMAN-APPEL, KATRIN: *Coping with Christian pictorial sources: What did Jewish miniaturists not paint?* [In]: Speculum, Vol. 75, Cambridge, MA, 2000. Pp. 816–858, illus., footnotes. [Deals with the ways Jewish medieval Sephardi and Ashkenazi illustrators dealt with the Christological pictorial sources and how these were translated into a Jewish pictorial language.]

39189. KOGMAN-APPEL, KATRIN: *Die Zweite Nürnberger und die Jehuda Haggada. Jüdische Illustrationen zwischen Tradition und Fortschritt.* Frankfurt am Main; New York, 1999. 495 pp., illus., footnotes, bibl., index. (Judentum und Umwelt, Bd. 69.) [Deals with two haggadot originating from Franconia between 1465 and 1470.]

39190. KORN, SALOMON. *Synagogen im Stilkonflikt: Über Sakralarchitektur als Spiegelbild einer Minderheit.* [In]: 'FAZ', Nr. 105, Frankfurt am Main, 6. Mai 2000. P. III, Beilage.

39191. KÜNZL, HANNELORE: *Die jüdische Kunst zwischen Mittelalter und Moderne: das 16. und 17. Jahrhundert.* [In]: Schöpferische Momente des europäischen Judentums in der frühen Neuzeit [see No. 38424]. Pp. 75–96, illus.

—— KÜNZL, HANNELORE: *Jüdische Kunst.* [See in No. 39141.]

39192. SABAR, SHALOM: *Masel tow. Illuminierte jüdische Eheverträge aus der Sammlung des Israel Museum.* Aus dem Engl. von Michael von Killisch-Horn. Berlin: Jüdische Verlagsanstalt, 2000. 199 pp., illus., plates, bibl. [Incl. also German marriage contracts.]

VI. ZIONISM AND ISRAEL

—— BODENHEIMER, MAX ISIDOR. THE CENTRAL ZIONIST ARCHIVES, ed.: *List of files of the papers of Max Bodenheimer and the Bodenheimer family.* [See No. 38670.]

39193. BOEHM, DAN/BEST, MICHAEL: *Schalom. Land der Väter. Erinnerungen eines deutschen Juden und israelischen Offiziers.* Berlin: Das Neue Berlin, 1998. 320 pp., illus., notes. [Memoirs of D.B., orig. Dieter B., b. 1921 in Dresden; dealing mainly with his life in Palestine/Israel; lives in Jerusalem.]

39194. BRUCKSTEIN, HANS J.: *Eine neue Generation – ein neuer Anfang: Geschichte eines deutschen Juden in Israel.* Berlin: Frieling, 1999. 191 pp. [Author, b. 1926 in Danzig, lives in Jerusalem.]

39195. COHEN, HERMANN. SHEAR-YASHUV, AHARON: *Darstellung und kritische Würdigung von Hermann Cohens Stellung zum Zionismus.* [In]: Aschkenas, Jg. 10, H. 2, Wien, 2000. Pp. 443–457, footnotes.

39196. DIVINE, DONNA ROBINSON: *Zionism and the transformation of Jewish society.* [In]: Modern Judaism, Vol. 20, No. 3, Baltimore, Oct. 2000. Pp. 257–276, notes. [Deals with early Zionism and its impact on the Diaspora, incl. German Jewry.]

39197. EDELHEIT, ABRAHAM/EDELHEIT, HERSHEL: *History of Zionism: a handbook and dictionary.* Boulder, CO: Westview Press, 2000. XVII, 672 pp., frontis., illus., facsims., tabs., maps, notes, bibl. (617–637), name index. [Cont. two parts: part I deals with the history of Zionism; part II is a dictionary of Zionist terms.]

39198. EVARD, JEAN-LUC: *Berlin, New York, Jerusalem.* [In]: Revue d'Histoire de la Shoah/le Monde Juif, Vol. 168, Paris, 2000. Pp. 175–188, notes. [Deals with the correspondence (dated 1926–1952) between Hannah Arendt and the Zionist leader Kurt Blumenfeld, with Zionism as a frequent topic.]

39199. FÖLLING-ALBERS, MARIA/FÖLLING, WERNER: *Kibbutz und Kollektiverziehung.* Entstehung – Entwicklung – Veränderung. Opladen: Leske + Buderich, 2000. 317 pp., bibl., gloss. (Reihe Kindheitsforschung, Bd. 13.) [Deals also with German precursors of the Kibbutz movement.]

39200. GELBER, MARK: *Melancholy pride: nation, race, and gender in the German literature of cultural Zionism.* Tübingen: Niemeyer, 2000. XVI, 309 pp., illus., fascims., footnotes, bibl. (291–302), index. (Conditio Judaica, 23.) [Cont. (titles condensed): Introd.: The parameters of German cultural Zionism: the possibility of a Jewish-national literature in German? I: The Jewish renaissance in Vienna and Berlin: a literature and art for the sake of Zion. II: The literary and cultural expressions of Jewish students and fraternity life at the turn of the century. III: Börries von Münchhausen and E. M. Lilien: the genesis of Juda and its Zionist reception. IV: The rhetoric of race and Jewish-national cultural politics: from Birnbaum and Buber to Brieger's René Richter. V: Feminist-Zionist expression: ideology, rhetoric, and literature. VI: Eroticism and masochism in cultural Zionism: Else Lasker-Schüler and Dolorosa. VII: Anti-semitism, philo-semitism, and the role of non-Jews in Jewish-national culture. Concl.: German cultural Zionism, Jewish difference, modern Jewish identity, and national creativity.] [Cf.: Review (Ritchie Robertson) [in]: Journal of Jewish Studies, Vol. 51, No. 2, Cambridge, Autumn 2000, pp. 360–363.]

—— HAMANN, BIRGITTA: *Lola Landau. Leben und Werk.* Ein Beispiel deutsch-jüdischer Literatur des 20. Jahrhunderts in Deutschland und Palästina/Israel. [See No. 39324.]

39201. HERZL, THEODOR. GOLOMB, JACOB: *"Ko amar Herzl…". Nietzsches Präsenz in der Welt des zionistischen Vordenkers.* [In]: Menora, Bd. 11, Berlin, 2000. Pp. 193–207, notes.

39202. HERZL, THEODOR. SEEWANN, HARALD: *Theodor Herzl. Vom Burschenschafter zum Vater des Judenstaates.* [In]: Einst und Jetzt. Jahrbuch für corpsstudentische Geschichtsforschung, Bd 45, Erlangen, 2000. Pp. 121–138.

39203. HÖXTER, NATHAN: *Jüdische Pionierarbeit.* Nach Kindheit und früher Jugend in Berlin: ein Leben im Kibbuz Geva und neue Brücken nach Deutschland 1916–2000. Hrsg. von Erhard Roy Wiehn. Konstanz: Hartung-Gorre, 2000. 142 pp., illus., footnotes. [Author, b. 1916 in Berlin, went in 1932 with a group of boys to Ben Shemen, Palestine, later lived in the Kibbuz Geva.]

39204. *Die Jeckes. Deutsche Juden aus Israel erzählen.* Hrsg. von Gideon Greif, Colin McPherson und Laurence Weinbaum. Mit einem Geleitwort von Dan Diner. Köln: Böhlau, 2000. XIV, 318 pp., ports., illus., gloss., indexes. [Incl. interviews with c. 80 persons made between 1994 and 1997;

also 5 introd. essays: Was ist ein Jecke? Jüdisches Leben in Deutschland vor 1933. Die braune Zeit. Einwanderung in Palästina. Zu Besuch in Deutschland.]

39205. LAQUEUR, WALTER: *My Jerusalem: recollections of Talbiyeh.* [In]: Partisan Review, Vol. 67, No. 1, Boston, Winter 2000. Pp.38– 48. [Author's memories of living in the Talbiyeh quarter of Jerusalem, which, before independence, was heavily populated by German Jews. W. L. compares his recollections of peaceful co-existence with the Arabs to those of Edward Said, the Egyptian author, whose autobiogr. was publ. recently.]

—— MEDOFF, RAFAEL/WAXMAN, CHAIM I.: *Historical dictionary of Zionismus.* [See No. 38692.]

39206. MIRON, GUY: *Autobiography as a source for writing social history – German Jews in Palestine/Israel as a case study.* [In]: Tel Aviver Jahrbuch für deutsche Geschichte, Vol. 29, Gerlingen 2000. Pp. 251–281, footnotes.

39207. RAN, DANIELA: *The contribution of Jewish-German immigrants to maritime development in Israel.* [In]: Mediterranean Historical Review, Vol. 15, No. 1, London, 2000. Pp. 94–101, notes.

39208. RUDEL, JOSEF NORBERT: *Sie kamen heim und schrieben deutsch. Der Verband deutschsprachiger Schriftsteller in Israel* [In]: Freiburger Rundbrief, N.F., Jg. 7, H. 2, Freiburg, 2000. Pp. 117–118.

39209. SIEGEMUND, ANJA: *Kassandrarufer? Robert Weltsch – eine Stimme des Verständigungszionismus.* [In]: Jüdischer Almanach 2001 des Leo Baeck Instituts, Frankfurt am Main, 2000. Pp. 108–126. [On W.'s role in the Brith Shalom in Germany and Palestine, which acknowledged the rights of the Arabs and favoured peaceful co-existence and willingness to share power.]

39210. SPECTOR, SCOTT: *Another Zionism: Hugo Bergmann's circumscription of spiritual territory.* [In]: Journal of Contemporary History, Vol. 34, No. 1, London, 1999. Pp. 87–108, footnotes.

39211. *Sprachbewahrung nach der Emigration – Das Deutsch der 20er Jahre in Israel.* Teil II: *Analysen und Dokumente.* Hrsg. von Anne Betten und Miryam Du-nour unter Mitarbeit von Monika Dannerer. Tübingen: Niemeyer, 2000. XIV, 481 pp., index. (Phonai, Bd. 45.) [A CD-rom is attached to the book. For part 1 (publ. 1995) see No. 33226/YB XLI.]

39212. STEGEMANN, EKKEHARD W., ed.. *100 Jahre Zionismus. Von der Verwirklichung einer Vision.* Mit Beiträgen von Jacob Allerhand [et al.]. Stuttgart: Kohlhammer, 2000. 247 pp. (Judentum und Christentum, Bd. 1.) [A collection of 23 papers given at an int. congress in Basle in Aug. 1997; essays are arranged under the sections: I. Der Zionismus als Nationalbewegung (17–94; contribs. by Shlomo Avineri, Miroslav Hroch, Gideon Shimoni, Anita Shapira, Yosef Gorny, Wladyslaw Bartoszewski, Shlomo Ben-Ami). II. Zionismus und Religion (95–163; contribs. by Aviezer Ravitzky, Albert H. Friedlander, Alex Carmel, Ekkehard W. Stegemann, Rolf Rendtorff, Hava Lazarus-Yafeh). III. Antisemitismus und Antizionismus nach der Schoah (163–209; contribs. by Yehuda Bauer, Irwin Cotler, Edna Brocke, Jacob Allerhand). IV. Das Erbe des Zionismus für jüdisches Selbstverständnis (209–244; contribs. by Eliezer Schweid, Haim J. Zadok, Shmuel Noah Eisenstadt, Arthur Hertzberg, Rita Thalmann, Eli Eyal).]

—— TEICHERT, CARSTEN: *Chasak! Zionismus im nationalsozialistischen Deutschland. 1933–1938.* [See No. 38977.]

—— URBACH, HEINRICH: *Herzl und Bialik.* [See in No. 38644.]

39213. WEINBAUM, LAURENCE/MCPHERSON, COLIN: *No milk and honey: the Yekkes and the Ostjuden.* [In]: The Jewish Quarterly, Vol. 47, No. 3, London, Autumn 2000. Pp. 25–30, illus.

39214. ZUCKERMANN, MOSHE: *Von Moses Hess bis David Ben Gurion: Widersprüche in der Ideologie des politischen Zionismus.* [In]: Jüdisches Leben und jüdische Kultur in Deutschland [see No. 38421]. Pp. 217–228, notes.

VII. PARTICIPATION IN CULTURAL AND PUBLIC LIFE

A. General

39215. BERNSTEIN, MICHAEL ANDRÉ: *Five portraits: modernity and the imagination in twentieth-century German writing*. Evanston, IL: Northwestern Univ., 2000. X, 150 pp., notes (125– 141), index. [Incl. Walter Benjamin and Paul Celan.]

39216. BLEKER, JOHANNA/SCHLEIERMACHER, SABINE: *Ärztinnen aus dem Kaiserreich*. Lebensläufe einer Generation. Weinheim: Deutscher Studien Verlag, 2000. 348 pp., tabs., footnotes. [Incl. chaps.: Zur Herkunft der frühen Ärztinnen (53–74; also on Jewish women, with an excerpt from the diary of Therese Oppler from Pleschen/Posen, later Breslau). Das Schicksal der "nicht-arischen" Ärztinnen der älteren Generation (127–158).]

39217. BRAUN, MICHAEL [et al.], eds.: *"Hinauf und Zurück/in die herzhelle Zukunft"*. *Deutsch-jüdische Literatur im 20. Jahrhundert*. Festschrift für Birgit Lermen. Bonn: Bouvier, 2000, 571 pp., illus., notes. [Incl.: Moderne und Judentum (Helmuth Kiesel, 51–79, bibl.; discusses the "contribution" of German and Austrian Jews to modern culture). "Shylock". Zur Geschichte seiner Wirkung im Spiegel zweier jüdischer Rezipienten (Johann Michael Schmidt, 131–146; deals with Heinrich Heine and Hermann Sinsheimer). Jüdisches in Walter Mehrings 'Ketzerbrevieren' (Hans-Peter Bayerdörfer, 161–175; on a pamphlet written in 1921). Spuren deutsch-jüdischer Vergangenheit in den kinder- und mädchenliterarischen Werken Else Urys (Gisela Wilkending, 177–188). Der deutsche Jude. Lion Feuchtwangers Roman 'Jud Süß' und Veit Harlans Verfilmung des "Jud Süß"-Stoffes (Peter J. Brenner, 215–240). "Sehnsucht und Sprache und Nacht der Toten". Zu einem frühen Gedicht von Tuvia Rübner (Hans Otto Horch, 241–251). Die Gestalt Jesu im Werk der jüdischen Dichterin Else Lasker-Schüler (Norbert Oellers, 253–263). Der Außenseiter und seine 'arme Freiheit'. Über Ludwig Marcuse (Dieter Lamping, 267–279). Hermann Brochs 'Pasenow oder die Romantik' und Matthias Grünewalds 'Die Menschwerdung Christi'. Zur Messiashoffnung in den 'Schlafwandlern' (Paul Michael Lützeler, 281–299). Das Deutsch Martin Bubers (Franz Pöggeler, 301–314). Bildreflexion, Lebensreflexion. Zu Paul Celans Gedicht 'Einkanter: Rembrandt' (Theo Buck, 325–351). Paul Celan – ein Schwellendichter (Klaus Manger, 353–369). Nelly Sachs und die jüdische Tradition: das Gebet und der religiöse Kalender in ihrer Dichtung (Mark H. Gelber, 371–388). "Ein selbstverständliches fragloses Judesein". Jenny Rosenbaum in Palästina/Israel (1939–1948) (Hartmut Steinecke, 389–401; on Jenny Aloni). 'Wenn du liebst – Zur Poetologie der späten Gedichte Rose Ausländers (Walter Schmitz, 403–426). 'Zwischen den Zeilen lesen'. Eine Computeranalyse von Gedichten Hilde Domins (Matthias Ballod et el., 427–452). "Hand in Hand mit der Sprache". Zu Hilde Domins Gedicht 'Älter werden' (Ulrike Pohl-Braun, 457–469). Barbara Honigmanns Weg "nach Hause in die Fremde" (Michael Braun, 471–486). Bukowina. Die lyrische Evokation einer Landschaft bei Moses Rosenkranz, Rose Ausländer und Alfred Gong (Reinhard Kiefer, 487–501). Zwischen Realität und Legende (Zu Friedrich Torbergs Erzählung 'Golems Wiederkehr' (Helga Abret, 521–541). Further essays are listed according to subject.]

39218. BUCKMILLER, MICHAEL/HEIMANN, DIETRICH/PERELS, JOACHIM, eds.: *Judentum und politische Existenz*. Siebzehn Porträts deutsch-jüdischer Intellektueller. Hannover: Offizin Verl., 2000. 420 pp., ports.

39219. BUNZL, MATTI: *Political inscription, artistic reflection: a recontextualization of contemporary Viennese-Jewish literature*. [In]: The German Quarterly, Vol. 73, No. 2, Riverside, CA, Spring 2000. Pp. 163–170, notes. [Discusses three young German-speaking Jewish writers: Daniel Ganzfried, André Kaminski, Doron Rabinovici. Also on the re-emergence in Austria of Jewish life in general.]

39220. DÜTTMANN, ALEXANDER GARCIA: *The gift of language: memory and promise in Adorno, Benjamin, Heidegger and Rosenzweig*. Transl. from the French by Arline Lyons. London: Athlone, 2000. VIII, 140 pp. New York: Syracuse Univ. Press, 2000. 224 pp., notes, bibl., index.

39221. EXILE. *Deutsche Intellektuelle im Exil*. Ihre Akademie und die "American Guild for German Cultural Freedom". Eine Wanderausstellung des Deutschen Exilarchivs 1933–1945/ Der Deutschen

Bibliothek. Red.: Brita Eckert unter Mitwirkung von Harro Kieser. Frankfurt am Main: Die Deutsche Bibliothek, 2000. 52 pp. [Focuses on Ernst Weiß, Ernst Bloch, Anna Seghers.]

39222. EXILE. DÜWELL, KURT: *Exil und Remigration von RWTH-Professoren (1933–1953)*. [In]: Zeitschrift des Aachener Geschichtsvereins, Bd. 102, 1999/2000, Aachen, 2000. Pp. 519–532, footnotes.

39223. EXILE. MEDAWAR, JEAN/PYKE, DAVID: *Hitler's gift: scientists who fled Nazi Germany*. London: R. Cohen Books, 2000. 261 pp., notes, bibl. [Incl. Max Born, Max Delbrück, Albert Einstein, Fritz Haber, Lise Meitner, Erwin Schrödinger. Also deals with the rescuers, notably the Hungarian physicist Leo Szilard who found homes for countless German-Jewish scientists.] [Cf.: The battle of science (John Cornwell) [in]: The Sunday Times, London, Aug. 13, 2000, pp. 35–36.]

39224. EXILE. PROSS, STEFFEN: *"In London treffen wir uns wieder". Vier Spaziergänge durch ein vergessenes Kapitel deutscher Kulturgeschichte nach 1933*. Frankfurt am Main: Eichborn, 2000. 224 pp., illus., maps, bibl., indexes. [Traces numerous German-Jewish refugees; deals also with the British refugee policy.] [Cf.: Anschnorrbar at Hallam Street (Benedikt Erenz) [in]: Die Zeit, Nr. 35, Hamburg, 24. Aug. 2000, p. 48.]

39225. EXILE. SCHERER, F. M.: *The emigration of German-speaking economists after 1933*. [In]: Journal of Economic Literature, Vol. 38, No. 3, Nashville, TN, 2000. Pp. 614–626, notes. [Discusses the impact the Nazi policy of dismissal of "non-Aryan" academics, incl. economists, had on the German and Austrian as well as on the Anglo-American economies.]

39226. EXILE. TORTAROLO, EDOARDO: *Historiker im Exil um 1933. Eine Problemskizze*. [In]: Deutsche Umbrüche im 20. Jahrhundert. Hrsg.von Dietrich Papenfuß und Wolfgang Schieder. Köln: Böhlau, 2000. Pp. 289–296, footnotes.

——— EXILE. WENDLAND, ULRIKE: *Biographisches Lexikon deutschsprachiger Kunsthistoriker im Exil*. [See No. 38699.]

——— EXILE LITERATURE. BOLBECHER, SIGLINDE/KAISER, KONSTANTIN: *Lexikon der österreichischen Exilliteratur*. [See No. 38686.]

39227. EXILE LITERATURE. GIGUERE, UNDINE G.: *Frauen im Exil: Untersuchung exilrelevanter Themenbereiche anhand der autobiographisch ausgewählten Texte von fünf Exilautorinnen (1933–1945)*. Ann Arbor, Mich.: UMI, 1999. VI, 406 pp. Zugl.: Albany, State Univ. of New York, Diss., 1997.

39228. EXILE LITERATURE. *Juni* H. 32 [with the issue title] *Dossier Emigration und Exil*. Mönchengladbach, 2000. 1 issue, notes. [Incl. (some titles abbr.): Editorial. Die Literatur im Exil (5–8). Positionsbestimmungen deutsch-jüdischer Schriftsteller im antifaschistischen Exil (Kerstin Schoor, 9–32). Arnold Zweig. Charme und Fluch der unentrinnbaren bürgerlichen Kultur (Gerhard Bauer, 33–46). Einsamkeit und Gemeinsamkeit – Lebensmotive Stefan Hermlins (Silvia Schlenstedt, 47–60). Spuren von Exilierung und Emigration im Werk von Anna Seghers (Sonja Hilzinger, 61–72).]

39229. EXILE LITERATURE. *Kleine Verbündete – Little Allies. Vertriebene österreichische Kinder- und Jugendliteratur/Austrian children's and juvenile literature in exile*. Hrsg. von Ursula Seeber in Zusammenarbeit mit Alisa Douer und Edith Blaschitz. Übers. ins Engl.: Karin Hanta. Mit 222 Abbildungen. Wien: Picus, 1998. 181 pp., illus., bibl., index. [Incl. (titles abbr.): Österreichische Kinder- und Jugendliteratur des Exils (Ursula Seeber, 9–18). Kinderleben im Exil (Edith Blaschitz, 19–42). Lebensbedingungen, Arbeitsmöglichkeiten, Verlagsgeschichten (Ursula Seeber, 43–53). Konzepte, Genres, Themen (Edith Blaschitz/Ursula Seeber, 54–88). Rückkehr und Neubeginn (89–110). Bio-Bibliografien (111–172). All texts also in English.]

39230. EXILE LITERATURE. SPALEK, JOHN M./FEILCHENFELDT, KONRAD/HAWRYLCHAK, SANDRA H., eds.: *Deutschsprachige Exilliteratur seit 1933*. Bd. 3: USA, Teil 1. Bern: Saur, 2000. X, 471 pp. [Incl. biographical articles on 28 writers.]

39231. EXILE MUSIC. GEIGER, FRIEDRICH/SCHÄFER, THOMAS, eds.: *Exilmusik. Komposition während der NS-Zeit.* Hamburg: von Bockel, 1999. 376 pp., footnotes, music. (Musik im "Dritten Reich" und im Exil, Bd. 3.) [Incl.: "Die mit Tränen säen …". Paul Dessaus '126. Psalm' – ein Exilwerk (Peter Petersen, 100–140). "Guilty Glory". Zum Verhältnis von ästhetischer Autonomie und biographischer Krise am Beispiel der 'Ode to Napoleon Buonaparte' op. 41 (1941) von Arnold Schönberg (Ferdinand Zehentreiter, 141–168). 'Ciaccona dei Tempi di Guerra' von Erich Itor Kahn (Juan Allende-Blin, 169–188). "Aus der Heimat hinter den Blitzen rot …". Hanns Eislers 'Dritte Sonate für Klavier' (Thomas Phleps, 189–231). "Battles, hopes, difficulties" – new battles new hopes no difficulties (Stefan Wolpes 'Battle Piece' (Thomas Schäfer, 232–266). Quellenkritische Anmerkungen zum Autograph der Oper 'Der Kaiser von Atlantis' von Viktor Ullmann (Ingo Schulz, 267–289). "Das Gegenteil von Pastorale". Anmerkungen zu Kurt Weills '2. Sinfonie' (Christian Kuhnt, 315–332).]

39232. FRANKFURT SCHOOL. DEMIROVIC, ALEX: *Das Institut für Sozialforschung. Ein Ort kritischer Gesellschaftstheorie.* [In]: Forschung Frankfurt. Wissenschaftsmagazin der Johann Wolfgang Goethe-Universität Frankfurt am Main, Jg. 18, H. 3: Sonderband zur Geschichte der Universität, Frankfurt am Main, 2000. Pp. 184–199, bibl., ports., illus.

39233. GOLLAND, LOUISE/SIGMUND, KARL: *Exact thought in a demented time: Karl Menger and his Viennese Mathematical Colloquium.* [In]: The Mathematical Intelligencer, Vol. 22, No. 1, New York, 2000. Pp. 34–45, illus., bibl. [Incl. numerous Jewish mathematicians.]

39234. GRAB, WALTER: *Zwei Seiten einer Medaille. Demokratische Revolution und Judenemanzipation.* Köln: Papyrossa, 2000. 382 pp., notes. [Cont.: 20 essays (previously publ.), some of which deal with Stephan Born, Theodor Lessing, Heinrich Heine, Johann Jacoby, Joseph Bloch, Kurt Tucholsky, Egon Erwin Kisch, Arnold Zweig; also one dealing with Jews in Vienna.] [Cf.: Obituaries Walter Grab (B.E.) [in]: Die Zeit, Nr. 1, Hamburg, 28. Dez. 2000, p. 52. Forschend nach Demokratie (Silvia Schlenstedt) [in]: Jüdische Korrespondenz, Jg. 11, Nr. 2, Berlin, Feb. 2001, p. 4.] [W.G., Feb. 17, 1919 Vienna – Dec. 17, 2000, Tel Aviv, prof. of history, emigr. 1939 to Palestine.]

39235. HAHN, HANS HENNING/STÜBEN, JENS, eds.: *Jüdische Autoren Ostmitteleuropas im 20. Jahrhundert.* Frankfurt am Main; New York: Lang, 2000. 546 pp., footnotes, indexes. (Mitteleuropa – Osteuropa, Bd. 1.) [Based on lectures given at Oldenburg Univ. 1997/1998. Selected essays (some titles abbr.) dealing with German-speaking authors: Oberschlesien und die Provinz Posen im Werk von Ulla Frankfurter-Wolff und Isaak Herzberg (Gabriele von Glasenapp, 19–60). Der "oberschlesische Orpheus". Aspekte des Werkes von Arthur Silbergleit (Detlef Haberland, 61–76). Der schlesische Maler und Dichter Ludwig Meidner (Idis B. Hartmann, 77–113). Arnold Zweig und das Ostjudentum (Karol Sauerland, 114–126). Das jüdische literarische Milieu in Prag (Wilma A. Iggers, 127–138). Religions- und Erziehungskritik in Efraim Frischs "Verlöbnis. Geschichte eines Knaben" (Andreas Herzog, 235–252). Joseph Roths Erzählung "Die Büste des Kaisers" (Burkhard Bittrich, 277–290). Zwei galizisch-jüdische Schicksale in Wien. Die Autobiographien von Manès Sperber "All das vergangene" und Minna Lachs "Warum schaust du zurück" (Maria Klanska, 291–312). Salcia Landmanns jüdische Identität im Spiegel ihrer galizischen "Erinnerungen" (Krzysztof Lipinski, 313–334). Elias Canetti – das Selbstbewußtsein eines Außenseiters (Johannes G. Pankau, 335–358). Paul Celans Weg vom "schönen Gedicht" zur "graueren Sprache". Die windschiefe Rezeption der "Todesfuge" und ihre Folgen (Wolfgang Emmerich, 359–384). Die literarische und dokumentar- literarische Reflexion des transnistrischen Holocaust (Klaus Werner, 385–428). Israelische Autorinnen und Autoren ostdeutscher und altösterreichischer Herkunft (Jens Stüben, 483–520). Also an essay about present-day Germany's nostalgic enthusiasm about the "Shtetl" (Michael Daxner, 161–172).]

—— HARTEWIG, KARIN: *Zurückgekehrt: die Geschichte der jüdischen Kommunisten in der DDR.* [See No. 39031.]

39236. *Jüdische Traditionen in der Philosophie des 20. Jahrhunderts.* Hrsg. von Joachim Valentin und Saskia Wendel. Darmstadt: Wiss. Buchgesellschaft, 2000. VI, 298 pp., notes. [A collection of 17 essays dealing with Jewish philosophers and sociologists, among them Franz Rosenzweig, Walter Benjamin, Max Horkheimer, Gershom Scholem, Leo Strauss, Theodor W. Adorno, Hans Jonas.]

39237. KEßLER, MARIO: *Exilanten und Remigranten.* Zwei Studien. Berlin: "Helle Panke" zur Förderung von Politik, Bildung und Kultur e.V., [1999]. 55 pp., footnotes. (Vielfalt sozialistischen Denkens, Ausgabe

6.) [Cont.: Albert Einsteins politisches Denken (7–30). Sozialisten jüdischer Herkunft zwischen Ost und West: Ernst Bloch, Hans Mayer, Alfred Kantorowicz, Leo Kofler, Josef Winternitz (31–55).]

39238. KREFT, GERALD: *Ornament und Programm: Zur Ästhetik der Goethe-Zitation bei jüdischen Neurowissenschaftlern in Frankfurt am Main.* [In]: Durchgeistete Natur: ihre Präsenz in Goethes Dichtung, Wissenschaft und Philosophie. Hrsg. von Alfred Schmidt und Klaus-Jürgen Grün. Frankfurt am Main; New York: Lang, 2000. Pp. 144–157, notes (302–306). [Deals mainly with Ludwig Edinger, Kurt Goldstein, M.M. Stern.]

39239. *Liebe Macht Kunst. Künstlerpaare im 20. Jahrhundert.* Hrsg. von Renate Berger. Köln: Böhlau, 2000. XII, 455 pp., notes. [Incl.: "… wird es mir eine Freude sein, Ihnen Ihren Weg zu zeigen". Irma Stern und Max Pechstein (Irene Below, 37–64). Doppelspiele – Über die fotografische Zusammenarbeit von Ringl + Pit alias Grete Stern und Ellen Auerbach (Katharina Sykora, 87–108).] [I.St., 1894 South Africa – 1966 Cape Town, daughter of German-Jewish immigrants, artist, lived in South Africa and Germany.] [G.St., 1904–1999, graphic artist, photographer, after 1933 emigr. to the UK, later went to Argentina.] [E.A., née Rosenbach, b. 1906, after 1933 emigr. via Palestine and the UK to the US; lives in New York.]

39240. RUBINSTEIN, W.D.: *Jews in the economic elites of western nations and antisemitism.* [In]: Jewish Journal of Sociology, Vol. 62, Nos. 1–2, London, 2000. Pp. 5– 35, tabs., notes. [Incl. German Jews and their economic contribution, families such as Bleichröder, Mendelssohn, Mosse, Rothschild.]

39241. SCHÜTZ, HANS J.: *"Euro Sprache ist auch meine": eine deutsch-jüdische Literaturgeschichte.* Zürich: Pendo, 2000. 494 pp., illus., bibl.

———— SCHWARZ, EGON: *"Ich bin kein Freund allgemeiner Urteile über ganze Völker".* Essays über österreichische, deutsche und jüdische Literatur. [See No. 39481.]

39242. *Sozialpolitik und Judentum.* Hrsg. von Albrecht Scholz und Caris-Petra Heidel. Dresden: Union Druckerei Dresden, 2000. 144 pp., illus., facsims., notes. (Medizin und Judentum.) [Incl. (some titles abbr.): Einführung (Werner F. Kümmel, 5–10). Sozio-politische Bestrebungen zur Hygiene der Juden im 18. Jahrhundert (Samuel S. Kottek, 11–21). Die Modernisierung der jüdischen Krankheitsvorsorge im 19. Jahrhundert am Beispiel Dresdens (Eberhard Wolff, 22–29). Sozialpolitisches Engagement bei jüdischen Neurowissenschaftlern in Frankfurt am Main (Gerald Kreft, 30–42; on Ludwig Edinger and Kurt Goldstein). Jüdische Ärzte in der Gesundheitsfürsorge in Berlin in den ersten Jahrzehnten des 20. Jahrhunderts (Manfred Stürzbecher, 43–53). Der Einsatz jüdischer Ärzte für die Klärung und Anerkennung von Arbeitsdermatosen (Albrecht Scholz, 54–64). Jüdische Frauenärzte und ihre sozialgynäkologischen Bestrebungen (Peter Schneck, 65–75; on Max Hirsch, Wilhelm Liepmann and Ludwig Fraenkel). Über den Anteil jüdischer Kinderärzte an der Entwicklung der Sozialen Pädiatrie (Eduard Seidler, 76–84; focuses on Eugen Neter und Else Liefmann). Der Berliner jüdische Kinderarzt Hugo Neumann (1858–1912) (Gerrit Kirchner, 85–91). Antisemitische Tendenzen in der ärztlichen Standespolitik der Weimarer Zeit? Das Deutsche Ärzteblatt und die jüdischen Mediziner 1918–1933 (Beate Waigand, 92–102). Das sozialpolitische Engagement der Familie Nelki (Wolfgang Kirchhoff, 103–111). Julius Tandler und das "Rote Wien" (Klaus Hödl, 112–120). Der Sozialhygieniker Alfons Fischer (1873–1936) und der Nationalsozialismus: Von der Anpassung zur Selbstaufgabe? (Klaus-Dieter Thomann, 121–134). Ärzte in Zwangslagen: Dr. Maximilian Samuel (1880–1943) (Daniel Nadav, 135–139; on a doctor deported from Cologne to Auschwitz). Also one contrib. on Henryk Makower and his wife and the Warsaw Ghetto. All contribs. with Engl. summaries.]

39243. STEINBACH, PETER: *Remigranten im deutschen Rundfunk.* [In]: Tribüne, Jg. 39, H. 155, Frankfurt am Main, 2000. Pp. 157–168.

39244. STIRN, AGLAJA: *Überleben und Auseinandersetzung mit dem Holocaust-Trauma in einer Auswahl literarischer Zeugnisse jüdischer Schriftsteller.* [In]: Kölner Zeitschrift für Soziologie und Sozialpsychologie, Jg. 52, H. 4, Köln, 2000. Pp. 720–760, footnotes. [Incl. also German-speaking authors.]

B. Individual

39245. ADLER, OSWALD. BERGEL, HANS: *Ein Südosteuropäer in der Landschaft Israels: der Maler und Graphiker Oswald Adler.* [In]: Südostdeutsche Vierteljahresblätter, Jg. 49, H. 1, München, 2000. Pp. 51–56, illus. [O.A., painter, b. 1912 in Békéscsaba in Austria-Hungary, emigr. 1960 from Romania to Israel.]

39246. ADORNO, THEODOR W. & HORKHEIMER, THEODOR. SEYMOUR, DAVID: *Adorno and Horkheimer: enlightenment and antisemitism.* [In]: Journal of Jewish Studies, Vol. 51, No. 2, Cambridge, Autumn 2000. Pp. 297–312, footnotes.

39247. AGNON, SHMUEL JOSEF. OZ, AMOS: *The silence of heaven: Agnon's fear of God.* Transl. from Hebrew by Barbara Harshav. Princeton, NJ.: Princeton Univ. Press 2000. X, 197 pp.

39248. ALONI, JENNY. STEINECKE, HARTMUT, ed.: *"Warum immer Vergangenheit?" Leben und Werk Jenny Alonis (1917–1993).* Münster: Ardey, 1999. 99 pp., illus., facsims. [J.A., née Rosenbaum, Sept. 7, 1917 Paderborn – Sept. 30, 1993, Ganei Yehuda, writer.]

39249. AMERY, JEAN. WOLF, SIEGBERT: *Jean Améry und die 'Tribüne'.* [In]: Tribüne, Jg. 39, H. 153, Frankfurt am Main, 2000. Pp. 162–179. [Incl. articles of J.A., publ. originally from the 1950s until the 1970s.]

39250. APPELFELD, AHARON. SUCHOFF, D.: *Kafka and the postmodern divide: Hebrew and German in A. Appelfeld's "The age of wonders".* [In]: The Germanic Review, Vol. 75, No. 1, Washington, DC, Spring 2000. Pp. 149–167.

39251. ARENDT, HANNAH. *Hannah Arendt revisited: "Eichmann in Jerusalem" und die Folgen.* Hrsg. von Gary Smith. Frankfurt am Main: Suhrkamp, 2000. 312 pp., notes. (Edition Suhrkamp, 2135.) Erstausgabe. [Cont.: Einsicht aus falscher Distanz (ed., 7–13). I. Anatomie einer Kontroverse: Rezeptionen des Eichmann-Buches (17–94; with contribs. by Amos Elon, Anson G. Rabinbach, Anthony Grafton, Stéphane Mosès). II. Geschichtsschreibung und der Eichmann-Prozeß (95–162; with contribs. by Seyla Benhabib, Dan Diner, Annette Wieviorka). III. Verstrickung und Verantwortung (163–230; with contribs. by Norbert Frei, Gabriel Motzkin, Avishai Margalit). IV. Moderne, Holocaust und die Paradigmen der Geschichtsschreibung (231–310; with contribs. by Dana R. Villa, Moishe Postone, Richard J. Bernstein).]

39252. ARENDT, HANNAH. STEINBERG, JULES: *Hannah Arendt on the Holocaust: a study of the suppression of the truth.* Lewiston, NY: Mellen, 2000. II, 290 pp., notes, bibl., index. (Symposium series, 62.)

39253. ARENDT, HANNAH. VILLA, DANA RICHARD: *Politics, philosophy, terror: essays on the thought of Hannah Arendt.* Princeton, NJ: Princeton University Press, 1999. X, 266 pp., notes.

39254. ARENDT, HANNAH. VILLA, DANA, ed.: *The Cambridge companion to Hannah Arendt.* Cambridge; New York: Cambridge Univ. Press, 2000. XVI, 304 pp.

39255. ARENDT, HANNAH. VOWINCKEL, ANNETTE: *Hannah Arendt und Jean-Paul Sartre: Zweierlei Interpretation des Antisemitismus.* [In]: Jahrbuch für Antisemitismusforschung 9, Frankfurt am Main; New York, 2000. Pp. 148–163, notes.

39256. ARENDT, HANNAH. WENZEL, RAINER: *Ein unabgeschlossener Prozess. Hannah Arendts "Eichmann in Jerusalem" in hebräischer Übersetzung.* [In]: Kalonymos, Beiträge zur deutsch-jüdischen Geschichte aus dem Steinheim-Institut, Jg. 3, H. 4, Duisburg, 2000. Pp. 11–17.

39257. ASCHER, SAUL. SCHULTE, CHRISTOPH: *Saul Ascher's 'Leviathan', or the invention of Jewish orthodoxy in 1792.* [In]: Leo Baeck Institute Year Book XLV, Oxford, 2000. Pp. 25–34, footnotes. [S.A., 1767 Berlin – 1822 Berlin, political journalist, early protagonist of the reform movement and pluralisation of Judaism.]

39258. AUERBACH, BERTHOLD. RADCZEWSKI-HELBIG, JUTTA: *Berthold Auerbach – Erfolgsautor der Dorfgeschichte.* [In]: Philippoff, Eva, ed.: La littérature populaire dans les pays germanique. Colloque franco-Autrichien des 12–13 décembre 1997 organisé par le Centre de recherches sur les pays de langues germaniques au XXe siècle avec le concours de l'institut autrichien de Paris. Villeneuve d'Asque (Nord): Université Lille 3, 1999. Pp. 105–114.

39259. BECKER, JUREK. ROCK, DAVID: *A Jew who became a German?* Oxford: Berg, 2000. XI, 186 pp., frontis., notes, bibl. (161–181). [J.B., Lodz 1937 – Berlin 1997, author, for data see No. 33305/YB XLI; book discusses both the person and his works.]

39260. BENJAMIN, DORA. SCHÖCK-QUINTEROS, EVA: *Dora Benjamin: "... denn ich hoffe, nach dem Krieg in Amerika arbeiten zu können." Stationen einer vertriebenen Wissenschaftlerin (1901–1946).* [In]: Barrieren und Karrieren. Die Anfänge des Frauenstudiums in Deutschland. Dokumentationsband der Konferenz "100 Jahre Frauen in der Wissenschaft" im Februar 1997 an der Universität Bremen. Hrsg. von Elisabeth Dickmann und Eva Schöck-Quinteros unter Mitarbeit von Sigrid Dauks, Berlin: Trafo-Verlag, 2000. Pp. 71–101. [D.B., economist, May 4, 1901 Berlin – Dec. 1942, Zurich; emigr. 1933 to France, escaped in Dec. 1942 to Switzerland.] [Incl. bibl. D.B.]

39261. BENJAMIN, WALTER. PHELAN, ANTHONY: *July days in Skovsbostrand: Brecht, Benjamin and antiquity.* [In]: German Life and Letters, Vol. 53, No. 3, Oxford, July 2000. Pp. 373–386. [On the Brecht/Benjamin meetings in 1938 when Brecht invited Benjamin to join him in Denmark.]

39262. BENJAMIN, WALTER. RICHTER, GERHARD: *Walter Benjamin and the corpus of autobiography.* Detroit: Wayne State Univ., 2000. 309 pp., illus., notes (247–279), bibl. (281–298), index. (Kritik: German literature theory and cultural studies.)

39263. BERADT, MARTIN. LEHNER, BEATE MARGARETE: *Martin Beradt – Jurist und Dichter in Berlin.* Hrsg. von Wolfgang Barthel. Frankfurt (Oder): Kleist-Gedenk- und Forschungsstätte, 2000. 15 pp., illus. (Frankfurter Buntbücher, 28.)

39264. BERENDSOHN, WALTER A.. *Zweifache Vertreibung: Erinnerungen an Walter A. Berendsohn, Förderer von Nelly Sachs.* In Verbindung mit Jakob Hessing und Helmut Müssener hrsg. von Hermann Zabel. Essen: Klartext, 2000. 268 pp., illus. (Beiträge zur Förderung des christlich-jüdischen Dialogs, Bd. 18.)

39265. BERNSTEIN, EDUARD. LÖWE, TERESA: *Der Politiker Eduard Bernstein. Eine Untersuchung zu seinem politischen Wirken in der Frühphase der Weimarer Republik (1918–1924).* Bonn-Bad Godesberg: Historisches Forschungszentrum, 2000. 157 pp. (Reihe Gesprächskreis Geschichte, H. 40.)

39266. CANETTI, ELIAS. ESFORMES, MARIA: *The sephardic voice of Elias Canetti.* [In]: European Judaism, Vol. 33, No. 1, London, Spring 2000. Pp. 109–117, illus., notes, bibl.

39267. CASSIRER, ERNST. MEYER, THOMAS: *Ernst Cassirer – Judentum aus dem Geist der universalistischen Vernunft.* [In]: Aschkenas, Jg. 10, H. 2, Wien, 2000. Pp. 459–502, footnotes.

39268. CELAN, PAUL. CELAN, PAUL: *Todesfuge.* Mit einem Kommentar von Theo Buck. Aachen: Rimbaud, 1999. 71 pp., illus., notes, chronol. (Texte aus der Bukowina, Bd. 7.) [Deals with Czernowitz and the poet's life, incl. chap. on a poem by Immanuel Weißglas, also a collection of different interpretations of 'Todesfuge'.]

39269. CELAN, PAUL. FRIEDLANDER, ALBERT H.: *In memoriam: Paul Celan, thirty years later.* [In]: European Judaism, Vol. 33, No. 1, London, Spring 2000. Pp. 149–153.

39270. CELAN, PAUL. *Gisèle Celan-Lestrange und Paul Celan.* Hrsg.: Stiftung Museum Schloss Moyland, Sammlung van der Grinten, Joseph Beuys Archiv des Landes Nordrhein-Westfalen. [Bedburg-Hau: Museum Schloss Moyland, 2000]. 74 pp., illus. [Exhibition catalogue.]

39271. CELAN, PAUL. MANGER, KLAUS: *Zeitenwende in der Lyrik Paul Celans.* [In]: Die politische Meinung, Nr. 362, Osnabrück, Jan. 2000. Pp. 77–82.

39272. CELAN, PAUL. *Paul Celan – Die Goll-Affäre. Dokumente zu einer 'Infamie'*. Zusammengestellt, hrsg. und kommentiert von Barbara Wiedemann. Frankfurt am Main: Suhrkamp, 2000. 925 pp., illus., footnotes, bibl., indexes. [Incl.: "Es ist eine lange, unglaubliche, bitter-wahre Geschichte". Claire Golls Angriffe auf Paul Celan: Gründe und Folgen (ed., 820–862). Book deals with accusations of plagiarism by Yvan Goll's widow Claire.]

39273. CELAN, PAUL. *Paul Celan. Biographie und Interpretation.* [Beiträge des am 11.-12. Oktober 1999 im Pariser Maison Heinrich Heine veranstalteten Colloquiums "Paul Celan – Biographie und Interpretation"]. Hrsg. von Andrei Corbea-Hoisie. Konstanz: Hartung-Gorre [et al.], 2000. 240 pp. (Colectia Ex libris mundi). [Cont. German and French contribs.]

39274. CELAN, PAUL. PÖGGELER, OTTO: *Der Stein hinterm Auge.* Studien zu Celans Gedichten. München: Fink, 2000. 195 pp., footnotes, index. [Analyses C.'s poetry in the context of his biography.]

39275. CELAN, PAUL & SACHS, NELLY. PETERSEN, JOAN: *"Some gold across the water": Paul Celan and Nelly Sachs.* [In]: Holocaust and Genocide Studies, Vol. 14, No. 2, Oxford, Fall 2000. Pp. 197–214, notes. [Poems about the Holocaust, also deals with the relationship of Celan with Sachs.]

39276. COHN, JONAS. HEITMANN, MARGRET: *Jonas Cohn: Jüdisches Denken als unendliche Aufgabe.* [In]: Menora, Bd. 11, Berlin, 2000. Pp. 299–312, notes. [J.C., Dec. 2, 1869 Görlitz – Jan. 12, 1947 Birmingham, philosopher, for further data see No. 38084/YB XLV.]

39277. DEINHARD, HANNA. BELOW, IRENE: *Unbekannte Kunsthistorikerinnen – Hanna Deinhard wiedergelesen.* [In]: Frauen Kunst Wissenschaft, H. 16, Marburg, 1999. Pp. 6–21, bibl. [H.D., née Levy, 1912 Osnabrück – 1984 Basle, art historian, emigr. 1934 to Paris, 1936 to Brazil, 1948 to the US; returned to Europe in 1973.]

39278. DÖBLIN, ALFRED. *Alfred Döblin. Im Buch. Zu Haus. Auf der Straße.* Vorgestellt von Alfred Döblin und Oskar Loerke. Mit einer Nachbemerkung von Jochen Meyer. Marbach: Deutsche Schillergesellschaft, 1998. 211 pp., frontis., ports. (Marbacher Bibliothek, 2.) [Incl.: Erster Rückblick (Alfred Döblin, 5–126). Das bisherige Werk Alfred Döblins (Oskar Loerke, 129–200). Nach siebzig Jahren (Jochen meyer, 201–211, footnotes).]

39279. DÖBLIN, ALFRED. *Der literarische Nachlaß von Alfred Döblin.* Schiller-Nationalmuseum – Deutsches Literaturarchiv, Marbach am Neckar [et al.]. Berlin: Kulturstiftung der Länder. 2000. 48 pp., illus. (Patrimonia, 148.)

39280. EDINGER, TILLY. KREFT, GERALD/KOHRING, ROLF: *"Ich bin also sozusagen ein auserwähltes Wesen …" Tilly Edinger (1897–1967), Begründerin der Paläoneurologie in Frankfurt am Main.* [In]: Forschung Frankfurt. Wissenschaftsmagazin der Johann Wolfgang Goethe-Universität Frankfurt am Main, Jg. 18, H. 3: Sonderband zur Geschichte der Universität, Frankfurt am Main, 2000. Pp. 158–165, ports., illus. [T.E., data see No. 34774/YB XLIII.]

39281. EHRENSTEIN, ALBERT. SCHUHMANN, KLAUS: *Albert Ehrenstein. Dichter und Lektor.* [In]: Aus dem Antiquariat [Beilage zum] Börsenblatt für den Deutschen Buchhandel, Jg. 167, Nr. 43, Frankfurt am Main, 30. Mai 2000. Pp. A 303–A 306, illus. [A.E., Dec. 23, 1886 Vienna – April 8, 1950 New York, writer, poet, brother of Carl E., worked for Kurt Wolff Verlag in Berlin, lived since 1932 in Switzerland, emigr. 1941 to the US.]

—— EINSTEIN, ALBERT. DEGEN, PETER A.: *Albert Einstein. Ein deutsch-jüdischer Physiker zwischen Assimilation und Zionismus.* [See No. 39462.]

39282. EINSTEIN, ALBERT. *The expanded quotable Einstein.* Collected and ed. by Alice Calaprice. With a foreword by Freeman Dyson. Princeton, NJ: Princeton Univ. Press, 2000. XLIII, 407 pp., illus. [Orig. publ. in 1996, this edn. contains about 375 new quotations by Einstein on many topics.]

39283. EISLER, HANNS. FISCHBACH, FRED: *Hanns Eisler: le musicien et la politique.* Franck Fischbach (ed.). Bern; New York: Lang, 1999. XII, 433 pp., footnotes, index, bibl. (Contacts, Sér. 3, Études et documents, Vol. 47.) [A collection of articles.]

39284. ENOCH, KURT. JAEGER, ROLAND: *Kurt Enoch (1895–1982) und der Gebrüder Enoch Verlag (1913–36).* [In]: Aus dem Antiquariat [Beilage zum] Börsenblatt für den Deutschen Buchhandel, Jg. 167, Nr. 43, Frankfurt am Main, 30. Mai 2000, Pp. A 288– A 300, illus., facsims., notes. [Deals with a publishing house in Hamburg; incl. list of its 147 publications 1913–1936.]

39285. FRANKL, VIKTOR. PYTELL, T.: *The missing pieces of the puzzle: a reflection on the odd career of Viktor Frankl.* [In]: Journal of Contemporary History, Vol. 35, No. 2, Beverly Hill, CA, 2000. Pp. 281–366, notes. [V.F., March 26, 1905 Vienna – Sept, 2, 1997, Vienna, psychotherapist, psychiatrist, author, survivor of Auschwitz.]

39286. FREUD, SIGMUND. BREGER, LOUIS: *Freud: darkness in the midst of vision.* New York; London: John Wiley, 2000. VIII, 472 pp., illus., notes, index.

39287. FREUD, SIGMUND. CHAMBERLAIN, LESLEY: *The secret artist: a close reading of Sigmund Freud.* London: Quartet, 2000. 322 pp., notes, bibl., index.

39288. FREUD, SIGMUND. TICHY, MARINA/ZWETTLER-OTTE, SYLVIA: *Freud in der Presse: Rezeption Sigmund Freud und der Psychoanalyse in Österreich 1895–1938. Mit einem Vorwort von Harald Leupold-Löwenthal.* Wien: Sonderzahl, 1999. 406 pp., bibl.

39289. FRIED, ERICH. PAPE, WALTER: *Papierkorb und Grammophon: Zur politischen Lyrik Erich Frieds und Wolf Biermanns.* [In]: German Life and Letters, Vol. 53, No. 3, Oxford, July 2000. Pp. 351–372, footnotes.

39290. GAY, PETER. BRACHER, KARL DIETER: *Deutsch-jüdische Erinnerung. Laudatio auf Peter Gay zur Verleihung des Geschwister-Scholl-Preises.* [In]: Die politische Meinung, Nr. 364, Osnabrück, März 2000. Pp. 7–14. [Held at Munich Univ. Nov. 22, 1999.]

39291. GERSON, HANS & OSKAR. *Hans und Oskar Gerson. Hanseatische Moderne.* Bauten in Hamburg und im kalifornischen Exil. Mit Beiträgen von Hartmut Frank und Ulrich Höhns. Hamburg: Dölling und Galitz, 2000. 128 pp., illus., notes. (Schriftenreihe des Hamburgischen Architekturarchivs.) [H.G., March 19, 1881 Magdeburg – Oct. 14, 1931 Hamburg; O.G. (later Oscar G.), July 11, 1886 Magdeburg – Dec. 25, 1966 Berkeley, CA, architects, lived in Hamburg since 1887. O.G. emigr. 1939 to the US.]

39292. GOLDBERG, OSKAR. GOETSCHEL, ROLAND: *Oscar Goldberg, "kabbaliste" berlinois.* [In]: les cahiers du judaisme, No. 1, Paris, 2000. Pp. 105–119, side notes. [O.G., data see No. 31025/YB XXXIX.]

39293. GOLDSCHMIDT, BERTHOLD. BUSCH, BARBARA: *Berthold Goldschmidts Opern im Kontext von Musik- und Zeitgeschichte.* Oldenburg: Bibliotheks- und Informationssystem der Universität Oldenburg, 2000. 498pp., frontis., facsims., music. [B.G., Jan. 18, 1903 Hamburg – Oct. 17, 1996 London, composer, emigr. 1935 to the UK.]

39294. GOLDSTEIN, EUGEN. HEDENUS, MICHAEL: *Eugen Goldstein und die Kathodenstrahlen. Mit Astrophysik im Labor wurde der Entdecker der "Kanalstrahlen" berühmt.* [In]: Physikalische Blätter, Jg. 56, Nr. 9. Weinheim, 2000. Pp. 71–73, notes, illus. [E.G., 1850 Gleiwitz – 1930 Berlin, physicist.]

39295. GOLDSTEIN, KURT. KREFT, GERALD: *"... weil man es in Deutschland einfach verschwiegen hat ...". Kurt Goldstein (1878–1965), Begründer der Neuropsychologie in Frankfurt am Main.* [In]: Forschung Frankfurt. Wissenschaftsmagazin der Johann Wolfgang Goethe-Universität Frankfurt am Main, Jg. 18, H. 3: Sonderband zur Geschichte der Universität, Frankfurt am Main, 2000. Pp. 166–177, illus., facsims., bibl. [K.G., data see No. 36834/YB XLIV.]

39296. GORAL-STERNHEIM, ARIE. DÖRR, THOMAS: *Von ferne ins Vergangene.* Topologien der Erinnerung bei Arie Goral. [In]: Mittelweg 36, H. 1, Hamburg, 2000. Pp. 29–48. [Incl. also autobiographical texts by A. G.-St.]

39297. GRAB, WALTER: *Zwei Seiten einer Medaille: Demokratische Revolution und Judenemanzipation.* Köln: Papyrossa, 2000. 382 pp., notes (349–379). [Cont. 19 articles previously publ. between 1974 and 1998.]

39298. GROSSMANN, HENRYK. SCHEELE, JÜRGEN: *Zwischen Zusammenbruchsprognose und Positivismusverdikt*. Studien zur politischen und intellektuellen Biographie Henryk Grossmanns (1881–1950). Frankfurt am Main; New York: Lang, 1999. 292 pp., footnotes, bibl. (267–292). (Europ. Hochschulschriften, Reihe XXXI: Politikwissenschaften, Bd. 398.) Zugl.: Marburg, Univ., Diss., 1997.) [H.G., April 14, 1881 Cracow – Nov. 24, 1950 Leipzig, prof. of economy, left Poland 1925, worked 1925–1933 in the Inst. für Sozialforschung (Frankfurt am Main), fled 1933 to France, emigr. 1936 to the UK, 1937 to the US, returned 1949 to Leipzig, GDR.]

39299. HABER, FRITZ. HAHN, RALF: *Gold aus dem Meer*. Die Forschungen des Nobelpreisträgers Fritz Haber aus den Jahren 1922–1927. Berlin: GNT-Verlag, 1999. 101 pp., frontis., illus., footnotes, bibl., index. [Incl.: Geleitwort (Lutz Haber, 7).]

39300. HECHT, OTTO. HERING, RAINER: *Nazi persecution and the pursuit of science: correspondence between Erich Martini and Otto Hecht, 1946–47*. [In]: Jewish Culture and History, Vol. 3, No. 1, London, Summer 2000. Pp. 95–124, footnotes. [For German version of article and details see No. 36840/YB XLIV.]

39301. HEINE, HEINRICH. BAUER, ALFREDO: *Die Stellung der Juden in der ersten Hälfte des XIX. Jahrhunderts und Heines Übertritt zum Judentum*. [In]: Heine-Jahrbuch 2000, Stuttgart, 2000. Pp. 184–191, notes.

39302. HEINE, HEINRICH. BETZ, ALBRECHT: *Wie Heinrich Heine die Massen entdeckte*. [In]: Die Neue Gesellschaft/Frankfurter Hefte, Jg. 47, H. 5, Frankfurt am Main, 2000. Pp. 163–166.

39303. HEINE, HEINRICH. HORST, CHRISTOPH AUF DER: *Heinrich Heine und die Geschichte Frankreichs*. Stuttgart: Metzler, 2000. XII, 434 pp., footnotes, bibl., indexes. (Heine-Studien.)

39304. HEINE, HEINRICH. PETERS, GEORGE F.: *The poet as provocateur: Heinrich Heine and his critics*. Rochester, NY: Camden House, 2000. XII, 227 pp., works cited (190– 192), bibl. (193–216), index of Heine's works. (Studies in German literature, linguistics, and culture.) [Discusses the critical reception of Heine from his own time to the present post-unification period, incl. Nazi antisemitism.]

39305. HEINE, HEINRICH. SCHLINK, BERNHARD: *"Schlage die Trommel und fürchte dich nicht!"* Rede zur Verleihung der Ehrengabe der Heinrich-Heine-Gesellschaft 2000. [In]: Heine-Jahrbuch 2000, Stuttgart, 2000. 230–237.

39306. HENSEL, FANNY. MITTAG, SUSANNE: *Vom Salon zum Konzertsaal. Musikerinnen im 19. Jahrhundert: Fanny Hensel und Clara Schumann. Eine Literaturschau*. [In]: Mitteldeutsches Jahrbuch für Kultur und Geschichte, Bd. 7, Köln, 2000. Pp. 115–122. [Review essay.]

39307. HEYM, STEFAN. ATTAR, K. E.: *The archive and the artist: the Stefan Heym archive revisited*. [In]: German Life and Letters, Vol. 53, No. 1, Oxford, Jan. 2000. Pp. 73–88, footnotes.

39308. HEYM, STEFAN. HUTCHINSON, PETER: *Stefan Heym – Dissident auf Lebenszeit*. Aus dem Engl. von Verena Jung. Würzburg: Königshausen und Neumann, 1999. 260 pp., bibl. (239–260). [For orig. edn. see No. 29789/YB XXXVIII.]

39309. HILFERDING, RUDOLF. SMALDONE, WILLIAM: *Rudolf Hilferding. Tragödie eines deutschen Sozialdemokraten*. Aus dem Amerik. von Christel Steinberg. Bonn: Dietz, 2000. 291 pp., footnotes, bibl. 273–286), index. (Reihe Politik und Gesellschaftsgeschichte, Bd. 55.) [For orig. edn. and data see No. 36854/YB XLIV.]

39310. HORKHEIMER, MAX. SCHÖLZEL, ARNOLD: *Kritische Theorie und Faschismus. Reflexionen Max Horkheimers vor 1933*. [In]: Rassismus, Faschismus, Antifaschismus [see No. 38922]. Pp. 137–145, notes.

39311. JACOBSOHN, SIEGFRIED. OSWALT, STEFANIE: *Siegfried Jacobsohn. Ein Leben für die Weltbühne*. Eine Berliner Biographie. Gerlingen: Bleicher, 2000. 293 pp., illus., notes, bibl., index. Zugl.: Potsdam, Univ., Diss., 1998.

39312. JACOBOWSKI, LUDWIG: *Gesammelte Werke in einem Band. Jubiläumsausgabe zum 100. Todestag.* Romane, Erzählungen, Lyrik, Dramatik. Kritische, essayistische und poetologische Schriften. Mit einer umfassenden Bibliographie der Primär- und Sekundärliteratur. Hrsg. und mit einem Nachwort versehen von Alexander Müller und Michael M. Schardt. Oldenburg: Igel, 2000. 1210 pp., bibl. [Incl.: Nachwort: Das Leben Ludwig Jacobowskis (Fred B. Stern, 1115–1159, footnotes.] [L.J., Jan. 21, 1868 Strelno (Posen) – Dec. 2, 1900 Berlin, lyricist, author, publicist.]

39313. JACOBY, EDUARD GEORG. ZANDER, JÜRGEN: *Eduard Georg Jacoby. Auf den Spuren des nach Neuseeland emigrierten Kieler Soziologen.* [In]: Zeitschrift der Gesellschaft für Schleswig-Holsteinische Geschichte, Bd. 124, Neumünster, 1999. Pp. 165–169, footnotes. [E.G. (later Peter)J., 1904 Breslau – 1978 Wellington, New Zealand, sociologist, demographer, emigr. 1938 to New Zealand.]

39314. JOACHIM, OTTO. JEAN, STÉPHANE: *The Otto Joachim fonds.* Numerical list. Ottawa: National Library of Canada, Music Division, 1999. 56 pp., illus. [O.J., orig. Joachimsthal, b. Oct. 16, 1910 in Düsseldorf, musician, composer, emigr. 1934 to Singapore, 1939 to Shanghai, 1949 to Canada; lives in Montréal.]

39315. KALISCHER, CLEMENS. *Clemens Kalischer. New York. Photographien 1947–1959.* Aachen: Museen der Stadt Aachen, [2000]. 96 pp., frontis. [Exhibition catalogue; incl. two biographical contribs. by Norbert Bunge and Sylvia Böhmer.] [C.K., b. 1921 in Lindau, photographer, after 1933 emigr. via Switzerland to France, escaped 1942 to the US, lives in Stockbridge, MS.]

39316. KESTEN, HERMANN. *"Ich hatte Glück mit Menschen". Zum 100. Geburtstag des Dichters Hermann Kesten.* Texte von ihm und über ihn. Stadtbibliothek Nürnberg. Hrsg. von Wolfgang Buhl und Ulf von Dewitz. [Nürnberg]: [Edelmann], 2000. 191 pp., illus. (Beiträge zur Geschichte und Kultur der Stadt Nürnberg, Bd. 24.)

39317. KLEMPERER, VICTOR. JACOBS, PETER: *Victor Klemperer. Im Kern ein deutsches Gewächs.* Eine Biographie. Berlin: Aufbau Taschenbuch Verlag, 2000. 381 pp., illus.

39318. KLÜGER, RUTH. DETERING, HEINRICH: *Tauziehen. Laudatio zur Verleihung des Thomas-Mann-Preises 1999 an Ruth Klüger.* [In]: Thomas Mann Jahrbuch, Bd. 13, Frankfurt am Main, 2000. Pp. 219–227.

39319. KOFLER, LEO. *Zur Kritik bürgerlicher Freiheit.: Ausgewählte politisch-philosophische Texte eines marxistischen Einzelgängers.* [Hrsg.: Christoph Jünke]. Hamburg: VSA-Verlag, 2000. 240 pp., footnotes, bibl. L.K. [Incl.: Freiheit wozu? Zur Einführung in Leben und Werk von Leo Kofler (1907–1995) (ed., 7–29).]

39320. KRACAUER, SIEGFRIED. KOCH, GERTRUD: *Siegfried Kracauer: an introduction.* Transl. by Jeremy Gaines. Princeton, NJ: Princeton Univ. Press, 2000. XII, 137 pp., notes (121– 130), (bibl. (131–132), index. [Orig. publ. in 1996.]

39321. KRAMER, THEODOR. *Chronist seiner Zeit. Theodor Kramer.* Hrsg. von Herbert Staud und Jörg Thunecke im Auftrag der Theodor Kramer Gesellschaft. Klagenfurt: Th. Kramer Ges.; Drava Verlag, 2000. 338 pp., notes. [A collection of 17 essays dealing with life and work of Th.K.] [Th.K., Jan. 1, 1897 Hollabrunn – April 3, 1958 Vienna, author, poet, emigr. 1939 to the UK, remigr. 1957 to Austria.]

39322. KRAMER, THEODOR. CHVOJKA, ERWIN/KAISER, KONSTANTIN: *Vielleicht hab ich es leicht, weil schwer, gehabt. Theodor Kramer 1897–1958.* Eine Lebenschronik. Wien: Theodor Kramer Gesellschaft, 1997. 118 pp., ports., illus., facsims., bibl. [Recent edns. of K.s poetry, hitherto party unpubl.: *Die Wahrheit ist, man hat mir nichts getan.* Gedichte. Hrsg. und mit einem Nachwort von Herta Müller. Wien: Zsolnay, 1999. 202 pp. *Der alte Zitherspieler.* Menschenbilder. Hrsg. von Erwin Chvojka. Vorwort von Elke Forisch. Wien: Club Niederösterreich, 1999. 159 pp., illus.] [Th.K., Jan. 1, 1897 Niederhollabrunn – April 3, 1958 Vienna, author, lyricist, emigr. 1939 to the UK, returned 1957 to Vienna.]

39323. KRAUS, KARL. GOLTSCHNIGG, DIETMAR: *Die Fackel ins wunde Herz. Kraus über Heine. Eine Erledigung?* Texte, Analysen, Kommentar. Wien: Passagen-Verl., 2000. 485 pp., notes 8347–448), chronol., bibl., indexes. (Passagen Literaturtheorie.) [Cf.: Besprechung (Joseph A. Kruse) [in]: Heine-Jahrbuch 2000, Stuttgart, 2000, pp. 247–248.]

39324. LANDAU, LOLA. HAMANN, BIRGITTA: *Lola Landau. Leben und Werk*. Ein Beispiel deutsch-jüdischer Literatur des 20. Jahrhunderts in Deutschland und Palästina/Israel. Berlin: Philo, 2000. 338 pp., illus., notes, bibl., index. (Studien zur Geistesgeschichte, Bd. 25.) [Incl. 18 interviews with German-speaking authors in Israel. See also No. 38933] [L.L., Dec. 3, 1892 Berlin – Feb. 3, 1990 Jerusalem, writer, in 1920 married Armin T. Wegner, emigr. 1933 via Sweden to the UK, 1935 to Palestine.]

39325. LANDAUER, GUSTAV. FRANZ, MICHAEL: *Skepsis und Enthusiasmus. Gustav Landauers 'Anschluß' an Fritz Mauthner*. [In]: Fritz Mauthner – Sprache – Literatur, Kritik [see No. 39339]. Pp. 163–174, footnotes.

39326. LANDAUER, ROLF WILLIAM. FOWLER, ALAN [et al.]: *Obituary Rolf William Landauer*. [In]: Physics Today, Vol. 52, Washington, DC, Oct. 1999. Pp. 104–105, port. [R.W.L., Feb. 4, 1927 Stuttgart – April 27, 1999 Briarcliff, NY, pioneer in the physics of information processing (IBM), emigr. 1938 to the US.]

39327. LANG, FRITZ. MINDEN, MICHAEL: *Fritz Lang's 'Metropolis' and the United States*. [In]: German Life and Letters, Vol. 53, No. 3, Oxford, July 2000. Pp. 340–350, illus., footnotes.

39328. LASKER-SCHÜLER, Else. *Else Lasker-Schüler. Schrift : Bild : Schrift*. Hrsg. vom Verein August Macke Haus. e.V. Mit Beiträgen von Margarethe Jochimsen [et al.]. Buch und Ausstellung: Ricarda Dick unter Mitarbeit von Volker Kahmen und Norbert Oellers. Bonn: Stollfuß, [2000]. 249 pp., illus., facsims., notes.

39329. LASKER-SCHÜLER, Else. ENGELMANN, SUSANNA: *"Ich ... mein Vater ... meines ... Vaters ... Vater und dessen Väter Väterväter. Else Lasker-Schülers 'Arthur-Aronymus'-Dichtung*. [In]: Jüdischer Almanach 2001, Frankfurt am Main, 2000. Pp. 127–144, notes. [On the book and play dealing with the family of E.L.-Sch.'s father Aron Schüler from East Westphalia.] [Also in this issue: Etwas von Jerusalem (Else Lasker-Schüler, 145–149; first publ. 1949). Else Lasker-Schülers Zimmer (Nehemia Cymbalist (Zori) (151–152). Hinter dieser Welt. Else Lasker-Schüler zum Gedenken (Lea Goldberg, 153–155; first publ. in Hebrew 1945). Gespräch mit Elsa Lasker-Schüler (Lea Goldberg, 156–159; first publ. in Hebrew 1952).]

39330. LASKER-SCHÜLER, ELSE. *Fäden möchte ich um mich ziehen. Ein Else-Lasker-Schüler-Almanach*. Hrsg. von Hajo Hahn und Hans Joachim Schädlich. Hrsg. von der Else-Lasker-Schüler-Gesellschaft. Wuppertal: Peter Hammer, 2000. 204 pp.

39331. LASSALLE, FERDINAND. *"Auf ehrliche und anständige Gegnerschaft". Ferdinand Lassalle und der F.A.Brockhaus-Verlag in Briefen und Kommentaren*. Hrsg. von Erhard Hexelschneider und Gerhild Schwendler. Wiesbaden: Harrassowitz [in Kommission], 2000. 195 pp.

39332. LASSALLE, FERDINAND. DOWE, DIETER: *Ferdinand Lassalle (1825–1864). Ein Bürger organisiert die Arbeiterbewegung*. Vortrag im Haus des Deutschen Ostens in München anläßlich des 175. Geburtstages von Ferdinand von Lassalle, am 10. April 2000. Bonn: Historisches Forschungszentrum, 2000. 29 pp. (Reihe Gesprächskreis Geschichte. H. 34.)

39333. LASSALLE, FERDINAND. STEIN, BRITTA: *Der Scheidungsprozeß Hatzfeldt (1846–1851)* München: Lit, 1999. XXV, 251 pp., illus. (Ius vivens: Abt. B, Rechtsgeschichtliche Abhandlungen, Bd. 9.) (Zugl.: München (Westfalen), Univ., Diss., 1998.).

39334. LESSING, THEODOR. KOTOWSKI, ELKE-VERA: *Feindliche Dioskuren. Theodor Lessing und Ludwig Klages. Das Scheitern einer Jugendfreundschaft (1885–1899)*. Berlin: Jüdische Verl.-Anst., 2000. 320 pp., illus., bibl. (Sifria, Bd. 3.)

39335. LOEB, JAMES. *James Loeb 1867–1933. Kunstsammler und Mäzen*. Bearb. von Brigitte Salmen. Murnau: Schloßmuseum des Marktes Murnau, 2000. 199 pp., frontis., illus., chronol., notes., bibl. [Catalogue of exhibition held in Murnau April 7 – July 9, 2000; documents L.'s numerous sponsorships of institutes and charitable institutions.] [J.L., data see No. 35625/YB XLIII.]

39336. LÖWENTHAL, LEO. JANSEN, PETER-ERWIN, ed.: *Das Utopische soll Funken schlagen … Zum hundertsten Geburtstag von Leo Löwenthal.* Frankfurt am Main: Vittorio Klostermann, 2000. 200 pp., frontis., facsims., footnotes (Frankfurter Bibliotheksschriften, Bd. 8). [Incl. contribs. on L.L. by Walter Greisner, Peter-Erwin Jansen, Helmut Dubiel, Rachel Heuberger, Udo Göttlich, Richard Wolin, Jochen Stollberg, Alessandra Sorbello Staub; also letters and other texts by L.L., bibl. L.L.] [L.L., Nov. 3, 1900 Frankfurt am Main – Jan. 21, 1993 Berkeley, CA, prof. of sociology, emigr. 1934 to the US.]

39337. LOWE, ADOLPH. DÖNHOFF, MARION GRÄFIN: *"… so wurde ich fast unmerklich zu einem kritischen Weltbürger erzogen." Laudatio für Adolph Lowe.* [In]: Forschung Frankfurt. Wissenschaftsmagazin der Johann Wolfgang Goethe-Universität Frankfurt am Main, Jg. 18, H. 3: Sonderband zur Geschichte der Universität, Frankfurt am Main, 2000, Pp. 144–147, ports., facsim. [Incl. also: Das wissenschaftliche Wirken von Adolph Lowe (Bertram Schefold, 147.] [A.L., orig. Löwe, March 4, 1893 Stuttgart – June 3, 1995 Wolfenbüttel; prof. of economics, 1933 emigr. to UK via Switzerland, 1940 to the US.]

39338. LUXEMBURG, ROSA. SCHMITTHENNER, CHARLOTTE: *Begegnung mit Rosa Luxemburg.* Auf der Spur des Schalom. Berlin: Frieling, 2000. 47 pp., illus. (Frieling Frauenliteratur.)

39339. MAUTHNER, FRITZ. HENNE, HELMUT/KAISER, CHRISTINE, eds.: *Fritz Mauthner – Sprache, Literatur, Kritik.* Festakt und Symposion zu seinem 150. Geburtstag. Tübingen: Niemeyer, 2000. VIII, 185 pp., facsims., footnotes, index. (Reihe Germanistische Linguistik, 224.) [Cont. 6 essays & discussion; also texts by F.M. Selected essays are listed according to subject.] [F.M., Nov. 22, 1849 Horzitz, Bohemia – June 29, 1923 Meersburg, journalist, philosopher, writer.]

39340. MEITNER, LISE. MORGENWECK-LAMBRINOS, VERA/TRÖMEL, MARTIN: *Lise Meitner, Otto Hahn und die Kernspaltung: eine Legende aus unseren Tagen.* [In]: Int. Zeitschrift für Geschichte und Ethik in den Naturwissenschaften, Technik und Medizin (NTM), N.S., Vol. 8, Basel, 2000. Pp. 65–76, notes. [Article alleges that Ruth Lewin Sime's biography of Meitner (see No. 34476/YB XLII) is fictitious and a distortion of the facts about the discovery of nuclear fission. In the same issue is R.L.S.'s reply: Whose legend? Some remarks on Vera-Morgenweck-Lambrinos and Martin Trömel: "Lise Meitner, Otto Hahn und die Kernspaltung: eine Legende aus unseren Tagen" (77–84). The two authors respond to this in 'NTM', Vol. 9, No. 1, 2001, pp. 29–30, notes.]

39341. MENDELSOHN, ERICH: *Gedankenwelten: unbekannte Texte zu Architektur, Kulturgeschichte und Politik.* Hrsg. von Ita Heinze-Greenberg und Regina Stephan. Ostfildern-Ruit: Hatje Cantz, 2000. 199 pp., illus. (Materialien zur Moderne.)

39342. MENDELSSOHN, FELIX. RICHTER, ARND: *Mendelssohn: Leben – Werke.* Zürich: Atlantis-Musikbuch-Verl., 2000. 449 pp., illus, music, discography, bibl. F.M.

39343. MENDELSSOHN, FELIX. SCHMIDT-BESTE, THOMAS: *Felix Mendelssohn Bartholdy und Heinrich Heine.* [In]: Heine-Jahrbuch 2000, Jg. 39, Stuttgart, 2000. Pp. 111–134, notes.

39344. MORGENSTERN, SOMA. WERNER, KLAUS: *Die galizische Vertikale. Soma Morgenstern im Kontext eines spezifischen Kapitels deutsch-jüdischer Literaturgeschichte.* [In]: Berichte und Forschungen, Jahrbuch des Bundesinstituts für ostdeutsche Kultur und Geschichte, Bd. 8, München 2000. Pp. 79–108, footnotes.

39345. MORGENSTERN, SOMA: *Dramen – Feuilletons – Fragmente.* Hrsg. und mit einem Nachwort versehen von Ingolf Schulte. Lüneburg: zu Klampen, 2000. 483 pp., notes. (Werke in Einzelbänden/Soma Morgenstern.)

39346. MOSSE, GEORGE. *George L. Mosse memorial symposium.* [Issue title of] German Politics and Society, Vol. 18, No. 4, Berkeley: Univ. of California, Winter 2000. 1 issue, notes. [Cont.: George

L. Mosse memorial symposium: introd. (Phyllis Cohen Albert and Alex Sagan, 1–2). Finding oneself in history and vice-versa: remarks on "George's voice" (Paul Breines, 3–17. Mosse's recasting of European intellectual and cultural history (Jeffrey Herf, 18–29). George Mosse and the culture of antifascism (Anson Rabinbach, 30–45). George Mosse and Jewish history (Steven E. Aschheim, 46–57). Bibl. of George L. Mosse (John Tortorice, 58.) [G.L.M., 1918 Berlin – 1999 Madison, WI., historian, for obits. see No. 39186/YB XLV.]

39347. MÜHSAM, ERICH. *Anarchismus und Psychoanalyse zu Beginn des 20. Jahrhunderts.* Der Kreis um Erich Mühsam und Otto Gross. Elfte Erich-Mühsam-Tagung in Malente, 2.-4. Juni 2000. [Lübeck: Erich-Mühsam-Ges., 2000.] 154 pp., frontis., illus., footnotes. (Schriften der Erich-Mühsam-Gesellschaft, H. 19.) [Incl.: Vorbemerkung (Jürgen-Wolfgang Goette, 5–7). 6 contribs., also excerpts from letters, diaries and other publs. of E.M.]

39349. MÜHSAM, ERICH. *Erich Mühsam und andere im Spannungsfeld von Pazifismus und Militarismus.* Zehnte Erich-Mühsam-Tagung in Malente, 14.-16. Mai 1999. [Lübeck: Erich-Mühsam-Ges., 2000]. 90 pp., illus., footnotes. [Incl.: Vorbemerkung (Jürgen-Wolfgang Goette, 5–6). Selected articles: Erich Mühsam im Ersten Wltkrieg – Pazifist? Patriot? Anarchist? (Kurt Kreiler, 7–18). "Sie töten den Geist nicht" – Kurt Tucholsky und der 1920 ermordete Pazifist Hans Paasche. Eine Collage (Michael Hepp, 19–49).]

39350. NASH, ERNEST. *Ernest Nash – Ernst Nathan: 1898 – 1974.* Photographie Potsdam, Rom, New York, Rom. Hrsg. von Maria R. Alföldi und Margarita C. Lahusen. Berlin: Nicolai, 2000. 239 pp., illus. [E.N., orig. Ernst Nathan, Sept. 14, 1898 Nowawes (Brandenburg) – May 19, 1974 Rome, jurist, art historian, photographer, fled 1935 to Italy, emigr. 1939 to the US, returned 1950 to Italy.]

39351. NEMITZ, KURT: *Die Schatten der Vergangenheit.* Beiträge zur Lage der intellektuellen deutschen Juden in den 20er und 30er Jahren. Oldenburg: BIS, 2000. 156 pp., illus. [A collection of 9 essays and speeches, publ. on the occasion of K.N.'s 75th birthday. On Jewish parliamentarians, Victor Klemperer, Julius Moses, Fritz (Perez) Naphtali, Martin Buber; other essays deal with resistance, antisemitism, Nuremberg laws.]

39352. NEUMARK, FRITZ. HÄUSER, KARL: *Der Remigrant vom Bosporus. Fritz Neumark und sein Einfluß auf die deutsche Finanzwissenschaft.* [In]: Forschung Frankfurt. Wissenschaftsmagazin der Johann Wolfgang Goethe-Universität Frankfurt am Main, Jg. 18, H. 3: Sonderband zur Geschichte der Universität, Frankfurt am Main, 2000. Pp. 138–143, notes, illus. [F.N., July 20, 1900 Hanover – 1991 Baden-Baden, political economist, prof. of finance, emigr. 1933 to Turkey, remigr. 1952 to Germany.]

39353. OFFENBACH, JACQUES. YON, JEAN-CLAUDE: *Jacques Offenbach.* Paris: Gallimard, 2000. 796 pp., illus., scores.

39354. ORLIK, EMIL. KUWABARA, SETSUKO: *Emil Orlik, ein Porträtist des geistigen Berlin.* Berlin: Gebr. Mann, 1998. 94 pp., frontis., bibl. [Incl.: Emil Orlik, ein Porträtist des geistigen Berlin (Setsuko Kuwabara, 7–16). Buch der Freundschaft und Spiegel der Zeit: Orliks Köpfesammlung (Eberhard Friese (17–26).]

39355. PAPANEK, ERNST. HANSEN-SCHABERG, INGE: *Die Wiener Schulreform und ihre pädagogische Umsetzung durch Ernst Papanek in den OSE-Kinderheimen in Frankreich.* [In]: Zwischenwelt [formerly: Mit der Ziehharmonika], Jg. 17, Nr. 2, Wien, Juli 2000. Pp. 10–14, illus., notes, bibl. [E.P., 1900 Vienna – 1973 Vienna, educator, Social democrat, emigr. 1938 to France, 1940 to the US.]

39356. PAPPENHEIM, BERTHA. KIMBALL, MEREDITH M.: *From "Anna O" to Bertha Pappenheim: transforming private pain into public action.* [In]: History of Psychology, Vol. 3, No. 1, Washington, DC, 2000. Pp. 20–43, notes.

39357. PAPPENHEIM, BERTHA. KREFT, GERALD: *Anna O. und/oder Bertha Pappenheim ...* Umschreibungen eines Desiderates anläßlich des nachgelassenen Manuskripts (1959) von Max Stern (1895–1982). [In]: Den Menschen zugewandt leben. Festschrift für Werner Licharz [see No. 39462.]. Pp. 205–237, footnotes, bibl. (228–237). [Article is preceded by Max M. Stern's essay on Bertha Pappenheimer (193–204), edited by Gerald Kreft.]

39358. PAULI, WOLFGANG ERNST. JACOBI, MANFRED: *"Von antimetaphysischer Herkunft"*. *Zum 100. Geburtstag von Wolfgang Ernst Pauli*. [In]: Physikalische Blätter, Jg. 56, Nr. 4, Weinheim, 2000. Pp. 57–60, bibl. [W.P., son of Wolf Pascheles, later Wolfgang Joseph Pauli, 1869 Prague – 1958 Zürich, physicist, Nobel prize winner, emigr. 1938 from Vienna to Zurich, lived 1940–1946 in the US, returned to his chair at the Zurich Techn. Univ. in 1946.]

39359. PERUTZ, LEO. SIEBAUER, ULRIKE: *Leo Perutz – "Ich kenne alles. Alles, nur nicht mich"*. Biographie. Gerlingen: Bleicher, 2000. 398 pp., illus., notes (299–367), bibl. (369–390), indexes. Zugl.: Regensburg, Univ., Diss., 1998. [Cf.: Von der Welt vergessen. Die sagenhaften Prager Geschichten des Leo Perutz (Stefan Berkholz) [in]: Die Zeit, Nr. 50, Hamburg, 7. Dez. 2000, p. 72.] [L.P., Nov. 2, 1884 Prague – Aug. 25, 1957 Bad Ischl, author, emigr. 1938 to Palestine.]

39360. POPPER-LYNKEUS, JOSEF. WAGNER, KARL: *Zwischen den Disziplinen: Josef Popper-Lynkeus im Kontext*. [In]: Hofmannsthal. Jahrbuch zur europäischen Moderne, Jg. 8, Freiburg i.Br., 2000. Pp. 247–272, footnotes.

39361. PORGES, LUCIE & PAUL PETER. *Lucie & Paul Peter Porges – style and humor*. Hrsg. von/ed. by Werner Hanak im Auftrag des Jüdischen Museums Wien/on behalf of the Jewish Museum Vienna. Wien: Jüd. Museum Wien, 2000. 104 pp., illus. [Catalogue book for exhibition; all texts in German and English.] [L.P., née Eisenstab, b. Nov. 23, 1926 in Vienna, graphic artist, fashion designer, emigr. via Cologne to Brussels, later to Southern France, escaped to Switzerland in 1942; P.P.P., b. Feb. 7, 1927 in Vienna, cartoonist, graphic artist, went with Kindertransport to France, in 1942 escaped from internment camp Rivesaltes to Switzerland; after liberation both lived in Paris, later USA, since 1994 partly in Vienna.]

39362. RADEK, KARL. LUBAN, OTTOKAR: *Karl Radek im Januaraufstand 1919 in Berlin. Drei Dokumente*. [In]: IWK, Internationale wissenschaftliche Korrespondenz zur Geschichte der deutschen Arbeiterbewegung, H. 3. Berlin: 2000. Pp. 377–397.

39363. REICH-RANICKI, MARCEL. *Marcel Reich-Ranicki. Sein Leben in Bildern*. Eine Bildbiographie. Hrsg. von Frank Schirrmacher. Stuttgart: Deutsche Verlagsanstalt, 2000. 288 pp., frontis., illus., facsims. [Incl.: Über Marcel Reich-Ranicki (ed., 7–14). Also texts by M.R.-R.] [Cf.: Ein Liebender, aber keiner, den die Liebe blendet: Marcel Reich-Ranicki, der vom Kritiker zum Schriftsteller wurde, zum achtzigsten Geburtstag (Ruth Klüger) [in]: 'FAZ', Nr. 140, Frankfurt am Main, 19. Juni 2000. P. 56, port.]

39364. RODE, WALTHER. BAUMGARTNER, GERHARD: *Es ist keine Schande, nichts oder wenig über Walther Rode zu wissen*. [In]: Zwischenwelt [formerly: Mit der Ziehharmonika], Jg. 17, Nr. 1, Wien, Mai 2000. Pp. 26–30, illus. [W.R., for data see No. 38197/YB XLIV.]

39365. ROSSI, HEDWIG. WALTER, INGRID: *"Mein Kopf muß jetzt auf verschiedenen Gleisen laufen"*. *Die Wiener Schriftstellerin und Dramatikerin Hedwig Rossi im amerikanischen Exil*. [In]: Zwischenwelt [formerly: Mit der Ziehharmonika], Jg. 17, Nr. 4, Wien, Dez. 2000. Pp. 14–17, illus., notes. [H.R., née Braun, 1891 Vienna – 1984 South Nyack, NY, author, emigr. 1939 via UK to the US.]

39366. SACHS, NELLY & AUSLÄNDER, ROSE. BOWER, KATHRIN M.: *Ethics and remembrance in the poetry of Nelly Sachs and Rose Ausländer*. Rochester, NY: Camden House, 2000. 280 pp., bibl. (251–273), index. (Studies in German literature, linguistics, and culture.)

39367. SAMUELY, NATHAN. OBER, KENNETH H.: *Nathan Samuely: a forgotten writer in a neglected genre*. [In]: Shofar, Vol. 18, No. 2, West Lafayette, IN, Winter 2000. Pp. 70–81. [Discusses the fact that through the Nazi suppression of Jewish writers a whole genre of ghetto literature was lost. N. Samuely (1847 Galicia – 1921 Baden near Vienna) is given as an example.]

39368. SCHLESINGER, GEORG. *Georg Schlesinger und die Wissenschaft vom Fabrikbetrieb*. Hrsg. von Günter Spur und Wolfram Fischer. Verfaßt von Günter Spur, Joachim Ebert, Sabine Voglrieder, Thorsten Klooster, Stefan Kleinschmidt, Christopher Hayes. Redaktionell bearb. von Yetvart Ficiciyan, Stefanie Finke. München: Hanser, 2000. X, 654 pp., illus., facsims., tabs., footnotes, bibl. (570–644), index. [Incl. chaps. on Ludw. Loewe & Co., Jewish professors, assistants and doctoral students at the 'Lehrstuhl für Werkzeugmaschinen und Fabrikbetriebe, Technische Hochschule Berlin', among them Hans D. Brasch, Franz Koenigsberger, Max Kronenberg, Max Kurrein.] [G.Sch. (1874–1949), mechanical engineer, for data see No. 36731/XB XLIV.]

—— SCHOEPS, HANS-JOACHIM. SCHOEPS, JULIUS H.: *"Nil inultum remanebit"*. *Die Erlanger Universität und ihr Umgang mit dem deutsch-jüdischen Remigranten Hans-Joachim Schoeps (1909–1980)*. [See: No. 39061.]

39369. SCHOEPS, HANS-JOACHIM: *Gesammelte Schriften*. Hrsg. vom Moses-Mendelssohn-Zentrum für Europäisch-Jüdische Studien in Verbindung mit Manfred P. Fleischer [et al.]. Nachdruck. Bd. 4: Abt. 1, Judenchristentum, Gnosis [et al.]. Bd. 7: Abt. 2, Geistesgeschichte. Was ist der Mensch?: philosophische Anthropologie als Geistesgeschichte der neuesten Zeit. Hildesheim: Olms, 1999. 2 vols., 88, XII, 324 pp. & 325 pp., bibl. [Publ. orig. 1956–1960.]

39370. SEGHERS, ANNA. BIRCKEN, MARGRID: *Im Kopf ein "rechter Turmbau zu Babel"*. *Die Bibliothek von Anna Seghers*. Erinnerung an den 100. Geburtstag am 19. November. [In]: Marginalien, H. 160 (4, 2000), Wiesbaden, 2000. Pp. 3–19, notes, port., illus.. [Also incl. in this issue: Welchen Eindruck Bücher auf mich gemacht haben (Anna Seghers, 1–8; letter written in 1954 to a Soviet functionary).]

39371. SEGHERS, ANNA. HILZINGER, SONJA: *Anna Seghers* Stuttgart: Reclam, 2000. 236 pp., illus., bibl. (199–226) (Universal-Bibliothek, Nr. 17623, Literaturstudium.)

39372. SEGHERS, ANNA. MYTZE, ANDREAS W.: *Von der negativen Faszination. Das westdeutsche Seghers-Bild*. Zum 100. Geburtstag von Anna Seghers am 19. November. Ein Text aus dem Jahre 1973. [In]: europäische ideen, H. 121, Berlin: 2000. Pp. 16–24.

39373. SEGHERS, ANNA. ROMERO, CHRISTIANE ZEHL: *Anna Seghers: eine Biographie. 1900–1947*. Berlin: Aufbau-Verl., 2000. 560 pp., illus., bibl. (528–542). [First publ. 1993, see No. 31126/YB XXXIX.]

39374. SEGHERS, ANNA. SCHUHMANN, KLAUS: *Der Kleist-Preis 1928 ging an eine Frau: Anna Seghers*. [In]: Aus dem Antiquariat [Beilage zum] Börsenblatt des Deutschen Buchhandels, Jg. 167, Nr. 69, Frankfurt am Main, 29. Aug. 2000. Pp. A 500–A 503, illus.

39375. SELIGMANN, RAFAEL. ROBERTSON, RITCHIE: *Rafael Seligmann's 'Rubinsteins Versteigerung': the German-Jewish family novel before and after the Holocaust*. [In]: The Germanic Review, Vol. 75, No. 3, Washington, DC, Summer 2000. Pp. 179–193, notes. [Deals with R. S., b. 1947 in Israel to German-Jewish immigrants, and his novel, which gives a very outspoken portrayal of Jewish life in post-war Germany and was met with considerable criticism when first publ.]

39376. SILBERMANN, ALPHONS. *Obituaries Alphons Silbermann*. Obituary (Joachim H. Knoll) [in]: Zeitschrift für Religions- und Geistesgeschichte, Jg. 52, H. 3, Leiden, 2000. Pp. 267–268, footnotes. "Wir danken für ein Leben namens Alphons Silbermann." (Fritz Pleitgen) & Rede zum Begräbnis von Alphons Silbermann (Julius H. Schoeps) [in]: Menora, Bd. 11, Berlin, 2000. Pp. 183–189; also publ. [in]: Jüdisches Leben und jüdische Kultur in Deutschland [see No. 38421]. Pp. 263–265.] [A.S., Aug. 11, 1909, Cologne – March 4, 2000 Cologne, sociologist.]

39377. SINGER, KURT. ALLERT, TILMAN: *Das gebrochene Pathos der Auserwähltheit. Zwischen Stefan George und Georg Simmel: Eine intellektuelle Biografie Kurt Singers*. [In]: Saeculum, Jg. 51, I. Halbband, Freiburg, 2000. pp. 100–107, footnotes. [K.S., 1886 Magdeburg – 1962 Athens, baptised, economist, sociologist, journalist, essayist, went in 1931 from Hamburg to Tokyo as a guest professor, dismissed from Hamburg Univ. in 1933, 1939 emigr. from Japan to Australia, 1940 interned, returned to Europe in 1957, from 1958 in Athens.]

39378. SPECHT, MINNA. *Erinnerung an Minna Specht*. Katalog zur Ausstellung. 21465 Reinbek: Arbeitskreis Frauengeschichtswerkstatt, 2000. 35 pp., illus. [Incl. contrib. by Inge Hansen-Schaberg.] [M.S., Dec. 22, 1879 Reinbek/Hamburg – Feb. 3, 1961 Bremen, educationalist, teacher, emigr. 1933 to Denmark, 1939 to the UK, where she continued to be active in education even during internment and worked from 1943 for the German Educational Reconstruction project; returned to Germany after the war.]

39379. SPERBER, MANÈS. HEMECKER, WILHELM/STANCIC, MIRJANA, eds.: *Ein treuer Ketzer: Manès Sperber – der Schriftsteller als Ideologe*. Wien: Zsolnay, 2000. 141 pp., bibl. (Profile, Bd. 6., Jg. 3.) [A collection of articles.]

39380. STEIN, EDITH. BATZDORFF, SUSANNE M.: *Edith Stein – meine Tante. Das jüdische Erbe einer katholischen Heiligen*. Mit einem Vorwort für die deutsche Ausgabe von Hanna-Barbara Gerl-Falkovitz. Würzburg: Echter, 2000. 213 pp., illus. [Cf.: Besprechung (Peter Maser) [in]: Beiträge zur ostdeutschen Kirchengeschichte, Folge 4, Düsseldorf, 2001, pp. 173–175.] [For orig. edn. see No. 38215/YB XLV.]

39381. STEIN, EDITH. BROCKE, EDNA/HENRIX, HANS HERMANN: *Zur Heiligsprechung Edith Steins*. Ein Briefwechsel. [In]: Neukirchener Theologische Zeitschrift, Jg. 14, H. 1, Neukirchen-Vluyn, 1999. Pp. 54–67.

39382. STEIN, EDITH. *Edith Stein Jahrbuch*. Bd. 6. Würzburg, 2000. 1 vol. [Section V, entitled 'Edith-Stein-Forschung', cont.: Edith Stein – von Auschwitz aus gesehen (Manfred Deselaers, 397–409). Die Vorträge Edith Steins aus den Jahren 1926–1930 (Maria Amata Neyer, 410–431). Die Heiligsprechung Edith Steins (Simeon Tomas Fernandez, 432–436). Englischsprachige Bibliographie von und über Edith Stein (John Sullivan, 437–446).]

39383. STERN, GERSON. KIECKBUSCH, KLAUS: *Der Schriftsteller Gerson Stern*. [In]: Jahrbuch für den Landkreis Holzminden, Bd. 18, Holzminden, 2000. Pp. 131–152, illus., bibl. [G. St., author, for data see No. 38399/YB XLV.]

39384. STERN, SELMA. SASSENBERG, MARINA: *The face of Janus: the historian Selma Stern (1890–1981) and her portrait of the Court Jew*. [In]: European History, vol. 33, No. 33, London, autumn 2000. Pp. 72–79, notes.

39385. STERNBERG, THEODOR. BARTELS-ISHIKAWA, ANNA: *Theodor Sternberg: einer der Begründer des Freirechts in Deutschland und Japan*. Berlin: Duncker & Humblot, 1998. 223 pp., frontis., footnotes, bibl. (Schriftenreihe zur Rechtssoziologie und Rechtstatsachenforschung, Bd. 79.)

39386. STERNBERG, THEODOR. *Post im Schatten des Hakenkreuzes*. Das Schicksal der jüdischen Familie Sternberg in ihren Briefen von Berlin nach Tokyo in der Zeit von 1910 bis 1950. Hrsg. von Anna Bartels-Ishikawa. Berlin: Duncker & Humblot, 2000. 270 pp., illus., facsims. [Incl. chaps. on the Sternberg family in Berlin and their fate during the Nazi era. The majority of letters were written between 1933 and 1941.] [Th.H.St., Jan. 5, 1879 Berlin – April 17, 1950 Tokyo, jurist, 1913–1919 prof. for German law at the Imperial Univ. in Tokyo, after 1921 lecturer at various Japanese universities, counsellor, 1921–1934 correspondent for 'Berliner Tageblatt'.]

39387. STORFER, ADOLF JOSEF: *Wörter und ihre Schicksale (1935) & Im Dickicht der Sprache (1937)* Berlin: Verlag Vorwerk 8, 2000. 2 vols., 384 & 303 pp. [Cf.: Wörter auf der Couch. A.J. Storfer, Psychoanalytiker und Freund Freuds, war ein ungewöhnlicher Sprachforscher (Michael Kohlstruck) [in]: Rheinischer Merkur, Nr. 50, Bonn, 2000, p. 8.] [A.J.St., after 1938 Albert J.St., Jan. 11, 1888 Botoschani, Bukowina – Dec. 2, 1944 Melbourne, publicist, psychoanalyst, etymologist, emigr. 1938 via Belgium to Shanghai, later to Australia.]

39388. STRAUSS, LEO. BATNITZKY, LEORA: *On the truth of history or the history of truth: rethinking Rosenzweig via Strauss*. [In]: Jewish Studies Quarterly, Vol. 7, No. 3, Tübingen, 2000. Pp. 223–251, footnotes. [Deals with Leo Strauss's interpretation of Rosenzweig.]

39389. TÄUBLER, EUGEN. SCHARBAUM, HEIKE: *Zwischen zwei Welten: Wissenschaft und Lebenswelt am Beispiel des deutsch-jüdischen Historikers Eugen Täubler (1879–1953)*. Münster: Lit, 2000. 136 pp., illus., bibl. (Münsteraner Judaistische Studien, Bd. 8.)

39390. TAL, JOSEF. LÜHE, BARBARA VON DER: *Ein Pionier der israelischen Musik*. [In]: Tribüne, Jg. 39, H. 155, Frankfurt am Main, 2000. Pp. 43–47.

39391. TAU, MAX. *"Ein symbolisches Leben"*. *Beiträge anläßlich des 100. Geburtstages von Max Tau (1897–1976)*. Im Auftrag der Stiftung Haus Oberschlesien hrsg. von Detlef Haberland. Heidelberg: Palatina, 2000. 330 pp., footnotes, index. [Incl. 17 contribs. dealing with M.T.'s life and work; also personal recollections and bibl. Max Tau. 2 essays are listed according to subject.] [M.T., Jan. 19, 1897 Beuthen (Upper Silesia) – March 13, 1976 Oslo, literary historian, journalist, editor, emigr. 1938 to Norway, escaped to Sweden, in 1946 returned to Norway.]

39392. TAUBER, RICHARD. JÜRGS, MICHAEL: *Gern hab' ich die Frau'n geküßt. Die Richard-Tauber-Biographie*. München: List, 2000. 430 pp., illus., bibl., index, CD-Rom. [R.T., May 16, 1891 Linz – Jan. 8, 1948 London, tenor, 1933 left Germany, 1938 left Austria, became British citizen in 1940.]

39393. TOEPLITZ, OTTO. HILDEBRANDT, STEFAN/LAX, PETER D.: *Otto Toeplitz*. Bonn: Mathem. Institut der Univ. Bonn, 1999. 210 pp., frontis., illus., facsims. (Bonner Mathematische Schriften, Nr. 319.) [Incl.: Otto Toeplitz in Bonn (Stefan Hildebrandt, 13–82, bibl.). The mathematical heritage of Otto Toeplitz (Peter D. Lax, 85–102). Ausgewählte Schriften von Otto Toeplitz (103–191). Briefe an Otto Toeplitz (193–209).] [O.T., Aug. 1, 1881 Breslau – Feb. 15, 1940, Jerusalem, mathematician, dismissed from Bonn Univ. in 1935, emigr. to Palestine 1939. See also No. 39452.]

39394. TUCHOLSKY, KURT. *Halb erotisch – halb politisch. Kabarett und Freundschaft bei Kurt Tucholsky*. Dokumentation der Tagungen der Kurt Tucholsky Gesellschaft Berlin 30.9. – 3.10.1999 [&] Triberg 9.6. – 11.6.2000. Hrsg. von Stefanie Oswalt/Roland Links im Auftrag der Kurt-Tucholsky-Gesellschaft. Oldenburg: bis, 2000. 202 pp., notes. [Cont. 10 essays, incl. one about Walter Mehring and one about Siegfried Jacobsohn.]

39395. TUCHOLSKY, KURT. *Kurt Tucholsky und die Justiz*. Dokumentation der Tagung der Kurt Tucholsky Gesellschaft vom 23. – 26.10.1997 in Berlin. Hrsg. von Michael Hepp im Auftrag der Kurt Tucholsky-Gesellschaft. Oldenburg: bis, 1998. 210 pp., notes.

39396. UECKERT, CHARLOTTE: *Margarete Susman und Else Lasker-Schüler*. Hamburg: Europ. Verlagsanstalt, 2000. 158 pp., ports. (Eva Duographien, Bd. 10.)

39397. WALLACH-FALLER, MARIANNE: *Die Frau im Tallit. Judentum feministisch gelesen*. Hrsg. von Doris Brodbeck und Yvonne Domhardt. Zürich: Chronos, 2000. 272 pp., frontis., bibl. M.W.-F. [Incl.: Vorwort (Eveline Goodman-Thau, 7–12). Biographische Einleitung (Marie-Theres Wacker, 13–16). Geleitwort (Albert Erlanger, 17–20).] [M.W.-F., 1942 Zürich – 2000 Zürich, feminist theologian.]

39398. WASSERMANN, JAKOB. KOESTER, R.: *Jakob Wassermann, anti-semitism, and German politics*. [In]: Orbis Litterarum, Vol. 53, No. 3, Las Vegas, 1998. Pp.179–190, notes.

39399. WEIL, GRETE. BAACKMANN, SUSANNE: *Configurations of myth, memory, and mourning in Grete Weil's "Meine Schwester Antigone"*. [In]: The German Quarterly, Vol. 73, No. 3, Cherry Hill, NJ, Summer 2000. PP. 269–286, notes. [Deals with W.s autobiographical novel about a Jewish woman who survived the Holocaust.]

——— WEILL, ALEXANDER. WEIß. GERHARD: *Alexander Weills "Sittengemälde aus dem elsässischen Volksleben" (1847): volkskundliche Zeugnisse, literarische Kunstwerke und emanzipatorische Botschaften*. [See No. 38614.]

39400. WEILL, KURT. FARNETH, DAVID (WITH ELMAR JUCHEM AND DAVE STEIN): *Kurt Weill: a life in pictures and documents 1900–1950*. Designed by Bernard Schleifer. Preface by Kim H. Kowalke. Foreword by Luciano Berio. Introd. by D. Farneth. London: Thames and Hudson; Woodstock, VT: Overlook Press, XV, 312 pp., frontis., chiefly illus., chronol. facsims., scores, appendix, bibl. (304–305), index of names, index of works by K.W. [Appendix cont. both transl. of documents and the German orig.]

39401. WEILL, KURT. *100 years of Kurt Weill*. [Issue title of] Theater, Vol. 30, No. 3. New Haven, CT: 2000. 1 issue, 136 pp., libretti. Special issue editor: Tom Sellar. [Incl. recently rediscovered and prev.

untranslated dramatic works by Weill, essays dealing with his legacy and influence, reviews and reports. Also first Engl. publ. of two major Weill libretti, transl. and introd. by Jonathan Eaton.]

39402. WEILL, KURT. *Kurt Weill.* [Issue title of] Neue Zeitschrift für Musik, H. 2, Mainz, März/April, 2000. 50 pp., illus., ports., notes, facsims. [Incl. contribs. by Konrad Boehmer, Gunther Diehl, Jürgen Schebera, Elmar Juchem, Andreas Hauff, Willem Breuker, Tom R. Schulz; also bibl. and discography K.W.]

39403. WEILL, KURT. *Kurt Weill: in memoriam 1900–2000.* Begleitheft zur Ausstellung des Deutschen Musikarchivs Berlin vom 10. Juli bis 8. September 2000/Die Deutsche Bibliothek, Leipzig, Frankfurt am Main, Berlin. Zusgest. von Bettina von Seyfried. Leipzig: Die Deutsche Bibliothek, 2000. 74 pp., discogr.

39404. WEILL, KURT. SCHEBERA, JÜRGEN: *"Mein ganzes Leben habe ich dem musikalischen Theater gewidmet". Zum 100. Geburtstag und 50. Todestag des Komponisten Kurt Weill.* [In]: Der Bär von Berlin. Jahrbuch des Vereins für die Geschichte Berlins, Jg. 49, Berlin, 2000. Pp. 129–148, illus.

39405. WEILL, KURT. SCHMIDT, MICHAEL: *Kurt Weill, der Opernaufklärer.* [In]: Die Neue Gesellschaft/Frankfurter Hefte, Jg. 47, H. 5, Frankfurt am Main, 2000. Pp. 309–315.

39406. WEININGER, OTTO. WOLFES, MATTHIAS: *Otto Weininger: "Geschlecht und Charakter". Das Werk und seine Wirkung.* [In]: Historische Mitteilungen. Jg. 13, Stuttgart, 2000. 76–93, footnotes.

39407. WEISS, PETER. HERMAND, JOST/SILBERMAN, MARC, eds.: *Rethinking Peter Weiss.* New York; Bern: Lang, 2000. IX, 199 pp., illus. (German life and civilization, vol. 32.)

39408. WERFEL, FRANZ. SPORIS, ERICH: *Franz Werfels politische Weltvorstellung.* Frankfurt am Main, New York: Lang, 2000. 225 pp., bibl. (Aspekte pädagogischer Innovation, Bd. 25.)

39409. WERTHEIMER, MAX. SARRIS, VIKTOR: *Max Wertheimers Frankfurter Arbeiten zum Bewegungssehen – die experimentelle Begründung der Gestaltpsychologie.* [In]: Forschung Frankfurt. Wissenschaftsmagazin der Johann Wolfgang Goethe-Universität Frankfurt am Main, Jg. 18, H. 3: Sonderband zur Geschichte der Universität. Pp. 120–126, notes, illus. [M.W., April 15, 1880 Prague – Oct. 12, 1943, New Rochelle, USA, founder of Gestaltpsychology, prof. of psychology, emigr. 1933 to the US.]

39410. WISCHNITZER, RACHEL. FEIL, KATHARINA S.: *Art under siege: The scholarship produced by Rachel Wischnitzer during her Berlin years 1921–1938.* [In]: Leo Baeck Institute Year Book XLV, Oxford, 2000. Pp. 121–133, footnotes. [For first part of article see No. 38240/YB XLIV.]

39411. WITTGENSTEIN, PAUL. KIM-PARK, SO YOUNG: *Paul Wittgenstein und die für ihn komponierten Klavierkonzerte für die linke Hand.* Aachen: Shaked, 1999. 199, XVII pp., footnotes, illus., music. (Berichte aus der Musikwissenschaft.) Zugl.: Karlsruhe, Univ., Diss., 1999.

39412. WOHL, JEANETTE. VETTER, EDITH: *Jeanette Wohl. Freundin und Mitarbeiterin von Ludwig Börne.* Bad Soden a. Ts.: Arbeitskreis für Bad Sodener Geschichte, 1998. 56 pp. (Materialien zur Bad Sodener Geschichte, H. 23.)

39413. WOLFF, JEANETTE. SEEMANN, BIRGIT: *Jeanette Wolff. Politikerin und engagierte Demokratin (1888–1976).* Frankfurt am Main: Campus, 2000. 141 pp., illus., footnotes, bibl. (123–139). [Incl. articles by J.W.] [J.W., née Cohen, June 22, 1888 Bocholt – May 19, 1976 Berlin, Social Democratic politician, in 1942 deported to Riga from Dortmund, after liberation continued her political career, active also in numerous Jewish organisations, i.e. Jüdischer Frauenbund.]

39414. WOLFF, THEODOR. SÖSEMANN, BERND: *Theodor Wolff. Ein Leben mit der Zeitung.* München: Econ Ullstein List, 2000. 360 pp., illus., bibl., index.

39415. ZUCKERMANN, RUDOLF & LEO. KIEßLING, WOLFGANG: *Absturz in den kalten Krieg. Rudolf und Leo Zuckermanns Leben zwischen nazistischer Verfolgung, Emigration und stalinistischer Maßregelung.*

Berlin: "Helle Panke" e.V. und Gesellschaftswiss. Forum e.V., 1999. 72 pp., footnotes (Hefte zur DDR-Geschichte, 57.).

39416. ZWEIG, STEFAN. HURTH, ELISABETH: *Tröstlicher Wahn. Stefan Zweigs Begegnung mit Albert Schweitzer.* [In]: Die Zeichen der Zeit/Lutherische Monatshefte, Jg. 3, H. 6, Hannover, 2000. Pp. 27–29, ports..

39417. ZWEIG, STEFAN. KLAWITER, RANDOLPH J.: *Stefan Zweig: an international bibliography.* Addendum I. Riverside, CA: Ariadne Press, 1999. 535 pp. [This addendum contains new material by and about Zweig publ. between 1990–1997, and also emendations and additions to the orig. bibl. publ. in 1991 (952 pp.) by the same publ.]

VIII. AUTOBIOGRAPHIES, MEMOIRS, LETTERS

39418. ADORNO, THEODOR W. ADORNO, THEODOR W.: *Kritik der Pseudo-Aktivität. Adornos Verhältnis zur Studentenbewegung im Spiegel seiner Korrespondenz. Eine Dokumentation.* [In]: Frankfurter Adorno-Blätter, Jg. 9, Frankfurt am Main, 2000. Pp. 42–116.

39419. BENJAMIN, WALTER: *Berliner Kindheit um neunzehnhundert.* Gießener Fassung. Hrsg. und mit einem Nachwort von Rolf Tiedemann. Frankfurt am Main: Suhrkamp, 2000. 131 pp., illus.

39420. BENJAMIN, WALTER: *Gesammelte Briefe.* Band VI, 1938–1940. Hrsg. von Christoph Gödde und Henri Lonitz. Frankfurt am Main: Suhrkamp, 2000. 629 pp., indexes. [Incl.: Gesamtregister (535–629).]

39421. BÖRNE, LUDWIG: *Briefwechsel des jungen Börne und der Henriette Herz.* Hrsg. von Ludwig Geiger. Unveränd. Nachdr. der Ausg. Odenburg, Leipzig, Schulze, 1905. Eschborn: Klotz, 2000. 201 pp. [Incl. letters written between 1802 and 1808.]

39422. BUBER, MARTIN. CUTTER, WILLIAM: *The Buber and Berdyczewski correspondence.* [In]: Jewish Social Studies, Vol. 6, No. 3, Bloomington, IN, Spring 2000. Pp. 160–204, notes. [M. J. Berdyczewski, Hebrew author, folklorist.]

39423. BUSCH, FELIX: *Aus dem Leben eines königlich-preußischen Landrats.* Hrsg. von Julius H. Schoeps. Berlin: Nicolai, 1999. 290 pp., illus., index. [Incl. short family history; also family trees.] [F.B., orig. Friedländer, 1871 Constantinople – 1938 (suicide) near Berlin, high Prussian civil servant, descendant of David Friedländer, grand-father of Julius H. Schoeps; memoirs were written 1934–1936.]

39424. CANETTI, ELIAS. BENDER, HANS: *Zum Briefwechsel mit Elias Canetti.* [In]: Sinn und Form. Beiträge zur Literatur. Jg. 52, H. 6, Berlin, 2000. Pp. 250–265.] [Incl. letters of E.C. and his German publisher Hans Bender.]

39425. *The correspondence of Sigmund Freud and Sandor Ferenczi, Vol. 3, 1920–1933.* Ed. by Ernst Falzeder and Eva Brabant, with collaboration of Patrizia Giampieri-Deutsch. Transl. by Peter T. Hoffer, with an introd. by Judith Dupont. Cambridge, MA: Harvard Belknap Press, 2000. 544 pp. [Last vol. of correspondence, ending with Ferenczi's death in 1933.]

39426. DÖBLIN, ALFRED: *Doktor Döblin. Selbstbiographie.* [Hrsg.: Erich Kleinschmidt.] Berlin: Friedenauer Presse, 2000. 13 pp. [On his life 1878–1918.]

39427. EHRENBERG, HANS: *Autobiographie eines deutschen Pfarrers.* Mit Selbstzeugnissen und einer Dokumentation seiner Amtsentlassung. [Hrsg.: Günter Brakelmann]. Waltrop: Spenner, 1999. 379 pp., docs., index (Schriften der Hans Ehrenberg Gesellschaft, Bd. 5.) [H.E., April 6, 1883 Altona – 1958, Protestant pastor, 1993 dismissed as a "Jew" from his church in Bochum, emigr. 1939 after deportation to Dachau to the UK; autobiography was orig. publ. in English 1943.]

39428. EHRENBERG, WOLF ZEEV: *Emigrationen: Lebensstationen eines Juden aus Deutschland.* Zürich: Chronos, 2000. 243 pp., illus., gloss. [Author, b. 1926 in Pforzheim, emigr. with his family in 1933 to Palestine, in 1946 went to Zurich to study engineering, still living in Switzerland.]

39429. FREUNDLICH, ELISABETH. *The traveling years*. Transl. from the German by Elizabeth Pennebaker. Riverside, CA: Ariadne Press, 1999. 177 pp., illus. [For German edn. and data of E. F. see No. 29884/YB XXXVIII.]

39430. HECHT, MANFRED. *My four lives: memoirs of a singing psychoanalyst*. Riverside, CA: Ariadne Press, 1999. 202 pp. [Author, born in Vienna, where he studied medicine, survived the war and went to the US, where he made a career as a singer and actor in Broadway shows, concerts and opera; served as cantor. Later became a psychoanalyst in New York.]

39431. HÖFLICH, EUGEN: *Eugen Hoeflich (Moshe Ya'akov Ben-Gavriel). Tagebücher 1915 bis 1927*. Hrsg. und kommentiert von Armin A. Wallas. Wien: Böhlau, 1999. 641 pp., facsims, ports., notes, indexes (245–552). [E.H., 1891 Vienna – 1956 Jerusalem, journalist, writer, Zionist, went to Palestine in 1927.]

39432. HOFMANNSTHAL, HUGO VON. GIACON, NICOLETTA, ed.: *Hugo von Hofmannsthal – Yella, Felix und Mysa Oppenheimer: Briefwechsel. Teil II: 1906–1929*. [In]: Hofmannsthal. Jahrbuch zur europäischen Moderne, Jg. 8, Freiburg i.Br., 2000. Pp. 7–155, illus. [For part I see No. 38139/YB XLV.]

39433. HÜMBELIN, LOTTE: *Mein eigener Kopf. Ein Frauenleben in Wien, Moskau, Prag, Paris und Zürich*. Zürich: Edition 8, 1999. 359 pp. [L.H., née Bindel, born 1909 in Vienna, Communist activist, lived between 1934 and eventual flight to the UK 1940 in Moscow, Prague, Vienna, Zurich.] [Cf.: Besprechung (Waltraud Seidel-Höppner) [in]: Beiträge zur Geschichte der Arbeiterbewegung, Jg. 42, H. 1, Berlin, 2000, pp. 128–131.]

39435. KEILSON, HANS: *"Sieben Sterne...". (Meine) Geschichte zur Sprache gebracht*. [In]: Deutsche Akademie für Sprache und Dichtung, Jahrbuch 1999, Göttingen, 2000. Pp. 74–86. [Personal memoirs.]

39436. KOLLISCH, EVA: *Girl in movement*. A memoir. Thetford, Vermont: Glad Day Books, 2000. 1 vol. [On the author's childhood in Vienna, Kindertransport and later life in New York among young Communist friends.] [Cf.: Trotzki und Eistee (Christine Forst) [in]: Aufbau, Vol. 66, No. 3, New York, Feb. 2001, p. 17.]

39437. KRAUS, KARL/LICHNOWSKY, MECHTILDE: *Briefe und Dokumente: 1916–1958. Karl Kraus und Mechtilde Lichnowsky*. [Hrsg. von Friedrich Pfäfflin und Eva Dambacher in Zusammenarbeit mit Volker Dahmen]. Marbach am Neckar. Dt. Schiller-Ges., 2000. 255 pp., illus., music. (Marbacher Katalog, 52; Beiheft, 3.)

39438. KREISKY, BRUNO: *The struggle for a democratic Austria: Bruno Kreisky on peace and social justice*. Ed. by Matthew Paul Berg in collaboration with Jill Lewis and Oliver Rothkolb. Transl. by Helen Atkins and M.P. Berg. With a preface by John Kenneth Galbraith. New York; Oxford: Berghahn Books, 2000. XXIX, 565 pp., illus., facsims., footnotes, bibl. (538–560), index. [Incl. chap. entitled 'Thoughts on antisemitism, "racial theories", and the future of the State of Israel'. Orig. edn. publ. 1986–1996.] [B.K. Jan. 22, 1911 Vienna – 1990 Vienna, Austrian statesman, foreign minister, then for 13 years chancellor of Austria.]

39439. MARX, KARL. BEER, MAX: *Karl Marx – eine Monographie*. 1. Aufl. Reprint [der Ausg.] Berlin, Verl. für Sozialwiss., 1918. Köln: Neuer ISP-Verlag, 1999. 108 pp., illus. (Edition 100 bei ISP, 15.)

39440. MOSSE, GEORGE L.: *Confronting history: a memoir*. With a foreword by Walter Laqueur. Madison: Univ. of Wisconsin Press, 2000. XV, 219 pp., illus., ports., facsims. [Cf.: Review (Stephen H. Garrin) [in]: Jewish Book World, Vol. 18, No. 3, New York, 2000, pp. 22–23.]

39441. MÜHSAM, ERICH: *Unpolitische Erinnerungen*. Mit einem Nachwort von Hubert van den Berg. Hamburg: Ed. Nautilus, 2000. 222 pp., illus., index. [Incl.: Zur Politik des Unpolitischen (Hubert van den Berg, 195–213); a collection of articles first publ. 1927 – 1929 in 'Unterhaltungsblatt der Vossischen Zeitung', later as a book running through 14 edns.]

39442. POSENER, JULIUS. *Julius Posener – ein Leben in Briefen*. Ausgewählte Korrespondenz 1929–1990. Hrsg. von Matthias Schirren und Sylvia Claus im Auftr. der Stiftung Archiv der Akademie der

Künste, Berlin. [Übers. aus dem Engl.: Karin Lelonek. Übers. aus dem Franz.: Frauke Dölp und Klaus Rupprecht]. Basel: Birkhäuser, 1999. 285 pp., illus.

39443. REICH-RANICKI, MARCEL. HAGE, VOLKER, ed.: *Golo Mann – Marcel Reich-Ranicki*. Ein Briefwechsel. Aufsätze und Porträts. Frankfurt am Main: S. Fischer, 2000. 291 pp. [Incl.: Vorwort (ed., 7–16).]

39444. ROVAN, JOSEPH: *Erinnerungen eines Franzosen, der einmal Deutscher war*. Aus dem Franz. von Bernd Wilczek. München: Hanser, 2000. 527 pp. [For orig. edn. and data see No. 38292/YB XLV.] [Cf.: Genie der Freundschaft. Joseph Rovan, einer der großen Vermittler zwischen Deutschen und Franzosen, hat seine Erinnerungen geschrieben (Klaus Harpprecht) [in]: Die Zeit, Nr. 51, Hamburg, 14. Dez. 2000, pp. 21–22.]

39445. SCHOLEM, GERSHOM: *Tagebücher nebst Aufsätzen und Entwürfen bis 1923*. 2. Halbband 1917–1923. Hrsg. von Karlfried Gründer, Herbert Kopp-Oberstebrink und Friedrich Niewöhner unter Mitwirkung von Karl E. Grözinger. Frankfurt am Main: Jüdischer Verlag, 2000. 734 pp., index.

39446. SERENY, GITTA: *The German trauma: experiences and reflections, 1938–2000*. London: Allen Lane, the Penguin Press, 2000. XXI, 377 pp., illus.,index. [G.S., born in Vienna, historian, worked with refugee children in France 1939–1940, fled to England, then US, returned to Germany with UNRRA in 1945 and worked with children in DP camps; later journalist and author.]

39447. SEGHERS, ANNA: *Hier im Volk der kalten Herzen*. Briefwechsel 1947. Hrsg. von Christel Berger. Berlin: Aufbau Taschenbuch Verlag, 2000. 281 pp., illus., notes (205–248), chronol., index. [Incl.: Nachwort (ed., 255–260).]

39448. STEIN, EDITH. *Edith-Stein-Gesamtausgabe (ESGA)*. Hrsg. im Auftrag des Int. Edith Stein Instituts Würzburg von Michael Linssen. Unter wissenschaftlicher Mitarb. von Hanna-Barbara Gerl-Falkovitz Bd. 2: Biographische Schriften 2. Selbstbildnis in Briefen I (1916–1933). Bd. 3: Biographische Schriften 3. Selbstbildnis in Briefen II (1933–1942). Einl., Bearb. und Anmerkungen von Maria Amata Neyer. Freiburg: Herder, 2000. 2 vols., 320 & 614 pp.

39450. STERN, HELLMUT: *Saitensprünge*. Die ungewöhnlichen Erinnerungen eines Musikers, der 1938 von Berlin nach China fliehen mußte, 1949 nach Israel einwanderte, ab 1956 in den USA lebte und schließlich 1961 zurückkehrte als Erster Geiger der Berliner Philharmonie. Berlin: Transit, 2000. 285 pp.,illus. [New edn.; first publ. 1990, see No. 27798/YB XXXIX.]

39451. STRAUSS, HERBERT: *In the eye of the storm: growing up Jewish in Germany, 1918–1943: a memoir*. New York: Fordham Univ. Press, 1999. XII, 262 pp., illus., ports., bibl., index. [For German edn. and data see No. 35745/YB XLIII.]

39452. TOEPLITZ, URI: *Und Worte reichen nicht. Von der Mathematik in Deutschland zur Musik in Israel*. Eine jüdische Familiengeschichte 1812–1998. Vorwort von Niels Hansen. Hrsg. von Erhard Roy Wiehn. Konstanz: Hartung-Gorre, 1999. 276 pp., frontis., illus., facsims., index. [U.T., b. 1913 in Kiel, son of the mathematician Otto Toeplitz (see No. 39393), mathematician, flautist, emigr. 1936 to Palestine, for decades 1st flautist of the Israeli Philharmonic Orchestra; lives in Tel Aviv.]

39453. TROLLER, GEORG STEFAN: *Meine Sammlung*. [In]: Aus dem Antiquariat [Beilage zum] Börsenblatt des Deutschen Buchhandels, Jg. 167, Nr. 43, Frankfurt am Main, 30. Mai 2000. Pp. A 313–A 316. [Autobiographical essay dealing with the author's collections of books and what became of them in the course of his life.] [G.St.T., born 1921 in Vienna, TV-journalist, film director; lives in Paris.]

39454. WEIL, ALISA: *Deutschland, Palästina und zurück*. Biographische Gespräche. Geführt und hrsg. von Carsten Teichert. Köln: Verlag Wissenschaft und Politik, 2000. 188 pp., illus. (Edition Zeitzeugen Europas, Bd. 1.) [A.W., née Levin, b. 1931 in Stettin, in 1937 emigr. with her Jewish father and non-Jewish mother to Palestine, in 1947 returned to Germany, married the painter Manfred Weil, now lives in Meckenheim.]

39455. WYSBAR, EVA: *"Hinaus aus Deutschland, irgendwohin ..."*. *Mein Leben in Deutschland vor und nach 1933.* Mit Vorworten von Maria Wisbar Hansen und Tania Wisbar und einem biographischen Nachwort von Detlef Garz. Lengwil: Libelle, 2000. 158 pp., illus., facsims. [First publ. of memoirs written 1939 as an entry in the Harvard University competition established by Gordon W. Allport (et al.).] [E.W., née Eva Theresa Krojanker, 1908 Berlin – 1984 New York, screen writer, film editor, journalist, after divorce from her non-Jewish husband in 1938 emigr. to US.]

39456. ZUCKER, RUTH: *Meine sieben Leben*. Autobiographie. München: Deutscher Taschenbuch Verlag, 2000. 260 pp., illus. Originalausgabe. [R.Z., née Koopmann, b. 1914 in Bonn, psychologist, graphologist, astrologist, emigr. 1934 illegally to Palestine, joined the Haganah. Lives in Haifa.]

39457. ZWEIG, STEFAN: *Briefe 1920 – 1931*. Hrsg. von Knut Beck und Jeffrey B. Berlin. Frankfurt am Main: S. Fischer, 2000. 696 pp., notes (329–645), indexes.

IX. GERMAN-JEWISH RELATIONS

A. General

39458. ALTFELIX, THOMAS: *The "post Holocaust Jew" and the instrumentalisation of philosemitism*. [In]: Patterns of Prejudice, Vol. 34, No. 2, London, April 2000. Pp. 41–56, footnotes. [Extreme philosemitism, mainly in post-war Germany, is seen as a post-Holocaust phenomenon and is compared to xenophobia.]

39459. BLOCK, RICHARD/FENVES, PETER, eds.: *"The spirit of poesy". Essays on Jewish and German literature and thought in honor of Géza von Molnár.* Evanston, IL: Northwestern Univ. Press, 2000. 1 vol. [Incl.: Non-Jewish Germans in the service of present-day Jewish causes. A footnote to German cultural history (Guy Stern, 233–246, notes).]

39460. COUDERT, ALLISON P.: *The impact of the Kabbalah in the seventeenth century. The life and thought of Francis Mercury van Helmont (1614–1698).* Leiden; Boston: Brill, 1999. XX, 418 pp. (Brill's series in Jewish studies, 9.) [Helmont, b. in Vilvorde near Brussels, lived in Sulzbach, a centre of Jewish scholars and Hebrew printers in the 17th cent.] [Cf.: Besprechung (Andreas Kilcher) [in]: Aschkenas, Jg. 10, H. 1, Wien, 2000, pp. 277–280.]

39461. CRAMER, ERNST: *Germany and the Jews at the turn of the millenium*. New York: Leo Baeck Institute, 2000. 16 pp. (The Leo Baeck Memorial Lecture 43.). [Incl. greeting sent by the German president Johannes Rau on the occasion of awarding the Leo Baeck Medal to Ernst Cramer.]

39462. *Den Menschen zugewandt leben. Festschrift für Werner Licharz*. Hrsg. von Ulrich Lilienthal und Lothar Stiehm. Osnabrück: Secolo, 2000. 280 pp. [Part 1 incl. contribs. on the Christian-Jewish dialogue by (a.o.) Ansgar Koschel, Winfrid Frey, Martin Stöhr, Albert H. Friedlander. Part II incl. (selected essays): Martin Buber und Albert Schweitzer. Geben, Nehmen, Miteinander 1901–1965 (Lothar Stiehm,). Albert Einstein. Ein deutsch-jüdischer Physiker zwischen Assimilation und Zionismus (Peter A. Degen). Further contribs. are listed according to subject.]

39463. DIEMLING, MARIA: *Chonuko – "kirchweyhe". Der Konvertit Antonius Margaritha schreibt 1530 über die Feier von Chanukka.* [In]: Kalonymos, Jg. 3, H. 4, Duisburg, 2000. pp. 1–3, notes. [Deals with M's life and his 'Der Gantz Jüdisch Glaub', publ. 1530 in Augsburg.]

39464. DUBIEL, HELMUT: *Niemand ist frei von der Geschichte. Die nationalsozialistische Herrschaft in den Debatten des Deutschen Bundestages.* München: Hanser, 1999. 304 pp., notes, index.

39465. *Freiburger Rundbrief.* Zeitschrift für christlich-jüdische Begegnung. Neue Folge. Hrsg.: Freiburger Rundbrief e.V. Jg. 7. Hauptschriftleiter: Clemens Thoma. Freiburg, 2000. 4 issues. [Incl. essays and book reviews pertaining to theological and historical aspects of Christian-Jewish relations. Selected contribs. are listed according to subject.]

39466. GLASENAPP, GABRIELE VON: *Zwischen Stereotyp und Mythos. Über das Bild des Hofjuden in der Deutschen Literatur des 19. und 20. Jahrhunderts.* [In]: Aschkenas, Jg. 10, H. 1, Wien, 2000. Pp. 177–201, footnotes. [Incl. also Jewish authors.]

39467. HENTGES, GUDRUN: *Schattenseiten der Aufklärung: die Darstellung von Juden und 'Wilden' in philosophischen Schriften des 18. und 19. Jahrhunderts.* Schwalbach/Ts.: Wochenschau-Verlag, 1999. 198 pp., footnotes, bibl. (286–298). Zugl.: Marburg, Univ., Diss.. 1998 u.d.T.: Antijudaismus, Antisemitismus und "Rassen"konstruktion in philosophischen Entwürfen des achtzehnten und beginnenden neunzehnten Jahrhunderts. [Incl. Kant, Fichte, Hegel.]

39468. HILTON, MICHAEL: *"Wie es sich christelt, so jüdelt es sich". 2000 Jahre christlicher Einfluß auf das jüdische Leben.* Mit einem Vorwort von Rabbiner Arthur Hertzberg. [Aus dem Engl. von Annette Böckler]. [Berlin]: JVB, [2000]. 319 pp., notes (289–307), gloss., bibl. [Orig. publ. 1994 with the title 'The Christian effect on Jewish life'; deals also with German developments.]

39469. HÖPPNER, REINHARD: *Christen, Juden, Israel aus der Perspektive der DDR-Wirklichkeit.* [In]: Neukirchener Theologische Zeitschrift, Jg. 14, H. 1, Neukirchen-Vluyn, 1999. Pp. 3–11.

39470. *The impact of the Holocaust experience on Jews and Christians.* Ed. by Michael A. Signer. Bloomington: Indiana Univ. Press, 2000. VIII, 461 pp., notes, index. [A collection of essays on different aspects of the Holocaust and contemporary responses in theology, literature, history, art and science. Part II incl. essays on Christian-Jewish theological debates in Germany related to the impact of the Holocaust, guilt, reconciliation by Hans Hermann Henrix, Berthold Klappert, Hanspeter Heinz; also contribs. on Austria and the Goldhagen controversy.]

39471. KAUFMANN, THOMAS: *Die theologische Bewertung des Judentums im Protestantismus des späteren 16. Jahrhunderts (1530–1600).* [In]: Archiv für Reformationsgeschichte, Vol. 91. Gütersloh, 2000. Pp. 191–237, footnotes. [Incl. English abstract.]

39472. KELLER, LUISE-LOTTE: *Kirche, Küche, Kinderzimmer. Im Spannungsfeld interkonfessioneller Interaktionen: Reflexionen über die Rolle der Dienstmädchen in jüdischen Familien.* [In]: Schmidt-Leutenschleier, Simone [et al.] eds.: Soziogramme, Soziolekte. Paradigmen weiblicher Orientierung im Fin-de-Siècle. Berlin: Ioculatrix, 2000. Pp. 73–81, footnotes.

——— KIRCHNER, PAUL CHRISTIAN: *Jüdisches Ceremoniell. Beschreibung jüdischer Feste und Gebräuche.* [see: No. 39174.]

39473. LOEWY, HANNO: *Deutsche Identitäten vor und nach dem Holocaust.* [In]: Jüdisches Leben und jüdische Kultur in Deutschland [see No. 38421]. Pp. 240–251, notes.

39474. MASSEY, IRVING: *Philo-semitism in nineteenth-century German literature.* Tübingen: Niemeyer, 2000. 199 pp., footnotes, bibl. (179–194), index. (Conditio Judaica, 29.) [Author defines philosemitic works of literature written by non-Jewish authors as those in which Jews and/or Judaism are presented in a favourable, or at least not unfavourable light. Traces in them both antisemitic and "philosemitic" views. Analyzes Bettina von Arnim, Annette von Droste-Hülshoff, Theodor Fontane, Gustav Freytag, Karl Gutzkow, Wilhelm Raabe, Marie von Ebner-Eschenbach.]

39475. MEINERT, JOACHIM: *Geschichte eines Verbots. Warum Primo Levis Hauptwerk in der DDR nicht erscheinen durfte.* [In]: Sinn und Form. Beiträge zur Literatur, Jg. 52, H. 1, Berlin, 2000. Pp. 149–165. [Essay is followed by a documentation of the debate 1981–1982 (166–194), resulting in the ban of Levi's book; incl. letters by Fred Wander.]

39476. NAVÉ LEVINSON, PNINA: *Aus freier Entscheidung. Wege zum Judentum.* Mit einem Geleitwort von Hermann Simon und einem Nachwort von Nathan Peter Levinson. Berlin: Hentrich & Hentrich, 2000. 200 pp. frontis., illus. [Book was completed after the author's death by Hermann Simon and Nathan Peter Levinson. Deals with conversions to Judaism in Germany and other countries. Incl. reprint of an article publ. 1955 by Nathan Peter Levinson on conversions in post-war Germany. Also numerous later testimonies of German converts.] [P.N.L., née Paula Jalowicz, April 3, 1921 Berlin – Aug. 3, 1998 Jerusalem, Judaist, theologian, lecturer.]

39477. OMRAN, SUSANNE: *Frauenbewegung und 'Judenfrage'. Diskurse um Rasse und Geschlecht nach 1900.* Frankfurt am Main; New York: Campus, 2000. 522 pp., footnotes, bibl. (479–516), bibl., index. [Deals also with antisemitism and Jewish "self-hatred"; incl. chap. entitled: Frauen- und Judenfrage bei Henriette Fürth (436–478).]

39478. REICHRATH, HANS L.: *Die "Judenfrage" in der Geschichte des Evang. Kirchenboten der Pfalz 1846 bis 1932.* Zweibrücken: [Privately printed], 2000. 96 pp. [Available at the Bibliothek Germania Judaica, Cologne.]

39479. REICHEL, PETER: *Wenn Auschwitz aufhört weh zu tun. Kontinuität und Wandel im deutsch-jüdischen Schuldverhältnis.* [In]: 'FAZ', Nr. 20, Frankfurt am Main, 25. Jan. 2000. P. 14. [On "Vergangenheitsbewältigung", remembrance and the history of memorial days.]

39480. SCHMITT, JEAN-CLAUDE: *Die autobiographische Fiktion: Hermann des Juden Bekehrung.* Trier: Arye-Maimon-Inst., 2000. 39 Pp. (Kleine Schriften des Arye-Maimon-Instituts, H. 3.) [Deals with a fictionalised text about a converted Jew, written in the 12th cent. by the canons of Cappenberg, today part of Bork, Southern Westphalia.]

39481. SCHWARZ, EGON: *"Ich bin kein Freund allgemeiner Urteile über ganze Völker".* Essays über österreichische, deutsche und jüdische Literatur. Hrsg. von Dietmar Goltschnigg und Hartmut Steinecke. Berlin: Erich Schmidt Verlag, 2000. 282 pp., footnotes, index. (Philologische Studien und Quellen, H. 163.) [Cont.: Vorwort (eds., 7–12). 14 essays, all but two previously publ., on Jewish contrib. to German literature, Jews depicted in German literature, antisemitism, also reviews.] [E. Schwarz, data see No. 31236/YB XXXIX.]

39482. SWACK, JEANNE: *Anti-semitism and the opera: the portrayal of Jews in the singspiels of Reinhard Keiser.* [In]: The Musical Quarterly, Vol. 84, No. 3, Oxford, 2000. Pp. 389–416., notes. [Deals with a few comic operas written by the 18th-century Hamburg composer R.K.; libretti (a.o.) by Praetorius, partly in Yiddish.]

39483. WEISS, YFAAT: *Deutsche, Juden und Weder-Nochs: Neuerscheinungen zum Thema deutsch-jüdische Mischehen.* [In]: Zeitschrift für Geschichtswissenschaft, Jg. 48, H. 1, Berlin, 2000. Pp. 73–82, footnotes. [Review essay.]

39484. WELZER, HARALD , [et al.], eds.: *"Was wir für böse Menschen sind!"* Der Nationalsozialismus im Gespräch zwischen den Generationen. Unter Mitarbeit von Martina Piefke. Tübingen: Ed. Discord, 2000. 224 pp., bibl. [Also on the persecution of Jews.]

B. German-Israeli Relations

39485. DACHS, GISELA: *Stabil, aber nicht normal.* Die deutsch-israelischen Beziehungen. [In]: Neukirchener Theologische Zeitschrift, Jg. 14, H. 1, Neukirchen-Vluyn, 1999. Pp. 12–19.

39486. FABER, KLAUS: *Israel und Ostdeutschland.* [In]: Tribüne, Jg. 39, H. 155, Frankfurt am Main, 2000. Pp. 168–174.

39487. HEPPERLE, SABINE: *Die SPD und Israel: von der großen Koalition 1966 bis zur Wende 1982.* Frankfurt am Main, New York: Lang, 2000. 499 pp. (Europäische Hochschulschriften: Reihe 3, Geschichte und ihre Hilfswissenschaften, Bd. 861.) Zugl.: München, Univ. der Bundeswehr, Diss., 1999.

39488. TIMM, ANGELIKA: *Views on Zionism and Israel in East Germany.* [In]: Shofar, Vol. 18, No. 3, West Lafayette, IN, Spring 2000. Pp. 93–109, notes. [Deals with the ideological background of attitudes to Zionism and Israel in the former GDR.]

C. Church and Synagogue

39489. ASCHOFF, DIETHARD: *"Alljährliche Karfreitagspogrome" in Westfalen und anderswo. Kritische Betrachtungen zur Synodalvorlage "Christen und Juden" der Evangelischen Kirche von Westfalen vor allem in historischer Sicht.* [In]: Jahrbuch für Westfälische Kirchengeschichte, Bd. 95, Bielefeld, 2000. Pp. 208–235, footnotes. [This article is followed in the same issue by: Gegen Relativierung und Verharmlosung. Zu Diethard Aschoffs "Kritischen Betrachtungen" der Synodalvorlage 1999 der Evangelischen Kirche von Westfalen (Günter Birkmann, 236–256), to which the author responds, also in the same issue: Eine neue Gretchenfrage? Antwort auf die Replik Pfarrer Günter Birkmanns (237–256).]

—— HEINRICHS, WOLFGANG E.: *Das Judenbild im Protestantismus des Deutschen Kaiserreichs.* Ein Beitrag zur Mentalitätsgeschichte des deutschen Bürgertums in der Krise der Moderne. [See No. 39511.].

39490. KAUDERS, ANTHONY: *Jews in the Christian gaze: Munich's churches before and after Hitler.* [In]: Patterns of Prejudice, Vol. 34, No. 3, London, 2000. Pp. 27– 45, notes. [Discusses the attitudes of the Catholic and Prostestant churches in Munich towards the Jews.]

39491. LOTTER, FRIEDRICH: *"Der Gerechte wird seine Hände im Blut des Gottlosen waschen". Die Reaktivierung des theologischen Antijudaismus im Psalmenkommentar des Bruno von Würzburg.* [In]: Aschkenas, Jg. 10, H. 1, Wien, 2000. Pp. 43–115, footnotes. [Bruno von Würzburg died 1045.]

39492. NIESNER, MANUELA: *Die Juden in den Teichnerreden.* [In]: Zeitschrift für deutsches Altertum und deutsche Literatur, Bd. 129, Stuttgart, 2000. Pp. 38–69, footnotes. [Analyzes the short sermons in rhyme written in the 2nd half of the 14th cent. by a layman intended at missionary work among laymen in Austria.]

39493. SCHRECKENBERG, HEINZ: *Die christlichen Adversus-Judaeos-Texte (11.-13. Jh.)* Mit einer Ikonographie des Judenthemas bis zum 4. Laterankonzil. 3., erg. Aufl. Frankfurt am Main; New York: Lang, 1997. 739 pp., frontis., index (659–710). (Europäische Hochschulschriften, Reihe XXII: Theologie, Bd. 335.)

39494. SCHRECKENBERG, HEINZ: *Christliche Adversus-Judaeos-Bilder.* Das Alte und Neue Testament im Spiegel der christlichen Kunst. Frankfurt am Main; New York: Lang, 1999. 469 pp., frontis., illus., gloss., bibl., indexes. (Europäische Hochschulschriften, Reihe XXII: Theologie, Bd. 650.)

39495. SCHWERHOFF, GERD: *Blasphemie zwischen antijüdischem Stigma und kultureller Praxis. Zum Vorwurf der Gotteslästerung gegen die Juden in Mittelalter und beginnender Frühneuzeit.* [In]: Aschkenas, Jg. 10, H. 1, Wien, 2000. Pp. 117–155, footnotes. [Also cites instances of blaspemy of Christians as a test case.]

39496. *Theologische Quartalsschrift.* Jg. 180, H. 2 [with the issue title] *Auf dem Weg zu einem christlich-jüdischen Dialog?* Tübingen, 2000. 1 issue. [Incl.: contribs. by Ernst Ludwig Ehrlich, Hans Hermann Henrix, K. Kienzler [et al.].

39497. THOMA, CLEMENS: *Der jüdisch-christliche Dialog.* Bilanz und Aussichten an der Jahrtausendwende. [In]: Judaica, Jg. 56, H. 2, Zürich, Juni 2000. Pp. 766–89, footnotes.

D. Antisemitism

39498. ALTERMATT, URS: *Katholizismus und Antisemitismus. Mentalitäten, Kontinuitäten, Ambivalenzen. Zur Kulturgeschichte der Schweiz 1918–1945.* Frauenfeld: Huber, 1999. 414 pp.

—— *Antisemitismus und Antizionismus nach der Schoah.* [Section III in: *100 Jahre Zionismus. Von der Verwirklichung einer Vision*; see in No. 39212.]

39499. *Antisemitismus unter Jugendlichen*. Fakten, Erklärungen, Unterrichtsbausteine. Hrsg. von Dietmar Sturzbecher und Ronald Freytag. Göttingen; Toronto: Hogrefe, 2000. 252; 29 pp., illus., docs., footnotes, tabs., graphs., chronol., bibl., index.

—— BENZ, WOLFGANG: *Antisemitismusforschung*. [See in No. 39141.]

39500. BERGER WALDENEGG, GEORG CHRISTOPH: *Antisemitismus: Eine gefährliche Vokabel? Zur Diagnose eines Begriffs*. [In]: Jahrbuch für Antisemitismusforschung 9, Frankfurt am Main; New York, 2000. Pp. 108–126, notes.

39501. BLASCHKE, OLAF/ALTERMATT, URS: *"Katholizismus und Antisemitismus"*. *Eine Kontroverse*. [In]: Schweizerische Zeitschrift für Geschichte, Vol. 50, Basel, 2000. Pp. 205–236, footnotes. [Authors discuss the accusations of plagiarism and their different approaches to antisemitism; see Nos. 35814/YB XVIII (1997) and 39498.]

39502. BLASCHKE, OLAF/MATTIOLI, ARAM, eds.: *Katholischer Antisemitismus im 19. Jahrhundert*. Ursachen und Traditionen im internationalen Vergleich. Zürich: Orell Füssli, 2000. VII, 383 pp., notes, index. [Cont.: Die Anatomie des katholischen Antisemitismus. Eine Einladung zum internationalen Vergleich (Olaf Blaschke, 3–54). Antisemitismus im 19. Jahrhundert (Helmut Berding, 57–75). Wie wird aus einem guten Katholiken ein guter Judenfeind? Zwölf Ursachen des katholischen Antisemitismus auf dem Prüfstand (Olaf Blaschke, 77–109). Das letzte Ghetto Alteuropas. Die Segregationspolitik der Papstkönige in der "heiligen Stadt" bis 1870 (Aram Mattioli, 111–144). Ritualmordgerüchte als Form von popularem Antisemitismus – Eine katholische Spezialität? (Christoph Nonn, 145–159). Die französischen Katholiken und die Erfindung der "jüdischen Gefahr" (Pierre Sorlin, 163–194). Antisemitismus, Kulturkampf und Konfession – Die antisemitischen "Kulturen" Frankreichs und Deutschlands im Vergleich (Johannes Heil, 195–228). Contribs. on Italy, the Netherlands and Poland by Carlo Moos, Theo Salemnik, Viktoria Pollmann. "So lange die Juden Juden bleiben". Der Widerstand gegen die jüdische Emanzipation im Grossherzogtum Baden und im Kanton Aargau (1818–1863) (Aram Mattioli, 287–315). Vom Agrarantisemitismus zum katholischen Antisemitismus im Vorarlberg des 19. Jahrhunderts (Hans Gruber, 317–335). Ultramontanismus und Antisemitismus in der Urschweiz – oder: Der Kampf gegen die Säkularisierung von Staat und Gesellschaft (1858–1878) (Josef Lang, 337–372).]

39503. BRONNER, STEPHEN ERIC. *A rumor about the Jews: reflections on antisemitism and the "Protocols of the Learned Elders of Zion"*. New York: St. Martin's Press, 2000. 177 pp., notes (155–169), index. [Incl. selected texts from the orig. Protocols.] [Cf.: Scholars contending with delusional ideology: historians, antisemitic lore, and 'the Protocols' (Ronald S. Green) [in]: Shofar, Vol. 18, No. 2, Winter 2000, pp. 82–100, footnotes.]

39504. BRONNER, STEPHEN ERIC: *Ein Gerücht über die Juden: 'Die Protokolle der Weisen von Zion' und der alltägliche Antisemitismus*. [Aus dem Amerik. von Klaus Dieter Schmidt und Hans-Ulrich Seebohm]. Berlin: Propyläen, 1999. 239 pp., notes, bibl., index. [Incl. excerpts from the "Protocols".]

—— BRUMLIK, MICHA: *Deutscher Geist und Judenhaß*. Das Verhältnis des philosophischen Idealismus zum Judentum. [See No. 39541.]

39505. FISCHER, JENS MALTE: *Richard Wagners 'Das Judentum in der Musik'*. Eine kritische Dokumentation als Beitrag zur Geschichte des Antisemitismus. Frankfurt am Main: Insel, 2000. 380 pp., illus., notes (359–370), bibl.

39506. FLECK, CHRISTIAN/MÜLLER, ALBERT: *Front-stage and back-stage: the problem of measuring post-Nazi antisemitism in Austria*. [In]: Modern Europe after Fascism 1943–1980s. Ed. by Stein Ugelvik Larsen with the assistance of Bernt Hagtvet. New York, 1998. Pp. 436–454, footnotes.

39507. GRUNBERGER, BÉLA/DESSUANT, PIERRE: *Narzißmus, Christentum, Antisemitismus: eine psychoanalytische Untersuchung*. Aus dem Franz. übers. von Max Looser. Stuttgart: Clett Cotta, 2000. 513 pp., bibl. (483–503).

39508. HAIBL, MICHAELA: *Zerrbild als Stereotyp: Visuelle Darstellungen von Juden zwischen 1850 und 1900.* Berlin: Metropol, 2000. 381 pp., illus., footnotes, bibl. (363–381). (Dokumente – Texte – Materialien, Bd. 26.) [Examines illustrated journals, joke books, illustrated broadsheets.]

39509. HARTSTON, BARNET P.: *Judaism on trial: antisemitism in the German courtroom (1870–1895).* San Diego: University of California, Diss., 1999. [Privately printed] XIV, 393 pp., bibl.

39510. HEILBRONNER, ODED: *From antisemitic peripheries to antisemitic centres: the place of antisemitism in modern German history.* [In]: Journal of Contemporary History, Vol. 35, No. 4, London, 2000. Pp. 559–576, notes.

39511. HEINRICHS, WOLFGANG E.: *Das Judenbild im Protestantismus des Deutschen Kaiserreichs.* Ein Beitrag zur Mentalitätsgeschichte des deutschen Bürgertums in der Krise der Moderne. Köln: Rheinland-Verlag, 2000. XIII, 851 pp., illus., footnotes, bibl. (733–837), index. (Schriften des Vereins für Rheinische Kirchengeschichte, Bd. 145.) Zugl.: Wuppertal, Univ., Habil.-Schr., 1996. [Deals mainly with Protestant antisemitism as reflected in archival material and numerous periodicals, pamphlets, and academic publications.]

39512. HESS, JONATHAN M.: *Johann David Michaelis and the colonial imaginary: orientalism and the emergence of racial antisemitism in eighteenth-century Germany.* [In]: Jewish Social Studies, Vol. 6, No. 2, Bloomington, IN, Winter 2000. Pp. 56–101, notes.

39513. HIRSCH, RUDOLF/SCHUDER, ROSEMARIE: *Der gelbe Fleck. Wurzeln und Wirkungen des Judenhasses in der deutschen Geschichte.* Essays. Köln: PapyRossa, 2000. 770 pp., illus., facsims., bibl., index.

39514. JÄGER, SIEGFRIED: *Das Sommerloch wird gefüllt. Rechtsextremismus, Rassismus und Antisemitismus.* [In]: Tribüne, Jg. 39, H. 156, Frankfurt am Main, 2000. Pp. 172–182, footnotes, bibl.

39515. JUST, DIETER: *Das gestörte Weltbild. Über die Funktion des Antisemitismus im völkischen Denken.* Berlin: Weidler, 2000. 361 pp., bibl.

39516. KLAMPER, ELISABETH: *Von den mittelalterlichen Wurzeln des modernen Antisemitismus.* [In]: Wiener Jahrbuch für jüdische Geschichte, Kultur & Museumswesen, Bd. 4, 1999/2000/5760, Wien, 2000. Pp. 123–134.

39517. *Kolloquium: "Antisemitismus und österreichische Literatur".* [In]: Zwischenwelt [formerly: Mit der Ziehharmonika]. Jg. 17, Nr. 1, Wien, Mai 2000. Pp. 18–23. [Documentation of a radio discussion on post-1945 Austrian antisemitism with Erna Wiplinger, Gerhard Scheit, Konstantin Kaiser, Doron Rabinovici, Vladimir Vertlib, Evelyn Adunka.]

39518. KOSZYK, KURT: *Tat gegen Traum. Wie das antisemitische Komplott gegen Dreyfus im republikanischen Frankreich um 1900 schließlich scheiterte.* [In]: Geist und Gestalt im historischen Wandel. Facetten deutscher und europäischer Geschichte 1789–1989. Festschrift für Siegfried Bahne. Münster, New York. 2000. Pp.: 167–178, footnotes. [Deals also with the reactions of Theodor Herzl, Theodor Wolff, Egon Erwin Kisch, Karl Kraus to the Dreyfus Affair.]

39519. KRAPF, MARTIN: *Kein Stein bleibt auf dem anderen. Die christliche Schuld am Antisemitismus.* Neukirchen-Vluyn: Neukirchener, 1999. VIII, 290 pp., footnotes, index. [Incl. prefaces by Elie Wiesel and Eberhard Bethge.]

39520. KREIS, RUDOLF: *Antisemitismus und Kirche.* In den Gedächtnislücken deutscher Geschichte mit Heine, Freud, Kafka und Goldhagen. Reinbek bei Hamburg: Rowohlt Taschenbuch Verlag, 1999. 333 pp., notes, index. (Rowohlts Enzyklopädie.) [Examines Christian antisemitism as reflected in the works of Heine, Freud, Kafka; incl. an essay on the Goldhagen debate.]

39521. LINDEMANN, ALBERT, S.: *Anti-semitism before the Holocaust.* Harlow, UK; New York: Longman, 2000. XX, 144 pp., docs., gloss., maps, bibl. (131–138), index. (Seminar studies in history.) [Deals with antisemitism in different countries and different eras. Sec. 3 incl.: The rise of Germany and Germany's 'special' anti-semitism; Wilhelm Marr, the 'patriarch of antisemitism'; 'respectable' anti-semitism; the Berlin movement; anti-semites' petition, 'peasant king'; the Belle Epoque: 1890–1914; Karl Lueger and 'insincere' anti-semitism; Nazism in the making?]

39522. MARIN, BERND: *Antisemitismus ohne Antisemiten.* Autoritäre Vorurteile und Feindbilder. Mit einer Einleitung von Gerhard Botz. Unveränderte Neuauflage früher Analysen 1974–1979 und Umfragen 1946–1991. Frankfurt am Main; New York: Campus, 2000. 875 pp., illus., tabs. (Wohlfahrtspolitik und Sozialforschung/Europäisches Zentrum Wien, Bd. 10.) [Deals with Austria.]

39523. NEIDHARDT, IRIT: *Antisemitic anti-fascism?: undercurrents of the German radical left.* [In]: The Jewish Quarterly, Vol. 47, No. 4, London, Winter 2000–2001. Pp. 73–76.

39524. NEIDHART, IRIT/BISCHOF, WILLI, eds.: *Wir sind die Guten. Antisemitismus in der radikalen Linken.* Münster: Unrast, 2000. 188 pp., illus. [Cont. 7 articles.]

39525. PFAHL-TRAUGHBER, ARMIN: *Antisemitismus, Populismus und Sozialprotest. Eine Fallstudie zur Agitation von Otto Böckel, dem ersten Antisemiten im Deutschen Reichstag.* [In]: Aschkenas, Bd. 10, H. 2, Wien, 2000. Pp. 389–415, footnotes.

39526. PFEIFFER, THOMAS: *Antisemitismus in Computernetzen.* Neue Kommunikationsmöglichkeiten für Rechtsextremisten. [In]: Sachor. Zeitschrift für Antisemitismusforschung, jüdische Geschichte und Gegenwart, Bd. 10, Essen, 2000. Pp. 131–146, footnotes.

39527. PÖTZSCH, HANSJÖRG: *Antisemitismus in der Region.* Antisemitische Erscheinungsformen in Sachsen, Hessen, Hessen-Nassau und Braunschweig 1870–1914. Wiesbaden: Kommission für die Geschichte der Juden in Hessen, 2000. IX, 413 pp., footnotes, bibl. (349–400), indexes. (Schriften der Komm. für die Gesch. der Juden in Hessen, 17.) Zugl.: Braunschweig, Techn. Univ., Diss., 1997.

39527. PULZER, PETER: *Judenfeindschaft in Wien und Österreich.* [In]: Projekt: Judenplatz Wien [see No. 39090]. Pp. 153–170.

39529. RAHDEN, TILL VAN: *Words and actions: rethinking the social history of German antisemitism, Breslau, 1870–1914.* [In]: German History, Vol. 18, No. 4, London, 2000. Pp. 413–438, footnotes.

Richard Wagner und die Juden. Hrsg. von Dieter Borchmeyer, Ami Maayani und Susanne Vill. [See No. 39560.]

39530. SCHNITZLER, NORBERT: *Judenfeindschaft, Bildnisfrevel und das mittelalterliche Strafrecht.* [In]: Bilder, Texte, Rituale. Wirklichkeitsbezug und Wirklichkeitskonstruktion politisch-rechtlicher Kommunikationsmedien in Stadt- und Adelsgesellschaften des späten Mittelalters. Hrsg. von Klaus Schreiner, Gabriela Signori. Berlin: Duncker & Humblot, 2000. Pp. 11–138, illus., footnotes. [Analyses medieval illustrations, among them several from Germany.]

39531. SCHEIT, GERHARD: *Verborgener Staat, lebendiges Geld. Zur Dramaturgie des Antisemitismus.* Freiburg: ca ira Verlag, 1999. 587 pp., notes. [Cf.: Der gespielte Jude (Ruth Klüger) [in]: Zwischenwelt, Jg. 17, Nr. 2, Wien, Juli 2000, pp. 8–9.]

39532. SHAPIRO, JAMES: *Oberammergau: the troubling story of the world's most famous passion play.* New York: Pantheon, 2000. X, 238, illus., notes, bibl. (226–236). [Deals with the history of the play from the 17th cent. through the Nazi era and the current attempts to cleanse the play of its blatant antisemitism.] [Cf.: Review (Paul Boyer) [in]: Dimensions, Vol. 14, No. 2, New York, 2000, pp. 42–45, illus.]

39533. SIRGES, THOMAS/SCHÖNDORF, KURT ERICH, eds.: *Haß, Verfolgung und Toleranz.* Beiträge zum Schicksal der Juden von der Reformation bis in die Gegenwart. Frankfurt am Main; New York: Lang, 2000. 211 pp., footnotes. (Osloer Beiträge zur Germanistik, Bd. 24.) [Cont. material from the the Germanic Institute, Univ. of Oslo, 1997. Incl.: Judenhaß und Toleranz im Spiegel von Flugschriften und Einblattdrucken des 16. Jahrhunderts (Kurt Erich Schöndorf, 11–46). Toleranz und Ausgrenzung. Antijüdische Implikationen der Geschichtsphilosophie in der deutschen Literatur um 1800 (Ludwig Stockinger, 47–72). Der Judenartikel in der norwegischen Verfassung von 1814 in der Sicht deutscher Kommentatoren (Ivar Sagmo, 73–88). Antisemitismus im Wiener Fin de siècle und der junge Hitler (Brigitte Hamann, 89–100). Antisemitismus in der Sprache des Nationalsozialismus (Kurt Erich Schöndorf, 101–118). Further contribs. are listed according to subject.]

39534. TABARY, SERGE: *Race, religion et projet religieux dans l'antisémitisme allemand au XIXe siècle.* [In]: Recherches germaniques, No. 30, Strasbourg, 2000. Pp. 85–103, footnotes.

39535. VIERHUFE, ALMUT: *Politische Satire? Fritz Mauthners Roman "Der neue Ahasver" und der Berliner Antisemitismusstreit.* [In]: Fritz Mauthner – Sprache, Literatur, Kritik [see No. 39339.]. Pp. 145–162, footnotes.

39536. WELSKOPF, RUDOLF/FREYTAG, RONALD/STURZBECHER, DIETMAR: *Antisemitismus unter Jugendlichen in Ost und West.* [In]: Jahrbuch für Antisemitismusforschung 9, Frankfurt am Main; New York, 2000. Pp. 35–70, notes.

39537. WISTRICH, ROBERT S., ed.: *Demonizing the other. Antisemitism, racism and xenophobia.* Amsterdam: Harwood Academic publishers, 1999. 1 vol. [Cont. 23 essays, some of them dealing with German antisemitism from the middle ages to the present by Saul Friedländer, Simon Epstein, Israel J. Yuval, Shulamit Volkov, Harumi Befu, Yaakov Schul, Henry Zukier, Ziva Amishai-Maisels, Shmuel Almog, Yael S. Feldman, Otto D. Kulka, Dina Porat, Philippe Burrin, Wolfgang Benz.] [Cf.: Besprechung (Doris Sottopietra) [in]: Zeitgeschichte, Jg. 27, H. 6, Salzburg, Nov./Dez. 2000, pp. 417–422, notes.]

——— ZIMMERMANN, PETER: *Die Nacht hinter den Wäldern.* [See No. 39581.]

E. Noted Germans and Jews

39538. BAUER, BRUNO. LEOPOLD, DAVID: *The Hegelian antisemitism of Bruno Bauer.* [In]: History of European Ideas, Vol. 25, London, 1999. Pp. 179–206, footnotes.

39540. BISMARCK, OTTO VON. HOPP, ANDREA: *Otto von Bismarck aus der Sicht des jüdischen Bürgertums.* Friedrichsruh: Otto-von-Bismarck-Stiftung, 1999. 33 pp., illus. (Friedrichsruher Beiträge, Bd. 5.)

39541. BRUMLIK, MICHA: *Deutscher Geist und Judenhaß. Das Verhältnis des philosophischen Idealismus zum Judentum.* München: Luchterhand, 2000. 351 pp., notes (321–346), index. [Cont. an introduction and 6 essays devoted to Immanuel Kant, Johann Gottlieb Fichte, Friedrich Schleiermacher, Georg Wilhelm Friedrich Hegel, Friedrich Wilhelm Schelling and Karl Marx.]

39542. BURCKHARDT, JACOB. MATTIOLI, ARAM: *Jacob Burckhardts Antisemitismus. Eine Neuinterpretation aus mentalitätsgeschichtlicher Sicht.* [In]: Schweizerische Zeitschrift für Geschichte, Vol. 49, Basel, 1999. Pp. 496–529, footnotes. [Incl. French summary.]

39543. FICHTE, JOHANN GOTTLIEB. VOIGTS, MANFRED: *Fichte as "Jew-hater" and prophet of the Zionists.* [In]: Leo Baeck Institute Year Book XLV, Oxford, 2000. Pp. 81–92, footnotes.

39544. FONTANE, THEODOR. MECKLENBURG, NORBERT: *"Ums Goldne Kalb sie tanzen und morden". Philo- und antisemitische Gedichte des alten Fontane.* [In]: Wirkendes Wort. Deutsche Sprache und Literatur in Forschung und Lehre, Jg. 50, Trier, 2000. Pp. 358–381, footnotes.

39545. GOETHE, JOHANN WOLFGANG VON. BATTAFARANO, ITALO MICHELE: *Goethe über Deutsche und Juden anno 1807.* [In]: Morgen-Glantz, Bd. 10, Bern; New York, 2000.

39546. GOETHE, JOHANN WOLFGANG VON. HOMANN, URSULA: *Weder Freund noch Feind. Goethe und die Juden: ein zwiespältiges Verhältnis.* [In]: Die Zeichen der Zeit/Lutherische Monatshefte, Jg. 3, H. 1, Hannover, 2000. Pp. 38–39, illus.

Bibliography

39547. GOETHE, JOHANN WOLFGANG VON. WASSERMANN, HENRY: *Goethe, Juden, Judentum.* [In]: 'MB', Jg. 68, Tel Aviv, März/April 2000, Nr. 153, Pp. 3–5.

39548. GOETHE, JOHANN WOLFGANG VON. WEBER, ANNETTE, ed.: *"Außerdem waren sie ja auch Menschen". Goethes Begegnung mit Juden und Judentum.* Berlin: Philo, 2000. 169 pp., notes (151–169). (Schriftenreihe des Jüdischen Museums Frankfurt am Main, Bd. 7.) [Incl. papers given at a symposium at Museum Judengasse, Frankfurt am Main, Sept. 1999; cont. (some titles abbr.): Vorwort (Georg Heuberger, 7–9). Einführung (Wilfried Barner, 11–17). Goethes Haltung zur Judenemanzipation und jüdische Haltungen zu Goethe (W. Daniel Wilson, 19–46). Die Judengasse in Frankfurt am Main (Gabriela Schlick, 47–66). Der junge Goethe zwischen religiöser Schwärmerei und Toleranz (Karl Dienst, 67–86). Goethe als Anwalt jüdischer Mandanten in Frankfurt 1771–1775 (Hans-Peter Benöhr, 87–88). Jüdisches im Werk des jungen Goethe (Jürgen Stenzel, 99–116). Die Juden und Goethe (Hans Otto Horch, 117–132). Die Entstehung eines nationalen Goethe-Bildes im 19. Jahrhundert und seine Rolle in antisemitischen Ausgrenzungsstrategien (Willi Jasper, 133–144). Zusammenfassung der Abschlußdiskussion (ed., 145–150).]

39549. HAUFF, WILHELM. DÜSTERBERG, ROLF: *Wilhelm Hauffs 'opportunistische' Judenfeindschaft.* [In]: Zeitschrift für deutsche Philologie, Berlin, Bd. 119, 2000. Pp. 190–212, footnotes.

39550. KANT, IMMANUEL. STANGNETH, BETTINA: *Antisemitische und antijudaistische Motive bei Immanuel Kant?* Der Philosophisch-Politischen Akademie in Berlin als Antwort auf die Preisfrage 'Antisemitische und antijudaistische Motive bei Denkern der Aufklärung'. Hamburg: [Typescript], 1999. 75 pp., footnotes. [Available at the Bibliothek Germania Judaica, Cologne.]

39551. KNIGGE, ADOLPH FREIHERR. GREIN, ALMUT: *Adolph Freiherr Knigge und die Juden.* Mannheim: Univ. Mannheim, Hist. Inst., Magisterarbeit, 1999. 97 pp., footnotes, bibl. [Available at the Bibliothek Germania Judaica, Cologne.]

39552. LUTHER, MARTIN. HAGEN, KENNETH: *Luther's so-called 'Judenschriften': a genre approach.* [In]: Archiv für Reformationsgeschichte, Vol. 90, Gütersloh, 1999. Pp. 130–158, footnotes. [Incl. German summary.]

39553. MANN, THOMAS. LEYERZAPF, GERHARD: *'Zur jüdischen Frage.' Eine verschollene Erstausgabe von Thomas Mann.* [In]: Aus dem Antiquariat [Beilage zum] Börsenblatt für den Deutschen Buchhandel, Jg. 167, Nr. 43, Frankfurt am Main, 30. Mai 2000. Pp. A 300–A 303, notes. [Deals with an article by Th.M. intended for publ. in 1921 in 'Der Neue Merkur', but withdrawn by him.]

39554. MÜNSTER, SEBASTIAN. BURNETT, STEPHEN G.: *A dialogue of the deaf: Hebrew pedagogy and anti-Jewish polemic in Sebastian Münster's 'Messiahs of the Christians and the Jews' (1529/39).* [In]: Archiv für Reformationsgeschichte, Vol. 91. Gütersloh, 2000. Pp. 168–190, footnotes, appendixes.

39555. NEUMANN, ELSA. VOGT, ANNETTE: *Elsa Neumann. Berlins erstes Fräulein Doktor.* Unter Mitarbeit von Annette Pussert. Berlin: Verl. f. Wissenschafts- u. Regionalgeschichte, 1999. 200 pp., footnotes, illus. [E.N., physicist, Aug. 23, 1872 Berlin – July 23, 1902 Berlin.] [Also on the fate of N.'s family in the Nazi period.]

39556. NIETZSCHE, FRIEDRICH. CANCIK, HUBERT: *Nietzsche – der Anti-Antisemit?* Ein Blick in die Dokumente. [In]: 'NZZ', Nr. 198, Zürich, 26./27. Aug. 2000. P. 54.

39557. REUCHLIN, JOHANNES. REUCHLIN, JOHANNES: *Recommendation whether to confiscate, destroy and burn all Jewish books.* A classic treatise against antisemitism. Transl., ed. and with a foreword by Peter Wortsman. Critical introd. by Elisheva Carlebach. New York: Paulist Press, 2000. V, 90 pp., illus., notes. (Studies in Judaism and Christianity.) [First publ. in 1510. Incl. bibl. of works relating to the Reuchlin and Pfefferkorn controversy.]

39558. SCHMITT, CARL. GROSS, RAPHAEL: *Carl Schmitt und die Juden. Eine deutsche Rechtslehre.* Frankfurt am Main: Suhrkamp, 2000. 442 pp., footnotes, bibl. (391–429), indexes (names, subjects). Zugl.: Essen, Univ., Diss., 1999. [Deals with the impacts of Schmitt's virulent antisemitism on his intellectual development and thinking.] [Cf.: Feinde des Politischen. Raphael Gross über Carl Schmitts Antisemitismus (Herfried Münkler) [in]: Die Zeit, Nr. 38, Hamburg, 14. Sep. 2000, p. 67. Besprechung (Ulrich Sieg) [in]: Zeitschrift für Geschichtswissenschaft, Jg. 49, H. 3, Berlin, 2000, pp. 268–270.]

——— WAGNER, RICHARD. FISCHER, JENS MALTE: *Richard Wagners 'Das Judentum in der Musik'*. Eine kritische Dokumentation als Beitrag zur Geschichte des Antisemitismus. [See No. 39505.]

——— WAGNER, RICHARD. FRIEDLÄNDER, SAUL/RÜSEN, JÖRN, eds.: *Richard Wagner im Dritten Reich. Ein Schloss Elmau-Symposion.* [See No. 38936.]

39559. WAGNER, RICHARD. FULCHER, JANE F.: *A political barometer of twentieth-century France: Wagner as Jew or anti-Semite.* [In]: The Musical Quarterly, Vol. 84, No. 1. Oxford, 2000. Pp. 41–57, notes.

39560. WAGNER, RICHARD. *Richard Wagner und die Juden.* Hrsg. von Dieter Borchmeyer, Ami Maayani und Susanne Vill. Stuttgart: Metzler, 2000. 354 pp., footnotes, index. [Papers given at a symposium in Bayreuth, Aug. 6–11, 1998; cont. (some titles abbr.): Einleitung (eds., 1–7). Bayreuth und der Erlösungsantisemitismus (Saul Friedländer, 8–19). Heinrich Heine – Richard Wagner. Analyse einer Affinität (Dieter Borchmeyer, 20–34). Richard Wagners "Das Judentum in der Musik" (Jens Malte Fischer, 35–54). Das ästhetische Motiv in Wagners Antisemitismus (Udo Bermbach, 55–78). Zur Frage antisemitischer Charakterzeichnung in Wagners Werk (Hermann Dauser, 79–102). Jüdische Theosophie in Richard Wagners "Parsifal" (Wolf-Daniel Hartwich, 103–122). "Nietzsche contra Wagner" und die Juden (Yirmiyahu Yovel, 123–143). Die Rassenlehre von Houston Stewart Chamberlain (David Clay Large, 144–159). Wagner, der Antisemitismus und die Auseinandersetzung zwischen der "traditionellen" und der faschistischen Rechten in Frankreich (Jane F. Fulcher, 160–179). Wieviel "Hitler" ist in Wagner? Anmerkungen zu Hitler, Wagner und Thomas Mann (Hans Rudolf Vaget, 178–206). Richard Wagners Bedeutung für Adolf Hitler und die nationalsozialistische Führung (Dina Porat, 207–222). Wagner und Hitler – nach dem Holocaust (Paul Lawrence Rose, 223–237). Wagner und der amerikanische Jude – eine persönliche Betrachtung (Joseph Horowitz, 238–250). Wagner aus psychoanalytischer Sicht (Peter Gay, 252–261). Die traumatische Beziehung Wagners zu Meyerbeer (Sieghart Döhring, 262–274). Die 'Propheten'-Aufführung in Paris und die Strategie der Diffamierung (Oswald Georg Bauer, 275–295). Mahler und Wagner – sichtbares und unsichtbares Theater (Susanne Vill, 296–309). Schönberg und Wagner (Ludger Arens, 310–327). Wagner in Israel. Vom Verbot bis zur Schaffung eines politischen Symbols, 1938–1997 (Na'ama Sheffi, 328–346).]

39561. WAGNER, RICHARD. WEINER, MARC A.: *Antisemitische Fantasien. Die Musikdramen Richard Wagners.* Aus dem Amerik. von Henning Thies. Berlin: Henschel, 2000. 477 pp., illus., notes (402–442), bibl. (444–472). [Orig. publ. 1995, see No. 33596/YB XLI.]

X. FICTION AND POETRY

39562. AGNON, SHMUEL YOSEF. *Only yesterday.* Transl. by Barbara Harshav. Princeton, NJ: Princeton Univ. Press, 2000. XXXI, 652 pp. [First English edn. of novel, orig. publ. in Hebrew in 1945.]

39563. APPELFELD, AHARON: *Roman.* Aus dem Hebr. von Anne Birkenhauer. Berlin: Alexander Fest Verlag, 2000. 284 pp. [Orig. publ. 1997; tells the story of a young couple from the Bukowina during Nazi occupation.]

39564. BERADT, MARTIN: *Die Straße der kleinen Ewigkeit.* Roman. Mit einem Essay und einem Nachruf von Eike Geisel. Frankfurt am Main: Eichborn, 2000. 369 pp., illus. (Die andere Bibliothek.) [Incl.: Das Scheunenviertel. Beschreibung eines Zenotaphs (Eike Geisel, 7–48; on Berlin and its Eastern Jewish population). Nachruf zu Lebzeiten (Eike Geisel, 355–370); novel set in Berlin, first publ. 1965; a 2nd and complete version publ. 1993 with the title 'Beide Seiten einer Straße', which incl. also the 'Nachwort' by E.G. (see No. 32447/YB XL).] [M.B., 1881 Magdeburg – Nov. 26, 1949 New York, lawyer, writer, emigr. 1939 via England to the US.]

39565. BRETT, LILY: *Collected stories.* St. Lucia: Univ. of Queensland Press, 2000. VI, 444 pp., illus. [Fictional stories about Holocaust survivors making a new life in Australia.]

39566. EICHNER, HANS: *Kahn & Engelmann.* Eine Familien-Saga. Wien: Picus, 2000. 367 pp. (Österreichische Exilbibliothek.) [Deals with Jewish families from Vienna and their fate in the 20th cent.] [H.E., born Oct. 30, 1921 in Vienna, prof. of German language and literature, emigr. 1938 via Belgium to the UK, 1950 to Canada, lives in Rockwood, Ontario.]

39567. GIORDANO, RALPH: *Morris. Geschichte einer Freundschaft.* Köln: Kiepenheuer & Witsch, 2000. 117 pp. [Incl. preface by the author; story was first publ. 1948, deals with the friendship between a non-Jewish and a Jewish boy in G.'s home town of Hamburg.]

39568. GRONEMANN, SAMMY: *Tohuwabohu.* Roman. Mit einem Nachwort von Joachim Schlör. Leipzig: Reclam, 2000. 376 pp. [Incl.: Tohuwabohu. Einige Klärungen und viel mehr Fragen (Joachim Schlör, 357–376, frontis., notes; biographical essay). Novel, set in the Eastern Jewish milieu of Berlin; 16 editions publ. between 1920 and 1925.] [S.G., data see No. 37129/YB XLIV.]

39569. HAMBURGER, MICHAEL: *In einer kalten Jahreszeit.* Gedichte (englisch/deutsch) und ein Essay. Aus dem Englischen von Peter Waterhouse. Wien: Folio, 2000. [Cf.: Im Wortgefängnis. Michael Hamburgers Holocaust-Gedichte (Harald Hartung) [in]: 'FAZ', Nr. 83, Frankfurt am Main, 7. April, Beilage, p. V.]

39570. HONIGMANN, BARBARA: *Alles, alles Liebe!* München: Carl Hanser, 2000. 179 pp. [Deals with Jewish intellectuals in the former GDR.] [Cf.: Aufbruch in ein neues Leben (Ludwig Harig) [in]: 'ndl', Jg. 47, H. 523, Berlin, Jan./Feb. 1999. Pp. 154–150.]

39571. KRESSMANN, TAYLOR: *Adressat unbekannt.* Hamburg: Hoffmann und Campe, 2000. [First publ. 1938; last American edn. 1995 with the title 'Address unknown'.] [Fictionalized correspondence between a German and an American Jew in the beginning of the Nazi era.]

39572. MITGUTSCH, ANNA: *Haus der Kindheit.* Roman. München: Luchterhand, 2000. 333 pp. [Deals with an Austrian born New York Jew claiming restitution of the house owned by his family in a small provincial town before 1938.]

39573. PARINI, JAY: *Dunkle Passagen.* Ein Walter-Benjamin-Roman. Aus dem Amerik. von Gerhard Beckmann. München: Albrecht Knaus, 2000. 447 pp. [Orig. publ. 1997 with the title 'Benjamin's crossing', see No. 37133/YB XLIV.]

39574. PERUTZ, LEO: *Nachts unter steinernen Brücken.* Roman. Hrsg. und mit einem Nachwort von Hans Harald Müller. Wien: Zsolnay, 2000. 296 pp. [Novel, set in Prague, written between 1943 and 1951 in Palestine, first publ. 1953; see also No. 39359.]

39575. RAUHUT-BRUNGS, LEAH: *Linkshändige Jüdinnen.* Erzählungen. Eichenau: Verl. Roman Kovar, 1998. 85 pp. [Stories deal with today's Jewish women in Germany and Switzerland and their lives overshadowed by the past.]

39576. REINEROVÁ, LENKA: *Zu Hause in Prag – manchmal auch anderswo.* Erzählungen. Berlin: Aufbau, 2000. 160 pp.

39577. SEIDEL, JÜRGEN: *Harry Heine und der Morgenländer.* Roman. Weinheim: Beltz, 1998. 236 pp. [Set in early 19th-century Düsseldorf, novel depicts Heinrich Heine's young years.]

39578. SEGAL, LORE: *Wo andere Leute wohnen.* Roman. Aus dem Amerik. von Sabine Illmer. Wien: Picus, 2000. 368 pp. (Österreichische Exilbibliothek.) [Autobiographical novel; tells the story of a young girl from Vienna, who went 1938 with a Kindertransport to the UK, 1948 to Sosua, Dominican Republic, 1951 to New York.] [L.S., née Groszmann, b. 1928 in Vienna, prof. of creative writing at American universities, went with Kindertransport to UK in 1938, 1951 she went to the US via the Dominican Republic.]

39579. TERGIT, GABRIELE: *Der erste Zug nach Berlin.* Novelle. Hrsg. und mit einem Nachwort versehen von Jens Brüning. Berlin: Das Neue Berlin, 2000. 192 pp., chronol. [Unpubl. autobiographical story, set in the early post-1945 years in Berlin; deals a.o. with the post-war antisemitism, and Holocaust denial.]

39580. WASSERMANN, JAKOB: *Die Juden von Zirndorf.* Roman. Mit einem Vorwort von Hilde Domin. München: Langen Müller, 1999. 303 pp. [First publ. 1897.]

39581. ZIMMERMANN, PETER: *Die Nacht hinter den Wäldern.* Roman. Wien: Deutecke, 2000. 301 pp. [Deals with the "ritual murder" of Polna (Moravia) 1899, resulting in the trial against Leopold Hilsner.]

Index to Bibliography

Aachen, 38905, 39222
Aalders, Gerard, 38894
Aargau, 39501
Abelein, Manfred, 38926
Abir-Am, Pnina G., 38666
Aboling, Sabine, 39166
Abraham Family, 38872
Abraham, Max, 38872
Abraham, Paul, 38482
Abrahamsohn Family, 38956
Abret, Helga, 39217
Academics, 38567
Acculturation, Assimilation, 38423, 38460, 38458, 38543
Ackermann, Bruno, 38751
Adams, Hermann, 38510
Adelson, Leslie A., 38899
Adler, Hermann, 39007
Adler, Oswald, 39245
Adorno, Theodor W., 38982, 39220, 39236, 39246, 39418
Adunka, Evelyn, 38616, 38686, 39064, 39517
Ages, Arnold, 38844
Agnon, Shmuel Yosef (Josef), 38432, 39247, 39562
Ahland, Frank, 38609
Ahr, Johan, 38745
Ahren, Yizhak, 39140
Ahrensbök, 38701
Ahrensfelde, 38908
Albany, Refugees,
Albers-Schönberg, Heinz, 38959
Albert, Phyllis Cohen, 39346
Albert, Pierre, 38651
Albrecht, Michael, 39126
Albrecht-Weinberger, Karl, 38628
Alexander, Isaak, 39098
Alföldi, Maria R., 39350
Allende-Blin, Juan, 39231
Allerhand, Jacob, 38628, 39212
Allert, Tilman, 39377
'Allgemeine' Jüd. Wochenzeitung, 39026, 39031, 39150
Allport, Gordon W., 38413, 39455
Almog, Shmuel, 39537
Aloni, Jenny, 39217, 39248
Alsace, 38565, 38612, 38613, 38614
Altenbockum, Jasper von, 39070
Altermatt, Urs, 38615, 39502
Altfelix, Thomas, 39458
Althaus, Hans Peter, 38461

Althoff, Gertrud, 38574
Altona, 38536
Altschul, Eleazar, 38639
Ambrose, Kenneth, 38956
Amery, Jean, 38950, 38982, 39249
Amishai-Maisels, Ziva, 39537
Amkraut, Brian David, 38702
Ammerich, Hans, 38437
Amsterdam, 38424
Anderl, Gabriele, 38984
Anders, Günther, 38982
Andrieu, Claire,
Andrzejewski, Marek, 38656
Anti-Judaism, 39491, 39492, 39493, 39494, 39495, 39519
Anti-Zionism, 39212
Antisemitism, 38419, 38458, 38491, 38631, 38685, 38687, 39016, 39200, 39212, 39240, 39246, 39256, 39323, 39398, 39474, 39477, 39490, 39500-39538, 39541, 39542, 39543, 39548, 39550, 39558, 39560, 39561
Antisemitism, Austria, 39014, 39152, 39517, 39528
Antisemitism, Christian (see also Anti-Judaism), 39478, 39519, 39520
Antisemitism, Defence, 38955, 39312
Antisemitism, Early Modern Period, 39510, 39512, 39557
Antisemitism, Imperial Germany, 38413, 39508, 39509, 39511, 39521, 39527, 39529, 39535
Antisemitism, Middle Ages, 39516, 39530
Antisemitism, Nazi Period, 38831, 38868, 38885, 38909, 38950, 38976, 38998, 39001
Antisemitism, Post-1945, 39023, 39499, 39514, 39522, 39524, 39526, 39536
Antisemitism, Research, 39141, 39507
Antisemitism, Switzerland, 38615, 38643, 38645, 38962, 38969, 39502
Antisemitism, Universities (see also University and Jews), 38767
Aplerbeck, 38703
Appelfeld, Aharon, 39250, 39563
Aptroot, Marion, 38465, 39141
Architecture, Jews in, 39291, 39341
'Archiv für Reformationsgeschichte', 39471, 39552, 39554
'Der Archivar', 38613
Archives, 38613, 38668
Arendt, Hannah, 38410, 38511, 38704, 38982, 39158, 39198, 39252-39257
Arens, Ludger, 39560

Argentina, Refugees, 38646
Armbrüster, Georg, 38947
Army, Jews in the, 38417, 38422, 38487
Arnim, Bettina von, 39474
Arnold, Klaus, 38651
Arnoldi, Udo, 38939
Arnstein, George E., 39182
Aronsen, Alex, 38780
Aronsfeld, C.C., 39153
Aronson, Shlomo, 38725
Art Historians, 38699, 39277, 39350, 39410, 39442
Art, Jewish, 39141, 39188, 39189, 39191
Art, Jews and Judaism depicted in, 39494, 39530
Art, Jews in, 38913, 39245, 39361
Aryanisation, 38571, 38700, 38705, 38718, 38724, 38739, 38760, 38824, 38872, 38891, 38894, 38985, 38986, 38987, 39003,
Ascher, Saul, 39257
Ascherson, Neal, 38842
Aschheim, Steven E., 38411, 39346
'Aschkenas', 38674; 38419, 38429, 38440, 38455, 38561, 38597, 39122, 39137, 39144, 39155, 39166, 39195, 39267, 39460, 39466, 39491, 39495, 39525
Aschoff, Diethard, 38498, 38566, 38574, 39489
Ash, Mitchell G., 38806
Assaf, David, 38628
Attar, K. E., 39307
Attenborough, Richard, 38860
Attias, Isaac, 38537
Auerbach, Berthold, 38423, 39258
Auernheimer, Georg, 38825
'Aufbau', New York, 38704, 39436
Aufgebauer, Peter, 38496
Augsburg, 38706
'Aus dem Antiquariat, (Börsenbl. f.d. Deutschen Buchhandel)', 39281, 39284, 39374, 39453, 39553
Auschwitz, 38707, 38711, 38722, 38749, 38802, 38864, 38866, 38870, 38872, 38882, 38893, 38898, 38910, 38916, 38927, 38950
Auschwitz-Birkenau, 38722, 38905
Auschwitz-Monowitz, 38712
Ausländer, Rose, 39143, 39217, 39366
Aussig, 38631
Australia, Immigration, 39565
Australia, Refugees, 38647, 38648, 38782, 39152
'Australian Jewish Historical Society Journal', 38648, 38782
Austria, 38432, 38617, 38624, 38627, 38629, 38713, 38717, 39016, 39173, 39470
Austria Judaica, 38673
Austria, Antisemitism, 39506, 39522, 39528, 39533
Austria, Emigration, 38650, 39229
Austria, Nazi Period, 38648, 38714, 38715, 38716, 38719, 38721, 38940, 39065
Austria, Post-1945, 38718, 38899, 39014, 39015, 39035, 39048, 39065, 39219, 39506

Austria, Refugees, 38667
Austria, Restitution, 39572
Autobiographies, Memoirs, Diaries, Letters, 38413, 39194, 39419, 39420, 39423, 39426, 39431, 39432, 39435, 39444, 39445, 39447, 39450, 39456,
Autobiographies, Memoirs, Nazi Period, 38735, 38749, 38853, 38862, 38999, 39578
Avineri, Shlomo, 39212
'Avotaynu', 39167
Ayalon, Moshe, 38521

Baackmann, Susanne, 39399
Baal Schem of Michelstadt see Wormser, Seckel Löb, 38561
Bacharach, Walter Zwi, 38725
Bachmann, Martin, 38895
Bachrach, Susan D., 38723
Backhausen, Manfred, 38564
Baden, 38472, 38507, 38569, 38816, 38906, 38935, 39501
Baden-Württemberg, 38437
Baeck, Leo, 39131
Bär, Ulrich, 38900
Bahne, Siegfried (Festschrift), 38438, 38742
Bai, Matt, 38942
Bajohr, Frank, 38705, 38724, 38725
Bakerde, 38513
Bakirdögen, Ayhan, 38658
Ballod, Matthias, 39217
Bamberger, Ernst, 38924
Bamberger, Fritz, 39114
Bankier, David, 38725
Banking, Jews in, 38534
Bar-Giora Bamberger, Naftali, 38568
Bar-Giora Bamberger, Naftali, Obit., 38568
Barck, Simone, 38821
Barkai, Avraham, 38668
Barkow, Ben, 38683
Barner, Wilfried, 39548
Barnett, Victoria J., 38758
Barta-Fliedl, Ilsebill, 38985
Bartels-Ishikawa, Anna, 39385, 39386
Bartfeld-Feller, Margit, 38633, 38634
Barthel, Wolfgang, 39263
Bartos, Josef, 38760
Bartoszewski, Wladyslaw, 39212
Bartov, Omer, 38745, 38810, 38832, 38899
Bartrop, Paul Robert, 38726
Barzel, Amnon, 38478
Barzilai, David, 39102
Basle, 38642
Bassewitz, Vanessa von, 38837
Bathrick, David, 38899
Batnitzky, Leora, 39388
Battafarano, Italo Michele, 39545
Battel, Franco, 38960
Battenberg, Friedrich, 38674
Batzdorff, Susanne M., 39380

Bauer, Alfredo, 39301
Bauer, Bruno, 39538
Bauer, Gerhard, 39228
Bauer, Leo, 38651
Bauer, Markus, 38727
Bauer, Oswald Georg, 39560
Bauer, Uwe F.W., 38579
Bauer, Yehuda, 38725, 39212
Baumann, Ulrich, 38472
Baumbach, Sybille, 38819
Baumgartner, Gerhard, 39364
Bavaria, 38611, 39017
Baviskar, Vera, 38467
Bayerdörfer, Hans-Peter, 39217
'Bayerische Blätter für Volkskunde', 38527
Bayreuth, 38728, 39560
Bechhofen, 38505
Beck, Evelyn Torton, 38667
Beck, Knut, 39457
Becker, Hans-Jürgen, 38579
Becker, Johannes, 38547
Becker, Jurek, 39259
Becker, Peter,
Beckmann, V., 38602
Beer, Max, 39439
Beer-Hofmann, Richard, 39147
Beese, Jürgen, 38593
Befu, Harumi, 39537
Behmer, Markus, 38651
Behrend, Susanne, 38649
Behring, Eva, 39163
Beinart, Haim, 38685
'Beiträge zur Gesch. d. Arbeiterbewegung', 38781, 39433
'Beiträge zur Nationalsoz. Gesundheits- und Sozialpolitik',
'Beiträge zur Ostdeutschen Kirchengeschichte', 38657, 39380
Beker, Avi, 38729
Belgium, Nazi Period, 38916, 39011, 39012
Belgium, Refugees, 38857
Bell, Anthea, 38801
Beller, Steven, 39152
Below, Hanna, 39277
Below, Irene, 39239
Ben Gurion, David, 39214
Ben-Ami, Shlomo, 39212
'Ben-Gavriel, Moshe Ya'akov, 39431
Ben-Shemen, 39203
Benbassa, Esther, 38612
Bender, Hans, 39424
Bendt, Vera, 38478
Benhabib, Seyla, 39251
Benjamin, Dora, 39260
Benjamin, Walter, 38899, 38982, 39099, 39110, 39139, 39149, 39215, 39220, 39236, 39261, 39262, 39419, 39420, 39573
Benjamin, Walter (Gesammelte Briefe), 39420
Benkendorf, Arne, 38604

Benöhr, Hans-Peter, 39548
Benz, Ernst, 38521
Benz, Ute , 38821
Benz, Wolfgang, 38684, 38730, 38731, 38821, 38882, 38922, 39141, 39537
Beradt, Martin, 39263, 39564
Berding, Helmut, 39501
Berdyczewski, Micha Joseph, 39422
Berenbaum, Michael, 38708
Berendsohn, Walter A., 39264
Berendt, Gzegorz, 38957
Berg, Hubert Van Den, 39441
Berg, Jimmy, 38721
Berg, Matthew Paul, 39438
Bergbauer, Knut, 39168
Bergel, Hans, 39245
Bergen-Belsen, 38732, 38870, 38904
Berger Waldenegg, Georg Christoph, 39500
Berger, Christel, 39447
Berger, Renate, 39239
Berger, Shlomo, 38465
Bergh, Magnus, 39164
Bergheim (Erft), 38473
Bergheim/Paffendorf, 38473
Berglind, Susanne, 38821
Bergmann, Armin, 38472
Bergmann, Herbert, 38945
Bergmann, Hugo, 39210
Bergmann, Peter E., 38809
Bergmann, Werner, 38684
Berio, Luciano, 39400
Berkel, Alexander, 38837
Berkholz, Stefan, 39359
Berlin, 38446, 38452, 38474-38480, 38483, 38733-38739, 38857, 38863, 39018, 39019, 39114, 39124, 39140, 39200, 39203, 39242, 39257, 39263, 39294, 39311, 39354, 39386, 39419, 39455, 39564, 39568, 39579
Berlin, Holocaust Memorial, 39066, 39067, 39095
Berlin, Jeffrey B., 39457
Berlin, Jewish Museum, 38477-38480, 39096
Berlin-Mitte, 38476
Berlin-Treptow, 38486
Berlin-Weissensee, 38487
'Berliner Tageblatt', 39414
Bermbach, Udo, 38936, 39560
Bern, 38643
Bernheim, Erhard, 38706
Bernkastel, 38488
Bernstein, Eduard, 38421, 39265
Bernstein, Michael André, 39215
Bernstein, Richard J., 39251
Berschel, Hugo, 38777
Bertman, Martin A., 39103
Bertsch, Franz, 39068
Best, Michael, 39193
Bethge, Eberhard, 39519
Bettelheim, Bruno, 38726
Betten, Anne, 39211

Betz, Albrecht, 39302
Beutin, Wolfgang, 38423
Beyer, Marcel, 38834
Bhatti, Anil, 38780
Biale, David, 38460
Bibliographies, Catalogues, Inventories, 38488, 38536, 38576, 38687, 38689, 38695, 38696, 39417
'Biblos', 38741
Biedermann, Klaus, 38655
Biege, Bernd, 38740
Biemann, Asher D., 39101
Bienenfeld, Franz Rudolf, 38616
Bier, Thomas, 38592
Biermann, Wolf, 39289
Bierwirth, Joachim, 38601
Biller, Maxim, 39161
Bilski, Emily D., 38474
Biman, Stanislaw, 38631
Binger, Werner, 39085
Biogr. Handbuch der deutschsprachigen Kunsthistoriker im Exil, 38699
Bircken, Margrid, 39370
Birkenhauer, Anne, 38675
Birkmann, Guenter, 39489
Biro-Bidjan, 39175
Bischof, Willi, 39524
Bismarck, Otto von, 38423, 39540
Bittrich, Burkhard, 39235
Black Death, 38431
'Blätter für Deutsche und Internationale Politik', 39021
Blaschitz, Edith, 39229
Blaschke, Olaf, 38901, 39501, 39502
Blasius, Rainer A., 38921
Blechhammer, 38864
Bleichröder Family, 39240
Bleker, Johanna, 39216
Blitzer, Hanna, 38821
Bloch, Ernst, 39221, 39237
Bloch, Joseph, 39234
Block, Ernst, 38587
Block, Richard, 39459
Blömer, Ursula, 38413
Blood Libel, 38511, 39501
Bloxham, Donald,
Blum, Isaak, 38507
Blumberg, Marina, 38486
Blumenfeld, Kurt, 39198
Blumenthal, W. Michael, 38477, 38478, 39069
Blumenthal-Weiss, Ilse, 38821
Blumesberger, Susanne, 38741
Boberach, Heinz, 38920
Bochum, 38742, 38939, 39427
Bock, Wolfgang, 39099
Bodenheimer Family, 38670
Bodenheimer, Max, 38670
Böckel, Otto, 39525
Böcker, Manfred, 38952

Böge, Wolfgang, 39089
Boehm, Dan, 39193
Böhmer, Konrad, 39402
Böhmer, Sylvia, 39315
Börne, Ludwig, 38418, 38423, 38429, 39412, 39421
Bohemia, 38630, 38631, 38637
Bohrmann, Hans, 38651
Boillat, Valérie, 38963
Bolbecher, Siglinde, 38686
Bolkosky, Sidney M., 38659
Boll, Günter, 38569
Bonavita, Petra, 38520
Bondy, Ruth, 38761
Bonn, 39393, 39456
Bookburning, 38847
Borchmeyer, Dieter, 38936, 39560
Borggräfe, Peter, 38580
Born, Max, 39223
Born, Stephan, 39234
Bornheim, 38489
Bornstein, Heini,
Boschung, Urs, 38643
Botany, 39166
Bothe, Rolf, 38478
Botz, Gerhard, 39522
Bouretz, Pierre, 39133
Bourgeois, Daniel, 38962
Bovenkerk, F., 38896
Bower, Kathrin M., 39366
Boyer, Paul, 39532
Brabant, Eva, 39425
Bracher, Karl-Dietrich, 39290
Brack, Viktor, 38744
Brämer, Andreas, 38533, 39100, 39112
Bräse, Stephan, 38834
Brakelmann, Günter, 38743, 39427
Bramann, Wilhelm, 38593
Brandenburg, 38428, 38490, 38818, 38908
Brasch, Hans D., 39368
Braun, Bernd, 38697
Braun, Helmut, 38641
Braun, Michael, 39217
Braunschweig, 39527
Brazil, Refugees, 38649, 38650, 38926
Brecht, Berthold, 39261
Brechtken, Magnus, 38744
Breckner, Roswitha, 39020
Breger, Louis, 39286
Breines, Paul, 39346
Breitman, Richard, 38725, 38785
Brenner, Henny, 38774
Brenner, Michael, 38414, 38415, 38432, 39141
Breslau, 38491, 38492, 38870, 39010, 39112, 39529
Brett, Lily, 39565
Bretzenheim/Nahe, 38579
Breuer, Isaac, 39101
Breuer, Mordechai, 38424

Breuker, Willem, 39402
Breysach, Barbara, 38746
Brieger (-Wasservogel), Lothar, 39200
Brinkmann, Annette, 39078
Brinkmann, Reinhold, 38936
Broch, Hermann, 39217
Brocke, Edna, 39212, 39381
Brocke, Michael, 38511
Brod, Max, 38640
Brod, Peter, 38631
Brodbeck, Doris, 39397
Brodenbach, 38493
Brodesser, Hermann-Josef, 39051
Bröskamp, Anke, 38917
Bronner, Stephen Eric, 39503, 39504
Browning, Christopher R., 38745
Bruch, Rüdiger vom, 38443
Bruchfeld, Stéphane, 39070
Bruchhäuser, Kurt, 38579
Bruckstein, Hans J., 39194
Brude-Firnau, Gisela, 38838
Brüderhof near Harksheide, 38908
Brülls, Holger, 38416, 38494, 38562
Brüning, Jens, 39007, 39579
Brumlik, Micha, 38834, 39021, 39138, 39541
Brunner, Alois, 38817
Bruno von Würzburg, 39491
Buber, Martin, 39102-39106, 39119, 39176, 39200, 39217, 39422, 39462
Bubis, Ignatz, 38926, 39025
'Buch und Bibliothek', 38682
Buchenwald, 38747, 38779, 38951
Buchholz, Ernst, 39082
Buck, Theo, 39217, 39268
Buckmiller, Michael, 39218
Budapest, 38632
Budde, Bernhard, 38423
Büttner, Ursula, 38725
Bugajer, Richard, 38749
Buhl, Wolfgang, 39316
Bukowina (see also Czernowitz), 38635, 39217, 39563
Bundesarchiv, 38920
Bunge, Norbert, 39315
Bunzl, Matti, 38432, 39219
Burckhardt, Carl J., 39542
Burg, 38494
Burgard, Friedhelm, 38689
Burgau, 38589
Burleigh, Michael, 38748
Burmeister, Helmut, 38545
Burnett, Stephen G., 39554
Burrin, Philippe, 39537
Busch, Barbara, 39293
Busch, Felix, 39423
Busch, Hans-Ulrich, 38563
Buschmann, Cornelia, 39126
Buss Family, 38956
Bussenius, Sieghard, 38908

'Les Cahiers du Judaisme', 39292
Calaprice, Alice, 39282
Canada, Refugees, 38667, 38755, 39314
Cancik, Hubert, 39556
Canetti, Elias, 39235, 39266, 39424
Caplan, Greg, 38417
Caplan, Jane, 38810
Caricatures, Jews depicted in, 39508
Carinthia, 38720
Carlebach, Elisheva, 39557
Carlebach-Preuss, Lotte, 39171
Carmel, Alex, 39212
Carnevale, Carla, 38667
Caruth, Cathy, 38900
Cassirer, Ernst, 39149, 39267
Castrop, 38495
Catalogues, of Exhibitions, 38453, 38556, 38571, 38897, 39221, 39270, 39361
Catholicism and Jews, 38615, 38631, 38901, 39044, 39501, 39502
Cattle Trade, 38493, 38742
Celan, Paul, 38641, 38982, 39215, 39217, 39235, 39268, 39269, 39270, 39271, 39272, 39273, 39274, 39275
Celan-Lestrange, Gisèle, 39270
Celle, 38496, 39081
Cemeteries, 38473, 38481, 38487, 38505, 38509, 38512, 38515, 38536, 38547, 38568, 38572, 38578, 38592, 38593, 38607, 38629, 39023
Central Zionist Archives, Jerusalem, 38670
Centralverein dt. Staatsbürger jüd. Glaubens (C.V.), 38668, 38885
Cernyak-Spatz, Susan E., 38707
Cesarani, David, 38860, 38871
Chamberlain, Houston Stewart, 39560
Chamberlain, Lesley, 39287
Chapman, Fern Schumer, 38750
Charguéraud, Marc-André, 38751
Chase, Jefferson S., 38418
Chemnitz, 38497
Chicago, Il, 38661
Children, 38655, 38747, 38953
Children, Nazi Period, 38820, 38916, 39229
Chotzen Family, 38738
Church, 38456, 3849, 38537, 38657, 38754, 39490
Church, Middle Ages, 39493, 39494
Church, Nazi Period, 38753, 38758, 39427 39472, 39492, 39520
Church, Post-1945, 39465, 39470, 39489
Chvojka, Erwin, 39322
Claus, Sylvia, 39442
Clemens, Detlev, 39091
Coburg, 38455
Coesfeld, 38498
Cohen, Daniel J., 38420
Cohen, Hermann, 39107, 39110, 39144, 39149, 39195
Cohen, Richard A., 39130

Cohen, Robert, 38900
Cohen, Susan Sarah, 38687
Cohn Family (Stralsund), 38595
Cohn, Dorrit Claire, 38667
Cohn, Frederick G., 38755
Cohn, Jonas, 39276
Colin, Amy, 38641
Colmberg, 38518
Cologne, 38499, 38502, 38756, 38757, 39172, 39242
Commemorations, 39093, 39097
'Commentary', 38852, 39050
Communists, 38730, 38888, 38990, 39020, 39031, 39237, 39298, 39433
Comparative Studies, 39501
Concentration and Internment Camps, Ghettos, see Name of Camp or Ghetto
Conversion from Judaism, Baptism, 38455, 38580, 39301, 39427, 39463, 39480
Conversion to Judaism, 39476
Coppi, Hans, 39008
Corbea-Hoisie, Andrei, 38636, 38641, 39273
Cordon, Cécile, 38641
Cornwell, John, 39223
Cotler, Irwin, 39212
Cottbus, 38503
Coudert, Allison P., 39460
Court Jews, 38430, 39384, 39466
Cramer, Ernst, 39022, 39461
Crane, Cynthia, 38759
Cresti, Silvia, 38419
'Crime Law and Social Change', 38896
Cronbach Family, 38956
Cronheim, 38505
Crowe, Cameron, 38660
Cutter, William, 39422
Cymbalist, Nehemia, 39329
Czapski-Holzman, Helene, 38849
Czechoslovakia (see also Bohemia, Moravia), 38637, 39024
Czechoslovakia, Nazi Period, 38631, 38705, 38722, 38760, 38761, 38762, 38763, 38764, 38882, 38918, 38928
Czechoslovakia, Post-1945, 38631
Czernin, Hubertus, 38986
Czernowitz, 38633, 38634, 38635, 38636, 39268

Dachau, 38765, 38882
Dachs, Gisela, 39485
Dämgen, Christine, 38512
Dahmen, Volker, 39437
Dalinger, Brigitte, 38622
'Damals', 38983
Dambacher, Eva, 39437
Damberg, Norbert, 38498
Damken, Martin, 39120
Dan, Joseph, 39141
Dancing, Jews in, 38867
Danks, Sigrid, 39260

Dannerer, Monika, 39211
Danuser, Hermann, 39560
Danzig, 38957
Darmstadt, 38506, 39032
Dausenau, 38579
'David', 38616
Davidovits, Daniela, 38624
Daxner, Michael, 39045, 39235
Dean, Martin, 38705
Decoste, Frederick , 38766
Deeters, Dorothea Elisabeth, 38511, 38657
Degen, Peter A., 39462
Degussa, 38705
Deidesheim, 38579
Deinhard, Hanna, 39277
Delbrück, Max, 39223
Demirovic, Alex, 39232
Demonizing the Other, 39537
Den Menschen zugewandt Leben, 39357
Denkler, Horst, 38423
Denman, Hugh, 38618
Denmark, 39261
Denmark, Nazi Period, 38908
Department Stores, 38503
Deportations, 38875, 38892, 38906, 38981
Deppe, Frank, 38825
'Der Bär von Berlin, Jahrbuch', 39404
Deselaers, Manfred, 39382
Dessau, 38553
Dessuant, Pierre, 39507
Detering, Heinrich, 39318
Determann, Andreas, 38596
Detroit, 38659
Dettmer, Frauke, 38582
Deuber-Mankowsky, Astrid, 39110
Deutsch-Krone, 38657
'Deutsche Akademie f. Sprache u. Dichtung, Jahrbuch', 39435
Deutsche Biographische Enzyklopädie (DBE), 38688
Deutsche Umbrüche im 20. Jahrhundert, 38427, 39005, 39226
'Deutsche Vierteljahrsschrift für Literatur und Geistesgeschichte.', 38992
'Deutsches Ärzteblatt', 39242
Deutsches Exilarchiv [Der Deutschen Bibliothek], 38671
Deutschkron, Inge, 38821
Deutz, 38455
Deventer, Jörg, 38544
Dewitz, Ulf von, 39316
Diamant, Adolf, 39023
Dick, Lutz Van, 38521
Dick, Ricarda, 39328
Dickmann, Elisabeth, 39260
Diehl, Gunther, 39402
Diemling, Maria, 39463
Dienemann, Max, 39111
Dienst, Karl, 39548
Diersburg, 38507

'Dimensions', 38913, 38942, 39532
Diner, Dan, 38768, 39150, 39204, 39251
'Diogène', 39135
Dipper, Christof, 38725
Dippold, Günter, 38516
Dirks, Christian, 38736
Dische, Irene, 39145
Dischereit, Esther, 39145, 39161
Displaced Persons, 38586, 39015, 39017, 39020, 39032, 39034, 39062, 39446
Disselnkötter, Andreas, 38769
Dithmarschen, 38508
Divine, Donna Robinson, 39196
Djuren, Andrea, 38413
Döblin, Alfred, 39278, 39279, 39426
Döhring, Sieghart, 39560
Dönhoff, Marion, 39337
Dörr, Karin, 38838
Dörr, Thomas, 39296
'Döw Jahrbuch', 38719
Dohle, Oskar, 38713
Dolbin, Benedikt Fred, 38651
Dolgesheim, 38770
Domhardt, Yvonne, 39397
Domin, Hilde, 39217, 39580
Dominican Republic, 39578
Domke, Petra, 38475
Dora-Mittelbau, 38722, 38772, 38773
Dorfman, Ben-Zion, 39024
Dorfman, Rivka, 39024
Dorhs, Michael, 38545
Dorner, Elke, 38479
Dortmund, 38703
Dosso, Diane, 38666
Douer, Alisa, 38549, 39222
Douglas, Lawrence, 38900
Dove, Richard, 38652
Dowe, Dieter, 38415, 39332
Dreessen, Wulf-Otto, 38462, 38468
Dresden, 38509, 38774, 39193, 39242
Dreyfus Affair, 39518
Drobner, Martina, 38557
Drohobyc, Ukraine, 38628
Droste-Hülshoff, Annette von, 38542, 39474
Drov, Dagmar, 39170
Du-Nour, Miryam, 39211
Dubiel, Helmut, 39336, 39464
Dülmen, 38775
'Dülmener Heimatblätter', 38775
Düren, 38776
Düsseldorf, 38777, 38778, 39577
Düsterberg, Rolf, 39549
Düttmann, Alexander Garcia, 39220
Düwell, Franz Josef, 38902
Düwell, Kurt, 39222
Duisburg, 38672
Dupont, Judith, 39425
Dutlinger, Anne D., 38978
Dvorak, Jiri, 38631

Dworkin, Susan, 38818
Dyson, Freeman, 39282
Dzialoszynski, Samuel, 38572

Early Modern Period (Pre-Enlightenment), 38454, 38455, 38523, 38542, 38566, 38596, 38597, 39191, 39460, 39472, 39533, 39552, 39554
East Friesland, 38510, 38514
East Prussia, 38511
Eastern Jewry, 38411, 38427, 38458, 38521, 38628, 38875, 38923, 38997, 38998, 39152, 39180, 39213, 39235, 39564, 39568
Eaton, Jonathan, 39401
Eber, Irene, 38675
Ebert, Joachim, 39368
Ebert, Sabine, 38593
Ebner-Eschenbach, Marie von, 39474
Eckert, Brita, 39221
Eckert, Rainer, 38762
Eckhardt, Albrecht, 38890
Economists, 39298, 39337, 39353, 39377, 39539
Edelheit, Abraham, 38708, 39197
Edelheit, Hershel, 39197
Edinger, Ludwig, 39238, 39242
Edinger, Tilly, 39280
'Edith Stein Jahrbuch', 39382
Education (see also schools), 38413, 38507, 38521, 38907, 39043, 39170, 39355, 39378
Egger, Franz, 38642
Ehrenberg, Hans, 38743, 39427
Ehrenberg, Wolf Zeev, 39428
Ehrenstein, Albert, 39281
Ehrlich, Abraham, 39071
Ehrlich, Ernst Ludwig, 38421, 39496, *Eichmann in Jerusalem*, 39252
Eichmann Trial, 39047, 39251
Eichmann, Adolf, 38744, 39252
Eichner, Hans, 38667, 39566
Ein Symbolisches Leben, 39391; 38591, 38941
'Einst und Jetzt', 39202
Einstein, Albert, 38643, 39223, 39237, 39282, 39462
Eisenstadt, Shmuel N., 39212
Eisler, Hanns, 39231, 39283
Eisner, Georg, 38643
Eke, Norbert O., 38423
El-Savador, Nazi Period, 38927
Elberfeld, 38512
Eley, Geoff, 38810
Elias, Bernd,
Elias, Buddy,
Elon, Amos, 39251
Elstner, Waltraud, 38697
Emancipation, 38442, 38451, 38494, 38543, 39234, 39297, 39501, 39548
Embacher, Helga, 38947
Emigration (see also name of country), 38521, 38662, 38664, 38656, 38869, 39038, 39225
Emmerich, Wolfgang, 39235

'Emsländische Geschichte', 38513
Emsland, 38513
Endres, Rudolf (Festschrift), 38436, 38516
Engel (Engel-Holland), Eva J., 39122, 39126
Engel, Reinhard, 38749
Engel, Walter, 38641
Engelmann, Susanna, 39329
Enlightenment (see also Haskalah), 38410, 38421, 38423, 38447, 38452, 38463, 38637, 39098, 39124, 39126, 39127, 39467, 39550, 39551
Enoch, Kurt, 39284
Enzer, Hyman Aaron,
Epstein, Simon, 39537
Erdheim, Claudia, 38628
Erenz, Benedikt, 39224
Erinnerung als Gegenwart, 38432
Erlangen, 39061
Erlanger, Albert, 39397
Erler, Hans, 38421
Ermland, 38511
Ernst, Petra, 39152
Esens, 38514
Esformes, Maria, 39266
Eshel, Amir, 38992
Essen, 38951, 39169
Ester, Matthias M., 38605, 39093
'Europäische Ideen', 39007, 39372
'European History Quarterly', 39056
'European Judaism', 38430, 39045, 39266, 39269, 39384
Euthanasia, 38719
Evan, Gershon, 38779
Evard, Jean-Luc, 39198
Exile (see also name of country), 38651, 38652, 38727, 38947, 39221, 39223, 39224, 39391
Exile, Art Historians, 38699
Exile, Historians, 39226
Exile, Journalism, 38704
Exile, Literature and Arts, 38646, 39227-39230
Exile, Music, 39231
Exile, Press, 38716
Exile, Sciences, 38666, 38806, 39222
Exile, Theatre, Film, 38660, 38717
'Exilforschung, Int. Jahrbuch', 38656, 38727
Exilmusik, 39231
Eyal, Eli, 39212

Faber, Klaus, 39486
Falzeder, Ernst, 39425
Farneth, David, 39400
Fassl, Peter, 38588
Fehn, Bernd Josef, 39051
Feil, Katharina S., 39410
Feilchenfeldt, Konrad, 39230
Feinberg, Anat, 38834
Feiner, Shmuel, 39121
Feldman, Gerald D., 39046
Feldman, Linda E., 39145
Feldman, Yael S., 39537

Felman, Shoshana, 38900
Fels Family, 38664
Fenske, Hans, 38577
Fenves, Peter, 39459
Ferenczi, Sandor, 39425
Fernandez, Simeon Tomas, 39382
Fernekes, William R., 39089
Fest, Joachim, 38936
Festschrift, Bahne, Siegfried, 38742
Festschrift, Endres, Rudolf, 38436, 38516
Festschrift, Koch, Ursula E., 38651
Festschrift, Molnár, Géza von, 39459
Festschrift (Festgabe), Neitzert, Dieter, 38496
Festschrift, Pätzold, Kurt, 38922
Festschrift, Lermen, Birgit, 39217
Festschrift, Moraw, Peter, 38600
Feuchtwanger, Lion, 38651, 39147
Feustel, Adriane, 38821
Fichte, Hubert, 39467
Fichte, Johann Gottlieb, 39541, 39543
Fichtner, Dietich, 38590
Ficiciyan, Yetvart, 39368
Fick, Norbert, 38701
Fiedler, Herbert, 38908
Fiedler, Martin, 38705
Film, Nazi, 38783, 38784
Final Solution (see also Holocaust), 38644, 38712, 38722, 38744, 38785
Finke, Stefanie, 39368
Finkelstein, Norman G., 38833
Finnane, Antonia, 38647
Fischbach, Franck, 39283
Fischbach, Fred, 39283
Fischer, Albert, 38725
Fischer, Alfons, 39242
Fischer, Barbara, 39146
Fischer, Elmar, 38965
Fischer, Gudrun, 38649
Fischer, Helmut, 38540
Fischer, Jens Malte, 38936, 39505, 39560
Fischer, Monika, 38964
Fischer, Wolfram, 38482, 39368
Fischer-Defoy, Christine, 38658
Fleck, Christian, 38666, 39506
Fleischer, Manfred, 38567, 39369
Flörsheim am Main, 38515,
Flüchtlingspolitik und Fluchthilfe, 38790
Fölling, Albers, Maria, 39199
Fölling, Werner, 39199
Fontane, Theodor, 39544
Forced Labour, 38705, 38712, 38714, 38722, 38736, 38745, 38772, 38773, 38802, 38824, 38864, 38882, 38897, 38922, 39017, 39052
Forisch, Elke, 39322
'Forschung Frankfurt', 38524; 39232, 39280, 39295, 39337, 39353, 39409
'Forschung. Mitteilungen der DFG', 38459
Forst Familiy, 38493
Forst, Christine, 39436

Index to Bibliography 449

Fortunoff Video Archive, 38836
'Forum Vormärz Forschung', 38423
Fowler, Alan, 39326
Fränkel, Daniel, 38725
Fränkel, Ludwig, 39242
Fraiman, Sarah, 38792, 39147
France, 38612, 39501, 39559
France, Nazi Period, 38651, 38816, 38914, 39012,
France, Refugees, 38781, 38863, 38884, 39309, 39446
Franconia, 38505, 38516-38519, 38549, 38611, 39189
Frank Family, 38661
Frank, Anne, 38798-801, 38896
Frank, Hartmut, 39291
Frank, Leonard, 38665
Frank, Meta, 38542, 38545
Frank, Otto, 38800
Frank, Werner L., 38661, 39182
Franke, Julia, 38781
Frankel, Zacharias, 39112
Frankenstein, Family, 38736
Frankenthal, Hans, 38802
Frankfurt am Main, 38455, 38507, 38520, 38521, 38522, 38523, 38525, 38999, 39242, 39548
Frankfurt am Main, Freies Jüdisches Lehrhaus, 39113
Frankfurt am Main, Philanthropin, 38525
Frankfurt am Main, Post-1945, 38521, 39025
Frankfurt am Main, University, 38524, 39280, 39295, 39337, 39353, 39409
Frankfurt an der Oder, 38428
Frankfurt School, 39232, 39298
'Frankfurter Adorno Blätter', 39418
'Frankfurter Allg. Zeitung' ('FAZ'), 38485, 39009, 39070, 39084, 39164, 39190, 39363, 39478, 39569
'Frankfurter Hefte' See 'Neue Gesellschaft/Frankfurter Hefte'
Frankfurter, Bernhard, 38707
Frankfurter-Wolff, Ulla, 39235
Frankl, Michal, 38981
Frankl, Viktor, 39285
Franks, Paul W., 39129
Franosch, Tilo, 39051
Franz, Michael, 39325
Franzos, Karl Emil, 38641
Freemasons, 38433
Freese, Werner, 38596
Frei, Norbert, 38709, 38722, 39046, 39251
'Freiburger Diözesan-Archiv', 38431
'Freiburger Rundbrief', 39465; 38925, 38930, 39153, 39165, 39208
Freies Jüdisches Lehrhaus, 39113
Freud, Sigmund, 39286, 39287, 39288, 39425, 39520
Freudenberg, 38526
Freudenheim, Tom L., 38478

Freund, Susanne, 38596
Freundlich, Elisabeth, 39429
Freyeisen, Astrid, 38947, 38948
Freytag, Gustav, 39474
Freytag, Ronald, 39499, 39536
Fried, Erich, 39289
Friedländer Family, 39423
Friedländer, Saul, 38899, 38936, 39537, 39560
Friedland, 38657
Friedland (Märkisch), 38511
Friedlander, Albert H., 38432, 39045, 39212, 39269
Friedlander, Elizabeth, 38912
Friedmann, Carl, 38834
Friedt, Gerd, 38473
Friese, Eberhard, 39354
Frisch, Efraim, 39235
Fritz Bauer Institut, 38705
'Fritz Bauer Institut, Newsletter', 38981
Fritz Mauthner – Sprache, Literatur, Kritik, 39339; 39325, 39535
Fröhlich, Elke, 38737
Fröndenberg, 38803
Frojimovics, Kinga, 38632
Fry, Varian,
Fürstengrube, 38701
Fürth, Henriette, 39477
Fürth, Jüdisches Museum Franken & Schnaittach, 38527
Fuhrmann, Horst, 38600
Fulcher, Jane F., 39559, 39560
Funkenstein, Amos, 38460
Furbach-Sinani, Maike, 38651
Furtado Kestler, Izabela Maria, 38650

Gabel, Gernot, 38682
Gabeli, Helmut, 38531
Gaines, Jeremy, 39320
Galicia, 38628, 39235
Gann, Christoph, 38804
Gans, Eduard, 38423
Gans, Salomon Philipp, 38496
Ganzfried, Daniel, 39219
Garbáty Family, 38736
Garbe, Detlef, 38897
Garrin, Stephen H., 39440
Garz, Detlef, 38413, 39455
Gawlick, Günter, 39126
Gay, Peter, 39290, 39560
Gechter, Marianne, 38499
Gehle, Holger, 38834
Gehring-Münzel, Ursula, 38662
Geiger, Abraham, 39148
Geiger, Friedrich, 39231
Geiger, Ludwig, 39421
Geis, Jael, 39027
Geis, Walter, 38499
Geisel, Eike, 39564
Geistingen, 38540

Gelber, Mark H., 39200, 39217
Gelderblom, Bernhard, 38538, 38539
Geldermann, Barbara, 38947
Gellmann, Jerome, 39104
Gemelli, Guiliana, 38666
'Genealogie', 39001
Genealogy, 39167, 39169, 39177, 39182, 39183
Genocide, 38883
Gera, 38805
Gerl-Falkovitz, Hanna-Barbara, 39449
Gerlach, Christian, 38722
Gerlach, Wolfgang, 38758
German Democratic Republic (GDR), 39058, 39059, 39088, 39415, 39019, 39020, 39031, 39047, 39469, 39475, 39488, 39570, 39488
'German Historical Institute London, Bulletin', 39074
'German Historical Institute Washington, D.C., Bulletin', 39094
'German History', 38433, 39044, 39529
'German Life and Letters', 38994, 39261, 39289, 39307, 39327
'German Politics and Society', 38848, 39346
'(The) German Quarterly', 39028, 39041, 39158, 39219, 39399
Germania Judaica, 38673
'(The) Germanic Review', 39250, 39375
Germany, Immigration, 38943, 39020, 39033, 39038, 39042
Germany, Post-1945, 38942, 39022, 39027, 39023, 39041, 39044, 39045, 39056, 39060, 39081, 39161, 39375, 39363, 39399, 39446, 39458
Germany, Remigration, see Remigration
'Geroldsecker Land', 38553
Gerson, Christianus, 38580
Gerson, Hans, 39291
Gerson, Oskar, 39291
Gerstenberger, Heide, 38725
'(Zur) Geschichte u. Kultur der Juden in Ost- und Westpreussen', 38511
'Geschichte und Gegenwart', 38617
'Geschichte und Gesellschaft', 38724
Geschichte und Kultur der Juden in Schwaben, 38588
Gesellschaft für Christl.-Jüd. Zusammenarbeit, 39082
Gesellschaft zur Erforschung der Geschichte der Juden, 38689
Gestapo, 38777, 38990
Giacon, Nicoletta, 39432
Giampieri-Deutsch, Patrizia, 39425
Giesing, Georg, 38493
Giessen, 38528
Gigue, 38774
Giguere, Undine G., 39227
Gillis-Carlebach, Miriam, 39171
Gilman, Sander L., 39028, 39145
Gingold, Etty, 38858
Giordano, Ralph, 39567

Gladbeck, 38807
'Gladbeck -Unsere Stadt', 38807
Glade, Felicitas, 38924
Glasenapp, Gabriele von, 39235, 39466
Glöckner, Olaf, 38678
Glogau, 38428
Glücksmann Family, 38778
Gödde, Christoph, 39420
Görgen, Hermann, 38926
Görtz, Heinz-Jürgen, 39159
Görtzen, Antje, 38646
Goethe, Johann Wolfgang von, 39545-39548
Götschel, Roland, 39292
Goette, Jürgen-Wolfgang, 39347, 39348, 39349
Göttingen, 38529
Göttlich, Udo, 39336
Goggin, Eileen Brockman, 38808
Goggin, James, 38808
Goldberg, Lea, 39329
Goldberg, Leonid, 38593
Goldberg, Oskar, 39292
Goldberg, Sylvie Anne, 38638
Goldhagen Debate, 38809, 38812, 38866, 38899, 38950, 39028, 39095, 39470, 39520
Goldhagen, Daniel J., 38809, 38810
Goldschmidt Family, 38813
Goldschmidt, Berthold, 39293
Goldschmidt, Günther, 38813
Goldschmidt, Helmut, 38501
Goldschmidt, Rosemarie, 38813
Goldsmith, Martin, 38813
Goldstein, Eugen, 39294
Goldstein, Kurt, 39238, 39242, 39295
Goll, Claire, 39272
Goll, Yvan, 39272
Golland, Louise, 39233
Golomb, Jacob, 39201
Goltschnigg, Dietmar, 39323, 39481
Gonen, Jay Y., 38811
Gong, Alfred, 39217
Goodman-Thau, Eveline, 39149, 39397
Goral-Sternheim, Arie, 39296
Gorcka, Cornelius, 38507
Gorny, Yosef, 39212
Gosewinkel, Dieter, 39046
Gott, Richard, 38830
Gottschalk, August, 38514
Gotzmann, Andreas, 39141
Goudsblom-Oestreicher, Maria, 38904
Gould, Melissa, 38432
Grab, Walter, 39234, 39297
Grab, Walter, Obituaries, 39234
Graetz, Heinrich, 38426
Graetz, Michael, 38424, 38447
Grafton, Anthony, 39251
Grandjonc, Jacques, 38884
Graphic Artists, 38651, 38912, 39239
Graz, 38432, 38617, 38720
Great Britain, Immigration, 38860

Great Britain, Nazi Period, 39224
Great Britain, Refugees, 38652, 38653, 38720, 38755, 38859, 38861, 38876, 39224
Great Plague, 38431
Green, Bea, 38821
Green, Ronald S., 39503
Greene, Joshua M., 38836
Greif, Gideon, 39204
Grein, Almut, 39551
Greisner, Walter, 39336
Grellert, Marc, 38453
Gremliza, Hermann L., 39014, 39095
Gries, Bernhard, 38573
Grobman, Alex, 38844
Gröbl, Lydia, 38673
Grözinger, Karl Erich, 38425, 38561, 38678, 39141, 39445
Grohs-Martin, Silvia, 38814
Gronemann, Sammy, 39568
Gross, Raphael, 39046, 39558
Grossbürger und Unternehmer, 38535, 38865
Grosser, Alfred, 39150
Grossman, David, 38675
Grossman, Jeffrey, 38463
Grossmann, Anita, 38810
Grossmann, Henryk, 39298
Grotum, Thomas, 38709
Gruber, Hans, 39501
Grübel, Monika, 38500
Grümme, Bernhard, 39128
Grünberg, Kurt, 39029
Gründer, Karlfried, 39445
Grunberger, Béla, 39507
Gruner, Wolf, 38705, 38714, 38725, 38815, 38922
Grunkin Family, 39075
Gruppe 3 Frankfurt a.M., 39052
Grzywatz, Berthold, 38827
Guang, Pan, 38947
Guggenberger, Günther, 38641
Gundacker, Felix, 38630
Gundlach, Christine, 39042
Gurs, 38816, 38875, 38906, 39012
Gut, Johannes, 38437
Gutschow, Mirjam, 38465
Guttmann, Julius, 39114
Gutwirth, Eleazar, 38424
Gutzkow, Karl, 39474
Gysler, Caroline, 39113

Haak, Angelika, 38531
Haas, Leo, 38979
Haas, Willy, 38780
Haase, Hugo, 38511
Haber, Fritz, 39223, 39299
Haber, Lutz, 39299
Haberland, Detlef, 39235, 39391
Habsburg, 38620
Hachshara, 38908
Häberlin, Mark, 38589

Häntzschel, Hiltrud, 38821
Häuser, Karl, 39353
Hafner, Georg M., 38817
Hage, Volker, 39443
Hagen, Kenneth, 39552
Hagen, William W., 38427
Haggadah, 39189
Hagner, Marc-Renée & Patrick, 38593
Hagspiel, Wolfram, 38501
Hahn, Fred, 38631
Hahn, Hajo, 39330
Hahn, Hans Henning, 39235
Hahn, Marie-Luise, 38671
Hahn, Ralf, 39299
Hahn-Beer, Edith, 38818
Haibl, Michaela, 39508
Haiger, 38530
Haigerloch, 38531
Haindorf, Alexander, 38423
Halevi, Yehuda, 39130
Halle, 38532, 39030
Haller, Annette, 39182
Halley, Anne, 38733
Halpert, Marta S., 39035
Halwer, Andreas, 38939
Hamann, Birgitta, 39324
Hamburg, 38533-38537, 38819, 38820, 39116, 39291, 39296, 39482, 39567
Hamburg-Harburg, 39073
Hamburger, Michael, 39569
Hameln, 38538, 38539
Hamkens, Wilhelm, 38924
Hammann, Brigitte, 39533
Hammerschlag, Richard, 38546
Hanak, Werner, 39361
Hansen, Antje, 38689
Hansen, Niels, 39452
Hansen-Schaberg, Inge, 38821, 39355
Hanslock, Andreas, 38428
Hanss, Karl, 38906
Hantsche, Irmgard, 38939
Harburg, 39073
Harck, Ole, 38943
Hardman, Anna, 38822
Harig, Ludwig, 39570
Harlan, Veit, 38784
Harpprecht, Klaus, 39444
Harran, Marilyn, 38690
Harris, Mark Jonathan, 38860
Harshav, Barbara, 39247, 39562
Hartenstein, Elfi, 38663
Hartewig, Karin, 39031
Hartman, Geoffrey H., 38900
Hartmann, Georg, 38912
Hartmann, Idis B., 39235
Hartmann, Moritz, 38423
Hartston, Barnet P., 39509
Hartung, Harald, 39569
Hartwich, Wolf-Daniel, 39560

Haskalah, 38452, 39121, 39124, 39127, 39257
Hass, Esther, 38552
Hass, Verfolgung und Toleranz, 38950, 39533
Hatzfeld, Sophie von, 39333
Hauff, Andreas, 39402
Hauff, Wilhelm, 39549
Hausleitner, Mariana, 38641, 38823
Havel, Vaclav, 38981
Hawrylchak, Sandra H., 39230
Hayes, Christopher, 39368
Hayes, Peter, 38705
Hecht, Manfred, 39430
Hecht, Otto, 39300
Hedenus, Michael, 39294
Hegel, Georg Wilhelm Friedrich, 39467, 39541
Heichelheim, Siegmund, 38528
Heid, Ludger, 38421, 38511
Heidegger, Martin, 39215, 39220
Heidel, Caris-Petra, 39242
Heidt, Günther, 38526
Heil, Johannes, 38429, 38684, 39501
Heilbronner, Oded, 39510
Heim, Susanne, 38725, 38806,
Heimann, Dietrich, 39218
'Heimatblätter des Rhein-Sieg-Kreises', 38489, 38563
Heine, Heinrich, 38418, 38429, 38614, 39217, 39234, 39301-39305, 39323, 39520, 39560, 39577
'Heine-Jahrbuch', 38614, 39301, 39305, 39323, 39343
Heinemann, Hartmut, 38541
Heinig, Paul-Joachim, 38600
Heinke, Ilse, 38413
Heinrichs, Wolfgang E., 39511
Heinrichsdorf, 38657
Heinz, Hanspeter, 39470
Heinze-Greenberg, Ita, 39341
Heitmann, Margret, 38511, 39276
Helas, Horst, 38476
Helgert, Heidrun, 38623
Heller, Marvin J., 38430
Heller, Peter, 38667
Helmarshausen, 38545
Helmont, Franciscus Mercurius van, 39460
Hemecker, Wilhelm, 39379
Hemmendinger, Judith, 38747
Henicke, Hartmut, 38486
Henisch, Peter, 39152
Henne, Helmut, 39339
Hennef, 38540
Hennenberg, Beate, 38624
Henrix, Hans Hermann, 39381, 39470, 39496
Hensel, Fanny, 39306
Hentges, Gudrun, 39467
Henze, Barbara, 38431
Hep-Hep Riots, 38436
Hepp, Michael, 38824, 39349, 39395
Hepperle, Sabine, 39487

Heppner, Harald, 38635
Herbert, Ulrich,
Herdemerten, Frank, 38951
Herf, Jeffrey, 39074, 39346
Hering, Rainer, 39300
Hermand, Jost, 38950, 39407
Hermann, Michael, 38531
Hermlin, Stefan, 39228
Herrmann, Max, 38681
Herskovic, Berl, 38979
Hertz-Eichenrode, Katharina, 38897
Hertzberg, Arthur, 38844, 39150, 39212, 39468
Herz, Henriette, 39421
Herzberg, Heinrich, 38734
Herzberg, Isaak, 39235
Herzfeld, Wilhelm, 38521
Herzig, Arno, 38423, 38438
Herzl, Theodor, 38644, 39201, 39202, 39212, 39518
Herzlake, 38513
Herzog, Andreas, 39235
Herzog, David, 38720
Herzog, Emmy, 38889
Herzog, Marvin, 38467
Herzogenberg, Johanna von, 38631
Heschel, Abraham Joshua, 39115, 39119
Hess, Jonathan M., 39512
Hess, Moses, 38421, 39214
Hess, Nicole, 38675
Hess, Rainer, 39033
Hesse, 38530, 38541-38546, 38555, 38590, 38770, 38825, 39032, 39525, 39527
Hessing, Jakob, 39264
Hettling, Manfred, 39075
Heuberger, Georg, 39548
Heuberger, Rachel, 39336
Heuer, Renate, 38691
Heumann, Pierre, 38644
Heurck, Jan van, 38665
Hexelschneider, Schwendler, Gerhild, 39331
Heyl, Matthias, 39089
Heym, Stefan, 39307, 39308
Heymann, Fritz, 38651
Heymel, Michael, 39115
Hieber, Jochen, 38993
Hilberg, Raul, 38954
Hildebrandt, Stefan, 39393
Hildermeier, Manfred, 39046
Hildesheim, 39081
Hilferding, Rudolf, 39309
Hilfrich, Carola, 39123
Hillebrecht, Sabine, 38658
Hilliard, Robert L., 39034
Hilsenrath, Edgar, 39151
Hilsner, Leopold, 39581
Hilton, Michael, 39468
Hilzinger, Sonja, 39228, 39371
Himmler, Heinrich, 38785

"*Hinauf und Zurück / in Die Herzhelle Zukunft*",
  39217; 38598, 38993
Hinkel, Hans, 38911
Hinrichsen Family, 38872
Hinrichsen, Henry, 38872
Hinzert, 38722
Hirsch, Fredy, 38905
Hirsch, Hans George, 39182
Hirsch, Max, 39242
Hirsch, Rudolf, 39513
Hirsch, Salomon, 38436
Hirsch, Werner, 38888
Hirschberg, Gerd, 38935
Hirschland Family, 39169
Hirt-Mannheimer, Aron, 39150
Historians, 39389
Historians' Debate, 38994
Historiography, 38424, 38429, 38445, 38448,
  38827, 39080, 39100, 39141
Historiography, Jewish, 38432, 39028, 39148
Historiography, Nazi Period (see also Goldhagen
  Debate), 38746, 38819, 38829, 38900, 39046,
  39077, 39094, 39252
'Historische Mitteilungen', 39406
'Historische Zeitschrift', 38439
'Historisches Jahrbuch der Stadt Linz', 38713
'Historisches Jahrbuch', 38829
'History Now', 38828
'History', 38745
'History of European Ideas', 39538
'History of Psychology', 39356
Hitler, Adolf, 38811, 38830, 38831, 38933,
  39533, 39560
Hochschule für die Wissenschaft des Judentums,
  Berlin, 39114
Hochstadt, Steve, 38947
Hödl, Klaus, 39152, 39242
Hödl, Sabine, 38432, 38673
Höflechner, Walter, 38720
Hoeflich (Höflich), Eugen (Moshe Ya'akov Ben-
  Gavriel), 39431
Höhns, Ulrich, 39291
Höppner, Reinhard, 39469
Hörstgen, 38551
Höxter, 38544
Höxter, Nathan, 39203
Hofbauer, Hannes, 38641
Hofer, Georg, 39152
Hoffmann, Christhard, 39141
Hoffmann, Peter, 38725
Hoffmann, Stefan-Ludwig, 38433
Hofgeismar, 38545
Hofmann, Michael, 39180
Hofmannsthal, Hugo von, 39432
'Hofmannsthal. Jahrbuch zur Europäischen
  Moderne', 39360, 39432
Hofmeister, Björn, 38443
Hohenems, 38618, 38619
Hohlstein, Michael, 38596

Holl, Bernhard, 38554
Holocaust (see also Final Solution), 38683,
  38690, 38698, 38754, 38822, 38832, 38836,
  38839, 38840, 38846, 38899, 38994, 38995,
  39470
'Holocaust and Genocide Studies', 38784, 38883,
  38903, 38940, 39275
Holocaust Denial, 38842, 38843, 38844, 38845,
  38922, 38957, 38989, 39579
'Holocaust Educational Trust', 38822, 38995,
Holocaust Memorial Museum, Washington,
  39089
Holocaust Trauma, 38821, 39244
Holocaust, Art, 38835, 39096
Holocaust, Children, 38953
Holocaust, Cult and Instrumentalisation, 38833
Holocaust, Film, 38835, 38837
Holocaust, Historiography (see also
  Historiography, Nazi Period), 38745, 38768,
  38809, 38828, 38954, 39253,
Holocaust, in Literature, 38769, 38841, 38942
Holocaust, Knowledge, 38644, 38934, 38949
Holocaust, Philosophical and Theological
  Impact, 38982, 39071
Holocaust, Remembrance (see also Memorials),
  38432, 39037, 39069, 39076, 39083, 39084,
  39086, 39087, 39088, 39097
Holocaust, Teaching, 38838, 39002, 39068,
  39070, 39078, 39089
Holsten, Nina, 38897
Holub, Robert C., 38848
Holzhausen (Hesse), 38546
Holzhey, Helmut, 39107
Holzman, Helene see Czapski-Holzman, Helene
Holzmann, Margarete, 38849
Homann, Ursula, 38490, 38575, 38585, 39030,
  39546
Homolka, Walter, 39116
Honigmann, Barbara, 38821, 39161, 39217,
  39570
Honigmann, Peter, 38613
Hoos, Hans-Helmut, 38606
Hoover Institution, 39091
Hopp, Andrea, 39540
Horb, 38547
Horch, Hans Otto, 38674, 39217, 39548
Horkheimer, Max, 39236, 39246, 39310
Horowitz, Bernhard & Laura, 38636
Horowitz, Joseph, 39560
Horst, Christoph auf der, 39303
Horwitz, Rivka, 39124
Hoss, Christiane, 38658, 38947
Hroch, Miroslav, 39212
Hübschen, Bettina, 38579
Hübschmann, Ekkehard, 38728
Hümbelin, Lotte, 39433
Hüppauf, Bernd, 38900
Huizinga, Kerstin, 38511
Huml, Ariane, 38821

Hummel, Nicole, 38413
(Hundert)100 Jahre Zionismus, 39212
Hundert, Gershon David, 38424
Hungary, 38823, 38910, 39024
Hungary, Nazi Period, 38632, 38804, 38932, 38975
Hunsrück, 38548
Hurth, Elisabeth, 39416
Hus, Jan, 38637
Hutchinson, Peter, 39308
Hájková, Alena, 38763

Idel, Moshe, 39133
Idelsohn, Abraham Zwi, 39108
Identity, Jewish, 39142, 39143, 39145, 39147, 39148, 39150, 39154, 39158, 39160, 39161, 39162, 39163, 39235
Iggers, Wilma Abeles, 39235
Ihrhofe, 38510
'Illustr. Neue Welt';, 38624
Immigration, see Germany, Immigration
Imperial Germany, 38413, 38443, 38458, 39216, 39508, 39511, 39525, 39529
Independent Committee of Experts, Switzerland, 38966, 38974
India, Refugees, 38780
Industrialists, 38486, 38567
Ingolstadt, 38549
Inowlocki, Lena, 39020
Institut für Geschichte der Juden in Österreich, 38673, 38674
'Int. Ztschrift. für Geschichte und Ethik der Naturwiss., Technik und Mathematik', 39340
'Internationale Schulbuchforschung', 39089
'Internationale Wissenschaftliche Korrespondenz', 38888, 38990, 39362
Internment Camps (see also name of camp), 38816, 38863, 38914
Irving, David, 38842, 38843, 38844
Isaak, Leopold, 38887
Israel (see also Palestine), 38779, 39083, 39199, 39204, 39207-39213, 39235, 39324, 39452, 39485, 39488, 39560
'Israelitisches Gemeindeblatt' (Cologne), 39172
'Israelitisches Wochenblatt', 38644; 38642, 39140
Italy, 39501

Jacobi, Manfred, 39358
Jacobowski, Ludwig, Gesammelte Werke, 39312
Jacobs, Jack, 39152
Jacobs, Peter, 39317
Jacobs, Robert A., 39126
Jacobsohn, Siegfried, 39311, 39394
Jacoby, Alfred, 38552
Jacoby, Hannelore, 38540
Jacoby, Johann, 39234
Jacoby, Peter (Eduard Georg), 39313
Jäckel, Eberhard, 38773, 38837
Jäger, Achim, 38464

Jäger, Gudrun, 38691
Jäger, Roland, 39284
Jäger, Siegfried, 39514
Jaffé, Robert, 39153
'Jahrb. des Hist. Vereins f.d. Fürstentum Liechtenstein', 38655
'Jahrbuch des Bergheimer Geschichtsvereins', 38473
'Jahrb. des Vereins f. Orts- u. Heimatkunde in der Grafschaft Mark', 38609
'Jahrbuch Extremismus & Demokratie', 39077
'Jahrbuch für Antisemitismusforschung', 38684; 38744, 38746, 38934, 39255, 39500, 39536
'Jahrbuch für den Kreis Cochem-Zell', 38564
'Jahrbuch für den Landkreis Holzminden', 39383
'Jahrbuch für Fränkische Landesforschung', 38436, 38454, 38516
'Jahrbuch für Westfälische Kirchengeschichte', 39489
'Jahrbuch Hochsauerlandkreis', 38560
'Jahrbuch Kreis Höxter', 38544
'Jahrbuch zur Geschichte und Wirkung des Holocaust;', 38705
'Jahrbuch, Landkreis Kassel', 38542, 38546
Jakl, Nina, 38686
Jakobovits, Immanuel, 39117
Jakobs, Hildegard, 38610
Jakov, Ben, 38882
James, Harold, 39046
Jammers, Antonius, 38681
Janesch, Jürgen, 39172
Jansen, Christian, 38722
Jansen, Peter-Erwin, 39336
Japan, 39385, 39386
Japan, Refugees, 38850
Jasper, Willi, 38678, 39548
Jeggle, Utz, 38531
Jehle, Manfred, 38697
Jena, 38851
Jens, Walter, 38658
Jensen, Uffa, 38491
Jersch-Wenzel, Stefi, 38421, 38697
'Jewish Book World', 38708, 39440
Jewish Councils, 38768, 38989
'Jewish Culture and History', 39300
'Jewish Journal of Sociology', 39240
Jewish National and Univ. Library, Jerusalem, 39106
Jewish Problem (see also Identity, Jewish), 39477
'(The) Jewish Quarterly', 38833, 39162, 39213, 39523
'Jewish Social Studies', 39096, 39422, 39512
'Jewish Studies Quarterly', 39106, 39388
Jewish Studies, Post-1945, 39141
'Jiddistik-Mitteilungen', 38461, 38462, 38468, 38470
Joachim, Otto, 39314
Jochimsen, Margarethe, 39328
Jochsberg, 38518

Johannisburg/Ostpreussen, 38511
John, Barbara, 38658
Johnson, Daniel, 38852
Jokiniemi, Miriam, 38838
Jonas, Hans, 38434, 39236
Jonas, Regina, 39181
Jonca, Karol, 38957
Jorde, Fritz, 38512
Josephu, Johanna, 39173
Jospe, Eva, 39130
'Journal of Contemporary History', 39148, 39210, 39285, 39510
'Journal of Economic Literature', 39225
'Journal of Historical Review', 38844
'Journal of Humanistic Psychology', 38938
'Journal of Jewish Studies', 38452, 39200, 39246
'Journal of Performance and Art', 38980
'Journal of Refugee Studies', 38877
Journalists, 38651, 38705, 39391, 39414, 39431, 39453
Juchem, Elmar, 39400, 39402
Jud Süss (Joseph Süss Oppenheimer), 38783, 38784
'Judaica', 39497
'Judaism', 38659, 39103, 39115, 39132
Judaism, Jewish History, in Teaching, 39079, 39089,
'(Der) Jude', 38419, 39176
(Die) Juden im Sudetenland, 38631
Juden in Berlin, 38736
Juden und Jüdische Kultur im Vormärz, 38423
Judenräte See Jewish Councils
Judson, Pieter, 38810
Jüdisch-Theologisches Seminar (Breslau), 39112
'Jüdische Korrespondenz', 39031, 39234
'Jüdischer Almanach', 38675; 38434, 39073, 39108, 39329
Jüdischer Frauenbund, 39413
Jüdischer Kulturbund, 38813
Jüdisches Kulturerbe, 38583
Jüdisches Leben und Jüdische Kultur in Deutschland, 38421; 39000, 39037, 39214, 39376, 39473,
'Jüdisches Nachrichtenblatt', 38736
Jülich (Kreis), 38776
Jünger, Ernst, 38899
Jünke, Christoph, 39319
Jürgs, Michael, 39392
'Juni', 39228
Jureit, Ulrike, 38853
Just, Dieter, 39515

Kabbalah, 39124, 39460
Kafka, Franz, 38410, 38640, 38982, 39145, 39250, 39520
Kahmen, Volker, 39328
Kahn, Erich Itor, 39231
Kaienburg, Hermann, 38705
Kaiser, Christine, 39339
Kaiser, Konstantin, 38686, 39322, 39517

Kaiser, Reinhard, 38849
Kaiser, Vladimir, 38631
Kaiser-Wilhelm-Gesellschaft, 38806
Kaisersesch, 38550
Kaiserslautern, 38664
Kalekin-Fishman, Devorah, 39020
Kalischer, Clemens, 39315
'Kalonymos', 39256, 39463
Kaminski, André, 39219
Kamp, 38551
Kamp-Lintfort, 38551
Kampmann, Christoph, 38436
Kangas, William, 39160
Kaniuk, Yoram, 38628
Kann, Hans-Joachim, 38599
Kant, Immanuel, 39138, 39467, 39541, 39550
Kantorowicz, Alfred, 39237
Kaplan, Marion, 38725
Kaplan, Yosef, 38424
Karlsbad, 38904
Karnagel, Gioia-Olivia, 38864
Karný, Miroslav, 38979, 38981
Kassel, 38545, 38552, 38876
Kater, Michael H., 38855, 38856
Katholischer Antisemitismus im 19. Jahrhundert, 39501
Kauders, Anthony, 39044, 39490
Kaufmann, David, 39134
Kaufmann, Doris, 38806
Kaufmann, Thomas, 39471
Kaufmann, Uri R., 38437
Kaufmann, Walter, 38780
Kavalli, Emine, 38593
Kayser,Max, 38438
Keil, Martha, 38456
Keilson, Hans, 39435
Keiser, Reinhard, 39482
Keller, Manfred, 38936
Kellerhals-Mäder, A., 38680
Kemper, Raimund, 38979
Keren, Nili, 39089
Kerler, Dov-Ber, 39466
Kernen, Jean-Marc, 38967
Kerr, Alfred, 38652
Kerschbaumer, Gert, 38987
Kershaw, Ian, 38830
Kersten, Lee, 38765
Kessler, Herbert Zwi, 38857
Kessler, Mario, 39237
Kesten, Hermann, 39316
Kibbutz Geva, 39203
Kibbutz Movement, 39199
Kieckbusch, Klaus, 39383
Kiefer, Reinhard, 39217
Kiefer, Ulrike, 38467
Kiel, 39313
Kienzler, K., 39496
Kiesel, Helmuth, 39217
Kieser, Harro, 39221
Kiessling, Wolfgang, 39415

Kieval, Hillel J., 38637
Kilcher, Andreas, 38693, 39133, 39155, 39460
Killius, Rosemarie, 38858
Killy, Walter, 38688
Kim-Park, So Young, 39411
Kimball, Meredith M., 39356
Kindertransport, 38735, 38859, 38860, 38861, 39162, 39436
Kinsbrunner, Josef, 38641
Kippenheim, 38553
Kirchberg, 38548
Kirchhof, Astrid M., 38648, 38782
Kirchhoff, Hans Georg, 38703
Kirchhoff, Wolfgang, 38825, 39242
Kirchner, Gerrit, 39242
Kirchner, Paul Christian, 39174
Kirtley, Karen, 38898
Kisch, Egon Erwin, 38640, 39234, 39518
Kittner, Alfred, 38641
Kitzmantel, Raphaela, 38628
Klages, Ludwig, 39334
Klamper, Elisabeth, 39516
Klanska, Maria, 39235
Klappert, Berthold, 39470
Klawiter, Randolph J., 39417
Klein, Anne,
Kleinheubach, 38554
Kleinschmidt, Erich, 39426
Kleinschmidt, Stefan, 39368
Klemmer, Clemens, 39186
Klemp, Stefan, 38803
Klemperer, Victor, 38852, 38996, 39317
Klenner, Hermann, 39126
Klessmann, Eckart, 38534
Klinger, Katherine, 38833
Klinkhammer, Lutz, 38752
Klooster, Thorsten, 39368
Klüger, Leo, 38862
Klüger, Ruth, 38667, 38950, 39318, 39363, 39531
Knapp, Alexander, 39187
Knapp, Gabriele, 38821
Kniesz, Jürgen, 38604
Knigge, Adolph Freiherr, 39551
Knight, Robert, 39016, 39048, 39065
Knilli, Friedrich, 38783
Knoll, Joachim H., 39376
Knopp, Guido, 38837
Knott, Marie Luise, 38704
Kober, Adolf, 38502
Koch, Erich (Festschrift), 38911
Koch, Gertrud, 39320
Koch, Ursula E. (Festschrift), 38651
Kocourek, Ludomír, 38631
Kocourkavá, Kvetoslava, 38631
Köln-Kalk, 38756
'Kölner Zeitschrift für Soziologie und Sozialpsychologie', 39244
Kölsch, Julia, 39076

König, Ernest, 38864
Königsberg, 38511
Königsberger, Franz, 39368
Köpke, Monique, 38863
Körbecke, 38607
Körner, Axel, 38899
Körner, Ruth, 38730, 38731
Körte, Mona, 38684
Köster, Rudolf, 39398
Kött, Martin, 38812
Kofler, Leo, 39237, 39319
Kogman-Appel, Katrin, 39188, 39189
Kohlbauer-Fritz, Gabriele, 38628
Kohlmannslehner, Dieter, 39032
Kohlstruck, Michael, 38947, 39387
Kohring, Rolf, 39280
Kolbe, Christian, 38700
Koller, Guido, 38680, 38968, 38970
Kollisch, Eva, 39436
Koltun-Fromm, Kenneth, 39148
Komoroczy, Geza, 38632
Komorowski, Manfred, 38672
Konitz, 38511
Koob, Manfred, 38453
Kopp-Oberstebrink, Herbert, 39445
Koppenfels, Johanna von, 38481
Kopper, Christopher, 38865
Korn, Salomon, 38453, 38521, 39025, 39036, 39037, 39190
Korte, Hermann, 38834
Kortner, Fritz, 38665
Kossert, Andreas, 38511
Koszyk, Kurt, 39518
Kotowski, Elke-Vera, 39334
Kottek, Samuel S., 39242
Kovach, Thomas, 39130
Kowalczuk, Ilko-Sascha, 39077
Kowalke, Kim H., 39400
Kracauer, Siegfried, 39320
Kralovitz, Rolf, 38951
Kramer, Helgard, 38866
Kramer, Theodor, 39322
Krammer, Reinhard, 39089
Kranz, Jarden, 39033
Kranzler, David, 38927, 38947
Krapf, Ernst, 39519
Krasa, Hans, 38980
Kraus, Karl, 39323, 39437, 39518
Kraus, Tomas, 38631
Krause, Kuno, 38867
Krause, Manfred, 38593
Krause-Vilmar, Dietfrid, 38552
Krauss, Reinhard, 38507
Krauss, Werner, 38996
Krebs, Gerhard, 38947
Kreft, Gerald, 39238, 39242, 39280, 39295, 39357
Kreiler, Kurt, 39349
Kreis, Georg, 38969, 38970

Kreis, Rudolf, 39520
Kreisky, Bruno, 39014, 39438
Krejcova, Heléna, 38631
Krell, Marc A., 39118
Krell, Robert, 38747
Kressmann, Taylor, 39571
Krieg, Robert A., 39470
Krings, Ulrich, 38499
Krist, Martin, 38988
Kristensson, Jutta, 39143
Krobb, Florian, 39154
Krochmalnik, Daniel, 38421, 39125, 39138
Kröger, Marianne, 38821
Krohn, Claus-Dieter, 38656, 38666, 38727
Krohn, Helga, 38521
Krois, Isabella, 39049
Kronenberg, Emil, 38593
Kronenberg, Max, 39368
Krug, Marina, 39156
Kruse, Andreas, 39039
Kruse, Joseph A., 39323
Kruse, Jürgen, 39038
Kruse, Sabine, 39348
Kuchenbecker, Antje, 39175
Küchler, Stefan, 39089
Kühn-Ludewig, Maria, 38868
Kümmel, Werner Friedrich, 39242
Künzl, Hannelore, 39141, 39191
Kugelmann, Cilly, 38432, 38521, 39035
Kugler-Weiemann, Heidemarie, 38879
Kuh, Anton, 39155
Kuhnt, Christian, 39231
Kukatzki, Bernhard, 38576, 38577, 38578
Kulka, Otto D., 38725, 39537
Kulturbund, Jüdischer, 38813
Kumar, Shiva, 38836
Kunne, Andrea, 39152
Kurrein, Max, 39368
'Kursbuch', 39054
'Kurtrierisches Jahrbuch', 38599
Kuschey, Bernhard, 38989
Kuwabara, Setsuko, 39354
Kwiet, Konrad, 38715, 38725

Laak, Dirk van, 39046
Labonté-Roset, Christine, 38821
Lachs, Minna, 39235
Lackmann, Thomas, 38479
Ladwig-Winters, Simone, 38725
Lässig, Simone, 38439
Lafontaine, Oskar, 38926
Lahnstein, 38579
Lahusen, Margarita C., 39350
Lambelet, Jean-Christian, 38971
Lammert, Norbert, 39066
Lamping, Dieter, 39141, 39217
Land-Weber, Ellen, 38928
Landau, Lola, 39324
Landauer, Gustav, 39325

Landauer, Rolf William, 39326
Lande, Peter W., 38958, 39182
(Die) Landjudenschaften in Deutschland, 38420
Landmann, Salcia, 39235
Landsberg, 39017
Lang, Birgit, 39152
Lang, Fritz, 39327
Lang, Josef, 39501
Lange, Nicholas de, 38435
Lange, Thomas, 39032
Langendernbach, 38555
Langer, Lawrence, 38900
Language and Culture Atlas of Askenazic Jewry, 38467
Lanzmann, Claude, 38900, 38979
Lappin, Eleonore, 38432, 39176
Laqueur, Walter, 38869, 39205, 39440
Large, David Clay, 38936, 39560
Lasker-Schüler, Else, 38512, 39156, 39200, 39217, 39328-39330, 39396
Lasker-Wallfisch, Anita, 38870
Lassalle, Ferdinand, 38421, 39331-39333
Latin America, Refugees, 38654
Lau, Jörg, 39040
Laub, Dori, 38900
Lauckner, Nancy A., 38838
Laurahütte, 38864
Lausch, Hans, 39126
Lawford-Hinrichsen, Irene, 38872
Lax, Peter D., 39393
Lazarus, Moritz, 39179
Lazarus, Nahida Ruth, 39179
Lazarus-Yafeh, Hava, 39212
Lederer, Herbert, 38667
Lee, Carol Ann, 38800
Legal History, 38420, 38440, 38442, 38508, 38566
Legal Professions, Jews in, 38616, 39385, 39386
Legerer, Anton, 38624
Lehberger, Reiner, 38820
Lehmann Family, 38863
Lehner, Beate Margarete, 39263
Leidinger, Paul, 38605
Leipzig, 38872
Leist, Klaus, 38979
Leitz, Christian, 38828
Lemke, Ute, 38716
Lennartz, Dirk S., 38526
Lenz, Wilhelm, 38873
Leo Baeck Institute New York, 38422
Leo Baeck Institute, 'Year Book', 38446, 38611, 38668, 38885, 39100, 39124, 39160, 39257, 39410, 39543
Leo Baeck Institute, London, 38677
Leo Baeck Institute, Memorial Lecture, 38484, 39461
Leo Baeck Institute, Occasional Papers, 38662
Leopold, David, 39538
Lermen, Birgit (Festschrift), 38598, 38993, 39217
Lerner, Markus, 39038

Leshchiner, Viatcheslav, 39089
Lessing, Theodor, 39146, 39234, 39334
Leuchter Report, 38844
Leupold-Löwenthal, Harald, 39288
Leutershausen, 38518
Leven Family, 38593
Levenson, Alan T., 39119
Leverton, Bertha, 38861
Levi, Primo, 39475
Levin, David J., 38936
Levine, Paul A., 39070
Levinson, Nathan Peter, 39476
Levinson, Pnina Navé, 39476
Lewald, Fanny, 38423
Lewis, Jill, 39438
Lewy, Günter, 38753
Lexandrowitz Family, 38879
Lexikon der Österreichischen Exilliteratur, 38686
Lexikon Deutsch-Jüdischer Autoren, 38691
Leyerzapf, Gerhard, 39553
Liberalism (Pol.), 38421, 38491
Libeskind, Daniel, 38477-38480, 39096
Librett, Jeffrey S., 39157
Licharz, Werner (Festschrift), 39357, 39462
Lichnowsky, Mechtilde, 39437
Lichtblau, Albert, 38432
Lieberman, Joseph I., 38927
Liebert, Elisabeth, 38874
Liechtenstein, 38655
Liedtke, Rainer, 38535
Liefmann, Else, 39242
Liepmann, Wilhelm, 39242
Lilien, Ephraim Moses, 39200
Lilienthal, Ulrich, 39462
Limina: a Journal of Historical and Cultural Studies', 38953
Lindemann, Albert, 39521
Lindner, Igor, 38507
Link, Olaf, 38593
Links, Roland, 39394
Linssen, Michael, 39448, 39449
Linz, 38713
Lipinski, Krzysztof, 39235
Lipstadt, Deborah, 38842
Listmann, Anja, 38586
Literature, Hebrew, 39127
Literature, Jews depicted in, 38511, 38741, 39152, 39154, 39466, 39474, 39480, 39481, 39549
Literature, Jews in, 38667, 38693, 38755, 38769, 39217, 39241, 39244, 39281, 39316, 39318, 39363, 39374, 39481
Lithuania, Nazi Period, 38849, 39009
Litt, Stefan, 38597
Loacker, Armin, 38717
Lodz, Ghetto, 38749
Löb, James, 39335
Loerke, Oskar, 39278
Lörrach, 38875
Löser, Hans, 38876

Löwe, Ludwig, 39368
Löwe, Teresa, 39265
Löwenthal, Leo, 39336
Loewy, Hanno, 39473
Loewy, Michael, 39135
Lohalm, Uwe, 38725
Lohrmann, Klaus, 38456, 38603, 38620, 38685
London, Louise, 38877
Longerich, Peter, 38995,
Lonitz, Henri, 39420
Lonyai-Kelemen, Piroska, 39035
Lordick, Harald, 38511
Lorenz, Dagmar C. G., 38838, 39041
Lorenz, Einhart, 38941
Lorraine, 38612, 38613
Lotfi, Gabriele, 38722
Lotter, Friedrich, 38440, 39491
Lotze, Siegfried, 38542
Lowe, Adolph, 39337
Lowenthal-Hensel, Cécile, 38681
Lower Saxony, 38556, 38813
Lozowick, Yaacov,
Luban, Ottokar, 39362
Luckner, Gertrud, 38929, 38930
Ludi, Regula, 38973
Ludwigshafen, 38878
Lübeck, 38879
Lüdtke, Alf, 38725
Lueger, Karl, 39521
Lühe, Astrid von der, 39126
Lühe, Barbara von der, 39390
Lühe, Irmela von der, 38834
Lütteken, Laurenz, 39126
Lützeler, Paul Michael, 39217
Luit, Riety van, 38465
Lustiger, Arno, 39009
Luther, Martin, 39552
Lutter, Walter E., 38607
Lutz, Carl, 38932
Luxemburg, Rosa, 39338
Lyons, Arline, 39220

'Maajan', 38568, 39177
Maayani, Ami, 39560
Macho, Thomas, 39133
Maciejewski, Marek, 38957
Madagascar, 38744
Mader, Ruth, 38501
Mächler, Stefan, 38880
Magin, Christine, 38421
Mahler, Gustav, 38898, 39560
'(Die) Mahnung', 38874
Maier, Johann, 38424
Maier, Louis, 38559
Maimon, Salomon, 39120, 39121, 39157
Mainz, 38428, 38557
Maiwald, Stefan, 38881
Mallmann, Klaus Michael, 38777
Malsch, 38559

Manes, Philipp, 38979
Manger, Klaus, 39217, 39271
Mankower, Henryk, 39242
Mann, Golo, 39443
Mann, Michael, 38883
Mann, Thomas, 39553, 39560
Mannheimer, Max, 38882
Mansbacher, Herta, 38579
Mantello, George, 38927
Manthey, Matthias, 38529
Manufacturers, 38706
Marburg an der Lahn, 38767
Marcuse, Carl, 38733
Marcuse, Edith, 38733
Marcuse, Ludwig, 38651, 38733, 39217
Marcuse, Paula, 38733
Margalit, Avishai, 39251
Margaritha, Anthonius, 39463
'Marginalien', 39370
Marienfeld, Wolfgang, 39079
Marin, Bernd, 39522
Markus, Edith, 38735
Marr, Wilhelm, 39521
Marriage Contracts, 39192
Marrus, Michael R., 38435
Mart, Erwin, 38643
Martin, Albrecht, 38579
Martini, Erich, 39300
Marum-Lunau, Elisabeth, 38884
Marx, Karl, 38421, 39439, 39541
Masaryk, Thomas G., 38637
Maser, Peter, 39380
'(The) Massachusetts Review', 38733
Massey, Irving, 39474
'(The) Mathematical Intelligencer', 39233
Mattenklott, Gert, 38678
Matthäus, Jürgen, 38711, 38885
Mattioli, Aram, 39501, 39542
Matzerath, Horst, 38756
Maul, Heinz Eberhard, 38850
Mauthausen, 38910
Mauthner, Fritz, 39325, 39339, 39535
May, Simon, 39116
Mayer, Hans, 39237
Mayer, Paul Yogi, 39178
'MB. Mitteilungsblatt des Irgun Olei Merkas Europa', 39547
Mcpherson, Colin, 39204, 39213
Mecklenburg, Norbert, 39544
Mecklenburg-Vorpommern, 39042
Medawar, Jean, 39223
Medicine, Jews in, 38825, 38946, 39216, 39238, 39295
Medicine, Nazi, 38855
Mediterranean Historical Review', 39207
Medoff, Rafael, 38692, 38886
Mehring, Walter, 39217, 39394
Meidner, Ludwig, 39235
Meiners, Uwe, 38976

Meinert, Joachim, 39475
Meinl, Susanne, 38705
Meirer, Albert, 38736
Meisel-Hess, Grete, 39152
Meitner, Lise, 39223, 39340
Memorials, 38629, 38835, 39073, 39081, 39085, 39090, 39097
Menasse, Eva, 38843
Menasse, Robert, 39152
Mendelsohn, Erich, 39341
Mendelssohn Family, 39240
Mendelssohn, Felix, 39342, 39343
Mendelssohn, Felix de, 39016
Mendelssohn, Moses, 38421, 39122, 39123, 39124, 39125, 39126, 39138
Mendes-Flohr, Paul, 38460
Menger, Karl, 39233
'Menora', 38678; 38425, 38449, 38457, 38487, 38494, 38532, 38622, 39069, 39083, 39086, 39087, 39088, 39097, 39109, 39186, 39201, 39276, 39376
Mercer, Ben, 38953
Mergen, Simone, 38521
Merrienboer, Johan Van,
Mertz, Peter, 38718
Meschede, 38560
Meshulash Berlin, 39018
Messianism, 38425, 38449, 38457, 39106, 39109, 39135, 39139
Métraux, Alexandre, 39080
Metschies, Kurt, 38697
Metz, 38612
Metzler Lexikon der Deutsch-Jüdischen Literatur, 38693
Metzler, Gabriele, 38829
Mexico, Refugees, 39415
Meyer, Ahlrich,
Meyer, Almut, 38628
Meyer, Beate, 38725, 38736, 38819
Meyer, Jochen, 39278
Meyer, Michael A., 38441, 38533
Meyer, Pierre-André, 38565
Meyer, Thomas, 39267
Meyerbeer, Giacomo, 39560
Michaelis, Johann David, 39512
Michelstadt, 38561
Middle Ages, 38424, 38428, 38429, 38431, 38440, 38456, 38462, 38464, 38499, 38502, 38566, 38603, 38623, 38685, 39188, 39189, 39463, 39480, 39491, 39492, 39493, 39495, 39516
'Midstream', 38627, 38844
Miethe, Ingrid, 39020
Milchram, Gerhard, 38456, 38621
Militarism, 38413
Minden, Michael, 39327
Mink, Peter-Josef, 38555
Miron, Guy, 39206
Mischler, Gerd, 38881
Misková, Alena, 38631
Mitchell, Paul, 38625

Mitgutsch, Anna, 39572
Mittag, Susanne, 39306
'Mitteilungen d. Inst. f. Österr. Geschichtsforschung', 38673, 39183
'Mitteilungen des Vereins für Heimatkunde, Birkenfeld', 38592
'Mitteilungen des Oberhessischen Geschichtsvereins Giessen', 38528
'Mitteilungen des Vereins für Geschichte der Stadt Nürnberg', 38519
'Mitteilungen Staatsbibliothek zu Berlin', 38739
Mittelbau-Dora (see also Dora-Mittelbau) 38772
'Mitteldeutsches Jahrbuch', 38416, 39306
'Mittelweg', 39296
Mittleman, Alan, 38442
Mixed Marriages, 38491, 38736, 38983, 39455, 39483
Mixed Marriages, Children of, 38706, 38759, 38819, 38922
'Modern Judaism', 38886, 38954, 39101, 39104, 39134, 39196,
'Modern Language Review', 38996
Möller, Horst, 38651
Möllers, H., 38775
Mönchengladbach, 38562
Mohr, Klaus, 38531
Molnár, Géza von (Festschrift), 39459
'Moment', 39055
Mommsen, Hans, 38855
Mommsen, Theodor E., 38443
Mondorf, 38563
Montgelas, Peter Janus Graf von, 38525
Moos, Carlo, 39501
Moravia, 38631, 38637, 39581
Moraw, Peter (Festschrift), 38600
Morgan, Michael L., 39129
'(Der) Morgen', 38419,
'Morgen-Glantz', 39545
Morgenstern, Matthias, 38521
Morgenstern, Soma, 38628, 39344, 39345
Morgenweck-Lambrinos, Vera, 39340
Morley, John F., 38929
Moruzzi, Norma Claire, 39158
Moselkern, 38564
Moselle, 38488, 38564, 38565
Moser, Rupert, 38643
Moses Mendelssohn Zentrum, 38678, 38694
Mosès, Stéphane, 39251
Moss, Christoph, 38778
Mosse Family, 39240
Mosse, George L., 38421, 39346, 39440
Mosselle, 38526
Mosès, Stéphane, 39133
Motzkin, Gabriel, 39107, 39251
Mühlberger, Sonja, 38947
Mühlheim (Main), 38887
Mühlstein, Jan, 39111
Mühsam, Erich, 39347, 39348, 39349, 39441
Mülheim/Moselle, 38579

Müller, Albert, 38666, 39506
Müller, Alexander, 39312
Müller, Arthur, 38486
Müller, Hans-Harald, 39574
Müller, Herta, 39322
Müller, Johannes, 38537
Müller, Reinhard, 38888
Müller-Commichau, Wolfgang, 39043
Müller-Elmau, Dietmar, 38936
Müller-Hill, Benno, 38806
Müller-Kampel, Beatrix, 38667
Münch, Hans Wilhelm, 38707
Münchhausen, Boerries Frhr. von, 39200
Münkler, Herfried, 39558
Münster, 38566, 38889
Münster, Sebastian, 39554
Münsterland, 38890
Müssener, Helmut, 39264
Munich, 38567, 38891, 38892, 39490
Murawski, Klaus-Eberhard, 38511
Museums, 38432, 38514, 38679, 38919
Music, Jewish, 39187
Music, Jews in, 38872, 39160, 39342, 39392, 39400, 39430, 39452
'(The) Musical Quarterly', 39482, 39559
Musicians, Composers, 38624, 38813, 39160, 39293, 39306, 39314, 39390, 39401, 39402, 39404
Musner, Lutz, 38899
Mutterstadt, 38579
Myschkow, 39017
Mysticism, 38622, 39103
Mytze, Andreas W., 39372

Nadav, Daniel, 39242
Nagel, Anne Christine, 38767
Nagold, 38547
Naor, Simha, 38893
Nash, Ernest, 39350
'Nassauische Annalen', 38555, 38606
Nationalism, 38448
Naumann, Michael, 38899
Nazi Crimes, Prosecution of, 38695, 38722, 38802, 38817, 38921, 39046, 39047, 39446, 38920
Nazi Period, in Film, Radio, Theatre, 38900
Nazi Period, Jewish Life in Germany, 38865, 38872, 38925
Nazi Period, Jewish Youth, 38907
Nazi Period, Teaching, 39078
Nazi Politics, 38940,
'NDL, Neue Deutsche Literatur', 39570
Neander, Joachim, 38772
Neidhardt, Irit, 39523, 39524
Neitzert, Dieter (Festschrift), 38496
Nelki Family, 39242
Nemitz, Kurt, 39351
Neter, Eugen, 39242
Netherlands, 38465, 39184, 39501

Netherlands, Nazi Period, 38814, 38894, 38895, 38896, 38928
Netherlands, Refugees, 38651, 38814, 38857, 38889,
Neubach, Helmut, 38511
Neuberg, Simon, 38469
Neubert, Andreas, 38497
'Neue Gesellschaft/Frankfurter Hefte', 39302, 39405
'Neue Jüdische Monatshefte', 38419
'Neue Praxis', 39185
'(Das) Neue Tage-Buch', Paris, 38651
'Neue Zeitschrift für Musik', 39402
Neuengamme, 38897
Neues Lexikon des Judentums., 38694
Neufeld, Michael, 38708
Neufreistett, 38935
Neugebauer, Wolfgang, 38719
'Neukirchener Theologische Zeitschrift', 39381, 39469
Neumann, Elsa, 39352
Neumann, Hugo, 39242
Neumann, Klaus, 39081
Neumann, Robert, 38467, 38652
Neumark, Fritz, 39353
Neumeier, Gerhard, 38567
'1999, Zeitschrift für Sozialgesch. des 20. und 21. Jahrhunderts', 38824, 38921
Neunkirchen (Austria), 38621
Neuro-Sciences, Jews in, 39238
Neutitschein, 38882
Neuwied, 38568
'New German Critique', 38899, 39157
'(The) New Republic', 38745
'New Statesman', 38830
New Zealand, Refugees, 39313
Newcastle-Upon-Tyne, 38653
Newman, Richard, 38898
'Newsweek', 38942
Neyer, Maria Amata, 39382, 39448
Nicosia, Francis R., 38839
Niedermeiser, 38545
Niesner, Manuela, 39492
Nietzsche, Friedrich, 39201, 39556, 39560
Niewöhner, Friedrich, 39122, 39445
Niewyk, Donald L., 38444, 38839
Nisko, 38764
Nittenberg, Joanna, 38624
'Non-Aryan' Christians (see also Mixed Marriages), 38778
Nonn, Christoph, 39501
Nonnenweier, 38569
Norway, 39533
Norway, Refugees, 39391
November Pogrom, 38728, 38807, 38872, 38901, 38902, 38917, 38989, 39076
November Pogrom, Remembrance, 39097
Nümbrecht, 38570
Nuremberg, 38571

Nuremberg Laws, 38873, 38881, 39000
Nuremberg Trials, 38900, 38903
Nussbaum, Laureen, 38838
'NZZ' (Neue Zürcher Zeitung), 38971, 38977, 39556

Obenaus, Herbert, 38725
Ober, Kenneth H., 39367
Oberammergau Passion Play, 39532
Obermoschel, 38579
Obschernitzki, Doris, 38884
'(The) Observer', 38842, 38913
Och, Gunnar, 38423
Oedl, Ulrike, 38686
Oellers, Norbert, 39217, 39328
Oertel, Christine, 39015
Oertel, W., 38560
Oesterle, Jenny Rahel, 38528
'Österreich in Geschichte und Literatur',
'Österreichische Zeitschrift für Politikwissenschaft', 38989
Oestreicher, Felix Hermann, 38904
Ofer, Dalia,
Offe, Sabine, 38679
Offenbach am Main, 39082
Offenburg, 38572, 38573
Oldenburg, 38890
Olfen, 38574
Olmütz, 38760
Olympic Games, 38723, 39178
Omran, Susanne, 39477
Ondrichová, Lucie, 38905
Oppenheimer Family, 39432
Oppenheimer, Deborah, 38860
Oppenheimer, Joseph Süß, 38783, 38784
Oppler, Therese, 39216
Oranienburg, 38888
'Orbis Litterarum', 39398
Orendi, Diana, 39145
Organisations, Nazi Period, 38925,
Organisations, Post-1945, 39057
Orlik, Emil, 39354
Ortelsburg/Masuren, 38511
Ortenau, 38507, 38906
'(Die) Ortenau', 38569, 38573, 38906, 38935
Orthodoxy, 38424, 39116, 39140
Ortmeyer, Benjamin, 38907
Osten-Sacken Peter von der, 39470
Ostermann, Dagmar, 38707
Ostjuden see Eastern Jewry
Oswald, Ingrid, 39020
Oswalt, Stefanie, 39311, 39394
Otten, Karl, 38652
Otto, Anton, 38631
Owings, Alison, 38737
Oz, Amos, 39247

Pabst, Manfred, 38691
Pätz, Andreas, 38908

Pätzold, Kurt (Festschrift), 38922; 39008, 39047, 39058, 39059, 39310
Palatinate, 38420, 38575, 38576, 38577, 38578, 38816, 38878, 39478
Palestine, 39193, 39199, 39205, 39206, 39209, 39211, 39213, 39428, 39454
Palestine, Immigration, 38779, 39203, 39204, 39456,
Pankau, Johannes G., 39235
Pankratius, Victor, 38593
Paoloni, Giovanni, 38666
Papanek, Ernst, 39355
Papanek, Hanna, 38821
Pape, Walter, 39289
Papen, Patricia von, 38909
Papenfuss, Dietrich, 38427
Pappenheim, Bertha, 39356, 39357
Parcer, Jan, 38709
Parini, Jay, 39573
Paris, 38781
Paris un Wiene, 38468
Parker, Clare, 38910
'Partisan Review', 39205
Pascheles, Wolf, 39358
'Patterns of Prejudice', 39016, 39458, 39490
Patzelt, Peter, 38911
Paucker, Arnold, 38725, 38947
Paucker, Pauline, 38912
Paul, Gerhard, 38777
Pauli, Wolfgang Ernst, 39358
Paulus, Helmut, 38728
Pechstein, Max, 39239
Pelli, Moshe, 39127
Pennebaker, Elizabeth, 39429
Peperkorn, Hella, 38879
Perels, Joachim, 38902, 39218
Performing Arts, Jews in, 38814
Perutz, Leo, 39359, 39574
Peters (Music Publishers), 38872
Peters, George F., 39304
Petersen, Joan, 39275
Petersen, Peter, 39231
Petropoulos, Jonathan, 38913
Petuchowski, Elizabeth, 38929, 38930
Pfäfflin, Friedrich, 39437
Pfahl-Traughber, Armin, 39525
Pfefferkorn, Johann Joseph, 39557
Pfeiffer, Thomas, 39526
Pforzheim, 39428
Pfuhlstein, Alexandra von, 38736
Phayer, Michael, 38754
Phelan, Anthony, 39261
Phiebig, Albert J., 39169
Philadelphia, 38664
Philanthropists, 38525, 38528, 38535, 39335
Philipp, Michael, 38947
Philippoff, Eva, 39258
Philippsburg, 38914
Phillips, Alastair,

'Philobiblon', 38912
Philosemitism, 39200, 39458, 39474
'(Die) Philosophin', 38417
Philosophy and Learning, Jews in, 39102, 39107, 39110, 39134, 39236, 39267
Philosophy, Jewish, 39114, 39129, 39138, 39141
Phleps, Thomas, 39231
Photographers, 39239, 39315, 39350
'Physics Today', 39326
'Physikalische Blätter', 39294, 39358
Pich, Henryk, 38595
Pingel, Falk, 39089
Piper, Ernst, 38882
Placzek, Adolf K., 38915
Pleitgen, Fritz, 39376
Pöggeler, Franz, 39217
Pöggeler, Otto, 39274
Poensgen, Aline, 38593
Poetry, 39274, 39322, 39366
Poetry, Holocaust, 39569
Pötzsch, Hansjörg, 39527
Pogroms, Middle Ages, 38431
Pohanka, Reinhard, 38626
Pohl, Dieter, 38840
Pohl, Johannes, 38868
Pohl-Braun, Ulrike, 39217
Pokorny, Siegfried, 38728
Poland, 38657, 39501
Poland, Nazi Period, 38656, 38722, 38928, 38957, 38998
'Polis', 38501
Politics, Jews in, 38438, 38511, 39265, 39413, 39423
'(Die) Politische Meinung', 39066, 39271, 39290
Polle, Theodor, 38513
Pollmann, Viktoria, 38695, 39501
Polna, 39581
Poloncarz, Marek, 38979
Poltorak, David, 39089
Pomerance, Aubrey, 38432
Pomeranz, Edith, 38636
Popper-Lynkeus, Josef, 39360
Porat, Dina, 39537, 39560
Porges, Lucie & Paul Peter, 39361
Posch, Herbert, 38985
Posen, 39235
Posener, Julius, 39442
Posner, Louis, 38916
Postone, Moishe, 39251
Potsdam, 38917
Potthast, Jan Björn, 38705
Pracht-Jörns, Elfi, 38583
Praetorius, Johann Philipp, 39482
Prague, 38423, 38469, 38637, 38638, 38639, 38866, 39235, 39574, 39576
Prague, Jewish Museum, 38919
Prague, Jüdisches Zentralmuseum, 38705, 38918, 38919
Prague, Nazi Period, 38705

Index to Bibliography 463

Prayer Books, 38610
Press, 38436, 38762
Press, Jewish, 38644, 38704, 38761, 39176
Press, Yiddish, 39152
Pressler, Mirjam, 38801
Prestes, Anita, 38649
Pribyl, Lukás, 38764
Primor, Avi, 39083
Pringle, Annette, 38696
Projekt: Judenplatz Wien, 39090; 38626, 38715, 38984, 38991, 39528
Prokasky, Judith, 38487
Prosecution of Nazi Crimes see Nazi Crimes, Prosecution of
Prosek, Zdenek, 38631
Pross, Steffen, 39224
Protestantism and Jews, 39471, 39511
Protocols of the Elders of Zion, 38643, 39503, 39504
Prucha, Martin, 38717
Prussia, 38511, 38596
Prutsch, Ursula,
Psychoanalysts, Nazi Period, 38808
Psychoanalysts, Psychologists, 38808, 39286-39288, 39295, 39409, 39430
Publicists, Journalists, 38651
'Publisher's Weekly', 38759
Publishers, Printers, 38872, 39284, 39424
'Publius', 38442
Pulzer, Peter, 39528
Purcell, Brendan, 39091
Purin, Bernhard, 38527
Pussert, Annette, 39352
Puto, Artan,
Putschke, Wolfgang, 38167
Pyke, David, 39223
Pytell, T., 39285

'Quellen und Forschungen aus Ital. Archiven und Bibliotheken', 38752
Quellen zur Gesch. der Juden in den neuen Bundesländern, 38697
Quinkert, Babette, 38802

Raabe, Wilhelm, 39474
Rabbinical Seminaries, 39112, 39140
Rabbis, 38459, 38573, 38720, 39098, 39100, 39112, 39140, 39171, 39181, 39184
Rabinbach, Anson, 39251, 39346
Rabinovici, Doron, 38989, 39152, 39161, 39219, 39517
Racism, 38881, 39001
Radczewski-Helbig, Jutta, 39258
Radek, Karl, 39362
Rademacher, Franz, 38744
Rahden, Till van, 38491, 39529
Ran, Daniela, 39207
Randt, Ursula, 38820
Rapoport, Tamar, 39020

Rappl, Marian, 38891
Raskin, Alexander, 38488
Rassismus, Faschismus, Antisemitismus, 38922; 39008, 39047, 39058, 39059, 39310
Rau, Johannes, 39461
Rauhut-Brungs, Leah, 39575
Raulff, Ulrich, 38460, 39084
Rauthe, Simone, 39067
'Ravensberger Blätter', 38602
Ravensbrück, 38814
Ravitzky, Aviezer, 39212
Rebhun, Ze'ev, 38923
'Recherches Germaniques', 39534
Rechter, David, 39152
Recklinghausen, 38580
Red Cross, 38740, 38979
Reform Judaism, 38533, 39111, 39112, 39148, 39184, 39257
Refugee Policy, Great Britain, 38877, 39224
Refugee Policy, Japan, 38850
Refugee Policy, Netherlands, 38896,
Refugee Policy, Scandinavia, 38941, 38950
Refugee Policy, Sweden, 38967
Refugee Policy, Switzerland, 38680, 38960, 38962, 38966, 38967-38972
Refugees see also Name of Country
Refugees, Czechoslovakia, 38762
Refugees, Great Britain, 39224
Refugees, Shanghai, 38948
Refugees, Spain, 38952
Regensburg, 39098
Rehn, Marie-Elisabeth, 38508
Reich, Jens, 39045
Reich-Ranicki, Marcel, 39363, 39443
Reichel, Peter, 39179
Reichrath, Hans L., 39478
Reichsvereinigung der Juden in Deutschland, 38736
Rein, Kurt, 38641
Reiner, Elchanan, 38639
Reinerová, Lenka, 39576
Reiter, Margit, 38947
Reitlinger, Gerald, 38954
Remembrance, Culture and Politics of, 39077
Remigration, 39031, 39061, 39222, 39243, 39353, 39415, 39454, , 38802
Remmler, Karen, 38838
Remy, Nahida (Nahida Ruth Lazarus), 39179
Rendsburg, 38581, 38924
Rendsburg, Jüdisches Museum, 38582
'Rendsburger Jahrbuch', 38582
'Rendsburger Jahrbuch' (Beihefte), 38924
Rendtorff, Rolf, 39212
Rensmann, Lars, 38925
Requate, Jörg, 39046
Rescue of Jews, 38722, 38734, 38804, 38926-38931
Resistance, 38867, 38990, 39008
Resistance, Jewish, 39007, 39011, 39012

Resistance, Non-Jewish, 39009
Restitution, 38802, 39050, 39051, 39052, 39053
Restitution, Austria, 38986, 39048, 39049
Reuband, Karl-Heinz, 38934
Reuchlin, Johannes, 39557
Reuling, Ulrich, 38541
Reuter, Fritz, 38579
Revolution and Jews, 38577
'Revue d'histoire de la Shoah: Le Monde Juif', 39198
'Revue des Études Juives', 38537
Rheinau, 38935
Rheinbischofsheim, 38935
'Rheinisch-Westfälische Zeitschrift für Volkskunde', 38562
Rheinz, Hanna, 39054
Rhineland, 38420, 38428, 38431, 38489, 38540, 38562, 38563, 38568, 38570, 38583, 38584, 38776
Richard Wagner und die Juden, 39560
Richter, Arnd, 39342
Richter, Gerhard, 39262
Ricken, Ulrich, 39126
Ridder, Thomas, 38608
Riegner, Gerhart M., 38644
Riga, 38738
Rilke, Rainer Maria, 39215
Riss, Heidelore, 38482
Rites and Ceremonies, 38543, 39174, 39463
Ritter, Wolfgang, 38514
Ritual Bath, 38499, 38578
Ritual Murder (see also Blood Libel), 38637
Robbins, Christopher, 39010
Robert Musil, 39215
Robert, Ludwig, 38423
Robertson, Ritchie, 38452, 39200, 39375
Rock, David, 39259
Rockenhausen, 38578
Rode, Walther, 39364
Röhrs, Christine-Félice, 39019
Römer, Gernot, 38706
Römer, Nils (Holger), 38426, 38445
Rogger, Franziska, 38643
Rohrbacher, Stefan, 39141
Rokahr, Gerd, 38514
Rolnick, Josh, 39055
Romania, 38823
Rome, 39501
Romero, Christiane Zehl, 39373
Rommelspacher, Birgit, 38821, 38866
Rommerskirchen, 38584
Ronell, Avital, 38900
Roschewski, Heinz, 38680
Rosé, Alfred, 38898
Rosé, Alma, 38898
Rose, Alison, 39152
Rose, Jonathan, 38847
Rosé, Justine, 38898

Rose, Paul Lawrence, 38936, 39560
Rosen, Evelyn Bodek, 38664
Rosenberg, Erika, 38931
Rosenberg, Leibl, 38571
Rosenberg, Richard, 39057
Rosenfeld, Alvin H., 38841
Rosengarten, Albrecht, 38552
Rosenkranz, Moses, 39217
Rosenthal, Hans, 38736
Rosenthal, Louis, 38545
Rosenzweig, Franz, 38421, 39118, 39128-39132, 39138, 39139, 39159, 39220, 39236, 39388
Roshwald, A., 39056
Rossel, Maurice, 38979
Rossi, Hedwig, 39365
Rossmeissl, Ralf, 38505
Rostock, 39042
Rotella, Mark, 38759
Roth, Joseph, 38797, 39180, 39235,
Rothauser, Therese, 38736
Rother, Dorothea, 38604
Rothkolb, Olivia, 39438
Rothschild Family, 39049, 39240
Rothschild, M. H., 38938
Rottenecker, Bernd, 38507
Rousso, Henry, 39046
Rovan, Joseph, 39444
Rovit, Rebecca, 38980
Rozett, Robert, 38698
Rubinstein, Ernest, 39131
Rubinstein, Sylvin, 38867
Rubinstein, W.D., 39240
Ruch, Martin, 38572, 38573
Rudel, Josef Norbert, 39208
Rudnick, Ursula, 38556
Rudof, Joanne Weiner, 38836
Rudolph, H., 38944
Rudzi, Margit Tamar, 38593
Rübner, Tuvia, 39217
Rürup, Reinhard, 38446, 38697, 39084
Rüsen, Jörn, 38936
Ruhr, 38939
Runge, Irene, 39019, 39031, 39058
Rupnow, Dirk, 38918, 38919
Rupprath, Gisela, 38540
Rural Jewry, 38472, 38493, 38507, 38515, 38526, 38546, 38550, 38588, 38589
Rychlo, Peter, 38641

Saar, 38420, 38526
Sabar, Shalom, 39192
Sabbatai Zvi, 39106
Sacharin, Rosa M., 38859
'Sachor. Beiträge zur Jüd. Gesch. und zur Gedenkstättenarbeit`, 38579
'Sachor. Ztschr. f. Antisemitismusforschung', 39526
Sachs, Nelly, 39217, 39264, 39275, 39366
Sachs, Shimon (Walter), 39170

Index to Bibliography 465

Sachsen-Anhalt, 38585, 39085
Sachsenhagen, 38813
Sachsse, Rolf, 38705
'Saeculum', 39377
Safrian, Hans, 38940
Sagan, Alex, 39346
Sagave, Pierre-Paul, 38651
Sagmo, Ivar, 39533
Said, Edward, 39205
Saint Sauveur-Henn, Anne, 38654
Sajak, Clauss Peter, 39165
Salemnik, Theo, 39501
Salier, Edward, 39182
Salmen, Brigitte, 39335
Salomon, Alice, 38821
Salons, 38483
Salzgitter, 39081
Salzschlirf (Bad), 38586
Salzwedel, 38587
Samen, M,, 38807
Samuel, Maximilian, 39242
Samuely, Nathan, 39367
Sanary-Sur-Mer, 38651
Sandmöller, Michael, 38593
Saphir, Moritz Gottlieb, 38418
Sarris, Viktor, 39409
Sartre, Jean-Paul, 39255
Sassenberg, Marina, 39384
Sassin, Horst R., 38593, 38594
Sauerland, Karol, 39235
Saxony, 39527
Scandinavia, Refugees, 38941, 38950
Schäbitz, Michael, 38736
Schädlich, Hans Joachim, 39330
Schäfer, Thomas, 39231
Schafranek, Hans, 38990
Schallner, Dieter, 38631
Schapira, Esther, 38817
Scharbaum, Heike, 39389
Schardt, Michael Matthias, 39312
Scharnholz, Lars, 38503
Schatz-Uffenheimer, Rivka, 39104
Schebera, Jürgen, 39402, 39404
Scheele, Jürgen, 39298
Schefold, Bertram, 39337
Scheichl, Sigurd Paul, 38423
Scheit, Gerhard, 39517, 39531
Schellack, Gustav, 38548
Schelling, Friedrich Wilhelm, 39231, 39541
Schellinger, Uwe, 38507
Schepua, Michael, 38878
Scherer, F. M., 39225
Scherg, Leonhard, 38517
Scheurenberg Family, 38736
Scheurig, Axel, 38507
Schieb, Barbara, 38736, 38738
Schiedel, Heribert, 39014
Schieder, Wolfgang, 38427
Schiele, Werner, 38515

Schiewitz, Lucian, 38591
Schindel, Robert, 38834, 39152, 39161
Schindler, Oskar, 38931
Schirren, Matthias, 39442
Schirrmacher, Frank, 38736, 39363
Schlant, Ernestine, 38942
Schleiermacher, Friedrich, 39541
Schleiermacher, Sabine, 39216
Schleifer, Bernard, 39400
Schlenstedt, Silvia, 38821, 39228, 39234
Schlesinger, Georg, 39368
Schleswig-Holstein, 38508, 38581, 38908, 38924, 38943
Schlick, Gabriela, 39548
Schlink, Bernhard, 39305
Schlör, Joachim, 38977, 39045, 39568
Schlüter, Margarete, 39141
Schmallenberg, 38802
Schmaltz, Florian, 38802
Schmeichel-Falkenberg, Beate, 38821
Schmeling, Anke, 38552
Schmid, Anton, 39007, 39009
Schmid, Martin A., 38623
Schmidt, Christoph, 39136
Schmidt, Gilya, G., 39105, 39130
Schmidt, Johann Michael, 39217
Schmidt, Michael, 39405
Schmidt, Walter, 39059
Schmidt-Beste, Thomas, 39343
Schmitt, Carl, 39136, 39558
Schmitt, Eric, 39039
Schmitt, Jean-Claude, 39480
Schmitthenner, Charlotte, 39338
Schmitz, Josef, 38584
Schmitz, Walter, 39217
Schneck, Peter, 39242
Schneider, Gabriele, 38423
Schneider, Hans, 38579
Schneider, Hans C., 38887
Schneider, Hubert, 38742, 38936
Schneider, Richard Chaim, 39060
Schneider, Wolfgang, 39095
Schnitzler, Norbert, 39530
Schochat, Asriel, 38447
Schocken (Department Store), 38503
Schöck-Quinteros, Eva, 39260
Schölzel, Arnold, 39310
Schön, Doris, 38625
Schönberg, Arnold, 38856, 39160, 39231, 39560
Schöndorf, Kurt Erich, 38950, 39533
Schöne, Lothar, 39161
Schönfeld, Gabriel, 39050
Schöpferische Momente des Europäischen Judentums, 38424; 38471, 38522, 38523, 38638, 38639, 39191
Schoeps, Hans Joachim (Gesammelte Schriften), 39369
Schoeps, Hans-Joachim, 39061, 39118, 39369
Schoeps, Julius H., 38651, 38678, 38694, 39023, 39061, 39086, 39150, 39376, 39423

Scholem, Gershom, 39104, 39133-39137, 39236, 39445
Scholz, Albrecht, 39242
Scholz, Dietmar, 38495
Schools, 38413, 38514, 38520, 38578, 38713, 38907, 38988
Schoor, Kerstin, 39228
Schorsch, Ismar, 39141
Schrader, Ulrike, 38593, 38610
Schreckenberg, Heinz, 39493, 39494
Schreiber, Birgit, 38866
Schreiber, Marion, 39011
Schreiner, Klaus, 39530
Schreiter, René, 38678
Schrijver, Emile G.L., 38465
Schröder, Bernd, 39170
Schröder, Frank, 39042
Schrödinger, Erwin, 39223
Schruff, Helene, 39161
Schubert, Klaus, 38531
Schubert, Kurt, 38456
Schuchard, Jutta, 38552
Schuder, Rosemarie, 39513
Schüler-Springorum, Stefanie, 38511
Schütte, Sven, 38499
Schütz, Chana C., 38736
Schütz, Hans J., 39241
Schütz, Siegfried, 38496
Schütze, Yvonne, 39020
Schüürmann, Herbert, 39169
Schuhmann, Klaus, 39281, 39374
Schul, Yaakov, 39537
Schulin, Ernst, 38448
Schulte, Christoph, 38449, 39257
Schulte, Diana, 38736
Schulte, Ingolf, 39345
Schulz, Armin, 38468
Schulz, Ingo, 39231
Schulz, Tom R., 39402
Schulz-Jander, Eva, 38552
Schumacher, Christina, 39181
Schumann, Clara, 39306
Schumann, Henry, 38565
Schwab, Hermann, 38651
Schwabach, 39062
Schwaben, 38531, 38588, 38589
Schwärzler, Monika, 38985
Schwara, Desanka, 39152
Schwarz, Egon, 38667, 39481
Schwarz, Esther, 38413
Schwarzschild, Leopold, 38651
Schweid, Eliezer, 39212
Schweiger, Andreas, 38720
Schweitzer, Albert, 39416, 39462
'Schweizerische Zeitschrift f. Geschichte', 38751, 38967, 38968, 38970, 38972, 39502, 39542
Schwelm, 38944
'Schwelmer Heimatbrief', 38944
Schwenk, Sebastian, 38593

Schwerhoff, Gerd, 39495
Schwerin, 39042
Schwersenz, Ruth, 38736
Sciences and Mathematics, Jews in, 38806, 39222, 39223, 39233, 39280, 39294, 39326, 39352, 39358, 39393
Scotland, Refugees, 38859
Sebek, Jaroslav, 38631
Sebnitz, 38945
Seeber, Ursula, 39229
Seemann, Birgit, 39413, 38691
Seewann, Harald, 39202
Segal, Lilli, 38858
Segal, Lore, 39578
Seghers, Anna, 39221, 39228, 39370-39374, 39447
Seibert, Hubertus, 38579
Seibert, Winfried, 38770
Seidel, Esther, 39114
Seidel, Jürgen, 39577
Seidel-Höppner, Waltraud, 39433
Seidler, Eduard, 38946, 39242
Seiler, Lukrezia, 38875
Seiz, Carola, 38521
'Selbstorganisation', 39139, 39149, 39159
Self-Hatred (see also Jewish Problem), 39477
Seligenstadt, 38590
Seligmann, Rafael, 39161, 39375
Sellar, Tom, 39401
Sellier, André, 38773
Sendtner, Florian, 38863
Sephardi Communities, 38536
Sereny, Gitta, 39446
Seyfried, Bettina v., 39403
Seymour, David, 39246
Sha'ary, David, 38635
Shaked, Gershon, 38432
Shalev-Gerz, Esther, 39073
Shanghai, Refugees, 38647, 38675, 38947, 38948, 39314
Shapira, Anita, 39212
Shapiro, James, 39532
Shapiro, Marc B., 39140
Shapiro, Robert Moses, 38846
Sharell, Esther, 39179
Shashar, Michael, 39117
Shear-Yashuv, Aharon, 39195
Sheehan, James J., 38913
Sheffi, Na'ama, 39560
Shermer, Michael, 38844
Shimoni, Gideon, 39212
Shoah Visual Foundation, 38871
'Shofar', 38765, 39105, 39367, 39488, 39503
Siebauer, Ulrike, 39359
Sieber, Peter, 38653
Sieg, Ulrich, 38450, 38767
Siegemund, Anja, 39209
Siegmund-Schultze, Reinhard, 38666
Sielemann, Jürgen, 38568

Sigmund, Karl, 39233
Signer, Michael A., 39470
Signori, Gabriela, 39530
Silbergleit, Arthur, 39235
Silberman, Marc, 39407
Silbermann, Alphons, 38949, 39087, 39376
Silbermann, Alphons (Obits.), 39376
Silbermann, Edith, 38641
Silesia, 38428, 38591, 39235
Sime, Ruth Lewin, 39340
Simon, Heinrich, 38423
Simon, Hermann, 38481, 38736, 39476
Simon, Josef, 39138
Simonsohn, Trude, 38866
Simsohn, Werner, 38805
Singapore, Refugees, 39314
Singer, Kurt, 39377
'Sinn und Form', 39424, 39475
Sinsheimer, Hermann, 39217
Sirges, Thomas, 38950, 39533
Smaldone, William, 39309
Smieszchala, A., 39093
Smith, Gary, 38460, 39251
Snopkowski, Simon, 39017
Social Sciences, Jews in, 39313, 39319, 39336
Social Welfare, Social Reform, 38497, 39170, 39185, 39378
Socialists, Social Democrats, 38438, 39237, 39298, 39309, 39332, 39362
Sösemann, Bernd, 39414
Sötern, 38592
Sokel, Herbert Walter, 38667
Solingen, 38593, 38594
Solotaroff-Enzer, Sandra,
Sommer, Margarete, 38734
Sommerfeld, Aloys, 38511
Sorbello Staub, Alessandra, 39336
Sorkin, David, 38435, 38451, 38452, 39126
Sorlin, Pierre, 39501
Sottopietra, Doris, 39537
South Africa, Refugees, 38675
Soviet Union, 38633, 38634
Soviet Union, Nazi Period, 38730, 38888
Soxberger, Thomas, 38470
Sozialpolitik und Judentum, 39242
'Sozialwissenschaftliche Literatur-Rundschau', 39168
Spain, Nazi Period, 38952
Spalek, John M., 39230
Specht, Minna, 39378
Spector, Scott, 38640, 39210
Spector, Shmuel, 38698
'Speculum', 39188
Speer, Albert, 39446
Speicher, Anja, 39098
Speitkamp, Winfrid, 38541
Sperber, Manès, 39235, 39379
Sperling, Maria, 38607
Speyer, 38428

Spiegel, Paul, 39011, 39025, 39063
Spielberg, Steven, 38871
Spindler, Carl, 38423
Spira, Henry, 38972
Spitzer, Shlomo, 38456, 38991
Spitzner-Jahn, Albert, 38551
Sporis, Erich, 39408
Sports, Jews in, 38723, 39178
Spuhler, Gregor, 38963, 38973
Spur, Günther, 39368
Sreberny, Annabelle, 39162
Staatsbibliothek zu Berlin, 38681
'Stammbaum', 39182; 38618
Stancic, Mirjana, 39379
Stangl, Franz, 39446
Stangneth, Bettina, 39550
Starck-Adler, Irene, 38675
Stargardt, Nicholas, 38953
Stark, Jared, 38900
Stauber, Roni, 38954
Staudinger, Barbara, 38673
Staudt, Michael, 39006
Stegemann, Ekkehard W., 39212
Stegmaier, Werner, 39138
Stein, Britta, 39333
Stein, Christine, 38528
Stein, Dave, 39400
Stein, Edith, 39380, 39381, 39382, 39448, 39449
Stein, Edith (Gesamtausgabe), 39448
Steinbach, Peter, 38955, 39243
Steinbacher, Sybille, 38709, 38710, 38722
Steinbeck, Udo, 38506
Steinberg, Jules, 39252
Steindling, Dolly (Adolf), 39012
Steinecke, Hartmut, 38423, 39217, 39248
Steiner, Elke, 38581
Steiner, George, 38913
Steinicke, Hartmut, 39481
Steinweg, Leo, 38889
Stemberger, Günter, 39141
Stendal, 38428
Stenzel, Jürgen, 39548
Stephan, Alexander, 38665
Stephan, Regina, 39341
Stern, Fred B., 39312
Stern, Gerson, 39383
Stern, Grete, 39239
Stern, Guy, 38651, 39459
Stern, Hellmut, 39450
Stern, Irma, 39239
Stern, Max M., 39238, 39357
Stern, Selma, 39384
Sternberg, Theodor, 39385, 39386
Sternheim, Walter G. see Goral-Sternheim, Arie
Stettin, 38956, 39454
Stiehler, Heinrich, 38641
Stiehm, Lothar, 39462
'Stimmen der Zeit', 39128
Stimpfig, Karl Ernst, 38518

Stirn, Aglaja, 39244
Stockinger, Ludwig, 39533
Stocksieker di Maio, Irene, 38423
Stoffel, Gisela, 38507
Stoffel, Manfred, 38548
Stoffer, Manfred, 38949
Stokes, Lawrence, 38701
Stollberg, Jochen, 39336
Stolleis, Michael, 39046
Storfer, Adolf (Albert) Josef, 39387
Stralsund, 38595
Strassberger, Erna, 39183
Strathausen, Carsten, 38899
Straub, Theodor, 38549
Strauss, Herbert A., 39451
Strauss, Leo, 39236, 39388
Struck, Gitte, 38595
Strümpel, Jan, 38834
Stuby, Gerhard, 38921
Stude, Jürgen, 38507
Studemund-Halévy, Michael, 38536, 38537
'Studia nad Fasczymem i Zbrodniami Hitlerowskimi', 38957
'Studia Rosenthaliana', 39184
Stüben, Jens, 39235
Stürmer, Michael, 39150
Stürzbecher, Manfred, 39242
Sturzbecher, Dietmar, 39498, 39499, 39536
Stutthof, 38722, 38958
Stutz, Hans, 38645
Styria, 38720
Suchoff, D., 39250
Suchy, Barbara, 38696
'Süddeutsche Zeitung', 38863
'Südostdeutsche Vierteljahresblätter', 39245
Sühlo, Winfried, 38681
Sullivan, John, 39382
Sulzbach, 39460
Sulzer, Salomon, 39187
'(The) Sunday Times', 39223
Sunshine, Andrew, 38467
Survival in Hiding, 38737, 38857, 38867, 38889
Survival, False Identity, 38818
Susman, Margarete, 39396
Swack, Jeanne, 39482
Sweden, Refugees, 39391
Sweet, Denis M., 39145
Switzerland, 38615, 38642, 38644, 38757
Switzerland (Jewish Assets), 38974
Switzerland, Antisemitism, 39501
Switzerland, Nazi Period, 38927, 38932, 38962, 38963, 38966, 38969, 38972, 38973, 38974, 39012,
Switzerland, Post-1945, 39428
Switzerland, Refugee Policy, 38973
Switzerland, Refugees, 38680, 38814, 38863, 38959, 38960, 38962, 38963, 38964, 38965, 38968, 38970, 38971
Sykora, Katharina, 39239

Synagogues, 38416, 38453, 38475, 38494, 38499, 38521, 38533, 38543, 38552, 38560, 38562, 38578, 38593, 38594, 38599, 38602, 38608, 38623, 39024, 39186, 39190
Szilard, Leo, 39223
Szita, Szabolcs, 38975
Szymeczek, Jozef, 38631

Taaks, Christian, 38947
Tabary, Serge, 39534
Taberner, Stuart, 38994
Tabori, George, 38950
Täubler, Eugen, 39389
Tal, Josef, 39390
Tandler, Julius, 39242
Tannenbaum, William Z., 38611
Tarsi, Anita, 38979
Taterka, Thomas, 39088
Tatzkow, Monika, 38486
Tau, Max, 38591, 39391
Tauber, Richard, 39392
Tautz, Joachim, 38976
Tegel, Susan, 38784
Teichert, Carsten, 38977, 39454
Teichner, 39492
'Tel Aviver Jahrbuch für Deutsche Geschichte', 39075, 39080, 39206
Telgte, 38596
Teplitz, 38631
Tergit, Gabriele, 39579
Teschen, 38631
Teuber, Werner, 38890
Tewarson, Heidi Thomann, 38423
'Text+Kritik', 38834
Thalmann, Rita, 39212
'Theater', 39401
Theatre, Cabaret, Cinema, Jews in, 38482, 38622, 39146, 39349, 39482
'Theologische Quartalsschrift', 39496
Theresienstadt, 38738, 38764, 38866, 38905, 38978, 38979, 38980
'Theresienstädter Studien und Dokumente', 38760, 38761, 38763, 38764, 38918, 38979
Thiel, Jens, 38482
Thiele, Frank, 38509
Thierling, Magda, 38546
Thoma, Clemens, 39465, 39497
'Thomas Mann Jahrbuch', 39318
Thomas, Michel, 39010
Thorson, Helga, 39152
Thumser, Regina, 38721
Thuringia, 38597, 38598
Tichauer, Ernst, 38711
Tichy, Marina, 39288
Tiedemann, Rolf, 39419
Tilly, Michael, 38579
'(The) Times', 38765
Timm, Angelika, 39047, 39488
Timm, Erika, 38471

Tiusanen, Juha, 38908
Tobias, Jim G., 39062
Toch Family, 39183
Toch, Michael, 38454, 38456, 39183
Toeplitz, Otto, 39393, 39452
Toeplitz, Uri, 39452
Toller, Ernst, 38730
Tollmien, Cordula, 38529
Tomann, Klaus-Dieter, 39242
Torberg, Friedrich, 39217
Tortarolo, Edoardo, 39226
Tortorice, John, 39346
Tosch, Karin, 38739
Tosello, Rosario J., 38666
Trade, Jews in, 38521
Traverso, Enzio, 38982
Tregenza, Michael, 38705
Treue, Wolfgang, 38455
'Tribüne', 38490, 38525, 38575, 38585, 38769, 38955, 39013, 39025, 39036, 39057, 39063, 39243, 39249, 39390, 39486, 39514
Trier, 38599
Trier, Walter, 38651
Trömel, Martin, 39340
Troki, Isaac Abraham, 38537
Troller, Georg Stefan, 39453
Tromm, Ulrich, 38908
'Trumah', 39125
Tschuy, Theo, 38932
Tucholsky, Kurt, 39234, 39349, 39394, 39395
Türcke, Christoph, 39150
Turkey, Nazi Period, 38658
Turkey, Refugees, 39353
Turniansky, Chava, 38522
Twardella, Johannes, 39137

Ueberschär, Gerd R. Ue!, 38921
Ueckert, Charlotte, 39396
Uhl, Heidemarie, 38432
Ukraine, 38675
Ullmann, Sabine, 38589
Ullmann, Viktor, 39231
Ungar, Elias, 38628
Ungar-Klein, Brigitte, 39035
Universities and Jews, 38524, 38643, 38767, 38851, 39061, 39200, 39216, 39352, 39393
UNRRA (United Nations Relief and Rehabilitation Administration), 39446
Upper Silesia, 38600, 39235
Urbach, Heinrich, 38644
Urban, Martina, 39106
Urban-Fahr, Susanne, 39013
Ury, Else, 39217
USA, 38663, 38813, 39230, 39315, 39436
USA, Holocaust, Reaction, 39004
USA, Immigration, 38661, 38662
USA, Nazi Period, 38665, 38886
USA, Refugees, 38659, 38667, 38704, 38876, 39221

Usingen, 38601

Vaget, Hans Rudolf, 38936, 39560
Valentin, Joachim, 39236
Varnhagen, Rahel, 38423, 38483
Vatican, 38754
Vechta, 38890
Veltri, Giuseppe, 39141
Vergangenheitsbewältigung, 38679, 38810, 38812, 38866, 38942, 39016, 39046, 39074, 39077, 39080, 39081, 39092, 39095, 39464, 39484
Versmold, 38602
Vertlib, Vladimir, 39517
'Vestische Zeitschrift', 38495
'Vestischer Kalender', 38580
Vestli, Elin Nesje, 38950
Vetter, Edith, 39412
Vidal-Naquet, Pierre, 38900
Vienna, 38423, 38603, 38622-38628, 38898, 38915, 38984-38988, 38991, 39152, 39200, 39234, 39235, 39242, 39323, 39430, 39436, 39528, 39533, 39566, 39578
Vienna, Jüdisches Museum, 38628
Vienna, Nazi Period, 38779, 38940, 38989, 38990, 39012
Vienna, Post-1945, 38624, 39064, 39090, 39219
Vierhaus, Rudolf, 38688
Vierhufe, Almut, 39535
'Vierteljahrshefte für Zeitgeschichte', 38815
Vill, Susanne, 39560
Villa, Dana R., 39253, 39254
Voegelin, Eric, 39091
Vögen, Hermann, 38917
Völter, Bettina, 39020
Vogel, Bernhard, 38598
Vogel, Hans-Jochen, 39092
Voglmayr, Anne, 38570
Voglrieder, Sabine, 39368
Vogt, Annette, 39352
Vogt, Bernhard, 38511
Voigt, Johannes H., 38780
Voigt, Wolfgang, 39291
Voigts, Manfred, 38457, 39139, 39543
Volcker, Paul A., 38974
Volkov, Shulamit, 38458, 39537
Vorarlberg, 39501
Voronkov, Viktor, 39020
Vorpommern, 38595
Vowinckel, Annette, 39255

Wachter, Clemens, 38519
Wacker, Marie-Theres, 39397
Wagener, Harald, 38550
Wagner, Bernd C., 38709, 38712, 38722
Wagner, Gottlieb, 38554
Wagner, Jens-Christian, 38722
Wagner, Johannes Volker, 38936
Wagner, Karl, 39360

Wagner, Nike, 38936
Wagner, Richard, 38936, 39505, 39559-39561
Waigand, Beate, 39242
Waite, Robert G., 38922
Waldauer Family, 38956
Waldheim Affair, 39065
Walk, Joseph, 38725
Wallach-Faller, Marianne, 39397
Wallas, Armin A., 39163, 39431
Wallenberg, Raoul, 38804, 38929, 38932
Wallet, Bart, 39184
Wallraff, Horst, 38776
Walser, Martin, 38994
Walser-Bubis-Debate, 38834, 38992, 38993
Walter, Ingrid, 39365
Walther, Peter T., 38484
Wandelt, Harald, 38495
Wander, Fred, 39475
Wandres, Thomas, 38845
Wannsee Conference, 38995
War and German Jews, 38422, 38450
Warburg Family, 38534, 38535
Waren, 38604
Warendorf, 38605, 39093
Warsaw, Ghetto, 39242
Waschk, Thomas, 38595
Washington, Holocaust Memorial Museum, 39089
Wassermann, Heinz P., 39152
Wassermann, Henry, 39547
Wassermann, Jakob, 39398
Wassermann, Rudolf, 39580
Watt, Roderick H., 38996
Wattenscheid, 38939
Waxman, Chaim I., 38692
Weber, Annette, 39548
Weber, Horst, 38936
Weck, Pia, 38593
Weerth, Georg, 38423
Wegner, Armin T., 38933
Wegner, Karl-Hermann, 38552
Weigel, Sigrid, 39133
Weil, Alisa, 39454
Weil, Grete, 39399
Weilburg (Lahn), 38606
Weill, Albert, 38553
Weill, Alexander, 38614
Weill, Kurt, 38553, 38856, 39231, 39400-39405
Weimar Republic, 38411, 38413, 38415, 38421, 38444, 39113, 39141, 39265, 39394
Weinbaum, Laurence, 39204, 39213
Weinberg, Arthur von, 38525
Weinberg, Jechiel Jacob, 39140
Weinberg, Robert A., 39182
Weindling, Paul, 38903
Weiner, Marc A., 38936, 39561
Weininger, Otto, 39406
Weinreich, Uriel, 38467
Weiser-Varon, Benno, 38627

Weiss, Ernst, 39221
Weiss, Karin, 38908
Weiss, Peter, 38950, 39164, 39407
Weiss, Volkmar, 39001
Weiss, Yfaat, 38725, 38997, 38998, 39483
Weissbecker, Manfred, 38922
Weissglas, Isak, 38641
Weissglass, Immanuel, 39268
Welskopf, Rudolf, 39536
'(Die) Weltbühne', 39311
Weltsch, Robert, 39209
Welz, Friedrich, 38987
Welzer, Harald, 38705, 39484
Wenck, Alexandra-Eileen, 38732
Wendel, Saskia, 39236
Wendland, Ulrike, 38699
Wenninger, Markus J., 38674
Wenzel, Rainer, 39256
Werfel, Franz, 38640, 38665, 39165, 39408
Wermuth, Henry, 38999
Werner, Klaus, 39235, 39344
Wertheim Family, 38757
Wertheim, Claus Albert, 38757
Wertheimer Family, 38569
Wertheimer, Max, 39409
West Prussia, 38511
Westerbork, 38904
'Western States Jewish History', 38661
Westerwald, 38530, 38555
Westphalia, 38566, 38596, 38605, 38607, 38608, 38803, 38890, 39329, 39480, 39489
Wetzel, Juliane, 38684, 38821, 39000
Wickerbach, 38515
Wickert, Christl, 38725
Widuwilt, 38464
Wieckhorst, Karin, 38736
Wiedebach, Hartwig, 39107, 39108, 39144
Wiedemann, Barbara, 39272
Wiedersbach, 38518
Wiehl, Reiner, 39138
Wiehn, Erhard Roy, 38508, 38633, 38634, 38636, 38805, 38816, 38857, 38904, 38914, 39203, 39452
'Wiener Jahrbuch für jüd. Gesch., Kultur & Museumswesen', 38456, 38623, 38625, 39516
Wiener Library, London, 38682, 38683
Wiese, Christian, 38434
Wiesel, Elie, 39180, 39519
Wiesenthal, Simon, 38932, 39090
Wieviorka, Annette, 39002, 39251
Wilder, Billy, 38660
Wildmann, Manfred, 38914
Wildt, Michael, 38725, 39046
Wilhelmy-Dollinger, Petra, 38483
Wilke, Carsten, 38421, 38459
Wilkending, Gisela, 39217
Wilkomirski, Binjamin, 38880
Willi, Gerhard, 38588
Wilna, 39007, 39009

Wilson, W. Daniel, 39548
Winkler, Ulrike, 39052
Winter, Jay, 38422, 39094
Winternitz, Josef, 39237
Wiplinger, Erna, 39517
'Wirkendes Wort', 39544
Wirth, Wilfried, 39051
Wirtz, Stefan, 38700
Wisbar Hansen, Maria, 39455
Wisbar, Tania, 39455
Wischnitzer, Rachel, 39410
Wismar, 39042
Wisse, Ruth R., 38846
Wissensbilder, 38460
Wissenschaft des Judentums, 38414, 39112, 39141
Wissenschaft vom Judentum, 39141
Wissmann, Friedrich, 38413
Wistrich, Robert S., 39537
Witte, Peter, 38981
Witten, 38609
Wittgenstein, Paul, 39411
Wittlich, 38488
Wlaschek, Rudolf M., 38631
Wogersien, Maik, 39053
Wohl, Jeanette, 39412
Wohlmann-Mayer, Claire, 38644
Wojak, Irmtrud, 39046
Wolf, Arnold Jacob, 39132
Wolf, Christa, 38821
Wolf, Siegbert, 38691, 39249
Wolfes, Matthias, 39406
Wolff, Claudia-Martina, 38489
Wolff, Eberhard, 39242
Wolff, Jeanette, 39413
Wolff, Theodor, 39414, 39518
Wolfhagen, 38545
Wolgast, Eike, 38523
Wolin, Richard, 39336
Wollenberg, Jörg, 38701
Wolzogen, Wolf von, 38521
Women, 38454, 38648, 38663, 38737, 38759, 38782, 38821, 38822, 38858, 39181, 39216, 39227, 39260, 39277, 39280, 39306, 39352, 39413
Women's Movement, 39477
Worms, 38428, 38455, 38579
Wormser, Seckel Löb, 38561
Wortsman, Peter, 39557
Würzburg, 38436
Wulff, Moses Benjamin, 38430
Wuliger, Michael, 39031
Wuppertal, 38610
Wurm, Siegfried, 39003
Wyman, David S., 39004
Wysbar, Eva, 39455

Yad Vashem, 38698, 38954
Yahil, Leni (Leny), 38725

Yekkes see Palestine, Israel
Yiddish (Western Yiddish), 38439, 38461-38471, 38522, 38618, 39141, 39172, 39184, 39482
Young, James E., 39073, 39096
Youth Aliyah, 38702
Youth Leader, 38905
Youth Movement, 39168, 39173
Youth Movement, Nazi Period, 38655
Yovel, Yirmiyahu, 39138, 39560
Yue-Dembski, Dagmar, 38947
Yuval, Israel Jacob, 39537

Zabel, Hermann, 39264
Zadok, Haim J., 39212
Zambelli, Paola, 38666
Zander, Jürgen, 39313
Zanthier, Agnieszka von, 39151
Zehentreiter, Ferdinand, 39231
Zehnpfennig, Barbara, 38831
'(Die) Zeichen der Zeit', 38718, 39030, 39416, 39546
Zeilitzheim, 38611
'(Die) Zeit', 39040, 39150, 39224, 39234, 39359, 39444, 39558
'Zeitgeschichte', 38650, 38654, 38716, 38721, 39537
'Zeitschrift des Aachener Geschichtsvereins', 39222
'Zeitschrift für Bayerische Landesgeschichte', 38567, 38891
'Zeitschrift des Bergischen Geschichtsvereins', 38594
'Zeitschrift für Deutsche Philologie', 39549
'Zeitschrift für Deutsches Altertum und Deutsche Literatur', 39442
'Zeitschrift für Geschichtswissenschaft', 38472, 38491, 38730, 38827, 38965, 39558
'Zeitschrift der Gesellschaft für Schles.-Holst. Geschichte', 39313
'Zeitschrift für Religions- und Geistesgeschichte', 38901, 39061, 39127, 39188
Zelinsky, Hartmut, 38936
Zelizer, Barbie, 38835
Zeller, Susanne, 39185
Zemke, Uwe, 38423
Zentralrat der Juden in Deutschland, 39026, 39040, 39057
Zentrum f. Antisemitismusforschung, Berlin, 38684
Ziatkowski, Leszek, 38492
Ziegerhofer, Anita, 38617
Ziegler, Dieter, 38865
Zielinski, Andrea, 39045
Zimmermann, Cornelia, 38532
Zimmermann, Moshe, 38432, 39005
Zimmermann, Peter, 39581
Zimmermann, Susanne, 38851
Zink, Wolfgang Se'ev, 38543

Zionism, 38410, 38670, 38692, 38908, 38977, 39101, 39176, 39195, 39196, 39197, 39198, 39200, 39201, 39209, 39210, 39212, 39214, 39488, 39543
Zippert Family, 38863
Zirndorf, 39580
Zohn, Harry, 38667
Zucker, Ruth, 39456
Zuckermann, Moshe, 39097, 39214
Zuckermann, Rudolf & Leo, 39415
Zukier, Henry, 39537
Zur, Yaakov, 38521
Zurek, Ralf, 38593
Zurich, 38644
Zweibrücken, 38579, 39006
Zweig, Arnold, 39228, 39234, 39235
Zweig, Stefan, 38652, 39416, 39417, 39457
Zwettler-Otte, Sylvia, 39288
'Zwischenwelt' (formerly: 'Mit der Ziehharmonika'), 38641, 38731, 38735, 38893, 39355, 39364, 39365, 39517, 39531

List of Contributors

BAADER, Maria Benjamin, b. 1959 in Giessen, Germany. Formerly a cabinet maker. Ph.D. candidate in Jewish History at Columbia University. Author of 'Die Deborah' in *Jewish Women in America: An Historical Encyclopedia* (1997); 'Zweierlei Befreiung' in *Nach der Shoah geboren: Jüdische Frauen in Deutschland* (1994). (Contributor to Year Book XLIII.)

BENHAR, Chanan, b. 1921 in Kroppenstedt, near Magdeburg, Germany. Formerly an electronics engineer and telecommunications teacher. Author of two pamphlets: *107 Tage mit der SH – 7* and *Ruth*.

EVANS, R. J. W., Ph.D., b. 1943 in Cheltenham, England. Regius Professor of Modern History and Fellow of Oriel College, Oxford. Publications include *Rudolf II and his World. A Study in Intellectual History, 1576–1612* (1973, latest reprint 1997); *The Making of the Habsburg Monarchy, 1550–1700* (1979, latest reprint 1991). Joint editor of *The Coming of the First World War* (1988, latest reprint 1998); *Crown, Church and Estates. Central European Politics in the Sixteenth and Seventeenth Centuries* (1991); *The Revolutions in Europe, 1848–9: From Reform to Reaction* (2000). Numerous articles on Central European history.

FERGUSON, Niall, D.Phil., b. 1964 in Glasgow, Scotland. Professor of Political and Financial History at Oxford University and Fellow of Jesus College. Publications include *Paper and Iron: Hamburg Business and German Politics in the Era of Inflation, 1897–1927* (1995); *The World's Banker: The History of the House of Rothschild* (1998); *The Cash Nexus; Money and Power in the Modern World, 1700-2000* (2000). Numerous articles on economic and financial history, including internet e-lectures.

HERTZ, Deborah, Ph.D., b. 1949 in St. Paul, Minnesota, USA. Professor of History, Sarah Lawrence College, New York. Author of *Jewish High Society in Old Regime Berlin* (1988); *Briefe an eine Freundin: Rahel Varnhagen an Rebecca Friedlaender* (1988). Forthcoming publications: 'Amalie Beer, High Culture Motherhood, and the Birth of Reform Judaism in Berlin' in *Der Differenz auf der Spur. Frauen und Gender im Aschkenasischen Judentum* (2001); 'High Culture Jews and their enemies in the days of Meyerbeer and Mendelssohn' in *Wiener Jahrbuch für Geschichte Kultur und Museumswesen* (2001). Numerous articles on conversion and Jewish women. (Contributor to Year Book XL.)

HERZOG, Dagmar, Ph.D., b. 1961 in Durham, North Carolina, USA. Associate Professor of History, Michigan State University. Author of *Intimacy and Exclusion: Religious Politics in Pre-Revolutionary Baden* (1996). Articles include '"Pleasure, Sex and Politics Belong Together": Post-Holocaust Memory and the Sexual Revolution in West Germany' in *Critical Inquiry* (1998); 'Sexuelle Revolution und Vergangenheitsbewältigung' in *Zeitschrift für Sexualforschung* (2000). Forthcoming publication on "Sex and Memory in Post-Nazi Germany". (Contributor to Year Book XL.)

KORMAN, Gerd, Ph.D., b. 1928 in Elberfeld, Germany. Professor Emeritus of History, Cornell University. Publications include *Hunter and Hunted: Human History of the Holocaust* (1974). Author of several articles in *American Jewish History*; 'Jews as a Changing People of the Talmud: An American Exploration' in *Modern Judaism* (2001).

LEVENSON, Alan T., Ph.D., b. 1960 in New York, USA. Associate Professor of Jewish History, Cleveland College of Jewish Studies, Ohio. Author of *Modern Jewish Thinkers: An Introduction* (2000). Numerous articles on several aspects of Jewish history and Judaism in *i.a. CCAR Journal, Shofar, German Quarterly Review*. (Contributor to LBI Year Book XL.)

MYERS, David N., Ph.D., b. 1960 in Scranton, Pennsylvania, USA. Professor of Jewish History, University of California, Los Angeles. Author of *Re-inventing the Jewish Past* (1995) and numerous articles on German-Jewish history. Co-editor of *From Ghetto to Emancipation* (1997); *The Jewish Past Revisited* (1998); *Jewish History and Jewish Memory* (1998); *Enlightenment and Diaspora: The Armenian and Jewish Cases* (1999). (Contributor to Year Book XXXIX.)

VAN RAHDEN, Till, Dr. phil., b. 1967 in Bremen, Germany. Wissenschaftlicher Assistent für neuere und Neuste Geschichte, Historisches Seminar, University of Cologne. Author of *Juden und andere Breslauer. Die Beziehungen zwischen Juden, Protestanten und Katholiken in einer deutschen Großstadt von 1860 bis 1925* (2000). Co-editor of *Bürger - Juden - Deutsche. Zur Geschichte von Vielfalt und Differenz seit dem späten 18. Jahrhundert* (Schriftenreihe wissenschaftlicher Abhandlungen des Leo Baeck Instituts, 2001). Articles include: 'Words and Actions: Rethinking the Social History of German Antisemitism – Breslau, 1870–1914' in *German History* (2000); 'Mingling, Marrying, and Distancing. Jewish Integration in Wilhelminian Breslau and its Erosion in Early Weimar Germany' in *Jüdisches Leben in der Weimarer Republik – Jews in Weimar Germany* (Schriftenreihe wissenschaftlicher Abhandlungen des Leo Baeck Instituts, 1998).

ROBERTSON, Ritchie, D.Phil., b. 1952 in Nairn, Scotland. Professor of German, St. John's College, Oxford. Main publications include *Kafka, Judaism, Politics, and Literature* (1985); *Heine* (Jewish Thinkers Series, 1988); *The Jewish Question in German Literature, 1749-1939: Emancipation and its Discontents* (1999). Editor of *The German-Jewish Dialogue: an anthology of literary texts, 1749-1993* (1999). Numerous articles on German literature. (Member of the London Board of the LBI.)

SAGARRA, Eda, Dr. phil., Litt. D., b. 1933 in Dublin, Ireland. Chairman of the Irish Research Council for the Humanities and Social Sciences. Formerly Professor of German, Trinity College Dublin. Author of *i.a. Tradition and Revolution* (1972), *A Social History of Germany 1648-1914* (1977), *Germany in the 19th century: History and Literature* (2001), and numerous articles on the social history of German and Austrian literature.

SOUSSAN, Henri, M.A., b. 1964 in Germany. D.Phil. candidate at the University of Sussex. Author of 'From Leopold Zunz to Leopold Lucas' (Centre for German Jewish Studies Research Paper 1999/2000).

TEMPEL, Ulrich, Staatsexamen, b. 1968 in Hoyerswerda, Germany. Archivist at the Topography of Terror Foundation, Berlin.

TIMMS, Edward, Ph.D., b. Windelsham, Surrey, England in 1937. Research Professor in German Studies and Director of the Centre for German-Jewish Studies, University of Sussex. Recent publications include co-editorship of *The German-Jewish Dilemma: From the Enlightenment to the Shoah* (1999); *Writing after Hitler: The Work of Jakov Lind* (2001). (Member of the London Board of the LBI.)

General Index to Year Book XLVI of the Leo Baeck Institute

Aachen, Congress of 1840, 12
Aaron, 4
Acculturation, 64, 164, 168
Adass Jisroel, 222, 234
Adler, Dr. (of Ges. z. Förd. d. Wiss. d. Jud.), 194
Adler, Samuel (rabbi), 167
Agudas Jisroel, 187
Ahrensdorf (agricultural concern), 307
Akademischer Verein für jüdische Geschichte und Literatur, 179
Akko prison, 321, 322, 324, 326, 330
Albach (Franciscan friar), 62
Alexander II (Tsar of Russia), 7
Alexander, Gabriel, 216n
Aliyah, 305–332
Alldeutscher Verband, 279
Allgemeine Real-Encyclopädie für das katholische Deutschland, 68
'Allgemeine Zeitung des Judentums', 175, 179, 186
Alliance Assurance Company, 21
Altmann, Eugen, 129, 139
American Jewish Joint Distribution Committee (Joint), 260, 270, 306
American Polish relief expedition, 260
American Red Cross, 252, 253, 255, 260, 269
Angoulême, Louis Antoine de Bourbon, Duc de (nephew of Louis XVIII), 33
"Antigone" (ship), 261
Anti-Jewish riots, August 1819, 16: in Frankfurt a. M., 16: in Würzburg, 16
Anti-Judaism, 161, 290–291
Antin, Mary (Russ.–Jewish migrant), 247, 250
Antisemiten-Petition, 282, 283, 284
Antisemitism, 17, 54, 60, 69, 70, 88, 106, 126, 129, 134, 152, 243–276, 277–301 *passim*: Jewish defence against, 238
Aoyama, Mitsu (w. of H. Coudenhove-Kalergi), 293, 297
Apple, John J., 245n
Apponyi, Rudolf (Austr. dipl.), 34, 36, 38
'Arbeiter Zeitung' (Yidd.-lang. paper), 250
Arbeitsgemeinschaft d. jüdischen Arbeitsnachweise, 230
Ardouin & Hubbard, 32n
Arendt, Hannah (social historian), 129–130, 160
Arndt, Ernst Moritz (politician), 16
Arnhold, Georg (merchant banker, philanthropist, pacifist), 278

Arnstein & Eskeles (bank), 36, 44, 58
Arnstein, Fanny v. (Vienna salon hostess), 5–6, 13
Arnstein, Nathan v. (Vienna banker, h. of Fanny), 12–13
Ashkenazi Jewry, 115
Aspey, Melanie, 19n
Assimilation, 81, 82, 125, 126, 147, 149, 161, 163
Athlit internment camp, 322, 329, 330
"Atlantic" (refugee ship), 313–330 *passim*
Auerbach, Anna (d. of W. Silbergleit), 134–135
Auerbach, Berthold (novelist), 87, 100, 102
Auslander, Leora, 156
Auspitz, Lazar (Brünn banker), 13
Ausschuß deut. Länder, 6, 7–8, 11, 14, 17
Austrian Jewry: contrib. to economy, 13: to education, 13: to military service, 13
Austro-Hungarian Empire, 4, 5, 8, 10, 11–12, 19–53 *passim*, 55, 59, 71, 72, 82, 90–91, 299: demography of Jews, 57–58: Jews in, 11–12, 27: Tolerance Edict 1782, 27

Baader, Maria, 153–154, 155, 157
Bacher, Wilhelm (orientalist), 184n, 187, 192, 194
Baeck, Leo (rabbi, scholar), 188
Baersche Dance School (Breslau), 137
Baja, Jewish community (Hungary), 81
Ballin, Albert (shipping magnate), 292
Balduin, (Archbp. of Canterbury), 75
Baneth, Eduard (talmudic scholar), 177n, 194
Bankers, Jewish, 19–54
Baptism *see* Conversions
Barings (bank), 22
Baron, Salo (historian), 5, 17
Barth, Jacob (orientalist), 185, 186
Barth, Karl (Prot. theologian), 204, 207
Bärwald, Dr. (of Ges. z. Förd. d. Wiss. d. Jud.), 194
Batthyany family, 58
Bauer, Bruno (Prot. theologian), 30
Baumann, Zygmunt, 291, 292
Bavaria, 6, 8, 69, 70: opposition to emancipation, 10, 14: Räterepublik, 286
Beck, Gad, 155
Beck, Karl (poet), 22, 26, 81–91
Beck, Siegfried (bapt., business man, bro. of Karl B.), 82
Beck, Willi (caricaturist, bro.of Karl B.), 82
Bees, Nikos (publisher), 190
Beller, Steven, 280

Belgrade, 311
Bendikowski, Tilmann, 172
Benjamin, Walter (lit. historian, author), 195
Beöthy, Ödön (Hung. lib. leader), 62, 63
Berendsohn, Walter Arthur (lit. historian), 278
Berlant, Lauren, 156, 157
Berlin, 89, 98, 105, 109, 111, 131, 139, 211, 286, 287, 292
Berlin Jewish community, 190, 215–240: school system, 234: and Palestine, 235–237
Berlin, Friedrich-Wilhelms-Universität, 16, 178, 202, 207, 282
Berliner Zionistische Vereinigung, 222
Bernays, Jakob (philologist), 201
Bernstein, Eduard (soc. polit.), 285, 300
Bethmann (bank), 36
Bethmann, Simon Moritz (Frankfurt banker), 23, 26
Bezerédj, István (Hung. lib. leader), 62
Biedermann family (Vienna bank), 58
Biggs, Hermann M (NY-chief of pathology), 251
Bismarck, Otto Fürst von (German statesman), 20, 91, 283
Blasius, Dirk, 129
'Blätter für literarische Unterhaltung', 100n
Bleichröder, Gershon v. (banker), 20
Bloch, Ivan S. (financier, economist, pacifist), 278
Bloch, Moses [Mor Ballagi], (theologian, linguist), 64
Bloch, Philipp (Poznan rabbi, historian), 184n, 187
Blue, Rupert (US Ass. Surgeon General), 266n, 271, 273
Bock, Leopold (friend of F. Lewald,), 108–109
Böckel, Otto (antisem. politician), 205
Bohemia, 55, 91
Börne, Ludwig (author), 21–22, 33–34, 53, 83, 84, 87, 89, 95
Bolzano, Bernhard (theologian, philos.) 72
Bornstedt, Luise v. (friend of A. Droste-Hülshoff), 69
Boyarin, Daniel, 113n, 170
Brann, Markus (historian), 182, 187, 194
Bratislava, 309
Braun, Otto (soc. polit.), 224
Bremen, 10, 11, 17, 23
Bremen Jewish community, 9, 11–12, 17
Breslau, 125–150, *passim*: University, 202
Breslau Jewish community, 125–150, 154: Jewish–Christian relationships, 125–150, 167
Breslauer, Benno (Breslau coachman), 148
Britain, immigrants to, 5
Brody, Heinrich (Orth. rabbi, scholar, 185n, 186
Broglie, Achille Charles Duc de (Fr. statesman), 38, 39
Brünn, 24
Brunner, Sebastian (antisem. priest), 56
Buber, Martin (philosopher), 195, 211, 212
Buchholz, Carl August (Lübeck lawyer), 9–10, 15
Budapest, 56, 57, 58, 63, 81, 82, 90, 310

Budapest Rabbinical Seminary, 185
Bulgaria (country of passage for immigr. ships), 311, 312, 317
Bund jüdischer Arbeitnehmer, 222, 223
Bund Neues Vaterland, 278, 285
Buol-Schauenstein, Johann Rudolf (Austr. dipl.), 23, 47, 48
Burschenschaften, 16
Butler, Judith, 155
Byron, George Gordon [Lord Byron] (poet), 81, 85, 87

Campe, Julius (publ.), 83
Capitalism, Jews and, 11
Carlebach, Joseph (Chief Rabbi Hamburg), 186
Carlebach, Julius (rabbi, sociologist), 175n
Carlsbad decrees 1819, 16
Cassirer, Ernst (philosopher), 196, 204, 210n
Castlereagh, Henry Robert Stewart, Marquis of Londonderry (Br. statesman), 7, 13
Catholicism, 82: and Jews, 67–79
Cemetry (Berlin-Weißensee), 229
Centralverein deutscher Staatsbürger jüdischen Glaubens (C.V.), 175, 216, 225, 235, 238, 281n: defence against antisemitism, 238
Centre for German-Jewish studies at Sussex Univ., 3
Chickering, Roger, 278
Chorin, Aron (maskil rabbi), 64
Chotek, Count (Archbp. of Olmütz), 45
Christian-Jewish relations, Germany, 17–18, 189–190, 192
Christians and Jews, 8, 9, 10, 14, 16, 17
Clark, Gordon Scott, 277n
Cofer, Leland E. (US physician), 257, 258, 259
Cohen, Friederike (mother of Hermann C., née Salomon), 200
Cohen, Gerson (father of Hermann C.), 200, 201, 214n
Cohen, Hermann (philosopher), 180, 184n, 186, 188, 194, 195–214
Cohn, Oskar (soc. politician), 223, 224–225, 230, 233, 234
Cohn, Willy (Breslau Zionist, diarist), 129, 137
Commercialism, Jewish, 7, 8
Communism, 11
"Concho" (ship), 252
Concordat of 1855, 67
Congress of Aix la Chapelle *see* Aachen
Congress of Verona (1822), 32
Congress of Vienna, 3–18, 47, 68, 106
'Constitutionel', 29
Conversations-Lexikon, 68
Conversions, 1, 2, 27, 95–172, 126, 130, 133, 145–146, 149, 177: to Judaism, 134, 147–148: and Judenkartei, Berlin, 98
Cooper, Fenimore (writer), 89
Cooper, Sandi, 285

Cortes (Span. and Port. parliament), 32, 33
Coswig (Anhalt-Bernburg), 199, 200, 201, 206
Coudenhove-Kalergi, Graf Heinrich v. (dipl., pacifist, polyglot), 277, 293–299
Coudenhove-Kalergi, Graf Richard Nikolaus (s. of Heinrich C-K., polit. writer, Pan-European), 294, 297–298, 299
'Courrier Français', 29
Cumming, H.S. (US Surgeon General), 271

Damascus Affair, 12, 48, 49, 89
Danz, (Frankfurt rep. on Ausschuß), 11
Danzig, immigration via, 243–276 *passim*: Troyl camp, 261, 269, 272: Gruppe camp, 261, 262, 266, 268, 269, 270
Darwinism, 249
David (rabbi) 185
Deák, Ferenc (lib. polit., lawyer), 62
Deak, Istvan, 278n
Deißmann, Adolf (Prot. theologian), 190
Dernburg, Bernhard (banker, polit.), 278
Derrida, Jacques (lit. philosopher), 199, 200, 214n
Dessau, 199, 200
Deutsch-Israelitischer Gemeindebund, 179, 190
Deutschkonservative Partei, 284
Deutsche Demokratische Partei, 284
Deutsche Friedensgesellschaft, 277, 278, 279, 299, 300, 301
Deutsche Volkspartei, 284
Deutscher, Isaac, 160
Deutscher Protestantenverein, 198
Disraeli, Benjamin [Earl of Beaconsfield] (Brit. statesman), 298
Dölzschen (nr. Dresden), 95
Dohm, Christian Wilhelm v. (Pruss. civil servant), 8
Dollinger, Roland, 101n
Donau-Dampf-Schiffahrtsgesellschaft (DDSG), 308, 310
Dresden, 83, 139
Dreyfus Affair, 289
Droste-Hülshoff, Annette v. (writer), 69
Dru, Alexander, 70
Duara, Prasenjit, 150
Dulon, Paul [v. Duelong], (law student), 284
Dunbar, Lee R. (US army physician), 260–261, 262

Eckmann family (of Breslau), 137
Eckmann, Leopold (f. of Mieze), 137
Eckmann, Mieze (w. of A. Riesenfeld), 137
Effenburger, Ruth (died on "Patria"), 305, 328, 329, 330
Edson, Cyrus (NY sanit. inspector), 254, 255–256
Edward I (King of England), 72
Ehrmann, Daniel, (writer), 64
Eichmann, Adolf (Nazi war criminal), 308
Einhorn, Ignaz [Ede Horn] (historian), 56, 64

Einstein, Albert (physicist), 266, 285, 286, 291, 298, 300
Eisenstadt Jewish community, 57
Eisner, Kurt (soc. polit., premier of Bavarian Räterepublik), 286
Elbogen, Ismar (historian, Judaist), 176, 184, 187, 192
Ellguth farm, 306
Ellis Island (US immigration centre), 245, 258, 271
Emancipation, 3–18, 8n, 20, 26, 72, 110, 113: Hungary, 57, 60, 61, 62, 65: discriminatory laws on, 7, 11, 18, 103: laws on 3–18 *passim*, 56, 70: Pruss. Edict 1812, 4, 71: of women, 166, 167, 168
Emigration, Jewish, from Germany, 305–332: to Palestine, 305–332: to USA, 243–276, 306
Emmendingen (Baden), 165
Endelman, Todd, 126, 130, 162
Engels, Friedrich (soc. theoretician), 81, 83, 84, 89
Englaender, Bernhard (municipal court judge, h. of R. Pringsheim), 133
England, 18
Engländer, Sigmund (editor), 82
Enlightenment, 10, 11, 18, 70, 71, 113, 117, 151, 164, 166, 168, 199
Eötvös Baron József (Hung. writer, statesman), 62, 65
Eppenstein, Simon (rabbi, scholar), 184, 187n
Errera, Marie (philanthropist), 191n
Eskeles, Bernhard v. (Vienna banker), 12–13, 49, 50
Eskeles, Cäcilie v. (Vienna salon hostess, w. of Bernhard E.), 13
Esterhazy family, 57
Esterhazy, Count (fl. 1844), 46
Esterhazy, Princess Marie, 29
Esterhazy, Paul (Austr. dipl.), 58
'Europa' (journal founded by A. Lewald), 100, 109

Falkenberg, Bertha (of Jüdischer Frauenbund), 225
Falkson, Ferdinand (of Königsberg, fl. 1840), 103
Felix, Arthur (bacteriologist), 273–274
Felix-Weil test (for typhus), 274
Ferdinand I (Emperor of Austr.), 42
Ferdinand I (King of Naples), 31
Ferdinand V and Isabella I (King and Queen of Castile), 72: expulsions of Jews, 72, 73–74: Jewish conversos, 72
Ferdinand VII (King of Spain), 32, 33
Ferguson, Niall, 89
Fischhof, Adolf [Abraham] (Austr. polit.), 55
Fichte, Johann Gottlieb (philosopher), 161
Fleischer, Kurt (surgeon, of Liberale Vereinigung), 225, 235, 238
Fontane, Theodor (novelist), 134
Foerster, Friedrich Wilhelm (philosopher, educationalist, pacifist), 277, 285–293 *passim*, 299

General Index

Foerster, Wilhelm (astronomer, f. of F.W. Foerster), 286
'Forward' (New York), 264n
France: 18, 20, 40: Napoleonic code, 11, 15: Napoleonic wars, 10–11, 15, 70, 99–106, *passim*, 114, and occupation of German cities, 10–11, 15, 16
Franco-Prussian War, 201
Frank, Erich (leader of refugee transport), 313–328 *passim*
Frankel, Zacharias (rabbi, rel. leader), 201
Frankfurt am Main, 11, 14, 15, 16, 22, 23, 25, 26, 46, 51, 89
Frankfurt am Main Jewish community, 4, 23, 46, 47, 105, 190
Frankfurt Institute for Social Research (Institut für Sozialforschung), 299
Frankfurt National Assembly, 7, 12, 15, 16, 18, 47, 82
'Frankfurter Zeitung', 284
Franz I (Emperor of Austria), 22, 27, 37, 44, 70, 71
Franz Joseph (Emperor of Austria), 28, 81, 90
Franzos, Karl Emil (novelist), 91
Freie Wissenschaftliche Vereinigung (FWV), 278n, 282, 301
'Freies Blatt' (Austr. Abwehrverein journal), 300n
Freimann, Aaron (historian), 182
French Revolution, 4, 151, 161
Freud, Jakob (f. of Sigmund), 91
Freud, Sigmund (founder of psychoanalysis), 91, 244, 245, 248
Freund, Ismar (Jewish functionary, historian), 236–237
Freytag, Gustav (novelist), 292
Fried, Alfred Hermann (publ., pacifist), 277, 279, 285, 299, 300n
'Friedensbewegung' (Die), 278, 297–298
Friedenthal, Dr. (physician on refugee ship "Pacific"), 319, 322
Friedländer, Israel (orientalist), 187n
Friedrich Wilhelm I (King of Prussia), 4
Friedrich Wilhelm IV (King of Prussia), 109
Friedrich Wilhelm Prince Hesse-Kassel (s. of Wilhelm), 204
Friedrich, Gerhard (antisem. author), 16
Fries, Friedrich (prof. nat. science), 16
Funk, Salomon, (Orth. rabbi, scholar), 185n
Funkenstein, Amos (philosopher), 197n
Fürth, 83

Galicia, 91
Geiger, Abraham (rel. philos.), 127, 167, 207
Geiger, Ludwig (ed. 'Allg. Z. J.', lit. historian, 185, 194
'Gemeindeblatt d. jüdischen Gemeinde Berlin', 218, 226
Gentz, Friedrich (Metternich sec.), 13, 14, 25, 26, 28, 36

Gerlach, Hellmut v. (lawyer, pacifist), 285, 300
German Committee *see* Ausschuß deutscher Länder
German constitution, 3, 5, 8, 11, 13, 16, 23
German Federation, 3, 4–7, 8, 10, 11, 12, 14, 15, 16, 18, 23, 36, 69
Germania Judaica (project), 182
Gesellschaft der Brüder, Breslau, 116
Gesellschaft der Freunde, Berlin, 116, 165: Königsberg, 116
Gesellschaft zur Förderung der Wissenschaft des Judentums, 175–194: Christian membership, 189: income and support, 190–191
Gestapo, 305–308
Geymüller (bank), 36, 44
Ghettos, 86, 91
Gilchrist, Harry L. (col., US army physician), 260–271 *passim*
Gilman, Sander, 101n, 162
Ginzburg, Louis (rabbi, scholar), 184
Goethe, Johann Wolfgang von (poet, dramatist), 83, 87
Goethe, Ottilie von (sister-in-law of Johann Wolfgang G.), 87
Goldmann, Moritz (of Berlin, h. of G. Riesenfeld), 136–137
Goldmark, Joseph (Austr. polit.), 55
Goldner (intermediary in illegal immigr. to Palestine), 316
Goldschmidt, Hermann (s. of Moritz G.), 29
Goldschmidt, Moritz (sen. clerk to S. Rothschild), 27, 28, 45, 51
Goldstein, Brigitte Maria, 285n
Gompers, Samuel (US labour leader), 245
Goslar, Hans (Pruss. civil servant), 219, 224, 238
Göttingen, 206
Göttingen University, 282, 284
Graetz, Heinrich (historian), 187, 201, 202, 205
Granby, Steffi [née Klinenberger] (d. of Breslau factory owner), 135
Grant, Hugh J (Mayor of NYC), 251
Gray, Victor, 19n
Greece (country of passage for immigr. ships), 305, 308, 319
Gregory IX (Pope), 74
Gregory XVI (Pope), 35
Grenville, John, 305
Greßmann, Hugo (Prot. theologian), 190
Grillparzer, Franz (novelist, dramatist), 67–79: and Jews and Judaism, 67–79
Gross, Heinrich (historian), 182
Groß-Glogau, (Lower Silesia), 194
Gross Isle (Canadian quarantine centre), 274
Grün, Anastasius (Austr. poet), 84
Grünstadt Jewish community (Rhineland-Palatinate), 117
Güdemann, Moritz (Chief Rabbi Vienna), 184n, 194
Guizot, François Pierre Guillaume (Fr. statesman), 39

Gumbel, Emil Julius (mathematician, pacifist), 278
Guttmann, Jakob (Breslau rabbi), 146, 187, 194
Gutzkow, Karl (novelist), 81

Haber (bank), 49
Habsburg Empire *see* Austro-Hungarian Empire
Haganah, 310–331
Haifa, 305, 320, 322, 324, 326, 327, 328, 330
Haertel, Emilie (w. of Th. Stahl), 134
Halakhah, 113, 119, 120, 122, 123, 164, 165, 166, 167, 168
Halevi, Lucienne (writer), 280
Hall, Stuart, 155
Haller, Joseph (gen., CO Polish Legion, 259, 261, 268
Hamburg, 10, 11, 247, 313
Hamburg Jewish community, 9, 11–12, 118, 66
Hanover, 8, 10
Hardenberg, Karl August Fürst v. (Pruss. statesman), 4, 6, 10, 11, 12, 14, 15, 18, 105
Harmann, Brigitte, 280
Harnack, Adolf v. (Prot. theologian), 178, 179, 204, 207
Harris, J.E. Holt (US medical scientist), 274n
Hartmann, Moritz (Austr. author, politician), 82, 89, 91
Haskalah, 64
Haynau, Julius Jakob Frh. v. (Austr. general), 90
Hebrew Immigrant Aid and Sheltering Society (HIAS), 267–273
Hebrew language, 119, 308
Hebrew University Jerusalem, 227
Hechaluz, 306, 312, 319,
Heidegger, Martin (philosopher), 196
Heidelberg University, 16
Heilberg (of peace movement), 278
Heimdorf, Alexander (physician, friend of A. Droste-Hülshoff), 69
Heine, Heinrich (poet), 22, 30, 41, 48, 53, 83, 84, 85, 87, 95, 100, 102, 162
"Helios" (refugee ship), 309, 311, 312
Herloßsohn, Georg Karl (Austr. author), 82
Hermann Cohen Archive Zurich, 196
Herrmann, Wilhelm (Prot. theologian), 204, 206, 207, 208
Hertz, Deborah, 152–153, 154, 155
Herz, Henriette (salon hostess), 89
Herz, Leopold v. (Vienna banker), 12–13
Herzl, Theodor (founder of Zionist movement), 279–280, 308
Herzog, Dagmar, 159, 160, 164, 169, 170, 171, 300
Herzogliches Gymnasium Dessau, 201
Heschel, Susannah, 207, 212
Hesse, 204, 205, 206
Hevrat Esrat Nashim of Emmendingen (assoc. for the help of women), 165
Hildesheimer, Esriel (historian), 187n

Hilliard, Kevin, 81n
Himmelauer (Austr. dipl.), 38
Hirsch, Max (polit., pacifist), 277
Hirsch, Samson Raphael (rabbi, leader of Orthodoxy), 122–123
Hirschberg, Felix (lawyer), 146
Hirschfeld, Otto (historian), 190
Historiography, German, 5, 69
Historiography, Jewish, 169, 170
Hoffmann, David (dir. Berlin Rabbinerseminar), 186
Hoffman Island (US quarantine centre), 247, 252
Holdheim, Samuel, (rabbi, Reform leader), 167n
Holl, Karl, 278, 300n
Holocaust, 197
Holt, Thomas, 156
Holy Alliance (Austria, Prussia, Russia), 21, 22, 29, 30, 35
Holzhey, Helmut, 196
Honvéd (Hung. army), 56
Horovitz, Joseph (orientalist), 184
Horváth, Mihály (Hung. historian, polit., bp.), 60
Hoser, Eleonore (fiancée of S. Lewald, 103n
Hughes, J. A., 3
Humboldt, Alexander Frhr. v. (natural scientist), 13–14, 286
Humboldt, Wilhelm Frhr. v. (Pruss. statesman), 4, 6, 9, 10, 13–14, 16, 71
Hungary, 55–63 *passim*, 81, 87: assembly, 56
Hunyady, József (Hung. landowner), 58
Hurban, Miroslav (Prot. cleric), 60
Hurter, Friedrich (Swiss historian), 74, 75
Hyman, Paula, 169

Identity, Jewish, 87, 91, 96, 98, 106, 169
Immigration, illegal to Palestine, 305–332
Imperial Germany, 125, Jewish women in, 126, 170
Innocent III (Pope), 74–75
Integration, 125, 126
Intermarriage, 64, 95–172, 125–150, 238: between Catholics and Protestants, 127: demographics: 11, 12, 126, 130, 131, 147, 148: divorce rate, 129, 146–147: dowries, 136–137, 138: economic background, 127–141 *passim*, 145, 149 historiography, 126–130 *passim*, 146: in Imperial Germany, 125, 130–150 *passim*: in Nazi Germany, opposition to, 10, 14, 16, 17 13–14, 17: religious aspects, 126, 148–149: sexuality, 129 138–139, 140–142 *passim*: social aspects, 126, 129, 130, 131–140 *passim*: statistics, 130–133, 141–145, 147–148: in Weimar Republic, 13–14, 125–126, 136 145, 147–148
International Peace Congress (The Hague, 1899), 279
Inzághy, Count (Austr. Lord Chancellor), 28
Isai, Paul (illegal immigr. on "Patria"), 328
'Israelit' [Der], 128, 186
Israelitisch-theologische Lehranstalt Vienna, 187

General Index

Israelitische Frauenkrankenkasse (Frankfurt), 117
Israelitische Kranken- und Verpflegungs-Anstalt und Beerdigungsgesellschaft (Breslau), 146

Jacobins, 16
Jacobson, Julius (ophthalmologist, f. of M. Quidde), 284)
Jacobson, Margarete (w. of L. Quidde), 284
Jacoby, Johann (physician, polit.), 110
Jahn, Friedrich Ludwig (Turnvater), 16
Jahrbuch für jüdische Geschichte und Literatur, 176 184, 188
Jakubczik, Gabriele (w. of F. Ungerleider), 146
Jaspers, Karl (philosopher), 176, 177
Jehuda [Juda] b. Samuel (13th-century Regensburg rabbi), 290
Jentes, Paul (leader of immigr. group), 307, 309, 314, 315, 317
Jewish Agency, 235, 236, 237, 330
'Jewish Chronicle' (London), 264n
Jewish disabilities/rights, 26, 27, 28, 46, 48, 53, 56, 59, 60, 63, 219
Jewish Question, 5, 17, 18, 277, 280–300 *passim*
Jewry, German, 164–172 *passim*: communual institutions, 113–123: communal politics, 215–240: communal voting patterns, 220–224: conversions, 95–172: demographics, 239: emigration, 243–276, 305–332: employment agencies, 229–233: historiography, 126: intermarriage: 95–172: mutual aid and benevolent associations, 113–123, 165, 166, 168: pacifism and, 277–301: religious practices, 113–123: social work, 168, 226–229: role of women, 95–172: and welfare, 239–240: and Zionism, 215–240, 305–332. *See also* Berlin, Bremen, Breslau, Frankfurt, Hamburg, Lübeck, Schnaittach Jewish communities
Jewry, Hungarian, 55–65: emancipation, 55–65; participation in army, 56
John XXIII (Pope), 69
Jordan, Silvester (jurist, politician), 204
Joseph II (Emperor of Austr.), 4, 13, 57, 59, 61
Judaism and Christianity, 195–214
Judaism, 86, 87, 89, 98, 99, 108, 111, 112, 113–123, 126, 146, 151, 164, 165, 177–193, 296, *passim*, 293: Hebrew prayer: 166–167, *Jüdin von Toledo (Die)*, 67–78
'Jüdisch-Liberale Zeitung', 220, 226, 232, 233
Jüdisch-Theologisches Seminar, Breslau, 185, 187, 201
'Jüdische Presse', [Die], 186
'Jüdische Rundschau', 215, 223, 226, 233, 238
Jüdische Volkspartei (JVP), 215–237 *passim*,
'Jüdische Volkszeitung', 141
Jüdischer Frauenbund, 223, 225
Jüdischer Schulverein, 227, 234
Jüdisches Museum Berlin, 217
Jungdeutscher Orden, 284

Kabbalah, 115
Kähler, Martin (Prot. theologian), 207
Kainz, Joseph (actor), 71n
Kant, Immanuel (philosopher), 199, 200, 202, 207, 209n, 210
Kaplan, Marion, 126, 169
"Karamania" (ship), 247, 250
Kareski, Georg (Zion. polit. Berlin community leader), 227, 234, 239, 240
Karpeles, Gustav (editor, lit. historian), 175–184n *passim*, 194, 277, 278, 300
Katz, Jacob (historian, Rector of Heb. University, Jerusalem), 301n
'Katzenmusik' (satirical paper), 82
Kaufmann, Jacob (polit., poet), 82, 83
Kayserling, Moritz Meyer (rabbi, scholar), 194
Kecskemét (Hung. market town), 59
Kellermann, Benzion (Berlin rabbi, philosopher), 213
Kessler, Harry Graf (pacifist, dipl.), 285–286
Ketteler, Wilhelm Emmanuel v. (Pruss. civil servant, bp. of Mainz), 75
Keren Hayesod [Hajessod] (Palestine foundation fund), 237
'Kibetzer' (Der) (NY Yiddish-lang. journal), 245, 247–248, 255
Kieval, Hillel, 82
Kinkel, Walter (philosopher), 196
Kinyoun, Joseph P. (US physician, health official), 252, 255
Kirchner (Austr. junior dipl.), 38
Kissinger, Henry, 5
Kladowo (internment camp), 311
Klatzkin, Jakob (philosopher), 196
Klee, Alfred (jurist, Ger. Zionist leader, 224, 225, 230, 232, 233, 237, 238, 239
Klein, Samuel (geographer, rabbi), 184, 185n
Kleinburg (near Breslau), 128
Klemperer, Victor (philologist, diarist), 95, 96, 112
Koch, Robert (bacteriologist), 256
Kocka, Jürgen, 164–165
Kohler, Kaufmann (rabbi, US theologian), 188
Kohut, Adolph (historian), 90
Kolowrat, Franz Anton Graf v. (Austr. minister), 29, 30, 36, 37, 42
Kompert, Leopold (author), 82
Königsberg, 98, 99, 108, 109
Kosch, Dr. (Königsberg physician, friend of F. Lewald), 110
Kossuth, Lajos [Louis] (Hung. polit), 55, 56, 61, 62, 63
Kotzebue, August Friedrich Ferdinand v. (dramatist), 16
Kraehe, Enno E., 5
Krauss, Samuel (talmudist), 184
Kronenberger (leader of refugee transport), 325, 326
Kroner (rabbi, scholar), 184n, 194
Krupina [Korpona; Karpfen] (Hung. town), 60

Kübeck, Karl Friedrich Frhr. v. Kübau (Austr. statesman), 34, 36, 50
Kühne, Ferdinand Gustav (journalist), 82, 90
Kugler, Bernhard v. (historian), 179
Kuh, Ephraim Moses (merchant, poet), 102
Kulturprotestantismus, 198, 212
Küng, Hans, 67
Kurunda, Ignaz (Austr. author, politician), 82

Laffitte (Paris bankers), 32n
Lagarde, Paul de (orientalist), 206, 212n
Lämel, Simon v. (Prague banker), 13, 14
Landau, Lola (author, w. of S. Marck and A.T. Wegner), 140, 145, 149, 154
Landau, Theodor (f. of L. Landau), 140
Landauer, Samuel (orientalist), 184
Lange, Friedrich Albert (philosopher), 203, 204
Laßberg, Jenny v. (sis. of A. Droste-Hülshoff), 69
Latour, Theodor Graf Baillet v. (Austr. war minister), 51
Laube, Heinrich (writer), 69
Lazarus, Moritz (philosopher), 194, 202
League of Nations, 263
Lehranstalt für die Wissenschaft des Judentums, 177n, 179, 186–187
Leipzig, 82, 83: book fair, 85
Leo Baeck Institute Year Book, 159
Lessing, Gotthold Ephraim (poet, dramatist), 67, 83
Lessing, Monae (Red Cross physician), 252–253
Lessing, Theodor (philosopher), 161
Levenson, Alan, 130
Lewald, August (actor, journalist, writer), 95–112, 152, 153, 155, 159, 160, 162–163
Lewald, David *see* Markus, David
Lewald, Fanny (writer), 95–112, 152, 153, 159, 162
Lewald, Kathi (w. of August L.), 100
Lewald, Salomon (uncle of August L.), 103
Lewald, Zippora see Markus, Zippora
Lewin, Louis (rabbi, historian), 186
Lewy (Grk. Hechaluz rep.), 319, 320
Liberaler Rabbinerverband, 185
Liberaler Verein (Breslau), 146
Liberaler Verein f. die Angelegenheiten der jüdischen Gemeinde Berlin, 222
Liberalism, German, 7, 95
Liebeschütz, Hans (philosopher, medievalist), 199, 208n, 210n
Liga für Menschenrechte, 278
Lieven, Dorothea Princess de, 29, 47, 48
Lilienthal, Arthur (jurist, gen. sec. of Reichsvertretung,) 236, 240
Linson, J.H (US physician), 265n, 271, 273
Liptzin, Solomon (lit. historian), 87
Littrow-Bischoff, August v. (assoc. of Grillparzer), 78
Loeb, Moritz A. (chairman of Verein z. Erhaltung d. überlieferten Judentums Berlin), 225, 226n, 227, 229, 232, 233

Loewe, Heinrich (historian, librarian, Zion. polit.), 224, 232
Löwenthal, Eduard (of peace movement), 278
London Jewish community, 23
London, Sally (C.V. member), 238
Lope de Vega *see* Vega Carpio
Louis Philippe (King of France), 39, 41, 50, 51
Lowenstein, Steven, 98
Lucas, Leopold (rabbi, historian), 179, 180, 184n, 185, 188, 194
Lübeck, 10, 11
Lübeck Jewish community, 9, 11–12
Luedtke, Alf, 156
Lueger, Karl (antisem. Mayor of Vienna), 280, 281
Luther, Martin (Prot. reformer), 87, 199, 200, 207, 210, 296
Lys, Bertran de (Spanish financier), 32–33

Macaulay, Thomas B. (historian), 89
McKinley, William (US president), 255
Maccabi-Hazair, 307
Magruder, George (US physician, health official), 252
Mahler, Moritz (journalist), 55
Maimonides, Moses [Rambam] (philosopher), 186, 187, 200, 209, 210
Mali (Herr) (organiser of emigration to Palestine), 308
Mannheimer Montag-Verein, 300
Manz (Cath. publ. firm), 68
Marburg, 200, 204, 205, 206
Marburg School, 203, 213
Marburg University, 196, 203, 204, 205, 208
Marck, Siegfried (of Breslau, h. of L. Landau), 139, 140
Marcus, Wilhelm (of Repräsentantenversammlung), 229
Marcuse, Max (sexologist), 128
Margot (friend of R. Effenberger on "Patria"), 328, 329
Maria Christina (Queen and Regent of Spain), 40
Maria Theresa (Empress of Austria), 57
Markel, Howard, 245, 254
Markus, David (banker, cousin of A. Lewald), 99, 108, 110n, 111
Markus, Samuel (merchant, f. of A. Lewald), 99
Markus, Zippora (w. of David M.), 99, 108, 111
Marx, Alexander (historian), 186
Marx, Karl Heinrich (founder of scientific socialism), 30, 53, 89
Mauritius, 330
Mauthner, Fritz (philosopher), 91
May, R.E. (businessman), 292n
Mayer, Dr. (of Ges. z. Förd. d. Wiss. d. Jud.), 194
Maynes, Mary Jo, 135–136
Mayr, Ernst, 249
Medici, Luigi de' (Neopolitan finance minister), 31, 32

Meiring, Kerstin, 126
Meissner, Alfred (Austr. author), 82
"Melk" (refugee ship), 312
Mendelssohn, Moses (philosopher), 10, 199
Mendizábal (Span. statesman), 40, 41
Menzel, Wolfgang (author), 86
'Menschheit', 287
Metternich, Klemens Wenzel Fürst v. (Austr. statesman), 3–18, 19–54, 71, 75: financial help from Rothschilds, 24: Brighton exile, 55: Plass estate, 24, 25
Metternich, Princess Melanie (3rd w. of Metternich), 25, 51–52
Metternich, Princess Pauline (d. of M. Sándor), 58
Michaelis, Georg (German chancellor), 288n
"Milos" (refugee ship), 313, 318, 320, 322, 325, 326
Mischehe see Intermarriage
Misrachi Ortsgruppe Berlin, 222, 224
Mittrowsky, Graf (head of Austr. treasury), 42
Mittwoch, Eugen (orientalist), 183, 187, 190
Mohl, Moritz (Prot. Württemberg deputy), 7
Moltke, Helmuth Graf v. (Pruss. field-marshal), 286
Mommsen, Theodor (lib. historian, jurist), 300
'Monatsschrift für Geschichte und Wissenschaft des Judentums', 183, 188
Montgomery, Robert (poet), 89
Moravia, 55, 28
'Morgenblatt für gebildete Stände', 86
Morgenstern, Lina (née Bauer, soc. scientist), 278
Moritz (Haganah memb. of Paderborn group), 327, 331
Mosse, George L. (historian), 201, 299
Mosse, Rudolf (publ.), 204
Mugdan, David (of Religiös-Liberal movement) 146
Mühlmann, Julie (w. of K. Beck), 90
Muhs, Rudolf, 82n
Müller, Nikolaus (Christ. theologian), 189–190
Münch-Bellinghausen, Eligius Frhr. v. (Austr. dipl.), 48
Münster, Graf (Hanovarian statesman), 47
Muniah (member of Haganah Haifa), 330, 331

Naples, Kingdom of, 29, 31, 32, 33
Napoleon I (Emperor of the French), 4, 11, 15, 70: return to France, 14
Nathan, Nathan, Max (Hamburg rabbi), 184
National Socialism, 126, 196
Nationalism, German, 15, 16
Nationalism, Hungarian, 2
Natorp, Paul, 196, 204, 206
Neo-Kantianism, 195–196, 202, 203, 204, 206, 213
Nesselrode, Karl Robert Graf v. (Russian foreign minister), 31
Netherlands, 15

Neuer jüdischer Gemeindeverein, 222
Neustadt, Adolf (journalist), 55
New York Academy of Medicine, 257
'New York Herald', 253
New York, immigration to, 243–276 passim: health depart. (division of contagious diseases), 250
'New York Times' (The), 247, 250, 252, 253, 264n
'New York World', 250n, 253
Nicholas I (Tsar of Russia), 36, 37, 50
Nicholas II (Tsar of Russia), 279
Nicholson, Harold (diplomat, writer), 5
Nicolai, Georg (physician, pacifist), 286
Nietzsche, Friedrich (philosopher), 199n, 298
Nobel, Alfred (chemist), 279
Nobel, Nehemia (rabbi, leader of Orthodoxy), 184–185
Nordau, Max (writer, Zion. leader), 280
'Nouvelle Revue', 280
Nuremberg, 83

Ofen, 23
Oppeln, 133,137
"Oristano" (emigr. ship), 274
Ortega y Gasset, José (Span. philosopher), 204
Orthodoxy, Jewish, 1, 7, 168
'Ost und West', 218
Ostberg, Hugo (anti-Zionist, of lib. Vereinigung), 233, 236n, 237

"Pacific" (refugee ship), 313–326
Pacifism, Jews and, 277–301
Paderborn group (immigr. to Palestine), 313, 314, 316, 325, 327
Palestina-Amt, 306
Palestine, German-Jewish commitment to, 235–237
Palestine, British Mandate, 235, 305–332: illegal immigration, 305–332
'Palestine Post', 325–326
Palmer, Alan, 5
Palmerston Viscount, Henry John Temple (Brit. statesman), 40, 51
Paris, 24, 29, 33, 35, 36
Paris Jewish community, 23
Parish, David, 22, 26, 31, 47
Pasternak, Boris (author), 204
"Patria" (refugee ship), 305–332: journey down Danube: 305–317
Patronka camp Slovakia (internment camp), 306, 308, 309, 310, 311, 316
"Pencho" (refugee ship), 311, 312
Pereira, Ludwig v. (banker), 44
Périer, Casimir (Fr. statesman, banker), 36
Pest see Budapest
Petőfi, Sandor (Hung. poet), 58

Philippson, Franz (consul general), 191n
Philippson, Ludwig (ed. 'Allgemeine Zeitung des Judentums'), 179, 277
Philippson, Martin (historian, s. of Ludwig), 179, 180, 181, 184n, 185, 186, 191, 194
Pickus, Keith, 300
Plass (Metternich estate), 24–25
Plato (Grk. philosopher), 139, 200, 202, 209
Poale Zion, 222, 223, 224
"Pocahantes" (ship), 261
Poetry, German, 81
Poetry, Jewish, 1–14
Pogroms, 26, 47, 56, 264, 281
Poland, 8
Poovey, Mary, 157
Pozzo di Borgo, Count Carlo Andreas (Russ. dipl.), 38
Prague Jewish community, 4: Hevra Qaddisha, 114n, 115
Prawer, Siegbert, 81
Pressburg [Pozsony], 56, 59
Pressburg Jewish community, 46
Preussischer Landesverband jüdischer Gemeinden, 223, 224, 227
Pringsheim, Rose (d. of Siegmund), 133
Pringsheim, Siegmund (banker, f. of Rose), 133
Prokesch, Graf Anton Graf v. Osten (soldier, Austr. dipl.), 34
Protestantism, 1: and Judaism, 195–214
"Protocols of the Elders of Zion", 262
Prussia, 4–6, 8, 9, 10, 11, 12, 13, 16, 23, 91, 104, 111, 204: emancipation Edict of 1812, 4, 11, 12, 71
Prussian Jewry, 4, 23, 46, 47, 99, 190, 215–240
Pückler-Muskau, Hermann Ludwig Fürst v. (writer), 21
Pulzer, Peter, 8

Quidde, Ludwig (lib. polit., historian, pacifist, Nobel Peace Prize winner), 277, 282–287, 299

Rabbinerseminar Berlin, 186, 187
Rabl, Hans (leader of refugee transport), 325, 326
Race theories, 248
Rade, Martin (Prot. theologian), 204
Radetzky, Graf Johann, Joseph (Austr. field-marshal), 52
Rahden, Till van, 154, 155, 157
Rathenau, Walther (statesman, philosopher), 292
Rau, Arthur (lawyer, Zion. polit.), 233
Rechberg, Graf Aloys v. (Bavarian min.), 6
Reform Judaism, 107, 120, 129, 167, 168, 207n, 297
Reformation, 199, 210
Reichsvereinigung der Juden in Deutschland, 308
Reifsche school of dance (Breslau), 137
Religiöse Mittelpartei (RMP), 222, 223, 227

Renan, Ernest (Fr. historian), 295–296
Repräsentantenversammlung, 215–240: elections to, 220–225 *passim*
Revolutions, 1848, 7, 49. 50, 53, 55, 56, 58, 59–60, 68, 72, 81, 82, 89, 91: in Hungary, 90
Rhineland, 4
Richard II (King of England), 75
Richarz, Monika, 129
Richelieu, Armand (Fr. statesman, cardinal), 53–54
Rickert, Heinrich (philosopher of history), 203
Riepel, Franz Xavier (prof., mining expert), 42, 44
Riesenfeld family (shipping magnates, of Breslau), 136–137
Riesenfeld, Adolf (of Breslau), 136–139
Riesenfeld, Grete (sis. of Adolf, w. of M. Goldmann), 136–137, 138
Riesenfeld, Samuel (of Oppeln, uncle of Adolf, and Grete), 136–137
Riesser, Gabriel (lib. politician, editor 'Der Jude'), 7, 18, 111, 153
Rigny (Fr. minister), 38
Rippner, Benjamin (rabbi, scholar), 179
Ritschl, Albrecht (Prot. theologian), 199n
Robespierre, Maximilian de (lawyer, revolutionary), 53–54
Romania (country of passage for immigr. ships), 305, 312, 314, 316, 317
Rome Jewish community, 48
Roosevelt, Theodor (soldier, US pres.), 251, 255
Rosenthal, Ferdinand (rabbi, scholar), 187n
Rosenthal, Moritz (lib. polit.), 238
Rosenzweig, Franz (philosopher), 195, 199, 200
"Rosita" (refugee ship), 316
Rothe, Richard (theologian), 198n
Rothschild family, 19–54, 87–88, 89: bankers to the Holy Alliance, 30: ennoblement, 27, 46: financial support for Metternich, 24, 25, 36: financial support for railways, 21, 41–46 *passim*: role in Spain, 31, 32, 33
Rothschild, Amschel Meyer Baron v. (Frf. banker), 24, 25, 26, 29, 46, 47, 48, 51
Rothschild, Anselm (s. of Amschel), 51, 52, 53
Rothschild, Anthony (neph. of Salomon and James R.), 25
Rothschild, Betty (d. of Salomon R.), 39, 53
Rothschild, Carl Mayer v. (banker), 24, 25, 31, 32, 39, 46, 51
Rothschild, Charlotte (d. of Carl R.), 51
Rothschild, Edmond de (banker, philanthropist), 191n
Rothschild, Evelyn de, 19n
Rothschild, James de (Paris banker), 22, 25, 29, 32, 35, 36, 39, 40, 41, 46, 47, 48, 49
Rothschild, Lionel (s. of Nathan R.), 27, 40, 41, 44, 49, 51
Rothschild, Mayer Amschel (founder of banking house), 21

General Index

Rothschild, Nat (s. of Nathan R.), 50
Rothschild, Nathan (London banker), 21, 24, 27, 32, 33, 38, 39, 40, 46, 50
Rothschild, Natty (grandson of Nathan R.), 27
Rothschild, Salomon Mayer Frh. v. (Vienna banker), 19–54 *passim* 58
Rubinstein, Richard, 291n
Rühs, Friedrich (historian), 16
Rupp, George, 198
Rürup, Reinhard, 17, 216, 240

Sabean, David, 140
Sachs, Margarete Rosalie (d. of S. Sachs, w. of Simundt), 131
Sachs, Ottilie [née Immerwahr] (w. of Siegmund), 131
Sachs, Siegmund (banker, f. of Margarete), 131
Salomon, Gotthold (Hamb. preacher, bible transl.), 121
Sand, Karl (killed Kotzebue), 16
Sándor, Móric (Hung. landowner), 58
Savigny, Carl v. (jurist, politician), 204
Saxe-Coburg, Leopold of (King of Belgium), 33, 35
Saxony, 5, 6, 8
Scheffler, Kitty (clerical assist. Troyl camp), 273n
Schiller, Friedrich v. (dramatist), 81, 83, 84, 87, 91
Schindler family (of Breslau), 139
Schindler, Johanna (friend of A. Riesenfeld), 139
Schlegel, Friedrich v. (littérateur, philosopher), 70
Schmidt, Michael, 100n
Schnabel, Franz (historian), 69
Schnapper, Anton (cousin of S. Rothschild), 27
Schnaittach Jewish community, 117–118
"Schönbrunn" (refugee ship), 312
Scholem, Gershom (philosopher), 161, 195, 197
Schomre Schabbes, 187
Schreiber, Emanuel (Reform rabbi), 127
Schuster ("Papa"), 322, 323
Schwarz, Adolf (talmudic scholar), 187, 194
Schwarzschild, Steven S. (philosopher, Judaist), 196
Scott, Joan, 157, 170
Sedgwick, Eve, 156
Self-hatred, 11, 160, 161–162
Seligmann, Caesar (Frankfurt liberal rabbi), 233
Sessa, Karl Alexander (Breslau physician, playwright), 105, 106
Sheppard, Eugene, 214n
Silbergleit, Wilhelm (industrialist, f. of A. Auerbach), 134
Simon, James F. (merchant, philanthropist), 281
Simon, Samuel (merchant, f. of Simundt), 131
Simonsen, David, J. (Chief Rabbi Copenhagen, orientalist), 187, 194
'Simplicissimus', 127
Simson, Eduard Martin (bapt., jurist, politician), 110

Simundt (Prot. lieutenant, h. of M.R. Sachs), 131
Sina (bank), 36, 44, 49
Slovakia (country of passage for immigr. ships), 306, 308, 309
Smidt, Johann (Bremen polit.), 10, 15, 17
Snidow, Robert C. (US army officer), 264–265
Sofia, 318
Sombart, Werner (economist), 128
Sonnemann, Leopold (banker, publ., lib. polit.), 278, 284
Sonnenfeld, Hugo (jurist, C.V. leader), 225
Sorkin, David, 5
Sorma, Agnes (actress), 71
Soult, Nichola Jean, Duke of Damaltia (Fr. marshal and statesman), 38
Sozial-Demokratische Partei Deutschlands (SPD), 225
Spanish-American War, and quarantine restrictions, 251–255
Spiel, Hilde (Austrian novelist), 5–7
Spindler, Max (historian), 69
Spinoza Baruch (philosopher), 87, 102, 296
Spranger, Eduard (philosopher, educationalist), 176
Springer, Gertrud Luise (w. of B. Breslauer), 148
Springer, Hermann (f. of Gertrud Luise), 148
Srbik, Heinrich v. (Austr. historian), 5, 16
Stachel, Peter, 72
Stadion, Johann Philipp Graf v. (Austr. finance minister), 31, 32
Stahl, Theodor (h. of E. Haertel), 133–134
Stahr, Adolf (lit. historian, writer, h. of F. Lehwald), 109
Stauf[f]er, (intermediary in illegal immigr. to Palestine), 316, 318
Steiner family (Vienna bank), 58
Steinschneider, Moritz (orientalist, bibliographer), 182
Steinthal, Heymann (philologist), 202, 205
Stern, Heinrich (jurist, of C.V.), 225, 229, 233, 235, 237,
Stern, Julius (teacher, chairman of Repräsentantenversammlung), 235
Sternberg fertiliser company (of Breslau), 137
Stoecker, Adolf (antisem. preacher), 283n, 288
Stoler, Ann, 157
Stolzenberg, Nomi Maya, 214n
Strehen, Martina, 114
Strauss, Leo (philosopher), 195, 197n
Strong, Richard P. (US physician, Red Cross rep.), 263
Stúr, L'udevit, (Slovak writer), 60
Suttner, Arthur Gundaccar v. (novelist, pacifist), 279, 280, 281, 300
Suttner, Bertha v. (née Kinsky, novelist, pacifist, Nobel Peace Prize winner), 277–281 *passim*, 299
Swinburne Island (US quarantine centre), 247, 250, 252
Synagogue (liberal, Berlin), 229, 233

Synagogue worship, 113–123
Szanto, Alexander (stenog. of Repräsentantenversammlung), 220, 225
Széchenyi, Count Istvan (reformer), 58, 60, 61

Tal, Uriel (historian, Judaist), 198n, 207n, 212
Talleyrand, Charles Maurice de (Fr. statesman), 7, 39
Talmud, 119, 122, 165, 166, 167, 169, 170, 206, 208,
Talmud Torah society, 113, 117, 118, 119, 120
Tänzer, Arnold (rabbi, historian), 128
Tatichev (Russ. ambassador in Vienna), 36
Theilhaber, Felix (sociologist), 128
'Theologische Literaturzeitung', 182, 192
'Theologische Rundschau' 192
'Theologisches Literaturblatt', 192
Thiers, Louis Adolphe (Fr. statesman, historian), 41, 49
Timms, Edward, 19n, 175n
Tivoli Programme, 284
Toller, Ernst (author, revolutionary), 298
Tommaso (Capuchin friar) *see* Damascus Affair
Torah, 119, 122, 164, 165, 166, 167, 169
Toreno (Span. polit.), 39, 40
Toury, Jacob (historian), 126
Traugott, Wilhelm (author), 8
Treitschke, Heinrich v. (historian), 179, 202n, 205, 283n
Trendelenburg, Friedrich Adolf (philosopher), 202
Trepp, Anne-Charlott, 135
Troeltsch, Ernst (Prot. theologian), 199n, 212, 213, 214
Trollope, Frances (m. of Anthony T., writer), 28
Türk, Moritz (leader of Repräsentantenversammlung), 225, 232, 234, 239
Tulcea, 313–319 *passim*
Turner, Victor, 171
Twain, Mark (writer), 89

Ullmann, Moritz (Pest merchant), 58
Ullstein, Hans (publ.), 284n
Unabhängige Sozialdemokratische Partei Deutschlands (USPD), 225
Ungerleider, Franz (h. of G. Jakubczik,), 146
United States Emergency Immigration Act (1921), 273
United States Marine Hospital Service, 247, 252
"Uranus" (refugee ship), 309, 310, 311, 312, 313, 314

Varnhagen von Ense, Rahel Levin (salon hostess), 96, 160n
Vaterländische Frauenvereine, 114
Vega Carpio, Lope Felix de (Span. poet, dramatist), 67, 71, 72, 73, 77

Verband der Literaturvereine, 179
Verein für Krankenpflege (Hamburg), 166
Verein zur Abwehr des Antisemitismus (Abwehrverein), 279, 281–282
Verein zur Förderung der Interessen des Judentums (Breslau), 146
Verein(e) für jüdische Geschichte und Literatur, 175, 177, 178, 179, 188, 190, 278
Vereinigung der Liberalen Rabbiner Deutschlands, 185, 187
Vereinigung für das liberale Judentum, 185, 225, 235
Versailles Treaty, 286, 289
Verwaltungsbericht d. jüdischen Gemeinde zu Berlin, 230
Vienna Jewish community, 4, 5, 308
Vienna, 12, 26, 27, 28, 29, 30, 31, 32, 33, 35, 36, 37, 40, 42, 44, 50, 52, 56, 58, 69, 63, 81, 82, 87, 90, 137, 182, 280, 292, 307–313 *passim*
Vienna University, 287
Villèle, Comte Joseph de (Fr. premier), 33, 34
'Völkischer Beobachter', 316
Vogelstein, Heinemann (Reform rabbi), 185, 194
Vormärz movement, 19, 60, 62, 82

Wagner, Richard (composer), 100
Waller, Kurt (pseud.) *see* Lewald, August
Warna, 317, 318
Wartburg 87
Wartburgfest 1817, 16
Wassermann, Oscar (banker, pres. Keren Hayesod), 286
Webber, Andrew, 81n
Wedel, Hans [HaWe] (lead. of Maccabi groups), 312, 317–328 *passim*
Wegner, Armin T. (author, 2nd. h. of L. Landau), 139–140, 149, 154
Wegner, Sybille (d. of L. Landau and A. Wegner), 149
Weimar Republic, 87, 125–126, 214, 215–240
Weinstock (intermediary in illegal immigr. to Palestine), 316, 317
Weismann, August W. (zoologist, geneticist), 249
Weiss family, 138
Weiss, Dora (factory worker Breslau, friend of A. Riesenfeld), 138
Weisse, Dr. (rabbi, of Ges. z. Förd. d. Wiss. d. Jud.), 194
Weisse, Samson (rabbi, RMP representative), 229
Wellhausen, Julius (Prot. theologian, 204, 206, 208
Wellington, Arthur Wellsley [Duke of] (Brit. soldier-statesman), 12–13, 22, 38
Werner, Dr. (rabbi, of Ges. z. Förd. d. Wiss. d. Jud.), 194
Wertheimstein, Leopold v. (sen. clerk to S. Rothschild), 27
White, John C. (US dipl.), 267

Wikoff camp, Montauk, LI (isolation camp), 251–270 *passim*
Wilhelm II (German Emperor), 284
Wilhelm, Kurfürst Hesse-Kassel, 204
Windelband, Wilhelm (philosopher), 203
Windischgrätz, Prince Alfred zu (Austr. field marshal, 52
Winz, Leo (co-founder 'Ost und West'), 218
Wissenschaft des Judentums, 113, 175–194
Wittenberg, 199
Wodianer, Samuel (Pest merchant), 58
Wolf, Joseph (Dessau preacher), 121
Wolff, Christian Frh. v. (philosopher, mathematician), 204
Women, Jewish, 95–172: emancipation, 166, 167: voluntary associations: 114, 168–169
World War I, 189, 191, 192, 198, 211, 285, 286, 297, 298
World War II, 290
Württemberg, 8: oppsition to emancipation, 7, 10, 14
Würzburg University, 16
Wyman, Walter (US surgeon general), 255, 258,

Yerushalmi, Yosef Hayim, 244
Yiddish literature, 116, 119
Yiddish bible, 119
Yugoslavia (country of passage for immigr. ships), 305, 306, 310, 311

Zay, Count Károly (Hung. nationalist, philosemite), 61
"Zena ur'ena", 119
'Zeitschrift für die elegante Welt', 83
'Zeitschrift für Völkerpsychologie und Sprachwissenschaft', 202
Zeller, Eduard (theologian), 179
Zionism, 129, 211, 215–240, 266, 279–280, 281n, 297, 298, 299, 305–332
Zionist Congress (XVI), 235, 236
Zionistische Vereinigung f. Deutschland (ZVfD), 224, 237, 238
Ziwa (Bielefeld illegal immigr.), 325–326
Zola (Fr. engineer, f. of Emile Z.), 42
Zunz, Leopold (scholar, headmaster), 180, 194
Zwahr, Hartmut, 144

Neu in der edition text + kritik

Exilforschung
Ein internationales Jahrbuch
Herausgegeben von Claus-Dieter Krohn, Erwin Rotermund, Lutz Winckler, Irmtrud Wojak und Wulf Koepke

Band 19/2001
Jüdische Emigration
Zwischen Assimilation und Verfolgung, Akkulturation und jüdischer Identität
etwa 250 Seiten
ca. DM 58,--/öS 423,--/sfr 52,50
ISBN 3-88377-672-6
Erscheint im September 2001

Das Schwerpunktthema des Bands bilden Fragen der jüdischen Identität und der Akkulturation im Exil und Nachexil. Die Beiträge befassen sich u. a. mit der Vertreibungspolitik der Nationalsozialisten, richten die Aufmerksamkeit auf die Sicht der Betroffenen und thematisieren Defizite und Perspektiven der Wirkungsgeschichte jüdischer Emigration.

FILMEXIL 14/2001
Filmkomponisten in der Emigration III
Herausgegeben vom Filmmuseum Berlin – Deutsche Kinemathek
etwa 60 Seiten, zahlreiche Abbildungen
DM 18,--/öS 131,--/sfr 17,--
ISBN 3-88377-676-9
Erscheint im Oktober 2001

In diesem Heft geht es ein weiteres Mal um ein zentrales Thema des Filmexils: die Tätigkeit von Filmkomponisten in der Emigration.
Diesmal stehen die Kompositionen von Kurt Weill zu G. W. Pabsts Film »Die 3-Groschen-Oper« und zu Fritz Langs ›Musical‹ »You and Me« im Mittelpunkt. Porträtiert wird darüber hinaus Franz Waxmann, einer der prägenden Filmkomponisten Hollywoods. Ein weiterer Essay stellt das filmische Werk von Robert Stolz, dem bekannten Operettenkomponisten, vor. Eine biografische Skizze rückt den nach Australien emigrierten Komponisten George Dreyfus ins Zentrum des Interesses.

edition text + kritik
Postfach 80 05 29 | 81605 München | Levelingstraße 6a | 81673 München
etk.muenchen@t-online.de | www.etk-muenchen.de

New Books from Mohr Siebeck

Michael Theunissen
Reichweite und Grenzen der Erinnerung
Scope and Limits of Remembrance
Edited by Eilert Herms
2001. 50 pages (est.) (Lucas-Preis 2001). ISBN 3-16-147475-1 paper DM 40.00 (est.) - November

Richard von Weizsäcker
Polnisch-deutsche Verständigung nach dem Zweiten Weltkrieg
Edited by Volker Drehsen
2001. 54 pages (Lucas-Preis 2000). ISBN 3-16-147545-3 paper DM 28.00

Steven Theodore Katz
Kontinuität und Diskontinuität zwischen christlichem und nationalsozialistischem Antisemitismus / Continuity and Discontinuity between Christian and Nazi Antisemitism
Edited by Volker Drehsen; translated by Alexandra Riebe
2001. 64 pages (Lucas-Preis 1999). ISBN 3-16-147544-5 paper DM 38.00

Michael Walzer
Exilpolitik in der Hebräischen Bibel
Politics of Exile in the Hebrew Bible
Edited by Volker Drehsen
2001. 128 pages (Lucas-Preis 1998). ISBN 3-16-147543-7 paper DM 58.00

Juden – Bürger – Deutsche
Edited by Andreas Gotzmann, Rainer Liedtke, Till van Rahden
2001. IX, 444 pages (Schriftenreihe wissenschaftlicher Abhandlungen des Leo Baeck Instituts 63). ISBN 3-16-147498-8 cloth DM 148.00

Selma Stern
Der Hofjude im Zeitalter des Absolutismus
Edited and translated from English into German by Marina Sassenberg
2001. X, 284 pages (Schriftenreihe wissenschaftlicher Abhandlungen des Leo Baeck Instituts 64). ISBN 3-16-147662-x cloth DM 128.00

Erika Bucholtz
Henri Hinrichsen und der Musikverlag C. F. Peters
2001. VIII, 367 pages (Schriftenreihe wissenschaftlicher Abhandlungen des Leo Baeck Instituts 65). ISBN 3-16-147638-7 cloth DM 78.00

Mohr Siebeck
Postfach 2040
D-72010 Tübingen

Fax 07071 / 51104
e-mail: info@mohr.de
www.mohr.de

TRIBÜNE

Unabhängig Objektiv Kritisch

seit 1962

Zeitschrift zum Verständnis des Judentums

Geschichte & Gegenwart
Wirtschaft & Wissenschaft
Kunst & Kultur

Neuerscheinung:

Sach- und Autorenregister der Jahre
1962 – 1999 (Hefte 1 – 152)
DM 19,80

Autoren von A wie Jean Améry bis Z
wie Walter Zadek – eine Bestandsaufnahme von knapp 40 Jahren Geschichte
in Deutschland, Israel und der Welt.

TRIBÜNE-Verlag
Habsburgerallee 72
D-60385 Frankfurt am Main
Tel.: +49 (0)69 943300-0
Fax: +49 (0)69 943300-23
e-mail: Tribuene_Verlag@t-online.de
www.tribuene-verlag.de

New Books

Irving Massey
Philo-Semitism in Nineteenth-Century German Literature

2000. VI, 199 Seiten. Kart. DM 98.– / € 50.11. ISBN 3-484-65129-6 (Conditio Judaica. Band 29)

The work begins with an attempt to understand the philosophy of Nazism and its attendant anti-Semitism, as a necessary prelude to the study of philo-Semitism, which also displays a continuous tradition to the present day. Most of the non-Jewish authors in Germany in the nineteenth century expressed both anti-Semitic and philo-Semitic views (as did most of the German-Jewish authors of that same time); the following work deals with philo-Semitic texts by the non-Jewish authors of the period. The writer who provides the largest body of relevant material is Leopold von Sacher-Masoch, but works by Gutzkow, Bettine von Arnim, Annette von Droste-Hülshoff, Hebbel, Freytag, Raabe, Fontane, Grillparzer, Ebner-Eschenbach, Anzengruber, and Ferdinand von Saar are also examined, as are several tales by the Alsatian authors Erckmann and Chatrian. There is a short chapter on women and philo-Semitism. The conclusion draws attention to the feelings of guilt that are revealed in a number of the texts.

Lebenswege und Lektüren
Österreichische NS-Vertriebene in den USA und Kanada
Herausgegeben von BEATRIX MÜLLER-KAMPEL unter Mitarbeit von CARLA CARNEVALE

2000. VI, 352 Seiten. 9 Abb. Kart. DM 88.– / € 44.99. ISBN 3-484-65130-X (Conditio Judaica. Band 30)

What was the driving force that motivated Austrians driven out of their homeland after 1938 and seeking refuge in the United States and Canada to devote their professional lives to the cultivation of literature in German, thus becoming intermediaries retilling the intellectual subsoil of the ›perpetrator cultures‹ Germany and Austria in their new home? Alongside practical considerations it was certainly a love of literature, of Kafka, Rilke, Werfel, Schnitzler, Stefan Zweig and their literary worlds, all of which held out the prospect of regaining a finer, more humane homeland. Throughout, however, their suspicion of German literary studies (a discipline which as early as the 1920s had vigorously supported the dissemination of nationalist and national socialist cultural ideology at Germany's universities) remained very marked indeed. At the same time, the analytic re-acquisition of literature, philosophy and art was a way of rebelling against the enforced abandonment not only of murdered friends, slaughtered relatives and confiscated property but also everything which had started to represent a home from home culturally, intellectually and emotionally.

Christoph Schmidt
Der häretische Imperativ
Überlegungen zur theologischen Dialektik der Kulturwissenschaft in Deutschland

2000. V, 189 Seiten. Kart. DM 104.– / € 53.17. ISBN 3-484-65131-8 (Conditio Judaica. Band 31)

The book describes the transformation of discourse in cultural studies, a discourse which after its inception around the turn of the century was also designed to salvage German-Jewish interculturality. This transformation manifests itself in a discourse on political theology (involving Carl Schmitt and Gershom Scholem) through which the disastrous dissociation of the two cultures took its final and irrevocable course.

Achim Jaeger
Ein jüdischer Artusritter
Studien zum jüdisch-deutschen »Widuwilt« (»Artushof«) und zum »Wigalois« des Wirnt von Gravenberc

2000. IX, 465 Seiten. 3 Abb. Kart. DM 196.– / € 100.21. ISBN 3-484-65132-6 (Conditio Judaica. Band 32)

This study examines the only extant Arthurian romance in German Jewish (»Widuwilt«/»Artushof«) and its links with Wirnt von Gravenberc's »Wigalois«. Central concerns are German-Jewish and Jewish-German literary transfer and aspects of the history of reception and impact of »Widuwilt« and »Artushof«. The protagonist was designed to figure as a ›Jewish Arthurian knight‹, which indicates that as early as the 14th/15th century there was a Jewish upper class using literature as a means of social participation and representation.

Max Niemeyer Verlag

Max Niemeyer Verlag GmbH · Postfach 21 40 · 72011 Tübingen
Tel 07071-98 94 94 · Fax 98 94 50 · E-mail order@niemeyer.de